Transportation Law

Contents

v

23. Pipeline Regulation, 439

24. Common Carrier Tariffs, 445

25. Schedules of Rates and Charges of Contract Carriers, 462

26. Rates and Charges, 471

27. Classifications, 523

pation in Rates by Carrier Necessary to Be Held Liable for Undue Preferences and Prejudices, 725; Tariff Provisions May Not Render Lawful a Practice Found to Be Unlawful by the Commission, 727; Equal Treatment, 728; Similarity of Circumstances and Conditions, 730; Rate Equalization, 732; Jones Amendment, 735

38. Unjust Discrimination against Shippers, 736

The Applicable Statutory Provisions, 736; Discrimination Defined, 736; Burden of Proof, 740

39. Unjust Discrimination between Carriers, 742

The Applicable Statutory Provisions, 742; Rail Carriers, 742; Water Carriers, 743

40. Commodities Clause, 751

Purpose of the Statute, 751; Prohibitions under the Statute, 752

41. Competition in Transportation, 766

Economic Policy in Favor of Competitive Enterprise, 766; Sections 1 and 2 of the Sherman Antitrust Act, 766; Historically Common Carriers Have Been Subject to the Antitrust Laws, 769; Exemptions from the Operation of the Antitrust Laws, 776; Proof of Damages, 782; Statutes Regulating Transportation Give Effect to the Public Policy of Preserving Competition, 783; Separation of Competing Forms of Transportation, 785; Dealings in Securities, Supplies or Other Articles of Commerce, and Contracts for Construction or Maintenance of Any Kind, 790; Interpretation of Words "Substantial Interest In" As Used in Section 10 of the Clayton Act, 791; Commission's Function, 791; Interpretative Cases, 792; Interlocking Directorate, 795; Robinson-Patman Act, 796

42. Unfair Methods of Competition by Air Carriers, 799

The Applicable Statutory Provisions, 799; Vindicating the Public Interest, 800; Power of the Board, 800

43. Primary Jurisdiction, 803

Expertise of Administrative Bodies and Need for Uniformity of Ruling, 803; Lack of Jurisdiction Concept, 805; The Doctrine of Primary Jurisdiction in Rate Cases, 808; The Doctrine of Primary Jurisdiction in Antitrust Cases, 811

44. Rate Making Agreements of Common Carriers and Freight Forwarders Subject to the Interstate Commerce Act, 829

Applicable Statutes, 829; Carriers of One Class, 832; Pooling or Other Matter or Transaction to Which Section 5 of the Act is Applicable, 834; The Right of Independent Action, 834; Standards Required by the Act, 842; National Trans-

56. Practice and Procedure before the Civil Aeronautics Board, 1120

57. Practice and Procedure before the Federal Maritime Commission, 1135

Preface

The first edition of this book was published in 1965 to meet the pressing need by members of the bar, and others intimately connected with and interested in transportation regulation, for a treatise on transportation law. The book was well received. The second edition was published in 1973. The purpose was not only to update the first edition but also to strengthen it.

There have been many developments in the field of transportation law in the intervening years since the publication of the second edition in 1973. These developments include the enactment of the Railroad Revitalization and Regulatory Reform Act of 1976. A revised edition is therefore essential. In addition to containing new developments in the interpretation and application of the transportation statutes and related acts, the revised edition is greatly enlarged.

In this book, many decisions are dealt with in order to bring a vast amount of material into focus. Principles of law arising from these decisions have been analyzed and discussed at length. The book is divided into principal subject headings, under which the law and discussion of law applying to each mode of transportation is found. This arrangement is in contrast with one which would have divided the book into sections treating each mode of transportation separately, resulting in a repetitious, cumbersome, and unwieldly presentation. It is hoped that the method used will simplify research by the reader who can find in one place without difficulty the discussion of the principle of law dealing with the particular mode of transportation with which he is directly concerned. At the same time, he will be able to compare or contrast application of legal principles relating to the mode of transportation with which he is directly concerned with that of other types. Since the regulatory statutes are related in many ways, and there is a relationship between the principles of law established by the administrative agencies and the courts pertaining to each of the modes of transportation, the advantage of the arrangement will readily be recognized. There are exceptions to the foregoing arrangement, but these were unavoidable.

Certain subject matters in the book are covered more thoroughly than others. Obviously, similar treatment could not be given to the many subjects falling within the ambit of the regulatory statutes and related acts, and still confine the material to the limitations of the book. In general, therefore, those subjects of principal, significance and importance are covered thoroughly; whereas other subjects, although given adequate coverage, are not dealt with as fully. This required an exercise of judgment and it is likely, therefore, that some readers may disagree with the selections made by the author of the subjects which are covered thoroughly. Because of the limitations of the book, it was necessary to evaluate for the reader the importance of each of the subjects, based upon the writer's training, experience and knowledge. In selecting the topics for full and complete coverage, special treatment also was given to those particularly complex problems which may require many hours of investigation for the research-minded reader.

John Guandolo
Washington, D.C.

Introduction

This revised edition of *Transportation Law* does not contain the changes, or a discussion of such changes, brought about by the enactment of the Revised Interstate Commerce Act, Public Law 95-473, October 17, 1978, and the Airline Deregulation Act of 1978, Public Law 95-504, October 24, 1978. The reason is the revision was on its way to completion before the enactment of the Revised Interstate Commerce Act and the Airline Deregulation Act of 1978, and it was too late because of printing deadlines to include the changes or a discussion of such changes.

However, as a matter of convenience to the reader in using the book we are including as appendixes a master disposition table showing the disposition of the prior provisions of the Interstate Commerce Act according to the United States Code citation (Appendix A), the text of the Revised Interstate Commerce Act (Appendix B), and the text of the Airline Deregulation Act of 1978 (Appendix C).

Regulation of Interstate and Foreign Commerce

Commerce Defined

Commerce has been defined by the Supreme Court on innumerable occasions since the early beginnings of the court. The following are examples of how the court has defined the word through the years. Commerce has been defined as comprehending intercourse for the purpose of trade in any and all its terms, including the transportation, purchase, sale, and exchange of commodities between the citizens of this country and the citizens and subjects of other countries, and between the citizens of different States;[1] as meaning commercial intercourse between nations and parts of nations in all its branches;[2] as including more than transportation, that is, embracing all the component parts of commercial intercourse among States;[3] as consisting of commercial intercourse and traffic among the citizens of States, in all the branches, including the transportation of persons and property;[4] as including commercial intercourse as well as the interchange of goods;[5] as meaning traffic but much more since it embraces also transportation and all the means and appliances necessarily employed in carrying it on;[6] as meaning commercial intercourse with one of its most essential ingredients being traffic;[7] as including commercial intercourse, transportation, communication, traffic, transit of persons, and the transmission

---

[1]*Welton v. State of Missouri*, 91 U.S. 275.
[2]*Henderson v. Mayor of New York*, 92 U.S. 259.
[3]*Foster-Fountain Packing Co. v. Haydel*, 278 U.S.1.
[4]*Gibbons v. Ogden*, 9 Wheat. 1; *State Tonnage Tax Cases*, 12 Wall. 204; *Gloucester Ferry Co. v. Pennsylvania*, 114 U.S. 196.
[5]*City of New York v. Miln*, 11 Pet. 102; *Philadelphia & R. Ry. Co. v. State of Pennslyvania*, 15 Wall. 232.
[6]*Chicago & N.W. R. Co. v. Fuller*, 17 Wall. 560.
[7]*Brown v. State of Maryland*, 12 Wheat. 419.

of messages;[8] as not being a technical conception but a practical one drawn from the course of business;[9] and as embracing every phase of commercial and business activity.[10]

Scope of the Regulatory Powers

The Commerce Clause on the Constitution[11] provides that Congress shall have the power "to regulate Commerce with foreign Nations, and among the several States."

The history of the times which immediately preceded the assembling of the Constitutional Convention demonstrates that the need of some equitable and just regulation of commerce was among the most influential causes which led to its meeting.[12] It is thus a matter of history that the purpose of the Constitution in committing to Congress power to regulate interstate commerce was to protect commercial intercourse from invidious restraints, to prevent interference through conflicting or hostile State laws, and to insure uniformity in regulation.[13]

In the exercise of sovereign powers it was customary in England from time immemorial and in this country from its first colonization to regulate, when necessary for the public good, the manner in which citizens used their own private property, thus common carriers, ferries, brickmen, bakers, millers, wharfingers and innkeepers were regulated and the power to regulate included the power to fix maximum charges.[14] The theory of such regulations rested upon the assumption of private property devoted to public use.[15] The principles of commerce law thus established in the regulation of common carriers and others engaged in commerce continued as precedents in the regulation of commerce after the adoption of the Constitution. There is no body of Federal common law separate and apart from the common law existing in the States; however, it is an entirely different thing to assert that there is no common law in force generally throughout the United States.[16] At the

---

[8]*Lottery Cases (Champion v. Ames)*, 188 U.S. 321.
[9]*Swift & Co. v. United States*, 196 U.S. 375.
[10]*Jordan v. Tashiro*, 278 U.S. 123.
[11]Const., Art. I. Sec. 8, clause 3.
[12]*Cook v. Pennsylvania*, 97 U.S. 566.
[13]*Commonwealth of Pennsylvania v. West Virginia*, 262 U.S. 553, aff'd 263 U.S. 350; *Bowman v. Chicago & N.W. Ry. Co.*, 125 U.S. 465; *Welton v. State of Missouri*, 91 U.S. 275; *Cook v. Pennsylvania*, 97 U.S. 556; *Cook v. Marshall County*, 196 U.S. 261.
[14]*Munn v. Illinois*, 94 U.S. 113.
[15]*St. Louis S. & P. R. v. Peoria & P. Union Ry. Co.*, 26 I.C.C. 226.
[16]*State of Kansas v. State of Colorado*, 206 U.S. 46.

time of the adoption of the Constitution, as pointed out, there was in existence a common law, and the adoption of the Constitution did not abrogate this common law. As to such matters as were committed to the control of the federal government there were applicable thereto the laws of nations, the maritime law, the principles of equity, and the common law.[17] In this regard for example, prior to the passage of the original Interstate Commerce Act, railway traffic was regulated by the several States under principles of common law applicable to common carriers. In some States legislation had been passed to secure the public against unreasonable and unjust discrimination, but the inefficiency of these laws and the evil which grew up under a policy of unrestricted competition suggested the necessity for legislation by Congress.[18] State regulation of rates had begun with railroad transportation; from the outset, in instances where railroads were chartered by the States, maximum rates for freight or passengers, or both, were prescribed.[19]

The plenary power of Congress over interstate commerce, derived from Article I, Section 8, Clause 3 of the United States Constitution was clearly recognized by the Supreme Court as early as 1824 in an opinion by Chief Justice Marshall in *Gibbons v. Ogden*.[20] The power of Congress under the Commerce Clause is complete in itself, may be exercised to its utmost extent, and acknowledges no limitations other than are prescribed in the Constitution.[21] The power to regulate commerce residing in Congress, which must determine its own policy, is so complete that it may shape that policy in the light of the fact that the interstate transportation, if permitted, would aid in the frustration of valid State laws for protection of persons and property.[22] Thus Congress may prevent interstate transportation from being used to bring into a State articles the traffic of which the State has Constitutional authority to forbid, and has forbidden in its internal commerce.[23]

The power to regulate commerce is thus the power to prescribe the rule by which commerce is to be governed.[24] To regulate commerce is to foster, protect, and control with appropriate regard for the welfare

---

[17]*Murray v. Chicago & N.W. Ry. Co.*, 62 Fed. 24, aff'd 92 Fed. 868.

[18]*I.C.C. v. Baltimore & O. R. Co.*, 145 U.S. 263.

[19]*Minnesota Rate Case*, 230 U.S. 352; *I.C.C. v. Cincinnati, N. O. & T. P. Ry. Co.*, 167 U.S. 479.

[21]*Kentucky Whip & Collar Co. v. Illinois Central R. Co.*, 229 U.S. 334, 345. See also *Brown v. State of Maryland*, 12 Wheat. 419; *Louisville & N. R. Co. v. Mottley*, 219 U.S. 467; *Starlock v. Alling*, 93 U.S. 99; *Adair v. United States*, 208 U.S. 161.

[22]*Ibid.*, p. 347.

[23]*Ibid.*, p. 348.

[24]*Gibbon v. Ogden*, 9 Wheat. 1; *Adair v. United States*, 208 U.S. 161; *Hammer v. Degenhart*, 247 U.S. 251.

of those who are immediately concerned, as well as the public at large, and to promote its growth and insure its safety.[25] The power to regulate includes the power to prohibit in cases where the prohibition is an aid of the lawful protection of the public.[26]

The commerce power extends to those activities intrastate which so affect interstate commerce, or the exertion of the power of Congress over it, as to make regulation of them appropriate means to the attainment of a legitimate end, the effective execution of the granted power to regulate commerce.[27] It is the effect upon interstate commerce or its regulation, regardless of the particular form which the competition may take, which is the test of federal power.[28] In the *Wrightwood* case it was held that competitive practices which are wholly intrastate may be reached by the Sherman Act because of their injurious effect on interstate commerce.

Exclusive Federal Powers

The power to regulate commerce is necessarily exclusive whenever the subjects of it are national in their character, or admit only of one uniform system or plan of regulation.[29] Especially is this so as regards any impediment or restriction upon such commerce.[30]

Instrumentalities of Commerce

The authority of Congress extends to every part of interstate commerce and to every instrumentality or agency by which it is carried on.[31] The subject matter of commerce may be things, goods, chattels, merchandise or persons; hence all of these may be regulated.[32] The operations of Constitutional provisions extend to new matters, as the mode of business and the habits of life of the people vary with each succeeding generation; they operate today upon modes of interstate commerce unknown to the framers and will operate with equal force

---

[25]*Second Employers' Liability Cases,* 223 U.S. 1; *Dayton-Goose Creek Ry. Co. v. United States,* 263 U.S. 456.

[26]*Bennett v. United States,* 194 Fed. 630, aff'd 227 U.S. 333.

[27]*United States v. Wrightwood Dairy Co.,* 315 U.S. 110.

[28]*Ibid.*

[29]*Robbins v. Shelby County Taxing District,* 120 U.S. 489; *Atlantic & Pac. Teleg. Co. v. Philadelphia,* 190 U.S. 160.

[30]*Walling v. Michigan,* 116 U.S. 446.

[31]*Minnesota Rate Case,* 230 U.S. 352; *Hopkins v. United States,* 171 U.S. 578.

[32]*McCall v. California,* 136 U.S. 104.

upon any new modes of such commerce which the future may develop.[33] The exclusive powers of regulation by Congress thus are not confined to the instrumentalities of commerce known today, but keep pace with the progress of the country and adapt themselves to the new developments.[34]

Retention by States of Nondelegated Powers

Whether a particular power has been delegated to one government or prohibited to the other by the Constitution depends on a fair construction of the whole instrument. The nature of the Constitution requires that only its great outlines should be marked, its important objects designated, and the minor ingredients which compose those objects be deduced from the nature of the objects themselves.[35] The grant in the Constitution of its own force, without action by Congress, established the essential immunity of interstate commercial intercourse from the direct control of the States with respect to those subjects embraced within the grant which are of such a nature as to demand that, if regulated at all, this regulation should be prescribed by a single authority. It other matters, admitting of diversity of treatment according to the special requirements of local conditions, the States may act within their respective jurisdictions until Congress sees fit to act.[36] When the subjects within the commercial power of Congress are local in nature or operation, or constitute mere aids to commerce, the States may provide for their regulation and management until Congress intervenes and supersedes their action.[37] When Congress has exerted its paramount authority over a particular subject of interstate commerce, State laws on the subject are superseded;[38] and failure to exercise the power of regulation, however prolonged, does not militate against its validity when exercised.[39]

State Regulation

When an Act of a State prescribes a regulation of commerce repugnant to and inconsistent with the regulation of Congress, the State

---

[33]*In re Debs*, 158 U.S. 564.

[34]*Mattingly v. Pennsylvania Co.*, 3 I.C.C. 592.

[35]*McCulloch v. State of Maryland*, 4 Wheat. 316.

[36]*Minnesota Rate Case*, 230 U.S. 352.

[37]*Cardwell v. American River Bridge Co.*, 113 U.S. 205; *Brown v. Houston*, 114 U.S. 622; *Gloucester Ferry Co. v. Pennsylvania*, 114 U.S. 196.

[38]*Northern Pac. Ry. Co. v. State of Wash.*, 222 U.S. 370; *Erie R. Co. v. State of New York*, 233 U.S. 671.

[39]*United States v. Delaware & H. Co.*, 213 U.S. 366; *German Alliance Insurance Co. v. Lewis*, 233 U.S. 389.

law must give way.[40] State legislation seeking to impose a direct burden on interstate commerce or to interfere with its freedom encroaches upon the exclusive burden of Congress.[41] The reasonableness or unreasonableness of a State enactment is always an element in the general inquiry, whether such legislation encroaches upon national authority over commerce or is to be deemed a legitimate exertion of the power of the State to protect the public interest or promote public convenience.[42]

The results of the pre-emption of the field by the federal government on State authority is demonstrated by the passage of the Motor Carrier Act of 1935. Since Congress adopted a comprehensive plan for regulating the carriage of goods by motor carriers in interstate commerce, and the federal plan of control was so all-embracing, the former power of States over interstate motor carriers was greatly reduced; no power at all was left in the States to determine what carriers could or could not operate in interstate commerce.[43] State authorities thus lacked power to issue interstate certificates of public convenience and necessity since it would resort, through State officials, to a test which is peculiarly within the province of federal action — the existence of adequate facilities for conducting interstate commerce.[44] Even under the all-

---

[40]*Sinnot v. Davenport,* 22 How. 227. See Section 28 of the I.C. Act which was added by the Railroad Revitalization and Regulatory Reform Act of 1976, 90 Stat. 54 ("4R Act"). Section 28 provides in part that,

"(1) Notwithstanding the provisions of section 202(b), any action described in this subsection is declared to constitute an unreasonable and unjust discrimination against, and an undue burden on, insterstate commerce. It is unlawful for a State, a political subdivision of a State, or a governmental entity or person acting on behalf of such State or subdivision to commit any of the following prohibited acts:

"(a) The assessment (but only to the extent of any portion based on excessive values as hereinafter described), for purposes of a property tax levied by any taxing district, of transportation property at a value which bears a higher ratio to the true market value of such transportation property than the ratio which the assessed value of all other commercial and industrial property in the same assessment jurisdiction bears to the true market value of all such other commercial and industrial property.

"(b) The levy or collection of any tax on an assessment which is unlawful under subdivision (a).

"(c) The levy or collection of any ad valorem property tax on transportation property at a tax rate higher than the tax rate generally applicable to commercial and industrial property in the same assessment jurisdiction.

"(d) The imposition of any other tax which results in discriminatory treatment of a common carrier by railroad subject to this part."

[41]*Hall v. De Cuir,* 95 U.S. 485.

[42]*Lake Shore & M. S. Ry. Co. v. Ohio ex rel Lawrence,* 173 U.S. 285.

[43]*Daniels v. United States,* 210 F. Supp. 942, 946.

[44]*Buck v. Kuykendall,* 267 U.S. 307; *George W. Bush & Sons Co. v. Maloy,* 267 U.S. 317; *Galveston Truck Line Corp. v. Allen,* 2 F. Supp. 488, aff'd 289 U.S. 708.

embracing plan of federal control over interstate motor carriage, the States may, however, in the absence of legislation by Congress dealing specifically with the subject, adopt regulations to promote safety upon the highways where the indirect burden imposed upon interstate commerce is not unreasonable,[45] and may impose a fair and reasonable nondiscriminatory tax as compensation for the use of its highways.[46]

Supremacy Clause

Where a State places a prohibition on the federal government, such as seeking authority over plans and specifications of a federal dam,[47] where State standards regulating contractors conflict with federal standards for those contractors,[48] or where a State seeks to exact a license requirement from a federal employee driving a mail truck,[49] the Supremacy Clause of the Constitution[50] may be invoked to resolve the conflict.[51] As Chief Justice Marshall said in *McCulloch v. Maryland*,[52] "It is of the very essence of supremacy to remove all obstacles to its action within its own sphere, and so to modify every power vested in subordinate governments, as to exempt its own operations from their own influence." A State thus is without power to provide the conditions on which the Federal Government will effectuate its policies.[53]

In *State of Maryland v. Wirtz*,[54] the State of Maryland filed an action, in which 25 other States intervened as parties plaintiff, asking for declaration that the 1966 amendments to the Fair Labor Standards Act insofar as they applied to employees of States were unconstitutional and seeking to enjoin enforcement of the Act against the States. A three

---

[45]*Buck v. Kuykendall*, 267 U.S. 307.

[46]*Aero Mayflower Transit Co. v. Board of Railroad Comm'rs*, 332 U.S. 495, 503. The imposition of a tax by a State was considered in *Complete Auto Transit v. Charles R. Brady, Jr. etc.*, 45 LW 4259, where the Supreme Court held that a Mississippi sales tax applied to an interstate activity—the transportation of automobiles to Mississippi from outside the State—for the privilege of doing business in the State did not violate the Commerce Clause. The *Complete Auto* case overruled *Spector Motor Service v. O'connor*, 340 U.S. 602. See also *Freeman v. Hewit*, 329 U.S. 249, in which the Court had held that a tax on the privilege of engaging in an activity in the State may not be applied to an activity that is part of interstate commerce.

[47]*Arizona v. California*, 283 U.S. 423.

[48]*Leslie Miller, Inc. v. Arkansas*, 352 U.S. 187.

[49]*Johnson v. Maryland*, 254 U.S. 51.

[50]Article 6, Clause 2.

[51]*Public Utilities Com. v. United States*, 355 U.S. 534, 544.

[52]4 Wheat. 316.

[53]*Public Utilities Com. v. United States, supra; United States v. Georgia Public Service Comm'n*, 371 U.S. 285.

[54]269 F. Supp. 826.

judge district court held that the minimum wage amendments extending coverage to, among others, nonprofessional, nonexecutive and nonadministrative employees of State public schools, hospitals and related institutions were not with respect to the minimum wage provisions unconstitutional and their enforcement against states would not be enjoined. The case is important in announcing the absolute supremacy of the power of Congress to exercise its authority to regulate commerce despite the defense of State sovereignty. The court rejected the argument that the commerce power is circumscribed by the State sovereignty. The court discussed certain cases where federal regulation under the Commerce Clause has been upheld even when applied to an essential State activity.[55]

In *United States v. State of California* the question was whether a terminal railroad owned and operated by a State for the purpose of facilitating the commerce of a port, all of the revenues of which were used to improve port facilities, could be subjected to the Federal Safety Appliance Act, so that the penalty prescribed by the Act for its violation could be recovered from the State of California. California urged these activities were not subject to the Act since the State was operating the railroad without profit, for the purpose of facilitating the commerce of the port, and was using the net proceeds of the operation for harbor improvements thus it was engaged in performing a public function in its sovereign capacity and for that reason could not constitutionally be subjected to the provision of the Act. The Supreme Court rejected the argument and sustained the imposition of the penalty. In *State of California v. United States,* an order of the Maritime Commission requiring elimination of preferential and unreasonable practices, i.e., excessive free time and non-compensatory charges for services, was held enforceable against California and the Board of State Harbor Commissioners for the San Francisco Harbor. California defended its noncompliance with the order on the ground that the Act under which it was issued had no application to public owners of wharves and piers. This question of statutory construction was decided against its contention. The court said that it was too late in the day to question the power of Congress under the Commerce Clause to regulate such an essential part of interstate and foreign trade as the activities and instrumentalities which were authorized to be regulated by the Mari-

---

[55]The principle authorities discussed, among others, were the following: *Sanitary District of Chicago v. United States,* 266 U.S. 495, 45 S. Ct. 176; *Board of Trustees of University of Illinois v. United States,* 289 U.S. 48; *Case v. Bowles,* 327 U.S. 92; *United States v. State of California,* 297 U.S. 175; *State of California v. United States,* 320 U.S. 577; *State of California v. Taylor,* 353 U.S. 553; and *Parden v. Terminal Ry. of Alabama State Docks Dept.,* 377 U.S. 184.

time Commission, whether they be the activities and instrumentalities of private persons or of public agencies.

In *State of California v. Taylor,* the question involved was whether the Railway Labor Act was applicable to the employer-employee relationship between California and its employees engaged in operating the Belt Railroad. Notwithstanding that California provided that its employees had no right to bargain collectively with it concerning terms and conditions of employment, the Railway Labor Act was held applicable on the principle that a State may not prohibit the exercise of rights which the Federal Labor Relations Acts protect. California asserted that the Act, if held to apply to it, invalidly interfered with its sovereign immunity. This argument was rejected by the court. The court held that California, by engaging in interstate commerce by rail, subjected itself to the commerce power so that Congress can regulate its employment relationships. A similar result was reached in *Parden v. Terminal Ry. of Alabama State Docks Dept.,* where Alabama's pleading of soverign immunity was rejected in a suit brought against it under the Federal Employers' Liability Act by an employee of a railroad which it owned and operated. The decision proceeded on the dual grounds that when Congress was empowered to regulate commerce, the States necessarily lost any portion of their sovereignty that would stand in the way, and that Alabama waived its protection against suit by an individual, as embodied in the 11th Amendment, by operating an interstate railroad for years after enactment of the Federal Employers' Liability Act.

Other decisions were cited by the court including *State of Colorado v. United States,*[56] where it was held that the Colorado State Board of Stock Inspection was subject to the registration requirements of the Packers and Stock Yards Act, and to the payment of penalties under the Act, the same as private persons or agencies, notwithstanding that inspection was conducted in its sovereign capacity as a State; and *N.L.R.B. v. Local 254, Building Service Employees International Union, A.F.L.-C.I.O.,*[57] holding that for purposes of the National Labor Relations Act, the Department of Education of the State of Massachusetts was a person engaged in commerce and an employee as defined in the Act.

Confiscation of Property

The Fifth Amendment to the Constitution of the United States provides that no person shall be deprived of his property without due process of law, and that private property shall not be taken for public

[56]219 F. 2d 474.
[57]376 F. 2d 131. See also *United States v. Feaster,* 330 F. 2d 671.

use without just compensation. The prohibition of this amendment has been held to constitute a restriction upon national action.[58] Its purpose is to give the same protection against Federal action as is afforded by the Fourteenth Amendment with respect to State action.[59]

The words "due process of law" means the same thing in both the Fifth and Fourteenth Amendments. In the Fifth Amendment the words constitute a limitation on Federal action, and in the Fourteenth a limitation on State action.[60] The constitutional requireemnt of due process of law, which embraces compensation for private property taken for public use, applies in every case of the exertion of governmental power. If, in the execution of any power, no matter what it is, the government, Federal or State, finds it necessary to take private property for public use, it must obey the constitutional injunction to make or secure just compensation to the owner.[61]

It cannot be doubted that the right of ownership of carrier property is entitled to the protection of constitutional guarantees.[62] Since the public power to regulate carriers and the private right of ownership coexist, and one does not destroy the other, the right of ownership of carrier property like other property rights, finds protection in constitutional guarantees.[63] Thus a regulation which is so unreasonable as to become an infringement on the right of ownership constitutes a violation of the due process clause of the Fifth Amendment.[64]

It has been settled by long practice and decisions that the right of private property may not be destroyed by the establishment of rates on a confiscatory basis.[65] Although the Constitution does not protect against all business hazards, there is a duty on the Commission to avoid establishing rates upon a basis which would compel use of property without just compensation.[66] For example, by compelling railroads to accept

---

[58]*Hunter v. Pittsburgh,* 207 U.S. 161, 176.

[59]*Tonawanda v. Lyon,* 181 U.S. 389, 391; *Cass Farm Co. v. Detroit,* 181 U.S. 395, 398; *Missouri Pacific R. Co. v. Nebraska,* 164 U.S. 403, 417.

[60]*Hurtado v. People of California,* 110 U.S. 516, 535.

[61]*Union Bridge Co. v. United States,* 204 U.S. 364, 396.

[62]*Western U. Teleg. Co. v. Pennsylvania R. Co.,* 195 U.S. 540, 570; *Atlantic C. L. R. Co. v. North Carolina Corp. Com.,* 206 U.S. 1, 20; *Missouri P. R. Co. v. Nebraska,* 217 U.S. 196, 206; *Northern P. R. Co. v. North Dakota Ex. Rel. McCue,* 236 U.S. 585, 595.

[63]*Atlantic C. L. R. Co. v. North Carolina Corp. Com.,* 206 U.S. 1, 20; *Ahnapee & W. Ry. Co. v. Akron & B. B. R. Co.,* 302 I.C.C. 265, 269.

[64]*Ahnapee & W. Ry. Co. v. Akron & B. B. R. Co., supra.*

[65]*Wilson v. New,* 243 U.S. 332.

[66]*Fifteen Percent Case,* 226 I.C.C. 41, 60; *Stonega Coke & Coal Co. v. Louisville & N. R. Co.,* 39 I.C.C. 523; *Great Northern Utilities Co. v. Public Service Comm.,* 52 F. 2d 802, 803.

inadequate compensation for the use of their freight cars, there would be imposed upon them and their properties burdens that are not incident to their engagements.[67]

The railroads, although dedicated to a public use, remain the private property of the owners, and their assets may not be taken without just compensation. Confiscation may result from a taking of property without compensation quite as well as from taking of the title. This was so held in *Chicago, Rock Island & Pacific R. Co. v. United States*,[68] where the Supreme Court said:

> . . . The use of railroad property is subject to public regulation, but a regulation which is so arbitrary and unreasonable as to become an infringement upon the right of ownership constitutes a violation of the due process of law clause of the 5th Amendment. . . . And certainly a regulation permitting the free use of property in the face of an express finding that the owner is entitled to compensation for such use cannot be regarded otherwise than as arbitrary and unreasonable.

If, as claimed, the earnings of the short lines are insufficient to enable them to make full payment of car hire costs, the Commission may be able to afford a remedy by increasing the rates, or by a readjustment of the division of joint rates. . . . It cannot be done by confiscating for their benefit the use of cars of other railroads. Short lines, as well as trunk lines, participating in joint rates, must furnish their share of the equipment. If they do not own cars, they must rent them. The Commission itself has pointed out very clearly the basis for this requirement. *Virginia Blue Ridge R. Co. v. Southern R. Co.*, 96 Inters. Com. Rep. 591, 593:

> "The per diem that complainant pays for car hire is merely equivalent to interest, depreciation, insurance, taxes, and other car-ownership costs which it would have to bear if it owned the cars used in interline traffic. The car owner incurs these costs in the first instance, and is reimbursed by complainant [a short line] through the per diem or rental charges, thereby relieving the latter of the necessity of investing in equipment for this service."

The case does not present a question of apportionment of car hire costs. The Commission undertook to determine, and did determine, what was a reasonable compensation for the use of cars, and definitely fixed that compensation on a per diem basis. It then, by its order, denied such reasonable compensation in certain cases. This is in no proper sense an apportionment of expense, but a plain giving of the free use of property for which, the Commission had concluded, the owner should be paid. . . .

[67]Cf. *Interstate Commerce Commission v. Oregon-Wash. R. & Nav. Co.*, 288 U.S. 14, 41.
[68]284 U.S. 80, 97-98.

The Question of Whether Commerce Is Interstate or Intrastate

It was held in *Baltimore & Ohio Southwestern R. Co. v. Settle,*[69] that the determinative factor as to whether a movement is interstate or intrastate is "the original and persisting intention of the shippers." In *Settle,* it was the original intention of the shippers, which was carried out, that a shipment move from the South to the freight station of Oakley, in Ohio, thence to the station of Madisonville, in Ohio. The Court, therefore, held that the second portion of the movement, from Oakley to Madisonville, was interstate. In a similar situation, where the first portion of a rail movement crossed a State boundary and the second portion occurred within a single State, *Western Oil Refining Co. v. Lipscomb,*[70] held that the second portion was interstate because the shipper intended from the beginning that the transportation should be continued beyond the first portion of the movement and to the ultimate destination. The Court wrote, at 349-49, that "this is not a case where at the time of the original billing the shipper had no purpose to continue the transportation beyond the destination then indicated."

Reconsignment, however, introduces an additional factor. As the entire Commission held in *Woodward & Son v. Southern Ry. Co.,*[71]

A general principle that the essential character of commerce, whether interstate or intrastate, for example, rather than the mere accidents of the billing, is controlling, and that a persistent original intent on the part of the shipper may be determinative of the question, has been laid down by the Supreme Court in *Chicago, M. & St. P. Ry. Co. v. Iowa*, 233 U.S. 334, *B & O.S.W.R.R. Co. v. Settle*, 260 U.S. 166, and other cases, but in none in which the principle was applied did a transit or reconsignment tariff come into play. The intent as to destination which enters into an original contract of carriage is not determinative in cases in which a tariff of either kind is in effect and expressly provides for changes in the original intent. The reconsignment tariff in this case so provides. By virtue of such a tariff, in effect when a shipment originates and duly complied with, movements to and from a reforwarding point, separate in fact, are in legal contemplation linked together in a continuous through movement, upon such rates and charges as the tariff provides therefor.

---

[69] 260 U.S. 166, 173-74. See *Leamington Transport,* 81 M.C.C. 695, 699, and *Alterman Transport Co., Inc., Extension,* 81 M.C.C. 781, holding that in determining the "essential character of the commerce," the factor most often relied on is the fixed and persisting transportation intent of the shipper at time of shipment, and such "character" is retained throughout the movement in the absence of significant interruption in the continuity thereof.

[70] 244 U.S. 346. See also *Gulf, Colorado and Santa Fe Ry. Co. v. Texas,* 204 U.S. 403.

[71] 156 I.C.C. 354, 356.

In *Woodward,* the first portion of a rail movement crossed a State boundary, the shipment was reconsigned at the original destination in the second State, and the second portion of the movement occurred entirely within that second State. The Commission held that the second portion of the movement was a continuation or extension of the preceding interstate movement, and that the entire through movement was interstate, and thus subject to the Commission's jurisdiction. Although the original intention of the shipper in *Woodward* was that the shipment cease at the original destination, and the second portion of the movement was not contemplated until the shipment arrived at the original destination, nevertheless, compliance with an effective reconsignment tariff rendered the second portion of the movement interstate.

In *Karr v. Louisville & N. R. Co.,*[72] the first portion of a rail movement crossed a State boundary, valid reconsignment instructions were given but improperly refused when the shipment reached the original destination in the second State, and so the shipment was rebilled and reshipped, instead of reconsigned, to its ultimate destination within the second State, moving entirely within that second State. The Commission found that the transactions at the original destination—the giving of valid reconsignment instructions and their improper refusal—constituted reconsignment, and held that the second portion of the movement was interstate.

In *Petroleum Products — Water — Motor — Inland Nav. Co.*[73] the Commission held that, tested by the criteria evidencing the intent of the shipper, motor transportation of petroleum products from barge line's bulk terminal storage to points in the same State over routes not crossing State borders was in intrastate commerce; and since continuity of transportation contemplated under the proposed joint rates would be broken at the storage points, subsequent motor transportation from those points to other points within the State was not subject to the Commission's jurisdiction. In *Osborne McMillan Elevator Co. v. M. St. P. & S. S. M. R. Co.,*[74] the Commission held that switching service performed by rail carriers in the movement of grain from complainant's elevator to a barge terminal, for transshipment to interstate destinations by contract barge-lines exempt from regulation under Section 303(b), although conducted exclusively within one State, was within the Commission's jurisdiction, since there was a continuing intention that the grain should be transported to other States and not come to rest at the barge terminal.

[72]151 I.C.C. 644.
[73]311 I.C.C. 219, 224-5.
[74]306 I.C.C. 155, 157-8.

In *Continental Oil Co. v. Kansas City Southern Ry. Co.*[75] the Commission said that detention of cars used to store off-specification coke pending marketing thereof was interstate in character; and complainant's contention that its original intention to ship to interstate destinations ended with discovery of the production malfunction and that, as ultimate destination of each car was unknown until shortly before final shipment, the shipments were intrastate in character at time assailed demurrage charges accrued, is without merit. The transportation began when the coke was placed in possession of the carrier, even though ultimate destination was then unknown, and ultimate disposition of the loaded cars determined the character of the transportation from the time the cars were appropriated for loading by the shipper. In *Direct Transport Inc. — Declaratory Order,*[76] the Commission held that transportation to or through a Government reservation which lies entirely within one State does not make an otherwise intrastate operation within that State subject to the Act; but where a State line passes through such reservation, if such operations extend at any point into the adjoining State the transportation is subject to the Act.

In *Monson Dray Line, Inc., Extension,*[77] the Commission said that transportation of shipments in bona fide operations between points in the same State, moving over an authorized regular route through another State, or through an authorized gateway point in another State to which the carrier is authorized to transport a given shipment from a point in a particular State, and from which it is authorized to transport the same shipment to a point in the same State, constitutes transportation in interstate commerce. In *Alabama Highway Exp., Inc. v. United States,*[78] the court held that transportation of aviation gasoline for the Government from barge terminal storage facilities in the State to other points in the same State was not interstate commerce; no shipments moved from out-of-State origins through the terminal to points beyond on a through bill of lading; shipments moved from the terminal on separate Government orders and on new and separate bills of lading.

While Section 203(a) (10) defines interstate commerce as including commerce between points in same State through another State, Section 202(b) emphasizes that the right to regulate intrastate commerce on its own highways remains in the State, and it has been held that

---

[75]311 I.C.C. 288, 289.
[76]83 M.C.C. 136, 137-8.
[77]83 M.C.C. 136, 137-8.
[78]175 F. Supp. 143, 145.

an attempted subterfuge to evade jurisdiction of a State might be inferred from a carrier's unreasonable interstate routing.[79] It was stated in the *Hudson* case (at 739) that while transportation under operating rights issued by the Commission of freight which is in continuous movement from or to points beyond a State can in no way impinge on the State's regulatory power as protected by Section 202(b), regardless of how it is routed between points in that State, it does not follow that all transportation performed pursuant to the technicalities appurtenant to such certificates is ipso facto interstate transportation, since it is possible for authority to be conceived for transportation of bona fide interstate traffic and thereafter abortively to be used to render service on intrastate traffic. It also was stated that transportation performed in an operation between points in one State through another State must not be in bad faith to escape the proper jurisdiction of the terminal State; and while circuitous interstate routing between points in a State is not in itself evidence of a bad-faith interstate operation, other factors coupled with circuitous routing may warrant such a conclusion.

The Commission said in the *Hudson* case (pp. 740-1) that since interstate routes through New Jersey utilized by defendants between considered Pennsylvania points were substantially longer than all-Pennsylvania routes normally used by intrastate carriers, no logical reason appears for such routing of intrastate traffic other than defendants' lack of intrastate authority to transport it, and officers of both defendants mitted that, in absence of any regulation of the challenged transportation, each would use the shorter or more geographically direct State routes; therefore, the only reason for such routing was so that defendants could participate in intrastate traffic purportedly under rights arising from certification issued by Commission; both defendants, by transporting freight moving between Pennsylvania points without a prior or subsequent interstate movement, attempted in bad faith to convert to interstate traffic freight which, but for such routing, was actually in intrastate commerce subject to the laws of Pennsylvania.

---

[79]*Pennsylvania Public Utility Comm. v. Hudson Transp. Co.*, 83 M.C.C. 729, 738. See *Hudson Transp. Co. v. United States* and *Arrow Carrier Corp. v. United States*, 219 F. Supp. 43, aff'd 375 U.S. 452; *Pennsylvania Public Utility Comm. v. Hudson Transp. Co.*, 88 M.C.C. 745. See also *Jones Motor Co. v. United States*, 218 F. Supp. 133, rehearing denied 223 F. Supp. 835, aff'd 377 U.S. 984, rev. *Penna. Public Utility Comm. v. Jones Motor Co.*, 89 M.C.C. 605. See also *Service S. & T. Co. v. Virginia*, 359 U.S. 171; *Service Trucking Co. v. United States*, CA No. 15249 (D. Md., 1965).

Investigations Involving State Regulation

Section 13(3) of the Interstate Commerce Act[80] provides:

"Whenever in any investigation under the provisions of this part, or in any investigation instituted upon petition of the carrier concerned, which petition is hereby authorized to be filed, there shall be brought in issue any rate, fare, charge, classification, regulation, or practice, made or imposed by authority of any State, or initiated by the President during the period of Federal control, the Commission, before proceeding to hear and dispose of such issue, shall cause the State or States interested to be notified of the proceeding. The Commission may confer with the authorities of any State having regulatory jurisdiction over the class of persons and corporations subject to this part or part III with respect to the relationship between rate structures and practices of carriers subject to the jurisdiction of such State bodies and of the Commission; and to that end is authorized and empowered, under rules to be prescribed by it, and which may be modified from time to time, to hold joint hearings with any such State regulating bodies on any matters wherein the Commission is empowered to act and where the rate making authority of a State is or may be affected by the action taken by the Commission. The Commission is also authorized to avail itself of the cooperation, services, records, and facilities of such State authorities in the enforcement of any provision of this part or part III."

Section 13(4),[81] as amended by the Railroad Revitalization and Regulatory Reform Act of 1976 (4R Act),[82] provides:

"Whenever in any such investigation the Commission, after full hearing, finds that any such rate, fare, charge, classification, regulation, or practice causes any undue or unreasonable advantage, preference, or prejudice as between persons or localities in intrastate commerce on the one hand and interstate or foreign commerce on the other hand, or any undue, unreasonable, or unjust discrimination against, or undue burdens on, interstate or foreign commerce (which the Commission may find without a separation of interstate and intrastate property, revenues, and expenses, and without considering in totality the operations or results thereof of any carrier or group or groups of carriers wholly within any State) which is hereby forbidden and declared to be unlawful, it shall prescribe the rate, fare, or charge, or the maximum or minimum, or maximum and minimum, thereafter to be charged, and the classification, regulation, or practice thereafter to be observed, in such manner as, in its judgment, will remove such advantage, preference, prejudice or discrimination. Such rates, fares, charges, classifications, regulations, and practices shall be observed while in effect by the carriers parties to such proceeding affected thereby, the law of any

---

[80]49 U.S.C. 13(3). Comparable provisions — Sections 205(f), 406(f) dealing with joint hearings and cooperation with States; and Sections 216(e) and 303(k), saving clauses as to intrastate rates and commerce.

[81]49 U.S.C. 13(4), Comparable provision — Section 406(f), saving clauses as to intrastate commerce. Sections 216(e) and 303(k).

[82]P.L. 94-210, 94th Cong., February 5, 1976, 90 Stat. 31.

State or the decision or order of any State authority to the contrary notwithstanding."

Section 13(5)[83] was added by the 4R Act. It provides:

"The Commission shall have exclusive authority, upon application to it, to determine and prescribe intrastate rates if—

"(a) a carrier by railroad has filed with an appropriate administrative or regulatory body of a State, a change in an intrastate rate, fare, or charge, or a change in a classification, regulation, or practice that has the effect of changing such a rate, fare, or charge, for the purpose of adjusting such rate, fare, or charge to the rate charge on similar traffic moving in interstate or foreign commerce; and

"(b) the State administrative or regulatory body has not, within 120 days after the date of such filing, acted finally on such change.

Notice of the application to the Commission shall be served on the appropriate State administrative or regulatory body. Upon the filing of such an application, the Commission shall determine and prescribe, according to the standards set forth in paragraph (4) of this section, the rate thereafter to be charged. The provisions of this paragraph shall apply notwithstanding the laws or constitution of any State, or the pendency of any proceeding before any State court or other State authority."

The right of the Commission to investigate and adjust interstate rates prior to any action by a State was recognized at an early date. It was held by the courts that the Commission had the power to establish intrastate rates in order to remove unjust discrimination and that it could constitutionally exercise this power at any time it found discrimination by intrastate rates against interstate commerce.

In the *Shreveport* case, *Houston, E. & W. T. R. Co. v. United States*,[84] the Supreme Court held that the antidiscrimination provisions of the I.C. Act made it unlawful for railroads to maintain intrastate rates which discriminated against interstate commerce and that the Commission was authorized to order the removal of the discrimination even though the rates had been required by State authority. In 1920, Section 13 of the I.C. Act was amended to make this power explicit under procedures prescribed for its exercise.

Section 13(4), as amended in 1958, clearly granted the Commission authority to investigate intrastate rates without awaiting State action on these rates. The 1958 amendment required the Commission, upon the filing of a petition by a carrier bringing into issue intrastate rates, to

---

[83] 49 U.S.C. 13(5).
[84] 234 U.S. 342. See also *Florida v. United States*, 282 U.S. 1994. *North Western-Hanna Fuel Co. v. United States*, 161 F. Supp. 714, 718, aff'd 356 U.S. 581.

"forthwith" institute an investigation into the intrastate rates "whether or not theretofore considered by any State agency or authority and without regard to the pendency before any State agency on authority of any proceeding relating thereto."[85] A carrier petition under the amendment was required to be considered and processed quickly by the Commission any time it was filed. This proviso was added to Section 13(4) in 1958 for the purpose of requiring the Commission to proceed promptly in protecting interstate commerce from discrimination and undue burdens caused by intrastate rates. It was added to the existing law because the Commission and the carriers had fallen into the practice of waiting for State action prior to acting under Sections 13(3) and 13(4). This is evident from the report of the House Conference Committee concerning this amendment.[86]

The 4R Act made certain changes in intrastate rate investigations and proceedings. However, the legislative history of the 4R Act indicates that Congress did not intend to diminish the Commission's authority by deleting certain language in Section 13(4)[87] and adding Section 13(5).[88] The intent of Congress appears to have been to make the Commission's authority over intrastate rates exclusive after the State has acted or after 120 days have elapsed if the State has not acted. The Commission's authority to act is postponed to ensure the State agency's ability to act on pertinent intrastate rate matters without the Commission's interference yet also to encourage prompt action by the State agency. Nevertheless, where a final decision is not rendered by the State agency within 120 days after the filing of a rate change, the Commission may act "notwithstanding the laws or constitution of any State, or the pendency of any

[85]See *Intrastate Freight Rates and Charges, 1969,* 339 I.C.C. 670, affm'd *sub nom. State of N. C. Ex Rel. North Carolina Utilities Com'n. v. I.C.C.* 347 F. Supp. 103, affm'd *sub nom. North Carolina Utilities Commission et al v. Interstate Commerce Commission, et al.,* 410 U.S. 919.

[86]See U. S. Code, Congressional and Administrative News, Volume 2, 85th Cong., 2nd Session, 1958, page 3485. In *Utah Citizen Rate Assn. v. United States,* 192 F. Supp. 12, 16-19, aff'd 365 U.S. 649, the court said that the 1958 amendment to Section 13(4) involved a matter of procedure rather than any substantive change in Congress' basic transportation policy. Addition of the words "or undue burdens on" added nothing to existing law but amounted merely to a codification of language used in prior court decisions. Similarly, the parenthetical addition, relating to the method of determination by the Commission of undue burden or discrimination cast upon interstate commerce by intrastate rates and charges, was partly a codification of prior decisional law; also the first phrase therein was merely permissive. There was nothing in the amendment inconsistent with the recognition that to rebut a prima facie presumption in favor of an order of the Commission, adjusting intrastate rates and charges found to cast an undue burden on interstate commerce, those claiming that intrastate commerce as a whole was not discriminatory could show as an affirmative matter favorable aspects of intrastate operations.

[87]49 U.S.C. 13(4).

[88]49 U.S.C. 13(5).

proceeding before any State court or other State authority." There is no basis in the new amendment or the legislative history to support the veiw that a State may now perpetuate unlawful intrastate rates simply by deciding a matter before the Commission's jurisdiction begins.

To support the conclusion that intrastate rates are unduly burdensome on interstate commerce within the meaning of Section 13(4), it must be shown that (1) existing intrastate rates are abnormally low and do not contribute a fair share of the railroads' revenue needs; (2) conditions surrounding the movement of intrastate traffic are not more favorable than those existing in interstate commerce; (3) increases in intrastate rates if ordered would yield substantial additional revenues; and (4) increases would not result in intrastate rates being unreasonable and would remove the existing discrimination against interstate commerce.[89]

In *Oregon Intrastate Freight Rates*[90] the Commission said that in a general revenue case, as distinguished from a proceeding concerning rates in detail on a specific commodity, it is unnecessary to establish for each item on each freight rate a fully developed rate case; the Commission's function in a general revenue proceeding under Section 13(4) is to determine whether the intrastate rates in issue are producing a fair proportionate share of the revenue, since increases authorized by the Commission are based on established need for additional revenues to assure adequate and efficient operation of both interstate and intrastate rail transportation; the Oregon intrastate rates, to the extent that they did not reflect those increases, failed to provide their fair share of the additional revenues needed and thus unjustly discriminated against and unduly burdened interstate commerce.

In *Idaho Intrastate Freight Rates and Charges,*[91] the Commission said that since increased operating costs, which general increases authorized by the Commission were designed to meet, were incurred on intrastate as well as interstate transportation in Idaho no more favorably than on interstate transportation in that and adjoining States, but the cost of handling intrastate traffic in local trains was substantially greater than the cost of handling interstate traffic in through trains, Idaho intrastate rates on sugar beets, and other commodities, in which the State commission declined to permit the increases, unduly burdened and discriminated against interstate commerce by failing to provide additional revenue commensurate with that provided by interstate traffic.

[89]*King v. United States*, 344 U.S. 254.
[90]311 I.C.C. 777, 783-4.
[91]309, I.C.C. 135, 137, 139, 144.

Foreign Commerce Defined

Commerce with foreign nations, the Supreme Court said, signifies transactions which, in some sense, are necessarily connected with nations, and is extraterritorial.[92] Commerce with foreign nations has also been defined by the Supreme Court as meaning commerce between citizens of the United States and citizens or subjects of foreign governments as individuals,[93] and as the transportation of persons and property between the States and foreign nations.[94]

As long ago as 1890, the Commission itself recognized that the only jurisdiction it had was that conferred by Congress. In it annual report to Congress of 1890, it said (at pp. 12-13):

> . . . A case of this nature was presented shortly after the organization of the Commission, the question being whether corporations doing an express business, and other corporations engaged in transportation by rail, but not expressly named in the act to regulate commerce and therein declared to be embraced by its provisions, were in fact embraced by implication so as to be subject to regulation by the Commission. It is very clear that no parties can, in respect to their business, be legally brought under supervision and control of a special regulating tribunal without authority of law delegated for the purpose, and had the Commission reached the conclusion that these corporations because of being auxiliary to the carriers named in the act were by implication embraced within its provisions, and therefore, subject to the regulation provided for, there would be no doubt that the matter would be open to judicial inquiry afterwards to the same extent as if no decision had been made. . . .

In *Propriety of Operating Practices — New York Warehousing,* [95] the Commission said:

> The Commission is a creature of statute, and its authority is derived from the act creating it. *New England Divisions,* 62 I.C.C. 513, affirmed, *New England Divisions* case 261 U.S. 184. Its jurisdiction is strictly statutory, and cannot be extended by implication over other subjects than those which the act defines. In *Re Express Company,* 1 I.C.C. 349. . . .

There is recognition by the courts that the Commission, as a statutory body, cannot assume powers plainly not granted. As stated in *Chicago, M., St. P. & P. R. Co. v. United States,*[96] "The Commission is

---

[92]*Veazie v. Moor,* 14 How. 568.
[93]*United States v. Holliday,* 3 Wall. 407.
[94]*Gloucester Ferry Co. v. Pennsylvania,* 114 U.S. 196.
[95]198 I.C.C. 134, 195.
[96]33 F. 2d 583, 587. See also *Palmer v. United States,* 75 F. Supp. 63; *United States v. Pennsylvania R. Co.,* 242 U.S. 208; *Interstate Commerce Commission v. Cincinnati, N. O. & T. P. R. Co.,* 167 U.S. 479; *Harriman v. Interstate Commerce Commission,* 211 U.S. 407; *United States v. Louisville & N. R. Co.,* 236 U.S. 318.

a body of limited jurisdiction. It may not directly exercise power, grant of which had been withheld by Congress. . . ."

Section 1(1) of the Interstate Commerce Act[97] makes the provisions of that Act applicable to common carriers engaged in the transportation of property by railroad "from or to any place in the United States to or from a foreign country, *but only insofar as such transportation . . . takes place within the United States.*" The language is unequivocal and its meaning is clear. The Commission has no power to regulate matters outside its own territorial jurisdiction.

While the original Act to Regulate Commerce[98] was applicable to carriers engaged in rail transportation "from any place in the United States to an adjacent foreign country," it is clear that it was not intended to give the Commission power to regulate transportation within adjacent foreign countries.[99]

The proviso in Section 1(1) reading "but only insofar as such transportation . . . takes place within the United States" was added by the Transportation Act of 1920[100] for the purpose of clarifying the understanding that the Commission was denied the power to regulate transportation within adjacent foreign countries. This is revealed by the following statement in H. Rep. No. 456, 66th Cong., 1st Sess., No. 10, 1919, p. 27:[101]

> . . . Section 400 amends the first five paragraphs of Section 1 of the Commerce Act, making minor corrections and clarifying the language in several respects, but makes no important change in policy. . . .

The limits of the Commission's authority under the statutory language was defined in numerous early decisions. Those cases consistently held that the extent of the Commission's authority in connection with transportation to an adjacent foreign country is over that portion within the confines of the United States.[102]

It is well settled also by numerous decisions since the Transportation

---

[97]49 U.S.C. 1(1).

[98]Act of Feb. 4, 1887, c. 104, Section 1, 24 Stat. 379.

[99]See 17 Cong. Rec. 3723, 3725-3726, April 22, 1886; 17 Cong. Rec. 7281, 7286, July 21, 1886; 17 Cong. Rec. 7753, July 30, 1886.

[100]Feb. 20, 1920, c. 91, Section 400, 41 Stat. 474.

[101]See 59 Cong. Rec. 888-890, Dec. 19, 1919.

[102]*International Paper Co. v. D. & H. Co.*, 33 I.C.C. 270; *Black Horse Tobacco Co. v. I.C.R.R. Co.*, 17 I.C.C. 588; *Humboldt S.S. Co. v. White Pass & Yukon Route*, 25 I.C.C. 136; *Fullerton Lumber & Shingle Co. v. B.B. & B.C. R.R. Co.*, 25 I.C.C. 376; *Good v. Great Northern Ry. Co.*, 48 I.C.C. 435; *Eastern Car Co. v. C.G. Rys.*, 51 I.C.C. 627; *Rates on Soda Ash and Other Commodities*, 28 I.C.C. 613; *The Canadian Pacific Passenger Rate Differentials*, 9 I.C.C. 71, 91; *Cist v. Michigan Central R. Co.*, 10 I.C.C. 217, 220.

Act of 1920 that the Commission has no extra territorial jurisdictional powers. This is true whether there is involved combination, proportional or joint through rates. See, e.g., *Elimination of Grand Trunk Ry. from Certain Routes*[103] (The Commission has no authority to require establishment of joint rates over Canadian routes or to prevent their cancellation.); *Atlantic Lumber Co. v. Louisville & N.R. Co.*[104] (The Commission has no authority to require changes in grouping of Canadian points.); *Clay Products Traffic Assoc. v. Akron, C & Y. Co.*[105] ("The complaint seeks joint rates to points in Canada. We are without jurisdiction to require the establishment of joint international rates. . . ."); *Peninsula Produce Exch. v. Pennsylvania R. Co.*[106] ("In the former of these cases we found the rates to certain Canadian destinations unreasonable in the past and awarded damages. We have, however, no jurisdiction to prescribe rates for the future to points in Canada and there is no evidence of record to warrant a prescription of rates to Canadian boder points applicable on traffic to Canada. No finding for the future will, therefore, be made with respect to Canadian destinations."); *Amsden v. Canadian National Rys.*[107] ("It is well settled that we are without jurisdiction to require the establishment of international joint rates."); *Animal Trap Co. of America v. New York Central R. Co.*[108] ("It is well settled that the Commission does not have authority to prescribe rates for the future on traffic from a point in the United States to a point in Canada."); *Washington Publishers' Assn. v. A.C. & H.B. Ry. Co.*[109] ("We may not prescribe joint rates for the future to Canadian points. . . ."); *Russell Fortune v. Baltimore & O.R. Co.*[110] ("We have no jurisdiction to prescribe joint rates from points in Canada to points in the United States. . . ."); *American Glue Co. v. Boston & M.R.*[111] (The Commission has no jurisdiction to prescribe rates from a Canadian origin.); *Pittston Paper Corp. v. Canadian National Ry. Co.*[112] (The Commission may not prescribe through routes or rates from points in Canada to points in the United States.);[113]

[103]15 I.C.C. 609.
[104]69 I.C.C. 3.
[105]160 I.C.C. 23, 27.
[106]160 I.C.C. 711, 723.
[107]176 I.C.C. 259, 260.
[108]229 I.C.C. 546, 547.
[109]104 I.C.C. 4, 9.
[110]177 I.C.C. 297, 298.
[111]191 I.C.C. 37, 38.
[112]165 I.C.C. 141, 144.
[113]See also *Cascade Timber Co. v. Great Northern Ry. Co.*, 172 I.C.C. 694.

Panels, Veneered, to Points in Canada[114] (The Commission is without authority to prevent Canadian lines from withdrawing from participation in joint rates or to prevent cancellation of the joint rates upon such withdrawal.); *Cutler-Hammer Mfg. Co. v. Director General*[115] (The factor of a combination rate applying over a line wholly within Canada, and not on file with the Commission, is not subject to the Commission's jurisdiction.); *Marine Engineering & Supp'y Co. v. Pacific Electric Ry. Co.*[116] (Movement at separately published rate, occurring wholly within Canada, is not subject to the Commission's jurisdiction.); *Elliott Packing Co. v. Duluth, W. & P. Ry. Co.*[117] (The Commission is without power to determine applicability or reasonableness of rates or charges from Canadian origins to the border points.);[118] *Watab Paper Co. v. Canadian N. Ry. Co.*[119] (Where a rate from a point in Canada to a destination in the United States is based on a combination of rates to and from a border point within the United States, the Commission's jurisdiction ordinarily extends only to the rate within this country.); *M. Crelinsten & Sons v. Railway Exp. Agency, Inc.*[120] (The Commission has no jurisdiction over transportation from the international boundary to Montreal.); *Gain Rates in United States and Canada*[121] (The Commission cannot compel representatives of Canadian railroads to appear before it with respect to rates between points in Canada or the conditions which govern such rates, and Canadian railways are not required by law to file tariffs with the Commission showing rates between points in Canada.); *Fruit Importers v. Atlantic Coast Line R. Co.*[122] ("We are without authority to prescribe joint rates to Montreal."),[123] *Castanea Paper Co. v. Algona Central & H. B. Ry. Co.*[124] (Assuming that undue prejudice exists in the practice of Canadian lines in according to the shipper at one point in the United States the Canadian manufacturers' scale on its inbound shipments of pulpwood while denying the like basis to the mill at another such point because that mill's products do not move over the Canadian lines, the Commission cannot correct it by a "cease and desist" order

[114]156 I.C.C. 465.
[115]88 I.C.C. 600.
[116]294 I.C.C. 276.
[117]292 I.C.C. 12, 13.
[118]See also *Western Peat Co. v. Illinois Central R. Co.*, 297 I.C.C. 273, 275.
[119]152 I.C.C. 265.
[120]201 I.C.C. 284.
[121]142 I.C.C. 755, 760.
[122]203 I.C.C. 139, 150.
[123]See also *J. R. Clogg & Co. v. Railway Exp. Agency, Inc.*, 215 I.C.C. 15, 17.
[124]177 I.C.C. 719, 729.

against the United States lines, the discrimination arising out of the action of the initiating Canadian lines.); *Bickett Rubber Prod. Corp. v. Chicago, M. St. P. & P. R. Co.*[125] (The Commission cannot prescribe a reasonable rate for future application over rail lines through Canada, as this would be asserting jurisdiction over foreign carriers and attempting to legislate regarding the regulation of transportation taking place partly outside the United States. The jurisdiction of the Commission applies only insofar as transportation takes place within the United States.). *Celon Co. v. Canadian Pac. Ry. Co.*[126] ("This Commission is without authority to require the establishment of international joint rates."); *Class Rate Investigation, 1939*[127] (Because of its limited jurisdiction the Commission is not empowered to prescribe specific through rates over differential lake-rail routes, part of which are in Canada.); *Thermoid Co., Southern Division v. Baltimore & O. R. Co.*[128] (The Commission has no jurisdiction to prescribe international rates for application partly within Canada.); *Board of Directors for Utilities v. Canadian Natl. Rys.*[129] (Where through rates assailed are combinations of rates to and from border points, the Commission has no jurisdiction over Canadian factors thereof or increases made therein.); *New York & Pennsylvania Co. v. Davis*[130] (". . . It is however, questionable whether the jurisdiction of the Interstate Commerce Commission is broad enough to include transportation occurring in a foreign country, and, indeed, the Interstate Commerce Commission has held [*Hale-Halsell Grocery Co. v. New Mexico Cent. R. Co. et al.,* 50 Interst. Com. Com's R. 262] that its jurisdiction over transportation to or from a foreign country is limited to that part of the transportation which takes place in the United States. . . ."); *Oil Country Iron or Steel Pipe, Midwest to Okla. & Tex.*[131] (The Commission's "jurisdiction extends over the transportation performed by railroads 'from or to any place in the United States to or from a foreign country, but only insofar as such transportation takes place within the United States,' under Section 1(1) of the Act."); *Citizens Gas & Coke Utility v. Canadian Natl. Rys.*[132] ("The Interstate Commerce Act, by its terms in Section 1, is applicable to transportation from or to any place in the United States, to or from

[125]163 I.C.C. 78.
[126]238 I.C.C. 407, 410.
[127]262 I.C.C. 447, 515.
[128]303 I.C.C. 743, 752.
[129]315 I.C.C. 471, 474.
[130]8 F. 2d 662, 663.
[131]332 I.C.C. 540.
[132]325 I.C.C. 527, 530.

a foreign country and to common carriers by railroad engaged in such transportation, but only insofar as such transportation takes place within the United States. Manifestly our jurisdiction must be so limited, for Congress could not confer upon us jurisdiction in respect of transportation wholly within a foreign country, and we do not have jurisdiction over rate factors in Canada. . . .[133]

In *Leamington Tranport*,[134] where a shipper manifested an original and continuing intention that traffic move without interruption from Canadian origin to United States destinations, the Commission said (p. 700) that the entire movement was that type of foreign commerce for which operating authority was required, and any portion thereof which traversed the United States was subject to full economic regulation by the Commission. The Commission said further (pp. 699-700) that Congress by amendment of Section 203(a) (11) did not intend to restrict, but rather to broaden, the scope of the Commission's jurisdiction in certain respects to embrace foreign carriers engaged in transportation in this country of shipments of foreign origin or destination.

In *Kingsway Transports — Purchase — Charles A. Kuhn Delivery*,[135] the Commission held that transportation between Detroit and points in New York of shipments moving in bond through Ontario was in foreign commerce within the meaning of Section 203(a) (11). In *Cartage Co. Extension*,[136] the Commission said that movement of import shipments of twine from a public warehouse at the port of Milwaukee, Wis., to points in Wisconsin was operation in foreign commerce subject to the Commission's jurisdiction; the shipper intended to move the twine, most of which was ordered by consignees before and during the sea voyage, through Milwaukee to final destination with as little delay as possible; the continuity of the movement was not interrupted by placing the goods in the warehouse to await customs clearance in view of the shipper's original and continuing intention to move his goods as soon as such clearances were obtained; and the fact that some twine was not sold prior to water shipment was immaterial. In *Alterman Transport Lines, Inc., Extension*,[137] the Commission said that single-State transportation of shipments that were at all times intended to move under storage-in-transit arrangements to Florida ports for export,

---

[133]See also *Kellogg Co. v. Abilene & S. Ry. Co.*, 273 I.C.C. 311; *Consolidated Mining & S. Co. of Canada v. B. & O. R. Co.*, 286 I.C.C. 313, 318; *Sulphur, Canadian Origins to East St. Louis, Ill.*, 326 I.C.C. 288, 292-293.
[134]81 M.C.C. 695, 699.
[135]85 M.C.C. 287, 300.
[136]81 M.C.C. 781, 786.
[137]81 M.C.C. 781, 786.

and that were readily identifiable prior to movement from the Florida origin, required authority from the Commission.

In *Consolidated Mining & S. Co. of Canada v. B. & O. R. Co.,*[138] a complaint was filed alleging that the applicable rail rates on lead and zinc articles from British Columbia, Canada, via routes through Portal, N.D., to points on and east of the Mississippi River and on and north of the Ohio River, were unreasonable and unduly prejudicial. The Commission was asked to require the defendant railroads to establish and maintain reasonable and non-prejudicial joint one-factor rates no higher than concurrent one-factor rates on these commodities from producing points in western United States. Canadian Pacific was willing to participate in the establishment of joint rates and, consequently, complainant maintained that the Commission's jurisdiction, insofar as the transportation takes place within the United States, was sufficient to bring about a proper adjustment of the assailed international rates. Division 2 commented (p. 317) that the "willingness or acquiescence of a foreign carrier does not and cannot provide us with jurisdiction that otherwise is lacking under the provisions of the Act. . . ." Division 2 added (p. 318) that the Commission "has jurisdiction to determine the lawfulness of these rates, insofar as the transportation takes place in the United States, and it may require the defendants subject to its jurisdiction to cease and desist from joining in the maintenance of rates that are unlawful for such transportation. . . ."

In *Conrad Fafard, Inc. v. Canadian National Rys.,*[139] a complaint was filed alleging that the rail rates charged on baled straw, in carloads, from points in Quebec and Ontario, Canada, to points in Ohio and Indiana, were unjust and unreasonable. Reparation and lawful rates for the future were sought. Canadian National appeared specially and moved that the complaint be dismissed as to that carrier for lack of jurisdiction. The shipments originated by Canadian National were interchanged with American carriers at the international boundary at Port Huron or Detroit, Michigan. The motion of Canadian National was granted, and the complaint as to that carrier was dismissed. (Canadian Pacific also was a defendant and the complaint as to that defendant was dismissed.)

Canada Packers v. A., T. & S. F.[140] and *H. K. Porter Co. v. Central Vermont R. Co.*[141] are important. It was held in *Canada Packers* that where a carrier performing transportation within the United States

[138]286 I.C.C. 313.
[139]302 I.C.C. 163.
[140]385 U.S. 182.
[141]366 U.S. 272.

enters into a joint through international rate covering transportation in the United States and Canada, the Commission does have jurisdiction to determine the reasonableness of the joint through rate and to order the carrier performing the domestic service to pay reparation in the amount by which the rate is unreasonable. There, certain railroads in the United States and their connecting carriers in Canada delivered a number of shipments of potash from New Mexico to points in Canada. The receiver was charged and paid a joint through rate which it later attacked as unreasonable in a reparation proceeding before the Commission. Finding the rate to be unreasonable, the Commission ordered reparation in the amount of the difference between the rate charged and the reasonable rate at the time the shipments were made. The railroads refused to pay part of this amount on the theory that it represented an overcharge for the Canadian portion of the trip over which they claimed the Commission had no jurisdiction. An action followed in the district court to collect the unpaid amount. On appeal from an award of reparation the court of appeals held that the Commission was without jurisdiction to determine the reasonableness of rates for transportation taking place in Canada, and, therefore, was without power to order reparation with respect to the Canadian portion of the movement. The Supreme Court reversed the decision of the court of appeals for the reason that the contrary view is one of long standing, citing among others, its prior decisions in *News Syndicate Co. v. New Central R. Co.,*[142] and *Lewis-Simas-Jones Co. v. Southern Pacific Co.*[143]

The leading case cited by the Supreme Court in support of its de-

[142]275 U.S. 179.

[143]283 U.S. 654. Initial carriers receiving property on through bills of lading for transportation to an adjacent foreign country are made liable for damage to goods occurring on the lines of connecting carriers. However, this has been done by express statutory language and not by implication. Under Section 20(11) of the Act, which requires common carriers receiving property for transportation from any point in the United States to a point in an adjacent foreign country to issue a receipt or bill of lading therefor, both the originating carrier and the delivering carrier are made liable for any loss, damage, or injury to shipments received by them for transportation. The section provides that claims may be filed with the originating or delivering carrier and the carrier with whom the claim is filed is made liable to the claimant for the full actual loss, damage, injury, regardless of whether or not the shipment was damaged while in its possession. Section 20(12) gives a carrier paying a claim the right to secure payment from the carrier responsible for the claim. Section 20(11) embodies what are commonly referred to as the Carmack and Cummins Amendments to the Act. The Carmack Amendment only imposed liability upon an initial carrier for damage to goods occurring on the lines of connecting carriers within this country. The Cummins Amendment extended this liability to initial carriers receiving property for transportation to a point in an adjacent foreign country when transported on a through bill of lading. *Mexican Light & Power Co. v. Pennsylvania R. Co.*, 33 F. Supp. 483.

cision in *Canada Packers* was *News Syndicate*. There the Supreme Court upheld a reparation order entered by the Commission upon a finding that the joint through international rate was unreasonable. The Supreme Court held that a shipper injured by having to pay unreasonable joint international rates is entitled to obtain reparation in an action filed against any one of the participating carriers. *News Syndicate* was followed in *Lewis-Simas-Jones*. There the Supreme Court also recognized jurisdiction of the Commission to award damages for unreasonable joint international rates. The case involved a joint through international rate from a point in Mexico to a point in the United States. In that case the court said (at p. 661), "The collection by a common carrier of exorbitant charges is a tort . . . and the general rule as to liability of joint tort-feasor applies where two or more connecting carriers combine to impose excessive charges for transportation over their connecting lines. . . ." The court added (pages 661-662):

> . . . While the act does not govern the joint through international rate, the demand for reparation is grounded upon the claim that the maintenance of that rate participated in by the American carrier and its violation of the act, in failing to maintain a just and reasonable rate for the transportation from the boundary to destination, operated to compel payment of the charges based on the excesive joint rate.

It is important to note that in *Lewis-Simas-Jones*, the court made it plain (at p. 660) that the Act "does not empower the Commission to prescribe or regulate" joint through international rates. It said that the Act applied to international commerce "only insofar that the transportation takes place within the United States." (The court noted that the Act "does not authorize or forbid the making of joint through international rates.")

In *Cyanamid and Cyanide from Niagara Falls*,[144] Division 4 in construing the language of the *News Syndicate* case said (p. 212):

> As we construe the language of the court quoted above we may consider the lawfulness of an international joint rate only for the ascertainment of damages sustained in consequence of the breach by the carriers subject to our jurisdiction of their statutory duty to publish a just and reasonable rate applicable to that part of the transportation within the United States. Accordingly it is our view that we are without jurisdiction to consider the lawfulness of an international joint rate for the future in either a complaint or suspension proceeding, except that we may require the carriers subject to our jurisdiction to establish and maintain for the future a just and reasonable rate applicable to that part of the transportation within the United States. We shall not require the latter, however, as in *Publication*

---

[144]151 I.C.C. 207.

of Rates Between United States and Canada, 148 I.C.C. 778, we reached the conclusion that we should not require any change in connection with the publication of rates on traffic between the United States and Canada until Congress had been afforded an opportunity to act upon recommendations concerning amendments to and changes in pertinent provisions of the act.

In *H. K. Porter,* American carriers established joint through rates on certain shipments from Canada to the United States that were lower than the rates available to other receivers of such shipments. The Commission, in finding the higher rates unjust and unreasonable, and unduly prejudicial and preferential, limited its order to transportation within the United States. The Supreme Court upheld the order. Since the order affected only the American part of the transportation, it had, as the Supreme Court emphasized, no extra-territorial effect.

The report and order of the Commission in F.D. No. 26106, *Penn Central Transportation Company Discontinuance of 34 Passenger Trains,*[145] served September 30, 1970, corrected October 15, 1970, is of interest. The report and order, served September 30, 1970, inadvertently referred to trains Nos. 14, 17, 52 and 351, as therein involved, as operating between Buffalo, New York, and Chicago, Illinois (via Canada). In the corrected order, served October 15, 1970, the Commission said:

> . . . These trains are, in fact operated between the indicated points, but the jurisdiction of the Commission was invoked in these proceedings only insofar as these trains are operated between Detroit, Mich., and Chicago, Ill. The discussion in the report makes it clear that with respect to the discontinuance proposed, consideration of these trains was limited to operations between Detroit and Chicago, and that the conclusions reached were directed to these operations only. . . .

Significantly, in Ex Parte No. 252 (Sub-No. 1), *Incentive Per Diem Charges — 1968,*[146] the Commission, in considering whether Canadian railways should be included in the incentive program under Section 1(14) (a) of the I.C. Act, said (p. 237) that it was not convinced that the inclusion of the Canadian railways "in the program on the same footing with United States carriers can as a practical or legal matter be accomplished." It added (p. 238) that Canadian railways "are subject

---

[145]This case was before the Supreme Court in No. 986, *Baker v. Pennsylvania.* The case was remanded by the Supreme Court to the district court with instructions to vacate its injunction and dismiss the action on the grounds of mootness.

[146]337 I.C.C. 217. On February 18, 1971, in *Florida East Coast Ry. Co. v. United States,* No. 70-574-Civ.-J., and *Seaboard Coast Line R. Co. v. United States,* No. 70-577-Civ.-J., the U.S. District Court for the Middle District of Florida, enjoined, annulled and set aside the Commission's order in Ex Parte No. 252 (Sub-No. 1), insofar as the same affected plaintiffs therein.

to our jurisdiction only to the extent they operate within the United States" and that they "do not file annual reports of their entire operations with us." By order served December 8, 1970, the Commission ordered that incentive per diem charges accrued on general service box cars owned by Canadian carriers be paid directly to those carriers; however, the Canadian carriers were required to retain the funds so collected in an escrow account in the United States until the further order of the Commission.

In *International Joint Rates and Through Rates*,[147] the Commission in prescribing new rules and regulations for filing and publishing both joint and combination rates over international-domestic through routes, made the following comments concerning the limits of its jurisdiction:

> Arguments concerning any possible conflicts between us and the Federal Maritime Commission are not germane. For a long time, we have regulated joint rates on traffic moving between the United States and Canada or Mexico and yet have never intruded upon the sovereignty of either of those nations. In the case of international joint rates involving countries other than Canada and Mexico we believe we can similarly exercise appropriate jurisdiction without intruding upon the jurisdiction of the Federal Maritime Commission.

> Canadian or Mexican carriers file with us, if they so desire, the tariffs establishing joint rates with our domestic carriers, and we do not thereby obtain jurisdiction over those foreign carriers. Similarly, under Section 216(c), water carriers subject to the jurisdiction of the Federal Maritime Commission file with us, if they so desire, tariffs establishing joint rates on motor-water movements between the mainland (48 States) and Alaska or Hawaii. We do not thereby obtain jurisdiction over those water carriers.

In *Canadian Pacific Limited v. United States*[148] the Canadian railroads had introduced a proposed tariff schedule for the purpose of encouraging Canadian shippers of potash to evenly distribute their shipments throughout the year and thus alleviate a shortage of hopper cars during peak potash shipping periods. The tariff was filed with the ICC "for information only." The ICC held that the tariff was inextricably intertwined with the joint through international rate and, therefore, the tariff was improperly filed without the assent of the U.S. carriers. The proposed schedule was ordered stricken from the files of the ICC. The court held that the ICC was without jurisdiction to take remedial or punitive action against the Canadian railroads for introduction of the proposed tariff schedule. It said that if in a subsequent proceeding the ICC should find that the new schedule results in an unreasonable joint

[147]337 I.C.C. 625, 632 (f'n. 6), 635 (f'n. 11).
[148]379 F. Supp. 128.

through international rate, it remains free to take corrective action such as assessing reperations from domestic U.S. carriers participating in such rate. The court made it plain that the ICC's jurisdiction is limited to holding domestic U.S. carriers responsible for reparations for past unreasonable international rates, and does not extend to direct control of the Canadian part of the transportation or to prescribing international rates for application partly within Canada and partly within the U.S.

2

Liabilities and Obligations of Carriers Subject to the Interstate Commerce Act, and Others

The Duty of a Common Carrier to Provide Transportation Service

Section 1(4) of the I.C. Act, which codifies the common law,[1] makes it the duty of every common carrier to provide and furnish transportation upon reasonable request therefor.[2]

The Commission's jurisdiction to enforce a common carrier's duty to provide and furnish transportation upon reasonable request therefor has been held to be limited when only Section 1(4) is involved.[3] However, in situations where other sections of the I.C. Act are involved in addition to Section 1(4) any jurisdictional obstacle is removed and the resolution of the Section 1(4) issue may be made by the Commission.[4]

---

[1]*American Trucking Associations, Inc. v. Atchison, Topeka & S.F. Ry. Co.*, 387 U.S. 397, 406; *Investigation into Limitation of Carrier Service on C.O.D. and Freight-Collect Shipments*, 343 I.C.C. 692, 721; *Johnson v. Chicago, Milwaukee, St. P. & P.R. Co.*, 400 F. 2d 968, 971-2.

[2]It is noted that railroads are preeminent among private instrumentalities affected with a public interest. They have acquired a unique status in our law. As expressed by the Supreme Court in *United States v. Trans-Missouri Freight Association*, 166 U.S. 290, 332-3: ". . . railways are public corporations organized for public purposes, granted valuable franchises and privileges among which the right to take . . . private property is not the least," and the business they do "is of a public nature, closely affecting almost all classes in the community . . . ." Owing a duty to the public of a very high nature, railroads cannot properly withhold essential transportation services simply because of an unwillingness on their part to provide such services.

[3]*U.S. v. Pennsylvania R. Co.*, 242 U.S. 208; *Cancellation of CRI&P & Soo Line Rates — Livestock*, 340 I.C.C. 463, 467.

[4]*Duralite Co., Inc. v. Erie Lackawanna Ry. Co.*, 339 I.C.C. 312, 314. See also *Livestock, South, Southwest, Central and Western Territories*, 346 I.C.C. 418, 434-5, 438-9; *Investigation into Limitations of Carrier Service on C.O.D. and Freight-Collect Shipments*, 343 I.C.C. 692, 721-31; *Investigation of Railroad Freight Service*, 345 I.C.C. 1223, 123-42; *Investigation into the Need for Defining Reasonable Dispatch (Perishable Commodities)*, 351 ICC 812, 824-29. Cf. *Director General v. Viscose Co.*, 254 U.S. 498.

But see F.D. No. 28412, *Winnebago Farmers Elevator Co. v. Chicago and North Western Transportation Co.*, decided March 29, 1978, where the I.C.C. held that it had jurisdiction to enforce the duty to provide adequate service under Section 1(4), and that long-standing I.C.C. precedents to the contrary are overruled.

In the past, the Commission has held that a common carrier may cease to hold itself out to transport a commodity if it proves that there is no present public need for it to transport the commodity and no reasonable prospect of such demand, particularly where the carrier would need to maintain special facilities incidental to the service.[5] In addition, the Commission has recognized that railroads may refuse to transport commodities that are proved not to be suited for common carrier rail service. The Commission has applied this exception for circuses and for goods of extraordinary value.

In *Transportation of Circuses and Show Outfits*,[6] the Commission recognized the peculiar nature of transporting circuses, including the difficulties with handling wild animals, the irregular scheduling requirements to meet show times, and the fact that circuses could not pay the much higher rates that would apply under regular freight service. In *Emporium v. New York Central Railroad Co.*,[7] the Commission upheld the railroads' refusal to accept and publish a rate for transporting silverware and goldware on the ground that these commodities "may be transported by parcel post, express companies, and steamers, and that these services are better equipped to transport commodities of high concentrated value than defendants."

The hazardous nature of a commodity is no excuse for a railroad not to transport it as a common carrier. The national interest that such commodities be transported on a reasonable and certain basis would otherwise be frustrated. A railroad must, for example, accept as a common carrier a shipment of explosives if the shipment is properly packaged in conformity with all applicable government regulations. In *Actiesselskabet Ingrid v. Central R. Co. of New Jersey*,[8] the court declared:

> A common carrier must transport freight (explosives) of this character over its lines . . .

---

[5]*Livestock, South, Southwest, Central and Western Territories*, 346 I.C.C. 418, 437.

[6]299 I.C.C. 330.

[7]214 I.C.C. 153, 154. See also Docket No. 36307, *Radioactive Materials, M-K-T*, decided Nov. 8, 1977.

[8]216 Fed. 72, 78, *cert. denied*, 238 U.S. 615.

In *Bruskas v. Railway Express Agency,*[9] it was stated:

> When the fireworks were packed and the character of the contents clearly stamped thereon as required by the Interstate Commerce Commission, the Express Company was under a legal duty to accept and transport the same. . .

In the absence of a question requiring the Commission's special competence, the courts do not hesitate to enforce the duty of a common carrier by railroad to provide transportation adequate to meet a shipper's needs on reasonable request therefor.[10]

In *Pacific Gamble Robinson Co. v. Minneapolis & St. Louis R. Co.,*[11] plaintiff shipper alleged that defendant, the only railroad operating switching facilities serving plaintiff's plant and warehouse, refused to furnish it with refrigerator cars for shipment of perishable groceries while furnishing them to other shippers in an adjacent market area. The railroad's defense was alleged intimidation by plaintiff's striking employees. The court issued a mandatory injunction on the basis that the case involved enforcement of the "plain duty" to provide service rather than a technical question calling for the Commission's expertise; such duty called for immediate action on the part of the railroad because of the threatened loss of perishable groceries, and the defense of intimidation was not borne out by the evidence.

In *Macon D. & S. R. Co. v. General Reduction Co.,*[12] the defense to refusal to provide service at the same rate as charged other shippers, was that the material tendered was not ground clay but fuller's earth. The court issued a writ of mandamus on the basis that the question

[9]172 F. 2d 915, 918. See also *Fort Worth & D.C. Ry. Co. v. Beauchamp,* 95 Tex. 496, 68 S.W. 502; *Walker v. Chicago, R.I. & P.R. Co.,* 71 Iowa 658, 33 N.W. 224. Insofar as air carriers are concerned see *Air Line Pilots Ass'n, et al. v. C.A.B.,* 516 F. 2d 1269, where the court denied petitions to review a Board order rejecting "embargo notices" filed by several carriers directed against the transportation of "hazardous materials." The court agreed with the Board that its embargo regulations only apply in situations in which a carrier is "temporarily unable" to transport freight and were inapplicable to the carriers' blanket refusal to carry hazardous materials.

[10]*Anderson v. Chicago, M. & St. P. Ry. Co.,* 175 N.W. 246; *Illinois Central R. Co. v. River & Rail Coal & Coke Co.,* 150 S.W. 641. The words "common carrier by railroad" as used in the Interstate Commerce Act, mean one who operates a railroad as a means of carrying for the public, not one whose shipments are carried by a railroad. *United States v. American Railway Express Co.,* 265 U.S. 425, 432-33. See also *Express Service at Borden, Campbellsburg, and Pekin, Ind.,* 286 I.C.C. 303, 306; *Oyler & Son v. American Ry. Express Co.,* 83 I.C.C. 160, 162; *Freight, All Kinds, L.C.L. Unitized Charges—U.S.A.,* 326 I.C.C. 594, 624; *In Re Express Rates, Practices, Accounts, and Revenues,* 24 I.C.C. 380; *Southeastern Express Co. v. American Ry. Express Co.,* 78 I.C.C. 123, 129-30.

[11]83 F. Supp. 860.

[12]44 F. 2d 499, cert. denied 283 U.S. 821.

was one "so plain as to require no action by the Commission," since the question was not one "involving rate making considerations," but whether the material, as a matter of common understanding, constituted "fuller's earth," and was of no general importance.

In *United States v. Louisville & N.R. Co.*,[13] the Louisville and Nashville R. Co. and Southern Railway Co. published joint and through routes with respect to coal car service from points that included plaintiff's location to southwestern territory and provided coal car service to other mines located in the same territory and transportation to the same destinations as those shipped to by plaintiff. But L&N, which owned the line adjacent to shipper's mines, and Southern, the line-haul carrier, jointly refused to provide car service to plaintiff's mines because of a dispute between them as to which had the duty to furnish cars. The court issued a writ of mandamus compelling the two to furnish car service, on the basis of their joint duty as common carriers, and deemed it unnecessary that the intercarrier dispute first be resolved. (Compare, *Rex Coal Co. v. Cleveland, C.C. & St. Louis Ry. Co.*,[14] in which refusal to assume jurisdiction was based on lack of a question involving a "plain duty . . . independent of administrative action," where plaintiff's claimed discrimination was railroad's refusal to furnish empty coal cars at, and transport loaded cars to, plaintiff's mines, where such mines were connected by plaintiff's own spur line to defendant's main line.)

Section 23 of the I.C. Act[15] provides that the writ of mandamus "shall be cumulative" to other remedies provided by the I.C. Act. The remedy is available on a satisfactory showing of violation of duty, irrespective of the availability of other remedies before the Commission, or elsewhere. "A shipper is not to be required to undertake an expensive litigation before the Commission in each disputed shipment in order to secure its acceptance at the proper published rate."[16] The *General Reduction Co.* case states:

> [Section 23] gives the court the power in a case like this, and in an unusual degree, for the mandamus is expressly declared to be cumulative of other remedies, and consequently not excluded by them. Assuming that a remedy under the Interstate Commerce Act may always be had before the Commission, even a more complete and satisfactory one, and that another remedy exists by paying the rates demanded and suing in court for overcharge, yet the fact remains that, by an amendment of the Act,

[13]195 Fed. 88 (Com. Ct.).
[14]9 F. Supp. 179. See also *Brownsville Navig. Dist. v. St. Louis, B. & M. Ry. Co.*, 91 F. 2d 502.
[15]49 U.S.C. 23.
[16]*Macon, D. & S. R. Co. v. General Reduction Co.*, *supra*, at p. 501.

Congress has provided mandamus as an expressly additional remedy. The rules as to the supplemental character of the remedy by mandamus, which apply elsewhere, have no place in this statute. (Id. at pp. 501-502).[17]

At common law, common carrier railroads were obligated to provide adequate transportation service on reasonable request therefor. As part of this duty, the railroad was expected to inform itself of shipper needs so that it could invest in sufficient transportation facilities to meet these needs.[18] A shipper states a cause of action, enforceable in state courts, if it alleges failure to provide cars on reasonable request.[19] Certain defenses have been recognized as available to the railroad at common law. These include such "extraordinary conditions that render performance impractical," such as a strike of railroad employees[20] and a sudden demand for cars, creating a temporary car shortage, which is a sufficient defense only if the railroad has adopted a rule for distribution of available cars without discrimination (the reasonableness of which is a question for the expertise of the Commission), or if a rule has not been "adopted," or the adopted rule is not followed, if distribution is without undue discrimination.[21]

Whether a defense is one of the relevance of which is peculiarly within the province of the Commission, is determined in Section 23 proceedings according to the same tests as in proceedings brought under Section 9 of the I.C. Act.[22] Thus in *Rex Coal Co. v. Cleveland, C., C. & St. L. Ry. Co.*,[23] in a Section 23 proceeding, railroad's defense held

---

[17]Section 22 provides that "nothing in this part contained shall in any way abridge or alter the remedies now existing at common law or by statute, but the provisions of this part are in addition to such remedies." See *Riss & Company v. Association of American Railroads*, 178 F. Supp. 438; *Consolidated Freightways v. United Truck Lines*, 330 F. 2d 522, cert. denied 359 U.S. 1001; *Hewitt v. New York, N.H. & H. R. Co.*, 29 N. E. 2d 641; *Pensick & Gordon, Inc. v. California Motor Express*, 323 F. 2d 769, cert. denied 375 U.S. 984; *Carr v. Maine Cent. R.R.*, 102 Atl. 532; *Montgomery Ward & Co. v. Northern Term. Co.*, 128 F. Supp. 475. As stated in the *Montgomery Ward* case, *supra*, at 496:
"The congress has never shown a disposition to destroy these original remedies or to repudiate the common law of the respective states relating to carriers. The common law remedies for breach of the obligations thereof were preserved by positive mandate and the statutory remedial devices were made additions thereto. Thus countenance was given to the basic principles then prevalent in the state systems and nationally observed in the public interest. The constant course of legislation has reiterated the common law responsibility of the carriers. It still subsists . . ."
[18]*Illinois Central Railroad Co. v. River & Rail Co. & Coke Co.*, 150 S.W. 641; *Anderson v. Chicago, M. & St. P. Ry. Co.*, 175 N.W. 246.
[19]*Ibid.*
[20]*Illinois Central Railroad Co. v. River & Rail Co. & Coke Co.*, *supra*.
[21]*Anderson v. Chicago M. & St. P. Ry. Co.*, *supra*.
[22]*Macon, B. & S. R. Co. v. General Reduction Co.*, 44 F. 2d 499.
[23]9 F. Supp. 179.

to make the case appropriate for Commission expertise was that its failure to furnish empty coal cars at, and transport full coal cars to, plaintiff's mines, over plaintiff's spur line, was to avoid according plaintiff an undue preference or a service not in railroad's tariffs. Similarly, Commission expertise is appropriate where the case raises questions falling within the Commission's rate making powers.[24] Because a defense raises a possible legal justification does not in itself deprive the court of jurisdiction under Section 23.[25]

The defense of weight and speed restrictions does not raise "technical" questions solely within the Commission's expertise and is not, at common law or under Sections 1(11) and 3(1), a legally sufficient one. A carrier has a duty at common law to maintain its tracks and other structures in order to provide service, on reasonable request, to shippers on its lines. This is necessarily implied in the duty of a railroad at common law "to provide itself with the instrumentalities and facilities necessary to carry on the business for which it is organized."[26] The duty to maintain cars so as to be able to provide car service answering shipper needs is implied in the duty to maintain a supply of cars sufficient to meet peak as well as through demand periods of shippers.[27]

The duty to maintain tracks in serviceable condition is implied in Section 1(11) of the Act: (See also Section 1(12) of the Act.)

> It shall be the duty of every carrier by railroad subject to this chapter to furnish safe and adequate car service and to establish, observe and enforce just and reasonable rules, regulations, and practices with respect to car service; and every unjust and unreasonable rule, regulation and practice with respect to car service is prohibited and declared to be unlawful.

There is no Commission-implemented policy applied in other than abandonment proceedings under Section 1a of the I.C. Act of excusing the duty to maintain tracks in serviceable condition on the grounds that exercise of such duty would entail substantially greater costs, because of previous dereliction, than ordinary maintenance costs. The Commission has indicated that it will not allow its jurisdiction to be evaded by a railroad's voluntary act. *Oregon Short Line R. Co. — Abandonment*[28] involved the question whether a line proposed to be abandoned was a "branch" line for which application under prior Section 1(18) was required, or a "spur" line over the abandonment of which the Commission

---

[24]See, e.g., *Macon, B & S. R. Co. v. General Reduction Co.*, *supra.*
[25]*Brownsville Navigation Dist. v. St. Louis, B. & M. Ry. Co.*, 91 F. 2d 502.
[26]*Anderson v. Chicago, M. & St. P. Ry. Co.*, *supra*, at pp. 251-252.
[27]See *Illinois Central R. Co. v. River & Rail Co. & Coke Co.*, *supra.*
[28]267 I.C.C. 633.

had no jurisdiction (prior Section 1(22)). The basis for railroad's claim that the line was a "spur" was that it had lately reduced service to points on such line, so that what had been a regular was now an irregular service. The Commission assumed jurisdiction, stating (at p. 635):

> If a carrier by voluntary reduction of service, with or without the approval of a State Commission, achieves the status of a particular line, our jurisdiction could be defeated entirely. Once having assumed a common carrier obligation subject to the jurisdiction of this Commission with respect to a particular line of railroad, that obligation remains until appropriate authority for abandonment is obtained.

Similarly, it would defeat both the policy of Sections 1(11) and 3(1), and a court's jurisdiction under Section 23, if a carrier could contend that the costs of righting previous derelictions of duty might create excusable circumstances, which it is the Commission's province to pass on. Court decisions imply that the costs to the railroad of fulfilling its duties as a common carrier is not a relevant consideration with respect to issuance of a writ of mandamus.[29]

The common law duty to provide car service on reasonable request, discussed *supra,* includes those "shippers located on branch or lateral lines of a railroad, and [such shippers] are entitled to the same kind of treatment as accorded to those whose business is on the main line of the railroad."[30]

By Sections 1(11) and 3(1) of the I.C. Act, Congress has made the common law duty to provide service on reasonable request, without undue discrimination, to all shippers, in the absence of the narrow context of abandonment, a duty of national concern, enforceable by a writ of mandamus under Section 23.[31] Therefore, whether the line falls within Section 1a, or outside of the context of abandonment, is immaterial. Even if the issue of "spur" versus "branch" line were relevant, such issue does not present a "technical" question requiring the Commission's expertise. Although in court review of Commission decisions, the benefit of the prior determination of the Commission with respect to this issue is required, it has been held that the courts have the "final say."[32] The question is a mixed one of law and fact.[33] Both the policy bases and the

---

[29]Cf. *Pacific Gamble Robinson Co. v. Minneapolis & St. L. R. Co.,* 83 F. Supp. 860; *United States v. Louisville & N. R. Co.,* 195 Fed. 88 (Com. Ct.); *Brownsville Navigation Dist. v. St. Louis, B. & M. Ry. Co., supra.*

[30]*Chicago, R. I. & P. Ry. Co. v. Sims,* 256 S.W. 33. See also Section 1(11) and 3(1), which apply to the most remote shippers on railroad's lines.

[31]See, e.g., *United States v. Louisville & N.R. Co.,* 195 Fed. 88 (Com. Ct.).

[32]See *City of Yonkers v. United States,* 320 U.S. 685; *United States v. State of Idaho,* 298 U.S. 103.

[33]*United States v. State of Idaho, supra.*

objective indices, have been set forth in numerous court and Commission decisions.[34]

The I.C. Act (Section 216(b)) imposes upon common carriers by motor vehicle the clear and unmistakable duty to provide adequate service, equipment, and facilities for the transportation of property in interstate or foreign commerce within the scope of their holding out to the public, and they are obligated to accept and transport all freight offered to them in accordance with the provisions of their tariffs. This duty is almost an absolute one.[35]

The Commission takes the position that if the public is to be adequately protected, common carriers must be held accountable for their performance. Certain occurrences, such as the intervention of acts of God and the common enemy, historically have been considered as appropriate excuses for the failure of common carriers to provide service indiscriminately. Other occurrences such as strikes, riots, or other disturbances attended by violence or such imminent threats thereof as to constitute the likelihood of damages to the carrier's employees or equipment, or rendering the operation of its vehicles impossible, are given consideration as possibly proper excuses for the refusal or failure of a carrier to discharge its duty to accept and transport. In all instances where the failure to provide service is claimed to be excusable the burden is upon the carrier to show that it did everything in its power to fulfill its obligations to the public and was prevented from doing so by circumstances beyond its control.

Self-Help Suits by Motor Carriers

Section 222(b) (2) of the Interstate Commerce Act[36] provides:

> If any person operates in clear and patent violation of any provisions of Section 303(c), 306, 309, or 311 of this title, or any rule, regulation, requirement, or order thereunder, any person injured thereby may apply to the district court of the United States for any district where such person so violating operates, for the enforcement of such section, or of such rule, regulation, requirement, or order. The court shall have jurisdiction to enforce obedience thereto by a writ of injunction or by other process, mandatory or otherwise, restraining such person, his or its officers, agents, employees, and representatives from further violation of such section or of such rule, regulation, requirement, or order; and enjoining upon it or them obedience thereto. A copy of any application for relief filed pursuant to

---

[34]See, e.g., *Atlanta & St. Andrews Bay Ry. Co., supra; United States v. State of Idaho, supra.*
[35]*Galveston Truck Line Corp. v. Ada Motor Lines, Inc.,* 73 M.C.C. 617, 626.
[36]49 U.S.C. 322(b) (2).

The Congressional concern with eliminating delay which prevents innocent parties from securing prompt and effective protection was manifest in the 1965 amendment. Thus, in discussing the amendment increasing the civil penalties, the House Report appropriately notes that: "Under existing law, procedures for dealing with certain motor carrier violations are often slow and cumbersome, and frequently ineffective." 1965 U.S. Code Cong. & Adm. News, Vol. 2, at p. 2929. Certainly one way of securing prompt and effective protection for innocent persons injured by the clearly illegal operations of other carriers is to give the injured persons the right to apply for injunctive relief independently of any Commission proceedings. § 322(b) (2) accomplishes this by allowing injured person to enjoin "clear and patent" violations.

Not only is a remedy provided therein, the words "clear and patent" are judiciously used to indicate jurisdiction separate and apart from the ICC's primary jurisdiction. Thus the House Report notes that, ". . . The words 'clear and patent' are used and are intended as a standard of jurisdiction rather than as a measure of the required burden of proof." 1965 U.S. Code Cong. & Adm. News, Vol. 2, at p. 2931. In order to regain primary jurisdiction of the controversy and also to prevent the use of § 322(b) (2) to harass carriers legitimately operating, the ICC may take jurisdiction of the matter under § 322(b) (3) and stay further action in the District Court. See 1965 U.S. Code Cong. & Adm. News, Vol. 2, at p. 2943. Thus it is clear that the court below did have jurisdiction of the ICC because while the ICC has intervened, it has not sought to stay under § 322(b) (3).

In passing Section 222(b), Congress was careful to ensure that matters formerly within the jurisdiction of the Commission remained so. This was accomplished by limiting district court jurisdiction to "clear and patent volation" as a standard of jurisdiction rather than a measure of the required burden of proof, and by providing in Section 222(b) (3) that the Commission can assure primary jurisdiction of the controversy by notifying the district court that it intends to consider the matter in a proceeding before the Commission. Upon the Commission's filing of such notice the district court must stay the judicial proceedings pending disposition of the proceeding before the Commission.[38]

The purpose for limiting district court jurisdiction to "clear and patent" violations, and for empowering the Commission, which may appear as a right in any Section 222(b) (2) action, to assume jurisdiction of a matter by notifying the district court that it intends to do so, was explicitly to provide for Commission determination of matters within its primary jurisdiction. Through these limitations Congress ensured that the Commission, rather than the courts, would initially determine important questions not clearly within the regulated areas.

[38]*Ibid.*, at p. 716. See 1965 U.S. Code Cong. & Admn. News, Vol. 2, at pp. 2930-31.

Loss and Damage

The applicable provisions of the Interstate Commerce Act relating to carrier liability for loss and damage are Sections 20(11)[39] and 20(12).[40]

The provisions of Sections 20(11) did not change the common-law doctrine in respect to a carrier's liability for loss occurring on its own line. Under common law a carrier, although not an absolute insurer, was liable, without proof of negligence, for all damage to goods transported by it, subject to certain exceptions.[41] Damage caused by the act of God, the public enemy, inherent, vice or nature of the property, the public authority, and shipper's act or default are recognized exceptions to that rule, conversely, and in absence of a contrary contract, a common carrier's liability for damage is limited to that occurring on its portion of the transportation.[42]

With respect to Section 20(11), the Supreme Court said in *Secretary of Agriculture v. United States:*[43]

It is conceded that § 20(11) codifies the common-law rule making a carrier liable, without proof of negligence, for all damage to the goods transported by it, unless it affirmatively shows that the damage was occasioned by the shipper, acts of God, the public enemy, public authority, or the inherent vice or nature of the commodity. . . .

To establish a carrier's common law liability for damages, claimant need only show initially the carrier's receipt of the property in apparent good order, its release thereof in damaged condition, and the amount of damages, thus establishing a prima facie case; the carrier then has the burden of proving otherwise or of showing that damage was due to an excepted cause.[44]

In *Missouri Pacific Railroad Company v. Elmore & Stahl,*[45] the Supreme Court said:

Accordingly, under federal law, in an action to recover from a carrier for damage to a shipment, the shipper establishes his prima facie case when he shows delivery in good condition, arrival in damaged condition, and

---

[39]49 U.S.C. 20(11). The provision is applicable under Sections 219 and 413.
[40]49 U.S.C. 20(12). The provision is applicable under Sections 219 and 413.
[41]*Helm's Express, Inc. v. United States,* 186 F. Supp. 521, 522.
[42]*United States v. Mississippi Valley Barge Line Co.,* 285 F. 2d 381, 388. See also *United States v. Reading Co.,* 289 F. 2d. 7, 9; Bills of Lading, 52 I.C.C. 671, 679; *Chesapeake & O. R. Co. v. Thompson Mfg. Co.,* 270 U.S. 416, 421-23; *Adams Express Co. v. Croninger,* 226 U.S. 491, 509; *Hall & Long v. Railroad Companies,* 13 Wall. 367, 372.
[43]350 U.S. 162, 165-66, f'n. 9.
[44]The prima facie showing of delivery of goods in good condition is made through a bill of lading, executed by a carrier, containing a recital to that effect.
[45]377 U.S. 134, 138.

the amount of damages. Thereupon, the burden of proof is upon the carrier to show both that it was free from negligence and that the damage to the cargo was due to one of the excepted causes relieving the carrier of liability. *Galveston, H & S. A. R. Co. v. Wallace*, 223 U.S. 481; *Chicago & E. I. R. Co. v. Collins (Products) Co.*, 249 U.S. 186; *Chesapeake & O. Ry. Co. v. A. F. Thompson Mfg. Co.*, 270 U.S. 416, 420-423; *Thompson v. James G. McCarrick Co.*, 5 Cir., 205 F. 2d 897, 900.

Thus once the shipper has proved a prima facie case, the burden of proof shifts to the carrier and remains there.

The *Stahl* case was applied in reaching the same conclusion in *L. E. Whitlock Truck Service, Inc. v. Regal Drilling Company*,[46] the court saying:

> Thus the Carmack Amendment codifies the common law rule of the carrier's liability, and the federal law applies. *Missouri Pacific R.R. Co. v. Elmore & Stahl*, 84 S. Ct. 1142 (1964); *Secretary of Agriculture v. United States, supra.* The Supreme Court has held that a carrier is not an absolute insurer, but is liable if the shipper makes a prima facie case and the carrier does not meet its burden to show both its freedom from negligence and that the loss was due to one of the causes excepted by the common law rule. The cases involving perishable goods are not distinguished from those where durable goods are transported. *Missouri Pacific R. R. Co. v. Elmore & Stahl, supra.*

The development of the presently applicable law on loss and damage claims was discussed by the Commission in *Loss and Damage Claims*[47] as follows:

> *Development of the presently applicable law.*—When the American Colonies inherited the common law of England, the body of principles included even then the rigid law governing the liability of common carriers. At the same time, this country simultaneously inherited many of the schemes carriers had conceived from time to time in an effort to limit their strict liability for loss and damage to cargo. Essentially, however, the rationale of a famous jurist. Lord Holt, has remained as a guiding light in determining carrier responsibility for loss or damage. In his often-quoted[48] ruling on bailments in the celebrated case of *Coggs v. Bernard*, 1 Smith's Leading Cases 369 (8th ed. 1885), Lord Holt there stated:
>
> > ° ° °The law charges this person thus intrusted to carry goods, against all events, but acts of God, and the enemies of the King. For though the force be never so great, as if an irresistable multitude of people should rob him, nevertheless he is chargeable. And this is a politick establishment, contrived by the policy of the law, for the safety of all persons,

[46]333 F. 2d 488, 491.
[47]340 I.C.C. 515, 520-23.
[48]The Commission has previously quoted the famous language of Holt when dealing with questions pertaining to carrier liability for claims. See *Bills of Lading*, 52 I.C.C. 671, 679.

the necessity of whose affairs oblige them to trust these sorts of persons, that they may be safe in their ways of dealing; for else these carriers might have an opportunity of undoing all persons that had any dealing with them, by combining with thieves, & c., and yet doing it in such a clandestine manner as would not be possible to be discovered. And this is the reason the law is founded upon in that point.

Despite this original clarity, however, the claims situation has since tended to become quite complex. The first of these complications seems to have appeared when the courts of the several States began to hand down decisions that were greatly dissimilar in their interpretations and applications of the common law. Thus, in a relatively short time, there developed great chaos in the transportation industry which increased even more as the industry began to expand. Any attempt then to determine common carrier liability on an interstate shipment was indeed a confusing and frustrating experience.

The more general rule, however, insofar as common carriers were concerned, seems at this point of time to have been that such carriers could not contract away or in any manner limit their liability for negligence; that they could by contract limit their liability as insurers of goods transported by them but that a consideration (usually in the form of a reduced rate) was required; and that a mere notice or printing on the face or back of a receipt was insufficient to bar a shipper's recovery for the full value of goods involved. Cf. *Railroad Co. v. Manufacturing Co.*, 83 U.S. (16 Wall.) 318 (1872); and *Railroad Co. v. Lockwood*, 84 U.S. (17 Wall.) 357 (1873).

The original Act to Regulate Commerce, enacted February 4, 1887, made no mention of a carrier's liability for loss and damage to the cargo transported. The statute also did not contain at the time of its initial adoption the provisions which conferred upon the Federal courts jurisdiction to decide controversies over claims for loss and damage arising out of interstate shipments. The later granting of that power to the Federal court system, however, failed to eliminate attempts by carriers to restrict their liability by various means. The Congress, therefore, included in the Hepburn Act of 1906 what is commonly called the Carmack Amendment (34 Stat. 595). This amendment was brought about, in part at least, by the conflict in judicial decisions as to the extent of the liability of the initial carriers on a through joint-line movement and the inconvenience to which shippers were subjected in proceeding against the intermediate or delivering carrier. The Carmack Amendment provided a uniform standard of liability for railroads and transportation companies and required them to issue bills of lading; it held them accountable for all damage to a shipment, including injuries that occurred beyond the line of the issuing carrier; and it also provided that no contract, receipt, rule, or regulation could exempt carriers from liability for the full actual loss sustained by the owner of the goods tansported.

Further complications in the processing of claims against carriers, however, arose when the Supreme Court held in *Adams Express Co. v. Croninger*, 226 U.S. 491, 509-510 (1913), that a carrier could under the

Carmack Amendment "by a fair, open, just and reasonable agreement limit the amount recoverable by a shipper in case of loss or damage to an agreed value made for the purpose of obtaining the lower of two or more rates of charges proportioned to the amount of the risk°°°." Following the *Croninger* case and other similar court decisions, many railroads began to publish reduced rates based on agreed values and prohibitively high rates based on actual values of commodities shipped. The net result of this was that shippers had no effective choice of rates and were denied full and fair recovery for shipments lost or damaged in transit.

The Congress unsuccessfully tried to correct the effects of the *Croninger* decision when in 1915 it enacted the law which came to be known as the First Cummins Amendment (38 Stat. 1197). That legislation provided that a common carrier was liable for the full loss, damage, or injury caused by it or any connecting carrier regardless of any agreement for a limitation of liability or value. The true objects and purposes of the Congress did not seem to materialize and so, in 1916, by the adoption of the Second Cummins Amendment (39 Stat. 441), the law was supplemented and carriers were authorized to limit their liability only by publishing released rates approved by this Commission. The purpose of the Second Cummins Amendment was, as stated in the report of the Senate Committee on Interstate Commerce: "°°°to restore the law of full liability as it existed prior to the Carmack Amendment of 1906°°°." Although there have been minor revisions from time to time since then, the law of full liability as it existed prior to the Carmack Amendment in 1906 has been in effect, and we have had the power, albeit indirect and limited (and quite sparingly utilized), to influence the amount of damages recoverable in claims when full liability is not imposed. Cf. *Released Rate Rules—National M. Freight Classification*, 316 I.C.C. 499, 508-509 (1962).

The substance of section 20(11) of the act, then, as it now applies to carriers[49] other than those by water (which will be considered next), represents a restatement of the common law rule that a common carrier is ordinarily a virtual insurer against loss, damage, or injury to property it accepts for transportation, and that only this Commission has the authority to modify this general rule by granting partial exemptions from full liability in cases where the applicable rates depend upon and vary with the declared or agreed values of the goods to be transported (released rates). Our exercise of this discretionary authority is conditioned on our finding that the released rates proposed are just and reasonable under all the circumstances.

Pursuant to section 20(11) of the statute, rail and motor carriers and freight forwarders are thus strictly accountable for the full actual loss or damage resulting from the transportation of property. The liability of water carriers, however, is not established by section 20(11); rather, that liability is primarily determined by the Harter Act (46 U.S.C. § 190-196, and 46 U.S.C. 181-184,

---

[49]The provisions of section 20(11) and related provisions in part I of the act are made applicable to motor carriers and freight forwarders by sections 219 and 413, respectively.

187), which generally limits or relieves completely in certain situations the liability of water carriers for loss or damage. For example, water carriers are not accountable for loss or damage due to faults or errors of navigation or management of the vessel, dangers of the sea, or from attempting to save life or property at sea. 46 U.S.C. § 192. Nor are such carriers liable for loss or damage due to fire to or on board the vessel unless the fire is by the design or neglect of the water carrier. 46 U.S.C. § 182. Obviously, however, water carriers are not relieved of all liability for loss or damage to property. They are still generally held accountable under the laws of negligence, 46 U.S.C. § 190; and they have a duty properly to handle and store property and to provide a seaworthy vessel and crew. 46 U.S.C. §§190, 191.

Although the liability of water carriers thus appears to be somewhat less than the strict accountability of rail and motor carriers and freight forwarders and is not governed by the Interstate Commerce Act, these carriers do, of course, have loss and damage claims filed against them and must process and settle such claims. It follows that, when operating in interstate or foreign commerce, and otherwise subject to the provisions of the Interstate Commerce Act, these water carriers have a duty to establish reasonable rules and regulations pertaining to the processing of loss and damage claims.

✿   ✿   ✿

Although the liability of a common carrier under the present law is effectively that of an insurer against the loss of or damage to property received for transportation, there are a few limited exceptions to this comprehensive liability. Carriers are not liable for an act of God, the public enemy, the inherent nature of the property shipped, the act of the shipper, or an act or mandate of public authority. Inasmuch as common carriers are liable as carriers and bailees, they are fully responsible for the consequences of their own negligence or want of skill and also for whatever else may happen (save the above exceptions and those applicable only to water carriers) to the property while it is in their possession. The rigid liability thus imposed may not arbitrarily or unilaterally be avoided by the carrier, but it may be limited for a consideration provided we give our prior approval under the released rates provision of section 20(11) of the act. . .

To establish the carrier's liability, it is necessary only for the claimant to show the carrier's receipt of the shipment in apparent good order, and the delivery or release of the shipment by the carrier in damaged condition. This being shown, the prima facie case is established and the burden is on the carrier to prove that the shipment was not delivered in good order, that it was delivered by it in good condition, or that the excepted causes were applicable, and it was free of negligence.

To recover for damages to goods in shipment there must be compliance with the provision in the bill of lading that the claim must be filed in writing with the carrier within a specified time after delivery; a verbal claim is not sufficient. That the carrier had actual notice of the damaged condition of the goods does not excuse the filing of the written claim; a carrier may not waive, or be estopped to assert, the requirements of bill of lading.[50]

Though the full actual loss occasioned when properties are damaged in transit by a carrier is usually determined by reference to the standard of market value of the damaged property at destination compared to market value of the property in an undamaged condition, the change in market value is not itself the statutory liability imposed, but is in most instances the obvious and fair method of determining actual loss. The nature of the property damaged may clearly indicate that change in market value does not compensate for actual loss, however, as in the case of household goods, heirlooms, and the like, which have a peculiar but recognized utility or intrinsic value to the owner; in such case the law will lean heavily on the subjective value to the owner excluding any fanciful or unduly sentimental valuation.[51] In an action against a carrier for damage to goods in shipment, the claimant is entitled to recover not only the value of the goods shipped but also the necessary expenses incurred in determining marketability and salvage value of the shipment.[52]

Released Rates

Although Section 20(11) provides that carriers shall be liable for the full, actual loss, damage or injury to property delivered to them, a carrier's liability may be limited by agreement upon a released value of a shipment, i.e., the value declared by the shipper.[53] Because the carrier's liability is limited and, in effect, the shipper becomes a co-insurer of the shipment, released value rates are lower than unreleased rates.

Express authorization of the Commission however is required under Section 20(11) for carriers to establish and maintain released value rates.

For years common carriers have sought, by provisions in shipping contracts, bills of lading, and tariff publication to limit their common law liability as insurers against loss or damage to property received by them for transportation. Prior to specific legislation, these efforts were largely unrestrained. One method was the so-called "release" whereby rates are maintained dependent upon the value of the property as declared by the shipper or as agreed upon by the shipper for the purpose of determining the rate to be applied. Upon such declaration or agreed

---

[50]*B. A. Walterman Co. v. Pennsylvania R. Co.*, 295 F. 2d 627, 628.
[51]*Olsen v. Railway Express Agency Inc.*, 295 F. 2d 358, 359.
[52]*Campbell Soup Co. v. Darling Transfer, Inc.*, 193 F. Supp. 408, 409.
[53]*Strickland Transportation Company v. United States*, 334 F. 2d 172, 174-175.

value, a shipper was generally estopped from collecting or receiving more than the value declared or agreed upon in case of loss or damage.

By adoption of the "Carmack amendment"[54] to the I.C. Act Congress provided that a common carrier receiving property for transportation in interstate commerce should issue a receipt or bill of lading and be liable to the lawful holder thereof for any loss, damage, or injury to such property caused by it or any common carrier to which such property might be delivered, or over whose lines such property might pass, and declared that no contract, receipt, rule, or regulation should exempt such common carrier from the liability thereby imposed. Problems developed in the interpretation and application of the Carmack amendment,[55] and that amendment was modified by the so-called first "Cummins amendment" to provide generally that where goods might be hidden from view by wrapping, boxing, or other means and the carrier was not notified as to the character of the goods, the carrier could require the shipper to specifically state in writing the value of the goods upon which the carrier would not be liable beyond the amount so specifically stated. This Commission was authorized to establish, publish, and maintain rates for transportation, dependent upon the value of the property shipped as specifically stated in writing by the shipper. The first "Cummins amendment" was faultily worded and in 1916 was amended by the so-called "Second Cummins" amendment,[56] which, among other things, expanded the use of released rates from goods which were merely hidden from view because of wrapping or boxing to baggage carried on passenger trains or boats, or trains or boats carrying passengers, and property, except ordinary livestock, received for transportation concerning which the carrier shall have been or shall hereafter be expressly authorized or required by the Commission to establish and maintain rates dependent upon the value declared in writing by the shipper or agreed upon in writing as the released value of the property. The effect was to limit liability and recovery to an amount not exceeding the value so declared. In this respect, the "Cummins amendment" was a codification of the common law rule of "full liability." However, the Commission was specifically empowered to order released rates in cases where rates based on a declared or released value would, in the opinion of the Commission, *be just and reasonable under the circumstances and conditions surrounding the transportation.* Therefore, the purpose of that amendment was not so much to restore the common law rule under which a carrier was forbidden to

[54]34 Stat. L. 595(1906).
[55]See *Adams Express Co. v. Croninger,* 226 U.S. 491.
[56]39 Stat. 6. 441 (1916).

limit its liability for negligence as it was to control the method by which it was effected. Consequently, no carrier may lawfully publish rates based on the declared or agreed value of the commodity shipped or limit the amount of its liability to the value so declared or agreed upon without specific authority from the Commission.

It was not until *Released Rates on Stone in the Southeast*[57] that the Commission laid down certain principles for administering the second Cummins Amendment. The Commission indicated that where the susceptibility to loss and damage is comparatively high and where the wide range in values for a commodity makes it difficult to estimate the amount of any claim, the carrier is at a disadvantage unless it is permitted to base its liability and its charges on a declaration of value obtained in advance from the shipper.

Therefore, in order to establish a prima facie case under the *Stone* criteria, an applicant must show: (1) a wide range in value of the commodity transported such that the amount of any claim which may arise would be difficult to estimate, (2) a comparatively high susceptibility of the commodity to loss or damage, (3) a relatively high ratio of monies paid in claims to revenues received, and (4) a high ratio of total claims to total shipments handled.[58]

In sum, Section 20(11) of the I.C. Act merely restates the common law rule that a common carrier is an insurer against loss, damage, or injury to property committed to it for transportation unless the carrier is otherwise relieved from full liability by the Commission.

The provisions of Section 20 (11) neither absolutely forbid nor absolutely compel the Commission to authorize released rates on a general application and by a general order, rather than by a commodity-by-commodity or other piecemeal process; whether to issue what amounts

---

[57]93 I.C.C. 90. The impact of the second Cummins amendment was considered in two earlier proceedings, namely, *Express Rates, Practices, Accounts, and Revenues*, 43 I.C.C. 510, and *Live Stock Classification*, 47 I.C.C. 335.

[58]These criteria have been recognized in subsequent released rates proceedings. Cf. *Fisher Supply Co. v. A & V. Ry. Co.*, 128 I.C.C. 215, 220; *General Electric Co. v. Aberdeen & Rockfish R. Co.*, 159 I.C.C. 327, 329; *Saalfield Publishing Co v. Atchison, T & S. F. Ry. Co.*, 274 I.C.C. 584, 587; *Released Ratings and Rates on Engines*, 47 M.C.C. 767 (the first formal proceeding in which an application for released rates was considered for a motor carrier); *Peoples Exp. Co.*, 311 I.C.C. 515, 517. *Wearing Apparel, Accessories, Piece Goods—Shulman Inc.*, 321 I.C.C. 1, 4-5; and *General Commodities — American Delivery Systems*, 351 I.C.C. 760, 764. The above four elements, however, are not exclusive since there are other circumstances and considerations such as compelling competitive need and the impact on shippers which are relevant and must be considered. See *General Commodities — American Delivery Systems*, 351 I.C.C. 760, citing *Rocky Mtn. Bureau, Released Val. Min. Charges*, 351 I.C.C. 505.

to a general released-rate order is for the Commission to determine upon the law and evidence adduced.[59] The power bestowed upon the Commission by the statute's proviso is not really an exception. It is a power reserved to the Commission, untrammeled save by the circumstances, to re-examine and readjust carriers' answerability for commodities not already enjoying released rates; the Congressional intention is clear, that, omitting baggage, the Commission is at liberty in exercising its reserve power, under justifying evidence, from time to time either to reduce the sweep of the statute's declaration of unlimited liability by expanding the field of limitation, or to make a change so far reaching as to eliminate one or the other entirely.[60] The Commission's discretionary power under Section 20(11) to authorize released rates is exercised sparingly, since it involves an exception to the general policy against any limitation of liability by a common carrier, thus before partial exemption from full liability may be approved, a showing must be made that susceptibility of the traffic to loss or damage is comparatively high and that the wide range in value of the commodity makes the amount of any claim that may arise difficult to estimate.[61]

While Section 20(11) prohibits common carriers from maintaining rates or charges based upon limitations of liability unless authorized or required by the Commission, it does not appear that that section would operate to preclude the granting and acceptance of a tender under Section 22 of reduced rates conditioned upon limited liability, absent a prior authorization therefor from the Commission.

Section 22(1) permits common carriers to provide transportation service free or at reduced rates for the United States, State or municipal governments, as well as other enumerated persons and groups, without regard to other provisions of the I.C. Act.[62]

The carriers may establish Section 22 quotations if they desire to do so, but they cannot be required to establish such quotations.[63]

As the Commission said in the *Tennessee Products* case (at p. 502), Section 22 makes it explicit and clear that it "is permissive, and a carrier cannot therefore, be forced to give a reduced rate thereunder," nor "can it be forced to give a similar reduction elsewhere simply because it has chosen to avail itself of the permissive treatment accorded by law."

Moreover, the Commission in the *Tennessee Products* case said (at

[59]*Southern Ry. Co. v. United States*, 194 F. Supp. 633, 638.
[60]*Ibid.*, pp. 636-8.
[61]*People's Exp., Co.* 311 I.C.C. 515, 519.
[62]*Southern Motor Carriers — Agreement*, 323 I.C.C. 396, 397.
[63]*Tennessee Products & Chem. Corp. v. Louisville & N. R.*, 319 I.C.C. 497.

p. 502) that a carrier "cannot be forced to raise the level of its Section 22 quotation or to cancel such a quotation voluntarily given; the plain language of Section 22 precludes such action." It recognized that Section 22, in effect, authorized discrimination in favor of the Federal Government, and that the quotations thereunder are not subject to the limitations in the I.C. Act.

A number of years ago the issue of the legality of these tenders was raised by DOD. At that time it concluded that such tenders were illegal. The conclusion of illegality was predicated upon the premises that Section 20(11) operates to preclude Section 22 reduced rates conditioned upon limited liability absent a prior authorization therefor from the Commission; and that Section 22 contemplates a pre-existing tariff rate or charge from which a reduction in whole or in part may be offered the United States, and that therefore in instances where carriers do not maintain released rates in published tariffs, there is no rate from which a reduction may validly be offered and accepted.

The question therefore was presented by the military to the Comptroller General of the United States for consideration. On May 18, 1959, the Comptroller General submitted his opinion (B-138736) to the Secretary of Defense in which he said, "In the absence of language clearly indicating that Congress intended so to limit the Government's freedom to contract for its transportation services, we believe this exemption ought not to be determined administratively to be affected by the proviso in Section 20(11) limiting released valuation rates and ratings to those authorized or required by the Interstate Commerce Commission." He also said, "There does not seem to be anything in the language of Section 22, by itself or when construed with the rest of the Act, which circumscribes the exemption so that it runs only to the level of rates, at least to the extent of requiring that tariff rates or charges for the contemplated services pre-exist the proposed Section 22 rates or charges." He added that frequently "carriers have offered and the Government has accepted and used Section 22 quotations providing charges for service not available to the public in tariffs," such as transit privileges not available to the public.

Section 413 of the Act requires a freight forwarder to issue a receipt or bill of lading when receiving property for transportation in its service, and specifically provides that the freight forwarder shall be deemed both the receiving and delivering transportation company for such purposes.[64] From the standpoint of the shipper, the freight forwarder, if

---

[64]*Acme Fast Freight, Inc. v. Western Freight Assn.*, 299 I.C.C. 315, 326.

used, is the "transportation company" upon whom responsibility is placed by Section 20(11) for issuance of a receipt or bill of lading and for any loss, damage, or injury to the property caused by it or by any common carrier, railroad or other transportation company to which such property may be delivered or over whose lines such property may pass.[65] Should a forwarder, subject to part IV of the I.C. Act, accept receipt of a shipment destined to a point beyond its authorized territory, it is operating unlawfully and is subject to the penalties provided therefor.[66]

Corporate Disclosure — Inquiry Into and Report on Carriers

Section 12(1) of the Interstate Commerce Act[67] was amended by the 4R Act. It provides as follows:

"(a) The Commission shall have authority, in order to perform the duties and carry out the objects for which it was created, to inquire into and report on the management of the business of all common carriers subject to the provisions of this part, and to inquire into and report on the management of the business of persons controlling, controlled by, or under a common control with, such carriers, to the extent that the business of such persons is related to the management of the business of one or more such carriers, and the Commission shall keep itself informed as to the manner and method in which the same are conducted. The Commission may obtain from such carriers and persons such information as the Commission deems necessary to carry out the provisions of this part; and may transmit to Congress from time to time such recommendations (including recommendations as to additional legislation) as the Commission may deem necessary. The Commission is hereby authorized and required to execute and enforce the provision of this part; and, upon the request of the Commission, it shall be the duty of any district attorney of the United States to whom the Commission may apply to institute in the proper court and to prosecute under the direction of the Attorney General of the United States all necessary proceedings for the enforcement of the provisions of this part and for the punishment of all violations thereof, and the costs and expenses of such prosecution shall be paid out of the appropriation for the expenses of the courts of the United States; and for the purposes of this part the Commission shall have power to require, by subpoena, the attendance and testimony of witnesses and the production of all books, papers, tariffs, contracts, agreements, and documents relating to any matter under investigation.

[65]*Movers' and Warehousemen's Assn. of America Inc., Petition,* 304 I.C.C. 517, 521.
[66]*Ibid.*
[67]49 U.S.C. 12(1). Comparable provisions, Section 204(a) (7); Section 316(a); Section 417(a).

"(b) Whenever the Commission determines, upon petition by the Secretary of an interested party or upon its own initiative, in matters relating to a common carrier by railroad subject to this part, after notice and reasonable opportunity for a hearing, that the application of the provisions of this part (i) to any person or class of persons, or (ii) to any services or transactions by reason of the limited scope of such services or transactions, is not necessary to effectuate the national transportation policy declared in this Act, would be an undue burden on such person or class of persons or on interstate and foreign commerce, and would serve little or no useful public purpose, it shall, by order, exempt such persons, class of persons, services, or transactions from such provisions to the extent and for such period of time as may be specified in such order. The Commission may, by order, revoke any such exemption whenever it finds, after notice and reasonable opportunity for a hearing, that the application of the provisions of this part to the exempted person, class of persons, services, or transactions, to the extent specified in such order, is necessary to effectuate the national transportation policy declared in this Act and to achieve effective regulation by the Commission, and would serve a useful public purpose."

In *Corporate Disclosure Regulations*,[68] the I.C.C. adopted specific items of corporate disclosures pertaining to (1) corporate structure, (2) affiliations of officers and directors, and (3) debtholding. It postponed adopting reporting regulations relating to voting stock ownership. In adopting the specific items of corporate disclosure, the I.C.C. discussed its authority to require the submission of the information called for by the first two sections. It said (pp. 35-41):

The appropriate starting point for an analysis of our statutory authority is at the beginning of the act, with the broad "declaration of policy" set forth in the "national transportation policy," added by Congress in 1940:

*   *   *

At the same time that Congress was broadening the purposes of the act in the general terms quoted above, specific grants of authority and directives to the Commission were added. The most significant, for our purposes here, was the amendment to section 12(1), which we have italicized below:

Section 12(1). The Commission shall have authority, *in order to perform the duties and carry out the objects for which it was created,* to inquire into *and report on* the management of the business of all common carriers subject to the provisions of this part and *to inquire into and report on the management of the business of persons controlling, controlled by, or under common control with, such carriers, to the extent that the business of such persons is related to the management of the business of one or more such carriers,* and the Commission shall keep itself informed as to the manner and method in which the same are conducted. The Commission may obtain from such carriers *and*

68354 I.C.C. 27.

persons such information as the Commission deems necessary to carry out the provisions of this part; and may transmit to Congress from time to time such recommendations (including recommendations as to additional legislation) as the Commission may deem necessary.° ° °

Section 204(a)(7), which is analogous to section 12(1) and relates to motor carriers, was also amended in 1940 to expand "the duty of the Commission" to include the duty "to inquire into ° ° ° the business of persons controlling, controlled by, or under common control with, motor carriers to the extent that the business of such persons is related to the management of the business of one or more motor carriers° ° °."

The following sentence was added to section 20(5) in the 1940 amendments to the act:

The Commission or any duly authorized special agent, accountant, or examiner thereof shall at all times have authority to inspect and copy any and all accounts, books, records, memoranda, correspondence, and other documents, of such carriers and lessors, and such accounts, books, records, memoranda, correspondence, and other documents, of any person controlling, controlled by, or under common control with any such carrier, as the Commission deems relevant to such person's relation to, or transactions with such carrier.

Finally, section 220(d) was amended in 1940 to extend the Commission's authority to inspect the books and records of motor carriers to include the books and records of "any person controlling, controlled by, or under common control with any such motor carrier."

With these series of amendments to the act, Congress could hardly have made it more clear that we have not only the authority, but the obligation, to concern ourselves with the activities of the persons controlling, controlled by, and sharing control with carriers. The amendments evidence a design to confer on us authority to gather information on these parties which is practically the same as our authority with respect to carriers.

In a case mentioned frequently in the responses, *Burlington Northern, Inc. v. Interstate Commerce Commission*, 462 F. 2d 280, *cert. denied*, 409 U.S. 891 (1972), the United States Court of Appeals for the District of Columbia described the congressional purpose for the amendment of section 20(5) quoted above:

the motivation for amending the section in 1940 was to permit the Commission to inspect and copy accounts, records, and explanatory material of controlling, controlled or jointly controlling persons in a manner similar to the inspection afforded in the case of regulated carriers. [462 F. 2d 280, 287.]

Thus, we are given the broad authority to inquire into the "management of the business" of these persons who are related to carriers in the same manner as we are to inquire into the "management of the business" of the carriers. The sole limitation imposed is that the inquiry be "related to the management of the business of" the carrier (sections 12(1) and 204 (a)(7)) and that the documents to be inspected be such "as the Commission deems relevant to such person's relation to or transactions with such carrier" (sections 20(5) and 220(d)).

If we relate the statutory directive to the information required by these sections of the proposed regulations, such information appears to us to come well within the parameters set by Congress. A minimal inquiry into the "management of the business" of an organization would include the naming of the organization and its principal officers and directors, a description of its business and certain limited financial information, such as a balance sheet and income statement. The occupations and affiliations of the principal officers and directors are properly called for by the regulations, since these individuals are, in most instances, controlling persons whose business is a proper subject of inquiry. Certainly, the financial condition and the management and control of the parents and subsidiaries of a carrier are "related to the management of the business of" the carrier. This is particularly true as to the business dealings between the carrier and officers and directors called for in the section entitled "Affiliations of Officers and Directors" as well as the interrelationships with the carrier to be described in "Corporate Structure."

The statutory provisions we are interpreting here must all be "administered and enforced with a view to carry out" the national transportation policy set forth above. We believe this requirement of the act reinforces our conclusion that we may require the reporting of the information in these sections despite the fact that the information will often come from persons other than the carrier. We have set forth above the background for the drafting and dissemination of these regulations. The subcommittee's representatives have testified as to many practices which would contravene the letter and spirit of the national transportation policy, and which may be remedied through the gathering of the requested data. Under that policy, we must strive to "foster sound economic conditions in transportation" and "eliminate unfair and destructive competitive practices." These regulations are a major step towards those goals.

Our exposition of the statutory support for the action taken herein will end with a recent example. In the Railroad Revitalization and Regulatory Reform Act of 1976 (the 1976 Act), the Commission is directed to study conglomerates and other corporate organizations within the rail industry:

> Sec. 903. The Commission shall undertake a study of conglomerates and of such corporate structures as are presently found within the rail transportation industry. The Commission shall determine what effects, if any, such diverse structures have on effective transportation, on intermodal competition, on revenue levels, and on such other aspects of national transportation as the Commission considers to be legitimate subjects of study. The Commission shall prepare a report with appropriate recommendations and shall submit its report to the Congress within 1 year after the date of enactment of this Act.

The congressional mandate to make such a broad study must be viewed as including the view of Congress that, under the statutes administered by this Commission, we are presently empowered to gather the necessary information.

Before discussing the objections to our authority based on the *Burlington Northern* case, we will briefly respond to those who concede that our power and duty to "inquire" pursuant to section 12(1) may be very broad, but contend that our authority to require the reporting of information is much more limited in scope.[69] We concede that there must be some limitations on our authority to require reports under section 12(1), which is expressed in the following sweeping language, "to require *** specific and full, true, and correct answers to all questions upon which the Commission may deem information to be necessary ***." Thus, that statute appears to give us unlimited discretion concerning the subject matter of reports.

We agree that there are limits to this discretion. We believe these limits have been well stated recently by the U.S. Supreme Court in *California Bankers Ass'n. v. Shultz,* 416 U.S. 21 (1974), which involved regulations requiring reports pursuant to the Bank Secrecy Act of 1970. The Court quoted from earlier Supreme Court decisions in formulating the constitutional limitations upon an administrative agency's power to require reporting of information. The reports are permissible when:

> ***the inquiry is within the authority of the agency, the demand is not too indefinite and the information sought is reasonably relevant. "The gist of the protection is in the requirement, expressed in terms, that the disclosure shall not be unreasonable." *United States v. Morton Salt Co.,* 338 U.S. 632, 652-653 (1950); see *Oklahoma Press Publishing Co. v. Walling,* 327 U.S. 186, 208 (1946). [416 U.S. 21, 67.]

We believe that we have demonstrated above that the information called for in these two sections is well without our broad authority to inquire; that the information required is limited in scope and clearly stated; and that the information is relevant to the responsibilities given to us by Congress. Accordingly, we have concluded that these reporting requirements meet the "reasonableness" test of the Supreme Court quoted above.

The case often cited by those questioning our authority in this area is *Burlington Northern, supra.* In that case, the courts refused to permit our agents to inspect a carrier's budget forecast data on the ground that such material did not constitute "accounts, books, records, memoranda, correspondence and other documents" within the meaning of section 20(5) of the act, and, therefore, the carrier was not subject to a fine for failing to comply with an investigative order calling for the forecasts. We should point out that the recording and reporting of forecast data was not then required by any Commission regulation.

---

[69]Several parties maintain that the last sentence of section 20(1), by referring to "an account of the affairs of the carrier," without mentioning affiliates, means no information on affiliates can be required. However, that sentence refers only to the "form and detail" of the report. Furthermore, the numerous 1940 amendments quoted above make it clear that many aspects of the business of those who control, are controlled by, or share control with, a carrier must be considered as part of the "affairs of the carrier."

Certain parties herein contend that *Burlington Northern* limits all our powers under section 20, not just the investigatory power under section 20(5), to the gathering of information which is related to, or explanatory of, required accounting and bookkeeping entries. We do not believe that this case can be interpreted so broadly. We will repeat here our view of the more sound interpretation of *Burlington Northern*, which appears in our report in Ex Parte No. 290, *Procedures Governing Rail General Increase Proc.*, 351 I.C.C. 544, served March 10, 1976, in which we required the submission by railroads of certain forecast data.

> We are convinced, however, that this limitation [of *Burlington Northern*] on our investigatory powers, which are ordinarily exercised through agents without issuance of formal orders by the Commission, and under which parties are subject to substantial forfeitures for refusing to allow inspection of material described in the statute, is not conclusive on our powers to require projection data. The case does not hold that the Commission is precluded from receiving forecasts under any circumstances; it applies solely to *inspection* of section 20(5) documentary materials by the Commission in the context of the forfeiture provisions of section 20(7). The Commission's power to require the filing of forecast data by regulation was not at issue. Since *Burlington Northern* applies only where the Commission attempts to inspect materials not required to be maintained by regulation, it imposes no limitations on the kind of accounting records the Commission may require to be maintained and submitted. [351 I.C.C. 544, 554-555.]

We note that *Burlington Northern* is even more easily distinguishable in the present case, in that we are not here concerned with any information relating to forecasts.

A decision of the District Court for the Northern District of Illinois, *C.A.B. v. United Air Lines, Inc.*, 399 F. Supp. 1324 (1975), which cited *Burlington Northern*, has also been cited in this proceeding as limiting our authority under section 20. The *C.A.B.* decision is consistent with *Burlington Northern* in that it limits the access of the C.A.B. to those "documents which were required to be kept or those documents kept which relate to the required records." 399 F. Supp. 1324, 1328. Again, however, the court was not presented with the question of an agency's power to require the recording or reporting of information. As the court stated:

> Not raised or decided here is the question of what records, or file system, Congress or C.A.B. might require, e.g., a carrier's parent's or subsidiary's activities, officers' positions on other boards of directors or employees' personal affairs.

Accordingly, we conclude that, while circumscribing our access to information not required to be recorded or submitted, *Burlington Northern* does not place any relevant limit on the information we may require carriers to report. As previously outlined, the limitations on our authority to require reports are: (1) relevance to our statutory purposes and obligations; and (2) the standard of "reasonableness," as enunciated in the *Bankers* case.

Statutory Authority for Actions by Shippers and Carriers

Section 16 of the Interstate Commerce Act[70] provides the authority for actions to be brought. Section 16(1) provides that "if after hearing on a complaint made as provided in Section thirteen of this part, the Commission shall determine that any party complainant is entitled to an award of damages under the provision of this part for a violation thereof, the Commission shall make an order directing the carrier to pay to the complainant the sum to which he is entitled on or before a day named." Section 16(2) provides that "if a carrier does not comply with an order for the payment of money within the time limit in such order, the complainant, or any person for whose benefit such order was made, may file in the district court of the United States for the district in which he resides or in which is located the principal operating office of the carrier, or through which the road of the carrier runs, or in any State court of general jurisdiction of the parties, a complaint setting forth briefly the causes for which he claims damages, and the order of the Commission in the premises. Such suit in the district court of the United States shall proceed in all respects like other civil suits for damages, except that on the trial of such suit the findings and order of the Commission shall be prima facie evidence of the facts therein stated, and except that the plaintiff shall not be liable for costs in the district court nor for costs at any subsequent stage of the proceedings unless they accrue upon his appeal. If the plaintiff shall finally prevail he shall be allowed a reasonable attorney's fee, to be taxed and collected as a part of the cost of the suit." Section 16(3) (a) provides that "all actions at law by carriers subject to this part for recovery of their charges, or any part thereof, shall be begun within *three years* from the time the cause of action accrues, and not after."

Section 16(3) (b) provides that "All complaints against carriers subject to this part for the recovery of damages not based on overcharges shall be filed with the Commission within *two years* from the time the cause of action accrues, and not after, subject to subdivision (d)." Section 16(3) (c) provides that "For recovery of overcharges action at law shall be begun or complaint filed with the Commission against carriers subject to this part within *three years* from the time the cause of action accrues, and not after, subject to subdivision (d),

[70]49 U.S.C. 16. Comparable provisions to paragraph (1) — Section 308(d); to paragraph (2), Section 308(e); to paragraph (3) (a), Sections 204a (1), 308(f) (1) (A), 406 a (1); to paragraph (3) (g), Sections 204a (5), 308(f) (4), 406a (5); to paragraph (3) (i), Sections 204a, 308(f), 406a; to paragraph (4) Section 308(g).

except that if claim for the overcharge has been presented in writing to the carrier within the *three year* period of limitation said period shall be extended to include six months from the time notice in writing is given by the carrier to the claimant of disallowance of the claim, or any part or parts thereof, specified in the notice." Section 16(3) (d) provides that "If on or before expiration of the *two year period* of limitation in subdivision (b) or of the *three year* period of limitation in subdivision (c) a carrier subject to this part begins action under subdivision (a) for recovery of charges in respect of the same transportation service, or, without beginning action, collects charges in respect of that service, said period of limitation shall be extended to include ninety days from the time such action is begun or such charges are collected by the carrier."

Section (16(3) (e) provides that "The cause of action in respect of a shipment of property shall, for the purposes of this section, be deemed to accrue upon delivery or tender of delivery thereof by the carrier, and not after." Section 16(3) (f) provides that "A complaint for the enforcement of an order of the Commission for the payment of money shall be filed in the district court or the State court within *one year* from the date of the order, and not after." Section 16(3) (g) provides that "The term 'overcharges' as used in this section shall be deemed to mean charges for transportation services in excess of those applicable thereto under the tariffs lawfully on file with the Commission."

Section 16(3) (i) provides that "The provisions of this paragraph (3) shall extend to and embrace all transportation of property or passengers for or on behalf of the United States in connection with any action brought before the Commission or any court by or against carriers subject to this part, *Provided, however,* That with respect to such transportation of property or passengers for or on behalf of the United States, the periods of limitation herein provided shall be extended to include *three years* from the date of (A) payment of charges for the transportation involved, or (B) subsequent refund for overpayment of such charges, or (C) deduction made under Section 322 of the Transportation Act of 1940 (49 U.S.C. 66), whichever is later." Section 16(4) provides that "In such suits all parties in whose favor the Commission may have made an award for damages by a single order may be joined as plaintiffs, and all of the carriers parties to such order awarding such damages may be joined as defendants, and such suit may be maintained by such joint plaintiffs and against such joint defendants in any district where any one of such joint plaintiffs could maintain such suit against any one of such joint defendants; and service of process against any one of such defendants as may not be found in the district where the suit is brought may be made in any district where such defendant carrier has its principal operating office. In case of such joint suit the recovery, if any, may be by judgment in favor of any one of such plaintiffs, against the defendant found to be liable to such plaintiff."

Section 16(3) is discussed in *Dow Chemical Co. v. Southern Pacific Transportation Co., et. al.,*[71] where the hearing officer said:

> Attention is directed to Section 16(3)(a) of the Interstate Commerce Act which requires that all actions at law by rail carriers for the recovery of transportation changes must be brought within three years from the date the cause of action accrues. Under Section 16(3)(e) of the Act the cause of action shall be deemed to accrue upon delivery or tender of delivery of the shipment by the carriers. Section 16(3)(b) requires that all complaints *against carriers* for the recovery of damages not based on overcharges shall be filed with the Commission within *two years* from the time the cause of action accrues subject to subdivision (d). Section 16(3)(d) provides that for recovery of *overcharges* action at law shall be begun or complaint filed with the Commission against the carrier within three years from the time the cause of action accrues subject to subdivision (d).

> Section 16(3)(d) provides that if on or before the expiration of the two-year period of limitation in Section 16(3)(b), or the three year period in Section 16(3)(c) a rail carrier begins action under Section 16(3)(a) for recovery of charges in respect of the same transportation service, said period of limitation shall be extended to include 90 days from the time such action is begun.

> The statute of limitations is not subject to waiver. The lapse of time not only bars the remedy, but it destroys the liability, whether the complaint is filed with the Commission or suit is brought in a Court of competent jurisdiction (*Feinstein v. New York Central Railroad Co.*, 159 F. Supp. 460, 465-67). Furthermore where statutes are a valid bar to recovery the defendants must *plead* them to avoid violations of the Interstate Commerce Act which prohibits undue preferences of advantage to any particular person. (Refer *Arma Corp. v. M & M Transp. Co.*, 61 M.C.C. 723; *Fedders-Quigan Corp. v. Long Transp. Co.*, 64 M.C.C. 581 (decided 1955)). The rail carrier defendants herein should be aware that their failure to plead the statutory bar to complainant's recovery herein lays them open to a charge of violating Section 3 Part I, of the Interstate Commerce Act. (*Phillips Company v. Grand Trunk W. Ry. Co.*, 236 U.S. 662, 667).

Right to Damages

To establish their right to damages, complainants must first show a violation of the I.C. Act, and thereafter must measure their dam-

---

[71]I.C.C. Docket No. 36048, Initial Decision served March 3, 1975.

ages. As the court pointed out in *United States v. Interstate Commerce Commission*,[72] the type of proof required to establish damages depends on the section of the I.C. Act allegedly violated. Specific proof of pecuniary loss is required if there are violations of certain sections of the Act. The cases cited by the court indicated that it was in this instance referring to violations of sections such as 2, 3 and 4 of the I.C. Act.[73] A finding that any of these sections of the Act has been violated does not necessarily mean that an excessive charge has been exacted; and reparation will not be awarded unless a specific loss is proved. The other manner in which damages may be proved is by a showing that the rate in question is unreasonable or excessive. If such a showing is made, then, as the court suggests in *United States v. Interstate Commerce Commission, supra,* no specific proof of loss need be made, for proof of a violation of the I.C. Act by the exaction of an unreasonable charge measures the damages. Since the complaint which initiated the proceeding before the court in *United States v. Interstate Commerce Commission, supra,* charged violations of both Sections 1 and 2, it pointed out that a finding of over-all reasonableness did not necessarily preclude an award of damages upon a showing of loss arising from, for example, a Section 2 violation.

Reparation

Suits for recovery of damages not based on overcharges, as pointed out above, must be filed within two years.[74] There can be a tolling of the statute by the filing of a special docket statement by the carriers which is deemed by the Commission to be the equivalent of an informal complaint filed on behalf of complaints. In *Alpha Portland Cement Co. v. Wabash R. Co.,*[75] a letter sent to Commission by a participating defendant, transmitting a statement of the billing on the shipments, and advising of complainant's claim for damages and of the reasons why defendant could not file a special-docket application within the statutory period, was sufficient to stay the statute. In *Carborundum Co. v. Louisville & N. R.,*[76] the Commission said that shipments concerning which claims were registered by the Commission at the request of a

---

[72]198 F. 2d 958, 973-5.

[73]See, e.g., *I.C.C. v. United States ex rel Campbell,* 289 U.S. 385, and *Davis v. Portland Seed Co.,* 264 U.S. 403.

[74]49 U.S.C. 16(3) (b); see *Anchor Petroleum Co. v. Chicago, R. I. & P. R. Co.,* 304 I.C.C. 500.

[75]308 I.C.C. 95, 96-97.

[76]309 I.C.C. 337.

defendant carrier pending submission by that carrier of an application for approval of a voluntary award of reparation, which the carrier subsequently declined to file, were not barred, since complaints were thereafter filed within the statutory period.

Where reparation is sought, the burden of proving by competent evidence that the rates involved are unjust and unreasonable rests upon the party seeking reparation; and the burden requires a showing that total rates exceed maximum reasonable levels.[77] The Supreme Court has held that a charge may be considered excessive only if it is excessive for the entire service performed; and that the whole line-haul rate, not a factor of it, must be found excessive and, therefore, unreasonable before reparation may be awarded.[78] In the *Great Northern* case, a shipper had sought reparations on the ground that a proportional rate, which was part of a through rate composed of several proportional rates, was unjust and unreasonable. The Supreme Court reversed an award of reparation by the Commission. The court held that in the absence of a claim or finding that the other proportionals or the total through rate were unjust or unreasonable, the through charges collected on the shipments must be deemed to have been just and reasonable. The court reasoned that since the shipper's only interest is that the charge shall be reasonable as a whole, the shipper was not damaged.

The *Great Northern* principle has been the subject of conflicting interpretations by the Commission.[79] However in the *Sterling Colorado Beef Company v. The Atchison, Topeka and Santa Fe Ry. Co.*,[80] the Commission resolved these conflicts, adopting the interpretation in *Auburn:*

> We believe the proper rule to be as follows: where a total rate or charge is challenged and is shown to embrace an unlawful factor, the total rate or charge is to be presumed unlawful to the extent such factor is demonstrated to be unlawful. Should a presumption of unlawfulness arise, defendants may of course present rebuttal evidence, or the Commission may further inquire as to actual impact of the unlawful factor in light of the pertinent transportation conditions.

Under Part I of the Act[81] shippers have long had a justiciable legal right to recover freight charges correctly calculated on the basis of rates

---

[77]*Consolidated Rendering Co. v. Atchison, T. & S. F. Ry. Co.*, 287 I.C.C. 673, 679, 300 I.C.C. 87, 91; *Yellow Jacket Boat Co., Inc. v. Atchison, T. & S. F. Ry. Co.*, 305 I.C.C. 113, 116.

[78]*Great Northern Ry. v. Sullivan*, 294 U.S. 458.

[79]See *Auburn Mills v. Chicago & A. R. Co.*, 222 I.C.C. 495 and *United States v. Beaumont, S. L. & W. Ry. Co.*, 301 I.C.C. 231.

[80]No. 35021, report and order served November 18, 1977. Sheet 15.

[81]49 U.S.C., Sections 1-26.

applicable and effective at the time the transportation was performed upon a determination that such rates were unreasonable. Part I gives the shipper alternative methods of vindicating this right. Under Section 9 he may either file suit in a United States district court or he may file a complaint with the Commission under Section 13 of the I.C. Act. If he elects the latter alternative the Commission is empowered under Section 16(1) of the Act, "after hearing on a complaint," to award him damages and issue an order directing the railroad to pay them.

In contrast to these provisions of Part I of the I.C. Act, Part II, originally enacted as the Motor Carrier Act of 1935, did not empower either a court or the Commission to determine the reasonableness of past motor carrier rates, and hence did not grant either a court or the Commission the power to award reparations to shippers. This also was true with respect to freight forwarders under Part IV of the I.C. Act.

In 1944, in *Bell Potato Chip Co. v. Aberdeen Truck Line*,[82] the Commission undertook a thorough reexamination of its jurisdiction to make an administrative determination of the lawfulness of rates charged on past motor carrier shipments. It therein recognized that Part II of the I.C. Act, unlike Parts I and III relating to rail and water carriers, conferred no authority upon the Commission to award reparation for damages to shippers sustained by the payment of charges based on unreasonable or otherwise unlawful motor carrier rates. After discussing prior proceedings (beginning with *W. A. Barrows Porcelain Enamel Co. v. Cushman M. Delivery*, 11 M.C.C. 365), it affirmed the view expressed in prior decisions that it had the requisite statutory authority to pass upon the lawfulness of past motor carrier rates charged, but that, generally, its jurisdiction should not be invoked in an adversary proceeding prior to the institution of a court action to obtain a money judgment predicated upon the unlawfulness alleged in the complaints to be filed with the Commission in and of the court. The preference expressed for the institution of a prior court action was based on the fact that the Commission's determination of an issue of past unreasonableness was not self-executing since it lacked authority to award reparation under Part II of the I.C. Act. It was also felt that such a procedure would serve to discourage the filing of frivolous or moot formal complaints.

Following the decision in *Bell Potato Chip, supra*, an informal, expeditious, and inexpensive motor carrier and freight forwarder reparation procedure was established by the Commission under which shippers

[82]43 M.C.C. 337.

could recover damages for unlawful charges on past shipments in un-contested cases. Uncontested cases are those in which the carrier admits that the charges applicable under the tariffs are unjust and unreasonable, and is willing to refund or to waive the differences between the charges collected, or to be collected, and those which it agrees are reasonable, after having amended the tariffs to establish the presumably lawful rates or other provisions. To safeguard against any collusion between carriers and favored shippers, the applicable rates, admitted by the carrier to be unlawful, were carefully examined to determine whether they were in fact unlawful under principles established by the Commission and court decisions before the carrier was advised that a refund or waiver could be made. In meritorious cases the carrier was advised by letter that the Commission would interpose no objection to the refund or waiver.

In *United States v. Davidson Transfer & Storage Co., Inc.,*[83] the Commission reaffirmed the position taken in *Bell Potato Chip, supra,* concerning its jurisdiction to make administrative determinations of the reasonableness of past motor carrier rates and charges in aid of pend-ing suits in the courts. However, in *T.I.M.E., Inc. v. United States,*[84] which embraced the *Davidson* case, *supra,* the Supreme Court held, in effect, that neither the Commission nor the courts had jurisdiction, either under the statute or under common law, to consider in post-shipment litigation, the reasonableness of a motor carrier's past charges applied in accordance with tariffs on file with the Commission.

In *Hewitt-Robins v. Eastern Freight-Ways,*[85] the Supreme Court said that the issue involved in the case was different than that in the *T.I.M.E.* case. The court said that the question involved in the *T.I.M.E.* case was whether a shipper of goods by a certificated motor carrier could chal-lenge in postshipment litigation the reasonableness of the charges which were made in accordance with the tariff governing the shipment, the court determining that the attack was foreclosed as being inconsistent with the statutory scheme of regulation. Here the court said, the chal-lenge is directed not to reasonableness of the rates but to the carrier's routing practices. This, the court said, has long been within the primary jurisdictions of the Commission. Unlike rate making, the court said, there is no statutory procedure by which routing practices may be challenged in advance of shipment, such as the 30-day notice provision and the power to suspend rates for seven months, nor is the shipper by truck

---

[83]302 I.C.C. 87.
[84]359 U.S. 464. See also *Columbus Coated Fabrics Corp. v. Wilson F. F. Co.,* 208 I.C.C. 49, 50; *Ford Motor Co. v. Standard Transp. Co. Inc.,* 308 I.C.C. 304.
[85]371 U.S. 84.

accorded even the right given the shipper by rail under 49 U.S.C. 15(8), to select and request a particular route of the carrier. Thus, the court said, the survival of a damage claim for misrouting "appears entirely consistent with the act." The court concluded by stating:

> Consistent with that decision, and Commission holdings in several subsequent cases that the Commission had no authority to determine the justness and reasonableness of motor carrier rates on past shipments, the informal handling of such matters in uncontested cases was discontinued.[86]

In *United States v. Garver*,[87] the Commission said that where rates charged on shipments lawfully transported by carrier under its interstate authority have been found applicable by a district court, the Commission, under the doctrine of the *T.I.M.E.* case may not consider their reasonableness. The Commission said that while the Supreme Court did not have before it in that case the question whether, or in what circumstances, the Commission is authorized to determine past charges for motor transportation in situations differing from the one there involved, its opinion indicates that the Commission has no authority to make such a determination solely in aid of a common-law action in court. Therefore, the Commission said, as Sections 216(b) and (d), 206 and 217, which are enforced through Sections 204(c), 212, and 222, confer on shipper no statutory right to recover damages for unreasonableness, and the Supreme Court has held that the common-law right is not preserved by Section 216(j), the Commission cannot determine the reasonableness of rates charged for performance of transportation beyond the scope of the carrier's authority.

Beginning in 1960, the Commission recommended annually enactment of legislation that would overcome the effects of the Supreme Court's decision in the *T.I.M.E.* case, *supra*, and, at the same time, make all four parts of the act uniform with respect to rate reparation by amending Parts II and IV thereof to permit shippers to recover damages for unlawful charges on past shipments in proceedings either before the Commission or in the courts in the same manner as they may seek redress for such damages against railroads and water carriers subject to Parts I and III, respectively. Legislation to this end was introduced in the 87th, 88th and 89th Congresses. In the face of vigorous opposition to them a compromise was struck in the 89th Congress and embodied in H.R. 5401, S. 1727 and ultimately in Public Law 89-170.

Public Law 89-170 created for the first time a justiciable legal right

[86]*Ford Motor Co. v. Standard Transp. Co., Inc.*, 308 I.C.C. 304.
[87]313 I.C.C. 139, 141-43.

to reparation against motor carriers and freight forwarders based on their failure to discharge their duty to establish and maintain just, reasonable and non-discriminatory rates. However, the remedy created by Public Law 89-170 falls far short of the remedy against railroads.

Section 6 of Public Law 89-170 amended Section 204a of the I.C. Act, applicable to motor common carriers, by adding the following new provision at the beginning of paragraph (2) thereof:

> (2) For recovery of reparations, action at law shall be begun against common carriers by motor vehicle subject to this part within 2 years from the time the cause of action accrues, and not after, ...

and by also adding the following new provision in a redesignated paragraph (5):

> (5) The term "reparations" as used in this section means damages resulting from charges for transportation services to the extent that the Commission, upon complaint made as provided in Section 216(e) of this part, finds them to have been unjust and unreasonable, or unjustly discriminatory or unduly preferential or unduly prejudicial.

Section 7 of Public Law 89-170 amended Section 406a, applicable to freight forwarders, in substantially the same manner.

The remedy of shippers and the authority granted the Commission by Public Law 89-170 is clear.[88] The sole remedy is to bring suit against a carrier for damages. The sole power of the Commission is purely ancillary to such a suit, namely to determine in aid of the court whether or not the rates paid were in fact unjust or unreasonable or unlawfully discriminatory, prejudicial or preferential within the regulatory standards of the Interstate Commerce Act. The Commission has no power to implement a determination of such unreasonableness or other unlawfulness by awarding damages or in any other way. That is the exclusive prerogative of the court.

The Commission's power is limited. First, it may deal only with rates in effect or proposed to be put into effect; second, the Commission may deal only with rates which are the subject of complaint in writing to it; third, the Commission may make no determination respecting a rate complained of except after hearing.

In *Informal Procedure for Determining Reparation,*[89] the Commis-

---

[88]See also Report No. 387, Senate Committee on Commerce, 89th Cong., 1st Sess., page 8; Hearings before the Surface Transportation Subcommittee of the Committee on Commerce, U.S. Senate, 89th Cong., 1st Sess., May 10, 11, 14, 19, and 20, 1965, page 62; and Hearings before the Committee on Interstate and Foreign Commerce on H.R. 5401, 89th Congress, 1st Sess., March 23 through 26, 1965, page 31.

[89]335 I.C.C. 403.

sion instituted a rule making proceeding on its own motion under Parts II and IV of the I.C. Act, particularly Sections 204a and 406a[90] and the Administrative Procedure Act,[91] for the purpose of determining whether and what, if any, procedure should be prescribed by which motor common carriers and freight forwarders may be authorized informally by the Commission to pay reparation to shippers, or to waive the collection of undercharges, on past shipments in uncontested cases. The informal procedure was initially sought to be established unilaterally by notice dated December 17, 1965, in a proceeding subsequently designated as Ex Parte No. 249, *In the Matter of Informal Procedure for Motor Carrier and Freight Forwarder Reparation.* Upon challenge by various carrier and freight forwarder interests, following denial of their petitions for reconsideration by order dated June 3, 1966, the matter was remanded by the court in *National Motor Freight Traffic Ass'n. v. United States.*[92] The remand was principally on the ground that interested parties were not accorded notice and opportunity to be heard in conformity with the provisions of the Administrative Procedure Act. The court did not reach the substantive issues raised concerning statutory authority under Parts II and IV of the Act to promulgate such informal reparation procedure. The original proceeding in Ex Parte No. 249 was thereafter discontinued, and a rulemaking proceeding in Ex Parte No. 249 (Sub-No. 1) was instituted.[93] In this case, the Commission held that it lacks jurisdiction to entertain reparation cases under Parts II and IV of the I.C. Act, and that it does not have jurisdiction to prescribe and establish an informal procedure whereby carriers subject to Parts II and IV of the I.C. Act may seek and obtain authority of the Commission to pay reparation to shippers, or to waive the collection of undercharges, for unreasonable rates charged on past shipments.

Overcharges

As pointed out above a three years' statute of limitations applies to suits for recovery of overcharges.[94]

The Act places the burden strictly upon the shipper to do one of two things. He must file a suit in court or file a complaint with the Commission within six months from the time the notice in writing was given by the carrier to the shipper of the disallowance of his claim in

[90]49 U.S.C. 304(a) and 1006(a).
[91]5 U.S.C. 552.
[92]268 F. Supp. 90.
[93]335 I.C.C. 403.
[94]49 U.S.C. 16(3) (c).

part or in whole. A resubmission of the claim by the shipper to the carrier within the six-month period would not toll the statute. Neither can the carrier pay the claim within the six-month extended period without the shipper's resorting to either one of the two courses of action stated. In fact, the initiative is squarely upon the shipper to take action within the six-month extended period in order to stay the period of limitations.[95]

Claims by or Against the Government

It is provided by 49 U.S.C. 66, as amended,[96] as follows:

"(a) Payment for transportation of persons or property for or on behalf of the United States by any carrier or forwarder shall be made upon presentation of bills therefor prior to audit by the General Services Administration, or his designee. The right is reserved to the United States Government to deduct the amount of any overcharge by any carrier or forwarder from any amount subsequently found to be due such carrier or forwarder. This does not affect the authority of the General Accounting Office to make audits in accordance with the Budget and Accounting Act, 1921, as amended (31 U.S.C. 41), and the Accounting and Auditing Act of 1950, as amended (31 U.S.C. 65). The term 'overcharges' shall be deemed to mean charges for transportation services in excess of those applicable thereto under tariffs lawfully on file with the Interstate Commerce Commission, the Civil

[95]It is well established, that a claimant may resubmit a claim for overcharge to the carrier within the statutory period and such claim remains alive, so that the additional 6-month period provided in the statute runs from the date of the first disallowance after the last resubmission within the statutory period. *Graves & Sons Co. v. Chicago, St. P., M. & O. Ry. Co.,* 177 I.C.C. at 732. See also W. A. *Riddell Corp. v Chicago, M., St. P. & P. R. Co.,* 269 I.C.C. 421; *Horn Mfg. Co. v. Illinois Central R. Co.,* 259 I.C.C. 609, 611; *Swift & Co. v. Canadian Pac. Ry. Co.,* 183 I.C.C. 137, 138; *Gauger-Korsmo Construction Co. v. Missouri Pac. R. Co.,* 183 I.C.C. 531; *Dunlop Tire and Rubber Corp. v. Transamerican Frt. Lines,* 62 M.C.C. 161, 162. In the *Dunlop* case, the Commission said that Part II contains the same statutory provisions as those contained in Part I of the I.C. Act and, therefore, it saw no reason why it should not apply the above principle uniformly in motor carrier and rail proceedings. *Republic Carloading & Distributing Co., Inc. v. B. & O. R. Co., et al.,* 284 I.C.C. 441-443, holds that claims for overcharges filed with carriers which are declined are not barred even though the complaint is filed more than 6 months after the expiration of the statutory period. Statutes of limitation do not apply to the United States in the absence of a clear and manifest intent that they shall apply. Congress, in amending Section 16(3) made the statute expressly applicable to the United States, and limited the Government's right of action to three years. *United States v. De-Queen E.R. Co.,* 271 F. 2d 597, 599-600.

[96]P.L. 93-604, 88 Stat. 1960, Jan. 2, 1975, amended like first sentence and the second proviso of subsection (a), and added subsection (b). Old subsection (b) is now (c) and old subsection (c) is now (d). See *United States ex rel. Skinner & Eddy Corporation v. McCarl, Comptroller General,* 275 U.S. 1, 4 (note 2); *McKnight v. United States,* 13 Ct. Cl. 292, 306, aff'd 98 U.S. 179; *United States v. Munsey Trust Company,* 322 U.S. 234, 239.

Aeronautics Board, the Federal Maritime Commission, and any State transportation regulatory agency, and charges in excess of those applicable thereto under rates, fares, and charges established pursuant to section 22 of the Interstate Commerce Act, as amended, or other equivalent contract, arrangement, or exemption from regulation: *Provided, however,* That such deductions shall be made within three years (not including any time of war) from the time of payment of bills: *Provided further,* That every claim for charges for transportation within the purview of this section shall be forever barred unless such claim shall be received in the General Services Administration, or by his designee within three years (not including any time of war) from the date of (1) accrual of the cause of action thereon, or (2) payment of charges for the transportation involved, or (3) subsequent refund for overpayment of such charges, or (4) deduction made pursuant to this section, whichever is later.

"(b) Nothing in subsection (a) hereof shall be deemed to prevent any carrier of forwarder from requesting the Comptroller General to review the action on his claim by the General Services Administration, or his designee. Such request shall be forever barred unless received in the General Accounting Office within six months (not including in time of war) from the date the action was taken or within the periods of limitation specified in the second proviso in subsection (a) of this section, whichever is later."

As authorized by 49 U.S.C. 66, a carrier's bills for transportation are paid upon presentation, in the amounts billed, prior to audit or settlement by the General Accounting Office. Such payments are necessarily tentative and the accounts are subject to audit by the General Accounting Office, the Government having the right to deduct overpayments from subsequent bills. In practice, upon completion of the General Accounting Office audit of a transportation bill, if an overpayment is found, the carrier is requested to refund the amount in question. If the refund is made, the account is closed. If the refund is not made, the overpayment is certified by the General Accounting Office to the agency which paid the bill originally, and in due course the amount in question is deducted from another bill due the carrier. In either case, the result is that the carrier's bill, originally paid in the amount billed, is reduced to the amount allowed by the General Accounting Office and the carrier has an underpayment on the bill as originally rendered.

An underpayment on a bill for transportation furnished the Government is different from an undercharge for transportation furnished a private shipper. It is not a violation of the Interstate Commerce Act if a carrier charges or collects from the Government less than the published tariff rate or fare, or accepts a settlement made by the General Accounting Office and writes off the outstanding balance. Whenever, therefore, a transportation bill against the Government has been finally audited and settled by the General Accounting Office and the carrier is not satisfied with the settlement and claims an underpayment, the position is simply that the carrier has a "claim" against the Government. In such a case, the carrier may ask the General Accounting Office to reconsider the matter by submitting a claim for the amount of the underpayment in the form of a supplemental bill, or the carrier may sue the Government in the Court of Claims or in one of the district courts. When suit is brought in the Court of Claims or one of the district courts to recover the balance alleged to be due on freight bills rendered for transportation of Government shipments; such courts have jurisdiction to determine the applicable charges.[97] The Court of Claims said in *Western Pac. R. Co. v. United States*[98] that it would not reach a result contrary to that reached by the Commission in a case involving applicability of rates and proper classification of commodity shipped unless the circumstances are very unusual, since the Commission has had wide experience in the area of transportation rates and is well qualified to handle such problems.

The statute of limitations on claims against the Government cognizable by the Court of Claims is 28 U.S.C. 262, which provides that such claims shall be forever barred unless filed "within six years after the claim first accrues." This Section ,however, does not apply to suits by carriers filed in the Court of Claims on account of Government transportation charges.[99]

For purposes of the statute of limitation, a claim "first accrues" the moment a suit may be brought on it. Generally, a claim for transportation charges accrues on the rendition of the service.[100] In addition, the running of the statute of limitations is not postponed by reason of provisions in the bill of lading prescribing the routine of settlement.[101]

The legislative history of 49 U.S.C. 66 makes it clear that Congress contemplated that the Government's protection against overcharges available under preaudit practice should not be diminished, and that the burden of the carriers to establish the correctness of their charges was to continue unabridged.[102] The burden of the carriers to establish the lawfulness of their charges is the same under 49 U.S.C. 66 as it was

---

[97]*Louisville & N. R. Co. v. United States,* 192 F. Supp. 557, 558, 561.
[98]279 F. 2d 258, 259.
[99]See 49 U.S.C. 16(3) (i).
[100]*St. Louis, Brownsville & Mexico R. Co. v. United States,* 63 Ct. Cls. 103; *Atlantic Coast Line R. Co. v. United States,* 66 Ct. Cls. 576.
[101]*Southern Pacific Co. v. United States,* 67 Ct. Cls. 414.
[102]*Ibid.*

under the superseded practice, i.e., to withhold payment until the carriers established the correctness of their charges.[103]

Orders of the Commission; Records Filed with the Commission

Section 16(5) of the Interstate Commerce Act[104] provides that "Every order of the Commission shall be forthwith served upon the designated agent of the carrier in the city of Washington or in such other manner as may be provided by law. In proceedings before the Commission involving the lawfulness of rates, fares, charges, classifications, or practices, service of notice upon an attorney in fact of a carrier who has filed a tariff or schedule in behalf of such carrier shall be deemed to be due and sufficient service upon the carrier, except where the carrier has designated an agent in the city of Washington, District of Columbia, upon whom service of notices and processes may be made, as provided in Section 6 of the Act of June 18, 1910 . . . *Provided,* That in such proceedings service of notice of the suspension of a tariff or schedule upon an attorney in fact of a carrier who has filed said tariff or schedule in behalf of such carrier shall be deemed to be due and sufficient service upon the carrier, and service of notice of the suspension of a joint tariff or schedule upon a carrier which has filed said joint tariff or schedule to which another carrier is a party shall be deemed to be due and sufficient notice upon the several carriers parties thereto. Such service of notice may be made by mail to such attorney in fact or carrier at the address shown in the tariff or schedule."

In the Commission's regulations governing the designation of process agents, providing that all motor carriers and brokers must observe the rules as set forth, "motor carrier" includes common and contract carriers operating under certificates and permits issued by Commission, common carriers operating under single-State exemption proviso of Section 206(a) (1), and any motor carrier subject to Part II (including private carriers) performing operations in the United States in the course of transportation between points in a foreign country or countries.[105]

Section 16(6)[106] provides that the Commission is authorized to suspend or modify its orders upon such notice and in such manner as it

---

[103]*Ibid.*, pp. 261-2. See *United States v. New York, N. H. & H. R. Co.*, 355 U.S. 253.

[104]49 U.S.C. 16(5). Comparable provisions — Sections 221(a), 315(a), 416(a). See also 49 U.S.C. 50.

[105]*Regulations Governing Designation of Process Agents*, 83 M.C.C. 561, 563.

[106]49 U.S.C. 16(6). Comparable provisions — Sections 315(c), 416(b). See Section 204(a) for general powers to make orders.

deems proper, and Section 16(7)[107] provides that it is the duty of every common carrier to observe and comply with the Commission's orders. Section 16(8)[108] provides for penalties for refusal to obey the Commission's orders. Recovery of forfeiture is provided for by Section 16(9).[109] Prosecution for the recovery of forfeitures is placed in the hands of the Attornel General under Section 16(10).[110] The Commission is empowered by Section 16(11)[111] to employ attorneys to aid the Commission in the conduct of its work including representation of the public interest in investigations and in representing the Commission in court.

Under Section 16(12)[112] it is provided:

> "If any carrier fails or neglects to obey any order of the Commission other than for the payment of money, while the same is in effect, the Interstate Commerce Commission or any party injured thereby, or the United States, by its Attorney General, may apply to any district court of the United States of competent jurisdiction for the enforcement of such order. If, after hearing, such court determines that the order was regularly made and duly served, and that the carrier is in disobedience of the same, such court shall enforce obedience to such order by a writ of injunction or other proper process, mandatory or otherwise, to restrain such carrier, it officers, agents, or representatives, from further disobedience of such order, or to enjoin upon it or them obedience to the same."

Section 16(13)[113] provides:

> "The copies of schedules and classifications and tariff of rates, fares, and charges, and of all contracts, agreements, and arrangements between common carriers filed with the Commission as herein provided, and the statistics, tables, and figures contained in the annual or other reports of carriers made to the Commission as required under the provisions of this part shall be preserved as public records in the custody of the secretary of the Commission, and shall be received as prima facie evidence of what they purport to be for the purpose of investigations by the Commission and in all judicial proceedings; and copies of and extracts from any of said schedules, classifications, tariffs, contracts, agreements, arrangements, or reports, made public records as aforesaid, certified by the secretary, under the Commission's seal, shall be received in evidence with like effect as the originals."

---

[107]49 U.S.C. 16(7). Comparable provisions — Sections 315(e) 416(d).

[108]49 U.S.C. 16(8). Comparable provisions — Sections 222(a), 317(a), 421(a).

[109]49 U.S.C. 16(9).

[110]49 U.S.C. 16(10).

[111]49 U.S.C. 16(11). Comparable provisions — Section 205(j), 319. See also Sections 18(1), general authority to employ, Section 19a, valuation employees; and Section 20(10) special agents or examiners.

[112]49 U.S.C. 16(12). Comparable provisions — Sections 222(b), 316(b), 147(b).

[113]49 U.S.C. 16(13). Provisions of Section 16(13) relating to public records are applicable under Part II, Section 204(d); comparable provisions — Sections 316(d), 417(d).

Unauthorized Disclosure of Information

Section 15(11) of the Interstate Commerce Act[114] provides:

"It shall be unlawful for any common carrier subject to the provisions of this part, or any officer, agent, or employee of such common carrier, or for any other person or corporation lawfully authorized by such common carrier to receive information therefrom, knowingly to disclose to or permit to be acquired by any person or corporation other than the shipper or consignee, without the consent of such shipper or consignee, any information concerning the nature, kind, quantity, destination, consignee, or routing of any property tendered or delivered to such common carrier for interstate transportation, which information may be used to the detriment or prejudice of such shipper or consignee, or which may improperly disclose his business transactions to a competitor; and it shall also be unlawful for any person or corporation to solicit or knowingly receive any such information which may be so used: *Provided,* That nothing in this part shall be construed to prevent the giving of such information in response to any legal process issued under the authority of any State or Federal court, or to any officer or agent of the Government of the United States, or of any State or Territory, in the exercise of his powers, or to any officer or other duly authorized person seeking such information for the prosecution of persons charge with or suspected of crime; or information given by a common carrier to another carrier or its duly authorized agent, for the purpose of adjusting mutual traffic accounts in the ordinary course of business of such carriers."

Section 15(12)[115] provides that "Any person, corporation, or association violating any of the provisions of the next preceding paragraph of this section shall be deemed guilty of a misdemeanor, and for each offense, on conviction, shall pay to the United States a penalty of not more than one thousand dollars."

The purpose of Section 15(11) is to curb the disclosure of commercial business information by a carrier or its agents to business competitors of the shipper or consignee, and the information of which disclosure is prohibited is that which may be used to the prejudice of such shipper or consignee.[116]

Payment of Freight as Prerequisite to Delivery

Under Section 3(2)[117] no carrier shall deliver or relinquish possession at destination of any freight or express shipment transported by it until

---

[114]49 U.S.C. 15(11). Comparable provisions — Sections 222(e), (f), 317(f), 421(f).

[115]49 U.S.C. 15(12).

[116]*National Freight, Inc., Extension,* 84 M.C.C. 403, 407.

[117]49 U.S.C. 3(2) Comparable provisions — Sections 223, 318, 414.

all tariff rates and charges thereon have been paid, except under such rules and regulations as the Commission may from time to time prescribe to govern the settlement of all such rates and charges and to prevent unjust discrimination. An example of the Commission's authority under Section 3(2) is demonstrated by *Regulations for Payment of Rates and Charges*,[118] where the Commission promulgated rules under which credit periods on carload traffic were extended to equalize those on less than carload traffic. The Commission said that this would be of some advantage ot the shipping public and was desirable to enable petitioning railroads to compete more effectively with motor carriers, which were authorized to extend more liberal credit privileges; and any disadvantage resulting from the reduction of petitioners' cash working capital would be offset by benefits derived. The Commission said further that as authority granted to broaden the credit regulations is permissive only, and other railroads experience similar competition with motor carriers, such findings are made applicable to railroads generally.

False Billing by Carriers and Shippers

Common carriers and others are by Section 10(2)[119] of the I.C. Act made subject to penalties for engaging in false billing and other devices to obtain transportation at less than the tariff rates. Section 10(3)[120] provides penalties for shippers and others engaging in false billing and other devices for obtaining or attempting to obtain transportation at less than the tariff rates. Section 10(4)[121] provides penalties for shippers and others inducing or attempting to induce common carriers to discriminate in their favor. Such shippers and others, together with the common carrier, are made liable, jointly or severally, in any action brought by shippers discriminated against for all damages caused by or resulting therefrom.

Performance Standards Governing Railroad Transportation

In Ex Parte No. 284, *Investigation into the Needs for Defining Reasonable Dispatch (Perishable Commodities)*, [122] the Commission adopted regulations establishing performance standards governing railroad trans-

---

[118]310 I.C.C. 391.
[119]49 U.S.C. 10(2). Comparable provisions—Section 222(c), 317, 421(b).
[120]49 U.S.C. 10(3). Comparable provisions—Section 222(c), 317(c), 421(c).
[121]49 U.S.C. 10(4). Comparable provisions—Section 222(c), 317(c), 421(c).
[122]355 I.C.C. 162.

portation of defined perishable commodities. These regulations require the publication of railroad tariffs setting forth operating schedules on the movement of these commodities between key points throughout the country. The adopted standards are designed to insure reasonably efficient and reliable transportation of perishables, and should be helpful to agricultural shippers.

3

Certificates of Public Convenience and Necessity for Railroads

EXTENSION OF RAILROAD LINES

The Applicable Statutory Provisions

The law formerly applicable to the extension of railroad lines was found in Section 1(18), (19), (20), (21), and (22) of the I.C. Act.[1] Paragraph (18) provided that a railroad desiring to build new track constituting an extension of its line required a certificate of public convenience and necessity from the Commission authorizing the construction. Paragraph (19) related to the procedure upon application for a certificate. Paragraph (20) stated that any construction contrary to provisions of the I.C. Act could be enjoined by any court upon the application of any party in interest. Paragraph (21) related to facilities for performing car service. Paragraph (22) provided that the jurisdiction of the Commission did not apply to the laying of a spur or industrial track.

The 4R Act repealed Section 1(19), (20), (21), and (22), and amended Section 1(18).

Section 1(18) (a) provides that no carrier by railroad shall (1) undertake the extension of any of its lines or the construction of any additional line of railroad, (2) acquire or operate any such extension or any such additional line, or (3) engage in transportation over, or by means of, any such extended or additional line of railroad, unless such extension or additional line is described in and covered by a certificate which is issued by the Commission and which "declares that the present or future public convenience and necessity require or will be enhanced by the construction and operation of such extended or additional line of railroad."

---

[1] 49 U.S.C. 1(18), (19), (20), (21), (22).

Section 1(18) (c) provides that the Commission may, upon petition or upon its own initiative, authorize any carrier by railroad "to extend any of its lines of railroad or to take any other action necessary for the provision of adequate, efficient, and safe facilities for the performance of such carrier's obligations" under Part I of the I.C. Act. No authorization shall be made "unless the Commission finds that the expense thereof will not impair the ability of such carrier to perform its obligations to the public."

Section 1(18) (d) provides that carriers by railroads may, notwithstanding Section 1(18) and without the approval of the Commission, "enter into contracts, agreements, or other arrangements for the joint ownership or joint use of spur, industrial, team, switching, or side tracks." The authority granted to the Commission under Section 1(18) "shall not extend to the construction, acquisition, or operation of spur, industrial, team, switching, or side tracks if such tracks are located or intended to be located entirely within one State, and shall not apply to any street, suburban, or interurban electric railway which is not operated as part of a general system of rail transportation."

Section 1(18) (e) provides that any construction or operation which is contrary to Section 1(18), of any regulations promulgated under Section 1(18), or of any terms and conditions of an applicable certificate, may be enjoined by an appropriate district court of the United States in a civil action maintained by the United States, the Commission, or the attorney general or the transportation regulatory body of an affected State or area. A civil penalty is provided (not to exceed $5,000) for each person who knowingly authorizes, consents to, or permits a violation of Section 1(18) or of the conditions of a certificate.

Extension Within The Meaning Of Section 1(18)

CONGRESSIONAL POLICY IN ENACTING SECTION 1(18) TO (22)
UNDER THE TRANSPORTATION ACT OF 1920

Prior to the adoption of the Transportation Act of 1920, the Commission had no authority to permit or to compel the extension of railroad lines, and such power as rested in the States in that behalf was not uniform — "statutory authority to order additions and extensions existed in some states and not in others."[2] As pointed out in the *Oregon-Washington* case (p. 23), "Congress was informed of this condition" by the Commission, and was "urged to exercise the federal power to promul-

---

[2]*I.C.C. v. Oregon-Washington R. Co.*, 288 U.S. 14, 32-3.

gate a uniform system of regulation of interstate commerce." This resulted in the enactment of legislation which first appears in the Transportation Act of 1920 giving the Commission jurisdiction over the extension of railroad lines.

In the course of interpreting the language of former paragraphs (18) to (22) inclusive, the courts explained repeatedly that consideration should be given not only to the words used in the statute, but also the purpose with which they were used by Congress in enacting the legislation, and, consequently, the object thereby sought to be accomplished. This engagement by the courts in the field of statutory construction necessarily has brought about an extensive case history of the legislative intent in enacting former paragraphs (18) to (22).

A review of the decisions reveals that Congress basically sought, by passing the Transportation Act of 1920, "to build up a system of railways prepared to handle promptly all the interstate traffic of the country," and to give the "railways an opportunity to earn enough to maintain their properties and equipment in such a state of efficiency that they can carry well this burden."[3] To achieve this purpose, the Court said (p. 478) Congress put the railroads "more completely than ever under the fostering guardianship and control of the Commission" which was authorized to supervise certain activities, including the "construction of new lines" and the "abandonment of old lines." The specific Congressional purpose in enacting former paragraphs (18) to (22) was expressed by Mr. Justic Brandeis in the celebrated case of *Texas & Pacific Ry. Co. v. Gulf, Colorado & Santa Fe Ry. Co.*[4] as follows:

> . . . A truer guide to the meaning of the terms extension and industrial track, as used in paragraphs 18 to 22, is furnished by the context and by the relation of the specific provisions here in question to the railroad policy introduced by Transportation Act, 1920. By that measure, Congress undertook to develop and maintain, for the people of the United States, an adequate railway system. It recognized that preservation of the earning capacity, and conservation of the financial resources, of individual carriers is a matter of national concern; that the property employed must be permitted to earn a reasonable return; that the building of unnecessary lines involves a waste of resources and that the burden of this waste may fall upon the public; that competition between carriers may result in harm to the public as well as in benefit; and that when a railroad inflicts injury upon its rival, it may be the public which ultimately bears the loss. See *Railroad Commission v. Chicago, Burlington & Quincy R.R. Co.*, 257 U.S. 563; *The New England Divisions Case*, 261 U.S. 184; *The Chicago Junction Case*, 264

---

[3]*Dayton-Goose Creek Ry. v. United States*, 263 U.S. 456, 478.
[4]270 U.S. 266, 277-8.

U.S. 258; *Railroad Commission v. Southern Pacific Co.*, 264 U.S. 331. The Act sought, among other things, to avert such losses.

Further insight into the underlying Congressional purpose in enacting the provisions contained in former paragraphs (18) to (22) is given in *Detroit & M. Ry. Co. v. Boyne City, G. & A. R. Co.*,[5] where the district court said (pp. 545-6):

> It is certain that the purpose actuating Congress in adding to the Interstate Commerce Act the provisions here involved was, as was pointed out by Interstate Commerce Commissioner Clark while speaking before the Committee on Interstate and Foreign Commerce of the House of Representatives, when such committee was considering the enactment of these amendatory provisions, and shortly before such enactment, "to prevent the building of duplicate lines of railroad because of keen rivalry of certain financial interests, or when the railroads so built will not serve the present or future convenience and necessity, and will simply depend for traffic upon that which they can get away from railroads already built, adding to the total burden of maintenance, capital returns, etc., which the public must pay."

> Congress had in mind and was endeavoring to correct the disastrous evils, to both the railroads and the public, which for many years had attended the construction of lines of railroad, main and branch, in ruinous competition with each other and with resultant injury to the public, which was compelled to bear the inevitable consequences of such a situation. The statutory provisions now under consideration substituted, as the underlying basis for the construction of new lines of railroad (main and branch), in place of the previously controlling policy of the private desires and ambitions of owners of railroads, the new test and rule of public convenience and necessity. . . .

That the fundamental purpose of the legislation was to prevent interstate carriers from weakening themselves by constructing and operating superfluous lines, and to protect them from being debilitated by another carrier operating in interstate commerce a competing line not required in the public interest, was announced in *Texas & New Orleans R.R. Co. v. The North Side Belt Ry. Co.*,[6] and re-expressed in *Union Pac. R. v. Denver & Rio Grande West. R. Co.*[7] New construction might prejudicially affect the public in many ways, such as financially hampering a carrier in performing its functions in furnishing adequate service by invading territory already adequately served by another carrier, thus injuring one or both of them, or by causing an increase in group rates.[8]

---

[5]286 Fed. 540.
[6]276 U.S. 475, 479.
[7]198 F. 2d, 854, 858.
[8]*Missouri-Kansas-Texas R. Co. v. Northern Oklahoma Rys.*, 25 F. 2d, 689, 691, cert. denied 278 U.S. 610.

The legislation enables "the Commission, in the interest of the public, to prevent improvident and unnecessary expenditures for the construction and operation of lines not needed to insure adequate service."[9]

THE ISSUE WHETHER TRACKS CONSTITUTE AN EXTENSION PRESENTS A JUDICIAL QUESTION

Whether certain trackage constitutes an extension or merely an industrial spur within the meaning of the statute "is a mixed question of fact and law left by Congress to the decision of a court — not to the final determination of either the federal or a state commission."[10] Hence, it is not incumbent upon the parties to have the ICC first decide the question.

The Supreme Court expressly decided in the *Texas & Pacific* case, *supra*, (pages 272-3), that the matter is properly for the courts, even though a railroad which proposes to lay tracks may, if it so wishes, first apply to the Commission for a certificate. Whenever an application is filed, the Commission, in order to determine whether it is authorized by the I.C. Act to consider the merits, "may pass incidentally upon the question whether what is called an extension is in fact such; for if it proves to be only an industrial track, the Commission must decline, on that ground, to issue a certificate." (p. 272) Unless the project is one covered by paragraph (18) of Section 1, the Commission is not authorized to consider whether the present or future public convenience and necessity require or will require the construction, and, for lack of jurisdiction to determine that question, it may deny the application. The mere fact that an application is filed with the Commission to construct new tracks does not necessarily mean that a carrier admits that the trackage constitutes an extension. A determination of the question may be secured by a carrier "without waiving any right, by asserting in the application that in its opinion a certificate is not required because the construction involves only an industrial track." (p. 273)

In either a suit to set aside an order of the Commission granting a certificate for extension of a line, or in a suit to enjoin a violation of paragraph (18), it is for the court and not the Commission to decide

[9]*Ches. & Ohio Ry. v. United States*, 283 U.S. 35, 42.
[10]*United States v. Idaho*, 298 U.S. 105, 109.

the question of whether the trackage constitutes an extension or an industrial spur.[11] In passing on the court's function, the Supreme Court said in the *Texas & Pacific* case, *supra*, (p. 273), that it "is a very different one from that exercised by the Commission" when "it grants or refuses a certificate." It was recognized by the court (p. 273) that it is the function of the Commission only to exercise administrative judgment on whether the project, assuming that it is one covered by paragraph (18), is in the public interest, and that the court "to construe a statutory provision and apply the provision as construed to the facts."

In *Long Island R. Co. v. New York Central R. Co.,*[12] the court said that while the enjoining of extensions or abandonment which the I.C. Act prohibits without a certificate is for the courts rather than the Commission, it hardly follows that Congress would not wish the courts to give heed to a long-standing and consistent interpretation by the Commission in discharge of duties confided to it; Section 1 (18) cannot be deemed wholly forbidden ground to the Commission, since often it must construe and apply that section correctly, as where an application is accompanied by a motion to dismiss for want of jurisdiction; nor is the Commission under a mandate to remain silent in an investigation and suspension proceeding as to whether the tariff contemplates action which the Commission believes it will be bound to seek to enjoin; so far as concerns the relative roles of the court and Commission, there is little distinction between Section 1 (18) and Section 20a, where also the decision whether Commission authorization is needed is ultimately for the courts, but where weight has been given not only to positive administrative construction but also to long-standing administrative inaction.

---

[11]*Powell v. United States,* 300 U.S. 276, 287. *City of Yonkers v. United States,* 320 U.S. 685, an abandonment of a railroad line case, held that the aid of the Commission need not be sought before jurisdiction of a court is invoked to enjoin violations of former Section 1 (18-22), and the fact that the Commission fails to make a finding of this given question obviously does not preclude the reviewing court from making that determination initially. The court said (p. 689), however, that it deemed it "essential in cases involving a review of orders of the Commission for the courts to decline to make that determination without the basic jurisdictional findings first having been made by the Commission." Insistence that the Commission make the jurisdictional findings before it undertakes to act, the court said (pp. 691-2), "gives added assurance that the local interests for which Congress expressed its solicitude will be safeguarded" and it also gives to the reviewing courts "the assistance of an expert judgment on a knotty phase of a technical subject."

[12]281 F. 2d 379, 383-4.

THE BURDEN IS ON THE DEFENDANT TO PROVE THAT THE PROPOSED TRACK IS NOT AN EXTENSION

In an action brought to enjoin the construction of an extension, the burden is upon the defendant to prove affirmatively that the proposed track is clearly within the exception. This was so held in *Lancaster v. Gulf C. & S. F. Ry. Co.*,[13] where the court said (pp. 491-2, 495):

> If, as I believe to be the case, paragraph 18 is the controlling portion of the act, and the purpose there expressed to make the public good, rather than the competitive instinct of railroad companies, the determining factor in the matter of whether substantial capital additions to existing railroads and substantial capital outlay in launching new roads shall be incurred, then in any case of complaint against the proposed addition to the capital account of a railroad company for the construction or extension of a line of road, which construction or extension is not sanctioned by a certificate of the Commission, an injunction ought to issue unless the constructor can satisfy the court that the construction is clearly within the exception to or limitation upon the statue, and is a side track, spur track, switch track, or industrial track, as contemplated and provided for in paragraph 22 of the act.
>
>   *   *   *   *   *
>
> It is my opinion that the affirmative is upon the defendant to prove that the track in this case is an industrial track, in order to defeat complainants' prima facie right to injunction upon the showing made, ...

THE FUNCTION OF THE COURT IN DETERMINING THE ISSUE WHETHER PROPOSED TRACKAGE CONSTITUTES AN EXTENSION OR A SPUR

In taking up the question of whether a proposed track constitutes an extension or merely a spur under the pertinent statutory provisions, the courts, it must be emphasized, have no concern with and no right to consider whether public convenience and necessity would be furthered by the proposed track, as that is a matter properly to be considered by the Commission in appropriate proceedings before it.[14] Thus, any factors bearing on convenience or necessity of the public would be irrelevant to the ultimate question to be determined. The task of the court, as stated in *Chicago, Rock Island & Pacific R. Co. v. Thompson, supra* (p. 48), is simply to characterize the trackage involved "as either an extension," in which case it cannot be built lawfully without authority from the Commission, "or spur or industrial trackage" with respect to which the Commission has no jurisdiction.

---

[13]298 F. 488, aff'd 270 U.S. 266.
[14]*Chicago, Milwaukee, St. P. & P. R. Co. v. Northern Pac. R. Co.*, 120 F. Supp. 710, 712, aff'd 225 F. 2d 840; *Chicago, Rock Island & Pacific R. Co. v. Thompson*, 135 F. Supp. 43, 48.

It was held in *Chicago, Milwaukee, St. P. & P. R. Co. v. Northern Pac. R. Co., supra* (p. 712), that courts are required by precedent to "give a liberal or broad construction to the word 'extension' and a limited or narrow construction to the words, 'spur' and 'industrial'" as applied in Section 1(18) to proposed railroad tracks." The statute as it is remedial legislation, should be given a liberal interpretation, and, for the same reason, exemptions from its scope should be narrowed and limited to effect the remedy.[15] To give the word "spur," as ued in the statute, a broad or comprehensive meaning rather than a limited or narrow construction would, in effect, negative the scheme envisioned by Congress in enacting Section 1(18).

It has been emphasized consistently by the courts that, in determining the issue, which is a mixed one of law and fact, there must be a full appraisal of the particular facts presented in each case in the light of the Congressional policy, and the detailed facts found by the court must be supported by substantial evidence.[16]

Line of Approach Employed and Factors Considered by the Courts

A reading of the cases in which injunctive relief has been sought readily reveals that the dominating question for determination is very narrow and limited. Basically, it is whether or not the track proposed to be built is an extension into territory new to that railroad and invading a field properly within or immediately adjacent to the area presently served by another railroad. In resolving the issue, the courts have considered a variety of tests or factors, not any of which has been held controlling in any given case, which distinguish a spur from an extension of lines. The reported decisions are more valuable in illustrating the lines of approach employed by the courts than in furnishing absolute rules to be followed.

Among these tests or factors are those indicated by the following questions:

1. Is the territory to be served by the proposed track within or adja-

---

[15]*Piedmont & Northern Ry v. Comm'n.*, 286 U.S. 299, 311-12; *Interstate Commerce Commission v. Piedmont & N. Ry. Co.*, 51 F. 2d 766, 774, aff'd 286 U.S. 299; *Lancaster v. Gulf C. & S. F. Ry. Co., supra*, (p. 494).

[16]*United States v. Idaho, supra*, (p. 109); *Marion & E. R. Co. v. Missouri Pac. R. Co.*, 149 N. E. 492, cert. denied 271 U.S. 661; *Chicago, Rock Island & Pacific R. Co. v. Thompson, supra* (pp. 49-50); *Chicago M. St. P. & P. R. Co. v. Chicago & E. I. R. Co.*, 198 F. 2d 8.

cent to a general area or community already being served adequately by another carrier?

2. Is it feasible or practicable for the entire area to be served and occupied by the carrier in the area?

3. Is the carrier in the area furnishing adequate service, and is it proposed to supply like facilities to other industries which may come into the area in the future?

4. Is it feasible for tracks to be constructed by the carrier in the area so as to serve future industries adequately?

5. Will the proposed line divert substantial revenues from the carrier already serving?

6. Will the proposed construction prevent the natural growth and expansion of the carrier already serving?

7. Will the proposed track connection provide service to a single customer similar to that provided other industries in the same area and similarly situated?

8. Will the proposed trackage serve only a single shipper?

9. Will the proposed track connection improve rail facilities required by shippers who are being served by other lines?

10. Will the proposed line cross the tracks of another railroad?

11. Will the proposed construction interfere with the efficient operation of another railroad?

12. Is the length of the construction so great as to be considered in the nature of a branch line?

13. Will the construction of the line necessitate a substantial outlay? Will special financing or condemnation proceedings be involved?

14. Is the cost of construction reasonable for an industrial spur in the light of the traffic involved?

15. Has service been requested by shippers?

16. Will the construction provide passenger, telephone, telegraph, or loading platform service?

17. Will there be present or absent stations, agents, line haul rates, billing by existing facilities, regular and continuous movement of trains, and other similar circumstances?

The leading federal court case in the field is *Texas & Pacific Ry. Co. v. Gulf, Colorado & Santa Fe Ry. Co., supra.* This case involved a proposed extension by the Santa Fe for the purpose of reaching some industries already being served by the Texas & Pacific. The Santa Fe took the position that the proposed trackage was an industrial spur, and for that reason commenced construction without obtaining a certificate of public convenience and necessity from the Commission. The Texas &

Pacific brought an action in the district court to enjoin further construction on the ground that the trackage constituted an extension within the meaning of the Act. The district court entered a final decree enjoining construction unless and until a certificate of public convenience and necessity was obtained from the Commission. The court of appeals reversed, but upon appeal to the Supreme Court the decision of the district court was affirmed.

In disposing of the case, Mr. Justice Brandeis cut through any effort to fashion the distinction between "extension" and "spur" by the use made of these terms in other connections, and projected the concrete situation against the broad transportation policy. At pages 277 and 278 of his opinion, Mr. Justice Brandeis said:

> When the clauses in paragraphs 18 to 22 are read in the light of this congressional policy, the meaning and scope of the terms extension and industrial track become clear. The carrier was authorized by Congress to construct, without authority from the Commission, "spur, industrial, team, switching or side tracks . . . to be located wholly within one State." Tracks of that character are commonly constructed either to improve the facilities required by shippers already served by the carrier or to supply the facilities to others, who being within the same territory and similarly situated are entitled to like service from the carrier. The question whether the construction should be allowed or compelled depends largely upon local conditions which the state regulating body is peculiarly fitted to appreciate. Moreover, the expenditure involved is ordinarily small. But where the proposed trackage extends into territory not theretofore served by the carrier, and particularly where it extends into territory already served by another carrier, its purpose and effect are, under the new policy of Congress, of national concern. For invasion through new construction of territory adequately served by another carrier, like the establishment of excessively low rates in order to secure traffic enjoyed by another, may be inimical to the national interest. If the purpose and effect of the new trackage is to extend substantially the line of a carrier into new territory, the proposed trackage constitutes an extension of the railroad within the meaning of paragraph 18, although the line be short and although the character of the service contemplated be that commonly rendered to industries by means of spurs or industrial tracks. Being an extension, it cannot be built unless the federal commission issues its certificate that public necessity and convenience require its construction. . . .

The Supreme Court of Illinois, in *Marion & E. R. Co. v. Missouri Pac. R. Co.*,[17] had before it the question whether or not a track which the Missouri Pacific proposed to construct would be an extension or a mere spur. The track proposed would be approximately one mile long, would cross the Marion Railroad, and would lead to a new coal mine

---

[17] 149 N.E. 492, cert. denied 271 U.S. 661.

to which the Marion Railroad already had constructed a switch track. At page 495 of the decision, the court said:

> . . . The proposed track, according to the answer of the Missouri Pacific Railroad Company, will be more than a mile in length, and will run from its line to a coal shaft under construction by the West Virginia Coal Company. Appellant has already constructed a switch track to this new shaft with the exception of the mine track, for which the material was on the ground. The new track, if built, will enter territory served by appellant, to and from which through routes and rates exist. While the answer avers that on the proposed track no line-haul rates will be established, nor regular continuous movements of trains made, nor a station erected, nor the billing of freight required, except through existing facilities, the effect of the construction of that track will be to afford railroad service in direct competition with appellant's road, on which, in connection with other railroads, through routes and rates have been established. The track, if laid, will be used in interstate as well as intrastate commerce. It will be an extension of the line of the Missouri Pacific Railroad rather than a spur, industrial, team, switching or side track, as defined in paragraph 22 of section 1 of the Interstate Commerce Act.

Other decisions in which the conclusion was reached that the track proposed for construction was an extension of the line of an interstate carrier, and that it could not be built without a certificate of public convenience and necessity from the Commission, are discussed below.

In *Missouri Pac. R. Co. v. Chicago R. I. & P. Ry. Co.,*[18] there was involved an appeal from a final decree granting a permanent injunction against the Missouri Pacific restraining it from constructing a railroad lead track approximately 3,700 feet long in Little Rock, Arkansas, across certain property and railroad tracks of the Rock Island. The court found among other things that both railroads were engaged in interstate commerce; that the territory of limited area into which the proposed construction would be projected already was occupied and served to a very considerable extent by the Rock Island; that it was entirely feasible for the whole territory to be occupied and served by the Rock Island whenever necessary; that the Missouri Pacific was neither occupying nor serving such territory, except with one spur track for a short distance; and that the introduction of the Missouri Pacific into this territory would prevent the natural growth of the business of the Rock Island in said territory, and very probably would lessen its present business there. Upon the foregoing facts stated, the court concluded that the proposed construction must be held to be an extension of the line of the Missouri Pacific within the meaning of Section 1(18).

---

[18]41F. 2d 188, cert. denied 282 U.S. 866.

A closely similar fact situation to the cases discussed is presented in *Chicago, Milwaukee, St. P. R. Co. v. Northern Pac. R. Co.*[19] The Northern Pacific sought to construct three miles of tracks with sidings and other subsidiary tracks from a main branch of its line to a 400-acre tract owned by it, which it proposed to develop for industry. Two firms had made commitments to locate on the tract if the proposed line were built. Under the plans for the proposed line, there would be no separate station or agent for the line and no regularly scheduled trains or passenger service thereon. The Milwaukee sought to enjoin the construction, its line being only one mile from the terminus of the proposed track of the Northern Pacific. The court stated that the basic issue was whether or not the proposed track was an extension into territory new to that railroad and invading a field properly within or immediately adjacent to the area presently served by the Milwaukee. The court so held and enjoined the construction.

In *Cleveland C. & St. L. Ry. Co. v. Commere Com'n.*,[20] a coal company sought to construct a railroad track from its mine to a point across the tracks of the Illinois Central and a second railroad to compel or force a connection with the right-of-way of plaintiff railroad. The Illinois Commerce Commission granted the requested permission. On appeal, the court held that the proposed track constituted an extension of the lines of the three railroads involved, and that the state authority was without jurisdiction to require the proposed construction. It was contended by plaintiff that even though the Illinois Commerce Commission provided in its order that the track, when built and connected with plaintiff's line, should not be used for any purpoose other than to serve the mine of the coal company, the track could not be viewed as a spur. Plaintiff was of the opinion that the order of the Illinois Commerce Commission had no validity for the reason that the track, when constructed, would become a public track and the state authority had no power to limit the use of it. The limitation placed on the track's usage by the state authority, according to plaintiff, had no effect upon the issue in the case. The court agreed with plaintiff's contentions (p. 612), stating that the limitation in the Illinois Commission's order was of no avail.

A fact situation paralleling the foregoing cases is presented in *Union Pac. R. Co. v. Denver & Rio Grande Western R. Co.*,[21] where the Rio Grande sought an injunction against the Union Pacific's proposed con-

---

[19]120 F. Supp. 710, aff'd 225 F. 2d 840.
[20]146 N. E. 606.
[21]198 F. 2d 854.

struction of a track about 9,000 feet in length which was to cross an interchange and spur track of the Rio Grande to reach a 265-acre area near Salt Lake City. The facts showed that the area was available for industrial development by the Rio Grande by means of spur tracks extending from its main line and interchange track, but it was not so available to the Union Pacific, as it was not feasible to reach the area; that the area constituted potentially and in the near future one of the best industrial traffic producing areas in Utah; and that the proposed trackage of the Union Pacific would result in traffic being diverted from the Rio Grande to the Union Pacific with substantial losses to the Rio Grande in freight revenues. The facts revealed also that the Union Pacific did not contemplate having freight stations, loading stations, or station agents within the industrial area; that it did not propose to operate trains therein under train orders; that it did not contemplate furnishing passenger, express, or mail service therein; and that it intended merely to furnish switching service within the switching limits to such industries as had spur tracks connected to the lead track. The court found (p. 859) that the proposed trackage would invade "new territory" not previously or presently served by the Union Pacific, and that it would result in loss of revenue to a competing line which had been furnishing adequate service to industries in the area, and was prepared to supply like facilities to other industries locating there in the future. The court held, therefore, that the proposed trackage constituted an extension.

In *Missouri Pac. R. Co. v. St .Louis, Southwestern Ry. Co.*,[22] a proposed track about one mile long from a railroad's main line to certain industrial plants was held by the court to be an extension and not a mere spur or industrial track, thus being within the pertinent provision of the I.C. Act requiring a certificate from the Commission. In order to construct the track, it would have been necessary for the Missouri Pacific to cross the tracks of its competitor located between the main line of the Missouri Pacific and the industrial area. The court held (p. 22) that the industries in question were amply and adequately served by two railroads now connected therewith, and that the proposed trackage "would invade" the territory. Following the language in the *Texas & Pacific* case, *supra*, which the court said was particularly applicable to the facts of the case, the conclusion was reached (pp. 22-3), "that the proposed extension, nearly a mile in length, into territory in which appellant has no trackage, and which territory is now and for the future

[22]273 F. 2d 21.

will be adequately served by other carriers, is an 'extension' of appellant's railroad within the contemplation of paragraph 18 of section 1 of the Interstate Commerce Act, and the same cannot be constructed without the consent of the Interstate Commerce Commission."

The fact that a railroad had partially completed a track and was proceeding vigorously with the construction to reach a 500-acre tract had no bearing on the ultimate decision of the court in *Southern Pac. Co. v. Western Pacific California R. Co.*[23] There were no industries located on the 500-acre tract, which was adjacent to a much larger industrial area not theretofore served by the railroad. An injunction granted by the lower court to halt the construction was affirmed on appeal. The Western Pacific previously had obtained a certificate from the Commission to extend its line into the industrial area involved, but had not commenced construction. The court found that the purpose of the Southern Pacific extending its line directly across the approximate proposed location and route of the Western Pacific trackage was to impede and, if possible, prevent the construction and operation by the Western Pacific of the line. This state of facts, the court said (p. 735) "does not indicate a need for the construction of spur tracks." Needless to say, the element of invasion was present in the case.

In *Chicago, Rock Island & Pacific R. Co. v. Thompson, supra* (p. 43), action was brought to enjoin the Missouri Pacific from constructing a railroad line to serve a single plant located in a planned industrial district on the theory that the proposed trackage constituted an extension of the defendant's line of railroad within the meaning of the I.C. Act. In its original complaint, the Rock Island, in addition to praying for the issuance of an injunction against the Missouri Pacific's proposed construction, prayed in the alternative that if the court determined that the trackage in question was not an extension but simply a spur, it should enter a declaratory judgment to the effect that the Rock Island was free to build trackage into and through the so-called planned industrial district.

Later, the Rock Island amended its complaint so as to set up a second alternative prayer for relief, namely, that if the court held that the Missouri Pacific trackage was a spur and if it found further that the Rock Island was not free to build a track to serve the entire industrial district without first obtaining a certificate, then a declaratory judgment must be entered to the effect that the Rock Island was free to build a track designed to serve the single plant planned to be served by the

[23]61 F. 2d 732.

Missouri Pacific. The court resolved the conflicting theories of the parties by holding that the track proposed to be constructed by the Missouri Pacific was a spur track, and that the track which the Rock Island proposed to lay to the same industrial plan or area was an extension. The court, in arriving at its decision, said (pp. 51, 54):

> When the facts above set forth are considered in the light of the principles announced in the decided cases that have been cited, we are satisfied that the Missouri Pacific's proposed construction is simply a spur or industrial track, rather than an extension of its line, and that no injunction should be issued. As stated, the present purpose of the Missouri Pacific is to serve the AMF plant alone, not the entire district; the proposed construction and service are typically spur or industrial track, as opposed to main or branch line; the distance between the Missouri Pacific's main line and the northeast corner of the AMF property is short, and the location is, in our opinion, within the defendant's normal service territory; the cost of the construction is small, comparatively speaking, and there will be no diversion of any business from the Rock Island.

❋   ❋   ❋   ❋   ❋

> From a reading of the decisions in *Texas & Pacific Railway Co. v. Gulf, C. & S. F. R. Co.* and *Union Pacific R. Co. v. Denver & R. G. W. R. Co.*, both supra, it seems clear that the national policy underlying the Transportation Act was twofold: first, to prevent wasteful or extravagant expenditures of funds by railroads for construction, and second, to prevent cutthroat competition. In our opinion, to declare that the Rock Island may build to the AMF plant without a certificate of public convenience and necessity would violate that policy in both respects. Although it may be conceded that in this particular instance the expenditure involved would not seriously affect a road as strong as the Rock Island, it must be remembered that particular instances can be multiplied, and that a carrier may weaken itself and dissipate its resources through many small extravagancies as well as by a few large ones. It was one of the purposes of Congress in passing the Act to prevent waste and extravagance in railroad construction; and we do not feel that the federal courts, in exercising the jurisdiction conferred upon them by paragraph 20, are called upon to determine relative degrees of waste or to attempt to draw any line between extravagancies that are serious and those that are not. Certainly, the courts are not concerned with balancing the expense of construction against the public convenience and necessity. Those are matters more properly addressed to the expert judgment of the I.C.C. But even if we assume for purposes of argument that wasteful construction is not a factor here, there is no question that to permit the Rock Island to build in to the AMF property would adversely affect the Missouri Pacific in its revenues.

> Under the facts presented here we are unable to find that the Rock Island's proposed construction to AMF is simply a spur or industrial track; on the other hand, it appears to us that said proposed construction would be an extension of the Rock Island's line of railroad which cannot lawfully be undertaken without the sanction of the Commission; . . .

Where proposed trackage has been held by the courts to be a mere spur rather than an extension, a review of the leading cases reveals factual situations existing which are far different from those appearing in the foregoing cases discussed.

In *Missouri Pac. R. Co. v. Union Pac. Ry. Co.*,[24] a 200-foot track of the Union Pacific over the right-of-way of the Missouri Pacific to connect with a track of the Chicago & Great Western was held to be within the exception of former Section 1(22). According to the evidence, however, the Union Pacific and the Chicago & Great Western interchanged business at the point involved for many years, using a piece of track belonging to a small railroad that formed a connecting link between their lines. Thereafter, the connecting link came into the possession of the Missouri Pacific.

In *Pennsylvania Railroad Co. v. Reading Co.*,[25] the conclusion was reached by the court that trackage proposed to be constructed by the Reading Company to serve an electric power plant constituted an industrial spur and not an extension, on the theory that the case had two important featuers of an industrial spur highlighted by Mr. Justice Brandeis in his opinion in the *Texas & Pacific* case, *supra*. The standards referred to were that tracks in the nature of an industrial spur either improve the facilities required by shippers already served by the carrier or supply facilities to others who, being in the same territory and similarly situated, are entitled to like service from the carrier. From the background of railroad transportation in the area, as outlined by the court in its decision, it is readily apparent that the Reading Company was not "invading" the territory of another railroad. As the court said (p. 622), the sum total of all the evidence indicates "that the construction involved incorporates all the features of an industrial spur only," and none of those involving an extension of lines.

Missouri K. & T. R. Co. v. Texas & N. O. R. Co.,[26] involved an action by M-K-T against the Texas & New Orleans to enjoin the latter from building certain tracks into an area characterized by the court as new territory. The Texas & New Orleans also sought an injunction by way of a cross-bill to stay the construction and operation of certain tracks by the M-K-T. The court held that the proposed tracks of the carriers were not extensions within the meaning of the I.C. Act, but mere spurs. In deciding the case, the court called attention to certain existing facts which distinguish it from the foregoing cases (pp. 770-1):

[24]60 F. 2d 126.
[25]132 F. Supp. 616, aff'd 226 F. 2d 958.
[26]172 F. 2d 768.

We do not think this case is like that of the *Texas & Pacific Ry. Co. v. Gulf, Colorado & Santa Fe Ry. Co.*, supra; or involves an "extension of [the] line of railroad" of either contestant. The obtuse angle of prairie land was originally bounded as much by the main line of the one as by the other. Each had a right to build spur tracks and industrial tracks from its main line into it. M.K. and T. built the first ones, and its longer one strategically paralleled the Texas and New Orleans. But neither that nor its other spurs pre-empted for the M. K. and T. the hinterland, still undeveloped but in easy reach of both railroads. Texas law permits the Texas and New Orleans to cross the highway as it has done, and to cross the extension of M.K. and T.'s spur as it has done, conceding the dispute about right of way to M.K. and T. as the district court decided. There is plenty room and opportunity for both railroads to serve. There is no serious raiding of any established traffic. The proposed expenditures are not unusual or very significant for these strong and extensive railroads to make. We see no need to strain to hold these tracks which are in form and in purpose and effect ordinary industrial tracks to be "extensions of the lines of railroads" of these two great carriers, which must be authorized by the Railroad Commission. We make no enquiry into any question of public convenience or necessity, which is not a function of the court, but rest the decision upon the grounds stated.

In *Chicago, M. St. P. & P. R. Co. v. Chicago & E. I. R. Co.*, *supra*, the court declined to enjoin the defendant from constructing trackage extending from an existing branch to an electric power plant and a coal mine, on the ground that the proposed construction was a spur for which a certificate from the Commission was not required. The decision of the court apparently rested upon the finding that there was no attempt being made to tap the territory already served by the plaintiff, and the defendant had in the past actually served the area immediately adjacent to the power plant. As the court said (p. 11), plaintiff does not "furnish service to any industry south of its present right-of-way," and as a matter of fact, the only industry in that territory "is served by the C. & E. I. R. R."

In *Jefferson County v. Louisville & N. R. Co.*[27] the court held that a proposed line to be constructed over three county highways to reach an electric company constituted a spur and not an extension. There suit was filed by Jefferson County, and not a railroad competitor, for an injunction to prevent the railroad from laying its tracks across the roads in question at grade level. The court recognized the guiding principles enunciated in the *Texas & Pacific* case, *supra*, upon which the county placed considerable reliance, but distinguished the two cases. As the court said (pp. 614-5), the controlling feature in the *Texas & Pacific*

[27]245 S. W. 2d 611.

case "was the fact that the proposed new line would be in direct competition with another railroad system, which was the complainant in the case," but, in the case under consideration, L. & N.'s competitor, Southern Railway, did not object "to the proposed construction," and both railroads had agreed with the electric company to connect their lines with the plant.

Trackage 1,300 feet in length which Detroit & Toledo Co. sought to enjoin New York Central from constructing was held to be a spur rather than an extension in *Detroit & Toledo Shore L. R. Co. v. New York Cent. R. Co.*[28] The facts reveal that it was not a case where one railroad was attempting to raid or invade the territory of another, as both railroads served the particular industrial area, and a request had been made by one of the shippers in the area for a spur connection. The facts also show that many years prior thereto a contract had been entered into between the Detroit & Toledo Co. and the New York Central's predecessor, Toledo, Canada, Southern and Detroit Ry. Co., authorizng the crossing of any portion of Detroit & Toledo Co's. tracks and right-of-way by the predecessor railway to reach the industrial area involved in the case.

A number of cases dealing with the question of railroad line extensions have been decided by the Commission, and the principles set forth in the *Texas & Pacific* case, *supra*, have been accepted as the guiding standards. In filing an application with the Commission under Section 1 (18), an applicant, as heretofore indicated, may at the same time file a motion to dismiss on the ground that the use to be made of the proposed line establishes it as an industrial spur or switching track, and that the Commission is without jurisdiction in the premises. In those instances, the Commission, in order to determine whether it is authorized to consider the merits, may pass incidentally upon the issue of whether or not an extension is involved. This has afforded the Commission guidance in dealing with the questions of its jurisdiction in similar proceedings. The decisions reveal that the Commission has not prescribed any concrete rules or formulas whereby a line of railroad in the nature of a spur, industrial, or switching track can be distinguished easily from a line that unquestionably is within the jurisdiction of the Commission. The jurisdictional questions involved appear to have been determined by the Commission in the light of the circumstances surrounding each case and by the standards set out in the *Texas & Pacific* case, *supra,* and other federal court decisions.

[28]233 F. 2d 168.

In *Chicago B. & Q. R. Co. Construction,*[29] two railroads filed separate applications for authority to construct short lines for the purpose of delivering coal to a large industrial plant which was being served by a third railroad. In discussing the scope of its jurisdiction in the case, the Commission said (p. 559) that where territory being served by one carrier is proposed to be invaded by another "our jurisdiction attaches even though the length of the line to be constructed may be short and its purpose may be to serve a single industry, and the track under other circumstances might be considered a spur or industry track."

Application Seeking a Certificate of Public Convenience and Necessity for the Extension of a Railroad Line

Issues Before the Commission

Where an application has been filed seeking a certificate of public convenience and necessity, pursuant to Section 1 (18), the Commission ordinarily is faced with two basic issues:

1. Is the proposed line of applicant an extension of its line of railroad so as to require a certificate of public convenience and necessity?
2. Assuming a certificate of public convenience and necessity must be obtained, does the record support the granting of such certificate?

We need concern ourselves only with the second issue as the first was discussed fully heretofore. Among other things, the matters to be considered in determining whether or not the public convenience and necessity require the construction and operation of a proposed line are the present or future needs for additional rail transportation facilities by the industries located, or to be located, in the industrial area; adequacy of the present service now being performed, or capable of being performed in the future, to meet the rail transportation needs of the industries in question; and the justification for the expenditure to provide the area with duplicate rail transportation facilities.

Justification for the Construction Must Be Established by Clear Proof That Public Convenience and Necessity Require the Proposed Line

Even though the Commission has held consistently in the past that it is undesirable, if not impossible, to lay down any general rule by

[29]282 I.C.C. 539.

which it can be determined whether or not certificates of public convenience and necessity should be issued for the construction of proposed railroad lines and that every case must be decided in the light of its own special circumstances,[30] the language used in prior cases is relied upon by the Commission in its consideration of similar problems. Thus principles established in the past though not inflexible are persuasive in, and underlie, subsequent decisions.

As pointed out heretofore, the Commission originally was given jurisdiction over railroad extensions by the enactment of the Transportation Act of 1920 in order to prevent wasteful and unwise railroad construction. It was one of the principal purposes of Congress in passing that law to curb invasion by one carrier of the territory of another merely for the purpoose of furthering the selfish interests of the invading line. The Congressional policy was voiced by the Commission in *Construction of Lines in Eastern Oregon*[31] where it said (pp. 45-6):

> The general principles which are to guide us are not difficult to establish. Congress has undertaken to develop and maintain, for the people of the United States, an adequate railroad system. It has recognized that as to individual carriers the preservation of their earning capacity and conservation of their financial resources is a matter of national concern; that the property employed must be permitted to earn a reasonable return; that the building of unnecessary lines involves a waste of resources, and that the burden of this waste may fall upon the public; that competition between carriers may result in harm to the public, as well as in benefit; and that, when a railroad inflicts injury upon its rival, it may be the public which ultimately bears the loss.

With the scheme envisioned by Congress, the Commission has stressed the point that certificates of public convenience and necessity for the extension of railroad lines will not be granted unless there is a "strong or urgent need" for the proposed service.[32] In holding as it did in the *Galesburg* case (p. 477) that the justification for construction of a railroad line "must be established by clear proof that the railroad is to be both a public convenience and a public necessity" and that the latter "implies a strong or urgent need," the Commission adopted the language used earlier in *Public Convenience Application of Utah Terminal Ry.*[33] where it said (pp. 93-4):

[30]*See Illinois Central R. Co. Construction and Operation*, 217 I.C.C. 615, 622; and *Construction by San Antonio & Pass Ry.*, 111 I.C.C. 483, 493.
[31]III I.C.C. 3.
[32]*Galesburg & G. E. R. Co. Construction*, 244 I.C.C. 470, 477.
[33]72 I.C.C. 89.

. . . "Public convenience and necessity" has been defined as "a strong or urgent public need." *Wis. Telephone Co. v. Railroad Com.*, 162 Wis. 383; 156 N. W., 614. A public need can hardly be predicated upon the demand of three shippers who may desire to introduce the element of competition in order to improve their position in their own competitive field. While one of the purposes of the transportation act, 1920, was to preserve competition between carriers, the provisions of paragraphs (18) to (20), inclusive, of section 1 negative any presumption that it was the purpose of Congress to permit the construction of new and competitive lines of railroad where existing facilities are adequate or can be made so by the exercise of available administrative remedies.[34]

The Commission has held uniformly in prior decisions relating to extension of railroad lines that sound economic conditions in the transportation industry require that carriers now serving a particular territory or locality normally should be accorded the right to transport all traffic therein which they can handle adequately, efficiently, and economically before a new authorization should be authorized. This conclusion is applicable not only with respect to existing traffic but also with respect to potential traffic.[35] When an existing line of railroad can meet the transportation needs of shippers, any outlay of funds to provide such shippers with the service of an additional railroad would be an economic waste. In a broad sense, it may be said that the construction, maintenance, and operation of unnecessary lines of railroad eventually must be borne by the public, the interests of which the Commission has a duty to protect.

A review of the cases which follow reveals that the Commission has been consistent in following the foregoing principle that carriers now serving a particular territory should be protected from unwarranted invasions, and should be permitted to furnish needed transportation facilities.

Chicago, B. & Q. R. Co. Construction, supra, two applicant trunk lines, C. B. & Q. and New York Central, in order to enhance their revenues and in response to requests of shippers, sought authority to extend their lines to Joppa, Illinois, a point on the north bank of the Ohio River, for the purpose of participating in a large volume coal movement

---

[34]The ultimate finding of the Commission in the *Utah Terminal* case was reversed on rehearing in a subsequent report (79 I.C.C. 187), and a certificate of public convenience and necessity was issued authorizing the construction of the railroad line involved; however, the amended report did not repudiate the language used in the original report but simply found that the facts of the case demonstrated a strong and urgent need for the service.

[35]*Operation of Lines by C. R. & E. Ry. Co.*, 94 I.C.C. 389; *Galesburg & G. E. R. Co. Construction, supra;* and *Chicago, B. & Q. R. Co. Construction*, 282 I.C.C. 725.

necessary for fuel requirements of steam electric stations which were to furnish electric energy to a plant of the former Atomic Energy Commission located ner Paducah, Kentucky. One of the steam electric stations, located at or near Joppa, was owner by a private concern; and the other, located at or near Chiles, Kentucky, about eight miles from Joppa and known as the Shawnee plant, was operated by Tennessee Valley Authority. Both Atomic Energy and T.V.A. intervened in the proceeding in support of the applications. The C. & E. I., which was serving the area, opposed the applications. The full Commission denied the applications, holding that the public convenience and necessity did not warrant the construction of new lines of railroad to serve these important national defense installations in the absence of any showing of inadequacy of existing service. Discussing the question of public convenience and necessity the Commission said (pp. 729-30):

> The principal questions for consideration in these proceedings relate to whether there is an existing public need for the railroad facilities and service of either or both the applicants at Joppa; to whether the existing carrier, the Eastern Illinois, may reasonably be expected to transport efficiently and without delay . . . all coal offered for movement to or through Joppa and under such conditions that the full and free movement of southern Illinois coal will not be retarded; to whether a carrier which had had a line into and has served a specific area for many years should be permitted to enjoy the increase of such area and be protected against competition, at least to the extent of affording it an opportunity to demonstrate that its transportation service is fully adequate and sufficient to meet the needs of the traffic; and to whether after a weighing of such factors it can be found as a matter of judgment upon the whole record that the public convenience and necessity require or will require the construction proposed.

The Commission in passing on the application recognized (pp. 730-1) that the C & E. I. had aided and encouraged the development of a market for southern Illinois coal on and south of the Ohio River and that its cooperation in providing a competitive rate was largely responsible for the location of the T.V.A. plant at or ner Chiles; and that the C. & E. I. had invested a large sum of money in rolling stock and other appurtenant facilities in contemplation of increased traffic over its lines, particularly that which it was instrumental in generating through Joppa. It was the Commission's opinion (p. 731) that, insofar as consistent with the factor of public need, "the investment" made by the C. & E. I. to render service at Joppa "should be protected."

The Commission held in *Southern Ry. Co. Construction*,[36] that the public convenience and necessity were not shown to require construction

[36]275 I.C.C. 792.

and operation by the Southern Railway of a branch line to enable it to reach and serve a plant of the former Atomic Energy Commission. The agency had arranged with a private concern for the construction and operation of the plant which was to be devoted to the production of atomic materials for use in national defense. The Atlantic Coast Line intervened in opposition to the granting of the application. In denying the application, the Commission stated (p. 796):

> The territory in which the plant is to be located is now served by two railroads, and should not be invaded by a competing railroad unless it be shown that the present and future public convenience and necessity require additional rail service which cannot be rendered by the present carriers. No such showing has been made. On the contrary, it is apparent from the record that the two carriers now in the territory are well equipped and ready to render satisfactory service to the proposed plant.

In *Galesburg & G. E. R. Co. Construction, supra,* the Commission denied an application for the construction of an extension into territory already served by other carriers on the ground that the proposed line would constitute an unnecessary duplication of railroad facilities. This conclusion was reached by the Commission even though the application was supported by coal mining industries and other interests in the territory tributary to applicant's line. There, the Galesburg Railroad sought to extend its line to a connection with the branch line of the Rock Island Railroad. The objective of the proposal was to reach a newly developed coal strip located closer to the Rock Island line than to the line of the C. B. & Q. with which applicant had its only connection. Applicant contended that the proposed extension would eliminate the C. B. & Q. as an intermediate carrier. In opposing the application, the C. B. & Q. argued that the joint through rates were available and therefore no material rate advantages would accrue to the shippers as a result of the proposed extension. The Commission in denying the application recognized that industries generally desire the convenience of as many direct trunk line connections as they can obtain, but held that this reason alone is not a justification for the construction of railroad lines in Interstate Commerce.

Where the contention was made by an applicant that the sole question to be determined in an application proceeding for the extension of a railroad line is whether there will be, in all probability, sufficient traffic to and from points on the proposed branch to justify its construction and maintenance, the Commission held in *Construction of Branch by St. L.-S. F. Ry.*[37] that the determining factor is not solely whether there is a probability of sufficient traffic to warrant construction,

---

[37]105 I.C.C. 768, 772-3.

but whether there is a need for a line of railroad in the territory to be served. Upon the facts presented in the case the Commission was unable to find that the present and future public convenience and necessity required or would require the construction of the branch line, stating that the territory involved was being served adequately. And in *Texas & P. N. Ry. Co. Proposed Construction,*[38] the Commission denied an application for authority to construct a railroad line where a large portion of the traffic would be drawn from carriers now serving the territory in question. The record showed that existing railroads already provided convenient access to the most important markets, and that the rail service was "supplemented by an extensive system of truck transport." (p. 70)

Upon the record made in *Toledo, P. & W. R. Operation and Construction,*[39] where the testimony showed that the existing carrier was serving satisfactorily all the industries established in the territory in question and was prepared to serve all those industries which may be established, the Commission denied part of an application for authority to construct an extension of a railroad line, stating (p. 113) that "applicant has not shown and the record does not indicate that the public interest requires the construction of the proposed line into the industrial territory mentioned." In *Construction by Piedmont & Northern Ry.,*[40] the Commission held, where the facts presented showed that there would have been an extraordinary paralleling of an existing line, "that the present and future public convenience and necessity is not shown to require the construction by the applicant of the lines of railroad described in the application." (p. 401) The Commission stated (p. 401) that the presumption against such paralleling as was proposed could not be overcome by the evidence presented in the case, and that "the investment proposed would not be justified."

A review of the cases also shows that in the course of deciding application for extension of lines cases the Commission in the past, though consistent in protecting the existing carriers from unwarranted invasion of territories, has recognized among other things that "(c)arriers have no legal right to exclusive occupancy of a territory."[41] In the *Louisville & N. R. Co.* case, the Commission said that carriers have no legal right to exclusive occupancy of a territory, and interests of a shipper may properly be considered in determining the question of public convenience and necessity; moreover, the added competition provided by the

[38] 184 I.C.C. 55.
[39] 162 I.C.C. 100.
[40] 138 I.C.C. 363.
[41] *St. Louis-S. F. Ry. Co. Construction,* 271 I.C.C. 282, 293; *Louisville & N. R. Co. Construction,* 312 I.C.C. 169, 176.

proposed construction can be in the public interest; the establishment of new markets and rate advantages flowing from service of a particular carrier are matters of substantial importance in determining whether public convenience and necessity require construction of a line of railroad or performance of service by one carrier or another.

The Commission has also said that it was not the purpose of Congress in regulating the construction of railroad lines "to put a stop to all competitive railroad building" and that the intention to preserve competition in rail transportation is manifest in other provisions of the I.C. Act;[42] that "the interests of a shipper properly may be considered in determining the question of public convenience and necessity";[43] that the interest of shippers are matters of substantial importance in determining the question of public convenience and necessity;[44] that shippers in any territory should not be denied the widest possible choice of markets and the ability to reach them over the shortest and most economical routes, if that can be avoided;[45] and that competition operates to stimulate better service and is in the public interest.[46] The Commission also has considered the benefits or advantages to be derived by proposed construction in the form of expedited delivery on rail traffic, a more abundant car supply, simplified negotiations on rate matters, and the stimulus of additional carrier competition;[47] in the form of savings in time and charges by the substitution of one-line haul for interchange arrangements;[48] and in the form of furnishing valuable alternate lines of transportation in time of emergency or in the event of a breakdown or interruption in service.[49]

Abandonment of Railroad Service

The authority of the Commission to regulate the abandonment and discontinuance of all railroad service is found in Section 1a of the I.C. Act which was added by the 4R Act.[50]

[42]*Construction by Ft. Worth & Denver South Plains Ry.*, 117 I.C.C. 233, 275.
[43]*St. Louis-S. F. Ry. Co. Construction, supra.*
[44]*Chesapeake & O. Ry. Co. Construction*, 267 I.C.C. 665, 681.
[45]*Levisa River R. Co. Construction*, 257 I.C.C. 203, 218.
[46]*Construction of Line by Wenatchee Southern Ry.*, 90 I.C.C. 237, 256-7.
[47]*Gulf, M. & O. R. Co. Construction*, 271 I.C.C. 541, 552.
[48]*Construction of Line by Prince George & C. Ry.*, 145 I.C.C. 788, 790.
[49]*Public-Convenience Application of Utah Term. Ry.*, 79 I.C.C. 187, 190; *Construction of Line by Prince George & C. Ry., supra; Northern Pacific Ry. Co. Trackage Rights*, F. D. 15925, unreported, decided September 28, 1948.
[50]49 U.S.C. 1a. For suspension, change, and revocation of certificates or permits see Section 210; for transfer of certificates or permits see Sections 212(b), 312; for abandonment of service of freight forwarders see Section 410; and for approval of abandonments of lines of railroads undergoing reorganization see 11 U.S.C. 205 (0).

Section 1a(1) provides that no carrier by railroad "shall abandon all or any portion of any of its lines of railroad . . . and no such carrier shall discontinue the operation of all rail service over all or any portion of any such line . . . unless such abandonment or discontinuance is described in and covered by a certificate which is issued by the Commission and which declares that the present or future public convenience and necessity require or permit such abandonment or discontinuance." The authority granted to the Commission under this section shall not apply to (a) abandonment or discontinuance with respect to spur, industrial, team, switching, or side tracks if such tracks are located entirely within one State, or (b) any street, suburban, or interurban electric railway which is not operated as part of a general system of rail transportation.[51]

Section 1a(4) provides that the Commission may (a) issue such certificate in the form requested by the applicant if it finds that such abandonment or discontinuance is consistent with the public convenience and necessity. In determining whether the proposal abadonment is consistent with the public convenience and necessity, the Commission shall consider whether there will be a serious adverse impact on rural and community development by such abandonment or discontinuance; (b) issue such certificate with modifications in such form and subject to such terms and conditions are are required, in the judgment of the Commission, by the public convenience and necessity; or (c) refuse to issue such certificate.

Section 1a(9) provides that any abandonment or discontinuance which is contrary to Section 1a, of any regulation promulgated under Section 1a, or of any terms and conditions of an applicable certificate, may be enjoined by an appropriate district court of the United States, the Commission, or the attorney general or the transportation regulatory body of the State or area. A civil penalty is provided (not to exceed $5,000) for each person who knowingly authorizes, consents to, or permits any violation of Section 1a or of any regulation under the section.

Section 1a(9) provides that in "any instance in which the Commission finds that the present or future public convenience and necessity permit abandonment or discontinuance, the Commission shall make a further finding whether such properties are suitable for use for other public purposes, including roads or highways, other forms of mass transportation, conservation, energy production or transmission, or recreation." If it is found that the properties proposed to be abandoned are suitable

[51]Added by Section 218(a) of the Rail Transportation Improvement Act, P.L. 94-555, October 19, 1976.

for other public purposes, the Commission "shall order that such rail properties not be sold, leased, exchanged, or otherwise disposed of except in accordance with such reasonable terms and conditions as are prescribed by the Commission, including, but not limited to, a prohibition on any such disposal, for a period not to exceed 180 days after the effective date of the order permitting abandonment unless such properties have first been offered, upon reasonable terms, for acquisition for public purposes."

An application for a certificate to abandon a line or to discontinue service must be filed with the Commission not less than 60 days prior to the proposed effective date of such abandonment or discontinuance. The applicant must serve notice of its intent to abandon upon the Governor of each State that would be directly affected by such action; post the notice in each terminal and station on the line to be abandoned; publish the notice in newspapers of general circulation in each county in which the line is located; and mail the notice, to the extent practicable, to all shippers who have made significant use of such line during the 12 months preceding the filing of the application.

During the 55 day period subsequent to filing of the actual application, the Commission must, on petition, or may, on its own initiative, cause an investigation to be conducted to assist it in determining what disposition to make of an application. If no investigation is ordered, the Commission is directed to issue a certificate within 60 days from the date of filing. If an investigation is ordered the Commission must postpone the effective date of the proposed abandonment for a reasonable time to allow for completion of the investigation. After an investigation, the Commission may grant, deny, or take other action on the application. If the Commission grants a certificate, actual abandonment or discontinuance may not take effect for 120 days after issuance of the certificate and must be in accordance with the terms of the certificate. However, if such certificate is issued without an investigation, actual abandonment of discontinuance may take effect, in accordance with such certificate, 30 days after the date of issuance thereof.

In reaching its decision, the Commission must consider whether there will be a serious adverse impact on rural and community development as a result of the abandonment or discontinuance. The Commission must make a further finding as to whether the properties involved are suitable for use for other public purposes. If the Commission finds that the properties are suitable for such purposes, it shall order that the properties may not be disposed of except according to terms and conditions prescribed by the Commission. One such condition must be a prohibition on any disposal of the properties for a period not to exceed 180 days after the effective date of the order permitting abandonment unless such properties have first been offered on reasonable terms of acquisition for public purposes.

Whenever the Commission finds that abandonment or discontinuance should be permitted, it must publish its finding in the Federal Register. If within 30 days of publication, the Commission finds that a "financially responsible person" (including a government entity) has offered financial assistance in the form of a "rail service continuation payment" which is likely to cover net avoidable costs and proved a reasonable return on investment or cover the cost of acquisition of the line, the Commission must postpone issuance of an effective certificate of abandonment or discontinuance for a reasonable time (not to exceed six months) to allow the parties to execute acquisition or operation agreements. Under certain conditions where a State makes the subsidy payment, it may be entitled to reimbursement of all or a portion of that payment from Federal funds. If an agreement is executed, the Commission will postpone the issuance of the abandonment certificate for so long as the agreement, including any extensions, is in effect.

The Commission has adopted regulations in Ex Parte No. 274 (Sub-No. 2), *Abandonment of Rail Lines and Discontinuance of Rail Service,* governing the abandonment of railroad lines and the discontinuance of rail service. (See *C & N W v. I.C.C.*, No. 76-2283, 7 Cir., decided May 30, 1978, remanding to I.C.C. for further proceedings covering certain regulations.)

The new regulations require each railroad to prepare a map of its rail system to be filed with the Commission and designated officials of each State where it operates. The system map must be separated into the following categories:

1. Lines which the carrier anticipates will be the subject of abandonment or discontinuance applications to be filed within a three-year period following the date in which the diagram is filed with the Commission.
2. Lines which the railroad has under study as candidates for future abandonment because it anticipates incurring operating losses or excessive rehabilitation costs;
3. Lines for which an application is pending before the Commission at the time the diagram is submitted;
4. Lines being operated under subsidy; and
5. All other lines which the carrier owns, and operates, directly or indirectly.

The railroads must provide for newspaper publication of the system map in each county in which a line in the first three of these categories is located.

The regulations outline procedures to be followed in giving public notice of the intention to abandon or discontinue service; detailed information required to be submitted in the application; the steps to be taken by those wishing to oppose the abandonment proposal; and the form and manner in which the Commission will handle the application. Also included in the regulations are standards for determining the cost of purchasing or subsidizing a money-losing line, and procedures to be followed by those wishing to provide financial support in order to retain their rail service.

MEANING OF LANGUAGE READING "LINE OF RAILROAD"

The following matters are taken into consideration in determining whether tracks constitute a "line of railroad": The language of the statute and it policy, the cases construing the statute, the character of the tracks, and the effect of the tracks on the public.[52]

The decisions of the Commission and the courts indicate that "line of railroad" is used in its ordinary sense to denote a permanent road providing a track for freight and passenger cars and other rolling stock, or the equivalent of such a road.[53] The term "railroad" as used in the I.C. Act includes "ferries used by or operated in connection with any railroad." Thus if the facilities are used by or in connection with interstate railroad operations the Commission has jurisdiction to consider and determine applications for permission to abandon such ferry operations.[54] Abandonments of operations under trackage rights are within the purview of the statute.[55] The Commission has no jurisdiction over abandonment of the spur, side, team or industrial tracks, but where such tracks are impressed with functions beyond those normally ascribed to them, as where they are the sole terminal facilities held out to the public for access to the main line, they are, for purposes of the statute, inseparable from the main line and may not be abandoned without a Commission certificate of convenience and necessity.[56] If a segment of branch line relegated to the status of an industrial spur or side track prior to the

---

[52]See e.g., *Piedmont & Northern Ry. v. Comm'n*, 286 U.S. 299, 311-12; *I.C.C. v. Memphis Union Station Co.*, 230 F. Supp. 456; *Texas & Pac. Ry. v. Gulf, C. & S. Fe. Ry. Co.*, 270 U.S. 266, 278; *Public Convenience Application of K.C.S. Ry. Co.*, 94 I.C.C. 691; *Abandonment By C.R.I. & P. Ry. Co.*, 131 I.C.C. 421, 429; *New Orleans Terminal Co. v. Spencer*, 366 F. 2d 160.

[53]*Boston Term. Co. Reorganization*, 312 I.C.C. 373, 379.

[54]*New York, P & N. R. Ferry Abandonment*, 290 I.C.C. 249, 266.

[55]*Thompson v. Texas Mexican Ry. Co.*, 328 U.S. 134.

[56]*Myers v. Jay Street Connecting R.*, 262 F. 2d 676, 678.

enactment of the statute has been continuously used in that manner, the Commission has no jurisdiction over abandonment of the segment.[57]

PROPER PARTY APPLICANT UNDER SECTIONS 1(18) AND 5(2)
OF THE ACT

The Commission (Division 3) in *City of Erie, Pa. Trackage Rights,*[58] concluded that it had jurisdiction under former Section 1(18) and Section 5(2) over the subject matter of an application filed under these sections by the City of Erie and that the city was a proper party applicant in the proceeding. In arriving at this conclusion, the Commission said (pp. 339-42):

> Our jurisdiction to entertain an application seeking approval of either proposal under Section 1(18) is in no way restricted by reason of the fact that the application is filed by the city of Erie and is opposed by the rail carrier involved. The primary concern of the statute requiring that a certificate must be obtained from us before operations over a line of railroad, or the line itself, legally can be abandoned is that proper consideration first be given to the question of public need. Section 1(18) does not prescribe the party or parties by whom application for the certificate is to be made, but the certificate obviously should run in the name of the person or persons charged with the duty of continuing service to the public unless and until legally relieved therefrom. *Chicago, S. & St. L. Ry. Co. Receiver Abandonment,* 236 I.C.C. 765, 771. The right of a State or municipality to bring action seeking such certificate of abandonment has been affirmed in other proceedings. Compare *Atchison, T. & S. F. Ry. Co. v. Railroad Comm. of Calif.,* 283 U.S. 380; *State of Okla., ex. rel. Dept. of Highways, Abandonment,* 324 I.C.C. 666. See also *Thompson v. Texas Mexican R. Co.,* 328 U.S. 134, 145 (1946), wherein the Supreme Court said:
>
> > There is no requirement in Section 1(18) that the application be made by the carrier whose operations are sought to be abandoned. It has been recognized that persons other than carriers "who have a proper interest in the subject matter" may take the initiative.
>
> Here, we conclude that the city of Erie has the requisite interest and is a proper party to seek the abandonment proposed under the provisions of Section 1(18), and that we have jurisdiction to entertain the application under such provisions.

[57]*New York; N. H. & H. R. Co. Abandonment,* 307 I.C.C. 705. See *State of Illinois v. United States,* 373 U.S. 378, affirming *per curiam* the lower court decision (213 F. Supp. 83) sustaining the Commission in permitting the Chicago, North Shore & Milwaukee Ry. to abandon its entire line. Plaintiff had contended that the North Shore was in interurban electric railway within the meaning of former Section 1(22) and thus, exempt from Commission regulation.

[58]328 I.C.C. 331.

The situation placed before us by the city of Erie is similar in many respects to that in the Los Angeles passenger terminal case which culminated in the Supreme Court's decision in *Atchison, T. & S. F. Ry. Co. v. Railroad Comm. of Calif.*, 283 U.S. 380 (1931). There the city of Los Angeles asked, among other things, that the Commission authority be given to certain railroads to construct connections and to extend or abandon certain lines and operations as necessary to provide service at a new location for the passenger terminal. There, as here, the railroads involved challenged the city's standing to make the request and the Commission's jurisdiction to grant the relief. Protracted litigation ensued before this Commission, State bodies and the courts; and in the final analysis the city's right to apply under Section 1(18-21) was sustained.

The Supreme Court in *Atchison, T. & S. F. Ry. Co. v. Railroad Comm. of Calif., supra,* premised its ruling on three preliminaries: (1) the State was deemed to have authority to compel railroads to construct such facilities as might be appropriate for serving certain localities, (2) the Interstate Commerce Act does not supersede that authority, and (3) a certificate of public convenience and necessity issued by the Interstate Commerce Commission is a *condition precedent* to the validity of any construction order on the part of the State Commission. [Emphasis added]

At page 394-395 of its report, the Supreme Court reviewed a number of decisions upholding the authority of a State of compel action on the part of carriers. . . .

It seems to us that the project espoused by the city of Erie might well be a matter within the power of the city or State to compel, and that the three premises employed by the Supreme Court in the Los Angeles case are equally applicable here. Dismissal of the application as requested by the protestants would require us to disregard the Supreme Court's reasoning upon the assumptions that the carriers are beyond the pale of State and local authority in the matter here involved, that Commission approval is not a condition precedent to the changes the city seeks to effect, and that, in any event, no provision of the Interstate Commerce Act is applicable to this situation. As indicated by our conclusions herein, we find these assumptions unwarranted.

In view of these conclusions, it is not necessary, for the purpose of disposing of the instant motion, to further consider whether the city of Erie is a proper "person" to make application for trackage rights under the provisions of Section 5(2) of the act. We would point out, however, that applicant's plan of rerouting N&W's trains over Central's line through the city under trackage rights is an incidental proposal urged by applicant as one means of accomplishing the basic plan of abandonment proposed. As such, it is an issue to be considered, in a Section 1(18) proceeding, in connection with the primary purpose of the application.

In abandonment proceedings of the type here presented, among the factors which the applicant is expected to develop for the record, and which we are required to consider, are the means by which the continuity of the affected rail carrier's line will be preserved in the event of the abandonment proposed. This may include proposals for the physical relocation of the line, the rerouting of trains over other carriers' lines under trackage rights arrangements, et cetera. While these are matters that go to the merits of the application and are not now before us for determination, they are issues which are vital to a favorable disposition of the application, if determined under the provisions of Section 1(18). Whether applicant will be able adequately to support its proposal in this vital area is a matter which must await final determination of the proposal after full hearing.

Assuming, however, as did the Supreme Court in *Atchison, T. & S. F. Ry. Co. v. Railroad Comm. of Calif., supra,* that the State has a repository of power through which the carriers may be compelled to conform their operations to the applicant's plan, and that, in exercising that power, the State orders an operation requiring a trackage rights arrangement, it would then be incumbent upon the carriers themselves to apply for authorization from this Commission under Section 5(2).

While it is sufficient, for the purpose of disposing of the motion, to conclude that the application may be entertained under the provisions of Section 1(18), we deem it appropriate to point out the possible applicability of Section 3(5) to applicant's proposed operating plan.
The pertinent provisions of Section 3(5) are as follows:

> If the Commission finds it to be in the public interest and to be practicable, without substantially impairing the ability of a common carrier by railroad owning or entitled to the enjoyment of terminal facilities to handle its own business, it shall have power by order to require the use of any such terminal facilities, including main-line track or tracks for a reasonable distance outside of such terminal, of any common carrier or other such carriers, on such terms and for such compensation as the carriers affected may agree upon, or, in the event of a failure to agree, as the Commission may fix as just and reasonable for the use so required, to be ascertained on the principle controlling compensation in condemnation proceedings.

While it cannot be definitely determined from the record herein whether applicant's overall plan contemplates that any of the Central facilities to be utilized by N&W are terminal facilities,[59] it appears that some use of such facilities may be involved. A proper showing by applicant regarding such use might possibly establish our jurisdiction to determine the proposal under the provisions of Section 3(5).

Section 3(5) is a highly remedial statute, intended for dealing with problems arising from traffic congestion in municipal areas, and available to any party having a sufficient interest, not necessarily carriers or shippers. Cf *City of Milwaukee v. Chicago & N. W. Ry. Co.,* 281 I.C.C. 311, 314.

---

[59]"Railroad facilities" are defined as "everything necessary for the . . . safety and prompt transportation of freight." *Hastings Commercial Club v. Chicago, M. & St. P. Ry. Co.,* 69 I.C.C. 489. See also, *Use by Erie of Niagara Junction Ry. Co. Terminals,* 269 I.C.C. 493. When used in terminal operations, they are terminal facilities.

Because of the aforementioned deficiencies in the record, we make no determination here of this jurisdictional question.

Issues Before The Commission

The national transportation policy requires that the interest of the public and that of interstate commerce be considered in each abandonment application. In considering such an application, the Commission has the duty to weigh the present and prospective needs for the line, and the resulting injury to the communities served by it if abandonment were authorized, against the burden that, presently and in the future, would be imposed upon the carrier and interstate commerce if operations were to continue.[60] The point at which abandonment shall be considered justified is a matter of sound judgment and must be determined by the circumstances of each case.[61]

To abandon within the context of the statute means to give up permanently, not merely to suspend.[62]

Principles which have been established in the determination of the question of public convenience and necessity include the following. A carrier cannot be expected to maintain railroad service at a continuing loss for the purpose of ensuring lower rates.[63] It is contrary to the abandonment provisions of the I.C. Act to require drains upon the revenue of an interstate carrier flowing from the operation of an unnecessary and unprofitable branch merely because system operations as a whole are profitable.[64]

Abandonment of applicant's branch line was permitted in *New York Central R. Co. Abandonment*,[65] the Commission stating that it was justified since passenger service over the branch had been discontinued, freight traffic on that segment had declined almost to the vanishing point, and none of the shippers served was solely dependent on rail service or would be seriously inconvenienced; all overhead traffic moved via another route.

In *Jay Street Connecting Railroad v. United States*,[66] a three-judge

---

[60]*Colorado v. United States*, 271 U.S. 153.

[61]*Chicago, M. St. P. R. Co. Abandonment*, 184 I.C.C. 687.

[62]*Akron & B. B. R. Co., Abandonment of Operation*, 239 I.C.C. 250, 254; *Zirn v. Hanover Bank*, 215 F. 2d 63, 69; *Williams v. Atlantic Coast Line R. Co.*, 17 F. 2d 17, 22.

[63]*Chicago, B. & Q. R. Co. Abandonment*, 193 I.C.C. 233.

[64]*New York Central R. Co. Abandonment*, 254 I.C.C. 745, 761. See also *State of Arizona v. United States*, 220 F. Supp. 337.

[65]312 I.C.C. 271, 272-3, 276.

[66]174 F. Supp. 609.

court upheld a Commission order permitting abandonment of a small connecting railroad which serviced industries whose properties adjoined its tracks in a small area. The Commission had concluded[67] that public convenience and necessity permitted abandonment where the railroad had been sustaining large and continuing operating losses without a substantial possibility of future improvement; and future operating revenues were not expected to cover the cost of providing safe facilities and continued transportation service.

Rejecting a contention by four plaintiff municipal corporations that railroad officials had promised that an acquired railroad would not be abandoned and that such promise estopped the railroads involved from later seeking authorization to abandon a portion of the acquired railroad's line, a district court sustained that portion of a Commission order which authorized the Savannah & Atlanta Railway Co. to abandon a 36-mile segment of its tracks, and operations thereover, between Waynesboro, Ga., and Sylvania, Ga.; the court held that such promise of the railroad officials, if made, could not foreclose the Commission from determining that public convenience and necessity permitted the proposed abandonment.[68]

Cessation of Operations Resulting from Conditions Over Which Railroad Has No Control

There are occasions when questions arise as to whether Commission approval is necessary where the cessation of operations will result not from the railroad but as a result of conditions over which the railroad has no control. This point is discussed below.

In *Town of Conway v. Atlantic Coast Line R. R. Co.*,[69] the town sought to compel the railroad to remove its tracks from a street where the town claimed it had no right to be. The court agreed that the railroad was not entitled to be where it was and granted the relief. In doing so the court spoke as follows in regard to the railroad's contention that the court could not order the removal until the Commission had passed on the matter (at p. 260):

> The theory of the defendant is that the Transportation Act, as construed by the cases referred to, constituted a new departure, and sought affirmatively to build up a system of railways prepared to handle promptly all

[67] *Jay Street Connecting Railroad — Abandonment — Entire Line*, 307 I.C.C. 137.
[68] *Burke County, Ga. v. United States*, 206 F. Supp. 586, sustaining *Central of Georgia Ry. Co., Abandonment*, 317 I.C.C. 184.
[69] 20 F. 2d 250.

the interstate traffic of the country, and that the power to order the abandonment of any track is now lodged solely in the Interstate Commerce Commission, and no change can be made without its consent. But I do not construe the act to apply to a case like the one at bar. The defendant does not seek to abandon a portion of its track. Nor does the town seek to compel it to abandon a portion where it has a legal right to remain. The act of Congress was intended to apply to those cases where the railroad company seeks to abandon a portion of its line of railroad, and possibly where it is sought to compel it to make such abandonment; but it was not intended to apply to those cases where the railroad is a trespasser, or where the railroad's occupancy is only by permission, and such permission has been revoked.

When the town in this case revoked the permission theretofore given to occupy the street, the railroad company then had no further right in the same. It may be doubted whether Congress could constitutionally deprive the town of its right to require the defendant to remove its track in such circumstances from its street, and certainly, if such a construction of the act as would render it unconstitutional can be avoided, it should be done. My view is that the act was not intended to apply to a case where the defendant's rights in the premises had ceased, and that no certificate from the Interstate Commerce Commission is necessary, and that this court has full jurisdiction to determine the rights of the parties, and to require the removal of the track if the railroad has no further legal right to keep it there.

My conclusion, therefore, is that the decree of the board of county commissioners is not to be deemed a grant of a franchise in perpetuity, and that, if so construed, it would be ultra vires, null, and void, but is to be deemed a mere temporary permission, which could be withdrawn, either by the board or their successor, the town of Conway, and that the ordinances above set forth of the town of Conway are valid insofar as they revoke the permission given by the decree of the board, and that the plaintiff is entitled to a mandatory injunction requiring the defendant to remove its track from Main street in the town of Conway within a reasonable time, and cease operating its trains along that street.

Zirn v. Hanover Bank,[70] involved a proceeding for repossession of locomotives from a railroad in accordance with the terms of equipment-trusts and leases entered into after commencement of reorganization proceedings, under which the railroad operated the locomotives. The lower court entered an order authorizing repossession. The bond-holders of the debtor appealed. In affirming the decision of the lower court, the court of appeals said (at p. 69):

> Nor, all else aside, is 49 U.S.C.A. § 1(18) relevant here. The district court's order did not permit the railroad or the bankruptcy-trustee to abandon either any part of its "line" or any "operation." To "abandon"

---

[70] 215 F. 2d 63.

in this context means, we think, to give up permanently, not merely to suspend operations for lack of physical equipment. No Commission approval is necessary where the cessation of operations results, not from the volition of the railroad or the bankruptcy-trustee, but from the exercise of the supervening rights, here recognized by the Bankruptcy Act, of third persons. See, e.g., Town of Conway v. Atlantic Coast Line R. Co., 4 Cir., 20 F. 2d 250, 259-260. . . .

In citing the *Town of Conway* case, the court noted (fn. 6) that there "it was held that absence of I.C.C. approval constituted no defense in a proceeding by a town to compel a railroad to remove a segment of its track, thus severing its line." In addition, the following comment was made by the court (fn. 7):

Although not the basis of our decision, we note the following in passing: (1) That the railroad is still operating goes to show that the orders did not authorize abandonment. (2) The bankruptcy-trustee stated that, if deprived of the diesel-electric locomotives, he can continue to operate by leasing steam locomotives.

We are not to be understood as indicating that, considering this railroad's prolonged grave financial condition and the failure to work out a reorganization plan, the court below, should not soon direct the bankruptcy-trustee to seek I.C.C. approval of abandonment of operation. Cf. Bankers Trust Co. v. Debhart, 2 Cir., 195 F. 2d 238, 240.

The *Town of Conway* case was cited as supporting the decision of the court in *City of Alexandria, La. v. Chicago, R.I.&P.R. Co.,*[71] but the court pointed out that it was not required to go as far as that court went. In the *City of Alexandria* case, involving an action by the railroad to enjoin enforcement of the city's pavement lien against the railroad's roadbed by execution proceedings through seizure and sale, the court said (at p. 825):

Rock Island and the City agree that they do not want the Alexandria railroad abandoned. Yet there is a solvent railroad which can remove any question of abandonment by the single expedient of paying a debt the Supreme Court of Louisiana has adjudged to be a just debt supported by a valid lien. We do not think that [the Interstate Commerce Act] contemplated that a creditor would have to initiate "abandonment" proceedings in order to collect a relatively small debt from a solvent railroad. "Abandonment" under the Act has a peculiar meaning, one that may even do violence to the ordinary acceptance of the term. But it is not that peculiar. If it is — and we say it is not — then the determination not to pay the just debt is entirely within the volition of the railroad. In the absence of any help from the statute on this point, the burden of going forward before the Commission ought to fall on the railroad.

[71]321 F. 2d 822.

The *Town of Conway* case is not supported by the weight of authority. Cases holding contrary to *Town of Conway* are discussed below.

In *Thompson v. Texas Mexican Ry. Co.*,[72] a railroad attempted to terminate and cancel a trackage contract with the trustee of a bankrupt road. After purportedly exercising this right, the lessor sought to obtain an increase in the payments for the use of the tracks. The trustee refused to pay anything higher than the contract rate. The difference of opinion led to a law suit in the state court in which the lessor asked for an injunction against the trustee's use of the tracks and recovery of $500 a day for past damages or, alternatively, the reasonable value of the use of the tracks. The state court awarded damaged but denied the injunction. The Supreme Court reversed, holding that the Commission should pass on all the terms and conditions of the trackage agreement, including the abandonment issue. The Supreme Court held that the entire arrangement was within the peculiar competency of the Commission and it should play its part in the affair before the courts intervened. It commented that the trackage agreement in all its ramifications vitally affected the goal of an orderly, integrated rail transportation system.

In *Smith v. Hoboken R. Warehouse & S. Connecting Co.*,[73] the Supreme Court decided that a bankruptcy court could not allow the forfeiture of a lease when the lessee had not obtained a certificate from the Commission permitting the railroad to abandon the lines covered. The lessor claimed under a provision providing for forfeiture in the event of assignment. In deciding that the forfeiture provision could not be enforced without the determination of the abandonment question by the Commission, the Supreme Court commented (at pp. 132-133):

> . . . Forfeiture of a lease in accordance with the provisions of § 70(b) may be wholly consistent with the preparation of a plan of reorganization under § 77. But, as we have said, the nature of the plan of reorganization to be submitted is entrusted primarily to the Commission. If forfeiture of leases can be decreed without prior reference of the matter to the Commission, it may be seriously embarrassed in preparing the plan which it deems necessary or desirable for the reorganization of the debtor. . . .

The Supreme Court was mainly concerned over the proper adjustment of the I.C. Act with the Bankruptcy Act. The court recognized that the primary responsibility for reorganizing railroads in financial difficulty lies with the Commission. The Commission should not be hampered in its operations by judicial decrees unduly encroaching into this territory.

---

[72]328 U.S. 134.
[73]328 U.S. 123.

(In the *Zirn* case, the court said that the doctrine in the *Hoboken* case could not apply to equipment-trust obligations which the bankruptcy court had authorized.)

In *Des Moines v. Chicago & N. W. Ry. Co.*,[74] the city, claiming that the railroad had violated an ordinance upon which its right to operate on the city's streets depended, decreed an ouster of the railroad from the city's street. It went into the state court demanding an injunction along the lines of its decree. The case was removed by the railroad to the federal court which dismissed the complaint. The appellate court remanded, directing the district court to retain jurisdiction pending disposition of the abondonment issue by the Commission. The court said (at p. 457):

> Regardless, however, of whether a valid forfeiture would have existed under the ordinance, a court could still not decree an ouster of the Railway from the street, so long as this might mean an abandonment or discontinuance of a portion of the Railway's line or operation in the interstate field. until the Interstate Commerce Commission gave its permission to such abandonment or discontinuance being made. *Thompson v. Texas Mexican Ry. Co.*, 328 U.S. 134, 66 S. Ct. 937, 90 L. Ed. 1132; *Smith v. Hoboken R.R. Warehouse & S.S. Connect. Co.*, 328 U.S. 123, 66 S. Ct. 947, 90 L. Ed. 1123.

> The City argues that 49 U.S.C.A. § 1, par. (18), supra, and the Thompson and Smith decisions cited, should not be regarded as having any application to such portions of a railroad's line as are located in public streets or highways — at least not where the railroad's occupancy has the status, as claimed here, of a trespass and a nuisance. We do not believe, however, that such an exception or exemption can impliedly be read into the language and purpose of § 1, par. (18), or into the expression or doctrine of Thompson and Smith opinions (although there were non-street situations), when the nature of the Interstate Commerce Act as a preemptive and comprehensive "scheme of regulation" is considered. And to the extent that *Town of Conway v. Atlantic Coast Line R. Co.*, D.C.E.D.S.C., 1926, 20 F. 2d 250, on which the City relies, gives recognition to such an exception or exemption in Interstate Commerce Commission domain, we must refuse to follow it.

The City of *Des Moines* case was cited in support of the decision of the court in *New Orleans Terminal Co. v. Spencer*.[75] There the court said (pp. 165-166):

> The judgment of the district court was, we think, predicated upon an erroneous conception of the distinction between "a line of railroad or extension thereof" and "spur, industrial, team, switching or side track."

---

[74]264 F. 2d 454.
[75]366 F. 2d 160.

If there are traffic movements which are part of the actual transportation haul from shipper to consignee, then the trackage over which the movement takes place is a "line of railroad or extension thereof," and there can be no abandonment of such trackage without obtaining a certificate of public convenience and necessity from the Interstate Commerce Commission. If, however, the trackage is used in the loading, reloading, storage, and switching of cars incidental to the receipt of shipments by the carrier or their delivery to the consignee, then such trackage is "spur, industrial, team, switching or side tracks" and as such not under Commission jurisdiction.

There are numerous Commission decisions which follow the doctrine in the above cases.[76]

There is a very real distinction which removes the *Zirn* and the *City of Alexandria* cases from the cases which hold that Commission approval is required where there is a cessation of operations by a railroad. This is the fact that in *Zirn* and *City of Alexandria* there was no actual or indeed threatened abandonment as there was, for example, in *City of Des Moines,* where the city was demanding that the railroad physically remove its main track from where it lay. In *Town of Conway* there definitely was a threatened abandonment, but the case stands alone.

It has been recognized that persons other than the carriers who have an interest in the matter may take the initiative to file an application with the Commission for abandonment of a line of railroad.[77]

Major and Minor Relocations

An abandonment (and relocation) application is required in order to effect a major relocation brought about by the exercise of the right of eminent domain by a federal agency in charge of flood control projects. The federal agency participates in the abandonment proceeding before the Commission in order to present its plan.[78] The Commission gives consideration to the expenditure necessarily incident to the relocation and the costs of operating the line to determine whether it is justified by the public convenience and necessity in taking action that will require the location of the line.[79]

---

[76]See e.g., *Duluth & I.R.R. Co. Control,* 224 I.C.C. 353, 356; *Chicago N. S. & N. Ry. Abandonment,* 290 I.C.C. 765, 771; *Clinchfield R. Co. Abandonment,* 295 I.C.C. 41, 49.

[77]See e.g., *Thompson v. Texas Mexican R. Co.,* 328 U.S. 134, 145; *City of Erie, Pa. Trackage Rights,* 328 I.C.C. 331.

[78]*Purcell v. United States,* 41 F. Supp. 309, aff'd 315 U.S. 381; *Los Angeles & Salt Lake R. Co.,* 212 I.C.C. 597; *St. Louis-San Francisco Ry. Co., Trustees-Abandonment,* 244 I.C.C. 485.

[79]*Confluence & O. R. Co., Abandonment,* 244 I.C.C. 451.

In *Purcell v. United States*,[80] the Commission asserted jurisdiction over the question whether the lack of profitability of the operation warranted the cost of relocation and increased maintenance cost arising therefrom, even though the application was only for abandonment, concluding that the public convenience and necessity required abandonment without relocation, even though the then former War Department, which was proceeding with the flood control project in question, was willing to compensate the railroad for all costs of relocation. The Commission held that it was immaterial who ultimately paid the cost of relocation. In *Purcell v. United States, supra,* the Supreme Court in sustaining the above decision assumed (fn 1, p. 383) the existence of power of the Commission to require relocations as a "condition" of abandonment. In *Central Pacific Railway Co., Abandonment,*[81] another abandonment caused by a flood control project, in which the application was merely to abandon, the certificate was conditioned so as to require applicant "to provide adequate rail transportation service to [the copper company on its line]."[82]

Commission decisions suggest that there is no necessity for an abandonment (and relocation) application in order to effect a minor relocation which involves no change in service to Shippers, and the cost of which clearly presents no question of undue burden on the railroad's interstate operations.[83]

Protection of Employees

The Commission has authority to impose conditions for the protection of employees.[84] However, the Commission generally has declined to impose conditions for protection of employees where an entire line of railroad was being abandoned. Where the railroad applicant was a subsidiary of another railroad, however, and that parent was considered to be the actual beneficiary of the proposed abandonment, labor pro-

[80]41 F. Supp. 309, aff'd 315 U.S. 381.
[81]271 I.C.C. 531.
[82]See also *Southern Pacific Co., Abandonment,* 267 I.C.C. 278, 286-87; *Abandonment by Fonda, Johnstown & Gloversville, R. Co.,* 158 I.C.C. 379.
[83]*Missouri Pacific R. Co., Trustee,* 282 I.C.C. 388; *Sacramento & N. Ry., Trackage Rights,* 290 I.C.C. 145.
[84]*Interstate Commerce Commission v. Railway L. E. Assn.,* 315 U.S. 373; *Chicago, B. & Q. R. Co. Abandonment,* 257 I.C.C. 700; see also *Smith v. United States,* 211 F. Supp. 66, sustaining retroactive imposition of conditions for protection of rail employees adversely affected by abandonment; and *C. & N.E. Ry. Abandonment,* 267 I.C.C. 139, 142; *Pittsburgh, S. & N. R. Co. Trustees Abandonment,* 267 I.C.C. 802; *Arkansas Valley Ry., Inc. Abandonment,* 252 I.C.C. 804; *Susquehana & N. Y. R. Co. Abandonment,* 252 I.C.C. 81; *Brotherhood of Locomotive Engineers v. United States,* 217 F. Supp. 98.

tective conditions have been imposed upon the parent.[85] Further, when there is an immediacy of relationship between one carrier and the employees of a second carrier, to such an extent that it can be said that the considered employee was in reality the joint or common employee of both carriers, such employee is to be considered affected by the transaction and entitled to protection under the employee-protective conditions imposed in the proceeding.[86]

---

[85]*Seaboard Air Line R. Co. Trackage Rights*, 312 I.C.C. 797, 801; *East Carolina Ry. Abandonment*, 324 I.C.C. 506, 521; *Washington & Old Dominion R. Abandonment-Virginia*, 331 I.C.C. 587, 602.

[86]*Atchison — Trackage Rights — Chicago*, 338 I.C.C. 778, 781.

4

Discontinuance or Change of Railroad Operations or Services

The Applicable Statutory Provisions

Section 13 a (1) of the Interstate Commerce Act[1] provides that a carrier or carriers "if their rights with respect to the discontinuance or change, in whole or in part, of the operation or service of any train or ferry operating from a point in one State to a point in any other State or in the District of Columbia, or from a point in the District of Columbia to a point in any State, are subject to any provision of the constitution or statutes of any State or any regulation or order of (or are the subject of any proceeding pending before) any court or an administrative or regulatory agency of any State, may, but shall not be required to, file with the Commission, and upon such filing shall mail to the Governor of each State in which such train or ferry is operated, and post in every station, depot or other facility served thereby, notice at least thirty days in advance of any such proposed discontinuance or change." Carrier "filing such notice may discontinue or change any such operation or service pursuant to such notice except as otherwise ordered by the Commission pursuant to this paragraph, the laws or constitution of any State, or the decision or order of, or the pendency of any proceeding before, any court or State authority to the contrary notwithstanding."

Upon filing notice "the Commission shall have authority during said thirty days' notice period, either upon complaint or upon its own initiative without complaint, to enter upon an investigation of the proposed discontinuance or change. Upon the institution of such investigation, the Commission, by order served upon the carrier or carriers affected thereby at least ten days prior to the day on which such discontinuance or change

[1] 49 U.S.C. 13a (1).

117

would otherwise become effective, may require such train or ferry to be continued in operation or service, in whole or in part, pending hearing and decision in such investigation, but not for a longer period than four months beyond the date when such discontinuance or change would otherwise have become effective. If, after hearing in such investigation, whether concluded before or after such discontinuance or change has become effective, the Commission finds that the operation or service of such train or ferry is required by public convenience and necessity and will not unduly burden interstate or foreign commerce, the Commission may by order require the continuance or restoration of operation or service of such train or ferry, in whole or in part, for a period not to exceed one year from the date of such order." The provisions of the statute do not supersede the laws of any State or the orders or regulations of any administrative or regulatory body of any State applicable to such discontinuance or change unless notice as provided in the statute is filed with the Commission. On the expiration of a Commission order after investigation requiring the continuance or restoration of operation or service, the jurisdiction of any State as to such discontinuance or change shall no longer be superseded unless the procedure provided by the statute shall again be invoked by the carriers.

The authority granted to the Commission by Section 13a is spelled out in *State of New Jersey v. United States,*[2] where a district court sustained the validity of section 13a (1) and refused to upset the Commission's determination not to institute an investigation pursuant to section 13a (1) into New York Central's proposed discontinuance of passenger ferries across the Hudson River. The holdings of the district court were that (1) Section 13a (1) confers no right to a hearing either to a State or to users of the service before discontinuance of the service; (2) that so construed, Section 13a (1) does not violate the due process requirement of the Fifth Amendment; (3) that the Commission's determination not to institute an investigation under Section 13a (1) is committed to its discretion and is not subject to judicial review; and (4) that even if its determination not to institute an investigation proceeding were reviewable to determine whether there had been an abuse of discretion, there was no showing of such abuse in this case.

---

[2]168 F. Supp. 324, aff'd 359 U.S. 27. Also see 168 F. Supp. 342. See *New Jersey v. New York, S and W. R.R. Co.,* 372 U.S. 1, upholding the Commission's order holding it had no jurisdiction under Section 13a (1) to consider a notice of proposed discontinuance where the train did not physically operate beyond the State boundaries except by connecting-line bus.

Factors to be Considered

Under Section 13a (1), the Commission's determination must be designed to protect interstate commerce from onerous burdens which may affect the carrier's ability to continue to provide efficient transportation service to the public generally; thus, in determining public convenience and necessity in such cases, the entire public, rather than the relatively few passengers who may use the considered trains, must be taken into consideration.[3] Among factors to be considered in a train-discontinuance proceeding are the populations of communities served, the public's use of the service sought to be discontinued, other means of transportation in the area, and financial losses sustained by the carrier in providing the service; but no one factor, standing alone, is decisive or in any manner controlling.[4]

Burden of Proof

In a proceeding under Section 13a (1), the burden of proof controls a decision on the merits only if no substantial evidence is adduced or if the evidence is equally balanced; otherwise it is of more theoretical than practical importance;[5] when neither of those conditions prevails, a carrier is not prejudiced because it is required to proceed initially with presentation of evidence to substantiate data submitted in required statements filed with notice of discontinuance;[6] but regardless of where the burden of proof lies, a carrier subject to regulation by the Commission is expected to aid in the disposition of a proceeding to which it is a party by making available all pertinent facts within its knowledge.[7]

[3]*Delaware, L. & W. R. Co. Discontinuance of Service,* 307 I.C.C. 627, 634; *Chicago & N. W. Ry. Co. Discontinuance of Service,* 307 I.C.C. 775, 782.

[4]*New Jersey & N.Y. R. Co. Discontinuance of Service,* 307 I.C.C. 532, 537; *Chicago, M. St. P. & P. R. Co. Discontinuance of Service,* 307 I.C.C. 565, 576; *Delaware, L. & W. R. Co. Discontinuance of Service, supra; Chicago & N. W. Ry. Co. Discontinuance of Service, supra; St. Louis S. W. Ry. Co. Discontinuance of Service,* 307 I.C.C. 639, 640.

[5]*Minneapolis & St. L. Ry. Co. Discontinuance of Service,* 307 I.C.C. 70, 81; *Louisville & N. R. Co. Discontinuance of Service,* 307 I.C.C. 173, 182; *Southern Pac. Co. Partial Discontinuance of Passenger Service,* 307 I.C.C. 209, 210.

[6]*Minneapolis & St. L. Ry. Co., supra.*

[7]*Chicago & N. W. Ry. Co. Discontinuance of Service,* 307 I.C.C. 462, 464; *Chicago & N. W. Ry. Co. Discontinuance of Service,* 307 I.C.C. 585, 586; *St. Louis S. W. Ry. Co. Discontinuance of Service,* 307 I.C.C. 639, 640.

Losses from Operation

The Commission said in *Minneapolis & St. L. Ry. Co. Discontinuance of Service,*[8] that although it was aware that the burden imposed on the carrier and ultimately on interstate commerce must be considered in direct relation to the public's need for service proposed to be discontinued, and that a substantial need and consistent use of a service might under some circumstances warrant its continuance at a loss, where passenger revenues continue to decrease and the losses to increase there must come a time when further operation is an undue economic waste; and in *Lehigh V. R. Co. Discontinuance of Passenger Operations,*[9] that a railroad cannot continue operations at a loss indefinitely, and substanial losses are bound to affect interstate and foreign commerce adversely, as if continued long enough they would eventually result in carrier's insolvency. Under certain circumstances, the Commission said in *Missouri Pac. R. Co. Discontinuance of Service,*[10] the prosperity of the carrier as a whole may be a factor to be weighed in a discontinuance proceeding, but in the absence of a demonstrated need for the service, the fact that a carrier's system operations are profitable is not controlling. The law does not require the Commission, in passing on proposed train discontinuance, to consider whether applicant's remaining trains are operating at a profit.[11]

In *Louisville & N. R. Co. Discontinuance of Service,*[12] the Commission said that the weight of the factor of undue burden of interstate commerce must be determined in regard to the general fiscal position of the carrier's system. There the carrier was a generally strong railroad whose prospects were relatively bright; the considered trains, after elimination of about 28 percent of the round-trip mileage, would incur less operating costs; and operating revenues would increase if an increase in the fair structure produced the desired results. The Commission said that there was reason to believe that annual operating results might at least approach the "breakeven" point, and operation of those trains would not unduly burden interstate commerce. Should that appraisal prove too optimistic, the Commission said, the carrier could exercise its right to file another discontinuance notice based on one year's experience of the reduced commuter train service.

---

[8]307 I.C.C. 79, 90. See *St. Louis S. W. Ry. Co. Discontinuance of Service,* 307 I.C.C. 639, 651.

[9]307 I.C.C. 239, 254.

[10]307 I.C.C. 787, 796.

[11]*Chicago, M. St. P. & P. R. Co. Discontinuance of Service,* 307 I.C.C. 675, 688.

[12]307 I.C.C. 173, 186-7.

In the computation of costs of providing the service, only those expenses which would be eliminated by discontinuance of considered trains should be included; maintenance-of-way and structures expenses are not properly includable as costs in such cases, nor are general and traffic expenses, since little if any savings in such items would result from discontinuance of particular trains.[13] Where utilization of trackage will continue, to consider as savings such expense items as track maintenance of way is unrealistic and therefore not acceptable in train discontinuance proceedings.[14] Joint facility expenses, however, are includable in cost in train discontinuance proceedings where the carrier's participation in use of such facilities will cease upon the discontinuance.[15] In *Chicago & N. W. Ry. Co. Discontinuance of Service*,[16] the Commission said that expenses for maintenance of ways and structures and general expense cannot be classified as costs that would be avoided as a consequence of discontinuance of certain passenger trains. While joint passenger terminal expense is properly chargeable to those trains, the total burden on interstate commerce would not be materially lessened when there would be no appreciable decrease in expense of the depots if those trains were discontinued, and principal effect thereof would be to shift their proportion of such expenses to other trains using the respective terminals.

Criticism of Service and Equipment

Whether considered passenger service would be used more if a carrier provided better equipment is not decisive in a Section 13a proceeding so long as the facilities appear to have been reasonably adequate for the type of service involved.[17] The Commission said in *Chicago & N. W. Ry. Co. Discontinuance of Service*[18] that criticism of equipment of the considered trains was not a decisive factor in passing on a proposed discontinuance so long as facilities furnished were reasonably adequate for the type of service rendered; experiments with modernistic equipment failed to attract passenger business, and other efforts of carrier to run special trains during vacation periods were unproductive, thus the use of expensive modern equipment on the run would not be justified.

---

[13]*Chicago & N. W. Ry. Co. Discontinuance of Service*, 312 I.C.C. 313, 315.
[14]*Lehigh Valley R. Co. Discontinuance of Service*, 312 I.C.C. 411, 415.
[15]*Lehigh Valley R. Co. Discontinuance of Passenger Service*, 312 I.C.C. 399 ,404.
[16]307 I.C.C. 585, 607. See also *Chicago & N. W. Ry. Co. Discontinuance of Service*, 307 I.C.C. 463, 471.
[17]*Chicago, M., St. P. & P. R. Co. Discontinuance of Service*, 307 I.C.C. 565, 577.
[18]307 I.C.C. 775, 782.

In *St. Louis S. W. Ry. Co. Discontinuance of Service*[19] the Commission said that a carrier was not shown to have purposely discouraged passenger traffic on considered trains when its direct solicitation thereof was discontinued because found to be ineffectual; reductions in service provided by the trains were made because of substantial losses and insufficient public use; and while equipment used was not of the latest design, it was adequate to meet existing need. The Commission said further that the carrier could not be said to be deliberately driving traffic off the line because it did not improve service and equipment in an unprofitable operation.

Availability of Other Service

Discontinuance of the carrier's only remaining trains, the Commission said in *St. Louis S. W. Ry. Co. Discontinuance of Service*,[20] would not unduly inconvenience the public when there was ample common carrier service in the area by other railroads, airlines, and motorbuses. The carrier would continue to provide adequate express service through substitute methods; and the Post Office Department had advised the carrier that plans had been made to handle mail by motor truck and other rail service. In *Chicago & N.W. Ry. Co. Discontinuance of Service*,[21] the Commission said that the proposed train discontinuance would not seriously inconvenience the public when passenger patronage had steadily declined and was relatively insubstantial; a multiplicity of common-carrier passenger transportation by bus, air, and other railroads was available in the area served, and none of the communities served would be left without passenger service. In *St. Louis-S. F. Ry. Co. Discontinuance of Service*,[22] the Commission said that continued operation of the carrier's train service would be unnecessary and wasteful when passenger patronage had been very light, due primarily to prevalence of private automobiles in the area, and operation had resulted in continuing substantial losses; and in view of the availability in the area of adequate substitute service, it did not appear that an extensive advertising campaign by the carriers would result in substantial increase of traffic. Discontinuance of the carrier's commuter service would not unduly inconvenience the public, the Commission said in *New Jersey & N. Y. R. Co. Discontinuance of Service*,[23] as passengers could by minor adjust-

[19]307 I.C.C. 639, 649-50.
[20]307 I.C.C. 639, 649-50.
[21]307 I.C.C. 463, 472-3.
[22]307 I.C.C. 477, 478, 484, 486.
[23]307 I.C.C. 532, 537-8.

ments in their schedules use one of carrier's other evening trains or use the numerous buses operating from and into the area served; the Commission said that it was significant that no public witness testified in opposition to discontinuance.

Feeder Value

The distinction between abandonment cases and train discontinuance cases is one of degree only, and the feeder-value theory is applicable to both.[24] Thus while feeder value of trains to a carrier's system or to other carriers is of some significance, it is not controlling as to a proposed discontinuance.[25]

Discontinuance of More than One Train

Section 13a is remedial in character and should be liberally construed; it applies to any train which meets the test provided therein, which could be one train, several trains, or all trains operated by a particular carrier.[26]

Employees

The Commission is not empowered by Section 13a to impose in proceedings thereunder conditions for the protection of employees who may be adversely affected by the proposed discontinuance of service.[27] Since Congress, in all other instances in which it has granted the Commission power to approve or disapprove proposals involving interest of the carriers' employees, has explicitly specified the power it intended to confer, it must be presumed that, in omitting from Section 13a any language expressly authorizing the imposition of terms and conditions, it did not intend such power to exist. There is thus no justification for assuming an implied power.[28] While the Commission is not empowered

---

[24]*New York Central R. Co. Discontinuance of Service,* 312 I.C.C. 4, 10-11.

[25]*Chicago & N. W. Ry. Co. Discontinuance of Service,* 307 I.C.C. 775, 783; *Chicago, M. St. P. & P. R. Co. Discontinuance of Service,* 307 I.C.C. 565, 576-7.

[26]*Lehigh V. R. Co. Discontinuance of Passenger Operations,* 307 I.C.C. 239, 241.

[27]*Minneapolis & St. L. Ry. Co. Discontinuance of Service,* 307 I.C.C. 79, 92; *Minneapolis, St. P. & S.S.M.R. Co. Discontinuance of Service,* 307 I.C.C. 125, 127; *Louisville & N. R. Co. Discontinuance of Service,* 307 I.C.C. 173, 174; *Southern Pac. Co. Partial Discontinuance of Passenger Service,* 307 I.C.C. 209, 219; *Lehigh V. R. Co. Discontinuance of Passenger Operations,* 307 I.C.C. 239, 253; *Texas & P. Ry. Co. Discontinuance of Service,* 307 I.C.C. 259, 263.

[28]*Missouri Pac. R. Co. Discontinuance of Passenger Service,* 312 I.C.C. 105, 117; *St. Louis S. W. Ry. Co. Discontinuance of Service,* 307 I.C.C. 639, 651.

by Section 13a to impose employee-protective conditions, in determining whether an operation involved in proceedings thereunder is required by public convenience and necessity consideration should be given to the probable adverse effect of discontinuance upon employees.[29]

Failure of State to Act

Section 13a (2)[30] provides that where "discontinuance or change, in whole or in part, by a carrier or carriers subject to this part, of the operation or service of any train or ferry operated wholly within the boundaries of a single State is prohibited by the constitution or statutes of any State or where the State authority having jurisdiction thereof shall have denied an application or petition duly filed with it by said carrier or carriers for authority to discontinue or change, in whole or in part, the operation or service of any such train or ferry or shall not have acted finally on such an application or petition within one hundred and twenty days from the presentation thereof, such carrier or carriers may petition the Commission for authority to effect such discontinuance or change." The Commission is authorized to grant such authority "only after full hearing and upon findings by it that (a) the present or future public convenience and necessity permit of such discontinuance or change, in whole or in part, of the operation or service of such train or ferry, and (b) the continued operation or service of such train or ferry without discontinuance or change, in whole or in part, will constitute an unjust and undue burden upon the interstate operations of such carrier or carriers or upon interstate commerce." When any petition is filed "the Commission shall notify the Governor of the State in which such train or ferry is operated at least thirty days in advance of the hearing provided for in this paragraph, and such hearing shall be held by the Commission in the State in which such train or ferry is operated; and the Commission is authorized to avail itself of the cooperation, services, records and

---

[29]*Southern Pac. Co. Partial Discontinuance of Passenger Service*, 307 I.C.C. 209, 220; *Minneapolis, St. P. & S. S. M. R. Co. Discontinuance of Service*, 307 I.C.C. 125, 126; *Louisville & N. R. Co. Discontinuance of Service*, 307 I.C.C. 173, 174; *Minneapolis, St. P. & S. S. M. R. Co. Discontinuance*, 307 I.C.C. 677, 694-5; *Chicago & N. W. Ry. Co. Discontinuance of Service*, 307 I.C.C. 775, 785; *Missouri Pac. R. Co. Discontinuance of Service*, 307 I.C.C. 787, 797-8; *Minneapolis & St. L. Ry. Co. Discontinuance of Service*, 307 I.C.C. 79, 92; *Texas & P. Ry. Co. Discontinuance of Service*, 307 I.C.C. 259, 263; *New Jersey & N. Y. R. Co. Discontinuance of Service*, 307 I.C.C. 532, 538; *Chicago M., St. P. & P. R. Co. Discontinuance of Service*, 307 I.C.C. 565, 579.

[30]49 U.S.C. 13a (2).

facilities of the authorities in such State in the performance of its functions under this paragraph."

The express language of Section 13a (2), confirmed by its legislative history clearly establishes that determination of a railroad's application to discontinue or change service of an intrastate train continues to reside with the State and the Commission's jurisdiction may be invoked only after the State has failed to grant the railroad's application within the prescribed 120-day period.[31] However, if the Commission once acquires jurisdiction in a case arising under Section 13a (2), such jurisdiction is not lost because of subsequent action by the State, although the State action may render the Commission's case moot.[32]

In conferring jurisdiction upon the Commission over discontinuance of intrastate service, Section 13a (2) represented a marked departure from the traditional separation of State and Federal authority in regulation of intrastate service, and it is reasonable to assume that Congress must have anticipated that creation of the right to invoke the Commission's jurisdiction would cause the States to take speedier and perhaps more favorable action on applications for intrastate train discontinuance.[33] In addition, the Commission may not properly consider a proposal for discontinuance or change of service differing substantially from that presented to the State; and where the railroad seeks authority to discontinue intrastate train service without providing, through its motor carrier subsidiary, the bus-truck highway service in the affected territory which it proposed to the State authority, the proposal submitted is materially different from that presented to the State and the Commission has no jurisdiction to approve it.[34] However, the issues before the Commission in a proceeding under Section 13a (2) are broader than that before the State Commission, since the Commission must also find, before authorizing a discontinuance, that continued operation of the service without change will constitute an unjust and undue buden on interstate operations of the carrier involved and upon interstate commerce.[35]

In *Missouri Pac. R. Co. Discontinuance of Passenger Service*,[36] it was stated that the I.C. Act provides that the Commission shall have jurisdiction of a proposed discontinuance of intrastate trains if the State authority has not finally acted on an application for such permission within 120 days "from the presentation thereof," thus a motion to dismiss carrier's

[31]*Northern Pac. Ry. Co. Discontinuance of Service*, 312 I.C.C. 150, 154.
[32]Id. p. 156.
[33]Id., pp. 154-5.
[34]Id., pp. 155-6.
[35]*New York Central R. Discontinuance*, 312 I.C.C. 4, 11.
[36]312 I.C.C. 105, 107-8.

petition for want of jurisdiction, on the theory that Congress must have intended "presentation" to mean something other than "duly filed," was overruled. In the proceeding, the protestants conceded that the State Commission did not finally dispose of carrier's application within 120 days from the date of its filing. The Commission said that under the dictionary definition of "file," as meaning to deliver a paper or instrument to the proper officer to be kept on file among the records of his office, and of "present," as to lay before or submit to a person or body for consideration or action, filing an application with the State Commission for authority to discontinue certain trains and laying an incidental request before that commission for its consideration and action are one and the same thing in the context of the statute; and that conclusion is supported by the legislative history of the Transportation Act of 1958 which added Section 13a to the Act.

The Commission is required to apply the same standard to interstate and intrastate operations in determining whether discontinuance of a train or service is justified. As the Supreme Court stated in *Southern R. Co. v. United States:*[37]

> All that need properly be considered under this standard, as both the language and history of Section 13a (2) thus make abundantly clear, is what effect the discontinuance of the specific train or service in question will have upon the public convenience and necessity and upon interstate operations or commerce. As the Commission has correctly summed up the matter in another case:
>
>> "The burden upon the carrier's interstate operations or upon interstate commerce, as expressed in Section 13a (2) . . . is to be measured by the injurious effect that the continued operation of the train purposed for discontinuance would have upon interstate commerce. As is indicated by its legislative history, the purpose of Section 13a (2) is to permit the discontinuance of the operation of services than 'no longer pay their way and for which there is no longer sufficient public need to justify the heavy financial losses involved.' (S. Rep. 1647, 85th Cong.) Nowhere in Section 13a (2) or elsewhere in the law is there any requirement that the prosperity of the intrastate operations of the carrier as a whole, or any particular segment thereof, must be given effect in determining whether the operation of an individual intrastate train imposes an unjust and undue burden on interstate commerce. To hold otherwise would be contrary to the apparent intent of the Congress." *Southern Pac. Co., Partial Discontinuance,* 312 I.C.C. 631, 633-634 (1961).

---

[37] 11 L. ed 541, 549.

5

Certificates of Public Convenience and Necessity for Motor Carriers

The Application

Section 206(b) of the Interstate Commerce Act[1] provides in part that "Application for certificates shall be made in writing to the Commission, be verified uner oath, and shall be in such form and contain such information and be accompanied by proof of service upon such interested parties as the Commission shall, by regulation, require." The filing of an application which fails to disclose the true nature of the proposed operation, whether intentional or not, does not give interested parties adequate notice thereof and is not condoned.[2]

Classification of Motor Common Carriers

In *Classification of Motor Carriers of Property*,[3] the Commission classified motor carriers into regular and irregular carriers for puposes of certifications and enumerated factors to be considered in determining whether or not a particular operation fell within one classification or the other. The reasonableness of the Commission's classification has been approved by the courts many times.[4]

Generally speaking regular service is service between fixed termini,

---

[1]49 U.S.C. 306(b). Comparable provisions — Sections 1 (19), 309(b), 410(b) as to form of application; and Sections 309(a), 410(a), 411(b) cover interim provisions.

[2]*Nelson Transport, Inc., Extension*, 79 M.C.C. 743, 747.

[3]M.C.C. 703.

[4]See *U.S. v. Maher*, 307 U.S. 148; *Crescent Express Lines, Inc. v. U.S.*, 320 U.S. 401; *Brady Transfer & Storage Company v. U.S.*, 80 F. Supp. 110, aff'd 335 U.S. 875; *Falwell v. U.S.*, 69 F. Supp. 71, aff'd 330 U.S. 807.

which is repetitive in character over more or less fixed routes. As stated by the Commission in *Classification of Motor Carriers of Property:*[5]

> As above stated, regular-route service is repetitive in character. It is necessarily marked by such periodic recurrence, as to become fixed in a pattern which is known to the public in contrast to on-call service which depends for its design wholly on the day to day needs of individual shippers. Regular-route service does not, however, depend upon the interval between offerings. Daily service is common but not necssarily the rule. Not infrequently regular-route "grandfather" rights have been granted on proof of only two or three services weekly over claimed routes. The essential thing is a service of such fixed and definite periodicity that it becomes known to and is relied upon by shippers and consignees generally. Where, however, daily service is shown it is obvious that it is strong evidence of a regular-route operation. A continuing course of daily service for a long time between specific points over substantially the same routes is not likely to be achieved in a bona fide on-call operation without any predetermined plan.

The Commission also classifies motor common carriers on a commodity basis. The commodity lists in the *Descriptions* case[6] were established primarily to permit carriers dedicated to serving particular industries to provide continuous and complete service in their respective fields, and to enable them to handle new products within the same generic classifications without opening the door for competition in other fields of service; and notwithstanding the statement therein that the prescribed lists were for use as guides in determining future grants of authority, it is clear from subsequent decisions that such lists may also be used as guides in ascertaining generally the commodities that may or may not be transported under previously issued certificates.[7]

Public Convenience and Necessity Defined

The term "public convenience and necessity" is spelled out and defined in *Pan American Bus Lines Operations,*[8] where the Commission said:

> Section 207(a) of the Motor Carrier Act is similar in general to Section 1(18) of the Interstate Commerce Act, above quoted, and both employ the expression "public convenience and necessity." The words "conveni-

---

[5]The salient parts of the Commission's report, setting up the classification and enumerating the criteria for determining whether or not a particular operation is either regular or irregular, are set forth in a note to the opinion *Brady Transfer & Storage Co. v. United States, supra* (note at page 117).

[6]61 M.C.C. 209.

[7]*E. Brooke Matlack, Inc. — Control — Reader Bros., Inc.,* 80 M.C.C. 349, 356.

[8]M.C.C. 190, 202.

ence" and "necessity" are used conjunctively, and we have found that they are not synonymous but must be given a separate and distinct meaning. Atlanta & St. A. B. Ry. Co. Application, 71 I.C.C. 784. Yet it is clear that the word "necessity" must be somewhat liberally construed, for there are comparatively few things in life which can be regarded as an absolute "necessity," and it was surely not the intent of Congress to use the word in so strict and narrow a sense.

Protestants direct attention to the following statement by division 4 in Utah Term. Ry. Co. Application, 72 I.C.C. 89, 93-94.

> So long as the available supply of coal can promptly reach the consuming public over existing lines, it is difficult to perceive how public convenience and necessity can be served by the establishment of competing facilities. "Public convenience and necessity" has been defined as "a strong or urgent public need." Wis. Telephone Co. v. Railroad Comm., 162 Wis. 383; 156 N.W. 614. A public need can hardly be predicated upon the demand of three shippers who may desire to introduce the element of competition in order to improve their position in their own competitive field. While one of the purposes of the transportation act, 1920, was to preserve competition between carriers, the provisions of paragraphs (18) to (20), inclusive of section 1 negative any presumption that it was the purpose of Congress to permit the construction of new and competitive lines of railroad where existing facilities are adequate or can be made so by the exercise of available administrative remedies.

This case involved the construction of a branch line of railroad strictly parallel with an existing line, both lines serving the same coal field. Division 4 denied the certificate, but its decision was reversed by the Commission in 79 I.C.C. 187. In San Antonio & A. P. Ry. Co. Construction, supra, at page 493, we said:

> It is undesirable if not impossible to lay down any general rule by which it can be determined whether or not certificates of public convenience and necessity should be issued for the construction of proposed new lines of railroad. Every case must be decided in the light of its own special circumstances.

Perhaps the best interpretation of the purpose underlying the "public convenience and necessity" provisions was by the Supreme Court in Texas & N. O. R. Co. v. Northside Belt Ry. Co., 276 U.S. 475, 479, as follows:

> The purpose of paragraphs 18 to 22 is to prevent interstate carriers from weakening themselves by constructing or operating superfluous lines, and to protect them from being weakened by another carrier's operating in interstate commerce a competing line not required in the public interest.

The question, in substance, is whether the new operation or service will serve a useful public purpose, responsive to a public demand or need; whether this purpose can and will be served as well by existing lines or

carriers; and whether it can be served by applicant with the new operation or service proposed without endangering or impairing the operations
of existing carriers contrary to the public interest.

Points Considered in Establishing Public Convenience and Necessity

In determining whether a proposed service is required by public
convenience and necessity, three major points have been considered in
the past: (1) would the new operation serve a useful public purpose responsive to a public demand or need; (2) can this public purpose be
served as well by existing facilities; and (3) could it be served by applicant without endangering the operations of existing carriers contrary to
the public interest.[9]

However, it is important to note that in determining the direction in
which the public convenience lies, the Commission often has stated that
adequacy of existing service is not the only measure and has frequently
considered the significance of competition; the courts also have recognized the relevance of increased competition in assessing the public
interest.[10]

Parties of Interest

Any carrier which can and will provide all or any part of the proposed service sought by an applicant may file a protest against the
application and participate in any proceeding held on such application
as a party of interest.

In *Auch Inter-Borough Transit Co., Extension,*[11] the role of brokers
of motor transportation was recognized and their familiarity with transportation conditions in the area and with the service proposed was
found to be a proper basis for recognizing them as parties of interest
to protest applications by motor carriers seeking to transport passengers
in special sightseeing and pleasure tours. However, the report also

---

[9]*Pan American Bus Lines Operation,* 1 M.C.C. 190; *D. C. Transit System, Inc.,
Extension,* 81 M.C.C. 737, 743; *Roadway Exp., Inc., Extension,* 82 M.C.C. 689, 701;
Martin Van Lines, Inc., Extension, 79 M.C.C. 767, 770.

[10]See e.g., the following court cases: *Bowman Transp. v. Arkansas-Best Freight
Sys.,* 419 U.S. 281; *Nashua Motor Express v. United States,* 230 F. Supp. 646, 652-
653; *Trans-American Van Servs., Inc. v. United States,* 421 F. Supp. 308, 321-324;
Lemmon Transp. Co. v. United States, 393 F. Supp. 838, 842. See also e.g., the
following I.C.C. cases: *Chicksaw Motor Line, Inc.,* 121 M.C.C. 476, 479, 499; *Arrow
Trucking Co.,* 121 M.C.C. 485, 488, 490; *Patterson Extension-York, Pa.,* 111 M.C.C.
645, 650; *M. R. & R. Trucking Co.,* 105 M.C.C. 69, 80; *Superior Trucking Co., Inc.,
Ext.-Agri. Machinery,* 126 M.C.C. 292.

[11]88 M.C.C. 455.

recognized that a broker's standing is not that of a carrier, and that consequently no consideration will be given to the adverse economic effects upon the broker which might result from the issuance of a certificate to the carrier.

Notice to Interested Parties

Notice of the filing of an application for authority is given by the publication of a summary of authority sought in the Federal Register.

In *Moffatt Trucking — Common Carrier Application*,[12] the application as filed and published in the Federal Register named two points as the proposed origins at which applicant desired to originate shipments. Just prior to or in the early stages of the hearing, applicant's counsel learned that the actual points of origin were the two plant sites located several miles from the two points mentioned in the Federal Register. In the recommended report, a request for an amendment, in effect, was allowed by reason of a grant of authority from the plant sites. In the circumstances, Division 1 required a republication in the Federal Register of the authority actually desired and stated (pp. 328-29) that it would "withhold the issuance of a certificate until the elapse of 30 days from the date of such republication, during which time any interested party may file a petition for further hearing."

In *North Creek Trucking, Inc. — Common Carrier Application*,[13] the requested authority was described and published in the Federal Register in an ambiguous, if not erroneous manner, easily capable of being misunderstood. Publication was in such manner that it might be interpreted that only authority from one point was sought whereas, in fact, additional points were involved. Nevertheless, the Commission granted the authority. The issuance of the certificate, however, was withheld pending republication in the Federal Register of the authority actually requested — an elapse of 30 days from the date of such republication during which period any proper party in interest could file a protest and petition for further hearing. Likewise, in *Tompkins Common Carrier Application*,[14] where the requested authority, through an error on the part of the Commission, was not published in a manner consistent with the application, the Commission granted the authority but withheld issuance of the certificate for a short period of time to permit republication.

---

[12]73 M.C.C. 327.
[13]72 M.C.C. 497.
[14]69 M.C.C. 427.

Broad Administrative Discretion is Exercised

The nature and extent of the authority of the Commission in matters arising under Section 207(a) of the Interstate Commerce Act[15] has been the subject of much litigation, extensive judicial consideration, and is well settled. The judicial determinations of the Commission's power under Section 1(18) prior to the enactment of part II of the I.C. Act constituted the precedence for later court interpretations of the Commission's authority under Section 207(a). In an early case, *Chesapeake & Ohio Ry. v. United States,*[16] the Supreme Court, recognizing the need for the expert body's determination in the field of transportation regarding public convenience and necessity, held:

> There is no specification of the considerations by which the Commission is to be governed in determining whether the public convenience and necessity require the proposed construction. Under the Act it was the duty of the Commission to find the facts and, in the exercise of a reasonable judgment, to determine that question.

Proceeding upon the same theory enunciated in the earlier cases, the Supreme Court in *Interstate Commerce Commission v. Parker,*[17] stated:

> Public convenience and necessity is not defined by the statute. The nouns in the phrase possess connotations which have evolved from a half-century experience of the government in the regulation of transportation. When Congress in 1935 amended the Interstate Commerce Act by adding the Motor Carrier Act, it chose the same words to state the condition for new motor lines which had been employed for similar purposes for railroads in the same Act since the Transportation Act of 1920, sec 402 (18) and (20), 41 Stat. 477. Such use indicated a continuation of the administrative and judicial interpretation of the language. Cf. *Case v. Los Angeles Lumber Co.,* 308 U.S. 106, 115. The Commission had assumed, as its duty under these earlier subsections, the finding of facts and the exercise of its judgment to determine public convenience and necessity. This court approved this construction. *Chesapeake & Ohio R. Co. v. United States,* 283 U.S. 35, 42. Cf. *Gray v. Powell,* 314 U.S. 402, 411-12. The purpose of Congress was to leave to the Commission authoritatively to decide whether additional motor carrier service would serve public convenience and necessity. Cf. *Powell v. United States,* 300 U.S. 276, 287. This, of course, gives administrative discretion to the Commission, cf. *McLean Trucking Co. v. United States,* 321, U.S. 67, 78-88, to draw its conclusion from the infinite variety of circumstances which may occur in specific instances. . . .

---

[15]49 U.S.C. 307 (a). Comparable provisions — Sections 1 (18)-(20), 309(c), 410 (c).

[16]283 U.S. 35, 42. See also *Texas & Pacific Ry. Co. v. Gulf, C. & S. F. Ry. Co.,* 270 U.S. 266, 273; *Colorado v United States* 300 U.S. 276, 287.

[17]326 U.S. 60, 65.

During the same term of the Supreme Court, it had occasion to deal with the same question in a case arising under part III of the I.C. Act relating to water carriers. The holding in *United States v. Detroit Navigation Co.*[18] further emphasizes the broad administrative and exclusive discretion vested in the Commission in matters involving the public convenience. In the *Detroit Navigation Co.* case, the Supreme Court, at page 241, had this to say:

> . . . The Commission is the guardian of the public interest in determining whether certificates of public convenience and necessity shall be granted. For the performance of that function the Commission has been entrusted with a wide range of discretionary authority. *Interstate Commerce Commission v. Parker*, 326 U.S. 60. Its function is not only to appraise the facts and to draw inferences from them but also to bring to bear upon the problem an expert judgment to determine from its analysis of the total situation on which side of the controversy the public interest lies. Its doubt that the public interest will be adequately served if resumption of service is left to existing carriers is entitled to the same respect as its expert judgment on other complicated transportation problems. See *Chesapeake & Ohio R. Co. v. United States*, 283 U.S. 35, 42; *Alton R. Co. v. United States*, 315 U.S. 15, 23. Forecasts as to the future are necessary to the decision. But neither uncertainties as to the future nor the inability or failure of existing carriers to show the sufficiency of their plant to meet future traffic demands need paralyze the Commission into inaction. It may be that the public interest requires that future shipping needs be assured rather than left uncertain. The Commission has the discretion so to decide. It went no further here.

A similar expression of the court is found in *United States v. Carolina Freight Carriers Corp.*,[19] where the court held, at page 489:

> We express no opinion on the scope of the certificate which should be granted in this case. That entails not only a weighing of evidence but the exercise of an expert judgment on the intricacies of the transportation problems which are involved. That function is reserved exclusively for the Commission (citing cases). Our task ends if the statutory standards have been properly applied.

And in *Wales v .United States of America*,[20] the court stated:

> We do not understand that the words, "convenience," "necessity," are to be bounded and limited by any authority, save and except the Interstate Commerce Commission.

[18]326 U.S. 236.
[19]315 U.S. 475. See also *Gateway Transp. Co. v. United States*, 173 F. Supp. 822, 826-7.
[20]108 F. Supp. 928, 932, affirmed per curiam 345 U.S. 954. See also *Capital Transit Co. v. United States*, D.C., 97 F. Supp. 614, 618; *St. Johnsbury Trucking Co. v. United States*, 99 F. Supp. 977, 981; cf. *A., B. & C. Motor Transp. Co. v. United States*, 69 F. Supp. 166, 169; *United States v. Pan American Petroleum Corp.*, 304 U.S. 156, 158.

And as was said in *Beard-Laney, Inc. v. United States:*[21]

> . . . It is for the Commission, not the court, to say what public convenience and necessity require and whether these will be better served by licensing an additional carrier than by permitting those already licensed to expand their facilities. . . .

Thus the issue of public convenience and necessity is a matter requiring particular exercise of the Commission's expert judgment in the field of transportation. No precise formula can be laid down with exactness by which the Commission's determination is to be governed in deciding whether additional motor carrier service would serve the public convenience and necessity.[22] As the court reiterated in *American Trucking Assns. v. United States,*[23] it is for the Commission to "weigh the advantages" of the granting of an application against the injury arising therefrom in order "to determine where public convenience and necessity lies." The Commission must give appropriate consideration to the consequence to the public of the proposals involved, as well as their bearing on the transportation agencies concerned.

Grandfather Rights

Following the adoption of the Motor Carrier Act of 1935, the Commission was literally inundated by applicants who sought to obtain certificates of convenience and necessity pursuant to the "grandfather" clause of that Act. As pointed out in *Gregg Cartage Co. v. United States,*[24] "the Commission had nearly 90,000 applications to pass upon under Section 206(a)." In its 51st Annual Report, issued on November 1, 1937, the Commission noted that 78,819 "grandfather" applications had been filed, that 75,819 of these applications had been referred to the field force, and that there were 24,541 applications on which field reports had been made.

The Commission further observed in its 51st Annual Report that in addition to the "grandfather" applications there were other applications. It noted that (p. 71) that these applications, "together with the 'grandfather' applications which have become too complicated or controversial to be handled in the manner described above, are heard formally by a joint board composed of representatives of the State commissions and assisted by one of our examiners, or by one of our examiners." It would

[21]F. Supp. 27, 32, aff'd 338 U.S. 803.
[22]*Norfolk Southern Bus Corp. v. United States,* 96 F. Supp. 756, aff'd U.S. 77, 86.
[23]326 U.S. 77, 86.
[24]316 U.S. 74, 84.

have been not only unfeasible but physically impossible for the Commission to determine all of these "grandfather" applications pursuant to a formal adversary proceeding. The Commission, therefore, in the exercise of the authority conferred upon it by Section 204(a) (6) to prescribe procedures for the administration of the Motor Carrier Act, adopted an "informal procedure," the only sensible approach to the matter. In its 51st Annual Report, the Commission described this procedure as follows (pp. 70-71):

> The year covered by this report is the second full year in which we have been receiving applications for certificates, permits, and licenses. In our last annual report we described by tabulation the applications received in that year. During the current year the number has grown from 85,636 to 89,456. The increase consists of 1,280 "grandfather" applications filed after February 12, 1936, 2,524 applications for authority to institute new operations, and 6 applications for determination of status.

> All applications for new operations and all applications for licenses required public hearings. "Grandfather" applications are being handled by an informal conference method to a very large extent. Only those which are too complicated or controversial for such handling are set for hearing. Most of the 78,819 "grandfather" applications filed on or before February 12, 1936, were prepared in haste and filed at the last moment. They did not, therefore, contain a record which would justify the issuance of a certificate or permit and, in any event, careful checking of the proof offered was necessary in most cases. Inadequate applications are referred to our field representatives for development through interviews with the applicants and protestants, if any. Upon receipt of sufficient information and evidence, this Section (Section of Certificates and Insurance) drafts, for our approval, an order granting or denying the application.

The Supreme Court itself has recognized that the summary or informal procedure that the Commission followed with respect to these "grandfather" applications was required by the mass of applications which flooded the Commission. Thus, in *Crescent Express Lines v. United States*,[25] specifically commenting on this procedure, the Supreme Court noted (pp. 404-405):

> However, under Section 306 the Commission was directed to issue the certificates to applicants under the grandfather clause without further proof of convenience or necessity and without further proceedings. Its routine practice was to refer the applications to its field force for investigation. The applicant appeared before this examiner prior to the first order of the Commission. The compliance order was made upon the application, the supporting affidavits and questionnaire. The mass of applications forced this summary procedure. The compliance order gave opportunity to the

[25]320 U.S. 401.

applicant or other parties in interest to protest its conclusions. Section 321 (b). This application was treated in the foregoing manner.

In order to obtain authority to serve all intermediate points on a regular route, a "grandfather" application was not required to show service at every point. If a sufficient number of intermediate points had been served, authority to serve all intermediate points would be granted.[26] In *Richards Common Carrier Application,* the Commission stated (p. 493):

> In cases such as this one, especially where the operations cover an extensive territory, we have not heretofore required proof of service to and from each point in the territory. Applicant has served every point embraced in the appendix from some other point in his territory, although he has not transported traffic originating at each point to every other point. For example, he has handled shipments between Philadelphia and Rochester, and between Rochester and New York, but has not transported any between Philadelphia and New York. We are of the opinion that applicant's operation to all points listed in the appendix is sufficient to entitle him to authority to operate in unrestricted service between these points over the routes prescribed.

The Commission summarized its decision in the *Richards* case in the following language (p. 494), which states the general rule followed in many other cases before and since:

> Applicant did not serve all of the intermediate points on all routes, but he did serve a number of them on most of his routes. Where we have found that there was a sufficient number of intermediate points served, authority to serve all intermediate points will be issued.

One of the early cases in which this rule was applied is *Pierce Auto Freight Lines Common Carrier Application,*[27] where, after summarizing the evidence, the Commission's Division 5 said (p. 420):

> The record clearly establishes by testimony of applicant's witnesses and by manifests submitted in evidence that applicant served on and subsequent to the statutory date a substantial number of the intermediate points between Portland and Medford. Any doubt, therefore, as to service at any particular point will be resolved in favor of applicant.

---

[26]*Roadway Express Application,* 51 M.C.C. 802; *Richards Common Carrier Application,* 27 M.C.C. 489. See *Al Renk & Sons, Inc. — Alaska "Grandfather" Application,* 89 M.C.C. 91, defining standards to be applied in determining the merits of motor carrier applications for Alaska grandfather authority under Section 206(a) (5) of the Act. The I.C. Act was construed as intending that Alaskan grandfather applicants be relieved of proving that their operations were as substantial and frequent as those operations which were required to be shown by applicants under previous grandfather legislation.

[27]11 M.C.C. 417.

The same case later came on for further hearing before the entire Commission, which in its decision, *Pierce Auto Freight Lines Common Carrier Application*,[28] affirmed the authorization to serve all intermediate points between Portland and Medford. That decision was assailed by a protesting carrier before a three-judge court and was upheld in *Mc-Cracken v. United States*.[29] The pertinent facts are stated and the view of the court is expressed in the following quotation from the opinion (pp. 446-447):

> A Division of the Commission issued a report favorable to authorization of the continuance of operations between Portland and Medford, Oregon, serving all intermediate points. . . . The full Commission affirmed the Division. . . . The basis of the attack is the alleged failure of the evidence to show that the Pierce Lines ever transported property between such intermediate points north of Drain and that the order is therefore unsupported by the evidence and is arbitrary and void.
>
> *   *   *
>
> There is no direct finding in the report of the Commission that the Pierce Lines transported property between points intermediate to Portland and Drain during the critical period. A review of the record also shows that the proof did not establish transportation between such points. There is, however, clear evidence that during this time goods were carried from points intermediate to Portland and Drain both to Portland and to points south of Drain, and were carried to said intermediate points from Portland and from points south of Drain.
>
> The order is, therefore, in this narrow respect, unsupported by the evidence. But it is contended by the United States and the Commission that the latter had power by statute to permit or compel Pierce Lines to carry property without limitation to and from such intermediate points.
>
> *   *   *
>
> The mere facts that the evidence does not show that Pierce Lines in the past had covered these intermediate points in all possible combinations and permutations did not prevent the Commission from imposing[30] on the carrier the necessity of transporting property between these intermediate points, as well as to and from such points, as a condition to the exercise of the privileges conferred by the certificate.

In *Riss & Co., Common Carrier Application*,[31] the facts were stated to be similar to those considered in the *Pierce Auto Freight Lines* case, and in the report by the entire Commission the following was said (p. 706):

[28]30 M.C.C. 629.
[29]47 F. Supp. 444.
[30]"If the Commission may order it may permit." *Myers Transp. Co. v. United States*, 49 F. Supp. 828, 830.
[31]44 M.C.C. 704.

In the instant proceeding, applicant has transported shipments to St. Louis and has transported freight through St. Louis in connection with its operations generally. Further, it solicited shipments from St. Louis and has transported shipments from that point since at least sometime in 1937. . . . We are of the view that applicant is entitled to "grandfather" rights to serve the intermediate point of St. Louis also without restriction. This conclusion seems necesary if a substantial parity is to be preserved as between applicant's future operations and its prior bona fide operations. *Alton R. Co. v. United States*, 315 U.S. 15; *United States v. Carolina Freight Carriers Corp.*, 315 U.S. 475.

In *Chicago, St. P., M. & O. R. Co. v. United States*,[32] the plaintiff railroads assailed an order of the Commission granting to one Styer a certificate under the "grandfather" clause to operate over described regular routes from the Twin Cities in Minnesota to certain points in South Dakota, contending that the portion of the order which authorized Styer to serve all intermediate points in Minnesota was without evidentiary support and in excess of the power of the Commission. On this phase of the case the court said (p. 253):

It must be true, however, that the Commission, in determining the nature and extent of the "grandfather" rights of a carrier in a particular case, is not required to do so with mathematical precision, and that, within reasonable bounds, its estimate of the character and scope of the carrier's bona fide operation on and prior to June 1, 1935, must be accepted by the courts, which cannot substitute their judgment for that of the Commission.

The Commission has, in effect, ruled in similar proceedings that proof of actual operations as a common carrier to and from termini and some intermediate points on a regular route, coupled with evidence of a holding out of service and of a willingness and ability to serve all points on the route whenever shipments are offered, will justify a finding of bona fide operation to and between all points on the route. . . . In the instant case, it is apparent that the Commission regarded the proof of actual service between termini and to intermediate points in South Dakota, together with the evidence which tended to prove that Styer was offering and was able to serve intermediate points, whether in Minnesota of South Dakota, on the "grandfather" routes, as sufficient to justify the grant which it made to Styer. Proper deference must be paid to the Commission's interpretation of the law which it enforces . . ., and if there is any warrant in the record for the judgment of the Commission, it must stand. . . .

Alton R. Co. v. United States,[33] involved an application for irregular-route rather than regular-route authority. The question considered was "as to the power of the Commission to authorize operation in an entire

---

[32]50 F. Supp. 249, aff'd 322 U.S. 1.
[33]315 U.S. 15.

State where only a few points in that State has been served" (p. 20). Upholding the Commission's power so to authorize, the court said, "While the test of 'bona fide operation' within a specified 'territory' includes 'actual rather than potential or simulated service' (*McDonald v. Thompson,* 305 U.S. 263, 266), it does not necessarily restrict future operations to the precise points or areas already served" (p. 21). Then, after reviewing the facts in the case and the Commission's conclusions, the court said, "That judgment is for the administrative experts, not the courts" (p. 23).

The Commission has, since the early days of Federal regulation of motor carriers, followed the rule that proof of service at a considerable number of intermediate points on a regular route is warrant for the issuance of authority to serve all intermediate points thereon; and the rule has been upheld by the courts, including the Supreme Court. These holdings have been in accord with the oft-repeated statement that the purpose of the "grandfather" clause was not to "freeze" the applicant's service "in its exact status on June 1, 1935, with no possibility for improvement or modification of the service given over the routes or in the territory served on that date to meet the changing requirements of public interest and demand."[34]

In this connection the Supreme Court, in *United States v. Carolina Carriers Corp.,*[35] used the following language in discussing the scope of the Commission's authority to issue certificates under the "grandfather" clause:

> Authority to operate within a specified "territory" may include permission to service all point in that area. On the other hand it may be restricted to designated points therein. Or as in the instant case, it may extend to all points in a part of that area and to selected localities in another part. The precise delineation of the area or the specification of localities which may be serviced has been entrusted by the Congress to the Commission.
>
> The judgment required is highly expert. Only where the error is patent may we say that the Commission transgressed. That is not this case.

To the same effect is *Noble v. United States,*[36] where the court again stated that the "precise delineation of an enterprise which seeks the protection of the 'grandfather' clause has been reserved for the Commission."

[34]*Byers Transp. Co. v. United States,* 49 F. Supp. 828, 830.
[35]315 U.S. 475, 480-482.
[36]319 U.S. 88, 93.

Grandfather Rights Involving Carriers of Exempt Commodities

Section 7 of the Transportation Act of 1958 amended Section 203(b) (6)[37] only to the extent that it (1) narrowed the area of that exemption by excluding specified commodities previously held to be exempt; (2) widened the area of exemption to include specified commodities previously held to be nonexempt; and (3) provided for "grandfather" rights on those commodities thereby made nonexempt.[38] Insofar as Section 203(b) (6) provides for the economic regulation by the Commission of certain motor transportation for hire of agricultural commodities formerly exempt from such regulation, those who were engaged in such transportation on or before May 1, 1958, and had so operated continuously since, were permitted to file "grandfather" applications and those who instituted such operations after May 1, 1958, but prior to August 12, 1958, were permitted to file "interim" applications; those who filed "grandfather" and "interim" applications on or before December 10, 1958, were permitted to continue the performance of the service without a certificate or permit pending determination of their applications.[39]

In essence, the purpose of the "grandfather" proviso of Section 7(c) of the Transportation Act of 1958 was to assure substantial parity between prior and future bona fide operations in transportation of the considered commodity, and the Commission has construed this to mean, in general, that applicant must establish by competent evidence a continuity of operations beginning at least on May 1, 1958, and continuing thereafter except for significant interruptions over which it has no control.[40]

The interim provisions of Section 7(c) of the Transportation Act of 1958 bestow a privilege on the carrier filing timely application thereunder and should be construed strictly.[41] Otherwise the carrier, by handling a few shipments of a single commodity for a single shipper, could claim to have instituted a service of transporting a whole class of similar commodities from and to a vast geographical area, thus building up under an alleged color of right an impressive list of shipments handled, which could in turn be submitted as proof of public convenience and necessity. Furthermore, such a carrier would receive the wind-

---

[37]49 U.S.C. 303(b) (6).

[38]*Various Commodities between Points and Places in U.S.*, 309 I.C.C. 573, 576. See *Milk Transport, Inc. v. United States*, 368 U.S. 5, affirming *per curiam*, 190 F. Supp. 350.

[39]*Insurance Compliance*, 79 M.C.C. 213.

[40]*Handy*, 83 M.C.C. 331, 333; *Harman*, 83 M.C.C. 341, 343-4.

[41]*H. C. Gabler, Inc., Extension*, 83 M.C.C. 274, 276-7.

fall of statutory permission to conduct operations pending final determination of its application.[42] Therefore, any authority granted pursuant to interim application filed under Section 7(c) of the 1958 Act must be restricted to service actually provided during the interim period from May 1 to August 12, 1958; and the statutory provision allowing continuance of service pending final determination of the application must be construed as referring only to operations actually conducted prior to the effective date.[43]

In proceedings under the "grandfather" clause, pertinent evidence is that dealing with the nature and extent of applicant's operations on and since the critical date and the good faith thereof.[44] Precedents arising from the "grandfather" sections of the Motor Carrier Act of 1935 are equally applicable to administration of the similar provisions of the Transportation Act of 1958; no attempt was made in administering the former act to set a rigid standard, applicable automatically in all cases, which would provide an absolute definition of "bona fide" operation or even of "substantial service."[45]

To establish past bona fide operation within the meaning of Section 7(c) of the Transportation Act of 1958 requires a showing of substantial and consistent service as distinguished from incidental, sporadic, or infrequent service; and the mere holding out of service or the intent to conduct operations, in the absence of actual movements, is insufficient to justify a finding of bona fide operations.[46]

Need for Service

Generally in cases in which a common carrier applies for a certificate of convenience and necessity, it must show that there is a need among shippers for the proposed service and that the resulting prejudice to existing motor carriers will not be such as to impair their ability to operate efficiently. (This is subject to the consideration of competition as a factor.) As usually stated, there must be an affirmative showing that the existing facilities are inadequate before the Commission is warranted in granting the new operating rights in a territory already served. Thus, in *Hudson Transit Lines v. United States*,[47] the court said:

[42]*Ibid.*
[43]*Ibid.*
[44]*Long*, 81 M.C.C. 689, 691.
[45]Id., p. 692.
[46]*Arthur Johncox & Son*, 83 M.C.C. 39, 41.
[47]82 F. Supp. 153, 157, aff'd 338 U.S. 802.

The Commission has frequently held that under Sec. 307, there must be an affirmative showing not only that a common carrier service is required in the convenience of the public but also that it is a necessity, and that the latter element includes a showing that present facilities are inadequate. *Pan-American Bus Lines, Operation,* 1 M.C.C. 190, 203; *Bluenose Bus Co., Ltd., Common Carrier Application,* 1 M.C.C. 173, 176; *Richard L. Richards, Extension of Operations,* 6 M.C.C. 80, 81; *Ohio Transportation Co., Common Carrier Application,* 29 M.C.C. 513, 520; *Royal Cadillac Service, Inc., Common Carrier Application,* 43 M.C.C. 247, 259. The courts, too, have recognized inadequacy of existing facilities as a basic ingredient in the determination (sic) of public "necessity." *Inland Motor Freight v. United States,* D.C.E.D. Wash. 60 F. Supp. 520, 524. See also: *Interstate Commerce Commission v. Parker,* 325 U.S. 60, 69, 70, 74, 65 S. Ct. 1490, 89 L. Ed. 2051 and dissenting opinion of Mr. Justice Douglas. This does not mean that the holder of a certificate is entitled to immunity from competition under any and all circumstances. *Chesapeake & O. R. Co. v. United States,* 283 U.S. 35, 51 S. Ct. 337, 75 L. Ed. 824. The introduction of a competitive service may be in the public interest where it will secure the benefits of an improved service without being unduly prejudicial to the existing service. *Interstate Commerce Commission v. Parker, supra.* No such finding has here been made, nor is there any evidence to support such a finding.

In *Inland Motor Freight v. United States,*[48] the court set aside an order of the Commission granting a certificate of convenience and necessity on the ground that the Commission made no finding that the existing service in the territory involved was inadequate. The court said (p. 524):

In the Order here under consideration, there is no finding to the effect that there was no existing service in operation over the area applied for or that such service was inadequate or that the existing carriers could not furnish and are not satisfactorily furnishing the service required. The state courts universally have recognized the necessity for some such conclusion as a basis for public convenience and necessity certificates under state statutes. . . . The Commission itself has recognized the rule enunciated by the state courts. *Bluenose Bus Company Application,* 1 M.C.C. 173, 176; *Pan American Bus Lines,* 1 M.C.C. 190, 203; *Richards Extension of Operation,* 6 M.C.C. 80, 81.

As stated in *Wales v. United States:*[49]

The Commission, through the application of its expert judgment and experience in, and knowledge of, interstate transportation matters, is the final arbiter upon whether or not additional motor carrier service is required.

[48]60 F. Supp. 520.
[49]108 F. Supp. 928, 933, aff'd 345 U.S. 954. See also *Lang Transp. Co. v. United States,* 75 F. Supp. 915; *Burlington Transp. Co. Ext.–Ill., Iowa and Mo.,* 43 I.C.C. 729, 736.

Public transportation is not something that can belong to an applicant. It is established and determined by proof of conditions which exist in the territory to be served.

In *L. A. Tucker Truck Lines v. United States*,[50] the court set aside an order of the Commission which had granted operating authority between two points by stating there was no evidence before the Commission. The court said (p. 649):

> There was no evidence before the Commission to sustain the need for granting additional service between St. Louis, Missouri, and Sikeston, Missouri, nor was there a showing that the present service was inadequate. While the routes over which Pemiscot Motor Freight operated required it to pass through Sikeston in order to render service to other points farther south granted in the certificate, this in the court's opinion is no justification for granting it authority to serve Sikeston.

In *McLean Trucking Co. v. United States*,[51] the court dismissed a complaint seeking to set aside an order of the Commission denying a portion of an application for a certificate on the ground that the plaintiff had not assumed its burden of proof. The court said:

> . . . For we conclude with the Commission that the privileges granted applicant on both applications are very substantial; that those denied are due to the applicant's failure to show the need for the service in some instances and in those where a demand exists the applicant has failed to show that existing authorized motor carriers are not able, ready and willing to perform the service.

In *Royal Cadillac Service, Inc. v. United States*,[52] the court, in dismissing a complaint seeking to set aside an order of the Commission denying a certificate of convenience and necessity, said:

> . . . The Commission, accordingly, was justified in concluding that the existing carriers were providing adequate and satisfactory services between the points sought to be served by the applicants and that the applicants accordingly have not established that public convenience and necessity require operations by them in the manner proposed.

> Public need is a fact and is not the exclusive property of any applicant, and having been proved by any one of several applicants for the same authority, or by all of them collectively, the public interest must control as to which shall receive the operation right.[53]

In the absence of proof of material deficiencies in the available service, the mere preference of a shipper for the proposed service does

[50]115 F. Supp. 647.
[51]63 F. Supp. 829, 831-2.
[52]52 F. Supp. 225, 226.
[53]*Ryder Tank Line, Inc., Extension*, 78 M.C.C. 409, 418; *Transport, Inc., Extension*, 69 M.C.C. 667.

not afford a sufficient basis upon which to predicate a grant of operating authority.[54] The fact that statements are made by various witnesses that there is need for additional transportation service in connection with the movement of their respective commodities should not be, and is not, accepted as conclusive by the Commission. It is a well established principle that public convenience and necessity should not be predicated wholly upon a shipper's preference or desires.[55] There can be no grant upon the basis of general and indefinite assertions of a need for service, but only upon an explicit showing of a need and that service of the type offered or its equivalent is not otherwise available. Even if the service of existing carriers is found to be inadequate to meet shipper's needs, an applicant for a certificate of public convenience and necessity would not be relieved of proving a need for such service.[56]

Nor is the fact that a number of witnesses advocate the services in question determinative of the issues in a proceeding involving the public convenience and necessity. The public interest demands that each case be decided on its merits. In *Southern Express, Inc., Common Carrier Application*,[57] the Commission, in denying certain applications there involved, said:

> We do not believe that the number of witnesses testifying in support of, or in opposition to, an application for authority to institute a new operation is of paramount importance. The public convenience and necessity, or lack thereof, is established by proof of the conditions existing at the points to be served, and it is our function to draw our own conclusions and form our own opinion from the proof offered, rather than to accept the consensus of opinion of witnesses upon the ultimate issue before us.

Where the shipper professes a need for the proposed service but has not tried all of the existing services available, the Commission denied an an application for additional authority.[58] In *Otto Pirkle Extension — Wisconsin*[59] the Commission stated at page 464 of its decision:

> There is no showing that any of the supporting shippers have actually suffered any loss of business or been materially inconvenienced through

---

[54]*P. B. Mutrie Motor Transp., Inc., Extension,* 79 M.C.C. 792, 794; *David Mongillo & Sons,* 82 M.C.C. 761, 765; *Bauman Extension,* 79 M.C.C. 547, 552; *Coastal Tank Lines, Inc., Extension,* 81 M.C.C. 600, 606; *Merchants Freight System, Inc., Extension,* 82 M.C.C. 293, 297; *Ruan Transport Corp., Extension,* 81 M.C.C. 467, 469-70.

[55]*Ford Brothers, Inc., Ext.—Hamilton Co., Ohio,* 52 M.C.C. 829 (not printed in full).

[56]*Inland Petroleum Transp. Co., Inc., Ext.—Oreg.,* 61 M.C.C. 726.

[57]10 Fed. Carrier Cases 32,835.

[58]*Walter C. Benson Co., Inc., Extension—N. Y., N. J. and Pa.,* 61 M.C.C. 128.

[59]54 M.C.C. 461

the use of existing service. While it may be that applicant could provide a somewhat faster service than is at present available, and in so doing the supporting shippers would receive certain benefits, these advantages alone are not sufficient reason here upon which to base a finding of public convenience and necessity. All things considered, we conclude that the application should be denied.

In *J. E. Fleming Common Carrier Application*[60] — in denying an application of a private carrier for a certificate of convenience and necessity, the Commission said:

Before we may grant authority for the institution of a new service of the type proposed, it is incumbent upon the applicant to establish that existing service is inadequate or in some respect unsatisfactory. This, applicant has failed to do. Although the supporting shippers have shown a desire to use his service to and from some of the involved points, there is no convincing showing that their reasonable transportation needs cannot be met by the existing carriers. Shippers have not acquainted themselves with, or utilized to any extent, the services of the authorized motor common carriers now operating in the considered territory. Preference or desire on the part of a shipper for an applicant's service is not sufficient to warrant a grant of the requested authority. We are not convinced that the evidence established any real need for the proposed service.

The Commission in *Claude A. Staats & Son, Inc., Common Carrier Application,*[61] stated:

. . . In this case, as in similar proceedings, it is incumbent upon the applicant to prove that the proposed service is required by the public convenience and necessity. Here, five shippers have expressed a desire for the services of a motor common carrier of stone from the described Indiana area. It appears from the record that some of the shippers have made unsuccessful attempts to locate the services of such a carrier. This seems to be the crux of applicant's case. We do not believe such facts are sufficient to support a finding favorable to applicant. . . . We must determine from the evidence of record whether, among other things, the public is presently receiving an adequate transportation service in the affected area. This includes rail service. The evidence shows that the supporting shippers have available the services of a number of rail carriers, which depend, substantially, upon the revenues derived from serving these very shippers. There appears to be no valid complaint concerning their services. Although the supporting shippers desire the service proposed by applicant, there is nothing definite of record to indicate that they would use the service to any great extent. A mere desire for an applicant's service will not, standing alone, satisfy the burden of proof placed upon the applicant.

[60] 9 Fed. Carrier Cases 32,377.
[61] 9 Fed. Carrier Cases 32,570.

In *Lester C Newton-Canned Goods,*[62] the Commission stated:

> . . . We are of the opinion that the evidence is insufficient to warrant
> a grant of authority to serve destination points and areas in the five
> states specified above. The testimony of the supporting witnesses is too
> general and indefinite to the basis of a finding that the present service
> offered by existing carriers is inadequate to meet the reasonable transpor-
> tation needs of shippers. It is noted that each witness emphasized that
> it was only during the canning season that the demand for service ap-
> peared to be greater than the existing carriers could supply. Moreover,
> the testimony shows that practically every example of allegedly unsatis-
> factory service cited by the witnesses occurred in the rush season. It is
> apparent that the granting of this application would not alleviate the sit-
> uation to any appreciable extent, however, because the ten vehicles which
> applicant operates also are kept busy during the rush season. At the same
> time it is inevitable that it would impair the operations of opposing car-
> riers, since friendly shippers would almost certainly employ applicant in
> preference to other carriers during the slack season. We have adhered
> to the view that the service of existing carriers would be deemed satisfactory
> if it were shown that the carriers were willing and able to meet the
> *reasonable* transportation needs of shippers. Here, there is no showing
> of any inability or unwillingness on the part of authorized carriers to serve
> particular points or shippers, but rather (a showing) in general (of)
> collective inability on the part of all carriers, within the limits of their
> respective authorities, to meet the unusual demand for service during the
> canning season. The purchase of sufficient equipment to meet the peak
> demand for service would be extremely wasteful. Since this would lead to
> operating inefficiency, it would be contrary to the public interest. The
> granting of this application would not benefit the public, since it is not
> pretended that the service in peak periods would be satisfactory if ap-
> plicant's services were available to shippers. At the same time it would
> prove harmful to the authorized carriers by permitting applicant to divert
> traffic from them during slack periods. Actually, what applicant has tried
> to do here is to show a need for additional service during the peak period,
> while proposing to provide such service only during the slack period, since
> it is admitted that all carriers are employed to full capacity during the rush
> season. We conclude, therefore, that the evidence is insufficient to sup-
> port the examiner's recommendation. . . .

The Commission is vested with great discretion in estimating future
requirements. This is clearly illustrated by the case of *United States v.
Detroit Navigation Co.*[63] In this case the Supreme Court was concerned
with an order of the Commission granting a certificate of convenience
and necessity to a steamship company to operate as a common carrier
in the transportation by water of motor vehicles from Detroit. The application was heard during the years of World War II when automobile

[62] 9 Fed. Carrier Cases 32,703.
[63] 326 U.S. 236.

production was almost completely curtailed. In granting the certificate the Commission considered the fact that production would be resumed after the termination of hostilities, which naturally was a matter of uncertainty, and took the prospect of the increase in the near future as one of the factors in determining the service. In sustaining the Commission's determination in this regard, the Supreme Court made the following observation concerning the Commission's duty and discretion in estimating future requirements.

> If the Commission were required to deny these applications unless it found an actual inability on the part of existing carriers to acquire the facilities necessary for future transportation needs, a limitation would be imposed on the power of the Commission which is not found in the Act. The Commission is the guardian of the public interest in determining whether certificates of convenience and necessity shall be granted. For the performance of that function the Commission has been entrusted with a wide range of discretionary authority, *Interstate Commerce Commission v. Parker*, 326 U.S. 60. Its function is not only to appraise the facts and to draw inference from them but also to bring to bear upon the problem an expert judgment and to determine from its analysis of the total situation on which side of the controversy the public interest lies. Its doubt that the public interest will be adequately served if resumption of service is left to existing carriers is entitled to the same respect as its expert judgment on other complicated transportation problems. See *Chesapeake & Ohio R. Co. v. United States*, 283 U.S. 35, 42; *Alton R. Co. v. United States*, 315 U.S. 15, 23. Forecasts as to the future are necessary to the decision. But neither uncertainties as to the future nor the inability or failure of existing carriers to show the sufficiency of their plans to meet future traffic demands need paralyze the Commission into inaction. It may be that the public interest requires that future shipping needs be assured rather than left uncertain. The Commission has the discretion so to decide.

In contemplating the imponderables of future needs, the agency is required to sift and segregate the practical from the impractical, reality from fancy, speculation from actuality. In short, the expectations for future need for services must be within the realm of possibility. The court in *American Air Lines v. Civil Aeronautics Board*[64] makes the following interesting comments on the function of regulatory agencies in issuing certificates of public convenience and necessity:

> . . . When a regulatory action contemplates a proposed development, new, not existing, a type of judgment is required which is wholly absent from the mere evaluation of past facts to ascertain a present or past fact. It is in the exercise of that sort of judgment that the much discussed expertise of administrative agencies finds its greatest value. Here is the field of uncertainties, imponderables and estimates. This is where the rule

[64]192 F. 2d 417, 420-1.

that a conclusion within the realm of national deduction or inference stands despite differences of opinion, has its greatest applicability.

❁ ❁ ❁

Since regulatory functions must necessarily contemplate the future, the law which is involved in those functions must be realistic enough to permit that scope. So, when a prospective rule is required to be upon evidence, that evidence must be construed to include estimates, or forecasts, or opinions, on future events. At the same time, governmental permissions for the future cannot be fashioned from pure fantasy, speculation devoid of factual premise. Public convenience and necessity in the sense of these statutes has a hard core of factual possibility, which can be ascertained and evaluated only upon the basis of present and past events and conditions. So the function of the agencies to which Congress has delegated these responsibilities is to examine the relevant past and present and then to exercise a rational judgment upon that data to ascertain the public convenience and necessity in the reasonably foreseeable future.

Tailoring of Grant of Authority to Evidence of Need

In numerous proceedings the Commission has recognized its obligation to conform and tailor its grant of authority to the evidence of need. In *Dahlen Transport of Iowa, Inc., Ext. Minnesota*[65] the Commission's rationale was set forth as follows:

> We conclude that the applicant has shown a need for service but not to the extent requested. We agree with the positions taken by protestants. Applicant has failed to make minimal showing of need regarding both the origin and destination territories sought. The supporting shippers actively seek applicant's service to points in Minnesota; however, their support to South and North Dakota points is only peripheral, and a need for service to Iowa points is not even mentioned. Accordingly, while broad commodity and territorial authority is requested, shippers' statements are not sufficient to support these broad requests. We are bound, when granting authority to have it conform to a reasonable showing of need.

Unopposed Cases

Even in entirely unopposed cases, the Commission has uniformly held that an applicant is required to establish by competent evidence that there is a public need for the service proposed. This position was set forth in typical language in *Hearin-Miller Transporters Ext. — Point Comfort, Tex.,*[66] wherein the Commission stated as follows:

---

[65]No. MC-105375 (Sub-No. 33), Rev. Bd. No. 2, sheet 4 report served May 9, 1968.
[66]100 M.C.C. 50, 55.

Applicants have the burden of establishing affirmatively, by substantial and competent evidence, that the present or future public convenience and necessity require their respective proposed operations. The lack of opposition on the part of existing motor carriers, standing alone, does not create a presumption of need for a proposed new service. See *Speed-Way Transports, Inc., Extension − Alabama,* 68 M.C.C.

Potential Need

Potential need as well as present need has long been recognized as a valid basis for grant of authority. As was stated in *Miller Transporters, Extension − Urea:*[67]

> Considering the evidence as a whole, we are compelled to the conclusion that a valid potential need has been shown for the proposed service by th supporting shipper herein. Potential need for a proposed service may be established by a showing that the supporting shipper has some definite plans upon which it can reasonably be found that the commodity sought to be transported will move in the future.
>
>   *   *   *
>
> The shipper has customers in the affected destination territory, ships its products to these customers, and is presently manufacturing a large volume of urea which is expected to increase in the near future. While the evidence as to the precise location of customers is somewhat general, we recognize that proof of a future need for service must necessarily be less certain and definite than proof of existing need.

As was commented in *Miller Petroleum Transporters, Extension − Petroleum Products:*[68]

> Although there were available to them the services of protestants in a portion of the territory authorized, which were then utilized by shippers for their production at the time of hearing herein, it was found that shippers' increase in traffic throughout a more extensive sales territory would justify the authorization of additional motor-carrier services.

Forecasts of large increases in traffic (such as in a particular industry) are given weight. For instance, in *D. L. Wartena, Inc., Extension − Texas,*[69] where the forecast involved the automobile industry:

> On the other hand, it is conceded by all that there will soon be a considerable increase in automobile traffic from all producing points to dealers throughout the country. The existing motor carriers from and to the points here involved are not presently equipped to handle this increased traffic. While they are preparing to re-engage on a large scale

[67]84 M.C.C. 684, 686-87.
[68]81 M.C.C. 443, 445.
[69]6 Fed. Carrier Cases 31,231.

in the transportation of automobiles from and to the points here involved and expect to acquire additional equipment and to be in a position to render better services than they did prior to the war, the evidence is convincing that there will be an unprecedented need for automobile transport facilities in this territory. Even with protestants' added facilities we are impressed that there will be a need for applicant's proposed service to the extent hereinafter indicated.

In a case involving an entirely new plant, a need was recognized for many additional carriers. In granting a multitude of applications, all seeking to serve the new facility at the same origin point, the Commission said in *C.P.T. Freight, Inc., Extension — Burns Harbor, Ind.*:[70]

> While the evidence as to precise location of potential customers is somewhat general in nature and relates basically to a future need, we recognize that the increase of Bethlehem's production and distribution is a gradual process, and that proof of a future need must necessarily be somewhat less certain and definite than proof of a present need.
>
>   ❂   ❂   ❂
>
> While the overwhelming portion of the motor traffic moving from and to Burns Harbor during the initial construction and operational phases between December 1962 and March 1965 was within the capabilities of existing carriers, the volume of traffic moved under these conditions is considerably below that which is expected to move when this integrated steel plant becomes operational and its marketing areas fully developed. In view of the foregoing, we conclude that additional motor carrier service is required to meet the supporting shipper's present and prospective needs; and that further, in the circumstances present here the quantum of service presently available is inadequate to meet Bethlehem's need.

Service of New Plant Facilities

In *Helm's Express, Extension, Mahwah, N. J.*,[71] the Commission authorized five applicants to serve the new plant facility of a major shipper in Mahwah, N. J., despite the opposition of a number of existing motor common carriers. The Commission's conclusions merit direct quotation:

> . . . There can be no question that carriers presently authorized to serve Mahwah will benefit by the increased tonnage which is destined to move to that point. In view of the benefits which will accrue to the presently authorized carriers by reason of the more than doubled volume of traffic, we are not convinced that authorization of the operations for which authority is sought will adversely affect the competitive position of other carriers to a material extent. On the other hand, we believe that denial of the applications would not only be detrimental to the public interest by depriving the shipper of a needed service but also harmful to applicants by

[70]100 M.C.C. 136, 145-46.
[71]67 M.C.C. 183.

depriving them of a substantial portion of their operations which have been devoted to the transportation of freight to the plant at Edgewater. In this instance, there is a compatibility of the public interest and that of individual carriers. Significantly, authorizing additional carriers to serve Mahwah will not enable them to solicit the traffic of other shippers to the detriment of existing carriers, since the evidence of record does not establish the existence of more than one other large industry at that point. Here, inasmuch as the grants of authority will not operate to permit service to and from a locality of heavily concentrated industry and population, the facts are distinguishable from those in *Smith & Solomon Trucking Co., Extension — Camden, N.J.*, 61 M.C.C. 748, where applicant was denied authority to serve a shipper's new plant.

Other cases following *Helm's Express* include: *Western Auto Transports, Inc., Extension — St. Louis County, Mo.;*[72] *Blain Driveaway System, Inc., Extension — Truckaway.*[73] See also, *C.A.B.Y. Transp. Co., Extension — Ohio,*[74] where the Commission, in granting a number of applications to serve a new producing point emphasized considerations of equity and public policy as follows:

> . . . In arguing that the applications should be denied, protestants overlook the fact that each applicant may now serve points located from 3 to 7 miles from Twinsburg. In our opinion, sound considerations of equity and public policy support the proposition that all carriers engaged in substantial operations in the general area of the new plant should be allowed, in the circumstances here presented, equal opportunity to exploit the new source of revenue. Each applicant meets this condition, and the extension of their services to the new plant seem only fair and reasonable in view of the fact that the new traffic source at Twinsburg has become available entirely by chance rather than as the result of promotional activity on the part of one or another of the existing carriers. Moreover, authorizing additional carriers to serve Twinsburg will not enable them to solicit the traffic of other shippers to the detriment of existing carriers, since the evidence does not stablish the existence of any other large industry at that point. In the circumstances, we conclude that the evidence establishes a need for the proposed operations to the extent set forth in our findings below. Compare *Helm's Exp., Inc., Extension — Mahwah, N.J.*, 67 M.C.C. 183, and the cases cited therein. (at p. 299)

Preference Alone is not a Basis for Granting Operating Authority

Preference alone is insufficient to warrant a grant of authority. As stated in *Clyde R. Sauers Extension*[75] — *East Cambridge, Mass.,* the Commission said:

[72]81 M.C.C. 291.
[73]62 M.C.C. 199.
[74]71 M.C.C. 295.
[75]61 M.C.C. 65, 67.

The record is devoid of any evidence that existing carriers' services are inadequate in any material respect. Furthermore, the circumstances under which the shipper will utilize the proposed service are not convincing that the shipper desires expedited or unique services not available by other means. It is apparent that the shipper's desire to have the proposed service available is based upon a preference for the service of a particular carrier without regard to the existence of other facilities capable of meeting their transportation requirements. The shipper has made little or no investigation of existing motor carrier services, and to the extent utilized, characterized them, together with rail service, as satisfactory. The burden is upon applicant affirmatively to show that the proposed service is one which existing carriers cannot or will not perform satisfactorily. No such showing has been made in this proceeding.

In *Oscar A. Corter*,[76] it was held as follows: "Furthermore, the evidence shows a mere preference on the part of the shippers for applicant's service. A mere preference or desire for applicant's service over that offered by existing carriers is insufficient in the absence of evidence showing that carriers now authorized cannot or will not render a reasonable service. In the circumstances, the application must be denied." In *Murrell Rucker, Extension*,[77] the Commission stated that, "In our opinion the evidence fairly establishes that Mitchell holds the necessary authority and is able and willing to meet the shipper's needs. While we recognize the desire of shippers to have its transportation needs handled by a single carrier whose services have proved particularly satisfactory in the past, the preference is not enough to warrant the granting of authority to applicant." In *Powell Bros. Truck Lines*,[78] the Commission held, "New operations cannot be founded upon the preference for a particular carrier in the absence of a showing that the proposed service is not reasonably obtainable." The same ruling was held in *Helm's Express, Inc.*[79] In that case the application was denied as follows: "There is no actual or convincing showing, by example, or by reference to particular shipments, that the available motor carrier service has been inadequate or deficient in any important element. It has been held, in cases too numerous to cite, that shippers should make a sincere effort to utilize the existing service, before they are in a position to support the claim that those services are either presently inadequate or that they will be inadequate to meet future needs, and that therefore, additional service is necessary. The

[76]74 M.C.C. 385.

[77]13 Fed. Carrier Cases 34,287.

[78]33 M.C.C. 93.

[79]71 M.C.C. 332, 333-34. See also *Home Transfer & Storage Co., Extension—Frozen Foods*, 63 M.C.C. 709, 726. *Clarke Robertson Transp., Extension — Petroleum Products*, 68 M.C.C. 611, 614. *Burlington Transp. Co., Extension*, 43 M.C.C. 729. *Kingsway Transports, Ltd.*, 84 M.C.C. 485.

mere desire of the shipper and receiver to have the proposed service available to meet some indefinite need based on their apprehension as to a future emergency situation is insufficient to warrant a grant of authority. In view of the present satisfactory utilization of an authorized motor carrier and the availability of several others, no need appears for the additional proposed service of applicant, and we conclude that the application should be denied."

In *Quality Carriers, Inc., Extension — Vegetable Oils,*[80] the Commission denied authority even where protestants did not solicit or participate in the traffic, saying, "that authority will not be granted unless the existing service is wanting in some material respect. The record discloses no such inadequacy."

See *Zuzich Truck Line, Inc.,*[81] where the following language appears: "The burden is upon an applicant affirmatively to establish that the proposed service is one which existing carriers either cannot, or will not, perform in a reasonably satisfactory manner."

In *John Bernerth*[82] and *Frank E. Lucki, Extension — Steel Brass and Aluminum,* the following is said: "The burden of proof is upon applicants to show affirmatively that a service is proposed which the existing carriers are unable, or unwilling to perform." In *The Brown Carryall Co.,*[83] the following is said: "The burden of proof is upon the applicant to show affirmatively that the operation for which it seeks authority will serve the useful public purpose responsive to a public demand and need which cannot or will not be met as well by existing carriers." In *Klein Contract Carrier Application,*[84] the Commission said: "When there are existing carriers, traffic should be offered to them, and only after their failure to perform the service, or perform it properly, can it successfully be argued that their services are inadequate."

Vague, General and Speculative Evidence

It has long been the Commission's policy not to grant applications which are based on vague and general testimony. As stated in *Consolidated Freightways Corporation of Delaware Extension — Frozen Foods:*[85]

[80]15 Fed. Carrier Cases 35,356.
[81]83 M.C.C. 625,637.
[82]Fed. Carrier Cases 31,580.
[83]43 M.C.C. 79.
[84]76 M.C.C. 196, 197. See also *Van Tassel, Inc., Ext.,* 86 M.C.C. 185, 187; *Vincent Montone Transp., Inc., Ext.,* 86 M.C.C. 253, 259; *Roadway Express, Inc., Ext.,* 88 M.C.C. 533, 537; *Mid-West Transfer Co., of Ill. — Purchase — A. & A. Trucking.* 87 M.C.C. 248, 256; *McKenzie Tank Lines, Inc., Ext.,* 88 M.C.C. 250, 252.
[85]83 M.C.C. 421.

On examining the evidence of record in all the proceedings, we are led inevitably to the factual conclusion that no real need for the proposed services, or for any one of them, was demonstrated by shippers. Their testimony as a whole is characterized by vagueness and lack of specificity throughout with regard to their present marketing patterns and the instances on which they allegedly have been unable to obtain adequate for-hire motor carriage or have received inadequate or unsatisfactory service. We are aware that in any area as large as that here involved, with as many commodities and shippers involved, and with the nature of the commodities in mind, there may be some inadequacies in the available for-hire motor carrier services. But unless we are specifically advised of such inadequacies by probative evidence, we cannot supply the essential elements of proof by resort to inference, grant blanket authority, and thereby burden the existing carriers with increased competition and dilution of their traffic. Focusing attention on each record separately, we do not reach any different result.

❋   ❋   ❋

The extent of existing motor service has been set forth in some detail in the various recommended reports and in the two prior reports, and we see no need to review it here. However, this evidence and the absence of any specific complaints and many admissions by shippers of adequacy of existing for-hire motor service, both joint and single-line, indicate to us that generally it is adequate to meet their reasonable transportation needs.

Thus, in *Southern Tank Lines, Inc., Extension — Fly Ash*,[86] the Commission stated:

It is well established that the burden is upon applicants to prove a need for proposed new services before authority therefor is granted. Here the evidence is indefinite and does not justify a grant of any authority. There has been no showing of the approximate volume of traffic which might reasonably be expected to move to any destination in the wide territory involved, nor has any data been furnished as to approximate locations where dams, locks, oil fields and highways are to be constructed. Indeed, any future demand by prospective users of fly ash from Louisville, many of whom are located at points far distant from the source of supply, would be dependent upon the shipper's ability to sell the product in competition with suppliers at closer points. In the circumstances we conclude that the evidence in support of the proposed operation is too speculative and vague and is insufficient to warrant grants of the authority sought; and that the applications should be denied.

So, too, in *Charles A. Kuhns, Extension — Bulk Commodities*,[87] the Commission stated:

Although the supporting shippers assert that the proposed motor carrier service is needed in order for them to market their products in the 11-

[86]MC-109637, Sub-No. 172, decided Oct. 27, 1961.
[87]72 M.C.C. 681.

State area and to compete with firms which have motor carrier service available, no specific evidence is adduced as to their volume of traffic to each of the destination States, the points in each to which shipments have been made in the past, and the frequency of movement. There also is no indication as to the volume of traffic which applicant would receive if the application is granted. Reliance is placed principally upon requests received by salesmen for motor carrier service, but the location of the customers or prospective customers who made these requests is not shown. Evidence of a very general character is clearly insufficient to sustain a grant of authority to serve the broad outlying territory sought here. Moreover, it confronts us with a situation where we must either grant a right to serve the entire outlying territory or deny the application in its entirety. In the circumstances, we conclude that the evidence lacks sufficient specificity to sustain applicant's burden of proof, and the application must, accordingly, be denied.

Identification of Commodities with Sufficient Particularity to Determine if they can be Handled by Existing Carriers

An applicant has the burden of identifying the commodities through its shipper witnesses with sufficient particularly to determine if they can be handled by existing carriers. This has been recognized by the Commission as an integral part of an applicant's burden of proof in cases of this kind.[88] Thus, if the volume of traffic that can be expected to move to specific destinations is withheld for competitive reasons and there is a refusal to describe the products moving for similar reasons, the Commission will not give weight to the shipper support.

In *Eldon Miller, Inc.. Ext.*,[89] the Commission denied an application supported by shipper testimony and noted as follows:

The burden of proof is upon the applicant seeking a certificate to show that the proposed service is or will be required by the present or future public convenience and necessity. In determining the issue of public convenience and necessity, the primary question, in substance, is whether

[88]*See Manfredi Motor Transit Company, Extension — Houston, Tex.*, 79 M.C.C. 501, *W. M. Chambers Truck Line, Inc., Extension*, 77 M.C.C. 602, *O-Boyle Tank Lines, Extension — Fish Oil*, 67 M.C.C. 504. In the *Manfredi* case, on further hearing to receive additional evidence as to the commodities involved, applicant declined to present further evidence and the Commission affirmed its prior ruling. See *Manfredi Motor Transit Transit Company, Extension — Houston, Tex.*, 82 M.C.C. 620. However, on reconsideration under the same title in 92 M.C.C. 471, the Commission concluded that this being an application for contract carrier authority the application should be granted for the reason that applicant had met all burdens of proof required for the issuance of such authority and that in this instance, it was unnecessary to determine if protestant's authorities enabled it to handle the same commodities. An applicant's burden of proof in a common carrier application was not changed by the final determination in that proceeding.
[89]79 M.C.C. 77.

the proposed operation will serve a public demand or need and whether such demand or need may as well be met by existing carriers. In our opinion applicant has failed to establish that a need exists for the proposed service. The transportation requirements of the supporting shipper are vague and indefinite. Its representative refused to divulge the exact nature of the involved commodity, and merely identifies it as a secret chemical compound used in the manufacture of medicine, the transportation of which requires the use of specially lined tank vehicles. In order to sustain his burden of proof, applicant should present evidence concerning the composition, manufacture, and use of the commodities it seeks to transport. . . . Moreover, the supporting shipper is unwilling to reveal the destinations to which the product might be shipped, although it does state that it has only one customer in Ohio and Iowa, and a prospective customer in Illinois; and it describes the volume to be shipped merely as "sufficient to keep one tank vehicle busy." Obviously it is not possible, in requesting transportation for a new product to pinpoint every possible destination and every gallon to be shipped, but in order to support a finding of public convenience and necessity, it is requisite that there be evidence sufficient to establish, with reasonable definiteness, that sufficient traffic will move to specific destinations points or areas to warrant the granting of the blanket authority sought. We cannot make an intelligent appraisal of the issues which we are required by statute to resolve unless we are furnished with reasonably complete factual data upon which to base our conclusions.

Inadequacy of Existing Service

In general before authority to institute a new service may be granted, applicant must establish that existing motor service is inadequate or in some material respect unsatisfactory.[90] Existing carriers normally should be accorded the right to transport all traffic they can handle adequately, efficiently, and economically in the territory served by them before additional authority is granted.[91] However, the facilitation of competitive market structure and performance is entitled to consideration.

See in this regard *Kingsway Transport, Ltd., Extension — Niagara Falls, N. Y.,*[92] wherein it was stated:

[90]*Marine Exp. Co., Inc., Extension.* 81 M.C.C. 155, 158-9.

[91]*Macy,* 79 M.C.C. 209, 212; *Oil Carriers Co. Extension,* 79 M.C.C. 41, 48; *Yiengst,* 79 M.C.C. 265, 267-8; *Transamerican Freight Lines, Inc., Extension,* 81 M.C.C. 161, 165; *Garrett,* 83 M.C.C. 795, 798; *Nelson Transport, Inc., Extension,* 79 M.C.C. 743, 748-9; *Guy Heavener, Inc., Extension,* 83 M.C.C. 216, 219-20; *Queen Extension,* 81 M.C.C. 471, 474; *Eldon Miller, Inc., Extension,* 79 M.C.C. 77, 79-80; *Zuzich Truck Line, Inc., Investigation of Permit,* 83 M.C.C. 625, 637; *Petroleum Carrier Corp., Extension,* 82 M.C.C. 727, 730; *Telischak Trucking, Inc., Extension,* 82 M.C.C. 109, 115; *Law & Ingham Transp. Co., Inc., Extension,* 82 M.C.C. 198, 200; *F. J. Boutell Driveway Co., Inc., Extension,* 79 M.C.C. 318, 320; *Smith Truck Lines Extension,* 79 M.C.C. 129, 133.

[92]84 M.C.C. 45.

The burden of proof is upon an applicant seeking a certificate to show that the proposed operation is or will be required by the present and future public convenience and necessity. In determining the issue of public convenience and necessity, the primary question, in substance, is whether the proposed operation will serve a public demand or need, and whether such demand or need may as well be met by existing carriers. In our opinion, applicant has failed to establish that need exists for the proposed service. The evidence in support of the application at most shows only a preference by some shippers and connecting carriers for the proposed service. Although those supporting the application express a need for the type of service which applicant proposes to render, significantly they have no specific complaints as regards the service rendered either by applicant or by the various protestants which stand ready, willing and able to meet their disclosed present and future requirements. There must be an affirmative showing of a need for the service based upon evidence of a consistent or recurring inability to secure adequate and satisfactory service from existing carriers. No such showing has been made here. Moreover, it is clear that the supporting shippers and carriers have not used all the existing services. We have repeatedly held that the existing carriers are entitled to transport within their territories all authorized traffic they can handle efficiently and economically before a new competitive service may be authorized therefor; and that the mere preference for a particular carrier is insufficient to support a grant of authority. We believe, therefore, that the application must be denied.

Similarly in the case of *Lester C. Newton Trucking Company*,[93] it was stated:

In the absence of a showing with specificity that the services of existing carriers have been tested and that such carriers have been found to be unable or unwilling to meet the shipping public's reasonable transportation needs within their respective authorized territories, such carriers are entitled at least to an opportunity to meet such needs before we can find a need for a new competitive operation.

In *Lester C. Newton Trucking Company Extension — Wilmington, Dela.*,[94] the Commission said:

Territorially, while a general pattern of distribution throughout the involved territory has been established, we are not convinced that applicant has shown a need for service to those points and areas served by protestants. There is nothing concrete of record herein to indicate that the supporting shippers' needs would exceed the ability of Service Trucking and Cowan to handle the considered traffic from Wilmington to points and areas which they are authorized to serve, or that Emery's recently authorized service would be found to be inadequate to the area which it has been authorized to serve. Both shippers have used the services of

[93]84 M.C.C. 157.
[94]M.C.C. 162.

Service Trucking, and although they had disputes with that carrier respecting freight charges, they failed to make any complaints of its service.

Moreover, they utilize the services of all available common carriers, and do not desire to assign all their shipments in a gievn area to any particular carrier. They have never used or investigated Cowan's service. Their support of the application primarily stems from applicant's satisfactory service from Newark, but a mere desire to continue the use of such service from a new shipping point does not provide a proper basis for the granting of authority for the institution of a new competitive service available from other carriers at the shipper's new location. See *Smith & Solomon Trucking Co. — Extension — Camden, N. J.* MC 59264, Sub 16, decided April 20, 1953, 9 F.C.C. 32, 789. In the absence of a showing with specificity that the services of existing carriers have been tested, and that such carriers have been found to be unable or willing to meet the shipping public's reasonable transportation needs within their respective authorized territories, such carriers are entitled, at least, to an opportunity to meet such needs before we can find a need for a new competitive operation. Compare *Dayton Transport Corp. — Ext. — Iron and Steel Articles,* 79 M.C.C. 713.

In *Smith & Solomon Trucking Co.,*[95] the Commission said:

In the proceeding now before us, applicant would have us grant it authority to follow a shipper to a new source of supply solely because it is faced with the loss of an allegedly substantial amount of its traffic as a result of shipper's change in origin points. In some cases the division has granted applications on such a showing. We have carefully considered this matter, however, and are compelled to conclude that a grant of authority on a mere showing of loss of traffic without proof of lack of adequate existing service in the new location would be contrary to law and to sound reasoning.

In *Seago, Inc., Contract Carrier Application,*[96] the Commission said:

In proceedings of this nature it is incumbent upon applicant affirmatively to show a need for the proposed operations and that existing carriers cannot or will not provide a reasonably adequate service before we may authorize a new competitive service. The evidence adduced herein is not, in our opinion, sufficient to establish that public convenience and necessity require the proposed operations.

As stated in *Kingsway Transport, Ltd. Extension — Niagara Falls, N. Y.:*[97]

---

[95] 9 Fed. Carrier Cases 32,789. See also *Safeway Trucking Corp. — Extension — Hackettstown, N. J.,* 69 M.C.C. 112, where the *Smith* and *Solomon* cases were followed.
[96] 77 M.C.C. 589, 591.
[97] 84 M.C.C. 45.

There must be an affirmative showing of a need for service based upon evidence of a constant or recurring inability to secure adequate and satisfactory service from existing carriers.

In *Quality Carriers, Inc., Extension — Vegetable Oils*,[98] it was stated:

In urging that it be granted authority to transport liquid adhesives from Chicago to Denver, applicant points out that protestant has neither solicited nor participated in the traffic. Protestant's outstanding authority, as noted above, and its physical ability to render an adequate service, are not questioned. The Commission has consistently held that authority will not be granted unless the existing service is wanting in some material respect. The record discloses no such inadequacy. In these circumstances this portion of the application must be denied.

In *P. B. Multrie Motor Transportation, Inc., Extension — Polystyrene*,[99] the Commission pointed out:

Existing carriers should be given a reasonable opportunity to demonstrate the adequacy of their service before additional authority is granted.

Competition

See the landmark decision of *Bowman, Inc. v. Arkansas-Best Freight System, Inc.*,[100] where the Supreme Court discussed the Commission's policies and administrative discretion regarding competition. It said:

The Commission's approach, on the other hand, was more congenial to new entry and the resulting competition. This is the Commission's prerogative in carrying out its mandate to insure "safe, adequate, economical, and efficient service," National Transportation Policy, preceding 49 U.S.C. § 1. The Commission was not compelled to adopt the same approach as the examiners. It could conclude that the benefits of competitive service to consumers might outweigh the discomforts existing certificated carriers could feel as a result of new entry. [Footnote omitted.] Our decisions have dispelled any notion that the Commission's primary obligation is the protection of firms holding existing certificates. ° ° °

A policy in favor of competition embodied in the laws has application in a variety of economic affairs. Even where Congress has chosen government regulation as the primary device for protecting the public interest, a policy of facilitating competitive market structure and performance is entitled to consideration. ° ° ° The Commission, of course, is entitled to conclude that preservation of a competitive structure in a given case is overridden by other interest, *United States v. Drum*, 368 U.S. 370, 374-375 (1962), but

---

[98]15 Fed. Carrier Cases 35,356.
[99]15 Fed. Carrier Cases 35,472.
[100]419 U.S. 281, 297-99.

where, as here, the Commission concludes that competition "aids in the attainment of the objectives of the national transportation policy" [citation omitted], we have no basis for disturbing the Commission's accommodation.

In *Patterson Extension — York, Pa.,*[101] the Commission stated its position on new competition as follows:

> Moreover, it now obtains that, if we do not find in a proceeding that the existing service is inadequate, we are not precluded from finding that the proposed operation is shown by other factors to be required. ° ° ° A carrier first in business has no absolute immunity against future competition. And even though the resulting competition from the institution of a newly authorized service will cause a decrease of revenue from a carrier presently providing service, the public interest and the national transportation policy may best be served, as they are here by the issuance of a new operating authority. ° ° ° Our function is not to preserve the *status quo* at all costs, denying augmentations in transportation service. The transportation industry should be dynamic, rather that static. [Citations omitted.]

In *Lester C. Newton Trucking Co. Common Carrier "Grandfather" Application,*[102] the Commission said:

> While we normally will not authorize a new service in the face of existing services not shown to be inadequate, circumstances may exist which compel us to depart from this policy. We cannot overlook the fact that, despite the services offered by protestants in the past, Newton's service has been largely utilized by the shippers from and to many of the points involved. Moreover, Newton has been free, during recent years, to acquire traffic on other than outbound movements and has realized revenue therefrom. Since protestants cannot be said to rely upon such traffic, and since the shippers have indicated that they will continue to use protestants' services as in the past, we do not believe that protestants will be injured seriously by a grant of authority enabling Newton to continue such service. We are of the opinion that Newton has established a need for the proposed service to the extent indicated in our findings. . . .

In *A. B. & C. Motor Transp. Co. v. United States,*[103] a three-judge court said:

> The Commission's decision that the transportation service proposed by the applicant is required by public convenience and necessity is not invalidated by the absence of a positive finding that existing carriers are not providing adequate transportation facilities. An increase in competition is not a reason for denying the Commission's authority to issue a certificate. [Citing *United States v. Pierce Auto Freight Lines,* 327 U.S. 515, 532.]

---

[101]111 M.C.C. 645, 650. See also *Trans-American Van Service, Inc., Ext.-Off-Highway Vehicles,* 126 M.C.C. 609; *Chem-Haulers, Inc. v. U.S.,* 536 F. 2d 610.
[102]84 M.C.C. 759, 770.
[103]69 F. Supp. 166, 169.

To the same effect is the decision in *Lang Transp. Corp. v. United States*:[104]

> . . . Lang Transportation Corporation takes the position that the Commission had consistently followed the principle that, in the absence of evidence of specific deficiencies in existing service, or of a showing of benefits from a new service, existing carriers should be accorded the right to transport all traffic which they can handle adequately, efficiently and economically in the territory served by them; but this line of reasoning is unsound and an adherence thereto would forever stifle healthy competition.
>
> From the foregoing authorities, extensively delineating the wide range of administrative discretion and judgment conferred upon the Commission, it was clearly proper for that expert body in the case at bar, to exercise its discretion and judgment and come to its conclusion, instead of adopting the arbitrary rule that an applicant should never be permitted to institute new service unless existing carriers already in the field had first been accorded an opportunity to furnish such additional service themselves.
>
> It is clear that under Federal law the carriers first in the field within a particular area do not enjoy legal protection against competition subsequently arising. The Interstate Commerce Commission has power to authorize any number of different carriers to operate within the same territory. . . .

In *United States v. Detroit Navigation Co.*[105] involving part III of the Act,[106] the Supreme Court said:

> If the Commission were required to deny these applications unless it found an actual inability on the part of existing carriers to acquire the facilities necessary for future transportation needs, a limitation would be imposed upon the power of the Commission which is not found in the Act. The Commission is the guardian of the public interest in determining whether certificates of convenience and necessity shall be granted. For the performance of that function the Commission has been entrusted with a wide range of discretionary authority. *Interstate Commerce Commission v. Parker*, 326 U.S. 60. Its function is not only to appraise the facts and to draw inferences from them but also to bring to bear upon the problem an expert judgment and to determine from its analysis of the total situation on which side of the controversy the public interest lies. . . .

Potential Loss of Revenue Resulting from an Applicant's Competition

In *P. C. White Truck Line, Inc., Ext. — Atlanta, Ga.*,[107] the Commission stated that protestants in application cases should normally be

[104]75 F. Supp. 915, 930-1.
[105]326 U.S. 236, 240-41.
[106]49 U.S.C. 901 et seq.
[107]129 M.C.C. 1, 9.

obligated to introduce more than merely evidence of the revenues they may lose to the applicant unless it is patently clear that the revenues amount to a significant percentage of the protestants' overall income. The Commission said further that the protestants should indicate specifically how the potential loss of revenue resulting from applicant's competition will affect their operations. In effect, protestants are required to establish that the loss of revenue as a consequence of applicant's competition will be so great that their operations will be jeopardized contrary to the public interest.

Protestants' Burden

Consideration should be given to the evidentiary burden imposed upon protestants in *Liberty Trucking Co., Ext.—General Commodities,* 130 M.C.C. 243, 246, the protest standards set forth in Ex Parte No. 55 (Sub-No. 26), *Protest Standards in Motor Carrier Application Proceedings,* served October 27, 1978, and the Commission's policy statement in Ex Parte No. MC-121, *Policy Statement on Motor Carrier Regulation,* served November 30, 1978. The policy statement in Ex Parte No. MC-121 indicates that competition is to be given more weight and less emphasis will be placed on protecting existing carriers in evaluating applications for new operating authority, thus reaffirming what the Commission has already said in several recent decisions. The *Liberty* case, on the other hand, sets forth the evidentiary burden that a protestant must satisfy if it is to prevail in a particular proceeding.

The *Liberty* case makes it incumbent upon applicant to initially demonstrate (1) that there is a public need for the proposed service, and (2) that existing carriers cannot satisfy the service needed by the supporting shipper and proposed by applicant. However, the Ex Parte No. 121 policy statement would eliminate the second required showing, although applicant would still be required to demonstrate a public need for its proposed service.

Considering the above, and particularly the *Liberty* decision, it is incumbent upon protestant once applicant has made a prima facie showing of public need to submit evidence that includes: (1) a detailed showing of how and why the proposed competitive service will lead to substantial revenue losses by protestant, and (2) sufficient explanation that the revenue loss caused by the proposed competitive service will materially jeopardize the existing carrier's ability to serve the public.

Where Collectively the Existing Carriers Can Provide the Service

The fact that no one carrier has all the authority requested by applicant is not determinative of whether an application for common carrier authority should or should not be granted where collectively the existing carriers can provide the needed service. As stated in *J. & M. Transport Co., Inc., Extension — Dawson, Georgia:*[108]

> In our opinion the evidence in both proceedings herein falls short of that required to establish public convenience and necessity. The alleged need for expedited service by applicant must be viewed in this light. The protesting carriers, both regular and irregular route, held substantial portions of the authority sought. Even though no single carrier can provide service to every point in Alabama and Florida, collectively, they are able to serve all points in the two states mentioned by the shippers supporting the application. The record indicates that the shippers' customers are dealers in their products and does not support the alleged need for single-line delivery to farm sites. It is well established that an applicant for common carrier authority has the burden of proving that existing service is inadequate in some material respect. In the absence of any showing that existing service has been tried and proved unsatisfactory, we cannot make a finding of inadequacy. Accordingly, we conclude in both proceedings that applicant has failed to sustain its burden of proof, and that the applications must be denied.

As stated in *Refrigerated Transport Co., Inc., Extension — Candy:*[109]

> Although now authorized motor carriers, singly or collectively, do not serve every point in the proposed destination territory, it does not necessarily follow that the operation proposed by applicant is required. There is no convincing evidence that present transportation facilities are not reasonably adequate to meet the requirements of the supporting shippers.

In *Refrigerated Transport Co., Inc. Extension—Southeastern States,*[110] it was stated:

> In any event, the mere fact that no motor carrier holds appropriate authority to operate from all points of origin to all destinations for any one shipper is not of itself sufficient upon which to base a grant of authority. The record does not establish that the presently available service is inadequate.

Other Modes of Transportation

When a motor carrier seeks to offer service where only rail transportation exists, it must still demonstrate a need for such service.[111] The

[108]MC-115311, Sub-No. 13, decided April 13, 1960.
[109]MC-107515, Sub-No. 80, decided October 19, 1951.
[110]MC-107515, Sub-No. 60, decided May 13, 1954.
[111]*California Express, Inc., Extension,* 77 M.C.C. 118, 119.

Supreme Court in *Schaffer Transportation Co. v. United States*,[112] held invalid an order of the Commission denying an application for a motor carrier certificate of public convenience and necessity. The Supreme Court held, among other things, that in determining matters involving applications for certificates of public convenience and necessity which are being contested by carriers of other modes of transportation, the Commission is applying the provisions of the national transportation policy must weigh the ability of one mode of transportation to operate with a rate lower than competing types of transportation, which is precisely the sort of inherent advantage that Congressional policy requires the Commission to recognize.

Volume of Traffic

Where traffic to be transported will be light in volume, justifying grant of authority to only one of two applicants, selection is based solely on the respective abilities of each to perform the proposed service, considering their present operations, and the effect upon each of a grant of authority to the other.[113] In requesting transportation for a new product, it is obviously not possible to pinpoint every possible destination and the amount of traffic to be shipped; but to support a finding of public convenience and necessity, there must be sufficient evidence to establish with reasonable definiteness that sufficient traffic will move to specific destination points or areas to warrant a grant of authority.[114] Where the record demonstrates that a substantial amount of traffic will develop and that a particular industry will continue to grow, adequate transportation should be made available to the industry as a whole.[115]

Past Operations

The Commission has many times held that evidence of past operations may properly be considered in determining whether there is a

---

[112]355 U.S. 83.

[113]*Hill Lines, Inc., Extension,* 81 M.C.C. 659, 665-6; *Roadway Exp., Inc., Extension,* 82 M.C.C. 689, 705; *Mason & Dixon Tank Lines, Inc. Extension,* 83 M.C.C. 159, 161-2.

[114]*Eldon Miller, Inc., Extension,* 79 M.C.C. 77, 80.

[115]*Everts' Commercial Transport, MC, Extension,* 78 M.C.C. 717, 761-2.

public need for continuance of the operations.[116] In *Crichton v. United States*,[117] the court said:

> . . . As the Commission stated in *Dougherty Storage & Van Co. Common Carrier Application*, 3 M.C.C. 427, 432, "Successful operation in the past creates a presumption that public convenience and necessity require a continuance of such operation." See also *Black & White Express Contract Carrier Application*, 6 M.C.C. 633, 634. Past operations standing alone, however, do not establish a need for service.[118]

The following statement was made by the court in *Inland Navigation Co. v. United States:*[119]

> . . . In the light of all the attendant circumstances, the nature of the waterway involved, the kind and volume of traffic available, and the transportation service, both exempt and non-exempt, performed by Tidewater, the question whether applicant has shown substantiality of performance of its holding out as a common carrier and the requisite bona fides of its operations is for the Commission to determine in the exercise of its expert judgment. The courts will not interfere with such a determination in the absence of patent error, and there is none here. . . .

Restrictive Amendments

Numerous restrictive amendments proffered by an applicant with a view towards eliminating opposition to the application rather than any consideration of the transportation requirements of the supporting shippers is against Commission policy; it precludes the acceptance of such amendments.[120]

Prior Denial

The fact that previous authority was sought by an applicant and denied does not control the disposition of a pending application.[121] The

---

[116]*Adkins — Purchase — Elliott and Ollis*, 38 M.C.C. 75, 78; *C. & D. Delivery Co. — Purchase — Elliott*, 38 M.C.C. 547; *Victory Coach Lines — Purchase — Indiana Motor Bus Co.*, 45 M.C.C. 575, 586; *Michigan Express — Purchase — Williams*, 45 M.C.C. 211, 216 ("We have repeatedly stated that the performance of service in the past is itself evidence of public need for continuance thereof in the future"); *Associated Truck Lines — Purchase — Adams*, 56 M.C.C. 287, 296; *Eastern Freight Ways — Merger*, 58 M.C.C. 7, 23; *Crawford*, 81 M.C.C. 793, 795.

[117]56 F. Supp. 876, 880, aff'd 323 U.S. 684.

[118]*Dean Van Lines, Inc., Extension*, 83 M.C.C. 323, 327.

[119]F. Supp. 567, 573.

[120]See *Sykes Transport Co. Common Carrier Application*, 83 M.C.C. 113; *Fox-Smythe Transp. Co., Extension—Oklahoma*, 106 M.C.C. 1, 21.

[121]*Monumental Motor Tours, Inc., Extension*, 77 M.C.C. 259, 262.

record in a pending application should reflect the needs of the traveling public and transportation facilities as they exist as of the time of the hearing of the application, and not those at the time of the prior proceeding; and, the doctrine of res judicata is not applicable in connection with the exercise of the Commission's quasi-judicial functions.[122]

Follow the Traffic Principle

The "follow the traffic" principle is merely an element of evidence comprising proof of public convenience and necessity along with other pertinent facts which are necessary.

The Commission, for the purpose of fostering sound economic conditions and the stabilization of the motor carrier industry on occasion has granted, in appropriate cases, operating rights to carriers which would permit them to follow an immediate or threatened loss of a substantial amount of traffic through no fault of the carrier. The circumstances giving rise to such a situation result from a relocation of a shipper's plant; the shifting of the sources of supply or point of distribution which manifests itself not only in such a material and adverse effect upon the carrier's ability to maintain the quality of the remaining service but may also jeopardize the carrier's continuance in business. However, in the final analysis this is merely evidence considered in connection with other evidence of a public need for the service.

In *Petroleum Transp. Co. Extension of Operations — Umatilla,*[123] which involved the movement of petroleum products in bulk, the Commission found that "where applicant, through no fault of its own, is faced with the possibility of losing a large percentage of its former business owing to the development of the Columbia River," it should be allowed to provide service from the new origin point. In the same case the Commission also found that no motor carriers were authorized to transport petroleum products from Umatilla prior to the hearing, and that the same situation confronted protesting carriers as that faced by applicant. In effect, the authority granted maintained the competitive *status quo.*[124]

In several early cases motor carriers were granted operating rights to afford transportation service to relocated shippers so that the carriers could recover or retain traffic otherwise lost through no fault of

[122]*Ibid.*
[123]19 M.C.C. 637, 639.
[124]See *Inland Petroleum Transp. Co., Inc., Extension — Umatilla,* 20 M.C.C. 757; *Pacific Transport, Inc., Extension — Umatilla,* 20 M.C.C. 761; *Lester Fellows Co., Extension — Burlington, N. J.,* 22 M.C.C. 131; *Becker Transp. Co., Inc., Extension — Waltham, Mass.,* 30 M.C.C. 355.

their own. These certificate extensions were granted on the peculiar facts presented in each instance and a general finding that a grant of the desired authority would not materially affect the status of existing competition between rail and/or motor carriers; that the proposed operation would be more economical than available service; that present service was inadequate, and that also a need was shown for the additional service.[125]

In *Ulrich Oil Co., Extension of Operations — Council Bluffs*,[126] the Commission said:

> As seen, applicant seeks authority to serve the same destination territory from Council Bluffs as it formerly served from origins in Kansas, or, in other words, to follow the traffic to the new source of supply at Council Bluffs. A carrier has no absolute right to follow particular traffic, but must make the showing required under the act. Here, applicant actually has customers at various destinations in northeastern Nebraska who desire to use its proposed service from Council Bluffs. These destinations are located within 150 miles of Council Bluffs, and are at least 200 miles closer to this origin than they are to the Kansas origins. Applicant's proposed service to these destinations would enable its customers to obtain petroleum products from a closer source of supply than that formerly patronized, thereby tending to eliminate wasteful transportation. Although authority is sought to serve a territory, the evidence establishes only a public need for the proposed service to specific points as named in our findings herein.

The conclusions of the Commission in the *Ulrich* proceeding and preceding cases are reflected in the decision of the Commission in *Herbert A. Voecks, Extension of Operations, Council Bluffs, Ia.,* [127] wherein applicant claimed the right to follow traffic from new origin points. The Commission cited the *Ulrich* case, *supra*, stating "We do not agree with applicant's contention that it should be allowed to follow its traffic to a new source of origin. A carrier has no absolute right to follow particular traffic, but must make the showing required under

---

[125]*Western Auto Shippers, Extension of Operations,* 3 M.C.C. 173, 174, 176; *Sober, Contract Carrier Application,* 3 M.C.C. 213, 216; *Nelson, Extension of Operations,* 6 M.C.C. 155, 157; *Sheriff Motor Co., Contract Carrier Application,* 6 M.C.C. 247, 251; *Kelly, Extension of Operations,* 6 M.C.C. 369, 370; *Austin, Extension of Operations — Kansas,* 7 M.C.C. 763, 764. Similar findings and conclusions were used in the following cases to justify grants of additional authority: *Overland Freight Lines, Inc., Contr. Car Application,* 29 M.C.C. 121, 124; *Thompson and B., Extension — Washington and Oregon Points,* 29 M.C.C. 633, 635, 637. See also *Commercial Carriers, Inc., Extension — Evansville, Ind.,* 12 M.C.C. 479; *Cassens Transport Co., Extension of Operations,* 18 M.C.C. 273; *Barton-Robison Convoy Co., Inc., Extension — Moffett, Okla.,* 19 M.C.C. 629.

[126]34 M.C.C. 147, 152.

[127]46 M.C.C. 819.

the Interstate Commerce Act." The application was denied in part for failure to prove a need for a portion of the proposed service.[128]

Despite the plea of "follow the traffic" invoked in many cases, the Commission has adhered consistently to the statutory command found in Section 207 (a) of granting operating rights only upon convincing evidence of public convenience and necessity. Many applications have been denied entirely or partially where the evidence lacked the basic element to justify a grant of authority to provide additional transportation service; i.e., proof of need for the service which could not be obtained from existing authorized carriers. An excellent example of the Commission's policy in this matter is found in *Becker Transportation Co., Inc., Extension — Manchester, N. H.* [129] In the case, Becker Transportation sought authority to transport petroleum in bulk, in tank trucks, from Boston, Mass., and points within 15 miles thereof, to Manchester, N. H. Applicant contended that it should be allowed to follow its shipper's traffic to the new source of supply at Revere, Mass. In denying the application the Commission declared:

> The cases cited by applicant contain no precedent on which the authority sought herein should be granted. In each of these cases there was more than a mere showing of an applicant's desire to follow the traffic of a particular shipper. Such other circustances for the grant of authority in those proceedings included a need for motor service and the absence of motor carrier opposition to the proposed operations, vehicles of the single opposing carrier were used to capacity and were not entirely suitable for the transportation of the commodity involved coupled with a possible loss of a large percentage of an applicant's traffic, the possible loss of the bulk of applicant's business together with no material adverse effect upon the single opposing carrier, and supply points new to all carriers and all carriers permitted to serve the new points. Applicant herein, has been similarly permitted to follow the traffic of its shipper where the circumstances justified a grant of authority. *Becker Transp. Co., Extension — Waltham, Mass.,* 30 M.C.C. 357, and *Becker Transp. Co., Inc., Extension — Dracut, Mass.,* 47 M.C.C. 836.

[128]See *Milek C Hess, Extension of Operations — Council Bluffs, Iowa,* 46 M.C.C. 867; *William A. Givens, Extension of Operations — Wadsworth, Ohio,* 46 M.C.C. 811; *R. J. Mulquinn, Extension — Wharton, N. J.,* 47 M.C.C. 828; *Blue Arrow Transport Lines, Inc., Extension — Grand Blanc, Mich.,* 47 M.C.C. 829; *Merchants Motor Freight, Inc., Extension — Hudson, Iowa,* 49 M.C.C. 852; *Joe J. Wilson, Extension — Nebraska,* 47 M.C.C. 870; *Fischbach Trucking Co., Extension — Fullerton,* 48 M.C.C. 857; *Hub Messenger Service, Inc., Common Carrier Application,* 48 M.C.C. 858; *Earl Houk, Extension — Refining and Distributing Points in Wyoming,* 49 M.C.C. 867; *St. George Trucking Corp., Contract Carrier Application,* 49 M.C.C. 890; *Johnson Transport Service, Extension — Sioux City, Iowa,* 52 M.C.C. 815; *Indianapolis-Kansas City Motor Express Co., Inc., Extension — Lake City, Mo.,* 53 M.C.C. 811; *Abe Ross, Extension — Garland, Texas,* 52 M.C.C. 811.

[129]51 M.C.C. 820.

*   *   *

Where, as here and in the *Gorey* case, existing motor carriers are able and willing to provide a proposed service from an established origin point of a particular commodity, we must be convinced that a denial of authority to permit such carrier to follow the traffic of its shipper would result in an irreparable injury to that carrier.[130]

Issuance of a Certificate of Public Convenience and Necessity to an Agricultural Cooperative

The Commission has held that it may issue a certificate of public convenience and necessity to an agricultural cooperative if a need for the proposed service is demonstrated.[131] This is in conformity with court decisions.[132]

Use of Rulemaking Power to Make a General Finding of Public Convenience and Necessity

In *Transportation of "Waste" Products for Reuse*,[133] the Commission adopted regulations which established procedures whereby carriers would be issued special certificates of public convenience and necessity, pursuant to a general finding that the present and future public con-

---

[130]*See Eastern Express & Haulage, Inc., Extension — Port Chester, N. Y.*, 26 M.C.C. 657, 659; *Empire Express, Inc., Extension — New Brunswick, N. J.*, 47 M.C.C. 727. The Commission said in the *Empire Express Case* (p. 730): Shippers and consignees frequently shift their sources of supply for particular commodities, but evidence of such a shift alone does not warrant a grant of authority to a motor carrier allowing it to follow the traffic. Where existing motor-carrier facilities are adequate, a carrier engaged in transporting general commodities from and to specified origins and destinations is not entitled to authority to extend its operations to new origins and destinations with every change in the flow of its customers' traffic. The following cases have not been printed in full: *Wm. Quits, Extension — Fargo, N. D.* 48 M.C.C. 846; *Shippers Dispatch, Inc., Extension — Illinois Points*, 49 M.C.C. 850; *Leamon Transportation Co., Inc., Extension — Corinth, N. Y.* 52 M.C.C. 827; *H. H. Rinker Transfer & Storage Co., Extension — Metal Castings*, 51 M.C.C. 801. In *Frank Dalzochio, Extension — Port of Redwood City*, 51 M.C.C. 819, it was said that the "threatened diversion of traffic is by no means an accomplished fact nor is it an event which is certain to take place within a definite time" and the "question is simply whether the present stage of the Port's development warrants the grant of an extension at the present time." In *Ft. Edward Express Co., Inc., Contract Carrier Application*, 51 M.C.C. 315, 52 M.C.C. 829, it was said that "Although the shipper does not support Davis' application, the fact that Davis has been transporting the traffic involved will be considered along with other factors"; *John A. Ralston Extension — Follansbee, W. Va.* 52 M.C.C. 828; *Indianhead Truck Line, Inc., Extension — Fargo, N. D.*, 51 M.C.C. 824; In *R. G. Watkins & Son, Inc., Extension — Chelsea*, 53 M.C.C. 820, it was said that "there is no showing that existing facilities are in any way inadequate to handle all requirements for service between such points."

[131]*American Farm Lines Common Carrier Application*, 114 M.C.C. 30, 37.

[132]*American Farm Lines v. Black Ball Freight Service*, 397 U.S. 532.

[133]124 M.C.C. 583.

venience and necessity require operation, in interstate or foreign commerce, by qualified motor carriers, between points as indicated in appropriately filed tariffs, in the transportation of "waste" products for reuse and recycling in the furtherance of recognized pollution control programs, subject to described terms, definitions, conditions, and restrictions. The Commission's use of rulemaking power to make a general finding of public convenience and necessity was judicially sustained in *Chemical Leaman Tank Lines, Inc. v. United States.*[134] The Court noted specifically that the proceeding did not itself issue a certificate of public convenience and necessity to any carrier, but rather merely defined the conditions under which the certificate will be granted. *Chemical Leaman, supra,* at 937. Of further interest, the Court commented that there was no statutory bar to the Commission issuing operating authority on a general nationwide basis if it determined that its responsibilities under the I.C. Act make it necesary or advisable. *Chemical Leaman, supra,* at 938.

Speculating in Certificates

A desire to obtain a certificate for purpose of sale is not ground for a grant of operating authority.[135]

Single Line for Joint-Line Service

The lack of single line service amounts to an inadequacy which the Commission has recognized in granting extension applications.[136]

When a carrier seeks to substitute single-line for joint-line service, the Commission focuses its attention primarily upon four factors: (1) adequacy and extent of applicant's joint-line service; (2) adequacy and extent of other competitive services; (3) beneficial and adverse impacts of the new improved operation upon applicant's competitors, including applicant's prior interline carrier; and (4) public benefits to be derived from fuel conservation and the promotion of economy and efficiency.

---

[134]368 F. Supp. 925. In *Nuclear Diagnostics Labs., Contr. Car. Applic.,* 129 M.C.C. 339, the Commission held that the word "property" as used in Section 202 of the I.C. Act is customarily used to designate something of value; therefore, since radioactive waste materials destined for burial have no real value and are analogous to garbage, refuse, and trash, which the Commission has determined are not within the meaning of the word "property" in Part II of the I.C. Act, they do not constitute property and it has no jurisdiction over the motor transportation of such waste.

[135]*Venco Trucking, Inc.,* 77 M.C.C. 775, 776.

[136]See *Midwest Transfer Company of Illinois Extension — Waukegan, Illinois,* 77 M.C.C. 675, 679; *Daniel Hamm Drayage Company Extension — Louisiana,* 78 M.C.C. 603, 607; *Carl Subler Trucking, Inc., Extension — Austin and Owatonna, Minn.,* 79 M.C.C. 365, 367.

Other factors may be considered, but they are usually of lesser importance.[137]

Heavy Demand Periods

It is recognized generally that certain industries are characterized by heavy demand periods at regular intervals during any given year. Where this demand, as in some industries, shows a reasonably consistent and determinable demand for additional motor carrier service this need will be recognized. Various prior Commission decisions support this principle. For instance, in *Ploof Transfer Company, Inc., Extension — Lumber*,[138] it was said:

> While normally peak period or emergency demands alone are not sufficient grounds upon which to predicate a grant of authority, that does not appear to be the situation here. Actually large quantities of lumber are shipped from numerous lumber mills in South Carolina to Florida wholesalers and retailers throughout the year, with the period of greatest demand on the so-called peak period extending from January through March or April of each year. Emergency demands for additional motor-carrier service occur throughout this 3- to 4-month period as well as during other times of the year. Accordingly, we are convinced that the evidence shows a reasonably consistent and determinable demand for additional motor-carrier service which does not depend upon the existence of extraordinary circumstances.

Broadly Based Multiple Carrier Service

A need for broad, complete and flexible service has often been recognized by the Commission, and grants of authority allowed on the basis thereof. In this regard in *H. C. Gabler, Inc., Extension — Cement*,[139] it was said:

> Turning next to the quantum of motor service for which a need has been shown, the evidence clearly establishes the present large scale utilization of cement in the considered areas and the rapidly increasing demand therein for motor-carrier service.
>
>   ✿   ✿   ✿
>
> The authorization of only one carrier to serve each such point would place a huge financial burden on the carrier selected, for vast quantities of suitable equipment must be purchased and appropriate facilities will have to be furnished. Satisfaction of the transportation needs of each shipper and its numerous customers, moreover, would then be totally dependent upon the services provided by a single carrier. While we do not

[137]*Chief Freight Lines Co. Ext. — Dallas*, 126 M.C.C. 794, 798.
[138]79 M.C.C. 215, 220.
[139]88 M.C.C. 447, 465.

doubt the ability of any of the applicants to expand their facilities and services in the manner required and to institute a reasonably adequate transportation service generally, we think that in situations such as this, where industry-wide changes in the marketing practices and distribution methods of a large shipper suddenly create an immediate and constant need for the movement by motor vehicle of great volumes of a single commodity from one or more origin points, the resultant impact upon the transportation industry should, in the public interest, be diffused among more than one motor carrier.

A Promise of Lower Freight Rates will not be Considered as Evidence of Public Convenience and Necessity

In a long line of cases the Commission has held that a promise of lower freight rates will not be considered as evidence of public convenience and necessity, or consistency with the public interest.[140]

The reason for the foregoing rule is obvious. If a mere promise to publish reduced freight rates should be held to constitute evidence sufficient to warrant the issuance of certificates, the Commission would be swamped with a flood of applications and all semblance of stability within the regulated common carrier industry quickly would be destroyed.

Schaffer Transportation Co. v. United States,[141] does not change that rule. The case involved a motor carrier application in which the applicant asserted that it could perform the service under consideration more economically than the protestant rail carriers and it appeared that the shipper witnesses supporting the application did so with the expectation that, if it were granted, they would obtain lower transportation costs. Following the same line of cases cited above, the Commission found that existing rail service was adequate, and that Schaffer's express or implied promise to provide the service at lower rates was not admissible to prove that the service proposed was required by the public convenience and necessity. Upon judicial review of the Com-

---

[140]See *Youngblood Extension of Operations — Canton, N. C.* 8 M.C.C. 193; *Wellspeak Common Carrier Application,* 1 M.C.C. 712; *Lindeman Common Carrier Application,* 29 M.C.C. 183; *Becker Transportation Co., Inc., Contract Carrier Application,* 26 M.C.C. 487; *Slagle Extension — Crete, Nebraska,* 26 M.C.C. 253; *Bos Freight Lines, Inc., Extension — Groceries,* 28 M.C.C. 61; *Naylor Extension — Carlsbad, Dallas,* 29 M.C.C. 483; *D. A. Beard Truck Lines Co. Common Carrier Application,* 34 M.C.C. 395; *Thompson Extension,* 34 M.C.C. 5; *Omaha & C. B. Ry. & Bridge Co. Common Carrier Application,* 52 M.C.C. 207; *Black Extension — Prefabricated Houses,* 48 M.C.C. 695; *Pomprowitz Extension — Packing House Products,* 51 M.C.C. 343; *Superior Trucking Co., Inc., Extension — Wisconsin,* 78 M.C.C. 51.
[141]355 U.S. 83.

mission's order, this holding was reversed by the Supreme Court which held:

> In these circumstances [intermodal competition] a rate benefit attributable to differences between the two modes of transportation is an "inherent advantage" of the competing type of carrier and cannot be ignored by the Commission.

> The ability of one mode of transportation to operate with a lower rate than competing types of transportation is precisely the sort of "inherent advantage" that the congressional policy requires the Commission to recognize.

It is to be emphasized that this was not a case in which, as between two carriers of the same type, both operating in the same manner, with identical facilities, and at comparable costs, one simply proposed to cut the rates of the other. To the contrary, the distinction made by the court was that these were carriers of different types, having different inherent characteristics, and that one of those inherent characteristics was the ability of Schaffer to perform the service more economically than the protesting rail carriers. This, the court held, was an inherent characteristic recognized and protected by the national transportation policy. This same rationale was reaffirmed by the Commission in *Best Transport, Inc., Contract Carrier Application.*[142]

Actually, the doctrine enunciated by the court in the *Schaffer* case and the Commission in the *Best* case was not a new one because it has been applied many times by the Commission in deciding water carrier applications. For example in *Sioux City New Orleans Barge Lines, Inc., Extension,*[143] the Commission expressly recognized that the lower cost of barge transportation is one of its inherent characteristics, and a factor to be considered in evaluating the public convenience and necessity for a proposed water carrier service. In that case, the Commission stated:

> While shippers and receivers of freight are not necessarily entitled to single-line barge service, applicant should be permitted to perform to some extent the proposed operation if shippers are to have the type of through water-carrier service they need. That shippers desire low transport charges is not fatal to a water-carrier application, as low-cost transportation is one of the primary reasons for utilization of water-carrier service.

Thus, comparative level of rate structures cannot be considered as basis for denial of authority sought any more than it could be so con-

[142]82 M.C.C. 407, 409.

[143]285 I.C.C. 463. For other similar water carrier decisions, see *Seatrain Lines, Inc., Extension — Savannah*, 285 I.C.C. 509; *Newtex S. S. Corp., Extension — Sulphur*, 285 I.C.C. 260; *Yazoo Barge Line, Common Carrier Application*, 305 I.C.C. 17; *S. C. Loveland Company, Inc., Extension — Tampa, Fla.*, 313 I.C.C. 121, aff'd Sub-Nom. *Atlantic Coastline R. Co. v. United States*, 202 F. Supp. 456.

sidered in support of a grant of authority.[144] Desire of shippers for still lower rates, in absence of showing that existing service itself is inadequate, is no real justification for grant of authority; if sole dissatisfaction stems from belief that rates of existing carriers are unjust or unreasonable, appropriate relief is available under other provisions of the I.C. Act.[145] Questions of rates are not material to issues presented in an application proceeding except where such rates amount to an embargo.[146]

In Ex Parte No. MC-116, *Consideration of Rates in Operating Rights Application Proceedings,* notice served September 19, 1978, the Commission said that parties should have the option of placing rate levels in issue in operating rights cases. It said that the ability of an applicant to offer the shipping public lower rates based on operating efficiencies is a factor that should be considered in determining whether there is a need for additional service.

Labor Difficulties and Other Emergencies

The mere possibility of an interruption in service arising from labor difficulties, or other causes, is an insufficient basis for an authorization which will place two additional carriers in the field.[147] In *Morgan Drive-Away, Inc., Extension,*[148] the Commission said that while shipper desires services of more than one carrier to enable it to cope with emergencies such as strikes, such situations, if they arise, may effectively be met by grants of temporary authority.

On the question of labor difficulties as a basis for authorization, the Supreme Court had the following to say in *Burlington Truck Lines v. U.S.*:[149]

> The difficulty with the order arises in connection with the findings and conclusions relevant to the choice of remedy. The assumption of the Commission was that the deficiencies of service made either of two remedies available — additional certification or entry of a cease-and-desist order — and that it had unlimited discretion to apply either remedy simply because either might be effective. It is unmistakably clear from the opinion of the Commission and from the fact-findings it made or adopted that the disruption in service resulted solely from refusals to serve, which in turn arose from union pressure applied to obtain union objectives. It is equally clear that absent union pressure there would have been no refusals to serve and that in such normal circumstances the facilities and the services of the

[144]*Freight Transit Co. Extension,* 78 M.C.C. 427, 432.
[145]*Carl Lubler Trucking Co., Inc., Extension,* 77 M.C.C. 707, 713.
[146]*Interstate Dress Carriers, Inc., Extension,* 77 M.C.C. 787, 790-1.
[147]*Mason & Dixon Tank Lines, Inc., Extension,* 83 M.C.C. 159, 162.
[148]77 M.C.C. 473, 476.
[149]371 U.S. 156, 165-168.

existing carriers were adequate. Moreover, the trunk-line carriers were operating below capacity, were in a position and anxious to transport additional traffic, and had been enjoying the previously interlined traffic which the grant would divert to Short Line. In this factual context we may put aside at the outset the authority which the appellees rely upon that holds that additional certification is the normal and permissible way to deal with generalized inadequacy in service. See, *e.g., Davidson Transfer Co. v. United States,* 42 F. Supp. 215 219-220 (E. D. Pa.), aff'd 317 U.S. 587. When, as here, the particular deviations from an otherwise completely adequate service (which has economic need for the traffic) consist solely of illegal and discriminatory refusals to accept or deliver traffic from or to particular carriers or shippers, the powers of the Commission under § § 204, 212, 217, bear heavily on the propriety of § 207 relief. And in such a case the choice of the certification remedy may not be automatic; it must be rational, and based upon conscious choice that in the circumstances the public interest in "adequate, economical, and efficient service" outbalances whatever public interest there is in protecting existing carriers' revenues in order to "foster sound economic conditions in transportation and among the several carriers" (National Transportation Policy, 49 U.S.C. preceding § § 1, 301, 901, 1001), and the other opposing interests.

There are no findings and no analysis here to justify the choice made, no indication of the basis on which the Commission exercised its expert discretion. We are not prepared to and the Administrative Procedure Act will not permit us to accept such ajudicatory practice. See *Siegel Co. v. Federal Trade Comm'n,* 327 U.S. 608, 613-614. Expert discretion is the life blood of the administrative process, but "unless we make the requirements for administrative action strict and demanding, expertise, the strength of modern government can become a monster which rules with no practical limits on its discretion." *New York v. United States,* 342 U.S. 882, 884 (dissenting opinion). "Congress did not purport to transfer its legislative power to the unbounded discretion of the regulatory body." *Federal Communications Comm'n v. RCA Communications, Inc.,* 346 U.S. 86, 90. The Commission must exercise its discretion under § 207 (a) within the bounds expressed by the standard of "public convenience and necessity." Compare *id.,* at 91. And for the courts to determine whether the agency *has* done so, it must "disclose the basis of its order" and "give clear indication that it has exercised the discretion with which Congress has empowered it." *Phelps Dodge Corp. v. Labor Board,* 313 U.S. 177, 197. The agency must make findings that support its decision, and those findings must be supported by substantial evidence. *Interstate Commerce Comm'n v. J-T Transport Company,* 368 U.S. 81, 93; *United States v. Carolina Carriers Corporation,* 315 U.S. 475, 488-489; *Chicago, M. St. P. & P. R. Co. v. United States,* 294 U.S. 499, 511. Here the Commission made no findings specifically directed to the choice between two vastly different remedies with vastly different consequences to the carriers and the public. Nor did it articulate any rational connection between the facts found and the choice made. The Commission addressed itself neither to the possible shortcomings of § 204 procedures, to the advantages of certification, nor to the serious particularly important in the present context and they should have been objections to the latter. As we shall presently show, these objections are taken into account.

Operating Economy

Proof of operating economy alone is insufficient to sustain applicant's burden of proving the existence of public convenience and necessity where a new service would result from the authority sought.[150]

Interchange

Grant of authority may not be premised on applicant's fear that interchange arrangements with protestants may be cancelled.[151]

Rejected Commodity

In order for a carrier to justify a movement as that of a rejected commodity, the following elements must have been present: (1) The carrier must have had authority to make the initial movement; (2) The commodity must have been rejected by the consignee, for whatever reason; (3) The rejection must have occurred prior to acceptance by the consignee; (4) The carrier must have had the commodity in its possession at the time of rejection; and (5) The movement must have been the subject of an appropriate provision in the carrier's tariff. In the absence of any of these elements, the movement is not one of a rejected shipment, but a separate, independent movement for which specific authority is required.

In motor carrier application cases, where the return movement was not made by a carrier having the goods in its possession at the time of rejection, the Commission has granted specific authority for the return; and in other instances, where the questioned movement was to be made by a carrier in possession of the commodity at the time of rejection, and the movement was provided for in the carrier's tariff, the Commission denied specific authority as unnecessary, referring to the carrier's inherent or implied authority to perform the service.[152]

[150]*Chesapeake Motor Lines, Inc., Extension,* 79 M.C.C. 175, 180.

[151]*Hughes Transp., Inc., Extension,* 83 M.C.C. 375, 378.

[152]*Eastern Delivery Service, Inc., Contr. Car. Application,* 83 M.C.C. 147; *Southwestern Frt. Lines, Inc., Ext. − Gypsum, Gypsum Products,* 86 M.C.C. 685, 687; *Whitfield Transp., Inc., Extension − Las Cruces, N. Mex.,* 83 M.C.C. 319, 322; *Speedway Transports, Inc., Ext. − Secondary Authority,* 76 M.C.C. 275, 278; *Central Dispatch, Inc., Extension − Vermont,* 79 M.C.C. 97, 99; *Western Auto Transports, Inc., Ext. − Hydraulic Hammers,* 72 M.C.C. 249, 252; *Glosson Motor Lines, Inc., Extension − Georgia,* 106 M.C.C. 147, 152; *J & J Trucking Co., Inc., Extension − New Furniture,* 111 M.C.C. 682, 690.

Complete Service

In *McKenzie Tank Lines, Inc., Extension Vegetable Oil*,[153] the Commission said:

> Regardless of whether or not the operating authorities of (the carriers) are as broad as these carriers allege, the evidence demonstrates that none of the protestants, either individually or collectively, hold commodity or territorial authority sufficient in scope to enable them to perform the operation proposed herein. Existing carriers normally are entitled to all available traffic and should be afforded an opportunity to participate in the movement therein before a new competitive service is instituted. The need of the supporting shipper here for a complete service, however, is paramount to the interests of opposing carriers which have not participated in the subject traffic and are unable to meet the demonstrated need for service.

Use of Operating Authority as an Incident to Carriage of Applicant's Own Goods and Business

In the *TOTO Purchasing & Supply Co., Inc.*,[154] the I.C.C. rejected the long-established *Geraci* rule[155] that motor carrier operating authority is not to be granted to an applicant who intends to use it primarily as an incident to carriage of its own goods and its own business. In the *TOTO* case, the I.C.C. said that motor carrier operating authority can be granted to such an applicant provided: (1) that the standard criteria for motor common carrier applications or motor contract carrier applications as the case may be, are met, and (2) that applicant is agreeable to the imposition of conditions requiring it to conduct its for-hire motor carrier activities and its other activities independently and to maintain separate records for each.[156] In overruling *Geraci*,[157] the I.C.C. felt that implementation of the new policy would enable private carrier applicants to provide for-hire service to shippers which do not have adequate for-hire service available, and will also provide for increased efficiency in the transportation system by filling up otherwise empty backhauls. The I.C.C. was convinced that the high cost of energy required it to pay close attention to the need for greater operating efficiency, not only in the for-hire sector, but in all interstate surface transportation.

---

[153]86 M.C.C. 536, 539.
[154]128 M.C.C. 873.
[155]*Geraci Contract Carrier Application*, 7 M.C.C. 369.
[156]Agreement will be assumed unless applicant's position is specifically expressed.
[157]7 M.C.C. 369.

Special Equipment

In *Coker Extension*,[158] the Commission said that the shipper's present method of shipping conduit pipe banded together in unitized containers requiring loading and unloading by forklifts and use of square nosed flat-bed trailers, justified grant of extension authority to applicant when existing motor carriers could not provide the necessary equipment; and the suggestion that protestant might acquire flat-bed equipment was too indefinite to warrant a finding that it presently was able to provide the needed service, which applicant had been furnishing satisfactorily under temporary authority. In *Daniel Hamm Drayage Co. Extension*,[159] the Commission granted authority to applicant because of its location and the availability of suitable equipment to meet a shipper's requirements for lowboy units which it was unable to obtain from other carriers.

Special Services

In *Martinez*,[160] the Commission granted authority where applicants would provide direct service with Spanish-speaking drivers for Latin-American agricultural workers between certain airports and farms in the considered areas. Most of the passengers who would use the proposed service did not speak English and had no knowledge of available transportation service; applicants would employ a representative in the Latin-American country who would advise such applicants of the departure of workers needing transportation to the farms; existing service was not adapted to meet the described transportation needs; and operations of opposing carriers would not be materially affected. The Commission in *Morgan Extension*,[161] granted an application in part, stating that the transportation of horses, other than ordinary, is highly seasonal, and when a horse show race, or other special event is scheduled, prompt and dependable service is essential. During such periods, horses are shipped between numerous and often far flung origins and destinations, creating a heavy demand for service on all carriers authorized to transport them; applicant's service was needed between certain points to meet this demand, particularly in view of protestants' apparent lack of interest in the traffic; but such service was not needed between other points where a number of carriers were authorized to operate since they are entitled to handle all the traffic they can without the added competition of a new carrier.

[158] 79 M.C.C. 255, 256-8.
[159] 78 M.C.C. 603, 607.
[160] 78 M.C.C. 25, 26, 29.
[161] 82 M.C.C. 116, 117-8.

One-Way Operations

The Commission granted authority in *National Cartage Co. Extension*[162] where need was shown for integrated and complete two-way operation; to require shippers to rely on a different carrier in each direction would result in an inefficient operation for both shippers.

Operation in Connection with Other Business

Ordinarily a carrier authorized to perform for-hire operations in conjunction with its private-carrier operations is required to conduct each operation separately in every respect from the other. However, the Commission said in *Stanley and Reedy*,[163] in view of the fact that the proposed common-carrier operations would be the only available service of that type, and that applicants' separate enterprises would not be interdependent or result in any unfair practices, the usual requirement that separate vehicles be used for the for-hire and private operations would not be imposed; but separate accounts and records must be maintained. In *Wright Motor Lines, Inc., Extension*,[164] the fact that applicant had been operating as both a dealer in, and carrier of, the considered commodity in the same area, and intended to continue to do so in the future, was no bar to the grant of authority sought; there was no evidence of unfair practices on applicant's part and it intended to discontinue private carrier operations in connection with its dealership in the States involved.

Affiliation of Motor Carriers with Sources of Traffic

Motor carriers have long been affiliated with sources of traffic,[165] and such affiliations cannot justifiably be condemned *per se*.

Congress would not give the Commission authority to divorce shipper interests from the transportation industry, and the courts would not permit it to step in without legislation. In *United States v. South Buffalo R. Co.*,[166] the Supreme Court said:

[162]78 M.C.C. 75, 77.
[163]82 M.C.C. 270, 271-2.
[164]77 M.C.C. 423, 426.
[165]For examples of affiliations, particularly with food businesses, see *Mid-States Freight Lines, Inc. — Consolidation*, 36 M.C.C. 1; *Alterman Transport Lines, Inc. v. Watkins M. Lines, Inc.*, 77 M.C.C. 407; *Lowrence "Grandfather" Application*, 91 M.C.C. 440; and *Winter Garden Freezer Co., Inc., Investigation*, 103 M.C.C. 513.
[166]333 U.S. 771, 784. See also *Beard-Laney v. United States*, 83 F. Supp. 27, aff'd 388 U.S. 803, which sustained No. MC-106119, *Associated Petroleum Carriers Common Carrier Application*, 47 M.C.C. 844; and *In Re Florida East Coast Railway Company*, 171 F. Supp. 512, 515-516.

Under the Government's theory, no other shipper or group of shippers any more than Bethlehem could own the road. Nor is it clear that any evils exist or are threatened which would be eliminated if this operation were transferred to control of one of the trunk-line railroads or to a pool of them. This road, despite its shipper ownership, is bound by both federal and state law to serve all shippers without discriminations or unreasonable charges. The Commission has power to exact compliance with these duties. The argument, however, is that a situation exists which presents opportunity and temptation for abuse and concealed evasions of duty. But to forestall possible abuses we are asked to apply a remedy which there is indication failed of Congressional approval because its application to many situations would be too drastic and would do greater injury to shipper and transportation interests than could result from its withholding. In the light of the history of this [commodities] clause . . . and the equitable considerations involved in this case, we decline to overrule the interpretation Congress has not seen fit to set aside.

In *Beard-Laney v. United States*[167] the principle that industrial control of a motor common carrier is merely "a matter to be weighed by the Commission along with other matters" was approved. The court concluded (at pp. 33-34):

In this connection it is to be noted that the prohibition of 49 U.S.C.A. §1(8) against transporting property owned by the carrier applies only to railroads and that an effort to amend it so as to make it applicable also to motor carriers was made when the Transportation Act of 1940 was under consideration by Congress but was abandoned. See *United States v. South Buffalo R. Co.*, 333 U.S. 771, 776, 790, and note 10 on page 790. There is nothing in the law, therefore, which forbids a motor carrier to transport commodities which it owns; and, even if there were, such provision would not prohibit the transportation of property owned by stockholders, *United States v. South Buffalo R. Co.*, *supra*, and would furnish no compelling reason which would preclude the granting of a certificate of convenience and necessity where in the opinion of the Commission the public interest required it.

Where an applicant and one of the supporting shippers are under common control, the burden is upon the applicant affirmatively to establish that a grant of common carrier operating authority cannot result (1) in favoritism, preference, and discrimination as between the commonly-controlled shipper and competing shippers, and (2) in unfair competition as between the applicant and other carriers.[168] Where the shippers other than the one affiliated with the applicant are aware of the affiliation, but nevertheless support the application, it has been found that the applicant has met its burden as to the first of the above

---

[167]83 F. Supp. 27, aff'd 388 U.S. 803.
[168]*Avondale Trucking Co., Inc., Common Carrier Application*, 68 M.C.C. 263; *Super Speed Transport, Inc., Common Carrier Application*, 96 M.C.C. 335.

conditions.[169] A finding favorable to an applicant with respect to the second condition can be made only where there is no service available from existing carriers and, hence, there is no competitive situation that can be affected by a grant,[170] or where the applicant and another carrier are fiercely competitive and the traffic available from the affiliated shipper is so minimal as to preclude the possibility of changing the competitive relationship.

In *Cousins, Inc., Common Carrier Application*,[171] the president and principal stockholder of the applicant for common carrier authority to handle malt beverages held all the outstanding stock of one of the shippers, a beer distributor. The Commission, in holding that applicant had failed to show that it was fit properly to conduct the proposed operation or to conform to the requirements of the I.C. Act and the rules and regulations thereunder, commented:

> We believe that applicant has here met its burden as to the first of the above conditions. The shippers other than City Beverage apparently mindful of the latter's affiliation with applicant, support the application. However, applicant has failed to show that a grant herein would not result in unfair competition as between applicant and protestant, Wolverine Trucking Company. Protestant currently provides a service in the transportation of malt beverages from Milwaukee to the destination points wherein a need has been shown. Since the principal support for the application comes from the affiliated shipper, applicant would have the built-in advantage of assured traffic upon its entrance into the competitive field with protestant. Moreover, the situation herein is distinguishable from that in the *National Trailer Convoy* case, *supra*. The traffic available to applicant from City Beverage is by no means so minimal as to preclude the possibility of changing the competitive relationship herein.
>
> The future of the affiliated shipper's transportation role is also unclear. Should City Beverage continue private carriage to its Oakland County consignees, Harold Cousins, as president of applicant and as owner of City Beverage, would be in a position to dominate and control the motor carrier operations of applicant and the private carriage of the shipper. This has been found inimical to the public interest. See *Watkins Motor Lines, Inc., Extension — Frozen Foods*, 49 M.C.C. 790, and *Watkins Motor Lines, Inc., Extension — Processed Nuts*, 51 M.C.C. 131. This possibility presents other opportunities for unfair practices prejudicial to the competitive interests of protestant. A situation conceivably might arise wherein a dual private-public transportation operation within a single territory would be created, resulting in a mixture of services and a mixture of traffic; it would be possible for applicant (controlled by Cousins) to aid or support one business with the other and to use the profits of the one

[169]*Super Speed Transport, Inc., Common Carrier Application*, 96 M.C.C. 335.
[170]*Ibid.; National Trailer Convoy, Inc., Ext. — Initial Movements*, 100 M.C.C. 101.
[171]102 M.C.C. 481, 484-85.

to competitive advantage in the other. We conclude, accordingly, that applicant has failed to establish that it is fit properly to conduct the proposed operation, and that the application must be denied. In view of this conclusion, other matters raised by the parties need not be considered.

Status of Applicant

The Commission held in *Bulk Motor Transport, Inc., Extension,*[172] that the question of common control must be considered in the application proceeding since applicant's controlling stockholder was also the controlling stockholder of another carrier; issuance of the certificate was conditioned upon applicant's controlling stockholder's obtaining approval under Section 5(2) of the I.C. Act to control the operation of applicant and the affiliate freight line and a written request by the affiliate for coincidental revocation of that portion of its certificate which duplicates the authority granted. In *Yale Transp. Corp. v. United States,*[173] the court held that granting a certificate of public convenience and necessity did not create a new control relationship which required approval under Section 5 of the I.C. Act; that a certificate was not an order subject to the 30-day notice provision of Section 221(b) of the I.C. Act; and that the 30-day notice provision of Section 221(b) of the I.C. Act applies only to the order granting the certificate and not to an order denying a petition for reconsideration of such an order.

Driveaway, Truckaway, Initial and Secondary Movements

In *Classifications of Motor Carriers of Property,* this group is described as consisting of motor carriers engaged in the transportation of new and used motor vehicles, including automobiles, trucks, trainers, chassis, bodies, and automotive display vehicles.[174]

The test as between "driveaway" and "truckaway" is whether the vehicles being transported are moved with motive power furnished by one or more of such vehicles in which case the service is driveaway; otherwise it is truckaway. Both driveaway and truckaway may include "towaway."[175]

The term "initial movement" embraces only the transportation of new vehicles from a place of manufacture or assembly for delivery to consignee or connecting carriers. Where the initial movement is interchanged, transportation by the subsequent or second carrier would fall

---

[172]79 M.C.C. 321, 325-6.
[173]185 F. Supp. 96, aff'd 365 U.S. 566.
[174]2 M.C.C. 703.
[175]*Hanavan Common Carrier Application,* 72 M.C.C. 477, 480.

within the term "secondary movement."[176] These terms therefore refer to the character of the movement.[177]

Single State Operation

The single state carrier can opt for an exemption from securing a certificate of public convenience and necessity as required by Section 206 and secure from the Commission a certificate of registration if it satifies the procedures outlined in Section 206(a) (6).[178]

Section 206(a) (6) provides in pertinent part as follows:

". . . no certificate of public convenience and necessity under this part shall be required for operations in interstate or foreign commerce by a common carrier by motor vehicle operating solely within a single State . . . if such carrier has obtained from the commission of such State authorized to issue such certificates, a certificate of public convenience and necessity authorizing motor vehicle common carrier operations in intrastate commerce . . . and such certificate recites that it was issued after notice to interested persons . . . of the filing of the application and of the desire of the applicant also to engage in . . . interstate . . . commerce within the limits of the intrastate authority granted . . . . that the State commission has duly considered the question of the proposed interstate and foreign operations and has found that public convenience and necessity require that the carrier authorized to engage in intrastate operations also be authorized to engaged in operations in interstate and foreign commerce within limits which do not exceed the scope of the intrastate operations authorized to be conducted . . . The termination restriction in scope, or suspension of the intrastate certificate shall have been renewed, reissued, or reinstated, or the restrict the right to engage in interstate or foreign commerce unless the intrastate certificate shall have been renewed, rissued, or reinstated, or the restrictions removed within said one hundred eighty-day period . . . any party in interest, who or which opposed in the State commission proceeding the authorization of operations in interstate or foreign commerce, may petition the Commission for reconsideration of the decision of the State commission authorizing operations in interstate or foreign commerce, and upon such reconsideration upon the record made before the State commission, the Commission may affirm, reverse, or modify the decision of the State commission, but only with respect to the authorization of operations in interstate and foreign commerce."

Under Section 206(a) (6) the Commission is authorized to issue certificates of registration provided that the State commission is permitted to issue certificates of public convenience and necessity in intra-

---

[176]*Morgan Drive-Away v. Mid-States Trailer Transport,* 105 M.C.C. 896, 900.
[177]See also *Morgan Drive-Away, Inc. Ext.,* 79 M.C.C. 11, 15; *Dealers Transit, Inc. Ext.,* 83 M.C.C. 779, 784; *Bell Transp. Co., Inc.,* 79 M.C.C. 721, 723-24; *Howard Lober, Inc., Ext.,* 83 M.C.C. 361, 366
[178]49 U.S.C. 206(a) (6).

state commerce; the State commission has duly considered the question of the proposed interstate operations; and the State commission has found that public convenience and necessity require authorization to engage in intrastate and interstate commerce.

Section 206(a) (6) established procedure for Federal and State cooperation in determination of the public necessity for proposed motor common carrier services in interstate or foreign commerce "which do not exceed the scope of the intrastate operations authorized to be conducted." Such coordinated Federal-State action is not a novel proposition.[179] The Section 206(a) (6) procedure for determination of the issue of need for proposed interstate service is similar to the procedure prescribed in Section 205(a) for determination of applications for motor common carrier service within three States or less. This section provides that the appropriate proceedings for determining public convenience and necessity shall be referred to a joint board composed of one member from each State within which operations are proposed. The recommendations of the Joint Board are filed with the Commission and made subject to the same rules as a recommendation by a hearing officer of the Commission.

Under Section 206(a) (6) the entire procedure by which a certificate authorizing operations in interstate commerce and foreign commerce is issued or the certificate is terminated is by operation of the Federal statute itself. The State commission does not have the power to issue a certificate, but only to make a finding of need which is subject to review by the I.C.C. after the filing of an appropriate application and only the I.C.C. can issue a certificate of registration authorizing the applicant to perform interstate service. Under the provisions of the statute, the I.C.C. reviews the proceedings before the State commission and, without regard to the findings of the State commission, may deny any recommendation for interstate motor carrier authority which is not based upon substantial evidence demonstrating public convenience. The State commission mere-

---

[179]In *Prudential Insurance Co., v. Benjamin,* 328 U.S. 408, the Supreme Court rejected a challenge to the constitutionality of coordinated federal-state action.

Section 202(b) (2), as amended by the Act of October 28, 1974, P.L. 94-496, 88 Stat. 1526, provides: "The requirement by a State that any motor carrier operating in interstate or foreign commerce within the borders of that State register its certificate of public convenience and necessity or permit issued by the Commission shall not constitute an undue burden on interstate commerce provided that such registration is accomplished in accordance with standards, or amendments thereto, determined and officially certified to the Commission by the national organization of the State commissions, as referred to in section 205(f) of this Act, and promulgated by the Commission."

ly performs the hearing function and determines initially the question of need for the proposed interstate service.

If the interstate service is terminated it is not the State commission which terminates the right to engage in interstate or foreign commerce. It is by operation of the Federal statute itself that the right is terminated.

Before the amendment of the statute in 1962 a single-state carrier could secure authority to operate in interstate or foreign commerce by simply registering its intrastate authority with the I.C.C. By enacting Section 206(a) (6) Congress narrowed the exemption by providing that the I.C.C. should review the findings of the State commission and issue a certificate only if there was substantial evidence of need. By so doing it diminished the influence of the State upon the rendition of interstate service by common carrier within a single State.

Foreign Commerce

In *Alterman Transport Lines, Inc., Extension,*[180] the Commission granted authority for transportation of hides and skins from Florida origins to four Florida ports for exports; the Commission held that the grant was warranted when existing contract carrier and the only common carrier-protestants who had evinced an interest in the traffic did not possess the type of equipment required; need of one supporting shipper for the proposed service was not too speculative although it had not yet exported hides, when it reasonably expected to market them in the near future in various Central American countries in which it had recently conducted an extensive sales campaign.

Fitness in General

In assessing an applicant's fitness, the Commission cannot ignore the fact that in a prior application proceeding it had found applicant unfit to conduct the service there proposed because of his willful and deliberate performance of unlawful operations.[181] The Commission said in the *Barrett* case that confronted with that finding, which rested upon facts and conditions continuing until the time the application was filed, it could not be found that an applicant who had demonstrated such complete disregard for the law was fit to perform the operations proposed. In *Lumber Haulers, Inc.,*[182] the Commission said that unlawful

---

[180]81 M.C.C. 781, 785.

[181]*Barrett Extension,* 81 M.C.C. 731, 735-6; *Halls Motor Transit Co. v. Buch Exp., Inc.,* 82 M.C.C. 139, 145.

[182]82 M.C.C. 373, 376; see also *Western Auto Transports, Inc., Extension,* 81 M.C.C. 71, 74-5.

transportation by an applicant, to the extent of its sole stockholder's participation therein, was a continuation of unlawful transportation performed by the stockholder which rendered him personally unfit to be granted interstate authority, and applicant's unlawful operations could not be condoned. Applicant was therefore found unfit to conduct the proposed operation.

This was discussed in *Beany Ext. — Ports of Entry Between U.S. and Canada,*[183] where it was said:

Applicant is an experienced operator of many years standing. That he transported commodities beyond the scope of his authority in good faith under color of right is a somewhat difficult premise to accept in the circumstances encountered here. The operations he performed were in violation of the terms of his certificate, contrary to numerous and consistent Commission pronouncements in the area, for 10 or more years, during which the legality of such services were challenged. He encroached upon the lawful operations of competing carriers to their detriment and despite their protests. He apparently sought a formal determination of the issue only when it became clear that he had no other choice if he intended to continue to engage in the challenged operations. In any event, applicant's consistent adherence to a position, however untenable, in asserting the legality of an operation being conducted under the mantle of an outstanding certificate, presents a problem which has already been disposed of in the proceeding in No. MC-11753 (Sub-No. 25). Applicant's use of evidence of past unlawful operations as a basis for attaining an extension of authority is a different matter and is the issue requiring resolution in this proceeding.

Past operations, even when conducted in good faith, are not necessarily determinative of the issue of a public need for the continuance thereof. *Peerless Stages, Inc., Investigation,* 86 M.C.C. 109, 119. Due consideration must be given to the interests of the carriers already authorized to provide the proposed service. In the instant case, it seems clear that applicant's claim of good faith service is of doubtful validity and little, if any, weight may be accorded to the evidence of applicant's past operations in support of a present and future public need for its continuance of such operations. Further, protestants, collectively, have the necessary authority and wherewithal to provide the proposed service, and the record does not contain evidence of sufficient probity, reflecting upon their inability to meet the reasonable transportation requirements of the involved shippers. The fact that denial of the application will foreclose applicant's participation in traffic it previously enjoyed for a number of years is not controlling. Protestants are entitled to all of the traffic they can handle economically and efficiently within the scope of their operating authorities. Compare *Floyd & Beasley Transfer Co., Inc., Ext. — Mill Supplies,* 79 M.C.C. 269; *Peerless Stages, supra; and C &H Transp. Co., Inc., Clarification of Certificate,* 88 M.C.C. 87. We agree with the examiner that the application should be denied.

[183]106 M.C.C. 243, 247-48.

Applicant cites two recent Commission decisions wherein grants of authority were, in part, premised on the past unauthorized operations of the respective applicants; namely, *Auto Driveway Co. Common Carrier Application*, 100 M.C.C. 724, and *AAA Con Drivers Exchange, Common Carrier Application*, 102 M.C.C. 393. The cases are not in point. Those proceedings dealt with operations which, prior thereto, were not clearly delineated to encompass transportation services requiring Commission regulation, and which existing carriers were not providing or were unable to provide at costs the traffic could bear. Such factors, which were controlling in those decisions, are not present here.

Applicant also refers to the proceeding in *Argo-Collier Truck Corporation Extension — Soaps*, docket No. MC-41404 (Sub-No. 72), wherein the examiner's recommended grant of authority to the applicant therein was adopted by one of our review boards. In that case, the subject application was unopposed and there was no evidence that the service for which authority was sought could be provided or was available from any established and duly authorized carrier. The facts herein are otherwise. The service for which authority is sought has been shown to be attainable from the opposing carriers which are fully authorized and eager to provide them upon reasonable request.

In *Carty*,[184] applicant knowingly operated unlawfully for many years until immediately prior to filing the pending application, despite his previously notifying the Commission that he had ceased operations. The Commission said that such willful and deliberate performance of unauthorized operations and contumacious flouting of the provisions of the I.C. Act warranted the conclusion that he was not fit to conduct the proposed operation; application was therefore denied. Regardless of whether a need had been established for either of the proposed services, the Commission said in *Haywood Trucking Co.*,[185] no authority could be granted because applicants' disregard for the requirements of the I.C. Act precluded a finding of fitness to conduct them. The record showed a consistent pattern of irregularities which, from their very repetitiveness, suggested strongly a willful defiance of the Commission's rules and regulations. Evidence of applicants' culpability was somewhat vague, and their unauthorized activities might have been minimized in the face of a demonstrated need for their services if their manager were a newcomer to the transportation field; however, their manager had been active in the trucking industry for more than 20 years, and the defense that their unauthorized operations were performed in a mistaken belief that no authority was needed, the Commission said, more than taxes credulity.[186]

---

[184]81 M.C.C. 420, 422; see also *Champ*, 79 M.C.C. 311, 315-6.
[185]81 M.C.C. 437, 441.
[186]Id., pp. 441-42.

In *Floyd & Beasley Transfer Co., Inc., Extension,*[187] the Commission said that since applicant was an experienced carrier of many years' standing, and was well aware that its authority to serve the considered territory was limited to transportation of textile products, but arbitrarily chose to interpret that commodity description in a manner most convenient and expedient to it, and unlawfully undertook an operation not authorized by its certificate; the fruits of such operation could not be permitted to redound to its substantial benefit. The Commission said that the prior report, in granting the authority sought, gave insufficient weight to the fact that applicant's service was conducted in flagrant disregard of its certificate and that much of the traffic thus unlawfully transported was undoubtedly obtained at the expense of existing carriers. The Commission said that such promiscuous disregard for regulation cannot be lightly considered. Applicant in *Johnson & Son, Inc.,*[188] although fully aware of certificate and permit requirements of the I.C. Act, willfully violated them by commencing unauthorized operations after filing the application and deliberately continuing those operations until a few days before the hearing. The Commission said that the claim that such service was performed at the request of a shipper was no justification, since compliance with the statutory requirements should not be subordinated to the needs of shippers who were implicated in applicant's unauthorized operations.

In *Mayer*[189] applicant had engaged in the trucking business for many years, held intrastate authority for many years, and provided interstate service for a number of years without authority; and although advised that his interstate operations were unlawful, he was still so operating at the time of the hearing. The Commission said that such willful and deliberate performance of unauthorized operations and contumacious flouting of the provisions of the I.C. Act require a conclusion that he was not fit properly to conduct the operation proposed. In *Gentry Extension,*[190] the Commission said that the applicant could not be found fit to conduct the proposed operations when, even after prosecution for unauthorized operations and safety violations and being enjoined from continuing such violations, he knowingly ignored requirements that he obtain operating authority and comply with safety and other regulations. That he previously had been found fit to conduct other operations and had been granted a certificate authorizing them, the Commission said,

[187]79 M.C.C. 269, 274.
[188]79 M.C.C. 362, 364.
[189]81 M.C.C. 57, 60.
[190]78 M.C.C. 473, 475.

was immaterial, since an applicant must establish his fitness in every application proceeding before he can be granted authority.

In *Hoyt Extension*,[191] the Commission said that in the absence of extenuating circumstances which would excuse his illegal operations, applicant could not be found fit to receive a certificate authorizing the proposed operations. The Commission said that applicant realized the necessity for authority to conduct such operations, failed to investigate the efficacy of his uncertified operations, and used evasive tactics to avoid the statute and the Commission's rules.

Where the facts and circumstances justified it, the Commission has granted authority notwithstanding unauthorized operations in the past. In *Howard Lober, Inc., Extension*,[192] applicant commenced considered operations under color of right, and while its continuance thereof after being informed that they were unauthorized could not be condoned, the Commission said, it did not intend deliberately to flout the statutory requirements, and a finding of unfitness was not warranted. In *Argo-Collier Truck Lines Corp., Extension*,[193] the Commission said that although applicant's past unauthorized operations were not condoned and it was admonished to discontinue them immediately if it had not already done so, they were conducted under a misinterpretation of its authority and did not require a finding of unfitness or bar grant of any authority. Applicant, after being informed that a certificate was not required for his formerly exempt transportation of bananas, entered into a purported lease arrangement with another carrier, under which he retained control of the leased equipment, thereby in effect conducting an unauthorized operation; such violation, while not to be condoned, the Commission said in *Crawford*,[194] did not bar a grant of authority for continuance of service shown to be needed in the absence of any willful purpose to evade the law.

In *Marine Exp. Co., Inc., Extension*,[195] the Commission said that applicant's past unauthorized operations, conducted under purported leasing arrangements, were not such as to justify finding that it was unfit to conduct the proposed service, when it was unaware of the impropriety of these arrangements and voluntarily ceased such practices. In *Clapps Extension*,[196] although applicants had conducted some operations between Torrington, Conn., and New York City over a proposed

---

[191]78 M.C.C. 437, 440.
[192]83 M.C.C. 361, 366; see also *Pettspiece Cartage & Builders' Supplies*, 79 M.C.C. 259, 264, and *Fletcher Extension*, 79 M.C.C. 164, 167.
[193]83 M.C.C. 63, 67, 72.
[194]81 M.C.C. 793, 794, 796.
[195]81 M.C.C. 155, 159-60.
[196]79 M.C.C. 370, 372-3.

alternate route without authority, they apparently had no intent to circumvent the I.C. Act. When notified of the unlawfulness they routed traffic through Hartford under the impression that they could tack their service routes at that point; and when informed that they could do so lawfully only at Glastonbury, a common point within the Hartford commercial zone, they operated thereafter through that point. The Commission said that while such past unauthorized operations were not condoned, they could be considered as evidence of applicant's competitive position and did not bar a grant of alternate route authority.

In *Standard Motor Freight, Inc., Extension — Off Route Points,*[197] the Commission considered the situation wherein the applicant had provided the service for a considerable period of years under the belief that it held the appropriate authority. The Commission held:

> A grant of the specific authority as herein sought will cure the situation and will permit the continuance of a service provided satisfactorily for many years. See *Jack Cole Co., Inc., Extension — Anniston Ordinance Depot,* 72 M.C.C. 691 and *Melton Truck Lines, Inc., Extension — Roofing,* 88 M.C.C. 735. Our action should not, of course, be construed as condoning such illegal activity. Inasmuch as applicant cannot on this record be classified as a new carrier entering the field and since protestants herein are not engaged in transporting the considered traffic, it does not appear that a grant of the requested authority will prove detrimental to the operations of protestant. *Compare Mattox Extension — Old Bridge, N.J.,* 77 M.C.C. 165.

Flagging Procedures

The Commission developed over the years certain internal procedures for handling of fitness matters. These procedures involved generally the determination of the question regarding fitness in a selected application proceeding, which, in turn, would affect the fitness finding of each of that carrier's other pending applications. The fitness question raised in the selected application proceeding could result in the flagging of each of the applicant's other pending applications thereby (1) causing the authority in the other pending applications to be withheld pending determination of the fitness question in the selected application, (2) causing permission to consummate the transaction of other pending applications to be withheld pending determination of the fitness question in the selected application, or (3) causing applicant's other pending applications to be denied upon adverse determination of the fitness question in the selected application.

These procedures for withholding final action on pending applications

---

[197]MC-16340, Sub-No. 4, decided Oct. 29, 1962.

other than the selected application proceeding had been determined in an ex parte manner, on the Commission's own motion. No hearing was held to allow the carrier to argue that its other pending applications should not have been flagged. These procedures were developed consistent with the view that a question regarding an applicant's fitness was all pervasive and affected the issue of fitness in every other pending application before the Commission. Individual applications were evaluated to determine their general relationship to the selected application proceeding and certain types of applications were traditionally excepted from the flagging process (i.e. gateway elimination applications, alternate route applications, and deviation route applications).

The flagging procedures were initiated in one of three ways: (1) by the Vice Chairman of the Commission, the Commission itself, or an appropriate Division thereof acting upon the recommendation of the Bureau of Investigations and Enforcement at the time of the institution of an investigation proceeding, (2) by the Bureau's participation in an application proceeding pursuant to the delegation of authority by the Commission allowing the Bureau to participate in an application proceeding upon the Bureau's determination that it had information tending to raise a significant question regarding the fitness of an applicant, and (3) by the appropriate Division granting leave to intervene to the Department of Transportation in a pending proceeding wherein DOT by petition alleged violation of the Federal Highway Administration's safety regulations.

When the fitness flagging procedures were initiated, one of an applicant's pending applications was designated the selected application proceeding. This procedure permitted all of applicant's other pending applications to go forward on all issues other than fitness (public need; operational fitness) while the overall concurrent, required statutory issue of the applicant's fitness was being resolved in the selected application proceeding. It was felt that the personnel requirements which would result in presenting the same evidence relating to an applicant's conformity fitness in every pending application proceeding clearly were beyond the staff capabilities of the Bureau, and no useful purpose would be served by repeating the same presentations in a number of pending applications nor should an applicant be put to the expense of rebutting the same evidence in successive hearings. In the same vein it was believed that consolidation of all pending applications with the fitness proceeding would be impractical because (1) that would involve interminable concurrent resolution of issues other than fitness, (2) not all applications are ripe for decision at the same time, and (3) not all applications are before the same decisional body at the same time (some may be required to be heard by a joint board, others may be more efficiently handled by modified procedure, and still others may be at an appellate level).

Experience has shown the Commission that the selection of one application for a determination of the fitness issue while flagging the others was, and is, the most realistic and administratively desirable way of resolving the issue of fitness. If a negative finding of fitness was made in the selected application proceeding (and that finding became administratively final), other flagged applications were denied on the basis of that negative fitness finding. Once an applicant had failed to show that it was fit to receive the authority sought, it had to re-establish affirmatively its fitness before any new applications would be granted.

The court in *North American Van Lines, Inc.*[198] and *North American Van Lines, Inc. v. United States*,[199] evaluated the Commission's prior procedure and held certain portions of it to be without the dictates of the Administrative Procedure Act and the I.C. Act. The court found (1) that the Commission may hold applications for new authority in abeyance pending all or part of a current fitness investigation as long as applicant is given the procedural protections (notice and hearing) of the Administrative Procedure Act, and (2) that the cross-relation (nexus) of a fitness investigation to the individual new authority application involves complex questions of fact and law and the Commission's expertise and experience in evaluating such cross-relevance deserves proper judicial deference.

In order to cure the defects found by the court in the *North American* cases the Commission in Ex Parte No. 55 (Sub-No. 23), *Fitness Flagging Procedures*, decided March 7, 1977, adopted fitness flagging rules.[200] Under the rules, the Bureau may no longer intervene in application proceedings on its own; instead the Bureau is required to make a request to participate in an application proceeding to the Commission or the appropriate Division which shall make a determination as to whether this request, if approved, could result in a negative fitness finding. If the Bureau is ordered to participate, an appropriate application is selected as the proceeding in which the issue of fitness is to be determined (this proceeding may be consolidated, if administratively possible, with an investigation or complaint proceeding involving applicant on the same issues). An order is then issued notifying all parties of the fitness participation. The applicant is, by an appropriate order, afforded an opportunity to show cause why its other pending applications should not be

[198]386 F. Supp. 655.
[199]412 F. Supp. 782.
[200]49 CFR 1067.

flagged (authority is not issued until resolution of the fitness issue in the selected application proceeding). The order also notifies applicant in general of the statutes, requirements, rules, and regulations allegedly violated and the general substance of the allegations made and identify all pending applications (called designated applications) in which flagging is to be considered. The Bureau or DOT is then required to advise applicant in writing of all matters of fact and law to be asserted with sufficient particularity to make clear the violations alleged and the nexus alleged to exist betwen those violations and other pending applications in which flagging is being considered. Applicant is afforded an opportunity to submit written representations to show why all or any of its pending designated applications should not be flagged, and the Bureau or DOT is given an opportunity to respond to those representations.

Failure of an applicant timely to respond in a show cause proceeding is construed as waiver of its right to hearing on the flagging issue and causes the pending designated applications to be flagged. The issuance of a show cause order or an order authorizing fitness participation with the described show cause requirements temporarily bars issuance of authority or consummation in any designated application proceeding until the issue of whether or not that designated application proceeding should be flagged is determined (there is a 70 day limit for determination) by the Commission or a Division thereof. The determination of the Commission or Division is made in an appropriate order. This order is subject to petitions for reconsideration under the Commission's rules of practice. Denial of the petition results in an order sufficiently final to be appropriate for judicial review. Pending applications not flagged are processed to final determination on all issues. These determinations (flagging of pending applications; the fitness issue itself) are expedited.

Applications subsequently filed by the same applicant are noticed and added to this list of designated applications in which the question of flagging has been raised in the show cause proceeding. If the show cause proceeding has already been resolved to flag pending applications, applicant is required to petition the Commission to have a new application excluded from flagging (failure to petition is construed as a waiver). An administratively final adverse fitness finding in the selected application results in denial of the application in the selected proceeding and all designated pending flagged applications. Thereafter, in subsequently filed applications, the applicant is required to establish its fitness as in any ordinary proceeding, except that the Commission may take official notice of the prior adverse fitness finding.

The fitness flagging procedure rules are not intended to codify the substantive standards for making determinations as to an applicant's fitness.[201] The Commission's purpose was to adopt regulations pertaining to flagging procedures, not fitness determinations.

Financial Fitness

In *Eyre Extension,*[202] applicant was found financially fit when he had operated at a profit for about 14 years and his capital was unimpaired; his financial statement, adjusted to exclude nontransportation items, showed no difficulty in meeting financial obligations shortly to become due. Although applicants' financial positions in *Wilson Extension,*[203] were not strong, applicants were solvent, operated profitably, and the proposed service would aid in improving their revenues; thus a finding of fitness was warranted. In *Marine Exp. Co., Inc., Extension,*[204] the Commission said that while applicant's current liabilities, which were due within one year, exceeded current assets, other factors should be weighed in determining its actual financial position. At the time of hearing, applicant had been conducting only limited operations for a comparatively short time; its net earnings for a ten-month period were small, but it conducted no operations during three of those months, and traffic available to it was limited during one month; its capital and surplus were not impaired; and it appeared capable of conducting opera-

---

[201]These standards have been enumerated in a series of adjudications, see for instance, *E & H Distributing Co. Contr. Car. Applic.,* 120 M.C.C. 731, *Peoples Express Co., Ext. — Empty Containers,* 118 M.C.C. 675, and *Ritter Trucking Co., Inc., Extension,* 111 M.C.C. 711.

It has long been held that where the record of an applicant's past conduct demonstrates a pattern of serious or continuing unlawfulness, the applicant has the burden of refuting the import of its past conduct in order to establish its fitness to receive additional authority. See *Kroblin Refrigerated Xpress, Inc. v. United States,* 197 F. Supp. *Fournier's Express, Inc., Ext.-Hartford, Conn.,* 108 M.C.C. 584; *Jones-Common Carrier Application,* 96 M.C.C. 100. On the general issue of fitness see *Sammons Trucking Ext. — Aberdeen, S. Dak.,* 124 M.C.C. 373; *Distributors Service Co., Ext. — Foods,* 118 M.C.C. 322; *Ritter Trucking Co., Inc., Ext.* 111 M.C.C. 771; *Eagle Motor Lines, Inc., Ext. — Lincoln, Ala.,* 107 M.C.C. 499; *L & M Express Co., Ext. — Crewe, Va.,* 106 M.C.C. 334.

The refusal of the Commission to issue a certificate on the basis of a finding of lack of fitness is not a punitive measure directed at past unlawful acts. It is, rather, the result of an evaluation of evidence as to applicant's willingness and ability to conduct its future operations lawfully. *Fournier's Express, Inc., Ext. — Hartford, Conn.,* 108 M.C.C. 584; *International Carriers Inc., Contr. Car. Applic.,* 112 M.C.C. 195; *McRay Truck Line, Inc., Ext.—Forty-Eight States,* 111 M.C.C. 602. It protects the public from the machinations of scofflaw carriers and those too careless of propriety to be trusted in public service. Its punishment of the carrier is only a secondary effect.

[202]81 M.C.C. 155, 159.
[203]77 M.C.C. 275, 280-1.
[204]81 M.C.C. 155, 159.

tions without financial difficulty. Under these circumstances, the Commission said, applicant was considered fit to conduct the proposed operation.

In *R. B. "Dick" Wilson, Inc., Extension*,[205] the Commission said that any finding that applicant was unfit to conduct limited extension operation authorized would be inconsistent with its demonstrated ability to perform its present service and the facts of record as a whole. This holding was made even though the most current financial information available at the hearing showed an operating loss. The Commission said in *Missouri, Kans. & Okla. Lines, Inc.*,[206] that the fact that applicant was controlled by persons in control of another interstate carrier was material and important in an application proceeding, since the Commission must, before granting any authority to a new corporation such as applicant, determine that it is fit, willing and able to perform the proposed operation and to conform with the Commission's rules and regulations. The Commission said that an applicant's financial structure and its relations with another carrier or other carriers are matters which affect its fitness and ability to function efficiently and consistently with the public interest. The Commission said (p. 107) that affiliated carriers, even though not standing in the relation of parent and subsidiary, are to some extent dependent upon each other or affected by the association. Moreover, reasons prompting formation of a separate corporation are of themselves of material importance in considering a grant of operating authority. In addition, it may be that existence of several different corporations under common control is for some reason undesirable in a given instance, or contrary to the public interest.

Solely because some of applicant's balance sheet items were not related to for-hire transportation activities did not establish that he was unfit to perform the proposed operations, the Commission said in *Sorensen Extension*.[207] The balance sheet items, the Commission said, were includable in order to reflect his over-all financial conditions, and such inclusion is required of class I motor carriers; his profit and loss statement was limited to for-hire transportation activities, and showed a moderate profit.

Temporary Authority

Section 210a (a) of the Interstate Commerce Act,[208] as amended, provides:

[205]79 M.C.C. 554, 556.
[206]78 M.C.C. 105, 106.
[207]78 M.C.C. 626, 629.
[208]49 U.S.C. 210a (a) Comparable provision — Section 311(b).

"To enable the provision of service for which there is an immediate and urgent need to a point or points or within a territory having no carrier service capable of meeting such need, the Commission may, in its discretion and without hearings or other proceedings, grant temporary authority for such service by a common carrier or a contract carrier by motor vehicle, as the case may be. Such temporary authority, unless suspended or revoked for good cause, shall be valid for such time as the Commission shall specify but for not more than an aggregate of one hundred and eighty days, and shall create no presumption that corresponding permanent authority will be granted thereafter. Note: For extension of temporary authority pending determination of permanent authority see the last sentence of §558(c) of the Administrative Procedure Act, 5 USC §558(c), infra."

Section 210a (b) provides:

"Pending the determination of an application filed with the Commission for approval of a consolidation or merger of the properties of two or more motor carriers, or of a purchase, lease, or contract to operate the properties of one or more motor carriers, the Commission may, in its discretion, and without hearings or other proceedings, grant temporary approval, for a period not exceeding one hundred and eighty days, of the operation of the motor carrier properties sought to be acquired by the person proposing in such pending application to acquire such properties, if it shall appear that failure to grant such temporary approval may result in destruction of or injury to such motor carrier properties sought to be acquired, or to interfere substantially with their future usefulness in the performance of adequate and continuous service to the public."

Section 558(c) of the Administrative Procedure Act[209] provides:

"When application is made for a license required by law, the agency, with due regard for the rights and privileges of all the interested parties or adversely affected persons and within a reasonable time, shall set and complete proceedings required to be conducted in accordance with sections 556 and 557 of this title or other proceedings required by law and shall make its decision. Except in cases of willfulness or those in which public health, interest, or safety requires otherwise, the withdrawal, suspension, revocation, or annulment of a license is lawful only if, before the institution of agency proceedings therefor, the licensee has been given—

(1) notice by the agency in writing of the facts or conduct which may warrant the action; and

(2) opportunity to demonstrate or achieve compliance with all lawful requirements.

When the licensee has made timely and sufficient application for a renewal or a new license in accordance with agency rules, a license with reference to an activity of a continuing nature does not expire until the application has been finally determined by the agency."

[209]5 U.S.C. 558(c).

Under the provisions of Section 210a of the I.C. Act, the Commission may not grant temporary authority or approval to an applicant beyond the 180 day limitation provided for therein. However an applicant who receives such temporary authority from the Commission automatically secures the rights conferred on licensees by Section 558(c) of the Administrative Procedure Act.

Section 558(c) in and of itself grants a special right to a licensee to operate under his temporary authority until such time as the Commission finally determines his application for permanent authority, provided only that the licensee complies with and meets the conditions specified in the last sentence of the said section. The Commission's function is simply to determine whether these conditions are fulfilled, and if it finds that they have been met it must, in compliance with the mandate of Section 558(c), authorize the licensee to continue to act under his temporary authority until it determines finally whether his application for permanent authority shall be granted or not. In carrying out the mandate of Section 558(c), and in determining whether the applicant meets the conditions there specified, the Commission decides whether the activity is of a continuing nature; whether the licensee has made timely application for a renewal or a new license; and whether the licensee has made sufficient application for a renewal or a new license.

From an early date after the adoption of the Administrative Procedure Act, the Commission has construed Section 558(c) as being applicable to temporary authorities or approvals issued pursuant to Section 210a, and it has consistently adhered to this interpretation over the intervening years.

Section 311(a) of the I.C. Act[210] is comparable to Section 210(a) except that it applies to water carriers. The Commission has often expressed the view that it has the power under this provision to grant temporary authority to the most suitable type of transportation for the proposed service, regardless of the fact that there may be other modes of transportation in existence which might physically be able to serve the particular point.[211]

In the *War Shipping Administration* case the Administrator shortly after the surrender of Japan had filed an application with the Commission under Section 311(a) for temporary authority to operate as a common and contract carrier between all ports on the Atlantic, Pacific, and

---

[210]49 U.S.C. 911(a).

[211]*Hudson River Day Line v. United States*, 85 F. Supp. 225; *Alabama Great Southern Ry. Co. v. United States*, 103 F. Supp. 223; *War Shipping Administration T.A. Application*, 260 I.C.C. 589.

Gulf of Mexico coasts by self-propelled vessels over ocean routes. In his application he pointed out that existing conditions prevented the immediate delivery of vessels to the coastwise and intercoastal carriers which were authorized to perform such services, and proposed that such temporary authority would be exercised only through such carriers as agents of the Administrator, pending the restoration of service by such agents in their own names. The railroads in protesting to the Commission argued that, as a prerequisite to the issuance of temporary authority, the Commission must find that there are no carriers — water, rail, motor, or other — capable of performing the desired transportation between the points or within the territory. This contention was predicated upon the view that only the availability of some means of physical transportation should be considered by the Commission, and that no consideration may be given to the desirability, in the interest of the commercial and industrial development of the affected areas, of encouraging full use of all practical means of transportation. The Commission rejected this argument and granted the authority requested.

A similar contention was made in *Alabama Great Southern R. Co. v. United States, supra,* and the court in affirming the view of the Commission, commented as follows (page 226):

> The Commission thought, and we agree, that the statute does not foreclose consideration of "the economic needs of commerce and industry" for water-carriers just because there are present motor, rail or air carriers "physically capable" of providing transportation service to and from the particular point. A more reserictive reading would mock the statute and the National policies. Scarcely is there a port in the United States without adequate rail service; therefore in actuality the provision for temporary authority would be meaningless if such authority were grantable only when other facilities were insufficient. Viability of water service was not to depend upon capability of other service. The latter was not to determine the creation or suppression of water service. Existence of other service is but one element to be considered. In this regard reason allows no distinction between temporary and permanent certificates.
>
> * o o
>
> Service, not simply transportation, is the stipulation of the statute. The Commission could not ignore these considerations. It would have erred had it reached its conclusion solely by measuring the physical ability of the existing rail service.
>
> It is upon the entire record this court must determine whether the Commission acted arbitrarily or capriciously. *Schenley Distillers Corporation v. United States,* 50 F. Supp. 491, at 496.

On the same point is *Pennsylvania Ry. Co. v. United States*[212] where a district court upheld a Commission order granting, over the protests

---

[212]13 Fed. Carrier Cases 81,256.

of railroads, temporary authorities to two motor carriers for the transportation of cement, in bulk, from the producers' plants in Martinsburg, W.Va., and Lime Kiln, Md., to points in several States. The protesting railroads contended that they had been handling this traffic for years without interruption, and that there was no basis for the Commission's finding that there was "immediate and urgent need" for the motor carrier service authorized as required by Section 210a (a). The court, in holding that there was substantial basis for the findings and conclusions, said that it was not the function of the court to weigh the "endorsements, protests, statements of fact and the like which were submitted to the Commission."

In *Pan-Atlantic Steamship Corp. v. Atlantic Coast Line Railroad Co.*,[213] the Supreme Court held that the Commission was authorized by the last sentence of Section 558(c) of the Administrative Procedure Act to extend temporary operating authorities issued under Section 311(a) of the I.C. Act beyond the period of 180 days, specified in the latter section, until the final determination of a timely and sufficient application for a permanent certificate, thereby confirming the Commission's interpretation of these statutes. The Court held that "license" as used in Section 558(c) includes temporary authorities; that Section 558(c) "is a direction to the various agencies"; and that there is no conflict between the 180 days' limitation upon the powers granted by Section 311(a) of the I.C. Act and the further grant of power by Section 558(c) of the Administrative Procedure Act. Although this decision, by its terms, applied only to grants of water-carrier temporary authorities under Section 311(a), the principle is equally applicable to motor-carrier temporary authorities issued under Section 210a (a) and to temporary acquisitions of motor-carrier and water-carrier operations under Sections 210(a) (b) and 311(b).

That operations under temporary authority can be considered to some extent in determining need for permanent authority is not open to dispute, although temporary operations alone are insufficient to form a basis for grant thereof and are of value only when there is other probative evidence.[214] Shipper's use of applicant's service under temporary authority cannot, standing alone, be the basis of a permanent grant of authority.[215] The granting of temporary authority does not give rise to any presumption that corresponding permanent authority is required.[216]

The standards for granting temporary authority under Section 210a

---

[213]253 U.S. 436.
[214]*Roadway Exp., Inc., Extension,* 82 M.C.C. 689, 703.
[215]*Marine Exp. Co., Inc., Extension,* 81 M.C.C. 155, 158.
[216]*Bulk Motor Transport, Inc., Extension,* 79 M.C.C. 321, 322.

are not the same as those demanded for the granting of permanent authority; the Commission has broader discretion and may act much more summarily thereunder. The administrative review process of grants of temporary authority calls for different legal evaluations than for permanent orders. Grants of temporary authority do not have to pass the same judicial muster as permanent orders. By the express language of Section 210a (a), a grant of temporary authority shall create no presumption that corresponding permanent authority will be granted thereafter. In short, the procedures for granting temporary and permanent authority are statutorily and legally separate and distinct.

Certain rules have been promulgated by the Commission to be used as guidelines in the handling of temporary authority applications. These rules are summarized below.

Under Section 210a (a) each application for temporary authority must be accomplished by a supporting statement(s) designed to establish an immediate and urgent need for service which cannot be met by existing carriers, except that when the Department of Defense is the shipper such support may be furnished directly to the Motor Carrier Board by the Washington office of that Department. Each such shipper's statement except those submitted by the DOD must contain a certification of its accuracy and must be signed by the person (or an authorized representative thereof) having such immediate and urgent need for motor carrier service. Any such supporting statement must contain at least the following information:

(1) Description of the specific commodity or commodities to be transported (where the transportation of property is involved).

(2) Points or areas to, from, or between which such commodities or passengers are to be transported. (If service is needed to or from a territory or area rather than a specific point or points, such territory or area must be clearly described and evidence must be furnished of a broad need to justify the territorial grant of authority requested.)

(3) Volume of traffic involved, frequency of movement, and how transported now and in the past.

(4) How soon the service must be provided and the reasons for such time limit.

(5) How long the need for such service likely will continue, and whether the persons supporting the temporary application will support a permanent service application.

(6) Recital of the consequences if service is not made available.

(7) The circumstances which created an immediate and urgent need for the requested service.

(8) Whether efforts have been made to obtain the service from

existing motor, rail, or water carriers, and the dates and results of such efforts.

(9) Names and addresses of existing carriers who have either failed or refused to provide the service, and the reasons given for any such failure or refusal.

(10) Name and address of motor carrier who will provide service and is filing application for temporary authority.

(11) If the person supporting the application has supported any prior application for permanent or temporary authority covering all or any part of the desired service, the carrier's name, address, and motor carrier docket number, if known, must be given, and a statement must be made as to whether such application was granted or denied which should include the date of such action, if known.

Emergency temporary authority is issued for periods of 30 days or less to meet an immediate and urgent need for service due to emergencies in which time or circumstances do not reasonably permit the filing and processing of an application for temporary authority.

Where the emergency is found to continue beyond the period of the initial grant, the emergency temporary authority may be extended only upon written request until disposition is made of the longer term temporary authority application.

Temporary authority is approved subject to compliance within 30 days, or within such additional time as the Commission may approve, with the applicable provisions of the statute and the requirements, rules, and regulations prescribed by the Commission thereunder governing the filing of rate and contract publications, the filing of acceptable evidence of security for the protection of the public and designation of agents for service of process.

If compliance is not made within the 30-day period, or within the time allowed in any extension thereof applicant will be notified that the temporary authority order is of no further force and effect. Where this occurs, applicant may make written request for reinstatement of the granting order if it so desires, provided (1) that such request is made within 20 days from the date of the notice, (2) that good cause can be shown as to why compliance was not made within the time allowed, and (3) that the request for reinstatement contains positive assurance that applicant is now able to and will comply immediately with all applicable requirements, if the order is reinstated.

Initial determination of temporary authority applications will be made by the Commission's Motor Carrier Board or by a Division of the Commission, acting initially. For purposes of administration, distinctions in the applicable grounds of approval and rate filings will be maintained as between temporary authority of not more than 30 days (ETA), and temporary authority of up to 180 days (TA). No successive grants of temporary authority shall exceed a total of 180 days, and, if a grant of an emergency authority results in a total of aggregate temporary authority grants of more than 180 consecutive days, such total, to the extent that it exceeds 180 days, will be reduced accordingly.

While a grant of temporary authority is neither a permit nor a certificate under the I.C. Act it nevertheless enables the applicant to provide service either as a common or a contract carrier, as the case may be. Consequently, an applicant for temporary authority to operate as a motor contract carrier must show that the operation proposed is that of a contract carrier by motor vehicle as defined in Section 203(a) (15); that is, that the applicant serves one or a limited number of shippers, and that the service proposed involves either the assignment of vehicles to the supporting shipper's exclusive use or the provision of a transportation service designed to meet the distinct needs of that shipper. No "dual operation" finding is necessary, however, where a grant of temporary authority to operate as a contract carrier is made to an existing common carrier and vice versa.

Since a grant of temporary authority is not a permit or certificate, none of the related rights, under the I.C. Act, such as the incidental charter rights of passenger carriers and the implied authority to perform terminal services at points within the commercial zone but beyond the corporate limits of named municipalities, is applicable. Temporary authority may not be tacked or joined with permanent authority held by the carrier for the purpose of performing through transportation, nor can through, joint-line service be performed thereunder. Where there is a need for such services which are not implicit in grants of temporary operating authority this fact should be stated specifically so that an appropriate authority description may be issued.

For administrative convenience, temporary authority to transport property will be considered to authorize the return transportation of shipper-owned trailers and of empty crates, barrels, bottles, hangers, pallets, bracing, dunnage, and other similar containers and shipping devices used in the outbound transportation covered by the temporary authority.

Grants of temporary authority shall only be made upon the establishment of an immediate and urgent need for the transportation of passengers, or of particular commodities or classes of commodities, from specified origin points or areas to specified destination points or areas, having no carrier service capable of meeting such needs. Requests for temporary authority involving service to or from entire States, counties, or other defined areas will warrant approval only when supported by evidence that there is a compelling need for service to or from a representative number of points in each such State, county, or area, that there is a reasonable certainty that such service will be utilized, and that there is no carrier service available capable of meeting such need. Otherwise, such grants will be limited in accordance with the evidence to point-to-point authorizations covering the immediate and urgent need for service.

Any need which is the basis of an operation authorized by a temporary authority to be conducted for a period of less than an aggregate of 180 days is presumed not to be of a "continuing nature" unless the Commission otherwise expressly determines. If the need for a particular service ceases and a temporary authority covering such need expires or is revoked, and a new or separate need arises subsequent to such expiration or revocation, additional temporary authority for the 180-day aggregate, or for a shorter period, may be granted to the same carrier for the service, notwithstanding the prior grant or grants. However, an application filed after an aggregate of 180 days temporary authority has expired or been revoked will be denied unless the facts clearly show that the application is in reality based on a new need and not a continuation of the need on which the prior grant of authority was based.

An immediate and urgent need justifying a grant of temporary authority will be determined to exist only where it is established that there is or soon will be an immediate transportation need which reasonably cannot be met by existing carrier service. Such a showing may involve a new or relocated plant, different method of distribution, new or unusual commodities, an origin or destination not presently served by carriers, a discontinuance of existing service, failure of existing carriers to provide service, or comparable situations which require new motor carrier service before an application for permanent authority can be filed and processed.

An immediate and urgent need justifying a grant of emergency temporary authority will be determined to exist only where it is established that existing carrier service is not capable of providing transportation service to meet immediate and actual emergencies, such as, for example, to prevent a plant shutdown, to move particular shipments in the interest of the national defense, to meet needs resulting from fires, floods, storms, or other disasters which affect the public health, safety, and welfare, disruption in existing carrier services by work stoppages, unexpected cessation of existing transportation service, lack of equipment capable of transporting the involved commodity, failure or lack of storage facilities and imminent spoilage of perishable commodities, or comparable situations which make it impracticable to afford the notice specified for temporary authority.

Generally, the desire of a shipper for single-line service in lieu of existing interchange or connecting-carrier service will not warrant a grant of temporary authority. A grant of temporary authority to effectuate single-line service will be authorized only when it is clearly established that the carriers providing multiple-line service are not capable of, or have failed in, meeting the reasonable immediate and urgent needs of shippers or receivers between the points or territories and in respect of the commodity or commodities involved.

Requests for temporary authority on the basis of "providing a complete service to a shipper," even though existing carriers are participating in the traffic and in many instances can provide a substantial part of the service, require special justification. Generally, in such instances, the applicant must establish with reasonable certainty that the existing carriers cannot adequately serve the shipper in their authorized territories, or that the supporting shipper has revised its distribution methods to such an extent that there actually is an immediate and urgent need for the complete service proposed.

Temporary authority may be granted where existing authorized carriers are unable or refuse to furnish equipment necessary to move passengers or the traffic of shippers in order to meet an immediate and urgent transportation need.

Except in unusual circumstances, temporary authority to operate over an alternate route will not be granted, even though the service route may be circuitous, since the carrier-applicant may now operate between the points involved.

Applications for temporary authority may be denied for the following reasons:

(i)   Failure to meet statutory standards.

(ii) Unfitness of the applicant.

A motor common carrier may not lawfully perform transportation until effective rates and provisions are published, posted, and filed with the Commission as required by Section 217 and the Commission's rules and regulations issued thereunder. Rates to be established upon less than 30 days' notice must not be less than existing motor common carrier commodity rates on the same commodities in like quantities from and to the same points, or in absence thereof not less than the motor common carrier commodity rates on the same commodities in like quantities from and to nearby points for similar distances. In the absence of existing motor common carrier commodity rates, the rates to be established on less than 30 days' notice shall not be less than the applicable motor common carrier class rates from and to the same points except as authorized.

A motor contract carrier may not lawfully provide transportation until executed transportation contracts, when required, and schedules of rates and charges are on file with the Commission as required by Section 218 of the I.C. Act and the Commission's rules and regulations issued thereunder. The filing of contracts covering transportation of passengers, currency, bullion, and certain other valuable articles is not required. Except as authorized, the rates proposed to be established upon less than 30 days' notice shall not be lower than as permitted above if applicant is a common carrier except that if any of the points of origin, destination, or territory to be served is at the time served by a contract carrier transporting the same commodities, the rates and charges may be made on the same or higher basis as those of such contract carrier, or those maintained by applicant between other points in the same area.

In most cases there is outstanding special permission authority to publish rates on less than statutory notice covering the substitution of motor for rail service. Most tariff publishing agents also have outstanding special permission authority to publish on short-notice scope of operating rights to be granted pursuant to a temporary authority application and to add new participating carriers to their tariffs. The temporary authority application must state who will make the tariff publication, and whether it is to be made on 30 days' notice or upon less than 30 days' notice.

If publication is to be made on short notice by the carrier filing the temporary authority application and it is not covered by the outstanding special permission authority, such temporary authority application must be accompanied by a special permission application setting forth the proposed rates clearly and completely. If the proposed provisions consist of rates, all points of origin and destination must be shown or definitely indicated. If permission is sought to establish a rule, the exact wording of the proposed rule must be shown. If relief from tariff circular rules is sought, the exact form of publication must be shown.

The special permission application must contain the names of motor carriers known to maintain competitive rates; charges, or rules between the same points or points related thereto, together with adequate identification of tariffs containing such rates, charges, or rules. It must also state whether such carriers have been advised of the proposed rates, charges, or rules and whether they have been advised that it is proposed to establish such provisions on less than 30 days' notice. The rates, charges, or rules proposed to be established should conform to competitive rate level standards. In the absence of effective commodity rates via competing carriers on the commodity or commodities to be transported, the Special Permission Board, upon a proper showing, may authorize the establishment of rates on a different level.

Each application for emergency temporary authority for 30 days or less, except those involving substitution of motor for rail service, shall be accompanied by a statement of the rates, charges, and rules to be filed under special permission for use in the event the authority sought is granted. Such statement shall contain the names of competing motor carriers transporting the same commodities and the rates of such carriers.

If the statement of the proposed rates submitted with the emergency temporary authority application contains rates or charges lower than existing rates by the named or other carriers, approval will not be recommended or authority granted. All emergency temporary authority will be expressly conditioned on establishing rates or charges no lower than those set forth in the application, and a "W" tariff naming rates lower than those set forth in the application will be rejected. Emergency authority will be revoked for failure to seasonably file a proper "W" tariff.

In every case the carrier shall state in its emergency authority application whether there is under suspension at the time any rates published for its account, or whether an application for special permission authority to file its rates on less than 30 days' notice has been granted or denied, covering the same traffic from and to the same points in connection with another temporary or permanent authority application. If the applicant has rates or other tariff matter under suspension, or has received or been denied special permission to file on less than 30 days' notice any rates not yet effective, covering the same traffic, the district supervisor will not recommend approval of the request nor will a grant be made of the emergency temporary authority.

If applicant carrier has rates under suspension covering the same traffic, it should file a special permission application requesting short notice authority to cancel the suspended matter and to file other rates, or in the alternative, stating that the suspended rates will be defended and requesting short notice authority to file rates to apply during the suspension period, such rates to expire at the end of the suspension period.

Each application by passenger carriers for emergency temporary authority must be accompanied by an application for special permission to publish fares and charges in connection therewith if they are proposed to be made effective on less than 30 days statutory notice. Such application shall be accompanied by a statement of the fares, charges, and rules to be filed if the authority is granted. Authority to file fares and charges on less-than-statutory notice will be granted only when the proposed fares and charges are on a level which does not undercut or disrupt the existing level of the fares and charges between the points involved maintained by competing motor carriers generally in the same territory.

The special permission application must contain the names of motor carriers known to maintain competitive fares, charges, or rules between the same or related points, together with accurate identification of the tariffs, by I.C.C. numbers, containing such fares, charges, and rules. It must also state whether such competing carriers have been advised of the fares and charges proposed to be established upon less-than-statutory notice.

Pursuant to and in accordance with the Commission's General and Special Rules of Practice, petitions for reconsideration of orders of (1) the Motor Carrier Board, and (2) a Division initially granting or denying temporary authority in proceedings not subject to prior determination by the Motor Carrier Board, may be filed by any interested person.

Replies may be filed by any interested person to such petitions; but if the facts stated in any such petition disclose a need for accelerated action, such action, in the discretion of the Commission, may be taken before expiration of the time allowed for reply. Replies received after accelerated action on petition will be treated as petitions for reconsideration of the accelerated action and given corresponding accelerated action.

The filing of a petition for reconsideration of an order of a Division or the Motor Carrier Board does not have the effect of automatically staying such order, and the grantee carrier may conduct the operations authorized by such order upon compliance with its tariff, insurance, and other requirements for the duration of the temporary authority, or until otherwise ordered.

Radial and Nonradial Operations

In *King Van Lines, Inc., Investigation of Certificate*,[217] the Commission said:

> It has been recognized consistently since the regulation of motor carriers that the words "on the one hand," and, "on the other" are words of extremity, and that they are used for the sole purpose of identifying the operators authorized as radial operations between a base point and other points in a described area, as distinguished from an unlimited nonradial operation between described points or all points within described areas. See *Classification of Motor Carriers of Property*, 2 M.C.C. 703, and *Gay's Exp., Inc. v. Haigis and Nichols*, 43 M.C.C. 277. It also has been well

[217]84 M.C.C. 269, 275.

established that the holder of a certificate authorizing radial irregular-route operations alone is not authorized to perform crosshaul operations between points in a radial origin or destination territory even though the service is performed through the base point. Compare *Akers Motor Lines, Inc., v. Malone Freight Lines, Inc.,* 53 M.C.C. 353 (356).

Terms and Conditions of Certificates

Section 208(a) of the Interstate Commerce Act[218] provides:

"Any certificate issued under section 206 or 207 shall specify the service to be rendered and the routes over which, the fixed termini, if any, between which, and the intermediate and off-route points, if any, at which, and in case of operations not over specified routes or between fixed termini, the territory within which, the motor carrier is authorized to operate; and there shall, at the time of issuance and from time to time thereafter, be attached to the exercise of the privileges granted by the certificate such reasonable terms, conditions, and limitations as the public convenience and necessity may from time to time require, including terms, conditions, and limitations as to the extension of the route or routes of the carrier, and such terms and conditions as are necessary to carry out, with respect to the operations of the carrier, the requirements established by the Commission under Section 204 (a) (1) and (6); *Provided, however,* That no terms, condition, or limitations shall restrict the right of the carrier to add to his or its equipment and facilities over the routes, between the termini, or within the territory specified in the certificate, as the development of the business and the demands of the public shall require."

A certificate which, by the terms, expires on a certain date is one containing a "condition"; a certificate may include reasonable terms, conditions, and limitations which are necessary for safe operation of motor carriers on the highways.[219] In the absence of compelling circumstances, grants of authority are not normally limited to a subdivided category or a specific type or types of a specified commodity, particularly where shipper produces various kinds;[220] nor is authority generally restricted to the site of a shipper's plant, since to confine an applicant's operations to service only the particular shipper would be inconsistent with its undertaking and duty as a common carrier to serve the public generally.[221] But while the Commission does not generally favor restricting a grant of common-carrier authority to a plant site, where such restriction provides the only suitable method of identifying the location where service is needed without granting countywide authority, it may be

[218]49 U.S.C. 308(a). Comparable provisions — Sections 309(d), 410(e).
[219]*Gateway Transp. Co. v. United States,* 173, F. Supp. 822, 825-7.
[220]*Dealers Transit, Inc., Extension,* 79 M.C.C. 26, 29.
[221]*Pettapiece Cartage & Builders' Supplies,* 79 M.C.C. 259, 264.

imposed.[222] As a general rule limited-term operating authorities are not favored, and will be issued only when the circumstances are compelling.[223] However, the Commission may issue limited-term certificates to carriers authorized to transport explosives; such action enables it to review the carrier's safety record when and if renewal of the authority is sought; limitation of such a certificate to five years is not unreasonable, arbitrary, capricious, or discriminatory, nor an abuse of the Commission's discretion; it promotes public interest and public safety on the highways.[224] Likewise, and for the same reasons, the Commission may impose limitation to a specified number of years on authority granted for the handling of other hazardous traffic.[225]

Authority for transportation of "truckloads only" is not ambiguous, but means a load of authorized freight to the carrying capacity of the vehicle, either by weight or by volume, composed of one or an aggregate mixture of items, moving from one consignor to one consignee at one time. While the Commission now normally declines to impose such a restriction, this is not due to its insusceptibility to common understanding, but rather to potential enforcement problems and to its inconsistency, in general, with the basic concepts of common carriage; but where such a restriction already exists, the Commission has declined to remove it without a showing of real need for the resulting service.[226] The Commission has found use of boundaries of political subdivisions more satisfactory than use of radial distances in defining authorized areas.[227] The use of mileage radii often present problems of interpretation.[228] An off-route point is one located off a described regular route and may be named specifically or identified as a point within a given distance of a regular-route point or within a specified area; service to and from such point may be made from the nearest regular route to which it is appurtenant, and must be performed in connection with good-faith operations over the regular route.[229]

In *Great Northern Ry. Co. — Modification of Certificates*,[230] the Commission held that removal of rail-auxiliary restrictions on applicant's routes in Montana and between Williston, N. D., and Montana was not

---

[222]*Wheeling Pipe Line, Inc., Extension*, 82 M.C.C. 229, 235.
[223]*Burks Motor Freight Line, Inc.*, 77 M.C.C. 303, 308.
[224]*Gateway Transp. Co. v. United States*, 173 F. Supp. 822, 826.
[225]*Tri-State Trucking Co. Extension*, 83 M.C.C. 247, 251.
[226]*Travelers M. Freight, Inc. — Definitions of Truckloads Only*, 83 M.C.C. 613, 616-7.
[227]*Huidsten Transport, Inc., Extension*, 83 M.C.C. 199, 204-5.
[228]*Kaw Transport Co. Extension*, 83 M.C.C. 207, 214.
[229]*Jasper & Chicago M. Exp., Inc., Extension*, 82 M.C.C. 171, 173.
[230]83 M.C.C. 345, 350-1.

warranted when supporting shippers' transportation requirements were vague and indefinite, the principal connecting carrier supporting the application admitted that joint-line service of certain protestants was "very good," and most if not all the small towns along applicant's routes were receiving regular and adequate service from one or more of the existing carriers.

Tacking

A carrier may tack or combine separate grants of authority (including tacking of regular with irregular route authority), not restricted against tacking, provided there is a point of service common to both authorities and physical operation is rendered through such common point, and the separate nature of each type of service is maintained.[231] It has not been the Commission's practice to restrict operating authority against joining or tacking unless there is some valid reason therefor.[232] In *Commercial Oil Transport Extension*,[233] the Commission said that it is reluctant to localize and isolate grants of common-carrier authority by encumbering them with restrictions aagainst tacking except for good cause shown. The Commission found in the *Commercial Oil Transport* case that there was no evidence that the opposing carrier would be adversely affected should applicant elect to tack the authority involved with any of its present authority, thus the condition against tacking would not be imposed. In *Monumental Motor Tours, Inc., v. Greyhound Corp.*,[234] the Commission said that since the earliest days of regulation it has been held that a common carrier of passengers, in order to provide through bus service, may tack separate grants of authority at a point of service common to both grants, therefore, complainant's contention that the joint route established by tacking the authorities of the two defendants was unlawful because there was no single certificate authorizing such service was without merit.

The Commission has imposed restrictions against tacking in both extension and purchase cases.[235] In *Direct Transport Co. of Kentucky, Inc.*

---

[231]*Clapps Extension*, 77 M.C.C. 683, 687; *T.S.C. Motor Freight Lines, Inc., Extension* 81 M.C.C. 619, 624.

[232]*Commercial Oil Transport Extension*, 76 M.C.C. 773, 778; *Manson Dray Line, Inc., Extension*, 77 M.C.C. 727, 736.

[233]77 M.C.C. 771, 773.

[234]79 M.C.C. 244, 247.

[235]*Pacific Intermountain Express Co. — Purchase — Keeshin*, 57 M.C.C. 341.

Extension,[236] the Commission restricted the certificate granted, stating:

> There is no merit to Liquid Transporters' contention that a restriction against joinder of any authority granted herein with its existing right is improper. The right of a carrier to operate over all combinations of its operating rights unless specifically restricted in its certificate is well settled. Our right, however, to impose restrictions against joinder where warranted is equally well established, and the imposition of such restriction here does not establish a new standard to be met by that applicant. Liquid Transporters indicated that it desired the prospective privilege of combining its present operating rights with any rights granted herein and any that may be hereinafter obtained. It established a need, however, for transportation service only between the origin and destination named below.

The right of a motor carrier to tack grants of authority requires either a specific authorization for joinder or their must be a point of service common to both operating authorities, and such authority must be authorized in a manner which would permit interchange at points common to both routes if the rights were in separate hands.[237] As stated in *Clapps, Extension — Alternate Route*[238] "a motor common carrier can tack or combine separate grants of authorities which are not restricted against tacking, provided that there is a point of service common to both authorities and the 'physical operations are rendered through such common point.'"

Where the common point of service is the "site" of a plant, does a motor carrier have the right to tack or combine separate grants of authorities which are not restricted against tacking? This question was resolved in *Petroleum Products, O'Boyle Tank Lines,*[239] where the Commission said:

> The only requirement is that there must be a point of service common to both operating authorities and the physical operation must be rendered through such common point. *Transport Corp. of Virginia Extension—Maryland,* 43 M.C.C. 716. and *Valley Motor Lines, Inc., v. Western Truck Lines,* 47 M.C.C. 718. Bolling Field is located within the Washington commercial zone and is a point common to both authorities considered herein. but Andrews Field is not so located and is not a gateway point. See *Washington, D. C., Commercial Zone,* 3 M.C.C. 243 and 48 M.C.C. 460. The extent to which a motor common carrier may operate within a military reservation to which service has been authorized is a matter which may be determined by the carrier and the military officials of the reservation.

[236] 68 M.C.C. 151, 156-7.
[237] *T.S.C. Motor Freight Lines, Inc., Extension — Alternate Routes,* 81 M.C.C. 619, 624.
[238] 77 M.C.C. 683, 687.
[239] 61 M.C.C. 48, 49-50.

Missouri Pac. Transp. Co. Extension—Fort Leavenworth, 41 M.C.C. 545. Therefore, the fulfillment here of the requirements that there must be a point of service common to both operating authorities and that operation must be performed physically through such common point, is contingent upon the approval by the governing officials for respondent to conduct physical operations through Bolling Field. *M. I. O'Boyle & Son, Inc., Interpretation of Certificate,* 52 M.C.C. 248.

Respondent has the approval of the governing officials to make deliveries at Bolling Field, but has been expressly prohibited from entering Bolling Field for the purpose of combining or tacking its separate operating authorities. It proposes to tack or combine the considered authorities by operating, and has operated, from and to the considered points, through or over an apron or driveway leading from the highway to an entrance gate at Bolling Field. A site is a plot of ground suitable or set apart for some specific use, and occupied for that purpose. In the certificate it is used to include the grounds within Bolling Field, and does not include adjacent streets, areas, or land in the vicinity. The operations conducted by respondent from and to the considered points have not been physically performed through Bolling Field, and a permanent injunction has been issued enjoining respondent from the conduct of such operations in *Interstate Commerce Commission v. M. I. O'Boyle & Son, Inc., doing business as O'Boyle Tank Lines, Civil No. 4027-52,* United States District Court, District of Columbia, from which respondent has noted an appeal. A motion to stay the issuance of such injunction was denied by the court.

The Interstate Commerce Act does not permit the filing of tariffs which contain rates for service which cannot be provided by the carrier, and in a number of proceedings, schedules covering service which the respondents therein could not lawfully render have been found unlawful and ordered canceled. See *Iron and Steel Articles, Central Territory,* 53 M.C.C. 769, and cases cited therein.

We find that the proposed schedules are unlawful because respondent may not now lawfully operate from and to the considered points.

In *Wheling Pipe Line, Ext. — Ethylene Dibromide,*[240] the Commission stated:

Gibbon holds no authority to operate from the El Dorado area to serve points in Kentucky and North Carolina, but it can serve a relatively large territory in southeastern Missouri by tacking at the site of a pipeline terminal at or near Conway, Ark. The right of motor common carriers to tack or combine separate grants of authority at common points limited to "the site of" military reservations and, by implication, industrial plants or installations was recognized in *M. I. O'Boyle & Son, Inc., Interpretation of Certificate,* 52 M.C.C. 248, and more recently in No. MC-86188 (Sub-No. 33), *Northland Petroleum Transport Co. Ext. — Paulsboro, N. J.* 79 M.C.C. 807 (not printed in full), decided March 9, 1959; and there is no

---

[240]82 M.C.C. 229, 234.

evidence here that Gibbon is unable to tack its operating authorities by physically operating through the site of the pipeline terminal near Conway.

In *M. I. O'Boyle & Son, Inc. v. E. Brooke Matlack, Inc.*,[241] the Commission held that a motor common carrier may tack separate grants of unrestricted authority if there is a service common to both authorities, provided that the operations are conducted through such common point and that the character of the service authorized is maintained. The Commission said that the common point must be a point "to which" the carrier is authorized to transport a given shipment under an authority and "from which" it is authorized to transport that same shipment under the joining authority. In the *O'Boyle* case, the defendant's certificate authorized the transportation from a refinery in Delaware to points in eleven states and the District of Columbia with a tacking restriction specifically limited to affect only through transportation to points in Virginia. Defendant contended that the restriction affected only shipments beyond Virginia into North Carolina. The Commission held (at p. 203) that there was no merit in the contention because such a construction would change the ordinary meaning of the language in the certificate. The Commission said that the movement of traffic to a point in Virginia for any purpose would constitute through transportation to that Virginia point.

In *John L. Muth Extension — Kentucky to Eastern States*,[242] the applicant, holding authority between points in a number of States for transportation of horses, applied for similar authority between points in two Kentucky counties and 13 states. The application was supported by seven shippers in the two-county area. Protestants argued (at p. 188) "that the grant recommended by the examiner will give applicant greater rights than those which he seeks, in that applicant will be able to tack his present authority into Ohio, Michigan, and Illinois to that recommended by the examiner, and thus provide a through service between points in those three states and points in the states involved in this proceeding." The Commission agreed with protestants, holding (at p. 189) that an appropriate restriction against tacking would be imposed in the authority granted. In *Eldon Miller, Inc., Extension — Memphis, Tenn., to three States*,[243] the hearing officer had recommended a grant of a certificate restricted against tacking with other authority to perform a through service. Applicant argued on exceptions that protestants failed to show a material adverse affect. Protestants replied (at p. 196) that the re-

[241] 81 M.C.C. 201, 202-3.
[242] 69 M.C.C. 187.
[243] 84 M.C.C. 195.

striction was justified "because applicant plans to operate services between points not embraced in the application by combinations of its authorities." The Commission held (at p. 200) that "In view of applicant's existing certificates which authorize transportation of specified acids and chemicals outward from various destination States, we believe that the grant of authority herein should be restricted against tacking or joining with such other authorities of applicant to prevent it from rendering services for which no need has been shown." *In Archer & Archer, Inc., Extension*[244] authority to transport agricultural machinery was restricted against tacking directly or indirectly with any other authority held by applicant for purpose of providing through service other than from and to the points authorized. In *Herrin Transp. Co., Extension,*[245] where authority for a given route did not authorize service at intermediate points, the Commission said that the carrier could not utilize an intermediate point thereon to tack its authority for that route with another route connecting at such point.

While the general rule regarding tacking is that separate grants of operating authority may be tacked at common service points, so long as the operation is performed through the common point and the separate nature of each type of service is maintained,[246] the rule has been modified with respect to tacking two separate grants of irregular route authority by the Commission's grateway regulations. Ex Parte No. 55 (Sub-No. 8) *Gateway Elimination.*[247] The requirement that the "separate nature" of each type of service be maintained means essentially that two grants of regular route authority cannot be bridged by a grant of irregular route authority because such operation would, in effect, result in conversation of the irregular route authority to regular route.[248] However, where two irregular route authorities are joined by a regular route authority, that prohibition does not apply since the nature of the opera-

---

[244]77 M.C.C. 782, 785.

[245]81 M.C.C. 683. For other cases where no-tacking restrictions were imposed see *W. M. Chambers Truck Line, Inc., Extension — Cement,* 83 M.C.C. 399, 404; *Eldon Miller, Inc. — Extension — Bulk Chemicals,* 76 M.C.C. 643, 645-6; *C & D Motor Delivery Co., Extension — Alternate Routes,* 74 M.C.C. 698; *Eldon Miller, Inc., Extension — Tulsa, Okla.,* 73 M.C.C. 149, 154; *Kulp & Gordon, Inc., Extension — Bridge Sites,* 73 M.C.C. 323; *Coastal Tank Lines, Inc., Extension — Delaware City,* 73 M.C.C. 189; *Chemical Tank Lines, Inc., Ext. — Wayne County, Mich.,* 71 M.C.C. 380; *Gardella Extension — New York, N.Y., Commercial Zone,* 71 M.C.C. 791; *Delcher Bros. Storage Co., Extension — California,* 68 M.C.C. 51.

[246]*M. I. O'Boyle & Son, Inc., Interpretation of Certificate,* 52 M.C.C. 248, 250; *Motor Common Carriers of Property—Routes and Service,* 88 M.C.C. 415, 420-421; *Lattavo Bros., Inc., Ext. — Neville Island Gateway Elim.,* 91 M.C.C. 643, 645.

[247]119 M.C.C. 530. See 49 C.F.R. §1065.

[248]*Falwell Fast Frt., Inc. — Pur. — Draper, and Evans Line, Inc.,* 40 M.C.C. 439, *Motor Common Carriers of Property — Rates and Service, Supra* at 420.

tions under the separate authorities would be identical. See *Red Arrow Frt. Lines, Inc. — Purchase — Galveston.*[249] In that proceeding, the Commission approved the purchase transaction where vendee's regular route authority would be surrounded on the north and south by vendor's irregular route authority, finding no violation similar to that contained in *Falwell, supra* and stating:

> Further, in numerous cases the unification of regular route with irregular-route operating rights has been found consistent with the public interest. See, for example, *B & E Transp. Co., Inc. — Purchase — Merchants Transp., Inc.,* 36 M.C.C. 561.

In 1973, in light of problems of economy, environment, and energy resources, the I.C.C. began scrutinizing tacking in cases which resulted in undue circuity. The I.C.C. tentatively decided that where the route via the gateway was considerably longer that the direct route motor carriers should be required to carry by the direct route, hopefully conserving much fuel in the process. The I.C.C. was faced, however, with the problem of how to implement a change in its tacking policy and how to gain more information to determine finally that a change was in the public convenience and necessity. Relying upon its authority under 49 U.S.C. §308(a), the I.C.C. determined that the most feasible manner in which to accomplish the requisite authorization of such necessary services is by means of a general rule of construction applicable to the carriers' outstanding certificates, based upon a finding of public convenience and necessity on a national scale and containing appropriate safeguards against the conduct of operations which result, or which are reasonably certain to result, in destructive competition.[250] The result was that in *Gateway Elimination*[251] rules and regulations[252] were promulgated

---

[249]104 M.C.C. 820, 825.

[250]The ICC relied in large part upon the decision in *Removal of Truckload Lot Restrictions,* 106 M.C.C. 455, aff'd, *Regular Common Carrier Conference v. United States,* 307 F. Supp. 941, for its authority to proceed under 49 U.S.C. §308(a).

[251]119 M.C.C. 170, 119 M.C.C. 530, aff'd in *Thompson Van Line Inc. et al. v. U.S. and I.C.C.,* CA No. 74-860, U.S. Dist. Ct. for D.C., April 28, 1975. The case presented two issues. The first was whether the gateway elimination rule constituted an amendment or revocation of certificates requiring an adjudicatory procedure or whether it was an example of a reasonable term or limitation which the ICC can from time to time impose as the public convenience and necessity require. Second, if the gateway elimination rule did effect an amendment or revocation of certificates, could the ICC nevertheless proceed by rule making under *American Airlines, Inc. v. CAB,* 359 F. 2d 624. The court found that where carriers have tacked their authorities in the past, absent express tacking authorization in the certificates, such tacking does not constitute such a part of their certificates that subsequent change of ICC policy constitutes an amendment or revocation of the carriers' certificates. Rather, that change of ICC policy, consistent with long-standing ICC interpretation, constitutes the exercise of the ICC's obligation under 49 U.S.C. §308(a) to attach reason-

for the elimination of gateways for irregular route motor common carriers. The rules enable irregular-route carriers to avoid gateways if the most direct highway distance between the points to be served is not less than 80 percent of the highway distance between these points over the carrier's authorized routing through the gateway. In other words, where a carrier by using the direct highway route can save up to 20 percent of its authorized-route mileage, then it may eliminate its gateway. As a corollary, gateway operations involving more than 20 percent circuity would have to be discontinued unless the carrier filed an appropriate application seeking direct-service authority which was granted by the I.C.C. An exception is made on movements of 300 miles or less.

Change in Route; Alternate Route; Elimination of Gateway

Section 208(b)[253] provides that "A common carrier by motor vehicle operating under any such certificates may occasionally deviate from the route over which, and/or the fixed termini between which, it is authorized to operate under the certificate, under such general or special rules and regulations as the Commission may prescribe." Under the deviation rules the Commission may refuse to permit deviation whenever a situation exists which is not in harmony with the general purpose and intent of those rules.[254]

The Commission and the courts have approved in special classes of cases a modified standard or lesser measure of proof of public convenience and necessity, and although the Commission has dispensed with the requirement of public evidence, alternate route applicants must meet af-

---

able terms and conditions to the privileges granted by the certificate. The court felt that the ICC must retain flexibility to reevaluate its policy and, where conditions require, to change that policy.

[252]49 CFR §1065. The proceeding was concerned only with irregular-route motor common carriers. A regular-route motor carrier operates according to a predetermined plan, habitually uses certain fixed routes, operates between fixed termini, has terminals devoted to the expeditious handling of traffic, maintains a constant periodicity in service, and observes definite or published schedules or their equivalent. *Transportation Activities, Brady Transfer & Storage Co.,* 47 M.C.C. 23, affirmed *Brady Transfer & Storage Co. v. United States,* 80 F. Supp. 110, affirmed per curiam 335 U.S. 875. *Fleetlines, Inc., v. Arrowhead Freight Lines,* 54 M.C.C. 279, affirmed, *Arrowhead v. U.S.,* 115 F. Supp. 537. Cf. *Century-Matthews Motor Freight, Inc. v. Thrum,* 173 F. 2d 454; and *Byers Transp. Co. v. United States,* 49 F. Supp. 828. In any event, regular-route carriers are permitted to traverse shorter routes under specific circumstances pursuant to the ICC's Superhighway and Deviation rules (49 CFR 1042) or by the filing of specific alternate-route applications. The rules are not applicable to carriers joining grants of irregular-and regular-route authority.

[253]49 U.S.C. 308(b).

[254]*Preston Trucking Co., Inc., Extension,* 82 M.C.C. 51, 63.

firmatively certain other well-established proof requirements that may be properly substituted for public evidence. An excellent expression of the doctrine underlying the alternate route theory is contained in *Cooper's Express — Extension — Alternate Route:*[255]

> We have consistently recognized a distinction between the measure of proof required to sustain the granting of an application seeking authority to improve an existing and competitively effective service and one seeking authority to institute a new service. In determining these so-called alternate route applications, the essential issue presented is whether applicant is actually engaged in the transportation of traffic, in substantial volume, between the termini of the proposed alternate or direct route and is at present in a position effectively to compete with other carriers for such traffic, or whether the new route will enable applicant either to institute a new service not theretofore conducted, or to institute a service so different from that theretofore provided as materially to alter the competitive situation to the injury of existing carriers. In the case of the former, we are justified in granting the authority sought solely upon proof that the proposed operation would result in operating economies, which, although primarily a benefit to the applicant, result in an indirect benefit to the public through the medium of more efficient service. In the latter case, however, where the use of the alleged alternate route would amount to the institution of a new service, or would provide applicant with a substantial competitive advantage not theretofore enjoyed, we must insist upon definite proof of a need for the proposed new service.

Historically, in motor carrier operations, routes that are ten per cent or more circuitous have been considered noncompetitive. This presumption has, in fact, been reduced to a regulation by the Commission in its rules governing deviations by motor carriers from their authorized regular routes or required gateways. It is, of course, recognized that in proper cases the presumption reflected by the regulations may be rebutted. However, the Commission itself has established that in practically no case can a reduction of twenty-five percent or more be tolerated. In *G. N. Childress, Elimination of Sanford Gateway,*[256] the Commission held that a reduction in mileage ranging from twenty-three per cent to twenty-nine per cent "would alter the competitive situation in instances where, as here, the one way movements are three hundred miles or more." The reasoning underlying the conclusion of the Commission in the *Childress* case is, of course, apparent. The Commission has simply recognized that through merger and route extensions many carriers now possess operating rights which theoretically authorize them, through tacking, to conduct unnatural or abnormal operations.

---

[255]51 M.C.C. 411. See *Riggs Dairy Express, Inc., Elimination of Gateway,* 66 M.C.C. 775; *Yale T. Corp. v. United States,* 210 F. Supp. 862, aff'd 373 U.S. 540.
[256]61 M.C.C. 421, 428.

Because of the complexity of carrier certificates the only valid test to be applied to alternate route or change in gateway proposals is that which determines whether the applicant is presently competitive over its existing service routes. If the applicant is competitive, other carriers cannot be adversely affected and a lesser standard of proof of public convenience may be imposed because, in fact, no new service is created. In determining competitiveness one of the elements or factors meriting consideration is profitability. If existing operations over presently authorized routes are shown to be profitable, and the applicant otherwise meets the standards of proof applicable in alternate route cases, it may be assumed no change in the competitive picture will result and no new service will be generated. Unless profitability is considered as an element it is possible for carriers to stimulate unnatural traffic movements over unnecessarily long and circuitous routes for the sole purpose of creating evidence in an attempt to meet the test of substantiality of operations.

Inherent in the question whether an applicant is effectively and efficiently competing with other carriers is the question whether an applicant's operations are bona fide. While the Commission ordinarily refers to an operation as impracticable because of the circuity involved, inherent in such a finding is the unprofitability of highly circuitous operations. That profitability is an issue in alternate route cases is established by the Commission's decisions in *Motorways, Inc., Extension — Alternate Route*[257] and *Pinson Transfer Company, Inc., Extension — Cincinnati, Ohio.*[258] In denying the application in the *Motorways* case, the Commission stated in part as follows:

> There is no evidence whatever that applicant ever transported any local traffic between Topeka and points on its line in Nebraska and, in consideration of the circuity of operation which would have been necessary, it is extremely doubtful whether such operations could have been conducted profitably. The distance between Topeka and Lincoln over applicant's presently authorized routes is 302 miles, as compared with 182 miles over the direct route here considered, and it is difficult to understand how applicant could effectivey compete with existing carriers over a route more than 66 per cent circuitous. Although the percentage of circuity is decreased when considering long-distance movement to or from points west of Denver, the fact remains that any operations conducted by applicant between Topeka and Lincoln over its authorized routes involved 120 miles of operation which would have been unnecessary had direct-route carriers handled the traffic. In this connection, it might be noted that applicant has consistently operated at a loss since it has been participating in the interline movement with Ringsby.

[257]MC-52912 (Sub-No. 17), decided June 18, 1952.
[258]71 M.C.C. 525.

There is little doubt that Ringsby could more economically operate between Denver and Topeka if permitted to use the route here proposed, but such fact alone is not controlling. Ringsby is not the applicant herein and we must consider the effect of the granting of the authority sought upon applicant's service. By the use of the proposed route, applicant or any carrier operating under applicant's certificate would be in a position to institute an entirely new service between Topeka and Nebraska points in competition with carriers with which it may not now effectively compete. A grant of authority for the institution of such a new service may not be justified on a showing of operating economies alone, and we find no basis for a finding that the proposed operation is required by the present or future public convenience and necessity. Compare *Cooper's Exp., Inc., Extension — Alternate Route*, 51 M.C.C. 411.

In the *Pinson Transfer Company, Inc.*, case,[259] — the applicant for alternate route authority was restricted on its service route to certain truckload averages due to highway limitations and topography of the routes, whereas higher truckload averages could be transported over the proposed alternate route. The contentions of protestants were presented in the decision as follows:

The O.K. Trucking Company, a common carrier of general commodities over regular routes, transports from 10 to 15 truckloads of freight a day between Cincinnati and Huntington, and 4 to 8 truckloads a day between Cincinnati and Ashland over U.S. Highway 52. It interlines an undisclosed number of tandem trailers at Cincinnati destined to Ashland and Huntington, and also at these latter points for Cincinnati. It does not consider applicant a competitor but feels that should the instant application be granted, applicant would definitely be in a competitive position by virtue of having their truckload capacity increased 50 percent, and having a route over which it could pull the large trailers used on interchange movements. Reinhardt Transfer Company, a regular-route general-Between Cincinnati and Ashland, over U.S. Highway 52. Among the com-commodity carrier, also operates between Cincinnati and Huntington, and modities it transports is steel from Ashland. It contends that applicant is not now in a position to compete profitably in this steel traffic, but would be if the proposed route is granted. The Maxwell Company holds contract-carrier authority to transport steel from Ashland and Huntington to Cincinnati, over irregular routes. It has many competitors for this traffic but does not consider applicant one of them.

After setting forth the tests usually considered in alternate route cases the Commission held:

Even though a grant of the proposed route would result in a saving to applicant by making available to it a shorter and safer route, in our opinion the evidence does not warrant a conclusion that applicant has satis-

[259]The contentions of protestants and the findings of the Commission are set forth at pp. 527-28 of the report.

factorily met the above tests. Its authorized service route is over highways that do not have the capability of handling the capacity which can be transported over the proposed route. The one opposing carrier which indicates its volume of traffic between Cincinnati, Ashland, and Huntington, over U.S. Highway 52, transports an estimated 14 to 23 truckloads daily, as compared to applicant's less than 0.5 truckload a day from Cincinnati to Huntington and Ashland. We do not feel that this represents effective competition. Furthermore if applicant is able to increase its unit load capacity to 50 percent, and is placed in a position to compete actively for interline traffic, competitive situation would not remain unchanged in this respect. Clearly the proposed route, if granted, would place applicant in a position whereby it would be afforded a substantial competitive benefit not previously enjoyed.

We find that applicant has failed to establish that the present or future public convenience and necessity require the proposed operation; and that the application should be denied.

The Commission recognized in the *Pinson* case, as it must whenever the issue is affirmatively raised, the question of the relative economic feasibility of past as against the proposed operations. Where there is doubt that past operations could have been conducted profitably and the evidence shows that the operations proposed would result in a substantial competitive benefit not previously enjoyed, then the new service must be denied in the absence of an affirmative showing of public need. As the Commission stated in *Cooper's Express, Inc., Extension — Alternate Routes:*[260]

> Where the use of the alleged alternate route would amount to the institution of a new service, or would provide applicant with a substantial competitive advantage not theretofore enjoyed, we must insist upon definite proof of a need for the proposed new service.

The sharp reduction in operating time that would result from a grant of alternate route authority to a carrier is, in itself, sufficient justification for denial of an application. In *England Bros. Truck Line, Inc., Extension — Alternate Route,*[261] the Commission denied an application for alternate route authority between Dallas, Texas, and Memphis, Tennessee. The Commission stated as follows at sheets 7 and 8 of its report:

> Even disregarding this aspect of the proceeding, it is our opinion that a grant of this authority would result in a change in the existing competitive situation. Applicant contends that operation over the alternate route would result in a decrease of its running time of about 2 hours, but this estimate is based on the assumption that there would be a 1 hour stopover at

[260]51 M.C.C. 411, 414-15.
[261]MC-29955 (Sub-No. 14), decided December 4, 1959.

Camden. We think it clear that use of this route, which is 115 miles shorter than the existing service route, would mean saving in transit time of closer to 3 than to 2 hours. Applicant now provides some next-morning service from Memphis to Dallas, but to do so it must dispatch its vehicles by 3:00 p.m. A saving of 3 hours would permit applicant to provide next-morning service on shipments dispatched in the early evening rather than in mid-afternoon. This would clearly increase the attractiveness of its service to shippers of freight destined to consignees at either Memphis or Dallas, and enable it to compete much more effectively for local freight, whereas the great majority of its present business consists of interline freight. This would have the effect of allowing applicant to institute a new service, without any showing of a need therefor.

In *Maryland Transp. Co. Ext. — Specified Commodities*,[262] the entire Commission affirmed that in a gateway elimination proceeding, "it must be shown that the proposing carrier is an effective competitor as to substantially all of the commodities and substantially all of the points within the scope of its pertinent outstanding authority." This has been uniformly interpreted as imposing upon applicant the burden of showing that it has provided a substantially complete territorial service through its gateway between all its authorized origins and destinations.[263] In order to effectuate this general policy, the Commission requires that applications seeking the eliminations of a gateway be granted or denied in the context of applicant's complete operations, and that the partial elimination of a gateway will not be sanctioned upon a mere showing of operating convenience.[264]

The general policy established in the *Maryland* case, *supra*, and subsequent related proceedings has been clearly interpreted as imposing upon applicant the burden of showing that it is an effective competitor as to substantially all of the points in its authorized territory, and that it is not enough for applicant to show that it has handled even a substantial volume of traffic if it has provided service only at selected points.[265]

In *Gordon's Transports, Inc., Extension — Alternate Route, Memphis and Birmingham*,[266] The Commission said:

[262]83 M.C.C. 451, 455.
[263]*Service Trucking Co., Inc., Ext. — Frozen Pies & Pastries*, 88 M.C.C. 697; *Yale Transport Corp., Elimination of Gateways*, 89 M.C.C. 527; and *Bowman Transp., Inc., Ext. — Substitution of Gateways*, 100 M.C.C. 314.
[264]*Overnite Transp. Co. Elimination of Gateway*, 103 M.C.C. 135; *Bowman Transp., Inc., Ext. — Substitution of Gateways, supra*; and *Atlas Van-Lines, Inc., Ext. — Elimination of Gateways*, 105 M.C.C. 156.
[265]*Youngblood Truck Lines, Inc., Elimination of Gateway*, 89 M.C.C. 541; affirmed 221 F. Supp. 809; *Dallas & Mavis Forwarding Co., Mc., Extension*, 106 M.C.C. 154.
[266]71 M.C.C. 93, 95.

Where proof of existing operations is shown only over an alternate route, the application must be denied . . . unless it can be found with assurance that the past service . . ., had there been no prior grant of alternative route, could have been performed with equal effectiveness competitively over the service route.

The Commission held in *Powell Truck Lines, Inc., Extension of Operations — Direct Routes:*[267]

The direct route would place it in a position to make first-morning delivery. The proposal here is neither a mere improvement of existing facilities, nor a realignment of highways of a route already operated, nor a minor extension within a territory already served. It is, in effect, the entering into a new field of transportation, and the institution of a class and quality of service made possible only by the acquiring of routes far outside a normal field of operations.

In *Pic-Walsh Freight Co.,*[268] it was held that a savings of 3.5 hours could result in a new service, depending upon the applicant's arrangement of its schedules. Since there was no evidence produced on this point the application was denied with the Commission holding (pp. 390-91):

Admittedly, it would experience a saving in transit time of at least 3.5 hours, and what effect this might have upon applicant's service we cannot say with assurance from the evidence of record. There is no evidence of its arrival and departure times, and thus we cannot determine whether by rearranging its schedule of operations applicant might improve its present service from generally second-day delivery to consistently second-morning delivery, or better. All things considered we are persuaded that applicant has failed to sustain its burden of proof and the application should be denied.

In *Great Southern Trucking Company — Extension,*[269] the Commission denied an application involving an improvement of transit time of four or less hours. There the Commission stated:

In No. MC-2900 (Sug-No. 80), the proposed alternate route between Baxley and Greenville would enable applicant to operate between Jacksonville and Charlotte in 13.4 to 14.2 hours instead of the present 17 to 17.8 hours. Its present operating time between Jacksonville and Greenville averages 14.6 to 14.8 hours. Approximately 13 percent of the shipments handled by applicant between Jacksonville and Charlotte are 1 day in transit, as are 46 per cent of the shipments between Jacksonville and Greenville. In the circumstances, if authority to operate over this proposed alternate route were granted, applicant's operating time between Charlotte and Jackson-

[267]33 M.C.C. 93, 100.
[268]83 M.C.C. 383.
[269]67 M.C.C. 467, reversed 69 M.C.C. 771.

ville would be less than its present time between Greenville and Jacksonville, enabling it to render a definitely improved overnight service on a substantially greater portion of its shipments between Charlotte and the latter 2 points in 11.3 to 12 hours, affording shippers regular overnight service, it seems clear that a new competitive service would result from granting the application. This obviously would alter the present competitive situation without a showing of public need therefor and is not warranted.

In *Houff Transfer, Inc., Extension — Virginia and West Virginia,*[270] the Commission stated as follows:

> Applicant's currently held authority is the result of a series of piecemeal purchases over a period of years. Any illogic in the consolidated authority is not of this Commission's making but rather the proposal of the consolidator. When purchases were made, applicant was charged with knowledge that unified operations would require observance of certain gateways and the resultant use of circuitous routes, if it chose to combine the authorities. It now seeks elimination of certain of these gateways; and at the same time, in the title proceeding it seeks substantial expansion of its presently held authority commodity-wise.

The requirement of bona fides of past operation was spelled out in *Cooper M. Lines, Inc., — Purchase — Parrish Dray Lines, Inc.,*[271] where the Commission on further hearing found that:

> Although vendor has held authority to transport general freight to and from points in Alabama for more than 10 years, its first shipment did not occur until January 13, 1949.

✿   ✿   ✿

> Applicants first negotiated for purchase of the considered rights in July 1949. Prior thereto, vendor's operations in Alabama consisted of but three shipments, transported from Birmingham to Sumter, and were practically nonexistent. Traffic developed subsequent to commencement of negotiations for sale of the rights or shortly prior thereto is entitled to little weight in determining the nature and extent of vendor's operations. Compare *Chicago Exp., Inc. — Purchase — Huck's Transfer, Inc.,* 58 M.C.C. 812 (not printed in full), decided November 5, 1951.

The Commission has consistently held that traffic development subsequent to commencement of negotiations for the sale of rights or shortly prior thereto is entitled to little weight in determining the nature and extent of vendor's operations, as the purchasers then obviously have a direct incentive in building up vendor's operations.[272]

---

[270]Docket No. MC-66900 (Sub-No. 19).

[271]58 M.C.C. 283.

[272]*P.I.E. — Purchase — Browning,* 58 M.C.C. 629, 637; *Star — Purchase — De-Beradinis,* MC-F-5275, July 2, 1953; *McCormick — Purchase — Lowell,* MC-F-5545, December 2, 1954.

Thus, at the risk of being repetitious, to justify grant of alternate route authority, applicant must show that it is transporting a substantial volume of traffic over a practicable and feasible route in effective competition with existing carriers; that use of proposed route will result in economies, increased efficiency, and flexibility of operation; and that the competitive situation between applicant and existing carriers will not be materially altered.[273] In applying these tests, traffic to be considered may be that moving between the termini or that moving through the termini to and from points beyond, but in either case it must be traffic transported under appropriate authority over a feasible route.[274]

Where applicant's present service operations are conducted over both irregular and regular routes, application for an alternate regular route will be considered as one for elimination of a gateway.[275] In an application seeking elimination of gateway by grant of authority to operate over more direct routes, convenience and necessity may be found in operating economies and efficiencies which will benefit applicant directly and the shipping public indirectly. In addition, however, applicant must establish affirmatively that it is transporting a substantial volume of traffic from and to points involved by operating in good faith through the gateway in effective competition with existing carriers, and that elimination of gateway will not enable it to substitute a new service or a service so different as to improve materially its competitive position to the detriment of existing carriers.[276]

A thorough discussion of the issues involved in change of gateway cases is found in *Bowman Transp., Inc., Ext. — Substitution of Gateways*,[277] there the Commission said (pp. 325-328):

> A gateway results from a motor carrier combining two grants of irregular-route authority at a point common to each—the gateway point— and conducting operations through from points authorized in one grant of authority to points authorized in the other. As a result of ensuing circuity, inadequate highways traversed, or for other reasons, certain operating inefficiencies *interior* to the carrier may well result from such a gateway operation. However, in the general interest of minimizing economic waste and promoting a stable, efficient, and economical transportation system, we will, in the absence of a showing of public convenience and necessity, authorize

---

[273]*Davidson Transfer & Storage Co. Extension*, 81 M.C.C. 447, 452; *Preston Trucking Co., Inc., Extension*, 82 M.C.C. 51, 54-5; *Hoover Motor Exp. Co., Inc., Extension*, 81 M.C.C. 93, 96.

[274]*Barber Transp. Co. Extension*, 79 M.C.C. 690, 693-4.

[275]*Chicago Exp. Inc., Extension*, 79 M.C.C. 384, 386.

[276]*Glotzman Extension*, 79 M.C.C. 227, 229. See also *Yale Transport Corp. v. United States*, 210 F. Supp. 862, aff'd 373 U.S. 540.

[277]100 M.C.C. 314.

a gateway carrier to perform more direct operations, on a showing that no substantial *exterior* advantages would result which would benefit it competitively vis-a-vis other carriers.[278] The crux of the matter is that if existing for-hire motor service is not shown to be inadequate, that is if the shipping public is not shown to need the improved service of the applicant, and if such improved service to reasonable appearances would dilute the traffic of existing carriers, applicant's improved service to that extent would be disruptive of the competitive situation and inimical to the general public interest in a stable and dependable for-hire transportation system.

When two separate grants of authority are joined at a gateway by a common carrier, a service results for which no public need has been demonstrated. The usual inefficiencies resulting from this type of operation are of the carrier's own choosing, and the mere fact of such operation is no assurance of need for such service or of economy and efficiency of operation. As a result, only when the elimination of whatever specific inefficiencies which may be involved is found not to present a substantial hazard to existing carriers, will we consider granting more direct authority. This was well stated in *Martin Van Lines, Inc., Extension — 12 States*, 79 M.C.C. 767, at 771, by division 1:

It must be noted that these gateways which applicant must observe are not a result of any grant of authority to applicant by this Commission, but are the result of applicant's voluntarily combining or tacking of several individual operating authorities which were granted by us to other carriers and purchased by applicant. There is no requirement of this Commission that applicant join separate operating rights and render service to the public from points in one authority to points authorized under another operating right. It is not our action that contemplates operation in a circuitous manner, but is a matter of operation undertaken by applicant on its own volition. To authorize applicant to conduct the proposed operations which it cannot now perform efficiently and effectively in competition with existing carriers, without any showing of need therefor, would be directly contrary to the mandate of the act.

° ° °

The criteria for elimination of a gateway were set forth firmly by division 5 in *Childress — Elimination Sanford Gateway*, 61 M.C.C. 421, at 428, as follows:

(1) whether applicant is actually transporting a substantial volume of traffic from and to the points involved by operating in good faith through the gateway and, in so operating, is effectively and efficiently competing with the existing carriers, and (2) whether the elimination of the gateway requirement would enable applicant to institute a new service or a service so different from that presently provided as to materially improve applicant's competitive position to the detriment of existing carriers. In the

---

[278]Essentially identical criteria govern alternate-route applications, wherein a carrier by joinder of two regular routes seeks a shortened alternate route between certain of the points served on its regular routes. See for example *Pacific Intermountain Exp. Co. Ext. — Los Angeles to Wichita, supra.*

former instance, a grant of the authority sought is justified solely upon proof that the proposed operation would result in operating economies, which although primarily a benefit to the applicant, indirectly benefit the public through the medium of more efficient and economical service. In the latter instance, however, where the elimination of the gateway requirement would allow a new service, or would provide applicant with a substantial competitive advantage not previously enjoyed, it is incumbent upon applicant to prove public convenience and necessity the same as in any other application for new authority.

*   *   *

The requirement that an applicant show that it has provided a substantially complete territorial service through its required gateway between all authorized origins and destinations was adhered to in *C & H Transp. Co., Inc., Ext. – Elimination of Tex. Gateway,* 71 M.C.C. 483, *Ace Lines, Inc., Extension – Elimination of Gateway,* 79 M.C.C. 685, *Martin Van Lines, Inc., Extension – 12 States, supra,* and *Yale Transport Corp. Elimination of Gateways,* 89 M.C.C. 527. Additionally, in *Ace Lines, Inc., Extension – Elimination of Gateway, supra,* division 1 unambiguously stated that a substantially complete service throughout applicant's authorized territory covering the full range of authorized commodities was also required (79 M.C.C. at 689):

In order to justify a grant of authority to eliminate a grateway between two irregular-route territories, it must be shown that as to substantially all of the commodities involved and the area which applicant is authorized to serve through the gateway it is an effective competitor. It is not enough to show that from selected points applicant has transported a segment of the considered traffic.

Also, in this report, division 1, as a matter of policy, refused to consider certain of applicant's gateway traffic which it failed to show was within the scope of its commodity authority. See 79 M.C.C. at 688-689, and *Home Transp. Co., Inc., Ext. – Removal Marietta Gateway,* 84 M.C.C. 671, 677.

Thereafter in *Maryland Transp. Co. Ext. – Specified Commodities, supra,* 83 M.C.C. at 455, the entire Commission affirmed that "°°°it must be shown that the proposing carrier is an effective competitor as to substantially all of the commodition and between substantially all of the points within the °°°pertinent outstanding authority," denying the application in the absence of such a showing. See also *Service Trucking Co., Inc., Ext. – Frozen Pies & Pastries, supra.* An apparently opposite conclusion that a partial elimination of a gateway had been authorized in *Bowman Transp., Inc., Elimination of Gateways,* 73 M.C.C. 341, was distinguished on the ground that public convenience and necessity had been shown therein for the grant of such authority.

The burden of proof in these cases rests clearly on applicant, and in the absence of applicant's negativing the apparent probability of resulting enhancement of its competitive position, its application must be denied. See

Pacific Intermountain Exp. Co. Ext. — Los Angeles to Wichita, supra, 84 M.C.C. at 414, and the cases cited above. (Footnotes eliminated.)

Superhighway Rules

The *Superhighway Rules — Motor Common Carriers of Property,*[279] enable a certificated regular-route motor common carrier of general commodities, with or without exceptions, to operate over superhighways (including highways connecting such superhighways with the carrier's authorized regular service route) between the point of departure from and the point of return to the carrier's authorized regular service route, provided that the operation is conducted within the guidelines specified *either* in the "25-mile" rule [section 1042.3(a)(1)] *or* the "85-percent" provision [section 1042.3(a)(2)]. Briefly, the "25-mile" rule requires that the superhighway route (including highways connecting such superhighway route with the carrier's authorized regular service route) between the point of departure from and the point of return to the carrier's authorized regular service route must (1) extend in the same general direction as the carrier's authorized regular service route, *and* (2) be wholly within 25 airline-miles of the carrier's authorized regular service route. The "85-percent" provision requires that the distance over the superhighway route (including highways connecting such superhighway route with the carrier's authorized regular service route) between the point of departure from and the point of return to the carrier's authorized regular service route must be not less than 85 percent of the distance between such points over the carrier's authorized regular service route. The "intermediate-point service provision" [section 1042.3 (b)] of the Superhighway Rules allows a carrier conducting superhighway operations under the above-described "25-mile" rule, which carrier is authorized to serve all intermediate points (without regard to nominal exceptions) on its underlying certificated regular service route between the point of departure from and the point of return to the said service route, to serve intermediate points on and within 1 airline-mile of the said superhighway route (and the highways connecting the said superhighway route with the carrier's authorized regular service route) in the same manner and subject to corresponding service limitations as de-

---

[279]49 CFR 1042.3. These rules, which were promulgated in *Motor Service on Interstate Highways—Passengers,* 110 M.C.C. 514, have been extensively clarified and interpreted by the Commission in *Property Motor Carrier Superhighway Rules.* 117 M.C.C. 119.

scribed in the pertinent certificate or certificates of public convenience and necessity.

The purpose of the superhighway rules is to expedite changeovers from antiquated authorized routes to new superhighways without upsetting the existing competitive balance preserved by ICC regulations.[280] The theory is that a motor carrier's original showing of public convenience and necessity can reasonably be expected to apply to a new route if the differences between the new route and the authorized route are sufficiently slight. The Commission's interpretation of the 25-mile rule[281] ensures that the superhighway route will not be drastically shorter than the authorized route, and it thereby prevents a carrier from taking advantage of the superhighway rules as to a way to enter new markets without having to apply to the Commission for a certificate of public convenience and necessity.

Transportation of Mail

The motor carrier licensing provisions of the Postal Reorganization Act[282] are found in Section 5215. It provides in part:

(a) Any person who was a contractor under a star route, mail messenger, or contract motor vehicle service contract on the effective date of this section (or successor in interest to any such person), shall, upon application to the [Interstate Commerce] Commission for the territory within which such contractor operated on or before the effective date of this section be issued a certificate of public convenience and necessity as a motor carrier for the transportation of mail by the Commission without the Commission's requiring further proof that the public convenience and necessity will be served by such operation and without further proceedings.

(b) Applications of persons who were not contractors on the effective date of this section shall be decided in accordance with applicable Commission procedure.

Star route contractors are transporters of mail operating in essentially local service under negotiated contracts with the Post Office Department for a term of 4 years. Some, however, are not "local" carriers, but perform operations over long distances, or within a rather vast territory. Mail

---

[280]*Motor Service on Interstate Highways—Passengers,* 110 M.C.C. 514, 528.

[281]The Commission has consistently interpreted the rules to require that the authorized route be wholly within 25 miles of the superhighway route. See *Commercial Motor Freight, Inc., Extension — Crawfordsville, Ind.,* 114 M.C.C. 500, 519-20; *Property Motor Carrier Superhighway Rules,* 117 M.C.C. 514, 150 n. 10; *Associated Truck Lines, Inc. v. Wolverine Express, Inc.,* 123 M.C.C. 206, 220.

[282]Public Law 91-375. 39 U.S.C. 5215.

messenger and contract motor vehicle service are similar types of local operations.

The Postal Act (Section 5212) provides for continuation by the Postal Service of star route contracting.

In *Implementation of Public Law 91-375*,[283] the Commission promulgated procedures to implement the "grandfather" certification provisions of Public Law 91-375 with respect to star route, mail messenger, and contract motor vehicle operators, in the transportation of mail by motor vehicle, in interstate or foreign commerce. The procedures comferred upon qualified star route, mail messenger, and contract motor vehicle operators status as common carriers by motor vehicle pursuant to the terms of the Postal Act and the provisions of the Interstate Commerce Act. Multi-State operators were permitted to achieve this status by applying for and receiving a Postal certificate of public convenience and necessity. Single-state operators had the choice of having such a certificate issued or electing the simpler procedure of being included within the terms of the General Postal certificate of exemption authorized in the report.

The Commission found that transportation of mail by motor carriers, holding contracts with the Postal Service as star route, mail messenger, or contract motor vehicle operators on the effective date of Section 5215 of the Postal Reorganization Act, in interstate or foreign commerce, and whose operations are conducted only within a single State, is in fact of such nature, character, or quantity as not substantially to affect or impair uniform regulation by this Commission of transportation by motor carriers engaged in interstate or foreign commerce in effectuating the national transportation policy; and that a general postal certificate exempting such operations should be issued.

[283]113 M.C.C. 14.

6

Certificates of Public Convenience and Necessity for Water Carriers

The Applicable Statutory Provisions

Section 309(c) of the Interstate Commerce Act[1] provides:

"Subject to section 310, upon application as provided in this section the Commission shall issue a certificate to any qualified applicant therefor, authorizing the whole or any part of the operations covered by the application, if the Commission finds that the applicant is fit, willing, and able properly to perform the service proposed and to conform to the provisions of this part and the requirements, rules and regulations of the Commission thereunder, and that the proposed service, to the extent authorized by the certificate, is or will be required by the present or future public convenience and necessity; otherwise such application shall be denied."

Section 309 (d)[2] provides:

"Such certificate shall specify the route or routes over which, or the ports to and from which, such carrier is authorized to operate, and, at the time of issuance and from time to time thereafter, there shall be attached to the exercise of the privileges granted by such certificate such reasonable terms, conditions, and limitations as the public convenience and necessity may from time to time require, including terms, conditions, and limitations as to the extension of the route or routes of the carrier, and such other terms, and conditions, and limitations as are necessary to carry out, with respect to the operations of the carrier, the requirements of this part or those established by the Commission pursuant thereto; *Provided, however,* That no terms, conditions, or limitations shall restrict the right of the carrier to add to its equipment, facilities, or service within the scope of such certificate, as the development of the business and the demands of the public shall require, or the right of the carrier to extend its services over uncompleted portions of waterway projects now or hereafter authorized by Congress, over the completed portions of which it already operates, as soon as such uncompleted portions are open for navigation."

[1]49 U.S.C. (909(c). Comparable provisions — Sections 207(a) and 410(c).
[2]49 U.S.C. 909(d). Comparable provisions — Sections 208(8) and 410(c).

Criteria Used in the Determination of Applications

Certain principles have been established in common carrier application proceedings which bear on the quantum of proof required to meet the statutory test to acquire authority — present or future public convenience and necessity for, and the fitness, willingness and ability to perform, the proposed service. These are set forth below.

An applicant for operating authority has a burden of showing that the proposed service is required by public convenience and necessity, and where service is already available from another carrier in the territory involved, it must be shown that the existing service is inadequate in some material respect.[3] Applicant must establish that existing water carriers cannot, or will not, meet the reasonable transportation requirements of the shippers between the points involved. Sound economic conditions in transportation require that carriers already serving a territory or locality be accorded the right to transport all traffic which they can handle adequately, efficiently and economically before a new operation is authorized.[4] So long as such carriers are ready, willing, and able to handle the traffic it would not be in furtherance of the national transportation policy to subject the carriers to unnecessary competition of a new service.[5] However, reasonable competition is in the public interest and regulated monopoly is not a complete substitute therefor.[6]

The fact that adequate service by other modes of transportation exists is no bar to a grant of operating rights.[7] Because of the inherent advantages of water transportation, including low transportation charges, it has been consistently found that the shipping public is entitled to

[3]*Calmar S. S. Corp. Extension,* 306 I.C.C. 765.

[4]*Union Barge Line Corp. Extension,* 311 I.C.C. 447, 465; *Moran Towing & Transp. Co. Inc. Ext. — Great Lakes,* 315 I.C.C. 591, 596; *Indian Towing Co., Inc., Contract Carrier Application,* 309 I.C.C. 473, 478.

[5]*Calmar S. S. Corp. Extension, supra.*

[6]*Narian,* 303 I.C.C. 529, 531.

[7]Consult *Sea-Land Service, Inc. Ext. — Pac. Coastline.* 329 I.C.C. 447, 456; *Coyle Lines, Inc., Ext. — Chattahoochee and Flint Rivers,* 323 I.C.C. 386, 392 *S. C. Loveland Co. Ext. — Tampa,* 313 I.C.C. 121, 126; *Yazoo Barge Line Com. Car. Application,* 305 I.C.C. 17, 19-20; *Woods Common Carrier Application,* 303 I.C.C. 158, 160; *Weyerhauser S. S. Co. Ext — Port Everglades,* 285 I.C.C. 765, 769; *Gulf Canal Lines, Inc., Ext. and Removal of Limitation,* 285 I.C.C. 291, 300; *Seatrain Lines, Inc., T.A. Applications,* 285 I.C.C. 83, 89; *Coyle Lines Inc., Ext. — Warrior River,* 265 I.C.C. 753, 757; *Yankton Barge Line Com. Car Application,* 265 I.C.C. 271, 276; *Inland Waters Corp. Ext. — Omaha,* 265 I.C.C. 207, 208; *Pan-Atlantic S.S. Corp. Ext. — Port St. Joe,* 265 I.C.C. 169, 176; *Canadian-Gulf Line Contr. Car. Application,* 260 I.C.C. 792, 795; *West Coast S.S. Co. Ext. — Crescent City,* 265 I.C.C. 577, 583; *McAllister Brothers, Inc., Extension-Steel,* 335 I.C.C. 52.

the transportation by water even though rail and motor transportation are available.[8]

In *McAllister Brothers, Inc., Extension — Steel*,[9] the Commission gave consideration to the position of railroad protestants that applicant had not demonstrated that its proposed service possessed any inherent advantages over rail service. The Commission said (pp. 54-55):

> In situations where a water carrier seeks authority to points presently served by rail carriers, we have repeatedly found that the availability of rail service does not preclude granting the application. Communities and shippers are entitled to adequate service by water as well as by rail because of the inherent advantage possessed by water carriers. *John I Hay Co. Extension — Malwaukee*, 285 I.C.C. 472; *Seatrain Lines, Inc., Temporary Authority Application*, 285 I.C.C. 83; *Bintliff Common Carrier Application*, 260 I.C.C. 727; *Canadian-Gulf Line Contract Carrier Application*, 260 I.C.C. 792; and *Yankton Barge Line Common Carrier Application*, 265 I.C.C. 271.

> We have long recognized certain inherent advantages in water transportation, but, without a doubt, the primary advantage, from a shipper's viewpoint, is that of low transportation charges. *Newtex S. S. Corp. Extension— Sulphur*, 285 I.C.C. 260; and *Woods Common Carrier Application*, 301 I.C.C. 158. In many instances the shipper support is predicated upon a mere expectancy of the lower transportation charges without positive evidence that such charges would actually result. In these circumstances we have found that the public is entitled to the benefits of water transportation including the advantage of low rates, if such be the case. *S. C. Loveland Co., Inc., Extension — Tampa, Fla.*, 313 I.C.C. 121, affirmed, *Atlantic Coast Line Railroad Company v. United States*, 202 F. Supp. 456. In application proceedings the desire by the shipper for a lower rate does not normally justify a grant of authority. However, we recognize that the expectancy of a lower rate is a factor for consideration when the proposed service is to be rendered by a water carrier when that mode has traditionally offered lower rates. *Seatrain Lines, Inc., Extension — Savannah*, 285 I.C.C. 509. Protestants argue that the record does not contain any cost data from which it may be determined that applicant's service will effectuate a lower transportation charge than that presently maintained by protestants. Such data is, of course, desirable, but not essential; its absence does not require that the application be denied. *Atlantic Coast Line Railroad Company v. United States, supra*, cf. *Bulk Food Carriers, Inc. — Exemption Application*, 326 I.C.C. 106. In numerous cases we have considered the possibility of lower transportation charges by applicants proposing an operation by water in instances where cost data were not submitted. E.g., *Yazoo Barge Line Common Carrier Application*, 305 I.C.C. 17; *Coyle Lines Inc. Ext. — Chattahoochee and Flint Rivers*, 323 I.C.C. 386; *Inland Waterways Corp. Extension of Operations — Omaha*, 265 I.C.C. 207; and *Pan-Atlantic S. S. Corp. Extension — Port Saint Joe*, 265 I.C.C. 169. In

[8]*Yazoo Barge Line Common Carrier Application*, 305 I.C.C. 17, 19-20.
[9]335 I.C.C. 52.

fact, in some instances where cost evidence was submitted in support of a lower rate in an application proceeding such evidence was disregarded as not conclusive and still the anticipated lower rates were given consideration. *Alaska Freight Lines, Inc., Common Carrier Application,* 285 I.C.C. 779; and *Sea-Land Service, Inc., Extension — Pacific Coastwise,* 329 I.C.C. 447.

The following cases demonstrate the criteria used by the Commission in determining the sufficiency of evidence presented to establish that public convenience and necessity require the service proposed. In *Union Barge Corp. Extension,*[10] where supporting shippers and members of public organizations were mainly concerned with additional water carrier service, the Commission denied the application stating that there was no showing of any material or substantial dissatisfaction on the part of the shipping public with the present services provided by other carriers, either by interchange with applicant or in their single-line services. In *Weyerhauser S.S. Co. Extension,*[11] the Commission said that shippers and communities were entitled to adequate transportation service by water with its inherent benefits and advantages upon proof of need, even though rail transportation was available. There, various receivers of green lumber in southern Florida needed additional water-carrier service if they were to compete with other receivers of lumber which obtained their supplies by water from Canadian or Pacific coast sources. Because of the inherent advantages of water transportation, including low transportation charges, the Commission has frequently held that the shipping public is entitled to water-carrier service where rail transportation is also available.[12]

In *S. C. Loveland Co., Inc., Extension,*[13] an application was granted by the Commission where applicant had demonstrated a public need for the proposed barge service between Atlantic coast points and Tampa; no water common-carrier service was available and the application was supported by shippers, water common carriers operating in the Gulf area, and by the local port authority. Although rail service was generally satisfactory, a large part of supporting shipper's present and future traffic was inherently suited to barge movement, and they were entitled to the benefits of water transportation; the Commission said that the authority granted would also enable applicant, through interline at Tampa, to

[10]304 I.C.C. 402, 409-10.
[11]285 I.C.C. 765, 769. See also *Sioux City & New Orleans Barge Lines, Inc., Extension,* 285 I.C.C. 463.
[12]*Woods,* 303 I.C.C. 158, 160; *Yazoo Barge Line,* 305 I.C.C. 17, 19.
[13]313 I.C.C. 121, 125-6; sustained in *Atlantic Coast Line R. Co. v. United States,* 202 F. Supp. 456.

provide a service not now available between the Atlantic coast area and ports in the Gulf area and along the Mississippi River. In *Oliver J. Olson & Co. Extension Tug and Barge*,[14] the Commission said that, in arriving at a conclusion on the weight of the evidence presented to establish that public convenience and necessity require the performance of a service with a different type of vessel in the transportation of the same commodities between the same ports previously authorized, consideration must be given to whether essentially the same or a new service is contemplated. The shipping public is entitled to a proposed service which would result in operating economies, primarily of benefit to the applicant, but also beneficial to the public through the medium of more efficient service.

In *Alaska Freight Lines, Inc.*,[15] the Commission refused to deny an application where there was considerable traffic available for regularly scheduled service even though protestants had been unable to augment their traffic at the particular ports involved. The Commission said that this did not necessarily establish absence of a need for additional water carriage and, furthermore, applicant proposed an entirely different type of operation from that of protestants. In *Garian*,[16] the Commission said that a public need existed for the service to be performed where applicant proposed to conduct a passenger service which catered to individuals and to small family groups, while protestant's present service was offered to larger groups on a charter-party basis; the involved resort area had a need for applicant's proposed service in addition to protestants present service in order to accommodate patrons in the area who desired lake cruise service.

Before an application can be approved by the Commission, an applicant must be found fit to conduct the proposed operations. This is demonstrated by the following cases. An applicant was selected in *Moran Towing & Trans. Co., Inc., Extension*,[17] as fit to conduct the freighting service authorized when it was a well-established, going concern, had considerable investment in various units of operating equipment, and had financial resources to acquire the necessary barges. An applicant was found fit to conduct the proposed operations in *S. C. Loveland Co., Inc., Extension*,[18] even though its capital was limited since its principal stockholder was able and willing to furnish additional funds as needed;

[14]285 I.C.C. 771, 777.
[15]285 I.C.C. 779, 788-9, 792.
[16]303 I.C.C. 529, 531.
[17]314 I.C.C. 287, 291-2.
[18]313 I.C.C. 121, 127. See also *Yazoo Barge Line*, 305 I.C.C. 17, 19.

the stockholder had many years' experience in barge transportation and had been applicant's president for many years. While applicant had not shown that the proposed operations would be successful, the Commission said that every new operation has the possibility of failure, and that alone does not warrant denial of the authority requested. An applicant was found financially fit in *Alaska Freight Lines, Inc.,*[19] where its past operations demonstrated an ability to perform the service proposed and its current assets were more than twice its current liabilities even though it was not in a position to make substantial profits because the entire income of an affiliate was derived from charter revenues.

Industrial Relationship

Industrial relationship with a carrier is not necessarily a ground for denying authority to conduct common (or contract) authority. While the Commission may give consideration to such a relationship in determining whether a particular transaction is consistent with the public interest, it is not a fact of controlling importance.[20]

Grant of a Certificate or Permit to a Private Water Carrier

The Commission following the decisions under Part II of the I.C. Act, has not in the past been willing to grant a certificate or permit to a private carrier to enable it to defray the expenses of one-way private carriage on the grounds that the grant of such authority would impair the competitive position of common and contract carriers.[21] There were instances in which the Commission acted favorably on applications even though carriers involved were carrying on substantial private carriage for their parent companies; however, such favorable action was taken principally under the grandfather clause.[22] In one case, *Ohio Barge Line, Inc., Extension — Coal,*[23] the Commission granted a permit to a wholly

---

[19]285 I.C.C. 779, 781.

[20]*Cornell Steamboat Co. — Purchase — Lowery,* 312 I.C.C. 55, 65. There are numerous water carriers industrially controlled and authorized to conduct operations under the Act. *Cornell Steamboat Co. — Purchase — Lowery, supra,* at p. 65.

[21]*Geraci Contract Carrier Application,* 7 M.C.C. 369; *Hardman Contract Carrier Application,* 48 M.C.C. 715; *American Coastal Lines, Inc.,* 285 I.C.C. 323; *Cornell Steamboat Co.,* 312 I.C.C. 55, 65; *Davison Chemical Corp. Applications,* 250 I.C.C. 291. The *Geraci* case was overruled in *TOTO Purchasing & Supply Co., Inc.,* 128 M.C.C. 873.

[22]*Warrior & Gulf Nav. Co. Control,* 250 I.C.C. 26; *Ohio Barge Line, Inc.,* 250 I.C.C. 57; *Weyerhauser Steamship Co. Application,* 250 I.C.C. 477.

[23]285 I.C.C. 506.

owned subsidiary of a steel company to transport coal between mines in West Virginia and Kentucky and Joliet, Illinois, and Gary, Indiana. The carrier had been transporting the coal in bulk in tows under the exemption provision of Section 303(b). One purpose of the application was to enable the carrier to transport a portion of its coal traffic in mixed tows with non-bulk commodities in order to improve efficiency of and bring about economies in operations. In another case, however, *A. L. Mechling Barge Line, Inc., Extension — Gulf Intra-Coastal Waterway*,[24] the Commission denied an application for a certificate to transport dry bulk commodities and grain and grain products in bags substantially along the same water routes that the carrier had been transporting the same commodities in bulk. The applicant had contended that the purpose of the application was to make the heretofore exempt operation more efficient and economical. In denying the application the Commission said that there was no public need shown for transportation by the carrier unencumbered by the Section 303(b) restrictions.[25]

The *TOTO* case, *supra*, reflects a more liberal policy on the part of the Commission in authorizing operating authority intended to be used primarily as an incident to carriage of applicant's own goods and its own business.

Effectuation of Operating Economies by Transporting Commodities in Mixed Tows

The fact that a carrier may be able to effect operating economies by transporting commodities in mixed tows when a certificate is granted instead of continuing to transport under the bulk exemption, is no bar to a grant of authority. *A. L. Mechling Barge Lines, Inc., Extension — Tampa.*[26]

Towage Service

Review of representative Commission reports discloses that "towage" service is generally described as the furnishing of the motive power by

---

[24]206 I.C.C. 223.

[25]Where there was no danger or undue competition between private towage and proposed common carrier operations, the commission granted an application in *Cornell Steamboat Co. — Purchase — Lowery*, 312 I.C.C. 55, for the transfer authority to transport general commodities along the same route and by the same means that the vendee was engaged in — performing transportation of crushed stone for its parent company.

[26]285 I.C.C. 743, 750.

tugboat for the movement of non-self-propelled vessels and other miscellaneous floating objects.[27] The Supreme Court has had occasion to describe the function of towage. In its opinion in *Stevens v. White City,*[28] the court stated:

> The supplying of power by a vessel, usually one propelled by steam, to tow or draw another is towage. Many vessels, such as barges and canal boats, have no power of their own and are built with a view to receiving their propelling force from other sources. And vessels having motive power often employ auxiliary power to assist them in moving about harbors and docks . . . .
>
> The tug does not have exclusive control over the tow but only so far as is necessary to enable the tug and those in charge of her to fulfill the engagement. They do not have control such as belongs to common carriers and other bailees. They have no authority over the master or hands of the towed vessel beyond such as is required to govern the movement of the flotilla. In all other respects and for all other purposes the vessel in tow, its cargo and crew remain under the authority of its master; and in emergency the duty is upon him to determine what shall be done for the safety of his vessel and her cargo. In all such cases the right of decision belongs to the master of the tow and not to the master of the tug. A contract merely for towage does not require or contemplate such a delivery as is ordinarily deemed essential to bailment.

Decisions of the Commission disclose that a "freighting" operation involves the transportation of general commodities by self-propelled vessels or by non-self-propelled vessels with the use of separate towing vessels; the carrier providing this service furnishes not only the motive power but also the vehicle for the cargo.[29]

It is apparent from the foregoing that the function and undertakings of a water carrier engaged in the performance of towage differ substantially from the functions and undertakings of a water carrier engaged in the performance of freighting. Whereas the former type of carrier is responsible merely for the propulsion of vessels from point to point, it is the latter's job to provide a complete transportation service. Stated differently, the primary purpose of a water carrier performing a freighting service is to transport commodities. That embraces the responsibility to furnish space for cargo in the shape of a vessel, to provide safe and

---

[27]*John L. Goss Corp.* 250 I.C.C. 101; *Cornell Steamboat Co.* 250 I.C.C. 301, aff'd *Cornell Steamboat Co. v. United States,* 321 U.S. 634; *Russell Bros. Towing Co., Inc.,* 250 I.C.C. 429; *Noran Towing* n *Transp. Co. Inc.,* 250 I.C.C. 541; *Card Towing Line, Inc.,* 250 I.C.C. 621; *Upper Mississippi Towing Corp.,* 260 I.C.C. 85.

[28]285 U.S. 195, 200.

[29]*Union Barge Line Corp.,* 250 I.C.C. 249; *McLain Marine Corp.,* 250 I.C.C. 297; *McLain Carolina Line, Inc.,* 250 I.C.C. 327; *John J. Mulqueen,* 250 I.C.C. 436.

adequate transportation of the cargo, and to provide the motive power for the vessel.

Early in its administration of water carrier provisions of the I.C. Act the Commission was called upon to decide this question, and in an application proceeding under Section 309,[30] *Eastern Transp. Co. Contract Carrier Application,*[31] held that a carrier possessing a certificate to engage in water transportation by non-self-propelled vessels with the use of separate towing vessels would not need additional authority to tow barges furnished by shippers when such carriers had contracted with the shipper for the transportation of specific commodities contained in barges furnished by the shipper.

In a later proceeding in which the same issue was presented for decision, the Commission explained its earlier holding in the *Eastern* case. In *Campbell Transp. Co. Contract Carrier Application,*[32] the Commission specifically held that the authority of a water carrier to engage in transportation of commodities generally by non-self-propelled vessels with the use of towing vessels did not authorize such carriers to perform a towage service. The Commission explained its ruling as follows:

> The question to be decided here is whether the terms "transportation of commodities by non-self-propelled vessels with the use of separate towing vessels" and "general towage" should be interpreted so as to include within the former, and exclude from the latter, the services of a carrier when, by the use of towing vessels, it provides for shippers only the propulsion of non-self-propelled vessels, either loaded or light, which they furnish and deliver to the carrier to be towed, and when under the contract for the service the carrier is liable for loss of or damage to the goods, or basis its charges for the service on the weight or volume of the commodities transported.

> Such interpretation of those terms (as used in the certificates and permits granted) would permit carriers whose authority is limited to freighting by barges and towboats to invade the field of carriers engaged in the performance of towage. Also, it would unduly limit the authority granted to the latter class of carriers as to the towage service, but on the other hand, it would mean that a carrier, which during the critical period furnished only towing vessels and performed only the service described above, should be authorized to perform for shippers the complete transportation usually offered by fully equipped barge lines. Carriers that have been granted authority to transport commodities by barges and towboats have been required to show that they were in bona fide operation in the performance of complete freighting service in which they furnished both types of vessels.

[30]49 U.S.C. 909.
[31]250 I.C.C. 505, 507-508.
[32]260 I.C.C. 107, 109-110.

The extent of a carrier's liability under admiralty or maritime law or its basis of charging does not affect the basic character of its services, and should not control its classification by this Commission under Section 304 (c) of the Interstate Commerce Act or the determination of authority granted under section 309. The service to shippers, as described above, is unquestionably towage, within the meaning of "general towage," rather than complete freighting service. Authority to perform such towage is not included in the authority granted to water carriers to engage in the transportation of commodities by non-self-propelled vessels with the use of separate towing vessels. Towage is a distinct type of service or field of operation. Many carriers perform only towage, and others which were engaged in freighting by barges and towboats did not perform such towage service for shippers during the "grandfather" period. Carriers whose certificates or permits do not specifically authorize the performance of towage are without authority to engage in such service.

Insofar as such a conclusion might be construed to conflict with its early decision in the *Eastern* case, the Commission, further explained its holding, as follows (p. 110):

To correct any misunderstanding of what we said relative to the use of towage of shippers' barges in our reports in *Eastern Transp. Co. Contract Carrier Application*, 250 I.C.C. 505, 635, it should be said here that a carrier authorized to engage in the transportation of commodities generally by non-self-propelled vessels with the use of separate towing vessels is not prohibited from using shippers' barges as a part of its equipment in performing such complete freighting service, provided the arrangements for such use are reasonable and otherwise lawful. The type of service performed for shippers by the carrier is different, however, when the carrier holds itself out to perform and actually performs only towage of commodities in shippers' barges. Although the physical use of the barges is the same in both cases, in the first instance they are used by the carrier in fulfillment of its obligation to provide the necessary equipment to transport a consignment of freight. In the latter instance, since the carrier performs only towage, the barges must be furnished by the shippers and are therefore used by them and delivered to the carrier as a part of the consignment to be towed.

The question as to what arrangement might be considered "reasonable and otherwise lawful," and the pertinency of Section 314 of the I.C. Act,[33] were further considered by the Commission in the *Dixie case*.[34] The question there was whether operations under a tariff provision by which allowances were made from commodity rates when the shipper furnished the scow, barge, or other vessel in which the commodity was transported, resulted in a transportation service covered by the certificate held by the water carrier involved.

[33]49 U.S.C. 914.
[34]278 I.C.C. 417.

In that case, it appeared that the Dixie line was the holder of a certificate of public convenience and necessity authorizing it to operate as a common carrier by water in the transportation of commodities generally by non-self-propelled vessels with the use of towing vessels; that it owned and used tugboats in such transportation for the propulsion of barges owned, leased, or rented by it, and in some instances barges or scows furnished by shippers whose products were contained therein; that Dixie published rates applicable to the transportation of various commodities when the same were transported in barges furnished by it (independent of whether the same were owned, leased, or rented by Dixie) and that certain deductions, expressed as allowances, from such rates were made applicable to the same commodity rates when the shipper furnished the vessel containing the commodity to be transported; that marine insurance was provided when commodities were transported under the first named rates; that transportation under the second set of rates was without marine insurance and the cost thereof was included as part of the allowance; and that when Dixie used a shipper's barge it had no authority to load cargo thereon in the return movement of the barge after discharge of the original cargo. From these facts the Commission concluded that Dixie was performing towage service, a service not authorized by the provisions of its certificate, and the carrier was, therefore, required to discontinue such operations.

In *Union Barge Line Corp. Applications*,[35] the Commission held:

> In our prior reports herein we found that applicant publishes standard rates under which it assumes common carrier liability; also rates lower than its standard rates covering transportation at owner's risk in the barges of shippers or others. The standard rates are intended to be enough higher than the last described rates to cover the use of the barge, insurance thereon, and insurance on the cargo therein, none of which items are included in the rates of freight in the barges of others. Service under the latter rates is towage only.

[35]260 I.C.C. 563.

7

Certificates of Public Convenience and Necessity for Air Carriers

The Applicable Statutory Provisions

Under Section 401(a) of the Federal Aviation Act,[1] "No carrier shall engage in any air transportation unless there is in force a certificate issued by the Board authorizing such air carrier to engage in such transportation."

Section 401(d) (1)[2] provides that the "Board shall issue a certificate authorizing the whole or any part of the transportation covered by the application, if it finds that the applicant is fit, willing, and able to perform such transportation properly, and to conform to the provisions of this Act and the rules, regulations, and requirements of the Board hereunder, and that such transportation is required by the public convenience and necessity; otherwise such application shall be denied." Section 401(d) (2)[3] provides that in "the case of an application for a certificate to engage in temporary air transportation, the Board may issue a certificate authorizing the whole or any part thereof for such limited periods as may be required by the public convenience and necessity, if it finds that the applicant is fit, willing, and able properly to perform such transportation and to conform to the provisions of this Act and the rules, regulations, and requirements of the Board hereunder." Under Section 401(i)[4] it is provided that "no certificate shall confer any proprietary, property, or exclusive right in the use of any airspace, Federal airways, landing area, or air-navigation facility."

Title IV of the FAA was amended by P.L. 95-163, Federal Aviation

[1] 49 U.S.C. 1371 (a).
[2] 49 U.S.C. 1371(d) (1).
[3] 49 U.S.C. 1371(d) (2).
[4] 49 U.S.C. 1371(i).

Act of 1958 — Insurance Risks, 91 Stat. 1284 by adding Section 418 at the end thereof. Section 418 provides:

(a) (1) Any citizen of the United States who has a valid certificate issued under section 401 (d) (1) of this title and who provided scheduled all-cargo air service at any time during the period from January 1, 1977, through the date of enactment of this section may, during the forty-five-day period which begins on the date of enactment of this section, submit an application to the Board for a certificate under this section to provide all-cargo air service. Such application shall contain such information and be in such form as the Board shall by regulation require.

(2) Any citizen of the United States who (A) operates pursuant to an exemption granted by the Board under section 416 of this title, and (B) provided scheduled all-cargo air service continuously (other than for inter-ruptions caused by labor disputes) during the 12-month period ending on the date of enactment of this section, or whose predecessor in interest provided such service during such period, may, during the forty-five-day period which begins on the date of enactment of this section, submit an application to the Board for a certificate under this section to provide all-cargo air service. Such application shall contain such information and be in such form as the Board shall by regulation require.

(3) After the three hundred and sixty-fifth day which begins after the date of enactment of this section, any citizen of the United States may submit an application to the Board for a certificate under this section to provide all-cargo air service. Such application shall contain such informa-tion and be in such form as the Board shall by regulation require.

✿   ✿   ✿

(b) (1) (A) Not later than sixty days after any application is submitted pursuant to paragraph (1) or (2) of subsection (a) of this section, the Board shall issue a certificate under this section authorizing the all-cargo air service covered by the application.

(B) No later than one hundred and eighty days after any application is submitted pursuant to paragraph (3) of subsection (a) of this section, the Board shall issue a certificate under this section authorizing the whole or any part of the all-cargo air service covered by the application unless it finds that the applicant is not fit, willing, and able to provide such service and to comply with any rules and regulations promulgated by the Board.

(2) Any certificate issued by the Board under this section may contain such reasonable conditions and limitations as the Board deems necessary, except that such terms and conditions shall not restrict the points which may be served, or the rates which may be charged, by the holder of such certificate.

(3) Notwithstanding any other provision of this section, no certificate issued by the Board under this section shall authorize all-cargo air service between any pair of points both of which are within the State of Alaska or the State of Hawaii.

(4) If any all-cargo service authorized by a certificate issued under this subsection is not performed to the minimum extent prescribed by the Board, it may by order, entered after notice and opportunity for a hearing, direct that such certificate shall, thereafter, cease to be effective to the extent of such service.

* * *

(c) Any applicant who is issued a certificate under this section shall, with respect to any all-cargo air service provided in accordance with such certificate, be exempt from the requirements of section 401 (a) of this Act, and any other section of this Act which the Board by rule determines appropriate, and any rule, regulation, or procedure issued pursuant to any such section.

* * *

(d) Any applicant who is issued a certificate under this section shall be an air carrier for the purposes of this Act, except to the extent such carrier is exempt from any requirement of the Act pursuant to this section.

* * *

Section 401(d) was amended by P.L. 95-163 to permit intrastate carriers in certain States to engage in through service with interstate or foreign carriers, and to establish joint fares, rates, and services for such through service.

Procedure Followed

In *C A B v. State Airlines*,[5] the Supreme Court said that the language of Section 401(d) (1) and (2) "unqualifiedly gives the Board power, after application and appropriate findings, to issue certificates for the whole or any part of transportation covered in an application. This manifests a purpose generally to gear the award of certificates to an application procedure." The court then pointed out that Congress made no attempt to define the full reach or contents of an application in Section 401(d) (1) and (2) and that the subsections did not even require an applicant to designate the terminal city or intermediate point a proposed route would serve. The only requirement, the court said, is found in Section 401(b) requiring an application to be in writing and verified, and that an application shall be in such form and contain such information as the Board by regulation may require.

Under Section 1001, the court said, Congress granted the Board authority to conduct its proceedings in such manner as will be conducive to the proper dispatch of business and to the ends of justice. The court concluded, "Thus, except for the statutory requirement of written and

[5]338 U.S. 572, 576.

verified applications, Congress plainly intended to leave the Board free to work out application procedures reasonably adapted to fair and orderly administration of its complex responsibilities."

In *Western Air Lines v. C A B,*[6] the following statement was made by the court of appeals as to the Board's duty under the Act:

> . . . It is the Board's duty under the [Federal Aviation] Act to ascertain, promote, and protect the public interest, as to which the Board is the "final arbiter." °°° Private litigants before the Board are primarily vindicating the public, not a private, interest °°° It would be strange indeed if we were enabled to oversee the administrative docket. The Board is an informed body and must necessarily have the widest latitude in the matter of how it goes about determining the public interest in what it believes to be the proper dispatch of the business before it. "Necessarily, therefore, the subordinate questions of procedure in ascertaining the public interest, when the Commission's licensing authority is invoked — the scope of the inquiry, whether applications should be heard contemporaneously or successively, whether parties should be allowed to intervene in one another's proceedings, and similar questions — were explicity and by implication left to the Commission's own devising, so long, of course, as it observes the basic requirements designed for the protection of private as well as public interest." *Federal Communications Commission v. Pottsville Broadcasting Co.*, 1940, 309 U.S. 134, 138 . . . .[7]

Public Convenience and Necessity Criteria

In determining under Section 401 whether an "applicant is fit, willing, and able" and that the service sought "is required by the public convenience and necessity," the Board must weigh all the criteria found in the Act which gives substance and vitality to the Congressional mandate of policy set forth in Section 2 of the Act.[8] Thus development, promotion and encouragement as expressed in the declaration of policy are matters of foresight which require a forward-looking function on the part of the Board. As the court of appeals said in *American Airlines v. C A B*,[9] "In that respect it differs markedly from a purely judicial or quasi-judicial determination of present or past rights." When action by the Board "contemplates a proposed development, new, not existing, a type of judgment is required which is wholly absent from the mere evaluation of past facts to ascertain a present or past fact. It is in the exercise of that sort of judgment that the much discussed expertise of ad-

---

[6]184 F. 2d 545. See also *United Air Lines, Inc. v. C A B,* 155 F. 2d 169, 173; *W. R. Grace & Co. v. C A B,* 154 F. 2d 271, 287.

[7]See also *F.C.C. v. WJR, The Goodwill Station, Inc.,* 337 U.S. 272.

[8]*Continental Southern Lines v. C A B,* 197 F. 2d 397, 402.

[9]192 F. 2d 417, 420.

ministrative agencies finds its greatest value. Here is the field of uncertainties, imponderables and estimates. This is where the rule that a
conclusion within the realm of national deduction or inference stands
despite differences of opinion, has its greatest applicability."[10]

The court of appeals said further (pp. 420-1) in the *American Airlines* case:

> The public convenience and necessity for which regulatory agencies issue
> certificates are the convenience and necessity of the future. The needs of
> yesterday require no fulfillment if they be not the needs of tomorrow.
> They may require recompense, but they need no regulation. Every new
> bus route, new airplane service, new radio station, new stock issue, new
> pipe line, new power project, and so on, seeks its permissive certificate
> upon the basis of future possibilities. If past or present events are indica-
> tive of such probabilities, they are useful as indices. But surely the future
> is not limited to or by the past. An application for a bus route could not
> be denied because there has been no bus service on that route; . . .

> Since regulatory functions must necessarily contemplate the future, the
> law which is involved in those functions must be realistic enough to permit
> that scope. So, when a prospective rule is required to be upon evidence,
> that evidence must be construed to include estimates of forecasts, or opin-
> ions, on future events. At the same time, governmental permissions for the
> future cannot be fashioned from pure fantasy, speculation devoid of factual
> premise. Public convenience and necessity in the sense of these statutes
> has a hard core of factual possibility, which can be ascertained and evalu-
> ated only upon the basis of present and past events and conditions. So the
> function of the agencies to which Congress has delegated these responsi-
> bilities is to examine the relevant past and present and then to exercise a
> rational judgment upon that data to ascertain the public convenience and
> necessity in the reasonably forseeable future.

The Board is required by the FAA to foster competition as a means of
enhancing the development and improvement of air transportation service on routes generating sufficient traffic to support competing carriers.[11]

"Factor Balancing" Approach in Determining what the Public Convenience and Necessity Require

The CAB's use of a "factor-balancing" approach in determining what
the public convenience and necessity require in various contexts was
affirmed in *United Air Lines, Inc. v. Civil Aeronautics Board.*[12] The

---

[10]*Ibid.* See also *United Air Lines v. C A B,* 155 F. 2d 169; *United States v.
Detroit & Cleveland Navigation Co.,* 326 U. S. 236.
[11]*Continental Air Lines v. C.A.B.,* 519 F. 2d 944.
[12]371 F. 2d 221.

court affirmed CAB orders entered in a proceeding styled *Detroit-California Nonstop Service Investigation,* which removed restrictions on the operating authority of the three carriers in the Detroit-Los Angeles and Detroit-San Francisco air travel markets, namely, American, Trans World, and United Air Lines. The court held that rigid adherence to criteria of public convenience and necessity for establishing new routes is not required in a restriction-removal case, and that the CAB has broad discretion to determine the relative weight the different factors are to be accorded in different types of proceedings.

Immediate Service

In *Continental Southern Lines v. C A B,*[13] the court of appeals affirmed an order of the Board which denied an application for a certificate since, under all the circumstances of the case, applicant could not furnish the immediate service which the public convenience and necessity required. The court said in affirming the order (p. 402) that there were so many foreseeable obstacles involved in the proceeding to ultimate approval of the application, which stemmed primarily from the fact that applicant had been acquired by a surface carrier, that "it was reasonable for the Board to question the willingness of Continental to risk the substantial investment necessary for the immediate activation of the routes."

Mutually Exclusive Applications

The Supreme Court held in *Ashbacker Radio Co. v. Federal Communications Commission*[14] that where the Communications Act provided in effect that applicants for licenses should have a right to a hearing before applications are denied, and two mutually exclusive applications were pending, that the Federal Communications Commission could not grant one application without a hearing of the other. The Supreme Court said, "For if the grant of one effectively precludes the other, the statutory right to a hearing which Congress has accorded applicants before a denial of their applications becomes an empty thing."

The *Ashbacker* doctrine was applied in *Delta Air Lines, Inc. v. C A B,*[15] where the court of appeals referred to the doctrine as "a practical conclusion of sound common sense. It is simply a realistic truth that,

---

[13]197 F. 2d 397, cert. denied 344 U.S. 831.
[14]326 U.S. 327, 330. See *R.E.A. v. United States,* 205 F. Supp. 831.
[15]275 F. 2d 632, 637, cert. denied 362 U.S. 969.

if only one of several applications can be granted, an award to one applicant is as effective a denial of all the others as would be a flat order of denial." The court of appeals spoke (pp. 637-8) of the general doctrine, based on economic considerations, that an operating license requires a finding of public interest, convenience and necessity, and that the public interest requires service for the public, thus if there be only enough business to support operation by one licensee there must be only one licensee. This, the court of appeals said, is commonplace of public utility regulation as was discussed at length in *Carroll Broadcasting Co. v. Federal Communications Commission*.[16] The court of appeals said further[17] (p. 638):

> The [Federal Aviation] Act requires notice and hearing on applications for certificates for new routes, and also requires notice and hearing upon petitions for modifications of existing licenses, which latter include extensions of existing routes. Under the Act . . . a finding of public convenience and necessity is a requirement for either the grant of a new certificate or the extension of an existing route. So the principles we have been discussing apply to air certifications. If the grant of one of several applications for a new route does, as a matter of economic necessity, preclude the grant of any other application, the doctrine of Ashbacker clearly applies. Likewise, if the forseeable traffic would support two carriers and there are, let us say, five applicants, the grant of any one is an effective denial of three of the remaining four applications, and Ashbacker applies.
>
> ❁   ❁   ❁
>
> The doctrine of Ashbacker also applies where a request for an extension of an existing route would preclude the grant of other pending applications for the entire route. If one certificate for a route exists, and if the grant of a second competitive route would as a matter of economic fact destroy or substantially reduce the rendition of the service required by the public interest, the public interest precludes the competitive grant. The Board has frequently recognized and applied the latter rule; as a matter of fact it almost always does so.

An important case involving the *Ashbacker* doctrine is *National Airlines, Inc. v. Civil Aeronautics Board*.[18] The Board had instituted five separate proceedings dealing with the southern transcontinental tier of States, each with its own focus on the service needs of specific points. Delta and National Airlines contended that this procedure would deprive them of comparative consideration of various applications in one

---

[16]258 F. 2d 440. See also *Federal Communications Commission v. RCA Communications, Inc.*, 346 U.S. 86; *Gerico Investment Co. v. Federal Communications Commission*, 255 F. 2d 893.

[17]See also *Southern Service to the West Case*, 18 C A B 234; *Transcontinental & Western Air, Inc., Detroit-Memphis Service*, 6 C A B 117.

[18]392 F. 2d 504.

proceeding which were allegedly mutually exclusive of applications being considered in another, and that the Board's procedure was in any event an abuse of discretion. The court held that *Ashbacker* does not necessarily require the Board to enlarge a proceeding to include abutting segments or prohibit the Board from considering in a separate proceeding an area that borders, or even lies wholly within, the area covered in another proceeding.

Another case involving a claim of denial of *Ashbacker* rights grew out of a proceeding to determine whether Western Air Lines' certificate of public convenience and necessity should be amended so as to designate Denver as a coterminal with Great Falls, Mont., on its existing Great Falls-Calgary route, thereby making possible nonstop Denver-Calgary service in accordance with a new Air Transportation Agreement between the United States and Canada granting to the United States a Denver/Great Falls-Calgary route.[19] The Board declined to consolidate into the proceeding Frontier Airlines' application for Denver-Calgary nonstop authority upon the grounds that the Air Transport Agreement prohibited the United States from designating more than one airline for the route at least for a short time; that Western (which had for some years been operating Great-Falls-Calgary under the prior agreement) had already been designated for the Great Falls-Calgary portion; and that the route is indivisible under the agreement. In a per curiam order, the court agreed with the Board that *Ashbacker* did not require consolidation of Frontier's application since no other carrier could be designated to serve the route, or any part of it, regardless of whether Western's application for Denver-Calgary nonstop authority was granted or denied.

In *Frontier Airlines, Inc. v. Civil Aeronautics Bd.,*[20] review was sought of the CAB's refusal to consolidate into a proceeding styled *Pacific Northwest-Southwest Service Investigation* the petitioners' mutually exclusive applications involving local service between Denver and Salt Lake City and points in the Northwest and Southwest. The court dismissed the petitions, holding that the CAB had properly found that the applications were not prima facie mutually exclusive and the Board had not abused its discretion in initially limiting the scope of its proceeding to long-haul service.

[19]*Frontier Airlines v. Civil Aeronautics Board*, C.A.D.C. No. 21, 670 (Mar. 1, 1968).
[20]349 F. 2d 587.

Terms and Conditions

Section 401(e) of the Federal Aviation Act[21] provides that certificates issued "shall specify the terminal points and intermediate points, if any, between which the air carrier is authorized to engage in air transportation and the service to be rendered; and there shall be attached to the exercise of the privileges granted by the certificate, or amendment thereto, such reasonable terms, conditions, and limitations as the public interest may require. A certificate "to engage in foreign air transportation shall, insofar as the operation is to take place without the United States, designate the terminal and intermediate points only insofar as the Board shall deem practicable, and otherwise shall designate only the general route or routes to be followed."

Section 401(e) provides further that any carrier holding a certificate for foreign air transportation shall be authorized to handle and transport mail of countries other than the United States; that no term, condition, or limitation of a certificate shall restrict the right of an air carrier to add to or change schedules, equipment, accommodations, and facilities for performing the authorized transportation and service as the development of the business and the demands of the public shall require; that no carrier shall be deemed to have violated any term, condition, or limitation of its certificate by landing or taking off during an emergency at a point not named in its certificate or by operating in an emergency under regulations which may be prescribed by the Board, between terminal and intermediate points other than those specified in its certificate; and that any "carrier may make charter trips or perform any other special service, without regard to the points named in its certificate, under regulations prescribed by the Board."

In proceedings in which the Board has concluded that the public interest requires two or more contiguous cities to be served at a single point it has specified one airport to best serve the entire area designated. The specification of one airport to serve has been accomplished under its power to impose reasonable terms, conditions, and limitations as the public interest may require when authorizing service.[22]

---

[21]49 U.S.C. 1371(e).

[22]*City of Dallas v. C A B*, 221 F. 2d 501, 504, cert. denied 348 U.S. 914; *Texas-Oklahoma Case*, 7 C A B 481, 539-40; *Trans-Texas Certificate Renewal Case*, 12 C A B 606.

Temporary Authority

Pursuant to its responsibilities under Section 2 of the Act,[23] the Board has experimented widely in authorizing new and largely uncharted operations for temporary periods, and its power to do so has been judicially affirmed.[24]

Abandonment of Route

It is provided by Section 401(j) of the Federal Aviation Act[25] that "No air carrier shall abandon any route, or part thereof, for which a certificate has been issued by the Board, unless, upon the application of such air carriers, after notice and hearing, the Board shall find such abandonment to be in the public interest. An interested person may file with the Board a protest or memorandum of opposition to or in support of any such abandonment. The Board may, by regulations or otherwise, authorize such temporary suspension of service as may be in the public interest."

Suspension-Substitution Arrangement

In *State of Maine v. C.A.B.*,[26] the court of appeals vacated and remanded a portion of a Board decision which deleted Bar Harbor and Rockland, Maine, from Delta's certificate. The court held that the Board was obligated to examine whether those points required a "suspension/substitution" arrangement. Under that arrangement Delta would retain certificate responsibility, but its obligation to provide the service itself would be suspended as long as it secured the substitute service of a non-certificated commuter air carrier. Such findings may not be required by the FAA, the court declared, but are necessary here because of the importance of that issue in the proceedings before the hearing officer because he found that such arrangements should continue.

In *Air Lines Pilots Ass'n, et al. v. C.A.B.*,[27] a court of appeals upheld a Board order authorizing Hawaiian Airlines to suspend service to Hana, Hawaii, conditioned on maintenance of replacement air taxi service.

---

[23]49 U.S.C. 1302.

[24]*American Airlines, Inc. v. C A B*, 192 F. 2d 417, 420; *Braniff Airways v. C A B* 147 F. 2d 152; *American Airlines v. C A B*, 178 F. 2d 903; *American Airlines, Inc. v. C A B*, 231 F. 2d 483; *Los Angeles Helicopter Case*, 8 C A B 92.

[25]49 U.S.C. 1371(j).

[26]520 F. 2d 1240.

[27]514 F. 2d 834.

Effective Date and Duration of Certificate

Section 401(f) of the Federal Aviation Act[28] provides that certificates "shall be effective from the date specified therein, and shall continue in effect until suspended or revoked as hereinafter provided, or until the Board shall certify that operation thereunder has ceased, or, if issued for a limited period of time under sub-section (d) (2) of this section, shall continue in effect until the expiration thereof, unless, prior to the date of expiration, such certificate shall be suspended or revoked as provided herein, or the Board shall certify that operations thereunder have ceased." However, "if any service authorized by a certificate is not inaugurated within such period, not less than ninety days, after the date of the authorization as shall be fixed by the Board, or if, for a period of ninety days or such other period as may be designated by the Board any such service is not operated, the Board may, by order entered after notice and hearing, direct that such certificate shall thereupon cease to be effective to the extent of such service."

Section 401(g)[29] provides that the "Board upon petition or complaint or upon its own initiative, after notice and hearings, may alter, amend, modify, or suspend any such certificate, in whole or part, if the public convenience and necessity so require, or may revoke any such certificate, in whole or in part, for intentional failure to comply with any provision of this title or any order, rule or regulation issued hereunder or any term, condition, or limitation of such certificate. No "certificate shall be revoked unless the holder thereof fails to comply, within a reasonable time to be fixed by the Board, with an order of the Board commanding obedience to the provision, or to the order (other than an order issued in accordance with this proviso), rule, regulation, term, condition, or limitation found by the Board to have been violated." Section 401(g) also provides that any "interested person may file with the Board a protest or memorandum in support of or in opposition to the alteration, amendment, modification, suspension, or revocation of the certificate."

As pointed out in *United Air Lines v. C A B*,[30] two separate areas are defined in Section 401(h) wherein the Board has authority to act with reference to existing certificates. One area involves the revocation of certificates for violations of the Act or Board regulations or orders, and the other involves alterations, amendments, modifications or suspen-

[28] 49 U.S.C. 1371(f).
[29] 49 U.S.C. 1371(g).
[30] 198 F. 2d 100, 105.

sions of existing certificates, in whole or in part, where the public convenience so requires. The court noted "that the power given to the Board to alter, amend, modify or suspend existing certificates is not punitive in character, but depends for its exercise upon the requirements of public convenience and necessity, which are the same standards under which the Board may grant certificate rights under Sec. 401(d) of the Act."

The court said further (p. 106) that the terms "alter," "amend" and "modify" connote some limitations. "In the larger aspect any changes ordered under the Board's authority to alter, amend, and modify must be partial and not total. Further, the Board cannot be permitted to do piecemeal or step-by-step that which it has not power to accomplish in one proceeding. However, the authority of the Board to alter, amend, or modify contemplates the power to make permanent though limited changes in existing certificates."[31]

The court in the *United Air Lines* case said further (p. 105) that although the statute permits the Board to suspend a certificate theretofore issued where the public convenience and necessity so require, "the determination of the meaning of the standards of public convenience and necessity is not left to the whim of the Board. That standard appears in nearly all public utility statutes, and, in addition, Section 2 of this Act provides that the Board shall consider a number of things as in accordance with public convenience and necessity." The court said (p. 106) that the "power to suspend depends upon the same factor of public convenience and necessity as does the power to alter, amend or modify. It contemplates the continued existence of the certificate right, and the possibility that the public convenience and necessity factors giving rise to the suspension may change or come to an end."

In *Western Air Lines, Inc. v. C A B*,[32] where the Board had suspended Western's service to certain points and had granted to another airline, a local type carrier, a route extension to provide service to the same points, the court held that it was the "merest speculation" to say that a suspension order was in substance a permanent revocation. The court said that the "Board may classify between types of air service and may find that one kind of air service is not appropriate during a certain time. To say that the Board could not substitute during that time another type of air service, required as a public necessity, would be an unreasonable

---

[31]In *Panagra Terminal Investigation*, 4 C A B 670, the Board recognized this limitation by holding that an alteration ordered pursuant to authority must not be such as to transform the essential character of the carrier's operations.
[32]196 F. 2d 933, 936.

limitation upon the Board's power to plot the air map, primarily in the public interest."

The Supreme Court had occasion to interpret the language of Sections 401(f), (g) in *C A B v. Delta Air Lines, Inc.*[33] The issue in the *Delta* case was narrow and can be stated simply: Has Congress authorized the Board to alter, without formal notice or hearing, a certificate of public convenience and necessity once that certificate has gone into effect? If not, should it make any difference that the Board has purported to reserve jurisdiction prior to certification to make summary modifications pursuant to petitions for reconsideration? The Supreme Court answered both questions in the negative. The court said (pp. 323-5) with respect to Section 401(f), (g):

> This language represents to us an attempt by Congress to give the Board comprehensive instructions to meet all contingencies and the Board's duty is to follow these instructions, particularly in light of the fact that obedience thereto raises no substantial obstacles. It is true, of course, that statutory language necessarily derives much of its meaning from the surrounding circumstances. However, we think that, while there is no legislative history directly on point, the background of the Aviation Act strongly supports what we believe to be the plain meaning of Section 401 (f) and (g). It is clear from the statements of the supporters of the predecessor of the Aviation Act — the Civil Aeronautics Act — that Congress was vitally concerned with what has been called "security of route" — i.e., providing assurance to the carrier that its investment in operations would be protected insofar as reasonably possible. And there is no other explanation but that Congress delimited the Board's power to reconsider its awards with precisely this factor in mind; hence the language that a certificate "shall be effective . . . until suspended or revoked as hereinafter provided," language which is absent from several of the Acts to which reference has been made. Thus, the structure of the statute, when considered in light of the factor persuading Congress, indicates to us that the critical date in the mind of Congress was the date on which the carrier commenced operations, with the concomitant investment in facilities and personnel, not the date that abstract legal analysis might indicate as the "final" date. In other words, it seems clear to us that Congress was relatively indifferent to the fluctuations an award might undergo prior to the time it affected practical relationships, but that Congress was vitally concerned with its security after the wheels had been set in motion. In light of this, we think the result we reach follows naturally: to the extent there are uncertainties over the Board's power to alter effective certificates, there is an identifiable Congressional intent that these uncertainties be resolved in favor of the certificated carrier and that the specific instructions set out in the statute should not be modified by resort to such generalities as "administrative flexibility" and "implied powers." We do not quarrel with those who would grant the Board great discretion to conjure

[33]367 U.S. 316.

with certificates prior to effectuation. But, we feel that we would be paying less than adequate deference to the intent of Congress were we not to hold that, after a certificate has gone into effect, the instructions set out in the statute are to be followed scrupulously.

The argument was made in the *Delta* case that even though the Board had allowed the certificate to become effective, the fact that a timely petition for reconsideration had been filed, which had not been ruled upon prior to the effective date of the certificate, permitted the Board to grant the petition and modify its order and the resulting certificate. In reply to this argument, the court said (pp. 329-32):

> Although we feel that the language and background of the statute are sufficiently clear so that affirmance can rest solely on that basis, it seems appropriate, in light of petitioners' vigorous assertion that policy reasons compel their result to discuss some of the ramifications of our decision. In the first place, it bears repetition that we are not deciding that the Board is barred from reconsidering its initial decision. All we hold is that, if the Board wishes to do so, it must proceed in the manner authorized by statute. Thus, for example, the Board may reconsider an effective certificate at any time if it affords the certificated carrier notice and hearing prior to decision; or, if it feels uncertain about the decision prior to its effective date, it may postpone the effective date until all differences have been resolved; and, if neither of these procedures seem practical in a given case, the Board may issue a temporary certificate set to expire on the date the Board prescribes for re-examination. (By provision of Section 401 (d) (2)). Indeed, with all these weapons at its command, it is difficult to follow the argument that the Board should be allowed to improvise on the powers granted by Congress in order to preserve administrative flexibility.
>
> ※   ※   ※
>
> In short, our conclusion is that Congress wanted certificated carriers to enjoy "security of route" so that they might invest the considerable sums required to support their operations; and, to this end, Congress provided certain minimum protections before a certificated operation could be cancelled. We do not think it too much to ask that the Board furnish there minimum protections as a matter of course, whether or not the Board in a given case might think them meaningless. It might be added that some-authorities have felt strongly enough about the practical significance of these protections to suggest that their presence may be required by the Fifth Amendment. See *Seatrain Lines v. United States*, 64 F. Supp. 156, 161; *Handlon v. Town of Belleville*, 4 N.J. 99, 71 A. 2d, 624; see also 63 Harv. L. Rev. 1437, 1439.

"Use-It-Or-Lose-It" Policy

In a case involving the "use-it-or-lose-it" policy,[34] it was found that the public interest required deletion of Pontiac and Cadillac-Reed City,

---

[34]*City of Pontiac, et al, v. Civil Aeronautics Board*, 361 F. 2d 810.

Mich., from the certificate of North Central Airlines. In affirming the Board's order, the appellate court held that while alleged deficiencies in the carrier's service must be weighed as a factor militating against decertification, the degree of importance to be attached to opposing factors falls within the "spacious domain" of policy matters which are entrusted to the Board's discretion.

In *New Castle County Airport Commission v. Civil Aeronautics Board*,[35] review was sought of CAB orders entered in a proceeding styled *Salisbury-Wilmington "Use-It-Or-Lose-It"* case. The Board amended Allegheny Airlines' certificate by deleting Wilmington, Del., as a separate intermediate point on one of the federally subsidized carrier's route segments. In response to New Castle's contention that the CAB's established approach precludes deletion of a point which meets the minimum-use test of five passenger enplanements per day, the court sustained the view that the "5 per day" factor is merely a guideline. The court noted that the Board properly considered reduction of subsidy cost and the proximity of alternative airports to Wilmington passengers as decisive factors in this decertification proceeding.

Exemption from Certification Requirements

Hughes Air Corporation v. C.A.B.[36] involved a challenge to certain Board regulations, granting an exemption from certification requirements to air taxi operators using aircraft having maximum capacities of 30 passengers and 7,500 pounds of payload. In affirming the regulations, the court of appeals rejected contentions that the Board was required to proceed by individual ad hoc proceedings, rather than rulemaking in exempting air taxi operations from applicable requirements of the FAA. It premised its rejection on the view that where the general regulation is based on a reasoned consideration of all the basic goals that might be compromised, the Board should be allowed to pursue the regulatory course it deems most advisable. The court went on to accept the Board's determination that the blanket exemption rules were in the public interest and that certification would be an undue burden on air taxis as a class because of the limited extent and pandemic financial instability of their operations.

Northwest Airlines v. C.A.B.[37] involved a challenge to the Board's grant of temporary exemption authority under Section 416(b)(1) to

---

[35]371 F. 2d 733, cert. denied 387 U.S. 930.
[36]492 F. 2d 567. See Section 416 of the F.A.A., 49 U.S.C. 1386.
[37]539 F. 2d 748.

permit the implementation of an agreement between TWA and Pan American routes operated by each, including exchanges of certain routes. The agreement was intended as a temporary response to the financial crisis threatening both carriers. On review, the court of appeals agreed with the Board that the severe financial distress of the two United States flag international carriers justified initial Board action under Section 416 (b)(1). It found, however, that the temporary changes should have been implemented only until such time as the Board could complete narrowly focused, expedited proceedings — including proper notice and hearing — looking toward a decision on permanent changes in certificate authority. As the Board had not instituted certificate proceedings during the exemption period, the court vacated the Board's order and remanded the case to the Board.

8

Permits for Contract Carriers by Motor Vehicle

The Applicable Statutory Provisions

Congress in 1957 enacted certain amendments to the Interstate Commerce Act which modified the definition of a contract carrier in Section 203(a) (15);[1] added to Section 209(b)[2] five criteria which must be considered by the Commission in deciding contract carrier application proceedings; and added Section 212(c)[3] which provided a procedure for the conversion from contract-to common-carrier status of contract carriers no longer able to qualify as such under the amended definition in Section 203(a) (15).

Section 203(a) (15) of the Interstate Commerce Act, as amended, states that the "term contract carrier by motor vehicle means any person which engages in transportation by motor vehicle of passengers or property in interstate or foreign commerce, for compensation (other than transportation referred to in paragraph (14) and the exception therein), under continuing contracts with one person or a limited number of persons either (a) for the furnishing of transportation services through the assignment of motor vehicles for a continuing period of time to the exclusive use of each person served or (b) for the furnishing of transportation services designed to meet the distinct need of each individual customer."

Section 209(b), as amended, provides that "a permit shall be issued to any qualified applicant therefor authorizing in whole or in part the operations covered by the application, if it appears from the application or from any hearing held thereon, that the applicant is fit, willing, and

[1] 49 U.S.C. 303(a) (15).
[2] 49 U.S.C. 309(b).
[3] 49 U.S.C. 312(c).

able properly to perform the service of a contract carrier by motor vehicle, and to conform to the provisions of this part and the lawful requirements, rules, and regulations of the Commission thereunder, and that the proposed operation, to the extent authorized by the permit will be consistent with the public interest and the national transportation policy declared in this Act; otherwise such application shall be denied."[4] In determining whether issuance of a permit will be consistent with the public interest and the national transportation policy declared in the I.C. Act, the Commission is required to "consider the number of shippers to be served by the applicant, the nature of the service proposed, the effect which granting the permit would have upon the services of the protesting carriers and the effect which denying the permit would have upon the applicant and/or its shipper and the changing character of that shipper's requirements."

Interpretation of Statutory Language

The background and applicability of this legislation was considered at length in *J-T Transport Co., Inc., Extension — Columbus, Ohio*,[5] which took up in detail the impact of the 1957 legislation on contract-carrier application proceedings and discussed the effect of the five criteria of Section 209(b); and *T. T. Brooks Trucking Co., Inc., Conversion Application*,[6] which laid down rules of general application with respect to Section 212(c) conversion proceedings.

In the application of the 1957 legislation to the disposition of individual contract carrier application proceedings, one of the most controversial issues which has had to be resolved has been the weight to be accorded the available services of opposing motor common carriers. In *J-T Transport Extension — Columbus, supra,* after pointing out that the Commission, in approaching contract-carrier applications, had always treated as a relevant factor the adequacy of existing common-carrier service, it was concluded that the new legislation did not require any substantial modification of the traditional method of treating this matter. In fact, in discussing the five criteria of Section 209(b), the Commission found (at p. 705) with respect to one of them — the effect

---

[4]The decision of the Supreme Court in *United States, v. Contract Street Carriers*, 350 U.S. 409, caused concern to the Commission which proposed amendments to the I.C. Act. There the Supreme Court held that a contract carrier rendering a specialized service, in the sense that it hauled only a limited group of commodities over irregular routes, did not become a common carrier because it reached for new business within the limits of its license.

[5]79 M.C.C. 695.

[6]81 M.C.C. 561.

which granting a permit would have on the services of protesting carriers — that there "is, in effect, a presumption that the services of the existing carriers will be adversely affected by a loss of 'potential' traffic, even if they may not have handled it before." This position was reiterated in *Reddish Contract Carrier Application*,[7] in which it was said, it "is clear that the authorization of a new carrier to transport traffic which a common-carrier protestant can efficiently handle would have an adverse effect upon the protestant." Upon review of the decisions in the *J-T Transport* and *Reddish* cases in *Interstate Commerce Commission v. J-T Transport Co.*,[8] the Supreme Court concluded that the standards employed by the Commission in disposing of those applications were improper in some respects. The Supreme Court said (at pp. 88-90):

> It seems clear from these provisions that the adequacy of existing service is a criterion to be considered by the Commission, as it is instructed to consider "the effect which granting the permit would have upon the services of the protesting carriers," as well as the effect of a denial upon the shippers. Or to put the matter otherwise, the question of the need of the shipping public for the proposed service necessarily includes the question whether the extent, nature, character, and suitability of existing, available service makes the proposed service out of line with the requirements of the national transportation policy. But the adequacy of existing facilities or the willingness or ability of existing carriers to render the new service is not determinative. The "effect which denying the permit would have upon the applicant and/or its shipper and the changing character of that shipper's requirements" has additional relevance. This is a phase of the problem reflected in the broadened definition of "a contract carrier by motor vehicle" — one who furnishes transportation services "designed to meet the distinct need of each individual customer." Section 203(a) (15). It means, we think, that the "distinct need" of shippers for the new contract carrier service must be weighed against the adequacy of existing services. The Commission indulged in "a presumption that the services of existing carriers will be adversely affected by a loss of potential traffic, even if they may not have handled it before." 79 M.C.C. 695, 705. The effect of the presumption is in substance to limit competing contract carriage to services "not provided" by existing carriers — a provision that the Commission sought unsuccessfully to have incorporated into the Act. We see no room for a presumption in favor of, or against, any of the five factors on which findings must be made under Section 209 (b). The effect on protesting carriers of a grant of the application and the effect on shippers of a denial are factors to be weighed in determining on balance where the public interest lies. The aim of the 1957 amendments, as we read the legislative history, was not to protect the status quo of existing carriers but to establish a regime under which new contract carriage

[7] 81 M.C.C. 35, 41.
[8] 368 U.S. 81. See *Moyer*, 88 M.C.C. 767; *Griffin*, 91 M.C.C. 801; *Umthun Ext.*, 91 M.C.C. 691.

could be allowed if the "distinct need" of shippers indicated that it was desirable.

We cannot assume that Congress, in amending the statute intended to adopt the administrative construction which prevailed prior to the amendment.

By adding the five criteria which it directed the Commission to consider, Congress expressed its will that the Commission should not manifest special solicitude for that criterion which directs attention to the situation of protesting carriers, at the expense of that which directs attention to the situation of supporting shippers, when those criteria have contrary implications. Such a situation doubtless exists in these cases, for granting the permits might well have produced some consequences adverse to the protesting carriers, while denying them may just as certainly prove burdensome to the supporting shippers. Had the Commission, having drawn out and crystallized these competing interests, attempted to judge them with as much delicacy as the prospective nature of the inquiry permits, we should have been cautious about disturbing its conclusion.

But while such a determination is primarily a responsibility of the Commission, we are under no compulsion to accept its reading where, as here, we are convinced that it has loaded one of the scales. By indulging in a presumption "that the services of existing carriers will be adversely affected by a loss of 'potential' traffic, even if they may not have handled it before," and by assigning to the applicants the burden of proving the inadequacy of existing services, the Commission favored the protestants' interests at the expense of the shippers in a manner not countenanced by anything discoverable in Congress' delegation to it of responsibility.

On the question of burden of proof, the Supreme Court said in the *J-T Transport* case (pp. 90-1) that it was improper to place the burden of proving inadequacy of existing service on applicants since the capabilities of the protesting carriers were peculiarly within their knowledge. The proper procedure was for applicant first to demonstrate that the proposed service was specialized and tailored to the shipper's distinct need. Protestants then would present evidence to show they had the ability as well as the willingness to meet that specialized need; if that were done, the burden would shift to applicant to show that it was better equipped than protestants to meet the shipper's distinct need. The standard is not whether the existing services are "reasonably adequate," but whether the shipper has a "distinct need" for a different, or more select, or more specialized service; thus the protesting carriers must show that they can fulfill that "distinct need" not that they can provide a "reasonably adequate" service.

In *Reddish v. United States*[9] a reviewing court held that whatever the

---

[9]188 F. Supp. 160, 167.

validity of the presumption that authorization of a new carrier to transport traffic which common carrier protestants could efficiently handle would have an adverse effect on their service, it is overcome by evidence which establishes that they not only have not handled the traffic involved but would not handle it if the permit were denied; and even assuming that some adverse effect would result from grant of the permit, no consideration was given to the special services which could not be supplied by a common carrier. Since the Commission's findings, in denying the contract-carrier permit, that service of existing common carriers was not shown to be inadequate, that denial would not adversely affect supporting shippers, and that grant of permit would adversely affect protestant common carriers' services were contrary to the preponderance of the evidence, the cause was remanded to the Commission for such further proceedings in conformity with the court's opinion as may be proper.[10]

The court said that it was not the intent of Congress that approval or disapproval of an application for contract-carrier permit should be determined solely by reference to whether or not the proposed service is provided by common carriers, or the service is one they are unwilling or unable to provide. Sufficient tests and safeguards to control granting of permits are contained in the law to protect common carriers without imposition by the Commission of a test which Congress deemed improper.[11] Nor may lower costs in form of rates be ignored in determining effect of denial of permit on shippers, since Congress has declared one of the goals of the national transportation policy to be the promotion of "economical" service. However, this does not mean that evidence of lower rates is always important, or determinative, when weighing evidence in support of a contract-carrier application against that presented by protestant common carriers; mere cost-cutting or profit-shaving need not be considered, but evidence of efficient operation must be heeded.[12] Where the lower rates result from economies and advantages inherent in contract carrier operation and there is a showing that efficient business operation requires the proposed tailored service, including the lower rates, the Commission may not disregard such evidence in evaluating the effect of denial on supporting shippers.[13]

Any proposed contract-carrier operation first must be examined to determine whether it meets the requirements of the 1957 contract carrier

[10]*Ibid.*, pp. 165, 167.
[11]*Ibid.*, p. 199.
[12]*Ibid.*, p. 167.
[13]*Ibid.*, p. 167.

definition in Section 203(a) (15). The operation must be one to be conducted under continuing contracts with one person or a limited number of persons either (a) for the furnishing of transportation services through the assignment of motor vehicles for a continuing period of time to the exclusive use of each person served, or (b) for the furnishing of transportation service designed to meet the distinct needs of each individual customer. In this connection, and although the Supreme Court emphasized in *J-T Transport, supra,* what may be termed the "distinct need" test, the "exclusive assignment of vehicle" requirement may not be disregarded; rather this test also must continue to be utilized and considered in appropriate circumstances. Where the proposed operation does not meet either test, however, the logical conclusion is that it is actually that of a common carrier as defined in Section 203(a) (14) of the I.C. Act, and the application must be considered and disposed of as are other applications for certificate of public convenience and necessity.

Once a proposed operation is determined to be contract carriage by reason of the "distinct need" or the "exclusive assignment of vehicle" test, the Commission next has the problem of weighing and balancing, within certain guidelines, the criteria embraced in Section 209(b). The Supreme Court made it clear in *J-T Transport, supra,* that, in so doing, the adequacy of existing services is to be considered. But, the Commission must bear in mind, as stated by the court,[14] that:

> though common carrier service is reasonably adequate and though another carrier is willing and able to furnish the service, a permit to a contract carrier to furnish this particular service still might be wholly consistent with the national transportation policy defined in the Act. For it is "the distinct need of each individual customer" that the contract carrier is designed to fill. 203(a) (15). And "the changing character" of the shipper's "requirements" is a factor to be weighed before denying the application. 209(b). Hence the adequacy of existing services for normal needs and the willingness and the ability of an existing carrier to render the service is not the end of the matter. The "distinct need" of the shipper may nonetheless not be served by existing services, if the new service is better tailored to fit the special requirements of a shipper's business, the length of its purse, or the select nature of the delivery service that is desired. The fact that the protesting carriers do not presently perform the service being tendered and that the grant of the application would not divert business from them does not necessarily mean that the grant would have no effect "upon the services" of the protesting carriers within the meaning of 209(b). But where the protesting carriers do not presently have the business, it would seem that the grant of it to a newcomer would have an adverse effect on them only in the unusual case.

[14]368 U.S. at pp. 92-93.

And in accomplishing these objectives, the various burdens of proof among applicant and protestants are to be allocated in accordance with the following expression of the court:[15]

> The proper procedure, we conclude, is for the applicant first to demonstrate that the undertaking it proposes is specialized and tailored to a shipper's distinct need. The protestants then may present evidence to show they have the ability as well as the willingness to meet that specialized need. If that is done, then the burden shifts to the applicant to demonstrate that it is better equipped to meet the distinct needs of the shipper than the protestant.

In applying the broad principles expressed by the court to the specific factual situations presented by individual applications, it also must be borne in mind, that the particular characteristics of whatever specialized need may be present will vary from case to case. Each will necessarily have to be decided on its own facts, in the light of the court's comments[16] upon the overall problem:

> Moreover, as we read the Act, as amended in 1957, the standard is not whether existing services are "reasonably adequate." It is whether a shipper has a "distinct need" for a different or a more select or a more specialized service. The protesting carriers must show they can fill that "distinct need," not that they can provide a "reasonably adequate service."

The court's conclusions in the *Reddish* case also add an additional factor which must be given consideration when the matter of lower rates or cost of service to the shipper is relied upon by an applicant, the court saying:[17]

> We think the matter of rates is one factor to be weighed in determining the need for a new service. . . . By analogy [to the court's decision in *Schaffer Transportation Co. v. United States,* 355 U.S. 83], contract carriage may be more "economical" than common carriage by motor or rail within the framework of the national transportation policy, as it is defined in the Act [footnote omitted] — "The Commission's guide" to the public interest. *McLean Trucking Co. v. United States,* 321 U.S. 67, 82. It would seem hardly contestable that if denial of the application meant, for example, that a shipper's cost of transportation would be prohibitive, the shipper had established a "need" for the more "economical" service. See *Herman R. Ewell Extension — Philadelphia,* 72 M.C.C. 645. This does not mean that the lawfulness of rates would be injected into certificate proceedings. This issue of whether or not the proposed service offers a rate advantage and if so whether such advantage established a "need" for the service that overrides counterbalancing considerations presents issues that fall far short of a rate proceeding.

[15]368 U.S. at p. 90.
[16]368 U.S. at pp. 90-91.
[17]368 U.S. at pp. 91-92.

Thus, when injected into a proceeding, the cost of service to the shipper is to be weighed by the Commission in reaching its ultimate findings.

It is important to note that the standing of common carrier protestants to oppose contract carrier applications cannot be seriously questioned. The Commission always recognized the right of existing carriers to appear in opposition to applications for both common- and contract-carrier authority; Section 205(e) of the Act requires that interested parties be given an opportunity to be heard; the provisions of Section 209(b) contemplate the appearance of opposing carriers; and the opinion of the court in *Interstate Commission v. J-T Transport Co., supra,* recognizes the right of common carriers to appear in opposition to a contract carrier application.

In spite of the fact that a given operation, as proposed by an applicant seeking a permit, is found to be that of a contract carrier as defined in Section 203(a) (15) it may be that there is nothing in the nature of the service proposed which would preclude its performance by common carriers. The only limitation by definition upon the transportation which may be provided by a motor common carrier is that it be held out to the public generally. Other than this requirement and those limitations contained in its certificate with respect to commodities, territories, and the like, no restriction is imposed upon the manner in which a common carrier may perform its physical operations, provided that the same service is made available to all who may desire to use it.[18] Thus a common carrier may provide a variety of specialized services and may even assign vehicles to the exclusive use of any customer desiring this kind of service, provided only that it offers to make available the same service to all. These factors must, obviously, be borne in mind when the Commission considers applications for contract-carrier authority and are faced with the task of determining whether protestants have the ability as well as the willingness to meet a shipper's specialized need.

In summary, all the facts relating to the statutory criteria, as well as any rate factor, must be weighed in determining, on balance, the ultimate conclusion where the public interest lies.

Issues Arising in Contract Carrier Cases

The Commission has attempted to clarify what constitutes a "limited number of shippers" within the meaning of the statutory definition of a contract carrier contained in Section 203(a) (15). Although it has been found to be impossible to arrive at a figure applicable to all situ-

---

[18]See *J-T Transport Co. Extension-Columbus, Ohio,* 79 M.C.C. 695, 700-701.

ations beyond which a contract carrier may not continue to add contracts, the Commission found in *Umthun Trucking Co. Ext. — Phosphatic Feed Supplements,*[19] that the applicant, upon execution of its seventh contract, reached the stage at which the addition of another shipper would place it in a position of serving more than a limited number of persons. The Commission noted that while the seventh contract would not be necessarily determinative in the operations of other contract carriers, the *Umthun* decision should serve as notice to contract carriers, whose services do not possess a high degree of specialization, that attempts to expand their operations to serve more than six or eight separate shippers will be carefully scrutinized to determine whether they are truly providing a service to a "limited number" of shippers.

In Ex Parte No. MC-119, *Policy Statement Regarding the "Rule of Eight" in Contract Carrier Applications,* served January 8, 1979, the Commission adopted a policy statement describing how it will apply that part of the statutory definition of "contract carrier by motor vehicle" which requires that these carriers serve no more than a "limited number" of persons. The statement provides that no fixed numerical ceiling will be used in defining the term limited number; describes certain situations in which it will be presumed that a contract carrier is serving no more than a limited number of persons; and adopts standards for determining when a contract carrier, because of a general holding-out of its services, may be found to have become, in fact, a common carrier.

The meaning and weight to be accorded "accessorial services," in connection with establishing that a proposed service is designed to meet the "distinct need" of a shipper within the statutory definition is another area of complexity. The Supreme Court, in the *J-T Transport* case, *supra,* pointed out that even though opposing common carriers are able to provide reasonably adequate service, a grant of contract carrier authority may be consistent with the public interest and the national transportation policy because the "distinct need" of the supporting shipper might not be as well served by protestants as by applicant. In line with this, in *Griffin Mobile Home Transporting Co. Contr. Car. Applic.,*[20] the Commission granted carrier authority where the protesting common carriers would not undertake to provide an "accessorial service," which shippers needed in order to obtain a complete service, and which applicant proposed.

In *Complete Auto Transit, Inc., Extension,*[21] the Commission granted an application where for 25 years applicant had served the supporting

[19]91 M.C.C. 691.
[20]91 M.C.C. 801.
[21]81 M.C.C. 445, 456-57, 459-60.

shipper exclusively in the transportation of various types of motor vehicles and was presently transporting trucks from one of shipper's plants
to all points in the United States. The shipper planned to manufacture
passenger cars at this plant and needed the services of a carrier which
could provide multiple deliveries of mixed shipments of cars and trucks
therefrom to points throughout the United States, and which would
work closely with the shipper in meeting its transportation needs. Such
service was not available from existing common carriers whose authorities for the combined transportation of cars and trucks were limited
to a few States and areas. Applicant through the years had become an
integral part of the shipper's operations; it altered its equipment to
accommodate the shipper's periodic model changeovers, and maintained
a terminal adjacent to the shipper's plant in order to provide service on
short notice. This, plus the fact that it served only this one shipper,
indicated that applicant was furnishing a "house carrier" service. Because of expansion at the shipper's plant and its need for transportation
of both trucks and cars, applicant would require additional authority for
passenger cars if it were to continue to render a complete service as it
had in the past.

While protestant motor common carriers which specialized in transportation service for the automobile industry could meet some of the
shipper's needs, and their operations and ability to render satisfactory
service was considered, in view of the fact they had never participated in
the considered traffic, any loss they might suffer as a result of the
grant of authority sought was limited to possible loss of potential traffic.
The Commission said, however, the advantages to the shipping public
from the grant to applicant outweigh such loss. The criterion in Section
209(b), as amended, concerning the effect denial of a permit would
have upon a shipper and "the changing character" of shipper's requirements refers to situations in which a shipper presently being provided
with a complete service by a contract carrier experiences a change in
such things as the marketing areas which it serves, the commodities
which it handles, or the location of its plants, which require that its
carriers acquire additional authority if it is to continue to render a
complete service.[22]

A grant of broader authority commoditywise was found justified in
Warren Transport, Inc.[23] to enable applicant, whose operations were
devoted to the shipper's exclusive use, to render a complete service, including multiple deliveries, in the transportation of other types of related
commodities which the shipper recently began to manufacture. No motor

[22]Id., p. 459.
[23]81 M.C.C. 393, 397-8.

carrier opposed the application, and rail protestants, whose services were not entirely adequate for shipper's needs, would not be deprived of their present share of traffic since the volume tendered to applicant would not be greater than that now being handled. In *E. Brooke Matlack, Inc.,*[24] a proposed contract carriage of dry cement from Cementon, N. Y., to New Jersey and Pennsylvania, in addition to destination territory previously authorized, was found to be required when supporting shipper's Martins Creek, Pa., plant did not produce certain grades or types produced at Cementon and used by consignees in those States; also, in cases of shortage of cement at the Martin Creek it would have to ship temporarily from Cementon. Although there was no complaint about available rail service apart from its inherent limitations, additional service by a motor carrier was required by changing competitive conditions. That supporting shipper was making a substantial investment for motor loading facilities was indicative of the need for such service; and there was no evidence that any motor carrier was ready, willing, and able to meet the shipper's need for service from Cementon to Pennsylvania and New Jersey, protestant's authority being limited territorially and commoditywise.

Where there were no opposing carriers authorized to perform the proposed service, intervener had no appropriate authority and would not be adversely affected by the grant of authority sought, and proposed extension of operation would meet the expressed distribution needs of a shipper of malt beverages, the Commission in *McCurdy Extension*[25] granted the application. In *Nuzzi Extension,*[26] the Commission said that the grant of extension authority to applicant would not adversely affect common carrier protestants when the only one which filed exceptions had not transported the traffic involved and the others were not in position to provide the complete and specialized service required by contracting shipper. In the *Nuzzi* case, since the contracting shipper, an air carrier, was converting its fleet from piston-engine to jet propulsion, entailing a corresponding change in the location of engine maintenace and repair facilities, the turbo engines involved were more valuable and more easily damaged than the piston type and required care during transit as well as a minimum of handling, and speed of delivery was essential for the airline to maintain a sufficient number of engines on hand for replacement because of premature failures or to meet governmental operational requirements, the Commission held that the grant of extension authority to applicant was necessary to enable it to continue the specialized ser-

[24]82 M.C.C. 377, 379-80.
[25]84 M.C.C. 227, 228-9.
[26]79 M.C.C. 590, 592-4.

vice considered by the shipper to be an integral and necessary part of the ground support of its air operations.

In *Leary Extension*,[27] the Commission said that while some traffic may be diverted from existing common carriers, the evidence fairly established that improvements in service would result in benefits to contracting shipper and its customers far outweighing any possible ill effects on protestants. Authority was granted applicant in *Dunbar Armored Service, Inc., Extension*[28] even though opposing carriers would be deprived of some traffic, both actual and potential, as any possible adverse effect on such carriers was outweighed by advantages to the shipping public from the proposed operation.

In *Atlantic Truck Lines, Inc.*[29] the Commission said that the grant of authority to applicant would not be inconsistent per se with the public interest and the national transportation policy merely because it was commonly controlled with its four principal supporting shippers, since a contract carrier is under no duty to render impartial service to the public and may serve only those with whom it has contracts. While applicant's past operations as a driver-employee of the supporting shipper suggested an unlawful subterfuge which could not be condoned, the Commission said in *Lyon*[30] that those operations should not operate as a bar to the grant of authority sought when they were conducted openly and with some color of support under the assumption that they were within the law; applicant's willingness to comply with the I.C. Act was evidenced by his filing of an application for authority.

Grants of authority, the Commission said in *Ruan Transp. Corp. of Kansas*,[31] to four applicants which were spun off one parent corporation, itself an affiliate of several other common and contract carriers, for the express purpose of providing a limited service for supporting cement shippers, would encourage multiple, corporate entities among carriers subject to the Commission's control, to the detriment of efficient regulation, and would operate to foster waste and inefficiency in transportation and to blur otherwise clean lines of motor-carrier responsibility.

Imposition of Conditions

The authority granted in *Contract Carrier Service, Inc., Extension*[32] was limited by the Commission to transportation service to be per-

[27] 81 M.C.C. 553, 559.
[28] 81 M.C.C. 710, 713.
[29] 83 M.C.C. 151, 156-7.
[30] 76 M.C.C. 735, 736-7.
[31] 83 M.C.C. 189, 194-5.
[32] 78 M.C.C. 301, 305. See also *Fuller* 77 M.C.C. 223, 226; and *Peck*, 79 M.C.C. 425, 429.

formed under a continuing contract or contracts with the two shippers named. In *Carl Subler Trucking, Inc., Extension*,[33] the authority granted was limited to transportation of traffic "not moving under refrigeration"; the phraseology "not requiring refrigeration," the Commission said, was indefinite and subject to varying interpretations. In *Wines from New York, N.Y. to Conn., N.J., N.Y., and Pa.*,[34] the Commission said that under its restricted permit, limiting persons with whom it could contract for transportation service to those "who operate wholesale grocery houses, the business of which is the sale of food," respondent did not have authority to transport wine from producer's plant; the wine producer was not a wholesale grocery house whose business was the sale of food.

While a restriction limiting contract carriers to service under contracts with named shippers is ordinarily included in permits, Section 209(b) does not require imposition of such a restriction in all cases. The Commission held in *Michigan Pickle Co.*[35] that since the proposed service was highly specialized, and the shippers to be served fell within a narrow grouping, the number of persons with whom applicant might enter into a transportation contract would be effectively limited; such a restriction or limitation was, therefore, omitted from the authority granted. Protestant's desire to handle only truckload traffic to the competitive portion of the destination area, the Commission said in *Beatty Motor Exp. Inc., Extension*,[36] was an insufficient reason for restricting the authority granted applicant to less-than-truckload shipments moving with other less-than-truckload shipments in split delivery service. The Commission said in *Fox-Smythe Transp. Co. Extension*[37] that although the service authorized would be limited to that to be provided for the two supporting shippers, a restriction limiting the proposed operation to a peddle service would not be imposed; such a restriction, the Commission said, would be impractical and difficult of enforcement. Here the restrictions would have been acceptable to all parties, but the Commission nevertheless did not impose them. The Commission held in *Pacific Motor Trucking Co., Extension*[38] that its authority to impose terms and conditions in permits issued under Section 209 is derived from

[33] 77 M.C.C. 633, 640.
[34] 305 I.C.C. 307, 308.
[35] 77 M.C.C. 549, 553.
[36] 83 M.C.C. 279, 281. See also *Beatty Motor Exp., Inc., Extension*, 79 M.C.C. 1, 3, where the Commission said that it has long been reluctant to impose load or weight restrictions in granting operating rights because such restrictions are impractical and administratively undesirable.
[37] 79 M.C.C. 279, 283.
[38] 77 M.C.C. 605, 621-3.

(b) thereof, and not from Section 5(2) (b); therefore the proviso in Section 5(2) (b) does not operate as a bar to the issuance of contract-carrier authority to an applicant railroad or an applicant railroad subsidiary. Considering the national transportation policy and the principles which underlie Section 5(2) (b), in accordance with prior holdings which apply in contract-carrier as well as common-carrier application proceedings, the Commission said that the permits issued to applicant would contain a territorial limitation of the service authorized to points which are stations on its parent railroad.

A permit was limited to a period of five years in *C. E. Lizza, Inc., Extension*[39] because the considered commodities were dangerous articles and would move in combined loads with explosives. The Commission said that it would be remiss in fulfilling its obligation to promote public safety if it ignored the hazardous nature of the commodities and the danger of transporting them without adequate policing, which necessarily included the opportunity for full review of applicant's safety practices at least every five years.

Keystone Restrictions

A Keystone restriction in a contract carrier's permit limits not the commodities which may be transported or the territory which may be served, but the persons or class of persons with whom the carrier may enter into transportation contracts. Such restrictions take their names from the application proceeding in which they were first imposed, *Keystone Transp. Co. Contract Carrier Application*.[40] The Keystone restriction was devised in order to enable the Commission to grant contract-carrier authority which was at once broad enough, with respect to the commodities authorized, to enable the carrier to provide a complete service for the shippers which it served, and, at the same time, would tie the carrier down to service for one specific industry or type of business enterprise, thus affording protection to carriers serving other classes of shippers from unwarranted competition.[41]

---

[39] 81 M.C.C. 372, 373.
[40] 19 M.C.C. 475.
[41] *T. T. Brooks Trucking Co., Inc. Conversion*, 81 M.C.C. 561.

9

Permits for Contract Carriers by Water

The Applicable Statutory Provisions

Section 309(f) of the Interstate Commerce Act[1] provides that no person shall engage in the business of a contract carrier unless he or it has an effective permit issued by the Interstate Commerce Commission authorizing such operation. Section 309(g)[2] provides that an application "for such permit shall be made to the Commission in writing, be verified under oath, and shall be in such form and contain such information and be accompanied by proof of service upon such interested parties as the Commission shall, by regulations, require. Subject to section 310, upon application the Commission shall issue such permit if it finds that the applicant is fit, willing, and able properly to perform the service proposed and to conform to the provisions of this part, and the requirements, rule, and regulations of the Commission thereunder, and that such operation will be consistent with the public interest and the national transportation policy declared in this Act. The business of the carrier and the scope thereof shall be specified in such permit and there shall be attached thereto at time of issuance and from time to time thereafter such reasonable terms, conditions, and limitations, consistent with the character of the holder of a contract carrier by water, as are necessary to carry out the requirements of this part or those lawfully established by the Commission pursuant thereto: Provided, however, That no terms, conditions, or limitations shall restrict the right of the carrier to substitute or add contracts within the scope of the permit, or to add to his equipment, facilities, or service, within the scope of the permit, as the development of the business and the demands of the carrier's patrons shall require."

[1]49 U.S.C. 909(f). Comparable provisions — Sections 209, 410(a), 411(b).
[2]49 U.S.C. 909(g). Comparable provisions — Sections 209(b), 410.

271

Principal Characteristics of Common and Contract Water Carriers

Principal Characteristics of Common and Contract Water Carriers

Section 302(d) and (e) of the I.C. Act[3] sets forth the common and contract carrier definitions.

Section 302(d) defines the term "common carrier by water" as meaning "any person which holds itself out to the general public to engage in the transportation by water . . . of . . . property or any class or classes thereof for compensation," and paragraph (e) of the above section defines the term "contract carrier by water" as meaning "any person which, under individual contracts or agreements, engages in the transportation (other than transportation referred to in paragraph (d) . . .) by water . . . of . . . property . . . for compensation."

The Commission gave consideration to the factors which distinguish common carriers from contract carriers in *American Range Lines, Inc., Contr. Car. Application.*[4] In doing so it described American Range's operations in essential part as follows (p. 364):

> Charter-party contracts with shippers were entered into by applicant, usually for a voyage only, but in some instances for more than 1 voyage or for a period of time. The application lists 71 contracts with 16 shippers during the period. . . . Two of these contracts were for periods of 9 months, 2 for 3 months, and 3 each for 2 voyages. The remaining contracts listed were for single voyages of full cargoes, or for quantities ranging, in most instances, from 1,000 to 4,800 tons. . . .

> Applicant did not maintain regular routes, or operate its vessels on fixed schedules, but moved from port to port as required by the individual contracts. . . . It does not advertise for freight, or employ freight solicitors. It neither owns nor leases piers or warehouses for the receipt and delivery of freight, facilities for the loading and unloading of cargoes being provided by the shipper or consignee.

Turning to the statutory definition for determining contract carrier status, the Commission said (pp. 367-68):

> Congress has specifically set forth the circumstances and conditions that constitute a water carrier a common carrier and a contract carrier, and specifically provided tests that distinguish them. The definitions of a common carrier and a contract carrier have one condition in common, namely, that the transportation be for compensation. A common carrier is further defined in part as one that holds itself out to the general public to engage in the transportation by water, in interstate or foreign commerce, of passengers or property. A contract carrier is defined in part as one that does not so hold itself out. Congress, however, went

[3]49 U.S.C. 909(d) and (e).
[4]260 I.C.C. 362.

further and added another condition to differentiate a contract carrier from a common carrier, namely, that it transport "under individual contracts or agreements."

The principal characteristics of a common carrier are holding out to carry for the general public. . . . Transportation for compensation necessarily implies some contract or agreement as to the amount thereof. The mere tendering of traffic to a common carrier and compliance with the carrier's rules . . . is the acceptance of the offer held out to the public and consummates [a] contract of carriage. . . .

Where there was no holding out, or in other words, no outstanding offer to the public generally . . . Congress provided that transportation by a contract carrier must be "under individual contracts or agreements." The reasonable interpretation of the word "individual" is that it was used as opposed to the general contract, arising by operation of law, of a common carrier and in its ordinary meaning of "only one," or as a contract or agreement negotiated with one shipper. The report [below] intimates that each contract of carriage by a common carrier is an individual contract. That is true to the extent that the contract is not consummated until the general offer is accepted and the acceptance is the act of an individual. It is significant, however, that Congress saw fit to incorporate the words "individual contracts or agreements" in the definition of a contract carrier and omit them from the definition of a common carrier. . . . Applicant here required an individual contract or agreement in every instance before it performed any transportation.

In conclusion, the Commission said (p. 369):

. . . [A]pplicant was engaged in the transportation of specific commodities, generally in full cargo lots, or large quantities, under individual contracts or agreements previously entered into. . . . It did not operate between fixed termini or over regular routes, but its vessels went to the ports and at the times called for by the individual contracts. We conclude, therefore, that applicant's operations were those of a contract carrier.

The Commission had considered a somewhat analogous problem in the field of motor carriage in *Contracts of Contract Carriers.*[5] For statutory and factual reasons which are instructive, the solution there evolved was of a different nature. The Commission said (p. 629):

The . . . object of Congress [in the Motor Carrier Act, 1935] is to protect . . . common carriers against cut-throat competition.

The rule evolved (p. 632) was—

that from and after the effective date of the order hereinafter entered, all contract carriers of property by motor vehicle, as defined in section 203(a) (15) of the act, shall transport under contracts or agreements

[5]1 M.C.C. 628. This was a rule making proceeding under §209(b) "to attach limitation to contract-carrier permits in order to forestall transgression upon common carriage." *Interstate Commerce Commission v. J-T Transport Co.*, 368 U.S. 81,97.

which shall be in writing, . . . [and] shall cover a series of shipments during a stated period of time in contrast to contracts of carriage governing individual shipments. . . .[6]

Water common carriers, by contrast, have never been barred from using requirements, voyage, or oral contracts or contracts "governing individual shipments."[7]

Not only is the permissible contract or arrangement different under Part III from Part II of the I.C. Act, but there is also an important difference in the requisites of carrier status in regard to equipment owned by others.

In *Dixie-Ohio Exp. Co. Common Carrier Application,*[8] the Commission evolved a control-and-responsibility test for determining "carrier" status in respect of transportation performed with owner-operated trucks. The Commission said:

> If the vehicles of the owner-operators, while being used by applicant, were operated under its direction and control, and under its responsibility to the general public as well as to the shipper, then its operations, in which such vehicles were employed, come within the phrase "or by a lease or any other arrangement" of section 203(a) (14), and applicant, as to such operations, was a common carrier by motor vehicle. The traffic transported in the vehicles of the owner-operators moved under bills of lading issued by applicant. The vehicles, while in applicant's service, were registered under applicant's operating authority and had applicant's name painted, or otherwise shown, thereon. Insurance covering them was arranged and paid for by applicant. Applicant's dispatchers or other employees directed the time and manner of the loading and unloading of the vehicles and also directed their movement over applicant's routes. We conclude that they were operated under applicant's direction and control and under its responsibility to the general public as well as to the shipper, and that applicant, as to its operations in which such vehicles were employed, was a common carrier by motor vehicle as defined in section 203(a) (14).

The requirements of *Dixie-Ohio* however were rejected by the Commission as a test of water carrier status in *Strittmatter Common Carrier Application.*[9] The question was thereafter considered again in *Bartenfeld Contract Carrier Application*[10] and in the first report in *Water Carrier*

---

[6]The regulation is presently codified.
[7]Commonly called "spot contracts" or "spot" shipments, see *Atwacoal Transp. Co. Contr. Car. Application,* 260 I.C.C. 409, 412; *Atwacoal Transp. Co. Minimum Rates,* 283 I.C.C. 647, 650; And generally see *American Range Lines, Inc., supra.*
[8]17 M.C.C. 735, 740.
[9]250 I.C.C. 639, 643-44.
[10]265 I.C.C. 33.

Service on Great Lakes, Nonowned Vessels.[11] The report on further hearing in the latter proceeding,[12] states the test succinctly as follows:

> The elements necessary to constitute McCarthy the carrier of this traffic were clearly stated in the prior report. Briefly, they may be summarized as follows: That *to constitute one a carrier by water it is necesary that he be in control of the transportation performed by a vessel through control of the cargo carried and the ports served;* that the control contemplated is the right, vested in one not owning a vessel, to *direct the transportation use* to which the vessel's cargo space shall be put, not merely that such space shall be used for a specific cargo previously agreed upon, but that it shall be available to him for the transportation of any suitable shipments or cargo he may desire carried. (Emphasis supplied.)

Sections 218(a) and 306(e) of the I.C. Act pertain to the rate schedules of, respectively, motor and water contract carriers. Sections 218(a) as amended prior to 1957, and 306(e) as enacted by the Transportation Act of 1940, were substantially the same.[13] Section 218(a) before 1957 required every motor contract carrier to file "schedules containing the minimum rates or charges of such carrier actually maintained and charged. . . ."[14] Similarly, Section 306(e) has consistently required each water contract carrier to file "schedules of minimum rates or charges actually maintained and charged. . . ."

In 1957 Section 218(a) was further amended however to require motor contract carrier schedules to show not "the minimum rates or charges . . . actually maintained and charged" but "the actual rates or charges of such carriers."[15] This change was made at the request of the Commission. In its statement of justification for the change the Commission said:

> There is no prohibition in the statute against a contract carrier discriminating amongst shippers as to rates. If, therefore, such a carrier has con-

---

[11] 285 I.C.C. 52.

[12] 285 I.C.C. 419, 422.

[13] "Subsection (e) [of Section 306] deals with contract carriers by water, and requires such carriers to file with the Commission and keep open for public inspection schedules of minimum rates actually maintained and charged. . . . It is comparable to Section 218(e) of Part II as amended." H. R. Rep. No. 1217, 76th Cong., 1st Sess. 23 (1939). Cf. *Filing of Contracts by Contract Carriers by Water,* 285 I.C.C. 450, 453, "recognizing that the phraseology of the parallel provisions in Parts II and III relating to the publication and posting by motor and water contract carriers of schedules showing rates and changes actually maintained and charged are substantially similar. . . ." See also administrative ruling WC No. 1, quoted in *Atwacoal Transp. Co. Minimum Rates,* 283 I.C.C. 647, 654.

[14] Transportation Act of 1940. ch. 722, § 23(a), 54 Stat. 925, 11 Interstate Commerce Acts Annotated 9563 (1942).

[15] Act of Aug. 18, 1957, Pub. L. 85-124, 71 Stat. 343.

tracts to perform identical services for more than one shipper, and different rates are charged the various shippers, the schedule filed with the Commission will show only the lowest charge made for such service.[16]

Since Sections 218(a) and 306(e) were the same in this respect at the time of the Commission's statement of justification, and 306(e) has remained unchanged, the above quotation constitutes a Commission recognition that a contract carrier by water lawfully may charge one shipper a higher rate than that named in its minimum rate schedule so long as at least one shipper is charged the minimum rate named therein. See also administrative ruling WC No. 1, quoted in *Atwacoal Transp. Co. Minimum Rates:*[17]

"[R]ates higher than the minimum rates and charges published may be charged other shippers . . . provided . . . those filed reflect the charges which are actually being collected from some shipper under a contract with such shipper."

As to these several forms of service discrimination collectively, it is pertinent to point out that a contract carrier is under no statutory obligation to provide service nor is it precluded by the I.C. Act from refusing to serve one shipper while choosing to serve another. The Part III requirement "to provide and furnish . . . transportation upon reasonable request therefor"[18] applies only to common carriers, as does the prohibition against "subject[ing] any . . . person . . . to any unjust discrimination. . . ."[19] These provisions have no application to contract carriers, nor is there any similar requirement elsewhere in the I.C. Act applicable to contract carriers. As stated in *American Range Lines, Inc., Contr. Car. Application:*[20]

Common carriers have a duty to serve the general public. They are required to handle traffic whether it is profitable to do so or not. They are also obliged to maintain a service they hold themselves out to perform. They must treat all shippers alike. The act does not place the contract carrier under such a duty. It may choose among shippers whom it will serve and what it will carry.

Applicable Criteria

Section 309(g) of the Interstate Commerce Act[21] authorizes the issuance of permits to water carriers upon the same statutory finding

---

[16]H. R. Rep. No. 895, 85th Cong., 1st Session, Appx. (1957).
[17]283 I.C.C. 647, 654.
[18]Section 305(a) of the I.C. Act.
[19]Section 305(e) of the I.C. Act.
[20]260 I.C.C. 362, 372 (Dissent).
[21]49 U.S.C. 909(g).

as required for the issuance of permits in motor carrier proceedings — consistency with the public interest and the national transportation policy. The only difference is that the Congress spelled out certain criteria of the public interest in its 1957 amendments of Sections 203(a) (15) and 209(b) pertaining to contract carriage by motor vehicle, while the provisions pertaining to water contract carriage have remained unchanged since the enactment of Part III in 1940. Under the contract carrier provisions of Part III, applications have generally been denied upon showings that existing carriers could provide the shipper with the type of service it requires.[22] On the other hand, contract carriers by water have been granted extensions of authority in cases involving shipper-owned carriers which gear their services to their parent companies in the interests of effeciency and economy.[23] Contract carrier authorities also have been granted where the showing is made that low-cost transportation would be provided by the applicant and that an applicant's equipment is especially adapted to the shippers' needs and protestant has not furnished a reasonably adequate service.[24]

For an application to be approved, it must be shown generally that opposing carriers cannot provide the shippers with the type of transportation service they require, and that applicant's proposed service would be superior to that which could be provided by the opposing carriers if the traffic were tendered to them. Unfavorable shipping experiences by the shippers would have to be shown.

In *Warrier & Gulf Nav. Co. Extension — Cape Canaveral*,[25] an application was filed seeking an amended permit authorizing operation, in interstate or foreign commerce, as a contract carrier by self-propelled vessels, and by non-self-propelled vessels with the use of separate towing vessels of numerous commodities (e.g., aluminum, canned goods, iron and steel articles, lumber, machinery, manganese ore paint) between points on the Atlantic Coast from Fort Pierce, Florida, to Cape Kennedy, Florida, as an extension of its present authority. Applicant was a wholly-owned subsidiary of a steel corporation, the supporting shipper. It was the successor in interest to another subsidiary water carrier which operated along the Gulf Intercoastal Waterways and had been granted a "grandfather" permit authorizing it to perform freighting services as a contract carrier in the transportation of most of the commodities for

---

[22]*Indian Towing Co., Inc., Contract Carrier Application*, 309 I.C.C. 473, 478.
[23]*Ohio Barge Line, Inc., Extension — Pig Tin*, 285 I.C.C. 5.
[24]*Marine Transport Lines, Inc., Extension — Los Angeles*, 285 I.C.C. 655; *Hanson Towing Co. Contract Carrier Application*, 311 I.C.C. 609; *McGehee Contract Carrier Application*, 285 I.C.C. 107.
[25]322 I.C.C. 261.

which new authority was being sought.[26] Applicant contended that it provided economical transportation coordinated to the needs of the shipper's production plants along the waterways it is authorized to serve and insisted that the single-line service it proposed to provide from the shipper's points to Cape Kennedy could be performed more economically than the joint-line services of existing carriers. The shipper stated that no other carrier by water offered it the complete, low-cost transportation service which applicant provided, and it believed that such service was necessary to meet its transportation needs to Cape Kennedy. The protestants contended that they could provide a through Kennedy service.

The Commission held that the showing made warranted the conclusion that a grant of authority would be consistent with the public interest and the national transportation policy. It said (pp. 265-66):

> . . . Clearly, applicant proposes to extend an efficient and economical service geared to meet the needs of its parent company and its divisions for the transportation of iron and steel articles to an additional consuming point. It is advantageous to the shipper to deal with applicant as its alter ego rather than two or more carriers in effecting the movement of its products from its mills to the consuming point. Although protestants are able to provide a through joint-line service which in some respects is similar to that of applicant, they have made no showing that such service would be as economical as that proposed by applicant, or so geared to the shipper's production schedules as to fully meet its overall needs. Nor does it appear that protestants would be materially affected by the authority granted herein since they made no showing that they handle any of the traffic here involved. In order that points between Fort Pierce and Cape Kennedy may be served by applicant should any movement of the shipper's traffic thereto arise, authority will be likewise granted to serve such points. However, no need for the transportation of commodities other than iron and steel articles has been shown and the authority will be limited accordingly.
>
> One additional matter requires comment. Under Section 310 of the Interstate Commerce Act, applicant may not hold a certificate and permit unless a finding is made that dual operations are consistent with the public interest and the national transportation policy. The proposed operation will not be competitive with operations under applicant's certificate No. W-654. Accordingly, the record supports a finding that the holding by applicant of its existing certificate and the proposed permit will be consistent with the public interest and the national transportation policy. However, such approval of dual operations at this time should not be construed as any waiver of the Commission's right, which is hereby expressly reserved, to reconsider this issue at any future date should the present situation change so as to bring about an improper competitive situation, discrimination, or preference.

[26]Applicant's corporate history, its past operations, and those of its predecessor are described in *Isthmian S.S. Co. Common Carrier Application*, 250 I.C.C. 359, 365.

The Commission in its interpretation of Section 309(g) has held that existing carriers are entitled to transport all of the traffic which they can handle adequately, efficiently, and economically without the competition of a new service in the considered territory.[27] In the *Indian Towing* case a permit was denied where carriers were ready and willing to charter shipper's waterproof barge to provide the required freighting service, or to tow it in interchange operations, thereby providing a through service without transfer of lading. As the shipper had not tendered its traffic to the available water carriers and had repeatedly been unwilling to charter its barge to any carrier but applicant, the Commission said that its support of the application was merely predicated on its preference for applicant's service.[28] In *Sause Bros. Ocean Towing Co., Inc., Extension,*[29] the Commission said that no doubt a grant of authority would aid applicant in obtaining balanced operations, but this is no valid reason for subjecting existing carriers to the added competition of the proposed operation, especially in absence of any clear need for such service.

The Commission said in *Hanson Towing Co.*[30] that to deny the application for a permit in the circumstances would be unrealistic. There the evidence established a need for transportation of scrap iron from Camden, Ark., to Baton Rouge and New Orleans, La., which could not be met by existing carriers; the railroads could not provide the type of service desired by the supporting shipper, and the protestant common-carrier barge line did not actually operate beyond a port 44 miles below Camden. The latter carrier, to handle the traffic, would have had to operate barges empty to Camden from perhaps as far away as New Orleans, and for several years it had maintained in its tariff a partial suspension of service between Camden and New Orleans. On the other hand applicant was already returning empty from Camden to Baton Rouge and was in position to offer a rate the shipper could utilize. The Commission said that while normally a shipper's desire for lower rates does not warrant a grant of authority here, however, it did not appear that protestant had any real interest in the considered traffic, and it was well aware of the fact that it would not move any of it at its present rates. Thus the offered rates were considered by the Commission in arriving at its determination.

[27]*Indian Towing Co., Inc.,* 309 I.C.C. 473, 478.
[28]*Ibid.*
[29]305 I.C.C. 311, 317.
[30]311 I.C.C. 609, 612.

Holding of Both a Certificate of Public Convenience and Necessity and a Permit

Section 310 of the Interstate Commerce Act[31] provides that a carrier may not hold a certificate and permit unless it is shown that both may be so held consistently with the public interest and the national transportation policy. If it is determined that operations as a common and contract carrier would be directly competitive because of such operations being conducted in substantially the same territory, thus presenting opportunities through dual operations for destructive competitive practices which Section 310 is designed to prevent, the conclusion would be arrived at by the Commission that the holding of both a certificate and permit is not consistent with the public interest and national transportation policy.[32]

---

[31]49 U.S.C. 910.
[32]*Warrier & Gulf Nav. Co. — Cape Canaveral,* 322 I.C.C. 261, 265-66.

10

Permits for Freight Forwarders

Freight Forwarder Defined

The term "freight forwarder" is defined by Section 402(a) (5) of the Interstate Commerce Act[1] as "any person which (otherwise than as a carrier subject to Part I, II, or III of this Act) holds itself out to the general public as a common carrier to transport or provide transportation of property, or any class or classes of property, for compensation, in interstate commerce, and which, in the ordinary and usual course of its undertaking, (a) assembles and consolidates or provides for assembling and consolidating shipments of such property, and performs or provides for the performance of break-bulk and distributing operations with respect to such consolidated shipments, and (b) assumes responsibility for the transportation of such property from point of receipt to point of destination, and (c) utilizes, for the whole or any part of the transportation of such shipments, the services of a carrier or carriers subject to Part I, II, or III of this Act."

The term "freight forwarders" was originally applied to persons who, without owning or controlling the actual means of carriage, such as ships, railroad cars, etc., arranged for the transportation of the goods of the consignor in the ships or vehicles of an actual carrier.[2] Later a different type of forwarding service was offered. The forwarder picked up a less than carload shipment at the shipper's place of business and engaged to deliver it safely at its ultimate destination, charging its rate covering the entire transportation and making its profit by consolidating

---

[1] 49 U.S.C. 1002(a) (5). Section 1010(a) (1) provides that it shall be illegal for any person to engage in the business of freight forwarding without first obtaining a permit from the I.C.C.

[2] *Mansfield v. Chicago Title and T. Co.*, 199 Fed. 95.

the shipment with others in carload quantities to take advantage of the spread between the carload rates paid by the forwarder and the higher rates, approximating less than carload rates, which the forwarder charged the owner of the shipment.[3] The definition of the term freight forwarder in Section 402(a) (5) shows that only the second type of freight forwarder[4] is within the coverage of the I.C. Act.[5]

The Supreme Court in *Chicago, M., St. P. & Pac. R. Co. v. Acme Fast Freight*,[6] spoke of the Freight Forwarder Act and the operations of freight forwarders in this fashion: The Freight Forwarder Act of 1942, which appears as Part IV of the Interstate Commerce Act, was designed to define freight forwarders, to prescribe certain regulations governing forwarder operations, and to bring the freight forwarder business within the control of the Commission. Freight forwarders consolidate less than carload freight into carloads for shipment by rail. Their charges approximate rail less than carload rates; their expenses and profits are derived from the spread between the carload and l.c.l. rates. Forwarders are utilized by l.c.l. shippers because of the speed and efficiency with which they handle shipments, the unity of responsibility obtained, and certain services which forwarders make available. Forwarders are required by Section 413 of the I.C. Act to issue bills of lading to their customers, covering the individual packaged shipments from time of receipt until delivery to the ultimate consignee. When the freight is consolidated into carloads, the railroad gives the forwarder its bill of lading in which the forwarder is designated as both consignor and consignee. The contents are noted as "one carload of mixed merchandise" and usually move under an "all-commodity" carload rate. The destination set out in the railroad bill of lading is the forwarder's break-bulk point. At the point the carload is broken up; some shipments may be distributed locally, some sent by truck to off-line destinations, and some consolidated into carloads for reshipment to further break-bulk points. The railroad has no knowledge of the contents of the car, the identity of the individual shippers, or the ultimate destinations of the consignment. The forwarder has an unqualified right to select the carrier and route for the transportation of the freight. The forwarder thus has some of the characteristics of both carrier and shipper. In its relations with its customers, a forwarder is subjected by the I.C. Act to many of

---

[3]*United States v. Chicago Heights Trucking So.*, 310 U.S. 344.
[4]For a full description of freight forwarder practices see *United States v. Chicago Heights Trucking Co.*, 310 U.S. 344; *Freight Forwarding Investigation*, 229 I.C.C. 201; *Bills of Lading of Freight Forwarders*, 259 I.C.C. 277.
[5]*Chicago, M St. P. & Pac. Ry. Co., v. Acme Fast Freight*, 336 U.S. 465.
[6]336 U.S. 465, 466.

the requirements and regulations applicable to common carriers. In its relations with these carriers, however, the status of the forwarder is still that of shipper.

Operations as a Freight Forwarder

All the elements delineated in Section 402(a) (5) must be proffered by a person in order to find that he is operating as a freight forwarder.[7]

The following pertinent findings were made by the Commission in the *Compass* case in arriving at a determination that freight forwarding operations were being conducted by the parties involved:

1. *Holding out to the general public* — It was found that the parties, through telephone listings, correspondence, advertising, and general solicitation, held themselves out to the general public to provide for-hire containerized services on shipments from Japan to the west coast ports of the U.S.
2. *Compensation* — There was a finding that the parties performed the services for compensation. This was based on an indirect compensation theory — measurable compensation for the considered services in direct proportion to the increased volume of shipments tendered to NYK and Japan Line.
3. *Assembly and consolidation* — A finding was made that the parties performed "assembly" and "consolidation" within the meaning of Section 402(a)(5).
4. *Break bulk and distribution* — A finding was made that the parties provided "break bulk" and "distribution" services within the meaning of Section 402(a)(5).
5. *Utilization of the services of a carrier subject to regulation by the I.C.C.* — Findings were made that the railroads were utilized from west coast ports to inland points, and that the railroads were paid on the basis of their tariff rates filed with the I.C.C. A finding was made also that the parties held out the performance of a through ocean-railroad service without the publication of governing joint rates.
6. *Assumption of responsibility for the transportation from point of receipt to destination* — Findings were made that the parties assumed responsibility to point of final destination, and there was no definite joint participation by several carriers in a through connecting service.

Consolidation or Distribution Service

While the I.C. Act does not limit forwarder operations to small shipments, it defines "freight forwarder" as a person who, among other things,

---

[7]*Compass, Nippon, and Transmarine-Investigation*, 344 I.C.C. 246, 262-63, rev. in *Japan Line, Ltd. v. United States*, 393 F. Supp. 131, on the ground that the parties did not perform the services for compensation.

assembles and consolidates shipments and performs or provides for performance of break-bulk and distribution service on such consolidated shipments; therefore, when a proposed volume rate contemplates truckload movements direct from shipper to consignee without any consolidation or distribution service, the transportation performed would not be a forwarder service and would be unlawful.[8] The I.C. Act also provides that rates and charges of a freight forwarder shall not be established to cover "the line-haul transportation between the principal concentration point and the principal break-bulk point," thus a freight forwarder must assemble and consolidate, and break-bulk and distribute.[9] Where shipments are tendered in cars loaded by shippers the operation would not be that of a freight forwarder.[10] To retain a freight forwarder status, however, it is not necessary to assemble and consolidate, and break-bulk and distribute as to every shipment handled as to so require would disregard the language in Section 402(a) (5), reading that the performance of the above should be "in the ordinary and usual course of its undertaking."[11]

Where one assembles and consolidates shipments and provides for the performance of break-bulk and distributing operations, and assumes responsibility for the entire transportation from point of receipt, the operation is that of a freight forwarder[12] since Section 402(a) (5) places upon a freight forwarder the responsibility for transportation of property "from point of receipt to point of destination."[13] The legislative history of Part IV does not establish that freight forwarders are restricted to handling of small shipments only, nor does Section 402(a) limit the maximum weight of shipments which may be handled by a forwarder.[14]

In *Forwarder Volume Commodity Rates, Transcontinental*,[15] the Commission said that there was nothing in the provisions of part IV or the legislative history thereof to establish that freight forwarders are, or were intended to be, limited in weight of shipments they may handle. The Commission said that even where rates are published on volume minima of 20,000 to 30,000 pounds, a partially loaded car would normally move to respondent's terminal for loading of additional shipments to

[8]*Boots or Shoes, Bel Camp, Md., to Boston and Providence*, 313 I.C.C. 137, 138.
[9]*Class Rates, Official Territory to Corpus Christi*, 303 I.C.C. 293, 298.
[10]*Ibid.*
[11]*Dinion Coil Co. v. International Forwarding Co.*, 304 I.C.C. 1, 3.
[12]*Parcel Warehouse, Inc., Freight Forwarder Application*, 285 I.C.C. 697, 701.
[13]*Acme Fast Freight, Inc. v. Western Freight Assn.*, 299 I.C.C. 315, 326.
[14]*Import Volume Forwarder Rates, Pacific Coast to East*, 310 I.C.C. 399, 401; *Eastern Central M. Carriers Assn. v. Baltimore & O. R. Co.*, 314 I.C.C. 5, 44.
[15]313 I.C.C. 773, 775-76.

make up as nearly as possible the 60,000 pounds average that respondent's experience showed could be loaded in a mixed carload; there was then no question that consolidation was practiced, and the fact that rules of underlying carriers (which were for their convenience) could at times obviate the handling that would otherwise be performed did not render respondent's operations unlawful; such operations were those of a forwarder as defined in the I.C. Act.[16]

In *Forwarder Volume Commodity Rates*,[17] the Commission held that under proposed volume rates where a forwarder contracted for 2 or more shipments (including 2 shipments each occupying a single trailer), tendered them at railhead to be shipped as a single carload, and made or arranged for distribution of each of the tendered shipments to its consignee, there was consolidation and distribution by the forwarder despite the fact that the railroad providing the underlying transportation physically placed the trailers on the flatcar and removed them from it at the termination of the line haul. However, in *Import Volume Forwarder Rates, Pacific Coast to East*,[18] the Commission said that since the stright volume shipments tendered in quantities equal to or exceeding the rail minimum would require no assembling or distribution, transportation thereof would not be a freight forwarder service as defined in Section 402(a) (5).

In *Sheiman*,[19] the Commission held that applicant's operation, which in all other respects conformed with the definition of a freight forwarder under Section 402(a) (5), was not removed from that category merely because the break-bulk, distribution, consolidation, and assembly services, in connection with inbound and outbound movement of campers' baggage and person effects, were performed physically by camp personnel at the campsites and not by applicant's employees; these services were performed in accordance with prior arrangements made by applicant with the camp management; and the transportation services undertaken by applicant, and for which he assumed full responsibility, were not completed until the baggage picked up at the campers' homes was placed at the individual camper's cabin or, on the return movement, placed at his home.

---

[16]*Ibid.*
[17]310 I.C.C. 199, 203.
[18]310 I.C.C. 399, 404.
[19]308 I.C.C. 665, 667-8.

The Applicable Statutory Provision for Issuance of Permit

Section 410(c) of the Interstate Commerce Act[20] provides that the "Commission shall issue a permit to any qualified applicant therefor, authorizing the whole or any part of the service covered by the application, if the Commission finds that the applicant is ready, able, and willing properly to perform the service proposed, and that the proposed service, to the extent authorized by the permit, is or will be consistent with the public interest and the national transportation policy declared in this Act; otherwise such application shall be denied. No such permit shall be issued to any common carrier subject to Part I, II, or III of this Act; but no application made under this section by a corporation controlled by, or under common control with, a common carrier subject to Part I, II, or III of this Act, shall be denied because of the relationship between such corporation and such common carrier." A permit is required under Section 410(a) (1).[21]

Public Interest and National Transportation Policy

Applicants for freight forwarder permits must show that the operations they propose will be consistent with the public interest and the national transportation policy; in making such a showing they must establish that the existing service is inadequate to meet the reasonable needs of the public in the same manner as those seeking certificated authority under Part II of the act. This latter requirement was effectively imposed when Section 410(d) of the I.C. Act was amended in 1957 for the specific purpose of eliminating the needless and uneconomical duplication of existing facilities which would result in the institution of additional freight forwarder service, absent such a showing.[22]

The burden is on applicant for forwarder permit to show by clear and convincing probative evidence that the proposed operations will be consistent with public interest and the national transportation policy; and generally speaking it is incumbent on the Commission, in the interest of sound and equitable regulation of the freight-forwarder industry and to avoid improvident and wasteful duplication of transportation services

---

[20]49 U.S.C. 1010(c). Comparable provisions — Sections 1(20), 207, 309(c) as to common carriers; Sections 209(b), 309(g) as to contract carriers; Section 211(b) as to brokers. As to competitive operation by commonly controlled carriers, see Sections 5(14)-(16), 210 and 310.

[21]49 U.S.C. 1010(a) (1).

[22]*Norman G. Jensen, Inc., F. F. Application*, 318 I.C.C. 719, 724.

and facilities, to require applicants to establish that existing service is unable or unwilling to meet reasonable needs of supporting shippers.[23]

The Commission may grant new or additional forwarder authority even though existing service is adequate, provided such a grant of authority is supported by proof of public interest factors of equal or dominant importance.[24] Adequacy of existing service therefore is not a controlling factor, but instead is only one of several elements to be considered. Other elements of importance may include the desirability of competition, the desirability of different kinds of service, and the desirability of improved service.[25] To establish a prima facie case, the Commission has held that supporting shippers "must show the commodities shipped or received, the points between which that traffic moved, the volume of freight to be tendered to applicant, the present transportation services used, and the deficiencies in existing services."[26]

If the evidence presented is too vague and hypothetical to permit a finding of any specific proposed service that could be valued in terms of the public interest and national transportation policy, the application will be denied.[27] The statute requires more than a commitment by the applicant seeking extension of its operation; there must be a clear-cut and definite description of the specific service or its territorial extent which applicant proposes to perform.[28]

Where an applicant admitted that the volume of forwarded traffic did not justify the expense of bringing shipper witnesses to the hearing, coupled with the testimony of existing carriers that the volume of available traffic was very small, the Commission in *Superior Fast Freight Extension*[29] denied the application, stating that serious doubts were raised as to the assurance of a continued stable operation if extension authority were granted. In *Flying Forwarding Co., Inc., Extension,*[30] the Commis-

---

[23]*West Coast Freight Co., Inc.,* 309 I.C.C. 123, 127.

[24]*Dow Co., Inc., Extension — Longview,* 322 I.C.C. 103; *Brinke Freight Forwarder Application,* 335 I.C.C. 861; *CTI-Container Transport International Freight Forwarder Application,* 341 I.C.C. 169; *D. C. Andrews & Co. of Illinois Extension — Baltimore, Md.,* 326 I.C.C. 743; *Aloha Consolidators Int. v. United States,* 395 F. Supp. 1006.

[25]*Nashua Motor Express, Inc. v. United States,* 230 F. Supp. 646; *Yellow Forwarding Company v. Interstate Commerce Commission,* 369 F. Supp. 1040.

[26]*John Novak Contract Carrier Application,* 103 M.C.C. 557; see also *Richard Dahn, Inc. v. I.C.C.,* 335 F. Supp. 337; *Acme Fast Freight, Inc. v. United States,* 146 F. Supp. 369.

[27]*ABC Freight Forwarding Corp. v. United States,* 169 F. Supp. 403, 404.

[28]*Ibid.,* pp. 405-6 See *Brinke Freight Forwarder Application,* 335 I.C.C. 867.

[29]306 I.C.C. 341-344.

[30]285 I.C.C. 794, 797.

sion said that where there is an abundance of service and no prospect of better service by the applicant, the service sought will be denied. In *West Coast Freight Co., Inc.*,[31] an application was denied where the applicant had failed to show any specific or substantive complaints or dissatisfaction of shippers with existing forwarder service; at best, supporting shippers showed only a preference for the proposed service, apparently stemming from their past satisfactory relations with applicant's president in another phase of the transportation business; this, the Commission said, is an insufficient basis for the grant of authority in the absence of evidence of some material deficiency in existing service. In this same proceeding, the Commission said that applicant's proposed free pickup service was not a new type of service which existing carriers were unable to provide, nor was that factor of proposed operation a sound or proper basis for issuance of new operating authority. If shippers believe that the failure or refusal of certain forwarders to provide unrestricted free pickup is an unjust or unreasonable practice, the Commission said, their remedy is in a complaint preceeding.[32]

An application was granted in *North Pacific Forwarders, Inc., Extension*,[33] the Commission stating that the grant was warranted when a substantial number of shippers in the involved States had shown need for a service to handle consolidation of their small-volume shipments to certain points, and their assurances that they would use the proposed service indicated that a sufficient volume of freight would be available to insure stability of the proposed operation. No adequate forwarder service was shown to be presently available, as the only authorized forwarder operating in that area was interested solely in a specific type of freight and, despite previous opportunity to do so, filed rates covering the type of operation proposed only after applicant had filed the pending application; also, it had handled no traffic between the points involved. The Commission granted authority in *Parcel Warehouse, Inc., Freight Forwarder Application*,[34] where applicant's service would supply a need for prompt transportation of parcels of merchandise from origin to points in certain States; no evidence was submitted by protestant and interveners of their services or that a service, such as proposed by applicant, was being supplied by existing freight forwarders or other carriers; and the proposed operation would facilitate the movement of mail-order

---

[31] 309 I.C.C. 123, 127.
[32] *Ibid.*
[33] 310 I.C.C. 316, 319.
[34] 285 I.C.C. 697, 702.

merchandise and would not have any material adverse effect upon existing carriers.

Availability of Other Modes of Transportation

The Commission has held that freight forwarders provide a service entirely different from that offered by other carriers so, despite the existence of other forms of transportation, if shippers desire to avail themselves of the advantages of this transportation medium they should be afforded an opportunity to do so; this is consistent with the national transportation policy.[35]

Terms, Conditions and Limitations

Under Section 410(e)[36] it is provided that any "permit issued under this section shall specify the nature or general description of the property with respect to which service subject to this part may be performed, and the territory within which, and the territories from which and to which, service subject to this part may be performed, under authority of such permit. At the time of issuance, and from time to time thereafter, there shall be attached to the exercise of the privileges granted by any such permit such reasonable terms, conditions, and limitations as are necessary to carry out the requirements of this part or those lawfully established by the Commission pursuant thereto; but no such terms, conditions, or limitations shall restrict the right of the freight forwarder to add to its equipment, facilities, or services within the scope of such permit, as the development of the business and the demands of the public shall require."

In *Sheiman*,[37] the Commission said that although camps of the operators supporting the application were situated at specific points in 3 of the 10 destination States sought, this was not sufficient justification for territorially limiting the authority granted; applicant had also served camps in 3 other States and, to enable him to perform a complete and well-rounded service, it was proper that he should be given authority to serve all points embraced in the application. In *Chi-Can Freight Forwarding*,[38] the Commission said that restriction of authority granted for

---

[35]*North Pacific Forwarders, Inc., Extension*, 310 I.C.C. 316, 319.
[36]49 U.S.C. 1010(e). Comparable provisions — Sections 208(a), 309(d) as to common carriers; and Sections 209(b), 309(g) as to contract carriers.
[37]308 I.C.C. 665, 669-70.
[38]310 I.C.C. 693, 698.

forwarder operation from four midwestern States to Ontario and Quebec, Canada, to traffic moving via Chicago would serve no useful purpose and should not be imposed. The Commission said that except in unusual circumstances, such a restriction is contrary to the general nature of freight-forwarder operations in that forwarders historically have exercised their discretion in routing their traffic.

In *Chain Deliveries Exp., Inc., Extension,*[39] applicant's existing authority being limited to parcels or packages not exceeding 100 inches length and girth combined, or 70 pounds weight, it sought removal of that limitation on traffic from New York City to District of Columbia and 5 States. The Commission said that since little or no other actual service on packages exceeding those limitations was available to North Carolina, Virginia, Kentucky, Tennessee, and certain points in Pennsylvania, provision of a complete forwarding service in that area would serve a useful purpose for supporting shippers, principally department stores, who should be able to rely on applicant for faster and more efficient service needed in handling the larger packages they were shipping within that territory; removal of the size limitations and increase of the maximum weight per parcel to 200 pounds was therefore justified. But the Commission said further that since forwarder service available from protestants generally on New York City traffic to Philadelphia and Washington, D.C., commercial zones, and from one of the protestants on wearing apparel, accessories, and piece goods to eastern Pennsylvania, appeared wholly adequate, and a new service competitive therewith would not serve the public interest, liberalization of the present size and weight restrictions on traffic to District of Columbia would be denied, and that which was authorized would be restricted to exclude traffic generally to the Philadelphia zone and Virginia points in the Washington zone, as well as wearing apparel, accessories, and piece goods, to Pennsylvania points.

Bills of Lading

The freight forwarder is required by Section 413 to issue bills of lading to its customers covering individual packaged shipments from time of receipt until delivery to ultimate consignee.

Contracts

Section 409 permits freight forwarders to enter into or to continue to operate under contracts with Part II common carriers governing the

[39]311 I.C.C. 569, 577-8.

utilization by freight forwarders of services and instrumentalities of such carriers and compensation to be paid therefor, provided that just, reasonable and equitable terms are established. Also where 450 miles or more are involved contracts shall not permit payment of compensation which is lower than would be received under rates or charges established under Part II.

Joint Loading of Traffic

Section 404(d) of the I.C. Act[40] provides:

Nothing in this part shall be construed to prohibit any freight forwarder from entering into an agreement with another freight forwarder for the joint loading of traffic between points in transportation subject to this part, except that the Commission may cancel, suspend, or require the modification of any such agreement which it finds, after reasonable opportunity for hearing, to be inconsistent with the national transportation policy declared in this Act.

The term "joint loading," as used in Section 404(d), connotes a common relation or interest in the operation; and that in order to be engaged in joint loading two or more freight forwarders, at least theoretically, must load their shipments together in the same car or other conveyance.[41] In *Twin City Shippers Ass'n. Freight Forwarder Application,*[42] the Commission held that pursuant to law a joint loader should pay only its proportion of the transportation charges. It also noted that if any terminal services are performed by the other freight forwarders for the joint loader, the latter's proportionate share of the terminal facility costs should be separate and distinct from the charges for transportation.

---

[40]49 U.S.C. 1004(d).
[41]*Kelly Freight Forwarder Application,* 40 I.C.C. 315, 322; *General Carloading Co., Inc., Freight Forwarder Application,* 260 I.C.C. 345.
[42]260 I.C.C. 307, 312-13.

11

Airfreight Forwarders

The economic regulations governing the classification and exemption of indirect air carriers and international airfreight forwarders provide that no person shall operate as an airfreight forwarder unless there is in force with respect to such person a document entitled "Operating Authorization" authorizing him to engage in air transportation pursuant to a general exemption.[1] Persons desiring to operate as airfreight forwarders or international airfreight forwarders must apply to the Civil Aeronautics Board for appropriate operating authorizations.[2]

No operating authorization will be issued to an applicant which fails to demonstrate, as part of its showing of capability, that it has such branch offices, associated companies, or agents as tend to establish the ability of applicant to perform pickup, delivery, and other necessary services to be performed in handling shipments.

In the event that operating authorization is sought through a subsidiary freight forwarder, the Board must approve of such control and of the interlocking relationships.

Each operating authorization shall be effective upon the date specified therein, and shall continue in effect, unless sooner suspended or revoked, during such period as the authority provided shall remain in effect, or if issued for a limited period of time, shall continue in effect until the expiration thereof unless sooner suspended or revoked. At the time of issuance, and from time to time thereafter, there shall

[1] 14 C.F.R. 296, 297.
[2] In *Railway Express Agency, Inc. v. CAB*, 345 F. 2d 445, the court upheld the Board's determination that REA was not entitled to perform certain indirect air carrier or airfreight forwarding services through the method of filing so-called "joint rates" between itself and the air carriers pursuant to Section 1003 of the Federal Aviation Act. Rather, the court said the CAB correctly determined that the operations required specific operating authority from the Board.

be attached to the exercise of the privileges granted by any operating authorization such reasonable terms, conditions, and limitations applicable to the person named therein as are necessary to carry out the requirements of the Act and the regulation prescribed thereunder.

An operating authorization shall be nontransferable and shall be effective only with respect to the person named therein or his successor by operation of law.

The Board's policy toward air freight forwarders has been one of free entry from the beginning of its regulatory history. However, special attention was paid to the problem of surface carrier interests controlling or dominating the infant industry. Where surface affiliations were not thought to be harmful to the promotion and development of air transportation they were permitted, but where an opposite result was anticipated surface control was prohibited. From 1948 to 1967, as the air freight forwarding industry matured, surface participation in the industry expanded until only long-haul motor carriers of general commodities were excluded from participation in domestic air freight forwarding.[3]

Motor Carrier — Airfreight Forwarder Investigation,[4] presented the question whether long-haul motor carriers of general commodities should be granted entry into the airfreight forwarding field. D. C. International, Inc., and Navajo Freight Lines, Inc., applied for domestic and international forwarding authority on their own behalf, and Consolidated Freightways, Inc., and Pacific Intermountain Express Co. requested similar authority through subsidiaries and applied for approval for the resulting control and interlocking relationships. After public hearings, the hearing officer issued an initial decision in which he concluded that the applicants should be granted authority to engage in airfreight forwarding, as requested, for an experimental, five-year period.[5] In essence, the hearing officer concluded that the applicants' authorizations would result in a substantial benefit to the public, would strengthen the airfreight forwarder industry over the long run, would not injure direct air carriers or cause any conflicts of interest adverse to the public, and would not lead to unfair competitive practices or other illegal activities. The Board

---

[3]See *Air Freight Forwarder Case*, 9 C.A.B. 473, affirmed in *American Airlines, Inc. v. C.A.B.*, 178 F. 2d 903; *Air Freight Forwarder Case (International)*, 11 C.A.B. 182; *Air Freight Forwarder Investigation*, 21 C.A.B. 536; *Railway Express, Airfreight Forwarder Application*, 27 C.A.B. 500; *Air Freight Forwarder Authority Case*, 40 C.A.B. 673; *Telstar Air Freight, Interlocking Relationships*, 43 C.A.B. 721; *Petition of Air Freight Forwarders Association of America*, Order 76-11-148, November 30, 1976.

[4]Order E-25725, September 1967.

[5]The recommendation was made subject to the approval of interlocking relationships of two of the carriers.

adopted the hearing officer's findings and conclusions, with certain modifications.

The Board recognized that the competition of these applicants as airfreight forwarders could divert some airfreight gathering and consolidating activities from other airfreight forwarders and from the direct air carriers themselves, but felt that applicants' activities might well increase the total volume of airfreight forwarding activity, and its public acceptance and use, to such an extent that the results would include net gains from the other airfreight forwarders and direct air carriers. In any event, the Board was of the opinion that the public interest in the availability of additional airfreight forwarding services would not permit it to forbid these services in order to protect existing airfreight forwarders and direct air carriers from this competition. Finally, the Board said that the participation in airfreight forwarding of motor carriers may well be necessary to achieve the full promise of air cargo.

The Board's order in *Motor Carrier-Airfreight Forwarder Investigation* was vacated and remanded in *ABC Airfreight Company v. CAB*,[6] for resolution of the ambiguity whether the Board had established a policy of entry for all truckers who wanted to act as airfreight forwarders or merely granted the applications that were before it.

On remand the Board reaffirmed[7] its previously authorized long-haul motor carriers to engage in air freight forwarding. The Board found that the applicants' authorizations would result in substantial public benefits, and that it appeared that the fears expressed by the independent forwarders of possible injury to the industry and to the promotion of air freight as a result of long-haul motor carrier entry were unfounded. Nevertheless, the Board determined to limit the authorizations to a period of five years and to "monitor the entry" of long-haul motor carriers during the period so that the Board could test on the basis of factual experience the contentions of the independent forwarders that the entry of long-haul motor carriers would result in deleterious conflicts of interest and would adversely affect continued operation by the independent forwarders.

In its opinion on remand in the *Motor Carrier* case, the Board had occasion to re-examine its policy with respect to the entry of surface carriers into the airfreight forwarding business. In making awards to three of the applicants, the Board summarized its findings and conclusions as follows:

[6]391 F. 2d 295.
[7]*Motor Carrier-Airfreight Forwarder Investigation,* Order 69-4-100, April 1969, mimeo. op. on remand, at pp. 3-4.

In brief, the Board finds that those applicants' authorization will result in substantial public benefits, will not result in conflicts of interest which will interfere with the promotion of air cargo, and will not reduce effective competition by the existing independent air forwarding industry. . . . And the Board believes that its policy should continue to be one of granting authorizations which will contribute to the growth and development of air cargo, rather than one of protecting existing forwarders from competition.

The Board emphasizes, however, that it is granting only the applications before it and not passing upon any others. For other applicants, the Board tentatively concludes only that it should not deem the size, geographical extent, or general commodity rights of a trucker's surface operations or authority — of themselves — as factors showing that the trucker should be barred from the airfreight forwarding business. But long-haul truckers of general commodities will not be granted air forwarding licenses routinely. Instead, each trucker applicant will be required to show that it will conscientiously promote air cargo and that its operations, either alone or in combination with others already licensed, will be in the public interest. The Board will not be satisfied with mere recitations; it will scrutinize each application (and any objection) to insure that these criteria are met. And the Board will maintain a close watch over the experiment through new and more detailed reporting requirements. As a final safeguard, the Board will reserve the power to suspend the processing of new applications and, if necessary, even to terminate outstanding licenses. This policy is being codified in proposed regulations issued concurrently with this order. For long-haul truckers who seek to become air forwarders, the rule will not be free entry, but monitored entry.

In the second challenge to the Board's decision, *ABC Airfreight Company v. CAB*,[8] the court held the ambiguity referred to in the first challenge was resolved and the Board might initiate this properly controlled experiment in the authorization of truckers as airfreight forwarders, with the limitations on the numbers and the reporting requirements an experiment would be expected to entail.

In 1974, the Board instituted the *Long-haul Motor/Rail Carrier Air Freight Forwarder Authority Case*[9] to determine whether the temporary authorizations for air freight forwarding held by certain long-haul motor carriers and railroads should be renewed and, if so, for how long. The Board first granted the authority to such carriers in 1969 on the condition that the authorization would be reviewed after a five-year trial period. The Board concluded that the affiliated corporations of long-haul carriers should be authorized to engage in air freight forwarding on the same basis as the so-called independent forwarders; and ended its

[8]419 F. 2d 154, cert. denied 397 U.S. 1066.
[9]Order 77-6-126, June 1977.

monitored entry program. It extended the temporary air freight authority for ten years. The Board said that the surface affiliations of the monitored entrants into air freight forwarding had not had an adverse effect in the independent forwarders or on the industry. Rather, the Board said, such affiliations have generally benefitted air transportation; it said furthur that the surface carriers had not dominated the market either in number or in their share of the market.

12

Licenses for Ocean Freight Forwarders

The Applicable Statutory Provisions

Section 44(a) of the Shipping Act of 1916, as amended,[1] provides that no person shall engage in carrying on the business of forwarding unless such person holds a license issued by the Federal Maritime Commission to engage in such business. However, a person whose primary business is the sale of merchandise may dispatch shipments of such merchandise without a license. A forwarder's license under Section 44(b)[2] shall be issued to any qualified applicant if it is found by the FMC that the applicant is, or will be, an independent ocean freight forwarder, is fit, willing, and able properly to carry on the business of forwarding and to conform to the provisions of the Act and the requirements, rules, and regulations of the FMC and that the proposed forwarding business is, or will be, consistent with the national maritime policies in the Merchant Marine Act, 1936; otherwise the application shall be denied.

A grandfather provision in Section 44(b) states that any independent ocean freight forwarder who, on the effective date of the Act, was carrying on the business of forwarding under a registration number issued by the FMC, may continue such business for a period of one hundred and twenty days thereafter without a license, and if application for such license is made within such period, such forwarder may, under such regulations as the FMC shall prescribe, continue such business until otherwise ordered by the FMC. The FMC is authorized by Section 44(c)[3] to prescribe reasonable rules and regulations to be observed by

[1] 46 U.S.C. 841b(a).
[2] 46 U.S.C. 841b(b).
[3] 46 U.S.C. 841b(c).

independent ocean freight forwarders. No license shall be issued or remain in force unless such forwarder shall have furnished a bond or other security approved by the FMC in such form and amount as in the opinion of the FMC will insure financial responsibility and the supply of the services in accordance with agreements, or arrangements therefor. Licenses, under Section 44(d)[4] shall be effective from the date specified therein and shall remain in effect until suspended or terminated. Any such license may, upon application of the holder thereof, in the discretion of the FMC, be amended or revoked, in whole or in part, or may upon complaint, or on the FMC's own initiative, after notice and hearing, be suspended or revoked for willful failure to comply with any provision of the Act or with any lawful order, rule, or regulation of the FMC promulgated thereunder.

Under Section 44(e),[5] a common carrier may compensate a forwarder to the extent of the value rendered such carrier in connection with any shipment dispatched on behalf of others when, and only when, such forwarder is licensed and has performed with respect to such shipment the solicitation and securing of the cargo for the ship or the booking of, or otherwise arranging for space for, such cargo, and at least two of the following services: (1) The coordination of the movement of the cargo to shipside; (2) the preparation and processing of the ocean bill of lading; (3) the preparation and processing of dock receipts or delivery orders; (4) the preparation and processing of consular documents or export declarations; (5) the payment of the ocean freight charges on such shipments. However, where a common carrier by water has paid, or has incurred an obligation to pay either to an ocean freight broker or freight forwarder, separate compensation for the solicitation or securing of cargo for the ship or the booking of, or otherwise arranging for space for, such cargo, the carrier shall not be obligated to pay additional compensation for any other forwarding services rendered on the same cargo. Before compensation is paid to or received by a forwarder, such forwarder shall, if qualified to receive such compensation, certify in writing to the common carrier by which the shipment was dispatched that he is licensed by the FMC as an independent ocean freight forwarder and that he performed the above specified services with respect to such shipment; such carrier shall be entitled to rely on such certification unless it knows that the certification is incorrect.

The term "carrying on the business of forwarding" is defined by Sec-

---

[4]46 U.S.C. 841b(d).
[5]46 U.S.C. 841b(e).

tion 1 of the Shipping Act of 1916, as amended,[6] to mean the dispatching of shipments by any person on behalf of others, by ocean-going common carriers; and "independent ocean freight forwarder" is a person carrying on the business of forwarding for a consideration who is not a shipper or consignee or a seller or purchaser of shipments to foreign countries, nor has any beneficial interest therein, nor directly or indirectly controls or is controlled by such shipper or consignee or by any person having such a beneficial interest.

Licensing Procedure

Requirements for licensing as an ocean freight forwarder include filing an application and bond in accordance with a prescribed form, publication of the application in the Federal Register, payment of certain fees, and assurance about fitness and ability to perform as such licensed freight forwarder.

It must be borne in mind that if an "all-water rate" is involved, the ocean freight forwarder need not obtain a freight forwarder permit from the I.C.C.. However, if intermodal movements are involved, where the underlying services of a railroad, or motor carrier, or water carrier subject to regulation by the I.C.C. under Parts I, II and III of the Interstate Commerce Act, respectively, are utilized the I.C.C. would assert jurisdiction and a permit would be required.

Function of the Freight Forwarder

The functions of a freight forwarder were outlined briefly in *Anglo-Canadian Shipping Co. Ltd. v. F.M.C.*,[7] where the court said that primarily "the freight forwarder prepares, processes and generally attends to the necessary shipping papers in connection with export ocean transportation, a function which he performs especially for the shipper. The freight forwarder looks after the booking of or arranging for cargo space for export shipments on ocean carriers, and performs a number of the other related functions including clearance of export shipments under government regulations and procuring certification of consular documents. Customarily also, when the freight forwarder books space on a vessel for a particular shipment, although he does so as an agent for the shipper, he generally collects freight brokerage from the carrier." In *Agreements and Practices Pertaining to Brokerage and Related Matters*[8]

[6] 46 U.S.C. 801.
[7] 310 F. 2d 606, 607-8.
[8] 3 U.S.M.C. 170, 172.

the term "forwarder" was defined as any person employed by shippers or consignees to dispatch shipments by ocean steamships and to take care of formalities.

Payment of Brokerage

In an action to annul and set aside an order of the FMC in *Atlantic & Gulf/West Coast v. United States*,[9] the court sustained findings made in *Agreements and Practices Pertaining to Brokerage and Related Matters*[10] "that forwarding activities have developed American commerce, that the forwarding industry is an integral part of the commerce of the United States, that forwarders, when collecting brokerage are doing so in return for services to the carrier and that agreements not to pay brokerage result in detriment to the commerce of the United States." Brokerage was defined (at p. 172) in *Agreements and Practices Pertaining to Brokerage and Related Matters* as compensation for securing cargo for the ship; it is "compensation paid by common carriers by water to brokers, including forwarders, and is generally measured in amounts equal to fixed percentages of gross revenues collected by the carriers from shippers who have employed the brokers or forwarders." In sustaining the order of the FMC, the court said (p. 142) in the *Atlantic & Gulf/West Coast* case that the "Commission's order directs merely that plaintiff's agreements not to pay brokerage be eliminated. Individual carriers are left free, subject to their own judgment and ordinary operation of lawful competition, to pay or not to pay." The court said that the "Commission's report did not go so far as to state that all agreements relating to the payment of brokerage would be disapproved, although it considered that an agreement to pay less than 1¼ percent would perpetuate the condemned detriment."

Section 44 of the Shipping Act, which provides for a system of licensing and regulating the business of forwarders, contains a provision stating that a water carrier may compensate a forwarder to the extent of the value rendered such water carrier in connection with any shipment dispatched on behalf of others when, and only when, such forwarder is licensed and has performed with respect to such shipment certain listed functions and duties. As the court pointed out in the *Anglo-Canadian case, supra* (p. 611), the Congressional enactment put an end to proposals to stop payments of brokerage.

[9]94 F. Supp. 138, 141. See also *Pacific Westbound Conference v. United States*, 94 F. Supp. 649.
[10]3 U.S.M.C. 170.

Ocean Common Carrier Serving as a Freight Forwarder

The laws on ocean freight forwarders were designed to prevent shipper control over a freight forwarder. The safeguards in the law, as expanded by regulation, against such control of freight forwarders do not apply to ocean common carriers. Accordingly, an ocean common carrier may serve as an ocean freight forwarder under U.S. shipping laws. Sections 1 and 44 of the Shipping Act, 1916, apply. In FMC General order 4,[11] "an oceangoing common carrier . . . may be licensed." Under the same authority an oceangoing common carrier may perform freight forwarding service without a license only with respect to cargo carrying under its own bill of lading.

Non-Vessel Operating Common Carrier

The non-vessel operating common carrier (NVO) is a common carrier which is required to file and observe tariffs with the FMC but need not go through a certification process by filing an application which must be published in the Federal Register concerning which interested parties may object requiring, if not a formal hearing, at least a considered inquiry by the FMC. As above, if an "all-water rate" is involved, the NVO subject to FMC regulation need not obtain a freight forwarder permit from the I.C.C. even though it otherwise meets the statutory definition of a freight forwarder in Section 402(a) (5). But if intermodal movements are involved, and the NVO makes use of the underlying services of a Part I, II, or III carrier, it becomes subject to the I.C.C.'s jurisdiction as a freight forwarder and a permit would be required.

[11]46 C.F.R. 510. 22(a).

13

Permits for Foreign Air Carriers

The Applicable Statutory Provisions

Under Section 402(a) of the Federal Aviation Act[1] "No foreign air carrier shall engage in foreign air transportation unless there is in force a permit issued by the Board authorizing such carrier so to engage." The Board is impowered under Section 402(b)[2] "to issue such a permit if it finds that such carrier is fit, willing, and able to perform such air transportation and to conform to the provisions of this Act and the rules, regulations and requirements of the Board hereunder, and that such transportation will be in the public interest." The Board under Section 402(e)[3] "may prescribe the duration of any permit and may attach to such permit such reasonable terms, conditions, or limitations as, in its judgment, the public interest may require." Section 402(f)[4] provides that any "permit issued under the provisions of this section may, after notice and hearing, be altered, modified, amended, suspended, canceled, or revoked by the Board whenever it finds such action to be in the public interest." Section 402(f) also provides that any "interested person may file with the Board a protest or memorandum in support of or in opposition to the alteration, modification, amendment, suspension, cancellation, or revocation of a permit."

[1] 49 U.S.C. 1372(a).
[2] 49 U.S.C. 1372(b).
[3] 49 U.S.C. 1372 (e).
[4] 49 U.S.C. 1372(f).

Executive Control

As pointed out in *Chicago & S. Lines v. Waterman S. S. Corp.*,[5] when a foreign air carrier asks for a permit to operate "or a citizen carrier applies for a certificate to engage in any overseas or foreign air transportation, a copy of the application must be transmitted to the President before hearing; and any decision, either to grant or to deny must be submitted to the President before publication and is unconditionally subject to the President's approval." The Supreme Court said (p. 109) that "when a foreign carrier seeks to engage in public carriage over the territory or waters of this country, or any carrier seeks the sponsorship of this Government to engage in overseas or foreign air transportation, Congress has completely inverted the usual administrative procedure." Thus, instead of acting free of executive control, "the agency is then subordinated to it. Instead of its order serving as a final disposition of the application, its force is exhausted when it serves as a recommendation to the President."

The court added (p. 109) that "Instead of being handed down to the parties as the conclusion of the administrative process, it must be submitted to the President, before publication even can take place. Nor is the President's control of the ultimate decision a mere right of veto. It is not alone issuance of such authorizations that are subject to his approval, but denial, transfer, amendment, cancellation or suspension, as well. And likewise subject to his approval are the terms, conditions and limitations of the order." The court said further (p. 109) that the "Presidential control is not limited to a negative but is a positive and detailed control over the Board's decisions, unparalleled in the history of American administrative bodies." It was the conclusion of the court (p. 114) that "orders of the Board as to certificate for overseas or foreign air transportation are not mature and are therefore not susceptible of judicial review at any time before they are finalized by Presidential approval." The court said further that after "approval has ben given, the final orders embody Presidential discretion as to political matters beyond the competence of the courts to adjudicate."

In *Diggs v. C.A.B.*,[6] there was involved a challenge to a Board order, approved by the President, which authorized a foreign air carrier under Section 402 to serve a new route between Johannesburg, South Africa,

---

[5]333 U.S. 103, 106.
[6]516 F. 2d 1248, cert. denied 424 U.S. 910.

and New York. The court of appeals dismissed the petition for appeal on the ground that Section 1006(a)[7] of the FAA expressly withholds court jurisdiction to review such orders. In *Sitmar Cruises v. C.A.B.*,[8] a district court dismissed an appeal from a Board order, approved by the President, which denied an application for a foreign air carrier permit under Section 402, on the ground that Section 1006(a) was intended to foreclose judicial review of such orders in any forum including district courts. In *Interamerican Air Freight Corp. v. C.A.B.*,[9] the court of appeals dismissed an appeal of a Board order granting a Section 402 permit to engage in international air freight forwarding, and denying an application to operate as a U.S. citizen international air freight forwarder, on the ground that the order had been approved by the President and was therefore exempt from judicial review.

[7]49 U.S.C. 1486(a).
[8]D.C.D.C., No. 75-1716, 1973.
[9]9 Cir., No. 71-3050, 1973.

14

Brokerage Licenses

The Applicable Statutory Provision

Section 211 of the Interstate Commerce Act[1] provides:

"(a) No person shall for compensation sell or offer for sale transportation subject to this part or shall make any contract, agreement, or arrangement to provide, procure, furnish, or arrange for such transportation or shall hold himself or itself out by advertisement, solicitation, or otherwise as one who sells, provides, procures, contracts, or arranges for such transportation, unless such person holds a broker's license issued by the Commission to engage in such transportation: provided, however, That no such person shall engage in transportation subject to this part unless he holds a certificate or permit as provided in this part. In the execution of any contract, agreement, or arrangement to sell, provide, procure, furnish, or arrange for such transportation, it shall be unlawful for such person to employ any carrier by motor vehicle who or which is not the lawful holder of an effective certificate or permit issued as provided in this part: And provided further, That the provisions of this paragraph shall not apply to any carrier holding a certificate or a permit under the provisions of this part or to any bona fide employee or agent of such motor carrier, so far as concerns transportation to be furnished wholly by such carrier or jointly with other motor carriers holding like certificates or permits, or with a common carrier by railroad, express, or water.

"(b) A brokerage license shall be issued to any qualified applicant therefor, authorizing the whole or any part of the operations covered by the application, if it is found that the applicant is fit, willing, and able properly to perform the service proposed and to conform to the provisions of this part and the requirements, rules and regulations of the Commission thereunder, and that the proposed service, to the extent to be authorized by the license, is, or will be consistent with the public interest and the national transpor-

---

[1] 49 U.S.C. 311. Comparable provisions to paragraph (a) — Section 410; to paragraph (b) — Section 410 (a) — (c); to paragraph (c) — Section 403(c); and to paragraph (d) — Section 220a, (d).

tation policy declared in this Act; otherwise such application shall be denied. Any broker in operation when this section takes effect may continue such operation for a period of one hundred and twenty days thereafter without a license, and if application for such license is made within such period, the broker, may, under such regulations as the Commission shall prescribe, continue such operations until otherwise ordered by the Commission.

"(c) The Commission shall prescribe reasonable rules and regulations for the protection of travelers or shippers by motor vehicle, to be observed by any person holding a brokerage license, and no such license shall be issued or remain in force unless such person shall have furnished a bond or other security approved by the Commission, in such form and amount as will insure financial responsibility and the supplying of authorized transportation in accordance with contracts, agreements, or arrangements therefor.

"(d) The Commission and its special agents and examiners shall have the same authority as to accounts, reports, and records, including inspection and preservation thereof, of any person holding a brokerage license issued under the provisions of this section, that they have under this part with respect to motor carriers subject thereto."

Section 203(a) (18) of the I.C. Act[2] provides:

"The term 'broker' means any person not included in the term 'motor carrier' and not a bona fide employee or agent of any such carrier, who or which, as principal or agent, sells or offers for sale any transportation subject to this part, or negotiates for, or holds himself or itself out by solicitation, advertisement, or otherwise as one who sells, provides, furnishes, contracts, or arranges for such transportation."

Section 221(c)[3] directs the Commission to prescribe "reasonable rules and regulations for the protection of travelers or shippers by motor vehicle, to be observed by any person holding a brokerage license," and provides that no license shall be issued or remain in force unless the licensee shall have furnished a bond or other security in such form and amount as will insure financial responsibility and the supplying of authorized transportation.

Section 204(a)(4)[4] provides that it shall be the duty of the Commission "To regulate brokers as provided in this part, and to that end the Commission may establish reasonable requirements with respect to licensing, financial responsibility, accounts, records, reports, operations, and practices of any such person or persons."

Section 204(b)[5] states that "The Commission may from time to time establish such just and reasonable classification of brokers *** as the

[2]49 U.S.C. 303(a) (18).
[3]49 U.S.C. 321(c).
[4]49 U.S.C. 304(a) (4).
[5]49 U.S.C. 304(b).

special nature of the services performed by such *** brokers shall require; and such just and reasonable rules, regulations, and requirements, consistent with the provisions of this part, to be observed by the carriers or brokers so classified or grouped, as the Commission deems necessary or desirable in the public interest."

Some of these provisions were discussed by the Commission in *Entry Control of Brokers,*[6] where it said:

> These provisions were but part of the general regulatory framework embracing motor carrier regulation as established by the Motor Carrier Act of 1935. The general sources for the legislative history and intent behind the Motor Carrier Act were this Commission's report on *Coordination of Motor Transportation,* 182 I.C.C. 263 (1932), and three reports of Commissioner Joseph B. Eastman in his capacity as Federal Coordinator of Transportation during the great depression, S. Doc. No. 188, 73d Cong. 2d Sess. (1934), S. Doc. No. 152, 73d Cong. 2d Sess. (1934), and H. R. Doc. No. 89, 74th Cong. 1st Sess. (1935). The Commission report in regards to passenger transportation took note of the brokerage problem, saying at 181 I.C.C. at 279-80:
>
> > With the development of long-haul motor transportation of passengers there has grown up in many cities the practice of selling transportation by agencies which do not represent any regular bus line. The practices of these agencies have given rise to many of the complaints registered by interstate bus passengers. The agencies advertise rates appreciably less than the fares of regular bus lines and then make arrangements with irregular operators, frequently the owners of private automobiles, to transport the passengers, the agency retaining a per cent of the fare collected as commission. ***
>
> The first of the two relevant reports of the Coordinator, S. Doc. No. 152, *supra,* at 45-49, 359, recommended regulation of "transportation agents or brokers" but said only that brokers should have to obtain a "permit," without specifying the standard. The second report, which recommended what became section 211, is more informative. It said, H.R. Doc. No. 89, *supra,* at 61-62:
>
> > Provision for more thorough-going regulation of brokers or transportation agents is made in the bill. To avoid confusion, the term "license" instead of "permit" is applied to the authority issued for brokerage operations. Licenses are required of all persons selling tickets or making contracts, agreements, or arrangements to provide transportation of persons or property in interstate or foreign commerce. Exemption of the agents of carriers holding certificates or permits is provided.
>
> > A showing of public interest and financial responsibility is a condition to the issuance of a license. The Commission shall make reasonable rules and regulations and require bond to protect the traveling or

[6]126 M.C.C. 476, 479-86.

shipping public. These licenses are subject to revocation, as provided in section 312 (49 U.S.C. 312).

A desirable control over transportation effected through brokerage operations is afforded by the provision which requires brokers to employ only carriers holding certificates or permits. If the broker or transportation agent himself performs any transportation, through agents or employees or by lease of equipment, he must secure a form of carrier authority, either a certificate or a permit, and take on the duties and responsibilities and subject himself to the regulation provided for motor carriers.

The Commission may prescribe the forms of brokers' accounts and require reports. It may also enforce appropriate penalties for unlawful operations.

Brokerage early became an incident of motor transportation. Its development is described in the following excerpt from the Commission's report in *Copes Broker Application*, 27 M.C.C. 153 (1940):

As is well known, the vast majority of motor carriers of freight are small operators with only a few pieces of equipment and neither a need for nor means to support a large organization including salaried solicitors. Many of them, particularly those offering specialized services such as household-goods carriers, provide an irregular-route service over extensive territory. Some offer services which are roving in character, while others tend to radiate out of a home base. Obviously, many of them cannot maintain even part-time solicitors at any significant portion of the points which they may be authorized to serve. Neither is it practical for them to "tramp" their vehicles from one shipper to another in search of available traffic. Nevertheless, economy and efficiency of operation require that they have some means of obtaining at points away from their home bases either return loads or lading for some other point.

Out of this situation there grew up, long prior to the adoption of the Motor Carrier Act, 1935, now part II of the Interstate Commerce Act, agencies independent of both carriers and shippers, devoted to the solicitation of traffic to be moved by carriers selected by them from whom they exacted a charge for their services. Concurrently, there developed, for somewhat similar reasons, another group of individuals engaged in arranging for or selling transportation of passengers over both regular-route and irregular-route carriers. In theory, the system was designed to work not only to the convenience of the carriers, but also to that of shippers and passengers, many of whom were not sufficiently informed or situated so that they could readily locate available motor-carrier service when desired, but the resulting dependence of both carriers and shippers or passengers on these independent transportation agents gave rise to abuses. Irresponsible persons exacted excessive charges for their services or engaged the services of unreliable and unqualified carriers, or both. Available traffic was held out to competing carriers, and the bids of each were used to beat down the price of others until all were reduced to a bare subsistence basis, and unconscionable commissions were obtained by the brokers.

Along the same line is the following from the second annual report of the Coordinator of Transportation (S. Doc. 152 73d Cong. 2d Sess.) which contained a proposal providing for the regulation of brokers:

> As noted earlier, a few states have enacted laws regulating the business of persons, usually termed "motor transportation agents" or brokers, who act as intermediaries between passengers or shippers and motor carriers but who, in general, are not themselves engaged in transportation. Ordinarily, their activities are confined to the sale of tickets or to the making of contracts and other arrangements for shipments of freight by truck. In some instances, however, such persons also sell motor vehicles on a deferred payment plan to the individual carriers engaged by them. In other instances, they operate or have an interest in so-called transportation or forwarding companies, which provide tonnage for carriers served by the transportation agent.

> The carriers also served are usually, if not always, of an irregular or unregulated type, lacking adequate financial responsibility. They, together with the unregulated motor transportation agent, are responsible for many of the evils, including the chaotic rate conditions, which characterize motor transportation for hire. Not infrequently passengers and shippers patronizing the transportation agent have been subjected to great inconvenience and substantial losses, without recourse, through failure of the carrier employed to fulfill the terms of the agent's agreement. Often the carrier, himself, is merely the dupe of the transportation agent who supplies him with business, takes a disproportionate share of the rate, and repossesses the equipment upon the carrier's failure to meet payments or his refusal longer to handle shipments under the conditions imposed upon him.

More particularly as to passenger brokers, the Commission noted in a 1928 examination of then prevalent industry practice, in *Motor Bus and Motor Truck Operation*, 140 I.C.C. 685, 704 (1928):

> There has grown in some cities the practice of brokerage in interstate transportation of passengers for hire by motor carriers. A so-called auto-travel agency owning no motor cars or busses will sell interstate transportation between certain points and then place the passenger in a motor car or bus owned by the driver who is answerable to no regulatory body for the proper conduct of his business. For this service the auto-travel agency deducts a certain percentage from the fare paid by the passenger as a commission and the owner of the car receives the balance.

> Transportation of this character is the source of complaints by passengers using such service. It is a practice that tends to disrupt service and business of regular lines, and is not conducive to giving the traveling public safe, adequate, and regular service. It should be prohibited.

Central to the policy issues raised in this proceeding is the intent of Congress in making brokerage of motor carrier services subject to the Commission's regulatory jurisdiction. The primary interpretation of this intent can be found in *Carla Ticket Service, Inc., Broker Application*, 94 M.C.C. 579, 580-581:[7]

°°°The legislative history of section 211 of the act clearly reveals that the primary purpose of Congress in regulating motor transportation brokers is to protect carriers and the traveling and the shipping public against dishonest and financially unstable middlemen in the transportation industry. Although this may be the primary objective of section 211 of the act, it does not follow that this is the sole objective of section 211. If financial integrity and stability were the sole aim of regulation in this area, it would have been sufficient for Congress to have formulated a statutory standard in section 211(b) of the act which would have limited our function in broker application proceedings to determining whether or not the applicant is fit, willing, and able to perform the proposed service. Instead, the statutory standard formulated by Congress in section 211(b), in terms of which all broker applications must be evaluated, requires us to find (1) that the applicant is fit, willing, and able to perform the proposed service, and (2) that the proposed brokerage operation is or will be consistent with the public interest and the national transportation policy. As a matter of statutory construction, no word or clause in a statute should be rejected as superfluous or meaningless, but must be given its due force and meaning appropriate to the context, albeit not a strained or unnatural meaning. *Cf. Keystone Transp. Co. Contract Carrier Application*, 19 M.C.C. 475, 492. The "public interest" aspect of the involved statutory standard obviously encompasses a broader range of deliberation than does the "fitness" aspect of the statutory standard. Therefore, it seems clear to us that Congress intended, by requiring consideration of the "public interest" in section 211(b) of the act, that our evaluation of broker applications on their merits not be limited to the issues of an applicant's fitness.

It is not clear from the legislative history as to whether or not the "public interest" aspect of the standard enunciated in section 211(b) requires some consideration of relevant competitive factors in our judging broker applications on their merits. However, we think it significant that when section 211(b) was enacted, although Congress was cognizant of the fact that Commission proceedings were [usually] adversary in nature entailing the development of evidence relating to competitive factors among others, we were not directed to deviate from this method of procedure. Despite changes in other language of this particular section and reconsideration of the entire act, Congress has not seen fit to change this standard or otherwise suggest that our prior interpretation of section 211(b) is in error. Moreover, the continued acquiescence of Congress in the Commission's interpretation since shortly after passage of the section is a strong indication of approval of that interpretation. The Commission's interpretation has been that competition is a factor to be considered. As early as 1938 a broker application was denied

---

[7]This interpretation met with approval in *Gray Line National Tours Corporation v. United States*, 380 F. Supp. 263 (S.D.N.Y. 1974).

because of possible adverse effect on competition even though the application was unopposed.[8] See *Interstate Ticket Sales, Inc., Broker Application*, 8 M.C.C. 483. Later decisions have been consistent with that approach. See e.g., No. MC-12596, *Hokay Broker Application*, 63 M.C.C. 814 (not printed in full), decided December 13, 1954, and No. MC-12610, *Ewing Broker Application*, 64 M.C.C. 815 (not printed in full), decided October 26, 1955. Under all circumstances we do not believe that Congress intended that the Commission be precluded from giving any consideration to competition in broker application cases.

Consistent with the legislative history of section 211 broker applicants are required to show that their services will contribute something of value or be of benefit to carriers or the public. Consideration of existing broker service is, therefore, relevant to broker applications for it is obvious that the creation of needless duplicative services will neither advance the primary purpose of section 211 nor be of benefit to anyone. [Footnote added.]

The standards of proof presently required by the Commission for a grant of broker authority are well settled. Consistent with the legislative history of section 211 of the Interstate Commerce Act, broker applicants are required to show that their services will contribute something of value or be of benefit to carriers or the public. While this burden is not as strict as the public convenience and necessity criteria, an applicant must nevertheless submit adequate and appropriate evidence. *Collette Travel Service, Inc., v. United States*, 263 F. Supp. 302 (D.R.I. 1966). For an applicant to establish that its proposed service will contribute "something of value" and not be needlessly duplicative of existing services, it must demonstrate that its operation will fulfill a felt public need which is not already being met. As stated in *Elegante Tours, Inc.—Broker Application*, 113 M.C.C. 156, 159 (1971):

> °°°Normally, an applicant makes such a showing through the testimony of interested members of the general public, although it is possible that under certain conditions a convincing plan of future operations presented by the applicant itself, together with the supporting evidence of existing motor carriers, would be sufficient to support a finding that a new brokerage service should be authorized. *White Rose Motor Club Broker Application*, 95 M.C.C. 101 (1964). Nebulous and general assertions by witnesses are unconvincing in the absence of more specific future plans and some indication as to a foreseeable public response to an applicant's proposed service, either from prospective tour patrons or from particular interstate carriers whose services would be utilized. Compare *Howard Tours, Inc., Broker Application*, 95 M.C.C. 405, 408 (1964). Moreover, in order for this Commission to give adequate consideration to any application proceeding, there must be a minimum amount of data submitted upon which a rational conclusion can be

[8]And as early as 1937, in *Acme Fast Freight, Inc., Common Carrier Application*, 2 M.C.C. 415, 430-432, reversed on other grounds, 8 M.C.C. 211 (1938), there is an intimation that competitive factors will be weighed.

drawn regarding a public need for service. See *Collette* case, *supra,* and compare *Novak Contract Carrier Application,* 103 M.C.C. 555 (1967). A broker applicant should not expect that these relatively less stringent standards will assure that a broker application will be granted as a matter of course. From the earliest days of regulation, broker applications have been denied in those instances where an applicant has failed to sustain its burden of proof.

Since the subject matter of this proceeding focuses on competitive, economic, and consumer protection factors, it is not necessary to analyze, as has been done on numerous occasions in the past, the precise nature of brokerage operations.[9]

A significant recent Commission decision has discussed at length competitive factors in a local area. In *Paragon Travel Agency, Inc., Ext.—Atlanta, Ga.,* 120 M.C.C. 1, 6-7 (1974), it was said:

> We first note that it is not conclusive with respect to this brokerage application that protestants offer tour services and that these tours may be adequate. Although the impact of applicant's proposal on the competitive situation must be considered, existing services are not entitled, as a matter of right, to have the tour market to themselves, particularly in a large metropolitan area embracing a population of varying interests. ***it appears to us to be important that the authority sought will introduce a new competitor which is independent of any motor carrier.*** a grant of brokerage authority to applicant would introduce into the Atlanta market the services of an experienced independent broker, which are not now available, that may be able to make more effective use of the various transportation services available in the Atlanta area than do protestants in the tour services which they offer.

Personalized local service was the touchstone of the decision in *Cook Broker Application,* 119 M.C.C. 709 (1974), where it was stated at 717:

> In considering the nature of the service proposed by applicant, we find

---

[9]See *Passenger Transportation in Special Operations,* 112 M.C.C. 160, 174-192 (1970), wherein is contained discussions of the leading cases in the field of passenger brokerage operations. The leading decision in the area of property brokerage which explains the rationale behind the regulatory framework pertaining to property brokers is *Practices of Property Brokers,* 49 M.C.C. 277 (1949), modified in 53 M.C.C. 633 (1951). We should note, however, the leading case in the field of passenger brokerage operations, *Tauck Tours, Inc., Extension—New York, N. Y.,* 54 M.C.C. 291 (1952), affirmed 63 M.C.C. 493 (1955), and *National Bus Traffic Association v. United States,* 143 F. Supp. 689 (D.N.J. 1956) where it was found:
> ***a group of persons who have joined a conducted all-expense tour whether preformed or assembled by applicant and who in writing accept and appoint applicant as agent, for the group collectively, for the purpose of arranging motor transportation, is a proper group for the purpose of obtaining charter transportation by motor vehicle and that applicant as broker-agent lawfully may on behalf of such group purchase for the group charter or group transportation, (1) provided that the contract negotiated with the carrier furnishing the motor transportation is one between it and the group members collectively, (2) provided the carrier is paid its full published fare, and (3) provided that applicant in arranging the motor transportation does not receive a commission from the carrier.

that a significant segment of the public in the vicinity of Fitchburg has come to depend upon applicant's personalized local service which includes a combination of service features unique to applicant's operation. His service includes the provision of meals for the tour price, high quality restaurant and hotel accommodations and unlimited choice of meals, the convenience of originating and terminating tours at Fitchburg, an uncommon desire to please expressed in individualized attention to personal detail, flexibility permitting last-minute changes in plans, a readiness to handle unscheduled developments, the provision of chaperones and registered nurses for high school tours and extended trips, ready refunds, and sufficient patronage to eliminate cancellations for lack of interest.

Applicant's operation, as generally evidenced by the high praise of supporting witnesses, appears to be well tuned to the specific needs of those who make up his clientele. It thus becomes apparent that notwithstanding the availability of other services in the region, applicant's tour operations are to a significant degree distinct from those other services, rather than duplicative of them. In our judgment, it is worthwhile to encourage efforts to provide a unique service directly aimed at serving a local market, and we find that authorization of the proposed service will contribute something of value to the public in the involved area.

The *Cook* and *Paragon* decisions indicate a tendency of the Commission in recent decisions to consider more factors than "adequate service" in a given area, in deciding whether or not there is a healthy, competitive situation in a local marketing area.

The final, and most crucial element, and prerequisite to any grant of broker authority, is whether an applicant has shown itself to be fit, willing, and able properly to perform the proposed service. For an early discussion of this, see *Cain Broker Application,* 2 M.C.C. 633 (1937). In *Cook,* supra, at 718, it was said that fitness in a brokerage proceeding involved four things: good general character, an ability to conduct the operations proposed in an appropriate manner satisfactory to patrons, willingness to comply with the various regulatory requirements, and the ability to obtain the required bond. In this connection, our previous requirement that a broker furnish a bond in an amount not less than $5,000 (see 49 CFR 1043.4) for the protection of the public before a license will be issued was designed to ensure the broker's continuing financial ability to operate properly. Safety requirements are normally inapplicable to brokers inasmuch as the actual transportation services must be provided by regulated motor carriers holding appropriate authority.

Distinction Between Agents of Carriers and Brokers

In *Practices of Property Brokers,*[10] the Commission considered the distinction between agents of carriers and brokers and concluded that

[10]49 M.C.C. 277, modified 53 M.C.C. 633.

one who was in a position to allocate shipments between competing principals was a broker, who required a license. On the other hand, an agent who devotes his service exclusively to a single carrier, is part of that carrier's organization and does not require a license.[11] It stated (at 299):

> Thus, the distinction between a broker and bona fide agent is one of fact, and it is obviously difficult to frame a hard and fast definition of a bona fide agent that would be determinative in all cases. However, we are convinced that the term "bona fide agent" is here used in a narrower sense than is usually connoted by the term agent, for otherwise it would be meaningless in view of the fact that in the broad sense of the word a broker is also an agent. We are of the opinion that the boda fide agent contemplated by the statute is one marked by a continuing relationship between the agent and carrier pursuant to a preexisting agreement between them whereby the agent functions as a normal part of the carrier's organization, performs his duties under the direction of the carrier in the status practically of an employee, and is precluded from exercising discretion in the awarding of traffic or otherwise acting with independence in respect thereof.

The Commission then concluded that the ability to allocate traffic between competing carriers was the controlling factor distinguishing a "broker" from a "bona fide agent," stating (at 301, 302):

> °°°The discretionary allocation of traffic as between competing carriers should be and under the rules herein approved will be conclusive on the question of broker versus agent status.

Entry

In *Entry Control of Brokers*,[12] the Commission examined into the question of whether there should be new entry control standards or procedures in the passenger broker and property broker areas.

The Commission's general conclusions with regard to passenger broker licenses was to ease entry controls. It felt that there was a need for more expedited and less complicated procedures, and that the public interest would be served with an expansion of the passenger broker services. A similar conclusion with regard to brokers of specified commodities (other than household goods) was reached by the Commission. A different conclusion was arrived at by the Commission with respect to brokerage of household goods.

---

[11]Section 203(a) (18) of the I.C. Act, which defines a broker, and section 211(a) which requires brokers to be licensed, both except a "bona fide agent."
[12]126 M.C.C. 476.

The Commission promulgated rules eliminate the fee for filing a broker license, (with the exceptions of applications for a household goods broker's license) raise the required amount of bonding to $10,000, and make a general finding that operation by qualified applicants, as brokers, in interstate or foreign commerce, of passengers and property (except household goods), between all points in the United States (including Alaska and Hawaii), will be consistent with the public interest and the national transportation policy. Generally, the procedure, because of the general finding, limits the examination of a broker license application to the issue of an applicant's fitness. This permits the expedited handling of broker applications, and offers greater ease of entry into the broker industry for qualified applicants. Household goods brokerage was excluded from this procedure, the Commission wishing to maintain the existing agency-carrier relationship in the household goods industry in its present form in order fully to protect the consumer.

15

Dual Operations

The Applicable Statutory Provision

Section 210 of the Interstate Commerce Act[1] provides:

"Unless, for good cause shown, the Commission shall find, or shall have found, that both a certificate and a permit may be so held consistently with the public interest and with the national transportation policy declared in this Act — (1) no person, or any person controlling, controlled by, or under common control with such person, shall hold a certificate as a common carrier authorizing operation for the transportation of property by motor vehicle over a route or within a territory, if such person, or any such controlling person, controlled person, or person under common control, holds a permit as a contract carrier authorizing operation for the transportation of property by motor vehicle over the same route or within the same territory; and (2) no person, or any person controlling, controlled by, or under common control with such person, shall hold a permit as a contract carrier authorizing operation for the transportation of property by motor vehicle over a route or within a territory, if such person, or any such controlling person, controlled person, or person under common control, holds a certificate as a common carrier authorizing operation for the transportation of property by motor vehicle over the same route or within the same territory."

Discrimination Resulting from Dual Operations

In Section 210 Congress evidenced a clear policy not to permit the same carrier or carriers under common control, to conduct both contract carrier and common carrier operations within the same territory, except upon a specific finding by the Commission that such dual operation

---

[1] 49 U.S.C. 310. Comparable provisions — Sections 310 and 410(c), (h). See Section 5(3) for applicability of U.S.C. 310 to noncarriers involved in acquisition of control authorized under Section 5(2).

would be consistent with the public interest and the national transportation policy. The prohibition is in recognition of the opportunity for discriminatory practices which is present when a carrier is authorized to offer both kinds of service to shippers. A shipper who is able to utilize both the common carrier and contract carrier services of a motor carrier, by assuring the carrier of certain of his traffic for transportation as a common carrier, is in a position to obtain special treatment on such of his traffic as would be transported under contracts. Conversely, the carrier, by giving the shipper special treatment in his contract operations, would have an undue competitive advantage over other common carriers in respect of such traffic as the shipper might have available for transportation by common carrier. By consenting to contract carrier charges lower than it would otherwise accept, the carrier would, in effect, accomplish a rebate of part of its common carrier charges.[2]

As the Commission said in the *Gallot* case, *supra.*, at pp. 4-5:

> . . . We do not imply that vendee herein would necessarily indulge in discriminatory practices, but the opportunity to do so would be present, and the policy of the statute is against the creation of the opportunity by permitting the conduct of dual operations. In determining proceedings arising under section 5, it is our duty to give effect to the letter and spirit of the statute by not approving transactions resulting in objectional dual operations. *Arco Auto Carriers, Inc. — Purchase — Automobile Convoy*, 37 M.C.C. 115, 121. In other words, we should not approve a transaction which would result in a situation where discrimination may be practiced, regardless of whether the dual operator has any intention of indulging in such practices. The fact that an opportunity to conduct such practices would be present is sufficient to warrant disapproval of the dual operations and a denial of the application. Otherwise, if the transaction is approved, it is doubtful whether we would be in a position to police the situation.

In numerous cases, the Commission has consistently held the evils inherent in a dual operating authority situation are such as to be contrary to the public interest and the declared policy of the I.C. Act.[3]

Even where the dual operations are different in nature, the Commission has held that such a situation would be inconsistent with the public interest and the national transportation policy. This issue was presented in the *Block* case, *supra.*, where the Commission said (at pp. 654-55):

---

[2]*Gallot — Purchase — Holst*, 45 M.C.C. 1.

[3]*Florman—Control—Automobile Convoy Co.*, 35 M.C.C. 521; *Block Common Carrier Application*, 49 M.C.C. 651; *Hunt — Purchase — Shideler*, 50 M.C.C. 683; *Shipley Transfer, Inc. — Purchase — W. T. Holt, Inc.*, 56 M.C.C. 96; *Crawford Transport Co., Inc. — Lease — Geo. F. Burnett Co.*, 56 M.C.C. 103; *La Casse Extension — Dairy Products*, 79 M.C.C. 222; *Dieckbrader Exp., Inc., Conversion Proceeding*, 83 M.C.C. 287; *Highway Transp. Corp. Conversion Proceeding*, 86 M.C.C. 169; *Hagerstown Motor Exp. Co., Inc. Transferee*, 87 M.C.C. 473.

Competition between commonly controlled common and contract carrier operations is not the significant consideration. In our administration of section 210 of the act, we are charged with carrying out the clear and unmistakable intent of Congress to preclude the opportunity for discriminatory practices which might well result from the simultaneous holding, by two commonly controlled carriers, of both a certificate and a permit. *Where the same shipper is or may be served in both capacities the door is open for objectionable practices even though the operations be wholly different.* It is not necessary to point out the many and complex situations, involving substantial injustices to shippers and carriers, which are potentially present when a single carrier, or two commonly controlled carriers, are in a position to offer both common- and contract-carrier service within the same territory. Neither is it necessary that we find the actual existence of such discrimination or even a probability thereof. We have consistently held that the mere possibility of discrimination warrants our refusal to relax the express prohibition contained in the statute.

In addition, even if the territory involved is not the same, the Commission is obliged "to scrutinize most carefully any proposal by a carrier or by affiliated carriers to serve the same shipper as both a common carrier and contract carrier and to disapprove any such proposal until the undesirable practice at which section 210 is aimed are negatived."[4]

As the terms of the statute show clearly, the prohibition of Section 210 is not absolute; however, to give effect to the mandate of Congress, opportunities for discrimination may not be created. This is borne out by the following cases.

In *Indianhead Truck Line, Inc., Ext. — Service Station Supplies,*[5] the Commission refused to sanction a dual operations situation where the applicant seeking contract carrier authority to transport packaged commodities used by gasoline service stations (applicant sought common carrier authority but the Commission found that what applicant was seeking was contract carrier authority) also conducted operations as a common carrier of bulk petroleum products in the same general territory serving the same shippers.

In *Hagerstown Motor Exp. Co. Inc., Transferee,*[6] the Commission held that the findings required by Section 210 could not properly be made on the record where the acquisition of common-carrier rights would, by use of Baltimore, Md., as a gateway, afford the transferee, engaged in approved dual operations, the opportunity to transport the same commodities from and to identical points, and the two kinds of operation would be conducted in a fairly compact geographical area. Applicants

---

[4]*Complete Auto Transit, Inc. — Extension — Willow Run,* 71 M.C.C. 383, 387. See also *Pacific Motor Trucking Co. Extension — Oregon,* 71 M.C.C. 561, 564.
[5]81 M.C.C. 715.
[6]87 M.C.C. 473, 477-78.

offered no plan for lessening the objectionable features, and it did not appear that any feasible plan would be effective.

In *La Casse Extension*,[7] the Commission said that dual operation by the applicant, as a contract carrier of dairy and related products, and by a commonly controlled common carrier of similar commodities in the same general territory as that sought by applicant, would place both carriers in a position to engage in discriminatory practices in such territory. Moreover, in view of the widespread variety of commodities applicant proposed to transport, the possible exclusion thereof from the authority of the common carrier would be impractical.

In *Dieckbrader Exp., Inc., Conversion Proceeding*,[8] the Commission held that respondent's holding of common carrier authority acquired in conversion and extension proceedings and contract carrier authority acquired by purchase would enable it to serve shippers in a dual capacity in the transportation of several commodities of similar nature within same area. The Commission said that while no implication that respondent would engage in discriminatory practices was intended, Congress, in enacting Section 210, intended to preclude any opportunity for discrimination, and such dual operations would be repugnant to that Section.

The holding of acquired permit and common carrier authority resulting from a conversion proceeding, the Commission said in *Highway Transp. Corp. Conversion Proceeding*,[9] would enable applicant to serve shippers both as common and contract carrier of several commodities in the same general area. Section 210 was intended to preclude any opportunity for such discrimination; operations under the considered authorities would be repugnant to the provisions of Section 210 and inconsistent with the public interest and the national transportation policy.

In *Complete Auto Transit, Inc., Ext. — G.M. Willow Run Plant*,[10] the authority granted duplicated that held by an affiliate, Square Deal Cartage Company, a common carrier of automotive vehicles. The Commission held that the approval of the resulting dual operations would not be justified unless Square Deal surrendered its duplicating authority for cancellation. It therefore required the surrender of duplicating authority as a condition precedent to a grant of authority. The Commission pointed out that the approval of the dual operations "should not be construed as any waiver of our right to reconsider this issue at any future date should

[7]79 M.C.C. 222, 225-6.
[8]83 M.C.C. 287, 289.
[9]86 M.C.C. 169, 170-1.
[10]81 M.C.C. 455.

the present facts change so as to bring about an improper competitive situation or result in improper discrimination or preference; and the permit issued this applicant will be subject to a condition which will reserve our jurisdiction in this matter." The dual operations of Complete, Square Deal, and Contract Cartage Company, a common carrier of automotive vehicles, had been considered at length previously in *Complete Auto Transit, Inc., Extension—Willow Run,*[11] and had been approved. In the *Willow Run* case, the Commission said that future applications involving the dual operations issue "will be carefully examined on its merits," and the applicant was admonished not to rely on past findings "for approval of additional dual operations."

That the prohibition of Section 210 is not absolute is demonstrated by the following cases.

In *Pacific Motor Trucking Co. Extension,*[12] the Commission held that dual operations by applicant, in addition to those approved in a prior report, occasioned by grants of other contract carrier authority, would not be such an aggravation of existing dual operations as to require disapproval. In *McCurdy Extension,*[13] the Commission said that under present and proposed contract-carrier authority applicants could originate malt beverage traffic only at Latrobe, Pa., while as a common carrier they could originate such traffic only at Milwaukee, Wis., and Baltimore, Md.; and that destinations which could be served under the two types of authority were also different, thus dual operations were approved. In *Everts' Chemical Transport, Inc., Extension,*[14] the Commission held that dual operations resulting from the grant of a certificate authorizing the transportation of certain chemicals, in bulk, in tank vehicles, to a carrier presently holding a permit authorizing the transportation of crude oil would be consistent with the public interest and the national transportation policy; although both crude oil and the considered chemicals would be transported in tank vehicles in the same general area, the same shipper was not shown to be involved in any of the various movements. Applicant's contract-carrier operations in *E. Brooke Matlack, Inc.*[15] were found not inconsistent with its obligations as a common carrier, since the commodities transported differed considerably, and applicant did not serve the same shipper as both a common and contract carrier and apparently could not do so because the shipper supporting the contract-carrier authority did not ship or receive any commodities applicant transported

[11]71 M.C.C. 383.
[12]77 M.C.C. 605, 624.
[13]84 M.C.C. 227, 229.
[14]78 M.C.C. 717, 764, 767.
[15]79 M.C.C. 761, 765.

as a common carrier. However, the permit included a condition reserving the right to impose any conditions found necessary should the situation change.

In *Eastern Delivery Service, Inc.*,[16] the Commission held that contract-carrier parcel delivery service by applicant commonly controlled with a common carrier could be approved when there was no duplication in the territorial scope of their services and only a remote possibility, if any, of discriminatory practices resulting from the dual operation. In *Cyrus Extension*,[17] the Commission approved the operation as a contract carrier of bulk petroleum products and as a common carrier of liquid grain fumigants and insecticides in bulk between the same points. The Commission said that while the applicant could serve the same shipper in a dual capacity, in view of the fact that the Commission reserved the right to reconsider the issue at a future date and of the fact that a conversion proceeding was pending whereby applicant's status could become that of a common carrier, the resultant operations were found to be consistent with the public interest and the national transportation policy. Where the contract-carrier status of one of two commonly controlled carriers had been confirmed, while the other was found in a conversion proceeding to be a common carrier, but the two served different classes of shippers and transported entirely different classes of commodities, the Commission held in *Lancaster & New York M. Freight Service, Inc., Conversion*,[18] that the resulting dual operation would be consistent with the public interest.

When the commodities being transported by applicant as a common carrier and those transported by an affiliated contract carrier were noncompetitive, the Commission held in *Smith Transit, Inc., Extension*,[19] that no opportunity for discrimination or other undesirable practices should arise, and that the resulting dual operation was not objectionable. The Commission held in *Oil Carriers Co. Extension*[20] that operation under an interim permit, or under a permanent permit if applicant's status were ultimately determined to be that of a contract carrier, from and to points entirely different from those authorized to be served by applicant as a common carrier, would entail no reasonable possibility that services opposed to the public interest or the national transportation policy might be rendered by it; however, such approval, the Commission said, should not be construed as a waiver of the Commission's right to reconsider

[16]83 M.C.C. 147, 149.
[17]82 M.C.C. 11, 16.
[18]83 M.C.C. 511, 513, 514,-5.
[19]82 M.C.C. 432, 433, 436.
[20]79 M.C.C. 169, 170.

the issue of dual operation at any future date should the facts change
so as to bring about an improper competitive situation or result in improper discrimination or preference. A district court in *Yale Tran. v.
United States*[21] upheld safeguards imposed by the Commission in
insulating applicant's contract from its common carriage, not only by
prohibiting common carriage from shippers utilizing contract carriage
as consignors but also by prohibiting common carriage to such persons
as consignees. The court held that it could not be said that there was
insufficient basis for the Commission's finding that the proposed dual
operations would be consistent with public interest and the national
transportation policy. The court said that the possibility of unfair rate
differentials resulting from the difficulty of keeping records accurately,
reflecting costs of the two types of cooperation, was a problem inherent
in any form of transportation where many different types of traffic are
handled in the same vehicle or a number of vehicles; however, the court
said applicant's maintenance of a formula for allocating costs to its
various services, and the Commission's reservation of jurisdiction were
adequate to enable it to order special cost studies whenever indicated.

In *Ryder System, Inc. — Control — Complete Auto Transit*,[22] the
Commission said (pp. 287-88):

> . . . We are convinced by both the evidence and our understanding of the
> auto haulers situation that small opportunity would exist for unlawful or
> discriminatory rate rebates should common control be authorized in this
> instance, the chief evil which the prohibitions of section 210 were de-
> signed to avoid. Nor would any attempt at such unlawful conduct be
> likely. The insignificant amount of traffic which Convoy has transported
> for General Motors in the past under special conditions should not be a
> bar to this transaction. Moreover, the possibility of any unlawful activity
> can be eliminated and the requirements of section 210 completely satisfied
> by the imposition of restrictions in the permits of Complete and the certifi-
> cates of Convoy, some of which are already so restricted, which would
> limit the former to and exclude the latter from the traffic of General Motors.
> Although restrictions in a common carrier certificate against the traffic of
> a particular shipper are not favored and are somewhat counter to the
> obligations of a common carrier generally, for reasons herein described,
> this should not be true with respect to a common carrier of automobiles. . .

In *Ryder* the Commission recognized that the mere presence of an
opportunity for discrimination does not automatically require denial of
a proposed transaction. This is in keeping with some prior Commission
decisions which state that neither the prohibition of Section 210 against
dual operations nor the principles upon which it is based are regarded

[21] 185 F. Supp. 96, 103.
[22] 109 M.C.C. 275.

as absolute and inflexible, and dual operations may be authorized where, in particular circumstances, good cause is shown therefor.[23]

The Commission issued a general finding in Ex Parte No. 55 (Sub-No. 27), *Dual Operations*, rule served April 6, 1978, that the holding of both common and contract carrier authority is consistent with the public interest and the national transportation policy. It adopted a rule which refers to this finding and provides that, as a result, the Commission will no longer consider the dual operations issue in applications for common or contract carrier operating authority unless there is a showing that rate or service preference is likely to be extended or that other discrimination is likely to be practiced. The rule is expected to remove artificial barriers to the seeking and obtaining of operating authority and to speed the handling of cases involving dual operations.

Relinquishment of Dual Operations

Where restriction of a carrier's authority to eliminate objectionable operations appeared to be impracticable, the Commission advised the carrier in *Dieckbrader Ex. Inc., Conversion Proceeding*[24] that it could elect whether to retain and operate under certificates to be issued in conversion, extension, and purchase proceedings and request cancellation of contract-carrier authority acquired in another purchase proceeding, or to retain the latter and seek cancellation of the common-carrier authority. It could divest itself of either the common or the contract-carrier authority by sale of that which it elected not to retain, or it could elect ot seek conversion of the purchased contract-carrier authority to common-carrier. The proceeding was held open for 90 days to permit respondent to elect which course to follow or to target other suitable action. Since the imposition of restrictions in a certificate resulting from a conversion proceeding and in an obtained permit which was not subject to conversion, so as to preclude applicant's transportation of similar commodities in the same general area as both a common and contract carrier, did not appear practicable, entry of an order in a conversion proceeding, *Highway Transp. Corp. Conversion Proceeding*,[25] was withheld for 90 days in order that applicant could elect which of three courses outlined it wished to follow in order to bring its operations into conformity with Section 210.

---

[23]See *Complete Auto Transit, Inc. − Extension − Willow Run*, 71 M.C.C. 383, 387; *United Parcel Service of New York, Inc., Com. Car. Applic.*, 79 M.C.C. 654, 655; *Estes − Purchase − Minton*, 80 M.C.C. 51, 53; *Cooper − Purchase − Transport Trucking Co.*, 70 M.C.C. 561, 564.

[24]83 M.C.C. 287, 289-90.

[25]96 M.C.C. 169, 171-2.

16

Conversion of Authority

The Applicable Statutory Provisions

Section 212(c) of the Interstate Commerce Act,[1] provides:

"The Commission shall examine each outstanding permit and may within one hundred and eighty days after this subsection takes effect institute a proceeding either upon its own initiative, or upon application of a permit holder actually in operation or upon complaint of an interested party, and after notice and hearing revoke a permit and issue in lieu thereof a certificate of public convenience and necessity, if it finds, first, that any person holding a permit whose operations on the date this subsection takes effect do not conform with the definition of a contract carrier in section 203(a) (15) as in force on and after the date this subsection takes effect; second, are those of a common carrier; and, third, are otherwise lawful. Such certificate so issued shall authorize the transportation, as a common carrier, of the same commodities between the same points or within the same territory as authorized in the permit."

Grandfather Rights, Lawfulness of Operations, Tacking of Rights Interchange, Substantial Parity, Dormancy

The legislative history of 212(c) indicates that it is essentially a "grandfather" provision pursuant to which those carriers whose operations on August 22, 1957, did not conform to the new defintion of a contract carrier, concurrently enacted, but were instead those of a common carrier and otherwise lawful, could without any showing of public need be issued certificates in lieu of their existing permits.

In *T. T. Brooks Trucking Co., Inc., Conversion*,[2] the Commission said that though no one in the hearings before the Senate and House com-

[1] 49 U.S.C. 312(c).
[2] 81 M.C.C. 561, 568-9.

mittees raised the questions of restrictions against tacking or interchange, dormancy, or the Keystone limitation, Congress apparently intended by its silence on such issues to permit the Commission to exercise its independent and expert judgment in the light of general legislative intent and the national transportation policy.[3] The commission said that those issues would not be resolved by consideration only of the last sentence of Section 212 (c). It said that the entire content of that paragraph would be considered, since it was plain that it speaks primarily of "operating authorities" as distinguished from "actual motor carrier operations," as the underlying basis for conversion. It added that while those terms are complementary and to some extent synonymous, where the operating rights of a carrier constitute the predominant language factor, as in Section 212(c), the scope and extent of the transportation a converted carrier shall be authorized to perform is not dependent on actual physical operations.[4] The Commission said further that this Section requires no showing of prior operations under a permit as a prerequisite to conversion; it merely provides for a restatement of the existing contract-carrier rights in the form of a certificate authorizing the converted carrier to perform the same transportation service it could formerly provide as a contract carrier.[5] It concludes that while Section 212(c) is essentially a "grandfather" clause, it differs from the "grandfather" clauses of the Motor Carrier Act, 1935, which required proof of past and continuous bona fide "operations" as basis for issuance of certificates and permits, and in connection with which the "substantial parity" test first arose.

In a number of decisions the Supreme Court held that the Commission had power to impose restrictions in "grandfather" certificates to insure substantial parity, and characterized the pattern of future operations as the product of the Commission's expert judgment based on evidence as to prior operations, characteristics of the type of carrier involved, and capacity or ability of the carrier to render service. And while Congress did not intend to penalize those contract carriers who had allowed their operations to become indistinguishable in most important respects from those of common carriers, in view of the past utilization of the substantial parity test and in absence of any Congressional expression to the contrary, the Commission was constrained to hold that Section

[3] 81 M.C.C. 561, 568-9; see *Tar Asphalt Trucking Co., Inc. v. United States*, 372 U.S. 596, affirming *per curiam* 208 F. Supp. 611, where the Commission's imposition of tacking restrictions in conversions under Section 212(c), interpretation of criteria in Section (a) (15) as applied to conversions, and the constitutionality of requiring involuntary conversions were sustained.

[4] *Ibid.*, p. 570.
[5] *Ibid.*, p. 570.

212(c) should be administered, on the basis of substantial parity with respect to conversion of operating authorities involved therein; and that certificates issued converted carriers should authorize transportation of the same commodities between the same points or within the same territories for which they held permits so as to insure that nothing was taken away from them commoditywise or territorially.[6] This did not mean that a contract carrier would be granted a certificate authorizing service so far beyond the scope of its previous service as to nullify the substantial parity test; mere conversion should not create for a converted carrier new common-carrier rights not substantially similar to those intrinsic in its old status or not within the normal operating framework of its existing permits.[7]

Whether the Commission had power to impose restrictions against tacking in certificates issued converted carriers was not controlled by absence of such restrictions on the face of existing permits, but rather by the scope of operating rights contained therein. Contract carriers have never been permitted to join separate segments of their authorities at common points to render a through service, and there was no warrant for a construction of the statute to the contrary so as to create new and additional rights beyond those formerly held by the converted carrier. Such a result would be contrary both to the wording of the statute and to its basic purpose.[8]

Restrictions against joinder were imposed in certificates issued in Section 212(c) proceedings where possibility of tacking separately stated rights existed. However, restrictions against tacking with any authority that could be obtained later were not imposed at the time of the conversion proceeding, propriety of their imposition was determined in the proceeding involving acquisition of such additional authority.[9]

Restrictions against interchange were not imposed in conversion certificates, as upon conversion the carrier assumed a new status with the duty to serve the public and the obligation to provide reasonable and adequate service, and privilege of establishing joint rates and interchange arrangements with other common carriers. The right of interchange stemmed from the carrier's new status and did not result from restatement of operating authority it previously held as a contract carrier. Nor were restrictions against interchange required either by the express terms of Section 212(c) or by the substantial parity test.[10]

[6]*Ibid.*, pp. 569, 571.
[7]*Ibid.*, p. 571.
[8]*Ibid.*, p. 572.
[9]*Ibid.*, pp. 572-3.
[10]*Ibid.*, p. 574.

Where permits contained Keystone restrictions, certificates issued in lieu thereof contained terms continuing, at least to some extent, the effectiveness of such restrictions. The certificate limitations were designed to enable performance of substantially the same service as a common carrier as was authorized as a contract carrier; only in this way could substantial parity between the permit and certificate authority be maintained.

The exact type of restriction imposed in conversion certificates were based on the facts in each case, the language employed in stating limitations depending on the form of restrictions in the existing permits.[11]

Contentions had been made occasionally in conversion proceedings that permit authority which had become dormant or under which only token operations had been conducted should not be converted, but should be revoked, and that conversion certificate should be issued only on proof of convenience and necessity or of past operations from which public need could be presumed. The Commission found such contentions without merit. The Commission, upon finding that a contract carrier was entitled to conversion, had no alternative but to issue a certificate authorizing performance, not of operations actually conducted on the "grandfather" date, but of the service authorized by the then outstanding permits; dormancy of operating rights was not an issue to be considered in determining conversion proceedings.[12] While it would be impossible to find that a carrier's operations were those of a common carrier and to authorize conversion when no service at all was provided, its status could be determined from consideration of its overall activities where only portions of its authority were dormant.[13]

In *Steel Haulers, Inc., Conversion,*[14] the Commission held that the authority held by a successor in interest to the holder of that authority on the date Section 212(c) was added to the I.C. Act could be converted under that Section. Since one purpose of the enactment of Section 203(a) (15), as amended, and Section 212(c) was to preserve the distinction between common and contract carriage, to deny conversion of a contract carrier's authority merely because the rights were acquired after the effective date of those amendments would defeat that purpose, and would also impose an unwarranted penalty upon a carrier which had obtained, in a lawful manner and in accordance with the Commission's regulations, authority under which its predecessor had operated and

[11]*Ibid.*, p. 576.
[12]*Ibid.*, p. 577.
[13]*Ibid.*, p. 577-8.
[14]82 M.C.C. 337, 339-40.

which, had application been filed by the predecessor, would result in issuance of a certificate in lieu of the presently held permit.

In the same case the Commission held that restrictions against interchange of traffic should not be imposed in certificates granted to converted carriers, since the right of interchange is a privilege stemming from, and incidental to, a converted carrier's new common-carrier status.[15] However, the Commission said, restrictions against tacking should be imposed in certificates issued to converted carriers, where possibilities for tacking separate authorities existed.

The fact that both applicant and its competitor had conversion applications under consideration with the Commission did not affect the Commission's conclusions in *Gene Adams Refrigerated Trucking Service, Inc., Extension,*[16] for it could not prejudge the determinations of those proceedings. The competitor's contention that should applicant's operations be certificated it would result in competitive injury to it was too speculative, the Commission said, to constitute an adequate basis for denial in the instant proceeding.

In *Nadeau Transport Conversion Proceeding,*[17] although applicant's employees were familiar with the handling of the considered commodity, and its equipment was well suited and used exclusively for transportation of that commodity, its services were similar to those offered by common carriers of the same article. Applicant had contracts with three shippers, but did not assign its vehicles to exclusive use of any particular shipper, and offered its services to any member of the shipping public. The Commission said that this service did not conform to the definition of a contract carrier as set forth in Section 203(a)(15), as amended. The Commission also said that the contention that applicant, a Canadian contract carrier, could not consistently be considered a contract carrier by the Province of Quebec and a common carrier by the Commission was without merit. The Commission said that applicant operated in two separate and independent jurisdictions which have different statutes, rules, and regulations; and since its operations within the United States

---

[15]While contract carriers have never been permitted to interchange freight moving beyond their own lines with other carriers, a contract carrier may participate in an operation closely resembling interchange by acting as agent of the shipper and as such turning the shipment over to another carrier at the common point of service. In such arrangements the contract carrier must be employed as agent "separately from the contract of carriage," the other carrier involved must collect its published charges for the service performed, and the bill of lading issued by it must show the shipper and not the contract-carrier agent as consignor. See *T. Brooks Trucking, Inc. Conversion* 81 M.C.C. 561, 573.

[16]77 M.C.C. 89, 90-1.

[17]82 M.C.C. 541-4.

did not conform to the definition of a contract carrier, but were the operations of a common carrier and were otherwise lawful, it was entitled to a certificate in lieu of its presently held permit.

The Commission also held that while the operations conducted on the critical date were controlling, evidence of operations conducted since that date gave support and credence to evidence of operations on and prior to that time. There was, therefore, no error in the joint board's consideration of applicant's operations as conducted and as intended to be conducted in the future. The certificate granted was not restricted against interchange, and, as applicant's permit was not susceptible to tacking, a restriction against joinder was also found unnecessary. Where applicant's operations in *Scott Trunk Line, Inc.*,[18] as conducted on and since the critical date had been those of a common carrier rather than a contract carrier, it was entitled, the Commission said, to be issued a certificate in a Section 212(c) proceeding.

Section 212(c) did not impose a strict test of fitness on a carrier as a condition to conversion; the purpose of the provision that a carrier's operations be found to be "otherwise lawful" was to ensure that only those operations lawfully conducted may be considered in determining whether it has been operating as a common or a contract carrier.[19] In the *Nelson* case where applicant's operations under all but six of 95 contracts had concededly been unauthorized, its status was determined by its lawful operations under the six contracts. The Commission held (pp. 263-4) that although applicant submitted no evidence of any operations under its authority for new and used household goods, its overall operations as actually conducted on the critical date entitled it to conversion, and that the certificate issued would authorize all service granted by its permit outstanding on that date.

In *Lewis Motor Service Conversion Proceeding*,[20] the Commission said that in requiring that operations of an applicant or respondent in a Section 212(c) proceeding he found "otherwise lawful," Congress did not mean to impose a strict test of fitness such as is required of applicants for additional authority. To find that unauthorized operations by a carrier or some breach of law or Commission's regulations, such as failure to collect correct charges, to file copies of contracts, or to keep drivers' logs, precluded issuance under Section 212(c) of a certificate in lieu of its outstanding permits, would leave the carrier in the anomalous position of being unable to operate lawfully unless it modified its

[18]82 M.C.C. 427, 429.
[19]*Andrew G. Nelson, Inc., Conversion Proceeding*, 86 M.C.C. 261, 263.
[20]83 M.C.C. 497, 499.

operations to conform with the new contract-carrier definition or took other steps to convert its permits to certificates, either of which courses might ultimately prove impossible. The net result might be that the carrier would be forced to cease operations altogether, surely too drastic a penalty to have been contemplated by such legislation. A finding in *J. B. Montgomery, Inc., Modification of Permit*[21] that petitioner's common carrier operations were "otherwise lawful" was not precluded because it or its predecessor transported certain traffic for one shipper without authority, since it was determined that it was actually entitled to grandfather authority for those operations.

In *Leslie J. Strawn, Inc., Conversion*[22] the Commision held that to authorize a converted contract-to-common carrier to perform a through service over a combination of its present routes would be akin to authorizing the transportation, as a common carrier, of traffic between points not previously authorized by the carrier's permits. Such a result, the Commission said, would be contrary to Section 212(c), and failed to ensure substantial parity between past and future operating rights; the Commission held that the certificates issued in lieu of the permit would be restricted against tacking, but such restriction would have no effect on any authority that may be obtained later. Likewise in *Scott Truck Line, Inc.*,[23] a conversion certificate was restricted to transportation of advertising matter and such general merchandise as is dealt in by wholesale, retail, and chain grocery and food business houses when moving from, to, or between warehouses and wholesale, retail, or chain outlets of grocery and food business houses in order to ensure substantial parity between past and future operations.

The Commission held in *J. B. Montgomery, Inc., Modification of Permit*[24] that where only portions of a carrier's operating authority were dormant, determination of its status should be made from consideration of its overall activities and conversion should be authorized where they are found to be those of a common carrier. Since petitioner's overall operations actually conducted on the critical date entitled it to conversion, the certificate issued authorized performance of all service authorized by the permit outstanding on that date. Likewise in *Steel Haulers, Inc., Conversion*,[25] the Commission held that where only portions of a

---

[21]83 M.C.C. 457, 463; set aside in part in *J. B. Montgomery, Inc. v. United States*, 206 F. Supp. 455.

[22]81 M.C.C. 758, 759.

[23]82 M.C.C. 427, 430.

[24]83 M.C.C. 457, 462; set aside in part in *J. B. Montgomery, Inc. v. United States*, 206 F. Supp. 455.

[25]82 M.C.C. 337, 338, 340.

carrier's authority were dormant, its status could be determined from the carrier's overall activities and conversion should be authorized where operations were found to be those of a common carrier. Since the overall operations of applicant and its predecessor entitled it to conversion, the certificate embraced rights authorized under the permit outstanding on the critical date, despite protestants' claim that portions of the rights acquired after that date had not been used by applicant. Since transportation of vegetable oils was found to be common carriage, the Commission held in *George Hillman Trucking Co., Inc., Conversion Proceedings*,[26] that the carrier was entitled to a certificate corresponding to its existing contract-carrier authority for such commodities notwithstanding the fact that it was conducting operations under a portion of such rights, since dormancy was not an issue in proceedings under Section 212(c).

There was nothing in Section 212(c) which compelled the Commission to convert a contract carrier to common-carrier status on the basis of its operations on the critical date if that carrier, within a reasonable time thereafter, modified its method of operation so as to bring it within the terms of the amended definition of a contract carrier. To hold otherwise not only would have deprived a carrier which wished to remain a contract carrier of the only opportunity it had of retaining its status, but also would have forced conversion of a carrier which, at the time the conversion became effective, was operating lawfully as a contrct carrier.[27] In *Frontier Delivery, Inc., v. Teoga Transport, Inc.*[28] the Commission said that while complainant common carriers insisted that the service provided by defendant contract carrier was no different than service they offered, it did not necessarily follow that defendant was a common carrier. Defendant's operations being in accordance with the definition of a contract carrier as set forth in Section 203(a) (15), as amended, it was entitled to continue operations under its existing permit; conversion under Section 212(c), therefore, was not justified and the complaint was dismissed. A conversion of contract-carrier authority held by applicant on the critical date was authorized in *Highway Transp. Corp. Conversion Proceeding*,[29] but the authority it subsequently acquired, confirmed as contract-carrier authority while in the hands of the transferor prior to the transfer but after the critical date, could not be subject to the conversion proceeding. Since acquisition of the latter rights gave rise to an issue of dual operations, which was not considered in the hearing officer's

---

[26]82 M.C.C. 389, 392.
[27]*Metz Conversion*, 82 M.C.C. 569, 571.
[28]82 M.C.C. 536, 539-40.
[29]86 M.C.C. 169, 170.

report in the pending proceeding or in the transfer order, the conversion proceeding was reopened to consider that issue.

Interim Permit

Where need for the proposed service was shown, in order not to delay disposition of the matter until a determination was made as to applicant's status as a common or contract carrier in a pending conversion proceeding, interim authority was granted in *Maxwell Co. Extension.*[30] In *Jacobsen Extension,*[31] the Commission said that since a proceeding had been instituted which could result in conversion of applicant's operations under outstanding permits to those of a common carrier, it would be inappropriate to issue permanent authority. The Commission held in *Lancaster & New York M. Freight Service, Inc., Conversion*[32] that as interim authority granted in an extension proceeding was not outstanding on the critical date, it was not subject to conversion in a proceeding under Section 212(c); in accordance with its own terms, the form of permanent authority to be issued would be determined in the extension proceeding. And in *Steel Haulers, Inc., Conversion,*[33] since the interim permit held by applicant was conditioned to expire upon final determination of the pending proceeding, the usual provision for revocation of existing authority concurrently with issuance of a new certificate was not included in the findings.

The Commission granted an interim permit pending final determination of applicant's status as a contract or common carrier under Section 212(c) in *Carl Subler Trucking, Inc., Extension.*[34] The Commission said in the *Subler* case that in view of the growing tendency in the food business for smaller inventories and more frequent deliveries, shippers of canned, prepared, or preserved foodstuffs require more expeditious, single-line, multiple drop off service; interline service is not satisfactory, thus the proposed service, designed to eliminate warehousing and redistribution costs, would be responsive to the need shown. Where the supporting shipper required for-hire transportation of canned, prepared, or preserved foodstuffs, previously moving in private carriage to the destination area sought, by a carrier able to provide multiple deliveries of l.t.l. lots, an interim permit was granted pending determination of

[30] 82 M.C.C. 23, 29.
[31] 79 M.C.C. 53, 55.
[32] 83 M.C.C. 511, 515.
[33] 82 M.C.C. 337, 341.
[34] 77 M.C.C. 633, 639-40.

applicant's status as a common or contract carrier in a conversion proceeding.[35]

In *Dahlsten Extension*,[36] the Commission said that the practice of granting interim permits pending determination of Section 212(c) applications had been developed in order to provide the public with needed transportation facilities pending determination of applicants' status; and the Commission had ample authority to grant such interim or conditional authorities.

Conversion Proceedings Under Section 207

In *Connell Transport Co., Inc., Conversion Application*,[37] the Commission articulated the general standard applicable in a conversion proceeding under Section 207 subsequent to the 1957 amendments. In accordance with *Connell* a carrier seeking conversion from contract to common carrier status is required to produce evidence of past lawful operations under the authority sought to be converted and to offer shipper testimony demonstrating a need for service as a common carrier rather than a contract carrier. The essential changes brought about by *Connell* in post-amendment cases are (1) a requirement of greater shipper support than was previously required by and (2) a more strict view taken regarding applicant's prior lawful activity.

Conversion of Irregular-Route to Regular-Route Motor Carrier Operations

Special rules of procedure were adopted by the Commission May 1, 1964, governing the conversion of irregular-route motor carrier operations to regular-route operations. The events which preceded the adoption of such rules and the intended purposes thereof are discussed in *Midwest Motor Exp., Ext., Intermediate Points*,[38] as follows:

Section 203(a) (14) of the Interstate Commerce Act, as amended, defines the terms "common carrier by motor vehicle" as "any person which

[35]*Beatty Motor Exp. Extension*, 83 M.C.C. 279, 281-2.

[36]81 M.C.C. 733, 776.

[37]95 M.C.C. 312. Application of a less stringent standard than Cornell in post-amendment cases is not without precedent. See: *T. T. Brooks Trucking Co., Inc.*, 86 M.C.C. 667; *Bankers Dispatch Corp., Conversion Application*, 110 M.C.C. 294.

[38]96 M.C.C. 402, 403-405. See No. MC-C-4366, *In the Matter of Declaration of Policy and Promulgation of Special Rules for Conversion of Irregular-Route to Regular-Route Motor Carrier Operations.* Notice of Proposed rule making published in 29 F.R. 1330, January 25, 1964, and effective by order published in 29 F.R. 5801, May 1, 1964.

holds itself out to the general public to engage in the transportation by motor vehicle in interstate or foreign commerce of passengers *or property* or any class or classes thereof for compensation, whether over *regular* or *irregular* routes. . . ." [Emphasis supplied.] Nowhere, however, does the act define regular- or irregular-route carriers, or set forth the particular or identifying characteristics of either class; and while the statutory dichotomy was recognized and generally described at the inception of Federal motor carrier regulation, no attempt was then made to trace definitely a line of demarcation between the two types of service. *Classification of Motor Carriers of Property,* 2 M.C.C. 703, 709. The Commission subsequently issued numerous certificates of public convenience and necessity authorizing the interstate transportation of property over either regular or irregular routes depending upon the operational pattern conducted or proposed and their apparent relation to the statutory distinction between such operations and services. Because of the absence of clear and definite standards by which to judge the essential character of the operations in question, however, much difficulty was encountered in distinguishing between regular- and irregular-route operations which frequently tended to overlap and shade into one another. This basic problem of definition was not resolved until the issuance in 1947 of the decision in *Transportation Activities, Brady Transfer & Storage Co.,* 47 M.C.C. 23. In that decision, the Commission, division 5, reviewed the matter as it then stood and, while recognizing the impracticability of establishing a rigid formula whereby the essential character of each operational method could be determined, it enunciated eight specific guidelines for use in distinguishing irregular-route operations from those performed by duly authorized regular-route carriers. These tests are as follows: (1) operation according to a predetermined plan or outline; (2) the movement in significant amounts of particular types of traffic; (3) the vigorous solicitation of this particular type of traffic and the holding out of particular types of service; (4) the maintenance at significant points of terminals devoted to, and designed for, the expeditious handling of certain traffic and the conduct of certain types of operations; (5) the habitual use of fixed routes; (6) operation between fixed termini; (7) a marked or constant periodicity in the service rendered; and (8) the observance of definite or published schedules or their equivalent.

Noting the natural tendency of irregular-route operations as conducted by motor common carriers of general commodities or of a wide range of diverse commodities, to gravitate toward and evolve into regular-route operations between certain terminals, the *Brady* case, *supra,* at page 40 discussed the procedure required to be followed by those carriers faced with this problem as follows:

> "Whenever, in the normal development and growth of an irregular-route service, the movement of traffic between particular points becomes so constant in point of time and of such volume as to suggest a public need for an added regular-route service between such points, the act provides a means by which appropriate authority for such an operation may be obtained. Noting a tendency for its operation to fall into regular routes, it is the obligation of every irregular-route

carrier either to check the tendency and preserve its status, or to obtain appropriate authority for the conversion. . . .

"A related argument that irregular-route carriers should be allowed to convert to regular-route 'upon a showing of past performance' without the introduction of testimony of shipper witnesses, merits only brief comment. To begin with, the reference to 'past performance' is not entirely clear in its meaning. If knowingly unlawful 'past performance' of unauthorized regular-route service is referred to, they are entitled to little, if any, weight. . . . If, on the other hand, reference is to an increasing and constant volume of lawful past operations in authorized irregular-route service, then clearly such operations are entitled to weight in the disposition of any application for authority to convert to regular-route service, but patently it cannot be said that past operations, standing alone, would in every case constitute sufficient proof of public need for regular-route service to justify a grant of authority to convert. Each such application must be determined upon its own particular facts."

Prior to the institution in 1959 of the rule making proceedings in Ex Parte No. MC-55, *Motor Common Carriers of Property — Routes and Service,* 88 M.C.C. 415, the motor carrier industry came to rely upon the *Brady* criteria and to obey its mandate that irregular-route general-commodity carriers seek conversion of their authorities in appropriate circumstances. As a result, the history of motor carrier regulation includes numerous individual application, investigation, complaint and other proceedings dealing with the distinction between regular- and irregular-route service. See, for example, *United Truck Lines, Inc., Extension — Missoula, Mont.,* 48 M.C.C. 71; *Masser, Extension — Gettysburg — Taneytown,* 51 M.C.C. 703; and the other cases cited in the report of division 1 in Ex Parte No. MC-55, *supra.* In an effort to alleviate the resulting administrative burden, the Commission, in 1959, initiated a rule making proceeding wherein it considered numerous industry proposals designed to obscure or eliminate the dichotomy between the two types of service. Ex Parte No. MC-55, *supra.* While irregular-route operations and services continued naturally to evolve into those of regular route operations, the Ex Parte No. MC-55 proposals, although ultimately rejected, resulted in an approximate 3-year hiatus or suspension in the filing and handling of appropriate conversion applications as well as in the institution of other proceedings. As an outgrowth of the Ex Parte No. MC-55 decision, it was foreseeable that the Commission would soon be confronted with a large number of application and other proceedings delayed during the pendency of Ex Parte No. MC-55. Thus it was to resolve the uncertainties and administrative problems created by this hiatus, and to make available a simplified and expedient procedure whereby irregular-route operations, which through the natural processes of evolution have developed into regular-route service between fixed termini, may be brought into harmony with both the letter and spirit of the act and the Commission's decisions thereunder, that the aforementioned special procedural rules were promulgated. These rules, which apply only to applications filed thereunder prior to March 1, 1965, envision the processing of conversion applications generally under modified procedure; are not to be utilized to obtain regular-route authority in addition to, rather than in lieu of, corresponding irregular-route authority; and do not contemplate the unwarranted broadening of a carrier's existing authority, either as to commodities or as to territory.

17

Interpretation of Operating Authorities

Power of the Commission

Sections 207(a), 208(a), 209, and 211 of the Interstate Commerce Act[1] empower the Commission to issue operating authorities, and such power implies the necessary power to review certificates and permits and formulate interpretive statements of general or particular applicability and future effect relative to them; and that it is within the Commission's province to interpret operating rights has been settled by the courts.[2] Thus, the Commission may in its discretion entertain a request for determination of service which may be rendered under a certificate it has issued.[3]

The task of construing a certificate has been placed upon the Commission by Congress and such construction will not be disturbed unless clearly erroneous.[4] Unless clearly erroneous, the Commission's interpretation of the meaning of words used in operating authority issued by it is controlling on the courts; and such interpretation, being simply a definitive declaration of what rights existed from the beginning under the authority granted, cannot be equated with modification.[5] Even though there is no patent ambiguity in a carrier's certificate, the Commission is not precluded from going behind it to examine the underlying background of the grant, its determination being reached independently by interpretation of the certificate at face value.[6]

---

[1]49 U.S.C. 307(a), 308(a), 309, and 311.

[2]*Interpretations, Operating Rights — Returned Containers*, 82 M.C.C. 677, 679-80; *Interpretation of Operating Rights — Alaska*, 81 M.C.C. 701, 705.

[3]*A. W. Hawkins, Inc., Interpretation of Certificate*, 82 M.C.C. 7, 9.

[4]*Denton Produce, Inc. v. United States*, 270 F. Supp. 402; *Dunkley Refrigerated Transport, Inc. v. United States*, 253 F. Supp. 891.

[5]*Sims Motor Transport Lines, Inc. v. United States*, 183 F. Supp. 113, 116-9.

[6]*Ibid.*, pp. 117-8.

It is only logical that the Commission, which is appointed by law and informed by experience to interpret the certificate issued by it, should be free to draw upon its own accumulative experience in reaching a decision. The weight to be accorded testimony of carrier's supporting witnesses is its exclusive function so long as it does not act arbitrarily, capriciously, or in clear error.[7] As was stated in *W. J. Dillner Transfer Co. v. United States,*[8] the interpretation of a certificate issued by the Commission is best left to the Commission. The court is bound by such interpretation unless it is persuaded that the Commission's interpretation is capricious or arbitrary, that it constitutes an abuse of discretion, or that it does violence to some established principle of law.[9]

The cardinal rule in interpreting motor carrier authority is that the carrier's certificate must speak for itself, and that consideration may ordinarily be given to the circumstances surrounding the grant of such authority only if the authority itself is patently indefinite or ambiguous. Absent these, and absent clerical errors and other ministerial mistake, it is the established rule that operating rights ordinarily must be construed according to their terms regardless of what may have been intended at the time of their issuance. This is so even though the effect is to confer more or less authority than intended originally.[10]

In *Holt Motor Express, Inc., Modification of Certificate, supra,* the Commission said (at 287) that the basic precepts in interpreting operating rights are as follows:

> . . . that the actual terms of the carrier's certificate or permit must be construed, and that matters extrinsic to such authority are not to be considered unless the authority itself is patently indefinite and ambiguous or when errors of a ministerial nature require correction. See *Mural Transport, Inc., Interpretation,* 111 M.C.C. 637, 640 (1970), and cases cited therein. Where there is no ambiguity in the language of the certificate as issued, it is neither necessary nor proper to examine the record which formed the basis for its issuance in order to determine what authority was granted. *Morehouse—Investigation of Operations,* 81 M.C.C. 614, 616 (1959). It is well settled that intentions or representations as to limitations of the type of service to be conducted, even when contained in reports under which certificates are issued, are of no significance in determinations of whether a service is being performed in accordance with the terms of

---

[7]*Ibid.,* p. 119.

[8]193 F. Supp. 823, 825-6, aff'd 368 U.S. 6.

[9]*Johnson Common Carrier Application,* 61 M.C.C. 783, 791.

[10]See *American Trucking Assn's. v. Frisco Co.,* 358 U.S. 133; *T. I. McCormick Trucking Co., Inc., — Investigation,* 110 M.C.C. 499; *Great Northern v. Standard Transportation and Elmer's Exp.,* 110 M.C.C. 35; *Holt Motor Express, Inc., Modification of Certificate,* 120 M.C.C. 282, 287.

the certificates. *Coastal Tank Lines, Inc., v. Charlton Bros. Transp. Co., Inc.,* 48 M.C.C. 289, 300-301 (1948) . . .

Descriptions in Motor Carrier Certificates

In the framing of motor carrier operating authorities, the Commission from the beginning of motor carrier regulation has been confronted with the necessity of avoiding undue and illogical fragmentation, or the granting of specific single or isolated commodities to the exclusion of others in the same class. On the other hand, when it came to avoiding fragmentation by grants of authority to transport classes of commodities, it encountered endless and recurring questions as to whether a particular commodity belonged in one class or another or possibly in both.

Even before Federal regulation, motor carriers came to be recognized as belonging to particular classes according to the classes of commodities they transported. On August 8, 1937, shortly after regulation got under way, the Commission, exercising its authority under Section 204(c) of the Act,[11] issued a report in *Classification of Motor Carriers of Property*,[12] in which it recognized 17 classes of motor carriers, all of which classes being dependent on the type of commodities transported. But not all carriers fitted into these 17 prominent classes, and it became the practice to grant motor carrier authorities in terms of other classes of commodities as seemed appropriate. After 15 years of this, the Commission found itself granting authority to transport certain classes of authority so frequently and so consistently that a listing of the specific commodities covered by certain class descriptions became desirable and it adopted a report, *Description in Motor Carrier Certificates*,[13] endeavoring (somewhat unsuccessfully) to list all the commodities covered by each of some 15 class descriptions.

But this was not the end of the problem for there still remained outstanding scores of operating authorities framed in terms of classes of commodities which were no place defined.

Commodity descriptions used by the Commission in certificates and permits have varied somewhat in the words actually used, but it has not in the past authorized a grant of authority to transport "shipments" as distinguished from "commodities," thus the individual commodity to be transported as contrasted to a shipment in the aggregate must be within the scope of the authority granted.[14] Many of the terms used in

[11]49 U.S.C. 304(c).
[12]2 M.C.C. 701.
[13]61 M.C.C. 209.
[14]*National Automobile Transporters Assn. v. Rowe Transfer*, 64 M.C.C. 229, 236.

certificates have been used either on the basis of industry customs and common understandings which may be at variance with strictly academic or literal definitions, or as the result of intentional resort to general terms or classifications in the interest of simplicity and reasonable regulation, and with the purpose and desire to describe in general terms all the service intended to be authorized.[15] Such general terms with well established meanings in a particular industry have been made the basis for claims of authority to render services partially or radically different from that originally intended or contemplated.[16] Authorities should be reasonably interpreted to accomplish the purposes for which they were issued, which purposes are well understood in the industry, and distorted and patently unwarranted and extravagant claims of authority and corresponding holding outs are not recognized by the Commission.[17]

Intended Use Test

The "intended use" test has been applied by the Commission in the past for determining whether a particular commodity comes within the terms of a certificate of public convenience and necessity. One example is *Fleetlines, Inc. v. Osbourn Trucking Company.*[18] In that case Osbourn Trucking Company held authority to transport building and construction materials, equipment and supplies, and mining equipment and supplies. In a complaint proceeding, the Commission found that Osbourn had been engaged in the transportation of a large number of commodities, such as floor wax, paper bags, clocks and door mats, and that such transportation to the extent indicated was not authorized. After discussing several similar cases in which the Commission had applied the "intended use" test, it was stated:

> The authority of defendant here is essentially the same as that in the cited proceedings, and interpretation thereof of necessity involves application of the same principles. Clearly, the broad interpretation of this authority as contended for by defendant cannot be adopted, since it would not limit the operations of defendant to the described industries, but would instead permit unlimited transportation contrary to the obvious intent of the certificate as granted. There can be no doubt that such a grant was not intended when the authority was originally granted, nor is it contended here that the authority actually granted was less than

[15]*Ibid.*
[16]*Ibid.*
[17]53 M.C.C. 277, 297. See *King,* 84 M.C.C. 269, 275.
[18]54 M.C.C. 221, 229-30; see also *Laverne W. Simpson v. United States,* 200 F., Supp. 372, aff'd 369 U.S. 526.

should have been granted. In the light of the precedents cited, and on principle also, defendant's right to transport any given commodity depends on whether "there is a then existing intent that the item be used in a manner to bring it within the scope of defendant's certificate." In other words, in order for the particular commodity or item offered for transportation to qualify as authorized mining equipment or as a mine supply, it must be of such character that it has virtually no other use, or, if it has some other normal use, it must be used there, or if it moves to any other consignee, as, for example, a mining equipment dealer or supply point it must be of such character, or must move under such circumstances, as to negative the probability of any future use other than as a mine supply. Defendant contends that this places an undue burden on it, but we do not agree. The method by which defendant determines that it may perform certain transportation is within its discretion; however, we believe that, if the shipper or consignee represents to the carrier that there is a definite "present intent" that the items which are offered for transportation shall be used in such a manner as to bring them within the authorized commodity description, that carrier has discharged its duty in this respect, unless it has reason to doubt the representation made to it and to believe that the shipments so offered "probably" will not be used in the manner represented. There are certain commodities that are of such a nature as virtually to have no uses other than those of a certain character. Such items may be said to be so closely associated with that activity that the carrier's transportation of them without investigation or inquiry as to their intended use would not appear unreasonable. The intended use of other items must be established with reasonable certainty. On the question of the intended use, the identity of the consignee may be significant either to establish or to negative a particular use, but in the end it is the "actually intended use rather than the identity of consignee that controls."

* * *

. . . The transportation of these items being established, the burden was upon defendant to show that they were transported under circumstances bringing them within its authority. Such information as is available in this record concerning the circumstances under which these particular items were transported, the consignees and consignors, and their intended use, does not disclose any facts about them to rebut the presumption that they were transported without authority.

Another similar case in which the Commission applied the intended use test is *England Transportation Co., Inc., Extension — Mississippi Points.*[19] The Commission held that authority to transport machinery, materials, supplies and equipment incidental to the construction of facilities for the development and production of natural gas did

---

[19] 49 M.C.C. 567. See also *Builders Express, Inc. — Interpretation of Certificate,* 51 M.C.C. 103, involving "contractors' materials, supplies and equipment"; *Greenberg — Investigation of Operations,* 52 M.C.C. 25; *Eastern Utah Transportation Co. Extension — Rangely, Colo.,* 51 M.C.C. 802; *Carroll Trucking Co. Interpretation of Certificate,* 52 M.C.C. 178.

not authorize the transportation of composition pipe intended to be used in a municipal waterworks. The Commission said (p. 571) that "In other words, the authority . . . is not unlimited, but is restricted to a certain kind of machinery and particular kind of materials, supplies, and equipment, which is identified by reference to their intended use."

MERCER DESCRIPTION

There is a widely held form of motor carrier operating authority, commonly known as the *Mercer* description from the decision in which it was originally formulated, *Mercer Extension — Oil Field Commodities.*[20]

The *Mercer* description authority reads as follows:

1. Machinery, equipment, materials, and supplies used in, or in connection with, the discovery, development, production, refining, manufacture, processing, storage, transmission, and distribution of natural gas and petroleum and their products and by-products, and
2. Machinery, materials, equipment, and supplies used in, or in connection with, the construction, operation, repair, servicing, maintenance, and dismantling of pipelines, including the stringing and picking up thereof.

The court in *Arrow Trucking Co. v. United States,*[21] said:

With reference to the *Mercer* description, the Commission held, that it is not controverted, that the consistent administrative interpretation thereof has been that it was intended to apply strictly to the oil and gas industry . . . This settled administrative interpretation is entitled to great weight (footnote omitted). No cogent reasons appear here for rejecting such administrative interpretation.

We agree with the Commission that clause (2) of the *Mercer* description must be read with clause (1), is limited to the oil and gas industry, and does not cover the movement of any commodities except when incidental to and used in various phases of the natural gas and petroleum industry.

The court's language tersely sums up what continues to be the Commission's position in this matter.

Heavy Haulers

The proper interpretation of the scope of the operating rights of the so-called heavy haulers (common carriers operating under the descrip-

[20]74 M.C.C. 459.
[21]181 F. Supp. 775, 778.

tion "commodities, the transportation of which because of size or weight requires the use of special equipment," or similar description) has always presented problems for the Commission. This is reflected in a number of cases involving the interpretation of the scope of the operating rights of heavy haulers.

In *St. Johnsbury Trucking Co., Inc., Extension — Heavy Hauling,*[22] the Commission said that the phrase "commodities which because of size or weight require special equipment'" enables the authorized carrier to render a complete service in the particular field of transportation "but, by the same token, restricts such carrier from invading the field of another type of service." In *McDade Interpretation of Certificate*[23] the Commission said that the word "require" does not necessarily mean that the commodities involved must be such that it is impossible to handle them without the use of rigging and erecting equipment, but it "is sufficient if the commodities are such that they are customarily, in ordinary trade usage, for reasons of economy and efficiency, handled with the use of rigging and erecting equipment." Special equipment refers to that type of equipment not normally utilized by authorized carriers providing an ordinary general freight service, and includes vehicles of odd or unusual design such as pole trailers, low-bed trailers, and those with additional equipment such as winch-equipment trailers; it is recognized that these vehicles are used solely by heavy haulers and there is no problem concerning their use.[24] The Commission, however, recognizes a trend in the motor carriers industry towards the use of larger sized "ordinary" vehicles capable of transporting heavier loads resulting from the continuing improvement in highway capabilities and the relaxation of the maximum weight limitations in many States.[25] In this regard the Commission has concluded that regular or so-called high flat-bed trailers as well as those described as heavy duty type, regardless of their bracing or reinforcing, are nevertheless ordinary in their design and ordinary in their usage and therefore not special equipment;[26] that both heavy haulers and general commodity carriers, under certain circumstances, may operate flat-bed trailers;[27] and that dropframe, bi-level floor units

[22]53 M.C.C. 401, 405.
[23]53 M.C.C. 401; see also *Schreiber Trucking Co., Inc. — Investigation of Operations,* 15 Fed. Car. Cases 35469.
[24]*Dallas & Mavis Forwarding Co., Inc., Ext. — Galion, Ohio,* 79 M.C.C. 28.
[25]*Ibid.* See *Schreiber,* 91 M.C.C. 91.
[26]*W. J. Dillner Transfer Co. — Investigation of Operations,* 79 M.C.C. 335, sustained *W. J. Dillner Transfer Co. v. I.C.C.,* 193 F. Supp. 823, aff'd 368 U.S. 6.
[27]*Schreiber Trucker Co., Inc. — Investigation of Operations, supra.*

may be used under certain circumstances by both heavy haulers and general commodity carriers.[28]

There is a twilight zone within which the same commodities may properly be transported by a general commodity carrier and a heavy hauler. In this regard the Commission said in *National Automobile Transporters Assn. v. Rowe Transfer:*[29]

> Thus, the line of distinction between general-commodity carriers whose authorities except "commodities requiring special equipment" and so-called heavy haulers who under appropriate authority offer special services and whose authority is limited to "commodities the transportation of which, because of size or weight, requires the use of special equipment" is not exact and despite it regulatory desirability cannot well be. The authorities though mutually exclusive in form are not so in fact and cannot practicably be so. The two fields of operation unavoidably tend to overlap and create a twilight zone wherein both may operate under certain circumstances and where the authority of the one or the other of the two classes of carriers in a particular instance depends upon the peculiar circumstances. First upon what, if any, special service or equipment is required by the inherent characteristics of the commodity to be transported and thereafter upon what is required of the carrier in the way of transportation including loading and unloading. As previously indicated, in certain circumstances the same commodity will fall within the authority of carriers in both classes. It is difficult to formulate a practiable rule of thumb by which to resolve all possible cases but the following test appears to cover most, if not all, those which have been brought to our attention:
>
> Where the commodity in question "requires" special equipment or special services for loading or unloading, or both, and only ordinary vehicular equipment for the over-the-road portion of the transportation, such commodity (1) is within the authority of a heavy hauler irrespective of whether or not the heavy hauler is required to provide such loading and unloading or service, and (2) is within the authority of a general-commodity carrier whose authority excepts "commodities requiring special equipment" provided the loading or unloading of both which necessitates the special equipment is performed by the consignor or consignee, or both.

In *Heavy & Specialized Carriers Section v. Wilson F.F. Co.,*[30] the Commission said that "weight and size regulations are a matter of local concern which, because of their local character and diversity, are necessarily left with the States" and that such "regulations are designed to meet the needs of a specific area and have a definite relationship to requirements to be met in operating over the particular Highways."

---

[28]*Ibid.*

[29]64 M.C.C. 229, 240. See also *Telischak Trucking, Inc., Ext. — Concrete Commodities,* 82 M.C.C. 109.

[30]79 M.C.C. 572, 574. See *Ohio Public Utilities Comm. v. Riss & Co., Inc.,* 72 M.C.C. 659, 672.

The Commission then added "that if special vehicular equipment is required and used to transport the involved lading through a certain area in the manner hereinbefore described, the resulting operation involves a service which carriers of general freight are not authorized to perform."

In *W. J. Dillner Transfer Co. — Investigation of Operation, supra,* certain criteria were established for determining the scope of operations which might be lawfully conducted by heavy haulers. In considering the question of bundling, aggregating or palletizing of individual commodities the Commission stated the general rule of construction as follows:

(1)   Reinforced or heavy-duty flat-bed vehicle of usual and ordinary design, with or without heavier boards, or other protections required by our safety regulations, are not special equipment as that term is used in the operating authorities here under consideration;

(2)   The so-called twilight zone approach as it relates to the construction of operating authorities of heavy haulers and general-commodity carriers, as summarized in the *Rowe case, 64 M.C.C. 229,* is well established, reasonable in its application, and will continue to be recognized;

(3)   In bundling, aggregating, or palletizing, it should be the general rule of construction (A) that the individual "commodity itself" is the controlling consideration as respects a carrier's authority; (B) that the limited exception which the *Black case, 64 M.C.C. 443,* represents, where commodities are bundled for protection or as otherwise required by their "inherent nature," must be maintained within its strictest limits; (C) that the minimum bundle which is required by the "inherent nature" of the commodity is the size or type of bundle which must be considered in any determination whether necessity exists for the use of special equipment; and (D) that in order reasonably to maintain these limits it shall be presumed, in the absence of a sound basis for concluding to the contrary, that commodities tendered to carrier, in bundles or aggregations, are within the general rule and not within the limited exception thereto;

(4) Heavy haulers, insofar as bundled or aggregated commodities are concerned, may transport only those which fall within the narrowly excepted group as described in (C) next above;

(5)   The usual type general-commodity carrier may transport bundled commodities within the excepted group set forth in (C) above *only* when loaded or unloaded by the consignor or consignee in accordance with the doctrine of the *Rowe* case, but the general-commodity carrier may transport other types of bundled or aggregated commodities so long as they are transported on ordinary equipment; and

(6)   Recognition is given to the principle enunciated in the concurrently decided *Dallas & Mavis case* (79 M.C.C. 285) that as a last-resort test, single-item shipments weighing 15,000 pounds or more even when loaded and unloaded under their own power and transported on ordinary equipment are within the authority of the unlimited heavy hauler, but are not

for this reason necesarily without the authority of the general-commodity hauler.

The following history of the interpretation of the scope of the operating rights of heavy haulers found in *Moss Trucking Co., Inc., Investigation of Operation*,[31] reflects the difficulties encountered in this area:

Heavy haulers as a class of carriers were first recognized by the Commission in *Classification of Motor Carriers of Property*, 2 M.C.C. 703, where they were termed "carriers of heavy machinery" and noted as being transporters of heavy machinery and equipment, including road machinery, structured steel, oilfield rigs, and oilfield equipment. It was also pointed out therein that certain auxiliary or accessorial services were also performed by such carriers, such as the dismantling and resetting of machinery, often requiring the use of rigging, skidding, and similar devices. The same decision characterized carriers of general freight as transporting commodities generally, "*except* such commodities as require special equipment or service." [Emphasis added.] Thus, it can be seen that at this very early stage of motor carrier regulation, the essential non-competitive nature of the two operations was impliedly recognized. The *Classification* case also set forth carriers of motor vehicles as a separate class, stating that such carriers were engaged in the transportation of new and used motor vehicles, including automobiles, trucks, trainers, chassis, bodies, and automotive display vehicles. (p. 101)

Subsequently, the definition of the nature of heavy-hauling service was refined on a case-by-case basis. Those elements or factors descriptive of typical heavy-hauling service were said to be (1) the ability and holding out to transport any large or heavy article almost wholly without regard to size, weight, or difficulty of loading, (2) the use and availability of loading machinery and devices and the services of riggers and other personnel necessary to remove such articles from buildings or to dismantle or assemble them at origin or destination points, and (3) the use and availability of vehicles especially constructed or equipped or otherwise made capable of transporting such articles. *St. Johnsbury Trucking Co., Inc., Extension — Heavy Hauling*, 53 M.C.C. 277, 285. In *Gallagher Common Carrier Application*, 48 M.C.C. 413, which concluded that ordinary flat-bed vehicles were not special equipment, an additional factor was added when it was determined that heavy hauling might be established when special equipment was required for loading and unloading, even though the actual haul was performed on conventional flat beds. Hence, special equipment can be either the vehicles utilized for over-the-road movement or the equipment used in loading and unloading. (p. 102)

This latter criterion caused considerable concern among ordinary common carriers, for, as it was developed in the *St. Johnsbury* case, *supra*, these carriers had been utilizing mechanical devices for loading and unloading such as forklifts and cranes, and were fearful lest such operation be

[31] 103 M.C.C. 91.

found to be unlawful. The problem brought to a focus in the *St. Johnsbury* case then became one of determining whether the fields of service of the heavy haulers and general commodity carriers were mutually exclusive. If, in other words, the general commodity carriers were flatly prohibited in the terms of their certificates from transporting commodities requiring the use of special equipment, they would not be authorized to continue the use of such devices. The problem was resolved by the Commission's decision to rely upon the mutually exclusive character of the language in the certificates and by its recognition instead of overlapping fields of service. The areas of overlapping were delineated in the "twilight zone" theory subsequently set forth in the *Rowe* case, *infra*. (p. 102)

Over the years the use of specifically named commodities (e.g., heavy machinery, et cetera) to describe the authority of heavy haulers began to fall into disuse. Instead, commodities were described in terms of the service to be provided for their transportation, e.g., "requiring the use of special equipment or handling." In *Descriptions in Motor Carrier Certificates, supra,* at pages 248-51, the lack of uniformity in heavy-hauler certificates was recognized, and a standard heavy-hauling description, adopted from an earlier case,[32] was set forth as a definition of heavy-hauling service to be utilized in future grants of heavy-hauling authority. (pp. 102-103)

In a later decision[33] it was noted by the Commission that the terms "machinery" and "equipment," such as had been used in earlier heavy-hauling grants, were difficult of exact interpretation and that a description phrased in terms of service rather than specific commodities should be utilized. With the benefit of hindsight it is now clear that this service-type description, although intended to simplify heavy-hauling certificates, has created problems of far greater scope and complexity than were forseen at the time the description came into general use. This is true because the description is phrased in terms (i.e., "special equipment" and "requires") which have an inherent flexibility with respect to the range of commodities authorized. (p. 103)

Over the course of years problem areas with respect to the field of heavy hauling continued to develop. In the *Dillner* case, *supra*, the Commission dealt with a number of these, affirming earlier findings that flat-bed trailers of ordinary design are not special equipment and that the "twilight zone" and "last resort" tests should continue to be utilized. In addition, the problem of aggregation was considered and the following rules established:

[32]*Osborne Common Carrier Application — Heavy Materials*, 47 M.C.C. 633. The description adopted was "commodities, the transportation of which because of size or weight requires the use of special equipment, and of related machinery parts and related contractors' materials and supplies when their transportation is incidental to the transportation of commodities which by reason of size or weight require special equipment."

[33]*Shea-Matson Trucking Co. Extension — Heavy Hauling*, 68 M.C.C. 269, at 271.

(3) In bundling, aggregating, or palletizing, it should be the general rule of construction (1) that the individual "commodity itself" is the controlling consideration as respects a carrier's authority; (2) that the limited exception which the *Black* case, 64 M.C.C. 443, represents, where commodities are bundled for protection or as otherwise required by their "inherent nature," must be maintained within its strictest limits; (3) that the minimum bundle which is required by the "inherent nature" of the commodity is the size or type of bundle which must be considered in any determination whether necessity exists for the use of special equipment; and (4) that in order reasonably to maintain these limits it shall be presumed, in the absence of a sound basis for concluding to the contrary, that commodities tendered to carrier, in bundles or aggregations, are within the general rule and not within the limited exception thereto; (4) Heavy haulers, insofar as bundled or aggregated commodities are concerned, may transport only those which fall within the narrowly excepted group described in (3) above;

(5) The usual type general-commodity carrier may transport bundled commodities within the excepted group set forth in (3) above only when loaded or unloaded by the consignor or consignee in accordance with the doctrine of the Rowe case, but the general commodity carrier may transport other types of bundled or aggregated commodities so long as they are transported on ordinary equipment. (pp. 103-104)

Subsequently, the *Dillner* case was subjected to court review in *W. J. Dillner Transfer Co. v. Interstate Commerce Commission*, 193 F. Supp. 823, and later affirmed *per curiam* in 368 U.S. 6. In dealing particularly with the Commission's finding that firebrick did not require palletization for its movement and hence was beyond Dillner's authority, the court noted that firebrick was, in fact, at times transported in an unpalletized form and that the convenience and economy were the main consideration for palletization, and therefore concluded:

Sufficient evidence was present to allow reasonable men to find that this commodity (firebrick) did not through its inherent characteristics demand that it be hauled only after it was placed on pallets. (p. 104)

It is axiomatic that one of the ideals of sound regulation should be that operating rights must be as clear and definitive as possible. If stability in the transportation industry is to be maintained, carriers and the shipping public should be able to ascertain, without the assistance of the celebrated "Philadelphia lawyer," the precise scope of operations authorized by the descriptions in our certificates. Experience has demonstrated, however, that if the phrase "special equipment" had a commonly accepted and precise meaning in the transportation industry at the time it first became a part of Commission certificates, that meaning has not remained static.[34] Further, the sense in which the word "requires" is to be understood in the context of the involved description has not been uniformly interpreted. See *McDade Interpretation of Certificate,* 53 M.C.C. 401, and later decisions discussed hereinafter. (p. 104)

While it is the Commission's responsibility to regulate in such a manner that operating rights will be as clear and unchanging as possible, it is also true that the development of new and improved methods and facilities for handling freight by regulated carriers should be encouraged within the framework of their certificates. This principle is applicable to all carriers, for the use of modern devices for the economical and expedient loading, unloading, and handling of freight should not be denied any class of carrier. *St. Johnsbury Trucking Co., Inc., Extension — Heavy Hauling, supra.* Our function is not to preserve the *status quo* in transportation service, but rather to assist in promoting the growth of a dynamic industry. *Cassens Transport Co. Extension — Three States,* 67 M.C.C. 410, 413. (pp. 104-105)

These two basic principles of transportation regulation, the need for preciseness and stability in the field of operating rights and the need for flexibility in the area of carrier and shipper operations through use of improved equipment, result in an apparent conflict in our interpretation of a commodity description which is phrased in terms of equipment and service, i.e., "commodities the transportation of which requires the use of special equipment." The obvious difficulty in this area of our regulation is how to provide for equipment which may have been considered "special" at some point in the past, but is not generally considered so today, and similarly, how to regulate impartially the movement of commodities which formerly were throught to "require" special equipment for their handling but today may be handled in ordinary common carrier service. In the history of our regulation of general commodity carriers we have not frozen such carriers into the use of the same type of facilities and equipment for loading, unloading, and transporting freight which they used at the outset of motor carrier regulation. Neither should we place such an unreasonable restriction upon heavy haulers. Further, to deprive heavy haulers of traffic once handled by use of required special equipment through a finding that such equipment is no longer "special" would be an improper deprivation of operating rights contrary to Section 212(a) of the act. (p. 105)

We believe that the only practicable solution to this seeming dilemma in our regulation of the involved classes of carriers, though not as clear-cut an answer as we might wish, must inevitably be a continuation of the same overall approach which we have utilized in the past. That approach has been in the nature of an accommodation, a recognition of overlap-

---

[34]See, for example, the history of the development of flat-bed trailers and the Commission's attempt to deal with the problem through the ill-fated 15,000-pound test, as described in *United Transports, Inc. v. Gulf Southwestern Transp. Co.,* 95 M.C.C. 443, 444-47.

ping areas of service, as is probably best exemplified by the "twilight zone" theory set forth in the *Rowe*[35] case. There it might well have been found that ordinary common carriers could not transport, in accordance with the literal terms of their certificates, commodities requiring special equipment for loading and unloading, even though those operations were performed by the shipper. In an accommodation to the general commodity carriers, however, such operations were found to be authorized, as long as the loading and unloading services were provided by the shippers and only ordinary flat-bed trainers used. At the same time the decision to allow the heavy haulers to transport items which were in fact loaded and unloaded by the shippers and consignees could be considered an accommodation to the heavy haulers, since they provided no special equipment for such movements. In the same vein the now defunct 15,000-pound test set forth in *Dallas & Mavis Forwarding Co., Inc., Ext. — Galion, Ohio*, 79 M.C.C. 285, was an attempt to preserve traffic historically considered to be that of the heavy haulers, even though special equipment was not always required for its movement. (pp. 105-106)

Thus, it may be seen that there is already considerable overlapping between the fields of service of the heavy haulers and ordinary general commodity carriers. A different approach to the problem, perhaps a "type-of-service" test as suggested in the dissent in the *Dillner case*, designed to make the services of the carriers more nearly mutually exclusive, might seem desirable, but we are persuaded that any radical change in approach at this time would not be feasible. To alter the scope and value of certificates by interpretive fiat at this late date would not be in the public interest, and we doubt that such action would be legally supportable. As we have said, a great deal of overlapping of service areas has already taken place, and we believe that the only way to allow both for the retention by the carriers of traffic which they have continuously handled and for the effectuation of their desire to utilize improved methods of freight handling is to continue to recognize a sphere of overlapping in the future. (p. 106)

Additional discussion is found in *Ace Doran Hauling & Rigging Co., Investigation*,[36] in which the Commission said (at p. 731) that a "delineation in reasonably explicit terms of the operations permissible under the imprecise heavy-hauler commodity description is far from an easy task." In the light of its discussion in the *Ace Doran* case, the Commission set forth the following summary of the major principles which should be followed in interpreting the heavy-hauler commodity description:

(1) With respect to bundled, aggregated or palletized commodities, the presumption described in the *Dillner* case, 79 M.C.C. 335, at 358 — that

---

[35]*National Automobile Transporters Ass'n. v. Rowe Transfer*, 64 M.C.C. 229, 240.
[36]108 M.C.C. 717. Aff'd in *Pittsburgh & New England Trucking Co. v. United States*, 345 F. Supp. 743, aff'd 409 U.S. 904.

such shipments, in the absence of a sound basis for a contrary conclusion, are outside the scope of heavy-hauler authority — is reaffirmed without modification.

(1a) That, again in accordance with *Dillner,* exceptions to the foregoing general rule will not be recognized when the use of aggregation is attributable *solely* to considerations relating to economy and efficiency; but, once a commodity's "inherent nature" is found to necessitate aggregation, the latter concepts must be taken into account in determining the minimum sized bundle required.

(2) That irrespective of whether they are tendered in aggregated or single-unit form, commodities such as classes A and B explosives, bulk commodities, or household goods, are likewise presumed in accordance with the *International Investigation* case, 108 M.C.C. 275, to be without the permissible scope of heavy-hauler service; and that in these cases exceptions will be recognized only when a clear basis is shown therefor.

(3) That future determinations as to whether the presumptions set forth in (1) and (2) above have been overcome as well as those regarding the status under size and weight authority of individuality shipped articles generally should be guided by a balanced consideration of the following factors: (a) the commodity's basic characteristics, (b) industry-wide (not individual shipper) practices with regard to its handling, (c) prior methods employed in shipment of the involved or an analogous commodity, and (d) its traditional sphere of carriage. (p. 757)

We do not pretend that the above represent a millenium with respect to clarity and stability of motor carrier operating rights. Nevertheless, upon viewing as a composite picture their application to the situations presented in this proceeding, we are satisfied that, properly implemented, the said guidelines will assure maximum fulfillment of the basic regulatory purposes set forth at the outset of our discussion. . . . (pp. 757-58)

Carriers of Aerospace Craft, Fully Assembled or Partially Dismantled, and of Aerospace Craft Parts

In its decision in *Dealers Transit, Inc., Extension — Missiles,*[37] the Commission determined generally that "missiles" were distinct from both "airplane" and "aircraft" for operating-rights purposes, and that the scope of the latter two terms should not be extended so as to embrace "missiles." Specifically, the Commission found that:

Aircraft are ordinarily considered to be craft capable of transporting humans which can be navigated in the air and which are supported by the buoyancy of their structures or the dynamic action of air against their surfaces. Airplanes are aircraft . . . but most certainly a missile is not an airplane. It is a much closer question whether *a missile* could be considered an aircraft. We believe, however, that even this term cannot

[37]86 M.C.C. 327.

be considered an appropriate description of *craft designed to operate in space as well as in the air, the navigation of which is limited to "some guidance which terminates in flight,"* and which are not supported by the buoyancy of their structures or the dynamic action of air against their surfaces. (86 M.C.C. 327, 334; Emphasis added.)

This determination was reiterated in *Baggett Transp. Co. Extension — Redstone Arsenal,*[38] and sustained by unanimous decision in *U.S.A.C. Transport, Inc. v. United States.*[39]

In addition to the type of "aircraft" as described in the *Dealers Transit* and *Baggett*[40] cases, *supra*, the aerospace industry produces a wide variety of items which fall generally into various categories. These categories are discussed in *U.S.A.C. Transport, Me., Extension — Missiles.*[41]

To cover the wide range of commodities manufactured by the aerospace industry, the Commission, in *U.S.A.C. Transport, Inc., Extension — Missiles,*[42] held:

In light of the foregoing, we conclude that for purposes of I.C.C. certification in the instant proceeding the term "aerospace craft" should be employed to refer to those commodities manufactured by the aerospace industry which operate within or beyond the earth's atmosphere, or which are equally adaptable for flight within either performance spectrum. This description is sufficiently flexible to accommodate new products and technological improvements in the industry, and, significantly, will be susceptible by applicant and its shippers of workable, day-to-day application.

The Commission, in keeping with its holding made the following grant in the *U.S.A.C. Transport* case:

We find that the present and future public convenience require operation by applicant, in interstate or foreign commerce, as a common carrier by motor vehicle, over irregular routes, of aerospace craft, fully assembled or partially dismantled, and of aerospace craft parts, restricted to the transportation of such described parts which because of their size, weight, or fragile character, require the use of special equipment or handling . . .

Tank Truck Carriers

Tank truck carriers confined themselves principally to the transportation of liquid-petroleum products during the early part of Federal motor

---

[38]88 M.C.C. 3.

[39]235 F. Supp. 689, aff'd *per curiam* 350 U.S. 450.

[40]In the *Baggett* decision, the Commission found, in part, that so-called "jet thrust units," used to propel "missiles and other similar craft," were not within the scope of authority to transport "aircraft parts," (or "explosives"), but properly fall within the purview of the commodity term "missile parts."

[41]103 M.C.C. 23, 26-27.

[42]103 M.C.C. 23, 35.

carrier regulation. However, with the country's industrial and economic growth, their activities expanded rapidly into new areas such as the transportation of liquid edibles, chemicals, acids, and many other commodities formerly moving in containers. Thus, whereas at the beginning of Federal motor carrier regulation generic and specific commodity authorizations used in operating authorities appeared to be appropriate for the traffic to be transported and the type of service to be rendered, they were found to be inappropriate subsequently when the transportation activities of the tank truck carriers expanded. This insufficiency resulted in an investigation being instituted by the Commission in *Descriptions in Motor Carrier Certificates*[43] for the purpose of promulgating proper and adequate commodity description for most classes of motor carriers.

In the *Descriptions case*, the Commission prescribed commodity descriptions with due regard to the classification and specialization of carriers. Included in the *Descriptions* case was a commodity description covering the activities of tank truck carriers reading "acids and chemicals, in tank vehicles." In the *Descriptions* case, where the prescribed commodity descriptions were headed by generic terms there were listed thereunder the specific items or articles embraced therein. Some of the lists contained the same items under different headings, which duplications later proved to be a source of difficulties. It was expected that, as new commodities were developed or discovered or new uses were discovered for existing commodities, there would arise the need for a method of procedure for adding commodities to the prescribed list. With the continued growth of the chemical industry and the additional utilization of tank vehicles for the transportation of liquid commodities, the prescribed commodity list of acids and chemicals became inadequate in many instances as a means of authorizing a complete and needed service. In an effort to correct this situation, a re-examination of the matter was made in *Maxwell Co. Extension — Addyston.*[44] There, in resolving the problem of defining "liquid chemicals," the most practicable solution was said to lie in adopting a definition or description of the terms which did not conflict with and was interpretative of the Commission's findings in the *Descriptions* case.

The term "liquid chemicals" was defined in the *Maxwell* case on page 681 as follows:

> Liquid chemicals, as used in motor-carrier operating authorities are those substances or materials resulting from a chemical or physical change induced by the processes employed in the chemical industry, including unit-

[43]61 M.C.C. 766.
[44]63 M.C.C. 677.

ing, mixing, blending, and compounding, except such finished or end products as are intended, at the time of transportation and without further processing, for packaging and sale to the general public.

The *Maxwell* case, in defining "liquid chemicals," departed from the practice utilized in the *Descriptions* case of listing the specific items embraced under generic headings and resorted to what was deemed a more practical method of identification. In an effort to clarify the application of the new chemical definition, there was excepted therefrom "such finished or end products as are intended, at the time of transportation and without further processing, for packaging and sale to the general public," thus providing what is termed the "intended-use" test. The definition in the *Maxwell* case was used extensively by the Commission in making new and additional grants of authority to transport liquid chemicals in numerous, subsequent proceedings. However, the *Descriptions* and *Maxwell* cases did not resolve the liquid chemical commodity description problem.

A long line of interpretative decisions followed the *Descriptions* and *Maxwell* cases, resulting in continued inconsistencies and confusion. This led to *Southern Tank Lines, Inc., Extension — St. Bernard, Ohio.*[45] There the Commission said that the chemical operating authorities embraced three stages. In the first stage, use was made of generic descriptions such as "chemical" and "liquid chemicals"; the second represented an effort to list all of the chemical items under a generic heading; and in the third, a specific definition of liquid chemicals was promulgated, which was used both as a commodity description and as a measure in construing previously chemical-operating authorities. The question confronting the Commission in the *Southern Tank* case was what could or should be done to clarify or modify the outstanding operating authorities and to provide a new, more adequate, and less controversial commodity description for future use.

In speaking of the *Maxwell* case, the Commission said on pages 138-40 in the *Southern Tank* case:

As we see it the *Maxwell* case definition may be said to place the following requirements upon a substance in order for it to be classified as a liquid chemical:

(1) It must result from a chemical or physical change induced by processes employed in the chemical industry. See *T. I. McCormack Trucking Co., Inc., Extension, supra,* at page 129, where it was emphasized that chemicals include those substances or materials resulting from a "physical" change induced by processes employed in the chemical industry, one of

which was indicated to be distillation, a method of separating the volatile components of a liquid by vaporization and subsequent condensation at temperatures reflecting the respective boiling and condensation points of each component. This case also illustrates the fact that the term "liquid chemicals" includes the chemical products of both analytical and synthetic chemistry. The decision in *Hearin Tank Lines, Inc., Extension — Pasadena, Tex.*, 81 M.C.C. 511, points out certain incompatibility of language in the Maxwell case and correctly concludes that the actual definition must be controlling in such case. Hence there is no literal requirement that a substance be for use "by industry in the manufacture or processing of other commodities" to qualitfy as a liquid chemical. The process need not be used in a chemical plant so long as it is a "chemical process."

(2)   The commodity must not be such a finished or end product which is intended, without further processing, to be packaged and sold to the general public. For the sake of clarity, this may be restated to the effect that the only chemically produced substances that are not within the description "liquid chemicals" are those which are intended for packaging and sale to the public in the retail trade; that is, are known to be moving to a distributor for packaging and retail sale to the public, inasmuch as they have assumed a separate and distinct identity of their own and are finished or end products. The *Maxwell* case specifically excluded substances in their raw or natural state, as was concluded with respect to liquid sulphur in *Robertson Tank Lines, Inc., Extension — Liquid Sulphur*, 79 M.C.C. 501.

To the foregoing observations, which we think represent reasonable interpretations of the definition set forth in the *Maxwell* case, common sense dictates that there should be added a separate category of commodities which, although logically they might come within the *Maxwell* case definition, cannot with reason be classified as chemicals because they are not by common usage considered as such. The type or class of commodity to which we have reference was considered in the *Reader Bros. case, supra,* wherein it was said at page 406:

Molasses is not a product of what is generally considered the chemical industry. While some processes employed in the production of molasses may be similar to processes which are used in the chemical industry and in the manufacture of products which are admittedly chemicals, this alone is not sufficient to classify molasses as a chemical. The definition of liquid chemicals established in the *Maxwell* case should not be extended to such an extent as to produce a result clearly at variance with common usage.

The same is true of finished potables such as the vodka involved in *Eldon Miller, Inc., Extension — Terre Haute, Ind.*, 77 M.C.C. 339. A number of other commodities doubtless may fall in this category, but it is neither necessary nor desirable that we undertake to specify them at this time. Inasmuch as this category amounts to a deviation from the general rules of interpretation set forth herein, its application should be limited to those products which have not in fact been produced by the chemical industry; that is, by companies engaged primarily in the manufacture of chemicals or by companies which produce chemicals as a by-product of a manufacturing process.

In the *Southern Tank* case, the following conclusion was reached by the Commission, at page 141-3, concerning a revised definition:

No one, it is believed, will disagree with the proposition that a broader and more realistic chemical commodity description is desirable, and if possible should be promulgated at this time. It likewise is clear that such a description should be one which also would permit the motor carriers to provide a full and complete service for the chemical industry; and the *Matlack* proceeding illustrates the wide range of chemically produced liquids distributed in motor service by a chemical plant which are intended, not only for further processing and use as ingredients in the manufacture of other products, but also for use as end products without further processing by those engaged in packaging and retailing to the general public, such as is done in the pharmaceutical industry. A serious deficiency in the *Maxwell* case definition is that all such products cannot be transported by carriers serving a shipper such as DuPont. In attempting to formulate a comprehensive commodity description which would cover such transportation, we are concerned primarily with service considerations; and we think it to be immaterial from a transportation standpoint whether a commodity which has been produced chemically is to be used as an ingredient in a different product, on the one hand, or on the other, is to be packaged and sold to the general public as a finished or end product. Regardless of their intended use, the transportation of such commodities is merely part and parcel of an overall service to the chemical producers. Motor carriers attempting to afford a complete service under specific or generic authority to transport chemicals and chemical products should hold such authority as will cover any of these commodities irrespective of their intended use or other considerations which often require hairsplitting distinctions.

All circumstances considered, we believe that an appropriate revised commodity description for motor carriers serving the chemical producers would be "liquid chemicals, in bulk, in tank vehicles," and that the following will be a reasonable and proper definition or interpretation of the commodities which are embraced in such description:

Liquid chemicals, as used in the foregoing commodity description, are those substances or materials resulting from a chemical or physical change induced by processes employed in the chemical industry, including uniting, mixing, blending, and compounding.

Simply stated, the revised definition is the same as the *Maxwell* case definition, minus the so-called intended use test. While it remains comprehensive in scope, it is intended to embrace those basic liquid chemicals and chemical products of the chemical industry and chemical producers, whether moving from a chemical plant or from storage and distribution points, without regard to their ultimate use. Although the definition is phrased in the term of chemicals, it is common knowledge that many acids, possibly all of them, are chemicals or classes of chemicals; and it is intended that the definition shall cover all acids which are, in fact, chemicals. Compare *Sprout & Davis, Inc., Extension — Liquid Chemicals, supra.*

On the other hand, we wish also to make clear that the revised definition is not intended to embrace such basic petroleum products as gasoline, kerosene, casinghead gasoline, fuel oil and lubricating oil. While many of the products of the petroleum industry result from chemical processes, the revised definition must be construed realistically so as not to include those petroleum items which customarily and ordinarily fall within the operating authorities of the transporters of petroleum and petroleum products, or more specifically gasoline, kerosene, fuel oil, et cetera. Nor do we intend at the same time to exclude therefrom the basic so-called petrochemical produced in the petroleum industry.

It is realized that the revised definition will not provide a panacea for every problem, past or future. Interpretative and other difficulties can be anticipated following its prescription. Obviously it will be necessary, as it is now, for use to decide in many instances whether a particular commodity is or is not a chemical within the meaning of the revised definition, since practically all liquid commodities lend themselves to the argument that they are produced through chemical processes. On the other hand, the revised definition should prove less controversial than the *Maxwell* case definition, and it will provide motor carriers with a commodity description flexible enough to meet the changing conditions of the chemical industry.

Aside from the foregoing, another equally important purpose of the revised definition is to provide a basis for the reformation of all outstanding chemical operating authorities. We believe that this definition should be made consistent throughout the operating rights of the chemical transporters in the interests of uniformity and the carriers' ability to provide a complete service for the chemical producers. The records before us, of course, do not provide a proper basis on which we would modify, without further proceedings, the outstanding certificates and permits so as to include the new description; and, if this end is to be finally achieved, the cooperation of the chemical carriers and other interested parties is required.

Household Goods' Carriers

Throughout the years of regulation there has been a steadfast adherence to the view that the scope of operating authority of the household goods carrier should be determined from the point of view of *service.*[46] The reason for this is that it is impractical to compile a list of articles which would apply to all household carriers under all situations.

[46]*American Red Ball Transit Co. Inc. v. McLean Trucking,* 67 M.C.C. 305, 313.

The definition of "household goods" prescribed in *Practices of Motor Common Carriers of Household Goods*,[47] is divided into three parts as follows:

1. Personal effects and property used or to be used in a dwelling when a part of the equipment.
2. Furniture, fixtures, equipment and the property of stores, offices, museums, institutions, hospitals, or other establishments when a part of the stock, equipment, or supply of such stores, offices, museums, institutions, hospitals, or other establishments.
3. Articles, including objects of art, displays, and exhibits, which because of their unusual nature or value require specialized handling and equipment usually employed in moving household goods.

Part 1 relates to a change in domicile of a household, and part 2 pertains to change in location of a store, office, museum, institution, hospital, or other establishment. Under these two the repetitive movement of items moving in channels of commerce from a dealer to a showroom or consumer and not as property of a householder, store, office, or similar establishment, even though such items may be eventually intended for such purpose, are not within the scope of authority of the household-goods carrier.[48] However, part 3, though not intended as a catchall grant of authority is not limited by the identity of the consignor or consignee, nor is the purpose for which the transportation takes place particularly relevant.

The distinction between the first two classes of household goods and the third was noted in the original report in *Practices of Motor Common Carriers of Household Goods, supra,* as follows:

> In issuing certificates of public convenience and necessity authorizing the transportation of household goods only, we do not intend to authorize the unrestricted transportation of a wide variety of commodities which do not by their nature require the specialized service rendered by household goods carriers. It is not intended, for example, to permit the transportation of new furniture from factory to store in competition with common carriers of that commodity. On the other hand, the transportation of objects of art, museum pieces, certain types of displays and exhibits, and other unusual objects, regardless of the identity of the consignee and consignor, is properly a part of the service of these carriers. Such articles, because of their high value, susceptibility to damage, or unique design, do not lend themselves readily to ordinary motor-carrier transportation but require the special care and handling which the household-goods carrier is qualified and equipped to give. In drafting the prescribed definition we have tried to preserve the inherent difference

[47]17 M.C.C. 467.
[48]*Practices of Motor Common Carriers of Household Goods,* 53 M.C.C. 177, and cases cited therein.

which exists between the household goods carrier and the common carrier of general or special commodities.

This position was reaffirmed in the report on further hearing in the same proceeding.

A comparison of the definitions of household goods by the Commission in 17 M.C.C. 467 with its more recent definition in *Practices of Motor Common Carriers of Household Goods*,[49] reveals no material differences. Nor does it make any material changes in prior interpretations of the household goods definition with respect to that portion under part 3 except to stress that crating or noncrating is not important with respect to articles actually embraced within part 3.

In *Neptune Storage, Inc., Extension — Tabulating Machines*,[50] the Commission said (at p. 330) that the real test is not whether the articles require specialized handling and equipment usually employed in moving household goods. In the *Neptune* case, the Commission said that the articles must necessarily be of such unusual nature, by reason of their fragility, delicateness, intrinsic value, or other characteristics that their transportation requires specialized handling and equipment usually employed in moving household goods.

The Commission has held that the transportation of X-ray machines require specialized handling and fall within the definition of household goods,[51] and microfilming equipment, television equipment, recording cameras, monitors, audio equipment, transmitting racks and other equipment, office equipment (including tabulators, punchers, sorters, wiring units and reproducers), office furniture (including cabinets, desks, and chairs), laboratory equipment (including tower assembly for a microwave portable test station), "portable carrier set" (consisting of cabinets with spare tubes and parts) for use in the transmission of telegraph messages fall either within part 2 or 3 of the definition of household goods.[52]

Express Service

The five indicia of express service are set forth in *Transportation Activities of Arrowhead Freight Lines*,[53] There the respondent's motor carrier certificate authorized the transportation of general commodities moving "in express service." The five indicia are set forth below:

[49]86 M.C.C. 293.
[50]67 M.C.C. 319.
[51]*Neptune Storage, Inc., Extension-X-Ray Machines*, 88 M.C.C. 25, 32.
[52]*Interstate Commerce Commission v. United Van Lines*, 110 F. Supp. 273, 276.
[53]63 M.C.C. 573, 581-582.

Succinctly stated the rendition of a bona-fide express service by property carriers with authority to transport general commodities requires such carriers (1) to provide a bona fide holding out together with the ability to transport any commodity which may be safely transported in ordinary van-type equipment, including those requiring a maximum degree of care or security or both, (2) to provide such care or security or both as the inherent characteristics of the commodities making up the shipments which are accepted may require, (3) to provide equally expeditious transportation and careful handling for all accepted shipments, regardless of their volume, special demands, or value, from the point of pickup to the point of delivery, (4) to perform actual operations between all authorized points upon firmly established schedules allowing minimum practicable highway transit time and providing fixed delivery times which are available to actual and potential shippers at authorized origins and which in practice are not changed except after substantial notice to the general public, and, (5) to use relatively simple billing, rate structures, and rate publications whereby the rates and charges for the services offered and performed may easily be determined with a minimum of delay.

Specialized Auto Haulers

In *Motor Vehicles — Idaho, Nevada, and Utah Origins*,[54] the principal issue involved the right of the respondent general commodity carriers, whose authorities excepted the transportation of commodities requiring special equipment, to transport multiple units of automobiles in special automobile "carry-all" equipment accommodating a number of automobiles. Although the transportation of an automobile *per se* does not require special over-the-road equipment, as an automobile can be carried on conventional trucking equipment, the Commission found respondents were not authorized under their existing authority to invade the field of the specialized auto haulers' by the use of the auto haulers' special "carry-all" equipment to transport multiple loads of automobiles. Such prohibition applies whether the special "carry-all" equipment used by respondents for multiple loads of automobiles was equipped with a permanent or removable type of superstructure.

Transportation of Component Part of an Authorized Commodity

In *U.S.A.C. Transport, Inc., Extension — Missiles,* [55] the Commission said:

[54]318 I.C.C. 859.
[55]103 M.C.C. 23, 35.

No specific authority is required for the transportation of component parts of any authorized commodity, when shipped in conjunction, and at the same time, with such commodity, in amounts consistent with their being of an incidental nature. Accordingly, this portion of the application should be denied. See the *Dealers Transit* case, *supra,* 86 M.C.C. 327, 333, and *East Texas M. Frt. Lines Interpretation of Certificates,* 62 M.C.C. 727.

18

Suspension, Revocation, and Change of Authority

MOTOR CARRIERS

The Applicable Statutory Provisions

Section 212(a) of the Interstate Commerce Act[1] provides:

"Certificates, permits, and licenses shall be effective from the date specified therein, and shall remain in effect until suspended or terminated as herein provided. Any such certificate, permit, or license may, upon application of the holder thereof, in the discretion of the Commission, be amended or revoked, in whole or in part, or may upon complaint, or on the Commission's own initiative, after notice and hearing, be suspended, changed, or revoked, in whole or in part, for willful failure to comply with any provision of this part, or with any lawful order, rule, or regulation of the Commission promulgated thereunder, or with any term, condition, or limitation of such certificate, permit, or license: Provided however, That no such certificate, permit, or license shall be revoked (except upon application of the holder) unless the holder thereof willfully fails to comply, within a reasonable time, not less than thirty days, to be fixed by the Commission, with a lawful order of the Commission, made as provided in Section 204(c), commanding obedience to the provision of this part, or to the rule or regulation of the Commission thereunder, or to the term, condition, or limitation of such certificate, permit, or license, found by the Commission to have been violated by such holder: And provided further, That the right to engage in transportation in interstate or foreign commerce by virtue of any certificate, permit, license, or any application filed pursuant to the provisions of Section 206, 209, or 211, or by virtue of the second proviso of Section 206(a) or temporary authority under Section 210a, may be suspended by the Commission, upon reasonable notice of not less than fifteen days to the carrier or broker, but without hearing or other proceedings, for failure to comply, and until compliance, with the provisions of Section 211(c), 217(a), or 218(a) or with any

[1] 49 U.S.C. 312(a). Comparable Provisions — Sections 312(a) and 410(f).

362

lawful order, rule, or regulation of the Commission promulgated thereunder."

Suspension and Revocation of Authority

Failure to comply with requirements to render reasonably continuous and adequate service generally constitutes grounds for revocation of authority.[2] In *Eagle Motor Lines, Inc. — Suspension or Revocation of Certificates*,[3] where the carrier had instituted corrective measures to comply with the Commission's safety regulations after a period of continued violations despite repeated advice and admonitions, the Commission said that suspension of the certificate was not warranted, but a cease and desist order would be entered to remain in effect for one year at the end of which time the carrier could petition the Commission for vacation of the order. In *Safeway Truck Lines, Inc., Suspension of Certificates*,[4] the Commission said that although the carrier's continued failure, even after admonition, to move satisfactorily toward full compliance with the Commission's safety regulations must be construed as "willful," and although it was not in compliance therewith, suspension of its certificates was unwarranted in view of its efforts to correct deficiencies in its safety program through which compliance could be achieved, thus instead of suspending the certificates the Commission would enter a cease and desist order.

Revocation of a permit may be effected after notice and hearing, or opportunity for hearing, for willful failure to comply with an order issued under Section 204(c).[5] Where the carrier in the *Rausch* case failed to comply with terms of two show cause orders, one instituting a proceeding under Section 204(c) to determine whether under Section 212(a) its permit should be revoked for failure to comply with the requirements of the I.C. Act and the Commission's rules and regulations, and the other requiring it to inform the Commission if an oral hearing were desired, it was deemed to be default and to have waived the right to such oral hearing. Considering the carrier's failure to answer either show cause order, and taking official notice of Commission records which indicate that respondent was not operating, owned no equipment or real estate, had no effective continuing contracts with any shipper on file, and had not filed evidence of insurance coverage, it was concluded that

[2]*Alterman Transport Lines, Inc. v. Yale Transport Corp.*, 78 M.C.C. 183, 186; *Monumental Motor Tours, Inc. v. Greyhound Corp.*, 79 M.C.C. 244, 247.
[3]77 M.C.C. 440.
[4]77 M.C.C. 443, 446.
[5]*Rausch Transp. Co., Inc. Conversion*, 82 M.C.C. 273, 276.

respondent was not engaged in operations authorized in its permit, and that such permit should therefore be revoked.

In *Cole's Exp. v. Homestead Bros.*,[6] the Commission said that inasmuch as there has been no demand for service, a showing that defendant had not actually performed service under its authority was insufficient to warrant a revocation thereof; complainants had failed to establish that defendant was not rendering a reasonably continuous and adequate service to the public under its certificate. In *John H. Eldred Trucking, Inc. — Investigation*,[7] the Commission said that it was the unequivocal duty of a motor carrier holding an outstanding permit or certificate from the Commission to supervise its operations in such a manner as to bring them into strict compliance with the I.C. Act and rules and regulations thereunder; failure to act positively in this respect is a consequence of the carrier's own voluntary acts of omission or commission, resulting from exercise of its own will and business judgment, or lack thereof; respondent's continuing pattern of violations after order requiring positive action to correct such defects established that the violations were willfully committed and respondent was unfit to assume the responsibilities imposed by the I.C. Act and rules and regulations thereunder. However, the Commission said as the successor carrier had taken active steps to correct the conditions resulting in violations enumerated, and it proposed to conduct operations in full compliance with the I.C. Act and rules and regulations, it would not be proper to revoke or suspend the considered operating authority, but the investigation would be continued so that in event of subsequent violations, consideration would be given to suspension or revocation forthwith, without another prolonged proceeding.

In a number of decisions relative to cessation of operations caused by financial difficulties the Commission has concluded that such cessation must necessarily be held to result from voluntary or willful acts of the carrier; and it is within the Commission's power to require the carrier to reinstitute such operations and thereafter to maintain reasonably continuous and adequate service.[8]

Modification of Certificates

If a carrier believes that its present authority does not accurately reflect the operations for which need was shown, its remedy lies in seeking modification thereof by appropriate petition.

---

[6]78 M.C.C. 79, 80.
[7]78 M.C.C. 9, 12-3.
[8]*Greyhound Corp. v. American Bus Lines*, 78 M.C.C. 384, 387.

The Commission had previously set forth two requirements to be met for obtaining modification of a "grandfather" certificate in the absence of shipper support. A petitioner had been required to show that (1) the specific authority under consideration was intended at the time of issuance to authorize a broader service than that encompassed in the terminology used under present-day interpretation, and (2) the authority has been continuously used to perform the broader service.[9] But in *D. B. Ford v. United States*,[10] a district court held that the second abovementioned requirement stated in the *North Penn* report was not necessary to be proved in order to obtain modification of a certificate. The district court stated at p. 1209, that:

> The continuity of operations requirement applies up to the time that the "grandfather" authorization is granted. ° ° °

> But cessation of operations has never been considered to be a bar to rights acquired prior to the hiatus. Such discontinuance cannot in itself result in the forfeiture of rights authorized as of the "grandfather" date. See Quaker City Bus Co. — Purchase — Blackhawk Line, Inc., 38 M.C.C. 603, 606 (1942). Once acquired, "grandfather" rights cannot be lost unless pursuant to the procedures and the for grounds set forth in §312(a) ° ° °.

In *Haggard Heavy Hauling, Inc., Petition for Modification*,[11] the Commission agreed that the district court's opinion in the *D. B. Ford* case sets forth a correct statement of the applicable law regarding modification of "grandfather" certificates. Therefore, in a proceeding in which modification of such a "grandfather" certificate is sought, a petitioner then needs only to meet the first of the two above-mentioned requirements set forth in the *North Penn* decision. It is not necessary for a petitioner to show continuous operations performing the broader service from the "grandfather" date to the time of filing of its petition for modification.

In *Kuntz & Joyce — Modification of Certificate*,[12] where the wording of grant of authority, as result of "grandfather" application was too narrow, and petitioners and their predecessors on, prior to, and since the original date had transported heavy machinery and heavy machinery parts and attachments, both together and separately, and when the parts and attachments were transported at the same time as the principal commodity, they were not necessarily a constituent of the machinery transported, the Commission said that petitioners were entitled to appropriate

---

[9]See *North Penn Transfer, Inc. — Petition for Modification,* 115 M.C.C. 207.
[10]380 F. Supp. 1202.
[11]128 M.C.C. 752, 757.
[12]78 M.C.C. 316, 317.

modification of their certificate to authorize transportation of heavy machinery and heavy machinery parts either separately or together.[13] In *Home Transp. Co., Inc., Extension,*[14] the Commission said that as testimony in the two proceedings, which resulted in the issuance of the considered authority, regarding the scope of the term "machinery" used in the authority, indicated that a broad interpretation was meant to be applied, and applicant and its predecessor had long been performing a heavy hauler type of service, applicant should be granted authority to transport commodities the transportation of which because of size or weight, required the use of special equipment.

Correction of Certificates

By Section 17(3) of the I.C. Act the Commission has power to modify the certificate so as to correct inadvertent ministerial errors. Section 212 does not prohibit such action although it makes issuance of a certificate the final step in the administrative process.[15] In the *Frisco Transportation* case, the Supreme Court, in reversing a district court decision, agreed with the Commission's conclusion that the administrative record being reviewed supported a finding that certain certificates of public convenience and necessity contained inadvertent errors which after notice and hearing could be modified to correctly reflect the proper authority granted. The Commission had approved the purchase of the operating rights involved subject to a reservation of power to restrict the operation to that which is auxiliary to or supplemental of train service, but the condition was inadvertently omitted from the several certificates. The lower court had held that the Commission's action was an attempt to revoke certificates duly issued, contrary to the provisions of Section 212 and was more than the mere correction of clerical errors.

Elimination of Key Point Restrictions

In this area the Commission has sought to strike a balance that would both safeguard the interest of independent motor carriers and, at

---

[13]See *Connell Transport Co. Extension,* 83 M.C.C. 143, 145; *Sims Motor Transport Lines, Inc. v. United States,* 183 F. Supp. 113, 119.

[14]77 M.C.C. 593, 598.

[15]*American Trucking Assns. v. Frisco Transp. Co.,* 358 U.S. 133, 145-6; *Axtell Extension,* 83 M.C.C. 571, 576. The I.C.C. has the power to correct or modify franchises obtained by virtue of fraud or misrepresentation, issued inadvertently, or issued without proper notice to interested parties. *Curtis, Inc., Extension — Meats Over Irregular Routes,* 113 M.C.C. 170, aff'd *Curtis, Inc. v. United States* (C.A. No. C-3498, D. Colo.)

the same time, enable railroads, through motor affiliates, to offer a more efficient and economical service. In *New York Central Transport Co. — Modification*,[16] a subsidiary of the New York Central asked that key point restrictions contained in certain of its certificates be eliminated and thus permit it to perform a substituted service on traffic theretofore handled by its parent. Such restrictions normally provide that no shipment shall be transported between any two of the named key points, or through, to, or from more than one such point. They are customarily attended by other conditions designed to insure that the proposed service is auxiliary to, or supplemental of, the railroad's operations. In the *New York Central* case there was abundant evidence of economies and improvements in service which could be achieved through a motor operation; but counterbalancing this was the deleterious effect which a total removal of key points would have upon the operations of existing motor carriers. Accordingly, the Commission conditioned their removal upon imposition in lieu thereof, of so-called key point zones which are territorial areas wherein all motorized substituted service may be conducted. Where an interzonal movement is proposed, a prior or subsequent rail haul still is required. This decision recognizes that not all situations lend themselves to any one concept of substituted service, and that key point zones may be established as an alternative to key points or to a prior or subsequent rail haul condition where such zones would be the most appropriate method of combining a more flexible operation with adequate protection of existing carriers.

Reinstatement of Operations

If a carrier has allowed its operations to remain dormant for many years in the past, it may by specific order be required to render reasonably adequate and continuous service in conformity with the terms of the certificate.[17]

Cease and Desist Orders

Where a carrier is conducting unauthorized operations or is exceeding its authority, the Commission has the power to issue cease and desist orders. For example, the Commission entered a cease and desist order in *Dealers Transit, Inc. v. Leonard Bros. Transfer & Storage Co., Inc.*[18]

---

[16]89 M.C.C. 389.
[17]*Hrnciar — Investigation and Revocation of Certificate*, 78 M.C.C. 467, 468, 470.
[18]78 M.C.C. 613, 616.

where the carriers engaged in the transportation of trailers containing electronic equipment when it had no authority for the transportation of trailers. A carrier was ordered to cease and desist, in *J. H. Nowinsky Trucking Co. — Investigation of Permits,*[19] from the unlawful transportation of building, roofing, and insulating materials under authority for farm supplies when such shipments were not in fact intended for use on a farm. A cease and desist order was entered in *Ace Lines, Inc. — Investigation and Revocation of Certificate,*[20] the Commission stating that authority to transport building materials did not include certain steel products unless at the time of movement they were in a form and condition to be used in the construction or repair of a building and were at such time intended to be so used.

WATER CARRIERS

The Applicable Statutory Provisions

Section 312a (1) of the Interstate Commerce Act[21] provides that "Certificates and permits shall be effective from the date specified therein, and shall remain in effect until suspended or revoked as provided in this section." Section 312a (2) provides that "Any certificate or permit issued under this part may, upon application of the holder thereof, in the discretion of the Commission, be amended or revoked, in whole or in part, or may, upon complaint, or on the Commission's own initiative, after reasonable notice and opportunity for hearing, be suspended, changed, or revoked, in whole or in part, for willful failure to comply with the provisions of Section 305(a) with respect to performing, providing, and furnishing transportation upon reasonable request therefor: *Provided, however,* That no such certificate or permit shall be suspended, changed, or revoked under this paragraph (except upon application of the holder) unless the holder therefor, fails to comply, within a reasonable time, not less than thirty days, to be fixed by the Commission, with a lawful order of the Commission, made as provided in Section 304(e) of this title, commanding obedience to the provisions of Section 305(a) with respect to performing, providing, and furnishing transportation upon reasonable request therefor."

The net effect of the addition of Section 312a is to grant the Commission the power to suspend or revoke water carrier operating author-

---

[19]83 M.C.C. 171, 174.
[20]78 M.C.C. 523, 528.
[21]49 U.S.C. 912a.

ities with procedures therefor. When part III of the I.C. Act was enacted in the Transportation Act of 1940, this power was not included therein.[22] For years the Commission recommended to Congress that provisions for revocation for nonuse of water carrier certificates and permits be added to Part III because of the dormancy of a number of outstanding certificates and permits.[23]

The language of Section 312a is similar in most respects to that used in Section 212(a) and Section 410(f) of the I.C. Act respecting motor carriers and freight forwarders, respectively. It provides that a water carrier certificate may be revoked after reasonable notice and opportunity for a hearing; but the revocation power thereunder is limited solely to the operating authority of a water carrier which has willfully failed to perform, provide, or furnish transportation upon reasonable request therefore as provided in section 305(a) of the I.C. Act. The revocation procedures, like those of motor carriers and freight forwarders, embody a proviso which provides that no certificate may be so revoked unless the holder thereof fails to comply with the stated requirements after a period of not less than 30 days.

The parallel provisions in Part II of the I.C. Act has been interpreted by the Commission as giving it "no power to compel a motor carrier to remain in business, whether or not its service is needed or used by the public, if it desires to discontinue its operations entirely."[24]

FREIGHT FORWARDERS

The Applicable Statutory Provisions

Section 410(f) of the Interstate Commerce Act[25] provides:

[22]*United States v. Seatrain Lines, Inc.*, 329 U.S. 442.

[23]The Commission's 61st annual report to Congress, dated November 1, 1947, first recommended inclusion of authority to revoke water carrier operating rights for nonuse. House bill, H.R. 5401 (89th Cong. 1st Sess.) originally proposed that the Commission may revoke a water carrier certificate "for willful failure to engage in, or to continue to engage in, the operation authorized by such certificate ° ° °". The Commission's Committee on Legislation supported the language and in a letter to the Senate dated June 1, 1965, stated:

"We wish to point out that even though the Commission may be given the power to revoke a certificate or permit, 'in part' we would not do so unless there was reason to believe that such willful failure to operate would continue indefinitely."

However, the proposal of the House and Senate conferees,—that a certificate may be revoked only for willful failure to perform, provide, or furnish transportation upon reasonable request therefore as provided in Section 305(a) of the act,—was ultimately enacted into law.

[24]See *Bekins Moving & Storage Co. — Purchase — Farrington*, 65 M.C.C. 56, 59.

[25]49 U.S.C. 1010(f).

"Permits shall be effective from the date specified therein, and shall remain in effect until suspended or terminated as herein provided. Any such permit may, upon application of the holder thereof, in the discretion of the Commission, be amended or revoked, in whole or in part, or may upon complaint, or on the Commission's own initiative, after notice and hearing, be suspended, modified, or revoked, in whole or in part, for willful failure to comply with any provision of this part, or with any lawful order, rule, or regulation of the Commission promulgated thereunder, or with any term, condition, or limitation of such permit: *Provided, however,* That no such permit shall be revoked (except upon application of the holder) unless the holder thereof fails to comply, within a reasonable time, not less than thirty days, to be fixed by the Commission, with a lawful order of the Commission, commanding obedience to the provision of this part, or to the rule or regulation of the Commission thereunder, or to the term, condition, or limitation of such permit, found by the Commission to have been violated by such holder: *Provided further,* That the right to engage in service subject to this part under authority of any permit or any application filed pursuant to the provisions of this section may be suspended by the Commission, upon reasonable notice of not less than fifteen days to the forwarder, but without hearing or other proceedings, for failure to comply, and until compliance, with the provisions of Section 405(a) or with any lawful order, rule, or regulation of the Commission promulgated thereunder or under the provisions of Section 403(c) or (d)."

The Commission has held that failure to provide service under a freight forwarder permit is sufficient to justify revocation of such authority.[26]

Section 410(i) of the I.C. Act provides in part that no freight forwarder which is controlled by, or under common control with, a common carrier subject to Parts I, II, or III thereof shall abandon all or any portion of its freight forwarder service unless and until there shall have been obtained from the Commission a certificate that such abandonment is consistent with the public interest and the national transportation policy. The legislative history of Part IV of the I.C. Act indicates that Section 410(i) was inserted in the I.C. Act principally for the purpose of protecting the public against the possibility that a common carrier might seek to use a controlled forwarder to discourage other forwarder service and then discontinue the controlled forwarder service, or, in other words, to use the controlled forwarder as a so-called "fighting ship" to discourage legitimate and normal competition of other forwarders.

In *Howard Terminal Freight Forwarder Application,*[27] involving a subsidiary of a company that was the sole stockholder of a Part I carrier,

---

[26]See *Acme Fast Freight, Inc. v. Interstate Exp., Inc.,* 298 I.C.C. 774, 776; *Aloha Consolidators v. Air-Sea Forwarders, Inc.,* 326 I.C.C. 559, 561-62.

[27]Docket No. FF-8, decided August 8, 1961.

the Commission found that abandonment of service as freight forwarder of canned goods from points in California to all other points in the United States would be consistent with the public interest and the national transportation policy; and that a certificate of abandonment would be issued, and the permit revoked. The facts showed that the freight forwarder was unable to obtain sufficient volume of traffic to enable it to perform the usual services of a freight forwarder, thus indicating that its operation no longer served a useful purpose, and that there was no public interest in the continuance of such service.

19

Industrial Lines

What tests are applied to determine the true character of an industrial line, i.e., whether the line is a plant facility merely or a common carrier?

The decision of the Supreme Court in the *Tap Line Cases*,[1] sheds light on this question. The *Tap Line Cases* involved appeals from decrees of the Commerce Court annulling orders of the Interstate Commerce Commission (The Commerce Court was established to review orders of the Commission; however, the court was abolished soon after its establishment.) refusing in whole or in part to compel certain trunk lines, which had filed schedules cancelling former schedules covering through routes and joint rates with a number of so-called tap lines, to establish or re-establish through routes and joint rates and to grant allowances and divisions to the tap lines. The Supreme Court affirmed the judgment of the Commerce Court.

The tap lines were owned by lumber companies and were engaged in moving logs from the timber regions to the mills and lumber from the mills to the trunk line connections. The tap lines served both proprietary and non-proprietary lumber companies. The report of the Commission held that the tracks and equipment of the tap lines were plant facilities and that the service performed for the proprietary lumber companies in moving logs to the mills and in moving lumber from the mills to the trunk line connections was not a service of transportation by a common carrier, but a plant service by a plant facility, and that any allowances or divisions of rates on that account were unlawful and resulted in undue and unreasonable preferences and unjust discriminations. The grounds of decision upon which the Commission proceeded

[1]234 U.S. 1.

were two: (1) That the tap lines were mere plant facilities; and (2) that they were not common carriers as to proprietary traffic. The Commission held that before incorporation they were plant facilities, and that after incorporation they remained as such.

It was contended before the Supreme Court that the tap lines were not common carriers because most of their traffic was in their own logs and lumber, and that only a small part of the traffic carried was the property of others. The court answered their contention by stating (p. 24), "But this conclusion loses sight of the principle that the extent to which a railroad is in fact used does not determine the fact whether it is or is not a common carrier." The court added, "It is the right of the public to use the road's facilities and to demand service of it, rather than the extent of its business, which is the real criterion determinative of its character." The court noted (p. 24) that this principle has been frequently recognized by the courts, citing *Union Line Co. v. Chicago & N.W.R. Co.*[2] It also noted (p. 25) that the Commission recognized this principle as applicable to tap lines, citing *Central Yellow Pine Asso. v. Vicksburg, S & P.R. Co.*[3] The court said (p. 26):

> Finally, these roads are common carriers when tried by the test of organization for that purpose under competent legislation of the state. They are so treated by the public authorities of the state, who insist in this case that they are such, and submit in oral discussion and printed briefs cogent arguments to justify that conclusion. They are engaged in carrying for hire the goods of those who see fit to employ them. They are authorized to exercise the right of eminent domain by the state of their incorporation. They were treated and dealt with as common carriers by connecting systems of other carriers, — a circumstance to be noticed in determining their true character. *United States v. Union Stock Yard & Transit Co.* 286 U.S. 286, 57 L. ed. 226, 33 Sup. Ct. Rep. 83. They are engaged in transportation as that term is defined in the commerce act and described in decisions of this court. . . .

The court said (p. 28) that it doubtless was true that abuses existed in the conduct and practice of these lines and in their dealings with other carriers, which resulted in unfair advantages to owners of some tap lines and in discrimination against the owners of others. It pointed out that because the conclusion was reached that the tap lines were common carriers of both proprietary and non-proprietary traffic, and as such entitled to participate in joint rates with other common carriers, it did not follow that divisions of joint rates might be made

[2] 223 U.S. 211, 221.
[3] 10 I.C.C. 193, 199.

with them at the will of the carriers involved and without power of the Commission to control the same. It said (p. 29):

> . . . It is not only within its power, but the law makes it the duty, of the Commission to make orders which shall nullify such practices resulting in rebating or preferences, whatever form they take and in whatsoever guise they may appear. If the divisions of joint rates are such as to amount to rebates or discriminations in favor of the owners of the tap lines because of their disproportionate amount in view of the service rendered, it is within the province of the Commission to reduce the amount so that a tap line shall reecive just compensation only for what it actually does.

There also are decisions of the Commission which throw light on this question. In *A.,T. & S.F. Ry. Co. v. Kansas City Stock Yards Co.*,[4] the Commision said, "The principal test of common carriage is whether there is a bona fide holding out coupled with the ability to carry for hire." In the original report of the Commission in the *Industrial Railways Case*,[5] it was held that all allowances to, or divisions of rates with, any of the so-called industrial lines were unlawful. No distinction was made between the industrial lines, although their physical characteristics and the conditions surrounding them varied widely. As a result of that report, although no order was entered, the line-haul carriers withdrew all allowances, divisions and demurrage and per diem arrangements with the industrial lines that were before the Commission in the proceeding, and also with other similar lines that were not before the Commission. After the original report was issued, the Supreme Court handed down its decision in the *Tap Line Cases*. The Commission therefore instituted an investigation on its own motion in *Industrial Railways Case*,[6] and modified its original report in 29 I.C.C. 212 in accord with the principles announced by the Supreme Court in the *Tap Line Cases*.

It modified the findings in the original report so as to permit the trunk lines to arrange, by agreement with such of the industrial lines as were common carriers under the test applied by the Supreme Court in the *Tap Line Cases* and which performed a service of transportation, for a reasonable compensation for such service in the form of switching charges or divisions of joint through rates. In modifying the original report, the Commission made the following comment (32 I.C.C. at pp. 132-33):

[4] 33 I.C.C. 92, 100. See also *Manufacturers Ry. Co. v. St. Louis I.M. & S. Ry. Co.*, 21 I.C.C. 304.
[5] 29 I.C.C. 212.
[6] 32 I.C.C. 129.

. . . We think that in the light of the decision of the Supreme Court in the *Tap Line Cases* it is our duty to so modify our findings in the original report herein as to permit the trunk line roads, if they so elect, to arrange by agreement with any of the industrial roads mentioned in our former report which are common carriers under the test applied by the Supreme Court in the *Tap Line Cases,* and which perform a service of transportation, for a reasonable compensation for such service in the form of switching charges or divisions of joint through rates. Each road that becomes party to such an agreement must file with us immediately upon the consummation thereof a full statement of the arrangement entered into showing specifically the allowances or divisions granted thereby. We shall, in the exercise of the duty pointed out by the Supreme Court, undertake at the earliest available opportunity to inquire carefully into any of these allowances or divisions which may seem to be unwarranted or unreasonable or to effect unjust discrimination.

The commodities clause of the act excepts timber and manufactured products thereof from the prohibition against the transportation by a railroad of any article or commodity manufactured, mined, or produced by it or under its authority, or which it may own wholly or in part, or in which it may have any interest, direct or indirect, except such articles or commodities as may be necessary and intended for its use in the conduct of its business as a common carrier. What we have here said relative to establishment of allowances or divisions with the industrial roads referred to is not to be understood as a finding by us that those industrial roads can resume these relations with the trunk line carriers without transgressing the provisions of the commodities clause. If infractions of that law come to our notice, we shall in the proper way bring them to the attention of the Department of Justice.

We shall expect the trunk line roads, under the modification here made of our original findings, to reestablish allowances, divisions, or demurrage or per diem arrangements with industrial roads only in instances in which the transaction is bona fide, and in which it is clearly lawful and proper. Each case must be judged by its own facts and merits. Each of the industrial railways is or is not a common carrier. If it is a common carrier, it is entitled to all the rights and subject to all of the limitations provided in the act.

In *Second Industrial Railways Case,*[7] the Commission conducted a further inquiry concerning the rates, rules and practices of trunk lines in connection with small lines of railways owned or controlled by industries. In order that the Commission might have before it all the facts concerning the history, operation, and practices of each of the lines involved, it distributed questions to each of the industrial lines. The information developed from the questions was as follows:

. . . Name and location of industrial line, its list of stockholders; complete statement of the history, ownership, and control of the industrial

[7] 34 I.C.C. 596.

line; its issues of capital obligations, if any, and the ownership thereof; a list of all of the industries located on the rails of the industrial line and the character of the business which each conducts; the aggregate length of tracks operated divided into main tracks and sidetracks and also as between length of track owned and track leased; a statement of the equipment operated; the length of haul between each trunk line interchange and each industry served; a map of the line; statement of the character of the service rendered and the compensation therefor; statements of the tariffs filed and the methods employed in waybilling freight, together with other transportation records kept; a statement of the passenger service, if any; the physical condition of the tracks; statements of general balance sheet, income account, and profit and loss account for the year ended June 30, 1913; analysis of traffic and revenues for the same year; analysis of the operating expenses; a statement of the extent to which officers of the industrial lines are identified with the controlling industrial company, and to what extent passes are interchanged with the trunk line connections; a statement of the aggregate length of tracks located outside of the plant inclosure of the controlling industry; and other facts pertinent to the general questions involved in this case.

Because of the varying nature of the operations of industrial lines and because each of them must be treated on the particular facts pertaining to it, the Commission felt that it should point out the principles and decisions which must guide those desiring to enter into joint rate arrangements and the limitations within which such arrangements may be made. It said (p. 600):

. . . There must be determined with respect to each of the lines, first, whether the instrumentality performing the service is a bona fide common carrier; second, whether the service which it performs between the point of interchange with the trunk line and point of placement on the line of the industrial road is plant service or public transportation; third, whether a charge should be made for such service in addition to the line-haul rate applicable to or from points on the rails of the trunk line at the junction. With these questions there is to be considered the larger economic problem whether part of the money paid to the trunk line carriers for public transportation service is to be used to defray the expense of particular shippers in conveying their traffic to and from the terminals of the truck line carriers. The *Industrial Railways Case* rests largely upon the principle of placing the cost of service where it properly belongs. In approaching the question whether the common carrier status of an industrial line is bona fide it must be borne in mind that there are interests of the industry beyond the mere question of rates in maintaining such a status. The recognition of such lines as common carriers in the association of railroads through which the interchange of cars is provided inures to the very great advantage of the controlling industry served by such a line in the way of remission of charges for the detention of cars.

The Commission found in *Second Industrial Railway Case* (p. 601) that many of the industrial lines owned no cars of their own and in some instances no locomotives, and maintained no stations other than loading and unloading docks within the plant. Their tracks were wholly on the line of the industry which they served, and access to them could be obtained only through the permission of the controlling industry. The Commission said (p. 601) that in such circumstances the holding out was not genuine. It said further, "The public cannot avail itself of such a line. Because of the location of many of them it is impossible to serve the public. In other cases there is no public to serve."

In treating the operations of each of the industrial lines in accordance with the facts relating to it, the Commission found (pp. 604-608) that the lines fell into more or less well-defined groups. As to each such group, the Commission indicated the consideration which should govern the making of joint rate arrangements.

The *first* group of lines had a very general merchandise and commodity traffic aside from the traffic of controlling enterprises. They were of a trunk line type and performed hauls ranging from 11 to 380 miles. This group presented no problem.

The *second* group were those extending from lumber mills to junctions of the trunk line carriers. The ownership or control of these lines was vested in the lumber companies which they served. The Commission said that in all respects they fell within the principles laid down in the *Tap Line Cases.*

The *third* group included those the physical operations of which were in all respects similar to those recited in *General Electric Co. v. N.Y.C. & H.R.R. Co.,*[8] and other cases where the industry attempted to compel the trunk line carriers to pay it for its service in switching cars from a reasonable interchange track to points of placement on its own system of tracks within its plant enclosure. In such cases it was held that the trunk line carrier could not lawfully compensate the shipper itself or indirectly through its incorporated plant railroad, for the use of its plant tracks or for switching the shipper's cars over them with its own motive power. The only essential difference between the lines in the third group and those in the cited cases was that the third group lines had been incorporated and held themselves out to be common carriers. In most instances the incorporated industrial line was first constructed as a system of plant tracks and in many instances the tracks were still owned by the industry and leased to the incorporated railroad. Usually the plant was located contiguous to the rails of the trunk line. The Commission said that insofar as this particular group is concerned there should be considered very carefully the test applied in

[8] 14 I.C.C. 237.

the *Tap Line Cases* regarding the bona fide character of the common carrier.

The *fourth* group resembled closely the lumber tap lines with the important exception that they could haul commodities other than lumber, and thus in some instances fell under the direct inhibition of the Commodities Clause. The history of these lines showed instances in which a system of plant tracks were constructed to serve an industry located immediately contiguous to trunk line rails, but because of various considerations, including a desire for an adequate car supply and a development of competition which could be used as a weapon to obtain divisions of the joint rate for the industrial line, the plant tracks were incorporated and connected with another trunk line located at a distance from the plant. The Commission questioned the manner in which joint rates were constructed by the carriers in this group because of possible discrimination. However, it appears that the Commission felt that these carriers were bona fide common carriers.

In the *fifth* group, the following conditions were shown: an industry had plant tracks which could under no conceivable conditions be considered as having common carrier characteristics. In order to give them such a status, a railroad was incorporated, the tracks of the plant were leased to it, and the trunk line granted trackage rights and even leased its rails to the industrially owned railroad corporation. The industrial railroad published tariffs, filed them with the Commission, made reports, and as a matter of form assumed the appearance of a common carrier. The trunk line afforded it divisions out of the rate applicable to the locality for the same service which the industry had previously performed without compensation. The Commission said that for a trunk line carrier to offer its facilities by lease or trackage rights to give an undue advantage to a single shipper is unquestionably such a device as is condemned by the I.C. Act.

The *sixth* group was composed of industrial plant tracks which were neither owned nor operated by common carriers and were not dedicated to public use, the ownership and right of use being in the controlling industries which operated them. Those in the sixth group asked that allowances be paid them upon the theory that they were performing a service of transportation which the trunk line was obligated to perform under the rate structure. The Commission did not enlarge upon the question of allowances to industries except to state that Section 15 of the I.C. Act was enacted to give the Commission a means of eliminating certain unjust discriminations.

In the *Second Industrial Railway Cases*, the Commission said (p.

606) that it would look to the trunk lines to reform their tariffs and file with it whatever arrangements they made with the industrial lines in light of its report.

It is clear that the Commission in the *Second Industrial Rai'way Cases* adhered to the following test applied by the Supreme Court in the *Tap Line Cases* regarding the bona fide character of a common carrier:

> It is the right of the public to use the road's facilities and to demand service of it, rather than the extent of its business, which is the real criterion determinative of its character.

The above test has been applied by the Commission in later cases. For example, in *Practices Affecting Dillonvale & S. Ry.*,[9] the Commission said that "one of the tests by which we sometimes judge whether or not a railroad is a common carrier" is "whether there is a bona fide holding out, coupled with the ability to carry for hire." The Commission also said (p. 693) that the right of the public to demand transportation service "rather than the degree to which it actually is used, is important."

In *Detroit Edison Co. Terminal Allowance*,[10] the Commission referred to and adopted its finding in *A., T. & S. F. Ry. Co. v. Kansas City Stock Yards Co.*,[11] where it said, "The principal test of common carriage is whether there is a bona fide holding out coupled with the ability to carry for hire."

There are two cases decided by the Commission which seem to narrow the "holding out" test applied in the *Tap Line Cases*. These are *Inland Ry. Co.*,[12] and *Bell Coal & Nav. Co. Application.*[13] In the *Inland* case the Commission said (p. 64), "while the extent to which the public uses the facilities of a railroad is not controlling, there must be some appreciable use of the railroad by the public or else the holding out to carry for all is merely an empty form." The Commission found (p. 64) that "with the exception of two carloads of junk shipped by employees of the salt company, the Inland has never handled shipments for shippers other than the salt company. The territory near it is barren, and there is no immediate prospect of future traffic other than that of the salt company."

---

[9]229 I.C.C. 687, 691. See also *Union Belt of Detroit Pooling of Revenues*, 201 I.C.C. 577, 581-82.
[10]209 I.C.C. 55.
[11]133 I.C.C. 92, 100.
[12]78 I.C.C. 59.
[13]223 I.C.C. 433, 436.

In *Bell Coal & Nav. Co. Application, supra,* at p. 436, involving an application to conduct service as a common carrier by water, the Commission said, "While a carrier may be a common carrier, even though most of its traffic consists of its own property, the extent to which the public uses its facilities not being controlling, nevertheless there must be some appreciable use or reasonably prospective use by the public or else the holding out to carry for all becomes merely an empty form," citing *Inland Ry. Co.*[14]

These decisions are not believed to be inconsistent with the test applied in the *Tap Line Cases.* The decisions simply state that mere expression of willingness to carry for others does not transform a private carrier into a common carrier. To constitute a common carrier, there must be a genuine holding out to carry for all, which implies, among other things, the availability of goods for carriage, and the existence, and ownership or control, of terminal and other facilities for such carriage.

If the true character of an industrial line is that of a plant facility, is it permissible for such a facility to receive switching allowances from the line haul carrier?

The obligation of carriers under Section 1(3) of the I.C. Act makes it their duty to perform interstate transportation at just and reasonable charges, which includes receipt and delivery of property transported. As stated in *United States v. Aberdeen & R. R. Co.,*[15] The problems involved in this statutory requirement have been many times resolved by this Commission, and so often been approved by the courts, as to provide firmly established principles governing the rendition of services, or payment of allowances in lieu thereof, by carriers concerned."

A carrier has the right to furnish whatever transportation service the law requires it to furnish. *Atchison, T. & S. F. Ry. Co. v. United States.*[16] A carrier may employ an agent to perform transportation service for it.[17] And a carrier may receive services from an owner for property transported or use instrumentalities furnished by the latter, in which cases the carrier is permitted to pay for such services subject to the restriction that the compensation be no more than is reasonable.[18] However, the demands upon a carrier which lawfully may be made are limited by its duty.[19]

---

[14]78 I.C.C. 59, 64.

[15]289 I.C.C. 49, 65.

[16]232 U.S. 199.

[17]*United States v. Fruit Growers Exp. Co.,* 279 U.S. 363.

[18]*United States v. Baltimore & O. R. Co.,* 231 U.S. 274.

[19]*National Industrial Traffic League v. Aberdeen & R. R. Co.,* 61 I.C.C. 120, 123; *Great Northern Ry. v. Minnesota,* 238 U.S. 340, 346.

It is well settled that carload freight may be delivered or received by carriers upon private industrial sidings. Under general custom and practice the line haul rate entitles a receiver to have its shipment delivered at a reasonably convenient place, whether this be within a plant, or upon a track agreed upon by it and the carrier. It is also clear that service beyond such reasonably convenient point is not service that the carrier is obligated to perform or pay for under its line-haul rates.[20]

The trunk lines need not, in the absence of unjust discrimination, make any allowances to the private line so long as they are ready to perform the switching wherever by custom and general usage the line haul rate covers that service.[21] Therefore, an allowance in excess of the cost to the trunk line of switching to and from the plant would be unlawful.[22]

As stated in the *Chicago, West Pullman & Southern* case (p. 414), "By granting more the trunk lines would in that measure be depleting their revenues. The allowance is further limited in that it may not exceed the reasonable cost to the industry of performing the service."

Service over private tracks or plant facility tracks by a carrier is neither compelled nor prohibited under the I.C. Act, and to furnish or withhold it lies within the discretion of the carrier.[23] The Commission is without power to prescribe rates from a point on the private line or to compel a common carrier to perform transportation service over that line or to grant an allowance for the performance of that service.[24] If a carrier operates over private tracks, it is because in its discretion it elects to do so, and its legal obligation in such operations extends no further than is covered by the compensation it exacts for the services performed. In other words, the obligation upon the carrier in such circumstances is measured by the compensation received and not by any definite duty otherwise placed on the carrier by the I.C. Act. Therefore, the payment by the carrier to a shipper for rendering services upon private tracks which are not contemplated by the charges of the carrier is prohibited.[25]

A carrier's duty to perform services under the line haul rate is discharged when it is prevented from performing service by the action

---

[20]*Operating Practices — Terminal Services, Propriety of,* 209 I.C.C. 11, 32-33.
[21]*Chicago, West Pullman & Southern R. R. Co. Case,* 37 I.C.C. 408, 414.
[22]*Chicago, West Pullman & Southern R. R. Co. Case, supra.*
[23]*American Fuel Co. v. A., T. & S. F. Ry. Co.,* 123 I.C.C. 101, 112; *Winnsboro Granite Corp. v. Southern Ry. Co.,* 176 I.C.C. 481, 483.
[24]*Winnsboro Granite Corp. v. Southern Ry. Co., supra.*
[25]*Propriety of Operating Practices — Terminal Services,* 209 I.C.C. 11, 29.

of the industry and where the service would not meet the needs and convenience of or be satisfactory to the industry.[26] In such circumstances there is no legal obligation upon the carrier to make an allowance to the industry for performing the service.[27]

No legal obligation exists upon a carrier to perform switching and spotting service solely at a shipper's convenience, and a shipper is not entitled to an allowance for these services if the carrier is ready and willing to perform them, but is not permitted to do so by the shipper.[28]

The above established principles were applied to the switching involved in *United States v. Aberdeen & R. R. Co.*,[29] where the Commission said:

> It is the right of every shipper including the Government as here concerned, to prohibit a carrier from performing switching upon private tracks, even though the carrier might be willing and able to perform the service. When so prohibited by the shipper, as was here done by the Army, the carrier's obligation to perform the service is discharged, and the payment of allowances to the shipper for its performance of the service, in whole or in part, would be unlawful, except as a voluntary concession of the carriers to the Government under section 22. Even if the Army had permitted the carriers to perform the service here involved, they could not do so, in the circumstances existing, at their operating convenience, in continuous movement, and without interruptions and interferences caused by shipper necessity and requirement. This would relieve the carriers of performing the service here involved under their line haul obligation. *United States v. American Sheet & Tin Plate Co.*, 301 U.S. 402.

If the common carrier status of an industrial line is bona fide, is it permissible for such a line to receive divisions of rates or switching allowances from a line haul carrier? If it is permissible, are there any limitations placed on the amount of divisions or switching allowances that can be received by the industry line from the line haul carrier?

If an industrial line is a bona fide common carrier of property subject to the I.C. Act, it may lawfully receive divisions of rates jointly established by it and its trunk line connections under appropriate tariff provisions.[30]

Where the service performed by the common carrier industrial line is interior plant service, compensation for such service should be made

---

[26]*Allowances to Gulf Sulphur Co.*, 96 I.C.C. 371.
[27]*Allowances to Gulf Sulphur Co., supra.*
[28]*Stewart Furnace Co. v. Pennsylvania R. Co.*, 68 I.C.C. 528.
[29]289 I.C.C. 49, 65-66.
[30]*Divisions Received by Brimstone R. R. & Canal Co.*, 68 I.C.C. 375, 386; *Chicago, West Pullman & Southern R. R. Co. Case*, 37 I.C.C. 408, 415.

by the industry served. When switching is performed by a common carrier industrial line between industries and connecting carriers, which may properly be regarded as a transportation service for which the connecting carriers may pay a division of the line haul rate, the trunk lines are not obliged to absorb the switching charges of the industrial lines.[31] The Commission, however, may require carriers to remove unjust discrimination occasioned by the absorption of switching charges in certain instances and not in others, under like circumstances and conditions.[32] The Commission also may require trunk lines to establish joint rates with connecting industrial lines lower than the combination on the junction point of the trunk line and the industrial line and may fix the divisions to be accorded the industrial line.[33]

The divisions of a common carrier industrial line should produce no more than an amount sufficient to cover the cost of its service and a fair return upon the property held for and used in the service of transportation for the public generally.[34] To the extent that the divisions exceed the cost of service and a fair return upon the property held for and used in the service of transportation, they amount to a rebate to the proprietary company.[35]

Where the cost of service performed by a common carrier industrial line varies substantially as between its different trunk line connections, the divisions of joint rates made by the trunk line to the industrial line must be based, so far as practicable, on the cost of the service in each case, plus fair return. Otherwise, if the divisions accorded for the greater service were reasonable, the same divisions accorded for a lesser service would amount substantially to a rebate to the proprietary company.[36]

In the *Chicago, West Pullman & Southern R. R. Co. Case, supra.,* the Commission established certain considerations that should prevail in arriving at the amount which trunk lines may allow common carrier industrial lines for switching. The Commission said (pp. 415-16):

> . . . In so far as the industrial line serves the plant in interplant switching and other purely plant service the cost of such service and the investment in facilities used exclusively to perform that service must be excluded in calculating the cost of the switching service to and from the trunk lines. The investment in facilities used both for plant service

---

[31]*Chicago, West Pullman & Southern R. R. Co. Case, supra., at* p. 415.
[32]*Ibid.*
[33]*Ibid.*
[34]*Divisions Received by Brimstone R. R. & Canal Co.,* 68 I.C.C. 375, 387-88.
[35]*Divisions Received by Brimstone R. R. & Canal Co., supra.* See also *Divisions of Joint Rates for Transportation of Stone,* 41 I.C.C. 321, 327.
[36]*Divisions received by Brimstone R. R. & Canal Co.,* 88 I.C.C. 62, 73.

and interchange switching can only be included in the proportion that they are used in interchange switching. Interior plant switching or any other service differing radically in nature from the general work of switching cars between industries and connections should be segregated as to investment and operating costs of the industrial line so far as this may be feasible. The engine hour will usually be found a safer guide than cars handled for making this general separation. For interior plant switching the industry benefited should be charged with the allocated capital and operating costs. The remaining operating and capital costs measure the maximum which may be received net for other switching, either in the form of switching charges or allowances, there being a minimum charge for the shortest switching and a somewhat higher charge for the longer distance switching. From its entire business the industrial line should not earn more than a fair return on the property devoted to the public use, less reserve for accrued depreciation, and including material and supplies in the investment. No abnormal divisions or allowances may in any case be made, for it is evident that, by paying or permitting to be paid more than would be just and reasonable for any service performed by the industrial line, the trunk lines may be giving the controlling industry a rebate.

As stated by the Commission in *Divisions of Joint Rates for Transportation of Stone,*[37] the allowances must be fair and reasonable and "free of concessions to the shippers controlling the roads." The Commission also said, "The total return from all interchange traffic must not exceed a fair return on the proportional value of the property devoted to public use, assignable to the handling of interchange traffic."

To what extent is an industry line having common carrier status subject to the Interstate Commerce Act?

Even though an industry line having common carrier status is located entirely within one state, it is subject to the I.C. Act so long as it engages in interstate commerce. In *Ligonier Valley R. R. Co.,*[38] a carrier which owned and operated 16 miles of single track and 10 miles of yard tracks and sidings, located in Pennsylvania, protested the valuation placed on its property by the Commission for rate making purposes on the ground that the Commission had no jurisdiction over such property. The carrier contended that it was not an interstate carrier and, therefore, was not subject to the jurisdiction of the Commission as its property was located entirely within Pennsylvania and its equipment did not leave its own line. The record, however, established that the carrier filed tariffs with the Commission covering interstate traffic and concurred in interstate tariffs filed by other carriers. Much of its traffic consisted of coal which moved to interstate destinations. The Commission held (p. 552),

[37]41 I.C.C. 321, 327.
[38]114 I.C.C. 551.

"It is clear the carrier engages in interstate commerce" and is therefore subject to the I.C. Act.[39]

If an industrial line is a common carrier, it is entitled to all the rights and subject to all the limitations provided in the I.C. Act.[40]

Will the separate incorporation of an industrial line transform a plant facility into a common carrier?

The answer is no. As the Commission said in *Inland Ry. Co.*,[41] "The mere fact of incorporation cannot transform a plant facility into a common carrier."

---

[39]See also *Stonega Coke & Coal Co. v. L. & N. R. R. Co.*, 23 I.C.C. 17, 22.
[40]*Industrial Railway Case*, 32 I.C.C. 129, 133.
[41]78 I.C.C. 59, 64.

20

Private Transportation

The Applicable Statutory Provisions

Section 203(a) (14) of the Interstate Commerce Act[1] provides:

"The term 'common carrier by motor vehicle' means any person which holds itself out to the general public to engage in the transportation by motor vehicle in interstate or foreign commerce of passengers or property or any class or classes thereof for compensation whether over regular or irregular routes, except transportation by motor vehicle by an express company to the extent that such transportation has heretofore been subject to chapter 1 of this title, to which extent such transportation shall continue to be and shall be regulated as transportation subject to chapter 1 of this title."

Section 203(a) (15)[2] provides:

"The term 'contract carrier by motor vehicle' means any person which engages in transportation by motor vehicle of passengers or property in interstate or foreign commerce, for compensation (other than transportation referred to in paragraph (14) of this section and the exceptions therein), under continuing contracts with one person or a limited number of persons either (a) for the furnishing of transportation services through the assignment of motor vehicles for a continuing period of time to the exclusive use of each person served or (b) for the furnishing of transportation services designed to meet the distinct need of each individual customer."

Section 203(a) (17)[3] provides:

"The term 'private carrier of property by motor vehicle' means any person not included in the terms 'common carrier by motor vehicle' or 'contract carrier by motor vehicle,' who or which transports in interstate or foreign commerce by motor vehicle property of which such person is the owner,

[1] 49 U.S.C. 303(a) (14).
[2] 49 U.S.C. 303(a) (15).
[3] 49 U.S.C. 303(a) (17).

lessee, or bailee, when such transportation is for the purpose of sale, lease, rent, or bailment, or in furtherance of any commercial enterprise."

Section 203(c)[4] provides:

"Except as provided in Section 302 (c) of this title, subsection (b) of this section, in the exception in subsection (a) (14) of this section, and in the second proviso in section 306(a) (1) of this title, no person shall engage in any for-hire transportation business by motor vehicle, in interstate or foreign commerce, on any public highway or within any reservation under the exclusive jurisdiction of the United States, unless there is in force with respect to such person a certificate or a permit issued by the Commission authorizing such transportation, nor shall any person engaged in any other business enterprise transport property by motor vehicle in interstate or foreign commerce for business purposes unless such transportation is within the scope, and in furtherance, of a primary business enterprise (other than transportation) of such person."

Section 209(a) (1)[5] provides:

"Except as otherwise provided in this section and in Section 310a of this title, no person shall engage in the business of a contract carrier by motor vehicle in interstate or foreign commerce on any public highway or within any reservation under the exclusive jurisdiction of the United States unless there is in force with respect to such carrier a permit issued by the Commission, authorizing such person to engage in such business." Section 204(c)[6] provides that "Upon complaint in writing to the Commission by any person, State board, organization, or body politic, or upon its own initiative without complaint, the Commission may investigate whether any motor carrier or broker has failed to comply with any provision of this chapter, or with any requirement established pursuant thereto. If the Commission, after notice and hearing, finds upon any such investigation that the motor carrier or broker has failed to comply with any such provision or requirement, the Commission shall issue an appropriate order to compel the carrier or broker to comply therewith. Whenever the Commission is of opinion that any complaint does not state reasonable grounds for investigation and action on its part, it may dismiss such complaint."

The "Primary Business" Test

As indicated above, Section 203(c) of the I.C. Act forbids any person to transport property by motor vehicle, in interstate or foreign commerce, unless there is in force with respect to such transportation a certificate or permit issued by the Commission, or unless the transportation is within

---

[4]49 U.S.C. 303(c).
[5]49 U.S.C. 309(a) (1). Comparable provision — Section 309 (f), 410(a).
[6]49 U.S.C. 304(c). Comparable provisions — Sections 13(1), (2), 304(e), 403 (f), 406(a) covering complaints; and Sections 15(1), 307 (h), 315(b), 406(b) covering orders.

the scope, and in furtherance, of a primary business enterprise other than transportation. This provision codifies the so-called "primary business" test as expressed in the decisions in *Lenoir Chair Co. Contract Carrier Application* (embracing *Schenley Distillers Corp. Contract Carrier Application*),[7] where the Commission said:

> If . . . the primary business of an operator is found to be manufacturing or some other non-carrier commercial enterprise, then it must be determined whether the motor operations are in bona fide furtherance of the primary business or whether they are conducted as a related or secondary enterprise with the purpose of profiting from the transportation performed. In our opinion, they cannot be both. A finding that a company is engaged in performing transportation for compensation with a purpose of profiting therefrom is inconsistent with and precludes a finding that the motor operations are conducted in bona fide furtherance of its other and primary commercial enterprise.

A number of criteria have evolved from past decisions of the Commission and the courts[8] to aid in determining "whether the motor operations are in bona fide furtherance of the primary business or whether they are conducted as a related or secondary enterprise with the purpose of profiting from the transportation performed."

Determination of What Constitutes Private Carriage

Although aware that common and contract carriers are continually faced with actual or potential competition from private truck operations, Congress nevertheless recognized the shipper's interest in furnishing its own transportation and limited the application of the licensing requirements to those persons who provide for-hire transportation; thus the Commission has had to decide whether a particular arrangement gives rise to that for-hire carriage which is subject to economic regulation in the public interest, or whether it is, in fact, private carriage as to which Congress determined that the shipper's interest in carrying its own goods should prevail.[9]

Two inquiries must be satisfied before an operation may be held to constitute private carriage. It would have to be found that no person other than the shipper has any right to control, direct and dominate the

---

[7]51 M.C.C. 65, aff'd *sub nom. Brooks Transportation Co. v. United States,* 93 F.S. 517, aff'd per curiam 340 U.S. 925. See *Burlington Mills Corp., Transp. for Compensation,* 53 M.C.C. 327. See also the earlier case of *Woitishek Common Carrier Application,* 42 M.C.C. 193.

[8]See e.g., *Red Ball Motor Freight v. Shannon* 377 U.S. 311. *Garland-Investigation of Operations and Practices,* 102 M.C.C. 437 and cases cited therin.

[9]*United States v. Henry E. Drum,* 368 U.S. 370.

transportation; and that no person before the Commission was, in substance, engaged in the business of transportation of property for hire. On the first question it was held in *H. B. Church Truck Service Co.*[10] that "Essentially the issue is as to who has the right to control, direct, and dominate the performance of the service. If that right remains in the carrier, the carriage is carriage for hire and subject to regulation. If it rests in the shipper, it is private carriage and not subject to regulation." It was the *H. B. Church* case which established the presumption that a lease of equipment results in for-hire carriage. The presumption was said to "yield to a showing that the shipper has the exclusive right and privilege of directing and controlling the transportation service as, for example, if the equipment were operated by the shipper's employee."[11] The control inquiry is supplemented by the test of substance and reality.[12]

In *Allen v. United States*,[13] the Commission held that in order to constitute private transportation, when equipment is supplied by a lessor, the shipper must have the exclusive right to direct and control the vehicle as well as the driver; thus when plaintiff, who was experienced in the transportation field, executed contracts with shippers under which he leased trucks for the shippers' use, selected drivers, made schedules and routing, and distributed amounts received from shippers between rental company, drivers, and himself, his operation was a "for-hire" operation, and the considered arrangement did not place plaintiff in the category of a private carrier. The Commission said that there was no substantial evidence that the shipper did anything other than inform plaintiff of need for service and the destination of shipments.[14] In *Vollbracht*,[15] the Commission said that the determination of whether, in the conduct of a particular enterprise, transportation performed is private or for-hire

[10]27 M.C.C. 191, 195.

[11]*Ibid.*, p. 196.

[12]See *Pacific Diesel Rental Co.*, 78 M.C.C. 161, 172-3. The courts have commonly articulated their plotting of the boundary between private and regulated carriage in leased equipment cases in terms of over-all substance, rather than simply in terms of "control." See *Georgia Truck System, Inc. vs. I.C.C.*, 123 F. 2d 210 212 ("(A)ppellant in substance and in reality, operates a transportation business."); *A. W. Stickle & Co. v. I.C.C.*, 128 F. 2d 155, 160, 161 (test of "substance and reality"); *Lamb v. I.C.C.*, 259 F. 2d 358, 360 ("Simply stated (the issue) . . . is who was transporting the goods in question."); *B & C Truck Leasing, Inc. v. I.C.C.*, 283 F. 2d 163, 165 (test of "substance and effect"); *I.C.C. v. Isner*, 92 F. Supp. 582; *United States v. La Tuff Transfer Service*, 95 F. Supp. 375; *I.C.C. v. Werner*, 106 F. Supp. 497.

[13]187 F. Supp. 625, 629.

[14]*Ibid.*, pp. 627-9.

[15]76 M.C.C. 761, 763.

carriage, must be made upon consideration of all the facts relating to the noncarrier and carrier part of each business, including the purpose for which the transportation is performed. If a person is engaged primarily in a noncarrier business, and the transportation is solely within the scope of and incidental or secondary thereto, and is only an instrument in furthering such business, such operations come within the definition of Section 203(a) (17), and no specific authority is required; however, where applicant's purpose in supplying the proposed transportation for the supporting shipper would be to profit directly therefrom, such transportation would not be primarily in furtherance of the business in which he is engaged and would be separate and distinct from such noncarrier activity, and would be that of a for-hire carrier.

In *Panhandle Eastern Pipe Line Co. Investigation*,[16] the Commission said that the pipeline company involved came within the first portion of the private carrier definition when it admittedly operated vehicles in interstate commerce transporting property of which it was the owner; and the transportation it performed was in furtherance of a commercial enterprise within the second portion of that definition. In *Northeastern-Malden Barrel Co., Inc.*,[17] the Commission said that the basic test of whether transportation is private or for-hire carriage is whether it is within the scope and in furtherance of a primary business enterprise other than transportation; and where the primary business of an operator is found to be some noncarrier commercial enterprise, it must then be determined whether the motor operations are in bona fide furtherance of the primary business or are conducted as a related or secondary enterprise for the purpose of profiting from the transportation performed.

The Supreme Court held in *Red Ball Motor Freight v. Shannon*[18] that the purchase of sugar to provide a backhaul in connection with outbound movements of livestock and other commodities was within the scope, and in furtherance, of the primary general mercantile business enterprise of appellees. The court stated that the record clearly established that appellees were in the general mercantile business buying and selling many items including sugar. The reasoning of the court was that Section 203(c) had merely codified the primary business test, and embodies no outright prohibition of backhauling practices.

---

[16]83 M.C.C. 9, 13.
[17]83 M.C.C. 705, 708. See also *Subler Transfer, Inc. — Investigation of Permit*, 79 M.C.C. 561, 569.
[18]377 U.S. 311.

Criteria of Buy-and-Sell Operations

The following criteria of buy-and-sell operations are set out in *Utley Lumber Co., Inc. — Investigation of Operations:*[19] (1) whether the carrier is the owner of the property transported; (2) whether orders for the property are received prior to its purchase by the carrier; (3) whether the carrier utilized warehousing facilities and the extent of this use as a storage place; (4) whether the carrier undertakes any financial risks in the transportation connected enterprise; (5) whether the carrier adds an amount identifiable as a transportation charge to the purchase price and its relation to the distance the goods are transported; (6) whether the carrier transports or holds out to transport for anyone other than itself; (7) whether the carrier advertises itself as being in a noncarrier business; (8) whether its investment in transportation facilities and equipment is the principal part of its total business investment; (9) whether the carrier performs any real service other than transportation from which it can profit; (10) whether the transportation of the considered products is coordinated with the movement in the opposite direction of other products so that empty vehicles are not ordinarily dispatched to pick up a load for a one-way haul; (11) whether the party at any time engages for-hire carriers to effect delivery of the products, as might be expected, for example, when it is called upon to fill an order and its own equipment is otherwise engaged; (12) whether the products are delivered directly from the shipper to the consignee (i.e. without intermediate warehousing); (13) whether the buying and selling of the considered products is undertaken in order to balance motor vehicle operations with a profit-yielding backhaul; and (14) whether the buying and selling cannot profitably be undertaken but for the availability of equipment which otherwise must be deadheaded incident to the transportation of other merchandise in the opposite direction.

[19]94 M.C.C. 458, 462-63. See slso *Wilson — Investigation of Operations,* 82 M.C.C. 651 where nine of the criteria of buy-and-sell operations were set forth. See also: *Church Point Wholesale Beverage Co. — Investigation,* 82 M.C.C. 457, aff'd 200 F.S. 508; *Morgan Packing Co., Inc. — Investigation of Operations,* 92 M.C.C. 48, 57; *Hofer — Investigation of Operations,* 84 M.C.C. 527, 540; *Stutzman-Investigation of Operations,* 81 M.C.C. 223.

21

Exempt Transportation

Railroads—Exempt Transportation

Section 207 of the 4R Act amended Section 12(1) of the I.C. Act by adding a new subdivision (b) which provides that the Commission, upon petition or on its own initiative, may exempt from regulation any person, class of persons, services, or transactions relating to transportation by railroad if it finds that regulation is not necessary to effectuate the national transportation policy, would be an undue burden on the person or class of persons involved or on interstate and foreign commerce, and would serve little or no useful public purpose.

Motor Carriers—Exempt Transportation

EXEMPTIONS UNDER SECTION 203(b) OF THE ACT
Section 203(b) of the Interstate Commerce Act[1] provides in part:

"Nothing in this part, except the provisions of Section 204 relative to qualifications and maximum hours of service of employees and safety of operation or standards of equipment shall be construed to include (1) motor vehicles employed solely in transporting school children and teachers to or from school; or (2) taxicabs, or other motor vehicles performing a bona fide taxicab service, having a capacity of not more than six passengers and not operated on a regular route or between fixed termini; or (3) motor vehicles owned or operated by or on behalf of hotels and used exclusively for the transportation of hotel patrons between hotels and local railroad or other common carrier stations; or (4) motor vehicles operated, under authorization, regulation, and control of the Secretary of the Interior, principally for the purpose of transporting persons in and about the national

---

[1]49 U.S.C. 303(b). Comparable provisions — Sections 303(b) — (d), (g), 402(b), (c). See also Section 418 for utilization by freight forwarder of vehicles exempt under Section 203(b) (7a).

parks and national monuments; or (4a) motor vehicles controlled and operated by any farmer when used in the transportation of his agricultural (including horticultural) commodities and products thereof, or in the transportation of supplies to his farm; or (5) motor vehicles controlled and operated by a cooperative association as defined in the Agricultural Marketing Act, approved June 15, 1929, as amended, or by a federation of such cooperative associations, if such federation possesses no greater powers or purposes than cooperative associations so defined, but any interstate transportation performed by such a cooperative association or federation of cooperative associations for nonmembers who are neither farmers, cooperative associations, nor feredations thereof for compensation, except transportation otherwise exempt under this part, shall be limited to that which is incidental to its primary transportation operation and necessary for its effective performance and shall in no event exceed 15 per centum of its total interstate transportation services in any fiscal year, measured in terms of tonnage: *Provided,* That, for the purposes hereof, notwithstanding any other provision of law, transportation performed for or on behalf of the United States or any agency or instrumentality thereof shall be deemed to be transportation performed for a nonmember: *Provided* further, That any such cooperative association or federation which performs interstate transportation for nonmembers who are neither farmers, cooperative associations, nor federations thereof, except transportation otherwise exempt under this part, shall notify the Commission of its intent to perform such transportation prior to the commencement thereof: *And provided further,* That in no event shall any such cooperative association or federation which is required hereunder to give notice to the Commission transport interstate for compensation in any fiscal year of such association or federation a quantity of property for nonmembers which, measured in terms of tonnage, exceeds the total quantity of property transported interstate for itself and its members in such fiscal year; or (6) motor vehicles used in carrying property consisting of ordinary livestock, fish (including shell fish), or agricultural (including horticultural) commodities (not including manufactured products thereof), if such motor vehicles are not used in carrying any other property, or passengers, for compensation: *Provided,* That the words 'property consisting of ordinary livestock, fish (including shell fish), or agricultural (including horticultural) commodities (not including manufactured products thereof)' as used herein shall include property shown as 'Exempt' in the 'Community List' incorporated in rules numbered 107, March 19, 1958, Bureau of Motor Carriers, Interstate Commerce Commission, but shall not include property shown therein as 'Not exempt': *Provided further, however,* That notwithstanding the preceding proviso the words 'property consisting of ordinary livestock, fish (including shell fish) or agricultural (including horticultural) commodities (not including manufactured products thereof)' shall not be deemed to include frozen fruits, frozen berries, frozen vegetables, cocoa beans, coffee beans, tea, bananas, or hemp, and wool imported from any foreign country, wool tops and noils, or wool waste (carded, spun, woven, or knitted), and shall be deemed to include cooked or uncooked (including breaded) fish or shell fish when frozen or fresh (but not including fish and shell fish which have been treated for preserving, such as canned, smoked, pickled, spiced, corned or kippered products); or (7) motor vehicles used exclusively in the distribution of newspapers; or (7a) the transportation of persons or property by motor vehicle when incidental to transportation by aircraft nor, unless and to the extent that the Commission shall from time to time find that such application is necessary to carry out the national transportation policy declared in this Act, shall the provisions of this part, except the provisions of Section 204 relative to qualifications and maximum hours of service of employees and safety of operation or standards of equipment apply to: (8) the transportation of passengers or property in interstate or foreign commerce wholly within a municipality or between contiguous municipalities or within a zone adjacent to and commercially a part of any such municipality or municipalities, except when such transportation is under a common control, management, or arrangement for a continuous carriage or shipment to or from a point without such municipality, municipalities, or zone, and provided that the motor carrier engaged in such transportation of passengers over regular or irregular route or routes in interstate commerce is also lawfully engaged in the intrastate transportation of passengers over the entire length of such interstate route or routes in accordance with the laws of each State having jurisdiction; or (9) the casual, occasional, or reciprocal transportation of passengers or property by motor vehicle in interstate or foreign commerce for compensation by any person not engaged in transportation by motor vehicle as a regular occupation or business, unless, in the case of transportation of passengers, such transportation is sold or offered for sale, or provided or procured or furnished or arranged for, by a broker, or by any other person who sells or offers for sale transportation furnished by a person lawfully engaged in the transportation of passengers by motor vehicle under a certificate or permit issued under this part or under a pending application for such a certificate or permit; or (10) the emergency transportation of any accidentally wrecked or disabled motor vehicle in interstate or foreign commerce by towing."

TRANSPORTATION OF SCHOOL CHILDREN AND TEACHERS

Section 203(b) (1) exempts motor vehicles employed solely in transporting school children and teachers to or from school.

Considering the dictionary definition of "school" as meaning "any place or means of learning" as well as an institution primarily devoted to educational development of children, "to and from school," as used in Section 203(b) (1), embraces transportation to or from any place where such transportation is directly connected with and contributes to the educational development of school children. Educational development in this context encompasses a broader area than mere classroom instruction in a school building; scope of the teaching process has widened, and classroom instruction is frequently supplemented with field and sightseeing trips to points of historical and cultural interest to provide students with firsthand knowledge of places, events, and techniques studied in the classroom. When such trips are sponsored and paid for by the school as official school functions, the transportation provided by a carrier whose vehicles are employed solely in transporting school children and teachers falls within purview of the exemption.[2]

TAXICABS

In giving consideration to Section 203(b) (2), the Commission has recognized that the essential characteristics of a bona fide taxicab service, as distinguished from special or charter service, which also need not be operated over a regular route or between fixed termini, is its inherently local nature. The former is ordinarily conducted within a municipality or a township and their immediate environs,[3] and is exempt.

TRANSPORTATION OF HOTEL PATRONS BETWEEN HOTELS AND LOCAL PASSENGER STATIONS

Motor vehicles owned or operated by or on behalf of hotels and used exclusively to transport its patrons to and from local passenger stations are confined to a large extent to municipalities, contiguous municipalities, or zones adjacent to and commercially a part thereof, and are thus exempt under Section 203(b) (3) of the I.C. Act.[4]

TRANSPORTATION OF PERSONS IN AND ABOUT THE NATIONAL PARKS AND NATIONAL MONUMENTS

Section 203(b) (4) exemption relates to motor vehicles operated principally for the purpose of transporting persons in and about the national parks and national monuments; thus when motor vehicles are operated exclusively for the transportation of property the exemption does not apply.[5]

AGRICULTURAL EXEMPTIONS

There are three exemptions which apply to agricultural transport. Section 203(b) (4a) exempts motor vehicles controlled and operated by any farmer when used in the transportation of his agricultural (in-

[2]*Keller Common Carrier Application*, 83 M.C.C. 339, aff'd 94 M.C.C. 238.
[3]*Dulgerian Common Carrier Application*, 53 M.C.C. 385, 387.
[4]*Motor Carrier Safety Regulations — Exemptions*, 10 M.C.C. 533, 538.
[5]*Garrett Freightlines, Inc., Ext. — Yellowstone Nat'l Park*, 49 M.C.C. 631, 632.

cluding horticultural) commodities and products thereof, or in the transportation of supplies to his farm. Section 203(b) (5) exempts motor vehicles controlled and operated by a cooperative association as defined in the Agricultural Marketing Act, approved June 15, 1929, as amended, or by a federation of such cooperative associations, if such federation possesses no greater powers or purposes than cooperative associations. Section 203(b) (6) exempts motor vehicles used in carrying property consisting of ordinary livestock, fish (including shell fish), or agricultural (including horticultural) commodities (not including manufactured products thereof), if such motor vehicles are not used in carrying any other property, or passengers, for compensation.

Section 203(b) (6) has the following provisos:

(1) That the words "property, consisting of ordinary livestock, fish (including shell fish), or agricultural (including horticultural) commodities (not including manufactured products thereof)" as used in the provision shall include property shown as "exempt" in the "Commodity List" 'incorporated in ruling administrative Ruling No. 7, dated March 19, 1958, but shall not include property shown therein as "not exempt."

(2) That notwithstanding the preceding proviso the words "property consisting of ordinary livestock, fish (including shell fish), or agricultural (including horticultural commodities (not including manufactured products thereof)" shall not be deemed to include frozen fruits, frozen berries, frozen vegetables, cocoa beans, coffee beans, tea, bananas, or hemp, and wool imported from any foreign country, wool tops and noils, or wool waste (carded, spun, woven, or knitted), and shall be deemed to include cooked or uncooked (including breaded) fish or shell fish when frozen or fresh (but not including fish and shell fish which have been treated for preserving, such as canned, smoked, pickled, spiced, corned, or kippered products).

Section 203(b) (5) has several provisions which are intended to restrict the transportation activities of cooperatives. These are as follows:

(1) Any interstate transportation performed by a cooperative association or federation of cooperative associations for nonmembers who are neither farmers, cooperative associations, nor federations thereof for compensation, except transportation otherwise exempt under the provision, shall be limited to that which is incidental to its primary transportation operation and necessary for its effective performance and shall in no event exceed 15 per centum of its total interstate transportation services in any fiscal year, measured in terms of tonnage.

(2) For the purpose of the provision, notwithstanding any other provision of law, transportation performed for or on behalf of the United

States or any agency or instrumentality thereof shall be deemed to be transportation performed for a nonmember.

(3) Any cooperative association or federation which performs interstate transportation for nonmembers who are neither farmers, cooperative associations, nor federations thereof, except transportation otherwise exempt under the provision, shall notify the Commission of its intent to perform such transportation prior to the commencement thereof.

(4) In no event shall any cooperative association or federation which is required to give notice to the Commission transport interstate for compensation in any fiscal year of such association or federation a quantity of property for nonmembers which, measured in terms of tonnage, exceeds the total quantity of property transported interstate for itself and its members in such fiscal year.

For the purpose of policing the activities of cooperatives, the Commission is permitted under Section 220(g) to have access to and authority, under its order, to inspect, examine, and copy any and all accounts, books, records, memorandums, correspondence and other documents pertaining to motor vehicle transportation of a cooperative association or federation of cooperative associations which is required to give notice to the Commission pursuant to the provisions of Section 203(b) (5). The Commission, however, has no authority to prescribe the form of any accounts, records, or memorandums to be maintained by a cooperative association or federation of cooperative associations.

DISTRIBUTION OF NEWSPAPERS

The interstate transportation of newspapers exclusively is exempt from economic regulation under Section 203(b) (7). However, where a motor carrier transports non-exempt commodities in addition to newspapers, the operation is subject to regulation in its entirety.[6]

TRANSPORTATION OF PROPERTY BY MOTOR VEHICLE WHEN INCIDENTAL TO TRANSPORTATION BY AIRCRAFT

Section 203(b) (7a)[7] exempts from economic regulation transportation of persons or property by motor vehicle when incidental to transportation by aircraft.

[6]*Clune Common Carrier Application,* 6 M.C.C. 799; *Monroe Common Carrier Application,* 8 M.C.. 183.

[7]Section 203(b) (7a) became law by virtue of the enactment of Section 1107 (j) of the Civil Aeronautics Act of 1938. The Civil Aeronautics Act was repealed in its entirety by the Federal Aviation Act of 1958, although provisions of the former Act were reenacted by the latter. The reenactment did not include Section 1107(j) nor any similar provisions.

Interpretation of the Statute

The legislative history of Section 203(b) (7a) provides virtually no assistance in its interpretation. The first Commission decisions to discuss at any length the incidental to aircraft exemption were *Sky Freight Delivery Service, Inc., Common Car. Application*,[8] which involved the transportation of property, and *Teterboro Motor Transp., Inc., Com. Car. Application*,[9] an application for authority to transport passengers. In these two cases, exemption was applied similarly to both passenger and property carriers. It was found that in either case motor transportation, to fall within the scope of the exemption, must be of passengers or property having an immediate prior or subsequent movement by air; that the length of the motor movement is not the sole determining factor; and that, because of the different circumstances present at various airports, no definite territorial limit to the exemption could be prescribed. The rationale of the *Sky Freight* and *Teterboro* cases was followed in *Picknelly, Extension of Operations — Bradley Field*,[10] involving the transportation of passengers, and in two cases involving the transportation of property, *Golembiewski, Com. Car. Application*,[11] and *Peoples Exp. Co., Ext. — Airfreight*.[12] A complete re-evaluation of the nature and scope of the incidental to aircraft exemption as it applies to property carriers was made in *Kenny, Ext. — Airfreight*.[13] It was there found (p. 595) that the transportation to come within the exemption must be "confined to the transportation in bona fide collection, delivery, or transfer service of shipments which have been received from, or will be delivered to, an air carrier as part of a continuous movement under a through air bill of lading covering in addition to the line-haul movement by air, the collection, delivery, or transfer service performed by motor carrier." This decision has been followed many times since its promulgation in 1953 in disposing of applications of property carriers.[14]

The Regulations

By a proceeding instituted October 4, 1961, in No. MC-C-3437, on its own motion, the Commission promulgated regulations substantially

---

[8]47 M.C.C. 229.
[9]47 M.C.C. 247.
[10]47 M.C.C. 401.
[11]48 M.C.C. 1.
[12]48 M.C.C. 393.
[13]61 M.C.C. 587.
[14]See e.g., *Fischer, Com. Car. Application*, 83 M.C.C. 229.

codifying the *Kenny* interpretation of the exemptive provision. The effective date of the rules was originally set as June 24, 1964. The rules are discussed in *Motor Transp. of Property Incidental to Air.*[15] The right of the Commission to issue such definitive regulations, though not their substance, was upheld in *Air Dispatch, Inc. v. United States.*[16] The regulations were also sustained in a collateral attack in *Wycoff Company v. United States,*[17] which in effect constituted a review of the order in *Wycoff Co., Inc. Extension — Airfreight.*[18] Similar regulations relating to air passengers were adopted in *Motor Transp. of Passengers Incidental to Air.*[19]

By these regulations, now appearing in 49 CFR 210.40, the Commission has set up the following three tests or conditions which must be met to be within the exemption:

1. It is confined to the transportation of shipments in bona fide collection, delivery, or transfer service performed within the *terminal area* of the direct air carrier or airfreight forwarder (indirect air carrier) providing the line-haul transportation, which terminal area, if the line-haul transportation is provided by a carrier subject to economic regulation under the Federal Aviation Act, has been described in a tariff filed with and accepted by the Civil Aeronautics Board.

2. It is confined to the transportation of shipments which have been received from or will be delivered to a direct air carrier or airfreight forwarder, *as part of a continuous movement* which if provided by an air carrier subject to economic regulations under the Federal Aviation Act, shall be provided for in tariffs filed with and accepted by the Civil Aeronautics Board.

3. Shall be performed on a *through air bill of lading* covering in addition to the line-haul movement by air the collection, delivery, or transfer service performed by the motor carrier.

At the time of the *Kenny* report, the CAB used as a "rule of thumb" for determining the reasonableness of an air carrier's terminal area (with the exception of a limited number of major air traffic points) a radius of 25 miles from the cities or airports served by the air carrier. In 1964, the CAB adopted regulations codifying, in effect, the 25-mile limits. These regulations were published in 14 CFR 222. In recognition of the CAB codification of the 25-mile terminal area as a general rule, the Commission in 95 M.C.C. 71 adopted the regulations which provide that the territorial scope of operations conducted pursuant to Section 203(b) (7a) is generally coextensive with the limits of an air carrier's terminal area as described in its tariff filed with and accepted by the

[15]95 M.C.C. 71.
[16]237 F. Supp. 450, aff'd *per curiam* 381 U.S. 412.
[17]240 F. Supp. 304.
[18]89 M.C.C. 369.
[19]95 M.C.C. 526.

CAB. These regulations specifically were adopted based upon the assumption that the CAB would not hesitate to reject any publication which would result in any unreasonable enlargement of an air terminal area. Under *Motor Transp. of Property Incidental to Air*, 131 M.C.C. 87, the I.C.C. recognizes an air terminal zone within 35 miles of a municipality's corporate limits.

The regulations adopted by the CAB and this Commission in 1964 were the result of interagency collaboration seeking to minimize the potential conflict arising out of the CAB's interpretation of "services in connection with . . . air transportation" within the meaning of Section 403(a) of the Federal Aviation Act, and the Commission's construction of services "incidental to transportation by aircraft" as contemplated by the exemption embodied in Section 203(b) (7a). The ensuing regulatory scheme has been judicially characterized[20] as a "system, devised to avoid interagency conflict while preserving agency sovereignty, . . . [according] the Board the first judgment, which shall be given non-conclusive respect by I.C.C."

Under the regulations promulgated in 95 M.C.C. 71, the Commission may upon its own motion or upon petition filed by any interested person, determine whether the area within which the transportation of property by motor vehicle, in bona fide collection, delivery, or transfer service, must be performed, in order to come within the provisions of the regulations, should be individually determined with respect to any particular airport or city authorized to be served by a direct air carrier or airfreight forwarder holding authority from the CAB.

While Tests 1 and 2 in 49 CFR 210.40 are required to be "described in" or "provided for" in the tariffs, Test 3 requires that the transportation be performed on a specified bill of lading. The question arises as to the meaning of "through air bill of lading."

Although the Commission's regulations require that the transportation must be performed on a *through air bill of lading*, covering, in

---

[20]*Law Motor Freight, Inc. v. CAB*, 364 F. 2d 139, cert. den., 387 U.S. 905. In this case, petitioner, an I.C.C.-certificated line-haul carrier, sought review of a CAB order which authorized Emery Airfreight Corp., a freight forwarder, to file a tariff for air cargo pickup-and-delivery service on the 34-mile trip between Nashua, N.H., and Boston, Mass. In affirming the Board's finding that the proposed service was truly "pickup and delivery" and thus was "in connection with air transportation," the court held that the extension of the pickup-and-delivery service beyond the 25-mile zone constituted a valid exercise of the Board's rulemaking power and that, accordingly, no prior hearing was required. Later, an appellate court affirmed *per curiam* a CAB order authorizing Emery to file tariffs for pickup-and-delivery service between Flint, Mich., and the Detroit airports, a distance of about 50 miles. *National Motor Freight Traffic Association v. Civil Aeronautics Board*, 374 F. 2d 266, cert. denied 387 U.S. 905.

addition to the line-haul movement by air, the collection, delivery, or transfer service, the term "through air bill of lading" is not defined in either the regulations themselves, the Federal Aviation Act, the Interstate Commerce Act, or the Bills of Lading Act. The term is employed in Section 20(11) of the I.C. Act, which is a comprehensive statutory scheme dealing with carrier liability for loss and damage. Section 15(8) establishes certain duties with respect to through routes and joint rates and issuance and observance of through bills of lading.

The absence from the Federal Aviation Act, of a provision such as Section 20(11) of the I.C. Act and the attendant problems in the field of common carrier liability is a statutory hiatus. Thus, there are no standards or guides to follow with respect to air common carrier liability. Because of the absence of standards or guides under the Federal Aviation Act, the Commission has followed the practice of employing terminology of special meaning under the Interstate Commerce Act in attempting to give some meaning to *through air bill of lading* when dealing with Section 203(b) (7a).

In many cases, prior to the issuance of its regulations, the Commission considered the nature of the bill of lading as one of the numerous facts considered in determining whether the transportation was "incidental to transportation by aircraft." Initially, questions of the scope of the Section 203(b) (7a) exemption, involved the geographical scope of the permissible area of exemption. The question of the air bill of lading was originally a determinative in aiding the Commission to distinguish between local collection and delivery service and line-haul transportation. Thus, in the leading *Kenny* case[21] (prior to the regulations), it was said in part:

> Motor transportation is "incidental" to transportation by air when that motor transportation is limited to a bona fide collection, delivery, or transfer service within a reasonable terminal area of the air carrier. Conversely stated, such motor transportation is not "incidental" to transportation by air when it is transportation having the character of a connecting-carrier line-haul service. Our past experience in proceedings such as this convinces us that the *modus operandi* of air carriers is sufficiently different from that of land carriers as to justify special consideration in the matter of terminal area limits which may or may not be somewhat larger than those of land carriers. . . .
>
> A more feasible and reasonable solution and one which, in our opinion, will solve or eliminate any now foreseeable problems, is to define the exempt motor transportation of property under this statutory exemption as that confined to the transportation in bona fide collection, delivery

---

[21]*Kenny Extension — Airfreight*, 61 M.C.C. 587, 595-96.

or transfer service of shipments which have been received from, or will be delivered to, an air carrier as part of a continuous movement *under a through air bill of lading covering in addition to the line-haul movement by air the collection, delivery, or transfer service performed by motor carrier.* This test, with its provision for a through air bill of lading and continuous movement from the pickup point to the point of delivery, would be self-limiting. Such a rule would in no way be inconsistent with the holding out of collection and delivery service by the air carriers within their established terminal area limits, within which such services are performed by motor carriers for the air carriers under air billing. . . . (Emphasis supplied.)

In *Panther Cartage Co. Extension — Airfreight,*[22] the Commission made clear that the areas or distances within which motor transportation of property for compensation is "incidental-to-air" within the meaning of Section 203(b) (7a), is not beyond the terminal area of an air carrier. To fall within the exemption, motor carrier movements must be confined to the terminal area of either the direct air carrier or airfreight forwarder (indirect air carrier).[23] On service to and from points beyond an air terminal area, a permit is necessary.[24]

In the *Panther Cartage* case, the Commission commented on the *Kenny* case as follows:

> . . . In *Kenny Extension — Airfreight*, 61 M.C.C. 587, division 5 found that motor transportation is incidental to transportation by aircraft when the motor transportation is limited to a bona fide collection, delivery, or transfer service within a reasonable terminal area of the air carrier as distinguished from a connecting-carrier line-haul service, and that a reasonable terminal area of the air carrier was found to be that established by the air carriers in their tariffs filed with the CAB. . . .

> . . . The answer to the second question is found in the reasoning in the *Kenny* case. This is to say, if the motor operations are confined solely to collection, transfer, delivery services between the terminal area points and the airport city named in the airfreight forwarder's tariff such operations will be considered to be legitimate collection, delivery, and transfer services, *if such pick up and delivery points are not beyond the limits of the terminal area established by the air carrier which performs the air portion of the line-haul transportation.* Conversely, if the motor operations extend beyond the limits of the terminal area established by the air carrier which performs the air portion of the line-haul transportation, such operations will be considered to be line-haul motor operations even though

---

[22]88 M.C.C. 37. See also *AB&W Transit Co. Ext.*, 88 M.C.C. 175; *Hatom*, 91 M.C.C. 725; *Kenny* 61 M.C.C. 587.
[23]*Panther Cartage Co. Extension — Airfreight, supra.*
[24]Ibid. See also *Nickerson Common Carrier Application*, 88 M.C.C. 186; *Special Delivery, Inc., Extension — Bradley Air Field*, 88 M.C.C. 275; *Air Cargo Terminal, Inc., Ext. — San Bernardino, Calif.*, 88 M.C.C. 468.

conducted to points named in the airfreight forwarder's tariff. . . . (Emphasis supplied

Another expression on whether transportation is being performed on a *through air bill of lading* is found in *Colorado Cartage Co., Inc. v. Murphy*,[25] where a finding was made that the defendant was transporting traffic moving in interstate or foreign commerce from Golden, Colo., to Stapleton International Airport, Denver, Colo., in violation of Section 206(a) of the I.C. Act. In the operations conducted, when tendered a shipment by the shipper at Golden the defendant received an air bill of lading for this shipment. The defendant transported the shipment, together with the air bill of lading, to the airport. Defendant had no bill of lading of his own, but marked the charges, which were commensurate with those set forth in the tariff filed by the air carrier with the CAB, on the air bill of lading as "charges advanced," and collected his share of the charges from the air carrier. The question raised was whether the above described operation was within the exemption of Section 203(b)(7a) of the Act. The Commision said (at pp. 749-50):

> We do not doubt that the complained of operations are confined to pickup service within the terminal area of an air carriers, that the terminal area has been accepted by the Civil Aeronautics Board, and that the operation is confined to shipments which will be delivered to an air carrier as part of a continuous movement provided for in tariffs filed with and accepted by the Civil Aeronautics Board.
>
> The issue then is whether the operation is performed on a through air bill of lading covering in addition to the line-haul movement by air, the collection service performed by defendant. We conclude it is not. The fact that the defendant has no bill of lading and marks his transportation charge on the air bill of lading does not mean that the shipment is moving on an air bill. On the contrary, there is no bill of lading covering defendant's operation since the air bill is only executed when the air carrier receives physical custody of the shipment. Thus, the air bill of lading does not cover the collection service of defendant and it is not transportation incidental to aircraft within the meaning of Section 203(b) (7a). *Con-Ov-Airfreight Service, Inc., Com. Car. Applic.*, 92 M.C.C. 526; and *Fisher-Common-Carrier Application*, 83 M.C.C. 229. We conclude, therefore, that defendant has been shown to have transported shipments from Golden to Stapleton Airport without appropriate authority

In determining the applications of motor carriers transporting airline passengers, the Commission follows the rather general guides of the *Teterboro* case. Unlike the transportation of property, which, to come within the incidental to aircraft exemption, must be performed

---

[25]100 M.C.C. 745.

under a through air line bill of lading and within the air carrier's terminal area, passenger transportation has been found to be exempt even though it was not arranged or paid for by the air carrier and is not provided under a through ticket embracing the line-haul air movement in addition to the motor movement. The Commission has, however, consistently found that the transportation to be incidental to transportation by aircraft may not involve a motor movement of too great a distance. In the *Picknelly* case the Commission found that the effect of the exemption on passenger operations may extend 13 miles; and in the *Teterboro* case and in *Hribar & Vickerstaff, Common Carrier Application*[26] the Commission found that the exemption would cover motor operations performed up to 25 miles from the airport. On the other hand, the exemption was found not to extend to movements up to 45 miles in *Di Lauro, Common Carrier Application;*[27] up to 75 miles in *Woodrum Field Airport, Lim. Service, Inc., Com. Car. Application;*[28] and up to 100 miles in *Airports City Limousine Service, Inc., Com. Car. Applic.*[29]

The transportation of either passengers or property between airports in emergencies, due to bad weather, for example has always been treated differently from the day to day transportation to or from airports. Emergency transportation was found to come within the scope of Section 203(b) (7a) exemption in *Graff, Common Carrier Applic.*[30] This finding was reaffirmed in the *Woodrum Field* case, and, with respect to the transportation of property, in *Motor Transp. of Property Incidental to Air,*[31] and, with respect to the transportation of passengers, in *Motor Transp. of Passengers Incidental to Air.*[32] In such circumstances, the emergency transportation is arranged and paid for by the carrier which finds itself in the position of having to move passengers by surface transportation because its planes, for some reason, cannot fly. The Commission has found in this type of cases that the distance of the motor movement is not of any particular significance in making a determination as to whether the application comes within the scope of the incidental to air exemption.

Examination of the decisions of the Commission and the courts discloses that the transportation of passengers having an immediately or subsequent movement by air by motor vehicle between an airport

[26]63 M.C.C. 822.
[27]84 M.C.C. 501.
[28]82 M.C.C. 647.
[29]68 M.C.C. 293.
[30]48 M.C.C. 310.
[31]95 M.C.C. 71. See *Fischer,* 83 M.C.C. 229, 234.
[32]95 M.C.C. 526.

and another point in the same state is not regarded as interstate commerce. In the cases where the issue has been specifically raised and dealt with (as distinguished from others in which authority may have been granted upon the assumption that interstate transportation was involved), the Commission has consistently held that regardless of the intentions of any passengers to continue or complete an interstate journey, the carrier of passengers operating wholly within a state, selling no through tickets, and having no common arrangements with connecting out-of-state carriers, is not engaged in interstate or foreign commerce.[33] This view is also supported by court decisions. The Supreme Court has held one-state operations to be intrastate in cases involving the transportation of passengers by taxi-cabs between their homes or hotels and the railroad station;[34] transportation of passengers by railroad between two rail points in the same State;[35] and transportation of passengers by taxicabs between a ferry landing and a hotel in the same State.[36] In all of the cases, the passengers' intentions to continue or complete an interstate journey were not deemed to be controlling.

Airport bus service which did not cross state lines was found to be intrastate in *Cederblade v. Parmalee Transp. Co.*[37] and airport limousine service was similarly classified in *Mateo v. Auto Rental Company.*[38]

Although a different result was reached in an earlier case, *Airlines Transp. v. Tobin,*[39] the court was no doubt influenced by the extraordinary degree of control which the airline company exercised over the motor operations. In that case, the limousine operator was an independent contractor by the terms of its agreement with the airline company, but under the same agreement the airline company controlled the limousine operation to the point of reserving the right to schedule the vehicles, discipline the drivers, and specify the uniform worn by the drivers. More than half the airline passengers used the limousine service with arrangements frequently made for them by airline personnel. The rate charge by the limousine operator could not be altered without the consent of the airline company.

---

[33]*Moore Service, Inc., Ext. — Migrant Workers*, 89 M.C.C. 180, 181; *Virginia Stage Lines, Inc. — Purchase — Southern Passengers*, 15 M.C.C. 519; *Spokane, Portland & Seattle Transp. Co., Com. Car. Applic.*, 26 M.C.C. 260; *Red Star Lines, Inc., Extension of Operations*, 3 M.C.C. 313, 314.
[34]*United States v. Yellow Cab Co.*, 332 U.S. 218.
[35]*New York Central R. R. Co. v. Mohney*, 252 U.S. 152.
[36]*Pennsylvania R. Co. v. Knight*, 192 U.S. 21.
[37]94 F. Supp. 965.
[38]240 F. 2d 831.
[39]198 F. 2d 249.

The Commission followed these principles in *Motor Transp. of Passengers Incidental to Air*,[40] stating (p. 537):

> We find no overriding necessity, rooted in the public interest, to claim the involved transportation as interstate commerce. We are already heavily burdened enough with regulatory responsibilities without casting about to expend our jurisdiction that specially required by law.

COMMERCIAL ZONES

The effect of Section 203(b) (8) is to exempt from economic regulation local motor transportation in interstate or foreign commerce, within commercial zones. An exception to the exemption is provided in Section 203(b) (8) when such transportation is under a common control, management, or arrangement for a continuous carriage or shipment to or from a point without such municipality, municipalities, or zone.

The term "commercial zone" is not defined in the I.C. Act. The function of determining the limits of commercial zones of municipalities was left to the Commission. This task began in 1944 in Ex Parte No. MC-37, *Commercial Zones and Terminal Areas*. The proceeding was decided in 1946 and reported in 46 M.C.C. 665. Since the original report in 1946, there have been numerous supplemental reports and subs defining specific commercial zones.

The purpose of the proceeding in Ex Parte No. MC-37 was not to create or establish any commercial zone, but simply to determine the limits of zones which already were in existence. As the Commission said, at page 672 of its report, the "existence of such zones is an economic fact."

A population-mileage formula was established in Ex Parte No. MC-37. Under the formula, except for those zones which had been individually considered and specifically defined, the zone contemplated by Section 203(b)(8) adjacent to and commercially a part of each municipality in the United States was said to consist of, and include, the following:

(a) The municipality itself;

(b) All municipalities which are contiguous to the base municipality;

(c) All other municipalities within the United States and all unincorporated areas which are adjacent to the base municipality as follows:

[40] 95 M.C.C. 526.

(1) When the base municipality has a population less than 2,500, all unincorporated areas within two miles of its corporate limits and all of any other municipality any part of which is within two miles of the corporate limits of the base municipality,

(2) When the base municipality has a population of 2,500 but less than 25,000, all incorporated areas within 3 miles of its corporate limits and all of any other municipality any part of which is within 3 miles of the corporate limits of the base municipality,

(3) When the base municipality has a population of 25,000 but less than 100,000, all unincorporated areas within 4 miles of its corporate limits and all of any other municipality any part of which is within 4 miles of the corporate limits of the base municipality, and

(4) When the base municipality has a population of 100,000 or more, all unincorporated areas within 5 miles of its corporate limits and all of any other municipality any part of which is within 5 miles of the corporate limits of the base municipality; and

(d) All municipalities wholly surrounded, or so surrounded except for a water boundary, by the base municipality, by any municipality contiguous thereto, or by any municipality adjacent thereto which is included in the commercial zone of such base municipality under the population-mileage formula.

In the application of the formula:

(a) Air-line distances or mileages about corporate limits of municipalities were used; and

(b) The population of any municipality was deemed to be shown for that municipality in the last census.

The following definitions were used for purposes of applying the formula:

(a) "Municipality" means any city, town, village, or borough which has been created by special legislative act or which has been otherwise, individually incorporated or chartered pursuant to general State laws, or which is recognized as such, under the Constitution or by the laws of the State in which located, and which has a local government. It does not include a town of the township or New England type.

(b) "Contiguous municipalities" means municipalities, which have at some point a common municipal or corporate boundary.

(c) "Unincorporated area" means any area not within the corporate or municipal boundaries of any municipality.

Recognizing that changes have occurred in the location of business and industrial activity since the development of existing commercial zone regulations in the mid-1940's, the Commission, on its own motion, instituted a rulemaking proceeding in Ex Parte No. MC-37 (Sub-No. 26), *Commercial Zones and Terminal Areas*[41] to scrutinize the population-mileage formula in light of changed demographic and industrial location patterns. This resulted in the following expansion of the population-mileage formula:

(1) When the base municipality has a population less than 2,500 all unincorporated areas within 3 miles of its corporate limits and all of any other municipality any part of which is within 3 miles of the corporate limits of the base municipality.

(2) When the base municipality has a population of 2,500 but less than 25,000 all unincorporated areas within 4 miles of its corporate limits and all of any other municipality any part of which is within 4 miles of the corporate limits of the base municipality.

(3) When the base municipality has a population of 25,000 but less than 100,000 all unincorporated areas within 6 miles of its corporate limits and all of any other municipality any part of which is within 6 miles of the corporate limits of the base municipality.

(4) When the base municipality has a population of 100,000 but less than 200,000 all unincorporated areas within 8 miles of its corporate limits and all of any other municipality any part of which is within 8 miles of the corporate limits of the base municipality.

(5) When the base municipality has a population of 200,000 but less than 500,000 all unincorporated areas within 10 miles of its corporate limits and all of any other municipality any part of which is within 10 miles of the corporate limits of the base municipality.

(6) When the base municipality has a population of 500,000 but less than 1 million, all unincorporated areas within 15 miles of its corporate limits and all of any other municipality any part of which is within 15 miles of the corporate limits of the base municipality.

(7) When the base municipality has a population of 1 million or more, all unincorporated areas within 20 miles of its corporate limits and all of any other municipality any part of which is within 20 miles of the corporate limits and all of any other municipality any part of which is within 20 miles of the corporate limits of the base municipality.

The Commission in Ex Parte No. MC-37 (Sub-No. 26) discussed certain fundamental principles to establish a suitable frame-work for its decision. In its discussion, the Commission said (Sheets 6-17):

Section 203(b) (8) established an exemption to Federal economic regulation of interstate transportation of passengers or property . . .

[41]Report of the Commission served December 30, 1976.

This statutory section exempts three types of local movements in urban areas: (1) that which is wholly within a municipality, (2) that which is between contiguous municipalities, and (3) that which is within a zone adjacent to and commercially a part of the base municipality. As defined by this Commission, the term "municipality" refers to a city, town, village, or borough which has been created by special legislative act, or otherwise individually incorporated or chartered pursuant to general laws, or which is recognized as such under the constitution or by the laws of the State in which located, and which has a local government.[42] *Commercial Zones and Terminal Areas*, 46 M.C.C. 665, 679 (1946). "Contiguous municipalities" are those which at some place have a common border, *Commercial Zones*, 46 M.C.C. at 681. It is apparent that once these terms are defined the geographic extent of the 203(b) (8) exemption for the first two types of local operation — within a municipality and between contiguous municipalities — is delimited. Our focus in this proceeding, however, is on the proper interpretation of the third type of exempt local operation, i.e., that which is "within a zone adjacent to and commercially a part of" the base municipality, and a simple definition of certain static terms will not suffice. Initially, this Commission directed its efforts toward defining the limits of commercial zones at particular municipalities, usually large population centers near or straddling State lines or near ports.[43] By the mid-1940's, however, it became apparent that the public interest would be better served if the Commission departed from this case-by-case approach and channeled its energies toward the development of a general method of establishing commercial zone limits at all cities. The considerations which led to this conclusion were articulated in the first report in Ex Parte No. MC-37, the rulemaking instituted in 1944 to consider this matter:

> Heretofore each determination of a commercial zone has been based on information as to particular facts affecting the extent of that commercial zone . . . . We do not now question the advantages inherent in this piecemeal approach to the problem but, carried to its logical extreme, it implies a special proceeding for the definition of the zone adjacent to, and commercially a part of, every municipality in the United States, and innumerable proceedings for the determination of the terminal areas of each carrier at each point served by it. Obviously, such a course would be prohibitively burdensome and wholly impracticable. Assuming that it could be accomplished the results would be

[42]This definition of "municipality" does not include unincorporated urban communities, *Commercial Zones*, 46 M.C.C. at 681, or New England-type towns, *Adams Trucking, Inc. — Revocation of Certificates*, 118 M.C.C. 567, 571-573 (1973) and 49 CFR 1048.100(a).

[43]See, *St. Louis, Mo.-East St. Louis, Ill., Commercial Zone*, 1 M.C.C. 665 (1937) and 2 M.C.C. 285 (1937); *New York, N.Y., Commercial Zone*, I M.C.C. 665 (1937); *Chicago, Ill., Commercial Zone*, 1 M.C.C. 673 (1937); *Los Angeles, Calif., Commercial Zone*, 3 M.C.C. 248 (1937); *Washington, D. C., Commercial Zone* 3 M.C.C. 243 (1937); *Philadelphia, Pa., Commercial Zone*, 17 M.C.C. 533 (1939); *Cincinnati, Ohio, Commercial Zone*, 26 M.C.C. 49 (1940); *Kansas City, Mo.,-Kansas City, Kans., Commercial Zone*, 31 M.C.C. 5 (1941); *Boston, Mass., Commercial Zone*, 31 M.C.C. 405 (1941); *Davenport-Rock Island and Moline Commercial Zone*, 41 M.C.C. 557 (1943).

ponderous, variable, and less desirable in important aspects than those produced by a more general approach. Actually, it is unlikely that any such program of individual proceedings could be carried beyond the point of determining the commercial zones of comparatively few municipalities, or the terminal areas of more than a few carriers at certain points, as special need arose. This is not enough. *Commercial Zones,* 46 M.C.C. at 670-671.

Noting that at most municipalities urban development spilled over the corporate limits and into the suburbs, former Division 5 stated that commercial zone bounds are established by various factors, including "trade practices, the uses to which the area is put, and geographical and political considerations." *Commercial Zones,* 46 M.C.C. at 672. After scrutinizing various alternative methods for defining commercial zones by general guidelines, it was determined that urban development normally radiates in all directions from the center city, and, consequently, commercial zones are "susceptible of reasonably accurate definition by the delineation of lines varying distances beyond the corporate limits, the distance used in any particular instance being dependent upon the population of the base municipality." *Commercial Zones,* 46 M.C.C. at 685. This rationale formed the basis for utilizing a population-mileage formula approach to defining commercial zones, and the following formula was adopted and remains unchanged to this time:

(1) When the base municipality has a population less than 2,500 all unincorporated areas within 2 miles of its corporate limits and all of any other municipality any part of which is within 2 miles of the corporate limits of the base municipality,

(2) When the base municipality has a population of 2,500 but less than 25,000, all unincorporated areas within 3 miles of its corporate limits and all of any other municipality any part of which is within 3 miles of the corporate limits of the base municipality,

(3) When the base municipality has a population of 25,000 but less than 100,000, all unincorporated areas within 4 miles of its corporate limits and all of any other municipality any part of which is within 4 miles of the corporate limits of the base municipality, and

(4) When the base municipality has a population of 100,000 or more, all unincorporated areas within 5 miles of its corporate limits and all of any other municipality any part of which is within 5 miles of the corporate limits of the base municipality.

It must be pointed out that the section 203(b) (8) exemption does not apply to local cartage operations performed under common control, management, or arrangement for the continuous carriage of a shipment to or from a point outside the limits of a particular municipality or its commercial zone. In other words, the "continuous carriage" exception to section 203(b) (8) provides that when the local transportation is part of or incidental to a linehaul service, the partial exemption of section 203(b) (8) is withheld. See, *Adams Cartage Limited Com. Car. Applic.,* 121 M.C.C. 115, 122 (1975), and *Commercial Zones,* 54 M.C.C. at 49.

The import of this observation is that our interpretation of the geographic scope of the exemption provided by section 203(b) (8), standing alone, has a real economic impact, in terms of our regulation, only at cities near or straddling State lines. At other cities, purely local operations—not part of a "continuous carriage" beyond the commercial zone — achieve their exempt status as intrastate movements without reference to section 203(b) (8). The geographic limits of commercial zones attain widespread economic significance primarily because they are used in the administration and implementation of other sections of the Act. More specifically, commercial zone limits are used (1) in determining the size of motor carrier and freight forwarder terminal areas, as used in section 202(c), and (2) in the construction of operating authorities issued pursuant to sections 207 and 209 of the Act.

Section 202(c), which was added by amendments to the Act in 1940 and 1942, speaks of "terminal areas" and complements the commercial zone exemption by excluding from direct economic regulation the transfer, collection, and delivery performed within the terminal areas of linehaul carriers in connection with linehaul services. The 202(c) exemption allows local cartage operators to contract with or act as agents for regulated linehaul common carriers — rail, express, motor, water, or freight forwarder — in incidental transfer, collection, and delivery service within terminal areas. Section 202(c) does not permit, however, the local carrier to participate in a through rate or to perform a through service with the linehaul carrier. More specifically, the exact dictates of section 202(c) are as follows:

> Notwithstanding any provision of this section or of section 203, the provisions of section 204 relative to qualifications and maximum hours of service of employees and safety of operation and equipment, shall not apply —
>
> (1) to transportation by motor vehicle by a carrier by railroad subject to part I, or by a water carrier subject to part III, or by a freight forwarder subject to part IV, incidental to transportation or service subject to such parts, in the performance within terminal areas of transfer, collection, or delivery services; but such transportation shall be considered to be and shall be regulated as transportation subject to part I when performed by such carrier by railroad, as transportation subject to part III when performed by such water carrier, and as transportation or service subject to part IV when performed by such freight forwarder;
>
> (2) to transportation by motor vehicle by any person (whether as agent or under a contractual arrangement) for a common carrier by railroad subject to part I, an express company subject to part I, a motor carrier subject to this part, a water carrier subject to part III, or a freight forwarder subject to part IV, in the performance within terminal areas of transfer, collection, or delivery service; but such transportation shall be considered to be performed by such carrier, express company, or freight forwarder as part of, and shall be regulated in the same manner as, the transportation by railroad, express, motor vehicle, or water, or the freight forwarder transportation or service, to which such services are incidental.

In the Sixth Supplemental Report to Ex Parte No. MC-37 former Division 5 considered the question of the proper demarcation of motor carriers' and freight forwarders' terminal areas.[44] Reasoning that "[i]f commercial zone limits mark the limits of industrial, business, or residential community, then they also mark the limits of the area which can be served in bona fide collection and delivery service and beyond which any service takes on the character of a line-haul or inter-community service," the Division adopted a rule of coextensive limits. *Commercial Zones,* 54 M.C.C. at 63 and 74. Thus it was found that the terminal area of a motor carrier or freight forwarder at a particular municipality is coextensive with the limits of the commercial zone of that municipality, although a carrier's or forwarder's terminal area may not extend beyond the territorial limits of the particular motor carrier's or freight forwarder's operating authority. See 49 CFR 1049.1.

The proper construction of operating authorities issued pursuant to sections 207 and 209 of the Act was also considered in the Sixth Supplemental Report. It was determined that a certificate or permit authorizing service at a particular municipality should be construed as conferring authority to serve all points and places which are within the commercial zone of that municipality. Of course, any territorial limitations or restrictions contained in the certificate or permit necessarily circumscribe the extent of authorized operations. See, *Commercial Zones,* 54 M.C.C. at 108 and 49 CFR 1041.20.

A few background comments concerning the historical treatment of transportation in and about unincorporated communities are appropriate at this juncture. Unincorporated communities[45] are not included within our definition of the term "municipality" as used in section 203(b) (8), and, consequently, they do not have "commercial zones." Nevertheless, in the original report in Ex Parte No. MC-37 it was stated that "[w]ithin and about each of these communities, purely local transportation of the type intended to be partially exempted from regulation by section 203(b) (8) is performed." *Commercial Zones,* 46 M.C.C. at 680. The original report left for possible future consideration the establishment of "commercial zone" limits at unincorporated communities, 46 M.C.C. at 681. As yet, this issue has not been raised again and remains untreated. Subsequent reports, however, have addressed the questions of (1) how to construe operating rights which authorize service at an unincorporated community,

---

[44]Originally, the findings of the Sixth Supplemental Report applied to all motor carriers, no distinction being made between carriers of property and carriers of passengers. In a subsequent decision, those findings were deemed inapplicable to the construction of certificates or permits issued to motor carriers of passengers or to the terminal areas of motor carriers of passengers, *Salem Transp. Co., Inc., Ext. — Pass. Vehicles,* 121 M.C.C. 331, 339 (1975) and *Commercial Zones and Terminal Areas,* 54 M.C.C. 615, 619-621 (1952).

[45]Unincorporated communities comprise those settlements or aggregations of homes or businesses which, although unincorporated, and without local governments or definite corporate limits, nevertheless, are similar from a transportation standpoint, to the cities, towns, villages, and boroughs, which are contemplated by the term "municipalities." *Commercial Zones and Terminal Areas,* 66 M.C.C. 541, 542 (1956).

and (2) how to determine terminal area limits for motor carriers and freight forwarders at an unincorporated community. See, *Commercial Zones*, 48 M.C.C. at 434-436 and 54 M.C.C. at 101-102. The rule that has emerged with respect to operating authority is that a certificate or permit authorizing service at a particular unincorporated community having a post office of the same name carries with it implied authority to serve all points within a described radius measured from said post office. This implied authority extends to service at any municipality any part of which is within the appropriate radius. The length of the radius is determined by reference to a population-mileage formula.[46] Where the unincorporated community has no post office of the same name, the service limits are measured from the generally recognized business center of the community. *Commercial Zones*, 54 M.C.C. at 109-110 and *Associated Truck Lines, Inc. v. Wolverine Exp.*, 123 M.C.C. 206, 224 (1975). Furthermore, terminal area limits for motor carriers and freight forwarders at unincorporated communities coincide with the implied service limits of their operating authorities and are described by reference to the same population-mileage formula, *Commercial Zones* 54 M.C.C. at 109 and 49 CFR 1049.2.

* * *

In the Interim Report in this proceeding, we noted that an appeal was pending with respect to our rulemaking dealing specifically with freight forwarder terminal areas, *Scope of Freight Forwarder Terminals*, 343 I.C.C. 565 (1973) (hereinafter referred to as *Forwarder Terminal Areas*). In that rulemaking, designated Ex Parte No. 266 (Sub-No. 1), we determined that the evidence of record relating to increased suburban economic activity did not justify a finding that the limits of "the single community" have expanded to encompass these outlying areas and that, consequently, we were constrained from expanding the geographic limits of the freight forwarder terminal area exemption. On February 27, 1976, the three-judge panel reviewing the rulemaking rendered a judgment which set aside our report and order in Ex Parte No. MC-266 (Sub No. 1) and remanded the proceeding to the Commission for further proceedings consistent with the court's decision. See *Freight Forwarders Institute v. United States*, 409 F. Supp. 693 (N.D. Ill. 1976). The opinion of the Court contains a thorough analysis of the deficiencies it perceived in our treatment of the freight forwarder terminal area exemption. Since the views of the court are of

[46]This formula is codified at 49 CFR 1041.22, which provides that " a certificate or permit issued to a motor carrier of property pursuant to the provisions of Part II of the Interstate Commerce Act (49 U.S.C. 301 et seq.) or to any freight forwarder under Part IV of the act (49 U.S.C. 1001 et seq.) authorizing service at a particular unincorporated community having a post office of the same name shall be construed as authorizing service at all points which are within the United States and not beyond the territorial limits, if any, fixed in such certificate or permit on the authority granted, as follows: (a) All points within 2 1/2 miles of the post office in such unincorporated community if it has a population of less than 2,500, within 4 miles if it has a population of 2,500 but less than 25,000; and within 5 1/2 miles if it has a population of 25,000 or more, (b) at all points in any municipality any part of which is within the limits described in (a) of this section and (c) at points in any municipality wholly surrounded, or so surrounded except for a water boundary by any municipality included under the terms of paragraph (b) of this section."

particular significance in the disposition of the issues now before us, a brief synopsis of the Court's reasoning is appropriate to set the stage for our evaluation of the evidentiary record and the proper implementation of the relevant sections of the Act.[47]

Since it was cognizant of the fact that the proper scope of freight forwarder terminal areas is being reexamined in the instant proceeding, the Court could have awaited the ultimate outcome of Ex Parte No. MC-37 (Sub-No. 26) before issuing a decision on the merits in the hope that our actions would dissipate the controversy before it. Nevertheless it felt compelled to address the merits of the situation for the following overriding reasons: to avoid the recurrence of the issues brought before the Court, to preclude the possibility that those issues would repeatedly escape proper judicial review, and to provide some guidance for this Commission in our handling of the issues presented by Ex Parte No. MC-37 (Sub-No. 26). *Freight Forwarders Institute v. United States*, 409 F. Supp. at 700. The Court concluded that the Commission specifically erred by adhering to a "statutory concept" of terminal areas coextensive with the limits of the single homogeneous community and by excluding factors relating to public need from a determination of the proper geographic scope of the terminal area exemption.

The Court noted that Congress did not specifically define "terminal area" in section 202(c) of the Act and surmised that it was Congress' intention that the Commission interpret, through an ongoing exercise of its expertise, the dynamic parameters of the exemption according to the prevailing conditions in the transportation market. This analysis by the Commission should not be constricted by concepts such as single community homogeneity, which is becoming rapidly irrelevant, but should consider industrial relocation to the suburbs and the changes in transportation patterns caused by modern expressways. The Court did not reject, however, the notions that the areas included within a terminal area should have a logical geographic relationship to each other and that the 202(c) exemption is essentially meant to cover local movements of traffic. Finally, the Court held that the National Transportation Policy requires the Commission to evaluate the proper limits of terminal areas in light of the needs of the general public, the needs of shippers, and the impact they have on affected carriers.

Interpretative Cases

Determination of commercial zone limits involves a situation existing as an economic fact as distinguished from the effect on individual parties or on adequacy or inadequacy of existing transportation services; the Commission does not "create" or "establish" a commercial zone — rather,

---

[47]By order served May 11, 1976, the Commission discontinued the Ex Parte No. 266 (Sub-No. 1) proceeding and stated that the matters raised by the reviewing Court would be dealt with in Ex Parte No. MC-37 (Sub-No. 26).

the zone surrounding a municipality within which motor transportation of the kind contemplated by Section 203(b) (8) is conducted already exists as a matter of trade practice, the uses to which the area is put, and physical and geographical considerations; and the Commission's function is to determine the limits of that zone.[48]

"Unincorporated urban community" means those settlements or aggregations of homes and business which, although unincorporated and without local governments or definite corporate limits, are similar, from a transportation standpoint, to the cities, towns, villages, and boroughs contemplated by the term "municipalities." However, every cluster of dwellings, residential or industrial settlement, collection of farms, housing project, or real-estate development is not within the meaning of "unincorporated community."[49]

In *Great Northern Ry. Co. — Control — Superior & D. Transfer*,[50] the Commission said that as Duluth and Superior are contiguous cities, part of their natural boundary being the Bay of St. Louis, with direct communication between them by motor vehicle via bridges and city streets, and their commercial zones overlap, the acquired carrier's transportation services between those cities for wholesale and retail merchants and their customers and for persons shipping their household effects were within the exemption of Section 203(b) (8) so long as there was no common arrangement for movement of such traffic to or from points beyond.

"The Commission's determination in *Commercial Zones and Terminal Areas*[51] that the term "municipality," as used in Section 203(b) (8) did not include towns or townships of the New England type, was upheld in *Palmer Lines, Inc. v. United States*.[52] The court said that the Commission's consistent construction of authority to serve a specifically named point in New England, which is the name of both a "town" and a community within that town, as conferring the right to serve all points in that township, but also as a territorially limited authority conferring no right to serve points beyond the township boundary under the commercial zone exemption, was neither clearly wrong nor arbitrary, and its finding must be upheld.

---

[48]*Commercial Zones and Terminal Areas (Lake Charles, La.)*, 83 M.C.C. 668, 671; *Commercial Zones and Terminal Areas (Baltimore, Md.)*, 83 M.C.C. 492, 495; *Washington, D. C. Commercial Zone*, 83 M.C.C. 471, 477-8, 83 M.C.C. 541.
[49]*Germann Bros. Motor Transp., Inc. v. Bargo*, 78 M.C.C. 791, 795-6. See also *Missouri-Arkansas Transp. Co. Extension*, 82 M.C.C. 311, 315.
[50]85 M.C.C. 401, 406.
[51]46 M.C.C. 665.
[52]179 F. Supp. 629.

In the earliest commercial zone proceeding, *St. Louis, Mo. — East St. Louis, Ill., Commercial Zones,*[53] the Commission said, "The zone adjacent to and commercially a part of a municipality and of contiguous municipalities will for convenience be referred to herein as the commercial zone." In *New York, N. Y., Commercial Zone,*[54] the Commission said, "Commercial zones defined under Section 203(b) (8) may include only those areas which are commercially a part of municipalities and contiguous municipalities and are adjacent thereto. By restricting the commercial zones to areas which are adjacent to municipalities and contiguous municipalities, it is presumed that Congress intended to restrict such zones to those areas in which transportation by motor vehicle is in the nature of an intraterminal movement." In *Commercial Zones and Terminal Areas,*[55] the Commission said, "The indicated conclusion is that any general definition of commercial zone boundaries should include all contiguous municipalities, but should make the inclusion of others depend upon their proximity to, and commercial unity with, the base municipality."

One of the earliest cases decided in regard to operations involving municipalities located on international boundaries was *Western Freight Lines Common Carrier Application.*[56] This case, in which applicant requested a determination of its status under Section 203(b) (8), involved the transportation of commodities generally, in foreign commerce between Detroit and the international boundary between the United States and Canada. The Commission said that "the record shows that, while applicant's operations in the United States are to be confined to the municipality of Detroit, freight carried by it will be under a common control, management, or arrangement for continuous carriage to or from points without the municipality of Detroit. The transportation in which applicant purposes to engage, therefore, does not fall within the exemption provided in Section 203(b) (8) of the act, and the application should be dismissed."[57] In *Ed Goyeau Contract Carrier Application,*[58] the Commission held that the evidence did not establish that the trans-

---

[53] 1 M.C.C. 656.
[54] 1 M.C. 665.
[55] 46 M.C.C. 665, 689.
[56] 3 M.C.C. 333.
[57] cf. *Transportes del Norte Sociedad Cooperativa Limitada Common Carrier Application,* 12 M.C.C. 759, where the Commission concluded that transportation performed within Laredo, Tex., is the part of a continuous haul to or from a point beyond the municipal area and a certificate is necessary for such an operation; authority was granted to transport passengers and baggage on city streets between Laredo and the international boundary between the United States and Mexico.
[58] 8 M.C.C. 359.

portation by applicant of automobile doors and fenders by motor vehicle from Detroit to the contiguous municipality of Windsor was an operation for which the I.C. Act requires a permit or certificate, and the application should be denied. The Commission said that "Detroit and Windsor are on opposite banks of the Detroit River. The two municipalities are joined by tunnel and bridge and are contiguous within the meaning of Section 203(b) (8) of the act. Some of the traffic transported by applicant moves to Detroit by another carrier, but applicant is compensated for the transportation from Detroit to Windosor solely by the contracting shipper. There is no evidence that applicant performs any interstate or foreign transportation under a common control, management, or arrangement with other carriers for a continuous carriage to or from a point beyond Detroit or Windsor. He is, therefore, not required to obtain a permit or certificate to perform the operation herein considered."[59]

In *Direct Winters Transport, Ltd. Application,*[60] the Commission granted authority to a Canadian carrier to transport general commodities between the boundary of the United States and Canada at Detroit, Mich., on the one hand, and on the other, Detroit, Mich., and between Detroit, Mich., on the one hand, and, on the other, points in Michigan within eight miles of Detroit. In *Charles Hinton, Sr. and Charles Hinton, Jr., Common Carrier Application,*[61] a certificate of public convenience and necessity was granted for transportation of household goods between points in Detroit as a part of a continuous carriage to or from points in Canada beyond the international boundary at Windsor. The Commission concluded that "While we agree with the result of the joint board's conclusion in respect of this operation between Detroit and Windsor, (that the carriage of general commodities, other than household goods, between Detroit and Windsor was exempt), it cannot be determined that such operation is exempt under the provisions of Section 203(b) (8) of the Act until it is established, in an appropriate proceeding for that purpose, that Windsor is or is not commercially a part of the city of Detroit for the purposes of motor carrier regulation. For this reason we make no finding concerning this phase of applicant's operation." In a proposed operation between points in the vicinity of Detroit, on the one hand, and, Windsor, on the other, the Commission found in *Earl S. Barnett Common Carrier Application,*[62] that the application failed to show that the

---

[59]See *Eugene Ethier Contract Carrier Application,* 14 M.C.C. 785; *Ernest Creasy Common Carrier Application,* 16 M.C.C. 47.
[60]MC-31918 (Sub-No. 1), decided October 16, 1940.
[61]28 M.C.C. 81.
[62]44 M.C.C. 578.

transportation for which authority is sought was transportation not within the partial exemption provided by Section 203(b) (8) and denied the application for a certificate subject to reconsideration when lines of the zone adjacent to and commercially a part of Detroit were definitely determined. The Commission pointed out that although transportation of automobile frames between points near Detroit and Windsor was probably conducted within the Detroit commercial zone, action on the application was complicated by the fact that Detroit commercial zone limits were not defined and that foreign commerce and an international boundary were involved. The certificate was denied since applicant failed to show that transportation was not within the partial exemption of Section 203(b) (8), without prejudice to reconsideration upon determination of the Detroit zone limits.

In *Dale Resler Extension of Operations, Juarez, Mex.*,[63] applicant sought authority to transport passengers in round-trip sightseeing or pleasure tours, beginning and ending in El Paso, Texas, including Juarez, Mexico, among other points. In discussing whether or not the operations fell within the exemption of Section 203(b) (8), the Commission stated, "We are satisfied that transportation service rendered by a single carrier between places in the United States and places in a foreign country does not fall within the exemption." Authority was granted to conduct operations between El Paso and the international boundary between the United States and Mexico. In *Commercial Zones and Terminal Areas*,[64] although the Commission found that any general definition of commercial zone boundaries should include all contiguous municipalities, it specifically stated that all municipalities, contiguous or otherwise, and all unincorporated areas, not within the United States, must be excluded from Section 203(b) (8). In *Commercial Zones and Terminal Areas*,[65] the commercial zone of Detroit was delineated and Windsor was not included therein. In a certificate proceeding, *Henry Bondy Common Carrier Application*,[66] the Commission again said that contiguous foreign municipalities did not come within the exemptions of Section 203(b) (8) stating "the partial exemption provided by Section 203(b) (8) accrues only to foreign commerce wholly within a municipality . . . or within a zone adjacent to and commercially a part of such municipality. The commercial zone of Detroit does not extend beyond the international border. The

[63] 44 M.C.C. 733.
[64] 46 M.C.C. 665, 668.
[65] 48 M.C.C. 95.
[66] 48 M.C.C. 132.

applicants' operations so far as they are performed within the United States, that is so far as they are subject to our jurisdiction, are confined to the commercial zone of Detroit, clearly does not operate to extend the exemption provided by the statute to operations which, in fact, go beyond the commercial zone and into a foreign country."[67]

In *Verbeem v. United States*,[68] the question before the court was whether the claimed exemption under Section 203(b) (8) was available to the plaintiffs. The court held that under the statute exempting transportation of passengers or property in interstate or foreign commerce between contiguous municipalities from jurisdiction of the Commission, operators of motor carriers engaged in transportation of property between Windsor and Detroit were exempt from the requirement that they obtain certificates of public convenience and necessity. The court said that "the plaintiffs operations therefore fit within the clear language of the second exemption, namely, that the plaintiffs are engaged in the transportation of property in foreign commerce between contiguous municipalities." The court reasoned that since Congress did not specifically restrict the exemption of domestic cities which were contiguous, that the Commission therefore had no power to exclude operations including a foreign contiguous city from being exempt.[69]

In line with the *Verbeem* case, the Commission held in *Autobuses Internacionales S. de R. L. Extension — Tornillo, Tex.*,[70] that the transportation of local passenger traffic moving between the contiguous communities of Juarez and El Paso is partially exempt from regulation, and no certificate is required therefor. The Commission spelled out the criteria which must be considered for delineating a commercial zone, as follows: "Actually, we do not 'create' or 'establish' any commercial zones, nor have we any power to 'extend' any exemption. A commercial zone about each municipality, within which motor transportation of the kind contemplated by Section 203(b) (8), is conducted, already exists by reason of trade practices, the uses to which the area is put, and geo-

[67]See also *Auto Transportes Del Norte, S. De R. L., Common Carrier Application*, 48 M.C.C. 671, involving operations between Laredo, Tex., and Nueva Laredo, Mex., and *Greenwood Transportation Co. v. Joe Lewels*, 51 M.C.C. 586, involving operations between El Paso, Tex., and Juarez, Mex.; *John E. Merrifield Common Carrier Application*, 61 M.C.C. 103; *Eugene Menard and Therese Menard Common Carrier Application*, 67 M.C.C. 365.
[68]154 F. Supp. 431, aff'd 356 U.S. 67.
[69]See *Soo-Security Motorways, Ltd., Extension — Pembina, N. D.* 184 M.C.C. 661.
[70]84 M.C.C. 216, *Soo-Security Motorways, Ltd., Extension — Pembina, N. Dak.*, 84 M.C.C. 661, cites the *Verbeem* case as authority for the proposition that Windsor is within the commercial zone of Detroit.

graphical and political considerations. The existence of such zones is an economic fact."

CASUAL, OCCASIONAL, OR RECIPROCAL TRANSPORTATION

Section 203(b) (9) exempts casual, occasional, or reciprocal transportation of passengers or property by motor vehicle in interstate or foreign commerce for compensation by any person not engaged in transportation by motor vehicle as a regular occupation or business.

This provision applies only when a person is not engaged in transportation by motor vehicle as a business. Thus, a person engaged in transportation in intrastate commerce by motor vehicle as a regular occupation or business is subject to the I.C. Act, if he also engages in the casual or occasional transportation of passengers or property in interstate or foreign commerce.[71]

In *Gross*,[72] the Commission held that applicant whose regular business was insurance, but who organized and conducted archeological ventures from Independence, Mo., to Mexico on a share-expense basis, soliciting patrons among, but not limiting them to, members of his religious organization, and operating only when enough persons were interested to make it likely that the tour would break even, was engaged in casual and occasional transportation within Section 203(b) (9); such tours were not conducted with any discernible pattern of regularity, and otherwise lacked characteristics normally associated with a special passenger operation of type intended to be regulated.

In *AA Auto Delivery, Inc.*,[73] the Commission said that while transportation involving a genuinely casual or occasional operation is exempt under Section 203(b) (9), and brokerage of such exempt transportation would require no authority as a broker from the Commission,, applicant's operation in driveaway service with drivers furnished, as actually conducted and in concept, were for-hire motor carrier operations by applicant and subject to the certificate provisions of the I.C. Act. In *Northeastern Malden Barrel Co., Inc.*,[74] the Commission said that since applicant's "buy-and-sell" operation was found to be in fact for-hire carriage, it was a person engaged in transportation by motor vehicle as a regular business and its "accommodation" transportation in emergencies for other dealers in steel barrels and drums was also for-hire carriage re-

[71]See Administrative Ruling No. 49, dated April 15, 1937.
[72]83 M.C.C. 541.
[73]77 M.C.C. 365, 372-73.
[74]83 M.C.C. 705, 709-709.

quiring appropriate authority and was not within the exemption of Section 203(b) (9), which extends to transportation of property only by those not engaged in motor transportation as a regular occupation or business.

ACCIDENTALLY WRECKED MOTOR VEHICLES

Section 203(b) (10), exempts emergency transportation of any accidentally wrecked or disabled motor vehicles in interstate or foreign commerce by towing.

This exemption does not apply to the towage of purchased wrecked and disabled motor vehicles, and the movement of wrecked and disabled vehicles from points other than the scene of the accident or disablement. This is not considered "emergency transportation."[75]

OPERATION WITHIN A SINGLE STATE — EXEMPTION CERTIFICATES

Section 204(a) (4a)[76] provides that it shall be the duty of the Commission:

"To determine, upon its own motion, or upon application by a motor carrier, a State board, or any other party in interest, whether the transportation in interstate or foreign commerce performed by any motor carrier or class of motor carriers lawfully engaged in operation solely within a single State is in fact of such nature, character, or quantity as not substantially to affect or impair uniform regulation by the Commission of transportation by motor carriers engaged in interstate or foreign commerce in effectuating the national transportation policy declared in this Act. Upon so finding, the Commission shall issue a certificate of exemption to such motor carrier or class of motor carriers which, during the period such certificate shall remain effective and unrevoked, shall exempt such carrier or class of motor carriers from compliance with the provisions of this part, and shall attach to such certificate such reasonable terms and conditions as the public interest may require.

"At any time after the issuance of any such certificate of exemption, the Commission may by order revoke all or any part thereof, it it shall find that the transportation in interstate or foreign commerce performed by the carrier or class of carriers designated in such certificates shall be, or shall have become, or is reasonably likely to become, of such nature, character, or quantity as in fact substantially to effect or impair uniform regulation

[75]*Skyline Diesel Sales & Service, Inc., Common Carrier Application,* 96 M.C.C. 430, 431.
[76]49 U.S.C. 304(a) (4a). Compare Section 303(e), (h) covering orders for exemption and revocation. See Section 418 for utilization by freight forwarders of carriers exempt under this Section.

by the Commission of interstate or foreign transportation by motor carriers in effectuating the national transportation policy declared in the Act.

"Upon revocation of any such certificate, the Commission shall restore to the carrier or carriers affected thereby, without further proceedings, the authority, if any, to operate in interstate or foreign commerce held by such carrier or carriers at the time the certificate of exemption pertaining to such carrier or carriers became effective. No certificate of exemption shall be denied, and no order of revocation shall be issued, under this subparagraph, except after reasonable opportunity for hearing to interested parties. Where an application is made in good faith for the exemption of a motor carrier under this subparagraph, accompanied by a certificate of a State board of the State in which the operations of such carrier are carried on stating that in the opinion of such board such carrier is entitled to a certificate of exemption under this subparagraph, such carrier shall be exempt from the provisions of this part beginning with the sixtieth day following the making of such application to the Commission unless prior to such time the Commission shall have by order denied such application, and such exemption shall be effective until such time as the Commission, after such sixtieth day, may by order deny such application or may by order revoke all or any part thereof as hereinbefore authorized.

"In any case where a motor carrier has become exempt from the provisions on this part as provided in this subparagraph, it shall not be considered to be a burden on interstate or foreign commerce for a State to regulate such carrier with respect to the operations covered by such exemption. Applications under this subparagraph shall be made in writing to the Commission, verified under oath, and shall be in such form and contain such information as the Commission shall by regulations require."

The purpose of Section 204(a) (4a) is to enable small local motor carriers engaged principally in intrastate commerce within a single State, usually centered on a town or city, to be relieved from the necessity of obtaining interstate certificates or permits and of otherwise complying with the provisions of Part II of the I.C. Act in instances where their interstate or foreign operation is a minor part of their entire operation and of little consequence or effect upon the transportation of other motor carriers which are engaged in interstate or foreign commerce in the territory and are fully subject to Commission regulations. Thus, where the main purposes of regulation can be fulfilled by State regulation of the predominant existing intrastate operation, any insignificant interstate traffic handled can be disregarded, thereby avoiding burdensome double regulation.[77]

---

[77]*Guanella Exemption Application,* 33 M.C.C. 379. See *Paulette Exemption Application,* 83 M.C.C. 438, where a proposed contract for the carriage of cosmetics and related articles between Shreveport and other Louisiana points within 125 miles thereof would be in a field already served by authorized common carriers. The physical circumstances were such that grant of the exemption certificate would substantially affect and impair uniform regulation of motor carriers engaged in interstate commerce. Therefore, the exemption was denied.

Where a motor carrier is lawfully engaged in operation solely within a single State and seeks a certificate of exemption under Section 204(a) (4a), the burden of proof is necessarily upon such application to establish that the transportation in interstate or foreign commerce which it is either performing or proposes to perform is, in fact, of such nature, character, or quantity as not substantially to affect or impair uniform regulation by the Commission of the transportation by other motor carriers engaged in interstate or foreign commerce in effectuating the national transportation policy.

TERMINAL AREAS

Section 202(c) of the Interstate Commerce Act[78] provides:

Notwithstanding any provision of the section or of Section 203, the provisions of this part, except the provisions of Section 204 relative to qualifications and maximum hours of service of employees and safety of operations and equipment, shall not apply (1) to transportation by motor vehicle by a carrier by railroad subject to Part I, or by a water carrier subject to Part III, or by a freight forwarder subject to Part IV, incidental to transportation or service subject to such parts, in the performance within terminal areas of transfer, collection, or delivery services; but such transportation shall be considered to be and shall be regulated as transportation subject to Part I when performed by such carrier by railroad, as transportation subject to Part III when performed by such water carrier, and as transportation or service subject to Part IV when performed by such freight forwarder; (2) to transportation by motor vehicle by any person (whether as agent or under a contractual arrangement) for a common carrier by railroad subject to Part I, an express company subject to Part I, a motor carrier subject to this part, a water carrier to Part III, or a freight forwarder subject to Part IV, in the performance within terminal areas of transfer, collection, or delivery service; but such transportation shall be considered to be performed by such carrier, express company, or freight forwarder as part of, and shall be regulated in the same manner as, the transportation by railroad, express, motor vehicle, or water, or freight forwarder transportation or service, to which such services are incidental."

The purpose of Section 202(c) is to permit all regulated carriers to use the services of pick-up and delivery carriers within the terminal area of the regulated carrier.

There is no definition of "terminal areas" in the I.C. Act. To meet this situation the Commission undertook to define the limits of terminal areas for motor carriers and freight forwarders in the sixth supplemental

---

[78]49 U.S.C. 302(c). Comparable provision — Section 303(f). See also Section 418 for carriers which may be utilized by freight forwarders.

report in Ex Parte No. MC-37, *Commercial Zones and Terminal Areas.*[79] In that proceeding, the Commission found (at pages 109-10):

(1) The terminal area within the meaning of Section 202(c) of any motor carrier or freight forwarder at any municipality authorized to be served by such motor carrier or freight forwarder, within which transportation by motor vehicle in the performance of transfer, collection, or delivery services may be performed by, or for, such motor carrier or freight forwarder without compliance with the provisions of the Act other than Section 204 consists of and includes, all points or places which are (a) within the commercial zone of such municipality as defined by the Commission and (b) not beyond the limits of the operating authority of such motor carrier or freight forwarder.

(2) The terminal area within the meaning of Section 202(c) of any motor carrier or freight forwarder at any unincorporated community having a post office of the same name which is authorized to be served by such motor carrier or freight forwarder, within which transportation by motor vehicle in the performance of transfer, collection, or delivery services may be performed by, or for, such motor carrier or freight forwarder without compliance with the provisions of the Act other than Section 204, consists of (a) all points or places in the United States which are located within the limits of the operating authority of the motor carrier or freight forwarder involved, and within 2½ miles of the post office at such authorized unincorporated point if it has a population less than 2,500, within 4 miles if it has a population of 2,500 but less than 25,000, or within 5½ miles, if it has a population of 25,000 or more; (b) all of any municipality, any part of which is included under the formula; and (c) any municipality wholly surrounded by any municipality included under the formula or so wholly surrounded except for a water boundary.

The terminal areas of railroads, express companies and water carriers are as published in their tariffs.

The terminal areas of motor carriers and freight forwarders at unincorporated communities served were changed in Ex Parte No. MC-37 (Sub-No. 26), *Commercial Zones and Terminal Areas, supra,* to cover all points in the United States which are located within the limits of the operating authority of the motor carrier or freight forwarder involved, and within 3 miles of the post office at such authorized unincorporated point if it has a population less than 2,500, within 4 miles if it has a population of 2,500 but less than 25,000, within 6 miles if it has a population of 25,000 or more.

Although the I.C. Act does not define "terminal area," and the terminal area of each form of transportation at any particular point must be

[79] 54 M.C.C. 21.

determined on the facts present, such determination must be made in conjunction with a reading of the I.C. Act as a whole; and the administration and enforcement of any provision of the I.C. Act must be made fundamentally with a view to carrying out the national transportation policy including recognition of the inherent advantages of each form.[80] Consideration of Section 202(c) in numerous past proceedings makes it clear that "terminal area" has a definite meaning in transportation parlance, and it is patent under the statute and the controlling decisions that a terminal area of a carrier, whether motor, rail, or water, or of a freight forwarder may not exceed the area within which bona fide collection, delivery, and transfer, as distinguished from line-haul service, is performed.[81] Thus, any service which goes beyond a single homogeneous community, identifiable as such by the factors of commercial and industrial integrity, population and business density, and existence of some reasonably compact limit to the geographical scope of community affairs and influence, is intercommunity in character and cannot be considered a bona fide collection, delivery, and transfer service.[82]

Where the terminal area of any carrier extends beyond the corporate limits, that area must be defined in applicable tariffs.[83] Since no general rule corresponding to that laid down for motor carriers and forwarders has been promulgated respecting terminal limits of water carriers, questions concerning the maximum permissible limits of such areas must be determined individually on the basis of the facts presented. But the view that the definition of terminal areas of motor carriers applies equally to water carriers, since the permissible limits of a terminal area depend largely on the character of the community served, finds support in prior decisions, which, while recognizing the need for permitting water carriers to change their terminal areas by tariff provision without seeking changes of their certificates, state that such flexibility was not intended to permit a water carrier to extend its terminal area into a territory which cannot be considered part of a single port.[84]

As in any case involving a carrier's right to perform incidental services, the operational features of a water carrier's primary function must be ascertained. Historically, the functional advantage of water carriage has been a more economic long-distance transportation service than any

---

[80]*Central Truck Lines, Inc. v. Pan-Atlantic S. S. Corp.*, 82 M.C.C. 395, 403.
[81]*Ibid.*, pp. 402, 404.
[82]*Ibid.*, p. 404.
[83]*Ibid.*, p. 401.
[84]*Ibid.*, p. 402.

form of overland transportation between the ports it serves; its functional disadvantages have been infrequency of schedules, comparative slowness in service, and inability to serve shippers or consignees at inland points without relying on an overland form of transportation.[85]

In the *Central Truck Lines case*, the defendant in an endeavor to maximize its advantages and minimize its inherent disadvantages, offered direct service to some inland points in its own vehicles, on the theory that, in view of its long-distance water operations, such service was merely a legitimate auxiliary or incidental terminal service within Section 202(c).[86] The defendant wanted to combine the advantages of its water operations and the operational features of a line-haul motor carrier to compete with other transportation media; however, the Commission said, "Section 202(c) does not give it a carte blanche exemption to perform motor service at all points where it can effectively compete with overland transportation; for the Commission to permit it to do so would be tantamount to failure to 'recognize and preserve' the inherent advantages of each mode; defendant's approach to formulating its so-called terminal areas and the result thereof is contrary to the provisions of the Act, most particularly those of the national transportation policy and Section 206."[87]

A Commission finding that a particular operation comes within the exemption of Section 202(c) does not destroy an operating right, or limit the carrier in its operation; it merely removes the pickup and delivery service from direct regulation and does not in any way alter the certificate of the carrier performing the service. Terminal carriers are still subject to direct regulation with respect to transportation to and from points beyond the terminal area.[88]

A motor carrier may establish a terminal area only at a municipality which it is authorized to serve specifically in its certificate; grant of authority to serve points in a particular territory is predicated on proof relating to a need for service in an area rather than at a specified municipality, thus a certificate authorizing service at a particular municipality contemplates service within the municipality and its commercial and industrial adjuncts which are, in fact, a part of the urban community.[89]

---

[85]*Ibid.*, p. 403.
[86]*Ibid.*, p. 403.
[87]*Ibid.*, pp. 403-4.
[88]*Advance Transp. Co. v. Allard*, 305 I.C.C. 751, 753.
[89]*Houff Transfer, Inc., Extension*, 78 M.C.C. 511, 515-16.

Water Carriers—Exempt Transportation

THE APPLICABLE STATUTORY PROVISIONS

Section 303(a) of the Interstate Commerce Act[90] provides that "In the case of transportation which is subject both to this part and Part I, the provisions of Part I shall apply only to the extent that Part I imposes, with respect to such transportation, requirements not imposed by the provisions of this part."

Section 303(b),[91] as amended by the Act of December 27, 1973, 87 Stat. 838, reads as follows:

"Nothing in this part shall apply to the transportation by a water carrier of commodities in bulk. This subsection shall apply only in the case of commodities in bulk which are (in accordance with the existing custom of the trade in the handling and transportation of such commodities as of June 1, 1939) loaded and carried without wrappers or containers and delivered by the carrier without transportation mark or count. This subsection shall not apply to transportation subject, at the time this part takes effect, to the provisions of the Intercoastal Shipping Act, 1933, as amended."

Section 303(c)[92] provides:

"Nothing in this part shall apply to transportation by a contract carrier by water of commodities in bulk in a non-ocean-going vessel on a normal voyage during which (1) the cargo space of such vessel is used for the carrying of not more than three such commodities, and (2) such vessel passes within or through waters which are made international for navigation purposes by any treaty to which the United States is a party."

Section 303(d)[93] provides:

"Nothing in this part shall apply to the transportation by water of liquid cargoes in bulk tank vessels designed for use exclusively in such service . . ." (the tank vessels are required to be certified under regulations approved by the Coast Guard.)

Section 303(e)[94] provides:

"(1) Notwithstanding any provisions of this part the Commission may, by order, from time to time, upon application, or upon its own initiative without application, exempt from the requirements of this part the transportation of passengers between points in the United States by way of a foreign port or ports, upon a finding that application of such requirements thereto

[90]49 U.S.C. 903(a). Comparable provisions — Sections 202(c), 203(a) (14).
[91]49 U.S.C. 903(b). Amended in 1970 by P.L. 91-590; 84 Stat. 1587. See Section 418 for utilization by freight forwarders of carriers exempt under Section 303(b).
[92]49 U.S.C. 903(c).
[93]49 U.S.C. 903(d).
[94]49 U.S.C. 903(e) (1) (2).

is not necessary to carry out the national transportation policy declared in this Act.

"(2) It is hereby declared to be the policy of Congress to exclude from the provisions of this part, in addition to the transportation otherwise excluded under this section, transportation by contract carriers by water which, by reason of the inherent nature of the commodities transported, their requirement of special equipment or their shipment in bulk, is not actually and substantially competitive with transportation by any common carrier subject to this part or part I or part II. Upon application of a carrier, made in such manner and form as the Commission may by regulations prescribe, the Commission shall, subject to such reasonable conditions and limitations as the Commission may prescribe, by order exempt from the provisions of this part such of the transportation engaged in by such carriers as it finds necessary to carry out the policy above declared. A carrier (other than a carrier subject, at the time this part takes effect, to the provisions of the Intercoastal Shipping Act, 1933, as amended) making such application prior to January 1, 1941, shall be exempt from the provisions of this part until a final determination has been made upon such application if such carrier or a predecessor in interest was in bona fide operation as a contract carrier by water on January 1, 1940, over the route or routes or between the ports with respect to which application is made and has so operated since that time (or, if engaged in furnishing seasonal service only, was in bona fide operation during the seasonal period, prior to or including such date, for operations of the character in question) except, in either event, for interruptions of service over which such carrier or its predecessor in interest had no control."

Section 303(f) (1), (2)[95] provides:

"Notwithstanding any provision of this section or of Section 302, the provisions of this part shall not apply —

"(1) to transportation by water by a carrier by railroad subject to Part I or by a motor carrier subject to Part II, incidental to transportation subject to such parts, in the performance within terminal areas of transfer, collection, or delivery services, or in the performance of floatage, car ferry, lighterage, or towage; but such transportation shall be considered to be transportation subject to Part I when performed by such carrier by railroad, and transportation subject to Part II when performed by such motor carrier.

"(2) to transportation by water by any person (whether as agent or under a contractual arrangement) for a common carrier by railroad subject to Part I, an express company subject to Part I, a motor carrier subject to Part II, or a water carrier subject to this part, in the performance within terminal areas of transfer, collection, or delivery services, or in the performance of floatage, car ferry, lighterage, or towage; but such transportation

[95]49 U.S.C. 903(f) (1) (2). Comparable provisions — Sections 202(c) (1), (2), 402(c). See also Section 418, carriers which may be utilized by freight forwarders.

shall be considered to be performed by such carrier or express company as part of, and shall be regulated in the same manner as, the transportation by railroad, express, motor vehicle, or water to which such services are incidental."

Section 303(g)[96] provides:

"Except to the extent that the Commission shall from time to time find, and by order declare, that such application is necessary to carry out the national transportation policy declared in this Act, the provisions of this part shall not apply (1) to transportation in interstate commerce by water solely within the limits of a single harbor or between places in contiguous harbors, when such transportation is not a part of a continuous through movement under a common control, management, or arrangement to or from a place without the limits of any such harbor or harbors, or (2) to transportation by small craft of not more than one hundred tons carrying capacity or not more than one hundred indicated horsepower, or to vessels carrying passengers only and equipped to carry no more than sixteen passengers, or to ferries, or to the movement by water carriers of contractors' equipment employed or to be employed in construction or repair for such water carrier, or to the operation of salvors."

Section 303(h)[97] provides:

"The Commision shall have the power to determine, upon its own motion or upon application of any party in interest, whether any water carrier is engaged solely in transporting the property of a person which owns all or substantially all of the voting stock of such carrier. Upon so finding the Commission shall issue a certificate of exemption to such carrier, and such carrier shall not be subject to the provisions of this part during the period such certificate shall remain in effect. At any time after the issuance of such certificate the Commission may by order revoke such certificate if it finds that such carrier is no longer entitled to the exemption under the foregoing provisions of this subsection. Upon revocation of any such certificate the Commission shall restore to such carrier, without further proceedings, the authority, if any, to engage in transportation subject to the provisions of this part held by such carrier at the time the certificate of exemption pertaining to such carrier became effective. No certificate of exemption shall be denied and no order of revocation shall be issued, under this subsection, except after reasonable opportunity for hearing."

Section 303(i)[98] provides:

"In the application of the provisions of this part to any carrier owned or controlled by the United States, no different policy, rule of rate making, system of accounting, or method of determining costs of service, value of property or rate of return shall be applied than is applied in the case of carriers not so owned or controlled."

[96]49 U.S.C. 903(g). Comparable provisions — Sections 203(b), 402(b), (c).
[97]49 U.S.C. 903(h). Comparable provisions — Sections 204(a), (4a).
[98]49 U.S.C. 903(i). See Section 307(f), note to Section 15(a) (2).

Section 303(j)[99] provides:

"Nothing in this part shall be construed to interfere with the exclusive exercise by each State of the power to regulate intrastate commerce by water carriers within the jurisdiction of such State."

Section 303(k)[100] provides:

"Nothing in this part shall authorize the Commission to prescribe or regulate any rate, fare, or charge for intrastate transportation, or for any service connected therewith, for the purpose of removing discrimination against interstate commerce or for any other purpose."

Section 303(1)[101] provides:

"Whenever transportation exempted under the provisions of subsection (g), or by order of the Commission under subsection (e), becomes subject to the provision of this part, the carrier may continue to engage in such transportation for a period of one hundred and twenty days without a certificate or permit covering such transportation, and, if application for a certificate or permit covering such transportation is made to the Commission within such period, the Commission shall, without further proceedings, issue to the carrier a certificate or permit, whichever is appropriate, authorizing such transportation previously exempted."

Applicable Law Relating to Commodities in Bulk

While under the legislative history of Section 303(b) there was no doubt that Congress intended to exempt transportation of commodities in bulk, such exemption was to apply only if not more than three bulk commodities were being transported in a single vessel or in two or more vessels being navigated as a single unit;[102] and where a carrier participated in through transportation under common arrangements with other carriers under circumstances not in conformity with the limitations imposed on the exemption, the entire transportation was subject to regulation.[103] Thus, if a carrier A, under a contract of affreightment with a shipper to transport bargeloads of bulk freight as exempt from regulation under agreed rates not published or filed with the Commission, turned the barges over to carrier B at an intermediate point for towage to destination and B continued the tow as one consisting of not more than three bulk commodities, the transportation was within the exemption

---

[99]49 U.S.C. 903(j). Comparable provision — Section 202(b).

[100]49 U.S.C. 903(k). Comparable provision — Section 216(e).

[101]49 U.S.C. 903(1). Comparable provision for restoration of previous authority following revocation of exemption, Section 204(a), (4a).

[102]*Mississippi Valley Barge Line Co. Exemption,* 311 I.C.C. 103, 107.

[103]*Ibid.,* p. 108.

and not subject to regulations as to any of the participating carriers. But if the tow beyond the intermediate point included nonexempt commodities or more than three bulk commodities, the transportation of all the commodities in the tow became subject to regulation.[104] Nonbulk commodities could not be included in a tow of bulk commodities, without subjecting the entire cargo to regulation, regardless of how the responsibility to shippers under bills of lading were divided among two or more carriers. This was held in *Commercial Transp. Corp. Exemption.*[105] The Commission said in deciding the case that Congress intended to exempt the transportation of commodities in bulk, but it intended to limit such exemption.

The views expressed by the Commission in the case were upheld by a district court in *Commercial Barge Lines, Inc. v. United States.*[106] The court said that in enacting Section 303b Congress intended to provide an exemption for a water carrier transporting commodities in bulk when no more than three bulk commodities are being transported, and this means that the unit must be considered in its entirety in order to appraise the impact of the statute upon it.[107] The court also said the Commission acted properly when it ruled that it makes no difference that the barge containing the nonbulk commodities would be towed for a regulated carrier under circumstances which would render the tower exempt from regulation with respect to the nonbulk commodities under the provisions of Section 303(f) (2).

Inasmuch as Congress considered transportation of commodities in bulk in volume as not competitive with service of regulated carriers, such transportation was exempted from regulations; and restrictions to which that exemption was made subject were intended to insure that regulated carriers would not be subjected to unfair competitive disadvantages. Thus the Commission said in *A. L. Mechling Barge Lines, Inc., Extension,*[108] the grant of authority sought would materially alter the competitive situation in applicant's favor, and defeat the restrictive purpose of Section 303(b) to protect regulated carriers from a form of transportation which is noncompetitive when conducted within the limitations of that exemption. The Commission said that it had consistently interpreted the limitation of the exemption provided in Section 303(b) to mean that barges operated in the same tow be considered as a single

---

[104]*Ibid.*, p. 107.
[105]300 I.C.C. 66, 71.
[106]166 F. Supp. 867, aff'd. 359 U.S. 342.
[107]*Ibid.*, pp. 871-2.
[108]306 I.C.C. 223, 228.

vessel, and, therefore, in order for a tow of traffic to be within the exemption it must consist of not more than three bulk commodities regardless of the number of barges in tow.[109] The Commission said furthur that the services of existing carriers were not unsatisfactory or inadequate in any respect; shippers' preference for applicant's service stems from a hope of eventual lower transportation charges rather than from a need for the proposed service or from any superior service that applicant would provide; while authority which would enable applicant to transport presently authorized traffic and other drybulk commodities in mixed tows, or in a single tow of more than three bulk commodities, might serve as a convenience to applicant and enable it to offer a more flexible service, no need therefor had been shown.[110]

The amendment of Section 303(b) in 1970 by P.L. 91-590 makes it plain that the exemption shall not be lost by the concurrent transportation in the same vessel of other commodities.

An essential finding to support a Commission order under Section 303(e)(2) exempting carrier from regulation on transportation of bulk petroleum in vessels which also transport regulated deck loads is that the exemption be not actually and substantially competitive with transportation by common carriers subject to Parts I, II, or III of the I.C. Act.[111] In *United Vintners Lines Exemption*,[112] the Commission held that although applicant's transportation of liquid cargoes in bulk for its parent company and others in a certified tanker was within the exemption of Section 303(d), its proposed transportation of bottled wine in dry-cargo compartments for the parent company was subject to all provisions of Part III; the carrier conceded that in such service it was a contract carrier within Section 302(e). A finding that applicant was not entitled to a certificate of exemption under Section 303(h) for transportation of bottled wine for the parent company in dry-cargo compartments of the tanker did not in any way subject the bulk transportation to any requirements of the I.C. Act.[113]

Ferry Operations

Authority to remove the exemption for ferries contained in Section 303(g2) is strictly limited by the terms of Section 303(g), and the Com-

---

[109]*Ibid.*, p. 225.
[110]*Ibid.*, pp. 226-8.
[111]*Seatrain Lines, Inc. v. United States,* 152 F. Supp. 619, 629.
[112]310 I.C.C. 81, 82, 85.
[113]*Ibid.*, p. 86.

mission may not properly remove the exemption without a specific finding and an order as spelled out therein.[114] In the *Black Ball* case, the Commission said that since the toll authority which operated the ferry held a certificate it was a carrier subject to Part III even though it had filed no tariffs, issued no bills of lading, and engaged only in operations of the type performed by exempt ferries; defendant had a dual status, both as a ferry and as a carrier subject to Part III of the I.C. Act. The Commission said that a public ferry, such as that operated by the toll authority, including the privately owned road or street approaches thereto, is a recognized "public way." It is but a substitute for a bridge and its purpose and use are the same; it is a link in the highway system; does not include transportation of goods and merchandise, or does not include for-hire transportation in the ordinary sense of the term, including the usual shipper-carrier relationship with its attendant mutual obligations.[115] The Commission said that a public ferry necessarily implies transportation for a relatively short distance, almost invariably between two points only, and is unrelated to other transportation; it thus presents a situation essentially local requiring regulation according to local conditions.[116]

Freight Forwarders—Exempt Transportation

The Applicable Statutory Provisions

Section 402(b) of the Interstate Commerce Act[117] provides that "The provisions of this part shall not apply (1) to service performed by or under the direction of a cooperative association, as defined in the Agricultural Marketing Act, approved June 15, 1929, as amended, or by a federation of such cooperative association, if such federation possesses no greater powers or purposes than cooperative associations so defined, or (2) where the property with respect to which service is performed consists of ordinary livestock, fish (including shellfish), agricultural commodities (not including manufactured products thereof), or used household goods, if the person performing such service engages in service subject to this part with respect to not more than one of the classifications of property above specified."

---

[114]*Black Ball Freight Service v. Acme Freight, Inc.*, 76 M.C.C. 5, 9.
[115]*Ibid.*, pp. 10-11.
[116]*Ibid.*, p. 11.
[117]49 U.S.C. 1002(b). Comparable provision — Sections 203(b), 303(g). See exemptions under Section 303(b)-(e).

Section 402(c)[118] provides that "The provisions of this part shall not be construed to apply (1) to the operations of a shipper, or a group or association of shippers, in consolidating or distributing freight for themselves or for the members thereof, on a nonprofit basis, for the purpose of securing the benefits of carload, truckload, or other volume rates, or (2) to the operations of a warehouseman or other shippers' agent, in consolidating or distributing pool cars, whose services and responsibilities to shippers in connection with such operations are confined to the terminal area in which such operations are performed."

A forwarder is not exempted from the provisions of Part IV, nor does it become subject thereto, at its own pleasure or option; the provisions of Section 402(b) are mandatory, and an applicant conducting an operation exempted thereby may not be granted a permit.[119]

PERFORMANCE OF SERVICE WITH RESPECT TO ONE CLASSIFICATION OF PROPERTY

It generally may be said that as long as a forwarder confines its service to "used household goods" and does not engage in forwarding any other property, it is exempt from regulation under Section 402(b)(2).[120] However, transportation of used household goods by a forwarder that is a subsidiary or affiliate of a regulated forwarder would not be exempt, since, as the subsidiary or affiliate would be directly or indirectly controlled by the parent company, operations of former would be considered as part of those of the parent company and not within the exemption.[121]

SHIPPERS' AGENT

If a forwarder's services are not confined to a terminal area which may be established by the facts, such as representations made to shippers and from the maintenance of insurance protection against loss and damage claims arising between receipt of property by forwarder and ultimately delivery to shippers' customers, the forwarder cannot be exempted as a shippers' agent under Section 402(c)(2).[122]

[118]Limited regulation or exemption of private carriage: Sections 204(a)(3), 303(h). Collection and delivery in terminal areas by carriers' agents: Sections 202(c)(2), 303(f)(2).

[119]*Ace Freight Forwarding Co.*, 310 I.C.C. 385, 386.

[120]*Movers' & Warehousemen's Assn. of America, Inc., Petition*, 304 I.C.C. 517, 519.

[121]*Ibid.*, p. 520.

[122]*Parcel Warehouse, Inc. Freight Forwarder Application*, 285 I.C.C. 697, 701.

22

Classification and Exemption of Air Carriers

The Applicable Statutory Provisions

Section 416(a) of the Federal Aviation Act[1] provides that the Board "may from time to time establish such just and reasonable classifications or groups of air carriers for the purposes of this title as the nature of the services performed by such air carriers shall require; and such just and reasonable rules and regulations, pursuant to and consistent with the provisions of this title, to be observed by each such class or group, as the Board finds necessary in the public interest."

Section 416(b) (1)[2] provides that the Board, "from time to time and to the extent necessary, may (except as provided in paragraph (2) of this subsection) exempt from the requirements of this title or any provision thereof, or any rule, regulation, term, condition, or limitation prescribed thereunder, any air carrier or class of air carriers, if it finds that the enforcement of this title or such provision, or such rule, regulation, term, condition, or limitation is or would be an undue burden on such air carrier or class of air carriers by reason of the limited extent of, or unusual circumstances affecting, the operations of such air carrier or class of air carriers and is not in the public interest." Section 416(b) (2)[3] provides that the Board "shall not exempt any air carrier from any provision of subsection (k) of Section 401 of this title, except that (A) any air carrier not engaged in scheduled air transportation, and (B), to the extent that the operations of such air carrier are conducted during daylight hours, any air carrier engaged in scheduled air transportation, may be exempted from the provisions of paragraphs (1) and (2) of such sub-

[1]49 U.S.C. 1386(a).
[2]49 U.S.C. 1386(b) (1).
[3]49 U.S.C. 1386(b) (2).

section if the Board finds, after notice and hearing, that, by reason of the limited extent of, or unusual circumstances affecting, the operations of any such air carrier, the enforcement of such paragraphs is or would be such an undue burden on such air carrier as to obstruct its development and prevent it from beginning or continuing operations, and that the exemption of such air carrier from such paragraphs would not adversely affect the public interest. Provided that nothing in this subsection shall be deemed to authorize the Board to exempt any air carrier from any requirement of this title, or any provision thereof, or any rule, regulation, term, condition, or limitation prescribed thereunder which provides for maximum flying hours for pilots or copilots."

Required Findings

Section 416(b) permits the Board to exempt an air carrier from the certificate requirements of Section 401 if it first finds that enforcement of those requirements would have certain specified results because of the existence of certain specified conditions. The Board must find that the operations of the air carrier seeking the exemption are either of limited extent or affected by unusual circumstances; aside from finding that one of these conditions is present, the Board must also find that the condition causes enforcement of the certificate requirements to work an undue burden on the carrier. Finally, the Board must find that enforcement of the requirement is not in the public interest. In the absence of any one of these findings the Board is not authorized to suspend the normal statutory requirements of notice, hearing and requisite findings for issuance of a certificate of public convenience and necessity.[4] Nor may these findings be merely a recital of Section 416(b); the Board must find that which the statute requires it to find, not in conclusory fashion in the statutory language but in such fashion that a reviewing court can test the validity of the finding.[5]

Supplemental Air Carriers

American Airlines v. C.A.B.[6] involved an order of the Board dealing with the problem of non-scheduled or irregular air carriers. The basic

---

[4]*Pan American World Airways v. C.A.B.*, 261 F. 2d 754, 757, cert. denied 359 U.S. 912.

[5]Ibid. See also *American Airlines, Inc. v. C.A.B.*, 235 F. 2d 845, 853, cert. denied 353 U.S. 905.

[6]235 F 2d 845, cert. denied 353 U.S. 905. Prior cases involving the background of the controversy include *Air Transport Associates v. C.A.B.*, 199 F. 2d 181, cert. denied 344 U.S. 922; *American Air Transport v. C.A.B.*, 206 F. 2d 423; *Eastern Airlines v. C.A.B.*, 185 F. 2d 426, vacated 341 U.S. 901; *New England Air Express v. C.AB.*, 194 F. 2d 894; *Large Irregular Carriers, Exemptions*, 11 C.A.B. 609.

requirement previously imposed by the Board upon the irregular carriers had been that they operate without any reasonable semblance of regularity as to schedule or route. The basic change wrought by the order was to remove this requirement of irregularity and to substitute in its place a maximum limitation upon the number of round trips permitted per month between any two points. The Board accomplished this by granting the carriers involved exemptions under Section 416(b) of the Act. Petitioners contested the validity of the order upon the grounds that the Act did not grant to the Board power to issue such an order; that the order was not supported by the findings required by the statute; and that the order was beyond the scope of the proceeding instituted to determine future policy with regard to irregular air carriers.

The Board had found that the services performed by the irregular carriers, including charter operations, individually ticketed coach flights, specialized services, and military air-lift, had proven of importance to both the irregular carriers and the public. It concluded that its policy should be directed toward their survival and healthy growth, and that the services rendered by the irregular carriers could not be rendered satisfactorily by the certificated carriers, which had fixed commitments to route and schedule operations. The Board found that the elimination of the restriction against regularity would help the public and strengthen the supplemental carriers, and that it would aid in the enforcement of regulations. The Board also said that the new scope of the supplemental operations would not open the door to unlimited competition, which would adversely affect the certificated carriers. The Board said that the supplemental carriers would not be permitted to combine and integrate their operations, and they would be restricted to needs they were designed to meet and if they posed a threat that they would have to face up to a prompt and effective dimunition in the maximum permissible flight frequencies.

The court of appeals on review stated (p. 851) that the judgment of the Board was a rational one which it must accept. Petitioners had argued before the court that the basic concept of the statute enacted by Congress for the regulation of air carriers was of a certificated system, and that Congress did not intend that the Board might, by use of the exemption provision of Section 416(b), destroy the elaborate basic requirements of the Act for a certificated system. The court agreed with this contention stating (p. 850) that "Despite the broad language of Section 416(b), we think it perfectly clear that the Congress did not set up so elaborate a series of provisions in respect to the certification of carriers, and the public interest, convenience and necessity therein involved, and at the same time grant its administrative agency power to destroy those elaborate provisions. We think there is and must be a boundary to the authority of the Board under its exemption power to impinge upon the certificated service." However, the court said (p. 850), the Board did not disagree with the foregoing and had declared that the main and basic transportation system should be a certified one.

Although the court in the *American Airlines*[7] case was of the opinion that the Board had demonstrated that the supplemental air carriers have a place in the national transportation system and that they should be authorized to operate, the case was remanded to the Board for furtheir proceedings. The remand was based on the failure of the Board to make findings on the question of whether the supplemental carriers should be exempted from certification altogether. It could not be ascertained from the Board's decision what undue burden the Board thought certification would be or why it thought certification of the supplemental service would not be in the public interest.

As the court said (p. 853), "the question now under consideration is whether they should be authorized by certificates, premised upon public convenience and necessity and specifying in some fashion the service which such carriers will be obligated to perform, or whether their operations may be authorized by a simple exemption from all the certification requirements of the statute." The court said that to validate an order of exemption the Board must comply with the statute. In conclusion the court held (p. 853) that the order issued was within the scope of the proceeding instituted by the Board's initial order.

[7]*Ibid.*, p. 853.

23

Pipeline Regulation

Scope of Regulation

Under Section 402(b) of the Department of Energy Organization Act[1] all functions and authority of the ICC or any officer or component thereof, where the regulatory function establishes rates or charges for the transportation of oil by pipeline or establishes the valuation of any such pipeline, were transferred to and vested in the Federal Regulatory Commission.

The ICC, however, retains its authority over transportation of commodities other than oil by pipeline.

The ICC was given jurisdiction over common carriers engaged in the pipeline transportation of oil and related products in interstate and foreign commerce by the following provisions of the I.C. Act.

The term "common carrier" is defined by Section 1(3) (a)[2] to "include all pipe-line companies; and the provisions of part I, by Section 1(1) (b)[3] apply to common carriers engaged in the "transportation of oil or other commodity, except water and except natural or artificial gas, by pipe line, or partly by pipe line and partly by railroad or by water." The national transportation policy also embraces carriers engaged in pipeline operations.

Many aspects of pipeline operations are not regulated, including mergers and consolidations, the granting of credit, the issuance of securities, and the formation of interlocking directorates. Nor must pipelines obtain

---

[1] 42 U.S.C. 7172. Under Section 306 of the Department of Energy Organization Act, 42 U.S.C. 7155, there was transferred to the Department of Energy such functions set forth in the I.C. Act and vested by law in the I.C.C. and members thereof as relate to the transportation of oil by pipeline.

[2] 49 U.S.C. 1(3) (a).

[3] 49 U.S.C. 1(1) (b).

certificates of public convenience and necessity to construct and abandon lines or to operate. The Commodities Clause does not apply to pipelines.

Pipelines, however, are subject to a number of provisions of the I.C. Act, such Sections as 1(4), 1(5), 2, 3(1), 4, 5a, 6(1), 6(7), 16(1,3,6,7), 19a(a) and 20(7b, 18). The Elkins Act applies. Section 7 of the Clayton Act applies.

Pipeline System Operations

A pipeline system is divided into the gathering system, which transports the oil from the wells to point of delivery within a gathering district or to a trunk line for transportation beyond the gathering district; and the trunk line system, which transports the oil that has been gathered from the wells, or has been received from connecting lines or vessels, and delivers it to connecting lines, to vessels, or into tankage provided by the consignee at the pipeline's terminal.[4]

Pipelines also handle refined products, which may move long distances and then be interchanged with other carriers for short hauls to final destination. The gathering system, a network of lines, must extend to all part of a field, which branches or feeder lines, to the leases of all producers; most areas are served by the gathering systems of more than one pipeline company.[5] The trunk line system is the main artery through which oil gathered in various fields is moved toward its ultimate destination; its operation is a complicated part of pipeline transportation.[6] Oil from different fields, and from different horizons in the same field, having fundamentally different physical and chemical characteristics, must be transported without contamination or adverse changes in characteristics.[7] The business of the petroleum industry may be done by integrated companies engaged in the combined activity of production, transportation, refining, and marketing.[8]

Since a refinery represents an outlay of millions of dollars in construction and operations, to safeguard this investment an adequate supply of crude petroleum must be assured and the refiner must have access to many sources of supply; it is also necessary to reach consuming areas conveniently and economically.[9] In the development of pipeline trans-

---

[4]*Reduced Pipeline Rates and Gathering Charges*, 243 I.C.C. 115, 116.
[5]*Ibid.*
[6]*Ibid.*
[7]*Ibid.*
[8]*Ibid.*
[9]*Ibid.*

portation, the parent or an affiliated company of an integrated system supplies the capital, the purpose being to assure an adequate supply of crude oil at all times at the system refineries.[10] Only in exceptional circumstances does the pipeline buy the oil it transports; crude oil is generally bought by a purchasing company or agent of the system, or by the refining unit itself, at the wells.[11] The pipeline has no direct market function itself, and frequently is integrated with the refiner who creates the demand for crude oil.[12] Many of the pipeline subsidiaries of integrated oil companies are also common carriers and compete with other common carrier pipelines for the transportation of crude oil or refined products for shippers who have available receiving facilities and meet the tariff requirements. The nonsubsidiary common carriers may serve not only independent companies but also integrated companies which own pipeline subsidiaries.

Tariffs

Pipeline companies are required by the I.C. Act to file tariffs showing all rates, charges, classifications, regulations and practices for transportation between all points on their systems (Section 6). The carriers are prohibited from demanding or collecting any different compensation for transportation than specified in their traiffs [Sections 2 and 6(7)]. Their rates, charges, and classifications must be just and reasonable [Sections 1(4), (5) and (6)] and must not subject any shipper, locality or territory to any undue or unreasonable prejudice or disadvantage (Section 3).

The tariff for a particular service must be filed at least 30 days before its effective date, except where by rule or by order in an individual proceeding there is provided a different notice period [Section 6(3)].

Matters Relating to Lawfulness of Tariff Rates

Upon the filing of a tariff, persons believing it to be unlawful in any respect may file complaints or protests, setting forth the grounds upon which they consider the tariff provisions to be in violation of the I.C. Act (Sections 13, 15). If the agency finds no basis for questioning the lawfulness of the tariff, it may simply deny the protest and allow the tariff to go into effect on the scheduled effective date. If, however,

[10]*Ibid.*
[11]*Ibid.*, pp. 118-19.
[12]*Ibid.*, p. 119.

either upon the basis of a protest or on its own motion, the agency believes that a hearing concerning the lawfulness of the tariff is warranted, it may institute an investigation and schedule a hearing [Section 15(7)]. Pending the hearing and decision, the agency may suspend the operation of the tariff for as long as 7 months [Section 15(7)].

If an investigation is instituted, with or without suspension of the tariff, the agency will conduct a full hearing as to the lawfulness of the tariff. Where initial rates are involved, those challenging the rates have the burden of proof.[13]

Pipeline revenues at a particular rate level are considered reasonable if they do not exceed the level necessary to cover operating expenses and income taxes, and provide a proper rate of return on the carrier's valuation.[14]

If the agency, after full hearing, finds that a rate is unjust or unreasonable, unjustly discriminatory, unduly preferential or prejudicial, or otherwise in violation of the I.C. Act, it may order the carrier to cease and desist from charging the rate, and may prescribe a just, reasonable and lawful rate for the future [Section 15(1)]. Finally, any person injured by the carrier's having maintained an unlawful rate may file a complaint seeking reparations or damages from the carrier (Sections 8, 9, 13, 16).

Valuation

The agency keeps abreast of the cost of pipeline construction and compiles an index of pipeline construction costs as an aid to its annual valuation of pipeline proporties. Under Section 19a of the I.C. Act the ICC was required to have a field inventory made of all the property owned and/or used in transportation service. These valuations were undertaken by the ICC during the 1930's. In conjunction with the field inventory each pipeline was required to submit a detailed paper inventory of its plant as called for by the ICC's valuation orders. Subsequent to the initial valuation the pipeline carriers are required to submit reports of annual property changes occurring in physical plant. These changes are reported in substantial detail by location.

Valuations of pipeline property are made from the data submitted by the pipeline carriers to be used for ratemaking purposes pursuant to the requirements of Section 19a of the I.C. Act. The elements considered in

---

[13]*Rail-Water, Grain in Bulk, Mo., Ill., and Ind. to Buffalo*, 321 I.C.C. 564.
[14]No. 35533, *Petroleum Products, Williams Brothers Pipe Line Company*, (served December 21, 1976).

such valuations are the original cost of the property, the cost of reproduction new, cost of reproduction less depreciation, present value of
lands and rights-of-way, working capital, and going concern value. The
valuations are not only based on valuation reports submitted by the
carriers, but also on audits by the agency's staff. The valuations do not
become final until after notice to the carrier and other persons of the
tentative valuation. In the event that a tentative valuation is protested,
an opportunity for hearing is provided before a final valuation is issued.

By preparing annual valuations of pipeline carriers, the agency has
available current in formation that permits a determination of the rates-
of-return being earned by pipeline carriers. The rates-of-return are based
on the valuation and classification of pipeline property by the agency
which, under Section 19a(i) of the I.C. Act, "shall be prima facie evidence of the value of the property in all proceedings under the Act . . . as
of the date of the fixing thereof, and in all judicial proceedings for the
enforcement of the Act . . . and in all judicial proceedings brought to
enjoin, set aside, annul, or suspend, in whole or in part, any order" of the
agency.

In the past an 8 percent return on valuation generally has been allowed for crude oil pipelines. A 10-percent return on valuation has been
allowed for pipelines transporting petroleum products.[15] However, a
judicial consent decree in 1941 allowed shipper-owners of pipeline carriers to receive dividends limited to 7 percent of the valuation of the
carrier's property. The allowable dividends were determined by taking
7 percent of the total valuation of the pipeline property and giving each
owner a proportion of the total dividends equal to the percentage of
stock owned in the pipeline. This method of limiting dividends based on
the valuation of the pipeline property was upheld by the Supreme Court
in *United States v. Atlantic Refining Co.*[16] because the language of the
consent decree had been interpreted in that way and had been adhered
to over many years by all the parties including the government officials
who drew up and administered the decree. The Court said (p. 24)
"where the trial court concludes that this interpretation is in fact the
one the parties intended, we will not reject it simply because another
reading might seem more consistent with the Government's reason for

[15]*Reduced Pipe Line Rates and Gathering Charges*, 243 I.C.C. 115; 272 I.C.C.
375. *Minnelusa Oil Corp. v. Continental Pipe Line Co.*, 258 I.C.C. 41. *Petroleum
Rail Shippers' Assn. v. Alton & S.R.*, 243 I.C.C. 589; *Petroleum Products, Williams
Brothers Pipe Line Company, supra.*
[16]360 U.S. 19.

entering into the agreement in the first place."[17] *Atlantic Refining* involved a complaint against major oil companies and their pipeline subsidiaries for violation of the Elkins Act and Section 6(7) of the I.C. Act. The action, as indicated above, was terminated by a consent decree.

[17]See *Fawcus Mach. Co. v. United States*, 282 U.S. 375, 378, where the Supreme Court said that "contemporaneous construction by those charged with the administration of the act . . . are . . . entitled to respectful consideration, and will not be overruled except for weighty reasons."

24

Common Carrier Tariffs

The Applicable Statutory Provisions

Section 6(1) of the Interstate Commerce Act[1] provides:

"That every common carrier subject to the provisions of this part shall file with the Commission created by this part and print and keep open to public inspection schedules showing all the rates, fares, and charges for transportation between different points on its own route and between points on its own route and points on the route of any other carrier by railroad, by pipe line, or by water when a through route and joint route have been established. If no joint rate over the through route has been established the several carriers in such through route shall file, print and keep open to public inspection as aforesaid, the separately established rates, fares and charges applied to the through transportation."

Section 6(1) provides further:

"The schedules printed as aforesaid by any such common carrier shall plainly state the places between which property and passengers will be carried, and shall contain the classification of freight in force, and shall also state separately all terminal charges, storage charges, icing charges, and all other charges which the Commission may require, all privilege or facilities granted or allowed and any rules or regulations which in any wise change, affect, or determine any part or the aggregate of such aforesaid rates, fares, and charges, or the value of the service rendered to the passenger, shipper, or consignee. Such schedules shall be plainly printed in large type, and copies for the use of the public shall be kept posted in two public and conspicuous places in every depot, station, or office of such carrier where passengers or freight, respectively, are received for transportation, in such form that they shall be accessible to the public and can be conveniently inspected. The provisions of this section shall apply to all traffic, transportation, and facilities defined in this part."

[1]49 U.S.C. 6(1) Comparable provisions — Sections 217(a), 218(a), 306(a), 306(e), 405.

Section 6(2)[2] provides:

"Any common carrier subject to the provision of this part receiving freight in the United States to be carried through a foreign country to any place in the United States shall also in like manner print and keep open to public inspection, at every depot or office where such freight is received for shipment, schedules showing the through rates established and charged by such common carrier to all points in the United States beyond the foreign Country to which it accepts freight for shipment; and any freight shipped from the United States through a foreign country into the United States the through rate on which shall not have been made public, as required by this part, shall, before it is admitted into the United States from said foreign country, be subject to customs duties as if said freight were of foreign production."

Section 6(3)[3] provides:

"No change shall be made in the rates, fares, and charges or joint rates, fares, and charges which have been filed and published by any common carrier in compliance with the requirements of this section, except after thirty days' notice to the Commission and to the public published as aforesaid, which shall plainly state the changes proposed to be made in the schedule then in force and the time when the changed rates, fares, or charges will go into effect; and the proposed changes shall be shown by printing new schedules, or shall be plainly indicated upon the schedules in force at the time and kept open to public inspection: Provided, that the Commission may, in its discretion and for good cause shown, allow changes upon less than the notice herein specified, or modify the requirements of this section in respect to publishing, posting, and filing of tariffs, either in particular instances or by a general order applicable to special or peculiar circumstances or conditions: Provided further, That the Commission is hereby authorized to make suitable rules and regulations for the simplification of schedules of rates, fares, charges, and classifications and to permit in such rules and regulations the filing of an amendment of or change in any rate, fare, charge, or classification without filing complete schedules covering rates, fares, charges or clasifications not changed if, in its judgment, not inconsistent with the public interest."

Section 6(4)[4] provides:

"The names of the several carriers which are parties to any joint tariff shall be specified therein, and each of the parties thereto, other than the one filing the same, shall file with the Commission such evidence of concurrence therein or acceptance thereof as may be required or approved by the Commission, and where such evidence of concurrence or acceptance is

[2]49 U.S.C. 6(2).
[3]49 U.S.C. 6(3) Comparable provisions — Sections 217(c), 218(a), 306(d), 306(e), 405(d).
[4]49 U.S.C. 6(4).

filed it shall not be necessary for the carriers filing the same to also file copies of the tariff in which they are named as parties."

Section 6(5)[5] provides:

"Every common carrier subject to this part shall also file with said Commission copies of all contracts, agreements, or arrangements with other common carriers in relation to any traffic affected by the provisions of this part to which it may be a party: Provided, however, That the Commission, by regulations, may provide for exceptions from the requirements of this paragraph in the case of any class or classes of contracts, agreements, or arrangements, the filing of which, in its opinion is not necessary in the public interest."

Section 6(6)[6] was amended by the 4R Act. It provides:

"The schedules required by this section to be filed shall be published, filed, and posted in such form and manner as the Commission by regulation shall prescribe. The Commission shall, beginning 2 years after the date of enactment of this sentence, require (a) that all rates shall be incorporated into the individual tariffs of each common carrier by railroad subject to this part or rail ratemaking association within 2 years after the initial publication of the rate, or within 2 years after a change in any rate is approved by the Commission, whichever is later, and (b) that any rate shall be null and void with respect to any such carrier or association which does not so incorporate such rate into its individual tariff. The Commission may, upon good cause shown, extend such period of time. Notice of any such extension and a statement of the reasons therefor shall be promptly transmitted to the Congress. The Commission is authorized to reject any schedule filed with it, which is not in accordance with this section and with such regulations. Any schedule so rejected by the Commission shall be void and its use shall be unlawful."

Section 6(7)[7] provides:

"No carrier, unless otherwise provided by this part, shall engage or participate in the transportation of passengers or property, as defined in this part, unless the rates, fares, and charges upon which the same are transported by said carrier have been filed and published in accordance with the provisions of this part; nor shall any carrier charge or demand or collect or receive a greater or less or different compensation for such transportation of passengers or property, or for any service in connection therewith, between the points named in such tariffs than the rates, fares, and charges which are specified in the tariff filed and in effect at the time; nor shall any carrier refund or remit in any manner or by any device any portion of the rates, fares, and charges so specified, nor extend to any shipper or

[5]49 U.S.C. 6(5) Comparable provisions — Sections 220 (a), 313(b), 409(b), 412(a).
[6]49 U.S.C. 6(6) Comparable provisions — Sections 217(a), 306(b), 405(b).
[7]49 U.S.C. 6(7) Comparable provisions — Sections 217(b), (d); 218(a), 306(c), (d); 306 (e), 405(c), (e).

person any privileges or facilities in the transportation of passengers or property, except such as are specified in such tariffs."

Section 6(9)[8] provides:

"The Commission may reject and refuse to file any schedule that is tendered for filing which does not provide and give lawful notice of its effective date, and any schedule so rejected by the Commission shall be void and its use shall be unlawful."

Section 6(10)[9] provides:

"In case of failure or refusal on the part of any carrier, receiver, or trustee to comply with the terms of any regulation adopted and promulgated or any order made by the Commission under the provisions of this section, such carrier, receiver, or trustee shall be liable to a penalty of five hundred dollars for each offense, and twenty-five dollars for each and every day of the continuance of such offense, which shall accrue to the United States and may be recovered in a civil action brought by the United States."

Filing of Rates, Fares and Charges

Section 6 of the Interstate Commerce Act[10] is clear in requiring every common carrier to publish and file with the Interstate Commerce Commission all of its rates, fares and charges for all services in connection with transportation subject to the Act.[11] Although both Section 6(6), authorizing the Commission to reject schedules not in compliance with Section 6 or regulations issued thereunder, and Section 6(9), authorizing it to reject any schedule lacking lawful notice of its effective date, provide that schedules so rejected shall be void, the Commission is not required to reject any schedule, and a schedule becomes void and its use unlawful only upon rejection. A schedule not rejected for noncompliance with Section 6 or the regulations is therefore valid, and under Section 6(7) carriers must strictly observe the rates contained therein.[12] Accordingly, the Commission said in the *Phillips Petroleum* case, that

---

[8]49 U.S.C. 6(9) — Comparable provisions — Section 217(a), 306(b), 405(b).

[9]49 U.S.C. 6(10). See general provisions for violation of regulations — Sections 222(a), 317(a), 421(a).

[10]49 U.S.C. 6.

[11]*C. B. & Q. R. Co. v. Chicago, & E.I.R. Co.*, 310 I.C.C. 349.

[12]*Phillips Petroleum Co. v. Akron, C. & YR Co.* 308 I.C.C. 257, 260. See also *Chicago & NW Ry. Co. v. United States*, 195 F. Supp. 708, 712-714. An agency is authorized to reject tariffs for defects of form and substance where the rate or tariff is an obvious nullity as a matter of substantive law. *United Gas Pipe Line Co. v. Mobile Gas Corp.*, 350 U.S. 332, 347; *Municipal Light Boards v. FPC*, 450 F. 2d 1341, 1345-46, *cert. denied*, 405 U.S. 989; *W. J. Dillner Transfer Co. v. United States*, 214 F. Supp. 941. *Cf Federal Power Commission v. Texaco, Inc.*, 377 U.S. 33, 44.

rates cannot be found inapplicable or unreasonable solely because filed on less than statutory notice without the Commission's prior consent. In *Bison Steamship Corp. v. United States*,[13] it was stated that any rates, thirty days after they are filed and published by participating carriers, unless overridden or altered by the Commission in the interim, are clothed with legality. While such rates are not Commission-approved, unless and until the Commission takes some positive action they continue to be effective.

Jurisdiction Cannot Be Conferred on the Commission by Tariff Reference on Matters Not Subject to the I.C. Act

A tariff of a port commission is neither required to be filed with the I.C.C., nor does the I.C.C. have authority to regulate any of the rates, charges, rules or regulations contained therein; thus, a tariff reference by a barge line to dockage charges, including those published by the port commission cannot operate to confer jurisdiction.[14]

Separate Statement of Charges Subject to the I.C. Act

The requirement of tariff provisions of the I.C. Act that charges for service subject to the Act must be filed with Commission has always been construed as necessitating statement of such charges separately from others not subject to the Act; therefore, the Commission said in *Petroleum Products — Water — Motor — Inland Nav. Co.*,[15] where barge transportation of bulk petroleum products to certain storage terminals was exempt under Section 303(b), charges for motor hauls beyond to ultimate destinations over routes crossing State borders, which were subject to Commission's jurisdiction had to be separately stated.

Proposed Rates Beyond Scope of Operating Authority

Proposed rates which are beyond the scope of the carriers' operating authority are unlawful.[16] When restrictions in a carrier's operating au-

---

[13]182 F. Supp. 63, 66.
[14]*Greater Baton Rouge Port Comm. v. American Barge Line Co.* 299 I.C.C. 736.
[15]311 I.C.C. 219, 225.
[16]*Coffee Beans other than green — Poole's Drayage Co.*, 308 I.C.C. 495, 496; *Castings and Forgings from Portland, Ore., to Illinois*, 306 I.C.C. 129, 130; *Union Barge Line Corp.*, 304 I.C.C. 402. 408; *Various Commodities between points and places in U.S.* 309 I.C.C. 573, 577-8; *Wines from New York, New York, to Conn., to New Jersey, New York, and Penn.*, 305 I.C.C. 307, 308.

thority preclude it from performing transportation service, the carrier's rates are considered unlawful and will be ordered cancelled.[17]

Intermediate or Nearest-Point Rule

The Commission's rules require that the names of places from and to which rates apply shall be clearly and explicitly stated, and that rate tariffs of regular-route carriers may include intermediate-point rules; under present regulations irregular-route carriers may not establish intermediate-point rules.[18] Irregular-route carriers may not maintain intermediate-point rules because over irregular routes use of such rules promotes uncertainty of tariff publication, and affords a great multiplicity of routes and opportunities for undue preference and prejudice.[19]

Purpose of Section 6

The purpose of Section 6 is to outlaw every subterfuge, plan, scheme, or device used by carriers to give rebates, concessions, advantages, and discriminations to shippers in interstate commerce; it is designed to strike down every such device regardless of how ingenious, and is intended to strike through all such pretenses and subterfuges to reach and eradicate the forbidden evil.[20] As was said in *Silent Sioux Corp. v. Chichgo & N. W. Ry. Co.*,[21] one of the prime reasons for enactment of Section 6 was to prevent discrimination resulting from either a higher or lower quotation of lawful rates.

A carrier's extension to a shipper of any privilege or facility in the transportation of property, without specifying same in its published tariffs, violates Section 6(7).[22] The tariff in effect when the shipment moves is binding unon the carrier and shipper alike, and an error in the publication of a rate therein affords no legal ground for a departure from the tariff provisions.[23] The carrier has no authority to waive the requirements of its tariffs relating to its functions as either a common carrier or a collection agent.[24] Under Section 6, carriers must abide by

---

[17]*Paper from Detroit, Michigan, to Chicago, Illinois,* 311 I.C.C. 444, 445-6; *Points in Rocky Mountain Territory,* 311 I.C.C. 555, 558-9.

[18]*Dairy Products, Rules, Riggs Dairy Exp., Inc.,* 302 I.C.C. 545, 546; *Tile and Related Articles from Okron, Ohio, to N.Y., N.J., and Pa.,* 308 I.C.C. 487, 488.

[19]*Basis of Rates to Unnamed Points, Middle Atl. Territory,* 314 I.C.C. 477, 480.

[20]*United States v. Union Pac. R. Co.,* 173 F. Supp. 397, 412.

[21]262 F. 2d. 474, 476.

[22]United States v. Union Pacific Railroad Co., 173 F. Supp. 397, 411.

[23]*Pittsburgh Plate Glass Co. v. Baltimore & Ohio R. Co.,* 305 I.C.C. 479, 480.

[24]*North Coast Mfg. Co. v. Union Pacific R. Co.,* 185 F. Supp. 287, 288.

the published rules just as they must abide by the published rates.[25] No act or omission of carrier can estop or preclude it from enforcing payment of the full amount of the tariff charges; nor may equitable considerations justify failure of the carrier to collect, or retention by shipper of, any part of lawful tariff charges. The lawful rate is that which carrier must exact and that which shipper must pay. The tariff, just as the bill of lading, has the force of a statute and cannot be varied under any pretext, nor can the carrier lawfully depart from its terms.[26]

The strictness with which the Commission has interpreted Section 6 and the reasoning behind such interpretation is demonstrated in *Louisiana A & T Ry. Co. Operation.*[27] That case grew out of an application by the LA&T for approval of a trackage right agreement with the Cotton Belt pursuant to which the LA&T would be given rights over tracks of the Cotton Belt between Greenville and Dallas, Texas, a distance of approximately 61 miles. The agreement in question called for the Cotton Belt to perform the actual operations as agent for the LA&T. The following significant observations were made by the Commission in denying the application:

> Section 6(7) of the Interstate Commerce Act, after providing that no common carrier subject to the Act shall engage in transportation unless its tariff schedules are duly filed with us, further provides that no such carrier shall —
>
> Charge or demand or collect or receive a greater or less or different compensation for such transportation of passengers or property, or for any service in connection therewith, between the points named in such tariffs than the rates, fares, and charges which are specified in the tariff filed and in effect at the time; nor shall any carrier refund or remit in any manner or by any device any portion of the rates, fares, and charges so specified, nor extend to any shipper or person any privileges or facilities in the transportation of passengers or property, except such as are specified in such tariffs.
>
> Under those provisions, when a carrier performs a transportation service, one rate is to be charged therefor and that the one filed and published in the manner pointed out in the statute. The carrier is expressly prohibited from departing from such rate in any manner for the benefit of any shipper or any person.
>
> Under the proposed arrangement the Cotton Belt, although actually performing the identical transportation service which it holds itself out to perform under its published tariffs, does not propose to collect for such service

[25]*Cargill, Inc. v. Atlantic Coast Line R. Co.*, 304 I.C.C. 480, 487.
[26]*Pennsylvania R. Co. v. Greene*, 173 F. Supp. 657, 659.
[27]170 I.C.C. 602, 608 — 11. Another case wherein a somewhat similar application was denied for comparable reasons is *C&EI Trackage Rights*, 254 I.C.C. 603.

its published tariff rates or its established divisions of such rates but to accept in lieu thereof, and without regard to the plain requirements of Section 6, special compensation under a contract.

As stated by the Supreme Court in *New Haven R.R. v. Interstate Commerce Commission,* 220 U.S. 361, 392:

"If a carrier has a right to disregard the published rates by resorting to a particular form of dealing, it must follow that there is no obligation on the part of a carrier to adhere to the rates, because doing so is merely voluntary. The all-embracing prohibition against either directly or indirectly charging less than the published rates shows that the purpose of the statute was to make the prohibition applicable to every method of dealing by a carrier by which the forbidden result could be brought about."

And as also stated by the Supreme Court in *Kansas City Southern Ry. Co. v. United States* (282 U.S. 760):

"A common carrier dealing with transportation that is subject to the act cannot escape its statutory obligations by calling itself a private carrier as to such transportation. This applies to transactions with other carriers."

While under certain circumstances one carrier may be regarded in a sense as acting as agent for another, as in the case of a switching or terminal carrier, not a party to the joint rate, which makes delivery of a shipment following line-haul transportation by another carrier, there can be, under the act, no unrestricted relationship of agency under which the line-haul carrier is left free to contract with the switching carrier as to the charge which the latter shall receive for its service, but the switching carrier is bound to collect its published tariff rate for the transportation service which it performs.

So far as the contract of transportation is concerned, the Cotton Belt would not be shown as a party to the transportation but the bill of lading would be issued in the name of the applicant on the theory that the applicant is the carrier "receiving the property for transportation," and that the Cotton Belt is merely its agent in performing the transportation. Such an arrangement would substitute a later connecting carrier for the actual initial carrier which is required by the act to issue the bill of lading and to assume responsibility to shippers for loss or damage occurring on its line or on the lines of any other carrier party to the through bill of lading. As above pointed out, however, there can be no valid contract of agency between carriers subject to the act which conflicts with, or tends to defeat, the purposes of the provisions of the act.

If the applicant's theory that a carrier can extend its operations over the line of a connecting carrier by employing it as agent for compensation and considerations specified in a special contract is sound as applied to the instant case, it is sound for wider application, and a line having several connections might have similar contracts, but specifying different considerations for the service, so that it would be performing transportation in part at tariff charges, if for its own account, and in part at varying compensations and considerations under its contracts as agents for connecting carriers. To uphold the doctrine of principal and agent to the extent contended for by the applicant would be to say that one carrier, by contracting to perform as agent of another carrier the same transportation service that it now performs, and will continue to perform, on its own account, can make a private service out of that which is in fact a common-carrier service and can thus make lawful that which would otherwise be unlawful.

There is every indication that the Commission would have approved a bona fide trackage right contract contemplating that the LA&T perform its own operations over the Cotton Belt trackage. In refusing to approve the application as filed, the Commission stated that the "finding is without prejudice to the filing by the applicant of an application for a certificate to permit actual operation by it over the tracks of the Cotton Belt." Obviously, it would also have been entirely proper for the Cotton Belt and the LA&T to have entered into joint through rates with divisions upon any mutually satisfactory basis.

Cases in which Commission approval has been given to arrangements of this nature have generally involved only switching or terminal operations or relatively limited movements within the coal fields. See, for example. *Missouri Pacific RR Co. Trustee Operation*[28] involving trackage rights over approximately five miles of track, the contract providing for switching of applicant's cars from and to the mine with grantor's power and crews, and that, while performing this service, the equipment and employees were to be considered as joint engines and crews of the railroads; and *Terminal Allowances at Minnesota Transfer*[29] wherein switching and interchange services performed at Minnesota Transfer, Minnesota, pursuant to a long-standing contract, without the publication of charges were found to be not in violation of Section 6. In this case the Commission went to some length to distinguish the specific situation there involved from those which it had condemned, for example, in *LA&T Ry. Operation*. A principal distinction, of course, was the "terminal or interchange" nature of the services.

Agreement Between Carrier and Shipper

Rates charged pursuant to an oral agreement between carrier and shipper, which rates are not disclosed by the carrier's tariff on file with the Commission when the shipments are made, are illegal;[30] the carrier is charged with knowledge that the agreed charges are illegal for failure

[28]242 I.C.C. 37.
[29]268 I.C.C. 5.
[30]*Northern Valley Transfer, Inc. v. I.C.C.*, 192 F. Supp. 600, 604.

to publish and file them as required by the I.C. Act.[31] The I.C. Act covers payments of rates in excess of tariff rates even though excess amounts are agreed to between carrier and shipper because of a strike at the shipper's plant in which pickets interfere with the movement of the freight.[32] By prohibiting a carrier from charging a greater or less or different charge than tariff charges on file with the Commission, the I.C. Act makes it the duty of carriers subject to its provisions to charge only just and reasonable rates, therefore, proof of actual discrimination is not necessary in actions charging violations of the I.C. Act.[33] In the *Schupper* case, the court said (p. 862) that the "impracticability of operation" clause of the carrier's tariff gave it only a right to refuse to enter the strikebound plant, not a right to declare such transportation an operation separate from the remainder of the journey and thus outside the rate restrictions included in the tariff.

Form and Effect of Tariff Publication

A principle expressed on the form and effect of publication of tariffs is that the terms of a tariff should be clearly stated so that misunderstanding can be avoided.[34] In the *Middlewest Motor Freight Bureau* case, the Commission said that since the tariffs provided lower rates on sheets and plates under the description of building and roofing materials than on iron or steel articles, resulting in application of different rates according to use or billing description, defendants should clarify them to eliminate such confusion.

In *Iron or Steel Articles over Barge Lines*,[35] the Commission said that while barge lines may, because of higher minimum weights among other things, find it necessary to provide different commodity groupings from those maintained by other modes of transportation, necessity for such larger or different groupings does not warrant failure to name specifically the articles comprising such groups; operational practices of water carriers which differ from those of other types of carriers in transporting freight afford no justification for lack of clarity in their tariffs.

---

[31]*Carlee Corp. v. Northern Valley Transfer, Inc.*, 304 I.C.C. 775, 778.
[32]*United States v. Schupper Motor Lines, Inc.*, 262 F. 2d 859, 861.
[33]*Ibid.*
[34]*Traylor Engineering & Mfg. Co. v. Lehigh Valley RR Co.*, 308 I.C.C. 529. See also *United States v. Associated Air Transport, Inc.*, 275 F. 2d 827, 833, 837; *Empire Petroleum Co. v. Sinclair Pipeline Co.*, 282 F. 2d 913, 916 — Not arising under the I.C. Act; *Middlewest Motor Freight Bureau v. Chicago B&QR Co.*, 309 I.C.C. 303, 305, 306.
[35]399 I.C.C. 481, 483.

The Commission said that carriers should specifically describe the commodities included in the generic descriptions when publishing commodity rates;[36] that a commodity description which leaves uncertain the commodities upon which the rates apply is unlawful and in violation of the Commission's tariff-publishing requirements, thus, the carrier was required either to describe fully and specifically the commodities included in the description "Iron and Steel Articles of Every Description" or to cancel the description in its entirety.[37]

Other principles concerning the form and effect of tariff publications are that specific routing in rate items takes precedence over general routing provided by reference to a territorial directory;[38] that it is the shipper's duty to pay and the carrier's duty to collect, charges on the articles actually shipped, regardless of their description in the shipping papers;[39] that it is the shipper's duty to state clearly and present truly the character of its shipment, and that it is entitled to no rate except that shown in the carrier's schedule for transportation of the commodity as tendered for shipment.[40] In construing tariffs, when two tariffs are equally appropriate, the one which provides the shipper with the lower rate is to be applied.[41] In the *Western Pacific* case, the court said that when two tariffs, one export and the other domestic, are equally appropriate, the export tariff naming the lower of two rates covers shipments to coast ports for export. In the *Western Pacific* case, both tariffs contained language to the effect that, on export tariff, a rate designated as an export rate would take precedence over other rates between the same two points.

In ascertaining the meaning of the language used in a tariff, the object sought to be accomplished is to be accorded full consideration, and if the language is fairly susceptible of the object sought to be accomplished, that construction must be placed thereon.[42] Language should be construed so as to carry out the intention of the parties, resolving any doubt as to meaning in favor of the shipper, and construction should be fitted to and controlled by the fact situation presented.[43] However, although doubt as to meaning of a tariff provision must be resolved in

---

[36]*Ibid.*
[37]299 I.C.C. 484.
[38]*Sulphur from Tioga, N. Dak., to Chandler, Ariz.*, 314 I.C.C. 337, 338, 339.
[39]*Traylor Engineering & Mfg. Co. v. Lehigh Valley RR Co.*, 308 I.C.C. 529, 534.
[40]Ibid. See also *Mead Corp. v. Baltimore and Ohio RR Co.*, 308 I.C.C. 790, 791.
[41]*Western Pacific RR Co. v. United States*, 279 F. 2d 258, 264.
[42]*Spreckels Sugar Co. v. Southern Pac. Co.*, 308 I.C.C. 783, 785; *General Motors Corp. v. New York Central RR Co.*, 306 I.C.C. 345, 347.
[43]*Union Pac. RR Co. v. United States*, 287 F. 2d 593, 598.

favor of shipper and against the carrier compiling the tariff, the doubt must be a reasonable one.[44]

Tariffs should be read in their entirety. All pertinent provisions of the tariff must be considered together, and if those provisions may be said to express the intention of the framers under a fair and reasonable interpretation that intention must be given effect.[45] In determining the rates on particular shipments, provisions of the governing tariffs in effect when the shipments moved must be considered; comparable provisions of other tariffs or subsequent amendments to the provisions under consideration, intent of the tariff framers, and symbols used in connection with the amendments may be considered for the purpose of shedding light on the meaning of unclear terms used in a tariff, but they may not be used to change such terms.[46] Terms used in the tariff must be taken in the sense in which they are generally understood and accepted commercially, and neither carriers nor shippers may be permitted to urge successfully for their own benefit a strained or unnatural construction.[47]

The nature and character of a commodity at time tendered for shipment determine its identity for transportation purposes. Facts which weigh heavily in making such determination are the producer's description of the commodity for sale purposes, the manner in which it is billed, its use and value, and how it is regarded in the trade.[48] A difference in freight rates may not lawfully be based solely on a difference in use to

[44]*Administrative Determination of Applicable Rate*, 310 I.C.C. 659, 662; *Arco Trading Corp. v. Missouri Pac. RR Co.*, 314 I.C.C. 225, 226, 227; *Berman and Specter v. Atchison T&SF RR Co.*, 308 I.C.C. 254, 255, 256; *Texas Gas Transmission Co. v. Alton & S. R.* 310 I.C.C. 207, 210.

[45]*Berman and Specter v. Atchison T&SF Ry. Co.*, 308 I.C.C. 254, 256; *Arco Trading Corp. v. Missouri Pac. RR Co.*, 314 I.C.C. 225, 227; *Spreckels Sugar Co. v. Southern Pac. Co.*, 308 I.C.C. 783, 785; *American Bread Co. v. Atchison, T&SF Ry. Co.*, 310 I.C.C. 196, 197, 198.

[46]*Northwestern Steel & Wire Co. v. Pennsylvania RR Co.*, 309 I.C.C. 470, 472.

[47]*Middlewest Motor Freight Bureau v. Chicago, B&QR Co.*, 309 I.C.C. 303, 305; *Texas Gas Transmission Corp. v. Alton & SR*, 310 I.C.C. 207, 210; *Arco Trading Corp. v. Missouri Pacific R. Co.*, 314 I.C.C. 225, 227; *Berman and Specter v. Atchison, T&SF Ry. Co.*, 308 I.C.C. 254, 256; *Administrative Determination of Applicable Rate*, 310 I.C.C. 659, 662.

[48]*Merrimac Leather Co., Inc. v. Boston & M.R.*, 306 I.C.C. 611, 613; *Hyman-Michaels Co. v. Chicago, R. I. & P. R. Co.*, 308 I.C.C. 339, 341; *Nobilium Products, Inc. v. Chicago B&Q R. Co.*, 308 I.C.C. 243, 244; *Virginia Crafts, Inc. v. Southern Ry. Co.*, 309 I.C.C. 56, 57; *Middlewest Motor Freight Bureau v. Chicago B&QR Co.*, 309 I.C.C. 303, 305. As stated in *Eliasberg Bros., Inc. v. Railway Exp. Agency, Inc.*, 302 I.C.C. 305, 307, the "provisions in the tariff of a common carrier on file with this Commission have the force and effect of a statute, and the carrier and shipper alike are charged with knowledge thereof and are bound thereby." See also *Farmers Potato Distr. Co., Inc. v. Atchison, T. & S.F. Ry.*, 318 I.C.C. 415, 419; *Liberty Industrial Salvage Co. v. Delaware, L. & W. R. Co.*, 262 I.C.C. 391, 395; *Kahn Mfg. Co. v. Boston & M.R.*, 276 I.C.C. 556, 559.

which an article is to be put; the same rate should apply regardless of the use to which it is put. However, even though a commodity may not be rated according to the different uses to which it may be put, nevertheless, the Commission in numerous reports has given weight to the use of an article in determining its nature and character.[49] As the Commission said in *Lockheed Aircraft Corp. v. Pan-Atlantic SS Corp.*,[50] while a single article may not be classified according to the use to which it is put, its use may be probative in the identification of the article shipped.

Obligations Under Tariffs

The tariff is treated as though it were a statute binding both the carrier and shipper to the rates, charges, rules and regulations published therein.[51] A carrier cannot waive or be estopped from collecting full charges prescribed by published tariffs.[52] The carrier is required to collect and the shipper to pay the full charges specified in the controlling tariff.[53] Both the shipper and the carrier are bound to take notice of such rates, and neither ignorance nor misquotation will justify the paying of less than the effective tariff rate. Neither misunderstandings nor agreements among shippers or receivers and carriers can affect the statutory provisions which obligate the carriers to collect and the shippers or receivers to pay amounts no different than the applicable rates.[54]

No concessions may be made contrary to the applicable tariff.[55] No oral contracts or agreements may supersede or vary the tariff as to permit such oral contracts or agreements would open the door to all manner of special contracts departing from the tariffs filed with the

---

[49]*Traylor Engineering & Mfg. Co. v. Lehigh Valley RR Co.*, 308 I.C.C. 529.

[50]308 I.C.C. 747, 748.

[51]*Pittsburgh & C. Ry. Co. v. Fink*, 250 U.S. 577; *Penna. R.R. Co. v. International Coal Co.*, 230 U.S. 184; *Miller v. Ideal Cement Company*, 214 F. Supp. 717, 720.

[52]*Union Pacific Railroad Company v. Higgins*, 223 F. Supp. 396, 401.

[53]*T & M. Transp. Co. v. S. W. Shattuck Chemical Co.*, 158 F. 2d 909, 910.

[54]*Fedders-Quigan Corp. v. Long Transp. Co.*, 64 M.C.C. 581, 587. No agreement, express or implied, can vary the terms of the tariff. *Northwest Potato Exc. v. Great Northern Ry. Co.*, 172 I.C.C. 671, 672; *Susskind v. Florida East Coast Ry. Co.*, 270 I.C.C. 239, 246; *Eliasberg Bros., Inc. v. Railway Exp. Agency, Inc.*, 302 I.C.C. 305. The carrier is required to adhere to the published tariff unless and until modified by the Commission to prevent discrimination between shippers and secret rebates and concessions. See *Thomson Phosphate Co. v. Atlantic Coast Line R. Co.*, 332 I.C.C. 641, 643-44.

[55]*United States v. P. Koenig Coal Company*, 270 U.S. 512; *Miller v. Ideal Cement Company, Supra.*

Commission.[56] Deviation from the lawful rates and charges duly published in the tariff is not permitted.[57] This is an unyielding and rigid rule, the purpose being to prevent every form of discrimination.[58]

A rule contained in the tariff is part of the tariff, and cannot be waived.[59] Thus if a certain period of free time is allowed for the detention of equipment under tariff rules the free time actually allowed by a carrier to a shipper or consignee must be limited to that specified in the tariff. Any free time beyond that specified in the tariff which is allowed by the carrier would be subject to the tariff charges. This is supported by the decisions applying to demurrage.

There is an analogy between the charges assessed for the detention of motor carrier equipment and demurrage charges assessed for the detention of railroad equipment. It has been held that demurrage charges are part and parcel of the transportation charges, and are covered by the same rules of law; they are a part of the tariff, and must be collected from the shipper or the consignees to the same extent as the charge for carriage.[60] A shipper must pay the published charges, including demurrage, strictly in accordance with the terms of the tariff.[61] The purpose of the law is to secure absolute equality between shippers.[62] Mistake, inadvertence, honest agreement, or good faith are alike unavailing if the demurrage charges are not collected by the carrier.[63]

Tariffs-Stipulations in Bills of Lading

No stipulation in a bill of lading can operate to defeat the provisions of Section 6 of the Interstate Commerce Act[64] Rates are governed by published tariffs and not by notations made on bills of lading.[65]

---

[56]*Atchison & C. Ry. Co. v. Robinson*, 233 U.S. 173; *Miller v. Ideal Cement Company, supra.*

[57]*Louis & Nash. R.R. v. Maxwell*, 237 U.S. 94; *Miller v. Ideal Cement Company, supra.*

[58]*T. & M. Transp. Co. v. S. W. Shattuck Chemical Co., supra.*

[59]*Gus Blass Co. v. Powell Bros. Truck Line*, 53 M.C.C. 603, 605; *Davis v. Henderson*, 266 U.S. 92, 93; *Bienville Warehouses Corp., Inc., v. Illinois Central R. Co.*, 208, I.C.C. 583, 585; *Natural Products Refining Co., v. Central R. Co. of N.J.*, 216 I.C.C. 105, 107.

[60]*Davis v. Timmonsville Oil Co.*, 285 Fed. 470, 472.

[61]*Central Iron & Steel Co. v. Pennsylvania R. Co.*, 237 I.C.C. 791, 793.

[62]*Davis v. Timmonsville Oil Co., supra.*

[63]*Davis v. Timmonsville Oil Co., supra.*

[64]*Brownyard v. Union P. R. Co.*, 148 I.C.C. 444, 447.

[65]*Pole Stock Lumber Co. v. G. & S. I. R. R. Co.*, 26 I.C.C. 451.

Master Tariffs

A master tariff is a separate tariff filed with the Commission to provide for a general increase in the level of all or substantially all rates and charges in individual tariffs of the railroads and their rate publishing agents. The Commission's tariff circular rules do not authorize the publication and filing of master tariffs. The Commission grants authority to file these tariffs by special permission orders issued in general revenue increase proceedings. These orders also permit the simultaneous filing of connecting-link supplements to individual tariffs to make them subject to the master tariff. These supplements provide the initial link that unites several thousand individual tariffs with a single master tariff.

Master tariffs obviously facilitate the railroads' task of initially publishing nationwide across-the-board rate increases. However, continued use of these tariffs over long periods of time runs counter to the goal of tariff simplification. Because of this, Congress amended Section 6(6) of the I.C. Act through the enactment of Section 209 of the 4R Act to legislate a solution to the problem of the proliferation of master tariff publications.[66]

The Commission instituted a proceeding in Ex Parte No. 326, *Regulations Governing the Transfer of General Increases from Master Tariffs into the Individual Tariffs of Railroads or Rail Ratemaking Organizations,* to amend tariff circular No 20[67] for the purpose of establishing regulations conforming to the statutory time limits within which general increases in rates and charges must be transferred from master tariffs into the individual tariffs of each railroad or rail ratemaking organization.

The following regulations will apply:

(1) A general increase shall be transferred from a master tariff to the basic tariffs: (i) within 2 years from the effective date of the master tariff if the Commission authorizes the general increase to become effective without suspension; or (ii) if the increase is suspended or an investigation is instituted within 2 years from the date of service of the Commission's final order authorizing the increase in whole or in part.

(2) If a general increase is under investigation by the Commission at the time a later general increase becomes effective, the date for compliance shall be determined by reference to the date of service of the

---

[66]The Commission for a number of years admonished the carriers to update their tariffs. See e.g. *Increased Freight Rates and Charges, 1973,* 344 I.C.C. 589, 620 and *Increased Freight Rates and Charges, 1975,* 349 I.C.C. 555, 575.

[67]Decided December 8, 1977. See 49 C.F.R. 1300.

Commission's final order relating to the prior increase. Thus, the date determined for transfer of the prior increase shall also govern transfer of the later increase.

Notice to Have Proposed Rate Change Considered by the Commission Pursuant to the "7 Percentum Increase or Decrease" Provisions of the 4R Act

The Commission by notice of February 17, 1976, announced that to satisfy the requirements of the statute and to facilitate the implementation thereof, any common carrier by railroad (or its tariff publishing agent) which desired to have any proposed rate change considered by the Commission pursuant to the "7 per centum increase or decrease" provisions of the 4R Act (Section 15(8) (b), (c) of the I.C. Act) should notify the Commission upon the carrier's (or publisher's) filing of the proposed tariff or schedule containing said changes. The notification to the Commission should include (1) the rate(s) in effect on January 1, 1976 (later January 1, 1977) and (2) verification that the information contained in said notice had been furnished to each subscriber of the tariff or schedule at the time said subscriber was furnished its copies of the publication as provided by the rules adopted in Docket No. 35613. This so-called "yo-yo" provision expired on February 5, 1978.

Timely Transmission of New Tariff Publications

In *Regulations-Transmission of Tariffs and Schedules,*[68] the Commission established new rules for the timely transmission of new publications to subscribers and for the furnishing of effective tariffs upon request. The new rules were promulgated because of the many problems that shippers have encountered in trying to get copies of the governing tariffs.

International Joint Rates and Through Routes

In Ex Parte No. 261, *International Joint Rates and Through Routes*[69] the Commission promulgated rules for the filing of international joint rates and through routes established by domestic rail, motor, and water

---

[68]349 I.C.C. 119.
[69]The fifth and final report is in 351 I.C.C. 490, aff'd in No. 76-1558, June 20, 1977, D.C. Cir.

carriers with ocean carriers. The Commission stated[70] that its purpose in promulgating rules concerning joint through rates was as follows:

"[I]t is our goal to facilitate the through transportation of freight by intermodal carriers between the United States and foreign countries. A shipper is benefitted when he can make a contract with the originating carrier which covers a movement through to the destination at a total charge published in a single tariff. Moreover, the national transportation policy should be fostered and the free flow of commerce spurred by encouraging the establishment of more economical and integrated transportation services between the United States and foreign countries."

The Commission had the following to say about the substantive regulation of the entire joint rate:[71]

In our consideration of the intermodal tariffs filed with this Commission, however, we do not intend to assert jurisdiction over or otherwise to engage in substantive regulation of the ocean portion of the rates pursuant to the Interstate Commerce Act.

Therefore, we wish to emphasize the fact that our jurisdiction will be invoked solely to accomplish substantive regulation of the domestic carrier's portion of the through rate and that any procedural requirements we may impose will be directed to this end.

Thus, from a procedural standpoint, a change in a joint through rate occasioned by a change in only the ocean portion of the rate will not provide grounds for suspension of either the entire rate or the ocean portion alone. When our suspension procedures are invoked, they will be limited to the divisions accruing to the domestic carrier and the relevant governing provisions.

From a substantive point of view, challenges to a joint through rate as inconsistent with the provisions of the Interstate Commerce Act will not be entertained unless directed to the domestic carrier's portion of the rate. Any determination of the lawfulness of the portion of a joint through rate accruing to the carriers subject to the jurisdiction of the FMC (ocean carriers) will be left to the FMC.

[70]337 I.C.C. at 627.
[71]351 I.C.C. at 491.

25

Schedules of Rates and Charges of Contract Carriers

Applicable Statutory Provisions

Section 203(a) (15) defines the term "contract carrier by motor vehicle" to mean any person which engages in transportation by motor vehicle of property in interstate or foreign commerce, for compensation, under continuing contracts with one person or a limited number of persons either for the furnishing of transportation services through the assignment of motor vehicles for a continuing period of time to the exclusive use of each person served or for the furnishing of transportation services designed to meet the distinct need of each individual customer."

Section 218(a), separated into its component parts, provides:

> (1) It shall be the duty of every contract carrier by motor vehicle to establish and observe reasonable minimum rates and charges for any service rendered or to be rendered in the transportation of property or in connection therewith and to establish and observe reasonable regulations and practices to be applied in connection with said reasonable minimum rates, fares, and charges.

> (2) It shall be the duty of every contract carrier by motor vehicle to file with the Commission, publish, and keep open for public inspection, in the form and manner prescribed by the Commission, schedules containing the actual rates or charges of such carrier for the transportation of property, and any rule, regulation, or practice affecting such rates or charges and the value of service thereunder. *Provided,* that any contract carrier serving but one shipper having rendered continuous service to such shipper for not less than one year may file reasonable minimum rates and charges unless the Commission in any individual case, after hearing, finds it in the public interest to require the filing of actual rates and charges.

(3) No contract carrier, unless otherwise provided, shall engage in the transportation of property unless the actual rates or charges for such transportation have been published, filed, and posted in accordance with the provisions of this section.

(4) Nothing in this section shall be so construed as to require such carriers to maintain the same rates, rules, and regulations for the same services for all shippers served.

(5) No reductions shall be made in any such charge either directly or by means of any change in any rule, regulation, or practice affecting such charge or the value of the service thereunder, nor shall any new charge be established, except after 30 days' notice of the proposed change or new charge filed in the aforesaid form and manner. The Commission may, in its discretion and for good cause shown, allow such change upon such less notice, or modify the requirements with respect to posting and filing of such schedules, either in particular instances, or by general order applicable to special or peculiar circumstances or conditions. Such notice shall plainly state the change proposed to be made and the time when such change will take effect.

(6) No such carrier shall demand, charge, or collect compensation for such transportation different from the charges filed, as affected by any rule, regulation or practice so filed, or less than the minimum rate or charges as may be prescribed by the Commission from time to time, and it shall be unlawful for any such carrier, by the furnishing of special services, facilities, or privileges, or by any other device whatsoever, to charge, accept, or receive compensation different from the actual rates and charges so filed, or less than the minimum charges so prescribed. Provided, that any such carrier or carriers, or any class or group thereof, may apply to the Commission for relief from the provisions of these provisions, and the Commission may, after hearing, grant such relief to such extent and for such time, and in such manner as in its judgment is consistent with the public interests and the national transportation policy.

Section 218(b), separated into its two principal parts, provides:

(1) Whenever, after hearing, upon complaint or upon its own initiative, the Commission finds that any minimum rate or charge of any contract carrier by motor vehicle, or any rule, regulation, or practice of any such carrier affecting such minimum rate or charge, or the value of the service thereunder, for the transportation of passengers or property or in connection therewith, contravenes the national transportation policy declared in this Act, or is in contravention of any provision of this part, the Commission may prescribe such just and reasonable minimum rate or charge, or such rule, regulation, or practice as in its judgment may be necessary or desirable in the public interest and to promote such policy and will not be in contravention of any provision of this part.

(2) Such minimum rate or charge, or such rule, regulation, or practice, so prescribed by the Commission, shall give no advantage or preference to any such carrier in competition with any common carrier by motor

vehicle subject to this part, which the Commission may find to be undue on inconsistent with the public interest and the national transportation policy declared in this Act, and the Commission shall give due consideration to the cost of the services rendered by such carriers, and to the effect of such minimum rate or charge, or such rule, regulation, or practice, upon the movement of traffic by such carriers.

Section 218(c) provides in part:

> Whenever there shall be filed with the Commission by any such contract carrier any schedule stating a charge for a new service or a reduced charge directly, or by means of any rule, regulation, or practice, for the transportation of passengers or property in interstate or foreign commerce, the Commission is hereby authorized and empowered upon complaint of interested parties or upon its own initiative at once and, if it so orders, without answer or other formal pleading by the interested party, but upon reasonable notice, to enter upon a hearing concerning the lawfulness of such charge, or such rule, regulation, or practice, and pending such hearing and the decision thereon the Commission, by filing with such schedule and delivering to the carrier affected thereby a statement in writing of its reasons for such suspension, may from time to time suspend the operation of such schedule and defer the use of such charge, or such rule, regulation, or practice, but not for a longer period than seven months beyond the time when it would otherwise go into effect; and after hearing, whether completed before or after the charge, or rule, regulation, or practice goes into effect, the Commission may make such order with reference thereto as would be proper in a proceeding instituted after it had become effective. If the proceeding has not been concluded and an order made within the period of suspension, the proposed change in any charge or rule, regulation, or practice shall go into effect at the end of such period.

Section 220(a) provides that the Commission may require any motor carrier "to file with it a true copy of any contract, agreement, or arrangement between such carrier and any other carrier or person in relation to any traffic affected by the provisions" of Part II of the Act. The statute also provides that the Commission shall *not* "make public any contract, agreement, or arrangement between a contract carrier by motor vehicle and a shipper, or any of the terms or conditions thereof, except as a part of the record in a formal proceeding where it considers such action consistent with the public interest." It is also provided that "if it appears from an examination of any such contract that it fails to conform to the published schedule of the contract carrier" the Commission may, in its discretion, "make public such provisions of the contract as the Commission considers necessary to disclose such failure and the extent thereof."

Section 222(c) provides:

> Any person, whether carrier, shipper, consignee, or broker, or any officer, employee, agent, or representative thereof, who shall knowingly offer,

grant, or give, or solicit, accept, or receive any rebate, concession, or discrimination in violation of any provision of this part, or who by means of any false statement or representation, or by the use of any false or fictitious bill, bill of lading, receipt, voucher, roll, account, claim, certificate, affidavit, deposition, lease, or bill of sale, or by any other means or device, shall knowingly and willfully assist, suffer or permit any person or persons, natural or artificial, to obtain transportation of passengers or property subject to this part for less than the applicable rate, fare, or charge, or who shall knowingly and willfully by any such means or otherwise fraudulently seek to evade or defeat regulations as in this part provided for motor carrier or brokers, shall be deemed guilty of a misdemeanor and upon conviction thereof be fined not less than $200 nor more than $500 for the first offense and not less than $250 nor more than $2,000 for any subsequent offense.

Regulations

A regulation was issued in *Contracts of Contract Carriers*,[1] requiring that contract carriers of property by motor vehicle shall tranport only under contracts or agreements. In *Filing of Contracts by Contract Carriers*,[2] a regulation was issued requiring the filing of a true copy of each contract required by 1 M.C.C. 628. In *Contract Carriers' Schedule of Minimum Rates*,[3] a regulation was issued requiring that all schedules of minimum rates or charges, and changes therein, be filed with the Commission.

Tariff Circular

Tariff Circular MF No. 4 contains regulations governing the construction, filing and posting of freight schedules of rates and charges of contract carriers.

Essential Requirement of the Statutory Definition of a Contract Carrier

An essential requirement of the statutory definition of a contract carrier is that it may not be a common carrier and shall perform transportation only under "individual contracts or agreements." In discussing the essential requirement of the statutory definition, the Commission said in *Government Freight, Contract Carriers by Motor Vehicle:*[4]

[1] 1 M.C.C. 628.
[2] 2 M.C.C. 55.
[3] 22 M.C.C. 343.
[4] 301 I.C.C. 551, 557.

While this Commission may modify the requirement respecting the form of the contracts, such as reduction to writing, retention of a copy by the carrier, etcetera, we may not dispense with the essentials affecting the legal status of contract carriers. It appears doubtful, therefore, that we have authority to waive the requirements of a bilateral agreement, imposing obligations upon both carrier and shipper, and covering a series of shipments during a stated period of time, promulgated for the purpose of effectuating the statutory distinction between common and contract carriers, and assuring that the latter do not trespass in the sphere of the former. . . .

In the *Government Freight* case, the question for determination was whether and the extent to which contract carriers should be granted relief from the provisions of Sections 218(a) and 220(a) and the Commission's rules and regulations promulgated thereunder, with respect to the filing of schedules of minimum charges and contracts, and the form and terms of such contracts, insofar as these matters relate to transportation performed under contracts with the Government. It was held that there was no sufficient factual or legal justification for granting the relief sought. The principal justification advanced for the requested relaxation of the regulation provided by the I.C. Act was that there should be complete equality and full freedom, as between common and the contract carriers, to compete for Government traffic. The Commission said (at pp. 556-57):

. . . This Commission on various occasions has recognized that one of the principal purposes of the act is to promote and protect adequate and efficient common-carrier service as the backbone of public transportation; that the regulation of contract carriage is designed and confined with that end in view; and that, for these reasons, the treatment of contract carriers differs from common-carrier regulation. It is because of this difference, under which contract carriers have certain advantages in competition with common-carriers, including the ability to pick and choose their traffic and shippers, that contract carriers are enabled to give a higher type of special and personalized service than is possible for common-carriers. It is the need and demand for this service which constitutes the chief justification for this class of carriers in the motor-transportation industry. . . .

Comparing the Charges in the Schedules
with Those in the Contracts

Contract carriers were required, as noted above, in *Filing of Contracts by Contract Carriers*,[5] to file with the Commission a true copy of each contract. Because of the difficulties in the administration of Section

[5] 2 M.C.C. 55.

218(a) requiring the filing of schedules containing minimum rates of contract carriers actually maintained and charged and the necessity of comparing the charges and the schedules with those in the contracts, that proceeding was reopened and, on reconsideration in 41 M.C.C. 527, 532, it was found:

> that in order properly to administer Section 218(a) of the Act, it is necessary to compare the minimum rates and charges stated in schedules of contract carriers of property, as defined in Section 203(a) (15) of the Act, with the rates and charges for the same service shown in the contracts between such carriers and shippers for whom they provide transportation, and that, in order to facilitate such comparison, and pursuant to Section 220(a) of the Act, all contract carriers . . . with each schedule naming minimum rates and charges for services not included in schedules and contracts on file with us, shall file with us at the same time a true copy of the actual contract or proposed contract covering the service for which the minimum rates and charges in said schedule are to apply, and showing the actual rates and charges therefor, or an amendment to a contract on file between such carrier and the same shipper showing such actual rates and charges. . . .

Obligations As Set Out in the Prior Language of Section 218(a)

Contract carriers under Section 218(a) were required to file with the Commission, publish and keep open for public inspection, in the form and manner prescribed by the Commission, schedules containing the minimum rates or charges of such carriers *actually maintained and charged.* The underlined phrase made it necessary to include in the schedules the lowest rates, fares, and charges which were actually assessed in order to give competing common carriers adequate notice of the true character of the competition by which they were confronted.[6] In the *Auto Transports case,* the Commission said (p. 603) that it "has consistently interpreted the provision in accordance with the intent of Congress." It added that the requirements in the Tariff Circular with respect to the publication, keeping open for public inspection, and filing of the minimum rates and charges actually maintained and charged for the transportation of property were promulgated to effectuate Section 218(a). Significantly, in the *Auto Transports* case, the Commission ordered the suspension of the right of the carrier to engage in transportation because it had failed to comply with its obligations, as set out in Section 218(a) and the requirements of the Tariff Circular and in failing to bring itself into full compliance with such requirements.

---

[6]*Auto Transports, Inc., Suspension of Permit*, 51 M.C.C. 600, pp. 682-83.

In *Shipman Bros., Contract Charges, California and Idaho*,[7] it was stated that schedules of contract carriers which fail to show the lowest rates or charges actually maintained for the transportation in the carriers' contracts are unlawful. See also *Atwacoal Transp. Co., Minimum Rates*,[8] holding the minimum rates and charges in the carriers' tariff not maintained or charged pursuant to existing effective contracts or agreements are unlawfully published and that to determine whether minimum rates are maintained pursuant to contracts or agreements there must be filed with the Commission true copies of contracts or agreements with shippers for the transportation of property or other services incidental thereto. In the *Atwacoal* case, the rates published were for substantially different transportation services than that indicated to come within the existing contracts, and the Commission was of the opinion that the contracts should be examined in order to determine whether, and to the extent to which, such contracts conformed with the published rates. The *Atwacoal* case related to a contract carrier by water and involved an interpretation of Sections 306(e) and 313(b). The wording of Section 306(e) is in all essential particulars the same as the wording of Section 218(a). The language in Section 306(e), therefore, was interpreted in the *Atwacoal* case in the same way as Section 218(a) was interpreted in the *Shipman* case.

Amendment of Section 218(a) in 1957

The objective of Congress in amending Section 218(a) was to equalize competitive opportunities by requiring contract carriers to make the same public disclosure of actual rates and charges that had for years been required of common carriers.[9] The long-familiar scheme of enforcement was likewise extended to contract carriers, outlawing attempts to recover charges higher than those duly filed and published.[10] In one respect, Congress relaxed the new requirements. Subject to the Commission's discretionary power to order the filing of actual rates in any particular case, it allowed a contract carrier serving but one shipper to file reasonable minimum rates and charges.[11]

A & F Trucking Corporation v. Liggett Drug Company,[12] *and Bowser and Campbell v. Knox Glass, Inc.*,[13] are important. The *A & F Trucking*

---

[7]30 M.C.C. 229.
[8]283 I.C.C. 647.
[9]*A & F. Trucking Corporation v. Liggett Drug Company*, 253 F. Supp. 699, 702.
[10]Ibid.
[11]Ibid., p. 702, f'n 3.
[12]253 F. Supp. 699.
[13]264 F. Supp. 522.

case involved an action by a contract carrier for claimed transportation charges. In accordance with Section 218(a), Plaintiff filed its initial schedule of contract rates with the Commission. Similarly, under Section 220(a), it filed the contract as a whole. Later the parties amended their agreement to provide for increased rates and this amendment was filed with the Commission. The contract recited that the rates were based upon the prevailing labor union contract wage scales and provisions, and upon the prevailing applicable common carrier charges of a rate bureau, and that rates were to be modified or adjusted accordingly if there were changes in either the labor scales or the bureau rates. The court held that a contractual escalation clause geared to labor scales and some other set of rates could not substitute for the rate filing the statute requires. The court said (at p. 702) that "The statutory end of disclosure would hardly be served by holding that an outside reader of the schedule should have been required to go to the contract (even assuming, contrary to 49 U.S.C., Section 320(a), that it was available), see what the schedule was said to be 'based upon,' and to know from this whether and how the actual rates, without a new filing, had been 'modified' or 'adjusted accordingly.'" The court stressed the fact that the contract was filed in accordance with Section 220(a), which statute does not provide for, but normally forbids publishing of contracts. It was obvious that the court felt that, since the contracts are not normally published, the prohibition against deviation from charges filed is not found in Section 220(a), but is found in Section 218(a) providing specifically for the filing and publishing of rates schedules.

In the *Bowser and Campbell* case, action was brought by a contract carrier against a shipper to recover alleged undercharges. The evidence showed that the written agreement and the schedule of charges incorporated therein did not express what the parties intended, and that what the parties intended was omitted therefrom inadvertently and by mistake. The carrier admitted this. The court held (at p. 526) that "Under the facts and circumstances of this case, we think the intentions of the parties expressed by the parol terms of their private contract, and the disclaimer of carrier, should prevail." The court said (pp. 526-27):

> Contract carriage is grounded on individual contracts between shippers and contract carriers. It is not based on a continuing offer to provide service to the general public, as is common carriage. Common carriage is regulated to protect the public from price discrimination; contract carriage is regulated to protect common carriers from cut-throat competition by contract carriers (§ 318(b), 49 U.S.C.A.). Subject to that limitation, contract carriage is special and individual; its purpose is to meet the needs of the particular shipper. Thus the shippers need not look at the rates

filed by the contract carrier, whereas the shipper by common carrier is absolutely bound by the filed tariff of the common carrier.

Since the rates actually charged Knox by Carrier were competitively comparable to those charged by common carriers operating in the vicinity, it is obvious why the I.C.C. expressed no concern in any action to enforce collection of the alleged undercharges. No common carrier was injured competitively by Carrier's mistake. On the other hand, if the rates mistakenly filed by Carrier were enforced by this court, not only would effect be given to Carrier's mistake and omission, but it would also enable Carrier to collect exorbitant rates for past services far in excess of those charged by common carriers offering similar services during the same period.

It is our opinion that in this action between parties to contract carriage, as distinguished from common carriage, contract principles should be applied in determining their rights and liabilities and not the rates filed in the erroneous Schedule of Charges. Accordingly, judgment will be entered in favor of Knox.

There were special facts and circumstances in the *Bowser and Campbell* case which tempers the decision somewhat. It appears that from the standpoint of equity the court was correct but in the process of arriving at a decision it misinterpreted the law. It is believed that the correct principle of law is that there can be no deviation from the schedules and contracts filed with the Commission.

26

Rates and Charges

The Applicable Statutory Provisions

Section 1(5) of the Interstate Commerce Act[1] was amended by the Railroad Revitalization and Regulatory Reform Act of 1976, 90 Stat. 34. Former Section 1(5) is now Section 1(5) (a); however, Section 1(5) (a) does not apply to railroads. Section 1(5) (b) is applicable to railroads Under Section 1(5) (b), each rate for any service rendered or to be rendered in the transportation of persons or property by railroads "shall be just and reasonable." A rate that is unjust and unreasonable is prohibited and unlawful. Section 1(5) (b) also provides as follows:

1. No rate which contributes or which would contribute to the going concern value of a railroad shall be found to be unjust or unreasonable, or not shown to be just and reasonable, on the ground that such rate is below a just or reasonable minimum for the service rendered or to be rendered.

2. A rate which equals or exceeds the variable costs of providing a service shall be presumed, unless such presumption is rebutted by clear and convincing evidence, to contribute to the going concern value of the railroad proposing such a rate.

    a. In determining variable costs, the Commission shall at the request of the railroad proposing the rate, determine only those costs of the railroad proposing the rate and only those costs of the specific service in question, except where specific data and cost information is not available.

    b. The Commission shall not include in variable costs any expenses which do not vary directly with the level of service provided under rate in question.

[1]49 U.S.C. 1(5) Comparable provisions — Sections 216 (a), (d), 305(a), 404(a).

3. No rate shall be found to be unjust or unreasonable, or not shown to be just and reasonable, on the ground that such rate exceeds a just or reasonable maximum for the service rendered or to be rendered, unless the Commission has first found that the proponent railroad has *market dominance* over such service. ("Market dominance" refers to an absence of effective competition from other carriers or modes of transportation for the traffic or movement to which a rate applies. Section 1(5) (c).).

   a. A finding that a railroad has market dominance over a service shall not create a presumption that the rate or rates for such service exceed a just and reasonable maximum.

4. A railroad is not prohibited from increasing a rate from a level which reduces the going concern value of the proponent railroad to a level which contributes to such a going concern value and is otherwise just and reasonable.

   a. For the above purposes, a rate increase which does not raise a rate above the incremental costs of rendering the service to which such rate applies shall be presumed to be just and reasonable.

Under Section 15(9) whenever a rate of a railroad is challenged as being unreasonable high, the Commission shall, upon complaint or upon its own initiative and within 90 days after the commencement of a proceeding to investigate the lawfulness of such rate, determine whether the carrier proposing such rate has market dominance over the service to which such rate applies. If the Commission finds that the railroad does not have market dominance, such finding shall be determinative in all additional or other proceedings under the I.C. Act concerning such rate or service, unless (a) such finding is modified or set aside by the Commission, or (b) such finding is set aside by a court of competent jurisdiction. Nothing shall limit the Commission's power to suspend a rate except that if the Commission has found that a railroad does not have market dominance over the service to which a rate applies, the Commission may not suspend any increase in rate on the ground that such rate as increased exceeds a just or reasonable maximum for such service, unless the Commission specifically modifies or sets aside its prior determination concerning market dominance over the service to which such rate applies.

However, it is noted that the above amendments made by the 4R Act do not (1) modify the application of Section 2, 3, or 4 of the I.C. Act in determining the lawfulness of any rate or practice; (2) make lawful any competitive practice which is unfair, destructive, predatory, or otherwise undermines competition which is necessary in the public interest; (3) affect the existing law or the authority of the Commission with respect to rate relationships between ports; or (4) affect the authority and responsibility of the Commission to guarantee the equalization of rates within the same port.[2]

In compliance with Section 202 of the 4R Act, the Commission instituted a rulemaking proceeding in Ex Parte No. 320, *Special Procedures for Making Findings of Market Dominance as Required by the Railroad Revitalization and Regulatory Reform Act of 1976*, to establish standards and procedures for making market dominance determinations. These standards and procedures were established by report and order of the Commission served October 1, 1976.[3] They provide in part as follows:

§1109.1 *Requirements and Procedures Relating to a Determination of Market Dominance with Regard to Rates Challenged as Unreasonably High*

(a) In order that the Commission may determine whether a rail carrier proposing a rate increase possess market dominance over the service to be rendered under a proposed rate, there shall be included in the carrier's statement notifying the Commission that it wishes to have the proposed rate considered pursuant to section 15(8)(c) of the Interstate Commerce Act, evidence upon which the Commission may base a determination with regard to market dominance, to the extent available, and including but not limited to the following information;

(1) Descriptions of involved commodities and full seven-digit STCC number(s);

(2) Descriptions of involved points or areas and mileage(s), stated in terms of short line mileage by rail;

(3) The variable cost of the service to which the rate applies;

(4) Whether and to what extent the rate in issue has ben docketed, discussed, considered, or approved before a rate bureau acting under an agreement filed with and approved by the Commission pursuant to section 5a or 5b of the Interstate Commerce Act; application number(s), date proposal docketed with rate bureau, and final disposition of proposal and date thereof; and the share of the market, or an estimate thereof, presently held by such participating carriers;

(5) Tonnage of the involved traffic transported between the involved points or areas by the proponent carrier and its affiliates during the preceding year, and the rates charged therefor during the same time period;

(6) Names of any known originating for-hire carriers of any mode offering interchangeable service between the involved points or areas, the

---

[2]Section 202(f) of the 4R Act.
[3]Aff'd except in one respect in No. 76-2048, Appls. D.C., May 2, 1978, *A. T. & S. Fe Ry. Co. v. I.C.C. and U.S.* See 49 C.F.R. 1121.

tonnage transported, and the rates charged therefor during the preceding year;

(7)   The extent to which the proponent rail carrier has taken general increases approved by the Commission in the preceding two years.

(8)   Any other relevant information.

(b)   In all proceedings involving a request for suspension of a proposed rate on the ground that it is unreasonably high there shall be included in the verified complaint seeking suspension of the schedule containing the proposed rate, evidence upon which the Commission may base a determination with regard to market dominance, including the information outlined in subparagraphs (a) (1)-(7), to the extent available and not previously furnished by the rail carrier, and including but not limited to the following information:

(1)   Characteristics of the involved traffic or movement affecting the case or difficulty with which transportation services of other carriers or modes may be substituted for the service to be performed under the rate in issue;

(2)   Tonnage of the involved traffic transported between the involved points or areas by any known for-hire carriers, other than those in subparagraph (a) (5), during the preceding year, and the rate charged therefor during the same time period;

(3)   Any other relevant information.

(c)   Any reply to a verified complaint seeking suspension should contain any information required by §1109.1(a) and (b), to the extent not previously furnished by complainant. Whether or not a reply to a verified complaint seeking suspension is filed, the proponent rail carrier on or before the due date for filing a reply, must provide the Commission with the information required by §1109.1(a) to the extent available and not previously submitted by another party.

(d)   A formal complaint containing an allegation that an existing rail rate is unreasonably high shall contain verified evidence upon which the Commission may base a determination with regard to market dominance, including, to the extent available, the information outlined in §1109.1(a) and (b.) The answer to a formal complaint shall be verified and shall contain the information outlined in §1109.1(a) to the extent not previously furnished. Replies limited to the issues of market dominance raised by any verified answer, may be filed within 10 days of the due date for the filing of such answer.

(e)   Upon notification of a proceeding instituted upon the Commission's own initiative to investigate whether an existing or proposed rate is unreasonably high, the interested carrier or carriers shall file, within 20 days from the service date of the order instituting said investigation, a verified statement containing, to the extent available and if not previously furnished by the carrier(s), evidence upon which a market dominance determination may be based, including but not limited to the information outlined in §1109.1(a) and (b). Replies, if any, directed to the issue of market dominance, should be field within 20 days of the due date for the filing of the carrier statement.

(f) In a proceeding involving a determination as to market dominance wherein the evidence adduced establishes that the rate in issue has been discussed, considered or approved under a rate bureau agreement filed with the Commission pursuant to section 5a or 5b of the Interstate Commerce Act, a rebuttable presumption will arise that a carrier participating in the rate or in such discussion or consideration does not provide effective competition to the proponent rail carrier for the involved traffic or movement.

(g) In a proceeding involving a determination as to market dominance wherein the evidence adduced establishes one of the following situations, a rebuttable presumption that the carrier whose rate is in issue has market dominance over the involved traffic or movement will arise:

(1) Where the proponent carrier has handled 70 percent or more of the involved traffic or movement during the preceding year; the market share of the proponent will be deemed to include the share of any affiliates, and of any carrier participating in the rate or with whom the proponent carrier has discussed, considered, or approved the rate in issue;

(2) Where the rate in issue exceeds the variable cost of providing the service by 60 percent or more; and,

(3) Where affected shippers or consignees have made a substantial investment in rail-related equipment or facilities which prevents or makes impractical the use of another carrier or mode.

Legal and Lawful Rate

The rates specified in tariffs, which carriers are required to charge, are known as legal rates. However, the legal rate is not necessarily a lawful rate. As stated in *Arizona Grocery Co. v. A., T. & S. F. Ry. Co.*,[4] a rate "was lawful only if it was reasonable . . . the shipper was bound to pay the legal rate; but if he could show that it was unreasonable he might recover reparation." In the case of rates prescribed by the Commission (as distinguished from carrier-initiated rates) there is "no difference between the legal or published tariff rate and the lawful rate."[5] But "the great mass of rates" are "carrier-made rates, as to which the Commission need take no action except of its own volition or upon complaint, and may in such case award reparation by reason of the charges made to shippers under the theretofore existing rate."[6]

[4]284 U.S. 370, 384.
[5]*Ibid.*, p. 387.
[6]*Ibid.*, p. 390.

The Meaning of the Words "Just and Reasonable"

The key words of the statute are "just and reasonable";[7] in other words a reasonable rate may be unlawful because it is unjust, and a just rate may be unlawful because it is unreasonable. The word "reasonable" implies a fair return for services rendered by the carriers; the word "just" implies that from the shipper's standpoint the rate must be fair to him in relationship to rates exacted from shippers of commodities under similar transportation conditions. The fact that a finding is made that a proposed rate schedule is not shown to be unlawful does not constitute an approval or prescription of the rates under suspension. They stand only as carrier-made rates.[8] Rates may lie within the zone of reasonableness and yet be unlawful.[9]

Burden of Proof

The proponent of a changed rate or schedule has the burden of showing that it is just and reasonable, in which a minimum requirement is a clear showing that it would be reasonably compensatory.[10] Likewise, the burden of proving that a proposed changed rule, regulation, or practice is just and reasonable is upon the proponent.[11] When an investigation into the reasonableness of rates is instituted after the rates have become effective, the burden of proof is not upon the respondent but upon the parties assailing the rates.[12] The statute does not place upon proponent

[7]The two words "just" and "reasonable" are not used in the I.C. Act as synonyms.
[8]*Cantlay & Tanzola v. United States*, 115 F. Supp. 72.
[9]*United States v. Illinois Cen. R. Co.*, 263 U.S. 515.In the absence of unlawful discrimination or of rates so low as to be a menace to the steady and efficient service called for by the statute a carrier is entitled to initiate rates and, in this connection, to adopt such policy of ratemaking as to it seems wise. *United States v. Chicago, M., St. P. & P. R. Co.*, 294 U.S. 499, 506; *United States v. Illinois Central R. Co.*, 263 U.S. 515, 522.
[10]*Rail-Trailer and Sea-Land Rates, East to Southwest*, 306 I.C.C. 795, 796, 797; *Radio and Television Sets, Ill., Ind., N.J. and N.Y.*, 302 I.C.C. 654, 656; *Garment on Hangers, N.Y. to Chicago and Detroit*, 309 I.C.C. 184, 186; *Petroleum Products-Water-Motor-Inland Nav. Co.*, 311 I.C.C. 219, 221, 223; *Radio and Television Sets, Ill., Md., D.C., Ind.*, 306 I.C.C. 207, 208, 209; *Insulation Material from Manville, N.J. to Virginia*, 309 I.C.C. 580, 582; *Building Material, Points in Central Territory*, 308 I.C.C. 324, 326; *Watson Bros. Transp. Co. v. United States*, 180 F. Supp. 732, 737, 738; *Acme Fast Freight, Inc. v. Western Freight Assn.*, 229 I.C.C. 315, 326; *Forwarder Rates from Niles, Ill. to Philadelphia, Pa.*, 300 I.C.C. 296, 298; *Class Rates, Providence — Philadelphia Dispatch, Inc.*, 302 I.C.C. 558, 560; *Clothing and Related Articles in Official Territory*, 306 I.C.C. 589, 590; *Work Clothing from Nixon, N.J. to Chicago, Ill.*, 306 I.C.C. 279, 280.
[11]*Stopoff Provision — Wilson Truck Co., Inc.*, 308 I.C.C. 159, 162.
[12]*Liquid Sugar to Ohio Points*, 306 I.C.C. 298, 299-300.

the burden of proving the justness and reasonableness of initial rates.[13] The burden of proving the unlawfulness of proposed initial rates rests with the protestants.[14]

Question of Reasonableness is for the Commission's Determination

A zone of reasonableness exists between maxima and minima within which a carrier is ordinarily free to adjust its rates.[15] However, the question of the reasonableness of a rate is essentially one of fact for the Commission's determination and the courts will not set aside findings that rates are reasonable if they are supported by substantial evidence.[16] As the Supreme Court said in *Illinois Commerce Commission v. United States:*[17]

> Whether or not the cost study was representative, whether the study should have been more refined, and whether it should have been supplemented as appellants desired, are questions of fact, the determination of which is within the competence of the Commission. The Commission reached its conclusion after full hearing and thorough consideration of all questions presented. As the record affords a sufficient basis for the Commission's determination, it is not subject to review in the courts.

In *Board of Trade of Kansas City v. United States,*[18] the Supreme Court said:

> Whether a preference or advantage or discrimination is undue or unreasonable or unjust is one of those questions of fact that have been confided by Congress to the judgment and discretion of the Commission . . ., and upon which its decisions, made the basis of administrative orders operating *in future,* are not to be disturbed by the courts except upon a showing that they are unsupported by evidence, were made without a hearing, exceed constitutional limits, or for some other reason amount to an abuse of power. *Manufacturers Ry. Co. v. United States,* 246 U.S. 457, 481; see

[13]*Malt Beverages from Golden, Colo., to Arizona,* 305 I.C.C. 91, 92; *Beer and Empty Containers – Transport Service, Inc.,* 305 I.C.C. 63, 65.

[14]*Livestock and Poultry Feed, Missouri to Arkansas,* 310 I.C.C. 13, 14; *Sugar from Idaho and Utah to Oklahoma and Texas,* 306 I.C.C. 271, 273, 273.

[15]*United States v. Chicago, M. St. P. & P. R. Co.,* 294 U.S. 499, 506; *Texas & P.R. Co. v. United States,* 289 U.S. 627, 636; *United States v. Illinois Central R. Co.,* 263 U.S. 515, 522; *Interstate Commerce Commission v. B. & O. R. Co.,* 145 U.S. 263; *Georgia v. Pennsylvania R. Co.,* 324 U.S. 439, 460, 461.

[16]*Illinois Central R. Co. v. Interstate Commerce Commission,* 206 U.S. 441, 445; *Interstate Commerce Commission v. Union Pacific R. Co.,* 222 U.S. 541, 550; *Virginian Ry. Co. v. United States,* 272 U.S. 658, 665.

[17]292 U.S. 474, 481.

[18]314 U.S. 534, 546.

Nashville, C & St. L. Ry. v. Tennessee, 262 U.S. 318, 322; *United States v. Chicago Heights Trucking Co.,* 310 U.S. 344, 352, 353.

The process of rate making is essentially empiric. The stuff of the process is fluid and changing — the resultant of factors that must be valued as well as weighed. Congress has therefore delegated the enforcement of transportation policy to a permanent expert body and has charged it with the duty of being responsive to the dynamic character of transportation problems. Cf. *Railroad Commission v. Rowan & Nichols Oil Co.,* 310 U.S. 573, 581, 582.

Test of Reasonableness

By the terms of the national transportation policy, the Commission is required to administer the Interstate Commerce Act so as to recognize and preserve the inherent advantages of each mode of transportation, and to encourage the establishment and maintenance of reasonable charges for transportation services, "without unjust discrimination, undue preferences or advantages, or unfair or destructive competitive practices." The policy further provides that "All of the provisions of this Act shall be administered and enforced with a view to carrying out the above declaration of policy."[19] Thus, the policy gives meaning and content to the standard, among others, of "just and reasonable" referred to in Section 1(5) of the I.C. Act. It is the yardstick by which the correctness of Commission action is measured.

A rate may be reasonable or unreasonable in relation to cost, in relation to rates on comparable shipments, or in relation to any other satisfactory standard which permits the Commission to measure and determine the factual question presented.[20] Thus the determination of the question of justness and reasonableness involves consideration of all given circumstances pertaining to the rate and the application of fairness and common sense.[21] In other words, all of the relevant circumstances

[19]See *Schaffer Transportation Co. v. United States,* 355 U.S. 83, 87, 88; *Eastern-Central Assn. v. United States,* 321 U.S. 194, 205-206; *McLean Trucking Co. v. United States,* 321 U.S. 67, 82, 83.

[20]*Chicago Board of Trade v. Illinois Central R. Co.,* 329 I.C.C. 529, 533; *Westinghouse Electric Corp. v. U.S.,* 388 F. Supp. 1309, 1317. A rate may be unreasonable per se, or intrinsically unreasonable — higher than justified by the service rendered by the carrier; or relatively unreasonable — unreasonable as compared with other rates on the same or similar commodities.

[21]*Albany Port District Com. v. Ahnapee & W. Ry. Co.,* 219 I.C.C. 151, 164; *Northwestern Steel & Wire Co. v. Pennsylvania R. Co.,* 305 I.C.C. 462, 464; *Chicago Board of Trade v. Illinois Central R. Co.,* 329 I.C.C. 529, 534.

surrounding such matters are to be evaluated in determining whether the resultant rate meets the standards of justness and reasonableness.[22]

The following discussion of some of the above-cited cases demonstrates that all the relevant circumstances surrounding the question of justness and reasonableness are considered by the Commission in rate cases.

In the *U. S. Steel* case, *supra*, complainant sought reparations on charges assessed by the railroads on shipments of iron or steel ingots from Geneva, Utah, to Fairfield, Alabama. At the time the shipments occurred, complainants' Fairfield facility was undergoing conversion from open-hearth to basic oxygen furnaces. During the conversion period complainant intended to meet Fairfield's ingot needs from other nearby mills. When those sources proved inadequate, an emergency situation developed which required complainant to make these interplant shipments from Geneva to keep the Fairfield mill operating near capacity. The single-car transcontinental rate was the only rate available from Geneva at the time the emergency developed. Therefore, a lower multiple-car commodity rate was proposed to provide complainant with a rate more in line with those for interplant movements in other territories. However, it became necessary to commence the movements before the lower rate became effective. Because of the particular circumstances involved and the fact that the rate applied to the subject movements was out of line with the rates on similar movements, the Commission found that the assailed charges were unjust and unreasonable.

In the *Valley Mould* case, *supra*, the railroads had agreed to publish a multiple-car rate on ingot molds which was $1.32 per net ton less than the single-car rate. Because of delays in publication, the reduced rate

---

[22]See e.g. *United States Steel Corp. v. Union Pacific R. Co.*, 355 I.C.C. 135; *Campbell Soup Co. — Petition for Declaratory Order*, 355 I.C.C. 504; *C. A. Wagner Construction Co. v. Chicago & N. W. Ry. Co.*, 208 I.C.C. 767; *C. A. Wagner Construction Co. v. Chicago, M. St. P. & P. R. Co.*, 219 I.C.C. 317; *Booth & Olson, Inc. v. Chicago, B & Q R. Co.*, 222 I.C.C. 569; *North American Cement Corp. v. Western Maryland Ry. Co.*, 235 I.C.C. 27, 28; *Valley Mould and Iron Corp. v. Norfolk and Western Ry. Co.*, Docket No. 34866 (not printed), report and order of ALJ served December 5, 1967, report and order of Review Board No. 4 served March 26, 1968; *E. I. DuPont DeNemours & Co. v. The Chesapeake and Ohio Ry. Co.*, Docket No. 36008 (not printed), initial decision of ALJ served October 3, 1974, Review Board No. 4 stay decision and order served April 28, 1975; *PPG Industries, Inc. v. The Alton and Southern Ry. Co. et. al.*, Docket No. 35121 (not printed) report and order of ALJ served April 6, 1970, effective May 6, 1970; *Derby Foods, Inc. v. Seaboard Coast Line Railroad Co. et. al.*, Docket No. 36471 (not printed), initial decision of ALJ served March 16, 1977, effective April 5, 1977.

did not become effective until after the movement of a number of cars had been completed. Complainant tendered the multiple-car shipments in accordance with the requirements of the multiple-car tariff, such as the number of cars, carload and shipment minimums, even though that tariff was not yet effective. Complainant contended that the rate assessed and collected was unjust and unreasonable to the extent it exceeded the multiple-car rate which later became effective. Upon consideration of the unusual circumstances, the fact that the traffic would not have moved but for the commitment of the railroads to establish the lower rate and the desirable nature of the traffic at rate comparisons with comparable traffic in the territory, the Commission found that the rate assessed was unjust and unreasonable.

In the *DuPont* case, *supra,* the railroad had published annual volume rates from and to Wurtland, Ky. and Petrolia, Pa., subject to certain tonnage requirements, and on condition that the shipper furnish an indemnity bond and notify the Eastern Weighing and Inspection Bureau of an intent to use the rates. Contemporaneously, the railroad maintained a higher carload commodity rate on the same commodity from and to the same points. The shipper met the tonnage requirements, but failed to meet the notice and bond conditions. Based upon the particular circumstances involved, and a comparison of the applicable non-annual volume rates with other rates, which non-annual volume rates were found to be higher than the compared rates, the assailed charges were found to be unjust and unreasonable.

In the *PPG* case, *supra,* single-car rates sought to be collected on shipments of vinyl chloride, in multiple tank carloads, from Lake Charles, La., to York, W. Va., were found applicable but unjust and unreasonable. Reasonable rates were determined. The shipments had moved under annual volume rates. The shipper met the annual volume tonnage requirements, but failed to furnish indemnity bonds and give notice of its intention to use the annual volume rates. It was found that the single-car rates were out of line with other rates and therefore were unjust and unreasonable to the extent that they exceeded the multiple-car annual volume rates.

In the *Derby Foods* case, *supra,* the railroads inadvertently increased their Plan II-1/4 rates by 7 percent whereas they had intended to increase such rates by only 3 percent. As a result the Plan II-1/4 rates were higher than the Plan II rates even though the railroads provided less service under Plan II-1/4 than under Plan II. It was held that the assailed Plan II-1/4 were unjust and unreasonable.

There are many established criteria which the Commission applies in evaluating the reasonableness of rates.[23] These include, *inter alia,* cost of service; value of service (what the traffic will bear); the existence of competition; the transportation characteristics of the commodity (weight, size, density); anticipated volume of shipments; the distance of the haul; the availability of return loads in the type of equipment used; the economic status of the industry served; the rate level required in order to move the traffic; comparison of the rate under consideration with established rates for comparable shipments in the territory involved; and other pertinent considerations.

As was said in *Interstate Commerce Commission v. Union Pacific R. Co.:*[24]

> The reasonableness of rates cannot be proved by categorical answers, like those given, where a witness may, in terms, testify that the goods were worth so much per pound, or the services worth so much a day. Too many elements are involved in fixing a rate on a particular article, over a particular road, to warrant reliance on such method of proof. The matter has to be determined by a consideration of many facts. *Smyth v. Ames,* 169 U.S. 466, 526; *Northern Pacific Ry. Co. v. North Dakota,* 236 U.S. 585, 596-597; *Intermountain Rate Cases,* 324 U.S. 476, 483-484; *Tripp v. Michigan Central R. Co.,* 238 Fed. 499, 453, cert. denied. 243 U.S. 648.

One of the best tests of reasonableness of a rate, the Commission has said, is a comparison with rates on a similar commodity between points in the same general territory.[25] The courts too have recognized that a comparison of other rates in the same general territory is proper in making a finding on the question of reasonableness.[26] In *Youngstown Sheet and Tube Co. v. United States,*[27] the Supreme Court in sustaining an order of the Commission said that "Comparisons of other rates in the same or adjacent territory, while not a conclusive test of reasonableness of a rate under investigation, have probative value." Comparisons of assailed rates, however, with other rates have little probative value

---

[23]See e.g. *Interstate Commerce Commission v. Union Pacific R. Co.,* 222 U.S. 541, 549. See also *Illinois Central R.R. Co. and Southern Ry. v. United States,* 101 F. Supp. 317, 324, 325; *El Dorado Oil Works v. United States,* 328 U.S. 12, 19.

[24]314 U.S. 534, 546.

[25]*Louisville & N. R. Co. v. United States,* 238 U.S. 1, 15; *Kansas City Structural Steel Co. v. A., T. & S.F. Ry. Co.,* 246 I.C.C. 13, 15; *Tidewater Associated Oil Co. v. A., T. & S.F. Ry. Co.,* 278 I.C.C. 586, 589; *Rheem Mfg. Co. v. Chicago, R. I. & P. Ry. Co.,* 273 I.C.C. 185, 190; *Charles A. Green & Son, Inc. v. Pennsylvania R. Co.,* 280 I.C.C. 357, 360; *Fairhurst Co. of Oregon v. Southern Pac. Co.,* 274 I.C.C. 435, 437; *Maple Island Farm, Inc. v. Chicago, B&QR Co.,* 280 I.C.C. 353, 356; *Asbestos Fiber, Canada to Middle Atlantic Territory,* 310 I.C.C. 729, 733, 734; *Panhandle Lbr. Co. v. Fort Worth & D.C. Ry. Co.,* 210 I.C.C. 353, 355; *Annisten Traffic Bureau v. Louisville & R. R. Co.,* 169 I.C.C. 741, 744.

[26]*State of New York v. United States,* 331 U.S. 284, 345.

[27]295 U.S. 476, 480.

without a showing of similarity in transportation conditions surrounding their establishment.[28] If there are different transportation characteristics between the two classes of commodities, the rates on such commodities cannot be properly compared to test the reasonableness of the assailed rates.[29]

The percentage relationships which rates bear to class rates, car-mile earnings, and ton-mile earnings are considered significant in testing rates.[30]

A mere showing of the existence of lower rates of a competing carrier at the time of publication of proposed rates does not establish the lawfulness of reduced rates to meet the competing rates.[31] This is especially true when the cost evidence indicates that the proposed rates would not be compensatory.[32]

The Commission has held that reduced rates which could reasonably be expected to spread throughout a particular rate structure disrupting rate adjustments of long standing with a consequent loss of revenue to carriers are unjust and unreasonable.[33] To upset or seriously menace a closely woven network of inter-related rates lawfully established may suffice to make proposed rates calculated to effect such a disruption unreasonable and unlawful.[34]

It has long been the rule, sanctioned by law and practical experience, that in establishing rates the Commission must have regard not altogether to particular carriers that may be most favorable or less favorably circumstanced, but to the whole situation, and its order must take into account its effect upon all carriers involved; this principle has applied throughout the history of the I.C. Act.[35]

[28]*General Commodities Between Chicago and New York*, 306 I.C.C. 243, 252; *Distribution Rates — Central Freight Trucking, Inc.*, 306 I.C.C. 769, 771; *Foodstuffs Between Rochester, N.Y., and Medina, Ohio*, 306 I.C.C. 646, 647.

[29]*Alcoholic Liquors from Boston, Mass. to Hartford, Conn.*, 308 I.C.C. 659, 660.

[30]*North American Aviation, Inc. v. Atchison T. & S.F. Ry. Co.*, 292 I.C.C. 257, 259; *Reduced Rates on Coal from the East to the Northwest*, 292 I.C.C. 119, 126-127; *Potash Co. of America v. Aberdeen & R.R. Co.*, 258 I.C.C. 109, 119-129. See also *North American Aviation, Inc. v. Atchison, T.&S.F. Ry. Co.*, 292 I.C.C. 257; *Reduced Rates on Coal, etc.*, 292 I.C.C. 119, 127; *General Commodity Rate Increases*, 233 I.C.C. 657, 676; *Potash Co. v. Aberdeen & R.R. Co.*, 258 I.C.C. 109, 126, in which the Commission has held that the earnings per car mile constitute an important element in passing on the question of what are maximum reasonable rates.

[31]*Candy Between Chicago and Cincinnati and Louisville*, 310 I.C.C. 799, 800.

[32]*Tapioca Flour from New York, N.Y., to Cincinnati and Hamilton, Ohio*, 306 I.C.C. 667, 668.

[33]*Grain and Grain Products to Eastern Points*, 122 I.C.C. 551, 564; *Chicago, Burlington & Quincy Railroad Co. v. C&EI Railroad Co.*, 315 I.C.C. 37.

[34]*Coal from Smithfield, Ohio to Ohio River*, 209 I.C.C. 399, 402; *Ex-Ohio River Coal to Ohio Points*, 185 I.C.C. 211, 219.

[35]*Increased Freight Rates*, 270 I.C.C. 403, 438.

Volume of traffic and regularity of movement are important considerations in determining reasonableness of proposed rates.[36]

Another element to be weighed in determining the reasonableness of a rate is the level of rates necessary to move a commodity.[37]

Where market competition is a factor, carriers may provide rates from competing origins which to some extent ignore relative distances;[38] maintenance of the same basis of rates is warranted when the competitive situation in one area is not shown to differ substantially from that in the other;[39] joint through rates which exceed the aggregate of intermediate rates are prima facie unreasonable and this presumption can be overcome only by a clear showing that the aggregate of the intermediate rates which would have applied in the absence of the through rate is below a maximum reasonable level;[40] a rate higher at an intermediate point than at a more distant point over the same route and in the same direction is prima facie unreasonable;[41] the prima facie presumption that rates to intermediate point which exceed the corresponding rates to more distant points over the same routes are unreasonable may be rebutted by a showing that the rate differences are warranted by differences in competitive conditions;[42] rates depressed to meet compelling competitive conditions are an improper standard by which to determine the reasonableness of rates under attack;[43] and compared

[36]*Boots or Shoes, Bel Camp, Md., to Boston and Providence*, 310 I.C.C. 769, 771; *United States Sugar Corp. v. Atlantic Coast Line R. Co.*, 277 I.C.C. 193, 201; *Snyder Chemical Co., Inc. v. A., T. & S. Fe Ry. Co.*, 294 I.C.C. 223, 225. In the *Snyder* case the Commission said, "It has long been a general rule of rate-making that rates may, and often should, decrease somewhat on a particular commodity as the volume of its tonnage increases, other transportation factors remaining constant" in *Ark-Mo Plant Food Co. v. Alabama, G.S.R. Co.*, 293 I.C.C. 707, 712, the Commission said, "Increased volume and heavy loading are significant factors in the determination of just and reasonable rates"; and in *Cigars from Jacksonville to Kansas City*, 313 I.C.C. 633, 636, the Commission said that ordinarily the difference between the carrier's rate and its cost between two points is substantially less on heavy movements of lower grade articles than on moderate shipments of high grade articles.

[37]*Penick & Ford v. Director General*, 80 I.C.C. 152, 156.

[38]*Building Materials, Waukegan to Omaha, Council Bluffs*, 310 I.C.C. 408, 410.

[39]*Meat and Packinghouse Products, Midwest to Coast*, 309 I.C.C. 551, 567, 568.

[40]*Sinclair Pipe Line Co. v. Transamerican Freight Lines*, 305 I.C.C. 772, 774.

[41]*Lynchburg Traffic Bureau v. Smith's Transfer Corp.*, 310 I.C.C. 503, 506.

[42]*Class Rates, Chicago, Ill. to Texas*, 311 I.C.C. 660, 662, 663.

[43]*Agsco Chemicals, Inc., v. Alabama Great Southern R. Co.*, 314 I.C.C. 725, 733; *Pittsburgh Metallurgical Co., Inc. v. American Barge Line*, 303 I.C.C. 686, 688. However, this does not mean that once a railroad reduces a rate for competitive purposes, that rate is forever thereafter insulated from comparison with other rates for the same commodity within the same interrelated network of rates. If this were the case, then, given the competitive pressures upon the railroads, many of the most sensitive rate relationships for numerous commodities would be beyond scrutiny. See No. 36114, *Pepco v. Penn Central Transportation Co.*, report served October 28, 1977.

rates depressed by reason of the competition of another mode of transportation are not an appropriate standard with which to measure maximum reasonableness of assailed rates not shown to be affected by such competition.[44]

In *North American Aviation, Inc. v. Atchison T. & S. F. Ry. Co.,*[45] the Commission stated:

> While the subsequent establishment of a lower rate creates no presumption of the unreasonableness of preexisting rates, that fact is entitled to consideration, along with other evidence, in determining whether the assailed rate was reasonable.

Some of the reasons for giving weight to value-of-service in rate-making is shown by the following quotation from the district court's opinion in *New York, New Haven and Hartford R.R. Co. v. United States:*[46]

> Value-of-service rate-making is a price-discrimination device, used either to maximize profit or to subsidize certain interests. As a maximizing tool, it can be used by a monopolist in the following way. M has a product — transportation — with two potential buyers, A and B. A uses it to ship industrial sand which he sells for $10 a ton, B to ship coal which he sells for $35 a ton; M's cost of shipment is the same for both. If he sets a uniform rate per ton of $2, B will ship but A will not — he will not be able to meet his competition at the market. If M sets his price at a uniform $1 per ton, both will ship — but M will lose a greater revenue which he could have garnered from B. And if M's out-of-pocket cost of carriage is $0.75 per ton, he will want A's $1 traffic. Early railroads thus developed the practice of charging $2 to B and $1 to A, cost of carriage notwithstanding.
>
> This value-of-service pricing is not necessarily unsound economically. Economists generally agree that:
>
> "Preferential rates relieve rather than burden other traffic if two conditions are fulfilled. These are (1) that the rate must more than cover the direct costs; and (2) that the traffic will not move at higher rates . . . ."
>
> And the ICC partly because this was the rate pattern prevailing when the Commission was established, and partly to maximize utilization of the railroads, adopted value-of-service as its own criterion of rate-making.
>
> The Commission, however, added factors of discrimination other than profit maximization. One of these is subsidization of certain commodities and/or producers, perhaps under political pressures. And of course, passenger traffic has been carried at a loss for some time. These losses are made up on other traffic. Other discriminations sometimes introduced by the ICC

---

[44]*Black Hills Glass & Mirror Co. v. C., M., St. P. & P. R. Co.,* 313 I.C.C. 333, 338.
[45]292 I.C.C. 257, 259. Cf. *Stauffer Chemical Co. v. Fort Worth & C. Ry. Co.,* 313 I.C.C. 393, 396.
[46]199 F. Supp. 635; judgment vacated 372 U.S. 744.

are attributable to its desire to act as an economic planner, see *e.g., Anchor Coal Co. v. United States,* 25 F. 2d 462, 470 (1928).

Cost of service is entitled to substantial consideration in determining the reasonableness of the rate which the carrier is seeking to assess. As early as 1911 in *Advances in Rates-Western Case,*[47] the Commission called attention to the importance of cost of service as an element in the prescription of rates. This was later reaffirmed in *Southern Class Rate Investigation,*[48] in the context of maximum reasonable rates. The Commission said that since the inception of Federal regulation of common carriers "cost of service has been recognized as one of the basic elements entering into the process of making and judging rates." The function of rate-cost comparisons as a standard of ratemaking was reiterated in *Hanna Mining Co. v. Missouri Pac. R. Co.*[49] More recently procedures adopted by the Commission to deal with general increase and rate cases place more and more emphasis upon cost-revenue relationships.[50] As the Commission said in *Rules to Govern Assembling & Presenting Cost Evidence, supra,* at 325-26, "Rate proceedings before the Commission generally require consideration of the relationship of relevant carrier costs to the rates."

Costs are most important in determining reasonableness where there is involved high volume, heavy loading traffic moving in multiple cars. The Commission has recognized that cost savings result from multiple-car movements.[51]

In ascertaining the cost of transportation of one out of numerous commodities handled by carriers it is impossible to attain precision. Mere lack of it, however, is not ground for objection to the evidence offered.[52] Thus average costs even though not identical with actual

---

[47]20 I.C.C. 307, 348.

[48]100 I.C.C. 513, 611.

[49]I.C.C. 166, 170. See also *Chicago Board of Trade v. Illinois Central R. Co.,* 329 I.C.C. 529, 533.

[50]See *Rules to Govern Assembling & Presenting Cost Evidence,* 377 I.C.C. 298; *New Procedures in Motor Carrier Revenue Proceedings,* 339 I.C.C. 324, 351.

[51]See e.g., *Grain in Multiple-Car-Shipments — River Crossings to the South* 325 I.C.C. 752; *Molasses from New Orleans, La., to Peoria and Pekin, Ill.,* 235 I.C.C. 485; *Coal from Ky., Va. and W. Va. to Virginia,* 308 I.C.C. 99; *Coal to New York Harbor Area,* 311 I.C.C. 355; Volume *Rates on Processed Meal — Midwest to Ports,* 322 I.C.C. 456, 485; *Asphalt to Iowa, Michigan, Minnesota and Wisconsin,* 316 I.C.C. 114, 124; *Multiple-Car Rates on Cement, Evansville, Pa., to N.J.,* 315 I.C.C. 672; *Limestone, Prairie Du Rocher, Ill., to Baton Rouge, Ia.,* 313 I.C.C. 71; *Rock Salt from New York to Del., Md., N.J., N.Y., and Pa.,* 313 I.C.C. 191; *Investigation of Railroad Frt. Rate Structure — Coal,* 345 I.C.C. 71, 332.

[52]*Baltimore & Ohio R. Co. v. United States,* 298 U.S. 349, 378.

costs, are the best approximation known to accountants.[53] Cost estimates made in accordance with acceptable cost-finding procedures are entitled to considerable weight.[54] That cost application made in strict accordance with acceptable cost-finding procedures has Commission support is made plain by its decision in *Iron or Steel Articles from the East to the Southwest*,[55] where it said:

> The railroads have a ready means of determining their costs on particular traffic: namely, the use of Rail Form A, a cost formula developed by our cost finding section, . . . Such cost formulas should be employed in establishing the compensativeness of rates in issue. Here . . . the margins by which the yields under the proposed rates would exceed the average earnings and expenses convinces us that the proposed rates would be reasonably compensatory.

See also *Lumber, California and Oregon to California and Arizona*,[56] where the Commission said:

> The protestants, particularly the water carriers and the Shippers Association, criticize the respondents' cost studies for failing to develop and present fully distributed costs. This is not fatal. Fully distributed costs computed in accordance with the method developed by our cost finding section, as protestants seem to think should have been submitted, would only represent the addition of a statistical apportionment of the constant costs to the variable costs, the results of which might not give effect to the competitive factors which must be considered in determining the justness and reasonableness of rates. We have said repeatedly that to be reasonably compensatory, a competitive rate must at least cover out-of-pocket costs, including the variable portion of a reasonable return after Federal income taxes, and make a contribution to the transportation burden. Out-of-pocket costs include those operating expenses, rents, taxes, and return which vary with changes in traffic volume and can be assigned directly to specific traffic movements. They are directly affected by the use of carrier facilities. The remainder or constant expenses are those incurred in connection with traffic as a whole, which, over a period of time, are generally unaffected by any increase or decrease in traffic volume, and, as they are incapable of direct assignment, must be fairly apportioned.

The following language, quoted from the Commission's decision in *Eastern Central M. Carriers' Assn. v. Akron, C. & Y. Ry. Co.*,[57] is pertinent:

---

[53]*Duplate Corp. v. Triplex Safety Glass Co.*, 298 U.S. 448, 458.
[54]*Rock Salt, Goderich, Ontario, to Illinois, Indiana, Mich., & Wis.*, 314 I.C.C. 327, 331.
[55]210 I.C.C. 587, 594.
[56]308 I.C.C. 345, 362.
[57]306 I.C.C. 61, 77, 78.

The revenue contribution studies prepared by our cost finding section are designed, in connection with past studies, to provide a comparison of carload revenues and costs by commodity classes and groups. Their broad purpose is to indicate the extent to which the revenues derived from the several commodity classes and groups exceed or fail to equal the out-of-pocket costs of handling the traffic. Detailed descriptions of the methods and definitions of the various statistical and cost concepts are matters of public record in the archives of the Commission, and need not be repeated in detail in this report.

By continuous study and development of cost-finding techniques, the Commission has been able to determine the compensativity of rates and charges by more definite standards than existed previously. The establishment of more definite ratemaking criteria, based on improved cost-finding methods has been advantageous in many ways. The regulated industry has been able to judge more precisely whether particular rates, their own or their competitors', would be found by the Commission to be just and reasonable. In addition, the resolution of intermodal rate controversies largely in accordance with impersonal cost standards has tended to allay fears that the Commission's decisions are arbitrary and capricious.[58]

Insofar as motor carrier costs are concerned, the Commission has said that a proposed reduced rate may not be approved without a positive showing that it would be reasonably compensatory; when no such showing is made, or that a competitive need exists for a reduction, the proposed rate will be disapproved.[59] In adjustments in which several carriers participate, costs developed on an average basis are entitled to weight, in absence of more specific data, in passing on the compensatory character of rates.[60] System average costs of a large group of carriers, reflecting costs of movement of a variety of commodities over a wide area with diverse operating conditions, cannot be accepted as decisive in determining reasonableness of particular rates on a specific commodity, especially where the proponent has been moving the traffic at rates the same as those proposed for several years under operating conditions similar to those attending the anticipated movement.[61] If proponent is primarily a hauler of less than truckload traffic, its system average operating expenses do not provide an adequate standard for measuring com-

---

[58]See *New York, New Haven & Hartford R.R. Co. v. United States*, 199 F. Supp. 635 (Appendix A), judgment vacated 372 U.S. 744, for an outline of the Commission's cost techniques.

[59]*Alcoholic Liquors from Boston, Mass., to Hartford, Conn.*, 308 I.C.C. 659, 660.

[60]*Cigarettes and Tobacco, Craig Trucking, Inc.*, 309 I.C.C. 267, 270.

[61]*Cotton Cloth, Canton, Mass., to New Jersey and New York*, 310 I.C.C. 675, 677; *Printing Paper from Holyoke, Mass., to Clayton, N.Y.*, 310 I.C.C. 652, 654.

pensativeness of proposed truckload rates.[62] The loading and unloading of truckload shipments by motor carriers promote efficient and convenient service, but they subject the carriers to additional expense which must be included in the line-haul rate.[63]

System average expense per vehicle-mile is valueless in ascertaining whether specific rates, such as those on fresh meats, are compensatory, since the vehicle-mile approach to costs falsely assumes that all expenses are caused by miles operated.[64] Operating ratios likewise have little value as cost data in support of rates, since an operating ratio is the result of comparing total operating expenses, taxes, and licenses with total revenues received from all rates, some of which may be much above costs and some barely meeting or possibly below costs.[65] Cost data based on territorial averages for one territory have no specific application to operation in another territory and thus are entitled to little weight in determining compensativeness of proposed rates in latter territory.[66] For cost purposes, where distances over actual routes of movement under proposed rates are not shown, an average percentage figure developed from studies by the Commission is added to the short-line distance to account for circuity.[67]

In dealing with freight forwarder rates, the Commission has said that there is nothing in the provisions of Part IV or the legislative history of that part which establishes that freight forwarders are, or were intended to be, limited in weight of shipments they may handle, or which prohibits their establishment of rates subject to volume minima; and if a forwarder can handle a heavier weighted shipment more economically than several small shipments of the same aggregate weight, the shipping public should receive the benefits flowing from that fact.[68]

Thus, so long as the rates yield substantially more than full cost plus a reasonable profit and would not constitute a destructive competitive practice they will be approved.[69] Differences in rates based on and accurately reflecting differences in costs and other transportation factors are lawful.[70] Rates are considered noncompensatory when

[62]*Green Coffee from New Orleans, La., to Atlanta, Ga.,* 310 I.C.C. 690, 691.
[63]*Allowance, Unloading Cement, Covered Hopper Cars-East,* 313 I.C.C. 743, 746.
[64]*Fresh Meat from the Midwest to the East,* 313 I.C.C. 345, 371.
[65]*Ibid.*
[66]*Paint and Chemicals between Ill., Mo., and Iowa,* 306 I.C.C. 42, 44.
[67]*Green Salted Hides, Pacific Southwest to the Midwest,* 309 I.C.C. 298, 299.
[68]*Forwarder Volume Commodity Rates, Transcontinental,* 311 I.C.C. 773, 775.
[69]*Ibid.,* p. 776. See also *Forwarder Volume Commodity Rates, Chicago and New York,* 308 I.C.C. 455, 456, 459-460 (310 I.C.C. 199, 201); *Eastern Express, Inc. v. United States,* 198 F. Supp. 256, 264.
[70]*Consolidation of Freight Forwarder Shipments,* 310 I.C.C. 191, 195.

they cover only the charges of the underlying assembly and distribution carriers and not the freight forwarder assumption of liability, handling of claims, cost of negotiating contracts with agents, publication of the rates, billing of the freight, and paying and receiving of the arbitrary charges.[71] Arbitrary rates of a freight forwarder, reflecting only its direct payments under contracts with motor carriers for performance of assembly and distibution service without regard to other overhead costs, are considered unjust and unreasonable because they are noncompensatory; the performance of service which is of value to shippers without adequate compensation therefor, as an inducement to secure their traffic, is an indirect form of illegal rebating.[72] The rule that where no single-factor rate for the through movement has been established the statute does not require each component to be compensatory so long as the total charge is just and reasonable is applicable to arbitrary rates published by a forwarder for assembly and distribution service; arbitraries are not unlawful when they exceed the freight forwarder's highest Section 409 contract rates.[73]

Prescription of Rates

Under Section 15(1),[74] the Commission is authorized to prescribe rates only after it finds that the existing rates are "unjust or unreasonable or unjustly discriminatory or unduly preferential or prejudicial, or otherwise in violation of any of the provisions of this chapter." Rate orders entered in the absence of such findings cannot stand.[75]

In the exercise of its power to prescribe just and reasonable rates the Commission is required by Section 15a(2)[76] to (1) give due con-

---

[71]*Acme Fast Freight, Inc. v. Western Freight Assn.*, 299 I.C.C. 315, 326.

[72]Ibid. See also *Arbitrary Rates, Los Angeles to Calif. Points*, 300 I.C.C. 117, 120.

[73]*Clipper Carloading Co., Inc. v. Western Freight Assn.*, 311 I.C.C. 653, 658.

[74]49 U.S.C. 15(1). Comparable provisions — Sections 216(e), 218(b), 307(b), (h), 315 (b), 406(b).

[75]See e.g., *United States v. Chicago, M., St. P. & P. R. Co.*, 294 U.S. 499, 504; *Central of Georgia R.R. Co. v. United States*, 379 F. Supp. 976, 979, aff'd 421 U.S. 957. The Commission has not hesitated to prescribe rates in the past notwithstanding that the rates found in violation of the I.C. Act were an integral part of a distinct rate pattern. See Docket No. 35786, *Feed Grains to New England*, decided Feb. 2, 1977, served Feb. 10, 1977; Ex Parte No. 270, (Sub-No. 1-A), *Investigation of Railroad Freight Rate Structure-Export-Import Rates and Charges-Pacific Coast*, 345 I.C.C. 423, 436-442, aff'd *Burlington Northern, Inc. v. U.S.A. and I.C.C.*, 549 F. 2d 83; *Board of Trade of the City of Chicago v. The Akron, Canton & Youngstown Railroad Co.*, 352 I.C.C. 881; aff'd *The Atchison, Topeka & Santa Fe Rwy. v. United States*, 549 F. 2d 1186.

[76]49 U.S.C. 15a(2). Comparable provisions — Sections 216(i), 307(f), 406(d). Compare also National Transportation Policy, Section 3(1a) (as to export rates on farm commodities) and Hoch-Smith Resolution, Section 55.

sideration, among other factors, to the effect of rates on the movement of traffic by the carrier or carriers for which the rates are prescribed; (2) the need, in the public interest, of adequate and efficient transportation service at the lowest cost consistent with the furnishing of such service; and (3) the need of revenues sufficient to enable the carriers, under honest, economical, and efficient management to provide such service.[77]

Competitive Ratemaking

Section 15a(3)[78] of the Interstate Commerce Act provides:

> "In a proceeding involving competition between carriers of different modes of transportation subject to this Act, the Commission, in determining whether a rate is lower than a reasonable minimum rate, shall consider the facts and circumstances attending the movement of the traffic by the carrier or carriers to which the rate is applicable. Rates of a carrier shall not be held up to a particular level to protect the traffic of any other mode of transportation, giving due consideration to the objectives of the national transportation policy declared in this Act."

Section 15a(4) and Section 15(5)[79] have been added by the 4R Act. Section 15a(4) provides:

> "With respect to common carriers by railroad, the Commission shall, within 24 months after the date of enactment of this paragraph, after notice and an opportunity for a hearing, develop and promulgate (and thereafter revise and maintain) reasonable standards and procedures for the establishment of revenue levels adequate under honest, economical, and efficient management to cover total operating expenses, including depreciation and obsolescence, plus a fair, reasonable, and economic profit or return (or both) on capital employed in the business. Such revenue levels should (a) provide a flow of net income plus depreciation adequate to support prudent capital outlays, assure the repayment of a reasonable level of debt, permit the raising of needed equity capital, and cover the effects of inflation and (b) insure retention and attraction of capital in amounts adequate to provide a sound transportation system in the United States. The Commission shall make an adequate and continuing effort to assist such carriers in attaining such revenue levels. No rate of a common carrier by railroad shall be held up to a particular level to protect the traffic of any other carrier or mode of transportation, unless the Commission finds that such rate reduces or would reduce the going concern value of the carrier charging the rate."

[77] By amendment under the 4R Act, Section 15a(2) does not apply to common carriers by railroad. See Section 15a(4),(5).

[78] 49 U.S.C. 15a(3). By amendment under the 4R Act Section 15a(3) does not apply to common carriers by railroad.

[79] 49 U.S.C. 15a(4), (5).

Section 15a (5) provides:

"The Commission shall, in any proceeding which involves a proposed increase or decrease in railroad rates, specifically consider allegations that such increase or decrease would change the rate relationships between commodities, ports, points, regions, territories, or other particular descriptions of traffic (whether or not such relationships were previously considered or approved by the Commission) and allegations that such increase or decrease would have a significantly adverse effect on the competitive position of shippers or consignees served by the railroad proposing such increase or decrease. If the Commission finds that such allegations as to change or effect are substantially supported on the record, it shall take such steps as are necessary, either before or after such proposed increase or decrease becomes effective and either within or outside such proceeding, to investigate the lawfulness of such change or effect."

The Commission pointed out in Ex Parte No. 343, *Nationwide Increased Freight Rates and Charges, 1977*, decided June 28, 1977, that the going concern value of the proponent railroad must be considered when a proposed rate is attacked as unreasonably low. Section 1(5)(b) provides that a rate cannot be held unreasonably low if it contributes or would contribute to the railroad's going concern value. Section 15a(4) provides that no rate of a railroad shall be held up to a particular level to protect the traffic of any other carrier or mode of transportation, unless the Commission finds that such rate reduces or could reduce the going concern value of the carrier charging the rate. Presumably rates which are at least equal to the variable cost of service contribute to going concern value. Thus a railroad is free to lower its rates in an effort to meet competition, so long as the reduced rate does not detract from the carrier's going concern value.

Rates Based on Seasonal, Regional, or Peak-Period Demand for Rail Service

Section 15(17) of the Interstate Commerce Act[80] was added by the 4R Act. It provides:

"Within 1 year after the date of enactment of this paragraph, the Commission shall establish, by rule, standards and expeditious procedures for the establishment of railroad rates based on seasonal, regional, or peak-period demand for rail services. Such standards and procedures shall be designed to (a) provide sufficient incentive to shippers to reduce peak-period shipments, through rescheduling and advance planning; (b) generate additional revenues for the railroads; and (c) improve (i) the utilization of the

---

[80]49 U.S.C. 15(17).

national supply of freight cars, (ii) the movement of goods by rail, (iii) levels of employment by railroads, and (iv) the financial stability of markets served by railroads. Following the establishment of such standards and procedures, the Commission shall prepare and submit to the Congress annual reports on the implementation of such rates, including recommendations with respect to the need, if any, for additional legislation to facilitate the establishment of such demand-sensitive rates."

The Commission instituted a rulemaking proceeding in Ex Parte No. 324, *Standards and Expeditious Procedures for Establishing Railroad Rates Based on Seasonal, Regional, or Peak-Period Demand for Rail Service,* under authority of Section 202(d) of the 4R Act to establish standards and expeditious procedures to promote the publication of rates which are intended to (1) provide sufficient incentive to shippers to reduce peak-period shipments, through rescheduling and advance planning; (2) generate additional revenues for the railroad; and (3) improve (i) the utilization of the national supply of freight cars (ii) the movement of goods by rail, (iii) levels of employment by railroads, and (iv) the financial stability of markets served by the railroads, as required by Section 15(17) of the Interstate Commerce Act.

The Commission adopted rules in Ex Parte No. 324[81] to facilitate the establishment of demand-sensitive rates principally by removing or reducing factors and concerns which may have inhibited such ratemaking in the past. Two such factors, for example, were (1) uncertainty with regard to evidentiary justification in the event the rate in challenged and (2) the problem of cancelling such a rate when it does not meet expectations, especially where shippers have come to rely thereon. In responses to these concerns the rules set forth: (a) the type of justification thought appropriate in the event such a proposal is assailed (although the rules leave the carrier free to tailor their justification to specific criticism); and (b) norms regarding the evidentiary weight to be accorded shipper reliance on a demand-sensitive rate which the carriers seek to cancel.

Under the rules, the Commission in considering tariffs filed under Section 202(d) of the 4R Act shall be guided by:

(1) The need to encourage the establishment of demand-sensitive rates and incentives to the shippers;

(2) The need to encourage ratemaking innovation by railroad management;

(3) The need to permit changes to or rescissions of a demand-sensitive rates as required by changes in the circumstances which prompted establishment of the rate;

---

[81]355 I.C.C. 521, amended by order served July 20, 1977; see 49 CFR 1109.10.

(4) The need to assist the railroads in attaining adequate revenue levels; and

(5) The need to improve (i) the utilization of the national supply of freight cars, (ii) the movement of goods by rail, (iii) levels of employment by railroads, and (iv) the financial stability of markets served by the railroads;

(6) the ability of the affected industry within a specific area to react positively to the proposed demand-sensitive rate consistent with statutory goals; and

(7) when the cancellation of a demand-sensitive rate is at issue, shippers' investment made for the purpose of availing themselves of the incentive offered thereunder will only be considered where:

(i) the rate has been in effect for at least two years without substantial change; or

(ii) the shipper can show that the carrier has made representations regarding the duration of the rate schedule and that the shipper has in fact relied on such representations to his detriment.

Distinct Rail Services

Section 15(18) of the Interstate Commerce Act[82] was added by the 4R Act. It provides:

"(18) In order to encourage competition, to promote increased reinvestment by railroads, and to encourage and facilitate increased non-railroad investment in the production of rail services, a carrier by railroad subject to this part may, upon its own initiative or upon the request of any shipper or receiver of freight, file separate rates for distinct rail services. Within 1 year after the date of enactment of this paragraph, the Commission shall establish, by rule, expeditious procedures for permitting publication of separate rates for distinct rail services in order to (a) encourage the pricing of such services in accordance with the carrier's cash-outlays for such services and the demand therefor, and (b) enable shippers and receivers to evaluate all transportation and related charges and alternatives."

The Commission instituted a proceeding under the authority of Section 202(d) of the 4R Act and the Administrative Procedure Act (5 U.S.C. 55, 559) in Ex Parte No. 331, *Expeditious Procedures for Permitting Publication of Separate Rates for Distinct Rail Services*, with the objective of facilitating the publication of separate rates for distinct rail services. The regulations[83] are meant to promote the objectives of Section 15(18) and to transmit to Congress the information required by

[82]49 U.S.C. 15(18).
[83]49 C.F.R. 1109.15. The regulations were adopted in 355 I.C.C. 683.

Section 202(g) of the 4R Act. In addition to assembling the information required by Congress, these regulations are designed to facilitate the prompt production of necessary evidence to resolve controversies that may result from the publication of separate rates for distinct rail services. In its notice of proposed rulemaking, served September 29, 1976, the Commission said:

> "This new section appears similar to the provision of section 6(1) of the Interstate Commerce Act relating to the publication of rates and specifically to that portion of 6(1) that provides that tariffs shall 'state separately all terminal charges, storage charges, icing charges, and all other charges . . .' In interpreting section 6(1), the Commission has permitted carriers to publish single factor rates which include all services performed in connection with the transportation of freight. However, when a carrier has proposed to separate from a single factor rate a service previously included and publish a separate charge for that service, as was the situation in *Inspection in Transit, Grain and Grain Products*, 349 I.C.C. 89, 92, the Commission has held that, not only must the separate charge for the distinct service be established to be lawful, but that, 'we have no alternative but to require that the line-haul rate, as increased through a diminution of service thereunder, be justified by appropriate evidence establishing that the aggregate charge for the through service is reasonable.'[84] Section 15(18) of the Interstate Commerce Act, while seeking to encourage the publication of separate rates for distinct rail services so as to present shippers and receivers with the option of selecting only those services they actually require, does not preclude the continued maintenance and publication of all-inclusive rate covering all services to be rendered in the transportation of certain type of freight. Further, section 15(18) does not appear to vary the holding in the *Inspection in Transit Case, supra,* in instances where reasonableness remains an issue, i.e. where the carrier proposing the charge has market dominance."

Rates Based on Capital Investment of One Million Dollars or More

Section 15(19) of the Interstate Commerce Act[85] was added by the 4R Act. It provides:

> "(19) Notwithstanding any other provision of law, a common carrier by railroad subject to this part may file with the Commission a notice of intention to file a schedule stating a new rate, fare, charge, classification, regulation, or practice whenever the implementation of the proposed schedule would require a total capital investment of $1,000,000 or more, indi-

---

[84]This holding was in accord with the Supreme Court opinion in *Atchison, T. & S. F. R. Co. v. Wichita Bd. of Trade,* 412 U.S. 800.

[85]49 U.S.C. 15(19). Reference to Section 1 was added to Section 15(19) by a technical amendment — P.L. 94-555.

vidually or collectively, by such carrier, or by a shipper, receiver, or agent thereof, or an interested third party. The filing shall be accompanied by a sworn affidavit setting forth in detail the anticipated capital investment upon which such filing is based. Any interested person may request the Commission to investigate the schedule proposed to be filed, and upon such request the Commission shall hold a hearing with respect to such schedule. Such hearing may be conducted without answer or other formal pleading, but reasonable notice shall be provided to interested parties. Unless, prior to the 180-day period following the filing of such notice of intention, the Commission determines, after a hearing, that the proposed schedule, or any part thereof, would be unlawful, such carrier may file the schedule at any time within 180 days thereafter to become effective after 30 days' notice. Such a schedule may not, for a period of 5 years after its effective date, be suspended or set aside as unlawful under section 1, 2, 3, or 4 of this part, except that the Commission may at any time order such schedule to be revised to a level equaling the variable costs of providing the service, if the rate stated therein is found to reduce the going concern value of the carrier."

To promote the filing of rates based on capital investment of $1,000,000 or more, the Commission adopted regulations under Section 15(19) in Ex Parte No. 327, *Rate Incentives for Capital Investments*.[86]

The regulations provide that notice of a carrier's proposal to file a capital incentive rate shall be given to concerned persons by publication of a summary of the proposal in the *Federal Register*. This summary is required to be submitted by the carrier to the Commission at the time the proposed tariff is submitted with the notice of intention to file. Protests must be filed within 25 days after the date of publication of the summary in the *Federal Register*. Upon receipt of a protest the Commission by order will immediately schedule a hearing to commence 30 days from service of the order. In any hearing pertaining to a capital incentive rate the burden of proof shall be upon the protestant.

Recyclable or Recycled Materials

Although Section 204 of the 4R Act does not include specific changes in existing law, it does, among other things, charge the Commission with the responsibility of conducting an investigation into the rail rate structures for the transportation of recyclable materials and for ordering removal from such rate structures any rates found to discriminate against recyclable materials. The Commission is also required to investigate the manner in which rail rate structures have been affected by succession general rate increases.

[86]353 I.C.C. 754; see 49 C.F.R. 1109.20.

The Commission instituted a proceeding by order served February 25, 1976 in Ex Parte No. 319, *Investigation of Freight Rates for the Transportation of Recyclable or Recycled Materials*, with the objective of investigating the rate structure for the transportation by common carriers by railroad of recyclable or recycled materials and competing virgin natural resource materials, and the manner in which such rate structure has been affected by successive general rate increases approved by the Commission for such carriers in order to determine whether such rate structure is just, reasonable, and non-discriminatory in whole or in part. In the order served February 25, 1976, the Commission noted:

> "Through the years the Interstate Commerce Commission has had a strong and continuing interest in the discovery and subsequent elimination of all forms of freight rate discrimination. Prior to and after the enactment of the Environmental Policy Act of 1969, the Commission, upon its own motion, upon the motion of others, and in response to various legislative enactments, has devoted significant time and effort to issues concerning the rate structures on recyclable materials. The Commission's recognition of the need to draw recyclable materials into the main stream of the economy is manifested in such proceedings as Ex Parte No. 270 (Sub-Nos. 5 and 6), *Investigation of Railroad Freight Rate Structure, Iron Ores & Scrap Iron and Steel*, Ex Parte No. 295 (Sub-No. 1), *Increased Freight Rates and Charges, 1973 — Recyclabe Materials*, Ex Parte No. 305-RE, *Increased Freight Rates and Charges, 1975 — Recyclable Materials*, and other general revenue proceedings. In furtherance of a just, reasonable and nondiscriminatory freight rate structure for recyclable materials, the Commission, in Ex Parte No. 306, *Public Law 93-236 — Freight Rates for Recyclables*, 346, I.C.C. 408, expeditiously responded to legislative direction by proposing and subsequently adopting appropriate rules to facilitate the elimination of discrimination against recyclable materials."

Section 22 Rates

Section 22 of the Interstate Commerce Act[87] provides "(1) That nothing in this part shall prevent the carriage, storage, or handling of property free or at reduced rates for the United States, State, or municipal governments, ..." This section permits a carrier to accord the government preferential rates. The section is discussed at length in *Interpretation of Govt. Rate Tariff — Eastern Central.*[88] In that case the following question was submitted to the Commission for decision in a petition for declaratory determination under the Administrative Procedure Act to remove uncertainty concerning the lawfulness of trans-

[87]49 U.S.C. 22.
[88]323 I.C.C. 347.

portation service performed at rates quoted according to the provisions
of Sections 22 and 217(b) of the I.C. Act where a commercial bill of
lading is used:

> May a common carrier subject to the Act charge or assess a shipper or
> receiver of freight, other than an agency or department of the Govern-
> ment, an amount less than that named in the tariffs published and filed
> by such carrier when the bill of lading contains an endorsement that
> the costs paid to the carrier by the shipper or receiver are to be reim-
> bursed by the Government?

Division 2 of the Commission held that the question presented should
be answered in the affirmative subject to certain qualifications. Division
2 stated (pp. 349-352):

> Section 22, which has been extended to apply to all forms of regulated
> common carrier surface transportation service, to the extent pertinent here,
> provides "(1) That nothing in this part shall prevent the carriage, storage,
> or handling of property free or at reduced rates for the United States, State,
> or municipal governments. . . ." The section thus allows a carrier to accord
> preferential rates for certain movements, if it so desires. It does not require
> such rates. *Nashville C. & St. L. Ry. Co. v. State of Tennessee*, 262 U.S.
> 318, 323 (1923); *United States v. Aberdeen & R.R. Co.*, 289 I.C.C. 49, 64
> (1953); *Tennessee Products & Chem. Corp. v. Louisville & N. R.*, 319
> I.C.C. 497, 502 (1963).

> An early opinion of the Attorney General, 25 Ops. Att'y Gen 408 (1905),
> declares that the applicability of Section 22 depends on whether the gov-
> ernment receives the entire benefit of the reduced rates, and that this is a
> question of fact. It further emphasizes (*Id*, at page 409) that:

>> the intention of Section 22 of the act . . . was to express sanction to
>> any arrangements between the United States, State, or municipal gov-
>> ernments and railroad companies by which those governments might
>> relieve themselves of the cost of transportation in whatever form it
>> might assume, and the section should be construed to give effect to
>> that intention. It is therefore immaterial whether the property trans-
>> ported belonged to the United States at the time of shipment or
>> whether it even subsequently became the property of the United States
>> in the particular shape in which it was shipped. It is sufficient that it
>> entered into the construction of a public work of the United States,
>> and that the cost of its transportation was a part of the final cost of
>> that work to the United States.

> This opinion was quoted and relied on in 40 Ops. Att'y Gen. 353 (1945),
> interpreting the scope of Section 3(2) of the Act which allows the ex-
> tension of credit in connection with shipments ". . . transported for the
> United States. . . ."

> The two opinions clearly construe the words "for the . . . governments"
> or "for the United States" as meaning for the benefit of the government.
> They specify that the benefit received must be total and direct. See also

C. B. Havens & Co. v. Chicago & N.W. Ry. Co., 20 I.C.C. 156; *Givens v. Louisville & N. R. Co.,* 140 I.C.C. 605; *accord. Sands v. Calmar S.S. Corp.,* 296 N.Y. Supp. 590, 592 (Sup. Ct. 1937). We agree with the reasoning of these opinions, and find nothing in the wording of the statute or in the legislative history to support a different interpretation. Therefore we conclude that Section 22 quotations are applicable on transportation services which are performed for the government, so long as the direct and entire benefit of the special rates accrues solely to the government. Whether it does so accrue is a question of fact.

The circumstances of the particular transportation determine whether the requirements of Section 22 have been met. For example, when a government bill of lading is issued, the fact is established that the transportation is performed for the government and that the full cost is borne by the government, giving it the entire benefit of any reduced rate. The same is true when a commercial bill of lading is used, to be exchanged for a government bill of lading at destination. Thus, use of a government bill of lading assures the carrier that the Section 22 rates will advantage only the government. We see no reason, however, why a government bill of lading should be a condition precedent to the use of Section 22 quotations. In this connection it should be noted that the government bill of lading referred to here is used by United States Government agencies and departments. But Section 22 allows reduced rates to be accorded also to State and municipal governments. To make a government bill of lading a *sine qua non* of reductions under the section would seem either to impose on these governmental units a form of documentation which may not comport with their established procedures or to deprive them of the benefit of the special rates. A carrier may, of course, choose to require a government bill of lading whenever the transportation service is performed for the Federal Government, but such a restriction cannot be read into the statute. See *Rocky Mountain Carriers — Agreement,* 314 I.C.C. 279, in which a carriers' agreement defined and somewhat narrowed the application of Section 22 quotations.

Section 22 does not apply only to movements of property of the government. *United States v. Georgia Public Service Commission* 371 U.S. 285 (1963). Cases cited in support of such an assertion concern land-grant rail rates which, by statute, applied on transportation of property of the United States. Such a requirement of ownership does not appear in Section 22.

Some of the parties argue that if a government bill of lading is not a condition to application of Section 22 rates, there is nothing to prevent any private shipper under contract with the government from using these quotations. This argument assumes that any form of benefit to the government, here supposed to be reflected in a reduced fixed contract price, qualifies the traffic for special rates. We do not agree with this construction. As stated before, the total benefit of special rates must accrue to the government. Therefore Section 22 rates are proper only where the government pays the charges or directly and completely reimburses the party which initially bears the freight charges. A government contractor operating under a fixed price contract would not be able to use Section 22 quotations. Even though the government might in fact receive the advantage of lower transportation charges through a lower contract price, the benefit would not be direct, nor necessarily total. On the other hand, a contractor working under a cost reimbursement contract, such as one calling for payment of costs-plus-fixed-fee, may claim freight charges under certain circumstances as a direct reimburseable cost. Where such a cost is both direct and allowable, under the appropriate procurement regulations, the government alone receives the benefit of any reduction and Section 22 rates would be applicable. The contractor must be, so to speak, a conduit for the payment of the freight charges by the government.

In the Armed Services Procurement Regulations, codified in 32 C.F.R., Section 15.205-45 (1961) describes transportation cost which is allowable under cost-reimbursement contracts. Where the cost can be readily identified with the items involved, it may be considered direct cost; where such identification cannot be readily made, the inbound transportation cost may be charged to appropriate indirect cost accounts. If reimbursable under the contract, outbound freight charges will be treated as a direct cost.

Indirect cost, as described in another section, 32 C.F.R. Section 15.203 (1961), is that which cannot be related specifically to a particular item because it is incurred for common or joint objectives of both the contractor and the government. Since the entire benefit does not accrue solely to the government, transportation which is considered a matter of indirect cost cannot be regarded as "for the government" so as to qualify for special rates under Section 22, even if the indirect cost item is allowable and an allocable portion is in fact paid by the government.

A subcontractor rarely has that contractual privity with the government which would give rise to direct reimbursement of such costs as transportation charges. See, for example, *Sullivan v. United States*, 129 Ct. Cl. 63, 68 (1954), and *General Elevator Co. v. United States*, 122 Ct. Cl. 467 (1952), and compare *Kern-Limerick v. Scurlock*, 347 U.S. 110 (1954), in which the contract specifically made the prime contractor agent of the government. Therefore, Section 22 quotations would seldom, if ever, be applicable on shipments for subcontractors.

There is no special magic in any particular formulation to be added to a commercial bill of lading which will automatically guarantee the carrier that the government alone will receive the benefit of the special rate. The endorsement constitutes a circumstance which the carrier may, or may not, consider sufficient assurance. Certainly nothing prevents the carrier from requiring whatever it considers adequate to show that the transportation service sought qualifies for the special rates which it is permitted, but not required, to establish. See *Rocky Mountain Carriers — Agreement, supra.* Therefore, our conclusion must not be construed as definitive approval of the endorsement language quoted earlier. Indeed, we consider that any endorsement might more appropriately specify that "the *actual, total* transportation cost paid to the carrier(s) by the shipper or receiver is to be *directly* reimbursed by the Government," in order to emphasize that the shipper or receiver is merely acting as a conduit for a benefit accruing to the government.

The petitioner's tariff provisions presently restrict application of Section 22 rates to movements for which a government bill of lading is issued. This limitation seems to afford the carriers the maximum assurance that the special rates are properly applicable. Such assurance is undoubtedly desirable, in view of the continuing statutory obligation on the carriers to collect charges based only upon the applicable rate, be it a Section 22 quotation or a published tariff rate. But neither the wording of the statute nor the apparent legislative intent to maintain the preferred position of governments in their transportation dealings allows us to limit the scope of the section by reading in such a restriction.

Freight Forwarder Rates

Section 408 of the I.C. Act[89] provides:

"Nothing in this Act shall be construed to make it unlawful for common carriers subject to part I, II, or III of this Act to establish and maintain assembling rates or charges and/or distribution rates or charges, and classifications, rules, and regulations with respect thereto, applicable to freight forwarders and others who employ or utilize the instrumentalities or services of such common carriers under like conditions, which differ from other rates or charges, classifications rules, or regulations which con-temporaneously apply with respect to the employment or utilization of the same instrumentalities or services, if such difference is justified by a difference in the respective conditions under which such instrumentalities or services are employed or utilized. For the purposes of this section (1) the term 'assembling rates or charges' means rates or charges for the transpor-tation of less-than-carload or less-than-truckload shipments into a point for further movement beyond as part of a carload or truckload shipment, and (2) the term 'distribution rates or charges' means rates or charges for the transportation of less-than-carload or less-than-truckload shipments moving from a point into which such shipments have moved as a part of a carload or truckload shipment. The provisions of this section shall not be construed to authorize the establishment of assembling rates or charges or distribution rates or charges covering the line haul transportation between the principal concentration point and the principal break-bulk point."

Under Section 408 of the I.C. Act, common carriers may establish as-sembling and distribution rates, applicable to freight forwarders and others who employ the carriers' services under like conditions, lower than the rates applicable to shippers generally. In commenting on this provision of the I.C. Act in *Freight Forwarders, Motor Common Carriers, Agreements,*[90] the Commission stated (p. 417):

[89]49 U.S.C. 1008.
[90]272 I.C.C. 413.

The authority in Section 408 to establish assembling and distribution rates is permissive. Common carriers by motor vehicle, railroad, and water subject to the Act are authorized to establish such rates at their discretion. These rates may not be established for the exclusive benefit of forwarders, but must be made available to "others who employ or utilize the instrumentalities or services of such common carriers under like conditions."

The decisions of the Commission establish that assembling and distribution rates applicable to freight forwarders and others will not be approved unless the difference between such rates and those applicable to shippers generally are justified by special conditions.[91]

Special justification for establishment of assembling rates on traffic of forwarders and others shipping under like conditions, lower than those available to shippers generally, includes reduced solicitation expense, lower costs in handling claims, and lower billing and collecting costs.[92] Compensatory yield of the rates, substantial cost savings, and demonstrated carrier competition provide justification for the establishment of the rates.[93] However, assembling and distribution rates differing from those contemporaneously applicable for similar services must be justified by a difference in the respective conditions under which the services of the carriers are employed; when no special conditions are shown to indicate a difference in the manner in which facilities and services would be utilized under proposed distribution rates, nor any showing of operational savings which would flow from such use, there is no justification for the substantial reductions below the normal rate level.[94]

In *Distribution Rates, Philadelphia to Del., N.J., and Pa.,*[95] the Commission disapproved proposed reduced distribution rates since they were not shown to be justified by any competitive necessity or by a difference in conditions under which the distribution services and normal services were performed; and the evidence was not convincing that the proposed rates would be compensatory or that they would not constitute a destructive competitive practice. Likewise in *Assembling and Distribution Rates — N.Y., N.J., and Pa.*[96] proposed assembling and distribution class rates were found not justified when they departed

---

[91]*Assembly Rates from Del., N. J., and Pa. to Philadelphia,* 310 I.C.C. 433, 436; *Assembling and Distribution Rates Between New England Points,* 318 I.C.C. 57; *Assembling and Distribution Rates Between Points in New York State,* 316 I.C.C. 606; *Distribution Rates — Pittsburgh to Ind., Ky., Mich., Ohio,* 316 I.C.C. 381.
[92]*Assembly Rates from Del., N.J., and Pa. to Philadelphia,* 310 I.C.C. 433, 436.
[93]*Ibid.*
[94]*Distribution Rates — Central Freight Trucking, Inc.,* 306 I.C.C. 769, 770.
[95]310 I.C.C. 9, 11-12.
[96]309 I.C.C. 362, 364.

from generally accepted rate-making principles in being lower in some instances than respondent's corresponding assembling commodity rates on freight, all kinds, and were not shown to be compensatory.

In *Assembling and Distribution Rates Between New England Points*,[97] the Commission found proposed schedules not shown to be just and reasonable which schedules involved less than truckload assembling and distribution class rates on traffic moving between Springfield, Mass., and points in Connecticut and Massachusetts. The proposed rates ranged from less than 50% to over 100% of the existing rates and were published in order to meet the competition of another carrier. Respondent stated that the traffic in question moved regularly, required no dock handling, occasioned a minimum of solicitation, billing and collection costs, caused no losses from bad debts, and was the source of a few loss and damage claims. Respondent also stated that handling this traffic afforded an opportunity to make the maximum use of equipment and personnel. The Commission held (p. 58) that many of the proposed rates were far below 85% of the regular class rates and the record was devoid of cost data from which the compensativeness of the rates might be determined. It also held that no shipper or receiver appeared in support of the proposal and that the only supporting evidence offered by the respondent consisted of general statements concerning the effectiveness of the traffic, and reference to the rates claimed to be competitive. In these circumstances, the Commission said that the suspended schedules may not receive its approval.

In *Assembling and Distribution Rates Between Points in New York State*,[98] the Commission found not shown to be just and reasonable proposed less-than-truckload assembling and distribution commodity rates between Syracuse and Utica, New York, on the one hand, and certain points in New York, on the other, applicable for freight forwarder traffic only. The Commission held that the rates could not be established for the exclusive benefit of the freight forwarders and must be made available to others; however, even if the rates were changed to conform to this requirement it could not on the record approve the proposed rates. The Commission held that under Section 216(g) the burden of proof is upon respondents to show that changed rates would be just and reasonable, and that a minimum requirement in that respect is a convincing showing that the proposed rates would be compensatory for the service to be performed thereunder. No such showing was made. Moreover, the Commission said, the authorization under Section 408 to initiate rates which

[97]318 I.C.C. 57.
[98]316 I.C.C. 606.

differ from other rates requires proof that such difference is justified by difference in the respective conditions under which the services are employed, and such showing was not made. Proposed distribution rates on freight, all kinds, and less-than-truckloads were found not shown to be just and reasonable in *Distribution Rates — Pittsburgh to Ind., Ky., Mich., Ohio.*[99] The Commission said (p. 382):

> The proposal involves distribution rates for freight consolidators. Section 408 of the Act authorizes a motor common carrier to establish distribution rates different from its normal rates if such difference is justified by a difference in the respective service. However, the respondent fails to show a difference in the respective services. Moreover, no attempt was made to show that the proposed rates would be compensatory. In the circumstances, the proposed schedules may not be approved. See *Distribution Rates — Central Freight Trucking, Inc.*, 306 I.C.C. 769, 770. Also compare *Distribution Rates, Newark, N.J. to N.J. and N.Y. Points*, 46 M.C.C. 745; and *Household Products Between Points in Indiana*, 304 I.C.C. 625, 630.

Although the schedules involved in the above cases were found not shown to be just and reasonable, the decisions reveal that there is no artificial bar in Section 408 to the establishment by common carriers of assembling and distributions rates so long as the defined criteria is met.

There is no reason why freight forwarders cannot make use of volume rates. On the question of volume rates, consideration should be given to *Corpus Christi Distributing Service, Inc., Ext. — Texas*,[100] in which a permit was sought under Section 410 of the I.C. Act authorizing operations as a freight forwarder of general commodities between various points through the use of the facilities of railroad, express, water, or motor carriers, but restricted to the use of water carriers on movements from consolidation points to distribution points. Applicant proposed to institute a freight forwarder barge operation between points in the areas along the Mississippi and Ohio Rivers, on the one hand, and points in Louisiana and Texas, on the other. It proposed to utilize motor or rail carrier service from the origin point to the consolidation point, and water service from there to the distribution point after accumulating a barge load. The supporting shippers generally maintained large inventories and were not interested in an expeditious transportation service but desired to obtain the most economical transportation possible. They were unable to use water carrier service, however, because they did

[99]316 I.C.C. 381.
[100]316 I.C.C. 542.

not individually ship in sufficiently large quantities to meet large load minimums. But collectively, they indicated that a large volume of traffic would be available. The traffic consisted of many different commodities including steel products, irrigation equipment, drilling equipment, electrical equipment, air conditioners, sisal, graphite, heat transfer cements, and industrial coatings. Division 1 concluded that the service by applicant would be consistent with the public interest and the national transportation policy. Division 1 said (p. 545):

> . . . the record indicates, however, that the supporting witnesses ship a large volume of traffic representing various different general commodities, between numerous points in the area proposed to be served. They desire to use water carrier service, rather than other modes of transportation, in order to obtain rate advantages, but they do not individually ship in sufficiently large quantities to meet the bargeload minimums. Applicant proposes to assemble numerous shipments of merchandise from individual shippers and consolidate them into volume lots for movement by water carriers. The ability of a particular mode of transportation to operate with a lower rate is an inherent advantage which must be considered, and shippers must be afforded an opportunity to use water transportation and to gain whatever benefits may accrue therefrom. The mere availability of common carriers should not bar the institution of freight forwarder service of a character not presently being offered. The evidence shows that no service of the type proposed is available to the public in the considered territories. . . . Considering all the circumstances, we believe that applicant has shown a substantial public need for the proposed service. . . .

Freight-forwarder volume commodity rates in connection with trailer-on-flatcar service were found just and reasonable and not otherwise unlawful by the Commission in *Forwarder Volume Commodity Rates, Chicago and New York*.[101] The proceeding involved a number of issues which were disposed of by the Commission as follows: (1) That the legislative history of Part IV does not establish that freight forwarders are restricted to the handling of small shipments only, nor does Section 402(a) of the I.C. Act limit the maximum weight of a shipment which may be handled by a forwarder (p. 459); (2) the fact that the proposed rates are subject to minimums ranging from 10,000 to 30,000 pounds does not automatically exclude the traffic from being handled by a freight forwarder (pp. 459-60); (3) the loading of trailers with different shipments prior to delivery to the line-haul carrier, including occasional instances where one of the trailers may be loaded with only one shipment from one consignor to one consignee constitutes an assembly and a consolidation of the shipment to be delivered to

---

[101]308 I.C.C. 455, sustained in *Eastern Express, Inc. v. United States*, 198 F. Supp. 256, aff'd 369 U.S. 37.

the carrier as one shipment (p. 460); (4) the trailers utilized in the operation conducted under the proposed rates are nothing more than containers filled with freight at their assembly station and loaded onto the railroad flat-cars for line-haul transportation to the break-bulk station and are not instrumentalities of transportation (pp. 460-62); (5) aside from the question of whether trailers when loaded upon flatcars are instrumentalities or containers, there is no contention that the ordinary shipper may not furnish the trailers under Plan III rates, and they likewise may be furnished by forwarders (p. 461); (6) it appears that the prohibition in Section 418 against the use of instrumentalities or services of carriers, other than common carriers, was designed to prevent forwarders from using contract carriers (p. 461); and (7) the proposed rates are just and reasonable and not otherwise unlawful. (p. 462).

On reconsideration in *Forwarder Volume Commodity Rates, Chicago and New York*,[102] the Commission affirmed its findings in the prior report[103] that freight forwarder volume commodity rates in connection with trailer-on-flatcar service are lawful. The Commission held (p. 203):

> . . . in our opinion, where a forwarder contracts for two or more shipments (including the case of two shipments each occupying a single trailer), tenders them at the railhead to be shipped as a single carload shipment, and makes, or arranges for, distribution of each of the tendered shipments to its consignee, there is consolidation and distribution by the forwarder despite the fact that the railroad which provides the underlying line-haul transportation physically places the trailer on the flatcar and removes them from the flatcar at the termination of the line haul. We conclude, upon the evidence, that under these rates, in the ordinary and usual course of their undertaking, the forwarders will perform the services of assembly, consolidation, and distribution as contemplated by Section 402(a) of the Act.

In *Eastern Express, Inc. v. United States*,[104] the court in sustaining the Commission's order in 308 I.C.C. 455 and 310 I.C.C. 199 said:

> From the foregoing, we conclude as a matter of law, that the defendant freight forwarders are not restricted by the Interstate Commerce Act, including the national transportation policy, to the handling of so-called small shipments or to the handling of shipments weighing less than 10,000 pounds or any other particular weight; nor are they so restricted to the publication of rates at minimum weights less than the minimum weights specified in the forwarder tariffs here involved. Nothing in that act and policy requires that freight rates of freight forwarders to the shipping

[102]310 I.C.C. 199.
[103]308 I.C.C. 455.
[104]198 F. Supp. 256, aff'd 369 U.S. 37.

public for shipments of more than 10,000 pounds shall be higher than the freight rates of the competing motor carriers for such shipments, or that they shall be no lower per hundred pounds than freight forwarder rates for smaller shipments. Nothing in that Act and policy gives, or was intended to give, to the motor carriers a right to exclude freight forwarders from competition with motor carriers for shipment of 10,000 pounds or more; nor does that Act and policy provide that competition of freight forwarders for such shipments shall be restrained by requiring freight forwarders to charge the public more for such shipments than is charged by motor carriers, or by requiring freight forwarders to charge for such shipments rates no lower per hundred pounds than the rates for smaller shipments. The legislative history of Part IV of the Interstate Commerce Act shows that Congress was well aware that freight forwarders handled shipments weighing in excess of 10,000 pounds, and further shows that Congress refused to restrict competition by adopting proposed provisions of Part IV which, if adopted, would have made it unlawful for freight forwarders to publish rates lower than the contemporaneous rates of common carriers by railroad or motor vehicle for a like kind and quantity of property between the same points.

Under their operations described in the reports of the Commission in connection with the handling of shipments to which these freight forwarder rates apply, the freight forwarders, in the ordinary and usual course of their undertaking, would perform all of the services contemplated by Section 402(a) (5) of the Interstate Commerce Act.

With respect to the plaintiffs' argument that the assailed forwarder service is in derogation of Section 418 of the Interstate Commerce Act, in view of the reasons stated in the Commission's initial report in these proceedings, which have been stated heretofore, we concur in the conclusion of the Commission that rail shipments by the freight forwarders of their trailers, loaded or empty, under the rail Plan III piggyback rates published by the railroads and available for the use of the shipping public, are not unlawful under said section.

In reaching its conclusions in this matter, the Commission gave due and careful consideration to, and properly applied the provisions of, the national transportation policy, as well as the other provisions of the Interstate Commerce Act. The record before the Commission amply justifies its conclusion that "The evidence does not permit a finding that the forwarder rates under consideration will produce a diversion of traffic sufficient to imperil the abilities of the motor carriers to survive and serve the public"; and the Commission's conclusion that "to refuse to permit the forwarders to maintain rates on the same level as those of the protestants would be tantamount to an attempt by us to apportion traffic artificially, and thereby to prevent normal, healthy competition and deny forwarders an opportunity to compete fairly with motor carriers, contrary to the national transportation policy" is a rational, proper and permissible judgment.

The decision of the Commission in this proceeding is consistent with its previous decisions. The Commission in previous decisions has approved the publication by freight forwarders of rates for volume shipments at various minimum weights over 10,000 pounds. *Consolidation of Shipments by Freight Forwarders*, 256 I.C.C. 305 (1943); *New England Motor Rate Bureau, Inc. v. Julius Bleich, doing business as New York-Philadelphia Dispatch*, 272 I.C.C. 133 (1948); *Prepared Flour from Los Angeles to Arizona*, 283 I.C.C. 92 (1951); *Barge Service Corporation Freight Forwarder Application*, 285 I.C.C. 249, 285 I.C.C. 309 (1953); *Freight Forwarder Commodity-Rates Westbound Transcontinental*, 296 I.C.C. 445 (1955); *Acme Fast Freight, Inc. v. Western Freight Association*, 299 I.C.C. 315 (1956); *Iron and Steel from Monaca, Pa. to Southern Points*, 305 I.C.C. 110 (1958); *Forwarder Volume Commodity Rates, Transcontinental*, 306 I.C.C. 535 (1959); *Radios, Boots, Etc. from the East to Texas*, 306 I.C.C. 615 (1959). Prior to the enactment in 1942 of Part IV of the Interstate Commerce Act, the Commission approved rail rates for the transportation of trailers of freight forwarders and other shippers and considered such trailers to be containers or articles of commerce. *Vehicle Container Rates in Southwest*, 196 I.C.C. 127 (1933); *Trucks on Flat Cars between Chicago and Twin Cities*, 216 I.C.C. 435 (1936). In *New England Motor Rate Bureau, Inc. v. Julius Bleich, doing business as New York-Philadelphia Dispatch*, 272 I.C.C. 133 (1948), the Commission, over the objections of competing motor carriers, approved rates of a freight forwarder at minimum weights up to 30,000 pounds, under which the freight forwarder shipped its loaded trailers by rail to the point from which delivery of the shipment was made direct to the consignee. In *Movement of Highway Trailers by Rail*, 293 I.C.C. 93 (1954), the Commission approved the use by freight forwarders of rail rates for the transportation of loaded trailers of the freight forwarders. As stated by the Commission in its reports herein, the Commission has held that the national transportation policy "does not mean that one transportation agency may be required to refrain from establishing rates which are reasonable and otherwise lawful in order to protect the traffic of a competing mode. E.g., *Cigarboxes from Newark, N. J. to Selma, Ala.*, 296 I.C.C. 68; *Various Commodities, − Mid-Atlantic and New England*, 63 M.C.C. 584; see *Mississippi Valley Barge Line Co. v. United States*, 292 U.S. 282 [54 S. Ct. 692, 78 L. Ed. 1260]." The Commission also has previously held that in ruling upon competitive transportation rates, it should exercise extreme care to avoid an attempt "to apportion the traffic artificially and thereby eliminate normal, healthy competition contrary to the national transportation policy." *Fabrics from Georgia and North Carolina to Okla. and Texas*, 63 M.C.C. 430, 434 (1955). By its reports and order in this proceeding, the Commission has properly recognized the right of the defendant freight forwarders to make available to the shipping public reduced rates to meet motor carrier competition on volume shipments, such reduced rates having been made possible through the use by the forwarders of the economical Plan III rates and transportation service instituted by the rail carriers in 1958, and the action of the Commission was in no way arbitrary or capricious.

In *Import Volume Forwarder Rates, Pacific Coast to East*,[105] the Commission said (p. 11) that the right of freight forwarders to main-

[105]313 I.C.C. 9.

tain volume commodity rates was determined in *Forwarder Volume Commodity Rates, Chicago and New York*, however, "a primary requirement of the Act is that a freight forwarder must assemble and consolidate shipments." The Commission added (pp. 11-12):

> . . . it is the duty of freight forwarders to determine type or types of shipments they can lawfully handle, to publish rates covering such traffic, and to refrain from accepting or publishing rates for shipments which they cannot handle as freight forwarders. In the absence of a restrictive provision in the tariff, the respondent is holding itself out to transport as a freight forwarder, under the rates named in the tariff, any and all shipments covered by such rates regardless of whether or not they could be handled as parts of consolidated shipments. There is thus a holding out in its tariff which goes beyond its operating authority.

> As stated, where the respondent is tendered a single shipment at the underlying carrier's minimum weight, the shipment is handled by it as a customs broker as agent for the shipper. The shipment then moves on a rail bill of lading showing the shipper as consignor or the customs broker as agent for the shipper, and apparently the respondent would assume no responsibility for the safe transportation of the shipment. If, as indicated, this is the respondent's intention, it should not object to a statement in the tariff limiting the volume rates, rules, and regulations so they will apply only on shipments which it, in the ordinary and usual course of its undertaking, assembles and consolidates, or arranges for the assembling and consolidating, and performs or provides for break-bulk and distributing operations with respect to such consolidated shipments, and for which it issues to the shipper its freight-forwarder bill of lading. Although the rates of other freight forwarders are not in issue before us and thus their lawfulness may not here be determined, nevertheless the same principle should apply to all who are similarly situated, and we shall expect such freight forwarders to insert substantially the same statement in their respective tariffs.

> Upon reconsideration, we conclude that the respondent's tariff should be amended as outlined above. In all other respects the findings in the prior report are affirmed. . . .

Is a freight forwarder required to perform all the functions it is required to perform in order to hold itself out as a freight forwarder? This question was answered in *National Motor Freight Traffic Ass'n. v. United States*.[106] In this case suit was brought to set aside and annul a decision of the Commission in *Forwarder Volume Commodity Rates, Transcontinental*,[107] approving a tariff published by a freight forwarder in which reduced rates were established for shipments of 20,000-30,000

---

[106]205 F. Supp. 592, aff'd 371 U.S. 223, petition for rehearing denied 372 U.S. 246.

[107]306 I.C.C. 535, 311 I.C.C. 773.

pounds moving from official territory to points on the Pacific Coast. Plaintiff attacked the tariff as unlawful insofar as under its terms freight forwarders need not perform specific forwarding duties which plaintiffs (all motor carrier associations) urged were required by Section 402(e) of the I.C. Act. It was argued that the freight forwarders under this tariff enter into destructive competition with the motor carrier industry contrary to established national transportation policy. The court pointed out (p. 595) that a forwarder ordinarily assembles the several different shipments at its terminals by having them brought in from the various consignor premises, usually by motor carrier; it consolidates the shipments into a proportion qualifying for the reduced carrier rate and in this form sees to their safe transport to destination; it breaks bulk at the destination point by restoring each shipper's merchandise in units for delivery to the consignee; and distributes the separated shipments or arranges for their distribution, again usually by motor carriers, to the premises of the various consignees not located in the destination terminal. The challenged tariff contemplated certain variations from these ordinary procedures when a shipper desires transportation of 20,000-30,000 pound loads, and it offered the shipper a reduced charge contingent upon what degree of variation occurs. Thus where a shipper delivers its own freight to the forwarder's loading facility or where it arranges to have the consignee pick up the freight at the carrier's destination terminal, or both, the freight charge will be correspondingly lower. The reduced rate flows from performing less service.

The essence of plaintiff's case was that a forwarder must actually perform all the functions it is authorized to perform: assemble, consolidate, break-bulk, and distribute the consignor's freight, and plaintiffs' claim that failing to do all four steps one cannot hold itself out as a forwarder. The court held (p. 597) that the forwarders proffer these services but that is the extent of their obligation under the certificate. "If some consignors or consignees wish to have less than the proffered service no statute and no public policy prevents such arrangements being authorized by the Commission." The court said (pp. 596-97):

> No reason appears to require a view that the break-bulk and distribution operations are always distinct, always occur in a certain order, and may never be consumated coincidentally or concurrently. We think it within the purview of statutory policy to consider that the freight forwarder has appropriately performed whatever his break-bulk and distribution functions may be when he has made a shipment available to a consignee at the destination terminal and, at consignee's option and request, relinquished control over the shipment to the consignee to do with it as the latter sees fit under the contract.

That aspect of the national transportation policy which seeks to promote more efficient service is clearly well served by the operations which may be undertaken under the freight forwarder rate schedule which the Commission has here approved. As the Commission said, "If a forwarder can handle a heavier weighted shipment more economically than it can handle several small shipments of the same aggregate weight, the shipping public should receive the benefits flowing from that fact." 311 I.C.C. 775. On the other hand, no destructive competitive effects appear of a proportion to offset the benefits of this improvement.

TOFC Service

In *Substituted Service-Piggyback*,[108] the Commission set forth through formal rules certain guidelines for TOFC service and practices for the purpose of furthering the growth of piggyback, standardizing industry practices, and insuring that piggyback is made available to all who are able to make effective use of it. Certain pronouncements made in the past were re-examined in the light of developments made. The proceeding was instituted on the Commission's own motion under the authority of the I.C. Act and Administrative Procedure Act, and constituted the first general investigation of TOFC service. The following plans were examined: (1) Railroad movement of trailers or containers of motor common carriers, with the shipment moving on one bill of lading and billing being done by the trucker; traffic moves under rates in regular motor carrier tariffs. (2) Railroad performs its own door-to-door service, moving its own trailers or containers on flatcars under tariffs usually similar to those of truckers. (3) Ramp-to-ramp rates based on a flat charge, regardless of the contents of trailers or containers,

---

[108]322 I.C.C., 301, remanded to Commission on other grounds in *Atchison T. & S. Fe Ry. Co. v. United States*, 244 F. Supp. 955. See Section 216(c). See also the following cases: *Motor-Rail-Motor Traffic in East and Midwest*, 219 I.C.C. 245; *National Auto. Transporters Assn. – Declaratory Order*, 91 M.C.C. 395; *Gilbert Carrier Corp. Extension – Kearny, N. J.*, 72 M.C.C. 204; *Substituted Freight Service*, 232 I.C.C. 683; *Trucks on Flat Cars Between Chicago and Twin Cities*, 216 I.C.C. 435; *Gordons Transports, Inc. v. Strickland Transp. Co.*, 318 I.C.C. 395, aff'd. *Strickland Transp. Co. v. United States*, 209 F. Supp. 618; *Substituted Rail Service by Red Ball Transfer Co.*, 52 M.C.C. 75 (303 I.C.C. 421); *Piggyback Traffic Statistics*, Docket No. 34364; *Ringsby Truck Lines, Inc., v. Atchison, T. & S. F. Ry. Co.*, 263 I.C.C. 139, 141; *Savage Application*, 265 I.C.C. 157, 167; *Greer Broker Application*, 23 M.C.C. 417; *Stone's Exp., Inc., Common Carrier Application*, 32 M.C.C. 525; *Substituted Service – Consolidated Freightways, Inc.*, 305 I.C.C. 301, aff'd. *Consolidated Freightways, Inc. v. United States*, 176 F. Supp. 559; *Movement of Highway Trailers by Rail*, 293 I.C.C. 93; *Eastern Central M. Carriers Assn. v. Baltimore & O. R. Co.*, 314 I.C.C. 5, 45-7, aff'd *Cooper-Jarrett, Inc. v. United States*, (C. A. No. 13496, W. D. Mo. 1964); *Motor Vehicles – Kansas City to Arkansas, Louisiana, and Texas*, 318 I.C.C. 301. In Ex Parte No. 230 (Sub-No. 4), *Investigation of Piggyback Service Regulations*, 355 I.C.C. 841, the circuitry provisions were abolished.

usually owned or leased by freight forwarders or shippers; no pickup or delivery is performed by the railroad. (4) Shipper or forwarder furnishes a trailer or container-loaded flatcar, either owned or leased; the railroad makes a flat charge for loaded or empty-car movement, furnishing only power and rails. (5) Traffic moves generally under joint railroad-truck or other combination of coordinated service rates; either mode may solicit traffic for through movement.

In *Substituted Service-Piggyback*, the Commission defined (at p. 327) trailer-on-flatcar (TOFC) service, as meaning "the transportation on a rail car, in interstate or foreign commerce, of (a) any freight-laden highway truck, trailer, or semitrailer (or the container portion of any highway truck, trailer, or semitrailer having a demountable chassis); or (b) any empty highway truck, trailer, or semitrailer (or the container portion of any highway truck, trailer, or semitrailer having a demountable chassis) when such empty equipment is being transported incidental to its prior or subsequent use in TOFC service as defined in subparagraph (a). . . ."

Trailer-on-flatcar operations are conducted under various plans which have attained general use in the transportation industry.[109] Under Plan I, the railroad moves trailers or containers of motor common carriers, with the shipment moving on one bill of lading and billing being done by the motor carrier; the traffic moves under rates in regular motor carrier tariffs. Under Plan II, the railroad performs its own door-to-door service, moving its own trailers or containers on flatcars under tariffs usually similar to the motor carriers. Plan II-¼ embraces a type of service whereby the rail carriers handle the freight in trailers or demountable trailer bodies furnished by the railroad from the carrier's origin ramp location to carrier's destination ramp location. Terminal services at either origin or destination (but not both) must be performed by the consignor, consignee or their agent at their expense. Plan II-½ embraces a type of service whereby the rail carriers handle freight in trailers or demountable trailer bodies furnished by the railroad from carrier's origin ramp location to carrier's destination ramp location. Terminal services at origin and destination must be performed by the consignor, consignee or their agent at their expense. Under Plan III, ramp-to-ramp rates on a flat charge are applied, regardless of the contents of the trailers or containers; the trailers or containers are usually owned or leased by freight forwarders or shippers and no pickup or delivery is performed by the railroads. Under Plan IV, shippers or forwarders furnish trailer or con-

[109]See *Substituted Service-Piggyback supra. at* 304-5.

tainer-loaded flatcars, either owned or leased; the railroads make a flat charge for loaded or empty-car movements, furnishing only power and rails. Under Plan V, traffic moves generally under joint rail-truck or other combination of coordinated service rates; either mode may solicit traffic for the through movement.

Trailer-on-Ship or Fishyback Service

There is no bar to motor carriers, if they hold the requisite authority, from entering into rate arrangements with maritime carriers to effect a substitution of water-for-motor service. (See Section 216(c).)

Contract Rates

Contract rates and agreed charges not designed to meet market competition but to meet carrier competition have been held by the Commission to constitute destructive competitive practices within the meaning of the national transportation policy, and held to be unjust and unreasonable.

In *Contract Rates, Rugs and Carpeting from Amsterdam, N. Y.,*[110] concerned with the lawfulness of a proposed rate on carpeting from Amsterdam, N.Y., to Chicago, conditioned upon the tender to the railroads by the shipper during the year of at least 80 percent of its traffic from and to those points, the Commission concluded that the proposed rate was unjust and unreasonable in that it constituted a destructive competitive practice. A three-judge court affirmed the Commission's report and order in *New York Central R. Co. v. United States.*[111] Interpreting the phrase "unfair and destructive competitive practices" in the national transportation policy in the light of earlier enactments using similar language, the court noted that among "the kinds of competitive practices that Congress authorized the Interstate Commerce Commission, in the exercise of its informed judgment, to decline to countenance" was that specified in Section 3 of the Clayton Act[112] as as an unlawful type of competition, namely, the fixing of a price charged "or discount therefrom, or rebate upon such price . . . on the condition, agreement, or understanding that the . . . purchaser thereof shall not use

[110]313 I.C.C. 247.
[111]194 F. Supp. 947.
[112]15 U.S.C. 14.

or deal in the goods, . . . (etc.), of a competitor or competitors . . . ,"
where the effect may be to substantially lessen competition or tend to
create a monopoly. The court noted that if the quoted provision of the
Clayton Act applied to services, the tariff therein considered would
plainly violate that statute, and continued:

> The effect of such a contract upon competition is quite different from
> that of mere reduction in charges. In the latter case a competitor who
> meets the reduction is in as good a position to compete as theretofore;
> here, even if he meets the contract tariff with a similar one, he has some
> initial handicap, and whichever competitor gets the traffic, the other is
> then in a poor position to compete. All this would be a valid consideration
> for the Commission if only competing railroads were involved; it is doubly
> so in view of Congress' direction in the National Transportation Policy "to
> recognize and preserve the inherent advantages of each" mode of transpor-
> tation.

In *Guaranteed Rates — Sault Ste. Marie, Ont., to Chicago, Ill.*[113] the
Commission said (page 322):

> The inevitable effect of a substantially exclusive patronage arrangement
> is to eliminate competition during the period it is in effect. During that
> period, and especially during the final months, the shipper's vested inter-
> est in the reduced rate would discourage acceptance of an offer of superior
> transportation service at an equivalent or lower rate, thus nullifying any
> inherent advantages of other transport agencies as a competitive factor. We
> are directed by the National Transportation Policy to "preserve" the inherent
> advantages of the several modes, not to approve arrangements which would
> prevent the effective assertion of those advantages. Moreover, the validity
> of the undertaking in the tariff schedule that no increase will be made in
> the rate during the period fixed for its duration, unless otherwise ordered
> by the Commission, even though changed conditions might warrant such an
> increase, appears to be inconsistent with the continuing obligation of com-
> mon carriers to establish and maintain just, reasonable and otherwise lawful
> rates.

The Commission further said (page 323) that "if this guaranteed
rate were approved other rates of like kind on the same and other
commodities would be established, and that competition could be expected to force the spread of such rates to most of the traffic moved
by carriers for hire in this country. The end result, in our judgment,
would be the destruction in large measure of what is in general a just,
reasonable, and otherwise lawful rate structure which is necessary to
the maintenance of an adequate National Transportation System."

[113]315 I.C.C. 311.

Volume Rates

The Commission has approved numerous volume rates including multiple-unit train and trainload rates.[114] In doing so the Commission recognized that cost savings and efficiencies are involved, and that the differences between such large volume service and conventional service are substantial. One of the principal problems which sometime arises in volume rate cases, are the annual volume or minimum tonnage requirements.

In *Coal from Ky., Va. and W. Va. to Virginia*[115] reduced rates on bituminous coal, conditioned upon the receipt by the consignee of a specified minimum tonnage during a stated period, were approved. The reduced rates were found necessary for the respondents to retain traffic which otherwise would have been lost by the construction of a mine-mouth generating plant by the utility using the coal for which the reduced rates were established. To the same effect is *Coal from Ill., Ind., and Ky. to Illinois and Indiana*[116] wherein approval was given to multiple-car rates on bituminous coal from midwestern mines to Chicago, Ill., and points grouped therewith. Also to the same effect is *Coal to New York Harbor Area*,[117] where the Commission approved reduced rates on bituminous coal to electric utilities conditioned upon the receipt of at least 500,000 tons annually, the reduction applying on amounts over specified volumes. Those rates were aimed at preventing the loss of important coal volume moving to such utilities, to offshore residual oil. In none of the foregoing proceedings did it appear that the approved rates would have a destructive effect upon other rates.

However, see *Great Lakes Ship Owners Assn. v. Chicago & N. W.*

---

[114]See e.g. *Natural Gas Pipeline Co. of America v. N.Y.C.R. Co.*, 323 I.C.C. 75; *Grain by Rent-A-Train, IFA territory to Gulf Ports*, 335 I.C.C. 111, 339 I.C.C. 579; *Grain in Multiple — Car Shipments — River Crossings to the South*, 325 I.C.C. 752; *Coal from Ky., Va. and W. Va. to Virginia*, 308 I.C.C. 99; *Coal to New York Harbor Area*, 311 I.C.C. 355; *Coal from Ill., Ind., and Ky. to Illinois and Indiana*, 308 I.C.C. 673; *Molasses from New Orleans, La., to Peoria & Pekin, Ill.*, 235 I.C.C. 485; *Eastern Coal to Chicago, Ill.*, 306 I.C.C.195; *Interstate Commerce Commission v. B. & O. Railroads*, 145 U.S. 263; *Huron Portland Cement Co. v. B. & O. R. Co.*, 332 I.C.C. 665; *Reduced Seasonal Household Goods Rates*, 335 I.C.C. 761; *Weekly Rates on Petroleum Products — from Sparks, Nev.*, 322 I.C.C. 541. See *Clay, Points in Georgia to Savannah & Port Wentworth*, 340 I.C.C. 377, on cancellation of existing multiple car rate on shipments of Kaoline clay.

[115]308 I.C.C. 99.

[116]308 I.C.C. 673.

[117]311 I.C.C. 355. Under a tariff allowing a lower rate to a shipper who meets stated requirements, the shipper is entitled to the lower rate only if all the requirements are met. *Louisiana & Arkansas Railway Co. v. Export Drum Co.*, 359 F. 2d 311, 316, affirming 228 F. Supp. 89.

Ry.,[118] where the principal question presented was whether the carrier's form of rate publication was a destructive competitive practice — specifically the condition requiring the shipper to tender 850,000 tons of coal annually from origin to destination in order to receive the $1.56 unit train rate. The Commission found that the annual volume requirement, conditioning the application of the unit train rate, constituted an unfair and destructive competitive practice contrary to the national transportation policy and hence was unjust and unreasonable under Section 1 of the I.C. Act.

In arriving at its conclusion, the Commission said (pp. 279-280):

> Where two or more commodities or geographic areas compete for the commerce to a given destination, we have termed that "market competition"; where two or more carriers compete for the same traffic, that has been called "carrier competition." Of course, in one sense there is little difference between the two since carriers are the conduit for the traffic to the markets. However, it is fundamental that the act contains less rigid standards governing market competition as opposed to carrier competition. Throughout the rate structure runs, among other things, the railroads' constant effort to maximize their flow of traffic by minimizing rate differences between competing localities, consistent with the overall rate structure. Section 15a(2) of the act enjoins the Commission to consider "the effect of rates on the movement of traffic by the carrier or carriers for which the rates are prescribed;" and generally encourages competition between ports and markets.
>
> For example, sections 3 and 216(d) clearly reflect the desire of Congress that the regulatory standards governing carrier competition should not apply to market competition. Both sections prohibit undue preference of any locality and both except from the prohibition "the traffic of any other carrier," i.e., the section does not restrict the carrier when only another carrier complains in a situation involving market competition. Similarly, under section 3 unjust discrimination between localities can be shown only if the same carrier or carriers serve the two points or effectively participate in the rates thereto. *Central R. Co. v. United States,* 257 U.S. 247, 259-60 (1921); *Texas & Pacific Ry. Co. v. United States,* 289 U.S. 627, 646 (1933); and *Albany Port District Comm. v. Ahnapee & W. Ry. Co.,* 219 I.C.C. 151, 170-173.
>
> In each of the three cases[119] which we have had dealing with annual-volume rates, the following factors were present:
>
> > (1) All three instances involved a movement of coal from mine to electric generating plant;

---

[118]341 I.C.C. 272.

[119]*Coal from Ky., Va. and W. Va. to Virginia,* 308 I.C.C. 99; *Coal to New York Harbor Area,* 311 I.C.C. 355; and *National Gas Pipeline Co. of America v. N.Y.C.R. Co.,* 323 I.C.C. 75.

(2) There was competition between the commodity to which the rate applied, coal, and another commodity, natural gas, residual oil or voltage transmission through power lines from a mine-mouth generating facility;

(3) The proponent rail carrier was faced with the likelihood that a substantial volume of its coal traffic would be lost due to the substitution of the competing commodity;

(4) No carrier subject to our jurisdiction was shown likely to be injured by the volume requirement; and

(5) There was no opposition by any shipper or consignee of the involved commodity. Shipper opposition was limited to shippers of different commodities.

Thus this complaint proceeding filed by certificated water carriers operating on the Great Lakes presents a question of first impression.

In another group of cases, the *Contract Rates* case and the *Guaranteed Rates case*, rate reductions were found unlawful because they were conditioned upon the shipper tendering no specific tonnage (such as 1 million tons), but rather 80 or 90 percent of its traffic (which could be 50 tons or 5 million tons) between two main points via the carrier's line. No competition between markets, commodities, or geographic areas was involved, but rather competition between regulated carriers. This we deemed destructive because it unlawfully deprived other modes of transportation of the opportunity to compete for particular traffic for the duration of the contract.

The Commission said further (pp. 283-285):

> However, in all material respects, the ultimate result of the volume condition is to prevent competition for 850,000 tons of traffic, which tonnage represents a substantial portion of the relevant market — the total traffic to Edgewater. In these circumstances, we are thus persuaded that the annual-volume requirement here in dispute comes within the ambit of the "initial handicap" doctrine as formulated by the Court in *New York Central R.R. v. United States, supra,* and adopted by us in the Guaranteed Rates case, *supra.* The Court stated at page 951:

> > The effect of such a contract upon competition is quite different from that of a mere reduction in charges. In the latter case a competitor who meets the reduction is in as good a position to compete as theretofore; here, even if he meets the contract tariff with a similar one, he has some initial handicap and whichever competitor gets the traffic, the other is then in a poor position to compete. All this would be a valid consideration for the Commission if only competing railroads were involved; it is doubly so in view of Congress' direction in the National Transportation Policy "to recognize and preserve the inherent advantages of each" mode of transportation.

And the basis for that doctrine can be found in our earlier decision in the *Contract Rates* case, *supra,* at page 253, where we stated:

> During the term of the contract, and especially during its final months, the shipper's vested interest in the reduced rate would discourage or

prevent acceptance of an offer of superior transportation service at an equivalent or lower rate, nullifying any inherent advantages of other transportation agencies as a competitive factor. We are directed by the national transportation policy to "preserve" the inherent advantages of the various modes not to approve contracts which prevent the effective assertion of those advantages.

Thus, there are certain practices, such as foreclosing other modes subject to the act from competing, which because of their pernicious effect on competition and a lack of any redeeming virtue are conclusively presumed to be unreasonable and therefore unlawful without elaborate inquiry as to the precise harm they have caused. Cf. *Northern Pac. R.R. v. United States*, 356 U.S. 1 (1958).

Defendant avers that complainants are not entitled to the protection of the national transportation policy, since they transport the vast preponderance of coal in unregulated movements pursuant to the bulk-commodities exemption in section 303(b) of the act. This argument, in the light of judicial expressions to the contrary, is unpersuasive. Each of the complainants holds a certificate of public convenience and necessity from this Commission and is thus subject to the act insofar as is necessary to receive the shelter of congressional policy. The protection of the national transportation policy is reserved to modes of transportation subject to the act which by definition means regulated carriers not regulated commodities or regulated rates. See *American Commercial Lines v. Louisville & Nashville R. Co.*, 329 U.S. 571, 593 (1968); *Dixie Carriers v. United States*, 351 U.S. 56 (1956); *ICC v. Mechling*, 330 U.S. 567 (1947); *Arrow Transport v. United States*, 176 F. Supp. 411 (N.D. Ala., 1959), affirmed *per curiam*, *sub nom. State Corporation Comm'n of Kansas v. Arrow Transport*, 361 U.S. 353 (1960); *James McWilliams Blue Lines v. United States*, 100 F. Supp. 66 (S.D.N.Y. 1951), affirmed *per curiam*, 342 U.S. 951 (1952).

Finally, as urged by the complainants, we may not ignore the policies of the antitrust and other statutes as a relevant factor in interpreting the objectives of the national transportation policy. See, *McLean Trucking Co. v. United States*, 321 U.S. 67 (1944), and the *New York Harbor* case, *supra*, at page 370. However, in view of our findings, it is unnecessary to consider the background of these other statutes except to the extent heretofore indicated.

One final comment seems appropriate especially since the issue in this proceeding has been designated of national transportation importance. The poor financial condition of many of the railroads is common knowledge. We have labeled their efforts to increase their traffic through the use of ratemaking and technological innovations as part of a current revolution in transportation techniques. Our conclusion that the annual-volume condition herein should be eliminated should be placed in its proper perspective. We have found nothing wrong with the concept of unit-train pricing which is so essential to the rail and coal industry, the electric utility market and the millions of customers which they serve. This proceeding need have no adverse effect on such unit-train arrangements since the annual-volume condition has not been shown essential to the unit-train operation or pricing technique. The level of the unit-train rate is the important consideration and it is apparently too low for the water carriers to compete, since on this record their rate offers were not accepted on two occasions since the unit-train rate of $1.56 became effective. Thus, there should be no impact on the rate levels, the minima, the unit-train service or the tonnage transported as a direct result of the elimination of the annual-volume condition. The only thing being condemned is the condition and related matters.

Rate Adjustments and Investigation and Suspension Proceedings

The ordinary rate adjustment or investigation and suspension ("I & S") proceeding usually involves the rates and charges upon one or a limited number of commodities, from one or a limited number of origin stations or points to one or a limited number of destination stations or points proposed by one or a limited number of carriers seeking an upward or downward rate revision. If ordered for examination by the Commission, the change will need to be justified by the proponent, and its burden of proof ordinarily will embrace the compensativeness of the resultant rates and charges, that is, whether they will cover the variable costs and/or the fully allocated costs of performing the service, and, if so, by how much. The proponent's case, moreover, normally will include comparisons with the rates and charges for similar movements such as those that apply on another commodity but one having similar transportation characteristics transported between the origins and destinations in question, all with a view to establishing the essential justness and reasonableness of the change. In turn, the opponent to the change in the rates and charges, whether it be a competing carrier or an affected shipper, in an ordinary rate adjustment or I & S proceeding, normally will counter that the carrier's earnings under the proposal will be inordinately low or unreasonably high; and will show the effect of the change upon the movement of the commodity, competing traffic, and the complainant, or show that the community in which it or another is situated will be unduly preferred or unjustifiably prejudiced, all as the case may be. The Commission's task is to determine whether the carrier has established the justness and reasonableness of the proposed rates and charges and their lawfulness otherwise; and, if it determines that it has not, it may order the proposal cancelled, leaving the existing rates and charges intact, or it may prescribe supplanting just and reasonable rates and charges or just and reasonable minima and/or just and reasonable maxima.

General Revenue Proceeding

The general rate case or general revenue proceeding[120] ordinarily relates to the rates and charges upon all or most of the commodities from all or most of the origin stations or points to all or most of the destination stations or points proposed by all or most of the carriers, if not throughout the country then most certainly in a large geographic area, such as Eastern Territory. It almost invariably entails an increase in the level of rates and charges, whether uniformly applied to all of the affected commodities, differentially related to broad groups of items, or subject to holddowns or maxima on specific articles or movements. If ordered for examination by the Commission, the changes will need to be justified by the proponent carriers, and their burden of proof normally is confined to establishing their overall revenue needs. Competing carriers ordinarily do not participate in general rate cases or general revenue proceedings, and the participation of affected shippers by and large is limited to efforts at disproving the carriers' overall revenue needs or attempting to establish that their freight, even without the sought increase, is contributing its fair share towards meeting whatever the carriers' revenue needs may be. The Commission's authorization of the requested increases, or some other increases, which it determines to be just and reasonable, in no way is an approval by it of the resultant rates and charges on specific articles and movements. It merely is an indication by the Commission that it is persuaded by the carriers' revenue requirements and that they may increase their rates and charges to the level authorized by the Commission to meet their demonstrated needs for increased revenues. It is for the very reason that Commission authorization in general rate cases or general revenue proceeding does not connote its sanction of any particular rate or group of rates as increased by the carriers.

Thus, the Commission does not attempt to determine whether the particular rates which result from the increases are maximum reasonable rates, nor does the order constitute a prescription of rates within the

---

[120]Although there was a broadly based freight rate increase as early as 1903, *In the Matter of Proposed Advances in Freight Rates*, 9 I.C.C. 382, the first nationwide general rate increase based on cost escalation and the need to improve earnings was approved in 1920. Ex Parte No. 74, *In the Matter of the Application of Carriers In Official, Southern and Western Classification Territories for Authority to Increase Rates*, 58 I.C.C. 220. The Commission's authorization of general rate increases has been interpreted and sustained through a long series of cases. *E.g., Aberdeen & R. R.R. v. SCRAP*, 422 U.S. 289; *United States v. SCRAP*, 412 U.S. 669; *United States v. Louisiana*, 290 U.S. 70; *New England Divisions Case*, 261 U.S. 184.

meaning of the decision in *Arizona Grocery Co. v. Atchison, T. & S. F. Ry. Co.*[121] If individual rates or groups of rates are believed to be unjust and unreasonable, a shipper or other interested persons has an administrative remedy available in the I.C. Act. General revenue proceedings are inappropriate forums for litigating such issues.[122]

Procedures Governing the Data and Information to Be Submitted by Carriers in General Revenue Proceedings

In a number of general rate increase proceedings a significant number of protestants criticized the adequacy of the carriers' case in support of the increase, and the Commission in various ways expressed dissatisfaction with the quality of the evidence submitted in support of these increases.[123]

In these proceedings the carriers had presented their case generally on the theory that all that was required to justify the increase was to show increases in operating expenses and to point to their rate of return. No attempt was made to present evidence showing the cost of performing the service involved. In this respect the record left much to be desired. Unless the Commission considers the cost of performing the services involved, there can be no real basis for a determination that the charges are the lowest consistent with the furnishing of such service and similarly no real basis for a determination that the increase authorized will not be unjustly discriminary or unduly perferential or prejudicial as between the various movements of traffic and services rendered.

The carriers had been on notice for some time that they have not been meeting their burden of proof. See e.g. *Increased Freight Rates, 1967,*[124] where the Commission had the following to say in regard to evidentiary deficiencies by carriers seeking general rate increases:

> We are reminded by some of the protestants that in a series of decisions starting in 1963, involving proposed general increases in freight rates for motor carriers, we have established the policy of requiring a different and heavier quantum of proof than in earlier proceedings. Some of these decisions are referred to in *Increased Class & Commodity Rates, Transcon-*

---

[121]284 U.S. 370.

[122]*Electronic Industries Assn. v. United States,* 310 F. Supp. 1286, 1289, aff'd mem., 401 U.S. 967; *Alabama Power Co. v. United States,* 316 F. Supp. 337, 338, aff'd by a divided court, 400 U.S. 73; *Increased Freight Rates, 1970 and 1971,* 339 I.C.C. 125; *Algoma Coke & Coal Co. v. United States,* 11 F. Supp. 487.

[123]See e.g. *Increased Freight Rates, 1970, and Increased Freight Rates, 1971,* 339 I.C.C. 125, 189-91 *Increased Freight Rates, 1967,* 332 I.C.C. 280, 286; *Increased Class & Commodity Rates, Transcontinental,* 329 I.C.C. 420.

[124]322 I.C.C. 280, 286.

tinental, 329 I.C.C. 420, which is cited by protestants. The implied suggestion is that in the present general revenue proceeding, which is the first to be brought by the railroads since 1960, we should, to be consistent, express dissatisfaction with the quantum of proof offered here, although it is in many respects substantially similar to that acted upon in Ex Parte 223 and prior rail proceedings. The factual situations are necessarily different, but the principle involved is essentially the same. While the evidence submitted, as hereinafter explained, is sufficient to justify the increases authorized, we shall expect the petitioning railroads in any future general revenue proceedings to make a more complete disclosure of the facts upon which they rely in support of the relief sought. As stated in *General Increases — Transcontinental,* 319 I.C.C. 792, 803, "in fairness, standards should not be changed without due notice." *This report will serve as such notice in regard to the evidentiary deficiencies discussed herein.*

Based on its experience with these rail proceedings and also certain motor carrier proceedings, the Commission arrived at the conclusion that the quality of the evidence could be improved. Therefore, the Commission in its report in *Increased Freight Rates and Charges, 1972*[125] advised and forewarned the carriers that its acceptance of annualized costs and other data of a type submitted in that and in prior general revenue proceedings was not an irrevocable commitment and that in the future it would require a much more varied data base to support an application for revenue relief. To this end it instituted a rulemaking proceeding (Ex Parte No. 290, *Procedures Governing Rail Carrier General Increase Proceedings*)[126] looking toward prescription of minimum evidentiary requirements in railroad general rate increase cases.

In Ex Parte No. 290, the Commission adopted procedures governing the submission of evidence in rail general increase proceedings. Those procedures require the filing and serving on each party of record in the last prior general increase proceeding, of verified statements presenting the full and entire evidential case relied upon by the carriers to support a proposed general increase, (minimum data requirements are set forth), at the same time that the schedules or petition seeking authority to publish such schedules are filed with the Commission. The rules requiring data and information concern five primary subjects, namely: application of the procedures; financial and revenue need data; cost and revenue data; employment, wage, productivity, and rate data; and the effect of affiliate transactions.

With respect to the motor carrier rate structure, the Commission has taken some significant actions in recent years. In a principal proceeding,

[125]341 I.C.C. 290, 312.
[126]351 I.C.C. 544, order served September 28, 1977 in Ex Parte No. 290.

Ex Parte No. MC-82, *New Procedures in Motor Carrier Revenue Proceedings,*[127] the Commission prescribed new procedures governing the data and information to be submitted by motor carriers of general commodities in revenue proceedings. This action stemmed from a general dissatisfaction with the quality of evidence submitted by the motor carriers in support of rate increases.

In sum, the procedures set forth in Ex Parte No. MC-82 provide as follows:

(1) Motor carriers are required to submit their evidence when they file the schedules. Special permission to file the schedules shall be conditioned on the publishing of an effective date at least 45 days later than the date of filing.

(2) A traffic study shall be submitted which covers the most current 12-month period available, and is based on the actual operations conducted during identical periods of time for each carrier included in the traffic study.

(3) A cost study shall be submitted. Highway Form B may be used for this purpose.

(4) Revenue need data on a combined basis shall be filed.

(5) Each individual traffic and cost study carrier (frame carrier) having transactions with affiliates shall submit appropriate data and analyses reflecting the effect on the parent carrier's profits of transactions with affiliates.

(6) The Commission will take official notice of all the proponent carriers' annual and quarterly reports.

(7) Service of submissions on each party of record is required.

(8) All underlying data used in preparation of submission shall be made available for inspection by any party of record and the Commission upon request therefor, and shall be made available at the hearing.

The Commission believes that the prescribed procedures will enhance the probability of accomplishing its previously announced goals of shortening the time necessary to dispose of motor carrier general rate increase proceedings, achieving greater uniformity and reliability in data submitted, and providing adequate notice of the minimum evidence deemed necessary to render a decision.

The significance of this recent development can be better appreciated in light of the historical development for determining revenue needs. Until 1965 motor carriers generally were able to obtain an increase in rates by pointing to their low operating ratios and complying with other requirements somewhat short of real economic justification. Between 1965 and 1971, the Commission moved toward more comprehensive data, thus showing progress toward developing criteria to be used in justifying rate increases.

[127]339 I.C.C. 324, 340 I.C.C. 1.

27

Classifications

Applicable Statutory Authority

It was not until the enactment of the Mann-Elkins Act of June 18, 1910, that carriers were expressly required to make or observe a classification of property. Although the Commission had no specific authority to prescribe classifications of property prior to 1910, the power was exercised from the beginning of regulation because it was deemed essential to the effective exercise of its specific powers over rates. The nature of the implied power asserted by the Commission was described in its First Annual Report to Congress (p. 31):

> It was, therefore, seen not to be unjust to apportion the whole cost of service among all the articles transported, upon a basis that should consider the relative value of the service more than the relative cost of carriage. Such method of apportionment would be best for the country, because it would enlarge commerce and extend communication; it would be best for the railroads, because it would build up a large business, and it would not be unjust to property owners, who would thus be made to pay some proportion to benefit received. Such a system of rate-making would in principle approximate taxation; the value of the article carried being the most important element in determining what shall be paid upon it.

Thus, when Congress enacted Section 1(6) of the Interstate Commerce Act[1] it confirmed a power which the Commission was already exercising under the Act to Regulate Commerce of 1887.

Section 1(6) of the I.C. Act, requires carriers "to establish, observe, and enforce just and reasonable classifications of property for transporta-

---

[1] 49 U.S.C. 1(6). Comparable provisions — Sections 216(a), (b), 305(a), 404(a).

tion, with reference to which rates, tariffs, regulations or practices are or may be made or prescribed.

Congressional policy requires just and reasonable classifications of freight for all ratemaking purposes — not just class rates. This is shown in the Hoch-Smith Resolution,[2] and in the analysis of that resolution by the Supreme Court in *Ann Arbor R. Co. v. United States.*[3] The second paragraph of that resolution directed the Commission to investigate the rate structure to determine the extent and manner that existing rates and charges imposed undue burdens or gave undue advantage as between, among other things, "the various classes of traffic, and the various classes and kinds of commodities." In commenting on that paragraph of the resolution, the Supreme Court referred to the substantive provisions therein which required consideration of the general and comparative levels in market value "of the various classes and kinds of commodities" as indicated over a reasonable period of years, a natural and proper development of the country as a whole, and the maintenance of an adequate system of transportation. These matters, the court emphasized, "have all been regarded as factors requiring consideration under existing laws." The basic statutory standards of lawfulness are substantially the same today. Just and reasonable classifications of freight are also clearly contemplated by Section 3(1), which prohibits undue preference or advantage to "any particular description of traffic, in any respect whatsoever."

Interstate Commerce Commission Has Exclusive Jurisdiction to Determine Effect Upon a Commodity of a Change of its Classification

That the Commission has exclusive jurisdiction to determine the effect upon a commodity of a change in its classification was the precise proposition decided in *Director General of Railroads v. Viscose Co.*[4] The court said:

> Without more, these references to the Interstate Commerce Act are sufficient to show that if the proposed change in the tariffs, and in a rule, which we are considering, constituted a change of classification or of regulation within the meaning of the Commerce Act, there was ample and

---

[2]49 U.S.C. 55.
[3]281 U.S. 658.
[4]254 U.S. 498, 502-4. The Director General of Railroads amended rule 3 of "Consolidation Freight Classification No. 1," having the effect of excluding silk therefrom. The Viscose Company, a shipper of silk, secured an injunction restraining the Director General from putting the amendment into effect. On appeal, the court of appeals certified to the Supreme Court the question of whether or not the district court had jurisdiction to grant the injunction.

specific provision made therein for dealing with the situation through the Commission, — for suspending the supplement or rule or annulling either or both if investigation proved the change to be unreasonable, and for providing for just treatment of shippers in the future.

❋ ❋ ❋

The importance to the commerce of the country of the exclusive, initial jurisdiction which Congress has committed to the Interstate Commerce Commission need not be repeated and cannot be overstated *(Texas & Pacific Ry. Co. v. Abilene Cotton Oil Co.*, 204 U.S. 426; *Baltimore & Ohio R.R. Co. v. Pitcairn Coal Co.*, 215 U.S. 481; *Morrisdale Coal Co. v. Pennsylvania R.R. Co.*, 230 U.S. 304; *Minnesota Rate Cases*, 230 U.S. 352; *Texas & Pacific Ry. Co. v. American Tie Co.*, 234 U.S. 138, 146; *Pennsylvania R.R. Co. v. Clark Coal Co.*, 238 U.S. 456, 469, and *Loomis v. Lehigh R.R. Co.*, 240 U.S. 43, 49), and, concluding, as we do, that this case falls plainly within that jurisiction, the question asked by the Circuit Court of Appeals must be answered in the negative.

Purpose of Freight Classification

The primary purpose of a freight classification is to assign each article, or group of articles, to a class according to well-known classification principles or elements which recognize distinctions from a transportation standpoint, along fairly broad lines, to meet the needs of commerce.[5]

Classification denotes the process by which the thousands of commodities tendered carriers are grouped for the pricing of their services. Classification has been defined in *Director General v. Viscose Co.*[6] as follows:

> Classification in carrier rate-making practice is grouping, the associating in a designated list, commodities, which, because of their inherent quality or value, or of the risks involved in shipment, or because of the manner or volume in which they are shipped or loaded, and the like, may justly and conveniently be given similar rates . . .

The Commission has variously defined the classification of freight a rate-making scheme devised for the purpose of according the same rate to all commodities of a like character from a transportation standpoint;[7] largely a matter of comparison of all the commodities that move as freight and the assignment of ratings such that each shall bear its

---

[5] *Class Rate Investigation, 1939*, 262 I.C.C. 447; *Vacuum Cleaners Mfgrs. Assn. v. Atchison A. & S.F. Ry. Co.*, 276 I.C.C. 783, 792.

[6] 254 U.S. 498, 503.

[7] *McCrory Stores Corp. v. Direction General*, 55 I.C.C. 423, 424; *Hires Condensed Milk Co. v. P.R.R. Co.*, 38 I.C.C. 441, 447.

fair share of the transportation burden;[8] and a determination of reasonable relations between commodities, with groupings of kindred articles.[9]

The factors that influence the freight's classification, the so-called transportation characteristics, are many and varied. In *Motor Carrier Rates New England*,[10] these characteristics were stated in the following terms:

The characteristics of the commodities which must be considered in fixing classification ratings are generally as follows:

1. Shipping weight per cubic foot.
2. Liability to damage.
3. Liability to damage other commodities with which it is transported.
4. Perishability.
5. Liability to spontaneous combustion or explosion.
6. Susceptibility to theft.
7. Value per pound in comparison with other articles.
8. Ease or difficulty in loading or unloading.
9. Stowability.
10. Excessive weight.
11. Excessive length.
12. Care or attention necessary in loading and transporting.
13. Trade conditions.
14. Value of service.
15. Competition with other commodities transported.

Transportation charges generally are assessed on the basis of the weight of the shipment that is, the rates are stated in terms of so many parts per 100 pounds. Under such a scheme of pricing, the shipper tendering a large shipment in terms of weight will pay more than the shipper tendering a light shipment. In other words, a shipper of a 1,000-pound box would be expected to pay more than the shipper of a 100-pound box. However, a carrier is limited in how much freight it can carry by the capacity of its equipment, and in any one piece of equipment it can carry a heavier load of freight having a low cubic displacement than it can shipments of high cubic displacement. Therefore, in determining the rate relationships of various commodities, that is, in grouping commodities for the assessment of transportation charges, carriers will rate freight of low density higher than freight of high density, all other things being equal.

[8]*Classification of Canned Goods*, 98 I.C.C. 166, 176.
[9]*National Electric Mfrs. Assn. v. Atchison, T. & S. F. Ry.*, 289 I.C.C. 125, 132.
[10]47 M.C.C. 657, 660-61. See also *All States Frgt. v. New York, N.H. & H.R. Co.*, 379 U.S. 343; *Class Rate Investigation, 1939*, 262 I.C.C. 447, 508; *Investigation and Suspension Docket No. 76*, 25 I.C.C. 442, 463, 472-73; and *Proctor & Gamble Co. v. C. H. & D. Ry. Co.*, 9 I.C.C. 440, 482.

In establishing the rate relationship between the many commodities they transport, the carriers assess a higher charge on freight more likely to be lost or damaged in transit than on freight not having such a tendency.[11]

Value is related to liability. If two packages of equal weight are lost in transit, the carrier incurs a greater monetary loss in paying the claim of the shipper of the more valuable freight than it does in paying any that may be submitted on the less valuable freight. Accordingly, in establishing the relationship of rates carriers assess the former a higher rate than the latter. In other words, as a measure of the risks assumed, value clearly is a transportation characteristic to be taken into account. Moreover, value is a factor in classification for the further reason that it generally is indicative of the ability of a commodity to pay the transportation charges.[12]

Ease or difficulty in loading or unloading, stowability, excessive weight, excessive length, and care or attention necessary in loading and transporting affect the costs incurred in performing the transportation and, accordingly, are considered by carriers in establishing the relationship of their transportation charges. For example, carriers receive greater compensation for a shipment of freight requiring extraordinary handling than one of equal weight that can be moved in the usual fashion.

Insofar as trade conditions are concerned, the conditions existing in an industry may be a proper factor to be considered in determining the reasonableness of the rates that apply on its products.[13]

Value of service relates to pricing in accordance with the elasticity of demand. The intensity and pervasiveness of competition have not diminished in any way the relevance of elasticity of demand as a matter to be taken into account in setting carrier rates and charges; the elasticity of demand for carrier service has increased greatly and shippers of

---

[11]Carriers are tantamount to insurers of the safe delivery of cargoes entrusted to their care for transportation. *Loss and Damage Claims,* 340 I.C.C. 515. See Section 20(11) of the I.C. Act, 49 U.S.C. 20(11).

[12]*Rates on Lumber and Lumber Products,* 52 I.C.C. 598, 615.

[13]*In re Transportation of Wool, Hides and Pelts,* 23 I.C.C. 151, 156, it was said, "If the condition of this industry is such that it can not flourish, that the traffic will not move for the reason that the wool itself will not be produced, that, certainly, is a circumstance which may be considered in comparing this rate with those upon other commodities." Again, in *Utah-Idaho Millers & Grain Dealers Assoc. v. Denver & Rio Grande R.R. Co.,* 41 I.C.C. 714, 726, it was concluded, "°°°the condition of an industry has an influence upon the ability of a commodity produced by that industry to bear a rate, which in turn may have a bearing upon the reasonableness of the rate charged." Accord: *Wool & Mohair Rates,* 276 I.C.C. 259, 269; *Livestock – Western District Rates,* 190 I.C.C. 611, 633; and *Rates and Charges on Grain & Grain Products,* 94 I.C.C. 105, 143.

freight will divert their traffic to alternative modes when confronted by increased charges by the mode of transportation they have been using.

Competition with other commodities transported is also an important characteristic which must be considered in fixing classification ratings.[14]

While any one of the transportation characteristics, considered alone, might appear to warrant a higher or lower classification rating of particular freight, all of them are taken into consideration, and no one of them is controlling.[15]

Effect of Competition Upon Ratings

Competition of different types of common carriers has had a material effect upon the relationship of classification ratings throughout the country just as it has had upon the level of freight rates themselves. In *Pacific Inland Tariff Bureau v. United States*,[16] plaintiff sought to enjoin an order of the Commission refusing to set aside an "all-commodity" classification rating. The purpose of the rating was to provide a lower rate to meet motor-carrier competition. The facts showed that important motor carriers maintained similar rate bases over wide areas, with minima either adapted to the size of their vehicles or larger, based upon competitive rail rates. There was a close analogy between carload all-commodity rates and container rates; the differences were chiefly those of size. The Commission had held that it was not persuaded that the requirements of law as to classification were contravened, and found that the proposed rates were not shown to be unlawful. The court held (pp. 379-80):

> These facts and circumstances among others disclosed by those reports, and the findings and reasons therefor contained in the above quoted language of the Commission, convincingly negative the plaintiff's claims of improper rate classification and of insufficiency and invalidity of the Commission's findings.

> ✿   ✿   ✿

> In its experienced judgment applied to factual bases and conclusions which in the nature of the case are sufficiently reasoned and stated, the Commission, considering the competitive and other conditions inherent in the

[14]*Motor Carrier Rates in New England*, 47 M.C.C. 657, 660-661; *Class Rate Investigation*, 1939, 262 I.C.C. 447, 508; *Investigation and Suspension Docket No. 76*, 25 I.C.C. 442, 472-473.

[15]*Vacuum Cleaner Manufacturers Assn. v. Atchison, T. & S. F. Ry. Co.*, 276 I.C.C. 783, 792; *Class Rate Investigation*, 1939, 262 I.C.C. 447, 508; *Nashville Traffic Bureau v. L. & N.R.R. Co.*, 68 I.C.C. 623, 626; *McCrory Stores Corp. v. Director General*, 55 I.C.C. 424, 424.

[16]50 F. Supp. 376. See also *Montgomery Ward & Co. v. Baltimore & Ohio R. Co.*, 209 I.C.C. 243, 249; *Mountain-Pacific Oil cases*, 192 I.C.C. 599, 636.

ratemaking process here has disagreed with plaintiffs' assertion of unjust discrimination under Section 2 and of undue and unreasonable preference and prejudice under Section 3 of the Act. . . . It was for the Commission to determine upon the evidence before it in this case whether such competitive conditions and merchandising needs and the circumstances attending the related transportation service justified the questioned change in rates, and this court is bound by such fact determination of the Commission.

Shipments Under Class Rates

The class rates are in the form of a schedule which shows the price per 100 pounds for moving first-class freight every possible distance it may be moved. The cost of shipment for a given commodity is determined by ascertaining its classification rating, the first-class rate per 100 pounds for the haul involved, and the percentage of the first-class rate to which the classification rating in question is subject."[17] However, class rates move but a small percentage of the traffic. Thus, they are sometimes called paper rates."[18] Where there is a substantial volume of traffic moving, it usually moves on another type of rate, which is ordinarily lower than the class rate which must theoretically be available for any sort of unusual shipment which might be tendered to a carrier. These were defined in *N.Y. v. U.S.* as follows:[19]

> "*Exception* rates are rates resulting from the transfer of a commodity out of its regularly assigned class in the classification and into another class.
> "*Commodity* rates are special rates established for particular commodities. For purposes of these rates a commodity is not given a classification rating; the result is that the commodity rates have no fixed percentage relationships to first-class rates.[20]

> "*Column* rates are fixed as definite percentages of first-class rates but like commodity rates they apply only to particular commodities and are assigned no regular class."

Reasonableness of a Class Rate

An attack upon the reasonableness of a class rate implies either (1) that the article is improperly classified, or (2) that, if properly classified,

[17]*N.Y. v. U.S.*, 331 U.S. 284, 290.
[18]*Ibid,*, p. 243.
[19]*Ibid.*, p. 290.
[20]Commodity rates are special rates "which ought to be made with reference to all the conditions surrounding the transportation of the particular articles between the particular points." In establishing commodity rates carriers take into account factors such as the volume of the movement in question, its regularity, duration, direction, and length. See *The Mississippi River Case,* 28 I.C.C. 47, 63; *Railroad Commission of Louisiana v. A. H. T. Ry. Co.,* 48 I.C.C. 312, 269.

the class rate, as such, is too high, or (3) that it moves in sufficient volume to entitle it to a commodity rate.[21] In that connection the Commission said in *H. Barschi & Son v. Baltimore & O.R. Co.*:[22]

> A freight classification "with reference to which rates are made" is a grouping of the commodities which move by freight into a limited number of classes. All commodities which are entitled under normal conditions of transportation to the same, or substantially the same rate, are assigned to the same class. For each group of commodities as thus classified, carriers must establish a class rate, which rate, likewise under normal conditions of transportation, must be reasonable for application to all the commodities in that class. A class rate may be unreasonably high, as such, i.e., in its application to the entire group of commodities made subject to it by the classification; or it may be unreasonably high in its application to a particular commodity, either because the commodity is rated too high in the classification, or because of the existence of special conditions affecting the transportation of that commodity between particular points or within a given territory less in extent than the whole classification territory. In the first situation correction should be made by reducing the class rate; in the second, by changing the classification and reassigning the commodity to its proper place therein; and in the third, by the establishment of commodity rates or a classification exception within the limited territory where the exceptional conditions obtain.

In *Underwood Veneer Co. v. Ann Arbor R. Co.*,[23] the complainant attacked the rating on veneer and built-up wood, and asked that the rating on lumber be applied. The Commission dismissed the complaint and said (p. 267) that "The fact that a classification has long existed and is accorded wide recognition is persuasive of its reasonableness. We do not feel that the complainant has established the contrary. That veneer loads as heavily as lumber and can be moved at the same cost is not controlling. On the other hand, veneer and built-up wood are more valuable than lumber, and move in much smaller quantities." In *American Wringer Co. v. N.Y. N.H. & H. R. Co.*,[24] the Commission dismissed a complaint attacking the reasonableness of a rating on hand wringers in official territory and said (p. 326) that "The rating assailed has been in effect for more than 18 years, and a presumption of reasonableness attaches to a rating long voluntarily maintained."

It is well settled that the mere comparison of similar commodities

---

[21]*Burson Knitting Co. v. Baltimore & O.R. Co.*, 91 I.C.C. 607, 608.
[22]155 I.C.C. 350, 351.
[23]332 I.C.C. 264.
[24]146 I.C.C. 325. See also *Dodge Cork v. Pennsylvania R. Co.*, 216 I.C.C. 281; *Pullman Laundry Co. v. Baltimore & Ohio R. Co.*, 186 I.C.C. 421, 422; *Triad Corp. v. Central of Georgia R. Co.*, 113 I.C.C. 663, 664; *McCrory Store Corp. v. Director General of Railroads*, 55 I.C.C. 423, 424.

covered by different ratings throws little if any light on the question of whether the higher rating is reasonable. Obviously, it may not be determined from such a limited test whether it is the higher or the lower rating that is unreasonable, if, indeed, either rating is unreasonable. In *Union Material Manufacturing Co. v. Atchison, Topeka & Santa Fe Ry. Co.*,[25] the complainant charged that the less-carload classification rating of one and one-half times first class on sheet-steel columns was unreasonable. The classification on steel pipe and tubing of the size of complainant's columns was second class. Complainant sought to have a second-class rating applied to columns and introduced the respective ratings in evidence. The Commission dismissed the complaint and said (p. 666):

> Complainant contends that there is little, if any, difference between sheet-steel pipe and columns from a transportation standpoint; and that steel pipe and columns of the same gage and diameter weigh the same, have the same density, and occupy the same amount of space in a freight car. Both articles require the same amount of labor to load and stow in a car, except that the columns, being crated, need not be blocked as is necessary for pipe shipments.

> The columns here considered are not sheet-steel pipe, and because these columns are hollow and tubular it does not follow that they are entitled to the ratings on sheet-steel pipe of comparable size. A mere showing of differences in ratings is insufficient to prove the rating assailed to be unduly high. *Leigh Banana Case Co. v. Director General*, 59 I.C.C. 113, 117.

Comparisons of ratings of a commodity in one territory different from the ratings of a similar commodity in another territory are not only subject to the same objection, but are also subject to the objection that transportation conditions, including the existence of competition, may be different in the two territories. In *Alloy Material Abrasives Co. v. Akron & Barberton Belt R. Co.*,[26] the Commission dismissed a complaint attacking a fourth-class less-carload rating of iron sand and other commodities within official territory. These commodities had an exception rating of 40 percent of first class between official territory and southern territory. The complainant sought rates produced by the lower rating. The evidence disclosed that the 40 percent exception rating was brought about to meet the competition of southern railroads. The Commission said (p. 462):

> The establishment of the 40 percent basis on chilled shot and iron sand from official territory to the South, as exceptions to the governing classi-

[25]237 I..C.C. 663.
[26]266 I.C.C. 460.

fication, was brought about by the southern carriers reducing the rates in southern territory on a number of commodities in less than carloads, including chilled shot and iron sand, to meet motor-carrier competition. The reduced rates on the latter commodities applied from northern gateways and points served by the southern carriers, who dominated the rates within the South. Thereafter, the carriers in official territory joined in their application on interterritorial traffic.

                      *   *   *

Competitive rates afford no proper basis for comparison as to the reasonableness of rates on noncompetitive traffic.

Even though the ratings assailed may be relatively higher than on articles in the iron or steel list, that fact does not of itself establish a basis for a finding of unreasonableness; such a showing may indicate that the compared ratings are too low, rather than that the assailed rates are excessive.

Likewise, a comparison, of itself, between the spread of ratings between carload and less-carload commodities in different territories is inadequate to establish the unreasonableness of the wider spread because the transportation characteristics of carload traffic and less-carload traffic are quite different. This difference was noted in *Interstate Commerce Commission v. Cincinnati H. & D. Ry. Co.*[27] In holding that it was improper to relate the reasonableness of a less-carload classification to that of a carload classification, the court said (pp. 561-2):

> The question presented is not one involving only the proper relation of soap in less than carload lots, to soap in carload lots, but also its proper relation to other articles in less than carload lots. Freight is carried either in carload lots, or in less than carload lots. This division of freight necessarily attends transportation by rail. Classification, within the meaning of the act to regulate commerce relates to these divisions separately. The classification of soap in less than carload lots is not controlled by the classification of soap in carload lots, nor its reclassification by the maintenance of the relative difference in rates between the two; but, on the contrary, the classification and reclassification of soap in less than carload lots should be controlled by the relation it bears to other articles in less than carload lots, — that relation to be determined by the degree in which, in comparison with such other articles, its handling and carrying is, or may be, affected by the cost of service, competitive and commercial conditions, volume, density, distance, value, and risk of loss or damage. It is true that these elements must also be considered in determining the classification of articles in carload lots, but from a different standpoint.

[27]146 Fed. 559, aff'd 206 U.S. 142. This was an action to enforce an order of the Commission requiring the defendant to cease and desist from departing from a reclassification rating of official territory on a less-carload commodity. Defendants contended that it was necessary to depart from this rating to maintain a relationship between carload and less-carload shipments theretofore existing.

Used, second-hand, or obsolete machinery parts, shipped for re-manufactured or rebuilding purposes only, are not entitled to lower ratings and rates than are maintained on the same articles when new.[28]

The Application of Section 1(6)

The maintenance of class rates is quite different from the classification of property required by Section 1(6) of the Interstate Commerce Act. While it was never intended that class rates must be applied on all traffic, the plain language of Section 1(6) requires the maintenance of a classification of property with the establishment of rates related thereto.[29] Exception rates and commodity rates do not represent departures from the classifications of property because such rates are established on specific commodities or groups of commodities to meet particular transportation conditions.[30] Thus, just and reasonable classifications for commodity rates may bear little, if any, resemblance to the classifications observed in orthodox class-rate adjustments, for the reason that commodity rates usually reflect material transportation circumstances and conditions, especially market and carrier competition, which are not reflected in class-rate structures.[31] Mixed shipments or variations thereof, moving at single rates and minimum weights, to which all-freight and all-commodity rates are closely akin, also are established to meet particular transportation conditions.[32] While such rates ignore to some extent the individual commodity classifications, they are a necessary and established part of the national rate structure, and thus may be regarded as a reasonable separate category of classification, provided always that such rates are so restricted as not to undermine seriously any just and reasonable rate adjustment.[33]

The issue presented in *All States Frgt. v. N. Y., N.H. & H. R. Co.*[34] was whether Section 1(6) is applicable to so-called all-commodity freight rates. The Commission had held[35] that Section 1(6) does apply and that the section was violated by the rate schedules in question. The district court held[36] that Section 1(6) requires "the maintenance in being of

---

[28]*Simmons Machine Tool Corp. v. Delaware & H. R. Corp.*, 269 I.C.C. 761, 763.
[29]*All Commodities — From New England to Chicago and St. Louis*, 315 I.C.C. 419, 423.
[30]*Ibid.*
[31]*Ibid.*
[32]*Ibid.*
[33]*Ibid.*
[34]379 U.S. 343.
[35]315 I.C.C. 419.
[36]221 F. Supp. 370, 374.

class rates" but does not prohibit "competitively compelled departures from classifications, within the established maxima, absent some other violation of the Act than mere departure from the classification." The Supreme Court agreed with the district court stating that both the legislative history and the course of the Commission's decisions "clearly impel the conclusion that Section 1(6) does not apply to all-commodity rates." The court added:

> In reaching this conclusion, we hardly need add that, as the Act is structured, these rates are subject to full policing by the Commission under other provisions. If a commodity rate is too high, the Commission may reduce it. If a commodity rate unjustly discriminates against a shipper, the Commission may order the discrimination removed. If a commodity rate results in an undue preference in favor of or an unreasonable prejudice against any person, locality, or description of traffic, the Commission may require that appropriate adjustments be made. If a commodity rate is unreasonably low, the Commission may order that it be increased.

In its consideration of the issue in the case, the Supreme Court noted the basic distinction between class rates and commodity rates, stating:

> Class rates were at the foundation of the railroad rate structure at the time of the enactment of the Interstate Commerce Act in 1887. Such rates are applied to traffic through two separate tariffs. One tariff, the "classification," assigns each of the many thousand commodities carried by rail to one of presently some 30 categories or classes, based upon the commodity's particular characteristics. A companion tariff specifies the rate at which each class of freight will be carried. By contrast, commodity rates, which were also in existence at the time of the original passage of the Interstate Commerce Act, are rates made specifically applicable for the carriage of a particular commodity or group of commodities from one designated point to another. The original function of commodity rates, which are generally lower than class rates, was to encourage the movement of bulk commodities, such as coal and grain. With the onset and rapid growth of intermodal competition, the railroads increasingly turned to commodity rates in an effort to prevent diversion of traffic to other modes of transportation. Since 1932, numerous all-commodity or all-freight rail rates have been established between various points throughout the country. Typically, such rates have not literally applied to all commodities, but to a broad number, and they have often applied only to mixed carload shipments. Today only a small fraction of rail carload tonnage moves on class rates; by far the major portion moves on commodity rates of some kind.

The court discussed the legislative history of Section 1(6) at length before reaching the conclusion that the reach of Section 1(6) was confined to class rates. The court said:

It is clear that § 1(6) gives the Commission power to require that carriers maintain just and reasonable classifications in conjunction with the setting of class rates. The question here posed is whether that section applies to commodity rates as well, and specifically whether it applies to all-commodity rates. No doubt the language of the statute, "just and reasonable classifications of property" and "just and reasonable regulations and practices affecting classifications" is susceptible of a construction which would embrace the rates in issue here. The rates do not apply to a single, uniquely identifiable article but to a large group of commodities, which could be described as a classification of property. But the fact that the terms of the statute can be interpreted broadly enough to encompass these rates without doing violence to the English language does not settle the problem. It remains to inquire whether the legislative history warrants or the statutory structure supports such a broad interpretation.

At the time of the enactment of the Interstate Commerce Act the vast preponderance of rail freight traffic moved on class rates. These classes as well as the rates applicable to them varied greatly among different railroads and different sections of the country. When the Interstate Commerce Act was formulated, consideration was given to empowering the Commission to prescribe classifications, but it was finally concluded that the provisions of the bill which required publication of rates and classifications, together with the provisions regulating unreasonable rates, would ultimately prove adequate to achieve the desired uniformity of classifications.[37] Beginning with its First Annual Report, however, the Commission expressed its concern with the continuing lack of uniformity in freight classifications,[38] and seven years later recommended that it be empowered to make a uniform classification.[39] In 1906 the Hepburn Act gave the Commission power for the first time to prescribe maximum reasonable rates,[40] but transportation charges could still be increased by changes in the classification of any commodity

The Commission had succeeded in exercising power over classifications in proceedings under §§ 1, 2, and 3 of the Act, and in many cases had declared classifications of particular commodities to be unreasonable.[41]

However; the power of the Commission to halt manipulation of the classification rate system had been thrown into serious doubt by a case decided in 1905.[42]

---

[37]S. Rep. No. 46, 49th Cong., 1st Sess., 188.
[38]First I.C.C. Ann. Rep. 30-32 (1887).
[39]Eighth I.C.C. Ann. Rep. 38-39. See also Fifth I.C.C. Ann. Rep. 33.
[40]34 Stat. 589, 49 U.S.C. § 15(1).
[41]*James Pyle & Sons v. East Tennessee, Virginia & Georgia R. Co.,* 1 I.C.C. 465 (1888); *Thurber v. New York Central & H. R. Co.,* 3 I.C.C. 473 (1890); see *National Hay Assn. v. Lake Shore & M. S. R. Co.,* 9 I.C.C. 264 (1902).
[42]*Interstate Commerce Commission v. Lake Shore & M. S. R. Co.,* 134 F. 942, aff'd by an equally divided court, 202 U.S. 613. In this case the court struck down a Commission order commanding the reclassification of hay and straw to a lower rated class.

It was against this background that § 1(6) was enacted in 1910 as part of the Mann-Elkins Act, which also gave the Commission power to find classifications unreasonable and to prescribe reasonable classifications for the future.[43] The immediate genesis of these provisions seems to have been a special message to Congress by President Taft rcommending ". . . that the commission shall be fully empowered, beyond any question, to pass upon the classifications of commodities for purposes of fixing rates, in like manner as it may now do with respect to the maximum rate applicable to any transportation."[44]

During the course of the debate on the proposed bill inthe House of Representatives, Congressman Russell, a member of the Committee on Interstate and Foreign Commerce, said:

[T]he shipper can be extorted from; he can by made to pay an unjust rate just as well through classification as he can through the fixing of a rate. The carriers can put an article in one classification, subject to a given rate, and if the Interstate Commerce Commission sees fit to declare that rate unreasonable, and reduce it, declaring what shall be a reasonable rate to take its place, the carrying corporation can obtain the same benefit and put the shipper under the same disadvantages by simply changing the classification of the article.[45]

Chairman Mann stated that "classification of freight is just as important as rates, because by moving a particular article from one class to another you affect the rates."[46] He added that "in the course of time undoubtedly the power of the Commission to have control of classifications will lead to greater uniformity and possibly to complete uniformity of classifications. . . ."[47] The Senate Report alluded only to the doubt which had been recently cast upon the Commission's power to deal with classifications.[48]

This legislative history makes it apparent that the object of § 1(6) was to give the Commission clear power to deal with the twin problems which had arisen in the administration of class rates — the possibility of their manipulation to avoid maximum rate regulation and their lack of uniformity. Those problems never affected commodity rates, because those rates were competitively compelled reductions from whatever class rates would otherwise be applicable, and because standardization of commodity

---

[43]36 Stat. 546, 551, 552, 49 U.S.C. §§ 1(6), 15(1), 15(7).
[44]H. R. Rep. No. 923, 61st Cong., 2d Sess., 3.
[45]45 Cong. Rec. 5142.
[46]45 Cong. Rec. 4578.
[47]*Ibid.*
[48]The Senate Report stated: "Some doubt has been raised as to whether, under the provisions of Section 15 of the existing Act, the Commission is empowered to review *classifications* of freight as well as rates, and to make orders dealing with improper classifications. (Judson on Interstate Commerce, Ed. of 1908, Secs. 209, 210.) By Section 9 of the bill, this doubt is removed and the power is expressly vested in the Commission," S. Rep. No. 355, 61st Cong., 2d Sess. 8 (1910). The authority primarily relied on by the Judson treatise was the *Lake Shore* case, note 12, *supra.*

rates would have been completely inconsistent with their basic function of accommodating specific particularized competitive conditions.

The court also reviewed the pattern of the Commission's decisions since Section 1(6) was enacted to confirm its conclusion. The court stated:

> The course of those decisions makes clear that the Commission has given full consideration to the question of whether § 1(6) applies to all-commodity rates, and has squarely decided that the section is inapplicable. All-commodity rates first came under scrutiny of the Commission more than 25 years ago. In 1937 and 1938, the Commission approved all-commodity rates on four different occasions without the slightest suggestion that the rates were subject to the provisions of § 1(6). The principal concern of the Commission's inquiry in these cases was to ascertain whether the rates were prejudicial to any person, locality, or description of traffic.[49] In a similar case decided in 1939, Commissioner Alldredge filed a dissent expressing the view that § 1(6) *did* apply to all-commodity rates, and that the rates in question violated that section by lumping into a single category articles which had traditionally been assigned to different categories under the customary classification criteria.[50] With Commissioner Alldredge's dissent putting in issue the applicability of § 1(6), it is clear that the Commission consciously rejected his position. Two years later, however, the view taken by Commissioner Alldredge prevailed in a two-to-one order by Division 3, which struck down all-commodity rates as violative of § 1(6).[51] With the decisions thus in conflict, the problem received consideration by the full Commission a year later in *All Freight to the Pacific Coast*, 248 I.C.C. 73. There the Commission squarely held that § 1(6) does not apply to all-commodity rates. Its report stated:
>
>> Respondents now maintain a full line of class rates governed by the western classification from and to all of the points involved in this proceeding, as required by Section 1(6) of the Interstate Commerce Act. They also maintain hundreds of lower rates as exceptions to the classification, including commodity rates, that are not subject to the classification ratings nor to rules as to mixing of commodities in carloads. . . . Class rates normally reflect the maximum of reasonableness on goods falling within the various classes of traffic. Commodity rates

[49]*Freight from Boston to East Hartford*, 223 I.C.C. 421 (Div. 4, 1937); *Commodities between Chicago, Ill., and the Twin Cities*, 226 I.C.C. 356 (Div. 3, 1938); *All Freight between Boston & Maine Railroad points*, 226 I.C.C. 387 (Div. 4, 1938); *All Freight from Chicago and St. Louis to Birmingham*, 226 I.C.C. 455 (Div. 3, 1938).

[50]*All Freight between Harlem River, N. Y., and Boston*, 234 I.C.C. 673 (Div. 3, 1939). See also Commissioner Alldredge's dissents in the following cases: *All Freight from Chicago and St. Louis to Santa Rosa, N. Mex.*, 243 I.C.C. 517 (Div. 2, 1941); *All Freight between Los Angeles and Albuquerque*, 28 M.C.C. 161 (Div. 3, 1941).

[51]*All Freight from Eastern Ports to the South*, 245 I.C.C. 207 (Div. 3, 1941). See also the decision under § 216(b) of the Interstate Commerce Act by Commissioners Alldredge and Johnson in *All Freight from Chicago and St. Louis to El Paso, Tex.*, 28 M.C.C. 727 (Div. 3, 1941).

are established, and necessary or desirable exceptions to the classification are made, when circumstances and conditions suggest that the class basis is too high for application on the traffic. We have approved this basis of ratemaking, and have never required commodity rates to conform to the ratings of the classification. [248 I.C.C., at 86-87.]

In a separate concurrence, Commissioner Eastman said:

> As is well known, the classifications of freight which the railroads publish are for the purpose of governing the application of their class rates. The latter are used when no rate has been published applying specifically to the movement in question, such specific rates being called commodity rates. The railroads carry, of course, a vast multitude of separate and distinct commodities, and the class rates are a convenient device for avoiding the publication of a like multitude of separate and distinct rates. . . . [248 I.C.C., at 88.]

Thereafter, the Commission rejected other challenges to all-commodity rates based on § 1(6) upon the authority of the *Pacific Freight* decision,[52] and the two-to-one decision based on § 1(6) which Division 3 had previously rendered was recalled and decided upon another ground.[53] In the years that followed, the *Pacific Freight* case was regarded as controlling, and all-commodity rate cases were decided without reference to the provisions of § 1(6).[54] Finally, it is significant that in approving the trailer-on-flatcar service instituted by the New Haven's rail competitors in 1958, the Commission did not discern any problem created by § 1(6).[55]

Exceptions Ratings

A presumption of unreasonableness attaches to any basis of rates which exceeds the classification basis since the latter normally reflects the maximum reasonable level.[56]

---

[52]*All Freight from Butte, Mont., to Spokane, Wash.*, 251 I.C.C. 291 (Div. 2, 1942); *All Freight to points in Southern Territory*, 253 I.C.C. 623 (1942).

[53]*All Freight from Eastern Ports to the South*, 251 I.C.C. 361 (1942).

[54]See *All Freight, Straight Carloads, to and from the South*, 258 I.C.C. 579 (Div. 2, 1944); *All-Commodity Rates between California and Ore., Wash.*, 293 I.C.C. 327 (Div. 3, 1954).

[55]*Eastern Central Motor Carriers Assn. v. Baltimore & O. R. Co.* 314 I.C.C. 5, 48-49. The trailer-on-flatcar rates, unlike the all-commodity rates involved in the present case, are subject to a mixing rule requiring that the lading consist of at least two commodities, no one of which shall exceed 60% of the total volume of the lading. But the New Haven points out that this mixing rule is satisfied whenever two straight trailerloads, each containing a different commodity, are tendered at the same loading platform under a single bill of lading, even though they may be consigned by different shippers and destined for different consignees.

[56]*Western Gillette, Inc. v. United States, et al.*, Civil Action No. 73-19-CC, U.S.D.C. C.D. Calif. (1974); *Line Material Co. v. Pennsylvania R. Co.*, 281 I.C.C. 749, 752; *Schenley Distillers, Inc. v. Cincinnati, N. O. & T. P. Ry. Co.*, 289 I.C.C. 709, 714; *Warner Chemical Co. v. Chesapeake & Ohio Ry. Co.*, 222 I.C.C. 103, 107;

It is a long standing principle that the classification ratings and the class rates governed thereby generally provide the highest rates and charges which an article should bear, and that an exceptions or commodity rate, which is higher than the corresponding class rate governed by the classification rating, is an anomaly requiring special justification.[57] Normally, if a rating in the general clasification is two low, the carriers should correct it by changing the general classification and not by providing exceptions ratings or commodity rates higher than the classification bases.[58]

This does not mean that an exceptions rating or commodity rate may not be established if (1) the transportation characteristics of the excepted article moving between certain points differ substantially from the common characteristics of similar articles generally, or where (2) special circumstances peculiar to a particular area warrant it.[59] However, it has been held that, once the complainant has shown that the defendants' exceptions rating exceeds the classification rating on the commodity under consideration, the defendants then have the burden of going forward with evidence to establish the reasonableness of the higher exceptions rating.[60]

New Process Gear Corp. v. New York Central R. Co., 250 F. 2d 569, 571, cert. denied 356 U.S. 959; *Feather and Down Association, Inc. v. Middlewest Motor Freight Bureau, et al.,* 340 I.C.C. 76; *Foodstuffs from New York to Baltimore and Washington,* 66 M.C.C. 682, 683; *Central Territory Motor Carrier Rates,* 12 M.C.C. 567, 568, and 19 M.C.C. 545, 575; *Foodstuffs or Beverages from Columbus, Ga. to the East,* 63 M.C.C. 795, 799; *Freight Forwarder Rates Within Official Territory,* 298 I.C.C. 536, 538; and *Assembling and Distribution Rates — N.Y., N.J., and Pa.,* 309 I.C.C. 362, 364; *United States v. Red Ball Motor Freight, Inc., et al.,* Docket No. 35254, order served May 25, 1972; *United States v. Red Ball Motor Freight, Inc., et al.,* Docket No. 35320, order served June 6, 1972; *United States v. Ryder Truck Lines, Inc., et al.,* Docket No. 35332, order served October 26, 1972; *United States v. Central Truck Lines, Inc., et al.,* Docket No. 35293, order served October 4, 1972.

[57]*Exceptions Ratings on Magnesium Metals,* 305 I.C.C. 318; *Page Belting Co. v. Boston & M.R.,* 294 I.C.C. 307. See also *Classification of Foodstuffs, Chips,* 62 M.C.C. 679, 687; *Kalte v. Central Motor Lines, Inc.,* 61 M.C.C. 529, 534; *Exceptions Ratings on Magnesium Metals,* 305 I.C.C. 318, 320; *Great American Industries, Inc. v. Brooks Transp. Co., Inc.,* 302 I.C.C. 259, 262; *E. I. DuPont de Nemours & Co. v. Super Service M. Frt. Co.,* 54 M.C.C. 481, 485; *Paint Material from Atlanta, Ga., to Memphis, Tenn.,* 54 M.C.C. 477, 480; *Aircraft and Automobile Glass — Middle Atlantic Territory,* 311 I.C.C. 650, 651; *Glama Dress Co. v. Mid-South Transports,* 335 I.C.C. 586, 595; *United States v. Mid-South Transports, Inc.,* et al., order served April 17, 1972, Docket No. 35453; *Westinghouse Electric Corp. v. P.R.R. Co.,* 323 I.C.C. 503, 507; *All States Frt. v. N.Y., N.H. & H. R.R. Co.,* 379 U.S. 343, 345-46, 353. Cf. *Director General v. Viscose Co.,* 245 U.S. 498, 502.

[58]*Classifications in Middle Atlantic States,* 42 M.C.C. 716, 720.

[59]*Ibid.,* p. 719.

[60]*E. I. DuPont Nemours & Co. v. Super Service M. Frt. Co.,* 54 M.C.C. 481, 485.

In *Rules Governing Publication of Exception Ratings*,[61] the Commission adopted a regulation requiring that tender to the Commission of any motor common carrier tariff provision which would result in a higher charge than would result from application of the classification rating and rules to the class rates be accompanied by a clear statement of the justification ruled upon to warrant the publication of such provision. In support of the regulation, the Commission said (pp. 725-29):

> This proceeding was instituted to consider the establishment of a rule which would govern the publication by motor common carriers of any tariff provision (*e.g.*, exceptions rating, commodity rate, charge, rule, et cetera) which would result in a higher charge than would otherwise apply under the classification basis. As proponents have noted, this Commission has consistently held that the classification ratings and the class rates governed thereby generally provide the highest rates and charges which an article should bear, and that an exceptions rating or commodity rate, which is higher than the corresponding class rate governed by the classification rating, is an abnormality requiring special justification. See *Classification in Middle Atlantic States*, 42 M.C.C. 716, 719 (1943); *Bell Potato Chip Co. v. Aberdeen Truck Line*, 43 M.C.C. 337, 348 (1944); *Kalte v. Central Motor Lines, Inc.*, 61 M.C.C. 529, 535 (1953); *Classification of Foodstuffs, Chips*, 62 M.C.C. 679, 687 (1954) and *Paint Material from Atlanta, Ga., to Memphis, Tenn.*, 54 M.C.C. 477, 480 (1952). This principle of longstanding has been upheld by the courts in such recent decisions as *T.I.M.E.-DC, Inc. v. United States*, Civil No. CA 5-75-17 (N.D. Tex., Sept. 30, 1975); *Central Truck Lines v. United States*, Civil No. 70-193-T.K. (M.C. Fla., March 5, 1975, appeal docketed No. 75-1955, 5th Cir. 1975); and *IML Freight, Inc. v. United States*, Fed. Car. Cas. 55, 460 (No. C-188-71, D.C. Utah 1972).
>
> ✿ ✿ ✿
>
> Central to our consideration of whether use of the presumption should be continued is section 216(b) which requires the carriers to publish reasonable classifications. A majority of the motor carriers discharge their duty of maintaining reasonable classifications by participating in either the National Motor Freight Classification or in the Coordinated Motor Freight Classification, or both, although some carriers maintain individual classifications. The classification is designed to reflect characteristics of the commodity transported; that is, to establish the relationship of a multitude of articles to each other in the rate structure, all to the end of insuring that relatively favorable or unfavorable transportation characteristics are appropriately reflected in the carriers' charges. Thus each article, or group of articles, is assigned to a class according to well-known classification principles or elements which recognize distinctions from a transportation standpoint, along fairly broad lines, in order to meet the needs of commerce. See *Classification Ratings Based on Density, supra* at 797, and *Class Rate Investigation, 1939*, 262 I.C.C. 447 (1945). Without a basic

[61]351 I.C.C. 716

unity in classification ratings throughout the country, it would be virtually impossible to maintain a just and reasonable relationship between competing commodities.

The class tariff, on the other hand, reflects the characteristics, not of the commodity, but of the haul; that is, it establishes a relationship between localities based upon weight and distance. By use of the classification in conjunction with the class tariff, it is possible for carriers to publish reasonable charges for transporting all articles of commerce between all points in the United States without the necessity of publishing billions of separate and distinct rates. *General Increases—Eastern Central Territory,* 316 I.C.C. 467, 483 (1962). Together the classification and the class rate tariff enable the motor carriers to comply with their duty under section 217(a) to publish tariffs containing all of their rates between all points.

The establishment of an exceptions rating on an article removes application of the rating thereon published in the classification, and it follows that such ratings tend to disrupt a commodity's relation to other commodities from a transportation standpoint. See *exceptions Ratings—Twin Cities—Minn., Wis., and N. Dak.,* 10 M.C.C. 511, 514 (1938), and *Exceptions Rating, Stove Canopies, Hoods, Central Ter.,* 309 I.C.C. 644, 646 (1960). Pursuant to our statutory responsibility to determine which rates and classifications are just and reasonable, this Commission has determined that exceptions ratings higher than classification ratings should have only a limited function. Accordingly, such ratings are allowed only when transportation characteristics of the excepted article moving between certain points differ substantially from common characteristics of similar articles generally, or where special circumstances peculiar to a particular area warrant special treatment.

Changes in the transportation characteristics of an article are seldom limited to one area as technology is rapidly dispersed throughout the country, and nationwide changes clearly demand an appropriate adjustment in the general classification and not just an exceptions rating. Thus, exceptions ratings are not the proper vehicle to remedy classification ratings which become too low because of universal changes in the transportation characteristics of an article. By the same token, higher exceptions ratings are not demonstrated to be just and reasonable simply because classification ratings, when applied to the class rates, are noncompensatory. If a classification rating is too low the carriers should correct it by changing the general classification and not by providing exceptions ratings higher than the classification basis. In this way the Commission has narrowed the occasions where such ratings will be approved. If higher ratings continue to be confined to proper circumstances, then the disruption in the classification system will be held to a minimum.

✿   ✿   ✿

Upon consideration of the evidence presented in this proceeding, we conclude that a statement of justification should accompany the filing of exceptions ratings higher than the classification ratings. We believe that the integrity of the classification system requires continued adherence to the principle that motor carrier exceptions ratings higher than the classification ratings are presumed unreasonable. Given the fact that such ratings are unjust and unreasonable absent special justification, we believe that the costs incurred by shippers and the Commission in monitoring tariffs and in litigating reparations claims are unnecessarily high. By the adoption of the proposed rule, these costs can be reduced substantially without any significant increase in costs for the motor carriers and rate bureaus. Moreover, the rule should also discourage the filing of exceptions ratings for improper purposes.

We also reaffirm the principle that commodity rates higher than the corresponding class rates are an abnormality requiring special justification. See, for example, *Page Belting Co. v. Boston & M.R.,* 294 I.C.C. 307, 309 (1955), *Glama Dress Co. v. Mid-South Transports,* 335 I.C.C. 586, 595 (1969), and *Feather & Down Assn., Inc. v. Middlewest M. Frt. Bur.,* 340 I.C.C. 76, 78 (1971). The rule should encompass both types of publications in order to prevent carriers from avoiding the justification requirement by publishing commodity rates in lieu of exceptions ratings. Our rationale holds true with respect to any exceptions rating, commodity rate, charge, rule, or other tariff provision, the application of which results in a higher charge than otherwise would result from application of the classification basis. Accordingly, we conclude that the filing of any tariff provision which would result in a higher charge than would result from application of the classification class or rating and rules to the class rates must be accompanied by a justification statement.

28

Suspension Proceedings

Applicable Statute

The power to suspend the effectiveness of carrier-made rates is entrusted by Section 15(7), (8) of the Interstate Commerce Act.[1] to the Interstate Commerce Commission. The Commission has no power, however, to suspend such rates for a longer period than seven months beyond the time when they would otherwise go into effect.[2] (ten months under Section 15(8) if the Commission makes a report to Congress).

By amendment under the 4R Act, Section 15(7) does not apply to railroad carriers. Section 15(8)[3] was added by the 4R Act to apply to railroad carriers. Under Section 15(8)(a), whenever a schedule is filed

---

[1]49 U.S.C. 15(7), 15(8); comparable provisions — Sections 216(g), 218(c), 307(g), 307(i), 406 (e).

[2]*Cantlay & Tanzola, Inc. v. United States*, 115 F. Supp. 72. See also *Freeport Sulphur Co. v. United States*, 199 F. Supp. 913; *Long Island Rail Road Co. v. United States*, 193 F. Supp. 795, 797-8; *Coastwise Line v. United States*, 157 F. Supp. 305; *Manhattan Transit Co., Inc. v. United States*, 24 F. Supp. 174, 177-8; *Merchant Truckmen's Bureau v. United States*, 16 F. Supp. 998, 999-1000; *National Water Carriers Ass'n. v. United States*, 126 F. Supp. 87, 90-91; *Luckenback Steamship Co. v. United States*, 179 F. Supp. 605, 610; *Bison Steamship Corp. v. United States*, 182 F. Supp. 63, 69; *North Carolina Natural Gas Corp. v. United States*, 200 F. Supp. 745; *Macauley v. Waterman Steamship Corp.*, 327 U.S. 540, 544-5; *Myers v. Bethlehem Shipbuilding Corp.*, 303 U.S. 41, 50-51; *State of New Jersey v. United States*, 168 F. Supp. 324, aff'd 359 U.S. 27; *M. P. & St. L. Express, Inc. v. United States*, 165 F. Supp. 677; *J. T. Transport Co. v. United States*, 191 F. Supp 593; *Panama Canal Co. v. Grace Line, Inc.*, 356 U.S. 309, 317; *Landsden v. Hart*, 180 F. 2d 679; *First National Bank v. First Federal Savings and Loan Assoc.*, 225 F. 2d 33; *American President's Lines v. Federal Maritime Board*, 112 F. Supp. 346; *National Motor Freight Traffic Assoc. v. United States*, C.A. No. 1689-60, U.S.D.C. Dist. of Col.; *Helm's Express, Inc., v. United States*, C.A. 17904, U.S.D.C. W.D. Pa.; *American Commercial Barge Line v. United States*, C.A. No. 60-751, U.S.D.C. W.D. Pa.; *Amarillo-Borger Express v. United States*, 138 F. Supp. 411; *Long Island Rail Road Co. v. United States*, 140 F. Supp. 823.

[3]49 U.S.C. 15(8).

with the Commission by a railroad stating a new individual or joint rate, etc. the Commission may, upon the complaint of an interested party or upon its own initiative, order a hearing concerning the lawfulness of such rate, etc. The hearing must be completed and a final decision rendered by the Commission not later than 7 months after such rate, etc. was scheduled to become effective, unless, prior to the expiration of such 7-month period, the Commission reports in writing to the Congress that it is unable to render a decision within such period, together with a full explanation of the reason for the delay. If such a report is made to the Congress, the final decision shall be made not later than 10 months after the date of the filing of such schedule. If the final decision of the Commission is not made within the applicable time period, the rate, etc. shall go into effect immediately at the expiration of such time period, or shall remain in effect if it has already become effective. Such rate, etc. may be set aside thereafter by the Commission if, upon complaint of an interested party, the Commission finds it to be unlawful.

Section 15(8)(b) and (c), which expired on February 5, 1978, provided a limited 7 percent zone of reasonableness, the Commission could only suspend rates published under that section if they appeared to violate Sections 2, 3, or 4, or to constitute a destructive practice, or if the Commission made a finding of market dominance. The provision could only be used for specific rate adjustments and not for general increases.

Under Section 15(8)(d), the Commission may not suspend a rate unless it appears from specific facts shown by the verified complaint of any person that —

1. Without suspension the proposed rate change will cause substantial injury to the complainant or the party represented by such complainant.

2. It is likely that such complainant will prevail on the merits.

The burden of proof shall be upon the complainant to establish the matters set forth above.

If a hearing is initiated with respect to a proposed increased rate, etc. and if the schedule is not suspended pending such hearing and the decision thereon, the Commission shall require the railroads involved to keep an account of all amounts received because of such increase from the date such rate, etc. became effective until the Commission issues an order or until 7 months (or 10 months) after such date, whichever first occurs. The account shall specify by whom and on whose behalf the amounts are paid. In its final order, the Commission shall require the railroad to refund to the person on whose behalf the amounts were paid that portion of such increased rate, etc. found to be not justified, plus interest at a rate which is equal to the average yield (on the date such schedule is filed) of marketable securities of the U.S. which have a duration of 90 days. With respect to any proposed decreased rate, etc. which is suspended, if the decrease or any part thereof is ultimately found to be lawful, the railroad may refund any part of the portion of such decreased rate, etc. found justified if such carrier makes such a refund available on an equal basis to all shippers who participated in such rate, etc. according to the relative amounts of traffic shipped at such rate, etc.

Under Section 15(8)(f), in any hearing the burden of proof is on the railroad to show that the proposed changed rate, etc. is just and reasonable. The Commission shall specifically consider, in any such hearing, proof that such proposed changed rate, etc. will have a significantly adverse effect (in violation of Sections 2 or 3) on the competitive posture of shippers or consignees affected thereby. The Commission shall give such hearing and decision preference over all other matters relating to railroads pending before the I.C.C. and shall make its decision at the earliest practicable time.

Review of Orders in Suspension Proceedings

Broad discretion in the exercise of the Commission's power of suspension has clearly been upheld and "judicial review of suspension action or inaction is most severely limited, if not forclosed."[4]

[4]*Aberdeen* & *Rockfish R. Co. v. SCRAP*, 409 U.S. 1207, 1208. See *Ferguson-Steere Motor Co. v. United States*, 126 F. Supp. 588, 591 where the court said that "it is certainly true that the making of the orders is confided to the discretion of the Commission, and that only upon the closest and most compelling showing that discretion was not exercised at all, or, if exercised was abused, would a court interfere with a suspension order; we think it clear that, considering the reason given by the Commission in this case in the light of this compelling principle, it cannot be said of it that it was no reason at all and that the Commission, therefore, entered the order not in the exercise of its discretion and in compliance with the statute but without the exercise of discretion and in defiance of the statute." See *Luckenback Steamship Co. v. United States*, 179 F. Supp. 605, aff'd in part and dismissed in part 364 U.S. 280, where a district court held that the Commission's action in declining to suspend the effectiveness of new reduced rail rates pending an investigation into the lawfulness of the rates was not reviewable since the denial of a suspension of a rate by the Commission is by law committed to agency discretion. In *United States v. Amarillo-Borger Express, Inc.*, 352 U.S. 1028, opinion below 138 F. Supp. 411, the Supreme Court vacated the judgment of a district court and remanded the case to it with directions to dismiss as moot a decision in which the lower court found that the Commission's interlocutory orders vacating prior suspension orders were subject to review. See also *Carlsen v. United States*, 107 F. Supp. 39; *Southern Bakers Assn., Inc. v. United States*, 124 F. Supp. 600, lower court judgment vacated per curiam 348 U.S. 941; *Coastwise Line v. United States*, 157 F. Supp. 305; *Freeport Sulphur Co. v. United States*, 199 F. Supp. 913, 915-6; *Arrow Transportation Co. v. Southern Ry. Co.*, 372 U.S. 658; *National Motor Freight Traffic Assn., Inc. v. United States*, U.S.D.C. for D.C., C.A. No. 1689-60 unreported).

Suspension Period Cannot Be Extended

The Commission is vested with exclusive power to suspend a change in a rate for a limited time thereby precluding jurisdiction to the courts to grant injunctive relief extending the statutory period. This was held in *Arrow Transportation Co. v. Southern Ry. Co.*[5] The Supreme Court held that if the courts extended the period of suspension, which Congress in its wisdom fixed, the courts would, in effect, be amending the statute and that is a matter beyond their control. Because the Supreme Court thoroughly surveyed the history of the suspension power in the hands of the Commission, its opinion is set forth at length below:

> The Interstate Commerce Commission was granted no power to suspend proposed rate changes in the original Act of 1887. The power first appeared among the 1910 amendments introduced by the Mann-Elkins Act. The problem as to whether the application of new rates might be stayed pending decision as to their lawfulness first emerged after the Commission was empowered by the Hepburn Act of 1906 to determine the validity of proposed rates. In the absence of any suspension power in the Commission, shippers turned to the courts for injunctive relief. The results were not satisfactory. The lower federal courts evinced grave doubt whether they possessed any equity jurisdiction to grant such injunctions and the availability of relief depended on the view of a particular court on this much controverted issue. The Interstate Commerce Commission was more concerned, however, with certain practical consequences of leaving the question with the courts. In its Annual Reports for the three years before 1910 the Commission had directed attention to the fact that such courts as entertained jurisdiction were reaching diverse results, which engendered confusion and produced competitive inequities.

> The large expense entailed in prosecuting an action and financing a substantial bond proved prohibitive for many small shippers of modest means. Even when a large shipper secured an injunction, the scope of its relief often protected only that particular shipper, leaving his weaker competitors at the mercy of the new rate. Therefore, the Commission reported to Congress, ". . . as a practical matter the small shipper who can not file the bond can not and does not continue in business under the higher rate." I.C.C. Annual Report, 1908, p. 12. As an equally serious consequence, the regulatory goal of uniformity was jeopardized by the diverse conclusions reached by different district courts — even, it appears, as to the reasonableness of a particular rate change. This resulted in disparity of treatment as between different shippers, carriers, and sections of the country, causing in turn "discrimination and hardship to the general public." I.C.C. Annual Report, 1907, p. 10.

> It cannot be said that the legislative history of the grant of the suspension power to the Commission includes unambiguous evidence of a de-

[5] 372 U.S. 658.

sign to extinguish whatever judicial power may have existed prior to 1910 to suspend proposed rates. However, we cannot suppose that Congress, by vesting the new suspension power in the Commission, intended to give backhanded approval to the exercise of a judicial power which had brought the whole problem to a head.

Moreover, Congress engaged in a protracted controversy concerning the period for which the Commission might suspend a change of rates. Such a controversy would have been a futile exercise unless the Congress also meant to foreclose judicial power to extend that period. This controversy spanned nearly two decades. At the outset in 1910, the proposal for conferring any such power on the Commission was strenuously opposed. The carriers contended that any postponement of rate changes would result in loss of revenue or competitive advantages fairly due them in the interim if the rates were finally determined to be lawful. But this opposition eventually took the form of efforts to limit the time for which suspension might be ordered by the Commission. The Mann-Elkins Act authorized a suspension for an initial period not to exceed 120 days with a discretionary power in the Commission to extend the period for a maximum additional six months. Ten years later the Esch-Cummins Act of 1920 cut the authorized period of extension from six months to 30 days, thus reducing from 10 to five months the overall period for which the Commission might order a suspension. Congress was aware throughout the consideration of these measures that some shipper might for a time have to pay unlawful rates because a proceeding might not be concluded and an order made within the reduced time. To mitigate that hardship the 1920 amendments authorized the Commission in such cases to require the carriers to keep detailed accounts of charges collected and to order refunds of excess charges if the Commission ultimately found the rates to be unlawful. The suspension provisions took their present form, vesting authority in the Commission to suspend for a maximum period of seven months, in the Act of 1927. The accounting and refund provisions of the 1920 law remained. Thus, as we have observed before, the present limitation was "formed after much experimentation with the period of suspension . . ." *Interstate Commerce Comm'n. v. Inland Waterways Corp.*, 319 U.S. 671, 689.

We cannot believe that Congress would have given such detailed consideration to the period of suspension unless it meant thereby to vest in the Commission the sole and exclusive power to suspend and to withdraw from the judiciary any pre-existing power to grant injunctive relief. This court has previously indicated its view that the present section had that effect. In *Board of Railroad Comm'rs. v. Great Northern R. Co.*, 281 U.S. 412, 429, Chief Justice Hughes said for the court: "This power of suspension was entrusted to the Commission only." The lower federal courts have also said as much. And the commentators on the matter have consistently supported the soundness of that view.

There is, of course, a close nexus between the suspension power and the Commission's primary jurisdiction to determine the lawfulness and reasonableness of rates, a jurisdicton to which this court had, even in 1910, already given the fullest recognition. *Texas* & *Pacific R. Co. v. Abilene Cotton Oil Co.*, 204 U.S. 426. This relationship suggests it would be anomalous if a Congress which created a power of suspension in the Commission because of the dissonance engendered by recourse to the injunction nevertheless meant the judicial remedy to survive. The more plausible inference is the Congress meant to foreclose a judicial power to interfere with the *timing* of rate changes which would be out of harmony with the uniformity of rate *levels* fostered by the doctrine of primary jurisdiction.

It must be admitted that Congress dealt with the problem as it affected the relations between shippers and carriers, making no express reference to the interests of competing carriers and their customers such as are involved in the instant case. We see no warrants in that omission, however, for a difference in result. Conflicts over rates between competing carriers were familiar to the Commission long before 1910, indeed, the struggle between competing barge and rail carriers has been going on almost since railroads came onto the national scene. Indeed, in another provision of the very same statute, Congress in 1910 dealt explicitly with the *reduction* of rates by railroads competing with water carriers: Section 4 (2) of the Act forbids a rail carrier competing with a water carrier to increase rates once reduced on a competitive service, unless " "after hearing by the Commission it shall appear that such proposed increase rests upon changed conditions other than the elimination of water competition." 49 U.S.C. Section 4 (2). In addition Section 8 of the Act, 49 U.S.C. Section 8 creates a private right of action for damages — based upon conduct violative of the Act — which might be available, though we have no occasion here to decide the question, to a competitor claiming that a proposed rate reduction had been grossly discriminatory. Our holding today therefore means only that the injunction remedy is not available to these petitioners, just as it is unavailable to shippers.

Our conclusion from the history of the suspension power is buttressed by a consideration of the undesirable consequences which would necessarily attend the survival of the injunction remedy. A court's disposition of an application for injunctive relief would seem to require at least some consideration of the applicant's claim that the carrier's proposed rates are unreasonable. But such consideration would create the hazard of forbidden judicial intrusion into the administrative domain. Judicial cognizance of reasonableness of rates has been limited to carefully defined statutory avenues of review. These considerations explain why courts consistently decline to suspend rates when the Commission has refused to do so, or to set aside an interim suspension order of the Commission. If an independent appraisal of the reasonableness of rates might be made for the purpose of deciding applications for injunctive relief, Congress would have failed to correct the situation so hazardous to uniformity which prompted its decision to vest the suspension power in the Commission, Moreover, such a procedure would permit a single judge to pass before final Commission action upon the question of reasonableness of a rate, which the statute expressly entrusts only to a court of three judges reviewing the Commission's completed task.

Nor is the situation different in this case if it be suggested that a court of equity might rely upon the Commission's finding of unreasonableness which preceded the Commission's suspension order. The Commission's consideration of the question, through its Suspension Board, involves only a brief and informal hearing. Automatic judicial acceptance of a finding reached in that way would delegate greater effect to such an administrative process than the process itself warrants. As the basis for a judicial decree of a single district judge, such a procedure would be inconsistent with Section 15 (1) of the Act, which provides that effective rates may be struck down as unlawful after a "full hearing" by the Commission.

The petitioners contend that in any event injunctive relief is authorized in this case to enforce the National Transportation Policy. They argue that when the rail carriers' rates go into effect the barge line will inevitably and immediately be driven out of business, contrary to the paramount concern of the policy for the protection of water carriers threatened by rail competition. Apart from the absence of any decisive showing that the barge line would suffer this misfortune, it is clear that nothing in the National Transportation Policy, enacted many years after the 1927 revision of Section 15 (7), indicates that Congress intended to revive a judicial power which we have found was extinguished when the suspension power was vested in the Commission. Cf. *United States v. Borden Co.*, 308 U.S. 188, 198-199. Indeed, if anything the policy reinforces our conclusion. The mandate to achieve a balance between competing forms of transportation is directed not to the courts but to the Commission. It is reasonable to suppose that had congress felt that balance to be in danger of distortion, it would have addressed itself to our problem directly by enhancing the powers granted the Commission to enforce the policy. Surely Congress would not have meant its silence alone to imply the revival of a judicial remedy the exercise of which might well defeat rather than promote the objectives of the National Transportation Policy.

29

Through Routes and Joint Rates

RAIL CARRIERS — THROUGH ROUTES AND JOINT RATES

Applicable Statute

Section 1(4) of the Interstate Commerce Act[1] provides that "It shall be the duty of every common carrier subject to this part to provide and furnish transportation upon reasonable request therefor, and to establish reasonable through routes with other such carriers, and just and reasonable rates, fares, charges, and classifications applicable thereto; and it shall be the duty of common carriers by railroad subject to this part to establish reasonable through routes with common carriers by water subject to Part III, and just and reasonable rates, fares, charges, and classifications applicable thereto. It shall be the duty of every such common carrier establishing through routes to provide reasonable facilities for operating such routes and to make reasonable rules and regulations with respect to their operation, and providing for reasonable compensation to those entitled thereto; and in case of joint rates, fares, or charges, to establish just, reasonable, and equitable divisions thereof, which shall not unduly prefer or prejudice any of such participating carriers."

Definition of Through Route

The Supreme Court has defined the statutory term "through route"

[1] 49 U.S.C. 1(4). Compare (as to through routes and joint rates) under Part II, § 216(a), common carriers of passengers by motor vehicle; § 216(c), common carriers of property by motor vehicle, Part III, § 305(b).
Duty to furnish transportation upon reasonable request, Part III, § 305(a); Part IV, § 404(a).

as follows:[2] A 'through route' is an arrangement, express or implied, between connecting railroads for the continuous carriage of goods from the originating point on the line of one carrier to destination on the line of another." The court has said that "the test of the existence of a 'through route' is whether the participating carriers hold themselves out as offering through transportation service."[3] Through carriage implies a "through rate," however, this "through rate" is not necessarily a "joint rate"; it may be merely an aggregation of separate rates fixed independently by the several carriers forming the "through route."[4]

In answering the question of fact as to the existence of a "through route," all the incidents and circumstances of the shipment must be taken into account.[5] As pointed out in the *Denver & Rio Grande* case:

> In considering the question of through routes under Section 15(4) we begin with our recent holdings and opinions in *Thompson v. United States*, 343 U.S. 549, 96 L ed 1134, 72 S. Ct. 978; *United States v. Great Northern R. Co.*, 343 U.S. 562, 96 L ed 1142, 72 S. Ct. 985. We there emphasized the purpose of Section 15(4) to bar the Commission from compelling railroads to establish through routes resulting in trunkline "short-hauls" without faithful observance of restrictive conditions imposed by that section. At the same time we recognized that Commission action is not necessary to the creation of through routes. We pointed out that a through route is ordinarily a voluntary arrangement, express or implied, between connecting carriers, and that the existence of such an arrangement depends on the circumstances of particular cases. We said in *Thompson v. United States, supra* (343 U.S. at 557), that "In short, the test of the existence of a 'through route' is whether the participating carriers hold themselves out as offering through transportation service." Findings of through routes can therefore be made on the basis of express agreements between carriers or on the basis of inferences drawn from continuous practices sufficient to show that through routes exist even though not provided for in formal contracts or tariffs. The question in each case is one of fact. Cf. *Through Routes and Through Rates*, 12 I.C.C. 163, 166, 167.

---

[2]*Thompson v. United States*, 343 U.S. 549, 556; *St. Louis Southwestern Ry. Co. v. United States*, 245 U.S. 136, 139.

A joint through rate is one that will apply on a through movement of cargo from a point or origin on the line of one carrier to a point of destination on the line of the other. See *Denver & R.G.W. RR. v. Union Pac. R.R.*, 351 U.S. 321, 327; *United States v. Great No. Ry.*, 343 U.S. 562, 573; *St. Louis S.W. RR. v. United States*, 245 U.S. 136, 139 n.4. Each participating carrier retains a division of the joint through rate agreed upon between the carriers. See, e.g., *Baltimore & O. Ry. v. Alabama Great So. Ry.*, 506 F. 2d 1265, 1266.

[3]*Thompson v. United States*, 343 U.S. 549, 557. See *Hausman v. Seaboard*, 32 M.C.C. 31, 37.

[4]*Thompson v. United States, supra.*

[5]*Through Routes and Through Rates*, 12 I.C.C. 163, 166; *Denver & Rio G. W. R. Co. v. Union Pacific R. Co.*, 351 U.S. 321, 327.

The decision of the Supreme Court in *Western Pacific R. Co. v. United States*,[6] is important because of its construction of the term "connecting line." In the *Western Pacific case,* the Supreme Court held that to qualify as a connecting line in the absence of a physical connection, for the purpose of filing a complaint alleging discrimination under Section 3(4) of the I.C. Act, a carrier need only show that it participates in an established through route, making connection at the point of common interchange, all of whose participants stand willing to cooperate in the arrangements necessary to eliminate the alleged discrimination. Thus, to qualify under Section 3(4) as a complainant "connecting line" no direct connections of line with the discriminating carrier is required.

Requirements of the Statutes

In the *Thompson* case, the Supreme Court stated that "Under the Interstate Commerce Act, a carrier must not only provide transportation service at reasonable rates over its own line but has the additional duty 'to establish reasonable through routes with such other carriers, and just and reasonable rates . . . applicable thereto.' Through routes may be and ordinarily are, established by the voluntary action of connecting carriers. Since 1906, through routes may also be established by the order of the Interstate Commerce Commission." Thus the duty contained in Section 1(4) to establish reasonable through routes with other carriers, and just and reasonable rates, fares, charges and classifications applicable thereto, is usually exemplified by, and continues to by the subject of 'voluntary action. However, in the absence of voluntary action, the Commission is empowered under Section 15(3) to compel the establishment of through routes.

Authority of Commission to Establish Through Routes and Joint Rates

Section 15(3) and (4) of the Interstate Commerce Act,[7] relating to the establishment of through routes, have gone through various changes and modifications. When we distill the end result sought by Congress in this legislation, we come to the conclusion, as did the courts in the cited cases, that it is the public interest, which includes that of the

---

[6]15 L. ed. 2d 294, 299-300.
[7]15 U.S.C. 15(3) (4); comparable provisions to 15(3) — Section 216(e) and 307(d). See *Penna R. Co. v. United States,* 54 F. Supp. 381, 385, aff'd 323 U.S. 588; *Mo. Pac. R. Co. v. United States,* 21 F. 2d 351, aff'd 378 U.S. 269 (also known as the *Subiaco* Case); *Thompson v. United States,* 343 U.S. 549.

carriers, which is to be served so that adequate, efficient and economical transportation may be provided.

Section 15(3) provides, in effect, that the Commission is authorized, "whenever deemed by it to be necessary or desirable in the public interest, after full hearing upon complaint or upon its own initiative without complaint," to establish through routes. A finding that through routes and joint rates are necessary in the public interest is essential under Section 15(3).[8] The Supreme Court has held also that " 'public interest' as thus used is not a concept without ascertainable criteria, but has direct relation to adequacy of transportation service, to its essential conditions of economy and efficiency, and to appropriate provision and best use of transportation facilities, questions to which the Interstate Commerce Commission has constantly addressed itself in the exercise of the authority conferred."[9] There can be no mistaken assumption that the stated criterion "public interest" is a mere general reference to public welfare without any standard to guide determination. The purpose of the I.C. Act, the requirements it imposes, and the context of the provision in question show the contrary.[10]

Short-Haul Provision

The Commission's power to establish through routes as provided in Section 15(3) of the Interstate Commerce Act is limited by Section 15(4) whenever such action requires carriers to short-haul themselves. Under that Section, carriers may be required to short-haul themselves only where their own lines make the existing through route "unreasonably long as compared with another practicable through route which could otherwise be established," or where the Commission makes special findings that a proposed through route "is needed in order to provide adequate, and more efficient or more economic transportation."

In considering the question of through routes, the Supreme Court in *Thompson v. United States*[11] emphasized the purpose of Section 15(4) to bar the Commission from compelling railroads to establish through routes resulting in trunk line short-hauls without faithful observance of restrictive conditions imposed by that section. As pointed out in *Missouri Pac. R. Co. v. United States*,[12] not only must the originating and delivering carriers be considered in the establishment of through

[8]*Virginian Ry. Co. v. United States*, 272 U.S. 658, 666.
[9]*New York Central Securities Corp. v. United States*, 287 U.S. 12, 25.
[10]*Ibid.*
[11]343 U.S. 549.
[12]21 F. 2d 351, aff'd 278 U.S. 269.

rates, but also intermediate carriers. That case also established the principle that the affected traffic need not be in the possession of a carrier to have its interests preserved. In other words, the right of an intermediate carrier whose traffic would be affected adversely or prejudiced by the creation of a new route, or which would be short-hauled, must be considered as an element of public interest although not necessarily an originating or delivering carrier or one which may have had earlier possession of the lading. Section 15(4) expressly states that no "through route and joint rates applicable thereto shall be established by the Commission for the purpose of assisting any carrier that would participate therein to meet its financial needs." This prohibition was expressly upheld by the Supreme Court in *United States v. Great Northern R. Co.*,[13] where the court said "Congress amended Section 15(4) to prohibit tinkering with through routes for the purpose of assisting a carrier to meet its financial needs."

The Supreme Court in *Penna. R. Co. v. United States*,[14] said that paragraphs 3 and 4 of Section 15 of the Act "have provided that the Commission may establish a through route if found to be 'in the public interest' but may not establish such a route which requires a carrier to short-haul itself unless it finds that the route will provide adequate, and more efficient or more economic, transportation." But the court also said this does not mean the two sections are redundant. The court noted that "It is conceivable that the Commission might refuse to establish many through routes as not required in the public interest where short hauling is not involved." The Supreme Court also held that the Commission lacks power to short-haul a carrier under the provisions or clause (b) of Section 15(4) without consideration of evidence tending to show that the routes sought to be established were needed in order to provide adequate, and more efficient or more economic, transportation and without making a specific finding to that effect.

A determination by the Commission in *Chicago, M., St. P. & P. R. Co. v. Spokane, P. & S. Ry. Co.*[15] that the short-haul protection of Section 15(4) of the I.C. Act applies where one railroad is jointly controlled by two other railroads, was upheld by the Supreme Court in *Chicago, Milwaukee, St. Paul & P.R.R. Co. v. United States.*[16] The Court referred to the fact that the short-haul exception of Section 15(4) originated in

---

[13]343 U.S. 562, 575.
[14]323 U.S. 588, 592.
[15]300 I.C.C. 453.
[16]366 U.S. 745.

the Mann-Elkins Act of 1910,[17] and that the crucial words "common management or control" were not defined. The court said:

> However, the overriding purpose of the Congress seems to have been the protection of the traffic of the controlling line. As Senator Elkins, a coauthor of the measure, stated to the Senate, the exception "is one which has always been recognized in the transportation business in the country. The road that initiates the freight and starts it on its movement in interstate commerce should not be required . . . to transfer its business from its own road to that of a competitor . . . when the commerce initiated by it can be as promptly and safely transported . . . by its road as by the line of its competitor." 45 Cong. Rec. 3475-3476. The same reasoning would apply equally here. Moreover, the Senate Report on the provision emphasizes the same purpose (S. Rep. No. 355, 61 at Cong. 2d Sess. 10).
>
> While the language of the section is framed in the singular, it appears to us that the reason for this exception is as valid and necessary in the case of two railroads owning a third as it is when only a single railroad and its subsidiary are involved. See *Louisville & N.R. Co. v. United States*, 242 U.S. 60 (1916), where this court, in construing the discrimination provisions of the predecessor of Section 3 (4) of the Act, stated, "(t)herefore, if either carrier owned and used this terminal alone it could not be found to discriminate against the Tennessee Central by merely refusing to switch for it . . . We conceive that what is true of one owner would be equally true of two joint owners . . ." At p. 73.

The Supreme Court then considered the phrase "operated in conjunction and under a common management or control" found in Section 15(4), and said that the phrase had not received prior judicial interpretation. However, the court said:

> . . . the decisions of the Interstate Commerce Commission support the view that control of the traffic policy of an affiliate is sufficient to constitute "control" or "management" within the meaning of Section 15(4). The Commission's conception of these terms was first expressed in a rate case, *Blackshear Mfg. Co. v. Atlantic Coast Line R. Co.*, 87 I.C.C. 654 (1924), in which the Commission stated that "the term 'carriers under the same management and control' . . . refers to carriers generally controlled through ownership, lease, or otherwise *to the extent of controlling traffic policy*, even though separate corporate entity may be maintained." At p. 664. (Emphasis added.) In subsequent rate cases the Commission has continued to apply this criterion to determine whether or not lines are under the same "management" or "control."[18]

---

[17]36 Stat. 539, 552.

[18]*Rates on Chert, Clay, Sand, and Gravel*, 197 I.C.C. 215; *Humbard Construction Co. v. Southern R. Co.*, 161 I.C.C. 38; *Justice Co. v. Holton Interurban R. Co.*, 153 I.C.C. 673; *Raleigh Freight Traffic Bureau v. Atlantic Coast Line R. Co.*, 107 I.C.C. 156; *Livestock To, From, and Between Points to the Southeast*, 101 I.C.C. 105; *Livestock To, From, and Between Points in the Southeast*, 91 I.C.C. 292.

In another line of rate-making cases, the Commission has held that there can be joint management and control of a third railroad.[19] In rates cases, the Commission generally prescribes a higher scale of distance rates for traffic moving over a combination of independent lines than it does for goods carried over a single line or over a parent-subsidiary system. The distinction is made because the latter are expected to result in economies of operation which should be passed on to the public. *Livestock to, From, and Between points in the Southeast,* 101 I.C.C. 105 (1925). For the same reason, short or "weak" lines are allowed arbitraries, i.e., differentially higher rates in addition to rate scales prescribed for general application whereas small railroads under the "management" or "control" of larger lines are not permitted the additional rates. *Rate Structure Investigation, Part 13, Salt,* 197 I.C.C. 115 (1933).

Unless the long haul of railroads, under joint management and control as interpreted by the rate-making cases, is protected by Section 15(4), the advantages which the Commission assumed existed, i.e., economies of operation, will be taken from them. The very reasons for applying the higher distance rates and denying arbitraries would cease to exist. Such a result, flowing from the failure to construe Section 15(4) as including joint control, would be clearly inconsistent with Commission policy in the rate-making cases. Therefore, the Commission has relied upon the same criteria in Section 15(4) cases. In *Alabama, T. & N. R. Co. v. Southern R. Co.,* 148 I.C.C. 708 (1928), the Commission specifically referred to its definition in *Blackshear, supra,* and applied the limitation of Section 15(4) to the three roads there involved. See also *Georgia & F. R. Co. v. Atlantic Coast Line R. Co.,* 191 I.C.C. 389 (1933). In fact, in seven separate proceedings involving the S. P. & S., the Commission has noted that for rate-making purposes it must be considered as part of the Northern Lines. In one of these proceedings, *West Coast Lumbermen's Assn. v. Chicago, M. & St. P. R. Co.,* 129 I.C.C. 363 (1927), joint through rates via Canada were sought to destinations served by the Milwaukee and the Northern Lines. It was urged that the joint rates, if they were prescribed, should be made over routes that would secure the long haul of these railroads. The Commission refused to establish the joint rates via the Canadian routes, holding *inter alia,* that the S. P. & S. "is considered for rate-making purposes a part of the Northern Pacific and Great Northern." At p. 364.

Likewise, the case of *Seaboard Air Line R. Co. v. Carolina & N. R. Co.,* 204 I.C.C. 416 (1934), applied the *Blackshear* definition to discrimination cases under Section 3(4) of the Act. The Commission held that under Section 3(3), the predecessor of Section 3(4), there could be no discrimi-

---

[19]This group of cases is bottomed on *Chicago, M. & St. P. R. Co. v. Minneapolis Civic & Commerce Assn.,* 247 U.S. 490, wherein this Court found that two competitive railroads owning a subsidiary coequally did, for rate purposes, each "directly control and operate" the subsidiary and that the latter must be treated as a part of each of the two owning carriers. See *Des Moines Union Ry. Switching,* 231 I.C.C. 631; *Blum Packing Co. v. Southern Pacific R. Co.,* 204 I.C.C. 93. *Russ Market Co. v. Northwestern Pacific R. Co.,* 171 I.C.C. 117; *Eriksen v. Ann Arbor R. Co.,* 102 I.C.C. 374; *Pacific Lumber Co. v. Northwestern Pacific R. Co.,* 51 I.C.C. 738.

nation where the roads involved were under a common management and control. The Commission found that the Carolina and Northwestern officials "determine the policy to be adopted with regard to traffic matters local to that carrier, but in matters of common interest between the Southern and the Carolina & Northwestern, the policy determined by the Southern prevails. It is apparent, therefore, that both carriers are operated under a common management control." At p. 420. Although not a Section 15(4) case, it is significant, as pointed out by the district court, because the Commission applied the *Blackshear* test and, upon finding the roads under common management and control permitted them to retain the long haul as protected by Section 15(4). The interrelationship between the two sections as applied by the Commission indicates the necessity for the use of the same criteria as to control in each.

Cancellation of Through Routes

Section 15(3) provides that if any tariff or schedule cancelling any through route or joint rate, fare, charge, or classification, without consent of all carriers, parties thereto or authorization by the Commission, is suspended for investigation, the burden of proof shall be upon the carrier or carriers proposing such cancellation to show that it is consistent with the public interest. It also provides by reason of amendment under the 4R Act as follows:

"With respect to carriers by railroad, in determining whether any such cancellation or proposed cancellation involving any common carrier by railroad is consistent with the public interest, the Commission shall, to the extent applicable, (a) compare the distance traversed and the average transportation time and expense required using the through route, and the distance traversed and the average transportation time and expense required using alternative routes, between the points served by such through route, (b) consider any reduction in energy consumption which may result from such cancellation, and (c) take into account the overall impact of such cancellation on the shippers and carriers who are affected thereby."

It is frequently in the public interest to cancel through routes.[20] Tariff simplification calls for such cancellations on certain occasions. The Commission has condemned so-called "open" routing, and has required carriers either to designate complete routing or definitely provide that the rates apply over all routes composed of lines of carriers parties to the tariff.[21] There are other reasons, too, why the cancellation of a through route is often in the public interest.

---

[20]See, e.g., *Cancellation of Rates and Routes Over Akron, C & Y. R.*, 276 I.C.C. 473, 481 ("Many of such routes are excessively circuitous and their elimination therefore is consistent with the public interest.")

[21]*Routing Soda Ash from Baton Rouge, La.*, 266 I.C.C. 323, 328.

When, under existing law, the cancellation of a through route is proposed as "consistent with the public interest," it is usually considered (assuming lack of agreement on the part of the participating carriers) in the following manner: (1) A tariff is filed, the effect of which is to cancel the route. (2) If the Commission does not suspend the tariff, the cancellation becomes effective. Sometimes the cancellation, although allowed to become effective, is made the subject of investigation, and the Commission may later order the restoration of the route. (3) If the Commission does suspend, the proponent of the cancellation assumes the burden of justifying it as "consistent with the public interest."

The burden of proof as to public interest is placed on the carriers proposing to cancel routes.[22] A district court set aside an order of the Commission which required the cancellation of certain schedules by which Southern Railway and its subsidiary proposed to eliminate through routes, embracing three other lines as intermediate carriers between two points. The court held that as to the routes embracing the three carriers the Commission's conclusion that Southern had failed to sustain the burden of showing that cancellation of the routes would be consistent with the public interest and that the proposed schedules were just and reasonable was not supported by findings sufficient to offset proof that such routes were wastefully circuitous.[23] In another case a district court upheld a Commission order which required cancellation of certain schedules by which Southern Railway and its system lines proposed to cancel through routes embracing the line of another railroad as an intermediate carrier. The court sustained the Commission, holding that the proponents of the schedules had not borne the burden of proving that the cancellation was consistent with the public interest, and that the schedules were just and reasonable.[24]

Restrictive Routing Provisions

In *Southern Ry. Co. v. United States*,[25] a district court upheld a Commission order requiring Southern Railway and its system lines to join in joint carload rates on fine coal from origin mines located on other railroad lines to destinations served by Southern over routes

---

[22]*Omaha Grain Exchange v. United States*, 194 F. Supp. 929, 936.

[23]*Southern Railway Company v. United States*, 166 F. Supp. 78.

[24]*Alabama Great Southern Ry. Co. v. United States*, 162 F. Supp. 614. See also *Atlantic Coast Line Railroad Co. v. United States*, 205 F. Supp. 360, sustaining *Routing, Coal from Origins on Louisville & N. R.*, 313 I.C.C. 752, aff'd 371 U.S. 6; and *Southern Ry. Co. v. United States*, 167 F. Supp. 747.

[25]153 F. Supp. 57, aff'd 355 U.S. 283.

embracing intermediate carriers which rates should not exceed the lowest joint carload rates on fine coal contemporaneously in effect over any route from and to the same points. By means of routing restrictions, Southern limited its participation in reduced rates to routes over which it received its longest haul, and declined to participate where the intermediate carriers were involved in the movement. As a result, the latter routes were denied the reduced rates and coal ceased to move over them. The district court sustained the Commission's findings that the routes over the intermediate carriers were existing through routes so that the Commission's power to prescribe just and reasonable rates over them was not limited by the provisions of Section 15(4), and the higher joint rates applicable over those routes were unjust and unreasonable to the extent that they exceeded the reduced joint rates applicable over the other routes from and to the same points.

Closing of Routes

The Commission entered an order which was based on a finding that it was unjust and unreasonable for Southern Railway to refuse to treat Boyce, Tennessee, as a point entitled to switching service from and to Chattanooga, at a switching charge, and for the maintenance of a provision which resulted in rates and charges to or from Boyce, when the line-haul routing to or from Chattanooga was over lines other than those of Southern, higher than those applicable when the routing embraced Southern as a line-haul carrier to or from Chattanooga.[26] The general effect of the railroad's action was to close through routes from Savannah, Ga., to Boyce. The Commission had found that the evidence did not show that it would be consistent with the public interest, as provided in Section 15(3), to close such routes. The Commission also found that the restoration of reciprocal switching would not require Southern to short-haul itself in violation of Section 15(4). The effect of the Commission's order was to require Southern to restore Boyce to the reciprocal switching limits of Chattanooga and to publish via its lines over open routes certain rates previously found reasonable.

The Transportation Service Must Be Subject to the I.C. Act

In *Petroleum Products-Water-Motor-Inland Nav. Co.*,[27] the Commission said that joint rates may not be made for a combination of

---

[26]*Cramet, Inc., v. Alabama Great Southern R.R. Co.*, 298 I.C.C. 439.
[27]311 I.C.C. 219, 225.

service subject to the I.C. Act and other service not subject to the I.C. Act; thus, proposed joint water-motor rates were ordered cancelled when, while the motor transportation to destination over routes crossing State lines would be subject to Commission's jurisdiction, the prior barge movement was exempt under Section 303(b).

MOTOR CARRIERS — THROUGH ROUTES AND JOINT RATES

Section 216(c) of the I.C. Act[28] provides:

"Common carriers of property by motor vehicle may establish reasonable through routes and joint rates, charges, and classifications with other such carriers or with common carriers by railroad and/or express and/or water; and common carriers of passengers by motor vehicle may establish reasonable through routes and joint rates, fares, or charges with common carriers by railroad and/or water. In case of such joint rates, fares, or charges it shall be the duty of the carriers parties thereto to establish just and reasonable regulations and practices in connection therewith, and just, reasonable, and equitable divisions thereof as between the carriers participating therein which shall not unduly prefer or prejudice any of such participating carriers. As used in this subsection, the term 'common carriers by water' includes water common carriers subject to the Shipping Act, 1916, as amended, or the Intercoastal Shipping Act, 1933, as amended (including persons who hold themselves out to transport goods by water but who do not own or operate vessels) engaged in the transportation of property in interstate or foreign commerce between Alaska or Hawaii on the one hand, and, on the other, the other States of the Union, and through routes and joint rates so established and all classifications, regulations, and practices in connection therewith shall be subejct to the provisions of this part."

The permission granted motor carriers by Section 216(c) to establish through routes and joint rates is not limited by anything contained in Section 217(a) except that the through routes and joint rates must be reasonable. Section 217(a) provides that motor common carriers shall file tariffs applicable to or from points it itself is not authorized to serve only when a through route and joint rate shall have been established. This cannot be interpreted to mean, however, that a through route and joint rate may be established only to or from points the motor carrier is not authorized to serve.[29]

Once through routes have been established, they remain open until shippers and other interested parties are placed on notice that they have been closed. The mere cancellation of joint rates does not close

---

[28]49 U.S.C. 316(c).
[29]*Lubbock-El Paso Motor Frt., Inc. Car. Appli.,* 27 M.C.C. 85; *Lubbock-El Paso Motor Frt., Inc.,* Ext. 29 M.C.C. 281; *Daniels v. Rose,* 43 M.C.C. 726.

the through routes over which they had previously applied.[30] Thus the through routes may exist without the maintenance of joint rates.[31] The discontinuance of joint rates would not preclude the Commission from passing upon the reasonableness of the resulting combination rates, and prescribing through rates which are reasonable and nondiscriminatory.[32]

The through rates which apply over through routes may be joint rates from origin to destination or combinations of rates made up of two or more factors to and from intermediate points. Thus in order to remove the availability of through combination rates it is necessary that each tariff in which the carrier withdrawing from a through route is a party, and in which there is a rate which could be used as a factor of a combination rate, contain a provision notifying the shipping public that the route is no longer open.

Differences Between Joint Arrangements by Motor Common Carriers and Those by Railroad and Water Common Carriers

Section 1(4) of the I.C. Act[33] imposes a duty on all carriers subject to Part I (railroads, express companies, and pipeline companies) to establish reasonable joint arrangements with other such carriers and, in the case of railroads only, with water carriers subject to Part III of the I.C. Act. There is a similar obligation imposed on water common carriers by Section 305(b) of the I.C. Act.[34] Authority is also given to the Commission by Sections 15(3) and 307(d) of the I.C. Act[35] to require the establishment of joint arrangements between Parts I and III carriers where necessary or desirable in the public interest, except that authority to prescribe such arrangements on an intermodal basis is limited to those between railroad and common carriers by water. This power of the Commission is limited, in the case of railroads, by Section 15(4) of the I.C. Act[36] whenever such establishment of joint arrangements would result in a carrier short-hauling itself. Therefore, in Parts I and III of the I.C. Act, there is imposed a duty on carriers to enter into joint arrangements and the Commission is empowered to require such arrangements.

There is no such similar duty imposed on motor common carriers of property to enter into joint arrangements with other such carriers

---

[30]*Restrictions, Riss & Co., and Eliminations, Hi-Way Motor,* 46 M.C.C. 290, 292.
[31]*Southeast Shippers Assn., Inc. v. Akers Motor Lines, Inc.,* 54 M.C.C. 770, 772.
[32]*Rocky Mt. Lines, Inc., — Elimination of Participation,* 31 M.C.C. 320, 321.
[33]49 U.S.C. 1(4).
[34]49 U.S.C. 905(b).
[35]49 U.S.C. 15(3), 907(d).
[36]49 U.S.C. 15(4).

or carriers of other modes. (A duty is imposed on motor carriers of passengers by Section 216(a) of the I.C. Act[37] to enter into joint arrangements.) Under Section 216(c) of the I.C. Act, motor common carriers "may" establish reasonable through routes and joint rates with other such carriers or with carriers of other modes; therefore, under Part II, unlike Parts I and III, the Commission is not empowered to require the establishment of joint arrangements.

In view of the express provisions for jurisdiction over interline arrangements for Part I and Part III carriers, the omission of that authority in Part II must be taken as explicit Congressional intention.

The Commission in the past had consistently held that Section 216(c) is permissive, i.e., that the section authorizes, but does not require, the establishment of through routes and joint rates. See *Transport Storage & Distr. Co. Ext. — Motor Vehicles*,[38] ("the establishing of joint through rates by rail and motor carriers is permissive and not mandatory under Section 216"); *Southeast Shippers Assn., Inc. v. Atlanta, C. A. Motor Lines*,[39] ("It is well established that the language of the act is permissive, and that we have no power to require motor common carriers to establish through routes or joint rates."); *Southeast Shippers Assn., Inc. v. Akers Motor Lines, Inc.*,[40] ("We find that the through routes under consideration have been closed and that the issues presented in this proceeding have, thereby, become moot. As the Commission has no authority to require the establishment of through routes nor any power to prevent the closing of such routes, the motion to dismiss the complaint is sustained."); *Restrictions, Riss & Co., and Eliminations, Hi-Way Motor*,[41] ("Under Section 216(c) of the Act, we may not require motor common carriers of property to establish through routes and joint rates. Not having the right to require their establishment in the first instance, we have no power to require the continued maintenance of through routes and joint rates voluntarily established."); *Strickroot v. Detroit & C. Nav. Co.*,[42] ("The voluntary maintenance in the past of through routes and joint rates, partly by motor vehicle and partly by water, does not give us jurisdiction to require their continuance or reestablishment."); *East South Joint Rates and Routes, Cancellation*,[43] (The provisions of Section 216(c) relating to the establishment of through routes and joint rates of

[37]49 U.S.C. 316(a).
[38]86 M.C.C. 519, 524.
[39]63 M.C.C. 491, 492.
[40]54 M.C.C. 770, 772.
[41]46 M.C.C. 290, 292.
[42]253 I.C.C. 535, 538.
[43]44 M.C.C. 747, 753.

motor common carriers of property "are permissive only," and we cannot, under this section, prevent the carriers "from closing through routes or require them to continue their participation in joint rates.") *Rayons Between Trunk Line and New England Territories*,[44] (The provisions of Section 216(c) "are not mandatory but are permissive"); *Hausman Steel Co. v. Seaboard Freight Lines, Inc.*,[45] (The permissive nature of the language of Section 216(c) "is emphasized by the provisions of Section 216(a) of the Act, relating to common carriers of passengers by motor vehicle, wherein it is made the duty of such carriers to establish through routes with other such common carriers and joint rates, fares, and charges."); *Gulf, M. & N. R. Co. Common Carrier Application*,[46] ("Furthermore we are without jurisdiction to compel coordinated service between carriers by rail and carriers by motor vehicle. It could only be accomplished through the medium of through routes and joint rates, and we have no power to require their establishment. Any such plan must be dependent upon their voluntary cooperation."); and *Freight, All Kinds, Chicago, and Mo., Mich., Ohio*,[47] (The Commission has no authority under Section 216(c) "to require carriers to establish through routes.")

However, in recent years the Commission has held that cancellation of presently applicable joint rates, through routes, and interchange agreements is unlawful if the cancellation is not shown to be just and reasonable.[48] Pursuant to this condemnation, such cancellations have been banned if they result in reductions of the quality or quantity of service offered to the shipping public.[49]

WATER CARRIERS — THROUGH ROUTES AND JOINT RATES

Section 305(b) of the I.C. Act[50] provides:

"It shall be the duty of common carriers by water to establish reasonable through routes and other such carriers and with common carriers by railroad, for the transportation of persons or property, and just and reasonable rates, fares, charges, and classifications applicable thereto, and to provide reasonable facilities for operating such through routes, and to make reasonable rules and regulations with respect to their operation and providing for

[44]44 M.C.C. 280, 282.
[45]32 M.C.C. 31, 35.
[46]18 M.C.C. 721, 726.
[47]322 I.C.C. 423, 427-28.
[48]See Ex Parte No. MC-77, *Restrictions on Service by Motor Common Carriers*, 111 M.C.C. 151, 198.
[49]See, e.g., *Interchange between McLean Trucking and Manning*, 340 I.C.C. 38, *aff'd sub nom, McLean Trucking Company v. United States*, 346 F. Supp. 349, *aff'd per curiam* 409 U.S. 1121.
[50]49 U.S.C. 905(b).

reasonable compensation to those entitled thereto. Common carriers by water may establish reasonable through routes and rates, fares, charges, and classifications applicable thereto with common carriers by motor vehicle. Common carriers by water subject to this part may also establish reasonable through routes and joint rates, charges, and classifications with common carriers by water subject to the Shipping Act, 1916, as amended, or the Intercoastal Shipping Act, 1933, as amended (including persons who hold themselves out to transport goods but who do not own or operate vessels) engaged in the transportation of property in interstate or foreign commerce between Alaska or Hawaii on the one hand, and, on the other, the other States of the Union, and such through routes and joint rates, and all classifications, regulations, and practices established in connection therewith shall be subject to the provisions of this part. In the case of joint rates, fares or charges it shall be the duty of the carriers parties thereto to establish just, reasonable, and equitable divisions thereof, which shall not unduly prefer or prejudice any of such carriers."

Under Section 307(d) of the I.C. Act,[51] it is provided in part:

"The Commission may, and it shall whenever deemed by it to be necessary or desirable in the public interest, after full hearing upon complaint or upon its own initiative without a complaint, establish through routes, joint classifications, and joint rates, fares, or charges, applicable to the transportation of passengers or property by common carriers by water, or by such carriers and carriers by railroad, or the maxima or minima, to be charged, and the divisions of such rates, fares, or charges as hereinafter provided, and the terms and conditions under which such through routes shall be operated. In the case of a through route, where one of the carriers is a common carrier by water, the Commission shall prescribe such reasonable differentials as it may find to be justified between all-rail rates and the joint rates in connection with such common carrier by water."

If the Commission deems the establishment of joint barge-rail rates to be the appropriate means for ending discrimination in ex-barge rates, it has a duty under Section 307(d) to prescribe joint rates at a level that will preserve intact the inherent advantages of water transportation.[52]

In *Lake Carriers' Assn. v. United States,*[53] a district court vacated an order of the Commission in *Lake Carriers' Assn. v. New York Central R. Co.,*[54] which had dismissed a complaint filed by water carriers against several railroads for refusing to establish unit train service and rates from coal mines in Ohio to Lake Erie ports on the same basis as the all rail

[51]49 U.S.C. 907(d). Comparable provisions — Sections 15(1), (3) 204(c), 216(e).

[52]*Dixie Carriers v. United States,* 351 U.S. 56; *Arrow Transp. Co. v. United States,* 176 F. Supp. 411, 420.

[53]399 F. Supp. 386.

[54]343 I.C.C. 491.

service between those mines and points in Michigan. The court held that discriminatory treatment was involved and, therefore, remanded the proceeding ot the Commission for prescription of reasonable joint or proportional rates between the mines and the ports. On remand the Commission prescribed proportional rates under the authority of Section 6(11)(b) of the I.C. Act.[55] Under Section 6(11)(b), the Commission is given authority to

> . . . establish proportional rates, or maximum, or minimum, or maximum and minimum proportional rates, by rail to and from the ports to which the traffic is brought, or from which it is taken by the water carrier . . .

This power is broad, and is not subject to the limitations (short-hauling) which Section 15(4) places on the Commission's authority to prescribe through routes and joint rates. The broad scope of Section 6(11)(b), and the inapplicability thereto of the limits of Section 15(4) has been stated clearly by both the Commission and the courts. For example, in *Baltimore and Carolina S. C. Co. v. A.C.L.R. Co.*,[56] the railroads contended, citing Section 15 of the I.C. Act, that the Commission was not empowered to establish through routes and joint rates between rail and water carriers where the effect was to short-haul the rail carrier, and that the same general results could not be attained by requiring the rail carriers to establish proportional rates to and from the port in connection with such water carriers. The Commission rejected that contention, stating (at 184) that:

> The limitation in section 15 refers specifically to railroads and apparently was intended to insure to the originating rail line as large a share as possible of the movement of freight by rail. That the limitation should be projected into section 6 so as to force a shipper to move his property by rail when he wishes to send it a portion of the way by water is utterly inconsistent with the policy of the Congress manifested in the passage of the Panama Canal act [section 6(13)][57]

In *White Star Line v. N. Y. C. R. R. Co.*,[58] the railroads opposed prescription of joint rates with a steam ship company operating from Detroit, on the ground that it would result in short-hauling those defendants reaching Detroit with their own rails. The Commission found this contention untenable as a matter of law, because the ". . . authority to require the establishment of through water-rail routes and joint rates

---

[55] No. 34822. Order served August 4, 1977.
[56] 49 I.C.C. 176.
[57] This statement was made prior to the 1920 addition to Section 15 of the specific exception for water carriers now found in the first sentence of Section 15(4).
[58] 83 I.C.C. 473.

is not subject to the limitation as to through routes and joint rates contained in section 15 of the general act."[59] (at 477)

The Supreme Court has affirmed the Commission's power to prescribe through rail-water routes which result in short-hauling. In *Chicago, R. I. & P. Ry. v. United States*,[60] the Supreme Court considered whether the Commission's order resulted in short-hauling the defendants' lines contrary to Section 15(4) of the I.C. Act. The Court did not decide whether the water carriers involved in the case fell within the exception in Section 15(4) because it found that the Commission's order could be sustained under "the later and broader provisions of paragraph (13) [now paragraph (11)] of §6." The Court went on to say (at 35) that what is now paragraph (11) "materially expands the jurisdiction of the Commission in respect of land and water transportation."

---

[59]This basic principle has been repeated in *Lake and Rail Class and Commodity Rates*, 205 I.C.C. 101, 177 and *Georgia Public Service Comm. v. Bush Term. R. Co.*, 310 I.C.C. 225, 238.
[60]274 U.S. 29.

30

Long-and-Short-Haul Provision

The Statute

Section 4(1) of the Interstate Commerce Act[1] provides:

"It shall be unlawful for any common carrier subject to this part or part III to charge or receive any greater compensation in the aggregate for the transportation of passengers, or of like kind of property, for a shorter than for a longer distance over the same line or route in the same direction, the shorter being included within the longer distance, or to charge any greater compensation as a through rate than the aggregate of the intermediate rates subject to the provisions of this part or part III, but this shall not be construed as authorizing any common carrier within the terms of this part or part III to charge or receive as great compensation for a shorter as for a longer distance: *Provided,* That upon application to the Commission and after investigation such carrier, in special cases, may be authorized by the Commission to charge less for longer than for shorter distances for the transportation of passengers or property; and the Commission may from time to time prescribe the extent to which such designated carrier may be relieved from the foregoing provisions of this section, but in exercising the authority conferred upon it in this proviso, the Commission shall not permit the establishment of any charge to or from the more distant point that is not reasonably compensatory for the service performed; and no such authorization shall be granted on account of merely potential water competition not actually in existence: *Provided Further,* that any such carrier or carriers operating over a circuitous line or route may, subject only to the standards of lawfulness set forth in other provisions of this part or part III and without further authorization, meet the charges of such carrier or carriers of the same type operating over a more direct line or route, to or from the competitive points, provided that rates so established over circuitous routes shall not be evidence on the issue of the compensatory character of rates involved in other proceedings: *and Provided Further,* that tariffs proposing rates subject to the provisions of

[1]49 U.S.C. 4(1).

this paragraph requiring Commission authorization may be filed when application is made to the Commission under the provisions hereof, and in the event such application is approved, the Commission under the provisions hereof, and in the event such application is approved, the Commission shall permit such tariffs to become effective upon one day's notice."

Section 4(2)[2] provides:

"Wherever a carrier by railroad shall in competition with a water route or routes reduce the rates on the carriage of any species of freight to or from competitive points it shall not be permitted to increase such rates unless after hearing by the Commission it shall be found that such proposed increase rests upon changed conditions other than the elimination of water competition."

Special Cases under Which Relief May Be Authorized

There are two major legal hurdles in the language of the Fourth Section itself which must be overcome before the Commission may authorized the relief sought. The first part of Section 4(1) of the I.C. Act is devoted to expressing the general prohibition against charging more for a shorter than for a longer haul over the same line or route, the shorter being included in the longer distance, and also against charging greater compensation as a through rate than the aggregate of intermediates. It is within the Commission's powers to relieve the carriers from the operation of this general prohibition upon proper application by them and investigation of the matter. but only in special cases and only after finding that the charge to the more distant point is reasonably compensatory for the service performed. While competition has always been the principal "special case" recognized in granting relief, other important cases have rested on circuity (before the 1957 amendment), need to protect recognized groups, importance of protecting weak lines, and other considerations of less common occurrence; but in every instance existence of a special case must be determined on facts of the particular situation.[3]

Of particular pertinence is the language of the Supreme Court in *United States v. Merchants etc. Assn.,*[4] where it said (at p. 187), that

---

[2]49 U.S.C. 4(2).

[3]*Class Rates on points East of Rocky Mountains,* 308 I.C.C. 293, 297. The burden on an applicant common carrier seeking special relief fom this section is a heavy one. *See, e.g., Mechling Barge Lines,* 376 U.S. at 385; *Louisville & N.R. Co. v. United States,* 225 F. 571, 581, *aff'd,* 245 U.S. 463.

[4]242 U.S. 178.

"The clause in Amended Fourth Section which declares 'That upon application to the Interstate Commerce Commission such common carrier may in special cases, after investigation, be authorized by the Commission to charge less for longer than for shorter distances' was designed to guard against the issue, by the Commission, of general orders suspending the long and short haul clause and to ensure action by it separately in respect to particular carriers and only after consideration of the special circumstances existing. Whenever such consideration has been given — 'the Commission may from time to time prescribe the extent to which such designated common carrier may be relieved from the operation of this section.'" And as stated by the Commission in *Commodity Rates East of the Rocky Mountains*,[5] it may grant carriers relief from general prohibitions in Section 4(1) only in special cases and only after finding that the charge to the more distant point is reasonably compensatory for service performed.

Since the decision in the *Transcontinental Cases of 1922*[6] it has been consistently held that the standards to be applied by the Commission in determining whether railroads have made out a special case to justify a long and short haul departure are that rates must cover and more than cover the extra or additional expenses incurred in handling the traffic to which it applies; be no lower than necessary to meet existing competition; not be so low as to threaten the extinction of legitimate competition by water carriers; and not impose an undue burden on other traffic or jeopardize the appropriate return on the value of the carrier's property generally, as contemplated by Section 15a.[7] It is the applicant and not the protestant who must meet the burden of making out a special case under Section 4.[8]

The I.C. Act is specific in its requirements that relief from the Fourth Section may be granted only in special cases, but the question of what constitutes a special case is difficult which, as just pointed out, must be determined on the facts of the particular situation. The following quotation from the Commission's decision in *Commodity Rates on Lum-*

[5]304 I.C.C. 535, 536, 539.
[6]74 I.C.C. 48, 71.
[7]See *Igert v. United States*, 211 F. Supp. 42, 44.
[8]*Ibid.*, p. 45. See also *Louisville & N.R. Co. v. United States*, 225 Fed. 571, aff'd. 245 U.S. 463; *Confectionary to Jacksonville, Fla.*, 272 I.C.C. 240; *Paper to Jacksonville, Fla.*, 245 I.C.C. 431; *Coke from Ohio River Points to Keokuk, Iowa*, 246 I.C.C. 609; 273 I.C.C. 122; *Anthracite Coal to New England Territory*, 277 I.C.C. 569; *Sulphur from La. and Texas to Nashville and Old Hickory*, 280 I.C.C. 423; *Pacific Coast Fourth Section Applications*, 264 I.C.C. 36; *Citrus Fruit from Fla. to North Atlantic Ports*, 266 I.C.C. 627.

ber and Other Forest Products[9] is particularly appropriate in demonstrating the considerations determinative of special cases:

> It may be taken as established, therefore, that in cases which may be distinguished from the generality by certain definite characteristics, we may grant relief dependent upon our judgment "in the exercise of a sound legal discretion as to whether the request should be granted compatibly with a due consideration of the private and public interests concerned and in view of the preference and discrimination clauses of the second and third sections," either upon the ground of competition or "for other adequate reasons."

As stated in a dissenting opinion in *Commodity Rates in Official Territory*[10] "The term (special case) refers not only to the rates but to the circumstances and conditions which affect the rates, regardless of the number of points between which they may apply."

In *Liquefied Chlorine Gas, Brunswick, Ga. to Tennessee*,[11] the Commission said that authority to charge a higher rate at an intermediate point than to a more distant point may be granted when in a special case it is shown that circumstances attending publication of the two rates are substantially dissimilar. Since the Fourth Section relief sought was ancillary to the establishment of the proposed rates, and competitive conditions compelling publication of the proposed rates were not present at intermediate points, a special case was presented affording support for the relief authorized. In *Newsprint Paper from Calhoun, Tenn., to Baton Rouge, La.*,[12] the Commission said that in view of actual water competition at more distant points which did not exist at intermediate points, a special case within the meaning of Section 4 was presented. Moreover, the rates from and to the intermediate points did not exceed those approved previously and the wide spread between yield and costs indicated that the proposed lower rates to the more distant destination were reasonably compensatory; relief, therefore, was granted. Where departures occurred within the territorial limits of the proposed reduced rates on fresh meats and packinghouse products resulting from the construction of rates on short-line distance formulas, grouping, use of short- and weak-line arbitraries, and application of intermediate rules, the

---

[9]165 I.C.C. 561. Relief from the unequivocal requirement of Section 6(1) has also been granted under a provision in Section 6(3) authorizing such action in "special or peculiar circumstances or conditions."

[10]209 I.C.C. 702.

[11]304 I.C.C. 545, 548, 550.

[12]310 I.C.C. 171, 176, 178, 180.

Commission held in *Meat and Packinghouse Products to the South*[13] that departures of that nature are usual in general adjustments incorporating those methods of rate making and constitute a special case justifying grant of the relief sought.

In *Class Rates of Points East of Rocky Mountains*,[14] the Commission said that in many instances where rates based on exceptions to the uniform classification are limited by competition encountered in one or more, but not all, of the defined rate making territories, a shorter route operates through an outside territory. Such routes are not the rate making routes and have no control over the rate making process, being to that extent in the same category as circuitous routes, which, however, no longer need relief to meet rates of the direct or rate making routes, but carriers in their managerial discretion may meet such rates without any limitations except those imposed by other sections of part I. Relief for the shorter outside routes to meet rates of the rate making routes at competitive points, without breaking down established adjustments within the outside territory not subject to the same competitive conditions, would afford them no greater relief than is enjoyed by the circuitous routes, and constitutes a special case.

Competition Has Been the Principal Special Case Recognized in Granting Relief

While competition has been the principal special case recognized in granting relief, existence of competition does not ipso facto entitle an applicant to relief; the competition upon which relief is based on must always be examined in relation to existing circumstances bearing in mind that relief may not be granted for rates violative of other sections of the I.C. Act, particularly Sections 2 and 3.[15] Applicant must affirmatively show: (1) that it has no control over the rate to or from the more distant competitive point that it desires to meet; (2) that in performing service to or from that point it is confronted with a handicap or disability not affecting the operation of the carrier or carriers controlling the rate to be met; (3) that the level of the more-distant-point rate is below the proper basis to intermediate points.[16] That test was met in *Iron or Steel Slabs*

[13]313 I.C.C. 464, 466. See also *Commodity Rates East of the Rocky Mountains*, 304 I.C.C. 535, 536, 539.

[14]308 I.C.C. 293, 295, 297.

[15]*Nepheline Syenite from Ontario, Canada, to the East*, 308 I.C.C. 561, 564-5; *Fine Coal to Eau Claire and Chippewa Falls, Wis.*, 308 I.C.C. 583, 588.

[16]*Iron or Steel Slabs to Riverdale, Ill.*, 308 I.C.C. 151, 154.

where the record clearly showed that applicant had no control over the cost of shipping by water to the most distant point; that in performing service to that point it was handicapped to the extent of the difference in cost of transportation by rail and by water; and that the water costs to that point did not afford a proper measure of rates to or from intermediate points on applicant's line.[17]

Permanent in lieu of temporary relief was granted in *Liquefied Petroleum Gas to and Within the South*[18] over existing through routes for reduced rates on liquefied petroleum gas within the South and from the Southwest and Zuni, N. Mex., to the South; relief was found justified to meet truck, barge, and pipeline competition. Relief was granted also for rates reduced to restore competitive relation of routes from the Southwest to certain Ohio and Maryland points via St. Louis and Memphis gateways. Such relief was warranted because departures at intermediate destinations were due to grouping, existence of short- or weak-line arbitraries, cross-country competition, or to the fact that rate making routes were not the direct tariff routes.

In determining whether water competition upon which relief was sought for establishment of proposed rate from considered origins was actual, as required by statute, the Commission said in *Ethylene Glycol from Texas to Clinton, Iowa*,[19] that the fact that there had been no movement by water was significant but not controlling. Since necessary facilities for water transportation were available, water competition actually existed, therefore relief was granted.

In *Iron or Steel Plates from Illinois*,[20] the Commission said that relief for reduced joint rates on iron or steel plate, plates, or sheets from East St. Louis and Granite City, Ill., to Belton and Temple, Tex., no lower than the cost to receiver of barge movement to Houston and truck movement beyond, was necessary to enable respondents to participate in the traffic when, except for emergency movements, none of it had moved by rail at the existing combination rates, and the competitive situation encountered at Belton and Temple differed materially from that at intermediate destinations.

Relief for combinations of proportional rates to and from Kankakee, Ill., on corn products from northern Illinois points on New York Central's Kankakee Belt Line to central, trunkline, and New England territories was found justified to meet barge-line competition via Chicago

---

[17]*Ibid.*, p. 154.
[18]309 I.C.C. 389, 391, 406.
[19]304 I.C.C. 531, 534.
[20]310 I.C.C. 47, 50-2.

in *Corn and Corn Products, Illinois to Official Territory.*[21] The competitive situation required an adjustment in the all-rail rates, and such adjustment required Fourth Section relief. While some diversion would necessarily result in developing rail movements of corn from the area contiguous to the rail line, and to that extent the barge movement would be adversely affected, the proposed rates nevertheless were found to be no lower than necessary to meet the barge competition. In *Iron or Steel Slabs to Riverdale, Ill.,*[22] the Commission said that while rail carriers have the right to establish rates to meet water-carrier competition, provided they do not contravene any provision of the I.C. Act, relief from the general prohibition of the long-and-short-haul clause may be granted for such rates only in special cases where it is shown that the water competition is actual and that the charge to and from the more distant point is reasonably compensatory for the service performed. The Commission said further that water competition was undoubtedly actual when the bulk of the traffic was currently moving over the water route, and relief was warranted when it appeared that the proposed rate would be fully compensatory over the relief route; that shipper-receiver was unwilling to pay more for rail than for barge service; that the slower service and higher minimum weight over the barge route were no inconvenience to it; and that at equal rates both applicant and barge lines would receive an equal share of the traffic. In absence of evidence of the barge line operating costs, it did not appear that the proposed rate would be competitively unfair or destructive.

Market competition has frequently been recognized as constituting a special case justifying Fourth Section relief. Thus, in *Iron or Steel Articles from East to the Southwest,*[23] where reductions of iron and steel rates from various producing points to Louisiana and Texas ports, and the impact of successive general increases, had resulted in changed relationships which placed other producing points not enjoying the benefit of reduced rates in a noncompetitive position, the Commission

---

[21]310 I.C.C. 151, 153-5. The Commission's order was upheld in *A. L. Meckling Barge Lines, Inc. v. United States,* 209 F. Supp. 744. Plaintiff contended in the court that the Commission had erred because it had considered the entire through rate in determining whether the proposed rate was reasonably compensatory without confining its deliberations to the 6-cent proportional rate factor which applied from origins to Kankakee on shipments distined beyond to points in official territory; and that the Commission had erred in failing to permit submission of evidence relating to section 3(4) violations. The court held that the Commission had properly based its deliberations on the entire through rate and that the Commission was not required to enlarge a Section 4 proceeding into an investigation of alleged discrimination under Section 3(4) which relates to discriminations between connecting carriers.

[22]308 I.C.C. 151, 153-5.

[23]310 I.C.C. 587, 593.

held that the proposed reductions from specified eastern producing points, which would restore as closely as possible the competitive relationships previously existing, appeared to be no lower than necessary for that purpose.

Reasonably Compensatory Rates as a Basis for Authorizing Relief

Prior to 1910 and the passage of the Mann-Elkins amendment, the Commission's enforcement of the Fourth Section against long-and-short-haul discrimination had been rendered ineffective by court action. The change which was brought about by the new legislation is exemplified by the language of the Supreme Court in *Intermountain Rate Cases*.[24] At page 485, the court stated:

> . . . it follows that in substance the amendment intrinsically states no new rule or principle but simply shifts the powers conferred by the section as it originally stood; that is, it takes from the carriers the deposit of public power previously lodged in them and vests it in the Commission as a primary instead of a reviewing function. In other words, the elements of judgment or so to speak the system of law by which judgment is to be controlled remains unchanged but a different tribunal is created for the enforcement of the existing law. This being true, as we think it plainly is, the situation under the amendment is this: Power in the carrier primarily to meet competitive conditions in any point of view by charging a lesser rate for a longer than for a shorter haul has ceased to exist because to do so, in the absence of some authority, would not only be inimical to the provision of the fourth section but would be in conflict with the preference and discrimination clauses of the second and third sections. But while the public power, so to speak, previously lodged in the carrier is thus withdrawn and reposed in the Commission the right of carriers to seek and obtain under authorized circumstances the sanction of the Commission to charge a lower rate for a longer than for a shorter haul because of competition or for other adequate reasons is expressly preserved and if not is in any event by necessary implication granted. And as a correlative the authority of the Commission to grant on request the right sought is made by the statute to depend upon the facts established and the judgment of that body in the exercise of a sound legal discretion as to whether the request should be granted compatibly with a due consideration of the private and public interests concerned and in view of the preference and discrimination clauses of the second and third sections.

From the foregoing it is clear that whereas prior to 1910 the carriers acted in the first instance to establish long-and-short-haul discriminatory rates and the Commission merely reviewed them, subsequent to the passage of the amendment the carriers had first to apply to the Com-

[24]234 U.S. 476.

mission for approval. Initially the Commission was satisfied if the departure rates met variable costs but since 1920, when the reasonably compensatory clause was added, the Commission required the rates to meet variable costs and to add something to the indirect or overhead costs. As a result, where previously the administration of the Fourth Section had been very flexible, the prohibition against approving other than reasonably compensatory rates tended to make it more rigid, although not completely so, for the Commission rejected the interpretation that to be reasonably compensatory a rate must bear its full share of indirect expenses. The amendment made mandatory, however, what theretofore had rested in the Commission's sound discretion as to compensation for the service performed to the more distant point and as to circuity. In *Transcontinental Cases of 1922,*[25] the Commission said:

> In the light of these and similar considerations, we are of the opinion and find that in the administration of the fourth section the words "reasonably compensatory" imply that a rate properly so described must (1) cover and more than cover the extra or additional expenses incurred in handling the traffic to which it applies; (2) be no lower than necessary to meet existing competition; (3) not be so low as to threaten the extinction of legitimate competition by water carriers; and (4) not impose an undue burden on other traffic or jeopardize the appropriate return on the value of carrier property generally, as contemplated in section 15a of the act. It may be added that rates of this character ought, wherever possible, to bear some relation to the value of the commodity carried and the value of the service rendered in connection therewith. We also find that where carriers apply for relief from the long-and-short-haul clause of the fourth section and propose the application of rates which they designate as "reasonably compensatory," they should affirmatively show that the rates proposed conform to the criteria indicated above.

Complaints

Rates established pursuant to a grant of Section 4 relief are not immune from attack under Section 15(1) of the I.C. Act.[26]

Comparison of Rates in Fourth Section Violations

It is fundamental that for Section 4 purposes like rates must be compared. In the *Whiterock* Case[27] an allegation of Section 4 long-and-

---

[25]574 I.C.C. 48, 71. See also *Rules to Govern the Filing of Fourth Section Applications,* 310 I.C.C. 275; *Igert v. United States,* 211 F. Supp. 42, 44-45.

[26]See *United States v. Merchants & M. Traffic Asso.,* 242 U.S. 178.

[27]280 I.C.C. 143. In other cases dealing with alleged differences in the nature or character of the rate the Commission has held that proportional rates lower than

short haul violation was based on the existence of a higher rate on lime (unqualified) at intermediate points and a lower rate on fluxing lime at the destination or more distant point. After noting that there were traditional diferences in the two types of lime, the Commission, at page 153, noted that "In determining violations of this section, rates and services of the same character must be compared." Hence, in *White-rock* the difference was in the nature of the commodity.

Aggregate of Intermediate Clause

The prohibition of Section 4 is against charging any greater compensation as a through rate than the aggregate of intermediate rates subject to the I.C. Act.[28] Thus in *Southern Iron & Metal Co. v. American Commercial Barge,*[29] where a one factor rate was charged, the Commission held that it was unreasonable to the extent that it exceeded the aggregate of intermediate rates published for application on like traffic over the same route between the same points in service of carriers which performed the transportation, when the service actually performed was no greater than would have been offered in case of separate local movements.

Intermediate Rule

In determining application of the intermediate rule at stations on indirect routes, the following rule is applied: When the governing tariff provides that the rates apply via "all" routes made by the use of the lines of "any" of the carriers parties to the tariff, the Commission has found in effect that this constitutes specific routing over all routes

---

local rates to intermediate points are not in violation of Section 4 (*Allowance on Oil Pipe at Texas Destinations,* 310 I.C.C. 709, 723); a joint through rate with storage in transit is unlike two local rates applying to separate moves to and from the transit point (*Proctor & Gamble Co. v. Alabama & V. Ry. Co.,* 153 I.C.C. 655, 656); export and domestic rates are unlike for Section 4 purposes (*Wenger-Armstrong Petroleum Co. v. Director General,* 64 I.C.C. 175, 176); and that a joint rail-water rate on lake-cargo coal from Illinois mines to Edgewater, Wis., lower than the railroad's local rate to Chicago does not violate Section 4, since the two rates are of different types (*Chicago B. & Q. R. Co. v. Chicago & E.I.R. Co.,* 310 I.C.C. 349, 372). In *Utah-Idaho Sugar Co. v. Chicago, M., St. P. & P. Co,,* 306 I.C.C. 599, 601-2, the Commission held that a Fourth Section violated over one route creates no presumption that the rate charged over another route between the same points in unreasonable, particularly where the route of movement is 30 percent longer than the more direct route.

[28]*Locarni Marble Corp. v. Missouri Pac. R. Co.* 314 I.C.C. 65, 69.
[29]309 I.C.C. 731, 733-4.

composed of lines of such carriers regardless of the degree of circuity; and when the tariff is silent as to routing the Commission has applied the reasonable route doctrine.[30] In no proceeding has the Commission established any precise formula regarding what may or may not be a reasonable or natural route in the case of open-routing tariffs involving the intermediate rule.[31] The Commission has held that a rate cannot be applied over any given route if any one of the carriers making up that route restricts the rate not to apply over its line.[32]

A. E. West Petroleum Co. v. Atchison, T. & S. F. Ry. Co.[33] supports the proposition that a "route" for intermediate-point rate purposes is subject to the limitation that it must not be unreasonable, and that "unreasonableness" depends upon the extent and direction of circuity and the commercial usage of the route. The *West Petroleum* case involved an action to recover an amount of a reparation award entered by the Commission in favor of plaintiff. The district court dismissed the complaint and plaintiff appealed. The court of appeals affirmed the decision of the lower court by holding that the construction of the tariff routing instructions by applying an intermediate destination rule so as to make Kansas City, Missouri, an intermediate point to Iowa stations was unreasonable, and plaintiff was not entitled to a rate based on such construction even though Kansas City would be an intermediate point in a possible route over lines of participating carriers. The court said (p. 821) "that the undisputed facts in this case convince that a route from Bradford through Kansas City as an intermediate-point to these Iowa stations is unreasonable and, therefore, is not a 'route' within the meaning of the . . . . tariff governing 'routes' and 'intermediate-point' rates." In reaching the conclusion which it did the court gave weight (at p. 816) to the fact that the claimed route "required a directional back haul" and that "no normal, customary, cognizable volume of shippers ever moved" over the route. Commenting on the tariff rules of the Commission, the court said (pp. 820-1):

> By rules of the Commission governing publication of freight tariffs (Rule 4(k) Circular No. 20 and Rule 27 in Supp. 5 thereto), the routing provisions involved here are required to be published as part of rate tariffs applicable to intermediate-point rates. When the expert ingenuity in cre-

---

[30]*Pure Oil Co. v. Alton & S.R.*, 284 I.C.C. 461.

[31]*Continental Steel Corp. v. New York, C. & St. L. R. Co.* 243 I.C.C. 775, 777; *Lustberg Nast & Co., Inc. v. New York, N.H. & H.R. Co.* 229 I.C.C. 684, 686; *Mid-West Fruit Co. v. St. Louis-S. F. Ry. Co.*, 203 I.C.C. 291, 293; *Miner Lumber Co. v. Pennsylvania R. Co.*, 161 I.C.C. 801, 803.

[32]*Great Atlantic & Pacific Tea Co. v. Baltimore & O.R.G.*, 311 I.C.C. 47, 51.

[33]212 F. 2d 812, 821.

ating imaginary routes . . . and the complexity of our vast railway systems and the nature of rate structures are considered, the extreme difficulty of any carrier complying with these Rules, as construed by the Commission, without danger to itself is clear — it would mean anticipation and specific exception as to every imaginable so-called "route." A definite ever present peril is that it could never know until too late, if it had underestimated the superior skill of the shipper's expert in devising a route no one else had dreamed of. Obviously, this would defeat the entire purpose and usefulness of the intermediate-point rate provisions in tariffs — to lessen the intricacy and bulk of rate tariffs.

In a number of other proceedings, the Commission has found that rates subject to an intermediate rule and without restriction as to routing do not apply over unnatural or unduly circuitous routes. As pointed out in the foregoing, no fixed rule has been observed by the Commission in regard to the degree of circuity considered as rendering a route unavailable. The Commission said in *Mid-West Fruit Co. v. St. Louis — S. F. Ry. Co.*:[34]

> In considering the application of rates over circuitous routes we have established no definitely settled rule to determine what is or is not a reasonable or natural route. Each case must be considered upon its merits. In some cases rates have been found inapplicable over unnatural route where the percentage of circuity was not great.

And in *Miner Lumber Co. v. Pennsylvania R. Co.*[35]

> In no case where the application of rule 77 has been considered have we established any definitely settled rule of what is or is not a reasonable or natural route. Every case has been decided on its own merits.

In *United States v. Interstate Commerce Commission*[36] the Government had originally brought action against the Commission to suspend, enjoin, set aside and annul an order in a proceeding known as *United States v. Southern Railway Co.*[37] but since the movement of the freight involved had ceased, the Government merely sought compensation by way of reparation on past shipments. The Government had been shipping large quantities of bauxite ore from the ports of New Orleans, Louisiana, to Bynum, Alabama, via Southern Railway. Section 22 rates were filed by Southern Railway with the Government which were rejected as being excessive. The charges sought were the lowest rates published by the railroad from Mobile to Lister Hill, Alabama, based on the so-called intermediate rule contained in the applicable tariff.

---

[34]203 I.C.C. 291, 293.
[35]161 I.C.C. 801, 803.
[36]142 F. Supp. 741.
[37]286 I.C.C. 203.

The rule in essence provided that points intermediate between the origin and a more distant point take the rate of the more distant point if lower than the rate to the intermediate point, and if the intermediate point is on a route permitted by the tariff to the more distant point. The rate sought by the Government was applicable over a route of Southern Railway described as follows: "Southern Railway (through Parrish, Alabama)." The court held (p. 742):

> Plaintiff cites *A. E. West Petroleum Co. v. Atchison T. & S. F. Ry. Co.* 8 Cir. 212 F. 2d 812, 821. We have no quarrel with the result in it. In it the court stated and properly so, that a *'route'* for *'intermediate-point'* rate purposes is subject to the limitation that it must not be unreasonable. The "unreasonableness" depends upon (a) the extent and direction of circuity and (b) the commercial usage of a "route." The Commission found a 22.5 percent circuity and no commercial usage. There is substantial evidence to support this finding and its ultimate conclusion that the Rule did not apply.

In *Firestone Tire & Rubber Co. v. Akron, C. & Y. Ry. Co.,*[38] rates charged on rubber in carloads, from Akron and Barbeton, Ohio, to destinations in the southwest were found by the Commission not to be unreasonable or otherwise unlawful where complaints had alleged that the rates charged were unreasonable to the extent that they exceeded a commodity rate contemporaneously maintained from Norwalk, Ohio, to Houston and Galveston, Texas, and other Gulf ports. The rate from Norwalk was not subject to any routing provisions. Complainants contended that Akron was intermediate to Norwalk over a route embracing the line of the New York Central to Cleveland thence Baltimore & Ohio to Akron. From Norwalk, the average distance to Southwest points (1,419 miles) was 7 percent in excess of the distance from Akron via the more direct route over which the shipments actually moved. Using distances to two representative points in the southwest, the indirect route exceeded the short line distance by 12.31 percent to one representative point and by 14 percent to another representative point. In finding the rates not unreasonable or otherwise unlawful the Commission said (p. 289):

> To construe the tariff as permitting traffic from Norwalk to be routed via Cleveland and Akron would be exceedingly unreasonable. A shipment so routed would not only begin its movement in a direction opposite to that of natural and logical routes, but upon reaching Cleveland would be about 56 miles farther eastward from the destination than when it started, and upon reaching Akron over the southeasterly route of the Baltimore & Ohio would be 66 miles farther away, over the short route from Nor-

---

[38]177 I.C.C. 287.

walk, before the movement westward would have begun. The record shows no movement of these or any other commodities from Norwalk over the Cleveland-Akron route. St. Louis is the natural gateway, through which nearly all of this traffic moved. To St. Louis the short-line distance from Norwalk is about 483 miles, and over the Cleveland-Akron route approximately 634 miles.

The Commission held in *Atchison, T. & S. Ry. Co. v. United States*[39] that in view of open routing, implied by absence of any routing provisions in the tariff naming a lower all-freight rate from Omaha to Pueblo, Colo., other than restriction against application via Kansas City or St. Joseph, Mo., that the rate applied under intermediate rules on shipments of bombs from Coplant, Nebr., to Avondale, Colo., by Union Pacific Railroad and Santa Fe, over a route on which the latter points were intermediate to the former, when that route was not shown to present any serious operating difficulties or to be in any respect impractical, circuity of 55.6 percent was not unusual for such hauls, and operating conditions over the circuitous route were not shown to be substantially more onerous than over route of movement giving originating carrier its long haul.

In the same case (at p. 684) the Commission held that since the shipments from Coplant, Nebr., to Avondale, Colo., were routed "via CB&Q-AT&SF," the lower rate from Omaha to Pueblo, Colo., could not be applied under the intermediate rule to those shipments handled by Chicago, Burlington & Quincy Railroad and Santa Fe when the only routes over which the former points were intermediate to the latter would have required the Burlington to interchange the traffic with carriers other than Santa Fe, contrary to the bill-of-lading routing.

Likewise in *Waggener Paint Co. v. Chicago G. W. Ry. Co.*[40] the Commission held that when no routes were available on the considered traffic from Minneapolis to St. Louis via Kansas City, the lower St. Louis rates did not apply to Kansas City under the intermediate rule and there was no violation of Section 4.

The Commission gives consideration to operating or other conditions in determining whether or not a route is an illogical or unnatural one over which a shipper could not reasonably expect transportation.[41] It is only where the carriers parties to the tariff take affirmative steps so

---

[39]310 I.C.C. 681, 683.
[40]308 I.C.C. 148, 149.
[41]*Olean Glass Co. v. Pennsylvania R. Co.*, 213 I.C.C. 229, 232; *Samuel P. Mandell Co. v. Pennsylvania R. Co.*, 298 I.C.C. 609, 613-14; *Swift & Co. v. Alabama G.S.R. Co.*, 263 I.C.C. 630, 632-3; *A. E. West Petroleum Co. v. Atchison, T. & S.F. Ry. Co.*, 212 F. 2d 812, 816.

as to provide specific routing by a provision absolute in its terms that consideration extraneous to the tariff have no place in interpreting routing instructions[42] In the *West Petroleum* case, the court, in finding that a "route" for intermediate point rate purposes is subject to the limitation that it must not be unreasonable, gave consideration to the fact that the records of the defendant disclosed that no normal, customary, or cognizable volume of shipments ever moved over the claimed route. In the *Swift & Co. case* (pp. 632-3), the Commission felt constrained to comment that the defendants failed to "show any of the factors extraneous to the tariffs, such as physical conditions, available facilities, operating arrangements, difficulties encountered at congested intermediate terminals, and additional switching, which usually are relied upon to show that a claimed open route is impractical, illogical and unnatural, and one over which an intermediate rate should not be found applicable."

In *Great Northern Ry. Co. v. Delmar Co.*[43] the Supreme Court said that where no affirmative routing is provided in the tariff in connection with a particular rate between specified points (open-routing tariff), such rate is not applicable over any circuitous route over which the application of such rate would result in violation of Section 4(1) provided that the application of the rate in question over the corresponding short-tariff route does not violate Section 4(1).

Quality Gas and Oil Co. v. Northern Pac. Ry. Co.[44] involved applicable rates on refined petroleum products in tank carloads from points in the Southwest to points in Minnesota. The rates were determined and found not unreasonable or otherwise unlawful. The consignee attempted to defeat the assessed rate by contending that his destinations were intermediate to lower-rated points in Wisconsin or Minnesota over circuitous segments of the Northern Pacific. The Commission found (page 398):

> The circuity of the longer route of the Northern Pacific from Minneapolis, the point of divergence of its lines to Carlton, through the destinations involved, is approximately 68 percent, while the entire route from the considered origins to Carlton, embracing the abovementioned line of the Northern Pacific, is approximately 9 percent circuitous. The question arises as to whether the circuitous route of the Northern Pacific is a direct one under a reasonable interpretation of the applicable tariffs. Indirect routes result from the desire of the carrier having the long route to compete with the line maintaining the short route. Under such circumstances,

[42]*Samuel P. Mandell Co. v. Pennsylvania Co., supra.*
[43]283 U.S. 686, 690-1.
[44]185 I.C.C. 395.

the shipper has the right to designate which of the competing routes shall be used. The preservation of a competitive status as between carriers may be regarded as justifying such a right. But where, as here, both the long and short route from point of divergence are parts of the same railroad, the element of competition disappears and with it any obvious reason, so far as this record shows, or public interest is concerned, for the asserted right of the shipper to specify routing. It must be assumed that the carrier will use its most economical route, and in view of the practical certainty of this, no reason appears why it should specify routes over its own lines. But where, as here, the carrier has gone so far as to limit routing to the "same direct line or route," there is no reason to doubt that it intended to designate other than the natural, shorter, and more economical route. The interpretation of the foregoing tariff provisions renders them inapplicable to the transportation here considered, and also removes the grounds for the fourth-section allegation.

The Commission made the point in the *Quality Gas* case that although a shipper must be accorded considerable latitude in designating which of several multiple-line competitive routes he chooses to use there is no justification for according to a shipper the right to specify the internal routing to be observed by a carrier over its own line.

The *Quality* case was cited with approval in *Interstate Fruit Co. v. Chicago, M. St. P. & P. R. Co.*[45] There reparation was sought on the movement of a mixed carload of foodstuff shipped from Galewood, Illinois, to Sioux Falls, South Dakota, on the basis of a commodity rate to Pipestone, Minnesota, by reason of an intermediate rule in the commodity-rate tariff on the major part of the shipment which came within the commodity description of canned goods. The short line distances from Galewood to Sioux Falls and Pipestone were 553.5 and 538.3 miles respectively. The distance to Pipestone via Sioux Falls was 606.8 miles, or 68.5 miles more than the direct route. The commodity tariff quoting the rate to Pipestone was unrestricted as to routing over defendant's lines. The Commission found (p. 565) that with higher class rates at Sioux Falls and several other stations intermediate to Pipestone, defendant could not lawfully maintain the adjustments sought over the longer route without appropriate Fourth Section relief. This left only the short route open for the movement of traffic under the commodity rate. Upon the basis of the facts the Commission held (p. 565) that it could not interpret defendant's commodity tariff in such a manner as to compel application of the aforementioned rate over a route which would result in a violation of the I.C. Act. The pertinent facts, the Commission said (p. 565), were similar to those in the *Quality Gas & Oil Co.* case since both cases deal with the question of routing over the lines of one carrier only. In

[45]195 I.C.C. 563.

accordance with the *Quality Gas & Oil Co.* decision the Commission held (p. 566):

> Upon reconsideration, we find that the circuitous route of defendant to Pipestone via Sioux Falls was not a natural or logical route that might properly have been designated by a shipper of traffic for that destination in the absence of definite routing provisions, that Sioux Falls cannot be considered intermediate to Pipestone over said route, and that the rate sought was not applicable under the tariff provision here considered.

Increase in Rates That Have Been Reduced under the Authority of a Fourth Section Order to Meet Water Competition

Skinner & Eddy Corp. v. United States[46] holds that Section 4(2) does not extend to instances where the reduction in rates to the water-competitive points is made with the approval of the Commission, its language in part reading (p. 568):

> . . . The specific purpose of the last paragraph of §4 is to insure and preserve water competition; to prevent competition that kills. A reduction made under the authority of a 4th section order after full hearing must have been found by the Commission to have been reasonably necessary in order to preserve competition between the rail and the water carrier. A reduction so made is not within the reason of the prohibition declared by the last paragraph. Transportation conditions are not static; the oppressor of today may tomorrow be the oppressed. And in order to preserve competition between rail and water carriers it is necessary that the Commission's power be as broad as it is to approve a modification in order to prevent unjust discrimination. Even a liberal reading of §4 would not require that the prohibition contained in the last paragraph be extended to reductions made with the approval of the Commission. . . .

See also *Anthracite Coal to New England Territory*[47] where the Commission, citing the *Skinner* case, said that an increase by a railroad of rates "that had been reduced, in competition with a water route or routes, under the authority of a fourth-section order after full hearing, is not within the reason of the prohibition declared in Section 4(2) of the Act."

---

[46]249 U.S. 557.
[47]277 I.C.C. 569, 571.

31

Division of Joint Rates, Fares, or Charges

The Applicable Statutory Provisions

Section 15(6) of the Interstate Commerce Act[1] was amended by the 4R Act by inserting "(a)" immediately after "(6)" and adding three other paragraphs. It provides as follows:

"(a) Whenever, after full hearing upon complaint or upon its own initiative, the Commission is of opinion that the divisions of joint rates, fares, or charges, applicable to the transportation of passengers or property, are or will be unjust, unreasonable, inequitable, or unduly preferential or prejudicial as between the carriers parties thereto (whether agreed upon by such carriers, or any of them, or otherwise established), the Commission shall by order prescribe the just, reasonable, and equitable divisions thereof to be received by the several carriers, and in cases where the joint rate, fare, or charge was established pursuant to a finding or order of the Commission and the divisions thereof are found by it to have been unjust, unreasonable, or inequitable, or unduly preferential or prejudicial, the Commission may also by order determine what (for the period subsequent to the filing of the complaint or petition or the making of the order of investigation) would have been the just, reasonable, and equitable divisions thereof to be received by the several carriers, and require adjustment to be made in accordance therewith.

"In so prescribing and determining the divisions of joint rates, fares and charges, the Commission shall give due consideration, among other things, to the efficiency with which the carriers concerned are operated, the amount of revenue required to pay their respective operating expenses, taxes, and a fair return on their railway property held for and used in the service of transportation, and the importance to the public of the transportation services of such carriers; and also whether any particular participating carrier is an originating, intermediate, or delivering line, and any other fact or circumstance which would ordinarily, without regard to the

[1] 49 U.S.C. 15(6). Comparable provisions — Sections 316(f), 307(e).

mileage haul, entitle one carrier to a greater or less proportion than another carrier of the joint rate, fare or charge.

"(b) Notwithstanding any other provision of law, the Commission shall, within 180 days after the date of enactment of this subdivision, establish, by rule, standards and procedures for the conduct of proceedings for the adjutment of divisions of joint rates or fares (whether prescribed by the Commission or otherwise) in accordance with the provisions of this paragraph. The Commission shall issue a final order in all such proceedings within 270 days after the submission to the Commission of a case. If the commission is unable to issue such a final order within such time, it shall issue a report to the Congress setting forth the reasons for such inability.

"(c) All evidentiary proceedings conducted pursuant to this paragraph shall be completed, in a case brought upon a complaint, within 1 year following the filing of the complaint, or, in a case brought upon the Commission's initiative, within 2 years following the commencement of such proceeding, unless the Commission finds that such a proceeding must be extended to permit a fair and expeditious completion of the proceeding. If the Commission is unable to meet any such time requirement, it shall issue a report to the Congress setting forth the reasons for such inability.

"(d) Whenever a proceeding for the adjustment of divisions of joint rates or fares (whether prescribed by the Commission or otherwise established) is commenced by the filing of a complaint with the Commission, the complaining carrier or carriers shall (i) attach thereto all of the evidence in support of their position, and (ii) during the course of such proceeding, file only rebuttal or reply evidence unless otherwise directed by order of the Commission. Upon receipt of a notice of intent to file a complaint pursuant to this paragraph, the Commission shall accord, to the party filing such notice, the same right to discovery that would be accorded to a party filing a complaint pursuant to this paragraph."

The Commission instituted a rulemaking proceeding in Ex Parte No. 322, *Expeditious Handling of Divisions of Revenue Cases* under Section 201 of the 4R Act to develop dules providing for the expeditious handling of division of revenue cases. The rules[2] were adopted by report and order served July 30, 1976.

In Ex Parte No. 322, the Commission in discussing the reasons for enacting Section 201 of the 4R Act said (pp. 1-2):

"The joint rates assessed and collected by common carrier railroads for the transportation of freight from a point on one line to a point on another line must be divided between the participating carriers. This division of revenue between carriers in the railroad transportation of freight is for the most part governed by private agreements, commonly referred to as division sheets, negotiated by the concerned carriers. When the carriers participating in a joint rate are unable to resolve their differences on how

²49 C.F.R. 1109.5.

the revenue is to be divided, they may, under the provisions of Section 15(6) of the Interstate Commerce Act, file a complaint requesting that the Commission prescribe just, able and equitable divisions. Interterritorial divisions disputes relate to procedures for revenue allocations between territorial rate bureaus which apply to all or a major portion of interterritorial interline traffic. The resulting divisions of revenue cases are among the most complex cases the Commission is called upon to decide. Major divisions cases involve literally hundreds of millions of dollars. For example, in the *Official-Southern Divisions* case the revenues as settled totaled nearly one-half billion dollars. *Official-Southern Divisions*, 325 I.C.C. 1, 50 (1965). Other divisions cases concerning only a limited number of carriers or commodities are nevertheless vitally important to those involved. In an attempt to expedite divisions of revenue proceedings, which have often required an extended period of time to resolve, Congress enacted Section 201 of the Railroad Revitalization and Reform Act (RRRRA).

"Section 201 of Railroad Revitalization and Reform Act amended section 15(c) of the Interstate Commerce Act by adding new provisions under paragraph '(b), (c), (d)' designed to expedite the handling of divisions of revenue cases. The prior provisions of section 15(6) are retained and designated paragraph '(a)'."

The rules adopted by the Commission in Ex Parte No. 322 provide in part as follows:

1. Prior to the filing of a notice of intent to file a complaint, or the filing of a formal complaint in a divisions case, it must be shown that the complainant or prospective complainant, during the 6-month period immediately prior to filing, willingly sought to negotiate the division arrangement in issue but failed.

2. The notice of intent to file a complaint shall specify in general terms (i) the traffic and joint rates concerning which an adjustment of divisions is sought; (ii) the territorial scope of the traffic involved; (iii) the railroads which participate in such joint rates; and (iv) the present and proposed divisional bases.

3. The party filing a notice of intent shall (i) indicate when the filing of a formal complaint is contemplated, (ii) exercise due diligence to meet such filing date, and (iii) file a formal complaint within a reasonable period of time after the filing of a notice of intent. In no event shall the filing of a formal complaint be greater than 18 months after the filing of a notice of intent unless the Commission shall first order extension of time upon good cause shown.

4. The party filing a notice of intent shall advise the Commission every 3 months of the anticipated date for the filing of a formal complaint. Letter replies by potential defendants will be permitted.

5. A party served with a notice of intent to file a formal complaint

shall within 30 days of such notice advise the Commission of its intent to file a cross complaint. If a party served with a notice to file a formal complaint does not intend to file a cross complaint no action need be taken.

6. Notice of intent to file a cross complaint shall be consolidated with a notice to file a complaint. The cross complaint must be filed within 30 days of the filing of the formal complaint. Failure to submit the cross complaint when due shall result in its dismissal and the affirmative relief sought may not be reinstituted until after the pending formal complaint is decided.

7. Defending carrier or carriers must within 30 days of service of the formal complaint file an answer.

8. Complainant must submit its case-in-chief at the time the formal complaint is filed and formally docketed. All underlying papers in support of a case-in-chief shall be made available to the other side, upon request.

9. If the formal complaint was preceded by a notice to file a complaint, then the case-in-rebuttal must be filed with the answer. All underlying papers in support of a case-in-rebuttal shall be made available to the other side, upon request.

Determination and Prescription of Divisions

In a proceeding to determine and prescribe divisions the Commission is not required or authorized to investigate or determine whether the joint rates are reasonable or confiscatory; the question whether it compiled with the requirements of the I.C. Act does not depend upon the level of the rates or the amount of revenue to be divided.[3] The purpose of Section 15(6) is to empower and require the Commission "to make divisions that colloquially may be said to be fair."[4]

In a very early case relating to divisions, *New England Divisions,*[5] the Commission said: "The thought dominates the law, as it is now framed, that a paramount consideration in determining the equitable share of the joint revenue which any carrier shall receive must be the relative amount and cost of the service which it renders . . . . the relative amount and cost under economical and efficient management of the service rendered is a prime factor in determining the fair and equitable share of joint revenue which each carrier shall receive."

---

[3]*Baltimore & O. R. Co. v. United States,* 298 U.S. 349, 356.
[4]*Ibid.* See *Akron, C & Y. v. Atchison T. & S. F.,* 321, I.C.C. 17.
[5]66 I.C.C. 196, 198-9.

Similar expressions are to be found in a number of later Commission decisions. However, it is well recognized that cost of service is not invariably of controlling importance in prescribing, divisions nor is any particular type of cost evidence indispensable for that purpose. Relative cost of service is not the only factor to be considered in determining just divisions.[6] There is no single test by which just, reasonable or equitable divisions may be ascertained; no fact or group of facts may be used generally as a measure by which to determine what divisions will conform to the standards of Section 15(6); considerations that reasonably guide to decision in one case may rightly be deemed to have little or no bearing in other cases.[7]

Judicial recognition of this principle is to be found in *Boston and Maine Railroad v. United States*,[8] where the court said that Section 15(6) does not establish cost of service as the primary criterion of fair divisions. The court said that "due consideration" is not the equivalent of "primary consideration," and that the importance to be given any of the factors enumerated in the I.C. Act must necessarily depend upon the case under consideration. The evaluation of the importance of the various factors in any given case, the court said, is peculiarly the function of the Commission. The court, citing *Interstate Commerce Commission v. Union Pacific R. R.*,[9] concluded that the question of divisions involves the making of practical judgment and cannot be solved as though it were a mathematical problem to which there could only be one correct answer.

---

[6]*United States v. Abilene & Southern Ry. Co.*, 265 U.S. 274, 284.

[7]*Baltimore & Ohio R. Co. v. United States, supra*, pp. 358-9.

[8]208 F. Supp. 661; aff'd 371 U.S. 26. The court dismissed a complaint which sought to set aside a Commission order in *L. & N. R. Co. v. Akron, C & Y. R. Co.*, 309 I.C.C. 491. The Commission under Section 15 (6) prescribed a basis for the primary division of joint rates on traffic (except coal and coke made from coal) moving between points in official territory and border points — those in a broader zone between official territory and southern territory. The order had the effect of completing the establishment of a uniform basis for the division of joint rates on interterritorial and border point traffic.

[9]222 U.S. 541, 550.

32

Rates and Practices of Air Carriers

Tariffs of Air Carriers

Section 403(a) of the Federal Aviation Act[1] provides that "Every air carrier and every foreign air carrier shall file with the Board, and print, and keep open to public inspection, tariffs showing all rates, fares, and charges for air transportation between points served by it, and between points served by it and points served by any other air carrier or foreign air carrier when through service and through rates shall have been established, and showing to the extent required by regulations of the Board, all classifications, rules, regulations, practices, and services in connection with such air transportation." Tariffs are required to be "filed, posted, and published in such form and manner, and shall contain such information, as the Board shall by regulation prescribe; and the Board is empowered to reject any tariff so filed which is not consistent with this section and such regulations. Any tariff so rejected shall be void."

Rates, fares, and charges shown in any tariff must "be stated in terms of lawful money of the United States, but such tariffs may also state rates, fares, and charges in terms of currencies other than lawful money of the United States, and may, in the case of foreign air transportation, contain such information as may be required under the laws of any country in or to which an air carrier or foreign air carrier is authorized to operate." Section 403(c)[2] provides that no "change shall be made in any rate, fare, or charge, or any classification, rule, regulation, or practice affecting such rate, fare, or charge, or the value of the service thereunder, specified in any effective tariff of any air carrier or

[1]49 U.S.C. 1373(a).
[2]49 U.S.C. 1373(c).

foreign air carrier, except after thirty days' notice of the proposed changed filed, posted, and published in accordance with subsection (a) of this section." The notice must "plainly state the change proposed to be made and the time such change will take effect." The Board may in the public interest, by regulation or otherwise, allow such change upon notice less than that specified, or modify the requirements of the Act "with respect to filing and posting of tariffs, either in particular instances or by general order applicable to special or peculiar circumstances or conditions." Section 403(d)[3] provides that "Every air carrier or foreign air carrier shall keep currently on file with the Board, if the Board so requires, the established divisions of all joint rates, fares, and charges for air transportation in which such air carrier or foreign air carrier participates."

In general the pattern of Section 403(a) follows the structure of the Interstate Commerce Act. The carrier is by statute and regulations obligated to file its schedules of rates, fares, and charges with the Board; the Board may reject them as improper or unreasonable, but if not so rejected they continue to be valid and enforceable until the question of their alleged invalidity or unreasonableness or otherwise is challenged by the Board or by interested parties before the Board, and held by the Board to be invalid.[4] Any interested person may file a complaint with the Board asking that a rule, regulation or tariff be declared unreasonable or unlawful; or the Board may investigate on its own initiative.[5] If the Board finds, after notice and hearing that any rule, regulation, or practice is unreasonable or unlawful, it may determine and prescribe more reasonable rules, regulations and tariffs. And in a suit against a carrier the tariff schedules must be accepted and applied by the courts in the litigation involved unless and until the Board has otherwise ruled.[6] Thus, for example, a provision in a tariff which requires timely notice of concealed damage of a shipment, which provision has not been rejected by the Board, must be accepted by the courts.[7] It is well established that a carrier's tariff on file with an administrative agency has an effect equivalent to law until declared unlawful by the agency, and that the provisions of the tariffs establish the legal relationships of the parties.[8]

---

[3]49 U.S.C. 1373(d).

[4]*Lichten v. Eastern Airlines*, 189 F. 2d 939; *Herman v. Northwest Airlines*, 222 F. 2d 326, cert. denied 350 U.S. 843; *Twentieth Century Delivery Service, Inc., v. St. Paul Fire & Marine Ins. Co.*, 242 F. 2d 292.

[5]*Killian v. Frontier Airlines*, 150 F. Supp. 17, 20.

[6]*Alco-Gravure Div. of Publ. Corp. v. American Airlines*, 173 F. Supp. 752, 755.

[7]*Ibid.*

[8]*Western Union Telegraph Co. v. Esteve Bros.*, 256 U.S. 566; *Boston & Maine R.R. v. Hooker*, 233 U.S. 97; *American Ry. Express Co. v. American Trust Co.*, 47 F. 2d 16; *Killian v. Frontier Airlines*, 150 F. Supp. 17, 19-20.

Lawfulness of Rates

Section 1002(d) of the Federal Aviation Act,[9] as amended by P.L. 95-163 provides that "whenever, after notice and hearing, upon complaint, or upon its own initiative, the Board shall be of the opinion that any individual or joint rate, fare, or charge demanded, charged, collected or received by any air carrier for Interstate air transportation of persons, air transportation of property within the State of Alaska, air tranportation of property within the State of Hawaii, or overseas air transportation or any classification, rule, regulation, or practice affecting such rate, fare, or charge, or the value of the service thereunder, is or will be unjust or unreasonable, or unjustly discriminatory, or unduly preferential, or unduly prejudicial, the Board shall determine and prescribe the lawful rate, fare, or charge (or the maximum or minimum, or the maximum and minimum thereof) thereafter to be demanded, charged, collected, or received, or the lawful classification, rule, regulation, or practice thereafter to be made effective." Section 1002(d) also provides "With respect to rates, fares, and charges for overseas air transportation, the Board shall determine and prescribe only a just and reasonable maximum or minimum, or maximum and minimum rate, fare, or charge." It provides further:

> Whenever, after notice and hearing, upon complaint, or upon its own initiative, the Board shall be of the opinion that any individual or joint rate or charge demanded, charged, collected, or received by any air carrier for interstate air transportation of property or any classification, rule, regulation, or practice affecting such rate or charge, or the value of the service thereunder, is or will be unjustly discriminatory, or unduly preferential, or unduly prejudicial, or predatory the Board shall alter such rate, charge, classification, rule, regulation, or practice to the extent necessary to correct such discrimination, preference, prejudice, or predatory practice and make an order that the air carrier or foreign air carrier shall discontinue demanding, charging, collecting, or receiving any such discriminatory, preferential, prejudicial, or predatory rate or charge or enforcing any such discriminatory, preferential, prejudicial, or predatory classification, rule, regulation, or practice.

Section 1002(f)[10] provides that "Whenever, after notice and hearing, upon complaint, or upon its own initiative, the Board shall be of the opinion that any individual or joint rate, fare or charge demanded, charge, collected, or received by any air carrier or foreign air carrier for foreign air transportation, or any classification, rule, regulation, or practice affecting such rate, fare, or charge, or the value of the service thereunder, is or will be unjustly discriminatory, or unduly preferential,

[9]49 U.S.C. 1482(d).
[10]49 U.S.C. 1482(f).

or unduly prejudicial, the Board may alter the same to the extent necessary to correct such discrimination, preference, or prejudice and make an order that the air carrier or foreign air carrier shall discontinue demanding, charging, collecting, or receiving any such discriminatory, preferential, or prejudicial rate, fare, or charge or enforcing any such discriminatory, preferential, or prejudicial classification, rule, regulation, or practice."

Under Section 1002(e) of the Act,[11] the rule of rate making, it is provided that in the exercise and performance of "its powers and duties with respect to the determination of rates for the carriage of persons or property, the Board shall take into consideration, among other factors," (1) the effect of such rates upon the movement of traffic; (2) the need in the public interest of adequate and efficient transportation of persons and property by air carriers at the lowest cost consistent with the furnishing of such service; (3) such standards respecting the character and quality of service to be rendered by air carriers as may be prescribed by or pursuant to law; (4) the inherent advantages of transportation by aircraft; and (5) the need of each air carrier for revenue sufficient to enable such air carrier, under honest, economical, and efficient management, to provide adequate and efficient air carrier service.

In *United Air Lines v. C.A.B.*,[12] the Court of Appeals affirmed a Board order rejecting tariffs filed by United Air Lines proposing new passenger fares for the U.S. Mainland-Hawaii market because they were inconsistent with the rates fixed by the Board in an outstanding rate order. On appeal, United argued that the Board lacked power to prescribe rates for the future; that tariffs filed by a carrier may be rejected only for failure to comply with procedural filing requirements; and that United was entitled to institution of a new ratemaking proceeding through the filing of tariffs proposing rates different from those which the Board had just fixed. In affirming the challenged order, the court held that the Board, like other regulatory agencies operating under statutes comparable to the FAA has the power to issue an order fixing rates for the future and to reject tariffs which are inconsistent with such Board-prescribed fares.[13]

Eastern Air Lines, Inc. v. C.A.B.[14] involved a review of an order of the Board by the court of appeals which order had terminated a Board initiated proceeding relating to a general passenger fare investigation.

---

[11]49 U.S.C. 1482(e).
[12]518 F. 2d 256.
[13]See 49 U.S.C. 15(1).
[14]294 F. 2d 235.

The investigation was to determine whether the fare and charges demanded, collected and received by each of the carriers named for the transportation of passengers were generally unjust or unreasonable, and if found to be unjust or unreasonable, to determine what overall percentage changes in the fares or charges should be permitted or required. After a lengthy hearing and other extensive proceedings, the Board entered its order without determining the justness and reasonableness of the existing passenger fares or the fares that would be just and reasonable. What the Board said was that the record before it was inadequate to permit the fixing of the fare level, but was adequate to permit it to formulate significant standards which would contribute to the regulation of fares. The Board stated that its difficulty in prescribing a just and reasonable fare level from the record was due to the fact that no forecasts of operations, revenues, and expenses had been submitted which would be used as reliable indicia of what the future results would be, and, in addition, there was an absence of data in the record presenting the experience of operations with new aircraft which were becoming an ever-larger element of the industry's operations. The standards formulated by the Board for passenger fare regulation related to four basic areas, profit element, rate base, depreciation, and taxes, which, the Board said, would be used in assessing future fare proposals of the carriers, and in assisting the Board in evaluating the reported results of the carriers so that it could determine when action on its own motion should be taken.

The principal argument on appeal was that the Board had failed to decide the question of justness and reasonableness of fares, the chief purpose for which the investigation had been instituted, and therefore the Board should be directed by the court to decide the case either upon the record made or upon the receiving of additional evidence. The court of appeals agreed (pp. 237-8) that the Act imposed a duty on the Board to prevent unjust and unreasonable rates and to fix reasonable rates in proceedings raising the issue of such rates, but said that this did not require the Board to perform this duty as a result of the investigation. The court said, "We cannot say that the Board decision not to decide the question of justness or reasonableness of the general level of trunkline fares requires this court to compel the Board to do so on this record or as it might be enlarged at this time, especially in view of the changes now under way in the industry. The Board's duty is to be performed in the context of particular proceedings. It is not mandatory in this one." Had the Board determined that the existing rates were unjust or unreasonable, the court said, the case would be different.

The court distinguished the *Eastern Air Lines* case from a prior decision in *Minneapolis Gas Co. v. Federal Power Comm.*[15] There the then Federal Power Commission, having a comparable duty as the Board under the Natural Gas Act, had terminated a proceeding and recited in its order that the result of the termination was to leave the proposed rates in effect. The order also recited that the proposed rates were just and reasonable. The court had concluded in the *Minneapolis Gas* case that in terminating the proceeding the Federal Power Commission had not rendered a decision and should actually have done so. The court said that having exercised its discretion to enter upon a hearing as to the lawfulness of the proposed rate increases, and to suspend them, rather than to permit the new rates to go into effect immediately, and having embarked on a hearing and all the procedings connected therewith thus arriving at a point of decision, to terminate the proceeding and fail to decide the case was inconsistent with the Federal Power Commission's obligation either to let the initial decision of the hearing officer stand or itself to render a decision. The court concluded that the point of no return in the exercise of the Federal Power Commission's discretion had been passed.

Carrier's Duty to Provide Service, Rates, and Divisions

Section 404(a) of the Federal Aviation Act[16] provides that "it shall be the duty of every air carrier to provide and furnish interstate and overseas air transportation, as authorized by its certificate, upon reasonable request therefor and to provide reasonable through service in such air transportation in connection with other air carriers; to provide safe and adequate service, equipment, and facilities in connection with such transportation; to establish, observe, and enforce just and reasonable individual and joint rates, fares, and charges, and just and reasonable classifications, rules, regulations, and practices relating to such air transportation; and, in case of such joint rates, fares, and charges, to establish just, reasonable, and equitable divisions thereof as between air carriers participating therein which shall not unduty prefer or prejudice any of such participating air carriers."

Section 404(a) has been construed to require a carrier to provide competitive service where it is authorized to provide such service, but has never attempted to comply, thus the fact that other carriers provide a market with minimally adequate service does not discharge the

---

[15]294 F. 2d 212.
[16]49 U.S.C. 1374(a).

offending carrier's obligations under its certificate.[17] The court of appeals said in the *Capital Airlines* case (pp. 51-2):

> We do not decide whether a certificated carrier can be required to undertake competitive service where it can show that the potential market is completely satisfied and that the service could only be instituted at a hopeless loss. That is not this case. Here the Board found, upon substantial evidence that, even if Capital's and United's combined service to Toledo is not legally inadequate, there is a potential demand for service between Toledo and New York, Chicago, and Philadelphia, which is not being fulfilled. Although the Board did not attempt to estimate the precise size of this potential market, we think it was fully justified on the record before it in concluding that the existence of more adequate Capital service, plus the expected improvement in United's service as a result of competition, would generate the demand necessary to sustain Capital's new flights.

The court also said (pp. 52-3) that the Board could not effectively order a delinquent carrier to provide more adequate service unless it could specify in detail what constitutes minimally adequate service, which it did in the *Capital Airlines* case, and that questions of adequacy turn on the details of available service and traffic needs in the particular market. The argument was made in the *Capital Airlines* case that the Board's order violated Section 410(e), which provides that no "term, condition, or limitation of a certificate shall restrict the right of an air carrier to add to or change schedules, equipment, accommodations, and facilities for performing authorized transportation." The court of appeals replied by stating (p. 52) that Section 401(e) must be read in harmony with the rest of the Act, thus the above argument would emasculate Section 404(a) and we are bound to avoid such an absurd result."

Through Air Transportation Service and Joint Rates, Fares and Charges

Section 1002(i)[18] provides that the "Board shall, whenever required by the public convenience and necessity, after notice and hearing, upon complaint or upon its own initiative, establish through service and joint rates, fares, or charges (or the maxima or minima, or the maxima and minima thereof) for interstate or overseas air transportation, or the classifications, rules, regulations, or practices affecting such rates, fares, or charges, or the value of the service thereunder, and the terms and conditions under which such through service shall be operated: Pro-

---

[17]*Capital Airlines, Inc. v. C.A.B.*, 281 F. 2d 48.
[18]49 U.S.C. 1482 (i).

vided, That as to joint rates, fares, and charges for overseas air transportation the Board shall determine and prescribe only just and reasonable maximum or minimum or maximum and minimum joint rates, fares, or charges." Section 404(a) of the Act[19] provides that every air carrier shall provide through service in connection with other air carriers and shall establish joint rates.

Section 404(a) was interpreted by the court of appeals in *Airborne Freight Corp. v. C.A.B.*[20] as not contemplating the establishment of joint rates by airlines and freight forwarders. It was contended by Airborne that since Section 412 provides that any agreement of an air carrier shall be filed with the Board that it could, therefore, make and file agreements with airlines by which it would pay lower rates for air transportation than the rates specified in effective tariffs. The Board's holding that Section 412 did not authorize the Board to approve agreements between air freight forwarders and airlines fixing rates for air transportation which would otherwise violate the rate-making provisions of the Act, was affirmed by the court. It is noted that the Board had pointed out that special reduced rates for air freight forwarders are not necessarily unlawful and a regulation prohibiting the filing of such rates would be premature.

Suspension of Rates

Section 1002(g),[21] as amended by P.L. 95-63, provides:

Whenever any air carrier shall file with the Board a tariff stating a new individual or joint (between air carriers) rate, fare, or charge for interstate or overseas air transportation or any classification, rule, regulation, or practice affecting such rate, fare, or charge, or the value of the service thereunder, the Board is empowered, upon complaint or upon its own initiative, at once, and, if it so orders, without answer or other formal pleading by the air carrier, but upon reasonable notice, to enter upon a hearing concerning the lawfulness of such rate, fare, or charge, or such classification, rule, regulation, or practice; and pending such hearing and the decision thereon, the Board, by filing with such tariff, and delivering to the air carrier affected thereby, a statement in writing of its reasons for such suspension, may suspend the operation of such tariff and defer the use of such rate, fare, or charge, or such classification, rule, regulation, or practice, for a period of ninety days, and, if the proceeding has not been concluded and a final order made within such period, the Board may, from time to time, extend the period of suspension, but not for a longer period in the aggregate than one hundred and eighty days beyond the

[19]49 U.S.C. 1374(a).
[20]257 F. 2d 210, 211.
[21]49 U.S.C. 1482(g).

time when such tariff would otherwise go into effect; and, after hearing, whether completed before or after the rate, fare, charge, classification, rule, regulation, or practice goes into effect, the Board may make such order with reference thereto as would be proper in a proceeding instituted after such rate, fare, charge, classification, rule, regulation, or practice had become effective. If the proceeding has not been concluded and an order made within the period of suspension, the proposed rate, fare, charge, classification, rule, regulation, or practice shall go into effect at the end of such period, except that this subsection shall not apply to any initial tariff filed by any air carrier. The Board shall not suspend any proposed tariff under this subsection because of the proposed rate, fare, charge, classification, rule, regulation, or practice stated therein unless the Board is empowered to find such proposed rate, fare, charge, classification, rule, regulation or practice unjust or unreasonable and empowered to determine and prescribe the lawful rate, fare, charge, classification, rule, regulation, or practice, or the lawful maximum or minimum, or maximum and minimum rate, fare, or charge.

Observance of Tariffs; Rebating Prohibited; Undue or Unreasonable Preference or Advantage Prohibited; Unjust Discrimination Prohibited

Section 403(b) of the Federal Aviation Act[22] provides that no "air carrier or foreign air carrier shall charge or demand or collect or receive a greater or less or different compensation for air transportation, or for any service in connection therewith, than the rates, fares, and charges specified in its currently effective tariffs; and no air carrier or foreign air carrier shall, in any manner or by any device, directly or indirectly, or through any agent or broker, or otherwise, refund or remit any portion of the rates, fares, or charges so specified, or extend to any person any privileges or facilities, with respect to matters required by the Board to be specified in such tariffs, except those specified therein." Nothing in the "Act shall prohibit such air carriers or foreign air carriers, under such terms and conditions as the Board may prescribe, from issuing or interchanging tickets or passes for free or reduced-rate transportation to their directors, officers, and employees and their immediate families; witnesses and attorneys attending any legal investigation in which any such air carrier is interested; persons injured in aircraft accidents and physicians and nurses attending such persons; and any person or property with the object of providing relief in cases of general epidemic, pestilence, or other calamitous visitation; and, in the case of overseas or foreign air transportation, to such other persons and under such other circumstances as the Board may by regulations prescribe." Any carrier, "under such terms and conditions as the Board may prescribe, may grant

[22]49 U.S.C. 1373(b).

reduced-rate transportation to ministers of religion on a space-available basis."

Section 404(b)[23] provides that "No air carrier or foreign air carrier shall make, give, or cause any undue or unreasonable preference or advantage to any particular person, port, locality, or description of traffic in air transportation in any respect whatsoever or subject any particular person, port, locality, or description of traffic in air transportation to any unjust discrimination or any undue or unreasonable prejudice or disadvantage in any respect whatsoever." Section 1002(h)[24] provides that "Whenever, after notice and hearing, upon complaint or upon its own initiative, the Board is of the opinion that the divisions of joint rates, fares, or charges for air transportation are or will be unjust, unreasonable, inequitable or unduly preferential or prejudicial as between the air carriers or foreign air carriers parties thereto, the Board shall prescribe the just, reasonable, and equitable divisions thereof to be received by the several air carriers." The Board is empowered to "require the adjustment of divisions between such air carriers from the date of filing the complaint or entry of order of investigation, or such other date subsequent thereto as the Board finds to be just, reasonable, and equitable."

Joint Boards of Interstate Commerce Commission and Civil Aeronautics Board

Section 1003(a) of the Federal Aviation Act of 1958[25] provides that the Civil Aeronautics Board and the Interstate Commerce Commission shall designate, from time to time, a like number of members of each to act as a joint board to consider and pass upon matters referred to such joint board. Under Section 1003(b)[26] air carriers are permitted to "establish reasonable through service and joint rates, fares, and charges with other common carriers; except that with respect to transportation of property, air carriers not directly engaged in the operation of aircraft in air transportation (other than companies engaged in the air express business) may not establish joint rates or charges with common carriers subject to the Interstate Commerce Act. In case of through service by air carriers and common carriers subject to the Interstate Commerce Act, it shall be the duty of the carriers parties

[23]49 U.S.C. 1374(b).
[24]49 U.S.C. 1482(h).
[25]49 U.S.C. 1483(a).
[26]49 U.S.C. 1483(b).

thereto to establish just and reasonable classifications, rules, regulations, and practices affecting such rates, fares, or charges, or the value of the service thereunder, and if joint rates, fares, or charges shall have been established with respect to such through service, just, reasonable, and equitable divisions of such joint rates, fares, or charges as between the carriers participating therein. Any air carrier, and any common carrier subject to the Interstate Commerce Act, which is participating in such through service and joint rates, fares, or charges, shall include in its tariffs, filed with the Civil Aeronautics Board or the Interstate Commerce Commission, as the case may be, a statement showing such through service and joint rates, fares, or charges."

Under Section 1003(c)[27] matters relating to through service and joint rates, fares, or charges may be referred by the Board or the Commission, upon complaint or upon its own initiative, to a joint board. Complaints may be made to the Commission or the Board with respect to any matter which may be referred to a joint board. Under Section 1003(d),[28] with respect to matters referred to any joint board, "if such board finds, after notice and hearing, that any such joint rate, fare, or charge, or classification, rule, regulation, or practice, affecting such joint rate, fare, or charge or the value of the service thereunder is or will be unjust, unreasonable, unjustly discriminatory, or unduly preferential or prejudicial, or that any division of any such joint rate, fare, or charge, is or will be unjust, unreasonable, inequitable, or unduly preferential or prejudicial as between the carriers parties thereto, it is authorized and directed to take the same action with respect thereto as the Board is empowered to take with respect to any joint rate, fare, or charge, between air carriers, or any divisions thereof, or any classification, rule, regulation, or practice affecting such joint rate, fare, or charge or the value of the service thereunder." Under Section 1003(e),[29] orders of the joint boards are enforceable and reviewable as provided in the Federal Aviation Act with respect to orders of the Board.

[27]49 U.S.C. 1003(c).
[28]49 U.S.C. 1003(d).
[29]49 U.S.C. 1003(e).

33

Rates and Practices of Ocean Carriers

Applicable Provisions in the Shipping Act

Section 18(a) of the Shipping Act of 1916, as amended,[1] provides the common carriers by water in interstate commerce "shall establish, observe, and enforce just and reasonable rates, fares, charges, classifications, and tariffs, and just and reasonable regulations and practices relating thereto and to the issuance, form, and substance of tickets, receipts, and bills of lading, the manner and method of presenting, marketing, packing, and delivering property for transportation, the carrying of personal, sample, and excess baggage, the facilities for transportation, and all other matters relating to or connected with the receiving, handling, transporting, storing, or delivering of property." Each of such carriers "shall file with the Commission and keep open to public inspection, in the form and manner and within the time prescribed by the Commission, the maximum rates, fares, and charges for or in connection with transportation between points on its own route; and if a through route has been established, the maximum rates, fares, and charges for or in connection with transportation between points on its own route and points on the route of any other carrier by water."

Section 18(a) provides further that no "carrier shall demand, charge, or collect a greater compensation for such transportation than the rates, fares, and charges filed in compliance with this section, except with the approval of the Commission and after ten days' public notice in the and manner prescribed by the Commission, stating the increase proposed to be made; but the Commission for good cause shown may waive such notice." Whenever a finding is made by the Commission "that any rate, fare, charge, classification, tariff, regulation, or practice, demanded,

[1]46 U.S.C. 817(a).

charged, collected, or observed by such carrier is unjust or unreasonable, it may determine, prescribe, and order enforced a just and reasonable maximum rate, fare, or charge, or a just and reasonable classification tariff, regulation, or practice." Paragraph (1) of Section 18(b)[2] provides that common carriers by water in foreign commerce and conferences of such carriers "shall file with the Commission and keep open to public inspection tariffs showing all the rates and charges of such carrier or conference of carriers for transportation to and from United States ports and foreign ports between all points on its own route and on any through route which has been established."

"Tariffs shall plainly show the places between which freight will be carried, and shall contain the classification of freight in force, and shall also state separately such terminal or other charge, privilege, or facility under the control of the carrier or conference of carriers which is granted or allowed, and any rules or regulations which in anywise change, affect, or determine any part of the aggregate of such aforesaid rates, or charges, and shall include specimens of any bill of lading, contract of affreightment, or other document evidencing the transportation agreement." Copies of tariffs are required to be made available to any person and a reasonable charge may be made therefor. The requirements of the section are not applicable to cargo loaded and carried in bulk without mark or count. Paragraph (2) of Section 18(b) provides that no "change shall be made in rates, charges, classifications, rules or regulations, which results in an increase in cost to the shipper, nor shall any new or initial rate of any common carrier by water in foreign commerce or conference of such carriers be instituted, except by the publication, and filing, as aforesaid, of a new tariff or tariffs which shall become effective not earlier than thirty days after the date of publication and filing thereof with the Commission, and each such tariff or tariffs shall plainly show the changes proposed to be made in the tariff or tariffs then in force and the time when the rates, charges, classifications, rules or regulations as changed are to become effective." The FMC, however, "may, in its discretion and for good cause, allow such changes and such new or initial rates to become effective upon less than the period of thirty days herein specified. Any change in the rates, charges, or classifications, rules or regulations which results in a decreased cost to the shipper may become effective upon the publication and filing with the Commission."

The term "tariff" is defined as including any amendment, supplement or reissue. Paragraph (3) of Section 18(b) provides that no "common

[2]46 U.S.C. 817(b).

carrier by water in foreign commerce or conference of such carriers shall charge or demand or collect or receive a greater or less or different compensation for the transportation of property or for any service in connection therewith than the rates and charges which are specified in its tariffs on file with the Commission and duly published and in effect at the time; nor shall any such carrier rebate, refund, or remit in any manner or by any device any portion of the rates or charges so specified, nor extend or deny to any person any privilege or facility, except in accordance with such tariffs." Paragraph (4) of Section 18(b) provides that the Commission shall by regulations prescribe the form and manner in which the tariffs shall be published and filed; and the Commission is authorized to reject any tariff field with it which is not in conformity with the Act and regulations. Upon rejection by the Commission, a tariff shall be void and its use unlawful. Paragraph (5) of Section 18(b) provides that the "Commission shall disapprove any rate or charge filed by a common carrier by water in the foreign commerce of the United States or conference of carriers which, after hearing, it finds to be so unreasonably high or low as to be detrimental to the commerce of the United States."

Applicable Provisions in the Intercoastal Shipping Act

Section 2 of the Intercoastal Shipping Act of 1933, as amended,[3] provides that common carriers by water in intercoastal commerce shall file with the FMC and keep open to public inspection schedules showing all rates, fares, and charges for or in connection with transportation between intercoastal points on its own route; and, if a through route has been established, all rates, fares, and charges for or in connection with transportation between intercoastal points on its own route and points on the route of any other carrier by water. Schedules filed and kept open to public inspection by carriers "shall plainly show the places between which passengers and/or freight will be carried, and shall contain the classification of freight and of passenger accommodations in force, and shall also state separately each terminal or other charge, privilege, or facility, granted or allowed, and any rules or regulations which in anywise change, affect, or determine any part of the aggregate of such aforesaid rates, fares, or charges, or the value of the service rendered to the passenger, consignor, or consignee, and shall include the terms and conditions of any passenger ticket, bill of lading, contract of affreightment, or other document evidencing the transportation agreement."

The terms and conditions as filed shall be framed under glass and

[3] 46 U.S.C. 844.

posted in a conspicuous place on board each vessel where they may be seen by passengers and others at all times. Carriers "in establishing and fixing rates, fares, or charges may make equal rates, fares, or charges for similar service between all ports of origin and all ports of destination, and it shall be unlawful for any carrier, either directly or indirectly, through the medium of any agreement, conference, association, understanding, or otherwise, to prevent or attempt to prevent any such carrier from extending service to any publicly owned terminal located on any improvement project authorized by the Congress at the same rates which it charges at its nearest regular port of call." Schedules shall be plainly printed, and copies shall be kept posted in a public and conspicuous place at every wharf, dock, and office of such carrier where passengers or freight are received for transportation, in such manner that they shall be readily accessible to the public and can be conveniently inspected. If the schedules include the terms and conditions of any passenger ticket, bill of lading, contract of affreightment or other document evidencing the transportation agreement, copies of such terms and conditions shall be made available to any shipper, consignee, or passenger upon request.

Terms and conditions, if filed and framed under glass and posted in a conspicuous place on board each vessel, may be incorporated by reference in a short form of the shipping document issued for the transportation by notice printed on the back of each document that all parties to the contract are bound by the terms and conditions as filed with the Federal Maritime Commission and posted on board each vessel. When "so incorporated by reference every carrier and any other person having any interest or duty in respect of such transportation shall be deemed to have such notice thereof as if all such terms and conditions had been set forth in the short form document."

Section 3 of the Intercoastal Shipping Act of 1933, as amended,[4] provides that whenever there is filed with the FMC "any schedule stating a new individual or joint rate, fare, or charge, or any new individual or joint classification, or any new individual or joint regulation or practice affecting any rate, fare, or charge," the FMC shall have authority, "either upon complaint or upon its own initiative without complaint, and if it so orders without answer or other formal pleading by the interested carrier or carriers, but upon reasonable notice, to enter upon a hearing concerning the lawfulness of such rate, fare, charge, classification, regu-

---

[4]46 U.S.C. 845. In October, 1974, the 93rd Congress approved Public Law 93-487. This law repealed Section 6 of the Intercoastal Shipping Act, 1933, which provided for the carriage, storage or handling of property free or at reduced rates, for the United States, States or Municipal Governments, or for charitable purposes.

lation, or practice: *Provided, however,* That there shall be no suspension of a tariff schedule or service which extends to additional ports, actual service at rates of said carrier for similar service already in effect at the nearest port of call to said additional port."

Section 3 provides further that pending hearing and decision thereon the FMC "upon filing with such schedule and delivering to the carrier or carriers affected thereby a statement in writing of its reasons for such suspension, may from time to time suspend the operation of such schedule and defer the use of such rate, fare, charge, classification, regulation, or practice, but not for a longer period than four months beyond the time when it would otherwise go into effect." After full hearing whether completed before or after the rate, fare, charge, classification, regulation, or practice goes into effect, the FMC is authorized by Section 3 to make such order with reference thereto as would be proper in a proceeding initiated after it had become effective. If the proceeding has not been concluded and an order has not been made within the period of suspension, the proposed change of rate, fare, charge, classification, regulation, or practice becomes effective at the end of such period. The FMC shall give preference to the hearing and decision of such questions and decide the same as speedily as possible; and nothing contained in the Section shall be construed to empower the FMC affirmatively to fix specific rates.

Determination of Lawfulness of Rates, Rules, Regulations and Practices

In rate cases the FMC determines the lawfulnes of rates by an examination of the assets, revenues and expenses of the dominant carrier in the pertinent trade area.[5] The dominant-carrier theory is applied after first examining the facts of the operations of all material services in the trade; the FMC, however, has never announced that the dominant-carrier theory will be inflexibly applied in rate proceedings.[6]

The FMC has the authority under Section 18 of the Shipping Act to determine the reasonableness of rules and regulations and practices of carriers relating to the issuance, form, and substance of tickets, bills of lading and receipts. The FMC has held in carrying out the above authority that the statute requires the publication in tariffs of any rules or regulations which in any way change, affect or determine any part of the aggregate of the rates, fares, charges or value of the service.[7] The FMC

[5]*Matson Navigation Co. — Rate Structure,* 3 U.S.M.C. 82, 83; *General Increases in Hawaiian Rates,* 5 F.M.B. 347, 349; *General Increases in Alaskan Rates and Charges,* 5 F.M.B. 486, 490.
[6]*Lee v. F.M.B.,* 284, F. 2d 577, 581.
[7]*Puerto Rican Rates,* 2 U.S.M.C. 117, 131.

has also said that the provisions of the bill of lading or other documents affecting rates or the value of service are not governing unless incorporated in the carriers published and filed tariffs.[8]

In *International Packers Ltd. v. Federal Maritime Commission*,[9] the court affirmed an order of the FMC which had upheld the legality of a surcharge imposed because of a longshoremen's strike. Rejecting the shipper's claims that the surcharge was illegal because it constituted a charge not expressly set out in the carrier's tariff and that the bill of lading rule, under which the surcharge was imposed, was not properly a part of the tariff, the court concluded: "This is clearly a question the resolution of which must be left primarily to the agency with expert experience in the everyday realities of the shipping industry, and to which Congress has entrusted primary responsibilty for effectuating the purposes of the Act."

It was held in *Alaska Steamship Company v. Federal Maritime Commission*,[10] that in the event the FMC decides to suspend newly filed rates under the provisions of the Intercoastal Shipping Act, 1933, the orders reflecting the FMC's action must be served prior to the effective date of the rates. The court also held that telegrams notifying the carrier of rate suspensions did not comply with the Act's requirement that the carrier be apprised of the suspension by being furnished with a written statement of the FMC's reasons for the suspension.

Jurisdiction of the Interstate Commerce Commission

Section 320(a) of the Interstate Commerce Act[11] has repealed the Shipping Act, 1916, and Intercoastal Act, 1933, insofar as they are inconsistent with any provision and insofar as they provide for the regulation of, or the making of agreements relating to, transportation of persons or property by water in commerce which is within the jurisdiction of the ICC; also repealed are other provisions of law insofar as they are inconsistent with any provision of Part III, of the Interstate Commerce Act. Not repealed, however, as provided in Section 320(b),[12] are (1) Section 205 of the Merchant Marine Act, 1936, as amended, or any provision of law providing penalties for violations of such Section 205; (2) part of Section 2 of the Intercoastal Shipping Act, 1933, as amended, as extended by Section 5 of such Act, or any provision of law

---

[8]*Alaskan Rates,* 2 U.S.M.C. 558, 584.
[9]356 F. 2d 808.
[10]362 F. 2d 406.
[11]49 U.S.C. 920(a).
[12]Section 320(b), 49 U.S.C. 920(b).

providing penalties for violations of such Section 2; (3) the provisions of the Shipping Act, 1916, as amended, insofar as such Act provides for the regulation of persons included within the term "other person subject to this Act," as defined in such Act; and (4) Sections 27 and 28 of the Merchant Marine Act, 1920, as amended.

Under Section 320(c)[13] nothing "shall be construed to affect the provisions of Section 15 of the Shipping Act, 1916, so as to prevent any water carrier subject to the provisions of this part from entering into any agreement under the provisions of such Section 15 with respect to transportation not subject to the provisions of this part in which such carrier may be engaged." Under Section 320(d)[14] nothing "shall be construed to affect any law of navigation, the admiralty jurisdiction of the courts of the United States, liabilities of vessels and their owners for loss or damage, or laws respecting seamen, or other maritime law, regulation, or custom not in conflict with the provisions of this part." Under Section 320(e)[15] it is provided that "Subsection (e) of Section 3 of the Inland Waterways Corporation Act of June 7, 1924, as amended (U.S.C., title 49, Sec. 153(e)), is hereby repealed as of October 1, 1940: *Provided, however,* That (1) any certificate of public convenience and necessity granted to any carrier pursuant to the provisions of such subsection (e) shall continue in effect as though issued under the provisions of Section 309 of the Interstate Commerce Act, as amended; and (2) through routes and joint rates, and rules, regulations, and practices relating thereto, put into effect pursuant to the provisions of such subsection (e) shall, after the repeal of such subsection (e), be held and considered to have been put into effect pursuant to the provisions of the Interstate Commerce Act, as amended."

The Shipping Act, as amended, conferred no jurisdiction on the FMC over carriers engaged in interstate transportation on rivers, bays, and intracoastal waterways which were not part of the "high seas," nor over contract carriers unless they engaged in transportation between ports in the United States by way of the Panama Canal.[16] Under Part III of the Interstate Commerce Act, the ICC has jurisdiction over both common and contract carriers operating over all such waterways when engaged in interstate or foreign commerce as those terms are defined in Section 302 of the Interstate Commerce Act.[17] Thus the ICC's jurisdiction over

---

[13]49 U.S.C. 920(c).
[14]49 U.S.C. 920(d).
[15]49 U.S.C. 920(e).
[16]*Status of Wharfingers*, 251 I.C.C. 610, 617.
[17]*Ibid.*

transportation by common and contract carrier by water, in interstate or foreign commerce, between ports in the United States is broader than that previously exercised by the FMC.[18]

Unfair Practices

Section 14 First of the Shipping Act of 1916, as amended,[19] provides that no common carrier by water shall directly or indirectly pay, or allow, or enter into any combination, agreement, or understanding, express or implied, to pay or allow, a deferred rebate to any shipper. The term "deferred rebate" is defined to mean "a return of any portion of the freight money by a carrier to any shipper as a consideration for the giving of all or any portion of his shipments to the same or any other carrier, or for any other purpose, the payment of which is deferred beyond the completion of the service for which it is paid, and is made only if, during both the period for which computed and the period of deferment, the shipper has complied with the terms of the rebate agreement or arrangement." Section 14 Second[20] provides that no such carrier shall use "a fighting ship either separately or in conjunction with any other carrier, through agreement or otherwise." The term "fighting ship" is defined to mean "a vessel used in a particular trade by a carrier or group of carriers for the purpose of excluding, preventing, or reducing competition by driving another carrier out of said trade." Section 14 Third[21] provides that no such carrier shall retaliate "against any shipper by refusing, or threatening to refuse, space accommodations when such are available, or resort to other discriminating or unfair methods, because such shipper has patronized any other carrier or has filed a complaint charging unfair treatment, or for any other reason." Section 14 Fourth[22] provides that no such carrier shall make "any unfair or unjustly discriminatory contract with any shippesr based on the volume of freight offered, or unfairly treat or unjustly discriminate against any shipper in the matter of (a) cargo space accommodations or other facilities, due regard being had for the proper loading of the vessel and the available tonnage; (b) the loading and landing of freight in proper condition; or (c) the adjustment and settlement of claims."

The Shipping Act is a comprehensive measure bearing a relation to

---

[18]*Ibid.*
[19]46 U.S.C. 812 First.
[20]46 U.S.C. 812 Second.
[21]46 U.S.C. 812 Third.
[22]46 U.S.C. 812 Fourth.

common carriers by water substantially the same as that borne by the Interstate Commerce Act to interstate carriers. In its general scope and purpose, as well as in its terms, the Shipping Act closely parallels the Interstate Commerce Act; and the two acts, each in its own field, should have like interpretation, application, and effect.[23]

The Supreme Court noted in *F.M.B. v. Isbrandtsen Co.*[24] that the Shipping Act was enacted after inquiries[25] had brought to light many predatory practices by shipping conferences designed to give the conferences monopolies upon particular trades by forestalling outside competition and driving out all outsiders attempting to compete. The court pointed out that the inquiries revealed that the crudest form of predatory practice was the fighting ship; the conference would select a suitable steamer from among its lines to sail on the same days and between the same ports as the nonmember vessel, reducing the regular rates to low level sufficient to capture the trade from the outside. The expenses and losses from the low level of rates were shared by all members of the conference. It was expected that through this method of operation the competitor would be caused to exhaust its resources and withdraw from competition.

More sophisticated practices, the court said, depended upon a tie between the conference and the shipper; the most widely used tie, since it was the most effective one, was the system of deferred rebates. Under this system a shipper signed a contract with the conference exclusively to patronize its vessels, and if it did so during the contract term, and for a designated period thereafter, a rebate of a certain percentage of the freight payments was made to the shipper at the end of the contract period. By this method, the shipper was under constant obligation to give its patronage exclusively to the conference lines or suffer the loss of this rebate, which often amounted to a sizeable sum of money. The court said that other predatory practices were found during the inquiries. Shippers who patronize outside competitors were denied accommodations for future shipments of freight even at full rates, or were discriminated against in the matter of lighterage and other services. Outside competition was also met by dual-rate contracts, by contracts with larger shippers at lower rates for volume shipments, and by contracts with railroads giving conference vessels preference in the handling of cargoes at the docks and delivering through shipments of freight to conference vessels.

Congress in enacting Section 14 "has flatly prohibited practices which

---

[23]*United States Navigation Co. v. Cunard S.S. Co.*, 284 U.S. 474, 480-1.
[24]356 U.S. 481, 487-9.
[25]H.R. 587, Hearings 62nd Cong.; H.R. Doc. No. 805, 63d Cong. 2d Sess.

have the purpose and effect of stifling the competition of independent carriers."[26] The deferred-rebate system and the fighting ship are specifically outlawed by Section 14; also prohibited is retaliation against any shipper by refusing space accommodations when such are available because the shipper has patronized any other carrier or filed a complaint charging unfair treatment, or for any other reason.[27] Also prohibited is the making of unfair or unjustly discriminatory contracts, based on the volume of freight offered, and unfair treatment in the matter of cargo space accommodations or other facilities, loading and landing of freight, and the adjustment and settlement of claims. Coordinate with the foregoing provisions, which are aimed at specific practices, is another provision in Section 14 couched in general language stating that a carrier may not "resort to other discriminatory or unfair methods." The court in the *Isbrandtsen* case said (p. 492) that the clause "resort to other discriminatory or unfair methods" constitutes a catchall clause by which Congress meant to prohibit other devices not specifically enumerated but similar in purpose and effect.

The characterizations "unjustly discriminatory" and "unjustly prejudicial" are also found in Sections 15, 16 and 17 where they "imply a congressional intent to allow some latitude in practices dealt with by those sections."[28]

Section 16 of the Shipping Act of 1916, as amended,[29] provides that it "shall be unlawful for any shipper, consignor, consignee, forwarder, broker, or other person, or any officer, agent, or employee thereof, knowingly and willfully, directly or indirectly, by means of false billing, false classification, false weighing, false report of weight, or by any other unjust or unfair device or means to obtain or attempt to obtain transportation by water for property at less than the rates or charges which would otherwise be applicable," and Section 16 First[30] provides that it "shall be unlawful for any common carrier by water, or other person subject to this Act, either alone or in conjunction with any other person, directly or indirectly" to make or give any undue or unreasonable preference or advantage to any particular person, locality, or description of traffic in any respect whatsoever, or to subject any particular person, locality, or description of traffic to any undue or unreasonable prejudice or disadvantage in any respect whatsoever." Section 16 also provides for

[26]*F.M.B. v. Isbrandtsen Co.*, 356 U.S. 481, 491-2.
[27]*Ibid.*
[28]*Ibid.*, p. 494.
[29]46 U.S.C. 815.
[30]46 U.S.C. 815 First.

the filing of protests with the FMC by a State, commonwealth or possession on the ground that a particular rate, rule, or regulation is unjustly
discriminatory, in which case a show cause order will be issued to the
conference involved.

Section 17 of the Shipping Act of 1916[31] provides that no "common
carrier by water in foreign commerce shall demand, charge, or collect
any rate, fare, or charge which is unjustly discriminatory between shippers or ports, or unjustly prejudicial to exporters of the United States as
compared with their foreign competitors." Whenever the FMC "finds
that any such rate, fare, or charge is demanded, charged, or collected it
may alter the same to the extent necessary to correct such unjust discrimination or prejudice and make an order that the carrier shall discontinue demanding, charging, or collecting any such unjustly discriminatory or prejudicial rate, fare, or charge." Section 17 also provides that
"such carrier and every other person subject to this Act shall establish,
observe, and enforce just and reasonable regulations and practices relating to or connected with the receiving, handling, storing, or delivering
of property." Whenever the FMC "finds that any such regulation or
practice is unjust or unreasonable it may determine, prescribe, and order
enforced a just and reasonable regulation or practice."

Absorption, transshipment, substituted service and overland/OCP
rates, while treated separately by the FMC, have a common purpose in
that they relate to the equalization to the shipper of the cost of shipping
through a more distant port rather than a port nearest the shipper. This
permits a carrier to compete for cargo at a port without calling there by
providing rates competitive with those provided by carriers that actually
serve the port.

In the past the FMC developed the naturally tributary concept to
prohibit equalization or absorption by carriers.[32] It has held equalization
practices violative of Sections 16 and 17 on the ground of the policy of
promoting and maintaining ports as expressed in Section 8 of the Merchant Marine Act of 1920. In recent cases, however, the FMC is lessening
the impact of the naturally tributary concept especially in view of inter-
modalism[33] or mini-bridge service.

Grace Line, Inc. v. F.M.B.,[34] involved a question of whether Grace
Line, a common carrier by water, violated Sections 14 Fourth and 16
of the Shipping Act by unjustly discriminating against shippers of ba-

---

[31]46 U.S.C. 816.
[32]See *Stockton Port District v. Pacific Westbound Conference,* 9 F.M.C. 12.
[33]See *Intermodal Service to Portland, Oregon,* 17 F.M.C. 106; *Investigation of
Overland and OCP Rates and Absorptions,* 12 F.M.C. 184, aff'd 429 F. 2d 633.
[34]280 F. 2d 790, cert. denied 364 U.S. 933. See also *Consolo v. Grace Line,* 4
F.M.B. 293.

nanas as to cargo space accommodations and by the unreasonable preference of certain shippers. Grace Line's position was that since it always carried bananas on a contract basis and had never held itself out as a common carrier that it had the privilege of allocating its cargo space, and confining its carriage to those shippers that it preferred. The FMC's holding that since Grace was a common carrier by water within the meaning of Sections 14 and 16, it could not evade those Sections as to any part of the goods that it lifted, but must give all shippers equal access to the ships, was affirmed by the court. In its decision (p. 792) the court said that Sections 14 and 16 should not be construed to give any common carrier the right to unjustly discriminate against any shipper in the matter of cargo space, or to give any undue or unreasonable preference or advantage to any particular person. The court added that it saw no reason to impute the limitation upon the definition of common carrier, urged by Grace, that the duties under Sections 14 and 16 are limited to common carriers while they are actually carrying goods as to which they have held themselves out as common carriers. The court concluded (p. 793) by saying that a common carrier "does not cease to be such because it chooses to make an exception as to a part of the goods that it accepts."

In the *Grace Line* case the court accepted the test (p. 792) that at common law a carrier becomes a common carrier only when it holds itself out as such. It also recognized that at common law a common carrier could on occasion carry by contract.[35] However, the court said, for the reasons given in deciding the case "we think that we need not decide in what circumstances, if at all, a carrier ever becomes subject to a common law duty of equal treatment of shippers of goods as to which it has never specifically held itself out as a 'common carrier.'[36] For instance, we need not express any opinion whether the privilege of carrying by

[35]In the *Express Cases,* 117 U.S. 1, railroads were permitted to choose their own express companies for the carriage of goods sent by express; and in *United States v. Louisville & Nashville Railroad Co.,* 221 F. 2d 698, a railroad was permitted to fix its charges against the United States for the transportation of silver electrical equipment which the freight classification rules provided it should not carry.

[36]Perhaps the court did not express an opinion because of the fact that there is always the danger of others reading too much into a court decision based on a comment made which is not necessary to arrive at a decision. As the Supreme Court said in *Cohens v. Virginia,* 6 Wheat 264, 399:

It is a maxim, not to be disregarded, that general expressions, in every opinion, are to be taken in connection with the case in which those expressions are used. If they go beyond the case, they may be respected, but ought not to control the judgment in a subsequent suit, when the very point is presented for decision. The reason of this maxim is obvious. The question actually before the court is investigated with care, and considered in its full extent. Other principles which may serve to illustrate it, are considered in their relation to the case decided, but their possible bearing on all other cases is seldom completely investigated.

'contract' is limited to those situations in which there are no competing shippers for the space granted to a preferred shipper, or to the cargoes of chartered ships, or to what other situations, if any." The *Grace Line* decision was followed in *Flota Mercante Grancolombiana v. F.M.C.*[37] in which an order of the FMC was affirmed on the ground that Flota was found to be a common carrier and that it had violated Section 14 Fourth and Section 16 First of the Shipping Act.

In *Brown & Williamson Tobacco Corp. v. The S.S. Anghyra,*[38] it was held that the ship involved in the case was a "tramp" vessel and therefore not subject to the provisions of the Shipping Act relating to preferences. The court said (p. 752) that tested by established principles the Anghyra met the definition of "tramp" vessel. The court referred to a definition of "tramp" vessel presented to Congress by the FMC in a report.[39] The report defined a "tramp" vessel as "a self-contained unit of transport. It is not attached continuously to any given trade route; it does not conduct its operations in concert with others. Its sailings are determined by no fixed plan. The function of the tramp, in short, is to fluctuate from one route to another according to the shifting requirements of the various trades. Its movements are determined by the law of supply and demand; it goes where its voyage will yield the greatest profit; and it undertakes no obligation beyond that involved in each particular venture." The report defined "tramp" vessel further by stating, "Often, however, it renders a service analogous to that of a common carrier, for when a tramp is placed 'on the berth,' the owner, operator, or agent announces that the vessel will sail for a given destination at a given time and he advertises for a full cargo or for smaller shipments to fill space not already contracted for."

Foreign Discrimination

Pursuant to Section 19 of the Merchant Marine Act, 1920,[40] the FMC is "authorized and directed in aid of the accomplishment of the purpose of this Act" to make rules and regulations affecting shipping in the foreign trade for the purpose of adjusting or meeting conditions unfavorable to shipping in the foreign trade which arise out of foreign laws, rules, or regulations or from competitive methods or practices employed by owners, operators, agents or masters of vessels of a foreign country.

[37]302 F. 2d 887.
[38]157 F. Supp. 737, aff'd in part, rev. in part 277 F. 2d 9, cert. denied 364 U.S. 879.
[39]H. Doc. No. 520 (1938), 3rd Sess., 75th Cong., pp. 2 and 4 of the report.
[40]46 U.S.C. 876.

In response to this mandate and because of certain existing laws and decrees of foreign nations which could give rise to conditions unfavorable to shipping in our foreign commerce, the FMC promulgated "Regulations To Adjust Or Meet Conditions Unfavorable To Shipping In the Foreign Trade."[41] The regulations set forth the conditions which are unfavorable to all shipping, not just U.S. shipping, in the foreign trade of the United States. In particular, it is noted that the reservation of cargo to national flag or any other vessels without equal access is considered an unfavorable condition. The order clearly indicates that any discrimination in the foreign trade of the United States is unfavorable and is subject to action or regulation by the FMC. Regulatory action will be taken by the FMC on its own motion or upon petition from any person.

Dual Rates

In the *Isbrandtsen* case, *supra*, the Supreme Court held that the dual-rate system instituted by the conference was for the purpose of curtailing competition, thus becoming a device made illegal by Congress in Section 14.[42] The Court said (pp. 492-3) that "Congress was unwilling to tolerate methods involving ties between conferences and shippers designed to stifle independent carrier competition. Thus Congress struck the balance by allowing conference arrangements passing muster under Section 15, 16 and 17 limiting competition among the conference members while flatly outlawing conference practices designed to destroy the competition of independent carriers. Ties to shippers not designed to have the effect of stifling competition are not made unlawful. Whether a particular tie is designed to have the effect of stifling outside competition is a question for the (FMC) in the first instance to determine."

After the decision in the *Isbrandtsen* case, Congress amended the Shipping Act of 1916 by adding Section 14b.[43] This Section provides that the FMC "shall, after notice, and hearing, by order, permit the use by any common carrier or conference of such carriers in foreign commerce of any contract, amendment, or modification thereof, which is available to all shippers and consignees on equal terms and conditions,

---

[41]General Order 33, effective December 2, 1974.
[42]The Supreme Court said that its decision was not foreclosed by the decisions in *United States Nav. Co. v. Cunard S.S. Co.* 284 U.S. 474 and *Far East Conference v. United States*, 342 U.S. 570, which held that the questions raised were within the primary jurisdiction of the agency. The court said (pp. 496-8) that the cases did not signify that the agency was free under the statute to approve or disapprove the types of agreements under attack.
[43]46 U.S.C. 813a.

which provides lower rates to a shipper or consignee who agrees to give all or any fixed portion of his patronage to such carrier or conference of carriers unless the Commission finds that the contract, amendment, or modification thereof will be detrimental to the commerce of the United States or contrary to the public interest, or unjustly discriminatory or unfair as between shippers, exporters, importers, or ports, or between exporters from the United States and their foreign competitors."

Under Section 14b the contract, amendment, or modification, (1) must expressly permit "prompt release of the contract shipper from the contract with respect to any shipment or shipments for which the contracting carrier or conference of carriers cannot provide as much space as the contract shipper shall require on reasonable notice"; (2) must provide "that whenever a tariff rate for the carriage of goods under the contract becomes effective, insofar as it is under the control of the carrier or conference of carriers, it shall not be increased before a reasonable period, but in no case less than ninety days"; (3) must cover "only those goods of the contract shipper as to the shipment of which he has the legal right at the time of shipment to select the carrier"; however "it shall be deemed a breach of the contract if, before the time of shipment and with the intent to avoid his obligation under the contract, the contract shipper divests himself, or with the same intent permits himself to be divested, of the legal right to select the carrier and the shipment is carried by a carrier which is not a party to the contract"; (4) cannot "require the contract shipper to divert shipment of goods from natural routings not served by the carrier or conference of carriers where direct carriage is available"; (5) must "limit damages recoverable for breach by either party to actual damages to be determined after breach in accordance with the principles of contract law," however, "the contract may specify that in the case of a breach by a contract shipper the damages may be an amount not exceeding the freight charges computed as the contract rate on the particular shipment, less the cost of handling; (6) must permit "the contract shipper to terminate at any time without penalty upon ninety days' notice"; (7) must provide "for a spread between ordinary rates and rates charged contract shippers which the Commission finds to be reasonable in all the circumstances but which spread shall in no event be more than 15 per centum of the ordinary rates"; (8) must exclude "cargo of the contract shippers which is loaded and carried in bulk without mark or count except liquid bulk cargoes, other than chemicals, in less than full shipload lots"; however, "upon finding that economic factors so warrant, the Commission may exclude from the contract any commodity subject to the foregoing exception";

and (9) must contain "such other provisions not inconsistent herewith as the Commission shall require or permit."

Section 14b provides further that the FMC "shall withdraw permission which it has granted under the authority contained in this section for the use of any contract if it finds, after notice and hearing, that the use of such contract is detrimental to the commerce of the United States or contrary to the public interest, or is unjustly discriminatory or unfair as between shippers, exporters, importers, or ports, or between exporters from the United States and their foreign competitors." A carrier or conference of carriers, under Section 14b, may on ninety days' notice terminate without penalty the contract rate system authorized, in whole or with respect to any commodity; however, "after such termination the carrier or conference of carriers may not reinstitute such contract rate system or part thereof so terminated without prior permission by the Commission in accordance with the provisions of this section."

Section 14b also provides that any "contract, amendment, or modification of any contract not permitted by the Commission shall be unlawful, and contracts, amendments, and modifications shall be lawful only when and as long as permitted by the Commission; before permission is granted or after permission is withdrawn it shall be unlawful to carry out in whole or in part, directly or indirectly, any such contract, amendment, or modification." The term "contract shipper" is defined by Section 14b to mean "a person other than a carrier or conference of carriers who is a party to a contract the use of which may be permitted under this section."

FMC approval is required for a dual rate contract under Section 14b or an anticompetitive agreement under Section 15. These contracts and agreements are required to be disapproved in the event that the FMC finds them to be discriminatory or unfair to shippers or ports, detrimental to the commerce of the United States, or contrary to the public interest.[44] Section 15 requires the FMC also to disapprove anticompetitive agreements if they are discriminatory or unfair to other carriers or which violate other provisions of the Shipping Act. Other specific provisions in Section 14b and 15, if violated, require prior approved agreements to be disapproved. Compliance with the statutory requirements is a prerequisite to the grant of antitrust immunity under Sections 14b and 15.

---

[44]See *FMC v. Aktiebolaget Svenska Amerika Linien*, 390 U.S. 238, regarding public interest. The FMC has held that the *Svenska* test applies to Section 14b agreements as well as Section 15 agreements. See *Latin America/Pacific Coast Steamship Conference and Proposed Contract Rate System*. 14 F.M.C. 172, aff'd in *Latin America/Pacific Coast Steamship Conference v. F.M.C.*, 465 F. 2d 542.

If a dual rate system has a legitimate commercial objective and meets the statutory requirements it generally will be approved by the FMC.[45] However, the FMC has denied approval of single dual rate systems which are designed to cover more than one trading area.[46]

Section 14b(7)[47] provides for a 15 percent maximum spread between contract and non-contract rates, and the FMC is required to approve only spreads which are reasonable in all the circumstances within the 15 percent limitation.

Wharfages, Docks, Warehouses, or Other Terminal Facilities

The activities of marine terminal operators are regulated by the FMC pursuant to the provisions of the Shipping Act, 1916. This entails the processing of terminal agreements, review of terminal tariffs, and policing and regulating terminal practices.

Section 1 of the Shipping Act of 1916, as amended,[48] defines the term "common carrier by water in foreign commerce" as "a common carrier, except ferryboats running on regular routes, engaged in the transportation by water of passengers or property between the United States or any of the Districts, Territories, or possessions and a foreign country, whether in the import or export trade; Provided, That a cargo boat commonly called an ocean tramp shall not be deemed such common carrier by water in foreign commerce." The term "common carrier by water in interstate commerce" means "a common carrier engaged in the transportation by water of passengers or property on the high seas or the Great Lakes on regular routes from port to port between one State, Territory, District, or possession of the United States and any other State, Territory, District or Possession of the United States, or between places in the same Territory, District, or possession." The term "common carrier by water" means "a common carrier by water in foreign commerce or a common carrier by water in interstate commerce on the high seas or the Great Lakes on regular routes from port to port." The term "other person subject to this Act" means "any person not

---

[45]*Pacific Westbound Conference Application to Extend its Exclusive Patronage Contract System to Include the OCP Territory,* 14 S.R.R. 1581, 1595.

[46]*U.S. Atlantic & Gulf/Australia-New Zealand Conference,* 9 F.M.C. 1; *Latin America/Pacific Coast Steamship Conference and Proposed Contract Rate System,* 14 F.M.C. 172.

[47]46 U.S.C. 813a(7). See *North Atlantic Portugal Freight Conference Exclusive Patronage (Triple Rate) System and Contract,* 10 F.M.C. 255, for disapproval of a proposed dual rate system which varied from the 15 percent spread.

[48]46 U.S.C. 801.

included in the term common carrier by water, carrying on the business of forwarding or furnishing wharfage, dock, warehouse, or other terminal facilities in connection with a common carrier by water." The term "person" means "corporations, partnerships, and associations, existing under or authorized by the laws of the United States, or any State, Territory, District or possession thereof, or of any foreign country." Section 33 of the Shipping Act of 1916[49] provides that the "Act shall not be construed to affect the power or jurisdiction of the Interstate Commerce Commission," nor to confer upon the FMC "concurrent power or jurisdiction, over any matter within the power or jurisdiction of such commission; nor shall this Act be construed to apply to intrastate commerce."

The Supreme Court said in *California v. United States*[50] that whatever may be the limitation implied by the phrase "in connection with a common carrier by water" which modifies the grant of jurisdiction to the FMC over those furnishing "wharfage, dock, warehouse, or other terminal facilities," there can be do doubt that wharf storage facilities provided at shipside for cargo which has been unloaded from water carriers are subject to regulation by the FMC.[51] The case of *Baltimore & Ohio R. Co. v. United States*[52] holds that a railroad providing maritime terminal operations is subject to regulation by both the ICC and the FMC, the former with respect to its full operations, the latter with respect to its maritime operations.

In *Port of Bandon v. Oliver J. Olson & Co.*,[53] it was held that the FMC has initial and primary jurisdiction to determine the lawfulness and reasonableness of provisions and practices under tariffs by a port operator so far as the same applies to shipping engaged in interstate commerce. The action was filed by a port operator against a shipowner to recover certain port charges allegedly due by reason of services performed for the shipowner. The court stayed the proceedings, stating (at p. 742) that "the respondent should be allowed a reasonable length of time and opportunity to apply for and obtain" from the FMC "its determination or ruling as to the 'lawfulness and reasonableness' of the pro-

---

[49]46 U.S.C. 832.

[50]320 U.S. 577, 586.

[51]See also *United States v. American Union Transport, Inc.*, 327 U.S. 437.

[52]201 F. 2d 795. The court noted that joint hearings have been held in the past between the ICC and FMC where there has been a clash of jurisdiction. See *Interchange of Freight at Boston Terminals*, 2 U.S.M.C. 671, involving a joint hearing where the FMC examined the railroads' wharf practices, and the ICC (253 I.C.C. 703) considered absorption of wharfage charges by the railroads in their rates.

[53]175 F. Supp. 736, 741. See *Contract Rates — Port of Redwood City*, 2 U.S.M.C. 727; *California v. United States*, 320 U.S. 577.

visions and practices" under the tariff.[54] Likewise, in *Rivoli Trucking Corp. v. New York Shipping Ass'n.*,[55] it was held that primary proceedings charging a defendant, who is subject to the Shipping Act, with a violation of the Shipping Act must be brought before the FMC.

Where a case presents no questions for determination by an agency of special competence to which Congress has committed questions requiring administrative expertise, and when all that remains is for the court to say what the plain words of the statute mean and whether the agency has acted, the doctrine of primary jurisdiction does not apply.[56] In regard to the issue before it in the *River Plate* case, the court said, "on the facts before us the question of approval is no more difficult than the score of yesterday's baseball game; the court can read the score as well as the (administrative agency)."

In *Pennsylvania Motor T. Ass'n. v. Port of Phila. M.T. Ass'n.*,[57] a district court held that it could determine whether a disputed provision was an "agreement," "modification" or "cancellation" as those words are employed in Section 15 of the Shipping Act without doing violence to the role of the administrative agency in the judicial process. The conclusion was predicated under the circumstances of the particular case and upon the fact that the decision called for in the controversy was in no way contingent upon the expertise of the FMC. The issues before the court in the suit for injunctive relief were: (1) Did the court have jurisdiction to enjoin the sudden imposition by pier operators of a compulsory loading and unloading regulation which abrogated a long standing practice of truckers' choice at the port where the only relief sought was the maintenance of the status quo pending an administrative determination on the merits of the regulations of the FMC, and (2) assuming such jurisdiction, upon a balancing of the equities had the plaintiff shown that irreparable harm would result without injunctive relief.

---

[54]See *Mitchell Coal & Coke v. Pennsylvania R. Co.*, 230 U.S. 247; *General American Tank Car Corp. v. El Dorado Terminal Co.*, 308 U.S. 422; *Thompson v. Texas Mexican Ry. Co.*, 328 U.S. 134, 147; *United States v. Western Pacific R. Co.*, 352 U.S. 59.

[55]167 F. Supp. 940, 167 F. Supp. 943. See also *United States Navigation Co. v. Cunard S.S. Co.*, 284 U.S. 474; *Far East Conference v. United States*, 342 U.S. 570; *United States v. Alaska S.S. Co.*, 110 F. Supp. 104; *American Union Transports, Inc. v. River Plate & Brazil Conferences*, 126 F. Supp. 91, aff'd 222 F. 2d 369.

[56]*River Plate and Brazil Conference v. Pressed Steel Car Co.*, 227 F. 2d 60, 63. Cf. *Great Northern Ry. Co. v. Merchants Elevator Co.*, 259 U.S. 285. See also *Isbrandtsen Co. v. United States*, 81 F. Supp. 544, appeal dismissed 336 U.S. 941; *West India Fruit & S.S. Co. v. Seatrain Lines*, 170 F. 2d 775, 779, cert. denied 336 U.S. 908; *United States Trucking Corp. v. American Export Lines, Inc.*, 146 F. Supp. 924, 925, 148 F. Supp. 61.

[57]183 F. Supp. 910.

In *Greater Baton Rouge Port Commission v. United States*,[58] a company licensed to operate a public grain elevator under the United States Warehouse Act[59] had entered into a lease with a certain port commission under which it received a right to operate a public grain elevator within the port area, and a first option on additional grain storage and handling facilities. A subsequent amendment to the lease required the grain company to furnish stevedoring service for vessels calling at the grain elevator, and allowed the grain company to condition the loading and unloading of vessels on the use of the grain company's stevedoring service exclusively. The original lease had not been filed with the FMC for approval, but after the amendment both the original lease and the amendment were filed. The original agreement was approved by the FMC, but the amended agreement was disapproved on the ground that it resulted in a monopoly of the stevedoring service detrimental to the United States.[60]

In contesting the validity of the FMC's order, the port commission conceded that it was subject to the provisions of the Shipping Act and to the jurisdiction of the FMC[61] but the grain company asserted that the Warehouse Act[62] vested in the Secretary of Agriculture exclusive jurisdiction over all activities of a licensed warehouseman, including stevedoring, wharfage, and dockage activities. Both the port commission and the grain company contended that the amended agreement did not come within the purview of Section 15 of the Shipping Act, and that the provisions in the agreement represented the exercise of the free right of managerial judgment by the port commission as owner and the grain company as operator of the property.

In upholding the FMC, the court in the *Greater Baton Rouge* case said (p. 95) that the grain company was subject to the jurisdiction of the FMC, whether or not it was licensed as a warehouseman by the Secretary of Agriculture, that the exclusive lease arrangement was within the scope of Section 15, that the FMC properly approved it, and that the amended lease was within the scope of Section 15 and the FMC properly disapproved it. The court said that if the original agreement came within Section 15 that the amended agreement, which broadened the original agreement to include stevedores, "clearly a maritime concern," came

---

[58]287 F. 2d 86, rehearing denied 293 F. 2d 959, cert. denied 368 U.S. 985.
[59]7 U.S.C. 241 et seq.
[60]See *Baker-Whiteley Coal Co. v. Baltimore & O. R. Co.*, 188 Fed. 405; *Donovan v. Pennsylvania Co.*, 199 U.S. 279; *Isbrandtsen Co. v. United States*, 211 F. 2d 51, 57; *McLean Trucking Co. v. United States*, 321 U.S. 67, 87.
[61]*State of California v. United States*, 320 U.S. 577, 585.
[62]7 U.S.C. 269.

within Section 15. The court said (p. 94) that "Stevedoring is traditionally maritime. Stevedoring of grain requires a close relation between the stevedore and the vessel, a careful inspection of the ship, a sound plan of storage, and skillful execution of the plan. There is a complete separation between the function of the elevator in delivering the grain and the function of the vessel in receiving it. There is no physical connection between vessel and elevator except guidelines to hold the spout discharging grain into a hatch. The elevator worker performs no services on the vessel; the longshoremen perform no services in the elevator or on the wharf."

The grain company argued that its obligation to perform stevedoring services in accordance with specified standards protected vessel owners and operators against unreasonable charges for stevedoring, thus removing any possibility that the agreement could be detrimental to commerce or in any way conflict with Section 17. The court said in reply (p. 95), "No matter how desirable an agreement may appear, no matter how beneficial the monopoly may appear, Congress has commanded that agreements limiting or destroying competition must first be approved by the (FMC) before they may be lawfully carried out. National policy favors free and healthy competition; monopoly is the exception."

In *Alabama Great Southern R.R. Company v. Federal Maritime Commission*,[63] the court affirmed FMC rules requiring the filing of tariffs for terminal services rendered by rail carriers and others who own or control port terminal facilities. The court held that the rules did not infringe upon the jurisdiction of the ICC and were permissible as a means of keeping the FMC informed as to matters within the latter's jurisdiction. The court noted that "at this point we would not be warranted in attempting to delineate the limits of such jurisdiction before any action has been taken or proposed by either Commission." The court concluded that the advance filing requirement in the rules "in no way militates against our conclusion that the Order has placed upon the Petitioners no unreasonable or unpermitted burden."

In *A. P. St. Philip, Inc. v. The Atlantic Land & Improvement Co. and Seaboard Coast Line R.R. Co.*,[64] a marine terminal operator's contract which conditioned access to its terminal facilities upon the exclusive use of a designated tugboat operator was found to be an unreasonable and unjust practice and constituted undue and unreasonable prejudice and disadvantage.

[63]D.C. Cir. No. 19,798, decided April 17, 1967.
[64]Docket No. 69-2, decided December 23, 1969.

34

Use of American Vessels in Coastwise Trade

Section 27 of the Merchant Marine Act of 1920[1] provides that "No merchandise shall be transported by water, or by land and water, on penalty of forfeiture thereof, between points in the United States, including Districts, Territories, and possessions thereof embraced within the coastwise laws, either directly or via a foreign port, or for any part of the transportation, in any other vessel than a vessel built in and documented under the laws of the United States and owned by persons who are citizens of the United States. . . ."

As its language clearly indicates, this clause was enacted to secure to American vessels the coastwise trade of the United States and prohibit the use of foreign vessels in such trade. The enactment clause is not applicable to arrangements falling within the excepting clause. The third proviso states that "this section shall not apply to merchandise transported between points within the continental United States, including Alaska, over through routes heretofore or hereafter recognized by the Interstate Commerce Commission for which routes rate tariffs have been or shall hereafter be filed with said Commission when such routes are in part over Canadian rail lines and their own or other connecting water facilities. . . ."

Section 883 of 46 U.S.C. has been interpreted by the Attorney General of the United States in opinions given to the Secretary of Commerce. In 34 Op. A.G. 355, the Attorney General gave the Secretary of Commerce an opinion on December 31, 1924, stating that the transportation of American grain from an American port to a Canadian port and thence to an American port, either consigned through to the American port or with a present existing intention on the part of those trans-

[1] 46 U.S.C. 883.

porting the grain that the same shall ultimately be transported to an American port, where any part of the transportation is in a foreign vessel, is a violation of 46 U.S.C. 883. In the same opinion, the Attorney General said that where American grain is transported in a foreign vessel from an American port to a Canadian port without existing intent on the part of those responsible for the transportation that the grain shall be transported to an American port and the grain is intermingled and its identity lost, such transportation becomes an exportation from the United States. Whether the subsequent transportation of such grain to an American port is a violation of 46 U.S.C. 883 must be determined by the existing facts in each case. The intention of the shipper, and not the contract of shipment, is the controlling factor in determining whether the transportation is in violation of the statute.

In 37 Op. A.G. 50, an opinion was given by the Attorney General to the Secretary of Commerce on January 23, 1933, relating to the administration and construction of 46 U.S.C. 883. The following question, among others, was submitted by the Secretary of Commerce to the Attorney General for answer:

> (2) Whether the transportation of merchandise on or by the vessels of the Central Vermont Transportation Company over that part of the route from New London, Conn., to New York, N. Y., the shipment of which began at Chicago, across to Canada, thence by Canadian railway lines to Montreal or Quebec, thence by Central Vermont Railway, Inc., to New London, thence from New London to New York by said vessels, a through route recognized by the Interstate Commerce Commission, for which the rate tariffs have been filed, constitutes a violation of [46 U.S.C. 883].

The facts reveal that Central Vermont Transportation Company was operating two vessels in the transportation of merchandise from New York City and New London, and the route of these vessels between these two points was part of the Canadian National-Central Vermont through route over which merchandise was transported between New York City and New England points in the East and Chicago and other points in the West in westward and eastward movements. A considerable portion of this through route passed through Canada with the Canadian National connection furnishing the Canadian rail line connection and the vessels constituting the connecting water facilities. The route was recognized by the Interstate Commerce Commission for which rate tariffs had been filed with said Commission. The stock of the owner of the vessel, Central Vermont Transportation Company, was owned by the Central Vermont Railway Company, a Vermont corporation, and the stock of the latter was, in turn, owned by Canadian National.

It was the opinion of the Attorney General that the route over which the vessels navigated was part of a through route from New York City across to Canada and thence by Canadian rail lines and subsidiaries to Chicago and return, and that rate tariffs for this through route had been filed with the Interstate Commerce Commission, and that the route had been recognized by said Commission. Consequently, the Attorney General said (p. 55), that the transportation referred to in the above question "clearly falls within the exception." The Attorney General concluded (at p. 55) that "the inhibition contained in the enactment clause thereof is not applicable thereto."

The meaning and purport of recognition of a through route by the Interstate Commerce Commission (the Commission has never undertaken to administer 46 U.S.C. 883 and has expressly disclaimed jurisdiction) is nowhere stated in the Merchant Marine Act. This question was discussed by the Commission in *Rail-Lake-and-Rail Rates Via Canada,*[2] wherein it was said:

> . . . If, as the Northern Company and the shippers contend, the receipt and placing in our files of tariffs constitutes recognition, we have recognized these routes. If, as the Transit Corporation and the shipping board contend, something more is necessary to constitute recognition we are nowhere advised what that something more is, or provided with a test or criterion by which to determine under what circumstances and in what cases recognition may be accorded, denied, or revoked.

> Under Section 27 of the Merchant Marine Act, 1920, recognition by us merely operates to stay the application of the section to merchandise transported in such manner as otherwise to be subject to penalty of forfeiture thereof. That section apparently provides that merchandise transported over the routes here considered would in the absence of recognition by us of these routes, be subject to forfeiture. Whether such merchandise is exempt from the penalty because we have recognized the routes is a question of fact to be determined by the court in which enforcement of that forfeiture may be sought. The duty of administering the Merchant Marine Act, 1920, does not rest upon us, and is not within our province to construe its provisions.

It appears from the language in *Rail-Lake-and-Rail-Rates Via Canada* that at least as far as the Commission is concerned, receipt and placing of the tariffs in the files of the Commission applicable to the through routes constitutes recognition.

[2] 93 I.C.C. 633, 642.

The exception in the third proviso relates only to shipments over (and not merely on some part of) the through routes and actually over a Canadian railroad. Thus a foreign-owned vessel is not permitted to carry merchandise in coastwise traffic, over routes wholly within the United States, by the expedient of filing tariffs showing participation in through routes extending over Canadian lines. This holding was made by the Supreme Court in *Central Vermont Co. v. Durning.*[3] In that case, a customs officers had seized merchandise which had been shipped over the Central Vermont from a point in Vermont to New London, Conn., and carried thence by Canadian vessel to New York City. It was contended that the merchandise transported by Canadian vessel was freed from the prohibition of 46 U.S.C. 883 by the proviso that it shall not apply to merchandise transported over through routes recognized by the Commission, where such routes are in part over Canadian rail lines. The Supreme Court answered this contention by stating (at p. 38):

> . . . It is true that all merchandise transported on petitioner's vessels between New London and New York is transported over a part of such through routes as are exempted by the proviso. But the proviso does not speak of transportation merely over a domestic segment of a through route which elsewhere embraces Canadian rail lines. The immunity which it grants is to merchandise transported "over" the through routes described. Even though the merchandise carried between points in New England and New York City by rail and water line might be said to be transported on a through route which embraces Canadian rail lines, it plainly is not transported over the route.
>
> The construction for which petitioner contends does violence to the words of the statute and would thwart its purpose.

---

[3]294 U.S. 33, affirming *Central Vermont Transp. Co. v. Durning,* 71 F. 2d 273.

35

Instrumentalities of Transportation and Services Connected with Transportation

Allowances

Section 15(5) of the Interstate Commerce Act[1] provides:

"If the owner of property transported under this part directly or indirectly renders any service connected with such transportation, or furnishes any instrumentality used therein; the charge and allowance therefor shall be published in this part and shall be no more than is just and reasonable, and the Commission may, after hearing on a complaint or on its own initiative, determine what is a reasonable charge as the maximum to be paid by the carrier or carriers for the services so rendered or for the use of the instrumentality so furnished, and fix the same by appropriate order, which order shall have the same force and effect and be enforced in like manner as the orders above provided for under this section."

Section 6(7) of the Interstate Commerce Act[2] provides:

"No carrier, unless otherwise provided by this part, shall engage or participate in the transportation of passengers or property, as defined in this part, unless the rates, fares, and charges upon which the same are transported by said carrier have been filed and published in accordance with the provisions of this part; nor shall any carrier charge or demand or collect or receive a greater or less or different compensation for such transportation of passengers or property, or for any service in connection therewith, between the points named in such tariffs than the rates, fares, and charges which are specified in the tariff filed and in effect at the time; nor shall any carrier refund or remit in any manner or by any device any portion of the rates, fares, and charges so specified, nor extend to any shipper or person any privileges or facilities in the transportation of passengers or property, except such as are specified in such tariffs."

[1]49 U.S.C. 15(15). Comparable provisions — Sections 225, 314 and 415.
[2]49 U.S.C. 6(7). Comparable provisions — Sections 217(b), (d); 218(a); 306(c), (d), (e); 405 (c), (e).

Under Section 1(3) (a) of the Interstate Commerce Act[3] the term "transportation" includes "locomotives, cars, and other vehicles, vessels, and all instrumentalities and facilities of shipment or carriage, irrespective of ownership or of any contract, express or implied, for the use thereof, and all services in connection with the receipt, delivery, elevation, and transfer in transit, ventilation, refrigeration or icing, storage, and handling of property transported." Transportation subject to regulation begins when the merchandise has been placed in the carrier's possession; and services in connection with transportation, as used in Sections 1(3), 6(7) and 15(15), has been uniformly construed to mean services rendered while a shipment is in custody and control of the carrier, or services which the carrier is legally obliged to perform.[4]

The definition of transportation in Section 1(3) (a) of the Interstate Commerce Act is broader than the pure transportation service of which common carriage consists; it includes services such as icing cars, weighing, storage, and loading and unloading, which may occur before or after actual carriage.[5] The purpose of having the Commission supervise these extra-carriage services was to prevent overcharges and discriminations made under pretext of performing such additional services, by including them in the single term "transportation" and thereby subjecting them to provisions of the I.C. Act respecting publication and reasonableness of charges.[6]

What constitutes a transportation service under the I.C. Act is a question of fact to be determined by the Commission.[7] It is well settled that under the I.C. Act the term "transportation" has a broader meaning than the mere carriage of persons or goods from place to place, since it embraces a variety of connected services as well.[8] Thus, it includes services performed at origin points, before a line-haul movement has been initiated, e.g., *Railroad Retirement Board v. Duquesne Warehouse Co.*;[9] services performed at intermediate points while a line-haul move-

---

[3]49 U.S.C. 1(3) (a). Comparable provisions — Sections 203(a) (19); 302(g), (h). See Section 303(g) for limitation of I.C. Act as to transportation intraharbor or by small watercraft. See *Long Island R. Co. v. Delaware, L. & W.R. Co.*, 183 F. Supp. 319, 323-4.

[4]*Eastern Central M. Carriers v. Baltimore & O. R. Co.*, 314 I.C.C. 5, 47. See also *Sugar from La. to Milwaukee and Battle Creek*, 305 I.C.C. 553, 558, stating that an allowance may not be made for a service which the carrier does not hold itself out to perform as a part of the transportation offered.

[5]*Republic Carloading & Distrib. Co. v. Missouri Pac. R. Co.*, 302 F. 2d 381, 388.

[6]*Ibid.*

[7]*United States v. Wabash R.R.*, 321 U.S. 403, 408; *United States v. American Sheet & Tin Plate Co.*, 301 U.S. 402, 408.

[8]See, *e.g.*, section 203(a)(19); *Boynton v. Virginia*, 364 U.S. 454, 459-60, 463-64; *Southern R. R. v. Prescott*, 240 U.S. 632, 637-38.

[9]326 U.S. 446, 453-55.

ment is in progress, e.g., *Boynton v. Virginia;*[10] *Baltimore & O. R. R. v. United States;*[11] and services performed at destination points, after a line-haul movement has been completed, *e.g., Cleveland, C. C. & St. L. Ry. v. Dettlebach;*[12] *Baggett Transp. Co. v. United States.*[13]

Under the I.C. Act an allowance shall be no more than is just and reasonable. There are two basic criteria for making this determination, namely, (1) the allowance must not exceed the cost of providing the service, and (2) the allowance must not exceed the shipper's cost of providing the service.[14] Whichever of these sums is the lower marks the maximum a carrier may pay.[15] An allowance which does not meet the above criteria would be an unlawful concession.

In *United States v. Lehigh Valley Railroad Company*[16] the defendant railroad paid a commission to a firm of forwarders whose business consisted of performing certain services for importers, which included the bringing of their goods from the place of purchase in Europe to their destination in the United States. Defendant railroad paid this firm a salary and commissions for sending goods over its lines. The lower court restrained the defendant from making these payments. The court first decided that, although the forwarders were not owners of goods, they were shippers. It then decided that the salary and commission payments constituted unlawful rebates.

It had been contended that the payment was authorized by 49 U.S.C. 15(15), but the court held that this was not a "service" or "instrumentality" connected "with transportation" within the meaning of the section. The court said:

> It is true no doubt that George W. Sheldon & Company in the performance of the services for which it is paid maintains offices here and abroad, advertising the railroad, solicits traffic for it, does various other useful things, and in short we assume, benefits the roads and earns its money, if it were allowable to earn money in that way. It is true also that in *Interstate Commerce Commission v. F. H. Peavey & Company,* 222 U.S. 42, an owner of property transported was held entitled under Section 15 of the Act to Regulate Commerce to an allowance for furnishing a part of the

[10]364 U.S. at 459-60, 463-64.
[11]305 U.S. 507, 513, 516-17.
[12]239 U.S. 588, 593-95.
[13]278 F. Supp. 912.
[14]See *Pickup and Delivery Allowance, St. Louis and Kansas City,* 64 M.C.C. 163. See also *Delivery Allowance in Central Territory,* 309 I.C.C. 187; *Pickup of Multiple Shipments at Rochester, N.Y.,* 309 I.C.C. 413.
[15]*Allowances for Privately Owned Tank Cars,* 258 I.C.C. 371.
[16]222 Fed. 685; affirmed 243 U.S. 444. The *Lehigh* case was cited with approval in *United States v. Chicago Heights Trucking Co.,* 310 U.S. 344, 353.

transportation that the carrier was bound to furnish. . . . But, that case goes to the verge of what is permitted by the act. The services rendered by George W. Sheldon & Company although in a practical sense "connected with such transportation," were not connected with it as necessary part of the carriage — were not "transportation service," . . . and in our opinion were not such services as were contemplated in the Act of June 29, 1906, 3591, Sec. 4, 34 Stat. 589, amending Section 15 of the original act. On the other hand, the allowance for them falls within the plain meaning of Section 2 of the Act of 1906, to which we referred above.

It is true that where a facility is furnished by a shipper in accordance with the authorization contained in Section 15(15), the Commission, in determining what is a just and reasonable charge or allowance for such facility, will permit a shipper to realize a fair rate of return on his investment in the facility.[17] However, the question involved in such situations is one of determining what is a just and reasonable rate when the section is admittedly applicable. The authorities cited have no application to a case where the question is whether any payment at all is authorized by the section.[18]

Union Pacific Railroad Company v. United States[19] involved payments, at the instance of the Union Pacific, by the City of Kansas City, Kansas, to induce tenants to move from the terminal market at Kansas City, Missouri. In framing the judgment in the case the court had to consider whether it would be proper to enjoin the payment of even the actual costs of the tenants moving from the Kansas City, Missouri, market to the new market in Kansas City, Kansas. The court refused to permit any such payments, saying:

> In prior sections of this opinion, it has been pointed out that any concession by any person or corporation in respect to transportation is forbidden by the federal transportation statutes. The paragraph of the injunction now under examination undertakes to apply this rule so that no cash payments or rental credits may be given. It is clear that insofar as such cash or credit is a "rebate, concession or discrimination" such an injunction is proper, but do all payments to induce dealers to rent space in the terminal fall in these classifications? The trial court said:
>
>> The proposed payments to Missouri dealers to induce them to move to a new market not being made to all tenants at the new market and being in the nature of bonuses the amount of which was not based on

[17]*Use of Privately Owned Refrigerator Cars*, 201 I.C.C. 323, 261 I.C.C. 291. See also *Mitchell Coal and Coke Co. v. P.B.R. o.*, 38 I.C.C. 40; *New Orleans Terminal Allowances*, 42 I.C.C. 748; *United Chemical and Organic Products Co. v. Director General*, 112 I.C.C. 687.

[18]It should also be noted that Section 15(13) requires that any charge or allowance permitted shall be published in the tariffs and schedules filed with the I.C.C.

[19]313 U.S. 450.

actual loss or expense, fall within the classification of discriminations prohibited by the Elkins Act.

The words of the injunction, however, go farther and forbid payments even though the payments are in all fairness and strictness limited to actual and necessary expenses and losses in moving an establishment. Consequently, in deciding the form of the injunction, we need to determine the breadth of language necessary "to suppress the unlawful practices" and preclude their revival. The district court summarized in findings of fact and conclusions of law the constant activity of the Union Pacific in pressing forward the idea of the Terminal. It had before it the testimony that the road sought, meticulously, to avoid conflict with the Elkins Act and yet gain the installation of the market; that the railway representatives acted with the City committees and talked with prospective tenants. Railroad influence pervaded each City action, and in those circumstances, the decree must be molded to meet the danger of subtle moves against the equality between shippers guaranteed by the Elkins Act.

Where, as here, the action of the City in giving cash and rental credits is, as we have decided, part of a plan in respect to transportation resulting in an advantage to shippers, we conclude that the giving of any cash, rental credit, free or reduced rents, to induce leasing of space in the Terminal is contrary to the Elkins Act. Even if we assume that nothing will be given except the actual costs of removal, the receipt of those costs would put the shipper in a preferred position to all other shippers using the facilities of an interstate carrier who did not receive such concessions. The act condemns any device "whereby any other advantage (than lower tariffs) is given. . . ." (pp. 469-471)

In *Manufacturers Railway Company v. United States*[20] the court recognized that unduly large allowances to a railway owned by a brewery-shipper would be equivalent to the payment of rebates to the brewery. In *Davis v. Cornell*[21] a shipper ordered empty cars for loading to be ready on a specified day. The cars were not shipped and the shipper sued the carrier on the ground that there had been an express contract to supply the cars on this day. The court found that "the obligation of the common carrier implied in the tariff is to use diligence to provide, upon reasonable notice, cars for loading at the time desired."

The contract to supply cars for loading on a day named provides for a special advantage to the particular shipper. . . . It was not necessary to prove that a preference resulted in fact. The assumption by the carrier of the additional obligation was necessarily a preference. . . . The paramount requirement that tariff provisions be strictly adhered to, so that shippers may receive equal treatment, presents an insuperable obstacle to recovery.

[20]246 U.S. 457, 486-487.
[21]264 U.S. 560.

Thus *In the Matter of Allowances to Elevators by the Union Pacific Railroad Company*[22] the Commission stated:

> It is true that under the terms of Section 15 of the amended act to regulate commerce a shipper may receive, in the rates charged, a just and reasonable allowance from a carrier for any service or instrumentality furnished by him in connection with the transportation of its own property. This provision, however, must be read in connection with the other provisions of the law forbidding and making unlawful any arrangement or practice that results in any undue preference or an unjust discrimination in favor of one shipper as against others, or that results in a rebate or other departure from the lawfully published rates. And, therefore, if the allowance involves a profit over and above the actual cost of the service rendered, it becomes, when made to a shipper, a rebate and an unlawful discrimination to the extent of the profit realized. It is not a rebate when it does not exceed the actual cost. But to avoid that fundamental objection, the actual cost of the service rendered must be the limit of the allowance.

And in *Use of Privately Owned Refrigerator Cars*[23] the Commission found that any allowances paid to the shipper-owner of private cars, including meat packers and their operating subsidiaries or agents, by the railroads as mileage in excess of the ownership cost, including a fair return on the investment, are unreasonable, unjustly discriminatory, and unlawful rebates and concessions.

In the Matter of Allowances to Elevators by the Union Pacific Railroad Company[24] carrier furnished "elevation" services consisting of unloading grain from cars or from grain-carrying vessels into a grain elevator and loading it out after a period of storage. Elevation is a service which a carrier may provide for the benefit of its shippers, and it may provide such elevation by constructing and operating an elevator of its own or by making arrangements with the owner of an elevator to furnish the service. The Union Pacific had made such arrangements with Peavey and Company, who besides operating elevators and furnishing this service to the carrier's shippers, was an extensive buyer, seller, and shipper of grain itself. The result was that practically all of the grain going into Peavey's elevators belonged to itself. It was held that to allow Peavey to make a profit on the elevation amounted to a rebate, the Commission saying (p. 89) "It is true that under the terms

[22]12 I.C.C. 85.

[23]201 I.C.C. 323. It has been held that carriers may reimburse shippers who furnish tank cars for movement of their products provided that such payments are the subject of published schedules and are "no more than is just and reasonable." *New York Central R. Co. v. United States*, 199 F. Supp. 955, 957.

[24]12 I.C.C. 85.

of section 15 of the amended act to regulate commerce a shipper may receive, in the rates charged, a just and reasonable allowance from a carrier for any service or instrumentality furnished by him in connection with the transportation of its property," but this provision "must be read in connection with the other provisions of the law forbidding and making unlawful any arrangement or practice that results in an undue preference or an unjust discrimination in favor of one shipper as against others, or that results in a rebate or other departure from the lawfully published rates." Therefore, the Commission commented, "if the allowance involves a profit over and above the actual cost of the service rendered, it becomes, when made to a shipper, a rebate and unlawful discrimination to the extent of the profit realized."

It is not a rebate when the allowance does not exceed the actual cost, but to avoid the fundamental objection, the actual cost of the service rendered must be the limit of the allowance. Accordingly, the Commission reduced the allowance to Peavey from 1¼ cents a hundred pounds to ¾ cents a hundred pounds which would "fully and amply cover the actual cost of the elevation contemplated in the law, without returning a profit and thus becoming a rebate." Significantly, the Commission, in the course of its decision, pointed out that the profit made on the elevation services had enabled Peavey to outbid its competitors in the purchase of grain from producers.

The Commission issued a cease and desist order in *Shaw Warehouse Co. v. Southern Ry. Co.*[25] based upon the premise that the carrier was engaged in a discriminatory practice by providing facilities to warehousemen and others at less than fair rental value. The case was sustained by a district court in *Southern Ry. Co. v. United States.*[26]

In *Southern Pacific Company v. H. Moffat Company*[27] the Southern Pacific entered into a written contract with the Western Likestock Service Company, owned by Swift and Armour, to operate certain corrals owned by the Southern Pacific for the purpose of feeding cattle in transit. The Service Company was paid by the railroad, which in turn collected for the service from the shippers. During the years 1938, 1939 and 1940, Swift received dividends from Service Company based on profits made after the feeding of cattle owned by the plaintiff. The question was whether the railroad could recover from the defendant more than the actual cost of the service to Service Company. It was held that it could not, because otherwise a profit would be made by Armour

---

[25]308 I.C.C. 609.
[26]186 F. Supp. 29.
[27]45 F. Supp. 924.

and Swift resulting in discrimination between shippers in violation of Section 2 of the I.C. Act. The court said:

> It is clear from the terms of the contract made with Western Livestock Service Company that plaintiff thereby effected a means by which Swift and Company, as a shipper of livestock through the Sparks Yards, could not only obtain service for rest, feeding and watering of its own livestock, so in transit, at actual cost but in addition thereto make a substantial profit, in the performance of similar required service, upon the part of plantiff, for other shippers of livestock. This presents a situation clearly in violation of the section of the statutes above quoted and the general principle of law controlling in transportation in interstate commerce.

In *Louisville and Nashville Railroad Company v. Mottley*[28] the Supreme Court held illegal a contract granting free passes to a passenger in release of his claim for damages for personal injuries caused by the carrier. The vice was that this was the sale of transportation for other than money. The court said:

> In our opinion, after the passage of the Commerce Act the railroad could not lawfully accept from Mottley and his wife any compensation "different" in kind from that mentioned in its published schedule of rates. And it cannot be doubted that the rates or charges specified in such schedule were payable only in money. They could not be paid in any other way, without producing the utmost confusion and defeating the policy established by the acts regulating commerce. The evident purpose of Congress was to establish uniform rates for transportation, to give all the same opportunity to know what the rates were as well as to have the equal benefit of them. To that end the carrier was required to print, post and file its schedules and to keep them open to public inspection. No change could be made in the rates embraced by the schedules except upon notice to the Commission and to the public. But an examination of the schedules would be of no avail and would not ordinarily be of any practical value if the published rates could be disregarded in special or particular cases by the acceptance of property of various kinds, and of such value as the parties immediately concerned chose to put upon it, in place of money for the services performed by the carrier.

In *New Haven Railroad v. Interstate Commerce Commission*[29] the Chesapeake & Ohio Railroad sold coal for delivery in Connecticut for $2.75 a ton. The cost of the coal to the Chesapeake & Ohio at the point of purchase plus the cost of shipment of the coal into Connecticut beyond its lines was $2.47 a ton. Therefore, for carrying the coal over its own lines the railroad realized 28 cents; but the tariff rate for such transportation over its own lines was $1.45 per ton. The question before the court was, as stated by the court itself, as follows:

[28]219 U.S. 467.
[29]200 U.S. 361.

Has a carrier, engaged in interstate commerce, the power to contract to sell and transport . . . when the price stipulated in the contract does not pay the cost of purchase, the cost of delivery, and the published freight rates?

It was held that the carrier had no such power because it resulted in a discrimination as against other dealers in coal, in violation of the I.C. Act. The Chesapeake & Ohio claimed it was acting in the dual capacity of dealer and common carrier. It contended that the difference between the price for which is bought the coal at the point of shipment plus the tariff rate for transportation of the coal over its lines and beyond its lines, and the price at which it sold the coal, constituted a loss borne by it as a dealer in coal, and hence, the full published rate for transportation over its lines was being paid. In answer to this contention the court said:

> . . . in view of the positive command of the second section of the Act, that no departure from the published rate shall be made, "directly or indirectly," how can it in reason be held that a carrier may take itself from out the statute in every case by simply electing to be a dealer and transport a commodity in that character? For, of course, if a carrier has a right to disregard the published rates by resorting to a particular form of dealing, it must follow that there is no obligation on the part of a carrier to adhere to the rates, because doing so is merely voluntary.

The pertinency of the *New Haven* case can be shown in still another way. The provisions in the I.C. Act against rebates, discriminations and concessions, including the provisions of the Elkins Act, are intended to prevent discriminations between shippers, since the effect of such discriminations is to give some shippers a competitive advantage over others unrelated to efficiency or any other factors entitling the favored shippers to a competitive advantage on any sound economic basis. In the *New Haven* case the Supreme Court refused to allow a sale at less than the various cost factors entering into the product plus the published freight rates by conclusively presuming that anything less than that received meant that the Chesapeake & Ohio, as a dealer in coal, was paying less than the published freight rates. The court thus insured that if a carrier did become a shipper it would not be a favored shipper.

The foregoing authorities involve practices which contain a degree of inherent discrimination. Such practices have received judicial disapproval, and the disapproval of the Commission, by being declared "devices" made unlawful by the Act to Regulate Commerce and the acts amendatory thereto, including the Elkins Act. As illustrated by *Davis v. Cornwell*,[30] such condemnation may properly be forthcoming even if the

[30] 264 U.S. 560.

discrimination is potential rather than actual. In the *Davis* case, Cornwell ordered of a station agent empty cars to be ready on a day certain. Failing to get the cars on the day specified, action was brought against the carrier. The obligation of the carrier implied in the tariff was to use diligence to provide, upon reasonable notice, cars for loading at the time desired.

A contract to furnish cars on a certain day thus imposed a greater obligation than that implied in the tariff. The contract therefore called for a discrimination in favor of Cornwell, was unlawful, and recovery was denied. The court said that it was not necessary to prove that a preference resulted in fact as the assumption by the carrier of the additional obligation was necessarily a preference. Thus it was immaterial whether the contract, if carrier out, would have in fact resulted in Cornwell's getting his cars sooner than other shippers.

Although the duty of unloading carload freight ordinarily rests with shipper or consignee, it is a transportation service within the definition of Section 1(3); the carrier, therefore, may under just and reasonable rules, assume obligation of unloading cars or pay a just and reasonable allowance therefor.[31]

Where motor carriers unload bulk cement from their trailers into consignee's silo without extra cost to consignee, the Commission, in *Allowance, Unloading Cement, Covered Hopper Cars — East, supra,* said (p. 745) that no valid reason appeared for permitting one mode of transport to perform the unloading and denying that right to the other, especially where its nonuse was causing a loss of traffic; it is no more an inherent feature of the one than of the other. In that case, the railroads, under the proposed schedules, held out to perform, or to assist in performing, the unloading service as a part of their obligations under

---

[31]*Allowance, Unloading Cement, Covered Hopper Cars — East,* 313 I.C.C. 743, 747, 744. If a carrier contracts with a shipper for the use of terminal facilities, if a shipper performs his own pickup or delivery service, if a shipper makes his own provision for a portion of the transportation, or if a shipper furnishes switching service or elevator service, and so long as the service or facility furnished is contemplated by the established tariff, a reasonable allowance to the shipper for furnishing the service or facility is permissible. *United States v. Baltimore & Ohio R. Co.,* 231 U.S. 274; *American Trucking Associations, Inc. v. United States,* 17 F. Supp. 655; *Mitchell Coal Co. v. Pennsylvania Co. v. Thompson,* 288 Fed. 167; *Interstate Commerce Commission v. Diffenbaugh,* 222 U.S. 42; *Union Pacific Railroad v. Updike Grain Co.,* 222 U.S. 215. See also *Delivery Allowance in Central Territory,* 309 I.C.C. 187, 188, where the Commission said that before an allowance to shippers for a carrier service may be approved, the shippers' average costs for that service when performed by or for shippers must be shown; *Forwarder Pickup Allowances, Los Angeles and Anaheim,* 310 I.C.C. 469, 471-2; *Pickup of Multiple Shipments at Rochester, N.Y.,* 309 I.C.C. 413, 415.

the line-haul rates, under arrangements that appeared practicable and lawful. The Commission held (p. 750) that there appeared to be no legal obstacle to their payment of a just and reasonable allowance where such services were performed by the consignee.

In an application for operating authority as a common carrier by motor vehicle to transport bulk liquid fertilizer in *Delaware Exp. Co. Extension — Liquid Fertilizers,*[32] applicant proposed to furnish the shipper's consignees with mobile storage tanks into which the fertilizer would be unloaded from the line-haul trailer. The opposing motor common carriers were willing to provide only the line-haul service and were not willing to furnish the storage tanks. Applicant's proposal was considered an integral part of the transportation service required by the shipper in instances in which consignees lacked storage facilities. Applicant proposed also to station self-propelled spreader tanks and crews to apply the fertilizer to the soil. This was held to be a nontransportation service and not relevant to the issue of public convenience and necessity.

When a carrier offers a lesser service for a lower rate than the rate for a complete service, and the offer at the lower rate is accepted by shipper, the carrier is not obligated to do more than it has offered to do for the lower rate, and no allowance can be made to the shipper for performing a service the avoidance of which is the consideration for the lower rate. Thus, if rates have been established for a complete, door-to-door TOFC service, carriers may also publish lower rates for service in which the shipper furnishes the trailer, loads and unloads it, and performs the drayage, and for service in which the shipper also furnishes the flatcar, without making allowances to the shipper.[33]

In *Central Railroad Company of New Jersey v. United States*[34] the defendant leased an entire railroad from a coal mining company, agreeing to pay the latter a certain rental each year and to transport the lessor's coal at reduced rates. In holding that to transport the coal at reduced rates would constitute an unlawful rebate, the court answered the contention that the reduced rates were payments for the use of an instrumentality of a commerce as follows:

> The defense that the allowances were merely payments for the use of an instrumentality of commerce . . . requires only a word. The Lehigh and Susquehanna Railroad is not an instrumentality furnished by the shipper, for whose use the carrier may lawfully make compensation. For all present purposes, the Lehigh and Susquehanna Railroad is not the property of the

[32]92 M.C.C. 718.
[33]*Eastern Central M. Carriers Assn. v. Baltimore & O. R. Co.,* 314 I.C.C. 5, 45-6.
[34]229 Fed. 501; cert. den. 241 U.S. 658.

Navigation Company, but is the defendant's own property, for the use of which it can make no allowance to a shipper.

Switching Services

The term "cross-town switching" is commonly known to mean a local transfer from one industry to another within the same switching district; it is synonymous with "intracity switching," that is, for example, a local transfer from one elevator or mill to another which takes place as an independent transaction after the inbound transportation is completed and before the outbound transportation begins. When the cross-town switching is over one line only it is called an intraterminal movement, and when over two or more lines are involved it is an interterminal movement; intradistrict switching is a complete service in and of itself having no relation to any road-haul movement.[35]

Intermediate switching includes all the elements of switching performed by a carrier which neither originates nor terminates the shipment nor performs a line-haul on it, the extent of the carrier's participation being only that of a connection between two other carriers.[36] Connection terminal switching includes all the elements of switching performed at origin and destination terminals by carriers, which as to the particular traffic do not provide line-haul service and do not provide intermediate switching service. This type of switching has been referred to frequently as reciprocal switching which is less descriptive than connection terminal switching.[37]

The Commission some years ago was concerned with the practice of railroads making payments to large industrial companies for the switching of cars within their yards under the assumption that it was the obligation of the railroads to perform this switching service and, hence, under Section 15(15) of the I.C. Act[38] — sometimes called the Shipper's Allowance Clause — that they could lawfully pay the industries for doing so. The railroads and industries in question contended that line-haul rates include delivery at destination and that delivery of cars at industrial plants is not completed until they are finally spotted or placed for unloading. But the Commission considered that payment for such services could well constitute rebating and the grant of preferential services to large industries maintaining railroad yards, tracks and locomotives, in

---

[35]*Enid Board of Trade v. Atchison, T. & S. F. Ry. Co.*, 256, I.C.C. 153, 154.
[36]*Intermediate Switching at Evansville, Ind.*, 256 I.C.C. 703, 704.
[37]*Intermediate Switching at Evansville, Ind.*, 256 I.C.C. 703 (footnote, p. 716).
[38]49 U.S.C. 15(15).

violation of Section 6(7) of the I.C. Act.[39] The Commission, therefore, instituted an investigation known as *Ex Parte 104, Practices of Carriers Affecting Operating Revenues or Expenses,*[40] *In United States v. American Sheet & Tin Plate Co.*[41] the scope of this investigation is outlined and the principles determined and summarized (pp. 404-405):

> Upon its own motion the Commission instituted an investigation known as "Ex Parte No. 104, Practices of Carriers Affecting Operating Revenues or Expenses." Part II of that proceeding had to do with terminal services. Voluminous evidence was adduced largely consisting of testimony by operating officials of carriers and traffic representatives of shippers touching the service of spotting cars at points upon the systems of plant trackage maintained by large industries. The Commission's report summarized its conclusions based on the evidence as to conditions at approximately two hundred industrial plants where spotting allowances were paid by the carriers and numerous plants where such services were performed by the carrier. The Commission found that line-haul rates had not been fixed to compensate the carriers for the performance of the service in question and that the railroads, after fixing their rates, had assumed a burden not previously borne by them. It found that § 15(13) of the Act permitting allowances by carriers to those performing a portion of the service of transportation had been made the instrument of abuse by the payment of unwarranted allowances and added: "When a carrier is prevented at its ordinary operating convenience from reaching points of loading or unloading within a plant, without interruption or interference by the desires of an industry or the disabilities of its plant, such as the manner in which the industrial operations are conducted, the arrangement or condition of its tracks, weighing service, or similar circumstances, . . . the service beyond the point of interruption or interference is in excess of that performed in simple switching or team-track delivery." In conclusion, the Report states that payment for or exemption of the cost of service performed beyond such points of interruption or interference is in violation of § 6, provides the means by which the industry enjoys a preferential service not accorded to shippers generally, dissipates the carriers's funds and revenues, is not in conformity with the efficient or economical management contemplated by the Interstate Commerce Act and is not in the public interest. . . .

Thus, as stated by the court, the principle announced by the Commission in *Ex Parte 104* is that the obligation of railroads to deliver cars at an industrial plant shall not extend beyond the point of inter-

---

[39]49 U.S.C. 6(7).

[40]209 I.C.C. 11.

[41]301 U.S. 402. No orders were made in this case upon the Commission's main report in *Ex Parte* 104; but thereafter a division made supplemental reports, and upon such reports issued cease and desist orders against appellee and five other industrial companies. Each of the appellees commenced action to set aside these orders and the causes were consolidate for hearing and were disposed of upon a single record in one opinion. 15 F. Supp. 711.

ruption or interference caused by the operations of the industry or the disabilities of the plant, and that the switching service required for delivery shall not exceed that performed in simple switching or team-track delivery. In *United States v. American Sheet & Tin Plate Co.*[42] the court concluded (p. 411):

> . . . It is sufficient now to say that in every case the Commission found, upon sufficient evidence, that the cars were, in the first instance, placed upon lead tracks, interchange tracks or sidings and subsequently spotted from these tracks; in each instance the spotting service involved one or more operations in addition to the placing of the car on interchange tracks, such as moving it to plant scales for weighing, or some additional burden, such as conformance to the convenience of the plant, supply of special motive power required by the plant's layout or trackage or some other element which called for excessive service greater than that involved in team track spotting or spotting on an ordinary industrial siding or spur. We are unable to say that the findings in respect of the individual plants lacked support in the evidence. We are, therefore, bound to accept them and to hold the orders lawful.

In *United States v. Pan American Petroleum Corp., supra*[43] the court said (p. 157):

> . . . The Commission held that, in the circumstances disclosed at each of the plants under consideration, the carriers' obligation of delivery was fulfilled by placing or receiving cars on interchange tracks and that the moving and spotting of cars in the industries' plants formed no part of the service covered by the line-haul rate. . . .

> . . . The orders should not have been set aside, and the decrees must be . . . *Reversed.*

In *United States v. U.S. Smelting, Refining & Mining Co., supra*[44] the court said (p. 197):

> Obviously the plant services at Leadville are different from those at Midvale, Garfield, and Murray under the 1938 tariff, which only emphasizes

---

[42]301 U.S. 402. See also *United States v. Pan American Petroleum Corp.,* 304 U.S. 156, 157; *Inland Steel Co. v. United States,* 306 U.S. 153; *Hanna Furnace Corp. v. United States, per curiam,* 323 U.S. 667; *Corn Products Refining Co. v. United States, per curiam,* 331 U.S. 790; *United States v. U.S. Smelting, Refining & Mining Co.,* 339 U.S. 186.

[43]An appeal from decrees of a three-judge court setting aside orders of the Commission in nine cases which were consolidated for a hearing and decided in a single opinion (18 F. Supp. 624). The orders commanded the railroads to cease and desist from the payment of allowances for switching services performed by the industrial companies.

[44]An appeal from judgment of a three-judge court setting aside orders of the Commission enjoining appellee railroads from performing various switching and spotting services as a part of line-haul transportation at three plants of American Smelting, Refining & Mining Co., and at one plant of U.S. Smelting & Mining Co.

the wisdom of Congress in empowering the Commission to fix the point where line-haul begins and ends with a view to giving all shippers equivalent service. The Commission has standardized such service as team track or simple placement switching. What we now hold is that the Commission has the power to fix the point at which line-haul carrier service begins and ends.

This is necessary because the need for switching varies from plant to plant; indeed, some plants may need no intraplant switching service Thus, unless the Commission can fix the beginning and ending point of the line-haul, some shippers would pay an identical line-haul rate for less service than that required by other industrial plants. See *Baltimore & Ohio R. Co. v. United States,* 305 U.S. 507, 526. A different point fixed by the carrier in its tariff gives service in excess of that accorded shippers generally as established in *Ex Parte* 104, and therefore amounts to an unlawful preferential service. . . .

In *A. O. Smith Corp. Terminal Allowance,*[45] the Commission held that where switching service is performed at an industry plant such service constitutes transportation service which the carrier is obligated to perform under it line-haul rates, and if the industry performs the switching service, an allowance, representing the carrier's minimum per-car cost, is a maximum reasonable charge to be paid by the carrier.

Where a carrier does not absorb switching charges to one industry while absorbing the cost of switching services to competitors and other industries where the switching service is greater, this amounts to an unreasonable practice in violation of Section 1(6).[46]

In *Department of Defense v. Southern Ry. Co.,*[47] the Commission said that providing switching service to industries without charge while refusing to do so at nearby military installations was not conclusive evidence of a violation of the I.C. Act; the refusal to perform switching service free of charge was not unreasonable when the service sought would substantially exceed that ordinarily rendered for industries generally in the area and was similar to that performed by the Government at other military installations throughout the South; and the total cost for performing the service substantially exceeded the amount assessed therefor. In *Department of Defense v. Northern Pac. Ry. Co.,*[48] the Commission said that defendants' refusal to perform switching at a military installation was not unreasonable when restricted clearances and hazardous crossings over which they had no control created dangerous operating conditions and would cause interruptions, delays, and breaks in service;

---

[45]313 I.C.C. 615, 622.
[46]*Albers Bros. Milling Co. v. Great Northern Ry. Co.,* 256 I.C.C. 491, 499.
[47]309 I.C.C. 699, 701-2.
[48]309 I.C.C. 691, 695-6.

and comparisons of requested service with switching practices of railroads within other military installations and industrial plants or with operations of railroads at highway crossings outside the industrial plants and military installations were neither relevant nor material.

Switch Connections

Under Section 1(9), it is provided that "any common carrier subject to the provisions of this part, upon application of any lateral, branch line of railroad, or of any shipper tendering interstate traffic for transportation, shall construct, maintain, and operate upon reasonable terms a switch connection with any such lateral, branch line of railroad, or private side track which may be constructed to connect with its railroad, where such connection is reasonably practicable and can be put in with safety and will furnish sufficient business to justify the construction and maintenance of the same; and shall furnish cars for the movement of such traffic to the best of its ability without discrimination in favor of or against any such shipper.

"If any common carrier shall fail to install and operate any such switch or connection as aforesaid, on application therefor in writing by any shipper or owner of such lateral, branch line of railroad, such shipper or owner of such lateral, branch line of railroad may make complaint to the Commission, as provided in section thirteen of this part, and the Commission shall hear and investigate the same and shall determine as to the safety and practicability thereof and justification and reasonable compensation therefor, and the Commission may make an order, as provided in section fifteen of this part, directing the common carrier to comply with the provisions of this section in accordance with such order, and such order shall be enforced as hereinafter provided for the enforcement of all other orders by the Commission, other than orders for the payment of money."

The Commission has on numerous occasions invoked its jurisdiction under Section 1(9) of the I.C. Act in order to require a railroad to provide a switch connection from its line to a lateral spur line or private side track where such connection is reasonably practical and is otherwise justified. However, in order for this section to apply, the party[49] would have to own the line to be connected by the switch.

---

[49]*Union Carbide Corp. v. Norfolk & Western Ry. Co.*, 323 I.C.C. 65. Cf. *J. K. Dering Coal Co. v. Cleveland, Cincinnati, Chicago & St. Louis Ry. Co.*, 96 I.C.C. 143; order sustained, *Cleveland, Cincinnati, Chicago & St. Louis Railway Company v. United States*, et al. 275 U.S. 404. See Section 6(11), physical connection between rail line and docks, and Section 1(21), rail carriers required to extend lines and provide themselves with safe and adequate car service facilities.

Lease of Rail Properties or Facilities to Shippers

The Commission has long held that lease of rail property or facilities to a shipper for that shipper's sole use does not come within the provisions of the I.C. Act, so long as the carrier is fully compensated by the rental payments.[50]

Authority Held by the Commission to Regulate Car Service of Railroads

Congress has granted the Commission authority to alleviate any car supply problem arising from poor utilization or distribution through car service directions or rules and regulations. Such orders may be issued requiring the prompt handling of cars by carriers, return of certain specific ownerships to owning lines, restricting the loading of certain cars to specified areas, imposing against shippers and receivers increased demurrage charges for detaining cars, restricting light loading of cars, reducing free time on cars held for unloading, restricting the circuitous routing of traffic, and many other items intended to improve utilization of the freight car fleet.

Prior to 1917 there was no governmental authority over the use and interchange of cars. In 1916, when an acute shortage developed, the Commission asked Congress for authority to prescribe rules and regulations governing interchange of cars, return of cars to the owning road, the conditions and circumstances under which such cars may be loaded on foreign roads, and the compensation which carriers shall pay to each other for the use of each other's cars. The result of the Commission's recommendation was the Esch Car Service Act of 1917, which added to the Interstate Commerce Act the paragraphs which now, after amendments in 1920 and 1940, appear as paragraphs 10 to 17 of Section 1.[51] These and certain other provisions of the I.C. Act give the Commission broad powers over car service.

Section 1(4) of the I.C. Act[52] makes it the duty of every common carrier by railroad, among other things, "to provide reasonable facilities" for operating through routes with other carriers.

By Section 1(10),[53] "car service" is defined to include the use, control, supply, movement, distribution, exchange, interchange, and return

---

[50]*Merchants Refrigerating Co. v. New York Central R. Co.*, 238 I.C.C. 599, 604, *Lake Coal Demurrage*, 232 I.C.C. 735, 779, *Leases and Grants By Carriers to Shippers*, 73 I.C.C. 671, 682.
[51]*Palmer v. United States*, 75 F. Supp. 63, 71-72 (D.D.C.).
[52]49 U.S.C. 1(4).
[53]49 U.S.C. 1(10).

of locomotives, cars, and other vehicles used in the transportation of property, including special types of equipment, and the supply of trains. By Section 8,[54] right of action for damages is provided to anyone suffering loss from excessive rate of hire for such use, since carriers are required by the I.C. Act to charge only reasonable compensation for use of their cars; the Commission is empowered by Section 13(1)[55] and Section 16(1)[56] to entertain complaints alleging excessive charges and to enter orders awarding damages resulting from past or present excessive car-hire charges and it has jurisdiction under the Administrative Procedure Act to enter a declaratory order with respect to the reasonableness of such charges.

Section 1(11)[57] makes it the duty of every common carrier by railroad "to furnish safe and adequate car service and to establish, observe, and enforce just and reasonable rules, regulations, and practices with respect to car service; and every unjust and unreasonable rule, regulation, and practice with respect to car service is prohibited and declared to be unlawful."

By reasons of Sections 1(4) and 1(11), the originating carrier has a duty to pass on, and the connecting carrier has the duty to accept, the former's cars where both are transporting a shipment on a through route. Section 1(12),[58]as amended by the 4R Act, provides in part:

"It shall also be the duty of every carrier by railroad to make just and reasonable distribution of cars for transportation of coal among the coal mines served by it, whether located upon its line or lines or customarily dependent upon it for car supply. During any period when the supply of cars available for such service does not equal the requirements of such mines it shall be the duty of the carrier to maintain and apply just and reasonable ratings of such mines and to count each and every car furnished to or used by any such mine for transportation of coal against the mine. . . . In applying the provisions of this paragraph, unit-train service and non-unit-train service shall be considered separate and distinct classes of service, and a distinction shall be made between these two classes of service and between the cars used in each class of service; questions of the justness and reasonableness of, or discrimination or preference or prejudice or ad-

---

[54]49 U.S.C. 8.
[55]49 U.S.C. 13(1).
[56]49 U.S.C. 16(1).
[57]49 U.S.C. 1(11). Comparable provision — Section 216(b). See *Shippers Car Supply Committee v. Southern Pacific Co.*, 292 I.C.C. 537; upheld in *Shippers' Car Supply Com. v. Interstate Commerce Com'n*, 160 F. Supp. 939, aff'd 358 U.S. 45.
[58]49 U.S.C. 1(12).

vantage or disadvantage in, the distribution of cars shall be determined within each such class and not between them, notwithstanding any other provision of section 1, 2, or 3 of this Act (49 U.S.C. 1, 2, or 3), and of section 1, 2, or 3 of the Elkins Act (49 U.S.C. 41, 42, or 43). Coal cars supplied by shippers or receivers shall not be considered a part of such carrier's fleet or otherwise counted in determining questions of distribution or car count under this paragraph or any provision of law referred to in this section. As used in this paragraph, the term 'unit-train service,' means the movement of a single shipment of coal of not less than 4,500 tons, tendered to one carrier, on one bill of lading, at one origin, on one day, and destined to one consignee, at one plant, at one destination, via one route."

Penalties are provided by Section 1(12) for failing to abide by the foregoing provision. Under Section 1(13)[59] it is provided that "The Commission is hereby authorized by general or special orders to require all carriers by railroad subject to this part, or any of them, to file with it from time to time their rules and regulations with respect to car service, and the Commission may, in its discretion, direct that such rules and regulations shall be incorporated in their schedules showing rates, fares, and charges for transportation, and be subject to any or all of the provisions of this part relating thereto."

Power of Commission When Emergency Exists

Section 1(15)[60] provides:

"Whenever the Commission is of opinion that shortage of equipment, congestion of traffic, or other emergency requiring immediate action exists in any section of the country, the Commission shall have, and it is hereby given, authority, either upon complaint or upon its own initiative without complaint, at once, if it so orders, without answer or other formal pleading by the interested carrier or carriers, and with or without notice, hearing, or the making or filing of a report, according as the Commission may determine: (a) to suspend the operation of any or all rules, regulations, or practices then established with respect to car service for such time as may be determined by the Commission; (b) to make such just and reasonable directions with respect to car service without regard to the ownership as between carriers of locomotives, cars, and other vehicles, during such emergency as in its opinion will best promote the service in

---

[59] 49 U.S.C. 1(13).
[60] 49 U.S.C. 1(15). Provisions of Section 1(15) are applicable to freight forwarders (Section 420). See Section 6(8), preference and expediting of military traffic during war, and no embargo in time of peace against shipments for the United States.

the interest of the public and the commerce of the people, upon such terms of compensation as between the carriers as they may agree upon, or, in the event of this disagreement, as the Commission may after subsequent hearing find to be just and reasonable; (c) to require such joint or common use of terminals, including main-line track or tracks for a reasonable distance outside of such terminals, as in its opinion will best meet the emergency and serve the public interest, and upon such terms as between the carriers as they may agree upon, or, in the event of their disagreement, as the Commission may after subsequent hearing find to be just and reasonable; and (d) to give directions for preference or priority in transportation, embargoes, or movement of traffic under permits, at such time and for such periods as it may determine, and to modify, change, suspend, or annul them. In time of war or threatened war the President may certify to the Commission that it is essential to the national defense and security that certain traffic shall have preference or priority in transportation, and the Commission shall, under the power herein conferred, direct that such preference or priority be afforded."

Section 1 (16)[61] was amended by the Regional Rail Reorganization Act of 1973, 87 Stat. 1021. It provides as follows:

"(a) Whenever the Commission is of opinion that any carrier by railroad subject to this part is for any reason unable to transport the traffic offered it so as properly to serve the public, it may, upon the same procedure as provided in paragraph (15), make such just and reasonable directions with respect to the handling, routing, and movement of the traffic of such carrier and its distribution over other lines of roads, as in the opinion of the Commission will best promote the service in the interest of the public and the commerce of the people, and upon such terms as between the carriers as they may agree upon, or, in the event of their disagreement, as the Commission may after subsequent hearing find to be just and reasonable.

"(b) Whenever any carrier by railroad is unable to transport the traffic offered it because—

(1) its cash position makes its continuing operation impossible;
(2) it has been ordered to discontinue any service by a court; or
(3) it has abandoned service without obtaining a certificate from the Commission pursuant to this section;

"the Commission may, upon the same procedure as provided in paragraph (15) of this section, make such just and reasonable directions with respect to the handling, routing, and movement of the traffic available to such carrier and its distribution over such carrier's lines, as in the opinion of the Commission will best promote the service in the interest of the public and the commerce of the people subject to the following conditions:

---

[61] 49 U.S.C. 1(16). Applicable to freight forwarders under Section 420.

"(A) Such direction shall be effective for no longer than 60 days unless extended by the Commission for cause shown for an additional designated period not to exceed 180 days.

"(B) No such directions shall be issued that would cause a carrier to operate in violation of the Federal Railroad Safety Act of 1970 (45 USC 421) or that would substantially impair the ability of the carrier so directed to serve adequately its own patrons or to meet its outstanding common carrier obligations.

"(C) The directed carrier shall not, by reason of such Commission direction; be deemed to have assumed or to become responsible for the debts of the other carrier.

"(D) The directed carrier shall hire employees of the other carrier to the extent such employees had previously performed the directed service for the other carrier, and, as to such employees as shall be so hired, the directed carrier shall be deemed to have assumed all existing employment obligations and practices of the other carrier relating thereto, including, but not limited to, agreements governing rate of pay, rules and working conditions, and all employee protective conditions commencing with and for the duration of the direction.

"(E) Any order of the Commission entered pursuant to this paragraph shall provide that if, for the period of its effectiveness, the cost, as hereinafter defined, of handling, routing, and moving the traffic of another carrier over the other carrier's lines of road shall exceed the direct revenues therefor, then upon request, payment shall be made to the directed carrier, in the manner hereinafter provided and within 90 days after expiration of such order, of a sum equal to the amount by which such cost has exceeded said revenues. The term 'cost' shall mean those expenditures made or incurred in or attributable to the operations as directed, including the rental or lease of necessary equipment, plus an appropriate allocation of common expenses, overheads, and a reasonable profit. Such cost shall be then currently recorded by the carrier or carriers in such manner and on such forms as by general order may be prescribed by the Commission and shall be submitted to and subject to audit by the Commission. The Commission shall certify promptly to the Secretary of the Treasury the amount of payment to be made to said carrier or carriers under the provisions of this paragraph. Payments required to be made by the Secretary of the Treasury from funds hereby authorized to be appropriated in such amounts as may be necessary for the purpose of carrying out the provisions hereof."

Carriers failing to obey strictly and conform promptly to the Commission's orders and directions as to car service and other matters referred to in Section 1(15), (16) are subject to penalties by the provision of Section 1(17) (a).[62] The section also provides that nothing therein shall impair or affect the right of a State, in the exercise of its police power, to require just and reasonable freight and passenger service for intrastate business, except insofar as such requirement is inconsistent with any lawful order of the Commission. By the provisions of Section 1(17) (b)[63] it is unlawful "to offer or give any cause or procure to be offered or given, directly or indirectly, any money, property, or thing of value, or bribe in any form whatsoever" to influence the supply, distribution, or movement of cars or other vehicles, or vessels, used in the transportation of property." Likewise, solicitation, acceptance, or receipt is made unlawful. Penalties are provided by Section 1(17) (b) for violations of the provisions.

The Commission, under Section 1(21) of the I.C. Act,[64] may, after hearing, in a proceeding upon complaint or upon its own initiative without complaint, authorize or require by order any carrier by railroad, party to such proceeding, "to provide itself with safe and adequate facilities for performing as a common carrier its car service as that term is used" in Part I of the Act.

In issuing a car service direction, the Commission does not support it with findings which are supported by evidentiary facts but merely expresses its opinion as to what it believes to be the existing conditions. In *United States v. Southern Railway Co.*,[65] the court held that absent a showing of fraud, wrong doing, or caprice, the Commission's "opinion" of whether there is an emergency will not be upset.

In its 80th annual report in 1966, the Commission noted that it has made extensive peacetime use of its emergency car service powers. It said (at pp. 92-93):

> . . . In service orders, we required railroads to expedite the handling of freight traffic by taking measures to prevent car delays at shipper locations and to reduce the idle time of cars in railroad yards and terminals. We also ordered increased demurrage rates on domestic traffic and re-

---

[62]49 U.S.C. 1(17) (a). By Section 420, the provisions of Section 1(17) (a) are made applicable ot freight forwarders. See Sections 202(b), 216(e), 303(j) for saving clauses as to reservation to States of power to regulate intrastate commerce; and Section 202(b) again as to State power to tax.

[63]49 U.S.C. 1(17) (b). Applicable to freight forwarders under Section 420.

[64]49 U.S.C. 1(21).

[65]364 F. 2d 86, 94. A service order promulgated without notice or hearing, which fixed demurrage charges during an emergency, was upheld by the Supreme Court in *I.C.C. v. Oregon Pacific Industries, Inc.*, No. 73-1210, decided February 19, 1975, as a power covered by Section 1(15). See *Turner Lumber Co. v. Chicago M. & St. P. R. Co.*, 271 U.S. 259; *Iversen v. United States*, 63 F. Supp. 1001, aff'd 327 U.S. 767.

duced free time at ports in order to discourage the use of cars for storage purposes by shippers. In addition, we authorized the use of substitute equipment in order to relieve some of the pressure of the boxcar fleet.

. . . The car distribution directions which were issued required carriers having more than their equitable share of the freight car supply to furnish weekly a specified number of empty cars of any ownership to carriers having less than an equitable share. By means of such direction it was possible in most instances to correct serious disparities in the nationwide car distribution pattern. In a few particularly critical situations, we found it necessary to take the unprecedented peacetime action of ordering all cars of certain railroads withdrawn from distribution and directly returned to the owning railroads, unless they would be promptly loaded and dispatched in the direction of the owning railroads.

Freight Car Rentals

Section 1(14) (a) of the Interstate Commerce Act[66] was amended by the 4R Act to read as follows:

"It is the intent of the Congress to encourage the purchase, acquisition, and efficient utilization of freight cars. In order to carry out such intent, the Commission may, upon complaint of an interested party or upon its own initiative without complaint, and after notice and an opportunity for a hearing, establish reasonable rules, regulations, and practices with respect to car service by common carriers by railroad subject to this part, including (i) the compensation to be paid for the use of any locomotive, freight car, or other vehicle, (ii) the other terms of any contract, agreement, or arrangement for the use of any locomotive or other vehicle not owned by the carrier by which it is used (and whether or not owned by another carrier, shipper, or third party), and (iii) the penalties or other sanctions for nonobservance of such rules, regulations, or practices. In determining the rates of compensation to be paid for each type of freight car, the Commission shall give consideration to the transportation use of each type of freight car, to the national level of ownership of each such type of freight car, and to other factors affecting the adequacy of the national freight car supply. Such compensation shall be fixed on the basis of the elements of ownership expense involved in owning and maintaining each such type of freight car, including a fair return on the cost of such type of freight car (giving due consideration to current costs of capital, repairs, materials, parts, and labor). Such compensation may be increased by any incentive element which will, in the judgment of the Commission, provide just and reasonable compensation to freight car owners, contribute to sound car service practices (including efficient utilization and distribution of cars), and encourage the acquisition and maintenance of a car supply

[66]49 U.S.C. 1(14) (a). Comparable provisions, Sections 204(a) (1) and 403(b).

adequate to meet the needs of commerce and the national defense. The Commission shall not make any incentive element applicable to any type of freight car if the Commission finds that the supply of such type of freight car is adequate. The Commission may exempt such incentive element from the compensation to be paid by any carrier or group of carriers if the Commission finds that such an exemption is in the national interest."

The Commission is authorized under Section 1(14) of the I.C. Act to establish the compensation to be paid and other terms of any agreement for the use of any car not owned by the carrier using it.

Rates for freight car rentals have been handled under uniform rules and regulations as early as 1867. A nationally uniform basis for freight car rentals was attempted in 1888; there was adopted a combined plan of per diem and mileage, but the plan was abandoned after a short trial. Prior thereto, rates for freight car rentals were fixed on an individual carrier basis under arrangements with connecting carriers. A per diem system was adopted in 1902. This system was revised in 1920 and at subsequent times. The earlier per diem rates were investigated by the Commission in *Rules for Car-Hire Settlement*,[67] and an order entered therein was sustained in *Chicago, R. I. & P. Ry. Co. v. United States*.[68] The proceeding in *Rules for Car-Hire Settlement* was reopened when a short line refused to recognize a ruling under railroad procedures regarding the continuation of a special agreement relating to free time and per diem reclaims, and was reopened from time to time when procedure for adjusting controversies between short lines and connecting trunk lines, (which was developed as a result of the Supreme Court decision in *Chicago, R. I. & P. Ry. Co. v. United States, supra*), failed to resolve various disputes.[69] Because of post-war car shortages the Commission began two proceedings to increase car utilization; one of the proceedings, *Car Service Freight Cars*,[70] involved an investigation of car service rules. The Commission found the car service rules not shown to be unlawful but stated that if the situation did not improve it might issue emergency car service orders under Section 1(15) of the I.C. Act or car service rules under Section 1(14) (a). In the other proceeding,

[67]160 I.C.C. 369; 165 I.C.C. 495.
[68]284 U.S. 80.
[69]262 I.C.C. 85; 277 I.C.C. 129; 283 I.C.C. 639; 287 I.C.C. 717.
[70]268 I.C.C. 687. Carriers were ordered to file with the Commission rules and regulations with respect to car service. This has been interpreted to include the filing of per diem rates as well as car service rules; however, it is not interpreted to be such filing as could be required under Section 1(13) — a tariff subject to suspension. See *B. & O. R. Co. v. New York, N. H. & H. R. Co.*, 198 F. Supp. 724 (footnote 734).

Increased Per Diem Charge on Freight Cars,[71] the Commission held that a penalty per diem rate would encourage greater efficiency in car utilization. However, in *Palmer v. United States*[72] it was held that the Commission did not have the power to establish a rate of per diem in excess of reasonable compensation to the owner for regulatory purposes, that is, to encourage greater efficiency in use of cars.

Privately owned cars are generally grouped into classes, cars owned by shippers, cars owned by private car lines, and cars owned by railroad-controlled car lines. Section 1(14) (a) authorizes the Commission to establish the compensation to be paid and other terms of any agreement for the use of any car not owned by the carrier using it.[73]

In 1946 the Commission was petitioned by certain short lines to find that the existing per diem rates were unreasonably high. A number of western lines subsequently petitioned the Commission to find the per diem rates unreasonably low. The Commission in *Alabama, T. & N. R. Co. v. Aberdeen & R.R. Co.*[74] held that the rates were neither too high nor too low. In 1949 the per diem rates were increased. Certain short lines refused to abide by the increase so some of the larger carriers filed a complaint with the Commission asking for a declaratory order under Section 5(d) of the Administrative Procedure Act.[75] Complainants disclaimed any intention of invoking the power of the Commission under Section 1(14) (a) of the I.C. Act to set per diem rates. The defendants in the proceedings requested the Commission to prescribe rates on a time-mileage basis, or a graduated system of rates, but the Commission held in *Chicago, B. & Q. R. Co. v. New York, S. & W. R. Co.*,[76] that this could not be done on the evidence before it. The Commission, instead, issued a declaratory order declaring that existing rates were reasonable and that any lower rates would not be compensatory. The Commission's order was attacked before a three-judge court in *Boston & Maine Railroad Co. v. United States.*[77] The court held that the Commission had the

[71]268 I.C.C. 659.

[72]75 F. Supp. 63 (D.D.C.).

[73]See *Mileage Allowances on Refrigerator Cars*, 218 I.C.C. 359, where a proposed reduction in mileage rates was found not to be justified; and *Use of Privately Owned Refrigerator Cars*, 201 I.C.C. 323, where certain mileage rates were found to be too high. See also *In Re of Private Cars*, 50 I.C.C. 652; *Keith Ry. Equipment Co. v. A.A.R.*, 64 F. Supp. 917; *Ahnapee & W. Ry. Co. v. Akron & B.B. R. Co.*, 302 I.C.C. 265; *through Routes and Joint Rates Between Inland Waterways Corp. and Other Common Carriers*, 174 I.C.C. 477.

[74]244 I.C.C. 383.

[75]5 U.S.C. 1004(d).

[76]297 I.C.C. 291.

[77]162 F. Supp. 289.

power to issue a declaratory order, but that it had erred in not giving sufficient consideration to the time-mileage formula advocated by one of the short lines. The court also criticized, by way of warning to the Commission for its future guidance, the failure of the Commission to investigate the cost of repairs in more detail, the use of reproduction value in calculating depreciations, and the use of a 20-year average for the car day divisor. An appeal to the Supreme Court was dismissed in *Boston & Main Railroad v. United States*.[78] The case was remanded to the Commission.

The Commission enlarged the remanded case with a view to prescribing per diem charges for the future under Section 1(14) (a), as well as rendering advice for the past. An extensive study of the costs of freight car ownership for the year 1960 was conducted under supervision of Commission cost accountants, with cooperation and participation by the railroads.

A decision was reached by the Commission on the remanded case in 1968[79] dealing with the amount of charges to be paid by railroads for their use of one another's cars.

In Ex Parte No. 334, *Car Service Compensation-Basic Per Diem Charges — Formula Revision in Accordance with the Regulatory Reform Act of 1976*,[80] the Commission, in order to implement the mandate of Congress set forth in the 4R Act to revise the Commission's rules, regulations, and practices with respect to car service to encourage the purchase, acquisition and efficient utilization of freight cars, developed a per diem formula which reflects consideration of the following factors:

1. The first factor is age and value brackets of the cars. The car hire rate table employs narrowband, $1,000 value brackets and one-year age brackets. This refinement in the classification of car types of age and value will produce per diem charges that more accurately reflect the true ownership costs for each individual car.

2. The second factor is depreciation. Rates of depreciation for each type of car are based on the average service life and salvage value determined from national railroad data. The rates are determined using statistical actuarial analysis of the data.

---

[78]358 U.S. 68.

[79]*Chicago, B. & Q. R.R. v. New York, S. & Western R.R.*, 332 I.C.C. 176. Two district courts, and the Supreme Court sustained the order of the Commission. See 297 F. Supp. 615, 300 F. Supp. 318, 396 U.S. 27.

[80]Decided August 1, 1977.

3. The third factor is repair costs. A 3-year moving average is used to develop average car repair costs while normalizing fluctuations in car repair activity resulting from inflation or deflation. It provides assurance that the car owner is reimbursed for an amount nearest to what it will cost to repair its cars.

4. The fourth factor is cost of capital. A discounted cash flow method and the resulting development of a current cost of capital will be used to compute the current cost of capital for car compensation rates. This method considers the economic costs to the firm of the return required to provide the debt investors their interest and the equity investors their earnings. The current cost of capital is that cost of acquiring funds during the current period and is used to judge asset acquisition decisions. As such, the current cost of capital is only concerned with incremental additions to the capital pool, and imbedded debt and equity costs are disregarded.

5. The fifth factor is transportation use. Pursuant to the 4R Act, the costs considered to determine the compensation for the use of freight cars must be related not only to the level and the adequacy of the national car supply but also to the transportation use of each type of car. Transportation use is a function of the time and distance in which cars are used, and adherence to it avoids compensation for any costs related to providing cars for other uses. A car-day divisor and a car-mile divisor are calculated and incorporated into the formula to reflect transportation use of each type of car.

In May 1976, while the *Per Diem* case was awaiting final decision, Congress amended Section 1(14) (a) of the I.C. Act. The existing provisions relating to "basic" per diem — payments by users designed to compensate the owner for costs of ownership — were unchanged. In addition to this compensation, however, the Commission was empowered to consider the nation's car supply and ownership, and to increase the compensatory rate for any type of car by such further "incentive" element as might, in the agency's judgment, "contribute to sound car service practices . . . and encourage the acquisition and maintenance" of an adequate car supply. No incentive element is to be added to the rate for any "type" of car found in adequate supply, and the Commission may exempt particular carriers or groups of carriers from any incentive requirement.

Shortly after this amendment, and in response to it, the Commission instituted a separate proceeding to determine whether an incentive element should be prescribed for any type of car on an interim basis pending further study. All railroads were made parties and were directed to file sworn statements indicating recommendations and any facts which the Commission should consider. After hearings, briefs and oral argument, the Commission concluded in October 1967 that "there is not available at this time reliable factual data" to justify addition of an interim incentive element.[81]

The Commission then instituted a proceeding looking to imposition of incentive charges on a more permanent basis.[82] In connection therewith, the agency conducted an extensive study of 1968 freight car operations. This investigation led to an imposition of an incentive charge.[83]

A complementary proceeding to the *Per Diem* and *Incentive Per Diem* case is Ex Parte No. 241, *Investigation of Adequacy of Railroad Freight Car Ownership, Car Utilization, Distribution, Rules and Practices.* In a September 1969 decision in this case,[84] the Commission, *inter alia*, required observance of certain industry-wide car service rules designed to increase the flow of cars from the users back to the owners, to enable the roads to determine shipper needs more precisely, and to produce more efficient practices in assignment of cars for shippers' exclusive use. The Commission spoke of its action in this *Investigation* case as meeting a problem in common with that of the pending *Incentive* case, and stated that prescription of mandatory rules would "facilitate the optimum use of the national car fleet. . . ."[85]

Allowances for Use of Privately Owned Cars

Section 1(14) (a) of the I.C. Act has been described by the Commission as conferring upon it the authority to prescribe the compensation to

[81]*Incentive Per Diem Charges,* 332 I.C.C. 11, 18.

[82]*Ex Parte No. 252 (Sub-No. 1), Incentive Per Diem Charges, 1968.* The proceeding was initiated by a notice of proposed rule making on December 15, 1967.

[83]See Ex Parte No. 252 (Sub-No. 1), *Incentive Per Diem Charges — 1968,* 337 I.C.C. 183; 337 I.C.C. 217, aff'd sub. nom. *United States v. Florida East Coast R. Co.,* 368 F. Supp. 1009, 410 U.S. 224; 343 I.C.C. 49; 349 I.C.C. 303; 350 I.C.C. 464; 353 I.C.C. 336; Ex Parte No. 252 (Sub-No. 1), *Incentive Per Diem Charges — 1968 (XF Cars),* 350 I.C.C. 11; Ex Parte No. 252 (Sub-No. 2), *Incentive Per Diem Charges — Gondolas,* 353 I.C.C. 612. See also *Ann Arbor Railroad Co. v. United States,* 368 F. Supp. 101.

[84]335 I.C.C. 264. Earlier proceeding, 323 I.C.C. 48. The proceeding in 323 I.C.C. 48 was instituted to obtain specific and current information on the "adequacy of freight car ownership," and to develop facts leading to the prescription of rules for alleviating the recurring problem of shortages of freight cars. Questionnaires were sent to the railroads and the returns thereto confirmed the existence of a substantial "inadequacy of ownership" in more than one category of freight cars throughout the country. See also *Car Service, Freight Cars,* 268 I.C.C. 687.

[85]335 I.C.C. at pp. 304, 308.

be paid by carriers and the rules and regulations relating thereto insofar as any car not owned by the carrier using it is concerned, including cars of private as well as of carrier ownership.[86] In the *Keith* case, the Commission proceeded under Section 1(14) (a) to determine a just and reasonable mileage allowance for tank cars utilized primarily by shipper lessees.

In proceedings under this section of the statute the Commission has clearly held that the appropriated elements to be considered are those items of ownership cost incurred by the owner of the car. Thus, in *Mileage Allowances on Refrigerator Cars,*[87] the Commission stated:

> The authority to prescribe the compensation to be paid by a railroad to a car owner for the use of a car owned by the latter carries with it the obligation to determine such compensation in an amount that will be reasonable to the owner. The compensation to be paid by a railroad for the use of cars of another, in order to be reasonable, must be at least sufficient to pay the expenses of car ownership, which include interest on the necessary investment in the cars, depreciation, insurance, taxes, expenses of repairs, and other costs directly attributable to car ownership. . . .

These same elements of cost were considered to be determinative in the *Keith* case. These costs, of course, are costs that are incurred by the owner-lessor, and are necessarily the relevant items of cost in this proceeding.

The rental paid by the shipper-lessee is not a relevant cost item to be considered in passing on the lawfulness of a tariff governing the use of privately owned cars. Based on the language of Section 15(13) and the so-called *El Dorado* litigation, *El Dorado Oil Works vs. U.S.,*[88] and *Allowances for Privately Owned Tank Cars,*[89] it might appear that the rental paid by the shipper-lessee would be a relevant cost item in determining the lawfulness of the tariff; however, Section 15(15), and the decisions of the Commission and the Supreme Court in the *El Dorado* litigation do not govern the prescription of a specific mileage allowance for future application on a general basis. Under the decisions of the Commission and the Supreme Court, the amount of the rental paid by the shipper-lessee operates merely as a restriction on the maximum amount which such an individual lessee may receive. It does not govern the nature of the obligation of the carrier insofar as the level of the mileage allowance payable to the owner of the car is concerned. This

[86]*Keith Railway Equipment Company v. The Association of American Railroads,* 268 I.C.C. 759.
[87]218 I.C.C. 359, 364.
[88]308 U.S. 422, 328 U.S. 12.
[89]358 I.C.C. 371.

distinction is clearly indicated by the following from the decision of the Supreme Court in the second *El Dorado case* (at p. 18):

> The Commission did not rule that a shipper-lessee would always be entitled to allowances equal to the cost to him of the cars he rented. The Commission's opinion makes it clear that a shipper-lessee is only entitled to receive a just and reasonable allowance for cars while they are actually used by the railroad, even though this allowance might be less than the car rent paid by the shipper. On that subject the Commission said:
>
> > In administering the provisions of Section 15(13) (now 15(15)) we have consistently adhered to two principles, bearing in mind that we were to prescribe the maximum amount which the carrier might pay: (1) The amount paid should not be more than was just and reasonable for the service or instrumentality furnished, and (2) that the amount which might be paid should not exceed the reasonable cost to the owner of the goods of performing the service or furnishing the instrumentality used. Whichever of these sums was the lower marked the maximum the carrier might pay.
>
> Here the Commission has applied these uniform criteria in such a way as to permit the shipper-lessee to receive as much as the full rental he paid. Were it not for these proceedings resulting from the Car Company's refusal to continue payments to the shipper, the railroad would have had to pay as it did pay 1½¢ per mile, which proved far in excess of the rental. It may be than in other cases a just and reasonable rate would fall below the rental. It may be that in this case the rental exceeded what would be a just and reasonable allowance with respect to the use of the cars by the railroad. But this would serve to further reduce the rate to which appellants were actually entitled; appellants, therefore, have no interest in challenging the Commission's order on this point.

Thus, although the amount of the rental may be significant for purposes of disposing of issues with respect to violations of the Elkins Act and related provisions of the Interstate Commerce Act proscribing rebates and discriminatory practices, the rental paid by shipper-lessee is not a relevant consideration in arriving at a reasonable allowance to be paid on a general and uniform basis to the owners of private cars used in railroad service.

This is consistent with the Commission's views of its jurisdiction under Section 15(15) of the I.C. Act. *In the Matter of Private Cars,*[90] the Commission stated:

> . . . the only power of the Commission to regulate payments by a carrier for an instrumentality of transportation furnished by the shipper was the

[90]50 I.C.C. 652, 680-81.

power given in Section 15 of the Act to determine what is a reasonable charge as the maximum to be paid by the carrier. This provision was directed to the prevention of rebates by way of excessive allowances to shippers, and has never been considered as granting power to fix a reasonable amount as an initial proposition as payment for the use of the car. . . .

Perhaps the most precise precedent on the matter is the Commission's decision in *Refrigerator Car Mileage Allowances.*[91] In that case the Commission was concerned with a petition for suspension of tariff items which would have reduced the compensation payable for certain types of refrigerator cars. In their reply to the petition for suspension the railroads asserted that the Commission was without jurisdiction to suspend a change in the compensation to be paid for the use of private cars not owned by shippers. The Commission found that the tariff provision in question related to cars owned by shippers and also to cars utilized by shippers on a lease basis and it proceeded to differentiate as to its authority with respect to these two categories. Its discussion of the matter is as follows (pp. 279-80):

> There seems to be no doubt that we have the authority to suspend a tariff item in which a change is proposed to be made in the allowance paid shippers for furnishing a transportation facility, as provided in Section 15(13) (now 15(15)) of the Act. Such an allowance affects directly the freight rates paid by such shippers, and under Section 15(7) the Commission is given authority to suspend any schedule which states a "new individual or joint regulation or practice affecting any rate, fare, or charge." In this connection, however, it should not be overlooked that the Commission has the power to fix only the maximum to be paid to the shipper furnishing such instrumentality, and therefore, as a practical matter, the right to suspend or to investigate would ordinarily be exercised only for the purpose of determining what such maximum reasonable allowance should be. The tariff item which is here suspended covers both allowances to shippers and compensation paid to private-car companies not shipper owned or controlled, "for the use of cars of private ownership." It carries a reference mark designating the change in the amount of the allowance as an "increase." The suspension of these schedules cannot, therefore, be said to have exceeded our authority.

> However, a review of the various provisions of the law which we administer leads us to the conclusion that the Commission is without authority to pass upon or to fix the compensation paid by railroads to private-car companies for the use of equipment furnished by them directly to the railroads. The relation between such companies and the railroads, as well as the Commission's power over such private-car companies was considered

[91]232 I.C.C. 276.

by the Supreme Court of the United States in *Ellis v. Interstate Commerce Commission*, 237 U.S. 434, in connection with the law as it stood prior to the enactment of the car-service provisions in 1917. In that proceeding the Commission sought to compel one Ellis, the vice president and general manager of the Armour Car Lines, to testify with respect to the ownership of the Armour Car Lines, a private refrigerator-car company, in order to determine whether or not the compensation paid for the use of its cars operated as a rebate to Armour & Company, a corporation using such cars in the shipment of packing-house products, and which it was thought might own and control the Armour Car Lines. The court said in the above-cited decision, at page 444:

If the price paid to the Armour Car Lines was made the cover for a rebate to Armour & Company or if better cars were given to Armour & Company than to others, or if, in short, the act was violated, the railroads are responsible on proof of the fact. *But the only relation that is subject to the Commission is that between the railroads and the shippers.* It does not matter to the responsibility of the roads whether they own or simply control the facilities, or whether they pay a greater or less price to their lessor. It was argued that the Commission might look into the profits and losses of the Armour Car Lines (one of the matters inquired about) in order to avoid fixing allowances to it at a confiscatory rate. *But the Commission fixes nothing as to the Armour Car Lines except under § 15 in the event of which we shall speak.* [Emphasis supplied.]

It is clear from the language quoted that the Commission at that time had nothing to do with the compensation paid to private-car companies, and we do not understand that the Congress broadened our power when it passed the car-service provisions in 1917. . . .

As a consequence of this determination that it did not have jurisdiction under Section 1(14) over allowances to private car companies not shipper-owned, the Commission held that it was improper for the tariffs to carry the allowance and the rules, regulations and practices with respect to cars leased by shippers. It ruled that "the tariff schedules concerned should, therefore, be promptly amended by striking therefrom all items covering the payment of compensation to private car companies, not shipper-owned or controlled, for the use of equipment furnished directly by them to respondents." (pp. 279-80)

It is clear from this decision that Section 15(15) of the I.C. Act does not give the Commission jurisdiction over the arrangements between the shipper-lessees and the car owners or between the lessors and the railroads. The jurisdiction over the allowance payable to non-shipper car owners arises only by reason of the amendment of Section 1(14) (a) after the decision of the Commission referred to above. The amendment of Section 1(14) (a) enlarged the jurisdiction of the Commission with respect to the arrangements between carriers and private car companies. It did not, however, affect the jurisdiction of the Commission insofar as the shipper-lessee is concerned.

While rental costs of a particular shipper may have some relevance in a proceeding where the issues concern the situation of an individual shipper with respect to rebates, and the maximum amount which such shipper may receive under Section 15(15), a proceeding to fix reasonable mileage allowances for the future for privately owned cars involves different considerations. This was recognized by the Commission in *Allowances for Privately Owned Tank Cars,*[92] where it emphasized that it was not fixing allowances for classes of cars, adding:

> Were we to attempt to determine the reasonableness of allowance for a "class" of tank cars such as these, we cannot tell how far reaching the investigation would have to be. Its result would be futile, because (1) there would be no way to compel restitution one way or the other, so as to conform to any figure we might determine, and because (2) since the amendment to the Interstate Commerce Act September 18, 1940, we have a jurisdiction as to the future with respect to matters such as are here considered, which is plenary and should be exercised directly and not as ancillary to a controversy concerning only past rights of parties to a contract entered into under pre-existing law.

The distinction between the issues which may arise under Sections 1(14) (a) and 15(15) of the I.C. Act were clearly stated by the Commission in *Keith Ry. Equipment Co. v. Assn. of American Railroads.*[93] Referring to Section 1(14) (a), the Commission stated (p. 472):

> The legislative history of an amendment embodied in the foregoing paragraph which became effective September 18, 1940, by which the words "(including the compensation to be paid) and other terms of any contract, agreement, or arrangement . . . (and whether or not owned by another carrier)," were inserted therein, . . . makes it plain that the intent was to confer upon the Commission the power to fix the specific or exact compensation which may be paid to the car owners. Such is the plain meaning of the words "the compensation." If the intent had been to confer authority to fix only the maximum compensation, the pattern set in Section 15(13) (now 15(15)) of the Act for expressing such an intent could have been readily followed.

The Commission then proceeded to determine the reasonableness of the mileage allowance paid to a tank car owner-lessor by reference to the cost of ownership factors. This is most precise authority for the propo-

[92]258 I.C.C. 371, 381.
[93]274 I.C.C. 469.

sition that the rentals paid by individual lessees are not relevant in a proceeding involving the prescription of a mileage allowance for private cars. While individual rentals may fix the maximum receivable by individual shippers under Section 15(15), the level of the allowance payable to tank car owners, shipper and non-shipper, is determined by other recognized cost of ownership factors.

The Commission has traditionally considered the allowance for railroad use of privately owned cars to be the means by which the carriers compensate the owner of the car for costs of ownership. Items such as return on investment, depreciation, repair costs and other costs of a like nature have been evaluated by the Commission for the purpose of fixing a compensatory allowance. The Commission has also recognized that the rental terms which appear in the lease agreements between the car owners and the shipper-lessees reflect a number of other considerations. This was most clearly indicated by the Commission in *Allowances for Privately Owned Cars*,[94] where the Commission stated:

> The record indicates that there is a substantial difference in the situation respecting the furnishing of cars to the railways by private car companies and shipper owners, and by shipper-lessees who obtain the cars from private car companies. With respect to the latter class, the principal cost is the rental paid by the shipper-lessees to the car companies, which varies with supply, demand and competition. Private car companies and shipper owners in furnishing cars to the railways, must consider investment, depreciation, maintenance, and certain related items of expense connected with ownership of the cars.

In *The Matter of Private Cars*,[95] the Commission referring to rentals paid by shipper-lessees stated: "The amount of the charge seems to be measured by the needs of the particular shipper." In *Use of Privately Owned Refrigerator Cars*,[96] the Commission also noted certain factors affecting rental rates which by their nature make such rates inappropriate in determining the level of a proper mileage allowance. The Commission stated: "Because of the extremely competitive conditions, the monthly charges for leased cars have steadily declined until, at the present time, they do not have any relation whatsoever to the cost of ownership."

In the same decision, however, the Commission recognized that the allowance to be paid by the railroads for the use of privately owned cars should reimburse the owners for appropriate ownership costs, stat-

---

[94]258 I.C.C. 371, 375-76.
[95]50 I.C.C. 652, 675.
[96]201 I.C.C. 367.

ing (p. 378), "A car line, whether it be shipper or not, cannot be expected to build, maintain, and supply cars to the railroads unless it may reasonably expect to obtain a fair return on its investment. In fact, they could not obtain the necessary capital under any other conditions."

Duty of Common Carriers by Railroad to Furnish Special Equipment for Transportation

Section 1(3) (a) of the Interstate Commerce Act defines the term "transportation" as including, among other things, vehicles and all instrumentalities and facilities of shipment or carriage. Section 1(4) provides that it shall be the duty of every common carrier "to provide and furnish transportation upon reasonable request therefor." The language of Sections 1(3)(a) and 1(4) indicates that the duty to furnish cars for transportation rests upon the carriers. Even though it may be considered that the duty to furnish cars rests upon the carriers, the following questions remain to be answered: (1) Whether the Commission has full authority to enforce the duty? (2) If it has authority to enforce the duty insofar as general equipment is concerned, can it be said that its power is broad enough to require special equipment to be furnished?

In *United States v. Pennsylvania R. Co.*,[97] the Supreme Court held that under the then existing I.C. Act the Commission lacked power, in the absence of discrimination, to require a carrier which owned no tank cars to obtain a supply of such cars for furnishing to shippers who desire to ship oil and other liquids in cars of that type. In that case, the Supreme Court gave consideration to *Transportation & Refrigeration of Fruits*,[98] in which the Commission said (p. 373) that it was of the opinion that it was the duty of railroads to furnish refrigeration cars for the transportation of fruits; that at one time carriers might have declined to provide this special kind of equipment, but that the trade had so grown that the carriers might as well decline to provide stock cars for the transportation of livestock as refrigerator cars for the carriage of perishable commodities." However, the Commission in *Transportation & Refrigeration of Fruits* added: "But this duty does not spring from the act to regulate commerce, nor has the Commission any jurisdiction of that matter. It arises out of the common-law liability of the defendant railway companies as common carriers, and redress for failure to fulfill it must be sought in the courts." After its discussion of *Transportation & Refrig-*

---

[97]242 U.S. 208.
[98]10 I.C.C. 360.

eration of Fruits, and an earlier case. *Scofield v. Lake Shore* & *M.S.R. Co.,*[99] the Supreme Court said (p. 222):

> This, then, was the view of the Interstate Commerce Commission of the duty of carriers and of its power over them; that is, that it was the duty of carriers to provide and furnish equipment for transportation of commodities, and that this duty might expand with time and conditions, the special car becoming the common car, and the shipper's right to demand it receiving the same sanction of law. But the Commission decided it was the sanction of the common law, not of the statute, and that the remedy was in the courts, not in the Commission. With this view we start as the first element of our decision.

In the *Pennsylvania* case, the carrier had alleged before the Commission that there was a tariff rule in effect which stated that the carrier would not assume any obligation to furnish tank cars. The Commission disagreed and contested the efficacy of the rule to divest the company of its duty as a carrier. The Supreme Court in reply to the position taken by the Commission said (p. 236), "This might be if there was a duty; but the United States seeks to establish the duty from the offer of the company, and must take the offer as made, and cannot, nor can the Commission, ignore its explicit qualification that the company assumed no obligation to furnish tank cars. The finding of the Commission, therefore, was one of law, and not of fact, and is reviewable."

The Commission gave consideration in *Matter of Private Cars,*[100] to the question whether carriers should be required to furnish cars of special types, such as refrigerator and tank cars to the exclusion of privately owned cars. The Commission determined (p. 671), "It is well settled law that the duty of a common carrier is to furnish equipment for transportation of articles it advertises to carry. The general duty of carriers at common law, and under the act, is to furnish such cars and other facilities as are reasonably necessary to enable them to fulfill their public obligations. It has been held that in the absence of discrimination the power to enforce the duty does not reside with the Commission." The Commission considered the Esch Car Service Act, which was enacted on May 29, 1917,[101] in *Matter of Private Cars,* stating (p. 672), "The Congress has thus recognized the use of privately owned cars in transporting the commerce of the countries, and has provided for their control by the Commission through (the) rules

[99]2 I.C.C. 67, 2 I.C.C. 90.
[100]50 I.C.C. 652.
[101]40 Stat. L. 101.

and regulations of carriers hauling them." It found that an important part of interstate commerce is transported in privately owned cars and that it is in the interest of the owners, carriers, and public that the operations should be continued, under such rules and regulations as will ensure their efficient handling without discrimination against any shipper or particular description of traffic. Recognition was given to the fact that the use of private cars was attended with abuses, and that the Commission was endeavoring by rulings and otherwise to lessen such abuses as far as possible.

The Esch Car Service Act was amended by Section 402 of the Transportation Act of 1920.[102] Under the Esch Car Service Act, Section 1(10) defined the term "car service" as including "the movement, distribution, exchange, interchange, and return of cars used in the transportation of property." Under the Transportation Act of 1920, and as it reads today, Section 1(10) defines the term "car service" as including "the use, control, supply, movement, distribution, exchange, interchange and return of locomotives, cars, and other vehicles used in the transportation of property, including special types of equipment, and the supply of trains." Under the prior legislation, Section 1(11) provided that it was the duty of carriers "to establish, observe, and enforce just and reasonable rules, regulations and practices with respect to car service, and every unjust rule, regulation and practice, with respect to car service is prohibited and declared to be unlawful." Under the Transportation Act, and as it reads today, Section 1(11) provides that it is the duty of carriers "to furnish safe and adequate car service and to establish, observe, and enforce just and reasonable rules, regulations and practices with respect to car service; and every unjust and unreasonable rule, regulation and practice with respect to car service is prohibited and declared to be unlawful."

Under the prior legislation, Section 1(14) provided that the Commission "shall, after hearing, on a complaint or upon its own initiative

---

[102]41 Stat. L. 476. The legislative history of Section 402 of the Transportation Act, 1920, makes it clear that the Commission was given broadened authority to order a common carrier to supply itself with equipment including special types of equipment. See House Report No. 456, 66th Cong. 1st Sess., submitted with H.R. 10453 on November 10, 1919; House Report No. 650, 66th Cong., 2d Sess., submitted with H.R. 10453 on February 18, 1920; Cong. Rec., Vol. 58, pp. 8309-8318, a speech by Chairman Esch of the House Committee on Interstate and Foreign Commerce; Hearings on H.R. 4378, July 22, 1919, Vol. I, pp. 114-15, Statement of Commissioner Clark of the Commission before the House Committee on Interstate and Foreign Commerce; Hearings on H.R. 4378, September 26, 1919, Vol. III, pp. 2919-20, Statement of Commissioner Clark of the Commission before the House Committee on Interstate and Foreign Commerce.

without complaint, establish reasonable rules, regulations, and practices with respect to car service, including the classification of cars, compensation to be paid for the use of any car not owned by such common carrier and the penalties or other sanctions for nonobservance of such rules." Under the Transportation Act, Section 1(14) provided that the Commission "may, after hearing, on a complaint or upon its own initiative without complaint, establish reasonable rules, regulations, and practices with respect to car service by carriers by railroads subject to this Act, including the compensation to be paid for the use of any locomotive, car, or other vehicle not owned by the carrier using it, and the penalties or other sanctions for nonobservance of such rules, regulations, or practices." Section 1(14) was amended by the Transportation Act of 1940 and is now Section 1(14) (a). As noted above Section 1(14) (a) also was amended by the 4R Act. The Commission has authority under Section 1(14) (a) to establish reasonable rules, regulations, and practices with respect to car service including the compensation to be paid and other terms of any contract, agreement or arrangement for the use of any locomotive or other vehicle not owned by the carrier using it. The authority conferred by Section 1(14) (a) thus includes cars of private as well as carrier ownership.

On its own motion in 1931, the Commission instituted a proceeding on an inquiry and investigation designated Ex Parte No. 104, *Practices of Carriers Affecting Operating Revenues or Expenses.* To facilitate the investigation, different phases were considered separately and assigned part numbers. Part V, *Private Freight Cars,* dealt with conditions surrounding and attending the use of cars owned or operated by persons or corporations, other than common carriers by railroad, but including carrier-controlled corporations. The investigation in *Private Freight Cars* was set down for hearing with an investigation and suspension proceeding, *Use of Privately Owned Refrigerator Cars,* and the records were consolidated so far as they dealt with refrigerator cars. In *Use of Privately Owned Refrigerator Cars,*[103] the Commission arrived at the following pertinent conclusions:

> It is well-settled law that it is the duty of common carriers by railroad to furnish such cars as may be reasonably necessary for the transportation of all the commodities they hold themselves out to carry. That duty, imposed by statute, necessarily implies that the carriers have the exclusive right to furnish such equipment. It is optional with them, whether they exercise that right by furnishing cars owned by them, cars owned by other carriers, or cars leased from independent contractors. Under

[103]301 I.C.C. 323.

modern conditions, refrigerator cars have become regular equipment. (p. 373)

A private-car owner, whether he be a shipper or not, has no right to have his cars used as a vehicle for the transportation of freight over the rails of any carrier without its consent. If the carriers have suitable cars and will furnish them on demand they may refuse to transport shipments in private cars. They are privileged to do so at any time they have, or will secure and furnish, suitable equipment to carry the commodities they hold themselves out to transport. *Armour & Co. v. El Paso & S. W. Co.*, 52 I.C.C. 240, 246. (pp. 373-74)

In *Atchison, T. & St. F. Ry. Co. v. United States*, 232 U.S. 199, 214, 215, the court said:

> Whatever transportation service or facility the law requires the carrier to supply, they have the right to furnish. They can therefore use their own cars and cannot be compelled to accept those tendered by the shipper on condition that a lower freight rate be charged.

The carriers, by the rule hereunder consideration, reserve the right to furnish exclusively all refrigerator cars ordered by shippers other than meat packers. But one of the grounds on which we are asked to find a rule not justified is that the use of private cars helps to hold traffic to the rails. We have no authority to require carriers to accept cars furnished by the shippers for that or any other purpose. Therefore, unless the proposed rule will result in violation of the act, it is our duty to find it justified. (p. 374)

✿   ✿   ✿

The carriers should give careful consideration to complying with their legal obligations to furnish suitable refrigerator cars of their own ownership or those with whom they have contractual relations for the transportation of perishable commodities which they hold themselves out to transport. This applies equally to the cars for the transportation of products of the meat packers. In the interest of efficiency and economy of operation and considering the seasonal needs of refrigerated cars a pooling of such cars under unified operation might well be considered. (p. 382)

The discussion herein has been herein confined almost entirely to refrigerator cars and the findings would be so restricted, *but the general principles enunciated apply equally to all other types of private cars.* (Emphasis supplied.) (p. 382)

✿   ✿   ✿

We do not undertake to say that the carrier may not accept private cars if it so desires, but if such cars are accepted the carriers may not acquiesce in arrangements under which mileage earnings accruing to the car owner are paid in whole or in part by such car owner to the shipper lessee which results in the payment by such shipper of charges less than the published tariff rate. (p. 383)

In *General Amer. T. Car Corp. v. El Dorado Term. Co.*, 308 U.S. 422 (1940), the Supreme Court said (at p. 428-30):

Freight cars are facilities of transportation as defined by the act. The railroads are under obligation, as part of their public service, to furnish these facilities upon reasonable request of the shipper, and therefore have the exclusive right to furnish them. They are not, however, under an obligation to own such cars. They may, if they deem it advisable, lease them so as to be in a position to furnish them according to the demand of the shipping public, and, if the carriers do so lease cars, the terms of which they obtain them are not the subject of the direct control by the Interstate Commerce Commission. If the carriers pay too much for the hire of such cars the Commission may, of course, refuse to allow them to reflect such excess cost in their tariffs. The lessor of such cars to a railroad, however, is not itself a carrier or engaged in any public service. Therefore its practices lie without the realm of the Commission's competence.

Cars thus leased and used by the carriers are to be distinguished from so-called private cars with which we are here concerned. Shippers, particularly those who require a specialized form of freight car for transportation of their products, may, and do, own cars adapted for the purpose. They may, and do, in lieu of owning such facilities, rent them from the owners. Car companies owning a large number of a special type of freight car, some affiliates or subsidiaries of railroads and others, like the petitioner, wholly independent and financed by private capital, have, for many years, been in the business of leasing cars to shippers. The practice has been well known and well understood. It is entirely lawful and the Commission has so held. But the practice cannot modify the requirements of paragraph (13) and Section 15, which governs the payment of allowances for private cars, and invests the Commission with authority to find and declare what allowances are reasonable.

o   o   o

From what has been said it results that the shipper in this case was permitted by law to furnish freight cars for the transportation of its products and to be paid a reasonable allowance for performing this portion of the public service which the carrier was bound to render, and that the law requires that the amount and conditions of payment of such allowance shall be set forth in a published tariff. If this is not done, the shipper may complain to the Commission, to the end that a proper allowance be ascertained and made effective by a schedule duly published.

Joint Use of Terminal Facilities

In order to grasp the breadth of the power conferred upon the Commission to order the joint use of terminal facilities it is important to consider Section 3(5) of the Interstate Commerce Act[104] in its historical setting. The Section in its present form had its origin in the Transportation Act of 1920. Prior to amendments in the Transportation

---

[104]49 U.S.C. 3(5).

Act of 1920, the antecedent section of the Interstate Commerce Act which related to the interchange of traffic between connecting carriers specifically provided that it should not be construed as requiring any common carrier to give the use of its tracks or terminal facilities to another engaged in like business. The amendment of 1920 reversed the policy of Congress and conferred upon the Commission direct and explicit power to require the use by one carrier of the full terminal facilities of another carrier upon certain terms and conditions.

In the light of the remedial character of the statute and the clear intent of Congress, the Commission, from the outset, adopted the policy of giving the section the broadest possible construction to the end that all of the privately owned rights and properties within a terminal area may be drawn upon for common use. As stated by the Commission in *Consolidation of Railroads.*[105]

> Generally speaking, the terminal railroad properties, wherever located, automatically fall into the aggregation of terminal properties of which they are a part. . . . All terminal properties should be thrown open to all users on fair and equal terms so that every industry on whatever rails shall have access to all lines radiating from that terminal, and every line carrier reaching that terminal shall similarly have access to all terminal tracks within the terminal area. . . .
>
> The unification of terminal properties everywhere should put an end to disputes . . . to the advantage alike of all railroads and all users of railroads. In the interest of efficient and economical operation and the free movement of traffic, restrictions in service and discrimination in charges which have arisen from differences in local terminal situations should cease to be a feature of railroad operation.

In carrying out the policy of the statute, the Commission has given the terms "terminal facilities" the broadest possible interpretation in a number of cases in which it has compelled the use by one railroad of the right-of-way and track of another.[106] The courts have recognized the broad powers conferred by Section 3(5) without exception. As stated by the Supreme Court in *Railroad Commission v. Southern Pacific Company.*[107]

[105]159 I.C.C. 522.

[106]*Hastings Commercial Club v. Chicago, M., St. P. & P. Ry. Co.*, 69 I.C.C. 489, 494; *Use by Erie of Niagara Junction Ry. Co. Terminals*, 269 I.C.C. 493, 497-498; *Chicago & N.W. Ry. Co. v. Ann Arbor R. Co.*, 263 I.C.C. 287; and *Erie R. Co. Acquisition*, 275 I.C.C. 679, 687.

[107]264 U.S. 343. See also, *Pittsburgh & West Virginia R. R. Co. v. United States*, 41 Fed. 2d, 806, 810; *El Dorado & Western Railroad Co. v. Chicago, Rock Island and Pacific Railroad Company*, 5 F. 2d, 799 (in this case, by way of *dictum*, the court observed that Section 3(5) gave the Commission power to order a cross-track over the right-of-way of an objecting railroad).

Paragraph 4 (Section 3, paragraph 5) provides that the Commission may in the public interest and without impairment of a carrier's power to handle its own business with its terminal facilities, require the use of its terminal facilities, including its main-line track or tracks for a reasonable distance outside of its terminal — for another carrier or carriers, upon such terms as may be agreed upon by the parties, fixed by the Commission or determined by suit as in condemnation proceedings.

It is obvious from the foregoing that Congress intended to place under the superintending and fostering direction of the Interstate Commerce Commission all increased facilities in the matter of distribution of cars and equipment and in joint terminals, in the exchange of interstate traffic and passengers between railways so as to make it prompt and continuous. It not only provides for the temporary expropriation of terminals and main track of one railway to the common use of one or more other railways in an emergency, but it also contemplates the compulsory sharing of one company's terminals with one or more companies as a permanent arrangement. This is a drastic limitation of a carrier's control and use of its own property in order to secure convenience and dispatch for the whole shipping and travelling public in interstate commerce. It gives the Interstate Commerce Commission the power and duty, where the public interest requires, to make out of what is the passenger and freight station of one interstate carrier, a union station or depot.

Continuous Carriage of Freight

Section 7 of the Act[108] provides that "it shall be unlawful for any common carrier subject to the provisions of this part to enter into any combination, contract, or agreement, expressed or implied, to prevent, by change of time schedule, carriage in different cars, or by other means or devices, the carriage of freights from being continuous from the place of shipment to the place of destination; and no break of bulk, stoppage, or interruption made by such common carrier shall prevent the carriage of freight from being . . . treated as one continuous carriage from the place of shipment to the place of destination, unless such break, stoppage, or interruption was made in good faith for some necessary purpose, and without any intent to avoid or unnecessarily interrupt such continuous carriage or to evade any of the provisions of this part."

Rail-Water Traffic

The Commission under Section 6(11) (a)[109] has jurisdiction over rail and water transportation and of the carriers "To establish physical

---

[108]49 U.S.C. 7.
[109]49 U.S.C. 6(11) (a). The last three paragraphs of Sections 5(15), (16), (17), and 6(11), (12) and parts of 49 U.S.C. 51 and 15 U.S.C. 31 are to be considered together.

connection between the lines of the rail carrier and the dock at which interchange of passengers or property is to be made by directing the rail carrier to make suitable connection between its line and a track or tracks which have been constructed from the dock to the limits of the railroad right of way, or by directing either or both the rail and water carrier, individually or in connection with one another, to construct and connect with the lines of the rail carrier a track or tracks to the dock. The Commission shall have full authority to determine and prescribe the terms and conditions upon which these connecting tracks shall be operated, and it may, either in the construction or the operation of such tracks, determine what sum shall be paid to or by either carrier: Provided, That construction required by the Commission under the provisions of this paragraph shall be subject to the same restrictions as to findings of public convenience and necessity and other matters as is construction required under Section 1 of the part." And under Section 6(11) (b)[110] "To establish proportional rates, or maximum, or minimum, or maximum and minimum proportional rates, by rail to and from the ports to which the traffic is brought, or from which it is taken by the water carrier, and to determine to what traffic and in connection with what vessels and upon what terms and conditions such rates shall apply. By proportional rates are meant those which differ from the corresponding local rates to and from the port and which apply only to traffic which has been brought to the port or is carrier from the port by a common carrier by water."

Section 6(12)[111] provides that "If any common carrier subject to this Act enters into arrangements with any water carrier operating from a port in the United States to a foreign country, through the Panama Canal or otherwise, for the handling of through business between interior points of the United States and such foreign country, the Commission may by order require such common carrier to enter into similar arrangements with any or all other lines of steamships operating from said port to the same foreign country."

Obtaining Equal Facilities for Shippers

By Section 23,[112] the federal courts have jurisdiction to order common carriers to move and transport traffic, or to furnish cars or other facilities for transportation, to any complainant establishing a violation

[110]49 U.S.C. 6(11) (b).
[111]49 U.S.C. 6(12).
[112]49 U.S.C. 23.

by a common carrier of any provision of the I.C. Act as prevents the complainant from having interstate traffic moved by the common carrier at the same rates as are charged, or upon terms or conditions as favorable as those given, by the common carrier to others for like traffic under similar conditions. An order may issue even though the compensation for the service is undetermined. The relief provided by Section 23 is cumulative and does not exclude or interfere with other remedies provided by the Act to which it is supplement.

Exchange of Services with Transmission Companies

Under Section 1(5 1/2),[113] it is provided that nothing in the I.C. Act is to be "construed to prevent any common carrier subject to this Act from entering into or operating under any contract with any telephone, telegraph, or cable company, for the exchange of their services."

Free Transportation

Under Section 1(7),[114] no common carrier may "directly or indirectly, issue or give any interstate free ticket, free pass, or free transportation for passengers, except to its employees, its officers, time inspectors, surgeons, physicians, and attorneys at law, and the families of any of the foregoing"; and except to certain classes of people designated therein.

Interchange of passes between common carriers is provided for by Section 1(7) as is the free carriage of passengers in cases of emergencies, and the exchange of passes or franks between common carriers and telegraph, telephone and cable operators. Section 1(7) also provides penalties for violations.

Transit

Transit is an accompaniment of, or supplementary advantage in connection with, existing rates; it is a rule, regulation or practice affecting the application of such rates, but it is not a rate itself.[115] That transit is merely an accompaniment of an existing rate, and not a reduction in rate, follows from the Commission's treatment of transit under the Inter-

---

[113]49 U.S.C. 1(5 1/2).

[114]49 U.S.C. 1(7), Cf. Section 22. See also Sections 217(b), 306(c), 32 U.S.C. 73, 39 U.S.C. 523, 45 U.S.C. 228r.

[115]*Great Northern Railway Co. v. United States,* 81 F. Supp. 921, 925, affirmed *Great Northern Railway Co. v. United States,* 336 U.S. 933; *Cooperative Mills, Inc. v. Alton & S. R.,* 278 I.C.C. 137, 141.

state Commerce Act. Under the original Act, the Commission held that it had no authority to require the establishment of transit, since Section 1(5) only outlawed unreasonable rates, and Section 15 applied only to rates.[116] Under the Hepburn Act of 1906, Section 15 was amended to permit the Commission to prescribe rates, and also, practices of regulations affecting rates. The Commission then held that it had authority over transit.[117] The Mann-Elkins Act of 1910 added paragraph 6 to Section 1, declaring unlawful all unreasonable rules, regulations, and practices affecting the application of rates. The Supreme Court has since held that transit may be required under Section 1, as amended. In *Central R. R. Co. of N. J. v. United States*,[118] the Supreme Court said:

> The Commission clearly has power under Section 1 of the Act to Regulate Commerce, as amended, to determine whether in a particular case a transit privilege should be granted or should be withdrawn. For that section requires, among other things, that carriers establish, in connection with through routes and joint rates, reasonable rules and regulations.

That transit does not amount to a reduction in the rates on transited traffic was also made clear by the Commission in *Thomas Keery, Inc. v. New York, O. & W. Ry.*,[119] where the Commission pointed out that if the proposition that transit did amount to a reduction in rates below normal or reasonable level, the carriers would be free to cancel the through rates and to establish, in lieu thereof, rates made by combination on the transit points — which the Commission considered as an inconceivable proposition. The Commission said (p. 591):

> It is a matter of common knowledge that transit arrangements of wide variety are authorized on a substantial portion of the traffic transported by the railroads in this country and that through rates, either voluntarily established by the carriers or prescribed by us, apply on this traffic. These rates and transit practices are an integral part of the rate structure of the country. If this traffic may not be regarded as through traffic, then unavoidable implications are that these rates, or at least a good part of them, are without warrant in law, that the carriers are at liberty to cancel them and to establish in lieu thereof rates made by combination on the transit points; a course of action so inconsistent with long-established practices and understandings, and so far reaching in effects upon the commerce

---

[116]*Re Iowa Barb Steel Wire Co.*, 1 I.C.C. 605; *Crews v. Richmond & Danville R. Co.*, 1 I.C.C. 703, 713; *Diamond Mills v. Boston & Maine R. Co.*, 9 I.C.C. 311, 316.

[117]*Re Transportation of Wool, Hides and Pelts*, 23 I.C.C. 151; *The Transit Case*, 24 I.C.C. 340, 343-344.

[118]257 U.S. 247, 257. See also *Tri-State Milling Co. v. Alameda Belt Line*, 303 I.C.C. 303, 309; *Thomas Keery Co., Inc. v. N. Y., O. & W. Ry. Co.*, 206 I.C.C. 585, 591, 211 I.C.C. 451.

[119]206 I.C.C. 585.

of the country, as to be not readily conceivable. The service accorded complainants' traffic at Cadosia is essentially no different in principle than encountered in innumerable other instances.

The Supreme Court held in *Interstate Commerce Commission v. Mechling*[120] that carriers may not increase the line-haul charges to cover the cost of transit at the expense of particular shippers. In *Central R. R. Co. of N. J. v. United States, supra,* the court said:

> Whether the privilege shall be granted or withheld is determined by the local carrier. If granted, the local carrier determines the conditions; and they are set forth in the local tariff. Although a joint through route with joint rates is established by concurrent action of several carriers, the transit privilege may thus be granted without the consent of, and without consulting, connecting carriers. And the whole revenue received for the use of the privilege is retained by the local carrier.

A carrier may provide for a transit privilege on its line by its individual tariff without the concurrence of other carriers and has a right to provide for such arrangement and subsequent shipment at lawfully established joint through rates from original origin to destination without concurrence of its connections, but it cannot establish a joint rate itself without such concurrence.[121] Transit privileges thus are treated as local to the carrier according them.[122] A carrier does not become responsible for the granting or withholding of transit privilege which is local to another carrier merely because it participates in the movement or concurs in joint rates.[123]

All provisions governing the application of a transit privilege must be strictly complied with to obtain the privilege.[124] In the *Union Pacific* case, the Commission said (p. 687) that since at the time of movement neither the storage-in-transit nor stoppage-in-transit tariff authorized application of transit balances on tonnage added to non-transit shipments stopped at storage point to complete loading, that the fact that the considered shipments would not be accorded transit under subsequently established provision for such consolidation did not warrant retroactive application thereof. Since transit service is of a special nature and local to the carrier that grants it, services accorded by different carriers need not be uniform in absence of undue preference or

---

[120]330 U.S. 567, 583. This holding was required by the prior pronouncements of the Supreme Court in *Central R. R. Co. of N. J. v. United States,* 257 U.S. 247, 255.

[121]*Allowances on Cottonseed at C & G Ry. Points,* 238 I.C.C. 309, 316.

[122]*Northern Milling Co. v. C. & N. W. Ry.,* 237 I.C.C. 235, 236.

[123]*Lynchberg Chamber of Commerce v. N. & W. Ry.,* 237 I.C.C. 408, 410.

[124]*Union Pac. R. Co. Petition for Declaratory Order,* 309 I.C.C. 683, 696.

prejudice.[125] While out-of-line or backhaul transportation has frequently been disapproved where an inadequate or no charge was made therefor, there are numerous instances where such transportation without additional charges has been approved or found not unlawful, particularly where the indirect routes did not appear unduly circuitous compared with the direct routes.[126]

Reconsignment and Diversion

The general rule respecting reconsignment and diversion in transit is that a separate charge for the service, based on cost and including a reasonable profit, is proper.[127] The Commission stated that a mere showing that certain railroads permit three free diversions for shipments of apples, without a showing that transit method of marketing apples is similar to that used by in-transit lumber dealers, is too meager for determining whether a departure from the general rule (that a separate charge based on cost and including a reasonable profit is proper) may lawfully be made on lumber. Charges made for reconsignment following inspection and sampling, which privilege involves additional clerical work and extra switching, beyond the charges made for the line-haul movement, are not unreasonable.[128] It is not unreasonable per se to apply a combination of local rates on a shipment which has been placed for unloading at the original destination, and which is subsequently reforwarded to a different destination.[129]

Routing and Misrouting

Section 15(10) of the Interstate Commerce Act[130] provides:

"In all cases where at the time of delivery of property to any railroad corporation being a common carrier, for transportation subject to the provisions of this part to any point of destination, between which and the point of such delivery for shipment two or more through routes and through rates shall have been established as in this part provided to which through routes and through rates such carrier is a party, the person, firm, or corporation making such shipment, subject to such reasonable exceptions and regulations as the Interstate Commerce Commission shall from

[125]*Beall Pipe & Tank Corp. v. Southern Pac. Co.,* 308 I.C.C. 139, 142.
[126]*Grain Transit at Concordia, Kans., Chicago, B. & Q. R. Co.,* 310 I.C.C. 573, 575.
[127]*Lumber, Free Time Allowance at Hold Points,* 310 I.C.C. 521, 526-7.
[128]*Minneapolis Traffic Assn. v. Great Northern Ry. Co.,* 269 I.C.C. 645.
[129]*Granite City Steel Co. v. Chicago & E. I. R. Co.,* 266 I.C.C. 300, 301.
[130]49 U.S.C. 15(10).

time to time prescribe, shall have the right to designate in writing by which of such through routes such property shall be transported to destination, and it shall thereupon by the duty of the initial carrier to route said property and issue a through bill of lading therefor as so directed, and to transport said property over its own line or lines and deliver the same to a connecting line or lines according to such through route, and it shall be the duty of each of said connecting carriers to receive said property and transport it over the said line or lines and deliver the same to the next succeeding carrier or consignee according to the routing instructions in said bill of lading: Provided, However, That the shipper shall in all instances have the right to determine, where competing lines of railroad constitute portions of a through line or route, over which of said competing lines so constituting a portion of said through line or route his freight shall be transported."

Under Section 15(10), the shipper's routing instructions must be obeyed.[131] The Commission has held that where a shipper's routing instructions are complete and the shipments move in accordance with such instructions, there is no misrouting.[132] When a shipper tenders to a carrier for execution a bill of lading with the route designated therein, and when no inconsistent rate is inserted or other evidence of error is apparent, it does not constitute misrouting by the carrier to move the shipment over the designated route even though a lower rate may be in effect over another route.[133]

Section 15(11) of the I.C. Act[134] provides:

Whenever property is diverted or delivered by one carrier to another carrier contrary to routing instructions in the bill of lading, unless such diversion or delivery is in compliance with a lawful order, rule, or regulation of the Commission, such carriers shall, in a suit or action in any court of competent jurisdiction, be jointly and severally liable to the carrier thus deprived of its right to participate in the haul of the property, for the total amount of the rate or charge it would have received had it participated in the haul of the property."

There is no liability if the carrier to which the property is diverted can show "that before carrying the property it had no notice, by bill of lading, waybill or otherwise, of the routing instructions."

Where traffic is not routed by the shipper, Section 15(12)[135] provides that "the Commission may, whenever the public interest and a fair distribution of the traffic require, direct the route which such traffic shall

---

[131]*New England Box Co. v. Boston & M. R.*, 305 I.C.C. 133, 135.

[132]*National Supply Co. v. Chicago B. & Q. R.*, 66 I.C.C. 604, 605.

[133]*New England Box Co. v. Boston & M. R., supra; American Sand & Gravel Co. v. Chicago & N. W. Ry.*, 148 I.C.C. 343, 345.

[134]49 U.S.C. 15(10).

[135]49 U.S.C. 15(12).

take after it arrives at the terminus of one carrier or at a junction point with another carrier, and is to be there delivered to another carrier."

Weighing

There is a legal obligation upon common carriers by railroad to ascertain the weights on carload traffic with sufficient accuracy to determine the freight charges thereon.[136]

As was stated in *Carrier Switching at Industrial Plants in the East.*[137]

> . . . It is the duty of a carrier to ascertain the weight of the freight carried by it where the weight so obtained is used by the carrier for billing purposes. Usually, carriers provide their own scales for this purpose. However, many industries, at their own expense, provide scales for weighing freight cars. Such scales are inspected periodically by the carriers to assure their accuracy, and the weights thus obtained are often used by them for billing purposes. Merely because the weight thus obtained may be desired or used also by the industry, is no reason in itself for precluding such service under the line-haul rate where a weighing of the car by the carrier on some scale is necessary in any event for its own purposes.

See *American Smelting & Refining Co. Terminal Services,*[138] noting that in *Carrier Switching at Industrial Plants in the East, supra,* approved tariff rules permit carriers "to perform the service of securing the weight of freight, irrespective of the ownership of the scales used, provided the weights obtained are used by the carrier for billing purposes." See also *Institute of Scrap Iron & Steel, Inc. v. Aberdeen & R. R.,*[139] where the following statements are made (at 774-76) concerning the responsibilities of carriers operating in Southern territory:

> The railroads are responsible for assuring that the weight is determined in a fair and accurate manner. To this end, railroad track scales are checked and tested by the Southern Weighing and Inspection Bureau, agent for the affected railroads. The Bureau employee who performs the weighing executes a sworn statement certifying that the weight is correct as noted . . .

>   ❊   ❊   ❊

> Subsections (4), (5), and (6) of section 1 are not violated by the terms of the weighing rule under consideration. It is neither unreasonable nor inequitable to require the shippers to rely upon certified destination weights

[136]*Checking, Marking, and Weighing Wool in the West,* 284 I.C.C. 697, 702; *Increased Switching Charges at Duluth, Minn.,* 309 I.C.C. 737, 770; *Anaconda Copper Mining Co. Terminal Service,* 226 I.C.C. 387, 391.
[137]294 I.C.C. 159, 164-65.
[138]294 I.C.C. 745, 749.
[139]341 I.C.C. 771, 346 I.C.C. 895.

found by authorized weighmasters operating industry-owned tracks. The privately owned equipment is regularly inspected and tested to assure accuracy in the same manner as railroad track scales . . .

As long ago as 1913 it was noted in *In Re Weighing of Freight by Carriers*,[140] that innaccuracies in weighing can result in discrimination between shippers as much as do differences in rates themselves. No order was entered in that proceeding, but subsequent thereto, and as a result thereof, a code of rules governing the weighing the reweighing of carload freight, incorporating many of the principles enunciated in the report in 28 I.C.C. 7, was adopted by the railroads. This code of rules was endorsed by the Commission and recommended for application to interstate transportation throughout the country subject to the Commission's right and duty, upon complaint, to inquire into the legality or reasonableness of any rule. Today charges, rules and regulations governing weighing and reweighing of carload and less than carload freight are published in tariffs.

Demurrage

Under Section 1(6) of the Interstate Commerce Act,[141] as emended by the 4R Act "Demurrage charges shall be computed, and rules and regulations relating to such charges shall be established, in such a manner as to fulfill the national needs with respect to (a) freight car utilization and distribution, and (b) maintenance of an adequate freight car supply available for transportation of property."

Charges for demurrage embrace compensation for the use of the cars and tracks and a penalty designed to prevent undue detention of cars and to insure their prompt return to public service.[142] Their purpose is to promote car efficiency by penalizing shippers for undue detention.[143] The dual nature of demurrage charges, the purpose of such charges, and their efficacy was clearly stated in *Commerce & Industry Assn. of N. Y., Inc. v. B. & O. R. Co.*:[144]

. . . Those charges are not primarily a source of added revenue to the carriers. They are designed to compensate the carriers for the shippers'

---

[140]28 I.C.C. 7. See *Smith & Duckworth v. C., C. & St. L. Ry. Co.*, 100 I.C.C. 300, 301.

[141]49 U.S.C. 1(6).

[142]*Chrysler Corp. v. New York Central R. Co.*, 234 I.C.C. 755; *Ford Motor Co. v. Chesapeake & O. Ry.*, 311 I.C.C. 559, 562; *Tildesley Coal Co. v. Norfolk & W. Ry. Co.*, 309 I.C.C. 275, 276. Detention is just a form of demurrage, *Continental Can Co., Inc. v. Pennsylvania R. Co.*, 270 I.C.C. 42.

[143]*Continental Oil Co. v. Kansas City Southern Ry. Co.*, 311 I.C.C. 288, 290.

[144]281 I.C.C. 655, 659-60.

use of cars for storage and, of equal importance as applied in rail transportation, are an incentive to compel release of carrier equipment. The necessity for demurrage is well recognized. Such charges serve the best interests of the railroads, the users of rail transportation, and the public in the maintenance of an adequate transportation service. Demurrage becomes increasingly important during periods of car shortages in order to maintain the available car supply to the best interests of all concerned. Toward that end, the Commission has, from time to time, exercised its authority by entering service orders which have increased the demurrage charges and alleviated car shortages under the exigencies of each particular situation.

It is a fundamental principle that a shipper or consignee is entitled to a reasonable time to load or unload his shipment. Demurrage charges accrue after the expiration of that reasonable period, referred to as free time. The carriers' primary duties and obligations to the public are for the carriage of goods. If a consignor or consignee elects to use a freight car or a railroad station to store his goods, he receives an extra service for which the carrier is entitled to additional remuneration. Widespread use of rail facilities for the storage of freight congests carrier facilities and causes delay in handling other shipments. It is necessary that demurrage, track storage, and storage charges ordinarily contain a penal element as an incentive for prompt release of equipment.

Likewise in *Balfour, Guthrie & Co. v. Chicago, M. St. P. & P. R. Co.*,[145] the Commission said:

> Demurrage charges are in part penalties for the undue detention of cars, and in part compensation for excessive use of cars as warehouses. What is said in the two preceding paragraphs about complainants' responsibility is particularly true so far as the compensation element of the charges is concerned, because the shipper has made use of the equipment and should pay reasonable rental therefor. . . . However, no definitely determinable portion of a demurrage charge can be said to represent either the compensation or penalty factor.

In various cases the Commission has stated that demurrage and other analogous charges arising after transportation has been completed are governed by the applicable tariffs in effect at the time the charges arise. For example, in *Getz Bros. & Co. v. Director General*,[146] the Commission stated:

> In *United Shoe Machinery Corp. v. Director General*, 55 I.C.C. 253, and *British Shoe Machinery Co. v. P.R.R. Co.*, 66 I.C.C. 661 . . . we held —
>
> That . . . track storage, and demurrage are controlled by the tariffs in effect contemporaneously with the accrual of these services, and therefore are subject to such charges as lawfully may be made in the applicable tariffs during the period of accrual.

[145]223 I.C.C. 441, 447.
[146]85 I.C.C. 673, 674.

A demurrage charge is no part of the rate or through charge in effect at the time the shipment is forwarded from point of origin; nor can it be incorporated therewith by calling it a contract.

Again in *Manassa Timber Co. v. L. & N. R. R. Co.*,[147] the Commission reviewed pertinent court and Commission proceedings in the following language:

> In our opinion demurrage charges have nothing to do with transportation rates. . . . Before a shipment is made it can not possibly be known what the demurrage charges will amount to or whether there will be any at all. If the cars are unloaded or reconsigned within the free time there will be none. In every case the question of whether or not there will be car service depends upon the consignee or owner or upon conditions which cannot possibly be known in advance. Demurrage charges are no part of and are separate from and distinct from transportation charges and do not arise, if at all, until the transportation has ended.

> The decision was affirmed by the United States Supreme ourt in *Berwind-White Co. v. Chicago & Erie R.R.*, 235 U.S. 371. Defendants point out that demurrage charges may be incident to transportation charges but are for an entirely different service. They cite *Krauss Bros. Lumber Co. v. Director General*, 92 I.C.C. 450, wherein we said:

> "But demurrage charges are no part of the rate or through charges in effect at the time the shipment is forwarded from point of origin. *Getz Bros. & Co. v. Director General*, 85 I.C.C. 673. Although they may follow the shipment and be collected together with the transportation charges, they are for a distinct and separate service."

The Commission has determined in numerous instances that penalty charges are unjust and unreasonable when the demurrage charges accrue from causes beyond the shipper's power to control.[148] The court held in the *St. Louis S.W. Ry. Co.* case that unreasonable interference with the cars by the carrier would preclude collection of demurrage to the extent that the delay in unloading was proximately caused by such interference. The court also said that the carrier might be required in the reasonable and ordinary course of its business to subject the cars to some disturbance, and that such reasonable interference would not operate to extend consignee's free time.

In *Ford Motor Co. v. Chesapeake & O. Ry. Co.*[149] the Commission said that where neither party was responsible for the severe weather

---

[147]115 I.C.C. 421, 425. See also *Chesapeake & Ohio Coal & Coke Co. v. Toledo & O. C. Ry. Co.*, 245 Fed. 917.

[148]*St. Louis S. W. Ry. Co. v. Mays*, 177 F. Supp. 182, 184; *Commerce & Industry Assn. of N. Y. v. B. & O. R. Co.*, 272 I.C.C. 7; and *Universal Carloading and Distributing Co., Inc. v. P. R. Co.*, 276 I.C.C. 145.

[149]311 I.C.C. 559, 562.

conditions that caused detention of the cars at defendant's Toledo dock, and complainant apparently used due diligence in forwarding cars to destination in all-rail service when it became apparent that Lake service could not be used, complainant would be entitled to reparation in any amounts included in the demurrage charges as a penalty. But since the per diem charge, plus a reasonable amount for administrative expenses, during the detention period aggregated at least as much as the $3.00 daily charge per car which accrued, that charge may not be said to have included any amount as a penalty. In *United Eastern Coal Sales Corp. v. Central R. Co. of N. J.*,[150] the Commission said that when the maximum demurrage charge assessed against or paid by any of complainants was $2.00 per car per day, it could not be found to contain any penalty element in view of numerous prior findings that the compensatory portion to be retained by carriers should be the existing per diem rate plus an amount for incidental expenses; a per diem rate of $2.40 had been established some years earlier.

In granting relief from penalty charges, the shippers have been held to a high degree of diligence by exercising prudent foresight in all the circumstances surrounding the transaction. Where the evidence discloses that the complainant failed to exercise due diligence, or where proximate cause of the car detention was found to be of the shippers' or consignees' own making, relief has been denied.[151]

The Commission in the *Continental Oil* case said that the ordinary economic vagaries and risks of doing business are not causes beyond control of a shipper in the same sense as occurrences that have been found to warrant exemption from penalty charges.[152] In *Arundel-Dixon Hunkin v. Baltimore & O. R. Co.*,[153] the Commission said that principles granting relief from demurrage on frozen lading should not be stretched to apply to instances where the considered articles themselves were not frozen and were physically susceptible of being unloaded but were not unloaded because they were to be used by a particular shipper only in a mixture with other commodities which were too frozen to be unloaded and used in the mixing process. In *Federal Chemical Co. v. New York*

---

[150]311 I.C.C. 199, 203.

[151]*Eagle Cotton Oil Co. v. Gulf, M. & O. R. Co.*, 268 I.C.C. 391; *Continental Can Co., Inc. v. Pennsylvania R. Co.*, 270 I.C.C. 42; *Apex Tire and Rubber Co. v. New York, N. H. & H. R. Co.*, 277 I.C.C. 1; and *Wells Fargo Carloading Co., Inc. v. Central R. Co., of N.J.*, 277 I.C.C. 797; *Continental Oil Co. v. Kansas City Southern Ry. Co.*, 311 I.C.C. 288, 290.

[152]See also *United Eastern Coal Sales Co. v. Central R. Co., of N.J.*, 311 I.C.C. 199, 201.

[153]308 I.C.C. 555, 557.

Central R. Co.,[154] while complainant had been unable to unload cars during a 6-day period following a severe storm, for which it was given relief from demurrage charges under tariff weather-interference rule and its average-agreement plan, detention of cars after that period was caused by its inability to unload for reasons peculiar to its business and not because of any reason covered by the tariff rule; having failed to exercise due diligence in avoiding or reducing the detention of these cars, the Commission said that the assailed demurrage charges were applicable and not unreasonable.

FREE TIME ON EXPORT TRAFFIC

From an early date export traffic has been given more free time than domestic traffic. The propriety of this difference in treatment between export and domestic traffic has been consistently recognized by the Commission in its decisions dealing with the subject. For example, in a case designated has *Export Free Time,*[155] Commission stated:

> It has long been recognized as a necessity of export business that sufficient time, within reasonable limits must be given to enable the export shipper to accumulate his cargo and arrange for its receipt by the vessel.

Again, in passing on the propriety of a railroad proposal to reduce free time at California ports, the Commission in summarizing the necessity for greater free time on export than on domestic traffic, said in *Decreased Free Time Allowance:*[156]

> It is clear from the record that detention at ports is not ordinarily intended by shippers, steamship companies, or respondents, and when it occurs is not of material benefit to them. The circumstances and conditions which are controlling in the case of traffic moving through ports are substantially dissimilar from those which obtain in connection with domestic traffic. Many of the factors which tend to delay traffic intended for ocean movement do not exist in the case of the domestic traffic.

Finally, in *Merchants and Planters Co. v. G.H. & H.R. Co.,*[157] the Commission made this observation:

> The differences between demurrage rules on domestic and export traffic have long been recognized as proper.

[154]308 I.C.C. 386, 387-8.
[155]47 I.C.C. 162, 179.
[156]67 I.C.C. 400.
[157]129 I.C.C. 477, 480.

Average Agreements

The Commission in *Seneca Coal & Iron Corp. v. Pennsylvania R. Co.*[158] Stated that average demurrage agreements are based on mutual gain and sacrifice by shipper and carrier, shipper being enabled thereby to escape payments which he would otherwise have to make by using unexpired free time on cars promptly released to offset demurrage on cars held beyond free time; and in recognition of such benefits, provisions whereby shippers waive exemption normally provided in connection with "straight" demurrage rules, from charges accruing because of bunching of cars by carriers, or due to weather interference, have consistently been found reasonable. The Commission said that while shippers have been relieved of demurrage charges where detention was clearly the fault of the carrier, in the absence of proven negligent action or inaction any delays of a few cars here or there during an extended period covered by an average agreement do not warrant remission of charges.

Water Carriers — Demurrage

Demurrage charges are compensation to the carrier paid by the consignor or consignee for the loss of the use of its barge and for administrative expenses incidental thereto; that is, the charges are assessed by the carrier for the detention of the barge beyond the free time allowed for loading and unloading.[159] However, penalty charges are unjust and unreasonable when demurrage charges accrue from causes beyond the shippers' power to control; in the granting of relief from such charges by the Commission, shippers have been held to a high degree of diligence, not only in minimizing delays by releasing or attempting to release the equipment, but also in the exercise of prudent foresight in all of the circumstances surrounding the detention. In the *Al Johnson* case, the Commission said that the shipper did not use prudent foresight in minimizing the accrual of the demurrage charges where strike-free and high-water-free facilities were available at a nearby port, thus the demurrage charges were not shown to be unjust and unreasonable.

---

[158]311 I.C.C. 795, 798.

[159]*Al Johnson Construction Co. v. Mississippi Valley Barge Line Co.*, 301 I.C.C. 561, 563-4.

Motor Carrier Vehicle Detention

In *Detention of Motor Vehicles — Nationwide*,[160] the Commission adopted uniform nationwide truckload and volume detention rules including prearranged scheduling and uniform nationwide charges for vehicles both with and without power.[161] The purpose of such rules are to discourage delays of carriers' vehicles and to eliminate unfair competitive advantages among shippers resulting from multiple rules or lack of rules. They are meant also to curtail unlawful concessions resulting from the failure of carriers to collect, and the failure of shippers to pay, proper detention charges.

Packaging of Commodities

The Commission has jurisdiction over the packaging of commodities for transportation, and has stated on various occasions that its purpose is to promote safety and economy of transportation, that is, to reduce loss or damage, or to facilitate handling or both.[162] Packaging requirements which promote neither of these ends have been held to be unreasonable.[163] For example, a manufacturer of pipe had shipments of used steel thread protectors for gas and oil well pipe returned from the field in open top cars for reconditioning and further use. Certain of the applicable tariffs carried packing requirements and the carriers invoked the classification 10-percent penalty rule for nonobservance. In view of the manner of transportation of the articles, as well as the fact that they were not susceptible to damage, the Commission found that it was unreasonable to require them to be packed for shipment.[164]

When packing requirements are not met, the carriers must reject that type of freight tendered to them, as required, for example, by Rule 5 under the Uniform Freight Classification. But when a carrier inadvertently accepts for transportation a package not meeting the requirements (and this has to be proven), penalty charges may be assessed.[165] However, when improperly packed articles are knowingly accepted for transporta-

---

[160]124 M.C.C. 680, 126 M.C.C. 803. aff'd *Ford Motor Co. v. U.S.*, 569 F. 2d 196; cert. denied by S. Ct., June 5, 1978. See also *Detention of Motor Vehicles — Middle Atlantic-New England Territory*, 325 I.C.C. 336.

[161]49 CFR 1307 35(e).

[162]*Elliot Co. v. Chicago, R.I. & P. Ry. Co.*, 100 I.C.C. 683, 684; *Victor Rubber Co. v. Detroit, T. & I. R. Co.*, 178 I.C.C. 145.

[163]*Valley Steel Products Co. v. Atchison, T. & S. F. Ry. Co.*, 255 I.C.C. 177, 180.

[164]*Valley Steel Products Co.*, supra, note 2.

[165]*Weifenbach Marble & Tile Co. v. N. P. Ry. Co.*, 140 I.C.C. 493, 496.

tion, the Commission has found that the higher charges imposed by the penalty rule are not applicable.[166]

Distribution Service by Line-Haul Motor Carrier

In *Local Cartage Natl. Conference v. Middlewest M. Frt. Bur.*,[167] it was held that there is nothing in the I.C. Act which specifically prohibits a line-haul motor carrier from offering a distribution service at a point which it is authorized to serve. "If it chooses to provide such a service, it must file a tariff in the form and manner prescribed" in the tariff regulations and it must establish rates and charges, and rules and regulations affecting such rates and charges, which are lawful. See also *Federal Glass Co. v. C., C. & C. Highway, Inc.*,[168] where it was held that shipments destined to points outside Detroit proper could be included in pool-truckloads destined to and breaking bulk in Detroit, so long as the points were named.

Motor Carrier Leasing Practices

The Commission, under Section 204(e) of the I.C. Act,[169] is authorized to prescribe, with respect to the use by motor carriers of motor vehicles not owned by them, regulations requiring that the lease, contract, or other arrangements be in writing and be signed by the parties, and shall specify the period during which it is to be in effect and the compensation to be paid, and regulations requiring that a copy of the lease, contract, or other arrangement be carried in each motor vehicle covered thereby. The Commission is also authorized to prescribe such other regulations as may be reasonably necessary in order to assure that motor carriers will have full direction and control of such vehicles and will be fully responsible for the operation thereof in accordance with applicable law and regulations, as if they were the owners of such vehicles, including the requirements with respect to safety of operation and equipment and inspection thereof, which requirements may include the promulgation of such regulations requiring liability and cargo insurance covering all such equipment. Exceptions to the foregoing provision are set forth in Section 204(f).[170] They include motor vehicles of a cooperative associa-

---

[166]*Watermelons from Southern Points to the U.S. and Canada*, 301 I.C.C. 461, 463.
[167]62 M.C.C. 239, 250.
[168]43 M.C.C. 721, 724.
[169]49 U.S.C. 304(e).
[170]49 U.S.C. 304(f).

tion or a federation of cooperative associations as specified in Section 203(b) (4a) or (5); of a private carrier as defined in Section 203(a) (17) and is used regularly in the transportation of property of a character embraced in Section 203(b) (6) or perishable products manufactured from perishable property of a character embraced in Section 203(b) (6), and such motor vehicle is to be used by the motor carrier in a single movement or in one or more of a series of movements, loaded or empty, in the general direction of the general area in which such motor vehicle is based; or where the motor vehicle so to be used is one which has completed a movement covered by Section 203(b) (6) and such motor vehicle is next to be used by the motor carrier in a loaded movement in any direction, and/or in one or more of a series of movements, loaded or empty, in the general direction of the general area in which such motor vehicle is based.

The Commission in its notice of proposed rulemaking in Ex Parte No. MC-43 (Sub-No. 3), *Lease to Regulated Motor Carriers of Vehicles with Drivers by Private Carriers*,[171] discussed the background of leasing as follows:

Leasing of vehicles by one carrier from another has long been a common occurrence in the motor transportation industry. In fact, during World War II that industry was encourage to lease equipment in order fully to utilize the Nation's resources to further the war effort. The advantages of leasing are plain: a carrier can obtain needed equipment to bolster its own supply, and the lessor can reduce his expenses by obtaining a load for his return trip that might otherwise be made without lading. There are disadvantages in the practice, however, among which are:

1. Non-compliance by carriers with safety rules, especially requirements dealing with the hours of service and qualifications of drivers. Such regulations have been more difficult to enforce in situations where equipment with a driver is leased for only a single trip.

2. The locus of liability. Prior to the present leasing regulations, there was often a question of who, as between the lessor or lessee, was liable in case of accidents. Much of this problem arose out of inadequately drafted and generally informal equipment-leasing agreements.

3. The fairness and adequacy of the compensation. A frequent cause of trouble in prior years was dissatisfaction with the money paid to owners of vehicles by carrier-lessees.

As a result of these advantages and disadvantages of equipment leasing, which are by no means exhaustive of the subject, this Commission's Bureau of Motor Carriers began, in 1940, a study of motor vehicle leasing practices. Although suspended during the war, that study was resumed in

[171]Served March 7, 1974.

1947 when tentative rules were proposed. Those tentative regulations were presented to the public and the motor carrier industry for their views and suggestions, but none was forthcoming. Thereupon, the Commission, on January 9, 1948, initiated a formal proceeding in Ex Parte No. MC-43, *Lease and Interchange of Vehicles by Motor Carriers*, to consider the lawfulness of equipment-leasing practices of motor common and contract carriers. On June 26, 1950, then Division 5 of this Commission issued its report (51 M.C.C. 461) determining that the leasing practices of motor carriers included many violations and evasions of part II of the Interstate Commerce Act. Although the Division accepted most of the proposed rules, it rejected two important principles—that the leases must be of at least 30 days' duration and that compensation should be on a basis other than a division of revenues—earlier recommended in the proceeding by the hearing officer.

Thereafter, following oral argument, the entire Commission issued on May 8, 1951, a report (52 M.C.C. 675) in which rules similar to those prescribed by Division 5 were adopted but which included the two basic points earlier recommended by the hearing officer. These specific rules were adopted for the stated reasons (a) that abuses by carrier managements—namely, the failure to keep control over operational safety and to meet their carrier responsibilities—were in need of correction; and (b) that this agency's ability to enforce certain economic regulation over the motor carrier industry would otherwise be diminished. This Commission's jurisdiction and authority to issue the rules were immediately questioned by certain agricultural interests and motor carriers, but were confirmed by the United States Supreme Court in *American Trucking Associations, Inc., v. United States*, 344 U.S. 298 (1953). The Court, though expressly not ruling on the wisdom of the adopted regulations, held that even though the Interstate Commerce Act does not specify a right in this agency to control vehicle-leasing practices, we nevertheless possess sufficient rule-making jurisdiction to promulgate rules governing the leasing of equipment. In addition, the Court decided that the rules adopted did not violate sections 208(a) or 209(b) of the Act which protect carriers' rights to augment their equipment, or section 203(b)(6) which exempts from this Commission's jurisdiction vehicles used in transporting livestock, fish, and unprocessed agricultural commodities. The latter section was not violated, the Court held, even though, in the face of the leasing regulations the cost of non-regulated transportation in such exempted vehicles might increase.

The leasing rules were to have taken effect on August 1, 1951, but because of objections registered by agricultural interests and certain motor carriers, and as a result of requests by certain committees of the Congress, that effective date was postponed. The main objection voiced by various groups against the adopted regulations was directed at the 30-day lease requirement. This portion was deemed to be extremely important because it would have effectively abolished much of the trip-leasing engaged in by carriers. As a result, transporters of agricultural commodities, livestock, and fish would no longer be able to obtain return loads by leasing their equipment. It was argued that empty return trips would prompt these carriers to increase their charges for hauling the above-mentioned products, thus increasing marketing costs and prices ultimately paid by consumers. As a House Report[172] stated:

> The economic loss involved in such wasteful use of equipment, manpower, and gasoline would be reflected in higher prices to consumers, or lower prices to farmers and other producers, or both. It is doubtful, indeed, whether exempt haulers of agricultural commodities, livestock, and fish would be able to survive under these conditions.

The 30-day rule was subsequently amended by this Commission so that it no longer applied to motor vehicles used in the transportation of agricultural commodities referred to in sections 203(b)(4a), (5), and (6) of the statute. Therefore, regulated carriers (common and contract) could trip-lease a motor vehicle with a driver, when that vehicle was either owned by a farmer or farmer cooperative or used in the for-hire transportation of commodities referred to in section 203(b)(6) of the Act after such vehicle had completed a movement exempted from regulation by reason of sections 203(b)(4a), (5) or (6) of the statute. The use of leased equipment under this exception, however, was restricted to a single movement in any direction, or a series of movements over reasonably direct routes in the direction of the general area in which the exempt movement originated, or in the direction of the area in which the equipment is based.

In 1956, the Congress withdrew, with respect to most vehicles used to haul agricultural commodities and certain related products, this Commission's power to regulate (1) the duration of equipment leases, and (2) the compensation to be paid for equipment used in the transportation of such commodities. The vehicles of certain private carriers, i.e., those whose vehicles regularly are used in the transportation of agricultural commodities (which was not permitted under the amended regulations), were allowed to be trip-leased. The House Committee stated its belief that limited trip-leasing by such private carriers would be:

> essential to the continuation of a flexible and efficient motor transportation service for the marketing of agricultural products and is in the public interest.[173]

This exemption of equipment hauling agricultural commodities was challenged in the courts and upheld in *Christian v. United States,* 152 F. Supp. 561 (D. Md., 1957). The court there held that the amendments were not discriminatory and did not constitute class legislation. The legislation enacted in 1956 represents the latest Congressional action on this matter. For subsequent Commission action in this area, see 64 M.C.C. 361 (1955), 68 M.C.C. 553 (1956), 79 M.C.C. 65 (1959), 79 M.C.C. 251 (1959), 84 M.C.C. 247 (1961), 86 M.C.C. 525 (1961), 89 M.C.C. 683 (1962), and 91 M.C.C. 877 (1963).

---

[172]House Report No. 2425, June 25, 1956 (to accompany S. 898), *U.S. Code Congressional and Administrative News,* 84th Congress, 2nd Sess., 1956, p. 4304.
[173]*Ibid.,* p. 4308.

Leasing practices of carriers have created problems from the inception of Federal motor carrier regulation. This is demonstrated by the following discussion in *Tischler Extension — Canned Goods:*[174]

> The so-called lease arrangement, in our opinion, is not a bona fide one as contemplated by our regulations promulgated in Lease and Interchange of vehicles by Motor Carriers, 68 M.C.C. 553. Rather it appears to be an unauthorized lease of operating rights. We note here that no written agreement exists, that "lessor" accepts and delivers the shipment, pays the drivers, retains responsibility for the freight, and prepares the billing. The equipment leased to Lerner is loaded for movement before applicant "leases" the vehicle to Lerner. Therefore, the equipment is unavailable to lessee to augment its fleet as contemplated by the leasing portion of the regulations. Lerner pays nothing for the privilege of leasing the equipment, and, in fact, he receives a portion of the revenue from applicant. We conclude that no lease of equipment actually exists, and that the ostensible lessee-carrier, Lerner, merely accepts a percentage of th revenues as consideration for permitting the ostensible lessor, applicant, to operate under the former's authority. We have repeatedly held that such arrangements are unlawful.

A district court upheld a Commission order in an investigation proceeding[175] which required that the respondents cease and desist from unlawful motor carrier operations performed by them under a purported lease arrangement; the respondent Allen held himself out to be a traffic consultant, and in conjunction with certain truck rental concerns and a drivers' organization, conceived and formulated a plan whereby they undertook to offer a full transportation service for shippers, without having obtained authority from the Commission. The court held, contrary to their contention, that the operation constituted "for hire" carriage. In *Steel Transp. Co., Inc., Extension,*[176] the Commission held that applicant's lease of loaded vehicles to another carrier for transportation of mixed shipments containing commodities not within the scope of its own authority was not a bona fide lease contemplated by regulations promulgated by the Commission, but an unauthorized lease of operating rights, when it was the "lessor" who accepted the freight, delivered the shipments, paid the drivers, retained responsibility for the freight, and on occasion prepared the billing; equipment leased was not available to "lessee" to augment its fleet as contemplated by the leasing section, as opposed to the interchange section, of the rules; "lessee" not only paid nothing for lease of the equipment, but received a portion of the trans-

[174]82 M.C.C. 179, 181-2.
[175]*Robert Allen — Investigation of Operations and Practices,* 79 M.C.C. 727.
[176]81 M.C.C. 637, 639. See also *John J. Casale, Inc. v. United States,* 208 F. Supp. 55, aff'd 371 U.S. 22.

portation charges as consideration for permitting applicant, the ostensible lessor, to operate under its authority.

The concept of common carriage utilizing vehicles which are not owned by the carrier, in essence requires only that the carrier exercise direction and control over leased equipment which it utilizes. In *P.B. Mutrie Motor Transp., Inc. v. Lang Storage & Transfer, Inc.*,[177] defendant was found exercising necessary direction and control, notwithstanding the fact that the shipper-lessor chose the particular trailer for its shipments, where leased trailers were not restricted to transportation to be performed by lessor, employees accompanying leased equipment were those of defendant, and where defendant insured, inspected, maintained and repaired leased trailers. Arrangement, whereby applicant leased vehicles to protestant, furnished drivers, maintained equipment, directed the placing of equipment at shipper's dock in response to requests for service, and received 75 or 80 percent of the gross revenues as compensation for use of its vehicles to transport traffic under protestant's authority, was found by the Commission in *Bennett*[178] not to be a violation of the leasing rules. In *Rock Island Motor Transit Co., Extension*,[179] the Commission held that protestant's lease of equipment through another carrier under a written agreement for a period exceeding 30 days, in which it hired and paid the owner as driver, caused its identification card and serial number to be affixed to the cab of the leased vehicle, and in general controlled the operation thereof, was a proper lease of equipment and not an unlawful lease of authority.

Utilization of Instrumentalities or Services of Common Carriers by Freight Forwarders

Section 418 of the Interstate Commerce Act[180] provides:

"It shall be unlawful, except in the performance within terminal areas of transfer, collection, or delivery services, for freight forwarders to employ or utilize the instrumentalities or services of any carriers other than common carriers by railroad, motor vehicle, or water, subject to this Act; express companies subject to this Act; air carriers subject to the Federal Aviation Act of 1958; common carriers by motor vehicle engaged in transportation exempted under the provisions of Section 203(b) (7a) of this

---

[177]84 M.C.C. 164, 167.
[178]82 M.C.C. 353, 354-5, 359.
[179]82 M.C.C. 491, 493.
[180]49 U.S.C. 1018. See Sections 202(c), (2), 303(f), (2) — performance of motor or water transportation in terminal areas for carriers of other types; and Section 409 for utilization by freight forwarders of common carriers by motor vehicles.

Act; common carriers by motor vehicle exempted under the provisions of Section 204(a) (4a) of this Act; or common carriers by water engaged in transportation exempted under the provisions of Section 303(b) of this Act."

The prohibition of Section 418 against the use of instrumentalities or services of carriers other than common carriers was designed to prevent forwarders from using contract carriers.[181] Section 418 does not prohibit forwarders from supplying an instrumentality of line-haul transportation; the prohibition is against their use of instrumentalities or services of other than common carriers, i.e., the line-haul transportation may not to be performed by the contract carriers.[182]

Section 409(a) of the Interstate Commerce Act[183] provides:

"Nothing in this Act shall be construed to prevent freight forwarders subject to this part from entering into or continuing to operate under contracts with common carriers by motor vehicle subject to part II of this Act, governing the utilization by such freight forwarders of the services and instrumentalities of such common carriers by motor vehicle and the compensation to be paid therefor: *Provided*, That in the case of such contracts it shall be the duty of the parties thereto to establish just, reasonable, and equitable terms, conditions, and compensation which shall not unduly prefer or prejudice any of such participants or any other freight forwarder and shall be consistent with the national transportation policy declared in this Act: *And provided further*, That in the case of line-haul transportation between concentration points and break-bulk points in truckload lots where such line-haul transportation is for a total distance of four hundred and fifty highway-miles or more, such contracts shall not permit payment to common carriers by motor vehicle of compensation which is lower than would be received under rates or charges established under part II of this Act." Section 409(b) of the Act[184] provides that "Contracts entered into or continued pursuant to subsection (a) of this section shall be filed with the Commission in accordance with such reasonable rules and regulations as the Commission shall prescribe. Whenever, after hearing, upon complaint or upon its own initiative, the Commission is of opinion that any such contract, or its terms, conditions, or compensation is or will be inconsistent with the provisions and standards set forth in subsection (a) of this section, the Commission shall by order prescribe the terms, conditions, and compensation of such contract which are consistent therewith."

It is mandatory that contracts supplemental to tariffs be filed with the Commission, thus, if such contracts are not filed with the Commission they can have no force and effect insofar as they attempt to change,

---

[181]*Forwarder Class Rates, Official and W.T.L. Territory*, 310 I.C.C. 785, 788.
[182]*Eastern Central M. Carriers Assn. v. Baltimore & O. R. Co.*, 314 I.C.C. 5, 44.
[183]49 U.S.C. 1009(a). Comparable provisions — Sections 6(5), 220(a), 313(b), 412(a), concerning the filing of contracts with the Commission.
[184]49 U.S.C. 1009(b).

modify, or vary the service to be rendered as set forth in the schedule.[185] While a forwarder may lawfully pass on to shippers some of the benefits it receives from entering into Section 409 contracts, that section does not relieve it from the requirements of Section 405(a) and (c) that it publish, file, collect, and receive charges no greater, less, or different than those lawfully on file and in effect in its tariffs.[186] Forwarders of goods within the purview of Section 402(b), not being subject to provisions of part IV, may not enter into contracts with motor carriers as contemplated by Section 409(a), but instead their relations with motor carriers are the same as those of any other shipper, and they are required to pay for motor-carrier services, on the basis of rates and charges in the latter's tariffs lawfully on file with the Commission.[187]

Transfer, collection, and delivery services on line-haul traffic, performed within terminal areas by a motor carrier as agent or under contractual arrangement for a freight forwarder, are exempt from the provisions of part II by Section 202(c), and thus are not services of "common carriers by motor vehicle subject to part II" within the provisions of Section 409 requiring filing with the Commission of contracts covering performance of service for forwarders by such carriers. This view is supported by Section 418, which distinguishes between transfer, collection, and delivery and services of common carriers by motor vehicle subject to the Act.[188] The Commission's regulations issued under Section 409 identify the services that must be covered by contracts as those "entered into pursuant to Section 409," and clearly do not apply to such terminal services.[189] Thus, the Commission said in the *Clipper Carloading* case, charges of railroad's motor carrier subsidiary for unloading a forwarder's freight from cars at Los Angeles and San Francisco and performing local deliveries at those points under agreement with that forwarder are not unlawful because not made public or available to complainant, a competing forwarder.[190]

---

[185]*Motor Rail Co. v. Cardinale Trucking Corp.*, 302 I.C.C. 707, 709.

[186]*Clipper Carloading, Inc. v. Western Freight Assn.*, 311 I.C.C. 653, 657.

[187]*Movers' & Warehousemen's Assn. of America, Inc., Petition*, 304 I.C.C. 517, 519-20.

[188]*Clipper Carloading Co., Inc. v. Pacific Motor Trucking Co.*, 310 I.C.C. 569.

[189]*Ibid.*

[190]*Ibid.*

36

Elkins Act

The Statute

The Elkins Act* makes it "unlawful for any person, persons, or corporation to offer, grant, or give, or to solicit, accept, or receive any rebate, concession, or discrimination in respect to the transportation of any property in interstate or foreign commerce by any common carrier . . . whereby any such property shall by any device whatsoever be transported at a less rate than that named in the tariffs posted and filed by such carrier . . . or whereby any other advantage is given or discrimination is practiced."[1]

Violation of the Elkins Act is made a misdemeanor and, in addition, it is provided that anyone who "shall knowingly by employee, agent, officer, or otherwise, directly or indirectly, by or through any means or device whatsoever, receive or accept from such common carrier any sum of money or any other valuable consideration as a rebate or offset against the regular charges for transportation of such property, as fixed by the schedule of rates provided for "in the Interstate Commerce Act," shall in addition to any penalties provided by this Act forfeit to the United States a sum of money three times the amount of money so received or accepted, and three times the value of any other consideration so received or accepted, to be ascertained by the trial court."[2]

---

*The chapters dealing with the Elkins Act, primarily administrative jurisdiction, and rate making agreements of common carriers and freight forwarders are expansions, by permission, of previous writings of the author.
[1] 49 U.S.C. 41(1).
[2] 49 U.S.C. 41(3).

Purpose of the Statute

Prior to the passage of the Act to Regulate Commerce in 1887, there were many serious complaints brought against the railroad industry by shippers and the general public[3] aimed at discriminations by the railroads between persons and localities; lack of uniformity in the classification of commodities; the granting of secret special rates, rebates, drawbacks, and concessions to favored shippers; and the refusal of carriers to enter into joint arrangements for the transportation of property over more than one railroad.

To eliminate many of the unfair and discriminatory practices of the railroads, especially with respect to rates and charges, Congress passed the Act to Regulate Commerce in 1887, which specifically prohibited unreasonable rates, unjust discrimination, undue preference, and undue prejudice; required common carriers to adhere to published tariffs; and required joint undertakings for the transportation of property over connecting railroads between interstate points. The provisions of Section 2 and Section 3(1) of the Interstate Commerce Act,[4] which prohibit unlawful and discriminations by common carriers, and Section 6(7) of the I.C. Act,[5] which requires common carriers to adhere to their published tariffs, are in substantially the same form as they appeared in the Act to Regulate Commerce of 1887.

While the Act to Regulate Commerce of 1887, together with the amendments of 1889, assured the publication and filing of rates and tariffs by common carriers and provided the Commission with the power to prevent any inequality of charges by carriers through resorting to secret concessions, it was the enactment of the Elkins Act in 1903[6] which really put teeth into the statute. It not only prohibited the granting by a common carrier but outlawed the receiving by a shipper of any rebate, concession, or discrimination in respect to the transportation of any property in interstate commerce. The Elkins Act was amendatory to and supplementary of the Act to Regulate Commerce, and was the first significant amendment to the original legislation of 1887.[7]

In 1906, Congress enacted the Hepburn Act which amended the Act to Regulate Commerce, as amended by the Act of 1889, and the Elkins Act of 1903.[8] The Hepburn Act, in addition to other penalties, subjected

---

[3]Rept. 46, part 1, (Cullom report), 49th Cong., 1st Sess., pp. 180-1; see also H. Doc. 363, 78th Cong., 1st Sess, pp. 91-92.
[4]U.S.C. 2, 3(1).
[5]U.S.C. 6(7).
[6]32 Stat. 847, c. 708.
[7]*Chicago & Alton R. R. Co. v. Kirby*, 225 U.S. 155, 165.
[8]34 Stat. 587, c. 3591; *United States v. Union Stock Yard*, 226 U.S. 286, 303.

shippers receiving rebates or offsets from the published tariff rates to a forfeiture of three times the amount of money or other valuable consideration so received or accepted.

The Statute Has Been Construed Broadly

For the purpose of effectuating its objectives, the Elkins Act has received a broad judicial construction, and in the process of applying the Act, the courts have been diligent in recognizing and eradicating rebating, unlawful discrimination, and undue preference. The courts made it clear at an early date that they will look at the substance of the transaction to determine whether there has been an adherence to the published tariff rates, and to determine whether a shipper has received, directly or indirectly, any refund, rebate, offset, concession, or discrimination from the published tariff rates.

By construing the Elkins Act to prohibit all rebates what ever the form they may take, the courts have been giving effect to the intent of Congress in enacting the legislation. The Elkins Act proceeds upon broad lines and was intended to effect the purpose of Congress to require that all shippers should be treated alike and that the only rate charged to any shipper for like service under similar conditions should be the one established, published and posted as required by law.[9] The intention of Congress in passing the Elkins Act, as expressed by the Supreme Court, was to prohibit any and all means that might be resorted to in order to obtain or receive concessions from the fixed and published rates;[10] to secure equality of rates as to all and to destroy favoritism by any means or device whatsoever;[11] and as expressed in *United States v. Koenig Coal Co.*[12] "to cut up by the roots and every form of discrimination, favoritism and inequality."

In *United States v. Union Pacific R. Co.,*[13] the court said that it is the purpose of the Interstate Commerce Act and the Elkins Act to outlaw every subterfuge, scheme, plan, or device of any person or corporation to give advantages, concessions, discriminations, and rebates to shippers in interstate commerce by carriers subject to the Elkins Act; the statutes were designed to strike down every device, regardless of how ingenious, by which those objectives are sought to be accomplished, and

[9]*Armour Packing Co. v. United States,* 209 U.S. 56, 72.
[10]*Ibid.*
[11]*United States v. Union Stock Yard,* 226 U.S. 286, 307; *New Haven R.R. v. Interstate Com. Com'n,* 200 U.S. 361, 391.
[12]270 U.S. 512, 519.
[13]173 F. Supp. 397, 412.

are intended to strike through all forms and subterfuges to reach and eradicate such forbidden evil.

The courts have found the statute effective to accomplish the destruction of discriminatory practices, whatever their form, as any and all means to accomplish the prohibited end are banned and favoritism which destroys equality between shippers, however brought about, is not tolerated.[14] To the extent of prohibiting secret departures from published tariffs and forbidding rebates, preferences and all other forms of undue discrimination the Act is "remedial and is, therefore, entitled to receive that interpretation which reasonably accomplishes the great public purpose which it was enacted to subserve."[15] If the public purpose which the statute was intended to accomplish be borne in mind, its meaning becomes clearer and its broad interpretation by the courts justified.

Since the courts have taken the position that they are bound to construe penal statutes strictly and may not extend them beyond their obvious meaning by strained inferences a serious question has been raised in the past as to how the Elkins Act, which contains penal provisions, should be construed. That the statute should not be construed so strictly as to defeat the obvious intention of Congress was held by the Supreme Court in the *Koenig Coal Co. Case, supra.* There the Supreme Court said (p. 519) that it would be contrary "to the general intent of the law to restrain the effect of the language use so as not to include acts exactly described, when they clearly effect discrimination and inequality." The court voiced the opinion that (p. 520) "(t)he general rule that criminal statutes are to be strictly construed has no application when the general purpose of the legislature is manifest and is subserved by giving the words used in the statute their ordinary meaning and thus covering the acts charged."

In *United States v. Hocking Valley Ry. Co.*,[16] the statute was said to accomplish "its end by directly and unmistakably condemning results, wherefore every devisable plan to produce the objectionable conditions is under its ban." Surely the judicial processes are "not so inept and feeble that a statute exhibiting a definite purpose to meet palpable mischiefs must be construed so narrowly as to oblige Congress from time to time to amend it so that its provisions may be kept, at the best, only in the immediate rear of a procession of new methods born of the fertility of human invention and designed to circumvent that legis-

---

[14]*Union Pacific Railroad Co. v. United States*, 313 U.S. 450, 461-2.
[15]*New Haven R.R. v. Interstate Com. Com'n, supra*, p. 391.
[16]194 Fed. 234, 251, aff'd 210 Fed. 735, cert. denied 234 U.S. 757.

lative will which it attempts by each amplifying amendment to express."[17]

Not being practicable for Congress to set a limit on human ingenuity in the initiation of schemes obnoxious to the I.C. Act by attempting a description of all possible methods, the Elkins Act made it unlawful to offer, grant, or give, or to solicit, accept or receive any rebate, concession, or discrimination whereby property "shall by any device whatsoever" be transported at less than the published tariff rates or whereby any other advantage is given or discrimination practiced. Thus the construction given to the statute has been achieved largely by a broad interpretation of the meaning of the term "device." In *Armour Packing Co. v. United States*,[18] the Supreme Court commented on the meaning of "device" as used in the statute by saying that the word was found to be "dissociated from any such words as fraudulent conduct, scheme or contrivance" thus a device necessarily need not be fraudulent, but it may "include anything which is a plan or contrivance." The inhibition of "any device whatsoever" that accomplishes the condemned results bans any possible invention by violators in this area. The manifest purpose of the statute, the court said in *United States v. Milwaukee Refrigerator Transit Co.*,[19] "is to strike through all pretense, all ingenious device, to the substance of the transaction itself."

Indirectness of Rebate

The decisions of the courts make it abundantly clear that no matter how indirect the device, if the result is to favor one shipper against another, it comes within the condemnation of the Elkins Act. The statute, it is noted, forbids a shipper to receive or accept a rebate from a carrier either "directly or indirectly." Performance of service which is of value to shippers without adequate compensation therefor, as an inducement to secure their traffic, is an indirect form of illegal rebating.[20] In *Union Pacific Railroad Co. v. United States*,[21] the Supreme Court furnished a striking illustration of how carefully the courts, in deciding cases under the Elkins Act, will trace the effect of a transaction in determining whether an unlawful rebate is involved; and the case demonstrates that the courts will construe the Elkins Act so that it will have the remedial

[17]*Ibid.*
[18]209 U.S. 56, 71.
[19]142 Fed. 247, 252, aff'd 145 Fed. 1007.
[20]*Arbitrary Rates, Los Angeles to Calif. Points*, 300 I.C.C. 117, 120; *Acme Fast Freight, Inc. v. Western Freight Assn.*, 299 I.C.C. 315.
[21]313 U.S. 450.

effect intended by Congress. If the result of the action is to put some shippers in a more favorable position than others, a device in violation of the Elkins Act is involved. The suit was one for injunctive relief and the unusual feature of the case was that the injunction ran not only against the Union Pacafic but also against Kansas City, Kansas, which had been active in promoting and developing a produce market. The Union Pacific had actively assisted in having a market built at Kansas City, Kansas, on land belonging to the city but at a location where the market necesarily would be served by it. In order to induce dealers to move from a market in Kansas City, Missouri, to the new market in Kansas City, Kansas, the carrier had the city make cash payments, offer free rentals, and offer reduced rentals for a limited period. The city's motive was to secure tenants. The carrier's motive was to secure additional traffic. There was no agreements between the shippers and the carrier and the payments and concessions were in all cases made by the city and not the carrier. The lower court held that since the tenants at the market, due to the nature of the leased premises, necessarily had to engage in interstate transportation, and since transportation over the lines of Union Pacific was a requirement growing out of absolute necessity due to the location of the market, a payment to some dealers to induce them to move to the Kansas City, Kansas, market when payments were not made to all dealers was a discrimination in violation of the Elkins Act.

The Supreme Court in affirming the lower court's decision stressed that the concessions were worked out cooperatively between the city and the carrier and that the railroad was the leading and dominant influence in the entire transaction, Although the payments and other inducements to the shippers were made by the city and not the carrier, and although the shippers did not make any formal agreements to use the carrier's facilities, nevertheless, looking at the transaction as a whole, some shippers were put in a favored position and there was, therefore, involved a device in violation of the Elkins Act.

The payments to induce dealers to move from the Kansas City, Missouri, market were to come out of rental income. In financing the market, the Union Pacific had bought three million dollars in bond which were to be retired with the rental revenues received from the property over and above operating revenues. Since making the payments to the Kansas City dealers necessarily would have the result of decreasing operating revenues and so leave less to retire bonds thus increasing the Union Pacific's risk, and since the Union Pacific had induced the city to make the payments, the court implied that this in itself involved an indirect rebate by Union Pacific to shippers in violation of the Elkins Act. In other words Union Pacific's assumption of increased risk for the benefit of some shippers was a discrimination by the carrier in favor of such shippers in violation of the Elkins Act. The court said at page 468 that "(i)t is impossible, and in our view immaterial, to determine from the evidence and findings whether the Union Pacific contributed indirectly to the fund for making payments to shippers."

In *United States v. Braverman*,[22] the defendant was indicted and charged with having violated Section 1 of the Elkins Act by having knowingly solicited from a motor carrier concessions and rebates respecting interstate shipments of goods so that, had the rebates been granted, goods would have been shipped at a lower rate than that named in the applicable tariffs filed with the Commission. The indictment did not allege, and all parties agreed that the Government did not intend to prove, that the rebate would have been for the benefit of the shipper. The district judge, believing that the Elkins Act applies only where some "advantage or discriminination is practiced in favor of the shipper," ruled that the indictment did not change an offense under the statute and therefore must be dismissed. In reversing the lower court, the Supreme Court held that an indictment under Section 1 of the Elkins Act states an offense when it charges that a person has solicited a rebate from a common carrier respecting the transportation in interstate commerce of a shipper's property, even though it is not alleged that the rebate was for the benefit of the shipper. The court commented that more "unequivocal language" as that contained in the Elkins Act "would be hard to imagine. It strikes at any and every kind of rebate, no matter by whom or to whom given. Nowhere does the section say or imply that rebates are unlawful only if they are give to or are for the benefit of a shipper. It is a rebate, to whomever given, which the statutory language proscribes."

The court said further:

> The legislative history of the Elkins Act bears out the conclusion that Congress intended to prevent any kind of departure from the published rates and to that end outlawed all rebates, without requiring a showing of benefit to any shipper. The original Interstate Commerce Act, passed in 1887, made it unlawful for any carrier to charge either more or less than the rate specified in its published schedule of rates. But the Interstate Commerce Commission, after a decade of experience with the Act, recounted in its Annual Reports to Congress between 1897 and 1902 the secrecy with which rebates were cloaked, the impossibility of enforcing tariffs when the Government had to prove not only a departure but also a

[22]10 L. ed. 2nd 444.

benefit to one shipper not received by another, and the pressing need to invoke penalties simply upon showing a departure from a published rate.

These urgings led to the passage of the Elkins Act. A Committee of the House of Representatives, in hearings on several bills proposing amendments to the Interstate Commerce Act, were told by the Chairman of the Interstate Commerce Commission that the existing law was "in some important respects . . . practically unworkable." In particular, he reported the virtual impossibility of showing that a rebate had resulted in an "actual discrimination" among shippers and agreed with a member of the Committee that "any departure" from the published rates should be made an offense.[23] In its favorable report on the bill which became the Elkins Act, the Committee observed that it was "practically impossible to show the discrimination" and recommended passage of its proposal making it "a penal offense to make any departure from the published rates whether there be a discrimination or not."[24]

This court has already held that the sanctions of the Act are not restricted to carriers or shippers and that "any person" as used in § 1 means "any person."[25] It was there recognized that, in order to ensure carrier efficiency, rates must be maintained unimpaired and that the Elkins Act no more intended to allow third persons to tamper with the statutory scheme than it intended to allow carriers and shippers themselves to do so. And in an analogous situation, this court has held that railroad employees who charge passengers more than the established rates are punishable under the Interstate Commerce Act even though they acted for their own gain and even though the railroad was not a party to their conduct.[26]

We have considered the statute before us in light of the salutary rule that criminal statutes should not by interpretation be expanded beyond their plain language.[27] But neither can we interpret a statute so narrowly as to defeat its obvious intent.[28] Congress, the Commission, and the public were concerned to make certain that, once a tariff had been published, no deviations whatever from that tariff would take place. Nowhere can we find support for the suggestion that some departures were to be checked while others were to be allowed. We would ignore the express language of the Elkins Act, the economic ills which gave rise to its passage, the objects which the framers of the statute had in mind, and the subsequent

[23]Hearings on H. R. 146, 273, 2040, 5775, 8337, and 10930 before the House Committee on Interstate and Foreign Commerce 197-199 (1902).

[24]H. R. Rep. No. 3765, 57th Cong., 2d Sess. 5 (1903). The bill passed the House by a vote of 250 to 6, 36 Cong. Rec. 2159 (1903), having already passed the Senate, 36 Cong. Rec. 1633-1634 (1903).

[25]*Union Pac. R. Co. v. United States* 313 U.S. 450, 463. The lower courts soon after the passage of the Elkins Act rejected the argument that the Elkins Act reached only the carrier and the shipper and held that it was immaterial that rebates were paid to someone other than the shipper. E.g., *United States v. Milwaukee Refrigerator Transit Co.*, 145 F. 1007, 1012; *United States v. Delaware, L. & W. R. Co.*, 152 F. 269, 273.

[26]*Howitt v. United States*, 328 U.S. 189.

[27]See *United States v. Resnick*, 299 U.S. 207, 209-210.

[28]See *United States v. Raynor*, 302 U.S. 540, 552.

judicial enforcement of the Act if we limited its operation to only some kinds of rebates or to only some people. Congress wanted rates to be published and honored. It wanted rebates stopped. It used fitting language to accomplish that end.

Forfeiture Provisions

That Congress may impose penalties in aid of the exercise of any of its enumerated powers is indisputed.[29] The Elkins Act provides a forfeiture to the Government of three times the amount of any rebates or offsets received by a shipper from a common carrier, and authorizes the Attorney General to institute a civil action to collect the sum so forfeited. In purpose and effect the forfeiture provisions is a sanction to enforce the regulatory provisions of the Elkins Act which prohibit the giving or receiving of rebates, and is in addition to the provisions for fine and imprisonment. This regulatory provision, which is clearly within the power of Congress under the commerce clause of the Constitution,[30] was held to be constitutional in *New York Central R. R. v. United States.*[31] The forfeiture provision is not excessive or confiscatory and is entirely a matter for legislative determination.

Due Process

In *United States v. Standard Oil Co. of Indiana,*[32] involving a conviction under the Elkins Act of 1903, it was contended by the defendant that the Elkins Act deprived the company of the right to make private contracts and that the defendant, therefore, had a right taken away without due process of law. Moreover, defendant contended that it was not within the power of Congress under its constitutional power to regulate interstate and foreign commerce to make the acceptance of rebates a criminal act, thereby subjecting a shipper to fine and imprisonment. In overruling the defendant's contention as to the Elkins Act denying the company due process of law, and upholding the power of Congress to make the acceptance of rebates criminal, the court said (p. 310) that in order to preserve uniformity, Congress "may prohibit the doing of any act or thing whatever by any person or corporation calculated to impair uniformity, and may enforce such prohibitions by such penal provisions as Congress may deem requisite."

[29]*Sunshine Coal Co. v. Adkins,* 310 U.S. 381, 393.
[30]Art. 1, Section 8, Clause 3.
[31]212 U.S. 481; 212 U.S. 500.
[32]155 Fed. 305.

Statute of Limitations

Paragraph 3 of the Elkins Act allows the United States to recover for rebates only if they are "received or accepted" during the period of six years prior to the commencement of the action, and in the trial of said action all such rebates or other considerations so received or accepted for a period of six years prior to the commencement of the action may be included therein.

Where there was no indication that separate conveyances were bargained for and contemplated but rather the entire deal was considered by the parties as one package, the court held in *United States v. General Motors Corporation*[33] that the transaction being unitary there could be no consummation of the arrangement until the entire agreement was either executed or terminated. Thus the statute of limitation did not begin to run until the negotiation bore final fruition, that is, only when the last necessary conveyance was made.

Reasonableness or Unreasonableness of the Published Tariff Rates

Refunds, rebates, offsets, concessions, and discriminations result from the transportation of property at less than the published tariff rates. Whether or not a payment results in a refund, rebate, offset, concession, or discrimination, within the meaning of the statutory prohibitions, is in no way connected with the reasonableness or unreasonableness of the published tariff rate charged. Thus it is wholly immaterial whether the published tariff rates are reasonable or unreasonable where action is brought under the Elkins Act. Of course the published tariff rate is necessary to constitute the standard, departure from which is the violation.[34] As the court said in *Chicago & A. Ry. Co. v. United States,*[35] under the statute "the standard of comparison is the published rate" thus "(i)t is only necessary to prove that the favored shipper has had his property transported at a less rate than that published and filed."

In *United States v. Vacuum Oil Co.,*[36] the court denied a defendant the right to litigate the legality of a rate as to its reasonableness or unreasonableness, and held that the testing of whether or not the defendant was criminally liable under the statute for giving a rebate was whether there had been a departure or deviation from the published rate. The court said (p. 540):

[33]226 F. 2d 745, 748.
[34]*United States v. Michigan Portland Cement Co.,* 270 U.S. 521.
[35]156 Fed. 558, 562 aff'd 212 U.S. 563.
[36]158 Fed. 536.

That Congress had power under the commerce clause of the Constitution to regulate commerce is conceded, and its purpose in enacting the statute forbidding unjust discrimination and preference to the end that all shippers shall secure uniform treatment is beyond question. How this object and purpose of Congress can be effectuate if a shipper receiving rebate, concession, or discrimination is permitted to question or litigate the legality of the rate as to its reasonableness or unreasonableness in a criminal prosecution charging him with having received a concession is difficult to understand. Indeed such a construction of the act would nullify its general scope, and render its strict enforcement wholly impracticable, for juries and judges in different jurisdictions would not be likely to reach a conclusion upon the subject of just or unjust tariff charges which would secure uniformity of rates. It is therefore clear that there can be no departure or deviation from the established rates except in the manner provided by the act, and such rate must be regarded as binding upon the shipper.

Speaking on the question of published tariffs, the court said in *United States v. Standard Oil Co.,*[37] that what Congress sought "was a fixed rate, absolutely, unvarying uniform, to be adhered to until publicly changed in the manner provided by law." That which was prohibited by Congress was a departure from the established "rate by any means whatsoever, whether direct between the parties or indirect by the employment of the most deviously circuitous subterfuge." (p. 721) It was urged by the defendant in the case that to require a shipper to adhere to a fixed published rate defeats the ultimate object of the legislation, that object being the transportation of property for a reasonable compensation. The court was unable to see that this result would follow, stating (p. 721):

> What Congress wanted to bring about was reasonable rates for all shippers, not simply for some shippers; and Congress knew that as an essential prerequisite to this preferences would have to be abolished. To abolish preferances, the law provides that the published rate shall be the only lawful rate. This does not mean that a rate once fixed and published shall never be changed, but it does mean that, when the change is made, it must be in the way provided by law, namely, by publication, to the end that the new rate may be available to all shippers at the same time, on equal terms.

Delay or Failure to Enforce the Elkins Act
Does Not Condone Its Violation

The "mere inaction, through failure of the Commission to institute proceedings . . . is not an administrative ruling and does not imply

[37]148 Fed. 719, 721.

decision."[38] Long continued practice and the approval of administrative authorities cannot alter statutory provisions that are clear and explicit when related to the facts disclosed, even though persuasive in the interpretation of doubtful provisions of a statute; and a failure to enforce the law does not change it.[39] As the Supreme Court said in *United States v. Sacony-Vacuum, Oil Co.*,[40] where defendants who had been indicted for violations of the Sherman Act asserted in defense that certain practices had been approved by agencies of the Government, "(t)hough employees of the government may have known of those programs and winked at them or tacitly approved them, no immunity would have thereby been obtained."

In *Merchants Warehouse Co. v. United States*,[41] the Commission by prior rulings had approved allowances to certain warehouses for services in handling freight at designated stations. These allowances had been and were published in the tariffs and the Commission had assumed that the warehouse facilities were part of the carrier's station facilities and that the warehouses had acted as the carrier's agent in handling freight. For many years this practice had gone unchallenged by any agency of the Government. Later, the Commission overruled its prior decisions and held that the allowances were in violation of the Act to Regulate Commerce and unlawful. The Commission ordered the tariffs cancelled. Suit was instituted to enjoin the order of the Commission requiring the cancellation of the tariffs which prescribed the unlawful allowances. In upholding the order of the Commission cancelling the tariffs, the Supreme Court said (p. 511) "(w)here a forbidden discrimination is made, the mere fact that it has been long continued and that the machinery for making it is in tariff form, cannot clothe it with immunity."

Power of Attorney General to Institute Proceedings

The statute makes it unlawful for any corporation to receive any rebate, concession or discrimination in respect to the transportation of any property in interstate commerce by any common carrier. It likewise subjects any corporation receiving a rebate from a common carrier to a forfeiture of three times the amount of money or value of any other consideration so received or accepted. The Attorney General may proceed to have the matter adjudicated by any court of the United States

[38]*Union Stock Yard & Transit Co. v. United States*, 308 U.S. 213, 224.
[39]*Louisville & Nashville Railroad Co. v. United States*, 282 U.S. 740, 759.
[40]310 U.S. 150, 226.
[41]283 U.S. 501.

of competent jurisdiction, and his decision to have the matter adjudicated may be even in direct conflict and disagreement with the views and opinion of the Commission. In *United States v. Milwaukee Refrigerator Transit Co.*,[42] unlawful rebating was brought to the attention of the Commission but it declined to take any action. The matter was then called to the attention of the Attorney General who, upon his own motion and without direction or investigation on the part of the Commission, instituted a proceeding in equity to restrain the rebating. In recognizing the right of the Attorney General of his own motion to institute a proceeding in equity to restrain rebating, the court said (p. 1010):

> The Attorney General, of his own motion, directed the institution of this proceeding. Defendants claim that a suit of this kind will not lie except upon the initiative of the Interstate Commerce Commission. Section 3 of the Elkins Act opens by providing for action by the Commission after investigation. The bill, as it passed the Senate and went to the House, evidently contemplated no other mode. In the House, the mandate that "it shall be the duty of the several district attorneys of the United States to institute and prosecute such proceedings" was amended by inserting after "United States" the clause, "whenever the Attorney General shall direct, either of his own motion, or upon the request of the Interstate Commerce Commission." Whatever doubt concerning the authority of the Attorney General to direct the bringing of this suit might arise from a mere reading of Section 3 is removed, we think, by noting the history of the bill.

Breadth of Commission's Power to Investigate

In *Southern Ry. Co. v. United States*,[43] the court held that the Commission did not disqualify itself from acting on a warehouse company's complaint when it authorized the Department of Justice to file a civil action seeking injunction to prevent the consummation of the carrier's sale plan and to avert its continuing failure to collect rents for use of terminal facilities involved; that action resulted in an agreement by the railroad to maintain the status quo respecting the sale plan pending determination of its validity in the complaint proceeding. Moreover, the court said, the Commission has a duty under Section 3 of Elkins Act to request the Department of Justice to institute such proceedings whenever it has reasonable ground for belief that a carrier is committing a forbidden discrimination, and that section provides that such proceedings shall not preclude any other action provided by the I.C. Act.

---

[42] 145 Fed. 1007. Parties injured are not precluded from bringing suit to recover damages or taking any other action provided by the Interstate Commerce Act.
[43] 186 F. Supp. 29, 41.

Persons within the Meaning of Section 2 of the Elkins Act

In *Hofer-Investigation of Operations*,[44] the Commission said that a producer of sugar and its brokerage agent who participated in unlawful carrier operations with full knowledge of every aspect thereof, and profited thereby, must be deemed to be interested in or affected by the considered practices within Section 2 of the Elkins Act. The Commission also said that the producer was responsible for the activities and knowledge of its brokerage agent. In *Mumby Investigation of Operations*,[45] the Commission held that respondent sugar refiners, brokers, dealers, and flour millers, who participated in unlawful for-hire transportation activities conducted by respondent carriers under the guise of buy-and-sell operations, were aware of the nature of such activities and benefited thereby, and therefore constituted persons interested in, or affected by, the practices under investigation within the meaning of Section 2 of the Elkins Act; a cease and desist order, therefore, was entered against all participating parties, including those who had discontinued their participation.

Discriminatory Practices in Leasing or Selling Property

Rebating, unlawful discrimination and undue preference will be recognized and eliminated not only with respect to rate-making and adherence to tariff charges, but also with respect to collateral commercial transactions such as the leasing or selling of property. Thus, as borne out by court and Commission decisions, to engage in discriminatory practices and hidden rebates in the leasing or selling of property to or from shippers constitutes a violation of the Elkins Act. Schemes or devices which have been recognized and eradicated by the courts and Commission have included such collateral commercial transactions, among others, as property leased by a carrier to a shipper at an inadequate rental in return for the shipper's agreement to transport commodities solely over the carrier's line — the shipper lessee was held to have received a concession in violation of the Elkins Act;[46] property leased by a carrier to a shipper in which part of the consideration for the lease was the shipper's agreement to route traffic over the carrier's lines — this was held to involve necessarily a lease to the shipper at less than a fair rental value, therefore, constituting a violation of the

[44]84 M.C.C. 527, 540-1.
[45]82 M.C.C. 237, 249.
[46]*Central of Georgia Ry. Co. v. Blount*, 238 Fed. 292; *Cleveland C., C. & St. L. Ry. Co. v. Hirsch*, 204 Fed. 849; *Freight Forwarding Investigation*, 229 I.C.C. 201.

Statute;[47] and property purchased or leased by a carrier from a shipper where the carrier at the same time agreed to reduce tariff charges to the shipper — it was held that a violation of the statute occurred.[48]

For a carrier to pay or to secure the payment of bonus to a shipper to build a plant at a location where the facilities of a particular carrier can be used in return for the shipper's agreement to use such facilities or, with or without such an agreement, at a location where the shipper necessarily has to use the carrier's facilities is in violation of the Elkins Act.[49] To understand by what standard transactions will be judged by the courts and Commission in determining whether a charge of unlawful concession has been met it will be necessary to review some of the decisions involving these matters.

The extent to which devices have been utilized for the purpose of engaging in discriminatory practices is demonstrated by *Northern Central Ry. Co. v. United States.*[50] There a carrier leased coal-producing land to a mining company for which the mining company was to pay stipulated royalties. The coal produced and sold by the mining company was distributed over the defendant's line at regular rates but for many years no royalties were paid by the shipper to the carrier. It was held that failure of the carrier to collect the royalties was evidence to support a finding by the jury that the carrier intended the coal company to receive a rebate and the conviction of the carrier under the Elkins Act was sustained.

In *Fourche River Lumber Co. v. Bryant Lumber Co.,*[51] the Bryant Lumber Company granted Fourche Railroad, a subsidiary of the lumber company, a right of way with the understanding that the Bryant Company's timber was to be carried over the line without discrimination. A dispute arose over whether the railroad should pay to the Bryant Company the sums received by the railroad on divisions of through rates on shipments of Bryant Company lumber. The railroad, after a board of arbitrators had found in favor of the Bryant Company, refused to pay them and the Bryant Company sued. It was held that for the railroad to pay such divisions to the Bryant Company would be an unlawful rebate; and they could not be regarded as part of the consideration for the right of way, the court saying (pp. 322-3) that carriers "cannot purchase land by rebating to the grantor a part of the freight

[47]*Wharfage Charges at Atlantic and Gulf Ports,* 157 I.C.C. 663.
[48]*Central R. Co. of New Jersey v. United States,* 229 Fed. 501; *Fourche River Lumber Co. v. Bryant Lumber Co.,* 230 U.S. 316.
[49]*United States v. Union Stock Yard,* 226 U.S. 286.
[50]241 Fed. 25, cert. denied 245 U.S. 645.
[51]230 U.S. 316.

rate on interstate shipments over the road built on the right of way, even though the amount of such rebate was much less than the value of the land thus acquired."

In *Central R. Co. of New Jersey v. United States,*[52] defendant leased a railroad from a coal mining company, agreeing to pay the lessor a certain rental each year and to transport the lessor's coal at reduced rates. No contention was made that the consideration for the lease was an unreasonable one. It was held that this involved an unlawful rebate, the court saying (p. 508) "whether or not this advantage be stated as a reduction in rates, or merely a part of the consideration for the lease, seems to be of little importance" as the parties to the lease, in the opinion of the court, "were right in regarding it as part of the consideration, and the government is also right in regarding it as an advantage to the Navigation Company by a reduction in rates." Assuming that the allowances complained of were rebates, they were forbidden in express terms by the statutes regulating commerce, and especially by the Elkins Act. (p. 509)

The authorities in the foregoing indicate that where a practice uniquely lends itself to a rebate, the practice will not be tolerated under any circumstances. It will be looked upon as a device to effect a rebate regardless of whether a rebate has in fact incurred in the immediate situation being considered. *Wharfage Charges at Atlantic and Gulf Ports*[53] is another illustration of this. It was there the Commission's view that any lease embracing a shipper's agreement to route traffic over the carrier's lines necessarily means a lease to the shipper at less than the fair rental value and is therefore in violation of the Elkins Act. The Commission referred with approval to an earlier decision, *Leases and Grants by Carriers to Shippers,*[54] as follows (p. 691):

> . . . we found among other things, that a provision in a lease of railway land whereby a shipper agrees to route over the lines of the lessor carrier or its connections all or any part of the traffic which the shipper is able to route amounts to an acknowledgment that the consideration for the making of the lease was in part the exchange of traffic by the shipper for the right to occupy the land; and that where it clearly appears that the traffic of the lessee is the part the consideration for the lease, the conclusion follows that the transaction amounts to a concession to the shipper-lessee, in violation of the Elkins Act and Sections 2 and 6 of the Interstate Commerce Act.

[52] 229 Fed. 501.
[53] 157 I.C.C. 663.
[54] 73 I.C.C. 671.

The conclusion follows irrespective of what the money consideration called for by the lease is. The arrangement is not saved if the money consideration is the full rental value.

Baltimore & Ohio Railroad Co. v. United States,[55] gives another example of a scheme by carriers to grant unlawful concessions. To get the rail transportation of large shippers, certain carriers sought them out and offered warehousing services and space below the rates of private warehousemen and below the cost to the carriers of the services rendered. It was not only a contest between carriers and private warehousemen but also between the carriers themselves. Traffic departments of the railroads became solicitors for warehousing business. Favored shippers were rented space by the carriers below compensatory figures. In regard to this situation, the court said (pp. 523-4):

> As the shippers of the Port of New York district can utilize, in many instances, commercial storage and other warehousing services in addition to rail transportation, a saving on the non-transportation services obviously figures out the same as a rebate on the transportation service. It is immaterial that the shipper pays fair value or the market price for the extra privilege he enjoys. Section 6(7) of the Act forbids the carrier to receive less than the published rates for transportation or to remit "by any device any portion of the rates." When services, not necessary for transportation, are furnished below cost in an effort to acquire rail transportation, as was done here, this provision is violated.

Thus there was expressed a requirement that full cost plus an adequate return should be realized to comply with the law, it being considered immaterial that the rentals exacted constituted fair value or were similar to the prevailing rents in general.

By concluding that "(i)t is immaterial that the shipper pays fair value or the market price for the extra privilege he enjoys" (p. 523) which, in this instance, meant the application of a cost measure in detecting the device used to grant unlawful concessions, the court did not pretend to establish a rigid rule that in all cases rentals must meet aggregate costs. This is evident from the language of the court where it states (p. 524) that "(t)his is not to say that for every situation it is necessary that the accessorial services should be rendered at not less than cost, rather than market or fair value . . . In other circumstances fair value and market have been recognized as legitimate bases." That a rigid rule was not established is demonstrated by the decision of the Supreme Court in *Union Pacific Railroad Co. v. United States,*[56] where

[55]305 U.S. 507.
[56]313 U.S. 450.

fair rental value rather than a compensatory return upon full value of the facilities was the standard by which the schedule of rates was judged, and in determining fair rental value the going rent for similar facilities in the area was considered significant as was the rental prospective tenants were willing to pay. In discussing the *Baltimore & Ohio* case, the court said (pp. 474):

> This is not the case for a rigid rule that aggregate rentals are to equal costs, such as was applied in *Baltimore & Ohio R. Co. v. United States,* 305 U.S. 507, 523-524, where this court approved an order of the Interstate Commerce Commission designed to root out competitive evils in discriminatory warehousing indulged in by carriers in an effort to acquire traffic. The City is entitled to develop its properties and location in accordance with the laws of Kansas for civic advantage, so long as it does not utilize its facilities in furtherance of a scheme to obtain customers for a carrier by the offering of concessions contrary to the Elkins Act. It was recognized in *Baltimore & Ohio R. Co. v. United States* that a charge of fair rental value for services accessorial to transportation would adequately protect even a carrier under proper circumstances. We are of the view that rental charges fixed upon that concept will avoid the discriminatory evils prescribed by the Elkins Act.

In *Southern Ry. Co. v. United States,*[57] the court said that the Elkins Act and the I.C. Act, being remedial in nature, are applicable to every method of dealing by a carrier whereby the forbidden discrimination can be brought about; and the Commission and the courts, in condemning discriminatory rental practices have considered those statutes to be in pari materia. Emerging from the *Baltimore & Ohio* case, the court said, is the rule that rents carriers charge for the purpose of attracting freight must be no less than prevailing market rents in the area, and no less than compensatory (including normal return on capital employed in like enterprises), whichever is higher; a carrier is prohibited from engaging in such noncarrier business on a more favorable basis than other business because it can offset any losses against carrier revenues; it cannot operate a noncarrier business as a means of securing freight free of statutory standards for carrier conduct,[58] and the *Union Pacific case,*[59] holding that rents at a joint food terminal of the city and the railroad need not be compensatory on the total investment, but because of the railroad's participation must be no less than "fair rental value," is not inconsistent with that rule.[60]

[57]186 F. Supp. 29, 36.
[58]Id., p. 37.
[59]313 U.S. 450.
[60]*Ibid.,* pp. 37-8.

The court said that the Commission in the instant case, in applying the tests prescribed in the *Union Pacific* case for determining the rent to be charged by the city, justifiably found that plaintiffs' rents for their terminal did not meet even that special standard, since they were substantially below the prevailing practice for similar facilities in the area, did not reflect overall costs and value of the properties, and on a comparative basis yielded an unduly low return on carrier's investment.[61] The court said that if the landlord were not a railroad leasing a freight-producing facility, there would be some logic to the carrier's position that it was not required to consider depreciation costs in fixing the rental charges, on the ground that under the agreement the tenants were obligated to purchase the facilities at undepreciated costs and its rental basis would treat all costs as not subject to depreciation in the same manner as prevailing market practice treats land; such a rental formula would be equivalent to an agreement by the railroad to postpone part of the rent to a future date, resulting in an unlawful loan or extension of credit similar to the extension of credit on delayed rent collection.[62] Though the Commission did not pass on the validity of the sales plan, inasmuch as the cost-price under that plan excluded the very costs which the Commission held could not lawfully be excluded from the rent base, the carrier could not complain of the Commission's action in adopting a rental plan which required application of a higher rental factor to depreciable items of cost.[63] The court said that under the ruling in the *Baltimore & Ohio* case, a railroad cannot justify its charging of lower rents because of the depressive effect of pre-existing market rents by its action in constructing facilities to be rented at a substantially lower rental;[64] and the inclusion in the prescribed rental base of the cost of spur tracks designed to service individual facilities of the terminal was not a taking of carrier's property without due process of law; carrier was not required to surrender the normal and usual control over such tracks, but merely to include their cost in those on which the rentals were based, just as any other landlord would do if it provided such facilities.[65]

In *United States v. General Motors Corporation*,[66] action was brought

[61]*Ibid.*
[62]*Ibid.*, p. 38.
[63]*Ibid.*, p. 39.
[64]*Ibid.*, p. 40.
[65]*Ibid.*
[66]226 F. 2d 745. See *United States v. Boston & M. R.*, 157 F. Supp. 218, 220, where the land proposed to be sold by the railroad had an appreciable value, and as part of the contract of sale, the carrier assumed direct financial obligations nearly twice the gross amount of the sales price. In return it received, if not a promise, at least a somewhat secured hope of substantial freight business. See also *United States v. Michael Schiavone*, 430 F. 2d 231.

by the Government against General Motors to recover under the Elkins Act three times the amount of alleged rebate received from the Baltimore and Ohio Railroad Company arising out of a transaction involving the sale of land for a plant site. On appeal from a judgment entered for General Motors pursuant to a jury verdict in its favor, the court held (p. 748) that the crux of the prohibition in the Elkins Act against rebates is the receipt of an advantage by the shipper and the receipt of advantages is to be tested by actual results and by intention. The court said that in *Union Pacific R. Co. v. United States*,[67] it was noted that contribution to a shipper's construction cost is forbidden, thus, assuredly, if a contribution to construction cost is barred so is contribution to the cost of the shipper's plant site as an inducement for the location of the plant on the railroad's line. The court pointed out that it is the contribution to the shipper and not the fair and reasonable price of that which the shipper receives which is critical; and it is of no consequence that the fair market value of the site is less than the price paid by the railroad.

The Commission also has applied a cost measure in the past for the purpose of determining whether illegal practices have been engaged in through the leasing of property by rail carrier. During an over-all investigation in *Freight Forwarding Investigation*,[68] the Commission had an opportunity to consider the leasing of freight house facilities by railroads to freight forwarders, which recognizedly occupy the dual status of shipper and common carrier. The Commission found during the investigation (pp. 216-7) that where facilities had been built by the railroads in behalf of the freight forwarders such facilities had been leased at rentals which failed to yield an adequate return on the value of the premises, and where existing facilities had not been constructed specially they had been leased at rentals accruing less than the total sum of taxes, maintenance, repairs and operating expenses. In both instances the Commission applied a cost measure, but in the first a recovery of full cost plus an adequate return was required whereas in the second out-of-pocket costs were required to be recovered.

Paying Less Than the Established Rate between Two Points

To pay less than the established rate between two points by including such lesser rate in a through rate was held to be a violation of

---

[67]313 U.S. 450.
[68]229 I.C.C. 201.

the Act in *Armour Packing Co. v. United States.*[69] There, oleo was shipped from Kansas City, Kansas, to a foreign country at the rate of 52.93 cents per hundred pounds. Twenty-three cents of this was for the shipment of the oleo from the Mississippi River to New York. The established rate from the Mississippi River to New York was 35 cents per hundred pounds.

Giving of Credit

Giving of credit to a shipper on tariff charges, even at interest, when such credit is not given to all shippers is a discrimination in violation of the Elkins Act.[70] In *Vandalia R. Co. v. United States*[71] a railroad organized a mineral company and the latter made a loan to a coal company at 2 percent interest. The coal company agreed that the railroad would be the exclusive carrier of all its coal. The money loaned to the coal company has been borrowed by the mineral company at 4 percent interest. It was held that the arrangement was a device for the payment of a rebate to a shipper, the coal company, and therefore in violation of the Elkins Act.

Rebate on Collateral Services

In *Spencer Kellog & Sons v. United States,*[72] the defendant was the owner of a grain elevator which was paid 1 cent a bushel by a carrier for lifting grain from the holds of lake vessels, storing it for a while, and then reloading the grain on to freight cars. The defendant paid 1/2 cent per bushel of this to shippers or consignees as an inducement to them to designate defendant's elevator to handle their grain. The defendant was held to be guilty of violating the Elkins Act because this practice resulted in the transportation of property at lesser rates than those in the tariffs published and filed by the common carriers transporting the grain. The case involved an indirect return to shippers of part of their transportation charges.

[69]153 Fed. 1; aff'd 209 U.S. 56.
[70]*United States v. Hocking Valley Ry. Co.,* 194 Fed. 234, aff'd 210 Fed. 735, cert. denied 234 U.S. 757, *United States v. Sunday Creek Co.* 194 Fed. 252, aff'd 210 Fed 747, cert. denied 234 U.S. 757.
[71]226 Fed. 713, cert. denied 239 U.S. 642.
[72]20 F. 2d 459, cert. denied 275 U.S. 566.

Insurance on Goods in Transit

It is a violation of the Elkins Act to give a shipper a greater insurance coverage than is provided for in the tariff schedule. *Duplan Silk Company v. American and Foreign Marine Insurance Company.*[73]

Failure to Charge and Collect Demurrage

Failure to collect from a shipper demurrage charges fixed by carriers is the grant of a concession to the shipper in violation of the Elkins Act.[74]

Free Franks

In *American Express Company v. United States,*[75] the issuance of franks permitting free transportation of personal packages for employees of express companies was held to be a violation of the Elkins Act.

Charging a Lesser Rate over One Through Route Than over Another

A railroad had entered into an arrangement with connecting carrier companies to transport property on a through route, and a joint rate for this was filed and published. The carrier transported property between the same termini at a lower rate over another route using other connecting carriers. This was held to be a violation of the Elkins Act in *United States v. Vacuum Oil Co.*[76]

Paying Shipper for a Service the Carrier Is Not Obligated to Perform

It is unlawful for a carrier to pay a shipper for the use of privately owned tracks which are used to get the shipper's shipment to the carrier's rails for transportation over the carrier's lines, if the published tariffs do not provide that the carrier will furnish the service involved.[77]

Paying or Receiving Rates on Commodities Not Entitled to Transit Privileges

In *Lewis, Leonhardt & Co. v. Southern Ry. Co.,*[78] the defendant was given a milling in transit privilege whereby it received the benefit of

[73]205 Fed. 724.
[74]*United States v. Standard Oil Co.,* 148 Fed. 719.
[75]212 U.S. 522.
[76]153 Fed. 598.
[77]*United States v. Chicago & A. Ry. Co.,* 148 Fed. 646, aff'd 156 Fed. 558 and 212 U.S. 563.
[78]217 Fed. 321, cert. denied 238 U.S. 618.

through rates instead of paying two local rates when unground oats and corn were shipped to Knoxville, milled, and then shipped to market. Such a milling in transit privilege of course is proper when provision is made for it in the carrier's tariffs, but it contemplates that the same commodity or an equivalent commodity will be involved in the two stages of the through shipment. In this case a product was shipped out which consisted of 50 per cent of oats and corn and 50 per cent of other ingredients. This was held to involve a rebate in violation of the Elkins Act, since it resulted in extending transit rates to ingredients not entitled to it — the 50 percent of the ingredients not consisting of oats and corn. In *Grand Rapids and I. Ry. Co. v. United States*,[79] transit rates were applied to certain shipments of lumber. However, the lumber shipped out of the transit point was not the same lumber shipped into the transit point, although the quantities were the same. For the carrier not to have collected two local rates was held to be a violation of the Elkins Act.[80]

In *Boone v. United States*,[81] the manager of a grain warehouse had used unused transit billings to get transit rates on certain cars of bulk corn. The transit billings permitted the loading and unloading of cars and did not require that the corn shipped out be identical to the corn shipped in. The corn actually shipped out had never been unloaded from the cars and, in and of itself, was not entitled to transit rates. It was held that a violation of the Elkins Act was involved, the court saying (p. 563) "(i)t is not practical to require that identity of each carload of grain be preserved but to the end that loose and fraudulent practices, the use of unlawful rates, unjust discrimination, undue prejudice and substantial revenue losses to the carrier may be prevented, it is unlawful to substitute or forward under the transit rate any commodity that does not move into the transit point at such rate." The foregoing illustrates the meticulous manner in which the courts examine any practice which in any way may involve a discrimination in favor of a particular shipper and, if any discrimination is found, declare the practice to be a device in violation of the Elkins Act.

Collecting a False Claim from a Carrier

In *United States v. Satuloff Brothers*,[82] the defendant surreptitiously removed eighteen barrels of turkeys from a carload assignment, claimed

---

[79]212 Fed. 577, cert. denied 234 U.S. 762.
[80]*Nichols & Cox Lumber Co. v. United States*, 212 Fed. 588, cert. denied 234 U.S. 762.
[81]109 F. 2d 560.
[82]79 F. 2d 846.

a shortage, and sued the carrier and recovered. It was held that this was a device for obtaining a rebate in violation of the Elkins Act.

Free Advertising

Where a railroad entered into a contract to grant transportation in exchange for advertising, the Supreme Court held such a scheme to constitute a violation of the Elkins Act and the Act to Regulate Commerce in *Chicago, Indianapolis and Louisville Railway Co. v. United States*.[83] In that case, the carrier contended that the money value of the advertising purchased under the contract was $500 as determined and fixed by the rate to the public, and that it was to pay therefor $500 in value of passenger transportation issued and based on regularly published rates, so that the money value of the advertising space purchased and the money value of the transportation furnished was the same.

This contention was held immaterial, the court saying (p. 496) the "decisive question" here is whether the contract is repugnant to the statutes regulating commerce. "In other words, could the company, in return for the transportation which it agreed to furnish and did furnish to the Munsey publisher over its interstate lines, and to his employes and to the immediate members of his and their families, accept as compensation for such service anything else than money, the amount to be determined by its published schedule of rates and charges?" The answer, the court said (p. 496) "must be in the negative." The acceptance by the railway company of advertising, not of money in payment of the interstate transportation furnished to the publisher, his employees and the immediate members of his and their families was in violation of the law. It was pointed out by the court (pp. 496-7) that the facts in the case show how easily the I.C. Act can be evaded and the object of Congress entirely defeated. "The legislative department intended that all who obtained transportation on interstate lines should be treated alike in the matter of rates, and that all who availed themselves of the services of the railway company . . . should be on a plane of equality. Those ends cannot be met otherwise than by requiring transportation to be paid for in money which has a certain value known to all and not in commodities or services or otherwise than in money."

[83]219 U.S. 486. See also *Union Pacific Railway Company v. United States*, 313 U.S. 450, 460, where the railroad made available to prospective shippers a certain amount of free advertising by interviewing the shippers on its radio program and allowing them to describe the kind and quality of their product; and *Use of Privately Owned Refrigerator Cars*, 201 I.C.C. 323.

Becoming a Dealer in a Commodity

In *New Haven R.R. v. Interstate Com. Com'n,*[84] a carrier sold coal in Connecticut at $2.75 a ton. The cost of the coal where the carrier bought it, plus the cost of shipping the coal beyond its lines to Connecticut, was $2.47. This meant that the carrier was getting 28 cents a ton for transporting the coal for that part of the transportation which took place over its own lines. The tariff rate for such transportation over its own lines was $1.45 per ton. This was held to be a discrimination in favor of the buyer in violation of the I.C. Act, the court regarding it as a case in which full tariff rates had not been collected.

Carload Rates on Less Than Carload Lots

In *Warehouse Company v. United States,*[85] certain warehouses were designed by carriers to be a part of their station facilities in Philadelphia. On outgoing freight, in order to make the use of their warehouses by shippers attractive, the warehouses accepted package freight in less than carload lots, combined such shipments into carload lots, and shipped them in carloads at carload rates. On incoming shipments, package freight in carload lots was received, the carloads were broken up, and were distributed to consignees in less than carload lots. This resulted in shippers getting carload rates on less than carload lots. This was held to be a rebate.

Payment of Unduly Large Allowances to a Subsidiary of a Shipper

In *Colonial Salt Company v. Michigan, Indiana & Illinois Line,*[86] the Commission found that a separately incorporated boat line and its facilities were actually the private transportation facilities of the salt company shipper-owner, and were not used in a common carrier capacity. The incorporation of the boat line was a mere device to evade the law and secure illegal refunds to the salt company through payments to the boat line by certain railroads of unreasonable divisions out of joint rates. These divisions were passed on by the boat line to the salt company on the form of dividends.

In condemning the method of operation as a means or device to accrue rebates though made in the form of dividends, the Commission said (pp. 366-7) "(t)he language of the Elkins Act is that it shall be

[84]200 U.S. 361.
[85]283 U.S. 501.
[86]23 I.C.C. 358.

unlawful to give or receive any rebates or concession with respect to the transportation of property whereby any such property shall by any device whatever be transported at a less rate than that named in the tariffs . . . or whereby any other advantage is given or discrimination practices"; and that the same thought is no less clearly expressed in Section 2 of the Act to Regulate Commerce. "In neither act is there any limitation of prohibition to some devices to accomplish the unlawful result, but the language comprehensively embraces all and any devices of whatever nature and form," and "bearing in mind the evils aimed at by the act there can be no doubt that this boat line, although incorporated and thus given a legal form and appearance, is a mere device by which grossly unlawful advantages are secured." Thus dividends, in the factual setting on which the Commission was passing, were held to constitute unlawful rebates in violation of the Elkins Act. The effect of the dividend is traced and if the ultimate result is to make the recipient a favored shipper, the dividend is a device to pay a rebate and is made unlawful by the Elkins Act.[87]

In the Matter of Division of Joint Rates and Other Allowances to Terminal Railroads,[88] the International Harvestor Company owned the capital stock of the Illinois Northern Railway Company, a terminal railroad connecting with the plant of International Harvester. To obtain traffic with International Harvester, certain carriers allowed the Illinois Northern Railway Company a division of $12.00 per car for performing a service in connection with the shipments by International Harvester when the service rendered was not worth over $3.00 a car. The Commission condemned the practice and said (pp. 400-2):

> We think these division, if not in violation of the expressed language of the second section of the original Act, are plainly within the prohibition of the Elkins Bill. When the Santa Fe Railway pays to the Illinois Northern Railroad $12.00 for the moving of a car loaded with the traffic of the International Harvester Company from the McCormick works to its Corwith yard . . . for the performance of which $3.00 is a reasonable compensation, which was never exceeded previous to January 1, 1904; and when it does this in order to obtain traffic of the International Harvester Company, it therefore grants that company in effect a rebate of $9.00 upon that carload of freight.

[87]*Divisions Received by Brimetone R.R. & Canal Co.,* 68 I.C.C. 375, 386-7, 88 I.C.C. 62, 73, 104 I.C.C. 415;*Allowances or Divisions Received by Texas Gulf and Sulphur Co.,* 96 I.C.C. 371, 376-7; and *Manufacturers Ry. Co. v. United States,* 246 U.S. 457, 486, where the Supreme Court recognized the unduly large allowances to a railway owned by a brewery-shipper would amount to the payment of rebates to the brewery, because "the Brewery's share of the profit accruing from them would amount to an indirect preference to the Brewery."
[88]10 I.C.C. 385, reaff'd at 10 I.C.C. 661.

°　　°　　°

It is urged that all this is simply an arrangement between two connecting railroads; that there is no negotiation with the shipper, and no payment to the shipper. This is a mere play upon words. The Illinois Northern Railroad Company and the International Harvester Company are one and the same thing. It is entirely immaterial whether the money goes in the first instance into the treasury of the International Harvester Company or that of its creature, the Illinois Northern Railroad Company. That subterfuges of this sort cannot avail has been often decided, and was affirmed within the year by the Supreme Court of the United States in *Interstate Commerce Commission v. Baird*, 194 U.S. 25, 48 L. ed. 860, 24 Sup. Ct. Rep. 563, in which it was held that it made no difference whether certain contracts were entered into with the railroad company itself or with a coal company the stock of which was entirely owned by the railroad company.

°　　°　　°

The manifest intention of the Act to Regulate Commerce, especially as expressed inthe Elkins Bill, is to strike through all pretense, all ingenious device, to the substance of the transaction itself. So, viewing this transaction, there is not the slightest doubt that the granting of these divisions is the allowance of a preference to the International Harvester Company, which is in violation of law.

Granting of Permits for Transportation During an Embargo

To grant permits for the transportation of hay and to deny it to others during an embargo, where no reason appears for differentiating between shippers, was held to be a violation of the Elkins Act in *United States v. Lehigh Valley Ry. Co.*[89]

Obtaining a Higher Priority During a Time of Car Shortages

An order of the Commission during a time of shortage set up certain priorities for the furnishing of coal cars. By reporting that the coal it was ordering was for a hospital when in fact it was for automobile manufacturer, defendant obtained a higher priority than it was entitled to. It was held that the defendant had thereby secured a discrimination in its favor in violation of the Elkins Act.[90]

Expedited Service or Delivery by a Specified Time

That a special contract to transport a car on a particular day is illegal when not provided for in the carrier's tariff was held in *Chicago & Alton*

---

[89]254 Fed. 332.

[90]*United States v. Koenig Coal Co.*, 270 U.S. 512. See also *United States v. Michigan Portland Cement Co.*, 270 U.S. 521; *United States v. Metropolitan Lumber Co.*, 254 Fed. 335.

R.R. Co. v. Kirby.[91] There the Supreme Court said (pp. 164-5) that the implied agreement of a common carrier is to transport safely and deliver at destination within a reasonable time, but it is otherwise when the action is for breach of a contract "to carry within a particular time, or to make a particular connection, or to carry by a particular train" where the carrier then becomes liable for the consequence of a failure to transport according to its terms. The court said that evidence of diligence would not excuse the carrier, and a showing that there had been no unreasonable delay would not be an answer as it would be in an action for common law carrier liability. Thus a carrier by entering into an agreement for expediting the shipment comes under a liability different and more burdensome than would exist if no special contract were made with a shipper. For such a special service and higher responsibility the carrier might clearly exact a higher rate, but to do so it must make and publish a rate open to all. The shipper in the *Chicago & Alton* case, it is plain, was contracting for an advantage which was not extended to all others, both in the undertaking to carry so as to give him a particular expedited service and a remedy for delay not due to negligence. The Supreme Court said (p. 165) that such an advantage, accorded by special agreement, which affects the value of the service to the shipper and its cost to the carrier should be published in the carrier tariffs, "and for a breach of such a contract, relief will be denied, because its allowance without such publication is a violation of the act" and is illegal also as "it is an undue advantage in that it is not one open to all others in the same situation."

The *Chicago & Alton* case was cited with approval in *Davis v. Cornwell*,[92] as supporting the proposition that a contract to furnish cars on a day certain imposes a greater obligation than that implied in the tariff because, "under the contract, proof of due diligence would not excuse failure to perform." The Supreme Court said (p. 562) that the *Chicago & Alton* case "settled that a special contract to transport a car by a particular train, or on a particular day, is illegal, when not provided for in the tariff." It is not necessary to prove that a preference results in fact. The assumption by the carrier of the additional obligation is necessarily a preference. The court added that "(t)he paramount requirement that tariff provisions be strictly adhered to, so that shippers may receive equal treatment, presents an insuperable obstacle to recovery."

Southern Ry. v. Prescott,[93] also cited the *Chicago & Alton* case with approval, stating that with respect to service governed by the I.C.

---

[91] 225 U.S. 155.
[92] 264 U.S. 560, 561-2.
[93] 240 U.S. 632, 638.

Act carriers and shippers are not at liberty to alter the terms of the service as fixed by the tariffs, this having been held repeatedly with respect to rates, "and the established principle applies equally to any stipulation attempting to alter the provisions as fixed by the published rules relating to any of the services within the purview of the Act." The court commented that the purpose of the statute is, "to shut the door to all contrivances in violation of its provisions against preferences and discriminations," and no carrier may extend any privileges or facilities except for those that have been duly specified.

An agreement to make delivery within a specified time or to expedite a shipment, when the published tariffs of the carriers contain no provision for such special service, has been recognized by the Commission as a discriminatory practice against shippers with whom no such agreement is entered into and, therefore, a violation of the Elkins Act and the I.C. Act. Pursuant to an order of investigation into the general subject of the form and substance of bills of lading, and of the practices of carriers in respect to their issuance, transfer, and surrender, the Commission had occasion to comment in *Bills of Lading*[94] on the granting of special or expeditious service to shippers when not open to all shippers alike.

In that proceeding there was under discussion a clause to be inserted in bills of lading providing that "(n)o carrier is bound to transport property by any particular train or vessel, or in time for any particular market or otherwise than with reasonable dispatch unless by specific agreement indorsed hereon.' The Commission (p. 732) said that while no objection was raised to the clause "we think that the reservation by the carriers of the right to grant expedited service by special agreement indorsed on the bill of lading, as contained in the words 'unless by specific agreement indorsed hereon' is objectionable." The Commission concluded that such language would make it "possible for certain favored shippers through special indorsements on their bills of lading to secure special and expeditious handling of their shipments, possibly to the undue prejudice and disadvantage of their less favored competitors," and for that reason "we are of the opinion these words should be eliminated."

Knowingly Undervaluating Property by a Shipper

In *United States v. North Carolina Granite Corp.*, [95] the court held that when a tariff provided rates based on value on crushed granite, a shipper obtained a lower rate than one based on the sale price of the

[94]52 I.C.C. 671.
[95]288 F. 2d 232, 233-4.

commodity less freight charges, thus procuring an unlawful rebate, when it consigned the shipments to itself, certifying on the bill of lading that actual value was less than $8.00 a ton, which value was based on cost of production, and by letter directed carrier's agent at destination to deliver the goods to the purchaser. The court said that the fact that the shipper for its own purposes chose to consign the goods to itself, thereby assuming the risk of loss, had no probative force, since there was no evidence that the circumstance would affect the sales price, and the shipper knew that the value of the goods at the time of delivery to the carrier exceeded the certified value in the bill of lading;[96] that the fact that the sales-price-less-freight formula for determining actual value would not apply to goods shipped by a manufacturer for storage or for its own use at another location, or would result in different values at different localities, owing to variations in freight rates or in market demand, the court said, did not undermine the propriety of that formula but merely showed the varying circumstances under which it might be applied.[97] The court also said that there was no substance to the contention that the penal statute was unconstitutional insofar as it was based on the tariff, because the term "actual value" used therein was too vague and uncertain to sustain a prosecution for crime; any uncertainty rests not in the meaning of the tariff but in the variety of circumstances to which it must be applied, a condition commonly encountered in applying a governing statute to the facts of a particular case.[98]

Ownership or Maintenance of Tracks inside a Plant for the Sole Benefit of a Shipper

A carrier's ownership or maintenance of tracks inside a plant violates the Elkins Act when such tracks are for the sole use or benefit of the industry, but not when they are not in fact plant facilities but are used primarily for carrier switching operations.[99]

Delay in Route for Benefit of Shipper

The Commission said in *Lumber, Free Time Allowance at Hold Points*[100] that a delay of several days, in route to hold points of lumber

---

[96]*Ibid.*, p. 235.
[97]*Ibid.*, p. 234.
[98]*Ibid.*, p. 235.
[99]*Ford Motor Co. Terminal Allowance*, 310 I.C.C. 297, 300.
[100]310 I.C.C. 521, 523. See also *Lumber, Free Time Allowance at Hold Points*, 308 I.C.C. 247, 249.

shipments moving over direct routes, at shippers' request to enable them to obtain buyers, violates Section 1 of the Elkins Act and Section 6(7) of the I.C. Act if no provision therefor is made in the carriers' tariffs and there is no charge for the service. In *United States v. Union Pacific R. Co.*,[101] the court held that a carrier's offering, agreeing on, and providing delayed lumber service to certain transit wholesalers and dealers in lumber, to induce them to ship over its lines to the exclusion of competitors, constituted a device for offering and giving rebates, concessions, advantages, and discriminations whereby those shippers were enabled to ship lumber at less than the published rates; the court said that such acts and practices of defendant violated the Elkins Act.

Unauthorized For-Hire Transportation

In *Mumby Investigation of Operations*,[102] where respondent shippers were beneficially interested in or affected by a carrier's unauthorized for-hire transportation, the Commission held that this constituted a violation of law.

Special Contracts of Carriage

In *Coal to New York Harbor Area*,[103] the Commission said that reduced rates on coal, conditioned on delivery of aggregate quantities which effectively restricted their use to traffic moving to an electric utility plant, were not "special contracts" of carriage contrary to law; those rates were published in lawfully filed tariffs and available to all who could comply with their provisions which fall far short of constituting a means of effecting rebates or refunds condemned by the Elkins Act.

Special Services

The Commission said in *Eastern Central M. Carriers Assn. v. Baltimore & O. R. Co.*, [104] that while there was evidence that in their piggyback operations, in which shippers furnished the equipment and performed or arranged for loading and unloading and pickup and delivery, certain railroads had been directly or indirectly leasing trailers and

[101]173 F. Supp. 397, 411, 413.
[102]82 M.C.C. 237, 249. See also *Wilson-Investigation of Operations,* 82 M.C.C. 651, 657-8.
[103]311 I.C.C. 355, 370.
[104]314 I.C.C. 5, 45-6.

cars to certain shippers and performing loading and unloading of trailers or furnishing drayage service at negotiated charges, and while furnishing of services which carrier did not hold out to perform could be the source of illegal rebating for which they could be liable to prosecution under Elkins Act, they were not barred from publishing rates for less than a "complete" service, since the differences in rates were entirely unlike allowance or rebates and were primarily a matters of managerial discretion, so long as they were lawful. The Commission said that while potential discrimination might be found in certain circumstances, the potentiality was inherent in the nature of the tariff publication and could not rest on speculation alone; the plans, openly published and available without collateral qualifications to all shippers at the same location, could not be found unjustly discriminatory because opportunity existed for the carriers, outside of the tariffs, to engage in criminal rebating.[105]

Loading and Unloading Services for Shippers or Receivers without Charge

The providing of loading and unloading services for shippers or receivers without charge, and the absence of such services from published tariffs, would constitute a violation of the Elkins Act.[106]

Claims

In *Loss and Damage Claims*,[107] the Commission said:

. . . In *Phillips v. Grand Trunk Ry.*, 236 U.S. 662 (1915), the Supreme Court stated, at page 667, that "The prohibitions of the statute against unjust discrimination relate not only ot inequality of charges and inequality of facilities, but also to the giving of preferences by means of consent judgments or the waiver of defenses open to the carrier." Although the Court there was addressing itself to the matter of the proper rate to be charged on a shipment transported by a rail carrier subject to part I of the act, we believe that the underlying principle is equally applicable to claims matters. Cf. *Georgia, Fla., & Ala. Ry. v. Blish Co.*, 241 U.S. 190, 196 (1916). It was also impliedly found by division 2, in *Arma Corp. v. M & M Transp. Co.*, 61 M.C.C. 723 (1953), to be applicable to motor carriers subject to part II of the act, and we can see no reason why the same logic should not hold true for other regulated carriers and the application of the concept to loss and damage claims. From a regulatory

[105]*Ibid.*, p. 49.
[106]Cf. *Acme Fast Freight, Inc. v. Western Freight Assn.*, 299 I.C.C. 315.
[107]340 I.C.C. 515, 529.

standpoint, therefore, we are also concerned that a rebate may be clandestinely granted by a carrier by the simple expedients of readily accepting a claimant's arguments in support of a claim, of consenting to a default judgment, of waiving available defenses, or even of failing to prosecute appeals when there is a reasonable basis for expecting to be successful if pursued.

To the extent, then, that regulated carriers voluntarily process or fail to process loss and damage claims filed by parties who, for one reason or another, are likely to sue or fail to sue, or who resort to litigation in one-State jurisdiction rather than another, we are also vitally concerned because we must see to it that they constantly are on guard and ready to explain to us, either informally or otherwise, why they have paid one claim and denied another whenever similar basic facts exist.

37

Undue or Unreasonable Preferences and Prejudices or Advantages and Disadvantages

The Applicable Statutory Provisions

Section 3(1) of the Interstate Commerce Act[1] is intended to protect shippers and not competing carrier. The section provides that it shall be unlawful for any common carrier "to make, give, or cause any undue or unreasonable preferences or advantage to any particular person, company, firm, corporation, association, locality, port, port district, gateway, transit point, region, district, territory, or any particular description of traffic in any respect whatsoever"; or to subject the foregoing "to any undue or unreasonable prejudice or disadvantage in any respect whatsoever." Section 3, however, "shall not be construed to apply to discrimination, prejudice, or disadvantage to the traffic of any other carrier of whatever description."

Intent of Section 3(1)

The preference and prejudice prohibited by Section 3(1) relate to preference and prejudice shown by one carrier or a combination of carriers between the entities named in Section 3(1) which are served by the one carrier or the combination acting as one. The prohibition of Section 3(1) is intended to prevent a carrier from giving preference or advantage, over which the carrier has control, to one of the entities named and not to another. Preference, not necessarily injurious in itself, affords opportunity to gain success over, and injure, the other party.

The mere existence of a difference in rates does not establish undue

---

[1] 49 U.S.C. 3(1). Comparable provisions — Sections 216(d), 305(c), 404(b), (c). See *Eastern Central M. Carriers Assn. v. Baltimore & O. R. Co.,* 314 I.C.C. 5, 50.

prejudice or preference. As stated by the Supreme Court in *United States v. Illinois Central R. R.*:[2]

> . . . to bring a difference in rates within the prohibition of § 3, it must be shown that the discrimination practiced is unjust when measured by the transportation standard. In other words, the difference in rates cannot be held illegal, unless it is shown that it is not justified by the cost of the respective services, by their values, or by other transportation conditions.

Elements to Be Demonstrated under Section 3(1)

The Commission expects five elements to be demonstrated under Section 3(1). They are (1) rate disparity, (2) competition between preferred and prejudiced origins, (3) control of the rates from the preferred and prejudiced origins by the rail defendants, (4) substantially similar transportation conditions, and (5) injury to the prejudiced origin.[3]

Burden of Proof

It is well settled that the burden of proof is on complainants before the Commission to establish that the carrier's rates are subjecting them to undue or unreasonable preference or prejudice.[4] When rates have been in effect for a long period of time there is a presumption of lawfulness, and the complainant must carry the burden of overcoming that presumption with clear and convincing evidence to the contrary.[5]

---

[2]263 U.S. 510, 524. See also *Black Hills Glass & Mirror Co. v. Chic., M., & St. P. R. Co.*, 313 I.C.C. 333, 339; *Malt Liquors, Mo., Ill., & Nebr. to Okla.*, 310 I.C.C. 93, 101; *United Lime Products Corp. v. A., T. & S.F. Ry. Co.*, 288 I.C.C. 293, 300; *Cinder Concrete Products, Inc. v. Colo. & S. Ry. Co.*, 279 I.C.C. 191, 194; *A. C. Jensen Block & Supply Co. v. Chic., M., & St. P. R. Co.*, 273 I.C.C. 399, 401; *Waggener Paint Co. v. Chicago G. W. Ry. Co.*, 308 I.C.C. 148, 150; *Commodity Credit Corp. v. Texas & P. Ry. Co.*, 306 I.C.C. 525, 533; *State Bd. of Equalization of Wyo. v. Abiline & S. Ry. Co.*, 305 I.C.C. 497, 513; *Southern States Cooperative, Inc., v. B. & O. R. Co.*, 323 I.C.C. 400, 408; *Southeastern Assn. of R. & Util. Comm. v. A., T. & S.F. Ry.*, 321 I.C.C. 519, 553; *United States v. Oklahoma City-ADA-Atoka Ry. Co.*, 319 I.C.C. 182, 186; and *Seattle Traffic Assn. v. CF, Inc.*, 306 I.C.C., 87, 92.

[3]See *Fresh Meats from Illinois, Indiana, Kentucky, Ohio & Missouri to Points in Florida*, 318 I.C.C. 5, 10; *Big River Industries, Inc. v. Aberdeen & R. R. Co.*, 329 I.C.C. 539; *Silica Products Co., Inc. v. Gulf, M. & O. R. Co.*, 329 I.C.C. 181; and *Corn and Corn Products, Illinois to Official Territory*, 332 I.C.C. 485; *Chicago & Eastern Ill. R.R. v. United States*, 384 F. Supp. 298, 300-01, aff'd mem., 421 U.S. 956; *Louis Dreyfus Corp. v. United States*, 401 F. Supp. 919, 926-27 & n.4.

[4]*Louisville & N. R. Co. v. United States*, 238 U.S. 1, 11; *Koppers Co. v. United States*, 166 F. Supp. 96, 99-100, 101-102.

[5]*Wallboard Between Southern and Official Territory*, 227 I.C.C. 235, 242; *Chamber of Commerce of Greenville, Ohio v. Akron, C. & Y. Ry.*, 203 I.C.C. 121, 124.

The legal principles governing the determination of whether an "undue preference or prejudice" exists are well established. Initially, it should be noted that it is only an "undue" or "unreasonable" preference or prejudice which is prohibited by the statute.[6] As the Supreme Court pointed out in the *Texas & Pacific Ry.* case, *supra*[7] "the mere circumstance that there is, in a given case, a preference or an advantage does not of itself show that such preference or advantage is undue or unreasonable within the meaning of the I.C. Act." The question of whether, in a given case, a preference or prejudice is undue or unreasonable is a question of fact, not of law.[8] The court pointed out in *Swayne & Hoyt, Ltd. v. United States, supra:*[9]

> Whether a discrimination of rates or services of a carrier is undue or unreasonable has always been regarded as peculiarly a question committed to the judgment of the administrative body, based upon application of all the facts and circumstances affecting the traffic.

Many factors are considered, compared, weighed, and valued by the Commission in reaching its decision in an undue preference and prejudice case,[10] and how much weight shall be given to the important factors involved must necessarily be left to the Commission.[11] The existence of alleged undue preference or prejudice at different places is a question of fact which must be proved.[12] It must be established that the rate disparity operates to the advantage of the competitors alleged to be preferred and to the disadvantage of the complainant. As was stated in *Young's Market Co. v. New York Central R. Co.:*[13]

> . . . It is well settled that a mere difference in rates is not sufficient to constitute undue prejudice. . . . Undue prejudice and preference must be established by a preponderance of evidence which must make it reasonably clear that the prejudice and preference complained of result from

---

[6]*United States v. Wabash R. Co.*, 321 U.S. 403, 411; *United States v. Illinois Central R.R.*, 263 U.S. 515, 521; *Texas & Pacific Ry. v. Interstate Commerce Commission*, 162 U.S. 197, 219-220; *State Corp. Commission of Kansas v. United States*, 184 F. Supp. 691, 698.

[7]162 U.S. at 219.

[8]*Board of Trade of Kansas City v. United States*, 314 U.S. 534, 546; *Swayne & Hoyt, Ltd. v. United States*, 300 U.S. 297, 304; *N. C. & St. L. Ry. v. United States*, 262 U.S. 318; *Manufacturers' Ry. v. United States*, 246 U.S. 457, 481; *United States v. Illinois Central R.R., supra*, 263 U.S. at 524; *Texas & Pacific Ry. v. United States, supra*, 162 U.S. at 219-220.

[9]300 U.S. at 304.

[10]Cf *Board of Trade v. United States, supra*, 314 U.S. at 536.

[11]*United States v. Illinois Cent. R.R.*, 263 U.S. 515, 524.

[12]Cf. *Board of Trade v. United States*, 314 U.S. 534, 546; *Duluth Chamber of Commerce v. St. P., M. & O. Ry. Co.*, 122 I.C.C. 739, 742.

[13]269 I.C.C. 297, 301. See also *United States v. Great Northern Ry. Co.*, 301 I.C.C. 21, 26-27.

the rate adjustment of which complaint is made. Undue prejudice and preference may not be assumed or left to inference. Moreover, general declarations as to competition or injury unsupported by evidentiary facts, do not warrant a finding of undue prejudice . . .

A distinction should be drawn also between the type of evidence required for individual shippers and territories. A showing of actual discrimination is required for individuals but where territories are concerned, a case might be impossible to make where trade barriers prevented the establishment of industries. In such circumstances it has been held that an inference of prejudice may be drawn from the discriminatory rate structure itself.[14]

Participation in Rates by Carrier Necessary to Be Held Liable for Undue Preferences and Prejudices

It is a well established principle that undue preference or prejudice may not be said to exist unless the same carrier serves the points or participates in the traffic, and the transportation conditions are shown to be substantially similar.[15]

Carriers that participate in joint rates are equally liable with carriers that publish the rates for undue preferences and prejudices that result therefrom.[16] In *Ayrshire Collieries Corp. v. United States*[17] the Supreme Court said (p. 585):

> The Milwaukee and Illinois Central were granting more favorable rates to some origins than to others in the same groups or districts. Their single-line rates from mines on their own lines were much lower than joint-line

[14]*New York v. United States*, 331 U.S. 284.

[15]*Westbound Rates on Meats*, 210 I.C.C. 13, 47; *Iron Ore Rate Cases*, 41 I.C.C. 181, 190-191; *Corn and Corn Products, Iowa, Nebr., Minn., So. Dak. to Ill.*, 318 I.C.C. 291, 296-297; *Interstate Commerce Commission v. B. & O. Railroad*, 145 U.S. 263, 283-284; *Lake Charles Harbor & Term. Dist. v. Atchison, T. & S. F. Ry. Co.*, 315 I.C.C. 485, 489-490; *State Corporation Comm. of Kansas v. United States*, 184 F. Supp. 691, 698; *Union Pac. R.R. Co. v. United States*, 132 F. Supp. 72, 80; reversed in part and affirmed in part in *Denver & Rio Grande West. R. Co. v. Union Pac. R. Co.*, 76, S. Ct. 982; *Central R. Co. of N. J. v. United States*, 257 U.S. 247, 259-260. If undue preference and prejudice are found the railroad is free to remove such preference and prejudice held to exist by reducing the rates from the prejudiced points, or by increasing the rates from the preferred points, or by any combination of the two. *Chrysler Corp. v. Abilene & S. Ry.*, 297 I.C.C. 589, 590.

[16]*Illinois Central R. Co. v. I.C.C.* 101 F. Supp. 317, 326-327. If two carriers refuse to act in concert to set a joint rate to a point which they can only serve jointly, because of a genuine divisions dispute, they cannot reasonably be said to be in control of the joint rate. However, the dispute must be genuine.

[17]335 U.S. 573. See also *A., T. & S. Fe Ry. Co. v. United States*, 218 F. Supp. 359, sustaining *Cudahy Packing Co. v. Akron, Canton & Youngstown R.R. Co.*, 318 I.C.C. 229.

rates from other mines in the same group to the same destinations. The latter are rates published by other carriers and in which Milwaukee and Illinois Central join. Milwaukee and Illinois Central therefore are parties to an arrangement which results in some mines getting lower rates than other mines in the same group on shipments to the same destinations.

It is settled, however, that carriers may not be held in violation of Section 3(1) of the I.C. Act because of undue preferences or prejudices caused by rate structures that they are powerless to remove. In *Texas & Pacific Ry. Co. v. United States*[18] the Supreme Court, in holding that New Orleans lines could not properly be held guilty of unjust discrimination against Texas ports in the absence of effective participation in the rates to them, said (p. 650):

> A carrier or group of carriers must be the common source of the discrimination — must effectively participate in both rates, if an order for correction of the disparity is to run against it or them. Where an order is made under § 3 an alternative must be afforded. The offender or offenders may abate the discrimination by raising one rate, lowering the other, or altering both.

It was said in *New York v. United States*[19] that the principle in the *Texas & Pacific Ry. Co.* case has full application "when the Commission is directing the carriers to remove discrimination."

Although the principle was established in *Texas & P. Ry. Co. v. United States*[20] that carriers made defendants in a proceeding involving undue prejudice and preference must be the common source of the unlawful discrimination sought to be corrected, the Commission's corrective power to prevent carriers from unduly preferring or prejudicing a point is not restricted to points reached by their own rails. Carriers are jointly and severally responsible for undue prejudice and preference where there is substantial and effective participation in both the prejudicial and preferential rates. Thus where a carrier is the delivering carrier to a certain point from two different origin points served by other carriers and the carrier effectively controls the rates causing the unlawfulness, the Commission would have power to prevent undue preference or prejudice.[21]

---

[18]289 U.S. 627.
[19]331 U.S. 284, 342.
[20]289 U.S. 627.
[21]*Fargo Chamber of Commerce v. Akron, C. & Y. R. Co.*, 306 I.C.C. 407; *Stauffer Chamical Co. v. Fort Worth & D. Ry. Co.*, 313 I.C.C. 393, 315 I.C.C. 63.

Tariff Provisions May Not Render Lawful a Practice Found to Be Unlawful by the Commission

Provisions of the tariff may not render lawful a practice found by the Commission to be unlawful. The Supreme Court had this very question for consideration in *United States v. U.S. Smelting, Refining & Mining Co.*[22] where it said (pp. 194-196):

> The court has emphasized that the preference involved in these proceedings is based upon an application oft he standards derived from *Ex Parte 104* to the unique conditions at particular plants, a preference necessarily resulting when a service is rendered "in excess of that which the carriers are obliged to perform by their tariffs." *United States v. Wabash R. Co.,* supra, 412, 413. In *Corn Products Refining Co. v. United States,* 331 U.S. 790, this court affirmed *per curiam* a decision upholding the exclusion, on the ground of irrelevancy, of evidence pertaining to the custom and practice of carriers in making delivery to other shippers. If custom may not be used to interpret "line-haul" after demarcation of transportation and industry service by the Commission, we think it follows that a carrier definition written into filed tariffs does not make impotent the Commission's authority to define the point.
>
> A tariff, effective June 25, 1938, is considered applicable only to the Midvale, Garfield, and Murray plants. By this tariff the "line-haul rate includes movement of loaded cars to track scales and subsequent delivery to any designated track within the plant which can be accomplished by one uninterrupted movement . . . from the road-haul point of delivery to the switching line." 266 I.C.C. at 353-354. There are additional charges for other services in the plants.
>
> If the Commission has the authority to fix the point at which line-haul begins and ends, and we have held that it has, and it designates Point X, obviously the carriers cannot by tariff fix line-haul at Point Y, a further point, and even add one subsequent movement. That would deprive the Commission of its right to determine the point. In the Commission's judgment, which is supported by the evidence, delivery to Point X is the equivalent of team track and simple placement service – the service other shippers receive under a line-haul rate. For the carriers to give the appellee-smelters service to Point Y plus 1 is to accord them service different from that given other shippers under *Ex Parte 104* and supplemental proceedings. By the orders in the instant cases, line-haul is translated, as it were, into the tariffs as beginning and ending where the Commission fixed it and not where the appellee-carriers fixed it by tariff. Thereafter, the charge for line-haul must be to the interchange tracks and not to the point fixed in the tariff. Transportation to the latter point at the line-haul rate would be preferential and would violate § 6(7).

[22]339 U.S. 186

Equal Treatment

Any difficulty encountered by a shipper in making beneficial use of rates or charges does not establish that such rates or charges are unduly prejudicial or unjustly discriminatory.[23] However in interpreting Section 3(1), the Commission has said:[24]

> The right of all shippers similarly situated to receive substantially equal treatment by carriers includes the right to reach competitive markets on relatively equal terms. A rate preference may not be accorded a shipper without a material difference in transportation conditions justifying the preference.

As the Commission said in *Mayo Shell Corp. v. Baltimore & O. R. Co.*,[25]

> The duty of a carrier to give substantially equal treatment to all shippers who are in a position to demand it includes the right to reach competitive markets on relatively equal terms. A rate preference may not be accorded a shipper without a material difference in transportation conditions justifying the preference. An unjustified difference in freight rates that are factors in the competition between shippers constitutes undue prejudice and preference where, as here, the rates are under the effective control of the participating carrier or carriers . . .

See *D. A. Stickell & Sons, Inc. v. Alton R. Co.*,[26] where the Commission said:

> It is not the province of railroads to determine what market shall be available to sellers or buyers, or, by their refusal to establish through routes or the maintenance of rate disadvantages, to restrict or circumscribe the opportunities of shippers located on other railroads to sell in markets served by them. It is their function to transport in the channels necessitated by trade conditions and not to fix limitations on commerce. The public interest demands that all shippers be accorded relatively equal opportunities to reach all reasonable available markets . . .

And see *Elk Cement & Lime Co. v. B. & O. R.R. Co.*,[27] where the Commission said:

> The duty imposed by law is to give equal treatment to all shippers, and this includes the right to reach competitive markets on relatively equal terms. Carriers . . . may not in any manner whatsoever unduly prefer one

---

[23]*Eastern Central M. Carriers Assn. v. Baltimore & O. R. Co.*, 314 I.C.C. 5, 50.
[24]*Fargo Chamber of Commerce v. Akron, C. & Y. R. Co.*, 306 I.C.C. 407, 412. See also *Citizens Gas & Coke Utility v. Chicago & N.W. Ry. Co.*, 314 I.C.C. 271, 274; *Paper Articles from Metuchen, N. J., to New York, N.Y.*, 308 I.C.C. 793, 794.
[25]297 I.C.C. 133, 135.
[26]255 I.C.C. 333, 337.
[27]22 I.C.C. 84, 88.

set of shippers entitled to treatment over another, or one locality over another.

In *Red River Milling Co. v. Great Northern Ry. Co.*,[28] where the Commission condemned the complained of rates as unduly prejudicial and preferential, it said:

A further defense is that the complainants have failed to prove actual damage resulting from the assailed switching charges. In Chrysler Corp. v. Akron, C. & Y. R. Co., 279 I.C.C. 377, 404, the Commission stated that although a complaining party may not prove actual damage, a finding of undue prejudice nevertheless is warranted upon a showing that competitors, by a preference not necessarily injurious in itself, are afforded an opportunity to gain success over and injure others. See also Northeast Kentuck Coal Bureau v. C. & O. Ry. Co., 206 I.C.C. 445, sustained in Chesapeake & O. Ry. Co. v. United States, 296 U.S. 187 . . .

In *Illinois Cent. R. Co., v. United States*,[29] the court said:

Plaintiffs next assert that there is no showing of an injury to interveners sufficient to provide the foundation for finding establishment of a discriminatory rate. Their position is that a mere difference in rates does not amount per se to discrimination. Injury must be shown to those allegedly discriminated against. Plaintiffs' premises are correct. However, the facts do not support their conclusion. The Commission affirmatively found that the lower rate accorded Ford and General Motors gave them a distinct financial advantage over their competitors due to the pricing system employed in marketing automobiles. It was shown that the practice in the industry is to price the cars on the basis of cost of production plus the rail freight charge from Detroit (or the primary manufacturing plant of the seller) to the retail dealer. Thus in the case of Ford and General Motors, due to the lower rates extended to them from their subsidiary plants, they realize an advantage over their competitors in that there is included in their price a sum greater than the actual cost of transportation. The Commission then reasoned that the correlative of this benefit must be a detriment or injury to the interveners. It said: "In a highly competitive market, in which competition will become even more severe when the abnormal demand for new automobiles is satisfied, those manufacturers having a lower level of rates are benefited and the manufacturers with the higher level of rates are injured. While at the present time the benefit is not reflected at the retail level because of the pricing methods of the manufacturers, it is present in the form of greater funds for use in the various manufacturing operations or for the payment of larger dividends to stockholders. It is clear that General Motors and Ford are benefited and the other manufacturers are injured by the differences in the levels of the rates from their respective plants." Although there may have been no affirmative evidence in terms of "injury" it seems to us that the Commis-

[28]289 I.C.C. 445, 454.
[29]101 F. Supp. 317, 323.

sion's ultimate conclusion in this respect was inescapable. Northeast Kentucky Coal Bureau v. C. & O., 206 I.C.C. 445, sustained in Chesapeake & Ohio R. Co. v. U.S., 296 U.S. 187, 56 S. Ct. 164, 80 L. Ed. 147, the ommission said: "Even though complainant's members may not be injured, their competitors are preferred. Preference, not necessarily injurious in itself, affords opportunity to gain success over and injure the other party. The act is specifically directed against undue preference and all other forms of unjust treatment of the shipping public." We think this is a correct analysis and applicable to the situation here.

In *Chesapeake B. O. Ry. Co. v. United States,*[30] the court in sustaining the Commission's decision in *Northeast Kentucky Coal Bureau v. Chesapeake & B. O. Ry. Co.,*[31] which is cited in the *Illinois Central* case, *supra,* said (p. 592) that the "mere fact that there was a discrimination in rates of itself would carry with it the presumption that the parties paying the higher rate were damaged."

In *Allen Mfg. Co. v. N., C. & St. L. Ry.,*[32]

Paragraph (1) of section 3 of the act forbids giving to any particular person, company, firm, corporation, or locality any undue or unreasonable preference or advantage, or subjecting it to any undue or unreasonable prejudice. The fact that Nashville has continued to compete with the other producing points despite its disadvantage in rates does not make the undue prejudice any the less unlawful . . .

Similarity of Circumstances and Conditions

In *Washington Potato & Onion Shippers Ass'n. v. U.P.R. Co.,*[33] the evidence showed that the prejudiced area had in recent years increased its volume of sales, while the shipments from the preferred area to the same markets had declined or showed a lesser percentage of increase. The Commission held that injury to the prejudiced shippers had nevertheless been established, stating (at pp. 551 and 555):

. . . The extent to which each of the many factors which affect the production and marketing of potatoes in these States contributed to these results is not shown, nor is such a showing essential to the determination of the issues.

Injury results when, as here, shippers, in selling in competitive markets, are compelled to absorb differences in rates greater than those which are warranted by the differences in service, measured by the transportation standard, as compared with those of their competitors. The fact that the

[30]11 F. Supp. 588, aff'd 296 U.S. 187.
[31]206 I.C.C. 445.
[32]98 I.C.C. 405, 407.
[33]300 I.C.C. 537.

burden of such injury may be mitigated or neutralized by circumstances of a non-transportation nature favorable to such shippers does not render the injury any less real.

In *Consolidated Mining & S. Co. of Canada v. N.Y. C.R. Co.*,[34] the Commission said (p. 244):

> . . . Nor does the fact, also stressed by defendants and interveners, that shipments have continued to move from Tadanac to the destination territory in substantial and increased volume despite the rate disparity complained of rebut the showing of undue preference and prejudice. A patent discrimination in rates is not to be condoned because other competitive advantages and disadvantages wholly unrelated to the service of transportation may favor a shipper complaining of such discrimination. When sales are made under keen competition in common markets, as they are here, the correlative of the advantage gained form the lower rate level must be a detriment or injury to a competitor who must ship on the higher level . . .

In making a determination of undue preference or prejudice, the Commission has held that a difference in rate treatment may be warranted because of competition from other modes of transportation. In *Newsprint Paper from Tenn. to Ala. to Houston, Tex.*[35] the Commission held that because of severe barge competition for movement of newsprint paper to Houston, but not at interior Texas points, conditions affecting the rail transportation to the interior points differed materially from those at Houston; and in those circumstances, undue preference or prejudice could not be found except to the extent that the rate proposed to Houston reflected a reduction greater than was warranted by the barge competition. In *Increased Rates on Fresh Fruits and Vegetables*,[36] the Commission held that the application of a proposed maximum increase of $2.00 per car on fruits and vegetables only to per-car rates within southern territory and from that territory to points on and east of the Missouri River would not unduly prejudice any shipper or area where rates on other units of shipment would be subjected to the full general increase; the difference in rate treatment was warranted by the more intense motor carrier competition on that traffic from Florida than from origins in any other section of the country.

[34]299 I.C.C. 231, aff'd sub nom. *Ores, United States and Canada Origins to Eastern, U.S.*, 303 I.C.C. 87. See also *Cudahy Packing Co. v. Akron, C. & Y. R. Co.*, 318 I.C.C. 229, 245-47, aff'd sub Nom. *Atchison, Topeka and Santa Fe Railway Co. v. United States*, 218 F. Supp. 359.
[35]313 I.C.C. 519, 529. See also *Seattle Traffic Assoc. v. United States*, C.A. No. 5349 (W. D. Wash.), sustaining *Seattle Traffic Assoc. v. Consolidated Freightways*, 301 I.C.C. 483, 306 I.C.C. 87, 310 I.C.C. 773; and *Class Rates Mountain-Pacific Territory*, 1295 I.C.C. 555.
[36]313 I.C.C. 519, 529.

Rate Equalization

In *Board of Trade of Kansas City v. United States*,[37] dealers at primary markets contended that the cancelling of a preferential rate deprived them of certain natural advantages. The Supreme Court, in apt language, refuted the contention (p. 548):

> What we have said sufficiently disposes of the suggestion that the orders of the Commission must be stricken down because they wipe out natural competitive advantages of the primary markets. A rate structure found to involve serious discriminations among shippers, carriers, and transit points alike, is hardly a manifestation of nature beyond the Commission's power to repair.

> Neither the Commission nor this court had held that lesser cost of service is a finding without which the Commission may not fix a charge, division of rate, or differential. On the other hand, the considerations just discussed were rightly taken into account by the Commission. We must not lose sight of the fact that the Commission has the interests of shippers and consumers to safeguard as well as those of the carriers. *Ayrshire Corp. v. United States*, 355 U.S. 573, 592. The accommodation of the factors entering into rate structures, including competition, is a task peculiarly for the Commission. *Id.*, at 593; *United States v. Pierce Auto Lines*, 327 U.S. 515, 535-536.

The difficult problem of equalizing an intricate rate structure (bituminous coal) in the interest of competition was referred to in *Ayrshire Collieries Corp. v. United States*[38] where the Supreme Court said:

> Rate structures are not designed merely to favor the revenues of producers and carriers. The Commission has the consumer interest to safeguard as well. And when it undertakes to rationalize the interests of the three, great complexities are often encountered. The economies of the bituminous coal industry have baffled even experts. We would depart from our competence and our limited function in this field if we undertook to accommodate the factors of transportation conditions, distance and competition differently than the Commission has done in this case. This is a task peculiarly for it. In fashioning what the Commission called a differentially related and finely balanced rate structure for this coal, there is no place for dogma or rigid formulae. The problem calls for an expert, informed judgment on a multitude of facts. The result is that the administrative rate-maker is left with broad discretion as long as no statutory requirement is overlooked. Yet that is, of course, precisely the nature of the administrative process in this field. See *Board of Trade v. United States*, 314 U.S. 534, 548; *New York v. United States*, 331 U.S. 284, 347-349.

[37]314 U.S. 534.
[38]335 U.S. 573, 592-593.

In *Port Arthur Cham. Comm. & Shipping v. Aberdeen & R. R. Co.*[39] equalization of export rates to certain ports was required and the Commission, at page 758, stated: "That we may permit equalization within reasonable limits is well established." The principle of port equalization has also been long recognized by the courts. See *Texas & Pacific Ry. Co. v. United States*[40] where it was said: "The legislative history of the Act demonstrates that Congress did not intend to forbid the equalization of export or import rates by lines serving several ports in order to meet competition."

In *Hillsborough County Port Authority v. Ahnapee & W. Ry.*[41] the Commission required a change in port rates based on undue prejudice. There, although the distances between Tampa and many interior points in the complaint territory were within the range of distance between the same points and competing Gulf and south Atlantic ports, the export-import rates between the latter ports and points in the complaint territory were lower than those to and from Tampa. The Tampa rates were found unduly prejudicial for the future to the extent that they exceeded the corresponding rates to and from Gulf and south Atlantic ports. However, the Commission said that a finding of undue prejudice in rates was not justified between other interior points and Tampa where the distances were generally in excess of the range of distances from the same points to Gulf and south Atlantic ports, and where the car-mile earnings under the rates sought would in practically all instances be below earnings under the rates to or from the most distant competitive Gulf or south Atlantic ports.

In *Sugar from Gulf Ports to Chicago*[42] the Commission said that carriers, in establishing rate groups, may not unduly deprive any point of the advantage of its geographical location, but they are not bound to recognize every shade of advantage by reason of distance or other factors of negligible consequence.

---

[39]169 I.C.C. 753. Earlier decisions involving the principle of port equalization, referred to by the Commission in the cited case, were: *Aransas Pass Channel & Dock Co. v. G. H. & S. A. Ry. Co.*, 27 I.C.C. 403; *City of Astoria v. S. P. & S. Ry. Co.*, 38 I.C.C. 16; and *Galveston Commercial Assn. v. G. H. & S. A. Ry. Co.*, 100 I.C.C. 110, 128.

[40]289 U.S. 627, 639.

[41]313 I.C.C. 691, 705, 706, aff'd *Alabama, Tenn. and Northern R.R. Co. v. United States*, C.A. No. 2747, U.S.D.C. S.D. Ala.

[42]299 I.C.C. 31, 34.

In *Boston and Maine R.R. v. United States*,[43] the court set aside a Commission order cancelling rate schedules filed by certain railroads in which they desired to reduce rates on export and import traffic between interior points and the ports of New York and Albany, N.Y., Boston, Mass., and Portland, Me., in order to place the rates on the traffic moving through the ports on a parity with rates on like traffic moving through the competing ports of Philadelphia, Pa., and Baltimore, Md., and Hampton Roads, Va., The Commission had disallowed the proposed rate schedule principally on the ground that the rates would violate Section (3)1 because of the distance disadvantage of the northern tier ports, and that the rates had not been shown to be reasonably related to the present rates on like traffic to and from the southern tier ports and would cause prejudice to those ports. The court held that in the light of the history of the differential existing between the two tiers of ports showing that the differential was established to place the northern tier of ports on a parity with respect to the aggregate of rail and ocean charges and no consideration was given to disparity in distance disadvantage, the Commission's position was difficult to understand.

The court pointed out that one of the purposes of Section 3(1) is to permit all ports and the carriers serving them to compete for all import traffic and thereby maximize the number of ports available; thus if the Commission's finding in the case is pressed to its ultimate conclusion it would result in traffic flowing only through the most distant favored port and, on the other hand, if applied only in this case, the decision is arbitrary and capricious. The court also said that the Commission had failed to distinguish between rates which carriers may voluntarily publish to meet competition pursuant to Section 15(8) and rates which carriers, on complaint under Section 3(1), may be required to change; under Section 15(8) the issue to be decided is whether the proposed rates are lawful and in a complaint proceeding under Section 3(1) the question is whether the existing rates are lawful and, if not, whether they should be required to be changed. The Commission regarded this as a "port" case not a "railroad" case; distance differences might be relevant insofar as they reflect differences in the cost and value

---

[43]202 F. Supp. 830, aff'd 373 U.S. 372. The Commission report is entitled *Equalization of Rates at North Atlantic Ports,* 311 I.C.C. 689, 314 I.C.C. 185. See also *Baltimore & Ohio v. United States,* 212 F. Supp. 13, and *New York Central v. United States,* 207 F. Supp. 483, for review of the Commission's decisions in *Iron Ore from Eastern Ports to Central Freight Assn. Points,* 312 I.C.C. 149.

(of the services but the Commission made no such cost or value) findings.

Jones Amendment

Section 3(1a) of the Interstate Commerce Act, which was inserted by the Jones Amendment in 1940[44] reads as follows:

> It is hereby declared to be the policy of Congress that shippers of wheat, cotton, and all other farm commodities for export shall be granted export rates on the same principles as are applicable in the case of rates on industrial products for export. The Commission is hereby directed, on its own initiative or an application by interested persons, to make such investigation and conduct such hearings, and, after appropriate proceedings, to issue orders, as may be necessary to carry out such policy.

The language of Section 3(1a) recognizes that agricultural and industrial products should be granted export rates on the same principles and without unjust discrimination. The directed application of principles the same "as are applicable in the case of rates on industrial products for export" contemplates the existence of similar circumstances.[45]

Section 3(1a) does not require that rates on farm commodities for export be lower than, or equal to, or bear any fixed relationship to the rates on farm commodities shipped for domestic consumption. As the court said in *Georgia Peanut Co. v. Interstate Commerce Com'n:*[46]

> It should be noted that Section 3(1a) of the Interstate Commerce Act makes no reference to domestic rates, agricultural or industrial. The section does not require that export rates on farm commodities bear any fixed relationship to domestic rates, or to either export or domestic rates on industrial products. The section requires only the equal application of rate-making principles in the fixing of rates for farm commodities shipped for export and the fixing of rates for industrial products shipped for export.

The teaching of this case is that Section 3(1a) "requires only the equal application of rate-making principles in the fixing of rates for farm commodities shipped for export and the fixing of rates for industrial products shipped for export," and that one seeking to invoke the policy of that section, per se or in aid of other provisions of the I.C. Act, must identify the claimed rate-making principle, and by substantial evidence, justify its application to the relief sought.[47]

---

[44]54 Stat. 902.
[45]*Georgia Peanut Co. v. Atlantic Coast Line R. Co.*, 284 I.C.C. 308, 311.
[46]110 F. Supp. 556, 558.
[47]*Chicago Board of Trade v. Illinois Central R. Co.*, 325 I.C.C. 412, 427.

38

Unjust Discrimination against Shippers

The Applicable Statutory Provisions

Section 2 of the Interstate Commerce Act,[1] similar to Section 3(1), is properly construed as being for the protection of shippers not carriers.[2] The section provides that if any common carrier "shall, directly or indirectly, by any special rate, rebate, drawback, or other device, charge, demand, collect, or receive from any person or persons a greater or less compensation for any service rendered, or to be rendered . . . than it charges, demands, collects or receives from any person or persons for doing for him or them a like and contemporaneous service in the transportation of a like kind of traffic under substantially similar circumstances and conditions, such common carrier shall be deemed guilty of unjust discrimination."

Discrimination Defined

To sustain a finding of discrimination under Section 2, it must appear that the transportation services are like and contemporaneous and performed under substantially similar circumstances and conditions, and that the property transported is like property.[3] Thus, when the transportation circumstances and conditions are substantially similar the rates cannot be different. In general, discrimination under Section 2 is a

---

[1] 49 U.S.C. 2. See comparable provisions — Sections 216(d), 305(c), and 404(b) covering unjust discrimination and Sections 217(b), 306(c) and 405(c) covering rebating. See also Elkins Act.

[2] *Texas & P. Ry. Co. v. Interstate Commerce Commission*, 162 U.S. 197; *Eastern Central M. Carriers Assn. v. Baltimore & O. R. Co.*, 314 I.C.C. 5, 50.

[3] See *Ayrshire Collieries Corp. v. United States*, 335 U.S. 573; *Corn from Michigan, Ohio, and Pennsylvania to Augusta and Portland, Maine*, 319 I.C.C. 344, 353.

personal matter, and the Commission has usually required the party alleged to be aggrieved to demonstrate that he is a shipper or receiver of a commodity which is also shipped or received by a competitor from and to the same points and that discrimination factually exists.[4]

One of the first cases dealing with this subject is *Wight v. United States*.[5] The court there held that where the transportation circumstances, the carriers involved, and the commodity being transported were the same, unequal treatment in the rates was a violation of Section 2. In *Wight v. United States* the Supreme Court said (p. 517):

> The wrong prohibited by the section is a discrimination between shippers. It was designed to compel every carrier to give equal rights to all shippers over its own road and to forbid it by any device to enforce high charges against one than another.

In an early case, *Interstate Com. Commiss. v. B. & O. Railroad*,[6] the Supreme Court pointed out that not all differences in rates are violations of Section 2. At page 276 the court stated:

> It is not all discriminations or preferences that fall within the inhibition of the statute; only such as are unjust or unreasonable. . . . Indeed, the possibility of just discriminations and reasonable preferences is recognized by these sections, in declaring what shall be deemed unjust.

In various other early cases, it was determined that whether the discrimination was unjust depended on the facts of the particular case. Therefore, in deciding the issue, reference to all of the factual circumstances is necessary. This is clearly stated in *Nashville Ry. v. Tennessee*:[7]

> Whether a preference or discrimination is undue, unreasonable or unjust is ordinarily left to the Commission for decision; and the determination is to be made, as a question of fact, on the matters proved in the particular case.

Section 2 was construed in *L. T. Barringer & Co. v. United States*[8] wherein it was held that the absorption of a carrier's loading charge of less-carload cotton in its through rate was not an undue discrimination against other shippers who shipped less-carload cotton from and between other points and whose loading charges were not absorbed (p. 6):

[4]*Pickup and Delivery — Official Territory — LCL & A.Q.*, 314 I.C.C. 313, 318; *Automobiles from Atlanta, Ga. to Norfolk, Va.*, 316 I.C.C. 99. However the following case indicates that competitive injury is not necessary: *A. Lindberg & Sons, Inc. v. United States*, 408 F. Supp. 1032.
[5]167 U.S. 512. Cf. *Ayrshire Collieries Corp. v. United States*, 335 U.S. 573, 583-84.
[6]145 U.S. 263.
[7]262 U.S. 318, 322.
[8]319 U.S. 1.

But differences in rates as between shippers are prohibited only where the "circumstances and conditions" attending the transportation service are "substantially similar." Whether those circumstances and conditions are sufficiently dissimilar to justify a difference in rates, or whether, on the other hand, the difference in rates constitutes an unjust discrimination because based primarily on considerations relating to the identity or competitive position of the particular shipper rather than to circumstances attending the transportation service, is a question of fact for the Commission's determination. Hence its conclusion that in view of all the relevant facts and circumstances a rate or practice either is or is not unjustly discriminatory within the meaning of § 2 of the Act will not be disturbed here unless we can say that its finding is unsupported by evidence or without rational basis, or rests on an erroneous construction of the statute.

As the Commission stated in *Whiterock Quarries, Inc., v. Pittsburgh & L. E. R. Co.*:[9]

> When there is no showing that different rail shippers are charged different rates for a like transportation service on like traffic from the same origin to the same destination, there is no violation of Section 2 of the act. *Mobile Traffic Assn. v. Georgia & F. R.*, 266 I.C.C. 483, 488.

Thus, a supportable Section 2 order not only contemplates the complaint of a *shipper*, but a situation presenting like and contemporaneous shipments from the same origin to the same destination at different rates or charges.

A factor to be considered in determining whether the circumstances under which the traffic is moving are similar is competition. In *Texas and Pacific Ry. Co. v. Interstate Commerce Commission*[10] it was said (p. 219):

> The very terms of the statute, that charges must be *reasonable,* that discrimination must not be *unjust,* and that preference or advantage to any particular person, firm, corporation or locality must not be *undue* or *unreasonable,* necessarily imply that strict uniformity is not to be enforced; but that all circumstances and conditions which reasonable men would regard as affecting the welfare of the carrying companies, and of the producers, shippers and consumers, should be considered by a tribunal appointed to carry into effect and enforce the provisions of the act.

> The principal purpose of the second section is to prevent unjust discrimination between shippers. It implies that, in deciding whether differences in charges, in given cases, were or were not unjust, there must be a consideration of the several questions whether the services rendered were "like and contemporaneous," whether the kinds of traffic were "like," whether the transportation was effected under "substantially similar circumstances and conditions." To answer such questions, in any case com-

[9]280 I.C.C. 143, 162.
[10]162 U.S. 197.

ing before the Commission, requires an investigation into the facts; and we think that Congress must have intended that whatever would be regarded by common carriers, apart from the operation of the statute, as matters which warranted differences in charges, ought to be considered in forming a judgment whether such differences were or were not "unjust." Some charges might be unjust to shippers — others might be unjust to the carriers. The rights and interests of both must, under the terms of the act, be regarded by the Commission.

Another case reaching a similar conclusion is *Koppers Co., Inc., v. Chesapeake & O. Ry. Co.*[11] There is was said (p. 101):

> A violation of Sections 2 and 3(1) of the Interstate Commerce Act is not established by proof that the rail rate for transporting like commodities between identical points varies depending on the primary origins or ultimate decisions of the commodities since rate variations under such circumstances are not per se illegal, but, on the contrary, are charcteristic of the rail rate structure. It is not necessarily unlawful to charge different rail rates, depending on the primary origins or ultimate destinations of the traffic, for performing the same physical transportation in moving like commodities between identical points.

The Commission has found that competition and volume of movement can create a dissimilarity in the circumstances and conditions underlying a particular movement of traffic. In *Coal from Ky., Va., and W. Va. to Virginia*,[12] the railroads were threatened with loss of coal traffic to a mine mouth generating plant which the utility companies proposed to construct. The railroads published a reduction conditioned upon the receipt by one consignee of an aggregate of at least 1.5 million tons of bituminous coal during a 12-month period. After finding that the proposed rates were no lower than necessary to meet the competition involved, the Commission held they would not result in unjust discrimination against or undue prejudice to other shippers or receivers of coal.

The Commission in *Coal to New York Harbor Area*[13] also approved reduced annual volume rates on bituminous coal. In this case, the competition was from residual oil. The reductions were generally 50 cents per ton lower than the single-car rates when specified minimum annual tonnages are received. In holding that there was no violation of Section 2 the Commission said, at pages 368 and 369:

> Neither this Commission nor the courts have followed the principle that a bare difference in the rates on the same commodity for the same service is sufficient to establish unlawful discrimination. Both prior to and

---

[11]301 I.C.C. 284 and 303 I.C.C. 383, upheld in *Koppers Company Inc. v. United States*, 166 F. Supp. 96.
[12]308 I.C.C. 99.
[13]311 I.C.C. 355.

subsequent to *Wight v. United States, supra,* such differences in rates, standing alone, have been found not unlawful. In *Interstate Commerce Commission v. Baltimore & O. R. Co.,* 145 U.S. 263, party rate tickets for 10 or more persons at a rate per person less than that charged a single individual for like transportation on the same trip were found not to contravene the provisions of Section 2, and also in *Texas & P. Ry. Co. v. Interstate Commerce Commission,* 162 U.S. 197, rates on traffic transported to a port for export lower than rates concurrently effective on the same traffic for local delivery at the port were found not unlawful.

❋　　❋　　❋

From the foregoing it is clear that a difference in the rates charged for the same transportation does not necessarily establish unlawful discrimination. In other words, a discrimination is not necessarily an unjust or unlawful discrimination; it can be unjust only where the circumstances affecting the transportation are substantially similar. . . .

❋　　❋　　❋

There is no evidence that the proposed rates are designed to create favoritism among shippers of like traffic, or that they are in fact creating or are likely to create favoritism. On the contrary, the only purpose of these rates is to prevent substantial traffic losses to the respondent railroads. As such, the discrimination resulting from the reduced rates may be considered as justified by the circumstances and conditions attending the particular transportation service. Such a conclusion is not precluded by *Wight v. United States, supra.* The competitive element presented, namely, the availability by means of nonregulated carriage of cheaper fuel oil in such quantities as to jeopardize a substantial segment of traffic essential to the well-being of the respondent carriers, is unlike any competitive factor considered by the courts in passing on issues raised under Section 2.

We are convienced that the danger of imminent loss to regulated transportation agencies of the coal traffic to the seaboard utilities, on which the porposed rates would apply, constitutes a major transportation circumstance which is substantially dissimilar from the circumstances surrounding the transportation by respondents of coal to other receivers in the same general area. Consequently, such discrimination as is reflected in the establishment of the proposed rates does not, in our opinion, constitute unjust discrimination under Section 2 of the Act.

Burden of Proof

It is incumbent upon the complainant before the Commission to assume the burden of proving the alleged violation of Section 2 of the Act, as well as the other alleged violations. This is the essential obligation of those who maintain the affirmative in any litigation and is applied in controversial proceedings before the Commission. In *Louisville and Nashville R. Co. v. United States*[14] the rule is stated (p. 11):

> Where an existing freight rate is attacked, the burden is on the complainant to establish that it is unreasonable in fact. This is especially so where, as here, the rate has been in force for a long period during which time the traffic greatly increased in volume. In order to carry this burden in the present case, the Traffic Bureau, while alleging that the rate was unreasonable in itself and by comparison with other like rates, does not seem to have attempted to prove the cost, or value of the carrier's service, but apparently relied largely on proof showing that the Nashville rate was higher than that charged for a similar haul to other points.

[14]238 U.S. 1; see *I.C.C. v. N. C. & St. L. Ry. Co.*, 120 Fed. 934, appeal dismissed, 195 U.S. 638; *Howitt v. U.S*, 150 F. 2d 182, affirmed 328 U.S. 189.

39

Unjust Discrimination between Carriers

The Applicable Statutory Provisions

Section 3(4)[1] provides that rail carriers "shall not discriminate in their rates, fares, and charges between connecting lines, or unduly prejudice any connecting line in the distribution of traffic that is not specifically routed by the shipper. As used in this paragraph the term 'connecting line' means the connecting line of any carrier subject to the provisions of this part or any common carrier by water subject to part III."

Rail Carriers

Section 3(4) is designed to discourage unequal treatment of connecting carriers at a given point. In *Western Pacific Rys. v. United States*[2] an intermediate carrier on a through route complained under Section 3(4) of discrimination by a railroad with which the complainant did not connect physically. The court rejected the Commission's narrow construction which would have required a complainant itself to "make a direct connection with the discriminating carrier, or be part of a through route that already includes the carrier." (at 242) In order to make plain that the facts of that case satisfied the requirements of Section 3(4), the court held "that to qualify as a 'connecting line,' in the absence of physical connection, a carrier need only show that it participates in an established through route, making connection at the point of common interchange, all of whose participants stand willing to cooperate in the arrangements necessary to eliminate the alleged discrimination." (at 245)

[1] 49 U.S.C. 3(4).
[2] 382 U.S. 237.

The equality of treatment between connecting carriers required by Section 3(4) is determined by similar circumstances and conditions. Thus where Southern Railway cancelled through routes from Louisville and Nashville coal mines to Georgia and Florida points via the Georgia Railroad and Atlantic Coast Line as intermediate carriers beyond Atlanta, while continuing the route via the Central of Georgia, the Commission held that there was no violation of Section 3(4).[3] The distance from Atlanta to the principal destination over Central of Georgia was only about 15 miles longer than over Southern's direct route, in contrast with 115 and 116 miles longer over the Georgia Railroad and Atlantic Coast Line. This, the Commission said, negatives any conclusion that the transportation conditions are similar.[4]

Water Carriers

Whenever a rail rate discrimination affects barge carriers it is necessary in applying the before-mentioned provision, as well as Section 2 to consider them in light of the National Transportation Policy.

The Supreme Court, relying on both the legislative history and express provisions of the Transportation Act of 1940 (including the Transportation Policy set forth in that Act), has recognized that one of the primary objects of Congress in passing this legislation was to insure that the inherent advantage of water transportation, namely, lower costs, be preserved.[5]

In *Interstate Commerce Commission v. Mechling*[6] the Supreme Court affirmed the judgment of the district court which set aside an order of the Commission authorizing railroads to charge generally three cents

---

[3]*Routing, Coal from Origins on Louisville* & *N. R.*, 313 I.C.C. 752.

[4]Id., p. 758.

[5]The legislative history of the Transportation Act of 1940 insofar as it pertains to the intent of Congress to protect barge carriers and shippers by barge, and to preserve the inherent advantage of such transportation is set forth in the opinion of the Supreme Court in *I.C.C. v. Mechling*, 330 U.S. 567, and in the dissenting opinion of Mr. Justice Black in *I.C.C. v. Inland Waterways Corp.*, 319 U.S. 671, 697 *et seq.* The concern of Congress for water transportation is revealed in the statement, dated August 7, 1940, of the managers on the part of the House on the Conference Report of the Senate and House recommending that the Congress pass the bill (which was later enacted as the Transportation Act of 1940) to amend the Interstate Commerce Act. It is there said:

> This legislation is a forward and fostering step for water transportation as well as national transportation. Heretofore, with limited exceptions, water transportation has not been within the fostering care of interstate regulation. This measure will place upon the Interstate Commerce Commission not only the power, but the duty to protect and foster water transportation and preserve its inherent advantages. House Report No. 2832, 76th Cong., 3rd Sess., p. 88.

per hundred pounds more to transport grain East from Chicago when the grain arrived in Chicago by river barge than when it arrived by rail. In holding that these rates violated Sections 2 and 3(4) of the I.C. Act, the Supreme Court stated (p. 577):

> The foregoing provisions flatly forbid the Commission to approve barge rates or barge-rail rates which do not preserve intact the inherent advantages of cheaper water transportation, but discriminate against water carriers and the goods they transport. Concretely, the provisions mean in this case that Chicago-to-the-east railroads cannot lawfully charge more for carrying ex-barge than for carrying ex-lake or ex-rail grains to and from the same localities, unless the eastern haul of the ex-barge grain costs the eastern railroads more to haul than does ex-rail or ex-lake grain. And § 307(d) authorizing the Commission to fix differentials as between through water-rail and through all-rail rates, does not authorize the Commission to neutralize the effective prohibitions of the other provisions which were strengthened in 1940 expressly to prevent a discrimination against water carriers.
>
> The basic error of the Commission here is that it seemed to act on the assumption that the congressional prohibitions of railroad rate discriminations against water carriers were not applicable to such discriminations if accomplished by through rates. But this assumption would permit the destruction or curtailment of the advantages to shippers of cheap barge transportation whenever the transported goods were carried beyond the end of the barge line.

The Supreme Court then rejected the argument that it was inequitable for the barges to charge a much lower rate for the inbound grain haul to Chicago than the competitive western railroads could afford to charge for the same haul. In this connection, the court said (p. 579):

> Furthermore, Congress has decided this question of equitable rates as between railroads and barges. It has declared in unmistakable terms that the "inherent advantage" of the lower cost of barge carriage as compared with that of railroads must be passed on to those who ship by barge. It is therefore not within the province of the Commission to adjust rates, either to equalize the transportation cost of barge shippers with that of shippers who do not have access to barge service or to protect the traffic of railroads from barge competition. For Congress left the Commission no discretionary power to approve any type of rates which would reduce

⁶330 U.S. 567. See also *Dixie Carriers v. United States*, 351 U.S. 56, and *American Barge Line Co. v. Alabama G. S. R. Co.*, 316 I.C.C. 759. Water carriers are entitled to the protection of Section 3(4) although transporting a bulk commodity exempt under Section 303(b). See *ICC v. Inland Waterways Corp.*, 319 U.S. 671, 697; *Valley Line Co. v. United States*, 390 F. Supp. 435, 438-39; *Seatrain Lines, Inc. v. United States*, 233 F. Supp. 199, 210; *Atchison, Topeka & Santa Fe Ry. v. United States*, 194 F. Supp. 438; *Arrow Transportation Co. v. United States*, 176 F. Supp. 411, 419, aff'd sub nom. *State Corporation Commission v. Arrow Transportation Co.*, 361 U.S. 353.

the "inherent advantage" of barge transportation in whole or in part. Cf. *Mitchell v. United States*, 313 U.S. 80, 97.

The Supreme Court concluded that only a greater cost would justify a railroad in charging more for transporting an ex-barge commodity than an ex-rail commodity, saying (p. 581):

> Carriage of ex-barge grain by eastern roads may conceivably entail more service and therefore greater costs than are involved in carrying ex-rail or ex-lake grain. If so, the eastern roads may, in certain circumstances, be justified in receiving an extra charge for that extra service wherever it is rendered. But the extra service must fit the extra charge and cannot justify lump sum rate increases which cut into the inherent advantages of cheaper barge transportation which Congress intended to guarantee to shippers.

In *Tennessee Valley Authority v. United States*[7] the district court set aside an order of the Commission which authorized railroads to charge higher rates for switching freight arriving at Knoxville, Tennessee, by water carrier than for switching similar freight arriving by rail, on the ground that the Commission had failed to make findings respecting the actual difference in cost in switching ex-barge and ex-rail freight and that a difference in charges had to be based on an actual difference in cost.

In overturning the Commission's order, the district court held that the Commission had misapprehended the requirements of the *Mechling* case. The court said (p. 415):

> Irrespective of whether this case may be distinguished from the Mechling case by contrasting the factual context of each, we believe that pertinent principles established by the court are dispositive of this review. We are constrained to the opinion that the Commission, in discussing the rule of the Mechling case, whether or not it conceded its applicability, misapprehended its requirements as to the basic findings essential to support a rate differential immediately affecting carriers both by rail and by water. Switching ex-barge freight entails more service and consequently involves more costs than are involved in switching ex-rail freight, the Commission found. We agree that there is substantial evidence in the record to support, even to demand such a conclusion. But the extra service must fit the extra charge and cannot justify lump sum rate increases which cut into the inherent advantages of cheaper barge transportation which Congress intended to guarantee to shippers.

The district court, after observing that "neither this court nor the Commission can afford to ignore the impact of the Transportation Act of 1940 on the statutory authority of the Commission," quoted the language of the *Mechling* case to the effect that the Commission had no

[7]96 F. Supp. 409.

discretionary power to approve any rate which would reduce the inherent advantage of barge transportation.

In *Alabama R. Co. v. United States*[8] the Supreme Court had occasion to reaffirm the principle of the *Mechling* case in upholding an order of the Commission which provided for differentials between corresponding all-rail rates and joint rail-barge rates. In rejecting the contention of the railroads that since the evidence failed to establish that it cost barge carriers less than railroads to furnish the particular transportation service there involved, the prescription of differentials deprived the railroads of their inherent advantages contrary to the National Transportation Policy and the doctrine of the *Mechling* case, the Supreme Court said (p. 227):

> In the *Mechling* case, the Commission had fixed a rate for transportation of wheat east by rail from Chicago at a rate higher if it arrived in Chicago by barge than if by rail or lake. This was a plain case of discrimination. There were different rates provided for equal service without any showing that any additional service was rendered for the additional charge. Here the question is whether the barge lines may charge less than the railroads for the different service they render. There is no unlawful discrimination here as there was in the *Mechling* case. The differentials providing a lower rate for barge service do not constitute an "unjust discrimination" by express proviso of § 305(c) of the Act. 54 Stat. 935, 49 U.S.C. § 905(c).

In light of the foregoing decisions, it is obvious that a railroad cannot lawfully charge more to transport a commodity simply because that commodity has moved or is to move partially by barge carrier rather than by all-rail, unless it can be shown that the higher charge is merely a reflection of the higher costs to the railroad in furnishing the transportation.

In holding that this discriminatory practice constituted a violation of Section 2 of the I.C. Act, the Supreme Court said (pp. 517-518):

> The wrong prohibited by the section is a discrimination between shippers. It was designed to compel every carrier to give equal rights to all shippers over its own road and to forbid it by any device to enforce higher charges against one than another. . . . But the service performed in transporting from Cincinnati to the depot at Pittsburgh was precisely alike for each. The one shipper paid fifteen cents a hundred; the other, in fact, but eleven and a half cents. It is true he formally paid fifteen cents, but he received a rebate of three and a half cents, and regard must always be had to the substance and not to the form. Indeed, the section itself forbids the carrier "directly or indirectly by any special rate, rebate, drawback or other device" to charge, demand, collect or receive from any person

[8]340 U.S. 216.

or persons a greater or less compensation, etc. . . . It was the purpose of the section to enforce equality between shippers, and it prohibits any rebate or other device by which two shippers, shipping over the same line, the same distance, under the same circumstances of carriage, are compelled to play different prices therefor.

The Commission itself, even prior to the passage of the Transportation Act of 1940, which placed water carriers under the regulatory power of the Commission, in several cases recognize the fact that if railroads can charge higher rates for traffic which moves partially by water rather than by all-rail, they would be in a position to destroy water carriers and to deprive shippers of the advantage of their location upon navigable waters.

In fact, the weight of the Commission's decisions supports the proposition that a difference in the type of transportation (whether rail or barge) used by shippers in an antecedent or subsequent haul does not present such a dissimilar circumstance or condition, within the meaning of Section 2, as would justify a difference in rates.[9]

In *Chattanooga Packet Co. v. Illinois Central R.R. Co.*[10] the Commission held that certain railroads had violated Section 2 by charging higher rates on traffic which had moved or was to move by unregulated water carriers than they charged on all-rail traffic. The Commission there stated (pp. 392-393):

> The shippers who desire to avail themselves of the water-and-rail route must be given equal treatment with those who ship all rail. Any discrimination which exists must not exceed that which is warranted by the differences in the circumstances and conditions of the haul over defendants' lines. *Sondheimer Co. v. I.C.R.R. Co.*, 17 I.C.C. 60.
>
>   ❋   ❋   ❋
>
> If carriers are permitted to apply higher rates for the same service on traffic routed over connecting water lines than on traffic via their all-rail connections, they will be in a position to destroy all water competition and to deprive shippers of the advantage of their location upon navigable waters.

---

[9]*Chattanooga Packet Co. v. Illinois Central R.R. Co.*, 33 I.C.C. 384; *Inland Navigation v. Wabash Ry. Co.*, 43 I.C.C. 588; *Restriction of Proportional Rates on Cotton*, 161 I.C.C. 113; *Ex-River Grain and Grain Products from Cairo and Metropolis, Ill., to Mississippi Valley*, 177 I.C.C. 206; *Raw Sugar, New Orleans to Gramercy and Reserve, La.*, 206 I.C.C. 231. Of course, because of the sanction of custom a railroad can lawfully charge less for transportation which is part of a longer through haul than for local transportation between the same points, since the difference in the origins or destinations of the traffic is considered to justify different rates. *I.C.C. v. Inland Waterways Corp.*, 319 U.S. 671, 684-685. See also discussion of Chairman Eastman in *Grain Proportionals, Ex-Barge to Official Territory*, 248 I.C.C. 307, 317 et seq.

[10]33 I.C.C. 384.

* * *

We are of the opinion and find that, by restricting their proportional rates to traffic routed over their southern rail connections, defendants are unjustly discriminating against complainant and against shippers yho desire to route their goods over complainant's boat line. . . . Defendants may make a reasonable charge to cover the additional expense, if any, of interchange with southern rail carriers.

In *Restriction of Proportional Rates on Cotton*[11] the Commission cancelled rail schedules under which the railroads proposed to restrict the application of proportional rates from Southeastern and Carolina points to Ohio and Missouri River crossings so that such rates would not apply to traffic which was to move by barge from the river crossings but would be applicable to traffic destined to move by rail from the crossings. The Commission there stated (p. 116):

> The real question at issue is whether the resulting rates would be unduly prejudicial to barge-line traffic under Section 3 of the interstate commerce act in comparison with rates upon similar traffic moving beyond the river crossings over rail lines, and also in comparison with rates to these destinations from New England territory. Manifestly, the barge line would be unable to secure any traffic from Cairo to Dubuque, originating at Atlanta, as the rail-and-river rate would exceed the all-rail rate by 11 cents. It appears that the cost of handling traffic by the southern carriers at the river crossings is no greater when delivered to the barge line than when it is delivered to their northern rail connections. If carriers are permitted to apply higher rates for the same service on traffic routed over connecting water lines than on traffic via their all-rail connections, they will be in a position to destroy all water competition and to deprive shippers of the advantage of the location upon navigable waters. *Chattanooga Packet Co. v. I.C.R.R. Co.*, 33 I.C.C., 384, 392.

In *Ex-River and Grain Products from Cairo and Metropolis, Ill., to Mississippi Valley*[12] the railroads proposed to restrict proportional rates on grain and grain products from Cairo and Metropolis, Illinois, to points in the Mississippi Valley territory so that they would apply only to traffic which arrived at these former points by rail and not by barge. In cancelling these schedules, the Commission said (p. 208):

> There is nothing in this record to indicate that the conditions under which ex-river traffic is or may be handled at Cairo are different from the conditions under which similar traffic is handled all rail. Respondents offered no testimony in justification of charging a higher rate on ex-river grain from Cairo than applies all rail. As hereinbefore stated, on traffic from St. Louis respondents publish the same proportional rate on grain regardless of whether the traffic into St. Louis moves ex-river or ex-rail.

[11]161 I.C.C. 113.
[12]177 I.C.C. 206.

Shippers who desire to avail themselves of the water-and-rail route must be given equal treatment with those who ship all-rail. An difference in rates must not exceed that which is warranted by the difference in the circumstances and conditions surrounding the transportation over respondents' lines. If rail carriers are permitted to apply higher rates on ex-river than on ex-rail traffic merely because of the different mode of transport employed prior to delivery to them, they will be in a position to destroy water competition and to deprive shippers of the advantage of their location upon navigable waters. See *Chattanooga Packet Co. v. I.C.R.R. Co.* 33 I.C.C. 384, 392.

In *Chicago I. & L. Ry. v. United States*[13] the Supreme Court held that the Commission would require a carrier to cease discriminating against another carrier even though there was no physical connection between the two. Mr. Justice Brandeis, speaking for the court, stated (p. 293):

> Direct physical connection with the carrier subjected to prejudice is not an essential. *St. Louis Southwestern Ry. Co. v. United States*, 245 U.S. 136, 144. Unjust discrimination may exist in law as well as in fact, although the injury is inflicted by a railroad which has no such direct connection. Wherever discrimination is, in fact, practiced, an order to remove it may issue; and the order may extend to every carrier who participates in inflicting the injury.

In *American Barge Line Co. v. Alabama G. S. R. Co.*[14] the Commission held that under the Supreme Court's decisions in *Interstate Commerce Commission v. Mechling*[15] and *Dixie Carriers v. United States*,[16] the carriers' assessment of local rates on ex-barge grain from Mississippi, Missouri and Ohio River trans-shipping points to interior destinations, while contemporaneously assessing lower proportional rates on ex-rail shipments, was discriminatory against the barge lines in violation of Section 3(4). The Commission also found undue prejudice to certain Tennessee River ports in violation of Section 3(1). The findings of the Commission were sustained in *Atchison, T. & S. F. Ry. Co. v. United States*.[17] The Commission's findings in a related case that the maintenance of all-rail single-factor joint rates afforded no Section 3(4) discrimination against barge lines not party thereto were, however, set aside and remanded in *Arrow Transportation Co. v. United States*.[18] The lower court said that the principle previously enunciated by the Supreme

---

[13]270 U.S. 287.
[14]306 I.C.C. 167.
[15]330 U.S. 567.
[16]351 U.S. 56.
[17]194 F. Supp. 438.
[18]176 F. Supp. 411; affirmed per curiam 361 U.S., 353 (*American Barge Line Co. v. Alabama Great Southern Railroad*, 296 I.C.C. 247, 303 I.C.C. 463, 306. I.C.C. 167).

Court in the *Mechling* case and *Dixie Carriers* was dispositive of the proceeding, and held that the I.C. Act requires the establishment of lawful, reasonable, and non-discriminatory ex-barge rail rates on the traffic involved. The district court also held that the Commission erred in refusing to receive evidence with respect to division received by the railroads on ex-rail traffic between the specific points, stating that the divisions received on ex-rail movements were prima facie evidence as to what charge should be assessed on ex-barge movements. The Commission issued a report in *American Barge Line Co. v. Alabama G. S. R. Co.*,[19] requiring that rail carriers hauling grain from Tennessee and Mississippi River crossings in the South remove the discrimination found to exist where the rates on such grain exceeded the divisions received by the defendants for corresponding service on all-rail grain. Previously, the Commission had required the same proportional rates on ex-barge grain as applied on all-rail grain from river crossings at which proportional rates were established.

[19]316 I.C.C. 759.

40

Commodities Clause

Purpose of the Statute

The purpose of the Commodities Clause[1] is to prohibit a railroad from transporting in interstate commerce any commodity, other than timber or the products manufactured therefrom, which is "manufactured, mined, or produced by it, or under its authority, or which it may own in whole or in part, or in which it may have any interest, direct or indirect, except such articles or commodities as may be necessary and intended for its use in the conduct of its business as a common carrier." The Commodities Clause excepts timber and manufactured products thereof from the prohibition.[2]

In the *Tap Line Cases,*[3] the Supreme Court said that while Congress, in enacting the Commodities Clause amending Section 1 of the I.C. Act sought to divorce transportation from production and manufacture and to make transportation a business of and by itself unallied with manufacture and production in which a carrier was itself interested, the debates in Congress, which may be resorted to for the purpose of ascertaining the situation which prompted this legislation, show that the situation in some of the states as to the logging industry and transportation was sharply brought to the attention of Congress and led to the exemption from the Commodities Clause of timber and the manufactured products thereof, thus indicating the intention to permit a railroad to haul such lumber and products although it owned them itself.

The enactment of the Commodities Clause was prompted by *New*

[1] 49 U.S.C. 1(8).
[2] *Industrial Railways Case,* 32 I.C.C. 129.
[3] 234 U.S. 1, 27.

Haven Railroad v. Interstate Commerce Commission,[4] and by other similar cases such as *Grain Rates of Chicago Great Western Ry. Co.*[5] Both cases held that a common carrier by railroad could not escape the prohibitions of the rebating statutes by owning a commodity which is transported. In the *New Haven* case, the Chesapeake & Ohio Railroad Company had entered into a contract with the New Haven Railroad Company whereby the Chesapeake & Ohio was to deliver sixty thousand tons of coal to a specified place at a definite contract price. This contract price was actually less than the purchase price of the coal at the place of purchase, plus the published tariff rates to the specified place. It was therefore obvious to the court that the prohibitions of the rebating statutes were being violated. The court destroyed this disclosed practice by upholding the injunctions granted by the lower court against both the Chesapeake & Ohio and the New Haven, stating:

> It is urged that if the requirement of the act to regulate commerce as to the maintenance of published rates and the prohibition of that act against undue preferences and discriminations be applied to a carrier when engaged in buying and selling a commodity which it transports, the substantial effect will be to prohibit the carrier from becoming a dealer when no such prohibition is expressed in the act to regulate commerce, and hence a prohibition will be implied which should only result from action by Congress. Granting the premise, the deduction is unfounded.

In a later case, *United States v. Delaware & Hudson Company,*[6] the Supreme Court commented on the *New Haven* case and corroborated the position of the court as follows (pp. 410-11):

> In that case, after much consideration, it was held that the prohibition of the Interstate Commerce Act as to uniformity of rates and against rebates operated to prevent a carrier engaged in interstate commerce from buying and selling a commodity which it carried in such a way as to frustrate the provisions of the act, even if the effect of applying the act would be substantially to render buying and selling by an interstate carrier of a commodity which it transported practically impossible.

Prohibitions under the Statute

The Commodities Clause applies four generic prohibitions, that is, it forbids a railroad carrier from transporting in interstate commerce

---

[4]200 U.S. 361. See also *American Brake Shoe & Foundry Co. v. A.G.S.R.R. Co.,* 26 I.C.C. 446 and *Arizona Rates, Fares and Charges,* 61 I.C.C. 572, 582, holding that one railroad may not transport free or at reduced rates the commodities for use as company material by another railroad being operated as an independent line even if a control relationship exists.

[5]7 I.C.C. 33.

[6]213 U.S. 366.

articles or commodities which it has manufactured, mined, or produced; which have been so mined, manufactured or produced under its authority; which it owns in whole or in part; and in which it has an interest, direct or indirect.

In the *Delaware & Hudson Company* case, the Supreme Court pointed out (p. 408) that the prohibitions which relate to manufacturing, mining or production, and the ownership resulting therefrom, are, if literally construed, not confined to the time when a carrier transports the commodities with which the prohibitions are concerned, and hence the prohibitions attach and operate upon the right to transport the commodity because of the antecedent acts of manufacture, mining or production. The two prohibitions concerning ownership, in whole or in part, and interest, direct or indirect, speak in the present and not in the past; that is, they refer to the time of the transportation of the commodities. These last prohibitions, therefore, differing from the first two, do not control the commodities if at the time of the transportation they are not owned in whole or in part by the transporting carrier, or if it then has no interest, direct or indirect, in them. The Supreme Court said that if the prohibitions as to manufacturing, mining or production be given their literal meaning, and therefore be held to prohibit, irrespective of the relation of the carrier to the commodity at the time of transportation, and a literal interpretation be applied to the remaining prohibitions as to ownership and interest, thus causing them to apply only if such ownership and interest exist at the time of transportation, the result would be to give to the statute a self-annihilative meaning.

This is the case, since in practical execution it would come to pass that where a carrier had manufactured, mined and produced commodities, and had sold them in good faith, it could not transport them; but, on the other hand, if the carrier had owned commodities and sold them it could carry them without violating the law. The consequence, therefore, would be that the statute, because of an immaterial distinction between the sources from which ownership arose, would prohibit transportation in one case and would permit it in another like case. For example: Carrier A mines and thus owns coal as a result thereof. It sells the coal to B. The carrier is impotent to move it for account of B in interstate commerce because of the prohibition of the statute. Carrier A at the same time becomes a dealer in coal — buying and selling coal and delivering it to B. This coal the carrier would be competent to carry in interstate commerce. The example not only serves to shown the incongruity and conflict which would result from the statute if the rule of literal interpretation be applied to all its provisions, but also serves to point out that as thus construed it would lead to the conclusion that it was the intention, in the enactment of the statute, to prohibit manufacturing and production by a carrier and at the same time to offer an incentive to a carrier to become the buyer and seller of commodities which it transported.

The contention was made in the *Delaware & Hudson* case by the Government that despite the literal sense of some of the prohibitions contained in the Commodities Clause, they should all be construed so as to accomplish the result intended by Congress to prohibit railroad companies engaged in interstate commerce from being at the same time manufacturers, etc., of commodities which they transport. Thus, their apparent divergence and conflict should be removed by construing them all as prohibiting transportation where certain conditions exist, irrespective of the particular relation of the railroad to the commodities at the time of transportation. After consideration of the foregoing arguments, and others, the court construed the statute as prohibiting a railroad company engaged in interstate commerce from transporting in such commerce articles or commodities under the following circumstances and conditions: (a) when the article or commodity has been manufactured, mined or produced by a carrier, or under its authority, and at the time of transportation the carrier has not disassociated itself from such article or commodity; (b) when the carrier owns the article or commodity to be transported, in whole or in part; (c) when the carrier at the time of transportation has an interest, direct or indirect, in a legal or equitable sense, in the article or commodity, not including articles or commodities manufactured, mined, produced or owned, etc., by a bona fide corporation in which the railroad is a stockholder. As thus construed, the court held that the statute was not unconstitutional.

In the next case in which the Supreme Court considered the Commodities Clause, *United States v. Lehigh Valley R.R. Co.*,[7] the court said that while its decision in *United States v. Delaware & Hudson Co.*, *supra*, expressly held that stock ownership by a railroad in a bona fide corporation, irrespective of the extent of such ownership, did not preclude a railroad from transporting the commodities manufactured, mined, produced or owned by such corporation, nothing in that conclusion foreclosed the right of the Government to question the power of a railroad to transport in interstate commerce a commodity manufactured, mined, owned, or produced by a corporation in which the railroad held stock and where the power of the railroad as a stockholder was used to

[7]220 U.S. 257.

obliterate all distinctions between the two corporations; that is to say, where the power was exerted in such a manner as to commingle the affairs of both as by necessary effect to make such affairs practically indistinguishable and, therefore, to cause both corporations to be one for all purposes.

The court said that the facts averred and other allegations contained in the proposed amended bill tended to show an actual control by the railroad company over the property of a coal company and an actual interest in such property beyond the mere interest which the railroad company would have had as a holder of stock in the company. The alleged facts, therefore, brought the railroad, so far as its right to carry the product of the coal company is concerned, within the general prohibitions of the Commodities Clause, unless for some reason the right of the railroad to carry such product was not within the operation of that clause. The argument was made that the railroad was so excepted because any control which it exerted or interest which it had in the product of the coal company resulted from its ownership of stock in that company, and would not have existed without such ownership. Answering the argument, the court said that defendant erred in "disregarding the fact that the allegations of the amended bill asserted the existence of a control by the railroad company over the coal corporation and its product, rendered possible, it is true, by the ownership of stock, but which was not the necessary result of a bona fide exercise of such ownership and which could only have arisen through the use by the railroad of its stock ownership for the purpose of giving it, the railroad company, as a corporation for its own corporate purposes, complete power over the affairs of the coal company, just as if the coal company were a mere department of the railroad."

In *Delaware, Lackawanna & Western R.R. Co. v. United States*,[8] a carrier was indicted for transporting 20 carloads or hay belonging to the carrier in alleged violation of the Commodities Clause. The trial disclosed that the defendant was not only chartered as a railroad but had also been authorized to operate coal mines. The hay referred to in the indictment had been purchased for the use of animals employed in and about the mines at Scranton, all the coal taken therefrom being sold for use by the public except the steam coal which was used as fuel for the company's locomotives. The defendant was found guilty. It carried the case to the Supreme Court where it insisted that the Commodities Clause violated the Fifth Amendment; deprived the company of a right to

[8]231 U.S. 363.

contract, and prevented it from carrying its own property needed in a legitimate intrastate business.

This contention was overruled on the authority of *United States v. Delaware & Hudson Co., supra.* While the decision in that case related to shipments of coal from mine to market, the court held (pp. 369-70) that the statute relates to all commodities except lumber owned by the company and included inbound as well as outbound shipments. "Both classes of transportation are within the purview of the evil to be corrected and, therefore, subject to the power of Congress to regulate interstate commerce." The court concluded that the exercise of that power is limited by the provisions of the Fifth Amendment, "but the Commodities Clause does not take property nor does it arbitrarily deprive the Company of a right of property." The statute deals with railroads as public carriers, and the fact that they may also be engaged in a private business does not compel Congress to legislate concerning them as carriers so as not to interfere with them as miners or merchants. If such carrier hauls for the public and also for its own private purposes, there is an opportunity to discriminate in favor of itself against other shippers in the rate charged, the facility furnished or the quality of the service rendered. The Commodities Clause was not an unreasonable and arbitrary prohibition against a railroad transporting its own useful property, but a constitutional exercise of a governmental power intended to cure or prevent the evils that might result if, in hauling goods in or out, the railroad occupied the dual and inconsistent position of public carrier and private shipper.

In *United States v. Delaware, Lackawanna & Western Railroad Company*,[9] a railroad engaged at the time of the passage of the Hepburn Act in the coal business. In order to divest itself of title after the coal had been mined and before transportation began, the railroad caused a coal company to be incorporated having stockholders and officers in common with itself. Thereupon the two corporations having a common management entered into a contract prepared by the railroad under which the railroad did not go out of the mining and selling business, but when the coal was brought to the surface it lost title by a sale of the coal company f.o.b. the mines. The carrier immediately thereafter regained possession of the coal and retained it until delivery to the coal company which subsequently paid the contract price. The price paid was a fixed percentage of the price at a stated terminal on the day of delivery at the mines, and the railroad agreed to sell all of the coal it produced

[9]238 U.S. 516.

or purchased from others to the coal company and the latter company agreed to buy only from the railroad and subject to the contract. The stockholders of the railroad were allowed to take pro rata the stock of the coal company and practically all availed themselves of the option, and the coal company declared a dividend on each share of stock sufficient to pay for the amount of stock alloted to the holder thereof.

The court held that it is not improper for a carrier engaged in mining coal to institute the organization of a coal company to buy or produce the coal so as to comply with the terms of the Commodity Clause and to give its stockholders an opportunity to subscribe to the stock, but it must dissociate itself form the management of the coal company as soon as the same starts business; mere stock ownership by a railroad company or by its stockholders in a producing company is not the test of illegality under the Commodity Clause but unity of management and bona fides of the contract between the carrier and the producer; the Commodity Clause and the Antitrust Act are not concerned with the interest of the parties, but with the interest of the public; and if a contract between a carrier and a producer is as a matter of law in restraint of trade, or if the producing company is practically the agent of the carrier, the transportation of the article produced by the carrier is unlawful; the contract in this case enables the railroad to practically control the output, sales and price of coal and to dictate to whom it should be sold, and as such is illegal under both the Commodity Clause and the Antitrust Act; in order to comply with the Commodity Clause in regard to the transportation of coal a carrier engaged also in mining coal must absolutely dissociate itself form the coal befor the transportation begins, and if it sells at the mouth of the mine, the buyer must be absolutely free to dispose of it and have absolute control, nor should a carrier sell to a corporation managed by the same officers as itself — that is contrary to the policy of the Commodity Clause; and while there might be a bona fide and lawful contract between a carrier mining coal and a buying company by which the latter buys all of the coal of the former, the contract to be not illegal must leave the buyer free to extend its business elsewhere as it pleases and to otherwise act in competition with the carrier.

In *United States v. Reading Company*,[10] the facts showed that throughout the period from December 1, 1896, to December 31, 1923, the Reading Company was a holding company which owned all the capital stock of the P & R Coal & Iron Company, a producer and ship-

---

[10]253 U.S. 26.

per of anthracite coal, and all of the stock of the Reading Railway Company, which transported a large tonnage of that coal. The Government alleged that the Reading Railway was transporting the anthracite coal in violation of the Commodities Clause. The district court held contrary to the contentions of the Government. The Supreme Court reversed the district court and said (pp. 60-2):

> The circuit judges, centering their attention upon the fact that the Reading Railway Company did not own any of the stock of the Reading Coal Company; that the two companies had separate forces of operatives and separate accounting systems; and upon the importance of maintaining "the theory of separate corporate entity" as a legal doctrine, concluded, upon the authority of *United States v. Delaware & Hudson Co.*, 213 U.S. 366, 413, that the evidence did not justify holding that, in transporting the products of the Reading Coal Company's mines to market, the Reading Railway Company was carrying a commodity "mined or produced by it or under its authority," or which it owned "in whole or in part," or in which it had "any interest, direct or indirect."

> But the question which we have presented by this branch of the case is not the technical one of whether ownership by a railroad company of stock in a coal company renders it unlawful for the former to carry the produce of the latter, for here the railroad company did not own any of the stock of the coal company. The real question is whether combining in a single corporation of the ownership of all of the stock of a carrier and of all of the stock of a coal company results in such community of interest or title in the product of the latter as to bring the case within the scope of the provisions of the act.

> The purpose of the commodity clause was to put an end to the injustice to the shipping public, which experience had shown to result from discriminations of various kinds, which inevitably grew up where a railroad company occupied the inconsistent positions of carrier and shipper. Plainly, in such a case as we have here, this evil would be present as fully as if the title to both the coal lands and the railroads were in the Holding Company, for all of the profits realized from the operations of the two must find their way ultimately into its treasury, — any discriminating practice which would harm the general shipper would profit the Holding Company. Being thus clearly within the evil to be remedied, there remains the question whether such a controlling stock ownership in a corporation is fairly within the scope of the language of the statute.

> In terms the act declares that it shall be unlawful for any railroad company to transport in interstate commerce "any article or commodity . . . mined or produced by it, or under its authority, or which it may own in whole or in part, or in which it may have any interest, direct or indirect."

> Accepting the risk of obscuring the obvious by discussing it, and without splitting hairs as to where the naked legal title to the coal would be when in transit, we may be sure that it was mined and produced under the same "authority" that transported it over the railroad. All three of

the Reading companies had the same officers and directors, and it was under their authority that the mines were worked and the railroad operated, and they exercised that authority in the one case in precisely the same character as in the other — as officials of the Holding Company. The manner in which the stock of the three was held resulted, and was intended to result, in the abdication of all independent corporate action by both the Railway Company and the Coal Company, involving, as it did, the surrender to the Holding Company of the entire conduct of their affairs. It would be to subordinate reality to legal form to hold that the coal mined by the Coal Company, under direction of the Holding Company's officials, was not produced by the same "authority" that operated the Reading Railway lines. The case falls clearly within the scope of the act, and for the violation of this commodity clause, as well as for its violation of the Antitrust Act, the combination between the Reading Railway Company and the Reading Coal Company must be dissolved.

In the foregoing cases, the railroad owned the stock of the industrial corporation or a holding company owned the stock of both the railroad and the industrial corporation. In none of these cases did the industrial corporation own the stock of the railroad. Such a situation was discussed by the Commission in *Campbell's Creek Coal Co. v. Ann Harbor R.R. Co.*[11] There at first the stock of the railroad was owned by the coal company and later at the time of the hearing the stock of the railroad had been distributed among the stockholders of the coal company so that both were then owned by the same persons. It was argued that this difference in the facts did not take the case outside the rule of *United States v. Lehigh Valley R.R. Co., supra.* The Commission said (pp. 691-2):

> . . . There would seem to be much to be said for this view assuming an identity in fact in the administration of the affairs of the two companies. It would appear from the opinion of the court in the *Lehigh Valley* case that it is not the fact of the ownership *by the railroad* of the stock of the producing company that constitutes a violation of the clause — indeed it was held in the earlier *Delaware & Hudson* case (213 U.S. 366) that mere stock ownership in the producing corporation by the railroad did not give the railroad the prohibited interest in the commodity transported — but it is rather its possible consequence, the commingling in administration of the affairs of the two companies so that they are virtually one. It would seem further, that since it is the fact of identity, the commingling of the affairs of the two companies which causes the prohibited interest, it is immaterial under what form of stock ownership the consequence may have been brought about. This view is not inconsistent with our earlier statements that mere ownership of a railroad by the principal shipper on its line is not prohibited by the act. In the same case the Commission further said (p. 693): . . . We may say, however, that whatever may be the doubt as to whether the letter of the law as it now stands will

[11]29 I.C.C. 682.

sustain this construction, there is no doubt in our minds that the central fact of the situation we have been discussing, namely, the ownership of the railroad by the producing corporation, or the common ownership of both corporations by the same persons, may just as easily be the means of a complete commingling of the affairs of the two companies as the ownership of the producing corporation by the railroad, and that, given the identity between the two companies, the evils which the commodities clause was designed to prevent would be no different or no less likely to ensue whether the identity was brought about in the one way or in the other.

In *Allowances to Kanawha, Glen Jean & Eastern*,[12] the Commission found that the railway had an indirect interest in the coal of the McKell Coal & Coke Company which it transported for the reason that the two companies had the same controlling stockholders, the same executive and managing officers and were conducted with little regard for the legal distinction between them. In that case the Commission said (p. 59): "(t)he commodities clause forbids common carriers by railroad to transport any articles or commodities, other than timber and the manufactured products thereof and company material, which they own; or in which they have any interest, direct or indirect; or manufactured, mined, or produced by them, or under their authority, from which they have not genuinely dissociated themselves before the act of transportation." The purpose of the commodities clause, the Commission added (p. 60), is to strike "at the possibility of discrimination and not merely at its actual effectuation."

In *United States v. Elgin, J. & E. R. Co.*,[13] the Supreme Court said (p. 501) that considering former rulings it was impossible to declare as a matter of law that every company all of whose shares are owned by a holding company necessarily becomes an agent, instrumentality, or department of the latter. "Whether such intimate relation exists is a question of fact to be determined upon evidence." It then said (pp. 502-3):

> If the evidence here showed the relationship between the holding company, the carrier, and the producing companies to be substantially as in the *Reading Co.* case, that opinion well might be regarded as controlling. But there is material difference and we must look elsewhere for guidance. Properly to appraise the situation now presented particular attention must be given to the following facts. All shares of appellee and the subsidiary producing companies have been owned by the United States Steel Corporation since 1901. The railroad has been under constant supervision of the Interstate Commerce Commission. *Re Alleged Rebates to the*

[12]41 I.C.C. 53.
[13]298 U.S. 492.

United States Steel Corporation, 36 Inters. Com. Rep. 557 (1915). It functions as a separate corporate carrier under immediate control of its own directors, no one of whom is on the board of the holding company; it owns all necessary equipment, makes its own contracts, manages its own finances, serves its patrons without discrimination and apparently to their satisfaction.

United States v. South Buffalo Ry. Co.[14] adhered to the construction placed upon the Commodities Clause by the *Elgin, Joliet and Eastern* case as not precluding a railroad whose stock is wholly owned by a parent company from carrying goods for another subsidiary of the parent company. The court said (p. 785):

> Bethlehem, as a stockholder, of course controlled South Buffalo. It did not, however, disregard in either the legal or economic sense the separate entity of its subsidiary or treat it as its own alter ego. On the contrary, it rather ostentatiously maintained the formalities of separate existence, choosing as directors several Buffalo citizens who were not interested in Bethlehem. We are not naive enough to believe that Bethlehem chose men for the posts whose interests or records left any fair probability that they would act adversely to Bethlehem in representing its interest as chief stockholder of the railroad. Nor has any instance been cited in which the best interests of the railroad would require them to do so. So long as Congress considers it inadvisable to extend the prohibition of the Commodities Clause to subsidiaries and affiliates, we see nothing that Bethlehem has done to incur liability for its violation. Of course, it could not expect the Commission or the courts to respect a corporate entity which Bethlehem itself disregarded; but that it has not done. The subsidiary would not have to establish its separate identity by a course of hostility to its sole stockholder or its chief customer. Its identity has been preserved in form and in substance — the substance of separate corporate existence being itself largely a matter of form. Under the *Elgin* Case and until Congress shall otherwise decide, this is sufficient.

The Commission had occasion to comment on the *Elgin, Joliet and Eastern* and the *South Buffalo* cases in *St. Marys R. Co. Construction*[15] where it said (pp. 689-90):

> The Seaboard claims that the relationship between the industry and the applicant is so close and the business of the two so commingled as to amount to contravention of the so-called commodities clause, Section 1 (8) of the act. The transportation of timber and the manufactured products thereof are exempt from the act. And, in *United States v. South Buffalo Ry. Co.*, 333 U.S. 771, the Supreme Court of the United States, following the decision promulgated in *United States v. Elgin, J. & E. Ry. Co.*, 298 U.S. 492, held in connection with the relationship existing between the Bethlehem Steel Corporation and its railroad subsidiary, that Section 1 (8)

---

[14]333 U.S. 771.
[15]295 I.C.C. 677, affirmed 312 I.C.C. 178.

of the act did not prevent a railroad from transporting commodities of a corporation substantially all of whose stock is owned by a holding company, which also owns substantially all the stock of the railroad, unless the control of the railroad is so exercised to make it the alter ego of the holding company, and the evidence in that case did not prove that Bethlehem, in either the legal or economic sense, disregarded the separate entity of its railroad subsidiary or treated it as its alter ego. We find nothing in the present proceeding that the relationship between Kraft and the applicant will involve a violation of Section 1 (8) of the act as interpreted by the Supreme Court, if the relationship is maintained as above described.

The Elkins Act was not suspended by the Commodities Clause. Nothing can be pointed to the Commodities Clause itself which indicates directly or indirectly, that the prohibitions of the Elkins Act making unlawful either the giving or receiving of rebates, concessions, or discriminations should not apply to the exception contained within the Commodities Clause itself, that is, railroads which transport timber or the products manufactured therefrom. In fact, the United States Supreme Court has ruled that the exception contained in the Commodities Clause, namely, a railroad which transports its own timber, was within the prohibitions of the rebating statutes.

In *Fourche River Lumber Company v. Bryant Lumber Company*[16] the Fourche Lumber Company and the Bryant Lumber Company were competing timber and cut-timber companies. Each company had mills and sawmill plants located some distance from the Rock Island Railroad. The Fourche Lumber Company and the Bryant Lumber Company entered into a contract whereby, in consideration for the right-of-way to lay down tracks and operate its railroad over the Bryant Lumber Company's land, the Fourche Lumber Company promised to haul the timber of the Bryant Lumber Company equally, impartially, and without discrimination so that each party would have a fair and equal opportunity to compete with each other in all respects in the purchase, hauling, and sale of land and timber or products thereof in that vicinity, or in the transportation of freight over the tap line. All differences were to be arbitrated. The Fourche Lumber Company then organized a separate corporate tap line railroad, known as the Fourche River Valley & Indian Territory R.R. Co., for the purpose of transporting its lumber to the interstate trunk line. It owned all of the stock of the railroad except one or two qualifying shares. However, each corporation kept separate books and records and, when the tap line railroad made profits, these profits were paid to the stockholders by means of dividends declared on the capital stock. The tap line railroad had a tariff arrangement with the

---

[16]230 U.S. 316.

interstate trunk line railroad embracing timber and cut-lumber, and the tap line railroad received a division of the through rate from freight originating on its lines.

Differences arose between the Fourche Lumber Company and the Bryant Lumber Company, and the latter demanded an arbitration. One of the differences between the companies was the demand by the Bryant Lumber Company for a division of allowances or differentials given by the interstate trunk line to the tap line railroad on shipments of timber and cut-lumber made by the Bryant Lumber Company. The arbitrators found that the Fourche Lumber Company had failed to pay the Bryant Lumber Company, in violation of its contract, the division of allowances or differentials which had been received by the tap line railroad from the interstate trunk line on shipments of timber and cut-lumber made by the Bryant Lumber Company. The terms of the award not having been complied with, the Bryant Lumber Company brought suit. The Fourche Lumber Company, as a defense to the Bryant Lumber Company's claim, urged that it would be a violation of the rebating statutes to pay a division of allowances or differentials to the Bryant Lumber Company. The lower court refused to allow this defense and the Arkansas Supreme Court sustained the lower court. On appeal to the Supreme Court of the United States, however, it was held that this was a valid defense to the claim of the Bryant Lumber Company. The court said (pp. 321-3):

> A judgment on the verdict rendered in accordance with this charge having been affirmed, the Fourche Lumber Company brought the case here, insisting that the charge and verdict were in violation of the Interstate Commerce Act, and, in effect, amounted to the giving of a rebate to the Bryant Lumber Company. The latter replies that the suit is against the Fourche Lumber Co. and that there is no law preventing one company from paying the whole or any part of the freight due by another. That may be true but not where that other party is sued as being in effect a common carrier engaged in interstate commerce. The arbitration was demanded and the award made on the theory that, inasmuch as the contract provided that there should be no discrimination, the Bryant Company was entitled to receive from the Fourche Lumber Company "the same freight concessions as are now enjoyed by the Fourche Lumber Company through its interest and the interest of its owners in the Fourche Railroad." This suit is based upon the assumption that the two companies are identical in fact, though different in name.

> Thus treating it, the case is as though the Bryant Lumber Company had sued the Fourche Lumber Company, doing business as the interstate carrier, for so much of the through rate as had been paid to it on the division by the Rock Island for hauling the Bryant Company's shipment of lumber. To state the proposition is to manifest its illegality, and to

show that thereby the Bryant Company would get a reduction on the through rate on all of its lumber originating on the Fourche line.

※   ※   ※

. . . On the other hand, if the Fourche Railroad was lawfully paid for such services [by the interstate trunk line] in hauling the lumber it would be illegal, directly or through a subsidiary to give to the shipper a part of such joint rate under any pretext whatever.

※   ※   ※

The Commerce Act prohibits the payment of rebates, and its command cannot be evaded by calling them differentials or concessions, nor by taking the money from the Railroad itself or from a company that is proved to be the same as the Railroad. Otherwise nothing would be easier than for lumber companies to charter a railroad, collect freight as a railroad, but pay it out as a lumber company to shippers.

In the later *St. Mary's R. Co. Construction* case[17] the Commission held that although 90 per cent of applicant's traffic was within the exemption of timber and products, it did and would transport non-exempt commodities shipped or received by the parent paper company, and if its relationship with the parent was such that it had a direct or indirect interest in those commodities it was operating in violation of the Commodities Clause and would probably do so over the proposed extension. The Commission said that the general policy of the law is to recognize separate corporate entities and not to disregard them where those in control have deliberately adopted the corporate form to secure its advantages and where no violence to the legislative purpose is done by treating the corporate entity as a separate legal person; and it is sufficient that the subsidiary railroad's identity has been preserved in form and in substance and that the control has not been so exercised as to make it the alter ego of the parent industry,[18] the separate corporate and legal entities of applicant and its parent were observed in all their activities, and protestant did not contend that it had dealt with applicant other than in the latter's individual capacity; neither the parent company nor the paper company which in turn controlled it treated the railroad as its alter ego, and the controlling industry treated its subsidiaries in their financial transactions as would any commercial lender; so long as applicant's relationship with the controlling companies is maintained on the present basis there will be no violation of Section 1(8) as currently interpreted.[19]

The Commission said further (p. 181) that whatever may have been

---

[17]312 I.C.C. 178, 181.
[18]Id., pp. 182-4.
[19]*Ibid.*, p. 184.

the primary purpose of exemption of timber and products from the commodities clause, it does not serve to restrict the plain meaning of the language used, which is not "lumber and products manufactured therefrom," but "timber and the products manufactured therefrom"; thus pulpwood, consisting chiefly of pine timber, and paper manufactured therefrom, are clearly within the exemption.

41

Competition in Transportation

Economic Policy in Favor of Competitive Enterprise

The Act to Regulate Commerce of 1887 is regarded as the first Congressional enactment of the economic policy in favor of competitive enterprise. The provisions of the Act of 1887 against monopolies were made applicable to all industries by the Sherman Act of 1890. In 1914, the Sherman Act was supplemented by the Federal Trade Commission Act and the Clayton Act.

Sections 1 and 2 of the Sherman Antitrust Act

The first two sections of the Sherman Act (15 U.S.C. 1 and 2) provide in substance that:

1. Every contract, combination in the form of trust or otherwise, or conspiracy, in restraint of trade or commerce among the several States, or with foreign nations, is hereby declared to be illegal. . . . Every person who shall make any contract or engage in any combination or conspiracy hereby declared to be illegal shall be deemed guilty of misdemeanor.

2. Every person who shall monopolize, or attempt to monopolize, or combine or conspire with any other person or persons, to monopolize any part of the trade or commerce among the several States, or with foreign nations, shall be deemed guilty of a misdemeanor. . . .

The sections are directed against the stifling and elimination of competition whereby a dominant or monopolistic position in any segment of trade or commerce may be acquired. The sections overlap as shown by decided civil cases[1] where the courts make no clear-cut statements

[1]*Northern Securities v. United States,* 193 U.S. 197; *United States v. Union Pacific Railroad Co.,* 226 U.S. 61, and *United States v. Southern Pacific Co.,* 259 U.S. 214. See *American Tobacco Co. v. United States,* 147 F. 2d 93, aff'd 328 U.S. 781, however, where clear-cut definitions of the Sections are made in criminal cases.

with respect to the separate violations under the sections. The monopoly prohibited by Section 2 is but a type of restraint of commerce prohibited by Section 1, and a violation of Section 1 may be but a step in the direction of a violation of Section 2. As stated in *United States v. Sacony-Vacuum Oil Company*,[2] "the two sections overlap in the sense that a monopoly under Section 2 is a species of restraint of trade under Section 1," in *United States v. Griffith*,[3] "for those things which are condemned by Section 2 in a large measure are merely the end product of conducts which violate Section 1," and *United States v. Columbia Steel Company*,[4] "Every attempt to monopolize must also constitute an illegal restraint under Section 1." What has been said with respect to Section 1 and 2 applies with equal force to Section 3 which relates to territorial commerce.[5]

When analyzed, it is found that the sections, although interrelated and usually applied together, have well-defined separate legal concepts. There are the various agreements and combinations in restraint of trade such as price-fixing, division of markets, group boycotts, and tying arrangements which fall strictly under the ban of Section 1. Such agreements need not be the part of a general design to monopolize, and in fact certain types of agreements are considered so pernicious by their intrinsic nature that they are held to be violations of the Sherman Act *per se*, even though it is not shown that they restrain or affect any substantial part of commerce.[6] The Supreme Court had occasion to state the reasoning lying behind *per se* violations in *Northern Pacific Railroad v. United States*,[7] where it is stated:

> However, there are certain agreements or practices which because of their pernicious effect on competition and a lack of any redeeming virtue are conclusively presumed to be unreasonable and therefore illegal without elaborate inquiry as to the precise harm they have caused or the business excuse for their use. This principle of per se unreasonableness not only makes the type of restraints which are proscribed by the Sherman Act more certain to the benefit of everyone concerned, but it also avoids the necessity for an incredibly complicated and prolonged economic in-

[2]310 U.S. 150, 226.
[3]334 U.S. 100, 106.
[4]334 U.S. 295, 518.
[5]*United States v. Sisal Sales Corp.*, 274 U.S. 268. See also *United States v. National Lead Co.*, 63 F. Supp. 513, aff'd 332 U.S. 319; *United States v. Timken Roller Bearing Co.*, 83 F. Supp. 284, aff'd 341 U.S. 593; *United States v. General Electric Co.*, 82 F. Supp. 753; *United States v. Aluminum Co.. of America*, 148 F. 2d 416, and *United States v. American Tobacco Co.*, 221 U.S. 106.
[6]*United States v. Griffith*, 334 U.S. 100, 105-106; *United States v. Masonite Corp.*, 316 U.S. 265, 275; *United States v. Patton*, 226 U.S. 525, 543.
[7]356 U.S. 1, 5; see also *Montague & Company v. Lowry*, 193 U.S. 38.

vestigation into the entire history of the industry involved, as well as related industries, in an effort to determine at large whether a particular restraint has been unreasonable — an inquiry so often wholly fruitless when undertaken. Among the practices which the courts have heretofore deemed to be unlawful in and of themselves are price fixing. *United States v. Socony-Vacuum Oil Co.*, 310 U.S. 150, 210; division of markets, *United States v. Addyston Pipe & Steel Co.*, 85 F. 271, aff'd 175 U.S. 211; group boycotts, *Fashion Originators' Guild v. Federal Trade Comm'n*, 312 U.S. 457; and tying arrangements, *International Salt Co. v. United States*, 332 U.S. 392.

It is well established that it makes no difference that the agreements were entered between parent and subsidiary corporations or that the prohibited result is accomplished by various interrelated corporate devices.[8]

There is a conspiracy to monopolize which falls strictly under the ban of Section 2. This is a factual concept based on the traditional common law idea of conspiracy, which entails the element of a design to accomplish a result though more often than not the existence of a design must be established inferentially. There is a concept of an attempt to monopolize which is likewise prohibited by Section 2. This concept is directed towards a series of acts done for the purpose of attaining a monopoly but which fall short of the accomplishment of the ultimate design. Lastly, there is the attained monopoly. This is a concept which is sometimes difficult to apply in particular situations.

As far as the definition and the legal principles surrounding a conspiracy to monopolize, an attempt to monopolize and a monopoly are concerned, the opinion of the Supreme Court in *American Tobacco Compan v. United States*[9] is considered definitive. In this case an information was filed under Sections 1 and 2 of the Sherman Act in connection with the practices in the purchase of tobacco on the tobacco markets and the marketing of cigarettes. The information contained four counts: conspiracy in restraint of trade, monopolization, attempt to monopolize, and conspiracy to monopolize. The defendants were convicted on all four counts, and, on appeal, vigorously attacked the charge of the lower court, particularly with respect to the monopoly and attempt to monopolize counts.[10] The instruction was as follows:

> Now, the term "monopolize" as used in Section 2 of the Sherman Act, as well as in the last three counts of the Information, means the joint

[8]*United States v. Timken Roller Bearing Co.*, 83 F. Supp. 284, aff'd 341 U.S. 593.
[9]328 U.S. 781.
[10]The defendants were not sentenced on the court charging "attempt to monopolize" because it was held that this court was merged into the broader one of "monopoly."

acquisition or maintenance by the members of a conspiracy formed for that purpose, of the *power to control and dominate interstate trade and commerce in a commodity to such an extent that they are able, as a group, to exclude actual or potential competitors from the field, accompanied with the intention and purpose to exercise such power.*

The phrase "attempt to monopolize" means the employment of methods, means and practices which would, if successful, accomplish monopolization, and which, though falling short, nevertheless approach so close as to create a dangerous probability of it, which methods, means and practices are so employed by the members of any group pursuant to a combination or conspiracy formed for the purpose of such accomplishment.

It is in no respect a violation of the law that a number of individuals or corporations, each acting for himself or itself, may own or control a large part, or even all of a particular commodity, or all the business in a particular commodity.

An essential element of the illegal monopoly or monopolization charged in this case is the existence of a combination or conspiracy to acquire and maintain the power to exclude competitors to a substantial extent.

Thus you will see that *an indispensable ingredient of each of the offenses charged in the Information is a combination or conspiracy.* (Italics supplied.)

The Supreme Court affirmed. It will be noted that a conspiracy to monopolize is an essential feature of an attempt to monopolize and of a monopoly. It will also be noted that the Supreme Court held that the two crimes involve a specific intent which would naturally flow from the conspiratorial activity.

Historically Common Carriers Have Been Subject to the Antitrust Laws

When the Sherman Act was passed, the country was served by only two types of common carriers, namely the railroads and the water carriers. Due to the monopolistic position of these carriers and the dependence of the public on them, the courts at the outset recognized that the antitrust laws applied to them with unusual force. Thus the second case under the Sherman Act, *United States v. Trans-Missouri Freight Association*[11] involved various agreements among railroads for the establishment of rates and classifications. The court emphatically stated at page 333:

The business which the railroads do is of a public nature, closely affecting almost all classes in the community — the farmer, the artisan, the manufacturer and the trader. It is of such a public nature that it may

[11]166 U.S. 290.

well be doubted, to say the least, whether any contract which imposes any restraint upon its business would not be prejudicial to the public interest.

Northern Securities Co. v. United States[12] involved the acquisition through a holding company of the controlling interest in the Northern Pacific and the Great Northern. These two systems operated roughly parallel lines originating in the Great Lakes area and terminating in the Pacific Northwest. They crossed the northern tier of states, the course of the Great Northern running in the extreme north and the Northern Pacific running through the southern portion of the tier. It appeared that the actual competition between the two lines was relatively small.[13] The court, in holding that the arrangement violated the antitrust act emphasized the great dependence of the public upon common carriers and stated (pp. 342, 343):

> If private parties may not, by combination among themselves, restrain interstate and international commerce in violation of an act of Congress, much less can such restraint be tolerated when imposed or attempted to be imposed upon commerce as carried on over public highways.

The court then clearly held that the common control of two common carriers which operated over roughly parallel routes and were thus natural competitors, constituted in and of itself a violation of the Sherman Act (pp. 326-327):

> No scheme or device could more cerainly come within the words of the act — "combination in the form of a trust or otherwise . . . *in restraint of commerce among the several states or with foreign nations,*" or could more effectively and certainly suppress free competition between the constituent companies. This combination is, within the meaning of the act, a "trust," but if not, it is a combination in restraint of interstate and international commerce; and that is enough to bring it under the condemnation of the act. *The mere existence of such a combination, and the power acquired by the holding company as its trustee, constitute a menace to, and a restraint upon, that freedom of commerce which Congress intended to recognize and protect, and which the public is entitled to have protected.* If such combination be not destroyed, all the advantages that would naturally come to the public under the suppression of the general laws of competition, as between the Great Northern and Northern Pacific Rail-

---

[12]193 U.S. 197.
[13]The defendants contended (p. 289) that no more than 3 or 4 percent of their interstate traffic would be affected. The Government contended simply that the lower court had found (p. 298) "that the roads are and in the public estimation have been regarded parallel and competing" but that "even if the roads only competed for 3 percent of their interstate business they would be competing lines." The Supreme Court stated, without detailed analysis (p. 320): "the two companies were engaged in active competition for freight and passenger traffic."

way Companies, will be lost, and the entire commerce of the immense territory in the northern part of the United States between the Great Lakes and the Pacific at Puget Sound will be at the mercy of a single holding corporation organized in a state distant from the people of that territory. (Emphasis supplied.)

The holding of the *Northern Securities* case was followed consistently throughout the years.[14] Thus in *United States v. Union Pacific Company*[15] the court held that the acquisition of control of the Southern Pacific by the Union Pacific in itself constituted an undue suppression of competition and was in violation of the Sherman Act. The routes of the two roads were widely divergent and the degree of actual competition was relatively small and the Supreme Court so stated (at page 88). It then said:

> The consolidation of two great competing systems of railroad engaged in interstate commerce by a transfer to one of a dominating stock interest in the other creates a combination which restrains interstate commerce within the meaning of the statute, because, in destroying or greatly abridging the free operation of competition theretofore existing, it tends to higher rates.

Again in *United States v. South Pacific Company*,[16] the court reaffirmed the doctrine. Briefly, the facts in this case were as follows. In 1898 the Southern Pacific had acquired the controlling stock interest in the Central Pacific Railroad, though not the entire interest. The Central Pacific linked with the Union Pacific at the Ogden gateway and ran down to the ports of California. The Government filed a complaint charging that the acquisition violated the antitrust laws, and asked that Southern Pacific divest its stock interest in Central. It does not appear from the opinion that the court gave any consideration to the extent of competition in terms of tonnage, dollar volume, or any other similar factors though it did emphasize the conflict of interest which would flow naturally from the Southern Pacific's effort to protect its long haul. In ordering divestiture, the court stated (page 230):

> Counsel for the defendants, evidently realizing this situation, make elaborate argument to distinguish the *Union Pacific* case. The claim is made

---

[14]The rule of reason which was developed in the classic case of *Standard Oil Co. v. United States,* 221 U.S. 1, in no way affected the basic doctrine of the *Northern Securities* case that the combination of common carriers operating parallel lines constituted a violation of the Sherman Act. In fact, the *Northern Securities* case was cited with complete approval in the *Standard Oil* case at page 69. The basic considerations were also applied to other carriers as well. See *Thomsen v. Calser,* 243 U.S. 66; *United States v. Pacific and A. Co.,* 228 U.S. 87.

[15]226 U.S. 61.

[16]259 U.S. 214.

that the decision there rested only on the fact that a then existing competition was restrained through the purchase by the Union Pacific of the control of the Southern Pacific in 1901; but the principle of that decision and of the previous cases upon which it rested was broader than the mere effect upon existing competition between the two systems.

Such combinations, not the result of normal and natural growth and development, but springing from the formation of holding companies, or stock purchases, resulting in the unified control of different roads or systems, *naturally competitive*, constitute "a menace to, and a restraint upon, that freedom of commerce which Congress intended to recognize and protect, and which the public is entitled to have protected." *Northern Securities Co. v. United States*, 193 U.S. 197, 327. This principle was restated and applied in *United States v. Union Pacific R. R. Co., supra;* it was reiterated and approved by the court as recently as the *October Term*, 1919, *United States v. Reading Co.*, 253 U.S. 26, 57, 58, 59.

In *Pearsall v. Great Northern Railway*[17] the court said:

Whether the consolidation of competing lines will necessarily result in an increase of rates, or whether such consolidation has generally resulted in a detriment to the public is beside the question. Whether it has that effect or not, it certainly puts it in the power of the consolidated corporation to give it that effect — in short, puts the public at the mercy of the corporation. There is and has been for the past three hundred years, both in England and in this country, a popular prejudice against monopolies in general, which has found expression in innumerable acts of legislation. We can not say that such prejudice is not well founded. It is a matter upon which the legislature is entitled to pass judgment. At least there is sufficient doubt of the propriety of such monopolies to authorize the legislature, which may be presumed to represent the views of the public, to say that it will not tolerate them unless the power to establish them be conferred by clear and explicit language. While, in particular cases, two railways, by consolidating their interests under a single management, may have been able to so far reduce the expenses of administration as to give their customers the benefit of a lower tariff, the logical effect of all monopolies is an increase of price of the thing produced, whether it be merchandise or transportation. Owing to the greater speed and cheapness of the service performed by them, railways become necessarily monopolistic of all traffic along their lines; but the general sentiment of the public declares that such monopolies must be limited to the necessities of the case, and rebels against the attempt of one road to control all traffic between terminal points. . .

In *United States v. Reading Co.*[18] the combination therein condemned was described as follows:

. . . in 1898 many of the independent coal operators in the Wyoming or Northern field became dissatisfied with the transportation and market

[17]161 U.S. 646, 676.
[18]226 U.S. 324.

conditions under which they were obliged to conduct their collieries. Many contracts for the sale of their coal to the defendant coal companies had expired or were about to expire, and they demanded either lower freight rates or better prices from the coal companies. A competing line of railway from the Northern or Wyoming zone of the anthracite region to a point on the Delaware River, where connection would be made with two or more lines extending to shipping points at New York harbor, was projected as a means of relieving the situation. The New York, Wyoming & Western Railroad was accordingly incorporated. Large subscriptions of stock were taken, the line in part surveyed, parts of the right-of-way procured, and a large quantity of steel rails contracted for.

* * *

The petition alleges that the construction of the projected independent railroad would not only have introduced competition into the transportation of anthracite coal to tide-water, but it would have enabled independent operators reached by it to sell their coal at distributing points in free competition with the defendant coal companies. *"Wherefore,"* avers the pleading, "the defendants, the Reading Company, owning the entire capital stock of the Philadelphia & Reading Railway Company, and the other carrier companies defendants herein, controlling collectively all means of transportation between the mines and shipping points at New York harbor, combined together for the purpose of shutting out the proposed railroad and preventing competition with them in the transportation of coal from the mines to other States, and the sale of coal in competition with their own controlled coal in the markets of other States." The plan devised was to detach from the enterprise the powerful support of Simpson & Watkins and the great tonnage which their cooperation would give to the new road, by acquiring for the combination the coal properties and collieries controlled by that great independent firm of operators. This would not only strangle the project, but secure them forever against new schemes induced by the large tonnage produced by these eight collieries, and secure not only that tonnage for their own lines, but keep the coal forever out of competition with that of their controlled coal-producing companies.

The scheme was worked out with the result foreseen and intended.

In *United States v. Joint Traffic Association*[19] the Supreme Court held that when competing railroads are involved "Congress is competent to forbid any agreement or combination among them by means of which competition is to be smothered." The agreement condemned provided for the fixing of rates, fares and charges.

The doctrine of the application of the antitrust laws in common carrier cases was further solidified in *United States v. Reading Co.,*[20] in which the court said:

[19]171 U.S. 505, 570.
[20]253 U.S. 26, 57.

Again, and obviously, this dominating power was not obtained by normal expansion to meet the demands of a business growing as a result of a superior and enterprising management, but by deliberate, calculated purchase for control.

That such a power, so obtained, regardless of the use made of it, constitutes a menace to and an undue restraint upon interstate commerce within the meaning of the Anti-Trust Act, has been frequently held by this court.

Thus, in Northern Securities Co. v. United States, 193 U.S. 197, 327, when dealing with a holding company, such as we have here, this court, in 1903, held:

No scheme or device could more certainly come within the words of the act — "combination in the form of a trust or otherwise . . . in restraint of commerce among the several States or with foreign nations," — or could more effectively and certainly suppress free competition between the constituent companies. . . . *The mere existence of such a combination and the power acquired by the holding company as its trustee, constitute a menace to, and a restraint upon, that freedom of commerce which Congress intended to recognize and protect,* and which the public is entitled to have protected. (Emphasis supplied.)

In *United States v. Lake Shore & M. S. Ry. Co.*[21] the court said:

Stress is laid both in the evidence and argument upon the economy of this interchange of facilities, since it secures easier grades over the Hocking Valley, as compared with those of the Toledo & Ohio Central, and avoids the necessity of building double tracks and of operating opposing trains over single-track roads with the usual sidings. These advantages may be conceded from an operating point of view; yet the logic of it all would in the end destroy competition between parallel roads generally.

In *United States v. Great Lakes Towing Co.*[22] the court said (page 733):

A combination which places the direct instrumentalities of interstate commerce in such a relation as to create a single dominating control in one corporation, whereby natural and existing competition in interstate commerce is unduly restricted or suppressed, is within the condemnation of the act.

It is not necessary to a violation of the Federal statute that a complete monopoly of all towing on the Great Lakes be effected. A monopoly in 14 ports is as offensive against the act as a monopoly in 50 ports.

The court said further (page 744):

The fact that the towing and wrecking service has been improved under the towing company's administration can not legalize the combination

---

[21]203 Fed. 312.
[22]208 Fed. 733.

if otherwise unlawful. Not only do good motives furnish no defense to a violation of the antitrust act, but we have no right to assume that the unsatisfactory conditions existing in 1899 could not have been eliminated by lawful and normal methods.

Whatever may be the views of individual economists, under the Federal statutory policy normal and healthy competition is the law of trade; and such evils as may result from such competition must be considered less than those liable to follow a complete unification of interests and the power such unification gives. The evil of unification lies in the temptation to higher rates and lessened regard for the public interests; and the tendency to this evil result must be recognized even though not in a given case yet realized in actual experience.

In *United States v. Pacific and A. Co.*[23] the Supreme Court stated:

The charge of the indictment is that the agreements were entered into not from natural trade reasons, not from a judgment of the greater efficiency or responsibility of the defendant steamship lines as instruments in the transportation than the independent lines, but as a combination and conspiracy in restraint of trade by preventing and destroying competition in the transportation of freight and passengers between the United States and Alaska and obtaining a monopoly of the traffic. . .

The transportation industry historically, as heretofore stated, has been subject to the antitrust laws. This has been true even though a part of the transportation may have been carried on outside the jurisdiction of the United States by companies operating within and pursuant to the laws of a foreign country.[24] Combinations of foreign or foreign and American steamship lines, whether formed in a foreign country or in the United States, affecting the foreign commerce of this country and the performance of the steamship lines' duties as common carriers to compete for the commerce between the United States and foreign countries, have been found illegal under the Sherman Act.[25] As was stated in *Hamburg-Amerikanische* (p. 807):

The prohibitions of the anti-trust statute apply broadly to contracts in restraint of trade or commerce with foreign nations. . . . We see nothing to warrant the contention that the act should be narrowly interpreted as prohibiting only contracts which are to be performed wholly within the territorial jurisdiction of the United States nor — if it were for us to consider — any reason for concluding that a broader construction would lead to international complications.

---

[23]228 U.S. 87, 104.
[24]*Ibid.*
[25]*Thomsen v. Cayser*, 243 U.S. 66, 89; *United States v. Hamburg-Amerikanische P-F-A-G*, 200 Fed. 806 (later dismissed without prejudice by the Supreme Court on the ground that the European war rendered the controversy moot, 239 U.S. 466).

. . . The vital question in all cases is the same: Is the combination to so operate in this country as to directly and materially affect our foreign commerce? . . .

In *Thomsen v. Cayser, supra,* it was said that it is the duty of common carriers to compete, not combine, and their duty subjects them in a special sense to the policy of the law. The court said further (pp. 86-88):

We have already seen that a combination is not excused because it was induced by good motives or produced good results, and yet such is the justification of defendants. They assert first that they are voluntary agencies of commerce, free to go where they will, not compelled to run from New York to Africa, and that "unlike railroads, neither law, nor any other necessity, fixes them upon particular courses"; and therefore, it is asked, "who can say that otherwise than under the plan adopted, any of the ships of the defendants would have supplied facilities for transportation of commodities between New York and South Africa during the time referred to in the complaint?" The resultant good of the plan, it is said, was "regularity of service, with steadiness of rates"; and that "the whole purpose of the plan under which the defendants acted was to achieve this result."

We may answer the conjectures of the argument by the counter one that if defendants had not entered the trade others might have done so and been willing to serve shippers without constraining them, been willing to compete against others for the patronage of the trade.

That the combination was intended to prevent the competition of the lines which formed it is testified, and it cannot be justified by the conjectures offered by counsel; nor can we say that the success of the trade required a constraint upon shippers or the employment of "fighting ships" to kill off competing vessels which, tempted by the profits of the trade, used the free and unfixed courses of the seas, to paraphrase the language of counsel, to break in upon defendants' monopoly. And monopoly it was: shippers contrained by their necessities, competitors kept off by "fighting ships." And it finds no justification in the fact that defendants' "contributions to trade and commerce" might "have been withheld." This can be said of any of the enterprises of capital and has been urged before to exempt them from regulation even when engaged in business which is of public concern. The contention has long since been worn out and it is established that the conduct of property embarked in the public service is subject to the policies of the law.

Exemptions from the Operation of the Antitrust Laws

It is settled law that regulated industries are not *per se* exempt from the antitrust laws.[26] It is also beyond question that while the I.C. Act

---

[26]*Georgia v. Pennsylvania Railroad Co.,* 324 U.S. 439.

extensively regulates carriers, such regulation is not so pervasive as to confer blanket immunity for any and all carrier activity.

Congress has expressly provided for relief from the operation of the antitrust laws in several narrow situations under the I.C. Act.[27]

One, where the ICC has approved a merger or other transaction under Section 5(2) such agreements are relieved from the coverage of the antitrust laws by Section 5(12) (formerly Section 5(11)).

Two, where the ICC has approved a pooling agreement under Section 5(1) such agreements are exempted from the antitrust laws.

Three, where the ICC has approved a rate conference agreement under Section 5a or Section 5b the making and carrying out of such rate agreement is immune from direct antitrust attack by Section 5a(9) and Section 5b(8).

In giving consideration to the approval and immunization powers of the ICC under Sections 5, 5a and 5b it is important to bear in mind the following principles:

(1) The approval and immunization powers under Sections 5, 5a and 5b are prospective only, and the ICC has no power to validate pre-approval action.

(2) The antitrust laws apply with their usual force unless the adminstrative procedure for the granting of immunity is strictly followed.

(3) Where congress carefully circumscribes the terms and conditions upon which persons receive antitrust immunity by operation of the regulatory statute, it is axiomatic that no greater immunity than that expressly granted is available. In other words, agreements which cover parties or terms not within the express language of the statute and, therefore, beyond the regulatory preserve are not immunized.

(4) Immunity from the antitrust laws may not be implied unless there is a plain repugnancy between the antitrust and regulatory provisions.[28]

A brief discussion of some cases will lend support to these principles.

United States v. Borden Co.,[29] involved indictments of milk producers, milk distributors, and others for engaging in an unlawful conspiracy

---

[27]Other regulatory statutes provide express immunity from the operation of the antitrust laws for certain conduct approved by the regulatory agency. E.g., Federal Aviation Act, 49 U.S.C. 1384; Federal Communications Act, 47 U.S.C. 221(a), 222(c) (1); The Shipping Act of 1916, 46 U.S.C. 814.

[28]See *United States v. Ass'n of Securities Dealers, Inc.*, 422 U.S. 694. See also *United States v. Philadelphia National Bank*, 374 U.S. 321, 350-51; *Gordon v. New York Stock Exchange*, 422 U.S. 659, 682.

[29]308 U.S. 188. See also *United States v. Socony-Vacuum Oil Co.*, 310 U.S. 150, 226-227; *Georgia v. Pennsylvania Railroad Co.*, 324 U.S. 439; *I.C.C. v. Parker*, 326 U.S. 60, 70.

under Section 1 of the Sherman Act. The dispositive issue before the Supreme Court was whether the Agricultural Marketing Agreement Act of 1937 and the Capper-Volstead Act had *per se* vested the Secretary of Agriculture with exclusive jurisdiction over the agreements which were the subject of the antitrust prosecution. Upon comparison of the Sherman Act and the Agricultural Act, the court found the former to be a broad enactment and the latter to be a limited statute with antitrust immunity provided for according to specifically enumerated conditions requiring prior approval of marketing agreements by the Secretary of Agriculture. Thus the agreements which were not approved under the specific terms of the regulatory act were fully subject to antitrust prosecution. A related principle was developed in the court's analysis of the effect of Capper-Volstead on Sherman Act jurisdiction. The Court found that the terms of the Capper-Volstead Act expressly premitted agricultural producers to combine for marketing purposes and to make contracts necessary for that collaboration. Section 6 of the Clayton Act relieved such agreements from the coverage of the antitrust laws. But the indictment charged not simply an agreement among producers, but rather their agreement with distributors, a union, city officials and others to control the milk market. As alleged in the indictment, the agreement was not the kind of arrangement covered by Capper-Volstead and, therefore, was outside the immunity afforded under the Act.

The Supreme Court reaffirmed the *Borden* decision in *Carnation Co. v. Pacific Westbound Conference.*[30] In that case a shipper brought a treble-damage action under the Sherman Act against two ocean shipping conferences whose members carried cargo in the United States-Far East Trades. The shipper alleged that the two had agreed to raise rates for the carriage of cargo to the Far East, and had carried the agreement out, charging the plaintiff the agreed-upon higher level of rates for a period of four years. The conferences moved to dismiss the case on the ground that the Shipping Act of 1916 *per se* repealed the antitrust laws insofar as they could be applied to industry rate-making activities. The Supreme Court found that Section 15 of the Shipping Act by its terms conferred antitrust immunity only over rate agreements approved by the FMC. Based on its prior decision in *Borden,* rejecting repeals of the antitrust laws by implication, the court held that the implementation of rate-making agreements which have not been approved by FMC is subject to the antitrust laws. The court was of the opinion that the language of Section 15 and its legislative history showed that Congress had intended

[30]383 U.S. 213.

to grant only limited antitrust immunity to certain types of agreements which had passed public scrutiny and examination by a governmental agency.

Marnell v. United Parcel Service of America,[31] involved a complaint charging United Parcel and its subsidiaries with conspiracy to restrain trade and monopolizing the retail parcel delivery service in the San Francisco area. The conspiracy was alleged to have been carried out by a number of methods including: The purchase of competitors; the acquisition from competitors of convenants not to compete and agreements not to protest defendants' applications for new operating authority; the maintenance of exclusive-use contracts with customers; and the establishment of unjustifiably low rates to induce new customers to sign exclusive-use contracts. Defendants moved alternatively to dismiss the complaint on exclusive jurisdiction grounds and to stay the action on primary jurisdiction grounds. The court denied both motions. The court rejected defendants' claims that the ICC had exclusive jurisdiction over motor carriers, basically on the reasoning of *Borden* and *Carnation*. The court found that the I.C. Act, like certain other regulatory acts, provided specifically for antitrust immunity only in limited areas. Since Congress had expressly limited antitrust immunity for motor carriers under the I.C. Act to specific situations, the court would not carve out a broader exemption by implication and judicial fiat. Nor did the ICC's power to control entry by the issuance of operating licenses or certificates compel a different result. The court found that on no occasion has the Supreme Court held that a federal regulatory act by implication completely displaced the antitrust laws.

American Mail Lines Ltd. v. Federal Maritime Com'n[32] involved a challenge to the authority of the FMC to approve an acquisition agreement under which two containership operators would become subsidiaries of the same corporate parent. The FMC approved the acquisition agreement on condition that the subsidiaries remain independent companies in competition with each other. The dispositive issue before the court was whether the FMC has jurisdiction to approve such an agreement under Section 15 of the Shipping Act of 1916 which requires all persons subject to that Act to file with the FMC every agreement within specified categories reached with any other person subject to the same Act. Of primary importance in the case is the express provision in Section 15 that approved agreements are exempt from the antitrust laws. The court held that the acquisition agreement was not the type of agreement

[31]260 F. Supp. 391.
[32]503 F. 2d 157, cert. denied, 419 U.S. 1070.

encompassed by Section 15 and that the FMC therefore lacked jurisdiction to approve the transaction. Again the court refused to carve out a broader exemption by implication and judicial fiat than that expressly limited by Congress.

California Motor Transport Co. v. Trucking Unlimited[33] makes it plain that extensive regulation by the ICC under the I.C. Act does not completely immunize parties from the antitrust laws. In *Trucking Unlimited,* the Supreme Court held that the institution of federal and State proceedings and actions to resist and defeat motor carrier applications for operating rights without probable cause and regardless of the merits of the case in furtherance of a conspiracy to exclude a competitor from a market are subject to challenge under the antitrust laws. In *Trucking Unlimited,* the use of State and federal agencies was a mere sham to cover what was nothing more than an attempt to interfere directly with the business relationships of a competitor and therefore the application of the antitrust laws was found to be justified.

The *Trucking Unlimited* case is therefore distinguishable from *Eastern Railroads Presidents Conference v. Noerr Motor Freight, Inc.,*[34] and *United Mine Workers v. Pennington.*[35] In *Noerr,* the court held that the antitrust laws do not forbid association for the purpose of influencing the passage of anticompetitive legislation, and recognized the First Amendment interests of association, assembly, and free speech involved in the case. In the *Noerr* case a group of truck companies and their trade associations sued under Section 4 of the Clayton Act for treble damages and injunctive relief against a number of railroads, a railroad association, and a public relations firm, charging them with conspiring to restrain trade in and to monopolize transportation of freight in alleged violations of Sections 1 and 2 of the Sherman Act. The gist of the conspiracy was that the railroads had engaged in a publicity campaign against the truckers designed to foster the adoption and retention of laws and law enforcement practices destructive of the trucking business, to create an atmosphere of distaste for the truckers among the general public, and to impair the relationship existing between the truckers and their customers. Specific charges were made as to particular instances in which the rail-

---

[33]404 U.S. 508.

[34]365 U.S. 127.

[35]381 U.S. 657. See also *Rush Hampton Industries v. Home Ventilating Institute,* 419 F. Supp. 19, 24; *Associated Radio Service Co. v. Page Airways, Inc.,* 414 F. Supp. 1089, 1096. The constitutional freedom "to petition the Government" does not extend to the petitioning of foreign governments, at least as far as the Sherman Act is concerned. *Cf. Occidental Petroleum Corp. v. Buttes Gas & Oil Co.,* 331 F. Supp. 92, 107-108, aff'd *per curiam,* 461 F. 2d 126, *cert. den.,* 409 U.S. 950.

roads had attempted to influence legislation by means of their publicity campaign including the use of so-called third-party technique, that is, the publicity matter circulated in the campaign being made to appear as spontaneously expressed views of independent persons and civic groups, when, in fact, it was largely produced for the railroads.

The Supreme Court held that such joint solicitation of government action with respect to the passage or enforcement of laws did not violate the Sherman Act, even if its purpose were to destroy competition and even if deceitful propaganda were used. Any other holding, the court said (pp. 137-8) would substantially impair the power of government to take actions through its legislature and executive departments; to hold that the government retains the power to act in a representative capacity and yet hold at the same time that the people cannot freely inform the government of their wishes would impute to the Sherman Act a purpose to regulate not business activity, but political activity, a purpose which would have no basis whatever in the legislative history of that Act. Further, the Supreme Court said, any other construction of the Sherman Act would raise important constitutional questions; the right of petition is one of the freedoms protected by the Bill of Rights.

In *Pennington* the Supreme Court held that a union and several large coal producers were not liable under the antitrust laws for successful lobbying which resulted in the Secretary of Labor's taking action adverse to small coal companies, and for the defendants' compliance with the resulting legislation. The court said (p. 670):

> Joint efforts to influence public officials do not violate the antitrust laws even though intended to eliminate competition. Such conduct is not illegal, either standing alone or as part of a broader scheme itself violative of the Sherman Act.

It is noted that in *Noerr* the Supreme Court in dicta (at p. 144) admonished that: "[t]here may be situations in which a publicity campain ostensibly directed toward influencing governmental action is a 'mere sham' to cover what is actually nothing more than an attempt to interfere directly with the business relationships of a competitor and the application of the Sherman Act would be justified." The effect of *Trucking Unlimited,* therefore, was to add dimension to the "sham" exception holding that concerted litigation and appeals from agency decisions designed to deter competitors from seeking new operating rights were not within the umbrella of the *Noerr-Pennington* protection, since such activities were not merely the exercise of defendant's right to petition, but were in reality efforts to deny their competitors equal opportunity to free and unimpaired right to access to the courts and administrative tribunals.

In sum, by denying their competitors access to such tribunals, defendants had usurped the decision-making process and made them the real regulators of the grants of rights, transfers, and registrations to plaintiffs.

In 1973 an indictment was returned against three mobile home carriers and certain individuals charging them with an unlawful conspiracy to restrain and monopolize trade and commerce in for-hire transportation of moble homes.[36] The indictment charged that defendants conspired to exclude competitors from the industry, to deprive their rate bureau members of the right of independent action, and to coerce others to join their rate bureau. In addition, the indictment charged the defendants had carried out their conspiracy by depriving others applying for authority to transport mobile homes of meaningful access to and fair hearings before federal and State agencies and courts. A motion to dismiss was filed on the ground of pervasive regulation. The motion was denied. In denying the motion the court believed that, as in *Trucking Unlimited*, agency action and procedures were used as a mere sham to cover anticompetitive behavior.

Proof of Damages

The *Noerr* decision was followed by the appellate court in *Association of Western Railways v. Riss & Company*, which reversed the judgment of the lower court.[37] Both the complaint and the evidence in the *Riss* case were largely though not entirely concerned with efforts of the defendants to influence legislative and administrative action. The judgment of the lower court was reversed for another reason also; it had erred in failing to accept the verdict first returned by the jury which found that some of the defendants had conspired but had not damaged the plaintiff. The lower court had asked the jury to return to the jury room to deliberate further after refusing to accept the no-damage verdict; and the jury subsequently brought in an altered verdict awarding damages. The lower court then trebeled the damages and allowed attorney's fees. The appellate court held that the finding that the conspiracy had not damaged plaintiff was also a finding that plaintiff had not proved its claims. Under Section 4 of the Clayton Act treble damages, costs and attorney's fees are allowed to a person who is "injured in his business or property by reason of anything forbidden in the antitrust laws."[38] The "gist of the action is

---

[36]United States v. Morgan Drive Away, et al., 1974 Trade Cases, Para. 74,888 (D.D.C., Cr. No. 697-73).
[37]299 F. 2d 133; cert. denied 370 U.S. 916.
[38]15 U.S.C. 15.

not merely the unlawful conspiracy . . . but is damage to the individual plaintiff resulting proximately from the acts of the defendant which constitute a violation of law."[39]

Proof of damages by plaintiff in an antitrust suit was discussed by the court in *Parmelee Transp. Co. v. Keeshin.*[40] There, plaintiff had failed to establish, prima facie, a *per se* violation of the antitrust law, thus, the court said, it was required to prove that the public at large had suffered or would suffer economic harm as a result of the alleged violation, the primary purpose of the statute being to protect the public from monopoly. In the light of these principles, Section 4 of the Clayton Act authorizing suits for treble damages places upon plaintiff the burden of establishing not merely his own damage but the actual or presumed harm to the public which is a prerequisite to a finding of Sherman Act violation; in that respect, allegations of a private claimant are no different than those required in a proceeding brought by the Government.[41]

Statutes Regulating Transportation Give Effect to the Public Policy of Preserving Competition

In addition to the antitrust laws, other legislation applicable to transportation has been enacted for the purpose of giving effect to the public policy of preserving competition. The statutes regulating transportation clearly embrace the principle of the preservation of healthy competitive conditions. Indeed, it has even been held that a new service may be authorized for the very purpose of providing the public with the benefits of competition. In *Chesapeake & Ohio Railway Company v. United States*[42] the Supreme Court said:

> In the absence of a plain declaration to that effect, it would be unreasonable to hold that Congress did not intend to empower the Commission to authorize construction of new lines to provide for shippers such competing service as it should find to be convenient or necessary in the public interest.

In *Davidson Transfer & Storage Company v. United States*[43] it was likewise held that "one of the weapons in the Commission's arsenal is the right to authorize competition."

---

[39]*Glenn Coal Co. v. Dickinson Fuel Co.,* 72 F. 2d 885, 887; *Keogh v. Chicago & N.W. Ry.,* 260 U.S. 156; *Hunter Douglas Corp. v. Lando Products, Inc.,* 235 F. 2d 631.

[40]186 F. Supp. 533, 538-9.

[41]*Ibid.,* p. 539.

[42]283 U.S. 35, 42.

[43]42 F. Supp. 215, 219, aff'd 317 U.S. 587.

The Commission has often considered the question of competition in connection with merger applications and applications for certificates of convenience and necessity.[44] In the *Santa Fe* case it was said:

Protestants cite many decisions of this Commission and other regulatory bodies to the effect that duplication of adequate existing service is unwarranted. In general the doctrine of these decisions is not questioned, but it can hardly be accepted without qualification, nor can it be said to be without exception. If we start with the question of what is an adequate existing service, we might very reasonably say that where there is ample traffic a dominant existing service without any effective competition is not all that experience has taught that the public needs for its best intersts and consequently is not for an adequate service. . . .

◦ ◦ ◦

The evidence indicates that by reason of the various mergers, acquisitions, contracts, and other arrangements heretofore referred to, the Pacific Southwest is threatened with a virtual monopoly in bus transportation. Such a situation would appear not to be in the public interest. Regulated monopoly is not a complete substitute for competition. The latter fosters research and experimentation and induces refinements in service which are not likely otherwise to be accomplished. Nor is it enough to say that rail and air service and the private automobile provide all the stimulus required, as vigorously contended by protestants. Bus travel no doubt makes its greatest appeal to a class of person who are either controlled by the element of cost or prefer to travel by highway and either do not own cars or do not care to drive their own cars long distances. It is questionable whether the air services or even the more expensive train services are real contenders for this patronage.

Competition from within the field of one's endeavor is one thing; that from without is quite another. Those inclined to patronize a bus service, for instance, may find its inherent advantages sufficiently attractive to induce them to use such service as is offered without demanding more. Thus, competition from without is met by the inherent advantages of a possibly inferior service, and the operator thrives while the patrons are denied that ultimate in service and convenience which they have a right to expect and which would be fostered by direct competition from within the field of endeavor.

It must be accepted then as an exception or qualification of the rule laid down in the cases above mentioned that an additional service may be required in the public interest even though an existing operator is supplying in quantum what appears to be a sufficient service, where there is lacking any worthy competitor of such operator in its own field and where the available business is ample to support another operation. (pp. 747-749)

---

[44]*Virginia Stage Lines, Inc. v. United States*, 48 F. Supp. 79, 81; *Santa Fe Trail Stages, Inc., Common Carrier Application*, 21 M.C.C. 725.

Separation of Competing Forms of Transportation

Section 5 of the Act to Regulate Commerce of 1887 was an absolute prohibition against the pooling of traffic of different and competing railroads, or any division of their earnings. This provision made it unlawful for any common carrier by railroad "to enter into any contract, agreement or combination with any other common carrier or carriers for the pooling of freights of different and competing railroads, or to divide between them the aggregate or net proceeds of such railroads, or any portion thereof."[45] Section 5 was amended by the Panama Canal Act of 1912,[46] which added a new paragraph making it unlawful "for any railroad company or other common carrier subject to the Act to regulate commerce to own, lease, operate, control, or have any interest whatsoever (by stock ownership or otherwise, either directly, indirectly, through any holding company, or by stockholders or directors in common, or in any other manner) in any common carrier by water operated through the Panama Canal or elsewhere with which said railroad or other carrier aforesaid does or may compete for traffic." Jurisdiction was conferred on the Commission "to determine questions of fact as to the competition or possibility of competition." The Commission was also given power to permit continuance of existing service which "will neither exclude, prevent, nor reduce competition on the route by water under consideration." It was under this provision that the Commission authorized continuance of railroad-owned steamship service between New York and various New England ports in *Steamer Lines on Long Island Sound.*[47] One Commissioner in dissenting, said:

> I agree with the conclusion that the service which the New Haven Railroad is providing through the steamship lines in question "is being operated in the interest of the public and is of advantage to the convenience and commerce of the people." Undoubtedly public opinion in New England strongly supports continued operation of these lines by the New Haven Railroad. If the public interest were the only standard prescribed by Congress for our guidance in this matter, I would have no difficulty in approving such continued operation. *But this is not the only standard. Congress also required, as a prerequisite to such approval, that we must find that the operation of the boat lines by the railroad "will neither ex-*

[45]24 Stat. 380.
[46]37 Stat. 566. President Taft in his message to Congress in December, 1910, had recommended legislation "prohibiting interstate commerce railroads from owning or controlling ships engaged in the trade through the Panama Canal." Papers relating to the Foreign Relations of the United States with Annual Message of the President Transmitted to Congress December 6, 1910, page XXXVII.
[47]50 I.C.C. 634, 183 I.C.C. 323, 349.

clude, prevent, nor reduce competition on the route by water under consideration." (Italics supplied.)

A finding was made, however, by the majority of the Commission that "performing of passenger service . . . *will neither exclude, prevent, nor reduce competition on the water route."* (Italics supplied.)

In an important case arising under the Panama Canal Act, *Lake Line Applications under Panama Canal Act,*[48] the Commission graphically depicted the consequences flowing from control of one type of transportation agency by another. The Commission there stated:

> These boat lines under the control of the petitioning railroads have been first a sword and then a shield. When these roads succeeded in gaining control of the boat lines which had been in competition with paralleling rails in which they were interested, and later effected their combination through the Lake Line Association, by which they were able to and did drive all independent boats from the through lake-and-rail transportation, they thereby destroyed the possibility of competition with their railroads other than such competition as they were of a mind to permit. Having disposed of real competition via the lakes, these boats are now held a shield against possible competition of new independents. Since it appears from the records that the railroads are able to operate their boat lines at a loss where there is now no competition from independent lines, it is manifest that they could and would operate at a further loss in a rate war against independents. The large financial resources of the owning railroads make it impossible for an independent to engage in a rate war with a boat line so financed.

Section 5 of the Transportation Act of 1920 gave the Commission the power to approve mergers and consolidations, and it was expressly provided that such approval would give immunity under the antitrust laws. The principle with respect to the separation of competing forms of transportation, however, continued to be maintained.

Congress wrote into the Motor Carrier Act of 1935 a proviso to Section 213(a) (1),[49] which was designed to preserve the motor carrier industry from domination or control by other forms of transportation which might use the control to curtail, strangle or hinder progress in highway transportation for the benefit of other competing transportation.

In the Transportation Act of 1940, Congress again affirmed its policy with respect to the separation of competing forms of transportation by re-enacting the restrictive provisions of the Panama Canal Act and of Section 213 of the Motor Carrier Act. Although fear was expressed that the slightly altered language of the two sections represented a

[48] 33 I.C.C. 700, 716.
[49] Stat. 555.

relaxation of the traditional Congressional policy,[50] the conferees in charge of the bill stated that the changes included in that Act were intended merely to clarify the earlier provisions and to leave the substance unchanged.[51]

Sections 211 and 212 of the Merchant Marine Act of 1936[52] are indicative of Congressional policy with respect to steamship participation in air transportation. It should be noted, however, that this Act was passed prior to the passage of the Federal Aviation Act and provided only for study by the Commission, and recommendation for further legislation, with respect to the applicability of the shipping acts to aircraft and the possible development of "super-liner" facilities, in connection with or in lieu of which transoceanic aircraft service might be used. This language of Sections 211 and 212 is obviously merely experimental or exploratory in its effect, and the actual growth of maritime facilities and of aviation has followed a somewhat different path than could have been envisaged in 1936.

The provisions of the I.C. Act relating to issuance of certificates authorizing institution of new service upon proof of public convenience and necessity are practically identical with those administered by the Civil Aeronautics Board in the field of air transportation. The same restrictions are found in the Federal Aviation Act as were found in the Motor Carrier Act of 1935. The second proviso of Section 408(b) of the Federal Aviation Act was patterned after the proviso contained in the Motor Carrier Act of 1935.[53] The terms of an earlier bill (H.R. 7273) had been extended to include not only air carriers but also *all* common carriers "in order to completely guard against the evils which may arise from such transactions."[54] That the Board may give effect to this policy and consider the requirements of Section 408(b) when

[50]Congressional Record, Vol. 86, pp. 10175-76, 10180-88, 11270-74, 11537-47, 11610-22, 11634-39, 11760-66.

[51]Congressional Record, Vol. 86, pp. 10175, 10188, 11270-74, 11543, 11546. In one instance a slight change of wording has had the effect of bringing about a different decision by the Commission in an acquisition proceeding, even though the conferees had stated that the two sections had the same force and effect. In *St. Johns River Line Company — Purchase — Edwards*, 25 M.C.C. 455, 36 M.C.C. 338, a water carrier was seeking to obtain control of a motor carrier. The application had been denied under Section 213(a) (1), but was granted under Section 5(2) (b), since the words "carrier other than a motor carrier" had been replaced in 1940 by the words "carrier by railroad."

[52]49 Stat. 1989-1990.

[53]Hearings before Committee on Interstate and Foreign Commerce on H.R. 5234, 75th Cong., 1st Sess.

[54]Hearings before Committee on Interstate and Foreign Commerce on H.R. 9738, 75th Cong., 3rd Sess.

passing upon applications for certificates of public convenience and necessity has been recognized by the courts.[55]

The Board announced in *American Export Airlines, Inc., American Export Lines — Control — American Export Airlines*[56] that the requirements of Section 408 would be deemed applicable in connection with the determination of public convenience and necessity under Section 401. The Board regarded it as clear,

> . . . that it must have been the purpose of Congress to prohibit, unless the conditions of Section 408, including its provisos, were met, the entry of carriers engaged in other forms of transportation into the air transportation field through wholly-owned subsidiaries irrespective of whether this was accomplished through the acquisition of a corporation engaged in an existing operation or of one about to inaugurate a new air transport service.
>
>   ❉   ❉   ❉
>
> In determining whether the "public convenience and necessity" require the granting of an application for a certificate by a carrier from another field of transportation, the Board must give substance to that term in accordance with the policy laid down by the Act as a whole. Therefore, in considering an application under Section 401 filled by a carrier other than an air carrier, we would not construe the public convenience and necessity as requiring the issuance of a certificate to such carrier unless the evidence indicates that the provisions of Section 408(b) are met.

Upon rehearing of this case, the Board said in *American Export Airlines, Inc., American Export Lines — Control — American Export Airlines:*[57]

> . . . after a reexamination of the record in light of the reargument, we are convinced that a construction of the . . . Act which rigidly limits the participation of the older forms of transportation in the air transport field is not only sustained by the language of the Act itself, but is also in harmony with well established Congressional policy, and will accomplish the national purpose in the particular manner which is prescribed by the second proviso of Section 408(b).
>
> The conclusion that there exists, and has existed for many years, a prevailing Congressional intent that the various forms of transportation should be mutually independent is well documented by legislative history.

A clear statement of the requirements which Section 408(b) makes with respect to the degree of integration and coordination necessary in order to constitute a common carrier service to which use of aircraft

---

[55]*Pan American Airways Company v. Civil Aeronautics Board,* 121 F. 2d. 810, 816.
[56]3 CAB 631, 637.
[57]CAB 104, 106.

is supplemental, auxiliary, or incidental was given by this Board in *American Export Airlines, Inc., American Export Lines — Control — American Export Airlines.*[58] In that case this Board said:

> . . . When the statute requires that the acquiring carrier shall be enabled by the acquisition "to use aircraft to public advantage in its operation" it obviously refers to its transport operations. As applied to the present case, the *phrase clearly refers only to Steamship Company's operations in a steamship service; and the aircraft involved, therefore, must be utilized in such steamship service.*
>
> *In view of the fact that the air service is not an integral part of the steamship operation but constitutes instead an alternative means of transportation to the steamship service from point of origin to destination, we are compelled to conclude that the requirements of the second proviso have not been met in this proceeding.* Nor can this conclusion be affected by the showing that (1) Steamship Company organized Airlines in lieu of constructing superliners in order to supplement its existing freight and tourist passenger steamship operations with a trans-Atlantic service for the deluxe passenger and fast express traffic, and thus enable it to compete with the superliner service of its competitors in other fields of steamship operations; or that (2) the control of Airlines by Steamship Company would enable Steamship Company to present to the public a full transport program and thus to maintain and improve its competitive position with foreign steamship companies; or that (3) the control of Airlines by Steamship Company would enable these two companies to coordinate communication, meteorological, and navigation facilities, and traffic and other operating functions in the manner shown by the record, with the alleged economies resulting therefrom.[59] (Italics Supplied.)

From the foregoing review of the authorities, it is clear that under the rulings established by previous decisions by the Board, the requirements of Section 408 must be met by surface carriers applying for a certificate of public convenience and necessity under Section 401. These requirements must be met whether the applicant is itself directly engaged in performing transportation as a carrier other than an air carrier, or whether such carrier puts forward a subsidiary or other affiliated company as applicant.

[58]4 CAB 104, 108-10.

[59]See also the Board's previous decision in the same case, 3 CAB 631. Compare the similar line of decisions by the I.C.C. under Section 5 of the I.C. Act, as amended (formerly Section 213 of the Motor Carrier Act of 1935). In *Pennsylvania Truck Lines, Inc. — Control — Barker Motor Freight, Inc.,* 5 M.C.C. 9, the Commission said:
> . . . Approved operations are those which are auxiliary or supplementary to train service. Except as hereinafter indicated, non-approved operations are those which otherwise compete with the railroad itself, those which compete with an established motor carrier, or which invade to a substantial degree a territory already adequately served by another rail carrier. (pp. 11-12)

Dealings in Securities, Supplies or Other Articles of Commerce, and Contracts for Construction or Maintenance of Any Kind

THE STATUTE

Section 10 of the Clayton Act[60] provides in relevant part:

> No common carrier engaged in commerce shall have any dealings in securities, supplies, or other articles of commerce, or shall make or have any contracts for construction or maintenance of any kind, to the amount of more than $50,000, in the aggregate, in any one year, with another corporation, firm, partnership, or association when the said common carrier shall have upon its board of directors or as its president, manager, or as its purchasing or selling officer, or agent in the particular transaction, any person who is at the same time a director, manager, or purchasing or selling officer of, or *who has any substantial interest in, such other corporation,* firm, partnership, or association, unless and except such purchases shall be made from, or such dealings shall be with, the bidder whose bid is the most favorable to such common carrier, to be ascertained by competitive bidding under regulations to be prescribed by rule or otherwise by the Interstate Commerce Commission. . . .[61]

The legislative history of Section 10 of the Clayton Act is recited in *United States v. Boston & Maine R. Co.,*[62] where the Supreme Court said:

> Section 10, indeed, has its roots in President Wilson's message to Congress of January 20, 1914, on the subject of "trusts," in which he denounced the abuses of "interlockings of the *personnel* of the directorates of great corporations." 51 Cong. Rec. 1962-1964; H. R. Rep. No. 627, 63d Cong., 2 Sess., pp. 17-18. Section 10 started as part of § 9 of the House bill and forbade certain types of interlocking office-holding. See S. Doc. No. 584, 63d Cong., 2d Sess., p. 10. The Senate made two main changes. First, it did not prohibit interlocking office-holding but seized rather on competitive bidding as the control. S. Rep. No. 698, 63d Cong., 2d Sess., pp. 47-48. Second, the Senate required competitive bidding not only when a director or other officer or agent of a common carrier was also a director or other officer of any firm with which the carrier had dealings to the amount of more than $50,000 in any one year, but also when the director or other officer of a common carrier had "any direct or indirect interest in" the other firm. S. Doc. No. 584, 63rd Cong., 2d Sess.,

---

[60]U.S.C. 20. Note that the statute uses the term "dealings" thus non-buying and selling transactions would be included such as, licenses and leases, just as they are under the Sherman Act. Note also that the term "articles of commerce" is used which would cover services.

[61]Even though there is compliance with the competitive bidding regulations it is possible to have a violation of Section 10 of the Clayton Act if there is involved a conspiracy to prevent meaningful bidding. *In re the Pittsburgh and Lake Erie Railroad Company Securities and Antitrust Litigation,* 378 F. Supp. 441.

[62]380 U.S. 157.

p. 13. The Conference changed the phrase "any direct or indirect interest in" to the present wording "any substantial interest in." *Ibid.*, pp. 13-14. As Senator Chilton, one of the Conferees, reported:

> It not only prevents corporations which are interlocked by officers and directors, but it says: "Or who has any substantial interest in such of them."

> The Senator will recall all we had before us, the ease by which interlocking directorates could be gotten around; in other words, you could have your son, or your cousin, or your lawyer, or your agent upon the corporation and accomplish the same thing as if you were on the board yourself. . . .

> They cannot dodge it by having a supply company, and even though they have discarded the form of interlocking directors, if there be the interest of the railroad or the common carrier in the supply company, as the Senator chooses to call it, then it is prohibited. 51 Cong. Rec. 15943.

Interpretation of Words "Substantial Interest In" As Used in Section 10 of the Clayton Act

The words "substantial interest in" as used in Section 10 of the Clayton Act[63] were interpreted by the Supreme Court in *United States v. Boston & Maine R. Co.* to mean an existing investment of some kind in the noncarrier company, or the creation of the noncarrier company by individuals for their use, or a joint venture or continued course of dealings, licit or illicit, with the noncarrier company for profit sharing. The court commented that while "history shows a rather wide pattern of railroad misconduct leading to Section 10, that section is a rather narrow prohibition applicable to activity that is conceptually within the antitrust philosophy" and the statute cannot be broadened to include a bribe "unless we attribute to Congress a purpose to make it a more general panacea for conflict of interest activities."

Commission's Function

The Commission's sole function under Section 10 of the Clayton Antitrust Act[64] is to furnish to the Attorney General the evidence it secures when it believes such evidence shows a violation of that Section together with its views or findings regarding the transaction involved.

---

[63]15 U.S.C. 20.

[64]*Automatic Train Control Devices,* 112 I.C.C. 259, 268; *Codman v. Boston & Maine R.R.,* 157 I.C.C. 552, 554; *Greyhound Securities,* 1939, 25 M.C.C. 365, 367.

It has no power to enforce Section 10 of the Clayton Act. Nor are other regulatory agencies given such power. Injunctive actions by private parties are not authorized.[65]

Interpretative Cases

There are a number of reported cases which interpret Section 10 of the Clayton Act.

In *Re Missouri Pacific R. R. Co.*,[66] involved the validity, in a railroad reorganization proceeding in bankruptcy, of contracts of that rail carrier for purchase from its affiliate, Terminal Shares, Inc., of capital stock of certain realty corporations, for the allegedly exorbitant price of $1,600,000 per year without competitive bidding. The court held that in view of the interlocking directorates between the rail carrier and Terminal Shares, Inc., and in view of the fact that competitive bidding is impossible when the subject matter consists of stock shares of other corporations, Section 10 of the Clayton Act absolutely forbade the dealings between the railroad and its affiliate. The trustees in bankruptcy were ordered to disaffirm the contracts and to take steps to recover from Terminal Shares, Inc., the money already paid under them by the railroad. The court stated (pp. 892-3):

> . . . I think it rather clearly provides that when interlocking directorates exist between a railroad which is engaged in interstate commerce, and another railroad, or corporation, then unless competitive bids are obtained, such corporations are forbidden to deal with each other. And if, as already said, in this situation existing here, no competitive bids are possible, then the statute forbids the deal absolutely. . . .

In *Beegle v. Thomson*,[67] one of the allegations against Sharon Steel Corporation, a manufacturer of railroad anti-splitting irons for railway ties, was that by Sharon's using its large volume of traffic to coerce purchases by the Pennsylvania Railroad of anti-splitting irons from Sharon in excess of $50,000 per year, without competitive bidding, in violation of Section 10 of the Clayton Act, plaintiff Beegle was precluded from selling his own anti-splitting irons to the railroad. The court held that as the plaintiff had not alleged any interlocking directorships or other agency relationships between Sharon and the railroad, the allegation in question could not be sustained on its face.

[65]*International T. & T. Corp. v. General T. & E. Corp.*, 351 F. Supp. 1153.
[66]13 F. Supp. 888.
[67]138 F. 2d 875, cert. den. 322 U.S. 743.

Independent Iron Works, Inc. v. U.S. Steel Corp.,[68] involved an action against a steel company on the ground that it conspired with a railroad which had a common director to prevent free and competitive bidding on railroad car underframes. The court held that the fact that the railroad accepted the steel company's bids on car underframes, although such bids were not in dollar amount the lowest bids submitted, would not support any inference of conspiracy of any wrongdoing by the steel company.

An interpretation of Section 10 was made by the Supreme Court in *Minneapolis St. Louis R. Co. v. United States,*[69] where it said:

> Section 10 of the Clayton Act is, of course, an antitrust law, and much of what we have just said relative to the problem of accommodation of Section 5(2) of the Interstate Commerce Act and the antitrust law is equally applicable to this contention. The evident purpose of Section 10 of the Clayton Act was to prohibit a corporation from abusing a carrier by palming off upon it securities, supplies and other articles without competitive bidding and at excessive prices through overreaching by, or other misfeasance of, common directors, to the financial injury of the carrier and the consequent impairment of its ability to serve the public interest.[70] But even if this purchase of securities might, under other circumstances violate Section 10 of the Clayton Act, Congress, by Section 5(11) of the Interstate Commerce Act, has authorized the Commission to approve if it finds that so doing is in the public interest. And Congress has expressly said that, upon such approval, the carrier shall be relieved "from the operation of the anti-trust laws . . ." a contrary view would, in effect, permit the Commission to authorize only those stock purchases which would not, in the absence of Section 5(11), offend the anti-trust laws. "As has been said, this would render meaningless the exemption relieving the participants in a properly approved (acquisition) of the requirements of those laws . . ." *McLean Trucking Co. v. United States, supra,* at 86.

Unless there is statutory language providing for exemption from the operation of the Clayton Act, such as is provided by Section 5(11) of the I.C. Act, the Commission is without power to grant any exemptions. The *Minneapolis St. Louis* case makes it plain that Section 5(11) gives power to the Commission to exempt carriers from the operation of the Clayton

[68]177 F. Supp. 743.
[69]361 U.S. 173, 190-1. See also *Cleary v. Chalk,* 488 F. 2d 1315, 1321.
[70]The legislative history of Section 10 of the Clayton Act, though meager, supports the view stated in the text. In fact, the language of the several drafts of Section 10, together with the types of abuses cited in support of its enactment, suggests strongly that the words "dealing in securities" were intended to cover only a carrier's dealings with related persons in its own securities. See H.R. Rep. No. 627, 63rd Cong., 2d Sess., p. 3; S. Rep. No. 698, 63rd Cong., 2d Sess., pp. 47-48; S. Doc. No. 585, 63rd Cong., 2d Sess., pp. 8-9; 51 Cong. Rec. 15943.

Act for transactions under Section 5(2) (a). On the other hand, *Securities of Western Pacific Railroad Co.*,[71] makes it reasonably clear that where a transaction comes within the scope of the Clayton Act, and there is no provision for exemption from the operation of the Clayton Act, the requirements of the Clayton Act must be met.

In *Securities of Western Pacific Railroad Company*, $800,000 of preferred capital stock of the Western Pacific was to be sold at par for cash to the Western Pacific Railroad Corporation, a Delaware holding company, which had directors in common with, and owned the capital stock of, the Western Pacific. The Commission said (p. 751):

> The sale is proposed to be made without compliance with Section 10 of the Clayton Antitrust Act. The Western Pacific claims that, in view of the plenary regulatory power conferred upon us by Section 20a of the Interstate Commerce Act over the issuance of securities by carriers subject to the Act, it is reasonable to conclude that it was the intention of Congress to give us sole and exclusive jurisdiction with regard to the issuance and disposition of all common-carrier securities to the exclusion of the provisions of Section 10 of the Clayton Antitrust Act pertaining to dealings in securities. This is a question which we do not undertake to decide. We are of the opinion, however, that in the sale of this stock the Western Pacific should comply with the provisions of Section 10 of the Clayton Antitrust Act, in so far as applicable. Our order will so provide.

In *Cleary v. Chalk*,[72] defendant D. C. Transit System had conveyed properties allegedly worth substantially more than the securities—the corporate stocks—received in return, and allegedly had divested itself of the earning power and the load value which those properties possessed. The court held that the transactions did not fall within the condemnation of Section 10 of the Clayton Act. In support of its holding, the court said (at p. 1322) that "[t]he literal wording of [a] statute is . . . not the sole index to legislative intent," adding

> We think the factor entitled to dominance in tightening the interpretation to be given Section 10 is the specific object which Congress had in mind in enacting it. What Congress sought, we repeat, was protection against the draining away of carrier assets by noncompetitive acquisitions for which the carrier pays too much, or by noncompetitive dispositions for which it nets too little. We turn, then, to the case at bar to ascertain whether the conveyances complained of impinged in that way on Section 10.

The court pointed out that at the time of each conveyance that each corporate conveyee was a wholly owned subsidiary of Transit. It said (p. 1322):

---

[71]145 I.C.C. 750.
[72]488 F. 2d 1315.

To be sure the conveyances effected a legal transformation of Transit's ownership of real estate to ownership of stock, but in the practical sense Transit's position hardly changed at all. Its complete ownership of the stock of the corporations having direct ownership of the realty was tantamount to continuing proprietorship of the realty. By virtue of its exclusive power to control the subsidiaries, Transit retained full dominion over the properties. Its economic relationship to the properties after the conveyances was virtually the same as it had been before.

In *Klinger v. Baltimore and Ohio R. Co.*,[73] the court held that B. & O. which, without competitive bidding, acquired another railroad's one-half interest in a jointly owned terminal had violated Section 10 of the Clayton Act but that it was not liable for damages.[74] The railroads had interlocking directors.[75] The court said (p. 512):

> The proper inquiry, therefore, is whether Section 10 imposes a duty upon any interlocked corporation dealing with a common carrier not to deal with that carrier except through competitive bidding. We find it does and that civil liability is imposed on one in B & O's position.[76]

It was argued in the *Klinger* case that the railroads were exempt from the operation of Section 10 of the Clayton Act by reason of Section 20a (12) of the I.C. Act. The court did not accept this implied immunity argument.

Interlocking Directorate

Section 20a(12)[77] provides in part as follows:

> After December 31, 1921, it shall be unlawful for any person to hold the position of officer or director of more than one carrier, unless such holding shall have been authorized by order of the Commission, upon due showing, in form and manner prescribed by the Commission, that neither public nor private interests will be adversely affected thereby.

---

[73]432 F. 2d 506.

[74]The court indicated that the evidence showed that the B & O actually paid more than the other railroad could reasonably have been expected to have been offered by any purchase solicited through competitive bidding.

[75]The court found that Section 10 of the Clayton Act was applicable to both horizontal and vertical interlocks.

[76]See *In re The Pittsburgh and Lake Erie Railroad Company Securities and Antitrust Litigation*, 378 F. Supp. 441, where the court (at p. 446) cited with approval the position taken by the dissent in the *Klinger* case where it was stated that the absence of competitive bidding as required by the first paragraph of Section 10 of the Clayton Act is per se injurious.

[77]49 U.S.C. 20a(12). Comparable statutes: Section 409(a) of the Federal Aviation Act, 49 U.S.C. 1379(a); Section 10 of the Clayton Act, 15 U.S.C. 20. Section 8 of the Clayton Act, 15 U.S.C. 19, prohibits interlocks between competing companies but carriers regulated by the Commission are exempted.

The statute affords no specific tests to be applied in determining whether public or private interests will be adversely affected.[78] However, the criteria which an applicant under Section 20a(12) must affirmatively satisfy has been outlined in *Chesapeake & O. Ry. Co. Purchase.*[79] In that case the Commission said (at p. 18):

> In determining whether an applicant had met the requirement of the statute we have held that (1) a showing of the absence of competition between the carriers involved is essential (*In re Rand,* 175 I.C.C. 587), and is even more important since the enactment of the Transportation Act of 1940 than prior thereto (*In re Coverdale,* 244 I.C.C. 567, 569); (2) even in the absence of direct competition of parallel tracks, if either carrier has an election, as between the other carrier and another road or roads, as to routing of traffic at interchange points, public and private interests will be adversely affected by an interlocking directorate (*In re Rand, supra, In re Coverdale, supra, In re Boatner,* 257 I.C.C. 369, 372); (3) the applicant must show that there are no existing or prospective conflicts between the interests of the respective carriers, e. g., if there are prospective negotiations between the carriers in question for consolidation of their properties, no person, regardless of his high character, should "be asked or permitted to sit on both sides of the table" *(In re Astor, supra);* (4) the applicant must show that the interlocking positions "will not tend to accomplish or effectuate the control or management in a common interest of the carriers" and "will not tend to interfere with the independence of those carriers" *(In re Coverdale, supra);* and (5) because of the importance of maintaining complete independence and impartiality between major railroad companies or systems and the possibility of competition and conflict of interest between such railroads or systems, a person should not be permitted to serve as officer or director of more than one such railroad or system, except in special circumstances *(In re Boatner, supra).*

Robinson-Patman Act

Mention should be made of Section 2(c) of the *Robinson-Patman Act,*[80] the so-called brokerage provision, since it has a relationship to the provisions found in the I.C. Act, Federal Aviation Act, and Shipping Act of 1916 pertaining to discriminatory practices and other unfair methods of competition. Furthermore, Section 2(c) is applicable to anyone engaged in commerce, thus if transportation agencies engage in activities as purchasers of supplies and equipment which are condemned by Section 2(c), they would fall within the reach of the statute.

Section 2(c) provides that it is "unlawful for any person engaged in

---

[78]*Boyd Application* Under Section 20a(12), 333 I.C.C. 815, 818.
[79]271 I.C.C. 5.
[80]15 U.S.C. 13(c).

commerce, in the course of such commerce, to pay or grant, or to receive or accept, anything of value as a commission, brokerage, or other compensation, or any allowance or discount in lieu thereof except for services rendered in connection with the sale or purchase of goods, wares, or merchandise, either to the other party to such transaction or to an agent, representative, or other intermediary therein where such intermediary is acting in fact for or in behalf, or is subject to the direct or indirect control, of any party to such transaction other than the person by whom such compensation is so granted or paid." The legislative history of Section 2(c) is set out in *Federal Trade Commission v. Henry Broch & Co.*[81] as follows:

> The Robinson-Patman Act was enacted in 1936 to curb and prohibit all devices by which large buyers gained discriminatory preferences over smaller ones by virtue of their greater purchasing power. A lengthy investigation revealed that the large chain buyers were obtaining competitive advantages in several ways other than direct price concessions and were thus avoiding the impact of the Clayton Act. One of the favorite means of obtaining an indirect price concession was by setting up "dummy" brokers who were employed by the buyer and who, in many cases, rendered no services. The large buyers demanded that the seller pay "brokerage" to these fictitious brokers who then turned it over to their employer. This practice was one of the chief targets of § 2(c) of the Act. But it was not the only means by which the brokerage function was abused and Congress in its wisdom phrased § 2(c) broadly, not only to cover the other methods then in existence but all other means by which brokerage could be used to effect price discrimination.
>
> The particular evil at which § 2(c) is aimed can be as easily perpetrated by a seller's broker as by the seller himself. The seller and his broker can of course agree on any brokerage fee that they wish. Yet when they agree upon one, only to reduce it when necessary to meet the demands of a favored buyer, they use the reduction in brokerage to undermine the policy of § 2(c). The seller's broker is clearly "any person" as the words are used in § 2(c) as clearly such a buyer's broker.

The Supreme Court said in a footnote to its analysis of the legislative history of Section 2(c) that "Congress had before it examples not only of large buyers demanding the payment of brokerage to their agents but also instances where buyers demanded discounts, allowances, or outright price reductions based on the theory that fewer brokerage services were needed in sales to these particular buyers, or that no brokerage services were necessary at all. . . . These transactions were described in the report as the giving of 'allowances in lieu of brokerage . . .' or 'discount[s] in lieu of brokerage'."

[81]363 U.S. 166, 168-170.

Violations of Section 2(c) of the Robinson-Patman Act, unlike Section 2(a), do not depend upon a showing of adverse effects flowing from the challenged transactions. Hence, the degree of control over the market by a respondent is irrelevant to a charge of a violation of Section 2(c). A functional discount is permitted under Section 2(a), that is, the section permits a price difference to buyers in different noncompetitive functional classes. On the other hand, Section 2(c) "expresses an absolute prohibition of the payment of brokerage or compensation in lieu thereof, to the buyer upon the buyer's own purchases";[82] and it is independent of Section 2(a).[83]

[82]*Great Atlantic & Pacific Tea Co. v. Federal Trade Commission*, 106 F. 2d 667, 673, cert. denied 308 U.S. 625.
[83]*Federal Trade Commission v. Henry Broch & Co.*, 363 U.S. 166.

42

Unfair Methods of Competition
by Air Carriers

The Applicable Statutory Provisions

Section 411 of the Federal Aviation Act[1] provides that the "Board may, upon its own initiative or upon complaint by any air carrier, foreign air carrier, or ticket agent, if it considers that such action by it would be in the interest of the public, investigate and determine whether any air carrier, foreign air carrier, or ticket agent has been or is engaged in unfair or deceptive practices or unfair methods of competition in air transportation or the sale thereof." Section 411 provides further that if "the Board shall find, after notice and hearing, that such air carrier, foreign air carrier, or ticket agent is engaged in such unfair or deceptive practices or unfair methods of competition, it shall order such air carrier, foreign air carrier, or ticket agent to cease and desist from such practices or methods of competition." The words in the statute reading "has been or is engaged in unfair . . . practices or unfair methods of competition," the Supreme Court said in *Pan American World Airways v. United States*,[2] plainly include practices started before the 1938 Act and continued thereafter. The court pointed out that the Sherman Act was applied to pre-1890 combinations,[3] and that in *United States v. DuPont & Co.*,[4] it was stated that the "test of a violation of Section 7 (of the Clayton Act) is whether, at the time of the suit, there is a reasonable

---

[1]4 U.S.C. 1381.
[2]9 L. ed. 2d 325.
[3]*United States v. Trans-Missouri Freight Assn.*, 166 U.S. 290. See also *Waters-Pierce Oil Co. v. Texas*, 212 U.S. 86, 107-8; *Cox v. Hart*, 260 U.S. 427, 435; *American P. & L. v. Securities & Exchange Comm'n*, 141 F. 2d 606, 625, aff'd 329 U.S. 90.
[4]353 U.S. 586, 607.

probability that the acquisition is likely to result in the condemned restraints."

Vindicating the Public Interest

The words "unfair practices" and "unfair methods of competition" are not limited to precise practices that can readily be delineated, but derive meaning from the facts of each case and the impact of particular practices on competition and monopoly. The words are derived from Section 5 of the Federal Trade Commission Act, and their meaning in the setting of that Act has been discussed by the courts.[5] The words do not embrace a remedy for private wrongs but only a means of vindicating the public interest.[6] As respects the "public interest" under Section 411, the Supreme Court in *American Airlines v. North American Airlines*[7] said that air carriers conduct their business under a regulated system of limited competition and the "business so conducted is of especial and essential concern to the public, as is true of all common carriers and public utilities."

In *Federal Trade Comm'n. v. Raladam Co.*,[8] the Supreme Court concluded that "unfair competition" was that practice which destroys competition and establishes monopoly. The court said further that the provisions of Section 5 of the Federal Trade Commission Act was designed to supplement the Sherman Act by stopping "in their incipiency those methods of competition which fall within the meaning of the word 'unfair'" and that Section 5, together with the Sherman Act and Clayton Act, "seek to protect the public from abuses arising in the course of competitive interstate and foreign trade."[9] No matter what unfair practice or unfair method is employed, Section 411 of the Federal Aviation Act, like Section 5 of the Federal Trade Commission Act, was designed to bolster and strengthen antitrust enforcement.

Power of the Board

Under the decision of the Supreme Court in *Pan American World Airways v. United States*,[10] it has been held that the power of the Board

---

[5]*American Airlines v. North American Airlines*, 351 U.S. 79, 82.
[6]*Federal Trade Comm'n v. Klesner*, 280 U.S. 19, 25-30.
[7]351 U.S. 79, 84.
[8]283 U.S. 643, 649-50.
[9]*Ibid.*, p. 647. See also *Federal Trade Comm'n v. Beechnut Co.*, 257 U.S. 441, 453-4; *Federal Trade Comm'n v. Keppel & Bros.*, 291 U.S. 304, 310-12; S. Rep. No. 597, 63d Cong., 2d Sess., p. 13.
[10]9 L. ed. 2d 325.

to issue a cease and desist order for a violation of Section 411 is broad enough to include the power to compel divestiture and that this power runs not only to air carriers but to others. The court called attention to the fact that there is no express authority for divestiture in either the Sherman Act or the Clayton Act, and said that the reasoning that supports such a remedy under those Acts is as applicable to the Board as it is to the courts, and it is as valid today as it was when originally stated in *Northern Securities Co. v. United States*.[11] There the Supreme Court had commented in regard to the Sherman Act that "All will agree that if the . . . Act be constitutional, and if the combination in question be in violation of its provisions, the courts may enforce the provisions of the statute by such orders and decrees as are necessary or appropriate to that end and as may be consistent with the fundamental rules of legal procedure."

The dissolution of unlawful combinations, when based on appropriate findings, thus is an historic remedy in the antitrust field, even though not expressly authorized.[12] The Supreme Court has previously related the power of administrative agencies to fashion appropriate relief to the power of courts to fashion Sherman Act decrees.[13] The Supreme Court has stated that authority to mold administrative decrees is like the authority of courts to frame injunctive decrees subject to judicial review.[14] Likewise, the power to order divestiture need not be explicitly included in the powers of an administrative agency to be a part of its arsenal of authority.[15]

The court emphasized in *Pan American World Airways v. United States*[16] that its holding in regard to the broad powers of the Board did not mean that there are "no antitrust violations left to the Department of Justice to enforce." The court said that apart from orders which give immunity from the antitrust laws by reason of Section 414, "the whole criminal law enforcement problem remains unaffected by the Act" and, moreover, "on the civil side violation of antitrust laws other than those enumerated in the Act might be imagined."[17] The court said that it hesitated to hold, as it did in comparable situations, that the regulatory

---

[11]193 U.S. 197, 344.

[12]*Shine Theatres v. United States*, 334 U.S. 110, 129-30; *United States v. Crescent Amusement Co.*, 323 U.S. 173, 189.

[13]*Federal Trade Comm'n v. Mandel Bros.*, 359 U.S. 385, 392-3.

[14]*Labor Board v. Express Pub. Co.*, 312 U.S. 426, 433, 436; *Labor Board v. Cheney Lumber Co.*, 327 U.S. 385.

[15]*Gilbertville Trucking Co. v. United States*, 371 U.S. 115. Cf. *Federal Trade Comm'n. v. Eastman Kodak Co.*, 274 U.S. 619.

[16]9 L. ed. 2d 325.

[17]*Ibid.*

scheme adopted for air carriers in 1938 "was designed completely to displace the antitrust laws — absent an unequivocally declared congressional purpose so to do."[18] The comparable situations noted by the court included *Georgia v. Pennsylvania R. Co.,* [19] holding that the Act was no bar to an antitrust suit against a carrier; *United States v. R.C.A.,*[20] holding that the Federal Communications Act was no bar to an antitrust suit; *United States v. Borden & Co.,*[21] holding that the Agricultural Adjustment Act did not displace the Sherman Act; and *California v. Federal Power Comm'n*[22] holding that the Clayton Act was not displaced by the Natural Gas Act.

[18]*Ibid.*
[19]324 U.S. 439.
[20]358 U.S. 334.
[21]308 U.S. 188, 195-99.
[22]369 U.S. 482; *see also Milk Producers Assn. v. United States,* 362 U.S. 458.

43

Primary Jurisdiction

Expertise of Administrative Bodies and Need for Uniformity of Ruling

Originally, two considerations were used by the Supreme Court in developing the doctrine of primary jurisdiction. The first of these considerations was that a uniformity of ruling was essential to comply with the purposes of the regulatory statute to be administered. Should courts be free to determine independently whether rates, rules or practices of carriers were reasonable or nondiscriminatory, uniformity, which was one of the objectives of Congress in enacting the Act to Regulate Commerce, would become impossible. Only if that Act were read as conferring on the Interstate Commerce Commission exclusive jurisdiction to decide these questions, could the desired consistency be attained and preserved. The alternative was a chaotic system of transportation which might lead to discrimination far worse than Congress had intended to legislate against. The second consideration was that the problems involved in the suit demanded the exercise of administrative discretion. There were required the special knowledge, experience and services of an administrative body to determine technical and intricate matters of fact not peculiarly within the judicial competence.

In the course of the development of administrative law greater reliance was placed on administrative agencies to determine questions which were essentially of fact and required competence and discretion in technical matters. Because a question is essentially one of fact does not necessarily mean that it is one within the special competence of the administrative body. As pointed out by the Supreme Court in *Pennsylvania Railroad Co. v. Puritan Coal Mining Co.*[1] an ordinary issue of fact such as that involved in the case would not require prior determination

[1]237 U.S. 121.

by the administrative agency. In that case, a railroad was sued by a shipper in a state court for damages caused by the failure on the part of the railroad to furnish an adequate number of freight cars required for the shipment of coal. The shipper did not challenge the railroad's tariff rule pertaining to the distribution of cars, but instead based its case on the failure to furnish cars equitably in accordance with the rule.

Reliance on this so-called expertise of administrative bodies finds expression in *Great Northern Railway Co. v. Merchants Elevator Co.,*[2] where Mr. Justice Brandeis, speaking for the Supreme Court, said (p. 291) that "(W)henever a rate, rule or practice is attacked as unreasonable or as unjustly discriminatory, there must be preliminary resort to the Commission." In some instances, the court said (p. 291) "this is required because the function being exercised is in its nature administrative in contra-distinction to judicial," however, "ordinarily the determining factor is not the character of the function, but the character of the controverted question and the nature of the enquiry necessary for its solution." If the question is to determine what rate, rule, or practice is to be deemed reasonable for the future there is involved a legislative or administrative function, but if the question is to determine whether a shipper has in the past been injured by the exaction of an unreasonable or discriminatory rate then it constitutes a judicial function.

In either event, the court pointed out (p. 291), preliminary resort to the administrative body is required "because the enquiry is essentially one of fact and of discretion in technical matters; and uniformity can be secured only if its determination is left to the Commission." The court recognized (p. 291) that such determinations are "reached ordinarily upon voluminous and conflicting evidence, for the adequate appreciation of which acquaintance with many intricate facts of transportation is indispensable; and such acquaintance is commonly to be found only in a body of experts." Dependence on the expertise of administrative agencies also finds expression in the decision of the Supreme Court in *Rochester Telephone Corp. v. United States*[3] where the court made reference (p. 139) to "the primary jurisdiction doctrine, firmly established in *Texas & Pacific Ry. Co. v. Abilene Cotton Oil Co.*, 204 U.S. 426," and declared that "matters which call for technical knowledge pertaining to transportation must first be passed upon by the Interstate Commerce Commission before a court can be invoked."

The doctrine of primary administrative jurisdiction as shown in the foregoing stems directly from the landmark case of *Texas and Pacific*

[2]259 U.S. 285.
[3]307 U.S. 125.

Ry. Co. v. Abilene Cotton Oil Co.,[4] which constituted the first expression by the Supreme Court upon the question. That case involved a suit brought by a shipper against a carrier in a state court subsequent to the enactment of the Act to Regulate Commerce to recover a part of the charge fixed by a tariff schedule and paid by the shipper on some carloads of cottonseed under an allegation that the tariff rate was unreasonable. The Supreme Court, in reviewing a judgment of recovery granted by the state court, reversed and remanded the case on the ground (p. 448) that the party challenging the reasonableness of the rates in the published tariff should "primarily invoke redress through the Interstate Commerce Commission, which body alone is vested with power originally to entertain proceedings for the alteration of an established schedule." As the celebrated opinion of Mr. Justice White (as he then was) makes clear, the decision of the court that the Commission had exclusive primary jurisdiction in cases involving the reasonableness of rates rested on a simple practical consideration (p. 440), "For if, without previous action by the Commission, power might be exerted by courts and juries generally to determine the reasonableness of an established rate, it would follow that unless all courts reached an identical conclusion a uniform standard of rates in the future would be impossible." It was this desire to assure uniformity and consistency in the regulation entrusted to the administrative agency which originally led the Supreme Court to enunciate the doctrine of primary jurisdiction.

Lack of Jurisdiction Concept

It would appear that the *Abilene* case was required to be read as holding that no jurisdiction existed in the courts to permit an action for reparations arising out of alleged unreasonable rates to be instituted until the Commission had *in limine* declared the charges to be unreasonable and illegal. This "no jurisdiction" concept, however, was considered again by the *Supreme Court* in *Southern Railway Co. v. Tift*[5] which was decided within a very short time after the ruling in the *Abilene* case. The *Tift* case involved a suit brought against a carrier for an injunction to prevent a new and higher tariff from being effectuated, which action was permitted by a federal court to remain in abeyance until the shipper had first resorted to the Commission for a determination of the unreasonableness of the new rate. Upon a declaration by the Commission that the new rate was unreasonable, the shipper was

[4] 204 U.S. 426.
[5] 206 U.S. 428.

allowed to seek reparations in the Federal court as one of the incidents in the proceeding still pending and was granted both injunctive relief and an award of damages, which decree and judgment were upheld by the Supreme Court.

It was recognized by the court that the *Tift* case presented serious questions in view of the *Abilene* case, but (p. 437) "(W)e are not required to say, however, that because an action at law for damages to recover unreasonable rates which have been exacted in accordance with the schedule of rates as filed, is forbidden by the Interstate Commerce Act, a suit in equity is also forbidden to prevent a filing or enforcement of a schedule of unreasonable rates or a change to unjust or unreasonable rates." To have recognized jurisdiction in the lower court to permit not only the filing, and holding in abeyance, of the suit for injunctive relief, but also the granting of subsequent judicial relief, by awarding damages, inescapably implied a clear departure from the lack-of-jurisdiction doctrine in the Abilene case despite the absence of any direct admission in the opinion of the Supreme Court.

In *Mitchell Coal and Coke Co. v. Pennsylvania Railroad Co.*,[6] the Supreme Court made a further retreat from the "no-jurisdiction" concept by giving implicit recognition to the right of a shipper to institute a judicial action for damages and have it held in abeyance pending resort to the Commission for a determination of the question of unreasonableness and illegality. There, a shipper sued a railroad for damages charging the payment of rebates by the railroad to competing shippers. The carrier defended on the ground that the allowances which were alleged to constitute rebates were for services performed by the competing shippers and that the action could not be maintained until their reasonableness had been determined by the Commission. The lower court dismissed the suit on the ground that it had no jurisdiction until the Commission had passed upon the legality of the allowances and the reasonableness of the amount paid to the competing shippers.

The Supreme Court held that certain of the payments were not for services rendered, and so constituted rebates which were clearly illegal. As to those payments, an action could be maintained without primary resort to the Commission. Other payments, however, were for services performed by the shipper and their validity could be determined only by the Commission. With respect to the disposition of this part of the case, the unsettled state of the law at the time the suit was begun and the failure of the defendant to make the jurisdictional point *in limine* so that the plaintiff could then have presented its claim to the Commission and obtained an order as to the "reasonable-

[6]230 U.S. 247.

ness of the practice or allowance," dismissal of the action should be stayed. This, the court said, would give the shipper a reasonable opportunity in which to apply to the Commission for a ruling as to the reasonableness of the practice and the allowance involved, and, if in favor of the shipper, it would have the right to proceed with the trial of the cause in the lower court, at which time the carrier would "have the right to be heard on its plea of the statute of limitations as of the time the suit was filed and any other defense which it may have" (p. 267).

The Supreme Court gave unstinted approval of the *Mitchell* case in *General American Tank Car Corp. v. El Dorado Terminal Co.*[7] involving not a suit for reparations under the statute, but one to recover a sum alleged to be due under the provisions of a car-leasing agreement, the payment of which was withheld by defendant on the ground that it would amount to the making of an illegal rebate. In reversing a judgment for the plaintiff, the Supreme Court said (p. 428) that the district court, although having jurisdiction of the subject matter and of the parties, "upon disclosure of the terms and operation of the lease contract, it should not have proceeded to adjudicate the rights and liabilities of the parties in the absence of a decision by the Commission with respect to the validity of the practice involved in the light of the provisions of the Interstate Commerce Act." It appeared here, as it did in the *Mitchell* case, that the question of the reasonableness and legality of the practices of the parties was subjected by the statute to the administrative authority of the Commission, the policy of the statute obviously being that (p. 432-3) "reasonable allowances and practices, which shall not offend against the prohibitions of the Elkins Act, are to be fixed and settled after full investigation by the Commission, and that there is remitted to the courts only the function of enforcing claims arising out of the failure to comply with the Commission's lawful orders." Since an administrative problem was involved, the Supreme Court held (p. 433) that the lower court "should have stayed its hand pending the Commission's determination of the lawfulness and reasonableness of the practices under the terms of the Act." and that there should not be a dismissal, but the "cause should be held pending the conclusion of an appropriate administrative proceeding."[8]

[7]308 U.S. 422.
[8]Cf. *Morrisdale Coal Co. v. Pennsylvania Railroad Co.*, 230 U.S. 304, 314-5, where no rights could be saved by retaining the cause but in which the Supreme Court gave implicit recognition to the right to institute an action for damages and have it held in abeyance pending resort to the Commission to determine the question of unlawfulness and unreasonableness; and *St. Louis, Brownsville & Mexico Ry. Co. v. Brownsville Navigation District*, 304 U.S. 295, 301, where the district court was asked to make an order which the Commission alone had authority to make.

A further retreat was made by the Supreme Court from the lack-of-jurisdiction doctrine in *Thompson v. Texas Mexican Ry. Co.*[9] where a lower court had granted recovery by plaintiff railroad in a suit for damages against the trustee of another railroad for use by the latter of tracks and other facilities of the former. Since a question of reasonableness of charges was involved, absent an existing agreement, and other issues of primary jurisdiction, the Supreme Court held (p. 151) that the lower court "should have stayed its hand and remitted the parties to the Commission for a determination of the administrative phases of the questions involved." As pointed out by the Supreme Court (p. 151), until the administrative problems were settled by the Commission it could not be known with certainty what issues for judicial decision would emerge, and therefore, "judicial action is premature." In reversing the judgment of the court below, however, the Supreme Court remanded the cause "so that the case may be held pending the conclusion of appropriate administrative proceedings." (p. 151)

The Doctrine of Primary Jurisdiction in Rate Cases

In *Norge Corporation v. Long Island R. Co.,*[10] defendant had charged a fourth-class rate on a shipment of refrigerators provided by a rating of "cooling boxes or refrigerators or cooling or freezing apparatus"; there was a rating provided fifth-class rates on "cooling or freezing machines, cooling boxes or refrigerators." The shippers contended that the fifth-class rate should have been charged and brought action for the alleged overcharge in a district court. Judgment for the shipper was entered and, on appeal, the court of appeals reversed judgment on the ground that the classification question was technical and that, hence, the Commission had exclusive jurisdiction to determine it. The court held that the doctrine applies when tariff schedules employ technical terms, the meaning of which must be determined upon evidence. The court said (pp. 314-15):

> It is the rule that, in order to secure uniformity and avoid discrimination between shippers, resort must first be had to the Interstate Commerce Commission, and in the absence of a determination by that expert body, a court is without jurisdiction to interpret the tariffs where there is a question of fact whether words in the tariff are used in their ordinary or in a peculiar, technical or trade sense, or where, because words are used in the latter sense, their interpretation requires a consideration of

[9]328 U.S. 134.
[10]77 F. 2d 312, cert. denied 296 U.S. 616.

evidence establishing special facts. Director General v. Viscose Co., 254 U.S. 498, 504, 41 S. Ct. 151, 65 L. Ed. 372. It is only where words of the tariff have an ordinary meaning only, and are employed in that sense so that their interpretation is solely a question of law, involving no issue of fact, that a court has jurisdiction in the first instance. Texas & Pacific Ry. Co. v. Amer. Tie & Timber Co., 234 U.S. 138, 34 S. Ct. 885, 58 L. Ed. 1255; Great No. Ry. Co. v. Merchants' Elevator Co., 259 U.S. 285, 42 S. Ct. 477, 66 L. Ed. 943; Standard Oil Co. v. United States, 283 U.S. 235, 51 S. Ct. 429, 75 L. Ed. 999; U.S. Nav. Co. v. Cunard S.S. Co., 284 U.S. 474, 481, 52 S. Ct. 247, 249, 76 L. Ed. 408; Davis, etc., v. Age-Herald Pub. Co., 293 F. 591, 592 (C.C.A. 5).

In Great Northern Ry. Co. v. Merchants' Elevator Co., supra, the court held that if the construction of the tariff presented solely a question of law, the court had jurisdiction, but if it involved a question of fact or of discretion in technical matters, the Commission had exclusive jurisdiction. In Texas & Pacific Ry. v. American Tie & Timber Co., supra, the issue was whether the general term "lumber" used in the carrier's classification included oak railway cross-ties which were not specifically listed therein, and the court held that it was a question of fact requiring preliminary resort to the Commission. In Davis, Director General, v. Age-Herald Pub. Co., supra, a question of overcharges regarding news print paper was presented and the dispute was whether a commodity rate upon "paper, viz., paper, printing, calendared or machine glazed" or a class rate upon "news print" paper was applicable. It was there held that the court did not have the jurisdiction until the Interstate Commerce Commission decided the question. In U.S. Nav. Co. v. Cunard S.S. Co., supra, it was said that the rule has become settled that: "Questions essentially of fact and those involving the exercise of administrative discretion, which were within the jurisdiction of the Interstate Commerce Commission, were primarily within its exclusive jurisdiction, and, with certain exceptions not applicable here, that a remedy must be sought from the Commission before the jurisdiction of the courts could be invoked." And referring to Great Northern Ry. Co. v. Merchants' Elevator Co., supra: "Such resort, it was said, must be had where a rate, rule, or practice is attacked as unreasonable or as unjustly discriminatory, and also where it is necessary, in the construction of a tariff, to determine upon evidence of peculiar meaning of words or the existence of incidents alleged to be attached by usage to the transaction. In all such cases the uniformity which it is the purpose of the Commerce Act [49 USCA § 1 et seq.] to secure could not be obtained without a preliminary determination by the Commission."

The application of the doctrine to a determination of carriers' classifications is well stated in *Director General of Railroads v. The Viscose Co.*[11] In this case the Director General of Railroads amended a consolidated classification so as to exclude the shipment of silk. A shipper brought original action in a district court to set aside and enjoin this

[11] 254 U.S. 498, 502-4.

order and the question of primary jurisdiction was certified to the Supreme Court. The Supreme Court held that the Commission had exclusive primary jurisdiction to determine the lawfulness of the classification, stating:

> Without more, these references to the Interstate Commerce Act are sufficient to show that if the proposed change in the tariffs, and in the rule, which we are considering, constituted a change of classisfication or of regulation within the meaning of the Commerce Act, there was ample and specific provision made therein for dealing with the situation through the Commission, — for suspending the supplement or rule or annulling either or both if investigation proved the change to be unreasonable, and for providing for just treatment of shippers in the future.
>
> * * *
>
> The importance to the commerce of the country of the exclusive, initial jurisdiction which Congress has committed to the Interstate Commerce Commission need not be repeated and cannot be overstated (*Texas & Pacific Ry. Co. v. Abilene Cotton Oil Co.*, 204 U.S. 426; *Baltimore & Ohio R.R. Co. v. Pitcairn Coal Co.*, 215 U.S. 481; *Morrisdale Coal Co. v. Pennsylvania R.R. Co.*, 230 U.S. 304; *Minnesota Rate Cases*, 230 U.S. 352; *Texas & Pacific Ry. Co. v. American Tie Co.*, 234 U.S. 138, 146; *Pennsylvania R.R. Co. v. Clark Coal Co.*, 238 U.S. 456, 469; and *Loomis v. Lehigh Valley R.R. Co.*, 240 U.S. 43, 49), and, concluding, as we do, that this case falls plainly within that jurisdiction, the question asked by the Circuit Court of Appeals must be answered in the negative.

In *Associated Grocers of Colo., Inc. v. Atchison, T. & S. F. Ry. Co.*[12] it was stated that it is not the court's province to usurp the exclusive primary jurisdiction of the Commission; the principle of limited jurisdiction of the courts in matters of tariff construction and interpretation is well entrenched in jurisprudence and well founded on sound reason and good judgment; and the courts must not only refrain from making tariffs for carriers but, under certain circumstances, must decline to construe them as well. In *Cornelli Seed Co. v. Union Pacific R. Co.*,[13] the court said that the doctrine of primary jurisdiction is one concerned with allocation of issues between the jurisdiction of the Commission and the courts; and it applies where a claim is equally cognizable in the Commission and the courts under the jurisdictional statutes, and is brought into play to assure that it is the Commission that decides the issue when it is one that "under a regulatory scheme" requires the special competence of the agency or a uniform result on certain administrative or factual questions.

The court held that it was required to accept the ruling of the Commission that the applicable tariff was reasonable because the subject

[12]191 F. Supp. 435, 436.
[13]263 F. 2d 127, 129-30.

matter was within the primary jurisdiction of the Commission. It held that not all questions of law are outside of the scope of the primary jurisdiction of the agency, particularly those requiring assertion of the expert and specialized knowledge of the agency members or questions involving the interpretation of terms used in a peculiar or technical sense. However, the court said, the determination of the question whether the shipper was in compliance with tariff rules governing transit privileges involved neither the factors of expertise nor language used in a peculiar or technical sense; the court thus had jurisdiction.

In *United States v. Western P. R. Co.*,[14] the Supreme Court said (pp. 69-70) that where the questions of tariff construction and reasonableness are so intertwined that the same factors are determinative of both issues, then it is the Commission which must first pass on them. The court said (pp. 66-7) that a tariff is not an abstraction but embodies an analysis of the costs incurred in the transportation of a certain article and a decision as to how much should, therefore, be charged for the carriage of that article in order to produce a fair and reasonable return; complex and technical cost-allocation and accounting problems must be solved in setting the tariff initially; thus to decide the question of the scope of a tariff without consideration of the factors and purposes underlying the terminology employed would make the process of adjudication little more than an exercise in semantics. The court said that there must be close familarity with the factors to answer the question.

The cases reviewed leave no basis to contend that a court is without jurisdiction to permit an action for damages or reparations to be instituted, and to be held in abeyance, merely because there is involved a question of reasonableness which must be referred to an administrative body for determination. It must be recognized, however, that a court may exercise its discretion to dismiss a suit if it appears that no useful purpose will be served by holding a suit in abeyance pending resort to an administrative body for determination of certain questions.[15]

The Doctrine of Primary Jurisdiction in Antitrust Cases

In the antitrust field, the doctrine of primary jurisdiction represents a method of accommodating the principle of free competition with the

---

[14]352 U.S. 59.

[15]Cf. *Far East Conference v. United States*, 342 U.S. 570, where the Supreme Court said (p. 576-7) that since a similar suit could be instituted conveniently later, if appropriate, "(w)e believe that no purpose would here be served to hold the present action in abeyance in the district court while proceeding before the Board and subsequent judicial review or enforcement of its order are being pursued."

principle that in some economic areas, regulation, restriction, or elimination of competition is required in the public interest.[16]

Development of the primary jurisdiction doctrine as applied in antitrust cases has varied according to the regulatory statute involved, the nature of the relief sought, and the type of violation alleged. The cases establish that the doctrine is properly applied where there is a clear possibility that the agency may immunize precisely that conduct which is the basis of the antitrust complaint, or where the agency is empowered to remedy anticompetitive practices under its own statute while immunizing some others, and is entrusted with enforcement of the antitrust laws themselves, even though its immunizing powers do not extend precisely to the conduct in question.

In the consideration of the application of the doctrine of primary jurisdiction to suits arising under the antitrust laws, *Keogh v. Chicago & Northwestern Railway Co.*[17] stands out as one of the leading cases. Here defendant railroads were sued by plaintiff shipper under the antitrust laws for triple damages on the ground that defendants had conspired to maintain unreasonably high rates. The challenged rates had been found to be legal in proceedings before the I.C.C. In affirming judgment for defendants, Mr. Justice Brandeis said (p. 162) "A rate is not necessarily illegal because it is the result of a conspiracy in restraint of trade in violation of the Anti-Trust Act" as "(w)hat rates are legal is determined by the Act to Regulate Commerce." Under the latter act the exaction of any illegal rate made the carrier liable to the person injured thereby for the full amount of damages sustained in consequence of any such violation, and provided for the recovery of such damages by complaint before the Commission or by a suit in a federal court. "If the conspiracy here complained of had resulted in rates which the Commission found to be illegal because unreasonably high or discriminatory, the full amount of the damages sustained, whatever their nature, would have been recoverable in such proceedings" (p. 162). To provide the shipper, from whom illegal rates have been exacted, with an additional remedy under the antitrust laws would defeat the paramount purpose of Congress in enacting the Act to Regulate Commerce, i.e., the prevention of unjust discrimination. If a shipper could recover under the antitrust laws "for damages resulting from the exaction of a rate higher than that which would otherwise have prevailed, the amount recovered might, like a rebate, operate to give him a preference over his trade

[16]See Denver Union Stockyards Co. v. Denver Live Stock Commission Co., 404 F. 2d 1055.
[17]260 U.S. 156.

competitors" (p. 163). The court reasoned that it is no answer to say that each of the trade competitiors could bring a similar action, as "(u)niform treatment would not result, even if all sued, unless the highly improbable happened, and the several juries and courts gave to each the same measure of relief." (p. 163)

In *United States Navigation Co. v. Cunard Steamship Co.*,[18] plaintiff, a corporation operating ships in foreign commerce, sought to enjoin defendant shipping companies from continuing an alleged combination and conspiracy in violation of the Sherman Antitrust Act[19] and of the Clayton Act.[20] The complaint charged that defendants had entered into and were engaged in a combination and conspiracy to restrain the foreign trade and commerce of the United States in respect of the carriage of general cargo from the United States to foreign ports, with the object and purpose of driving plaintiff and others not parties to the combination out of, and of monopolizing, such trade and commerce.

The complaint also charged that defendants had established a general tariff rate and a lower contract rate, the latter to be made available only to shippers who agreed to confine their shipments to the lines of defendants; and that the differentials thus created between the two rates were not predicated upon the volume of traffic or frequency or regularity of shipment, but were purely arbitrary and wholly disproportionate to any difference in service rendered, the sole consideration being their effect as a coercive measure. The complaint charged further that defendants had put into effect what is called a scheme of joint exclusive patronage contracts, by which shippers were required to agree to ship exclusively by their lines, and to refrain from offering any shipments to plaintiff, and unless they so agreed, the shippers were forced to pay the far higher general tariff rates; and that other means were used to exclude plaintiff entirely from the carrying trade between the United States and foreign ports, such as granting rebates, coercion, threats, and spreading false rumors.

The Supreme Court found that the complaint standing alone charged a violation of the Sherman Act and stated a case for injunctive relief, and that the sole question to be determined was whether the effect of the Shipping Act of 1916 was to confer on the Shipping Board jurisdiction over the subject matter of the complaint. The court affirmatively answered the question, holding that the matters charged in the complaint were within the exclusive primary jurisdiction of the Shipping

[18]284 U.S. 479.
[19]15 U.S.C. 1 *et seq.*
[20]15 U.S.C. 12 *et seq.*

Board and that the evident purpose of the Shipping Act was demonstrative of this conclusion. The court stated (p. 485) that a comparison of the enumeration of the wrongs charged in the complaint with the provisions of the Shipping Act conclusively shows "that the allegations either constitute direct and basic charges of violations of these provisions or are so interrelated with such charges as to be in effect a component part of them." The court concluded (p. 485) that "the remedy is that afforded by the Shipping Act, which to that extent supersedes the antitrust laws." Since the Shipping Act embodied a remedial system that was complete and self-contained and plaintiff was seeking the same relief obtainable from the Shipping Board, the court determined that jurisdiction should lie in the Board.

There was no expansion of the doctrine of primary jurisdiction in the *Cunard* case, but merely a reaffirmation of the doctrine by the court. In it decision (p. 480-1), the court referred to the Shipping Act as "a comprehensive measure bearing a relation to common carriers by water substantially the same as that borne by the Interstate Commerce Act to interstate common carriers by land." The Shipping Act, in its general scope and purpose, as well as in its terms, closely paralleled the I.C. Act, and the court was of the opinion that the conclusion would not be escaped "that Congress intended that the two acts, each in its own field, should have like interpretation, application and effect." (p. 481)

When the Shipping Act was enacted, "the Interstate Commerce Act had been in force in its original form or in amended form for more than a generation," and its "provisions had been applied to a great variety of situations, and had been judicially construed in a large number and variety of cases." (p. 481) From these cases developed the settled rule "that questions essentially of fact and those involving the exercise of administrative discretion, which were within the jurisdiction of the Interstate Commerce Commission, were primarily within its exclusive jurisdiction." (p. 481) It follows, reasoned the court (p. 481), "that the settled construction in respect of the earlier act must be applied to the later one, unless, in particular instances, there be something peculiar in the question under consideration, or dissimilarity in the terms of the act relating thereto, requiring a different conclusion."

The *Cunard* case was followed in the Supreme Court by *Central Transfer Co. v. Terminal Railroad Association of St. Louis*[21] and *Terminal Warehouse Co. v. Pennsylvania Railroad Co.*[22] In the *Central Transfer* case, there was involved a suit by a transporter of interstate freight

[21]288 U.S. 469.
[22]297 U.S. 500.

against an association of interstate rail carriers having terminals in St. Louis and East St. Louis, to restrain an alleged violation of the Sherman Act. For many years before the suit was filed, the rail carriers had maintained certain off-track stations for receipt and delivery of less-than-carload freight, and by the employment of transfer companies had provided for the transportation of such freight by motor carrier between such stations and their on-track stations, and between each of the on-track stations. Tariffs filed with the I.C.C. designated all such off-track stations and fixed line-haul rates for the transportation of freight between such stations and points on the rail carriers' lines. The off-track stations generally were places of business of local transfer companies, including plaintiff. In this case, the Commission had approved certain rate schedules which entailed abandoning certain off-track stations and the employment by the carriers of a single transfer company, also named as a defendant, to do interstation hauling. The carriers proceeded to make an agreement to carry out the program which had been submitted to the Commission and which was later approved by it.

The suit brought by plaintiff was to enjoin performance of the contract on the ground that it created a monopoly in violation of the antitrust laws. The Supreme Court held that the suit was barred by Section 16 of the Clayton Act.[23] The court pointed out that the purpose of Section 16 was "to preclude any interference by injunction with any business or transactions of interstate carriers of sufficient public significance and importance to be within the jurisdiction of the Commission, except when the suit is brought by the Government itself" (p. 475). The court added that (p. 476) "a contract may precede and have existence apart from the several acts required to perform it, and conceivably all of those acts might be done if no contract or agreement to perform them had ever existed," but "when they are done in performance of an agreement, there is no way by which the agreement itself can be assailed by injunction except by restraining acts done in performance of it." It was not because the contract was within the jurisdiction of the Commission that Section 16 of the Clayton Act precluded the private party to maintain the suit "but because the acts done in performance of it, which must necessarily be enjoined if any relief is given, are matters subject to the jurisdiction of the Commission" (p. 476).

The policy behind the restrictions to use placed on private parties by Congress was aptly presented in the *Terminal Warehouse* case,

---

[23] 15 U.S.C. 26.

where the Supreme Court, relying on prior decisions, including the *Keogh* and *Cunard* cases, said (p. 513) "(i)f a sufferer from the discriminatory acts of carriers by rail or by water may sue for an injunction under the Clayton Act without resort in the first instance to the regulatory commission, the unity of the system of regulation breaks down beyond repair." On the other hand, if the regulatory body "has issued a 'cease and desist' order, an injunction under the Clayton Act is inappropriate and needless." (p. 514)

The court continued by saying that the "same considerations are applicable, and with undiminished force, where the suit under the Clayton Act is not for an injunction but for damages," and a finding of undue discrimination by the regulatory body is a necessary preliminary to a suit in a district court. (p. 514) The court pointed out that the I.C. Act provided the means for ascertaining the existence of a preference, and gave a cause of action for damages against not only the carrier but also others who have incited or abetted. For the wrongs that it denounces, the I.C. Act "prescribes a fitting remedy" which "was meant to be exclusive." (p. 514) If another remedy is sought under cover of another statute, the court said (p. 514), there "must be a showing of another wrong, not canceled or redressed by the recovery of damages for the wrong explicitly denounced."

The *Cunard* decision was reaffirmed by the Supreme Court in *Far East Conference v. United States*,[24] a case in which there were involved the same considerations as those in the *Cunard* case. There, an action was brought by the Government under the Sherman Act to enjoin a dual-rate system enforced in concert by steamship carriers engaged in foreign trade. Under the established dual system of rates, called the contract and non-contract rate system, shippers who agreed to deal exclusively with members of the Far East Conference paid one rate, and those who did not bind themselves by such exclusive patronage contract paid a fixed higher rate. This system of two levels of freight rates was admitted by defendants, but they moved that the complaint be dismissed on the ground that the nature of the issues required that resort must be first had to the administrative body before a district court could adjudicate the Government's complaint.

In dismissing the complaint of the Government, the Supreme Court commented that there was no reason to depart from its decision in the *Cunard* case as it answered the problem. "The sole distinction between the *Cunard* case and this," asserted Mr. Justice Frankfurter for

[24]342 U.S. 570.

the court, "is that there, a private shipper invoked the Antitrust Acts and here it is the Government." (p. 576) The Government had argued that it should not be forced to go first to the administrative body because the United States may not be deemed a "person" who under Section 22 of the Shipping Act may file a complaint. The court answered this argument by stating (p. 576) that the administrative body had "consistently treated the United States as a 'person' within its rule for intervention"; that the United States is one of the largest shippers in the Far East trade; and that the matter seems to be disposed of by *United States v. Interstate Commerce Commission*,[25] involving similar provisions of the I.C. Act. Upon reaching the conclusion that the large question in the case ought not to turn on such a debatable point, the court then discussed why it was unnecesary to depart from the decision in the *Cunard* case (p. 574):

> The court thus applied a principle, now firmly established, that in cases raising issues of fact not within the conventional experience of judges or cases requiring the exercise of administrative discretion, agencies created by Congress for regulating the subject matter should not be passed over. This is so even though the facts are they have been appraised by specialized competence serve as a promise for legal consequences to be judicially defined. . . . Uniformity and consistency in the regulation of business entrusted to a particular agency are secured, and the limited functions of review by the judiciary are more rationally exercised, by preliminary resort for ascertaining and interpreting the circumstances underlying legal issues to agencies that are better equipped than courts by specialization, by insight gained through experience, and by more flexible procedure.

That the foregoing antitrust cases constitute but a continuous thread in the fabric of the doctrine of primary administrative jurisdiction, and not an expansion of the doctrine, is demonstrated by the factors which determined the cases. The same considerations which prompted the Supreme Court to first give expression to the doctrine in the *Abilene* case, and later developed it in other cases, are apparent in the antitrust cases.

Turning now to *Georgia v. Pennsylvania Railroad Co.*,[26] where we find factors different from those which determined the antitrust cases discussed above and where the court was not asked to encroach on the domain of the administrative body, there was no prior resort to the administrative body. In the *Georgia* case, the State of Georgia invoked the original jurisdiction of the Supreme Court under Article III, Section 2, of

[25]337 U.S. 426, 430 *et seq.*
[26]324 U.S. 439.

the Constitution to bring suit against twenty railroads by a bill of complaint in which the State, suing as *parens patriae* and in its proprietary capacity, sought injunctive relief under the antitrust laws.

The essence of the complaint in the *Georgia* case was a charge of a conspiracy among the defendant rail carriers in restraint of trade and commerce among the States. It charged that the railroads had fixed arbitrary and noncompetitive rates and charges for transportation of freight to and from Georgia; that rate organizations had been utilized to fix these rates; that no railroad could charge joint through rates without the approval of the private rate-fixing agencies; that the private rate-fixing machinery, which was not sanctioned by the I.C.C. and was prohibited by the antitrust laws, had put the effective control of rates to and from Georgia in the hands of the defendants; that the practices complained of in purpose and effect gave shippers in the North an advantage over shippers in Georgia; that the rates fixed were much higher than the rates and charges for transportation of like commodities for like distances between points in the North; and that the defendants who had lines wholly or principally in the South were generally dominated and coerced by the defendants who had northern roads, and therefore that, even when the southern defendants desired, they could not publish joint rates between Georgia and the North when the north carriers refused to join such rates.

It was argued by the defendants that the complaint failed to state a cause of action. It was pointed out that no action for damages on the basis of unjust, unreasonable, or discriminatory railroad rates could be maintained without prior resort to the Commission; that an injunction could not be granted to restrain rates alleged to be unreasonable or discriminatory where there had been no prior determination of the matter by the Commission and that the only way that a judical determination of the legality of a rate could be obtained was by review of the Commission's order; that damages under the antitrust laws could not be recovered against railroad carriers though the rates approved by the Commission were fixed pursuant to a conspiracy; that persons other than the United States were barred from enjoining violations of the antitrust laws by virtue of Section 16 of the Clayton Act; and that Georgia could not maintain an action on common law principles based upon a conspiracy among carriers to fix rates.

The court said that it was clear from the *Keogh* case that Georgia could not "recover damages even if the conspiracy alleged were shown to exist" (p. 453); that a suit in the Supreme Court could not be maintained to review, annul, or set aside an order of the Commission as

Congress had "prescribed the method for obtaining that relief" and it was "exclusive of all other remedies" (p. 454); and suit could not be maintained where the basis for attacking an order of the Commission was a violation of the antitrust laws, as Section 16 of the Clayton Act which gives relief by way of injunction "provides that no one except the United States shall be entitled to bring such suits against common carriers subject to the Interstate Commerce Act 'in respect of any matter subject to the regulation, supervision, or other jurisdiction' of the Commission." (p. 454) In this suit, however, Georgia was seeking relief to eliminate from rate-making the influence of an unlawful conspiracy alleged to exist, and there was no administrative control over the combination. As the court pointed out (pp. 455-7):

> The relief which Georgia seeks is not a matter subject to the jurisdiction of the Commission. Georgia in this proceeding is not seeking an injunction against the continuance of any tariff; nor does she seek to have any tariff provision cancelled. She merely asks that the alleged rate-fixing combination and conspiracy among the defendant-carriers be enjoined. As we shall see, this is a matter over which the Commission has no jurisdiction. And an injunction designed to put an end to the conspiracy need not enjoin operation under established rates as would have been the case had an injunction issued in *Central Transfer Co. v. Terminal R. Assn.*, *supra*.

> These carriers are subject to the Anti-trust laws. *United States v. Southern Pacific Co.*, 259 U.S. 214. Conspiracies among carriers to fix rates were included in the broad sweep of the Sherman Act. *United States v. Trans-Missouri Freight Assn.*, 166 U.S. 290; *United States v. Joint Traffic Assn.*, 171 U.S. 505. Congress by Sec. 11 of the Clayton Act entrusted the Commission with authority to enforce compliance with certain of its provisions 'where applicable to common carriers' under the Commission's jurisdiction. It has the power to lift the ban of the antitrust laws in favor of carriers who merge or consolidate (*New York Central Securities Corp. v. United States*, 287 U.S. 12, 25-26) and the duty to give weight to the antitrust policy of the nation, before approving mergers and consolidations. *McLean Trucking Co. v. United States*, 321 U.S. 67. But Congress has not given the Commission comparable authority to remove rate-fixing combinations from the prohibitions contained in the anti-trust laws. It has not placed these combinations under the control and supervision of the Commission. Nor has it empowered the Commission to proceed against such combinations and through cease and desist orders or otherwise to put an end to their activities. Regulated industries are not *per se* exempt from the Sherman Act. *United States v. Borden Co.*, 308 U.S. 188, 198 *et seq.* It is true that the Commission's regulation of carriers has greatly expanded since the Sherman Act. See *Arizona Grocery Co. v. Atchison, T. & S. F. R. Co.*, 284 U.S. 370, 385-386. But it is elementary that repeals by implication are not favored. Only a clear repugnancy between the old law and the new results in the former giving way and then only

pro tanto to the extent of the repugnancy. *United States v. Borden, supra,* pp. 198, 199. None of the powers acquired by the Commission since the enactment of the Sherman Act relates to the regulation of rate-fixing combinations. Twice Congress has been tendered proposals to legalize rate-fixing combinations. But it has not adopted them. In view of this history we can only conclude that they have no immunity from the anti-trust laws.

Defendant rail carriers argued that under Section 1(4) of the I.C. Act[27] it was the duty of every common carrier subject to the Act to establish reasonable through routes with other such carriers, and just and reasonable rates, fares, charges, and classifications applicable thereto, thus, collaboration was contemplated. The court noted in its opinion that the "collaboration contemplated in the fixing of through and joint rates is of a restrictive nature,"[28] and that it could find no warrant in the I.C. Act and the Sherman Act for stating "that the authority to fix joint through rates clothes with legality a conspiracy to discriminate against a State or a region, to use coercion in the fixing of rates, or to put in the hands of a combination of carriers a veto power for rates proposed by a single carrier." (pp. 457-8) It was added that the "type of regulation which Congress chose did not eliminate the emphasis on competition and individual freedom of action in rate-making," and that the I.C. Act "was designed to preserve private initiative in rate-making, as indicated by the duty of each common carrier to initiate its own rates" (pp. 458-9). The court then said (p. 459) that if a combination of the character described in the complaint were immune from suit, "freedom of action" disappears, "coercive and collusive influences of group action takes its place," and a "monopoly power is created under the aegis of private parties without Congressional sanction and without governmental supervision or control."

The court also gave consideration to the authority lodged in the Commission under Section 3(1) of the I.C. Act[29] to remove undue or unreasonable preference or advantage in rates. In considering this provision as a bar to suit, the court said (pp. 459-60) that Georgia did not seek to have the court act in the place of the Commission in removing undue or unreasonable preference or advantage in rates, but sought "to remove from the field of rate-making the influences of a combination which exceed the limits of the collaboration authorized for the fixing of joint through rates," and sought "to put an end to discriminatory and

---

[27]49 U.S.C. 1(4).
[28]No attempt was made by the court to delineate the legitimate area in which such collaboration may operate.
[29]49 U.S.C. 3(1).

coercive practices." In granting leave to the State of Georgia to file suit, the court said (pp. 460-1):

> It must be remembered that this is a suit to dissolve an illegal combination or to confine it to the legitimate area of collaboration. That relief cannot be obtained from the Commission for it has no supervisory authority over the combination. It is true that the injury to Georgia is not in the existence of the combination *per se* but in the rates which are fixed by the combination. The fact that the rates which have been fixed may or may not be held unlawfully by the Commission is immaterial to the issue before us. The *Keogh* case indicates that even a combination to fix reasonable and non-discriminatory rates may be illegal. 260 U.S. p. 161. The reason is that the Interstate Commerce Act does not provide remedies for the correction of all the abuses of rate-making which might constitute violations of the anti-trust laws. Thus a "zone of reasonableness exists between maxima and minima within which a carrier is ordinarily free to adjust its charges for itself." *United States v. Chicago, M., St. P. & P. R. Co.*, 294 U.S. 499, 506. Within that zone the Commission lacks power to grant relief even though the rates are raised to the maxima by a conspiracy among carriers who employ unlawful tactics. If the ratemaking function is freed from the unlawful restraints of the alleged conspiracy, the rates of the future will then be fixed in the manner envisioned by Congress when it enacted this legislation. Damage must be presumed to flow from a conspiracy to manipulate rates within that zone.

The opinions of the lower courts in *Seatrain Lines v. Pennsylvania R. Co.*[30] and *Slick Airways v. American Air Lines*[31] point the same way as the Supreme Court decision in the *Georgia* case by permitting action to be brought under the antitrust laws where the relief sought was not a matter subject to the jurisdiction of the administrative bodies. In each of these cases, as in the *Georgia* case, whatever relief was appropriate under the antitrust laws, whether by injunction or the award of damages, could be granted without encroachment upon any area of concern of the administrative bodies. The cases demonstrate that the division of jurisdiction, in the interest of orderly administration, between court and administrative agencies does not deprive a litigant of the privilege of seeking judicial relief under the antitrust laws when the court can consider and act without invading the administrative province.

In *S.S.W., Inc. v. Air Transport Ass'n of America*,[32] the court of appeals was called upon to consider in an antitrust suit the effect of the antitrust laws upon a regulated industry, the problem being one

[30]207 F. 2d 255.
[31]107 F. Supp. 199, appeal dismissed 204 F. 2d 230, cert. denied 346 U.S. 806.
[32]191 F. 2d 658, cert. denied 343 U.S. 955. See *Slick Airways v. American Airlines, supra; Apgar Travel Agency v. International Air Trans. Ass'n.*, 107 F. Supp. 706.

involving the interrelation of two statutory schemes. The court compared the allegations of the complaint with the provisions of the Federal Aviation Act and found that the provisions covered the dominant facts alleged in the complaint as constituting a violation of the antitrust laws. As a result, the court said (p. 662) that the plaintiff must first seek relief from the Civil Aeronautics Board. The court said (p. 664) that it thought that "accommodation of the two statutes and of the remedial provisions thereof can best be accomplished" by having the district court retain jurisdiction of the antitrust suit while relief was sought from the Board by plaintiff. The court said that the "proceedings before the Board will result in a determination by it of the extent of its jurisdiction over the subject matter. In addition, they will produce a record, findings of fact and conclusions of law as to whether the specific practices complained of are legal or illegal" under the Act, "all of which will be subject to judicial review."

The court said that the lower court, "which will meanwhile have retained jurisdiction of the antitrust suit, will have the benefit of these proceedings in determining the issue of antitrust violations." The court added that whatever damages might ultimately be awarded by the lower court would be treble damages for violation of the antitrust laws, not specific damages under the Federal Aviation Act.[33] and whatever injunctive relief is ultimately granted by the lower court "with regard to matters determined by the Board to fall outside its jurisdiction would be under the antitrust laws," not the Federal Aviation Act. The court concluded by stating (p. 664) that although such a procedure certainly makes the court and the agency collaborative instrumentalities of justice,[34] it may also make for considerable delay, but "absent specific congressional action to deal with the problem, we see no other way in which to accommodate these conflicting statutory schemes and the principles which follow in their wake."

In *Federal Maritime Board v. Isbrandtsen Co.,*[35] a dual-rate contract case, petitioners argued that the Court was bound by the decisions in *United States Nav. Co. v. Cunard S.S. Co.*[36] and *Far East Conference*

---

[33]Where specific damages are provided by a regulatory statute, it has been held that there can be no recovery of treble damages under the antitrust laws and this even in a statute such as the I.C. Act, which contains a clause saving all pre-existing remedies at common law or by statute. *Terminal Warehouse v. Pennsylvania R. Co.,* 297 U.S. 500, 514; *U.S. Navigation Co. v. Cunard S.S. Co.,* 284 U.S. 474, 484-5; *Keogh v. Chicago, N.W. Ry. Co,* 260 U.S. 156, 163-4.

[34]See *Montana-Dakota Utilities Co., v. Northwestern Public Service Co.,* 341 U.S. 246.

[35]356 U.S. 481.

[36]284 U.S. 474.

v. United States,[37] and that if the court in the earlier cases had thought that Section 14 of the Shipping Act of 1916[38] in any way makes dual rates *per se* illegal and thus not within the power of the administrative body to authorize, it would not have found it necessary to require that the administrative body first pass upon the claims. The Supreme Court replied (p. 498) that these earlier cases, while holding that the administrative body had primary jurisdiction to hear the case in the first instance, did not signify that the statute left the administrative body free to approve or disapprove the agreements under attack; rather "those cases recognized that in certain kinds of litigations practical considerations dictate a division of functions between court and agency under which the latter makes a preliminary, comprehensive investigation of the facts, analyzes them, and applies to them the statutory scheme as it is construed."

The court said further that "It is recognized that the courts, while retaining the final authority to expound the statute, should avail themselves of the aid implicit in the agency's superiority in gathering the relevant facts and in marshalling them into a meaningful pattern. Cases are not decided, nor the law appropriately understood, apart from an informed and particularized insight into the factual circumstances of the controversy under litigation." The court said (pp. 498-9) that the action in the *Cunard* and *Far East Conference* cases should be taken as a deferral of what might come to be the ultimate question, the construction of Section 14 Third rather than an implicit holding that the administrative body could properly approve the practices there involved. The holding that the administrative body had primary jurisdiction, in short, was a device to prepare the way, if the litigation should take its ultimate course, for a more informed and precise determination by the court of the scope and meaning of the statute as applied to those particular circumstances. Since Section 14 Third strikes down dual rate systems only where they are employed as predatory devices, then precise findings by the administrative body as to a particular system's intent and effect would become essential to a judicial determination of the system's validity under the statute. The court said that in neither *Cunard* nor *Far East Conference* did it have the assistance of such findings on which to base a determination of validity.

In *Pan American World Airways v. United States,*[39] the Supreme Court held that the narrow questions presented in a complaint charging

[37]342 U.S. 570.
[38]46 U.S.C. 812. See 46 U.S.C. 813 a, 814.
[39]9 L ed. 2d 325.

violations of Section 1, 2 and 3 of the Sherman Act,[40] which suit was instituted by the United States at the request of the Civil Aeronautics Board, had been entrusted to the Board by provisions for economic regulation in the Civil Aeronautics Act of 1938 (re-enacted without change in the Federal Aviation Act of 1958), thus the complaint should have been dismissed by the lower court. The court said that the acts charged in the civil suit as antitrust violations, including division of territories, allocation of routes and combinations between carriers and other common carriers, are basic in the regulatory scheme, and that these are the precise ingredients of the Board's authority in granting, qualifying, or denying certificates to air carriers, in modifying, suspending, or revoking them, and in allowing or disallowing affiliations between common carriers and air carriers.

The case, the court said, is unlike *Georgia v. Pennsylvania R. Co.,*[41] where a conspiracy among carriers for the fixing of through and joint rates was held to constitute a cause of action under the antitrust laws, in view of the fact that the Commission had no power to grant relief against such combinations.[42] The court said that under Section 414 of the Federal Aviation Act, the Board, in the prospective application of the Act, could give a carrier immunity from the operation of the antitrust laws insofar as may be necessary to enable the carrier to do anything authorized, approved, or required by an order under Section 408 permitting an affiliation between an air carrier and a common carrier of another mode of transportation.

Further, the Board under Section 411 could investigate and bring to a halt all unfair practices and all unfair methods of competition including those which started prior to the passage of the Act in 1938. Thus, the court said, Section 411 leaves to the Board all questions of injunctive relief against the divisions of territories or the allocation of routes or against combinations between air carriers and common carriers of other modes. Furthermore, the court said, many of the problems presented by this case, which pertained to air routes to and in foreign countries, may involve military and foreign policy considerations that the Act, as construed in *Chicago & Southern Airlines v. Waterman S.S. Co.,*[43] subject to presidential rather than judicial review.

In *Luckenbach S. S. Corp. v. United States,*[44] the court said that the

---

[40]15 U.S.C. 1, 2, 3.
[41]324 U.S. 439.
[42]The court said that the result reached in the *Georgia* case might be different today because of Section 5a (and 5b) of the I.C. Act.
[43]333 U.S. 103.
[44]179 F. Supp. 605, aff'd in part and dismissed in part 364 U.S. 280.

doctrine of primary jurisdiction requires that where there is an administrative body, particularly knowledgeable in a specialized area, preliminary resort should be had to that body if some phase of the matter has been especially committed to it, even if that agency has no jurisdiction to grant the relief sought; that agency action should precede court review where machinery for such procedure is provided is especially true in the field of transportation. The court said (pp. 610-14) that the allegations that a reduced rail rate violated the antitrust laws in that it was designed to eliminate plaintiff water carrier as a competitor, that the railroads' action also violated the national transportation policy in attempting to monopolize the traffic involved, and that the Commission's action in permitting the reduced rate to become effective constituted the final step resulting in injury to plaintiff, should be initially considered by the Commission under the doctrine of primary jurisdiction, since under Section 5a (now 5b) the Commission has jurisdiction over antitrust exemption agreements pursuant to which defendant railroads were operating.

In *Carnation Company v. Pacific Westbound Conference*,[45] the appellate court held that the antitrust laws are superseded where the Shipping Act, 1916, provides a remedy for conduct which is violative of both the antitrust statutes and the Shipping Act. Carnation Company began an antitrust treble damage suit against the Pacific Westbound Conference and Far East Conference for damages arising from the implementation of secret agreements which had not been approved by the FMC pursuant to Section 15 of the Shipping Act. The lower court had dismissed the complaint on the ground that the Shipping Act provided an adequate remedy. The Supreme Court in *Carnation Company v. Pacific Westbound Conference*[46] reversed the decision in 336 F. 2d 650. The Supreme Court held that actions taken pursuant to agreements which have not been filed with or approved by the FMC are subject to the treble damage remedies provided by the antitrust laws. The court also held that an action for treble damages under the antitrust laws should be stayed pending a determination by the FMC as to the legality under the Shipping Act of the Conferences' actions.

In *United States v. RCA*,[47] the Supreme Court refused to find primary jurisdiction in the Federal Communications Commission which did not have statutory power to grant antitrust immunity, although Section 7 of the Clayton Act itself exempts transactions approved by the FCC.

[45]336 F. 2d 650.
[46]383 U.S. 213.
[47]358 U.S. 334.

RCA allegedly had compelled Westinghouse to transfer a Philadelphia television station to the NBC network. FCC approved the transfer despite the objection that the transfer was compelled. The FCC refused to make any determination on the antitrust question, and generally did not regard competitive factors as an integral part of its regulatory function.

In *California v. Federal Power Commission*,[48] the government charged two natural gas carriers with violations of Section 7 of the Clayton Act when El Paso acquired almost all the stock of Pacific Northwest. El Paso then applied to the FPC for approval of the acquisition under Section 7(c) of the Natural Gas Act,[49] and both the court and the agency were petitioned to allow the other to proceed. The court finally deferred to the agency, but on review of the final FPC decision, the Supreme Court held that primary jurisdiction was in the court and that the agency should not have acted while the transaction was being challenged in the court even though it did so with express permission.

Section 7 of the Clayton Act excepts from its coverage transactions authorized by the FPC, but the FPC had no explicit jurisdiction to enforce the Clayton Act nor did the Natural Gas Act specifically provide for grants of antitrust immunity. The Natural Gas Act empowered the FPC to authorize acquisitions of the assets of other natural gas companies, but it did not cover stock acquisitions in companies with such assets. The court noted that there was no provision similar to Section 5(11) of the I.C. Act which specifically provides for grants of immunity for carriers mergers, and emphasized (at p. 485) that "there is no pervasive regulatory scheme including the antitrust laws that has been entrusted to the Commission." The court pointed out several possible conflicts between the exercise of jurisdiction by both the court and the agency, and said that the orderly procedure was for the court to proceed to decision first.

The Supreme Court refused to apply primary jurisdiction in *Philadelphia National Bank v. U.S.*,[50] where the banking agencies had approved the merger in question. The Bank Merger Act of 1960 directed the bank agencies to consider competitive factors in granting such approval, but it contained neither enforcement nor immunizing powers. The court said (pp. 351-52) that the range and scope of administrative powers under the Bank Merger Act bears little resemblance to those involved in the *Pan American* case. The court said, moreover bank regu-

---

[48]369 U.S. 482.
[49]15 U.S.C. § 717f(c).
[50]374 U.S. 321.

lation is in most respects less complete than public utility regulation, to which interstate rail carriers, among others, are subject. It added (at p. 353) that the doctrine requires abstention in cases where protection of the integrity of a regulatory scheme dictates preliminary resort to the agency which administers the scheme.

In *Riss & Company v. Association of American RR's*,[51] it was held that an antitrust case must continue unabated where only some of the conduct alleged as part of the antitrust violation is subject to agency review and antitrust immunity. Riss involved an alleged railroad conspiracy to drive a competing motor carrier out of business in violation of the Sherman Act. The complaint alleged that the conspiracy was carried out by various means including the institution of a rate reduction for the purpose of excluding plaintiff from the explosives traffic. Defendants moved to refer the issue of reasonableness of rates to the I.C.C. The court denied the motion, giving several reasons for the decision. The court, in following the guidelines for referral established in *Atlantic Coast Line R. Co. v. Riss & Co., Inc.*,[52] believed that the reasonableness of the reduced rate was not the "sole or dominant issue" in the antitrust case. It felt that the alleged rate practices, involving questions of purpose and effect as well as reasonableness were an integral part of the alleged conspiracy, and, therefore, could not be evaluated apart from the other allegations in the complaint. Moreover, even if the reduced rate were itself lawful and, therefore, by itself immune from the antitrust laws, it could nevertheless be charged as one of a number of means used by defendants to effect an unlawful conspiracy.[53] The court found that referral to the I.C.C. would likely delay the antitrust litigation for years.

---

[51] 170 F. Supp. 354, cert. denied 267 F. 2d 659, 361 U.S. 804. A jury verdict in this case favorable to the plaintiff was reversed basically because the complaint and evidence were concerned with defendants' lobbying activities — matters held to be outside the scope of the antitrust laws. Association of *Western Rys. v. Riss & Company*, 299 F. 2d 133, cert. denied 370 U.S. 916.

[52] 267 F. 2d 657.

[53] See *American Tobacco Co. v. United States*, 328 U.S. 781, and *Atchison, Topeka & S.F. Ry. Co. v. Aircoach Trans. Ass'n.*, 253 F. 2d 877, 887-88. In *Aircoach*, the sole issue of the antitrust case concerned the purpose and effect of defendant railroads' rate practices. The court of appeals held that even in such a narrow case the district court may proceed immediately to decide whether the purpose of the rate reductions was to "destroy competition." This is so because even immunized rate agreements are subject to the antitrust laws when part of a larger conspiracy. As the court of appeals said (pp. 887-88):

> Even though it should be found in the end that the practices as such have been validly immunized by section 5a approved agreements, nevertheless if they are part of an effort by railroads in combination or conspiracy to eliminate the competition of *Aircoach*, rather than used merely to meet that competition, the practices would be removed from the protection of section 5a(9).

Since there was no guarantee that the I.C.C. would act at all much less act promptly, and since I.C.C. action would have no bearing on the larger antitrust issues, referral would be contrary to sound judicial discretion. Finally, the court stressed the danger to plaintiff's case which would likely result from further delay in that this would add to the difficulty of obtaining witnesses and would further dim memories of facts essential to all parties.

As indicated above, the application of the doctrine of primary jurisdiction frequently arises when conduct seemingly within the reach of the antitrust laws is also at least arguably protected or prohibited by another regulatory statute enacted by Congress because the regulatory statute grants the relevant agency authority to enforce the statute's distinct standards, which may or may not include antitrust considerations of free and unrestrained competition. Thus is borne out by the decision in *Ricci v. Chicago Mercantile Exchange,*[54] which involved an action brought by a former member of the Chicago Mercantile Exchange against the Exchange and others for conspiring to restrain his business by transferring his membership in the Exchange without notice and a hearing. The practices were alleged to have been violative of the Exchange rules, the Commodity Exchange Act, and the antitrust laws. The Supreme Court held that it was proper to stay the action pending prior reference to the Commodity Exchange Commission, on the grounds that it would be essential for the court to determine whether the Commodity Exchange Act or any of its provisions were incompatible with the maintenance of an antitrust action; that the Commodity Exchange Commission had statutory jurisdiction to consider and resolve some aspects of the dispute between Ricci and the Exchange; and that the adjudication of the dispute by the Commodity Exchange Commission promised to be a material aid in resolving the question of immunity.

In *United States v. Navajo Freight Lines, Inc.,*[55] the court applied the primary jurisdiction doctrine where there was a clear possibility that the I.C.C. would immunize precisely the conduct which was the basis of the antitrust complaint, where it was empowered to remedy anticompetitive practices under the I.C. Act while immunizing some others, and where it was entrusted with enforcement of the antitrust laws, even though its immunizing powers did not extend precisely to the conduct in question.

[54]409 U.S. 289.
[55]339 F. Supp. 554.

44

Rate Making Agreements
of Common Carriers
and Freight Forwarders
Subject to the Interstate Commerce Act

Applicable Statutes

Section 5a of the Interstate Commerce Act[1] was amended by the 4R Act by eliminating common carriers by railroad from its application. Section 5b[2] was added by the 4R Act to cover common carriers by railroad.

Common carriers and freight forwarders subject to Parts I (other than a common carrier by railroad), II, III, or IV of the Act are authorized by Section 5a to apply to the Interstate Commerce Commission for approval of any agreement between two or more such carriers[3] relative to rates, fares, classifications, and certain other traffic matters or procedures for the joint consideration, initiation, or establishment thereof. Parties to any agreement approved by the Commission are relieved from the operation of the antitrust laws with respect to the making and carrying out of the agreement in conformity with its provisions and such terms and conditions as may be prescribed. The Commission is directed to approve such agreement if it finds that by reason of the furtherance of the national transportation policy declared in the Act, exemption from the application of the antitrust laws should apply. The Commission may not approve any agreement between or among carriers of different classes unless limited to matters relating to transportation under joint rates or over through routes; any agreement which concerns a pooling, division or other matter or transaction to which Section 5 is applicable; or any

[1]Enacted June 17, 1948, as Public Law 662, 62 Stat. L. 472, 49 U.S.C. 5b. Commonly referred to as the Reed-Bulwinkle Act.
[2]49 U.S.C. 5c.
[3]The term "carrier" means any common carrier subject to parts I, II, or III, or any freight forwarder subject to part IV of the Act. (Paragraph (1) (a) of Section 5a.)

agreement which does not accord to each party the free and unrestrained right to take independent action either before or after any determination arrived at through the procedure established by the agreement.

This particular section of the I.C. Act is permissive only and it is optional with carriers to apply or not to apply for relief as to the making and carrying out of an agreement as to joint action coming within its scope. "It confers no initial jurisdiction upon the Commission beyond the terms and provisions of particular agreements which carriers may voluntarily submit."[4]

Under paragraph (8) of Section 5a "No order shall be entered under this section except after interested parties have been afforded reasonable opportunity for hearing."[5] In conformity with this provision, the Commission's rules and regulations governing applications under Section 5a, as amended, for authority to establish or continue agreements between or among carriers provide[6] that "A public notice will be issued by the Commission and filed with the Director of the Federal Register stating the fact that an application has been filed under these rules and indicating how a hearing on such application may be obtained."[7]

By the enactment of Section 5a, Congress did not intend that the powers and duties conferred on the Commission by the I.C. Act should in any way be diminished.[8] Nor is there anything in Section 5a which would justify the abandonment of the fundamental principle of the I.C. Act that competitive initiative must characterize and give dynamic force to rate initiation. This underlying premise continues in effect.[9] Except as modified by Section 5a, the I.C. Act imposes a duty on each carrier to initiate its own rates.[10] Section 5a, in providing for approval of proced-

---

[4]*Eastern Railroads — Agreement*, 277 I.C.C. 279, 287. See also the report of the Special Master in *Georgia v. Pennsylvania Railroad Co.*, 324 U.S. 439 (S. Ct. No. 10, Original, Vol. 1, p. 33).

[5]"This requirement is applicable not only as to orders with respect to original applications for approval of agreements, but also as to orders terminating or modifying approval of agreements, or modifying terms and conditions upon which agreements were approved." (H.R. Report No. 1100, 80th Cong., 1st Sess., p. 16.)

[6]Section 3.3 (d).

[7]See *Central States Motor Freight Bureau, Inc. — Agreement*, 278 I.C.C. 581, 582, where no request for public hearing had been received from applicants, and where no other party to the proceeding supported the application.

[8]Cong. Rec., Vol. 94, No. 111, June 17, 1948, pp. A-4219-4222.

[9]*Georgia v. Pennsylvania Railroad*, 324 U.S. 439, 459; *United States v. Chicago, Milwaukee, St. Paul and Pacific Ry.*, 294 U.S. 499; *Texas and Pacific Railway Co. v. United States*, 289 U.S. 627; *Arizona Grocery Co. v. Atchison, Topeka and Santa Fe Ry. Co.*, 284 U.S. 370.

[10]*Georgia v. Pennsylvania R.R., supra; Arizona Grocery Co. v. Atchison, Topeka and Santa Fe Ry. Co., supra.*

ures for the joint consideration, initiation or establishment of rates and other related matters did not undertake to change the design of the I.C. Act to preserve the individual carrier's initiative in rate-making, but provided for approval of joint action by all the carriers involved therein. Further, the I.C. Act's emphasis on individual freedom of action is strengthed by the requirement in paragraph (6) that no agreement shall be approved which fails to preserve full independence of action by each carrier. In addition the words, "joint consideration, initiation or establishment" in paragraph (2) of the section and the words "through joint consideration" in paragraph (6) manifestly connote participation and the exercise of responsibility by each carrier.

Section 5b of the Act, which supersedes section 5a with respect to ratemaking agreements of rail common carriers, provides more restrictive statutory prohibitions governing the approval of such agreements by the Commission.

Section 5b authorizes common carriers by railroad subject to Part I of the Act to apply to the Commission for approval of any agreement between or among two or more such carriers relating to rates, classifications, and other specified matters, or procedures for the joint consideration, initiation, or establishment thereof. The parties to an agreement approved by the Commission are relieved from the operation of the antitrust laws with respect to the making and carrying out of such agreement in conformity with its provisions and such terms and conditions as we may prescribe. The Commission is directed to approve such agreement if it finds the agreement to be in furtherance of the national transportation policy and not prohibited by Section 5b. Paragraphs (4) and (5) of Section 5b prohibit the Commission from approving any agreement (1) with respect to a pooling, division, or other matter or transaction to which Section 5 is applicable, or (2) which does not accord to each carrier party the free and unrestrained right to take independent action without fear of any sanction or retaliatory action, at any time, before or after any determination arrived at through the procedure established by the agreement. In addition, limitations are provided that no conference, bureau, committee, or other organization established or continued pursuant to any agreement approved by the Commission under Section 5b shall (i) permit participation in agreements with respect to, or any voting on, single-line rates, allowances, or charges established by any carrier; (ii) permit any carrier to participate in agreements with respect to, or to vote on, rates, allowances, or charges relating to any particular interline movement, unless such carrier can practicably participate in such movement,[11] or (iii) permit, provide for, or establish any procedure for joint consideration or any joint action to protest or otherwise seek the suspension of any rate or classification filed by a carrier of the same mode pursuant to section 15(8) where such rate or clasification is established by independent action. However, the limitations cited in (i), (ii), and (iii) above are not applicable to (1) general rate increases or decreases if the agreement accords the shipping public, under specified procedures, adequate notice of at least 15 days of such proposals, and opportunity to present comments thereon, in writing or otherwise, prior to tariff filing of such increases or decreases with the Commission, or (2) broad tariff changes of general or substantially general application throughout the territory within which such changes apply.

As explained by the Commission in *Railroads Per Diem, Mileage, Demurrage — Agreement:*[12]

> . . . Commission approval of a proposed agreement under section 5b of the act, must consider apart from the specific prohibitions 5b(5)(a), whether the agreement is in furtherance of the national transportation policy. If a finding cannot be made that a proposed agreement is consistent with this policy and contributes to its effectuation then the agreement must be disapproved. Determination of the foregoing necessitates a broad examination of conditions which affect the public interest, the interests of the carriers, the needs of commerce, and the national defense. . . .

Carriers of One Class

In determining whether an agreement between or among two or more carriers relating to rates and other traffic matters can be approved,

[11]The original Senate bill provided that no carrier organizations could permit any carrier to participate in discussions or agreements, or to vote on rates of an interline movement, unless the carrier could practicably participate in the movement. *Senate Conference Report*, No. 94-595, in *U.S. Code Congressional and Administrative News*, 94th Cong., 2d Sess. 168 (1976). The language was intended to permit "[o]nly those railroads which could actually handle the movement of traffic under the rate as an origin, destination or intermediate carrier" to join in the proceedings relating to that rate. *Senate Report*, Committee on Commerce, 94-499 in *U.S. Code Congressional and Administrative News*, 94th Cong., 2d Sess. 69 (1976). The House bill allowed non-participating carriers to discuss rates but not to vote or enforce such rates. See *Senate Conference Report, id.* at 169. The Conference Committee decided that the Act should permit discussion with respect to joint line rates as provided in the House Bill. In *Southern Ports Foreign Frt.—Agreement*, 355 I.C.C. 216, the Commission approved a ratemaking agreement which defined "practically participate" as follows: Carrier can practically participate in a movement involved in a proposal if such carrier participates in a route as published in a tariff on file with the I.C.C. from an origin involved in the proposal to a destination involved in the proposal.

[12]353 I.C.C. 673. 684.

the Commission must consider the specific prohibitions against approval contained in paragraphs (4), (5) and (6) of Section 5a.[13]

Under paragraph (4) of Section 5a, the Commission may not approve "any agreement between or among carriers of different classes unless it finds that such agreement is of the character described in paragraph (2)" and "is limited to matters relating to transportation under joint rates or over through routes." For purposes of paragraph (4), "carriers by railroad, express companies, and sleeping car companies are carriers of one class; pipe-line companies are carriers of one class; carriers by motor vehicles are carriers of one class; carriers by water are carriers of one class; and freight forwarders are carriers of one class."[14]

In *New England Motor Rate Bureau, Inc. — Agreement,*[15] the Commission dismissed an application submitted by a group of common carriers by motor vehicle because it was found that approval of the agreement was prohibited by paragraph (4). Among the applicant signatories to the agreement submitted to the Commission for approval were three freight forwarders. The freight forwarders participated in the bureau's classification and were permitted to file proposals and take part in public hearings, but did not have a vote in the determination of classification matters. It was contended by those in opposition to approval of the agreement that the inclusion of the freight forwarders as applicants and as participating parties contravened paragraph (4) of Section 5a. Under special permissions from the Commission, the three freight forwarders had been allowed to concur in the freight classification published by the bureau in order that their individual tariff rates could be governed by that classification. But these special permissions were unrelated to the matter of participation in an agreement submitted for approval under Section 5a. The Commission, in holding that paragraph (4) forbade approval of the agreement so long as freight forwarders were parties thereto, said (p. 15):

> Public Law 881, Eighty-first Congress, second session, approved December 20, 1950, amended Section 409 of the Act in certain respects and authorized freight forwarders and common carriers by motor vehicle to continue to operate under joint rates and charges until the expiration of 9 months after the date of such enactment, or until September 20,

---

[13]*Western Traffic Assn. — Agreement,* 276 I.C.C. 183, 209.

[14]Representative Bulwinkle, one of the sponsors of Section 5a, in commenting on paragraph (4), said that the paragraph "prohibits 'mixed' conferences . . ." Thus railroads may not be part of the same conference with motor carriers, nor either of them with carriers by water, or any of these with freight forwarders or pipe lines. (Cong. Rec., Vol. 94, No. 111, June 17, 1948, pp. A4219-4222.)

[15]287 I.C.C. 9.

1951. By order of the Commission, division 2, of the latter date, all concurrences issued by motor common carriers of property authorizing freight forwarders to publish and file joint forwarder-motor rates pursuant to Section 409(b) of the Act were stricken from the Commission's files. Since that date freight forwarders and motor common carriers have been without statutory authority to enter into or maintain joint rates. Apart from this, however, the nature of classification ratings is such that they are not susceptible of separate consideration and determination with respect to their application in connection with joint rates as distinguished from other rates.

In *Pacific Motor Tariff Bureau, Inc. — Agreement*,[16] the Commission said that although all existing members of the rate bureau were motor common carriers, membership was not limited to such carriers, the bylaws providing that qualified applicants found eligible by the secretary could become members; nor did the record establish any requirements respecting membership qualifications or eligibility. To meet the standards contemplated by Section 5a, the bylaws should be amended to set forth requirements providing that any motor common carrier operating under authority of Commission and engaged in transportation within the bureau's territorial jurisdiction may become a member on the same terms and conditions as existing members.

Pooling or Other Matter or Transaction to Which Section 5 of the Act is Applicable

Under paragraph (5) of Section 5a, the Commission may not approve "any agreement which it finds is an agreement with respect to a pooling, division, or other matter or transaction, to which Section 5 of this Act is applicable." This is to make it clear that matters to which Section 5 now relate "are to continue to be subject to the appropriate provisions of Section 5, and that the new Section 5a is intended to apply only to agreements not already covered by Section 5."[17]

The Right of Independent Action

By paragraph (6) of Section 5a, the Commission may not approve an agreement "unless it finds that under the agreement there is accorded to each party the free and unrestrained right to take independent action either before or after any determination arrived at through" the prescribed procedure.

[16]313 I.C.C. 406, 407.
[17]H.R. Report No. 1100, 80th Cong., 1st Sess., p. 5.

The meaning of the phraseology used in paragraph (6) was considered in *Western Traffic Assn. — Agreement*.[18] The independent action provision there under consideration was cast in the words of the statute, and reserved to each member of the association the "free and unrestrained right to take independent action either before or after any determination" arrived at under procedure established by that agreement. The Commission there indicated that the purpose and effect of this phraseology was to guarantee that each party to an agreement shall have the right to elect whether it will "(1) place a proposal in channels for consideration under bureau or committee procedure, (2) proceed by independent action to establish the proposed rate or charge without regard to bureau procedure, or (3) to take independent action during or after bureau consideration." In other words, as held in *Central States Motor Freight Bureau, Inc. — Agreement*,[19] "the member carrier is to be accorded the right to take independent action at any time, whether before, during, or after consideration pursuant to procedures established by the particular agreement to which it is a party."

In the *Central States Motor Freight Bureau* case, applicants took the position that in view of the disjunctive "or" in the language of paragraph (6), their agreement did not run afoul of the paragraph if the member carriers' right of independent action were limited to the period preceding or the one following bureau action.[20] Protestants shared the view that paragraph (6) required that there be preserved the free and unrestrained right of any member carrier to take independent action at any time, whether before, during, or after consideration pursuant to procedures established by the particular agreement. The Commission found that approval of the agreement was prohibited by paragraph (6) and dismissed the application which had been filed.

The agreement in *Columbia Tariff Bureau — Agreement*[21] also failed to accord each party thereto the free and unrestrained right to take independent action during the period in which a proposal was being processed under bureau procedures. By the terms of the agreement, opportunity to act independently was restricted to the time preceding submission of a proposal or following the close of the docket meeting where it was considered. The Commission, citing its decision in the *Central States Motor Freight Bureau* case, dismissed the application.

The Commission dismissed an application field in *Independent Mov-*

---

[18]276 I.C.C. 183, 210.
[19]278 I.C.C. 581, 584.
[20]In this instance, to the period "after" such action.
[21]284 I.C.C. 436.

ers' & *Warehousemen's Assn.* — *Agreement*[22] where the agreement failed
to provide for "the free and unrestrained right to take independent action
either before or after any determination." The Commission said (pp.
232-233):

> Protestant contends, in substance, that Section 5a, paragraph (6), pro-
> vides that a specific guarantee to each member of the right of indepen-
> dent freedom of action must be spelled out in the agreement as a condi-
> tion precedent to approval of the agreement by us. That contention is
> sound. The oral evidence is to the effect that it is the custom and prac-
> tice of the association to publish rates, rules, and regulations for account
> of, and as desired by, individual members, as well as for the members of
> the association as a group. Notwithstanding this, ... the agreement
> provides, in part, that "the members of this Association shall automatically
> participate in the tariffs published by this Association for the transporta-
> tion of household goods. . . ."

> The issue before us concerns the agreement as filed, and no oral explana-
> tion or interpretation of the agreement can be accepted as constituting,
> in any respect, a modification of the agreement. The provisions . . . .
> taken together, indicate the possibility that the agreement does bind the
> members so that they are not accorded the free and unrestrained right
> to take independent action either before or after any determination ar-
> rived at through the procedure outlined in the agreement. At the hearing
> counsel for applicants offered to amend the agreement by incorporating
> in the bylaws a specific provision to the effect that each member shall
> have the free and unrestrained right to take independent action in regard
> to tariff matters, if the Commission should consider such a provision
> obligatory. Any amendment to the bylaws must first be approved by a
> majority of the members . . . . While we are authorized to prescribe such
> terms and conditions as may be necessary to enable us to grant approval
> of an agreement in accordance with the standard set forth in paragraph
> (2) of Section 5a, paragraph (6) provides that the Commission shall
> not approve any agreement which does not accord each party "the free
> and unrestrained right to take independent action either before or after
> any determination. . . ." There is no such provision in the agreement.
> In the circumstances, we conclude that approval of the agreement is pro-
> hibited by paragraph (6).

In *Western Carriers Tariff Bureau* — *Agreement*,[23] the Commission
reiterated that it looked with disfavor on any language in Section 5a
agreement that may be susceptible of misinterpretation; thus, although
the rules established under the proposed agreement apparently assured
each member the right to act independently in publication of its own
rates, to avoid any question which might arise in that respect, the
Commission said that the agreement should be amended to provide

---

[22]277 I.C.C. 229.
[23]310 I.C.C. 334, 337.

specifically that each party is accorded the free unrestrained right to take independent action in publication of rates, rules, and regulations, either before or after any determination arrived at through bureau procedure, and to provide a reasonable time limit within which such independent actions will be published. In *Transcontinental Refrigerated Carriers, Inc. — Agreement,*[24] the Commission said that a provision of bylaws that a carrier may exercise its right of independent publication only as to rates submitted for consideration through procedures of the association was in violation of prior findings of the Commission and was objectionable as an infringement of a carrier's right to act independently.

In determining whether an agreement filed under Section 5a accords to carrier parties the free and unrestrained right to take independent action, even though the language of the agreement is cast in the language of the statute, the Commission appraises the whole agreement. This was demonstrated in *Central States Motor Common Carriers — Agreement,*[25] where the Commission found that approval of the agreement submitted was prohibited by paragraph (6) because of a provision therein which authorized the rate bureau to be the exclusive publishing agent of its members. Protestants had directed attention to a provision in the agreement filed by members of Central States Motor Freight Bureau, Inc., which provided in effect for exclusive publication by the bureau of its members' rates and charges. They contended, generally, that the preclusion of the right of a carrier to publish its own rates is a substantial impairment of the right of independent action.

Applicants asserted, however, that the language of paragraph (6) relates the right of independent action directly to determinations arrived at under procedures established by agreements among carriers, and that no mention is made of the publication of tariffs in that paragraph of Section 5a. They argued that the publication of tariffs is not an activity within the purview of section 5a and that the requirement in the bureau's bylaws that all tariffs of each member, including tariffs giving effect to independent action, shall be published through the bureau cannot in fact be a restraint upon a carrier's right to determine independently what the rate shall be, particularly in view of the provisions in the agreement expressing each member's right of rate determination. The Commission rejected applicants' contention by stating (pp. 524-525):

[24]308 I.C.C. 193, 196.
[25]289 I.C.C. 517. This was the second agreement submitted by members of Central States Motor Freight Bureau, Inc.

. . . We are unable to agree with applicant's contention that the quoted language is limited to determinations and does not apply to provisions of the agreement relating to the publication of tariffs. The coverage of Section 5a extends to procedures for the "joint consideration, initiation or establishment" of rates. Tariff publication is necessary to the establishment of rates, and the provisions of the agreement governing such publication are within the scope of that section. Furthermore, the phrase "unrestrained right to taken independent action" in connection with the establishment of a proposed rate in our opinion clearly includes the choice by the individual carrier of assigning publication of its determination to an agent or of making its own publication. Unless the carrier has that choice, it does not have the free and unrestrained right contemplated by the statute. The agreement in its present form, modified as proposed by the applicants, will not permit this independence of action. Approval of the agreement is prohibited, therefore, by paragraph (6) of Section 5a.

"Complete freedom of independent action embraces," the Commission said in *Columbia River Tariff Bureau — Agreement*[26] "the right of a carrier to publish its own tariffs without risk of forfeiting its membership." In the *Columbia River* case, the agreement provided that each carrier member of the bureau covenanted and agreed to have its tariffs published by the bureau, and that failure to comply with the terms of the agreement would be sufficient cause for forfeiture of membership.

It had been contended by protestants in various Section 5a proceedings that the practice of rate bureaus filing petitions with the Commission for suspension of rates, whenever independent action is taken by a member carrier, amounts to an unwarranted interference with, and a restraint upon, the free and unrestrained right of a carrier to take such action. It had been argued that parties to a Section 5a agreement are not accorded the right of independent action, free and unrestrained, when a rate bureau or conference holds over them the threat of a suspension proceeding. The Commission considered this problem in *Middle Atlantic Conference — Agreement*,[27] stating:

> We recognize that this practice is of advantage and aid to the Commission in the administration of the act and the prevention of destructive rate cutting such as has required the issuance of minimum-rate orders in the Middle Atlantic and other territories. It is manifestly impossible, as a practical matter, for the Commission to scrutinize each and all of the multiplicity of tariffs and rate changes that are constantly being filed. So far as concerns motor-carrier rate matters, the practice is one which is governed and sanctioned by Sections 216 (e) and (g) of the act. Section 216 (e) provides that "Any person, State board, organization or body politic" may make complaint against any rate in effect or proposed to be put into effect, and Section 216 (g) provides that the Commis-

26284 I.C.C. 436, 440.
27283 I.C.C. 683, 688-690.

sion may suspend the operation of any proposed rate "upon complaint of any interested party. . . ." We do not believe that approval under Section 5a is a prerequisite to the free exercise of this statutory right. It is our view and we conclude that such a group activity is not one pertaining to the "joint consieration, initiation, and establishment" of rates and charges within the purview of paragraphs (2) and (9) of Section 5a, and accordingly that provision for such a practice has no proper place in an agreement submitted for approval under that section. It follows that we may not impose a condition of approval prohibiting the exercise of this statutory right, as sought by the shipping interests, and further that our approval of the agreement, subject to the conditions hereinafter indicated, will not encompass this practice.

In *New England Motor Bureau, Inc.,*[28] the Commission held that a provision in an agreement authorizing the bureau to engage in litigation as a party complainant against its members and others by seeking the suspension of proposed rates or by assailing rates established and in effect was "in conflict with the views expressed and determination made in" the *Middle Atlantic* case "and for reasons there stated should be stricken from the agreement."[29] In *Pallets, Platforms, or Skids, Central Territory,*[30] the contention was made that under the principles of Section 5a, there is serious question as to the propriety of a rate bureau's actively contesting schedules which it publishes in behalf of a member carrier as its agent. There, the Commission said:

> This proceeding does not bring in issue the question of the scope and application of Section 5a in relation to the practice to which objection is made. The question raised by the respondents, at most, is collateral to the issue presented by the proposed schedules. The propriety under Section 5a of such practice by bureaus should be determined, therefore, only in proceedings under that section which present the question directly for decision. We express no opinion here on the merits of this practice.

The Commission, however, had in the past cautioned rate bureaus operating under Section 5a agreements for protesting rate proposals and then failing to submit supporting evidence. Such a practice, the Commission had said, was an harrassment which could lead to depriving an

---

[28]287 I.C.C. 9, 14.

[29]That provisions authorizing rate bureaus to protest the establishment of proposed rates have no proper place in Section 5a agreements also was held in *General Tariff Bureau, Inc., New Furniture — Agreement,* 288 I.C.C. 578, 581; *Eastern Motor Freight Conference, Inc., — Agreement,* 286 I.C.C. 791, 796; *Columbia River Tariff Bureau — Agreement,* 284 I.C.C. 436, 439; *Chicago Suburban Motor Carriers Assn., Inc. — Agreement,* 288 I.C.C. 415, 419-420; *Central State Motor Common Carriers — Agreement,* 289 I.C.C. 517, 528-529; *Tobacco Transporters Freight Traffic — Agreement,* 288 I.C.C. 517, 520, *National Motor Freight Traffic Agreement,* 292 I.C.C. 45, 52.

[30]52 M.C.C. 282, 283.

individual carrier of its free and unrestrained right to take independent action guaranteed by Section 5a(6).[31]

Rate bureaus are now prohibited entirely from protesting proposals of carrier members. This prohibition was announced in *Rate Bureau Investigation.*[32] This finding in *Rate Bureau Investigation* overturned earlier I.C.C. decisions, such as *Middle Atlantic Conference—Agreement, supra.*[33] In reversing its past decisions, the I.C.C. said (pp. 459-62):

> . . . Upon reevaluation of the entire matter on the record before us, and in the light of our greater knowledge and experience in administering section 5a, we found in the prior report that the reasoning of those decisions is incorrect and must be reversed.[34] For the reasons enunciated below, we conclude that our decision prohibiting rate bureau protests of member carriers' independent actions is a necessary and proper function of this Commission under the section 5a statute.

> Paragraph (2) of section 5a confers upon the Commission authority to grant approval of carrier (not bureau) agreements "only upon such terms and conditions as the Commission may prescribe as necessary to enable it to grant its approval in accordance with the standard above set forth in this paragraph." The standard set forth in paragraph (2) requires that the approval not be prohibited by other provisions of section 5a and that the agreement be in furtherance of the national transportation policy. Paragraph (7) of section 5a further authorizes the Commission to investigate and determine whether any previously approved agreement is in conformity with the standard of paragraph (2). It is apparent that the Commission, in administering section 5a of the act, has the authority to impose conditions and prescribe standards for carrying out the mandate of the statute.

> In order to prevent any threat to the free and unrestrained right of carrier independent action, the public interest and furtherance of the national transportation policy require that we condition our approval of an agreement against bureau protests of members' independent action proposals.

> We cannot emphasize too strongly that the right of a carrier member of a ratemaking bureau to take independent action before or after the collective ratemaking process is absolute under section 5a(6) of the act. This means that, contrary to the petitioners' arguments, we must not only inquire whether a bureau's procedures protect the carrier's right of independent action but also examine how practices by the agent bureau affect the exercise of that right. Furthermore, this examination cannot be limited to determining whether the bureau intends to restrict the independence of its carrier members, for the statute does not provide that only intentional

---

[31]*Feed from Kansas City, Mo., to Indianapolis, Ind.,* 304 I.C.C. 411; *Groceries from Chicago, Ill., to Ia. and Minn.,* 304 I.C.C. 437, 439.

[32]351 I.C.C. 437.

[33]See also *Central States Motor Common Carriers — Agreement,* 299 I.C.C. 773, 777; and majority report in *Arbet Truck Lines, Inc. v. Central States Motor Freight,* 321 I.C.C. 460, 463-466.

[34]The I.C.C. has authority to reverse past decisions when it has sound reasons to do so. See *American Trucking v. A. T. & S. F. R. Co.,* 387 U.S. 397, and *Atchison, Topeka & Santa Fe R. Co. v. Wichita Board of Trade,* 412 U.S. 900.

infringement of a carrier's freedom is to be banned. If a practice restricts or tends to restrict the right of carrier independent action, the statute requires that it be prohibited. On this record, we have become convinced that bureau protests are a deterrent to individual members carriers' free and unrestrained right of independent action.

We disagree with petitioners allegations that approved section 5a rate bureaus have a statutory right to protect independent action proposals which the Commission may not infringe. Petitioners disregard the fact that the enactment of section 5a of the act was an accommodation between two conflicting policies the antitrust laws and collective ratemaking practices. (See the legislative history of section 5a, House Report 1100, 80th Cong., 1st Sess., at p. 12 and the detailed discussion thereof in *Western Traffic Assn.–Agreement*, 276 I.C.C. 183, 185.) In the statutory accommodations of both policies, carriers were placed in a unique position of being able to engage in collective ratemaking exempt from the antitrust laws so long as their actions were taken in accordance with section 5a. The exemption from the antitrust laws must be strictly construed in order to make certain that carrier competition remains viable. Abuses such as instances shown on this record where it is apparent that rate bureaus and not their members determined what rates were to be maintained by member carriers can no longer be sanctioned. The protests by the rate bureaus of independent action proposals does inhibit competition. The Commission has pointed out "° ° °" that the failure of some bureaus operating under section 5a agreements to submit supporting evidence after having protested rate proposals tends to deprive an individual carrier of its right of independent action, guaranteed by paragraph 6 of section 5a of the Act." *Junk from Davenport, Iowa, to Chicago*, 302 I.C.C. 39, 40; *Feed from Kansas City, Mo., to Indianapolis, Ind.*, 304 I.C.C. 411. We take official notice of the fact that since our prohibition became effective on July 15, 1975, there has been a substantial increase in the publication of independent action proposals and a decrease in the number of protests filed. The general language of section 216(e) of the act, relied upon by motor rate bureaus as conferring a right to protest member carrier independent action, cannot be used to defeat the authority of the Commission to condition its approval or continued approval of carrier ratemaking agreements to achieve the express statutory standards of section 5a(2) and the prohibition of section 5a(6) of the act.

As the Commission explained in *Eastern Railroads–Agreements*, 277 I.C.C. 279, 287: "Section 5a is permissive only and it is optional with carriers to apply or not to apply for relief as to the making and carrying out of an agreement as to joint action coming within the scope of that section." However, if carrier groups seek the protection of section 5a, they must be prepared to accept such conditions as the Commission may prescribe for approval of the carrier agreements to comport with the statutory standards of section 5a. While a rate bureau seeking continued approval of its agreement under section 5a is by our decision, here affirmed, prohibited from protesting independent action proposals, member carriers are still able to protest those proposals individually or jointly, so long as the joint action does not constitute an "attempt to interfere directly with the business relationships of a competition." See *California Motor Transport Co. v. Trucking Unlimited, supra.*

The authority to initiate protests rests with the member carriers themselves, not the bureau. Several individual carriers assert they do not have the personnel and resources at hand to develop traffic and cost data within the time available for filing protests and seek the continued participation of rate bureaus in this process. Although we are cognizant of the role played by rate bureaus in providing many transportation related services for their member carriers, such as continuing traffic studies of carrier operations as well as compilations and analyses of carrier costs for performing transportation, we have concluded that the bureaus' role must be limited if the right of independent action is to remain absolute and viable. Fairness dictates that the data compiled and maintained by rate bureaus should be equally available to all member carriers, proponents and protestants alike. Thus, our decisions will permit the furnishing of data to any member carrier upon specific request. Parties are advised that the furnishing of data by rate bureaus does not in any manner limit our prior holding that any attempt by rate bureaus "to continue the same practice with the charade of a change of name of protestant only or any other device" will not be tolerated.

Contrary to suggestions made by petitioning rate bureaus, it is the Commission and not the rate bureau that has the statutory duty to make certain that the rate structure is lawful in all respects. Petitioners' fears that the curtailment of their "policing" activities will result in the proliferation of below-cost rates are misplaced. The Commission in the exercise of its tariff supervision has established a Consumer to bring to its attention nonprotested proposals which may require action on the Commission's own motion. This unit is being expanded to provide greater surveillance in connection with unreasonable rate filings. Again we emphasize that, whatever the advantages of rate bureau protests, they must yield to the mandate of section 5a that a carrier's right of independent action be free and unrestrained.

Standards Required by the Act

Under paragraph 2 of Section 5a of the act, the Commission may not approve an agreement unless it finds that, by reason of the national transportation policy declared in the I.C. Act, relief from the operation of the antitrust laws should apply.[35] Paragraph 2 of Section 5a requires two

---

[35]The direction that the Commission shall approve the application upon the making of the finding above referred to is subject, however, to the qualification that approval is to be granted upon such terms and conditions as the Commission may prescribe as necessary to enable it to grant its approval in accordance with the standard set forth in the paragraph." (H.R. Report No. 1100, 80th Cong., 1st Sess., pp. 14-15.) The authority granted to the Commission to impose terms and conditions in connection with approval of agreements is necessary, as pointed out in H.R. Report No. 1100, "for protection of the public interest"; and by imposing such terms and conditions, "the Commission will be able to qualify and limit its approval so that the agreement, subject to such qualifications and limitations will meet the standard or test for approval prescribed in paragraph (2)."

findings: (1) That the agreement will be in furtherance of the national transportation policy, and (2) that the agreement will so further the transportation policy as to outweigh the agreement's disadvantages to the public interest to be guarded against by the antitrust laws.[36] Provisions having a similar purpose as Section 5a are to be found in Section 15 of the Shipping Act of 1916;[37] Section 5 of the I.C. Act, as amended;[38] and Section 412 and 414 of the Federal Aviation Act of 1958.[39] Each of these, like Section 5a, provides for relief to the parties involved from the operation of the antitrust laws upon approval of a subject by the administering body.

National Transportation Policy

Basic to any consideration which must govern the determination of the Commission's approval or disapproval of any agreement presented under Section 5a of the act, apart from the specific prohibitions contained in that section, is whether the particular agreement submitted for approval is in furtherance of the national transportation policy. The national transportation policy formulated and declared by Congress was designed to provide for fair and impartial regulation of all modes of transportation subject to the provisions of the Interstate Commerce Act, and —

> to promote safe, adequate, economical, and efficient service and foster sound economic conditions in transportation and among the several carriers; to encourage the establishment and maintenance of reasonable charges for transportation service, without unjust discriminations, undue preferences or advantages, or unfair or destructive competitive practices; to cooperate with the several States and the duly authorized officials thereof; and to encourage fair wages and equitable working conditions;— all to the end of developing, coordinating, and preserving a national transportation system by water, highway, and rail, as well as other means,

[36]Enactment of Section 5a followed several years of controversy before Congress over the merits of the collective rate-making practices of private groups of carriers. In its report on the bill which was passed in substantially the same form in which it was reported (H. Report 1100, 80th Cong., 1st Sess., P. 12), the House Committee on Interstate and Foreign Commerce said that Congress had in its legislation embodied two important policies. One is the policy set forth in the antitrust laws, that restraint of commerce is not in the public interest, and the other is the policy set forth in the I.C. Act, particularly in the national transportation policy. The conclusion was arrived at in the report that "in the field of transporation the two policies cannot both be applied in full measure," so there "must be some accommodation between them."

[37]46 U.S.C. 814.
[38]49 U.S.C. 5.
[39]49 U.S.C. 1382 and 1384.

adequate to meet the needs of the commerce of the United States, of the Postal Service, and of the national defense.

All provisions of the act are to be administered and enforced with a view to carrying out the declaration of policy. This is expressly designated as the general standard by which agreements submitted under Section 5a are to be approved or disapproved. If a finding cannot be made that any proposed agreement harmonizes with this policy and contributes to its effectuation then the agreement must be disapproved.[40] As was explained by the Commission in the *Western Traffic Assn.* case (p. 211):

> This necessitates a broad examination of conditions which affect the public welfare, the interests of the carriers, and the needs of commerce of the postal service, and of the national defense. Those parts of the policy, however, most directly pertinent here call for the promotion of "adequate, economical and efficient service," for the fostering of "sound economic conditions in transportation," and for encouraging the establishment and maintenance of "reasonable charges for transportation service, without unjust discrimination, undue preferences, or avantages, or unfair or destructive competitive practices."

In *Wearing Apparel Carriers — Agreement*,[41] the Commission found that because of certain deficiencies in the agreement it would not be in furtherance of the national transportation policy. In dismissing the application of the common carriers by motor vehicle, the Commission said (p. 487):

> An examination of the agreement reveals various defects, mainly of omission. The agreement is deficient in failing to provide specific procedures for the joint consideration, initiation, or establishment of rates which will adequately preserve the rights of the individual carriers as well as shippers in conformity with the national transportation policy. While we do not assume the task here of setting forth in detail every provision that should be contained in the proper agreement of this type, we note that the submitted agreement fails to: (1) specify the number of members in the rate committee, how they are designated, what constitutes a quorum thereof, and how the committee votes or takes action; (2) provide for the submission of proposals by shippers as well as member carriers; (3) provide for notice of proposals and of dispositions to member carriers and interested shippers; and (4) afford member carriers and interested shippers an opportunity to present their views, either orally or in writing, in support of or in opposition to any proposal. Pertinent here is the view expressed in *Independent Movers' & Warehousemen's Assn. — Agreement*, 286 I.C.C. 651, 654, in denying the application, that "An agreement under which joint procedures are to be followed should specify the pro-

[40]*Western Traffic Assn. — Agreement*, 276 I.C.C. 183, 211.
[41]288 I.C.C. 486.

cedures." Furthermore, the agreement fails to outline the geographical scope of operations of the carriers parties thereto, or to provide for the admission or participation of other certificated motor carriers upon the same terms as existing parties to the agreement. See *Waterways Freight Bureau — Agreement*, 277 I.C.C. 593, 597.

In *Independent Movers' & Warehousemen's Association — Agreement*[42] the Commission made the following comment with respect to an agreement which failed to make clear steps taken in the processing of a rate proposal:

> An agreement under which joint procedures are to be followed should specify the procedures. . . . We must conclude, therefore, that the agreement, as amended, through failure to provide adequate joint procedures, does not meet the standard of Section 5a, and accordingly that we are precluded from finding that the carrying out of the agreement would be in furtherance of the national transportation policy.

> We find that the agreement, as amended, will not be in furtherance of the national transportation policy . . .

Relief Provided from the Operation of the Antitrust Laws

Under paragraph (9) of Section 5a, parties to any agreement approved by the Commission and other persons are, if the approval of such agreement is not prohibited by paragraph (4), (5), or (6), "relieved from the operation of the antitrust laws with respect to the making of such agreement, and with respect to the carrying out of such agreement in conformity with its provisions and in conformity with the terms and conditions prescribed by the Commission." Any action of the Commission under Section 5a in approving an agreement submitted, denying an application for such approval, terminating or modifying it approval of an agreement, prescribing the terms and conditions upon which its approval is to be granted, or in modifying such terms and conditions, "shall be construed as having effect solely with reference to the applicability of the relief provisions of paragraph (9)."[43]

The scope of relief provided by Section 5a(9) is demonstrated by the decision in *Baltimore & O. R. Co. v. New York, N. H. & H. R. Co.*,[44]

---

[42]286 I.C.C. 651, 654.

[43]Paragraph (10). This provision "makes it clear that, while approval of an agreement will result in antitrust law relief, the Interstate Commerce Act and other applicable provisions of law will be fully operative with respect to action taken or failures to act in connection with the carrying out of engagements which are approved by the Commission under the section." (H.R. Report No. 1100, 80th Cong. 1st Sess., pp. 16-17.)

[44]196 F. Supp. 724, 748.

where the court said that even if the illegality of a per diem agreement, as a price-fixing agreement, were assumed, since in the case it was entered into pursuant to legislative edict (Esch Car Service Act) and further immunized by Section 5a of the I.C. Act, its enforcement would not be precluded by the antitrust laws; for where a restraint is based on valid governmental action as opposed to private action, no violation of the Sherman Act can be made out.

Even if the Commission finds that an agreement is in furtherance of the national transportation policy there can be no approval until a finding is made that the agreement furthers the policy in such manner and to such extent that relief from the antitrust laws should apply.[45] In considering the agreement, the Commission must give weight to each of the two established policies, and determine where the public interest lies after the accommodation and comparative evaluation of those policies. The Commission's task of "accommodation" implies that it shall give effect to both policies to the maximum extent practicable. One of these policies may be subordinated to the other only where there is (1) an actual conflict or incompatibility between the two policies, and where (2) the advantages flowing from the one policy are substantial and certain, while those flowing from the other are negligible and uncertain.

Any departures from the principles of the antitrust laws must be strictly construed, and immunity is obtainable only by precise compliance with the specific conditions prescribed by Congress.[46] Thus, where dispensation from the antitrust laws is involved, every provision is an immunizing agreement should be clear, definite, specific and complete. No device or subterfuge should be permitted which would enable carriers, under the shield of immunity granted by the Commission, to take action without the knowledge of the Commission and going beyond the limits of the precise terms approved after full disclosure of the surrounding circumstances.

In this connection, the language of the Special Master in *Georgia v. Pennsylvania Railroad Co.*[47] appears to be extremely pertinent in point-

---

[45]The Special Master is *Georgia v. Pennsylvania Railroad Co.*, 324 U.S. 439 (S. Ct., No. 10, Original, p. 5 of abstract of report) made it clear that Section 5a does not give the Commission authority to find that an agreement either violates or does not violate the antitrust laws. The Commission's approval of an agreement simply relieves the parties from the operation of the antitrust laws in carrying out the agreement according to its terms and conditions.

[46]*United States v. Frankfort Distilleries*, 324 U.S. 293; *United States v. Masonite Corp.*, c16 U.S. 265, 280; *United States v. Sacony-Vacuum Oil Co.*, 310 U.S. 150; *United States v. Borden Co.*, 308 U.S. 188, 198.

[47]324 U.S. 439. Abstract of principal points in Special Master's Report to the Supreme Court (No. 10, Original, pp. 10-11.)

ing out some of the devices which should be guarded against in any immunizing agreement:

> The territorial rate associations, considered only as forums for the discussion of rate proposals in advance of any filing with the I.C.C., are essential, because of the effects which rate changes have on other rates and on the intersts of competing shippers and localities, and because of the railroads' duty under the Interstate Commerce Act to initiate rates that are reasonable and nondiscriminatory. . .

> The defendants, however, in establishing and maintaining their territorial associations, have agreed upon more than the mere provision of forums for discussion. They have agreed upon procedures and structures which are designed to check the scope and frequency of rate reductions by (i) guarding railroads against the importunities of their customers (through secret ballot votes and the confidentiality of proceedings); (ii) bringing the influence of adverse majority votes (including the votes of railroads not directly concerned with the given proposal) to bear on the proponent of a rate reduction and on any roads disposed to join with the proponent; (iii) vesting authority in paid officials to hold up favorable majority action (or threatened independent action against unfavorable majority action) by means of an appeal to a higher body when these officials deem the reduction inimical to the best interests of the railroads as a whole; and (iv) providing separate organizations of Vice Presidents and Presidents to each of which such appeals may be taken. In addition, there is a common understanding that, while each member reserves the right, at every given stage of rate association proceure, to take independent action, either as the initiator of a rate change or as a joint participant in it, the members will rarely exercise that right when appeals are taken or the votes go against the proposal, realizing that if the appeal provisions and majority votes were disregarded with much frequency the system would tend to break down, to the financial injury of all.

> These agreements and understandings do not destroy the right of independent action, but to some extent they dampen down the frequency of its use and serve as a deterrent, self-imposed and non-coercive, to the freedom of rate-making.

Conformance of the Agreement to Limitations Recited in the Statute

To be approved by the Commission, an agreement submitted under Section 5a must conform to the limitations recited in the statute. The agreement must relate specifically to rates, fares, classifications, divisions, allowances, or charges, and rules and regulations pertaining thereto, and the procedures for the joint consideration, initiation or establishment thereof.[48] "Anything outside the scope of these specified

---

[48]E.q. In Section 5a Application No. 61 (Amendment No. 3), *National Classification Committee — Agreement,* decided November 29, 1977, the Commission held that procedures for the processing of claims for loss and damage were not within the scope of Section 5a.

objectives would be ultra licitum."[49] However, while many of the agreements approved by the Commission under Section 5a have dealt with rate-making procedures, the scope of that section is not so limited; the language of the section specifically embraces an agreement between carriers relating to charges and other matters specified in the I.C. Act.[50] Section 5a was amended in conference by the Senate and the House to make it absolutely clear that joint action shall be strictly confined to the foregoing matters. Senator Reed, one of the sponsors of Section 5a, in reporting to the Senate on behalf of the conferees, compared the broad language of the bill as originally introduced and the bill as reported by the conferees and later passed by Congress. He emphasized[51] that "the version of the bill on which the conferees have agreed is limited virtually to rates, fares, and charges, and joint rates and through routes." The Commission has no jurisdiction under Section 5a to consider and approve agreements which deal with matters other than those specified in paragraph (2) of Section 5a. This was recognized by Senator Reed, who, in his conference report, said: "One of those things (rates, fares, etc.) must be the subject matter of the agreement in order to lay it before the Interstate Commerce Commission and obtain approval."[52]

The scope of section 5a was considered by the Commission in *Michigan Motor Carriers Conference, Inc. — Agreement*,[53] where it was found that an agreement between and among motor common carriers was not one relating to rates and other traffic matters within the meaning of the statute because it merely delegated to the rate conference, among other things, the functions of carrier management with respect to tariff compilation, publication, and filing with regulatory bodies. The Commission said (pp. 329-330):

> The Department [of Justice] contends in effect, among other things, that the agreement is not one within the purview of Section 5a of the Act. There is merit to this contention. By Section 5a, common carriers subject to the act may apply to the Commission for approval of any agreement between or among two or more such carriers relative to rates, fares,

---

[49]*Western Traffic Assn. — Agreement*, 276 I.C.C. 183, 212.
[50]*National Motor Equipment Interchange — Agreement*, 305 I.C.C. 196, 199; *Western-Traffic Assn. — Agreement*, 309 I.C.C. 280.
[51]Cong. Rec., Vol. 94, No. 97, May 28, 1948, p. 6820.
[52]Eliminated from Section 5a are "agreements dealing with time schedules, routes, the interchange of equipment, the settlement of claims, the promotion of safety, or the promotion of adequacy, economy, or efficiency of operation or service." (Cong. Rec., Vol. 94, No. 84, May 11, 1948, 5769.) See also Cong. Rec. Vol. 94, No. 110, June 16, 1948, A 4183. See *National Motor Equipment Interchange-Agreement, supra*, relating to "charges" pertaining to the interchange of equipment.
[53]288 I.C.C. 327.

classifications and certain other matters, hereinafter called rates, or procedures for the joint consideration, initiation, or establishment thereof. The Commission is directed to approve any such agreement unless it falls within certain prohibitions, and if it finds that by reason of furtherance of the national transportation policy relief from the antitrust laws should apply with respect to the making and carrying out of the agreement. The issue concerns the scope of the agreement as filed, and no explanation or interpretation thereof, written or oral, can be accepted as constituting, in any respect, a modification of the agreement.

In substance, this agreement, among other things, merely delegates to the conference the functions of carrier management with respect to tariff compilation, publication, and filing with regulatory bodies . . . the members may request the conference to publish rates for their account, and are to compensate it in the form of dues or special assessments for the services rendered. The Commission has long recognized that these functions may be performed by agents under appropriate powers of attorney from the carriers. *F. S. Johnson & Co. v. Atchison, T. & S. F. Ry. Co.*, 21 I.C.C. 637. No other functions or duties with respect to rates appear to have been delegated or assigned to the conference in either the articles of incorporation or the bylaws; nor have any additional functions or duties with respect to rates been assigned to the conference. . . . This interpretation of the agreement is indirectly admitted by applicants. . . . None of the provisions of the articles of incorporation, or of the bylaws insofar as they specify the duties or functions of the conference, its board of directors or officers, discloses any rule of procedure between or among the carriers relating to the joint consideration, initiation, or establishment of rates as contemplated by Section 5a.

Supervisory Function of the Commission

Paragraph (3) of Section 5a provides that each conference, bureau, committee, or other organization established or continued, pursuant to any agreement approved by the Commission[54] shall maintain such accounts, records, files, and memoranda and shall submit such reports to the Commission, as may be prescribed. All such accounts, records, files, and memoranda shall be subject to inspection by the Commission or its duly authorized representatives.

The Commission considered the requirements of paragraph (3) in *Western Traffic Assn. — Agreement*,[55] where it emphasized that not

[54]What is submitted under Section 5a to the Commission is the basic agreement establishing the rate bureau and defining the nature and scope of its activities and mode of operation. It is not the rates or other collective actions resulting from the rate bureau procedures that are submitted.

[55]276 I.C.C. 183, 215. See also *Middle Atlantic Conference-Agreement*, 283 I.C.C. 683, 690-691, where the Commission said, "We shall, however, undertake to keep ourselves informed as to whether operations under the agreement are carried on in a manner to meet the standards of Section 5a and merit the continuance of our approval of the agreement."

only did it have knowledge of the procedures set up in the agreement submitted for approval, but that it could keep itself "informed as to their observance and their effects." The Commission concluded by saying, "We particularly shall keep ourselves informed as to the functioning of the right of independent action provided in the agreement."

In *Railroad Interterritorial Agreement*,[56] common carriers by railroad sought approval of an agreement between and among themselves relating to interterritorial traffic matters or proposals between points in the United States. There it was contended that the carriers had failed to establish a central office for the maintenance of accounts, records, files, and memoranda. The Commission said at page 709:

> Finally, we do not believe that the failure to establish a separate interterritorial organization with a "central record-keeping place" will tend to obstruct the Commission in performing its supervisory functions relating to the carrying out of the agreement, as contended by the Department [of Justice]. We have already expressed the view that utilization of territorial organizations, and of their experience in both territorial and interterritorial matters, will further the maintenance of a proper balance between territorial and interterritorial adjustments. It will be necessary for each territorial group to maintain records of each interterritorial proposal which it considers or acts upon, and we shall expect that each such organization will have complete records of the territorial group action on each proposal initiated by it. Thus, the Commission may inspect the records of interterritorial actions and related territorial actions at the same sources. Should any difficulties arise in this or any other connection, however, the matter of the procedures established by the agreement will be subject to further consideration on the Commission's own motion or on representations by any interested parties.

Investigation by the Commission

By paragraph (7) of Section 5a, the Commission is authorized, upon complaint or upon its own initiative, to investigate and determine whether any agreement previously approved by it under the section, or terms and conditions upon which approval was granted, "is not or are not in conformity with the standard set forth in paragraph (2), or whether any such terms and conditions are not necessary for purposes of conformity with such standard." After any such investigation, "the Commission shall by order terminate or modify its approval of such agreement if it finds such action necessary to insure conformity with such standard, and shall modify the terms and conditions upon which such approval was granted to the extent it finds necessary to insure conformity

[56]287 I.C.C. 701.

with such standard or to the extent to which it finds such terms and conditions not necessary to insure such conformity." This provision was deemed necessary by Congress in order that the public interest, as involved in the case of agreement to which Section 5a relates, would be protected adequately. It "is necessary that interested parties have the right to complain to the Commission, and that the Commission have the right to institute proceedings upon its own initiative, in order to correct situations which may develop through the operation of agreements in ways which were not foreseen at the time of the original grant of approval."[57]

Paragraph (7) also provides that the "effective date of any order terminating or modifying approval, or modifying terms and conditions, shall be postponed for such period as the Commission determines to be reasonably necessary to avoid undue hardship." While this provision appears to be unnecessary, it was considered "advisable to give recognition to the fact that undue hardship might result if such orders were to go into effect without giving the parties to agreements appropriate time to make necessary readjustments in their activities."[58]

Amendments to Agreements

While it may be recognized that an agreement properly may provide a method for its amendment, any approval of the agreement as submitted does not constitute approval of subsequent changes therein. As the Commission pointed out in *Western Traffic Assn. — Agreement:*[59]

> . . . Should any change in the rules of procedure of those bureaus be made effective without prior submission to and approval by us, the agreement will be subject to further investigation and consideration pursuant to the provision of paragraph (7) of Section 5a, for the purpose of determining whether the approval herein granted should be modified or terminated. Whether such change without our prior approval would deprive the parties of the relief from operation of the antitrust laws accorded in paragraph (9) is a question as to which we express no opinion. For the reasons indicated, therefore, we see no occasion for attaching a condition of approval requiring deletion of the provisions in question from the agreement.

[57]H.R. Report No. 1100, 80th Cong., 1st Sess., p. 16.
[58]*Ibid.*
[59]276 I.C.C. 183, 217. See also *Perishables Tariff Bureau — Agreement,* 308 I.C.C. 651, 654-5; *Pacific Motor Tariff Bureau, Inc. — Agreement,* 313 I.C.C. 406, 410; *Western Motor Tariff Bureau, Inc. — Agreement,* 310 I.C.C. 53.59.

In *National Bus Traffic Assn., Inc. — Agreement*,[60] it was contended by protestants that applicants were seeking approval of a right lodged in themselves to amend the agreement at any time without applying to the Commission for approval of the amended agreement. There, the Commission said:

> . . . To the extent that any changes in the rate and fare procedures are made effective without prior submission to and approval by the Commission, the matter would be subject to further investigation and consideration under Section 5a (7) of the Act for the purpose of determining whether a prior approval should be modified or terminated. In any event, the relief provided in paragraph (9) of Section 5a will not apply to such changed procedures unless and until an agreement establishing them is submitted to and approved by the Commission.

Admission, Participation and Expulsion of Carriers

As a condition of approval of Section 5a agreements, the Commission has required that such agreements provide "for the admission and participation of other carriers."[61] As expressed in *National Bus Traffic Assn., Inc. — Agreement*,[62] the agreement should provide that any carrier "shall be admitted to membership, as of right, upon the same terms as existing members." And in *Atlantic-Gulf Coastwise SS Freight Bureau — Agreement*,[63] the Commission said that "Admission to membership should be as a matter of right and anything less would be inconsistent with our prior decisions."

In *Western Motor Tariff Bureau, Inc. — Agrement*,[64] the Commission said that a provision for assessing participation charges based on a proportional relationship of individual carrier's gross common-carrier revenue earned within the scope of the bureau's tariff to total revenue of all carriers participating in that particular tariff, which charges would be determined by the board of directors, did not set forth with sufficient definiteness the charges to be made. The Commission said that charges should be based on gross revenues, with a specific charge for each gross-revenue bracket.

The Commission also has found that "Expulsion of a member for any other reason" than for a failure to pay dues would not "be an act coming

---

[60]278 I.C.C. 147, 155. See also *Chicago Suburban Motor Carriers Assn., Inc. — Agreement*, 288 I.C.C. 415, 421.

[61]*Waterways Freight Bureau — Agreement*, 277 I.C.C. 593, 597.

[62]278 I.C.C. 147, 154. See also *Middle Atlantic Conference — Agreement*, 283 I.C.C. 683, 690.

[63]284 I.C.C. 751, 755.

[64]311 I.C.C. 547, 548.

within the coverage of our approval of the agreement."[65] In *Western Motor Tariff Bureau, Inc. — Agreement,*[66] the Commission said that a provision in the bylaws for expulsion of bureau members for violation of rules or regulations prescribed by board of directors would militate against the member carriers' right to take independent action and should be stricken. Causes of suspension or expulsion should be limited to failure to pay dues, fees or charges owed the bureau under the agreement. In *National Bus Traffic Assn., Inc. — Agreement,*[67] the Commission again said that causes for expulsion of a carrier from a rate bureau should be limited to failure to pay financial obligations incurred under the agreement. The Commission said that the proposed amendments, to the extent they subjected members to suspension or expulsion for violating any of the provisions of the bylaws or for failing to cure a breach or obligation other than one involving payment of money owed to the association, unduly restrains the freedom of action of individual members, and must be stricken before the agreement, as amended, would be approved.

Joint Interterritorial Arrangements

In *Eastern Railroads — Agreements,*[68] the Commission considered certain provisions in the agreement submitted by railroad carriers which contemplated consideration and action by eastern carriers jointly with those in other territories. No procedures had been provided in the agreement. The Commission said that the provisions appeared "to have been included by applicants merely in anticipation of joint interritorial arrangements yet to be effected," but "In any event, the relief provided in paragraph (9) of Section 5a will not apply to such joint consideration and action unless and until an agreement establishing such procedures is submitted to and approved by this Commission."[69]

In *Chicago Suburban Motor Carriers Assn., Inc. — Agreement,*[70] the Commission expressed itself in this fashion:

Although the agency and rate agreements would be between associations, as distinguished from direct arrangements between and among common

[65]*National Bus Traffic Assn., Inc. — Agreement, supra,* pp. 154-155.
[66]310 I.C.C. 53, 56.
[67]308 I.C.C. 33, 36.
[68]277 I.C.C. 279, 290.
[69]The same finding was made by the Commission in *Central States Motor Common Carriers — Agreement,* 289 I.C.C. 517, 528; *New England Motor Rate Bureau, Inc. — Agreement,* 288 I.C.C. 450-451; *Chicago Suburban Motor Carriers Assn., Inc., — Agreement,* 288 I.C.C. 415, 420-421; *Southern Ports Foreign Freight Committee — Agreement,* 284 I.C.C. 775, 779, 780.
[70]288 I.C.C. 415, 420, 421.

carriers themselves, nevertheless the association here concerned, acting through its chairman, can only enter into such agreements with the authorization, approval or ratification of the board of directors, who are the duly authorized representatives of the member carriers. Such agency and rate agreements, which could affect the aforementioned collective rate-making procedures and practices of the applicants herein, may therefore be within the purview of Section 5a. Approval of the instant agreement, however, will not extend the relief provided in paragraph (9) of Section 5a to any procedures or practices resulting from such agency and rate agreements. See *Eastern Railroads — Agreement*, 277 I.C.C. 279, 290.

Operational Procedures

The Commission, in approving agreements submitted under Section 5a, has prescribed certain terms and conditions in the operational rate-making procedures of rate bureaus. The Commission has required that there be eliminated from agreements all provisions which accord bureau employees the right to docket for review by higher committees traffic matters which have received the consideration of member lines or which have been the subject of a recommendation by a lower ranking committee;[71] that the agreements include provisions that notice of intention to permit the expiration of rates bearing expiration dates which have been in effect for 15 months or longer shall be placed on the public dockets;[72] that determinations of rate committees be made by majority vote rather than by three-fourths vote;[73] that public notice through recognized traffic journals of national circulation be given of docketed proposals, hearings and recommended and final dispositions;[74] that direct notice be given of rate proceedings to all interested parties;[75] that notice of all actions taken by rate bureaus on traffic matters shall be given in the same manner and to the same extent as docket proposals;[76] that if shortened procedure is invoked shippers and other interested parties not

---

[71]*Western Traffic Association — Agreement*, 276 I.C.C. 183, 218; *Southern Freight Assn. — Agreement*, 283 I.C.C. 245, 252; *Eastern Railroads — Agreements*, 277 I.C.C. 279, 293; and *Illinois Freight Assn., — Agreement*, 283 I.C.C. 17, 26.
[72]*Ibid.*
[73]*Eastern Railroad — Agreements*, 277 I.C.C. 279, 293; *Illinois Freight Assn. — Agreement* 283 I.C.C. 17, 26; and *Central States Motor Common Carriers — Agreement*, 289 I.C.C. 517, 527. Protestants contended in these proceedings that the three-fourths rule provided the dominant carriers with veto power over rate adjustments desired by the majority of the membership. See also *Western Motor Tariff Bureau, Inc. — Agreement*, 310 I.C.C. 53, 56.
[74]*Central States Motor Common Carriers — Agreement*, 289 I.C.C. 517, 525; and *Illinois Freight Assn. — Agreement*, 310 I.C.C. 53, 56, 311 I.C.C. 547, 548.
[75]*New England Motor Rate Bureau, Inc. — Agreement*, 288 I.C.C. 450, 451-452; and *Chicago Suburban Motor Carriers Assn., Inc. — Agreement*, 288 I.C.C. 415, 422.
[76]*Inland Water Carriers' Freight Assn. — Agreement*, 278 I.C.C. 756, 760.

members of the conference should be provided with notice of filing of such matters, an opportunity to present their views for or against the matter, and notice of disposition thereof;[77] that there be eliminated from agreements open end provisions which permit use of procedures not provided in the agreement;[78] that approval of an agreement is restricted to the portions that concern rates and other matters subject to the Commission's jurisdiction and does not include intrastate matters;[79] that a general geographical description setting forth the territorial limits of rate-making is desirable in the interest of clarity;[80] that the agreement may provide for the publication of schedules containing or limited to quotations or tenders of rates and/or charges to the United States Government under Section 22 of the I.C. Act;[81] and the imposition of a condition in an agreement, that nothing therein or in action take thereunder shall relate to or circumscribe the duty or right of any carrier in the use of vehicles to serve its shippers in accordance with its duties under its tariffs and under the statute, is unnecessary since those duties and rights remain paramount and would not be affected by the Commission's approval of the agreement.[82]

Rate Bureau Investigation

In Ex Parte 297, *Rate Bureau Investigation*,[83] the Commission instituted a proceeding to inquire into the activities of ratemaking organizations operating pursuant to approved Section 5a agreements for the purpose of determining whether it should require any of these agreements to be amended in any respect. As a result of this proceeding the I.C.C. made the following findings (pp. 466-67):

[77]*Southern Illinois Motor Rate Conference — Agreement*, 311 I.C.C. 45, 46.
[78]*Movers' & Warehousemen's Assn. — Agreement*, 308 I.C.C. 421, 423-4.
[79]*General Tariff Bureau, Inc., New Furniture — Agreement*, 288 I.C.C. 578, 582; *Pacific Motor Tariff Bureau, Inc. — Agreement*, 313 I.C.C. 406, 408; *Western Motor Tariff Bureau, Inc. — Agreement*, 311 I.C.C. 547; *Ohio Motor Freight Tariff Committee, Inc. — Agreement*, 311 I.C.C. 127, 128. In *Western Motor Tariff Bureau, Inc. — Agreement*, 310 I.C.C. 53, 55, the Commission said that all references in the agreement to intrastate commerce or rates should be eliminated; "commerce," as pertinent to a Section 5a proceeding, is defined in the antitrust laws as "trade or commerce among the several States"; rates applicable exclusively to intrastate commerce are not within purview of Section 5a, and since the Commission has no jurisdiction thereover under that section, antitrust immunity could not be granted with respect thereto.
[80]*Transcontinental Refrigerated Carriers, Inc. — Agreement*, 308 I.C.C. 193, 196.
[81]*Movers' & Warehousemen's Assn. — Agreement*, 308 I.C.C. 421, 423-4. Section 5a, by amendment of Section 22, is made applicable to tenders or quotations arrived at through bureau procedures.
[82]*National Motor Equipment Interchange — Agreement*, 305 I.C.C. 196, 200.
[83]351 I.C.C. 437.

1. Rate bureaus assist the making of appropriate rates.

2. Procedural changes would foster actions more favorable to bureau members, shippers, and the general public; such changes being contained in the body of the report.

3. The right of independent action does not adversely affect the rate structure.

4. A system need not be established by the I.C.C. to monitor public hearings before rate bureaus, but that formal minutes, and not verbatim transcripts, are required of rate committee proceedings.

5. I.C.C. representatives may attend all rate bureau meetings; but that copies of correspondence and documents concerning all rate bureau meetings need not be filed with the I.C.C.

6. A uniform system of accounts for rate bureaus will be promulgated.

7. Rate bureaus are not prohibited from furnishing technical and professional services to other bureaus or nonmembers provided that the limitations expressed in the report are observed.

8. Rate bureaus may not invest in another commercial business, whether related or unrelated to its primary function of processing and publishing rates and related matters for member carriers.

9. Rate bureaus are prohibited from acquiring other rate bureaus without prior I.C.C. approval.

10. Rate bureaus should not be profitmaking enterprises.

11. A carrier member of a bureau, which carrier is affiliated in any way with a shipper, may not serve on a bureau's board of directors, general rate committee, or any other committee which has an effect, either directly or indirectly, on the ratemaking function of the bureau without specific prior I.C.C. approval.[84]

12. A maximum period of 120 days should be prescribed for the processing of proposals to final disposition.

13. Public notice of proposals need not identify the proponent.

14. Rate bureaus are prohibited from broadening the territorial or commodity scope of an individual rate proposal without prior adequate notice.

---

[84]A "shipper-affiliated carrier" was defined in Ex Parte No. 297, by order served August 25, 1975, as a common carrier which

(1) is wholly or partially controlled or managed by an individual, company, or other business enterprise and for whom the carrier performs transportation services; or,

(2) wholly or partially controls or manages a company or other business enterprise for whom the carrier performs transportation services; or,

(3) is controlled or managed in a common interest with a shipper or receiver of freight for whom the carrier performs transportation services and/or shares common facilities, however such result is attained, whether directly or indirectly by use of common directors, officers, or investment company or companies, or in any other manner whatsoever.

The court in *Motor Carriers Traffic Assn. v. U.S. and I.C.C.*, No. 76-1329, 4 Cir., decided July 21, 1977, said that the Commission acted within its authority under Section 5a(7) in prohibiting carriers that are in any way affiliated with a shipper from serving on a bureau's board. See also *United States v. Chesapeake & Ohio Ry. Co.*, 44 LW 4869-4878 (decided June 17, 1976); *United States v. Allegheny-Ludlum Steel*, 406 U.S. 742, 755.

15. Adoption of shortened special procedures involving proposals covering special docket applications are not warranted.

16. Section 22 quotations require special bureau procedures limiting notification to members and the governmental agency.

17. Docketing of rate bureau proceedings with respect to general rate increase proposals need not be mandatory.

18. The I.C.C. need not obtain and publish reports of the deliberations within the industry concerning the matter of general increases.

19. The various rate bureaus need not join in seeking general rate increases.

20. The various rail rate bureaus are not required to substantiate general increases on a regional basis only, but the regional costs should be presented in a more explicit manner.

21. Rate bureaus are prohibited entirely from protesting proposals of carrier members, and are not merely limited to instances in which the proposed rate is less than long-term variable cost or any other specific instance.

22. Rate bureaus should be prohibited from discouraging independent action proposals of member carriers in any way, including the protesting of the filing of any rates pursuant to such action.

23. Rate bureaus should be prohibited from discouraging members from publishing individual tariffs.

24. Immunity from antitrust laws shall be continued.

25. Immunity from the antitrust laws shall continue to be extended to agreements with respect to proposals of single-line movements.

26. Additional legislation is not necessary, and need not be sought, to better effect the goals for which Section 5a was enacted.

45

Pooling or Division of Traffic, Service, or Earnings of Carriers Subject to the Interstate Commerce Act

Purpose of the Act

Section 5(1) of the Interstate Commerce Act[1] provides as follows:

Except upon specific approval by order of the Commission as in this section provided, and except as provided in paragraph (16) of Section 1 of this part, it shall be unlawful for any common carrier subject to this part, Part II, or Part III to enter into any contract, agreement, or combination with any other such common carrier or carriers for the pooling or division of traffic, or of service, or of gross or net earnings, or of any portion thereof; and in any case of an unlawful agreement for the pooling or division of traffic, service, or earnings as aforesaid each day of its continuance shall be a separate offense: *Provided,* That whenever the Commission is of opinion, after hearing upon application of any such carrier or carriers or upon its own initiative, that the pooling or division, to the extent indicated by the Commission, of their traffic, service, or gross or net earnings, or of any portion thereof, will be in the interest of better service to the public or of economy in operation, and will not unduly restrain competition, the Commission shall be order approve and authorize, if assented to by all the carriers involved, such pooling or division, under such rules and regulations, and for such consideration as between such carriers and upon such terms and conditions, as shall be found by the Commission to be just and reasonable in the premises: *Provided further,* That any contract, agreement, or combination to which any common carrier by water subject to Part III is a party, relating to the pooling or division of traffic, service, or earnings, or any portion thereof, lawfully existing on the date this paragraph as amended takes effect, if filed with the Commission within six months after such date, shall continue to be lawful except to the extent that the Commission, after hearing upon application or upon its own initiative, may find and by order declare that such

---

[1] 49 U.S.C. 5(1). Pooling agreements subject to Section 5(1) are not to be approved under Section 5a. For the authorization of pooling of traffic in reorganization of railroads, see Section 77(f) of the Bankruptcy Act (11 U.S.C. 305(f)).

contract, agreement, or combination is not in the interest of better service to the public or of economy in operation, or that it will unduly restrain competition.

Competing Carriers

Section 5(1) contemplates approval by the Interstate Commerce Commission of any arrangement whereby competing carriers seek to pool their traffic, their services, or their revenues. The primary purpose of such provision is that of guarding against actions by competing carriers which would tend to reduce competition.

The Commission and the courts have consistently held that Section 5(1) is applicable only to arrangements between competing carriers which arrangements present at least the possibility of a lessening of competition contrary to the public interest. In order to avoid a lessening of competition in situations wherein such would be adverse to public interest, the authority of the Commission must be sought as a condition precedent to any such pooling arrangement by the competing carriers. For example, if two railroads which both operate from point A to point B were to decide that the traffic of both could be physically transported in the trains of one of them with resultant over-all operating savings, and that the net revenues or profits of such operation should be divided between the two railroads, that would be a pooling as contemplated by Section 5(1). Similarly, if it were to be agreed between the two railroads that each should operate only on alternate days, the carrier operating on a given day to move the traffic of both on that particular day, such would be a Section 5(1) pooling.

In *Petition, Dining Car, Nashville, C. & St. L. Ry.*,[2] the Commission reiterated a previous holding in *Application of Pullman Company*,[3] stating:

> We conclude that the provisions of Section 5(1) which were primarily designed to protect competition in the transportation field are still so designed and are thus limited. There must be competition between the carriers involved in order to activate the statute.

Like recognition as to the vital element of a competitor's relationship between the carriers is to be found in *Railroad Freight Traffic, Everett and Bellingham, Wash.*[4] The Commission, at page 522, observed that the applicants were "competing for the traffic, thus activating the pro-

[2]292 I.C.C. 783, 785.
[3]259 I.C.C. 41, 47.
[4]298 I.C.C. 521.

visions of Section 5(1) of the Act." Similarly, in *Boston & M.R. Pooling Application,*[5] the Commission stated that in order to bring an agreement within the purview of Section 5(1) there must be an actual competitive relationship between the carriers involved in. In *Application of Pullman Co.,*[6] the Commission stated:

> There is nothing in the legislative history of the 1940 act to envince an intention on the part of Congress to depart from the long-continued provision limiting the effect of the prohibition to competing carriers and to bring under the control of the Commission any contract dealing with the subject matter of the section regardless of a competitive relation between the parties. On the contrary, that such was not the intent is indicated by the fact that we are still required to find in applications under this section that the pooling or division will not unduly restrain competition. The fact that the adjectival phrase "different and competing" in describing the carriers affected was omitted is of no significance. The word "pooling" itself contemplated a competitive relationship between the parties to the pool.

In *Railroad Freight Traffic Between Everett and Bellingham, Wash.,*[7] CMStP&P and GN applied under Section 5(1) for approval of a pooling of service arrangement whereby the GN would transport loaded and empty freight cars moving in the service of CMStP&P between Everett and Bellingham, which was a segment of its line from Seattle to Vancouver, B.C., Canada. The CMStP&P had a line of railroad, unconnected with any of its other lines, from Bellingham to Glacier, Wash., known as the Glacier Branch. The CMStP&P traffic between Seattle, Wash., on the one hand, and Bellingham and points on the Glacier Branch on the other, was moved by barge. Most of the barges in this service were owned by the CMStP&P, and they were moved by a towing company. The barges continued to be used in emergencies and in instances of unusually heavy movements. The applicants maintained connections with each other and had interchange facilities at Everett and Bellingham. The CMStP&P paid GN 35 cents a car mile for each loaded or empty car. GN estimated out-of-pocked costs of 10 cents a car mile for handling CMStP&P cars. CMStP&P estimated it would save about $5.00 per car over its cost by barge, which resulted in an annual savings in excess of $40,000. The Commission found that applicants were competing for the traffic, thus activating the provisions of Section 5(1); the arrangement, assented to by the carriers, would not unduly restrain such competition as they would continue to solicit

[5]298 I.C.C. 703, 709.
[6]259 I.C.C. 41, 45.
[7]298 I.C.C. 520.

traffic over their respective routes; the arrangement would be in the interest of better service to the public; the arrangement would promote economy in operation; the terms and conditions thereof were just and reasonable; and the agreement was a contract for the pooling of service within the purview of Section 5(1).

Absence of Competition

In *Southern Pacific Co. v. Interstate Commerce Commission*,[8] the Supreme Court held that a contract between railroads, connecting but not competing, which reserved the right of routing shipments, was not a pooling agreement within the purview of Section 5(1). The Supreme Court in the *Southern Pacific* case rested its conclusion as to the inapplicability of Section 5(1) upon the absence of competition. The court observed (p. 559) that the "various roads were really not competing roads within the meaning of the fifth section of the Commerce Act, when the facts are carefully examined." The lower court's observation on the same point was as follows:[9]

> That act (Section 5(1)) prohibits only pools of competing railroads, and the sole object of suppressing such pools was to protect the competing relation, and any and every arrangement or device intended to destroy, and which does destroy, that relation, whether expressly named in the act or not, contravenes its policy.

Pooling Arrangement as Contemplated by Section 5(1)

In *Express Contract, 1920*,[10] the Commission indicated that Section 5(1) embraces all agreements or arrangements between carriers that tend to restrain competition or potential competition with respect to traffic or service or which involve a division of revenues from such traffic or service on some basis other than the individual performance of the carriers involved.

Pooling of Railroad Earnings and Service, Pullman Co.,[11] involved an application filed by the railroads for approval under Section 5(1) of the purchase of the sleeping car ownership and servicing business

---

[8]200 U.S. 536. Also see *Atchison, T. & S. F. Ry. Co. v. Denver & N. O. R. Co.*, 110 U.S. 667.

[9]*Interstate Commerce Commission v. Southern Pac. Co.*, 132 Fed. 829, 841.

[10]59 I.C.C. 518, 521-22. See also *Joint Passenger Train Service*, 302 I.C.C. 355; *Pooling, Less Than Carload Freight Service, New York and Philadelphia to Macon*, 283 I.C.C. 158; *Pooling of Merchandise Traffic, St. Louis, Mo., to Los Angeles*, 276 I.C.C. 424.

[11]268 I.C.C. 473.

of Pullman.[12] The application was field after Pullman was ordered in an antitrust suit to confine itself to the manufacturing phase of its business and to divest itself of its sleeping car ownership and servicing business. The application was opposed by the Department of Justice on the ground that no pooling was involved and on the basis that approval was not justified because of the undue restraints on competition inherent under the argeement. The Commission found that the arrangement involved pooling and it approved it on the ground that the arrangement would provide improved sleeping car service and would promote economy in operation. It also concluded that the arrangement involved no undue restraint of competition.

Express Contract, 1920,[13] involved an application by American Railway Express Company and the railroads for approval of an operating agreement between them. Under the agreement, the express company was to receive a certain percentage of any profits derived from the express business and the remainder of the profit, or any losses, would be divided among the railroads based on some formula that had been worked out. The Commission found that the agreement involved a division of earnings, and therefore was a pooling agreement under Section 5(1). (Because of the dominance of the express business by Railway Express Company, the Commission expressed doubt as to whether there was any competition foreclosed by the agreement. It found, however, that foreclosure of potential competition might be involved.)

Relying on the 1920 decision, the Commission found in *Securities and Acquisition of Control of Railway Express Agency,*[14] that an agreement by the railroads to form Railway Express Agency, Inc., for the purpose of acquiring and operating the business of Railway Express Company involved a pooling of earnings within the meaning of Section 5(1). The Commission approved the agreement. The exclusive agency provision in the agreement was challenged by the Department of Justice in an antitrust suit in *United States v. Railway Express Agency, Inc.*[15] The district court referred the matter to the Commission for a determination of whether the exclusive agency provision was a necessary part of the pooling agreement. The Commission found that the provision was a necessary part of the agreement and approved it. It found that the exclusive agency provision contributed to economy in operation and there was no undue restraint involved. The district court dismissed the anti-

---

[12]The sale was approved by the district court in *United States v. Pullman Co.*, 64 F. Supp. 110, aff'd 330 U.S. 806.

[13]59 I.C.C. 518.

[14]150 I.C.C. 423.

[15]101 F. Supp. 1008.

trust suit on the ground that the Commission's approval of the agreement immunized it from attack under the antitrust laws.

In *Boston & M. R. R. Pooling Application*,[16] and *Geitz Storage & Moving Company, Inc. — Investigation of Control*,[17] the Commission found that agreements which tend to restrict the freedom to solicit business by a carrier constitutes pooling within Section 5(1).

The *Fifteen Per Cent Case, 1931*,[18] involved the grant by the Commission of a general rate increase of 15 percent for the railroads. However, the Commission conditioned the increase to provide that the proceeds from such an increase would be pooled and made available to financially distressed railroads. The railroads contended that this pooling arrangement was not within the purview of Section 5(1) because the participating railroads did not all compete with one another. The Commission agreed with the contention of the railroads and instead of exercising control over the agreement under Section 5(1) did so through its power to impose conditions in approving the rate increase.

In *Application of Pullman Co. Under Section 5(1)*,[19] Pullman and Canadian National agreed to apportion sleeping car service and earnings on through runs between Canada and the United States in accordance with the mileage in the respective territories. It was agreed that the earnings on this service above a certain amount would be divided equally. The Commission held that the agreement did not involve pooling on the ground that Pullman and Canadian National did not compete.

In *Riter v. Oregon Short Line R. R.*,[20] an association was formed by Western railroads to validate return excursion passenger tickets for the member lines. A fee for the service was charged the passengers and revenues were distributed among the member lines in proportion to their respective track mileage. The arrangement was attacked on the ground that it constituted illegal pooling. The Commission held that it was unable to see how there was anything amounting to a pooling or a division of earnings involved.

In *Freeport Fast Freight, Inc., and Liberty Trucking So. — Pooling*,[21] the Commission said that the commingling by two motor carriers of less than truckload shipments not exceeding certain weights in any one day, regardless of the number of shipments, for transportation in vehicles

---

[16]298 I.C.C. 703.
[17]55 M.C.C. 649.
[18]179 I.C.C. 215.
[19]259 I.C.C. 41.
[20]19 I.C.C. 443.
[21]85 M.C.C. 577, 578-79.

of one between Chicago and Freeport, Ill., the operating carrier to receive 85 per cent of net revenue accruing to the billing carrier, was a pooling arrangement which met the requirements of Section 5(1).

In *T.E.K. Lines, Inc.*[22] it was held that pooling contemplates the mutual surrender of traffic by one competitive carrier to another without regard to individual performance.

The question of what is a pooling arrangement as contemplated by Section 5(1) was discussed at length in *Consolidated Freightways Corp. of Del., Pooling,*[23] a case which also contains a discussion of the history of that statute. In *Consolidated Freightways,* the Commission said (pp. 600-605, 606-607):

> The question of whether the considered agreement is properly a pooling arrangement as contemplated by Section 5(1) of the Act is fundamental. No definition of pooling appears in that section, nor elsewhere in the act. See *Chicago & N. W. Ry. Co. v. Peoria & P. U. Ry. Co.,* 201 F. Supp. 241 (1962). The examiner found that the agreement provided for a pooling of service. A pooling of service is sufficient under the act. The initial question therefore, is whether the proposed agreement is a "contract, agreement, or combination . . . for the pooling or division of traffic, or of service, or of gross or net earnings, or any portion thereof" within the meaning of Section 5(1) of the Act.

> As originally enacted in 1887, the Act to Regulate Commerce, 24 Stat. 380, prohibited all agreements to pool freight or to divide earnings of rail carriers. Prior to the enactment of that legislation, the courts generally held that such agreements limiting competition were contrary to public policy and refused to enforce them. *Chicago M. & S. P. R. Co. v. Wabash St. L. & P. R. Co.,* 61 Fed. 993 (1894).

> Subsequent to enactment of the act of 1887, opposition to pooling was beginning to be counterbalanced by sentiment for legalizing such agreements if they were in the public interest; and the Commission was given power effectively to regulate them. See our 1892 annual report, pages 47-55. The most significant factor which prompted legalization of certain pooling was the experience gained from the Government's operation of the railroads during World War I. "Under such operations it was found that certain pooling or division of traffic and revenue, although inherently restraining competition to some extent, resulted in more economical operations for the carriers and provided a better service to the shipping public, . . ." *Terminal Cartage Corp.—Pooling,* 70 M.C.C. 199, 203 (1956). We recommend in our 1919 annual report, at page 4, that the Congress consider a revision of the limitations upon united or cooperative activities among common carriers by rail and by water, whereby wasteful or unduly expensive competition in rates or service would be eliminated.

[22]286 M.C.C. 139, 147-48.
[23]109 I.C.C. 596.

Subsequently, Congress approved Section 5(1) of the Transportation Act of 1920, 41 Stat. 48, which amended the earlier act by legalizing those agreements among common carriers "for the pooling of freights of different and competing railroads or to divide between them the agreegate or net proceeds of the earnings of such railroads or any portion thereof" which are approved by order of the Commission, after a hearing. Section 5(1) provides that before we can approve such agreements, we must find that the division of traffic or earnings will be in the interest of better service to the public, or economy in operation, and will not unduly restrain competition. If favorable findings are made, the Commission is authorized to approve the division of traffic or earnings, if assented to by all the carriers involved, under such rules and regulations, and for such consideration as between such carriers and upon such terms and conditions, as shall be found by us to be just and reasonable.

The act of 1920 did not apply to motor carriers, and the Motor Carrier Act of 1935, 49 Stat. 543, contained no prohibition against pooling. Subsequently, however, the provisions of the 1920 act relating to pooling and applying only to rail carriers were revised somewhat and were made applicable to motor carriers in the Transportation Act of 1940, 54 Stat. 905. Comparing the 1920 and 1940 provisions, we expressed the opinion in our 54th annual report, 1940, at page 3, that "former Section 5 with respect to pooling is not materially changed, except that it is extended to cover common carriers subject to Parts II and III as well as Part I, ..." Also, in *Atlantic Greyhound Corp.–Pooling*, 37 M.C.C. 543, 55 (1941), we expressed the view that "there was no intent, in enacting the amendment, to change essentially the former intent of the paragraph as to the nature of contracts, agreements, or combinations declared unlawful." The changes made by the 1940 act must be kept in mind when considering the present proposal. The act removed the phrases, "of freights of different and competing railroads or to divide between them the aggregate or net proceeds of such railroads, or any portion thereof," and substituted in lieu thereof the phrases, "or division of traffic, or of service, or of gross or net earings, or any portion thereof."

Although legislative treatment of pooling agreements thus dates back to the act of 1887, no specific definition of pooling appears in any of the applicable legislation. Furthermore, there are few Federal court decisions applying and construing Section 5(1). *Chicago & N. W. Ry. Co. v. Peoria & P. U. Ry. Co., supra.* As noted by the examiner at page 9 of his reoprt: "What cases there are, however, generally appear to contemplate a mutuality of interest in a common cause arising out of an agreed upon exception to normal operation by carriers subject to the act. . . .'" There are also, as shown in protestants' arguments, cases which say that for an agreement to be a pooling agreement, the division of revenue among parties must be based on something other than individual performance. See, for example, *Atlantic Greyhound Corp.–Pooling, supra,* where it is stated at page 550:

> To come within the provisions of the paragraph, the arrangement between the carriers must provide for a pooling or division of traffic, to which each participating carrier contributes, and int he revenues

from which each shares according to some agreed formula otherwise than according to individual performance.

It should be noted, however, that the above quotation treats the pooling or division of traffic *and* the pooling of revenues as conjunctives even though Section 5(1) clearly states them in the disjunctive.

Analysis of several cases indicates that a pro rata division of revenues may qualify as a pooling agreement within the meaning of Section 5(1) if it embodies a pooling of service or traffic. In *Canada Coach Lines and Niagara Scenic Bus—Pooling*, 45 M.C.C. 555 (1947), a pooling agreement was approved which provided basically that each of the two participating carriers would provide equal shares of the service and equipment, and receive equal shares of the net revenues. Also supporting this position is *Freeport Fast Frt., Inc., and Liberty Trucking Co.—Pooling*, 85 M.C.C. 577 (1960), which approved an agreement whereby two motor carriers would pool certain shipments moving to or from two Illinois points, with the operating carrier receiving 85 percent ofthe net revenue accruing to the billing carrier. Also, in *Pooling, L. C. L. Freight Service, New York to Miami*, 283 I.C.C. 171 (1951), in approving an arrangement under which loaded less-than-carload cars would move over alternate roads in Alternate weeks, it was stated at page 173:

> . . . There is no pooling of revenue. Each carriers participating in the arrangement receives its proportionate share of a common through rate on each commodity transported pursuant to established divisional arrangements.

As in the foregoing cases, the present proposal involves a pooling of service rather than a pooling of revenue; thus, a division of revenues based on individual performance would not preclude a finding that it is the type of agreement contemplated by Section 5(1) of the Act. Because each of the multi-State carriers agrees that their traffic covered by the agreement will be transported to and from the involved service points only by Ryan, the proposed agreement is one for the pooling or for the division of service. Protestants, however, argue that a *correlative* surrunder or division of traffic is also a requisite, and that such surrunder or division is lacking on the part of Ryan. As noted by the examiner at page 11 of his report, however, what is required "is a correlative surrender or contribution, *Atlantic Greyhound Corp. et al.—Pooling*, 37 M.C.C. 543, 551 (1941), and Ryan's contribution is that it will perform the work." Based upon the foregoing analysis, we find that the proposed agreement is of the type described in Section 5(1).

With respect to one of its minor features, to come within the purview of Section 5(1), the agrement must be among carriers subject to Part II of the Act. Thus, unless the service performed by Ryan under the proposal is within the Commission's jurisdiction, it would seem that Ryan could not properly be considered a common carrier subject to Part II of the Act for purposes of applying Section 5(1) to the proposal. To the extent that Ryan could perform only terminal area operations within the Ardmore (or Oklahoma City) terminal zone, its operations under the agreement would be exempt under Section 202(c) (2). See *Interchange of Traffic at Point of Origin*, 46 M.C.C. 623 (1946), and *Ric's Transfer Co., Inc., Extension—Seattle, Wash.*, 96 M.C.C. 366 (1964). Since Ryan would not be acting as a line-haul carrier in a commercial zone, the proposed agreement should be revised to clearly provide that the service to be performed by Ryan at Ardmore (or Oklahoma City) shall include only that service over which the Commission has jurisdiction.

Under Section 5(1), our approval may be given only if it can be found that the proposed pooling or division will be in the interest of better service to the public or of economy in operation, will not unduly restrain competition, and is assented to by all the carriers involved. The record supports the conclusion that the pooling arrangement would result in economy in operation, both financially and otherwise. Because of the small number and size of shipments in the involved area, the multi-State carriers generally must operate at a loss in handling the traffic which is the subject of the proposal. Operations pursuant to the agreement would result in diminution of operating expenses, thus enabling these carriers to at least minimize such losses. Furthermore, the shipping public would be offered more frequent and more expeditious service than is presently available. From the record, it is apparent that the proposal would be in the interest of better service to the public and of economy in operation.

The examiner's approach to the question of restraint upon competition is both reasonable and necessary. Because he determined that approval of the agreement as proposed by applicants could cause an unfair competitive situation to arise between pool and nonpool carriers, he conditioned approval herein upon applicants' permitting any suitably authorized line-haul carrier to become a party to the agreement. He recognized that if all suitably authorized carriers became parties, there would be no pickup and delivery competition whatever at the pool points, and determined that it would be more advantageous to shippers and receivers to have pool service of only one carrier available to them than merely to continue the present level of service. Additionally, there is presently no real competition at the proposed pool points inasmuch as carriers do not find it economically feasible to serve these points and have reduced service to minimum levels, thereby leaving the involved segment of the shipping public with a lack of competition among carriers. Approval of the agreement and subsequent rendition of service in accordance with its terms should raise the level of service. Shippers would be protected from any possible abuses inasmuch as we would be authorized under Section 5(9) of the Act to issue orders supplemental to those made under Section 5(1). The order will also retain broad jurisdiction to enter any further order we may in the future require in the public interest. On this basis, we believe that the agreement should be approved subject to the condition that all appropriately authorized carriers be permitted to become parties, to it, to the conditions set forth below, to appropriate modifications with regard to service at Ardmore, and to assent of all participating carriers.

* * *

It is also imperative that thorough consideration be given to the question of the agreement's implications with regard to motor carrier operating rights and the duties inherent in those rights. The most fundamental opposition to approval of the agreement stems from the argument that approval of the involved arrangement would, in effect, permit motor carriers to bypass their duty to provide reasonably continuous and adequate service to and from their authorized service points in violation of the duty imposed by Section 216(b) of the Act. This position relies on cases such as *Buhr—Revocation of Certificate*, 62 M.C.C. 774 (1954), wherein it was stated at page 776:

> In our opinion, carriers holding operating rights issued by us should render the service authorized and should not be permitted to retain authority unless they intend to and do render such service. The failure of a common carrier to operate may be regarded as a violation of the terms of its certificate and of the provisions of the act and of the Commission's rules and regulations promulgated thereunder, and constitute grounds for the Commission's calling upon the carrier to resume operations under penalty of havingt he certificate revoked. . . .

See also *Central States Transit Lines—Revocation of Certificate*, 66 M.C.C. 325 (1956). However, these and other similar cases applying the above-quoted principles involved situations in which common carriers had completely ceased solicitation of traffic and operations and did not, as here proposed, attempt to fulfill their certificate obligation through the use of an agent, and to combine to serve shippers at their authorized points. Where we have examined the situation in the light of current conditions and a concrete proposal to continue and even improve operations under a pooling-of-service arrangement which would benefit both the carriers involved and the shipping public, we can find that the active and continued interest and participation by carriers in such a pooling arrangement can be considered to have met the duty imposed by Section 216(b). Such a finding, we emphasize, does not imply that any carriers may casually abandon its duty to render an active and continuous service under its certificates.

Belated Applications for Approval of Pooling Agreements

There have been many instances in which the Commission has approved belated applications for approval of pooling agreements.[24]

Change in the Pooling Arrangement

In *Increased Express Rates and Charges*,[25] the Commission said that

---

[24]*Contracts for Protective Services*, 253 I.C.C. 18; *Pooling of Refrigeration Earnings*, 258 I.C.C. 24; *Juan de la Cruz Guerra Common Carrier Application*, 49 M.C.C. 657; *Puget South-Portland Joint Passenger Train Service*, 169 I.C.C. 244; *Pooling Passenger Train Revenues and Service*, 223 I.C.C. 343; *Freeport Fast Freight, Inc. and Liberty Trucking Co. — Pooling*, 85 M.C.C. 577; *North American Van Lines, Inc. — Investigation of Control*, 55 M.C.C. 649; 65 M.C.C. 257.

[25]266 I.C.C. 369.

a change by the railroad owners of Railway Express Agency in apportioning revenues and expenses from a monthly to a yearly basis and a simplification of the apportionment calculations constituted a change in the pooling arrangement that required Commission approval.

It was held in *Pooling of Railroad Earnings and Service, Pullman Co.*,[26] that a carrier having an interest in the Pullman Company was not required to secure Commission approval when it discontinued sleeping car service by Pullman and undertook to provide such service on its own. This ruling was based on the ground that the above was a withdrawal from and not the formation of a pooling agreement.

Enforcement of Section 5(1)

Section 5(8)[27] provides that district courts shall have jurisdiction upon the complaint of the Commission alleging violation of Section 5(1) or disobedience of any order issued by the Commission thereunder, to provide for injunctive relief, mandatory or otherwise, as may be necessary to restrain a violation of that provision or to compel obedience to such order. Section 8 provides that in case any common carrier subject to Part I shall do, cause to be done, or permit to be done any act, matter, or thing in such part prohibited or declared to be unlawful ,or shall omit to do any act, matter, or thing in such part required to be done, such common carrier is made liable to the person or persons injured thereby for the full amount of damages sustained in consequence of any such violations, together with reasonable attorney's fees. Penalties are provided in Section 10 for violations of the provisions of Part I.

[26]306 I.C.C. 138.
[27]49 U.C.C. 5(8).

46

Pooling and Other Agreements
of Air Carriers

The Applicable Statutory Provisions

Section 412(a) of the Federal Aviation Act[1] provides that air carriers must "file with the Board a true copy, or, if oral, a true and complete memorandum, of every contract or agreement (whether enforceable by provisions for liquidated damages, penalties, bond, or otherwise) affecting air transportation and in force on the effective date of this section or hereafter entered into, or any modification or cancellation thereof, between such air carrier and any other air carrier, foreign air carrier, or other carrier for pooling or apportioning earnings, losses, traffic, service, or equipment, or relating to the establishment of transportation rates, fares, charges, or classifications, or for preserving and improving safety, economy, and efficiency of operation, or for controling, regulating, preventing, or otherwise eliminating destructive, oppressive, or wasteful competition, or for regulating stops, schedules, and character of service, or for other cooperative working arrangements."

Section 412(b)[2] provides that the Board is authorized to "disapprove any such contract or agreement, whether or not previously approved by it, that it finds to be adverse to the public interest, or in violation of this Act, and shall by order approve any such contract or agreement, or any modification or cancellation thereof, that it does not find to be adverse to the public interest, or in violation of this Act; except that the Board may not approve any contract or agreement between an air carrier not directly engaged in the operation of aircraft in air transportation and a common carrier subject to the Interstate Commerce Act, as

[1]49 U.S.C. 1382(a).
[2]49 U.S.C. 1382(b).

amended, governing the compensation to be received by such common carrier for transportation services performed by it."

Criteria Governing Action by the Board

The Board is directed to approve contracts or agreements filed pursuant to 49 U.S.C. 1382 unless they are adverse to the public interest or in violation of the Act. The section was patterned after Section 15 of the Shipping Act of 1916, which was interpreted by the Federal Maritime Commission in *Rates in Canadian Currency*,[3] where it said that conference relationships should not be disturbed without "compelling reasons and a reasonable certainty that any cancellation or modification of an agreement it might order under authority of Section 15 would be of practical benefit." The Board, following the precedent set by the FMC in interpreting Section 15 of the Shipping Act, has recognized the principle that certain air carrier agreements should not be disturbed unless it is otherwise demonstrated that they will result in substantial harm to the public interest.[4]

In *Southern Service to the West Case*, the Board said that it "would presently be inclined to approve an interchange agreement of the latter type (one requiring no certificates for new routes) unless it were affirmatively shown that the operation of the interchange would otherwise result in substantial harm to the public interest" and that it had in the past "consistently approved such interchange with little hesitation where there was little or no evidence of possible adverse effect on the public interest." Thus a contract or agreement falling within the purview of 49 U.S.C. 1382 must be examined in the light of the criteria of the public interest provided by the Act and if any provision of the contract or agreement is found to be in contravention of such criteria it must be held to be adverse to the public interest.[5] The term "public interest" as used in the section is not a mere general reference to the public welfare, but has direct relationship to the statutory objectives in the Act.[6] In deciding whether a contract or agreement is adverse to the public interest, the Board cannot ignore the question of whether such contract or agreement runs counter to the principles of the antitrust laws. Since approval exempts an agreements from the operation of the antitrust laws, it is the duty of the Board in determining the effect of a

---

[3]U.S.S.B. 264, 281.
[4]*Southern Service to the West Case, Reopened*, 18 CAB 790, 197.
[5]*Pan American-Matson-Inter-Island Contract*, 3 CAB 540, 549.
[6]*Air Freight Tariff Agreement Case*, 14 CAB 424, 425.

contract or agreement on the public interest to evaluate the contract or agreement in the light of the antitrust policies and principles.[7] Where a contract or agreement has among its significant aspects elements which are plainly repugnant to established antitrust principles, approval should not be granted unless there is a clear showing that the contract or agreement is required by a serious transportation need or in order to secure important public benefits.[8]

Imposition of Conditions

In applying the test of public interest to an agreement, the Board has held that it can attach reasonable conditions to its approval, nullifying objectionable provisions and prescribing the basis upon which the agreement will acceptably meet the test of public interest.[9] In the *Air Cargo* case, the Board considered an argument that the imposition of a condition to an agreement amounted to a revision and therefore was illegal. The Board said in reply:

> Under such circumstances we have the alternative of either disapproving the agreement or imposing a condition to nullify objectionable provisions. The argument that we can use only the alternative of disapproval, whatever its academic legal merits, would appear to be an unrealistic approach tot he problems of administrative regulation under Section 412. It would impose unwarranted burdens on parties to an agreement and defeat the accomplishment of many worthwhile objectives. It would appear to be a much sounder regulatory approach to give the parties to an agrement the opportunity of the performance under the agreement in accordance with standards of public interest determined by us where that is a practical possibility, rather than to disapprove the who agreement outright. Since we can always disapprove an agreement if a condition imposed upon an order of approval under Section 412 is violated, the legal result will be the same whether we impose a condition in the first instance or disapprove an agreement until it is amended to remove provisions that are adverse to the public interest. In the administration of Section 412 we are concerned with the fulfillment of the policy objectives laid down in Section 2, particularly those relating to competition. We believe that those objectives are better fulfilled by the imposition of a condition, where required, as in the agreement before us, than by disapproval of th agreement.

Scope of Agreement

The language of Section 412 encompasses all contracts and agreements between air carriers for pooling services or for preserving ef-

---

[7] *Local Cartage Agrement Case,* 15 CAB 850, 852-3.
[8] *Ibid.*
[9] *Air Cargo, Inc., Agreement, Petitions,* 9 CAB 468, 471-2.

ficiency of operation. Thus, in *McManus v. CAB*,[10] the court of appeals sustained an order of the Board approving a conference resolution which provided for the establishment of an agency committee with which applications would be filed by potential ticket agents; only if the committee approved of the applicant would his name be entered on the conference agency list from which members were required to select their agents. The Board held that the plan was not adverse to the public interest since it would, if properly administered, bring about a rise in the standards of agency representation. As a result of the approval, carriers acting under the resolution were, by reason of Section 414, exempted from the operation of the antitrust laws. The court of appeals said (p. 419) that "It may well be that Congress did not intend to cover so broad an area by enacting Section 412, and that the airlines should not be permitted to exercise concerted control which is immune from antitrust regulation over some related industry such as that of ticket agencies. But there is no indication in either the words of the statute or its legislative history that would justify our reading Section 412 and 414 narrowly to insulate airlines from antitrust liability to other airlines only and not to protect (them) from suits by those engaged in affiliated services by an agreement among airlines." The court said further (p. 419):

> Nor is there any merit to the petitioner's contention that the Board, once having approved an agreement, could not act on its own to investigate and conditionally disapprove. The exemption from the operation of the antitrust laws is valid only so long as the Board believes that the agreement is not adverse to the public interest. Section 412(b) clearly provides that one decision on an agreement does not bind the Board as to later agreements, and that it may disapprove an agreement "whether or not previously approved by it." If complaints regarding the operation of a system established by the approved resolution come to its attention the Board is justified in reopening the case and considering the agreement anew. Nor is the Board bound to approve or disapprove agreements in their entirety. It is true that Section 15 of the Shipping Act of 1916, 46 U.S.C. 814, on which Section 412 of the Civil Aeronautics Act was modeled, provides that the Federal Maritime (Commission) may "disapprove, cancel, or modify any agreement," whereas Section 412 says only that the Board may "by order disapprove." However, the power to condition its approval on the incorporation of certain amendments is necessary for flexible administrative action and is inherent in the power to approve or disapprove. We would be sacrificing substance to form if we held invalid any conditional approval but affirmed an unqualified rejection accompanied by an opinion which explicitly stated that approval would be forthcoming if modifications were made.

The court of appeals also held (pp. 419-20) that the procedure established by the Act did not amount to an unconstitutional delegation of

---

[10]286 F. 2d 414, cert. denied 366 U.S. 928, rehearing denied 366 U.S. 978.

legislative power. The court said that although the activity approved is insulated from the operation of the antitrust laws, the Board may approve only such agreements as are not adverse to the public interest. This standard, the court said, is definite enough to withstand constitutional attack,[11] and the exemption from regulation of such concerted activity as, in the opinion of the regulatory public agency, meets the standard, is not unlawful.[12]

In *Air Line Pilots Ass'n v. C.A.B.*[13] the court of appeals affirmed the Board's interim 6-month approval of an agreement among American Airlines, Trans World Airlines, and United Air Lines which decreased the number of flights operated by those airlines between New York-Los Angeles, New York-San Francisco, Washington-Los Angeles, and Chicago-San Francisco. In its petition for review, the Air Line Pilots Association argued without success that the Board cannot grant interim approval to a capacity-reduction agreement without holding an evidentiary hearing to determine whether the anticompetitive effects of the agreement outweighed other public interest considerations, and that the Board should have required labor protective arrangements as a condition for interim approval. Both arguments were rejected by the court.

United States v. C.A.B.[14] involved a challenged to two Board orders approving two short term intercarrier agreements to reduce capacity in 24 markets on the basis of the need to conserve scarce supplies of aviation fuel. The court of appeals upheld the first agreement as justified by the emergency presented by the Arab oil embargo and the resultant fuel allocation program. It set aside the second because, in the court's view, the emergency had passed and there was no factual support for the Board's determinations respecting (1) the probable behavior of air carriers if required to make unilateral capacity reductions and (2) the effect of such behavior on the public interest. At the same time, however, the court rejected the contention of the Department of Justice that an anticompetitive agreement cannot be approved unless it is impossible to achieve the end sought by any other means.

---

[11]*New York Central Securities Corp. v. United States,* 287 U.S. 12.
[12]*Sunshine Anthracite Coal Co. v. Adkins,* 310 U.S. 381, 396.
[13]509 F. 2d 964.
[14]511 F. 2d 1315.

47

Conference and Pooling Agreements

The Applicable Statutory Provisions

Section 15 of the Shipping Act of 1916, as amended,[1] provides that common carriers by water, or other person subject to the Act, shall file immediately with the Federal Maritime Commission a true copy, or, if oral, a true and complete memorandum, of every agreement, or modification or cancellation thereof, to which it may be a party "fixing or regulating transportation rates or fares; giving or receiving special rates, accommodations, or other special privileges or advantages, controlling, regulating, preventing, or destroying competition; pooling or apportioning earnings, losses, or traffic; alloting ports or restricting or otherwise regulating the number and character of sailings between ports; limiting or regulating in any way the volume or character of freight or passenger traffic to be carried; or in any manner providing for an exclusive, preferential, or cooperative working arrangement." The term "agreement" includes understandings, conferences, and other arrangements.

The FMC is authorized upon notice and hearing to disapprove, cancel or modify any agreement, or any modification or cancellation thereof, whether or not previously approved, "that it finds to be unjustly discriminatory or unfair as between carriers, shippers, exporters, importers, or ports, or between exporters from the United States and their foreign competitors, or to operate to the detriment of the commerce of the United States, or to be contrary to the public interest, or to be in violation" of the Act, and shall approve all other agreements, modifications or cancellations. No agreement shall be approved or continued

[1] 46 U.S.C. 814.

approval be permitted for any agreement "(1) between carriers and members of the same conference or conferences of carriers serving diffrent trades that would otherwise be naturally competitive, unless in the case of agreements between carriers, each carrier, or in the case of agreements between conferences, each conference, retains the right of independent action, or (2) in respect to any conference agreement, which fails to provide reasonable and equal terms and conditions for admission and readmission to conference membership of other qualified carriers in the trade, or fails to provide that any member may withdraw from membership upon reasonable notice without penalty for such withdrawal." The FMC is authorized upon notice and hearing to disapprove any agreement "on a finding of inadequate policing of the obligations under it, or of failure or refusal to adopt and maintain reasonable procedures for promptly and fairly hearing and considering shippers' requests and complaints."

Section 15 provides further than any agreement and any modification or cancellation of any agreement not approved, or disapproved, by the FMC shall be unlawful, and shall be lawful only when and as long as approved by the FMC. Before approval or after disapproval it shall be unlawful to carry out in whole or in part, directly or indirectly, any such agreement, modification, or cancellation; except that tariff rates, fares, and charges, and classifications, rules, and regulations explanatory thereof, including changes in special rates and charges covered by Section 813a which do not involve a change in the spread between such rates and charges and the rates and charges applicable to noncontract shippers, agreed upon by approved conferences, and changes and amendments thereto, if otherwise in accordance with law, shall be permitted to take effect without prior approval upon compliance with the publication and filing requirements of Section 817(b) and with the provisions of any regulations the FMC may adopt.

Required Filing of Agreements

At all times Section 15 of the Shipping Act has provided that common carriers by water are required to file with the FMC copies of every agreement with other carriers by water, and the section provides that the FMC shall by order after notice and hearing, disapprove, cancel, or modify any agreement, whether or not previously approved by it, that it finds to operate to the detriment of the commerce of the United

States.[2] So long as approved by the FMC agreements under Section 15 are exempted from the antitrust laws.[3]

The Publication and Filing of Tariffs

In the past the FMC construed the words "every agreement" in Section 15 as not to include routine operations relating to curent rate changes and other day-to-day transactions,[4] and the words "routine operations" were interpreted by the FMC to include conventional rate changes. Thus issuances and modifications of tariffs pursuant to an approved basic agreement were not considered new agreements requiring prior Section 15 approval.[5] This interpretation by the FMC of Section 15 was held by the court in *Empire State Highway Transp. Ass'n. v. F.M.B.*[6] to be reasonable. The court said (p. 339) that "Thousands of rate changes have been agreed upon in concert by conference members in the maritime and related industries under the authority of approved conference agreements, and we are cited to no instance in which conventional rate changes have been held by(FMC) or court to be unlawful because unaccompanied by prior (FMC) approval." The court said that

---

[2]*Anglo-Canadian Shipping Co. Ltd. v. F.M.C.*, 310 F. 2d 606, 608-9. See also *F.M.B. v. Isbrandtsen Co.*, 356 U.S. 481, 490.

[3]*Trans-Pacific Frgt. Conf. of Japan v. F.M.B.*, 302 F. 2d 875, 876. See approval by FMC of rate agreements in *Rate Agreement Gulf Mediterranean Trade*, 7 F.M.C. 495; *Agreement 8900 — Rate Agreement United States/Persian Gulf Trade*, 8 F.M.C. 712; *Interconference Agreements U.S./Mediterranean Trades*, 11 F.M.C. 183. *American Mail Line Ltd., et al. v. F.M.C. et al.*, No. 73-1252, D.C. Cir. 1974, dealt with court of appeals review of an FMC order conditionally approving R. J. Reynolds Tobacco Company's acquisition of the United States Lines, Inc., which was to be held and operated in competition with another Reynolds subsidiary, Sea-Land Service, Inc. In vacating the FMC's order, the court found that Section 15 of the Shipping Act did not give the FMC jurisdiction over mergers or acquisitions by steamship companies even though such transactions may include some "ongoing" or continuing obligations, nor could the FMC establish jurisdictional authority over such acquisitions by the imposition of continuing covenants requiring FMC supervision.

[4]*Section 15 Inquiry*, 1 U.S.S.B. 121, 125. See *Volkswagenwerk Aktiengesellschaft v. FMC*, 390 U.S. 261, where it was held that an agreement among the members of the Pacific Maritime Association was an agreement required to be filed with and approved by the FMC pursuant to Section 15 of the Shipping Act, 1916. The association's agreement provided for the funding of the costs of a "mechinization and modernization" agreement between the association, and the International Longshoremen's and Warehousemen's Union. This latter agreement was a significant departure from previously existing management-labor practices in that the Union permitted automation in return for financial guarantees that its members would not be penalized by such automation.

[5]*Empire State Highway Transp. Ass'n. v. American Export Lines*, 5 F.M.B. 565, 585-6.

[6]291 F. 2d 336, 339, cert. denied 368 U.S. 931.

the "long administrative practice is unusually impressive." Furthermore, the court said, "rates are subject to Section 17 of the Shipping Act regarding the observance of just and reasonable regulations and practices and, additionally, that when a conference has engaged in conduct violative of the fair and reasonable standards of the Act the (FMC) may withdraw approval of the basic agreement itself, or require its modification."[7]

Today, by reason of Section 18(b), carriers by water in foreign commerce and conferences of such carriers are required to publish and file tariffs with the FMC. Schedules do not become effective earlier than thirty days after publication except that they may become effective on less than thirty days by permission; schedules which decrease costs to shippers may become effective upon publication and filing of tariffs; and the FMC is empowered to disapprove rates or charges which are "so unreasonably high or low as to be detrimental to the commerce of the United States."

Interim Injunctive Powers

In *Trans-Pacific Frgt. of Japan v. F.M.B.*,[8] the court held that the FMC had no power to issue an order during the pendency of a hearing on a conference agreement filed under Section 15, directing those against whom the order was issued to show cause why they should not be ordered to cease and desist *pendente lite* from taking certain action under the agreement. The Section 15 agreement, which had been approved by the FMC previously but was being extended to another carrier, permitted the parties thereto to combine to fix rates and trade practices, and set out a code of business practices. The agreement also contained a schedule of monetary penalties, payable to the conference, for violating various provisions. As a means of enforcement, the agreement provided for the employment of a neutral body, empowered to investigate the complaint of any member line and to impose a fine upon discovery of an infraction of the agreement.

One of the offenses for which a fine could be imposed was the refusal of a member to make its business records available to the neutral body on demand. The order of the FMC was directed to the members

---

[7]See *Edmond Weil, Inc. v. Italian Line, "Italia,"* 1 U.S.S.B. 395, 398, holding that an unreasonably high rate is clearly detrimental to the commerce of the United States, and upon a showing that a conference rate in foreign commerce is unreasonably high a reduction in the rate to a proper level will be required, and, if necessary, approval of the conference agreement will be withdrawn.

[8]302 F. 2d 875.

to cease and desist from collecting fines and from using a neutral body to investigate and to impose the fines. The court said (p. 879) that neither Section 15 nor Section 22 supports the order as issued by the FMC, and that its conclusion was reinforced by administrative interpretation placed on the Shipping Act. The court said that in the past the FMC had not asserted that it possessed the kind of interim injunctive powers exercised in the case, and that the FMC had on several occasions expressly disclaimed such authority.[9] In fact, the court said (p. 879) Congress had been requested by the FMC to give it the power to enter cease and desist orders of an interlocutory nature prior to completion of full evidentiary hearing. The court added (p. 880) that "Congress has repeatedly demonstated that it knows how to make an express delegation of authority to issue interim cease and desist orders when it so desires"; and that frequently "Congress has expressly provided that an agency can obtain this form of relief by applying to an appropriate district court." The court concluded (p. 880) that the power which the FMC "now claims is in many ways a drastic one, and in fact more akin to judicial injunctive power than the power which Congress has given some agencies to issue cease and desist orders against conduct deemed in violation of the law."

The court added that the "order here is not a directive to comply with existing law" or an existing FMC regulation. On the contrary, the court said, "It seeks to prohibit one party (in what is at this stage essentially a private dispute) from enforcing an agreement previously approved" by the FMC, "made with another private party." The court said that the FMC is not a court and cannot rely for its action on the powers of a court of equity. "On the contrary, the law is settled that an administrative agency can exercise only those powers conferred on it by Congress."[10]

Rules Requiring the Filing of Minutes and Reports of Concerted Activities

The FMC has the responsibility of insuring that parties to agreements approved under Section 15 of the Shipping Act, 1916, as amended, are complying with the requirements of their agreements, and that their operations under such agreements are not detrimental to the commerce

---

[9]See *Isbrandtsen Co. v. United States*, 81 F. Supp. 544, 547, appeal dismissed sub. nom. *A/S J. Ludwig Monwinckels Rederi v. Isbrandtsen Co.*, 366 U.S. 941; *West India Fruit & Steamship Co. v. Seatrain Lines*, 170 F. 2d 775, 776.

[10]See *CAB v. Delta Air Lines*, 367 U.S. 316; *United States v. Seatrain Lines*, 329 U.S. 424; *Alaska Airlines v. CAB*, 257 F. 2d 229.

of the United States, contrary to the public interest or otherwise in violation of the Act.

Rules have been promulgated by the FMC in order that it may be kept informed of the manner in which parties to agreements are carrying out their activities.[11] These rules require that conference agreements, agreements between or among conferences, and argreements whereby the parties are authorized to fix rates, state (1) the manner in which the joint business of the parties may be carried out; i.e., full conference meeting, agents' meeting, principals meeting, owners' meeting, through committees or subcommittees, telephone or oral polls, or through any other procedure by which the business of the joint parties may be conducted; (2) quorum requirements and the types of vote necessary to take various actions; and (3) that there shall be filed with the FMC within 30 days after each meeting of the conferences or parties to the agreement, a report of matters within the scope of the agreement which are discussed or taken up at any such meeting and the action taken with respect to each such matter.

In *Pacific Coast European Conference v. Federal Maritime Commission*,[12] the court upheld the use of the FMC's rulemaking authority derived from Section 43 of the Shipping Act, 1916, in promulgating rules concerning admission to, and withdrawal and expulsion from, steamship conferences. The FMC had ordered that approval of the conference's agreement be withdrawn, unless compliance with its rules was forthcoming. If affirming the order, the court rejected the conference's contention that the FMC could not withdraw approval of a conference agreement for noncompliance with the FMC's rules, stating: "This contention has the antique virtues of simplicity and straight-forwardness. The difficulty is that it is a doctrinal archaism in modern administrative law. It comes, indeed, at a time when many knowledgeable voices have been urging the agencies to make greater, rather than less, use of their rulemaking authority in the interest of more precise definition of decisional standards."

Self-Policing of Section 15 Agreements

The pertinent provisions of the Shipping Act, 1916, as amended, provide that "The Commission shall disapprove any such agreement, after notice and hearing, on a finding of inadequate policing of the obligations under it, ..." The FMC has adopted self-policing rules under this

[11]See 46 CFR 537.
[12]376 F. 2d 785, 789.

statutory requirement.[13] The rules require that conference and other rate making agreements between common carriers by water in the foreign and domestic offshore commerce of the United States shall contain a provision describing the method or system used by the parties in policing the obligations under the agreement, including the procedure for handling complaints and the functions and authority of every person having the responsibility for administering the system.

In Docket No. 1095, the FMC established certain principles regarding self-policing of Section 15 agreements.[14] These principles are as follows:

(1) Determinations made under a neutral body type of self-policing system, which combines both investigative and adjudicatory functions, must be subject to a *de novo* review by an impartial and disinterested panel of arbitrators;

(2) to give effect to the principle that an accused should not be subject to punishment on the basis of secret evidence, arbitrators must be furnished only with such evidence as has been disclosed to the accused line and which the accused line has had an adequate opportunity to rebut or explain; and

(3) a review *de novo* by a panel of arbitrators does not require a new trial but merely a new evaluation of the record established before the neutral body.

Exemption of Nonexclusive Transshipments Agreements from Section 15 Approval

Section 35 of the Shipping Act, 1916, as amended, provides that the FMC, upon application or on its own motion, may by order or rule exempt for the future any class of agreements between persons subject to the Act, or any specified activity of such persons from any requirements of the Shipping Act, 1916, or the Intercoastal Shipping Act, 1933. The exemption can only be extended by the FMC when it finds that such exemption will not substantially impair effective regulation by the FMC, be unjustly discriminatory, or be detrimental to commerce.

Rules have been published by the FMC[15] exempting nonexclusive transshipment agreements from Section 15 approval requirements. The FMC by appropriate safeguards, through the requirement of filing for information but not for approval, and by implementation of tariff filing

---

[13]See 46 CFR 528.

[14]The Commission decided Docket No. 1095 after remand of the case from the court of appeals in *States Marine Lines, Inc. v. Federal Maritime Commission*, 376 F. 2d 230.

[15]See 46 CFR 524.

requirements in Section 18(b) of the Shipping Act, 1916, as amended, is able to exercise its authority to exempt nonexclusive transshipment agreements from formal consideration and processing under Section 15. In this way transshipment agreements may be more readily negotiated and expeditiously put into operation.

Pooling Agreements

Pooling agreements as a rule involve revenue and cargo pools to meet economic market conditions, or provide for equal access to government controlled cargo and the pooling of cargo or revenue in response to government cargo preference laws.

Pooling agreements are considered a *per se* violation of the Sherman Act,[16] and are *prima facie* subject to disapproval under the public interest standard of Shipping Act Section 15.[17] Approval is only possible if its anticompetitive features have been sufficiently justified. A sufficient justification is a showing that the arrangement is *necessary* to meet a serious transportation need, to secure important public benefits, or to further a valid regulatory purpose of the Shipping Act, or the agreement is otherwise found to be in the public interest. The burden of making the required showing falls squarely on the parties to the agreement.[18]

[16]See *Citizen Publishing Company v. United States*, 349 U.S. 131, 135-36; *United States v. Topco Associates*, 405 U.S. 596, 608-09.

[17]46 U.S.C. 814. See *Mediterranean Pools Investigation*, 9 F.M.C. 264, 290-291; *Federal Maritime Commission v. Aktiebolaget Svenska Amerika Linien*, 390 U.S. 238.

[18]*Canadian-American Working Arrangement*, 16 SRR 733, 736-737. See *Nopal Line v. Moore McCormack Lines*, 8 F.M.C. 213, where the FMC disapproved a pooling agreement which allocated market shares on a basis discriminatory to third flag carriers.

48

Consolidation or Merger, Purchase, Lease or Contract to Operate, and Acquisition of Control

Statutory Authority

Section 5(2) of the Interstate Commerce Act,[1] as amended by the 4R Act, provides in part as follows:

> Under the premerger notification provisions of the Clayton Act (12 U.S.C. 12 et seq.) no person shall acquire any voting securities or assets of any person unless notification is given to the government if the following is involved:
>
> (1) the acquiring person, or the person whose voting securities or assets are being acquired, is engaged in commerce or in any activity affecting commerce;
>
> (2) (a) any voting securities or assets of a person engaged in manufacturing which has annual net sales or total assets of $10,000,000 or more are being acquired by any person which has total assets or annual net sales of $100,000,000 or more;
>
> (b) any voting securities or assets of a person not engaged in manufacturing which has total assets of $10,000,000 or more are being acquired by any person which has total assets or annual net sales of $100,000,000 or more; or
>
> (c) any voting securities or assets of a person with annual net sales or total assets of $100,000,000 or more are being acquired by any person with total assets or annual net sales of $10,000,000 or more; and
>
> (3) as a result of such acquisition, the acquiring person would hold—
>
> (a) 15 per centum or more of the voting securities or assets of the acquired person, or.

---

[1] 49 U.S.C. 5(2). Transfer of certificate or permit authorized under Part II (except as provided in Section 5), by Section 212(b); Part III, by Section 312; and Part IV, by Section 410(g). See Part IV, Section 411, for control of carrier by freight forwarder and of freight forwarder by common carrier. For temporary authority pending proceedings upon application, see Part II, Section 210a(b); Part III, Section 311(b).

(b)   an aggregate total amount of the voting securities and assets of the acquired person in excess of $15,000,000.

However, the following transaction, among others, is exempt: a transaction specifically exempted from the antitrust laws if approved by a federal agency, if copies of all information and documentary material filed with such agency are contemporaneously filed with the Federal Trade Commission and the Antitrust Division of the Department of Justice.

"(2)(a)   It shall be lawful, with the approval and authorization of the Commission, as provided in subdivision (b) or paragraph (3).

"(i)   for two or more carriers to consolidate or merge their properties or franchises, or any part thereof, into one corporation for the ownership, management, and operation of the properties theretofore in separate ownership; or for any carrier, or two or more carriers jointly, to purchase, lease or contract to operate the properties, or any part thereof, of another; or for any carrier, or two or more carriers jointly, to acquire control of another through ownership of its stock or otherwise; or for a person which is not a carrier to acquire control of two or more carriers through ownership of their stock or otherwise; or for a person which is not a carrier and which has control of one or more carriers to acquire control of another carrier through ownership of its stock or otherwise; or

"(ii)   for a carrier by railroad to acquire trackage rights over, or joint ownership in or joint use of, any railroad line or lines owned or operated by any other such carrier, and terminals incidental thereto.

"(b)   Whenever a transaction is proposed under subdivision (a), the carrier or carriers or person seeking authority therefor shall present an application to the Commission . . . If the Commission finds that, subject to such terms and conditions and such modifications as it shall find to be just and reasonable, the proposed transaction is within the scope of subdivision (a) and will be consistent with the public interest, it shall enter an order approving and authorizing such transaction, upon the terms and conditions, and with the modifications, so found to be just and reasonable: *Provided,* That if a carrier by railroad subject to this part, or any person which is controlled by such a carrier, or affiliated therewith within the meaning of paragraph (6), is an applicant in the case of any such proposed transaction involving a motor carrier, the Commission shall not enter such an order unless it finds that the transaction proposed will be consistent with the public interest and will enable such carrier to use service by motor vehicle to public advantage in its operations and will not unduly restrain competition.

"(c)   In passing upon any proposed transaction under the provisions of this paragraph (2), the Commission shall give weight to the following considerations, among others: (1) The effect of the proposed transaction upon adequate transportation service to the public; (2) the effect upon the public interest of the inclusion, or failure to include, other railroads in the territory involved in the proposed transaction; (3) the total fixed charges resulting from the proposed transaction; and (4) the interest of the carrier employees affected.

"(d) The Commission shall have authority in the case of a proposed transaction under this paragraph (2) involving a railroad or railroads, as a prerequisite to its approval of the proposed transaction, to require, upon equitable terms, the inclusion of another railroad or other railroads in the territory involved, upon petition by such railroad or railroads requesting such inclusion, and upon a finding that such inclusion is consistent with the public interest.

"(e) No transaction which contemplates a guaranty or assumption of payment of dividends or of fixed charges, shall be approved by the Commission under this paragraph (2) except upon a specific finding by the Commission that such guaranty or assumption is not inconsistent with the public interest. No transaction shall be approved under this paragraph (2) which will result in an increase of total fixed charges, except upon a specific finding by the Commission that such increase would not be contrary to public interest.

"(f) As a condition of its approval, under this paragraph (2), or paragraph (3), of any transaction involving a carrier or carriers by railroad subject to the provisions of this part, the Commission shall require a fair and equitable arrangement to protect the interests of the railroad employees affected . . ."

The pertinent provisions of the 4R Act regarding rail consolidations, etc. are: Section 401 enlarges the role of the DOT by allowing the Secretary of Transportation to "develop and make available to interested persons possible plans, proposals, and recommendations for mergers, consolidations, reorganizations, and other unification or coordination projects for rail services . . ." Section 401 authorizes the Secretary to conduct a study of any merger proposals subject to the jurisdiction of the Commission and to appear before the Commission with respect to such application. Section 401 also authorizes the Secretary to hold conferences with respect to proposed unification or coordination projects, provides that the Secretary may mediate any disputes that arise and grants antitrust immunity to persons participating in the conference. Section 402 revises Section 5 of the Interstate Commerce Act by adding a statutory timetable and procedures to which the Commission must adhere in rail unification and consolidation proceedings. The "standard" merger procedure (Section 5(2) of the I.C. Act) must be completed by statute within 31 months from the day the application is filed with the Commission. If the Commission, for some reason, is unable to issue a decision within the statutory time frame, it must notify Congress and advise it of reasons for the delay. Section 402 authorizes the Secretary to propose modifications to the application to the Commission and to appear before the Commission in support of such proposals. Section 403 provides an alternate procedure (Section 5(3) of the I.C. Act) whereby railroad merger, consolidation, unification, coordination projects, joint use of tracks and facilities, or acquisition or sale of assets may be proposed. Under this "expedited merger procedure," applicants have the option of developing consolidation proposals with the Secretary which the Secretary files before the Commission or applicants may file directly with the Commission. Under either option, the Secretary must prepare and submit to the Commission a nine point study in advance of the time frame designated for the Commission to process its portion of a Section 5(3) application. The Commission must give due weight and consideration to the Secretary's report. The Commission then notifies the public and conducts public hearings and oral argument prior to rendering a final decision. The entire process within the Commission must be completed within 24 months. Section 309 established the Rail Services Planning Office as a permanent office in the Commission and assigned to the Office the duty of long-range planning. This amendment also charged the Office with the responsibility of assisting the Commission in studying and evaluating any merger, consolidation, unification or coordination projects, joint use of tracks or other facilities, or acquisition or sale of assets.

Regulations Promulgated Under the 4R Act

The Commission instituted a general rulemaking proceeding by notice published in the *Federal Register on* May 26, 1976, in Ex Parte No. 282 (Sub-No. 1), *Railroad Consolidation Procedures,* in order to revise its regulations[2] pertaining to the contents and procedures for applications involving railroad transactions under Section 5 of the I.C. Act (mergers, controls, leases, acquisitions, coordination projects and trackage rights to which the term "consolidation" is generally applied). The revision of the consolidation regulations was deemed necessary because of the amendments to Section 5 contained in Sections 402 and 403 of the 4R Act. Principally, these sections added a new subdivision (g) to Section 5(2) and a new paragraph (3) to Section 5. In general, Section 5(2) (g) provides new procedures and strict time limits for Commission action on consolidation applications. Section 5(3) provides a new mechanism for the submission of applications under which consolidation proposals are first considered or developed by the Secretary of transportation and then submitted on an expedited basis.

[2] 49 C.F.R. 1111.

The Commission in Ex Parte No. 282 (Sub-No. 1), *Railroad Consolidation Procedures,*[3] adopted regulations which generally provide for the complete submission of all pertinent evidence at the time a consolidation application is filed. This will ensure timely consideration of the proposed transaction by the Commission to obtain a complete initial understanding of the scope and effect of a proposed railroad consolidation.

The regulations contain the following reclassification of rail consolidation applications in a declining order of significance and data requirements.

1. Application involving two or more class I railroads, except for those applications involving trackage rights, joint use, or joint ownership of a line or coordination project.

2. Applications involving two or more class II railroads, or a class I and class II railroad, except for those applications involving trackage rights, joint use, or joint ownership of a line or coordination project.

3. Applications involving trackage rights, joint use, or joint ownership of a line or coordination project, except for those applications which result in a major market extension for the applicant.

Under the regulations, all petitions for inclusion and inconsistent applications responsive to a Section 5(2) application must be filed within 90 days of publication in the *Federal Register* of a notice that an initial application was filed. This filing provision reflects the requirements of Section 5(2)(g)(iv) of the I.C. Act. Additionally, the regulations stipulate various data and filing requirements for petitions and inconsistant applications. Notably, such filings are required to contain basically all the information in the exhibits required for the proposed transaction. For example, in the event that inconsistent applicant seeks a merger with one of the carriers to the initial application, then the inconsistent applicant is required to meet the filing requirements for a merger.

The regulations adopt an approach which requires the submission, to the fullest extent practicable, of all exhibits and information within the 90-day period. In the event that all required materials are not capable of production, then the Commission may, upon good cause shown for specified materials, afford an additional 90 days to file such specified materials. A request for additional time to submit specified materials will not suspend the requirement of filing petitions or applications within the initial 90-day period. To ensure that a petitioner or inconsistent ap-

[3]348 I.C.C. 771.

plicant will have access to the necessary data contained in the initial applications, the Commission has also provided that applicants will furnish copies of their applications upon request. Hence, if carriers considering the filing of an inconsistent application or petition for inclusion request a copy of the initial application upon its filing, they will be able to afford themselves the additional time provided for Commission review of the application under Section 5(2)(g)(i) before the 90-day time period commences.

Probability sampling is adopted by the regulations as the exclusive method in the preparation of traffic diversion studies. The reason for this is that the Commission believes first that probability sampling yields knowledge of the precision of estimates, while judgmental studies do not. Secondly, the random selection of elements eliminates sampling biases which may occur in judgmental studies. In addition, it supplies formulas for the estimates which give proper weightings of the sample elements of the study. Judgmental studies have often been unweighted, and this factor can lead to biased results in the traffic study. Moreover, the sampling units in a probability study are usually individual waybills, or lines on monthly interline abstracts of waybills, whereas judgment studies cover broad categories of traffic often lacking details concerning individual car movements. While these broad categories cover movements which are actually diverse, the traffic expert appearing in support of judgmental survey decides the issues as if the groups of traffic under consideration were homogeneous. Based on the records developed in prior railroad consolidation proceedings, it has been the Commission's experience that this factor is one of the greatest weaknesses in the judgmental survey.

The regulations require a narrative summary of the proposed transaction and the proposing party's reasons and public interest justification therefor. The Commission feels that a properly devised narrative summary could serve dually as part of the notice in Section 5(3) cases, while also providing valuable details to interested parties regarding transactions arising under both Sections 5(2) and 5(3). The narrative summary must contain the following information: (1) a brief summary of the proposed transaction, with the names of applicants; (2) the proposed time schedule for the consummation of the transaction; (3) the objectives of the transaction, such as operating savings, reduction of excess facilities, extension of markets, and greater financial strength; (4) the nature and amount of any new securities to be issued or other financing contemplated; (5) a brief summary of the proposing party's reasons and public interest justifications in support of the application;

(6) any other brief supporting or descriptive statements the applicants believe to be material; and (7) reference to the exhibits which are the underlying data for each statement therein.

The regulations require employee information to be presented in order to permit the Commission to assess better the impact of a transaction upon employees. It will also permit the Commission to ascertain more accurately the savings flowing from a transaction — an area which has proven to have caused some difficulty in prior rail merger proceedings.

Since intermodal competitive issues have been, and will continue to be of great significance in Section 5 proceedings, the regulations require the submission of such intermodal data that is within the purview of applicants.

In Ex Parte No. 282 (Sub-No. 2), *Railroad Consolidation Procedures,* the I.C.C. issued the following general policy statement (49 CFR Part 1111) describing how it will treat certain aspects of applications seeking approval of the merger or common control of major railroad systems under Sections 5(2) and 5(3). The policy statement addresses criteria to be applied in determining applications; means of identifying public interest considerations and economic impacts; inclusion of other railroads into a merged railroad; labor protection and procedural matters.

(a) *General.* — The I.C.C. encourages the rationalization of railroad facilities and the reduction of excess rail capacity through the merger of existing railroad companies where operating efficiencies will result, marketing opportunities will be enhanced, essential rail services will be retained, and competition will not be unnecessarily diminished. The I.C.C. also encourages other means of attaining these ends, including the joint use of rail facilities and the use of run-through trains. It does not favor rail industry restructuring through the exercise of managerial and financial control unless the controlling entity assumes full responsibility for carrying out the operating railroad's common carrier obligation to provide service upon reasonable demand.

(b) *Merger Criteria.* — The I.C.C. considers the following to be among the most significant factors in determining whether a particular rail merger proposal should be approved:

(1) Retention of essential rail services, whether provided by the merging companies or by other railroads which may be affected by the merger.

(2) Increased opportunities to achieve operating efficiencies.

(3) Elimination of redundant facilities.

(4) Enhanced ability of the merged system to attract new business.

(5) Financial viability of the merged company.

(6) The maintenance of effective intra-modal competition, wherever economic realities make this possible.

(7) Minimum adverse impact on the environment of the region served.

(8) Adequate provision for the protection of railroad labor.

(c) *Public Interest Considerations.* — An important factor in determining whether a proposed merger is in the public interest is the impact which it will have on essential rail services and upon the socioeconomic aspects of the environment of the region served. In order to make every effort to assure a fully developed record on the questions of what are essential services and of what potential socioeconomic impacts a proposed merger would have, the I.C.C. will—

(1) Encourage participation in merger proceedings of other government departments and agencies, and particularly those with direct responsibility for issues related to the nation's rural and urban areas, employment policies, and business development.

(2) Encourage participation by State and local governments and regional and local planning bodies.

(3) Permit intervention by interested persons proposing to address these issues.

(4) Assure that these issues are fully addressed in the course of the I.C.C.'s review of the environmental impact of the proposed merger.

(5) Provide in appropriate cases for the intervention of I.C.C. staff to develop the record on these issues.

(d) *Essential services, economic impact* — . . .

(e) *Inclusion of Other Carriers Pursuant to Section 5(2)(d).* — The I.C.C. does not visualize the merger process as a means for preserving intact the systems of financially weak and marginal railroads, or as a means for protecting these carriers from the necessity for undergoing reorganization under the bankruptcy laws. On the contrary, the I.C.C.'s concern is with the preservation of service, not of companies or railroad systems. The I.C.C. will, therefore, use its powers to condition approval of a merger upon the involuntary inclusion of all or parts of other railroad systems only when it can be shown that there is no other reasonable alternative for preserving essential services; that the facilities to be included fit operationally into the merged system; and that inclusion can be accomplished without endangering the financial success of the merged company. Application of these criteria will mean that requests for inclusion of an entire railroad system are less likely to be successful than those offering more limited, and clearly identified, facilities for acquisition by the merger partners.

Notwithstanding the foregoing, the I.C.C. recognizes that a particular merger of strong carriers could have the effect of worsening the condition of other railroads to the extent that they could not survive. In such a situation, the I.C.C. will attempt to assess the impact of a particular carrier's being forced into reorganization or having to terminate service. If it appears that the end result of the proposed merger would be the permanent cessation of essential services by some other railroad, the I.C.C. is prepared to deny the merger application or to condition its approval upon the willingness of the applicants to restructure their proposal.

(f) *Labor Protection* — The I.C.C. encourages voluntary negotiation of labor protective conditions in individual rail merger proceedings. The I.C.C. will, however, review negotiated agreements to assure that they provide adequate protection for railroad employees and do not jeopardize the future viability of the merged company. In the absence of a negotiated settlement, labor protective conditions will normally provide for protection at the level mandated by law.

(g) *Merger Procedures.* —

(1) In order to expedite the disposition of rail merger proceedings, the I.C.C. will normally consider applications on an individual basis, and will not consolidate two or more pending applications for disposition. The I.C.C. recognizes, however, that there may be situations in which it has before it simultaneously merger proposals which are mutually exclusive or which are so closely interrelated that only consolidation or simultaneous disposition would permit adequate consideration.

(2) The I.C.C. will not accept petitions for inclusion in rail merger proceedings governed by Section 5(3). If, however, the record in such a proceeding shows that a transaction can be found to be in the public interest only if some portion of another carrier's system is included to preserve essential rail services, the I.C.C. will consider conditioning its approval of the proposed transaction upon inclusion of that portion of the system.

(3) The I.C.C. will entertain applications for the control of a rail carrier under Section 5(3) if the arrangement is likely to reduce costs and improve rail service.

(4) The I.C.C. interprets the public interest tests under Sections 5(2) and 5(3).

History of Railroad Consolidations

The history of railroad consolidations is divided into the following periods: (1) That prior to the enactment of the antitrust laws; (2) the period following the enactment of the antitrust laws up to 1920; (3) the period between 1920 and 1940 in which emphasis was placed on the Commission's responsibility for promoting an overall plan for rail mergers; (4) the period between 1940 and the enactment of the 4R Act in 1976; and (5) the period since the enactment of the 4R Act.

Under Section 5 of the original Act of 1887, agreements between railroads for the pooling of freight or revenues were prohibited and railroads were fully subject to the antitrust laws.[4] In *St. Joe Paper Co. v. Atlantic Coast Line R. Co.*,[5] the Supreme Court succinctly described the national railroad policy as it existed prior to 1920 with the terse statement that "competition was the desideratum of our railroad economy."

In the aftermath of World War I, Congress conceived the theory

---

[4]*United States v. Freight Association,* 166 U.S. 290; *United States v. Joint Traffic Association,* 171 U.S. 505; *Northern Securities Co. v. United States,* 193 U.S. 197.
[5]347 U.S. 298, 315.

that the health of our railroads could best be protected by merging into fewer systems the great number of railroads then in existence. In furtherance of this purpose, the Congress enacted the Transportation Act of 1920, which conferred upon the Commission, for the first time, exclusive and plenary jurisdiction over railroad mergers.

The Transportation Act of 1920 terminated wartime federal control of the railroads and provided for a return of railroad properties to their owners and for operation by them. The legislation also contained far-reaching changes in the legislative policy of the United States concerning railroad construction, operation, combinations, rates, and capitalization, which made a new departure in federal regulation of railroads.[6] In passing the legislation, Congress had before it information on all phases of the railroad problem collected during years of hearings and investigations. Congress acted also with the advantage of experience of unified operation of railroads on a nationwide scale. In enacting the Transportation Act of 1920, Congress had before it such questions as these: whether the experiment of Government operation had not shown that there were advantages, economies, efficiencies resulting from large-scale operation of railroads which, under appropriate legislation, might be continued under private operation; whether the experience of the railroads in the past did not call for some relief, under proper safeguards, from the prohibitions and restraints of existing laws; whether, for instance, it was not in the public interest that some means should be provided for relieving the railroads from the rigid prohibitions and the uncertainties of the antitrust laws. Thus, one of the questions with which Congress was confronted was whether the experience of the past and changes in conditions affecting railroad transportation did not show a change in the public interest respecting the application of existing antitrust laws to railroads and require a change in the legislative policy on the subject.

Congress in enacting the Transportation Act of 1920 did not repeal the antitrust laws as they apply to railroads, but provided the machinery whereby the Commission in its administrative discretion could withdraw any particular transaction from the operation of such laws. The conclusion indicated as to the effect of the provisions of the Transportation Act is confirmed by the report of the House Committee in charge of the bill that went from the House to the Conference Committee, whose labors resulted in the Transportation Act of 1920. The Chairman of the House

---

[6]*Railroad Commission of Wisconsin v. Chicago, B. & Q. R. Co.*, 257 U.S. 563, 585.

Committee in his report[7] summarized the provisions of the House Bill as follows:

Consolidation and mergers — Section 407 amends the first paragraph of Section 5 of the commerce act so as to confer jurisdiction upon the Commission to authorize the unification, consolidation, or merger of two or more carriers engaged in transportation of passengers or property, or of the ownership and operation of their properties, or the pooling of their traffic, earnings, or facilities, if the Commission finds that such unification, consolidation, merger, or pooling will be in the interest of better service to the public or economy in operation or otherwise to the advantage of the convenience and commerce of the people. The approval by the Commission is to be given under such rules and regulations and upon such terms and conditions, including consideration as between the carriers, as the Commission may find just and reasonable. The carriers receiving such authority from the Commission are relieved from the operation of the anti-trust law and other State or Federal restraints insofar as necessary to enable them to effect the unification, consolidation, merger, or pooling.

The Transportation Act of 1920 directed the Commission to prepare and adopt a plan for the consolidation of the railway properties of the United States into a limited number of systems. Although railroads were not permitted to consolidate their properties into single corporations except in accordance with the Commission's completed plan, they were authorized to move toward consolidation while the plan was pending. Both pooling and acquisition of control of other railroads, by lease or share interests, could be carried out with Commission approval. All forms of consolidation effected under the legislation were exempted from the antitrust laws and all other restraints or prohibitions by law, State or Federal. In the words of the Supreme Court:[8]

As a result of the enactment of the Transportation Act in 1920, consolidation of the railroads of the country, in the interest of economy and efficiency became an established national policy, and the effective consolidation of the railroads in conformity to the provisions of the Act and the plan of consolidation which the Commission was directed to prepare became a matter of public interest.

The master-plan approach itself created serious difficulties. The Commission was of the opinion that the process of consolidation should be permitted to develop, under the guidance of the Commission, in a normal way. The Commission repeatedly asked Congress to relieve it

---

[7]H. R. No. 456, 66th Cong., 1st Sess., p. 28.
[8]*U.S. v. Lowden*, 308 U.S. 225, 232. With specific references to the 1920 Act, the Supreme Court, in *Texas & P. Ry. Co. v. Gulf, C. & S. F. Ry. Co.*, 270 U.S. 266, 277 observed, "that competition between carriers may result in harm to the public as well as in benefit."

of the duty to prepare a plan, being of the opinion that the task was impossible.[9] In 1929, the Commission published its plan of consolidation under which any consolidation had to conform to the system outlined in the plan and be in the public interest.[10] The proposed consolidated systems never got off the ground and only a small number of railroad consolidations were effected during the existence of the Act.

Thus, by 1940, it had become apparent to both the Commission and the Congress that "the ambitious nation-wide plan of consolidation was not bearing fruit" and "that it was a case where the best was an enemy of the good, and waiting for the best official plan was defeating or postponing less ambitious but more attainable voluntary improvements."[11]

Before the enactment of the Transportation Act of 1940, a committee consisting of three railroad executives and three members of railway labor organizations were appointed to consider the transportation problem and recommend legislation. With respect to the matter of railroad consolidations and mergers, the committee made the following findings and recommendations:[12]

> Historically, the large railroad systems of the United States have developed through the consolidation of numerous small roads. Economies of operation have thus been secured, and a more satisfactory transportation service has been afforded to the public. It is our belief that other economies may be effected and that added improvement may be made in the service rendered the public through further consolidations. . . .
>
> No objection could be urged today against consolidation that could not have been urged with much greater force against the actual consolidations of the past. Yet without the consolidations of the past there would be no major rail systems of today. The progress and accomplishments of the past are indicative of the possibilities of accomplishments of the same sort that may be realized in the future.
>
> The fact that consolidation of railroads has not been carried out to an even greater extent is, in our opinion, ascribable to two factors. Prior to 1920 it was retarded by the prohibitions of the anti-trust acts. Since that date it has been hampered by the unduly restrictive provisions of Section 5 of the Interstate Commerce Act with their requirement for a rigid plan developed in accordance with a prescribed formula, which militates against any results that are not highly artificial and unattractive.

---

[9]39 I.C.C. Annual Rep. 13-14 (1925); 40 I.C.C. Annual Rep. 13, 76-77 (1926); 41 I.C.C. Annual Rep. 65, 80 (1927); 42 I.C.C. Annual Rep. 60-61, 81-82 (1928).

[10]*In the Matter of Consolidation of the Railway Properties of the United States into a Limited Number of Systems,* 159 I.C.C. 522.

[11]*Schwabacher v. United States,* 334 U.S. 182, 193.

[12]See pp. 30-32 of the committee's report filed in December, 1938.

We recommend legislation repealing those portions of the Interstate Commerce Act which make the regulatory body responsible for the prescription of a general plan of consolidation for railroads, and substituting therefor provisions which will restore to the carriers all initiative in the matter, with requirement of the approval of the Transportation Board before any proposed consolidation may lawfully be made effective, such approval to be granted or withheld in accordance with the considerations hereinbefore suggested, and, when granted, to carry with it relief from all restraints or prohibitions imposed by State or Federal law.

The Transportation Act of 1940, which embodies Section 5(2) generally in its present form, relieved the Commission of its duty to promulgate a master plan. Instead, it authorized the Commission to approve carrier-instituted, voluntary plans of merger or consolidation provided that the plans met the public interest test prescribed therein.[13] In addition to the test of public interest, the merger terms must be found to be just and reasonable as to stockholders. As the Supreme Court stated in *St. Joe Paper Co. v. Atlantic Coast Line R. Co., supra*, at 310, "the very heart of Section 5 is that a merger of two carriers may be approved by the Interstate Commerce Commission only if it originates as a voluntary proposal by the merging carriers." Thus, the initiative to formulate and present for approval specific merger proposals was left entirely to the railroads.[14] It should also be observed that the 1940 Act retained the provision immunizing mergers from the operation of the antitrust laws, but deleted the requirement of the 1920 Act relating to the preservation of competition.

While the initiative to present merger proposals to the Commission for approval rests with railroads, the Commission may grant such approval only if it finds upon the basis of the record that such proposal will be in the public interest. The Commission, however, is not restricted to the specific proposal advanced by the applicants, but must afford full recognition to the evidence adduced by opposing parties and determine the modifications, if any, that are required to meet the public interest test. On this point, it is significant that the express authorization to impose conditions provided by Section 5(2) is "not limited to conditions proposed or favored by the carriers."[15] In each instance the consummation of a transaction whether approved in its original form or as modified by the Commission is permissive and not mandatory.

It was the purpose of Congress in enacting the 4R Act to provide

---

[13]*Schwabacher v. United States, supra.*

[14]See *St. Joe Paper Co. v. Atlantic Coast Line R. Co., supra*, at p. 315 for outline of the history of the consolidation provisions of the Act.

[15]*New York Central Securities Corp. v. United States*, 287 U.S. 12, 28.

the means to rehabilitate and maintain the physical facilities, improve the operations and structure, and restore the financial stability of the railway system of the United States, and to promote the revitalization of such railway system, so that this mode of transportation will remain viable in the private sector of the economy and will be able to provide energy-efficient, ecologically compatible transportation services wth greater efficiency, effectiveness, and economy, in part through the encouragement of efforts to restructure the system on a more economically justified basis, including planning authority in the Secretary of Transportation, an expedited procedure for determining whether merger and consolidation applications are in the public interest, and continuing reorganization authority.[16]

The Commission Power to Effect a Transaction

The law is clear that the Commission does not have the power to require the transfer of railroad property from one railroad to another in the absence of an application to effect such a transaction.

In *Gulf, M. & O. R. Co. Purchase, Securities*,[17] the Commission found:

> This assumes that under the provisions of Section 5(2) we have the authority to require the transfer of railroad property from one person to another if we find that such transfer would be consistent with the public interest. That section confers no such authority on us. Under the provisions of Section 5(2) we have authority by our order to approve a transaction coming within those provisions only upon application of a carrier or other person, and our order is permissive, not mandatory.

The Supreme Court in *St. Joe Paper Co. v. Atl. Coast Line R. Co.*[18] had this to say about involuntary mergers which applies equally as well to all transactions under Section 5 of the I.C. Act.

> Suffice it to say here that one clear thread which runs through a course of legislation extending over a period of twenty years, as well as through the various commentaries upon it, is that only mergers voluntarily initiated by the participating carriers are encompassed by that statute and sanctioned by it. From the initial enactment in the Transportation Act of 1920, 41 Stat. 456, 480, to the most recent comprehensive reexamination of these provisions in the Transportation Act of 1940, 54 Stat. 898,

---

[16]Section 101(a) of the 4R Act.

[17]267 I.C.C. 265, 269-70.

[18]347 U.S. 298, 305-10. Cf. *Central Freight Lines, Inc. Control — Alamo Freight Lines, Inc.*, 70 M.C.C. 610, 75 M.C.C. 731, 90 M.C.C. 96, 90 M.C.D. 246, sustained in *Walker v. United States*, 208 F. Supp. 388, aff'd 372 U.S. 526. (See also 204 F. Supp. 918), where the Commission indicated that it had jurisdiction to entertain a unilateral application for control in the face of a contractual dispute.

905, Congress has consistently and insistently denied the Interstate Commerce Commission the power to take the initiative in getting one railroad to turn over its properties to another railroad in return for assorted securities of the latter. The role of the Commission in this regard has traditionally been confined to approving or disapproving mergers proposed by the railroads to be merged. And this adamant position taken by Congress has not been for want of attempts to secure relaxation. Advocacy of giving the Commission power to propose and enforce mergers has been steady and, at times, strong, but it has consistently failed in Congress.

The reasons for this hostility to mergers imposed by the Commission derive largely from the disadvantages attributed by Congress to such far-reaching corporate revampings. Employees of the constituent railroads would, it has been feared, almost certainly be adversely affected. Shippers and communities adequately served by railroad A may suddenly find themselves unfavorably dependent upon railroad B. Investors in one railroad would, contrary to their expectations, find their holdings transmuted into securities of a different railroad. As the Commission in its 1938 Annual Report said of consolidations:

> Projects of this character cannot be crammed down the throats of those who must carry them out or conform to them. Legal compulsion can be used with advantage to bring recalcitrants and stragglers into line, but not to drive hostile majorities into action. (p. 23)

We therefore conclude that the Commission does not have under Sec. 77 of the Bankruptcy Act a power which Congress has repeatedly denied it under the Interstate Commerce Act, namely to initiate the merger or consolidation of two railroads. In light of the continuously and vehemently reiterated policy against endowing the I.C.C. with such a power under Sec. 5 of the Interstate Commerce Act, it is inconceivable, wholly apart from the consistency clause, that such was the *sub silentio* effect of Sec. 77, an emergency statute hurriedly enacted with scarcely any debate. The consistency clause serves but to strengthen this natural presumption against such a tacit grant. It would require unambiguous language indeed to accomplish a contrary result; yet nowhere in the committee reports and the debates on the original Sec. 77, nor in any of the legislative materials relating to the thorough reexamination of that statute in 1935, can we find so much as one word which conveys the impression that as to mergers under the Bankruptcy Act, Congress stealthily designed to jettison its long-standing and oft-reiterated policy against compulsory mergers. (347 U.S. 305-308) . . .

All this of course is not to say that mergers cannot be carried out in the course of a Sec. 77 reorganization. It merely means that if they are, they must be consummated in accordance with all the requirements and restrictions applicable to mergers under the Act primarily concerned with railroad amalgamations, the Interstate Commerce Act. So far as here relevant, that means that the merger must be worked out and put before the Commission by the merging carriers. It also means that one carrier cannot be railroaded by the Commission into an undesired merger with another carrier.

In short, the consistency clause of Sec. 77 incorporates by reference Sec. 5 of the Interstate Commerce Act, as amended. And the very heart of Sec. 5 is that a merger of two carriers may be approved by the Interstate Commerce Commission only if it originates as a voluntary proposal by the merging carriers. (298 U.S. 309-310)

In *Wheeling & L. E. Ry. Co. Control*,[19] the Commission said:

The New York Central filed in the Section 5 proceeding a petition requesting that it be included in the transactions there proposed in the following respects: (1) Protection of through routes and joint rates at present maintained with the Wheeling, . . . and (3) granting by the Wheeling to the New York Central of new trackage rights which will give the latter access to mines on rails of the former . . .

         o   o   o

The applicants contend that we are not authorized to require one carrier to grant trackage rights over its line to another, except as provided in Section 3(5) of the Interstate Commerce Act, relying on a dictum in *Construction by Alabama, T. & N. R. Corp.*, 124 I.C.C. 114, a matter arising under Section 1(18), and decided in 1927. They point out correctly that the trackage rights here sought by the New York Central are not intended to accomplish common use of terminals, as contemplated by Section 3(5). The New York Central contends that express statutory authority exists for imposition of the trackage condition which it requests.

         o   o   o

Our right to impose the conditions requested by the New York Central is seriously questioned, but in view of our conclusions herein it is unnecessary that we pass upon that question.

In *Baltimore & O. R. Co. Operation*,[20] the Commission said:

We are without power to compel the Pere Marquette to grant trackage rights over its line, *Alabama T. & N. R. Corp. Construction*, 124 I.C.C. 114, and we think the situation here is essentially different from that in *Chicago & Alton R. Co. v. Toledo P. & W. Ry. Co.*, 146 I.C.C. 171, cited by one of the interveners as authority for us to compel the continuance of the present operation on the same terms, because, in that case, insofar as is pertinent here, it was found merely that an operation under trackage rights may not be abandoned without our authority. We are of the opinion that the contract between the Baltimore & Ohio and the Pere Marquette, based upon the clearly expressed intention of the parties and their understanding thereof, the necessary legal effect of the agreement as a whole, and the method of operation actually followed, is one providing for a joint traffic arrangement and not for an operation under trackage rights.

[19]267 I.C.C. 163, 186-188.
[20]261 I.C.C. 535, 544-545.

In *Detroit, T. & I. R. Co. Control*,[21] the Commission said:

> *Trackage Rights.* — At present the Baltimore & Ohio operates passenger service under trackage rights over a line of the New York Central between Toledo and Detroit. It does not, however, have a direct freight service between those points. In its petition for leave to intervene herein, the Baltimore & Ohio contends, among other things, that approval of the instant application would eliminate all competition at present existing between the applicants, on the one hand, and Ironton, on the other, and that the only manner by which active and effective competition in the public interest could be fully preserved would be for us to impose a condition to such approval, the grant of trackage rights to the Baltimore & Ohio over the main line of Ironton between Leipsic and Detroit, including the joint use of terminal facilities. Under the proposal all industries now served by Ironton also would be served by Baltimore & Ohio. No investigation or study was made as to the cost or the feasibility of the trackage operation requested, or to what, if any, extent such operation would result in duplication of service. The applicants, Ironton, New York Central, and Youngstown are opposed to the trackage operation proposed by Baltimore & Ohio. Youngstown contends that it could not compete with Baltimore & Ohio single-line service into Detroit, especially in connection with the rubber traffic moving thereto from Akron.

> Our right to impose the condition requested by the Baltimore & Ohio in this case is seriously questioned. See *Wheeling & L. E. Ry. Co. Control,* 267 I.C.C. 163, 188.

The Proposal before the Commission

Under Section 5(2), the Commission is not in a position to consider whether an acquisition of control in some manner other than that proposed, or by some other carrier than the applicant, would better serve the public interest; the question which the Commission must determine is whether the acquisition of control proposed is in the public interest.[22] A somewhat different problem is found in *Toledo, P. & W. R. Co. Control*,[23] where the Commission had before it two applications requesting authority to acquire control of the same carrier. The Commission considered the first application filed in point of time, not because it was in any way bound to consider the first application filed, but because the first represented a transaction capable of being consummated upon approval, and the second would require further steps before the plan could

[21]275 I.C.C. 455, 484-5.
[22]*Clinchfield Ry. Lease,* 90 I.C.C. 113, 132.
[23]295 I.C.C. 523, 546-7.

be consummated and under no circumstances could it be consummated without the first being denied.

Hearing Is Not Required in All Instances

The Commission has held that a public hearing is not necessary in the public interest where approval and consummation of a proposed transaction under Section 5 will not adversely affect existing transportation service to the public and will afford an improved transportation service to the public.[24]

Accommodation with the Objectives of the Antitrust Laws

The effect of the provisions of Section 5(12), formerly 5(11), excepting Commission-approved mergers from the antitrust laws, was considered by the Supreme Court in *McLean Trucking Co. v. United States.*[25] Commenting upon the nature of the power and duty delegated to the Commission, the Supreme Court, in *McLean Trucking Co. v. United States*, said:

> To secure the continuous, close and informed supervision which enforcement of legislative mandates frequently requires, Congress has vested expert administrative bodies such as the Interstate Commerce Commission with broad discretion and has charged them with the duty to execute stated and specific statutory policies. That delegation does not necessarily include either the duty or the authority to execute numerous other laws. Thus, here, the Commission has no power to enforce the Sherman Act as such. It cannot decide definitively whether the transaction contemplated constitutes a restraint of trade or an attempt to monopolize which is forbidden by that Act. *The Commission's task is to enforce the Interstate Commerce Act and other legislation which deals specifically with transportation facilities and problems. That legislation constitutes the immediate fram of reference within which the Commission operates; and the policies expressed in it must be the basic determinants of its action.* (Emphasis supplied.)

[24]*Rockdale S. & S. R. Co. Operation and Control* 282 I.C.C. 297, 298; *Arkansas & L. M. Ry. Co. Control*, 282 I.C.C. 564, 565; *Valdosta S. R. Purchase*, 282 I.C.C. 705, 706. The Commission has held in cases that the failure to produce a witness or witnesses qualified to testify and stand cross-examination concerning the situation of the vendor carrier does not require the Commission to dismiss the application or permit the Commission to refuse to decide the application on its merits. *Mercury Motor Express, Inc., − Consolidation − Carolina Southern Motor Express, Inc.*, 60 M.C.C. 427; *Raymond Brothers Motor Transportation, Inc., − Purchase − Berzel*, 15 M.C.C. 477; *Falwall Fast Freight, Incorporated − Purchase − Draper*, 40 M.C.C. 127; *Kenosha Auto Transport Corp. − Purchase − Frey*, 55 M.C.C. 76; *Marion Trucking Company, Inc. − Purchase − Harwood Trucking, Inc.*, 50 M.C.C. 613.
[25]321 U.S. 67.

But in executing those policies the Commission may be faced with over-lapping and at times inconsistent policies embodied in other legislation enacted at different times and with different problems in view. When this is true, it cannot, without more, ignore the latter. The precise adjustments which it must make, however, will vary from instance to instance depending on the extent to which Congress indicates a desire to have those policies leavened or implemented in the enforcement of the various specific provisions of the legislation with which the Commission is primarily and directly concerned. (pp. 79-80)

The court then proceeded to find in the transportation statutes the aforementioned Congressional intent. It found that the national transportation policy was the guide by which the Commission must be governed and concluded that:

The history of the development of the special national transportation policy suggests, quite apart from the explicit provision of Sec. 5 (11), that the policies of the anti-trust laws determine "the public interest" in railroad regulation only in a qualified way. And the altered emphasis in railroad legislation on achieving an adequate, efficient, and economical system of transportation through close supervision of business operations and practices rather than through heavy reliance on the enforcement of free competition in various phases of the business, cf. *New York Central Securities Corp. v. United States*, 287 U.S. 12, has its counterpart in motor carrier policy. (p. 83)

This, in turn, led the court to state that:

. . . there can be little doubt that the Commission is not to measure proposals for all-rail or all-motor consolidations by the standards of the anti-trust laws. Congress authorized such consolidations because it recognized that in some circumstances they were appropriate for effectuation of the national transportation policy. It was informed that this policy would be furthered by "encouraging the organization of stronger units" in the motor carrier industry. And in authorizing those consolidations it did not import the general policies of the anti-trust laws as a measure of their permissibility. (pp. 84-85)

In explaining the duty of the Commission, the court said:

Congress however neither has made the anti-trust laws wholly inapplicable to the transportation industry nor has authorized the Commission in passing on a proposed merger to ignore their policy. Congress recognized that the process of consolidating motor carriers would result in some diminution of competition and might result in the creation of monopolies. To prevent the latter effect and to make certain that the former was permitted only where appropriate to further the national transportation policy, it placed in the Commission power to control such developments. The national transportation policy requires the Commission to "promote . . . economical . . . service and foster sound economic conditions in transportation and among the several carriers; to encourage the establishment and maintenance of

reasonable charges for transportation services, without unjust discriminations, [or] undue preferences or advantages. . . .” The preservation of
independent and competing motor carriers unquestionably has bearing on
the achievement of those ends. Hence, the fact that the carriers participating in a properly authorized consolidation may obtain immunity from prosecution under the antitrust laws in no sense relieves the Commission of
its duty, as an administrative matter, to consider the effect of the merger
on competitors and on the general competitive situation in the industry in
the light of the objectives of the national transportation policy. (pp. 86-87)

In summary, the court explained:

> In short, the Commission must estimate the scope and appraise the ef-
> fects of the curtailment of competition which will result from the pro-
> posed consolidation and consider them along with the advantages of
> improved service, safer operation, lower costs, etc., to determine whether
> the consolidation will assist in effectuating the over-all transportation pol-
> icy. Resolving these considerations is a complex task which requires ex-
> tensive facilities, expert judgment and considerable knowledge of the
> transportation industry. Congress left that task to the Commission “to the
> end that the wisdom and experience of that Commission may be used not
> only in connection with this form of transportation, but in its coordination
> of all other forms.” 79 Cong. Rec. 12207. “The wisdom and experience of
> that commission,” not of the courts, must determine whether the proposed
> consolidation is “consistent with the public interest.” (pp. 87-88)

Historically, the Commission has considered in control or consolidation
proceedings the impacts of various proposals on interrailroad competition.[26]

The Supreme Court also has ruled that in determining merger and
acquisition proceedings under Section 5, the Commission is required to
give consideration to the competitive consequences of such proposals.
The Supreme Court, in *Minneapolis & St. L. v. United States*,[27] relying
upon its previous holding in *McLean Truck Co. v. U.S.*,[28] stated:

> . . . the problem is one of accommodation of Section 5(2) and the anti-
> trust legislation. The Commission remains obligated to estimate the scope
> and appraise the effects of the curtailment of competition which will result
> from the proposed [acquisition] and consider them along with the advan-
> tages of improved service [and other matters in the public interest] to
> determine whether the [acquisition] will assist in effectuating the over-
> all transportation policy.

[26]*Consolidations and Combinations of Carriers*, 12 I.C.C. 277, 304-305; *Denver
& Rio Grande Investigation*, 113 I.C.C. 75, 87; *Construction by Western Pacific
R. R.*, 138 I.C.C. 779, 784-785; *Western Pacific R. R. Co. Construction*, 170 I.C.C.
183, 207; *Construction of Lines in Eastern Oregon*, 111 I.C.C. 3, 37-38, 117 I.C.C.
737, 124 I.C.C. 529, 138 I.C.C. 99; *Great Northern Ry. Co. Construction*, 166 I.C.C.
3, 33-35, 39-40, 170 I.C.C. 399, 175 I.C.C. 367 and 175 I.C.C. 513.
[27]361 U.S. 713.
[28]321 U.S. 67.

❄ ❄ ❄

Against this background no other inference is possible but that, as a factor in determining the propriety of [railroad acquisitions] the preservation of competition among carriers, although still a value, is significant chiefly as it aids in the attainment of the objectives of the National Transportation Policy.

Effect upon competition continues to be one of the important factors to be weighed in considering the public interest. Thus, Union Pacific, in *Spokane International R. Co. Control*,[29] was authorized to acquire control of Spokane International Railroad, while participation in control by Great Northern and Northern Pacific was denied, in order to preserve interrailroad competition in the territory involved. *Spokane International R. Co. Control*.

And, in the first case involving the Frisco's efforts to secure approval of its control of Central of Georgia, *Central of Georgia Ry. Co. Control*,[30] the Commission observed:

. . . We think it important that the Frisco and the Central do not compete in the ordinary sense, but are geographically complementary and will provide an efficient traffic channel between the Southeast and the Southwest . . .

That the Frisco was subsequently denied the authority it sought because it had violated 5(5), formerly 5(4), in acquiring control of the Frisco without approval does not detract from the validity of this quoted expression, or its applicability.

Competition was also evaluated in *Louisville & Nashville R. Co. Merger*,[31] where it was pointed out that, while there was a limited degree of competition between the carriers involved, the record pointed to no important effect to be expected from termination of that competition. Stressing that no carrier opposed the merger because of any adverse impact on competition, the Commission said:

. . . The resulting localized reduction in competition must be considered in the light of the effect of competition by the system as a whole. . . . We conclude from the record that the merger would strengthen the resulting system and make it more capable of rendering effective competition with the other railroads serving the South Atlantic coastal area.

The Commission, in *Norfolk & W. Ry. Co. Merger*,[32] and *Erie R. Co. Merger*,[33] in testing for consistency with the public interest, carefully reviewed the effects on interrailroad competition. The fact that in each of these proceedings the Commission sanctioned combinations

[29]295 I.C.C. 425, 437-438.
[30]295 I.C.C. 563, 579.
[31]295 I.C.C. 457, 488.
[32]307 I.C.C. 401.
[33]312 I.C.C. 185.

which resulted in elimination of a certain degree of interrailroad competition cannot be taken as an indication that this factor is no longer considered significant. On the contrary, these cases mean only that maintenance of interrailroad competition, while important, may in some instances be outweighed on the scales of the public interest by other overriding factors.

In the *Norfolk & Western* case, for example, the Commission was confronted with a situation probably unparalleled in the railroad industry. While the lines of Norfolk & Western and Virginian would have appeared, as a result of their generally close proximity, to compete with each other vigorously, such was not at all the case. The Virginian was not only a "one commodity" but also a "one-way" railroad. By far the greater part of its traffic was eastbound coal. Norfolk & Western was also a heavy coal carrier, but merchandise constituted a much larger percentage of its total traffic than of Virginian's. In approving the merger, the Commission observed (p. 440) that "The Norfolk & Western and the Virginian serve different areas of the Appalachian coalfields and, therefore, there is no direct competition between them for their principal traffic. Such competition as does exist for coal traffic is in the nature of market competition between mines, and this will not be affected by the merger." And, with respect to other traffic, the opinion continued, "As to traffic other than coal, the record shows, that while the two lines do have competitive through routes from and to commonly served points, there is little direct competition between them."

The Commission concluded on this aspect of the case:

> *While there may be some slight lessening of competition* as a result of the proposed merger, we do not regard that fact as of controlling significance. The evidence establishes that, after the merger, strong competition will still be afforded by other forms of transportation. We conclude that the public interest would not be adversely affected by any lessening of competition which may result from the proposed merger. (Emphasis supplied.)

In the *Erie* case the consequences of the merger on interrailroad competition were stated in these words (at p. 245):

> The merger of the Lackawanna into the Erie would eliminate the present direct competition each with the other for the same traffic, but would not reduce the competition which confronts the applicants because of the availability to the public of the services of various connecting railroads and other forms of transportation, and in effect, would not substantially lessen such competition or tend to create a monopoly.

Moreover, the Erie-Lackawanna merger was a move made by two roads so weak financially that in recent years neither had income sufficient to meet fixed charges and contingent interest.

In passing on any proposal under Section 5(2), the Commission is to consider, along with other matters affecting the public interest, the effect which consummation of the proposal will have on other carriers and whether such effect would be to "jeopardize the capacity of [such carriers] to maintain adequate transportation service to the public."[34] The Commission has also held that "(w)here a part of the public would benefit by the proposed transaction and other parts would be injured, the question is whether the benefits outweigh the injuries.[35]

In summary, the congressional purpose in enacting Section 5(2) is to facilitate mergers and consolidations in the national transportation system.[36] In administering Section 5(2), the Commission is not to "measure proposals for all-rail or all-motor consolidations[37] by the standards of the antitrust laws." However, it may not disregard the policy underlying the antitrust laws even though carriers participating in a merger are relieved by Section 5(12) from the operation of such laws.[38] Its primary task is to reconcile the objective of "preventing injurious waste and in securing more efficient transportation service,"[39] with the general concern of Congress "that tendencies toward concentration in industry are to be curbed in their incipiency, particularly when those tendencies are being accelerated through giant steps striding across a hundred cities at a time."[40] In short, the "problem is one of accommodation of Section 5(2) and the antitrust legislation."[41]

In *Schwabacher v. United States, supra,* at 198, the court said that the Commission "must look for standards in passing on a voluntary merger only to the Interstate Commerce Act," which in "matters within its scope . . . is the supreme law of the land." As indicated, these standards have been prescribed by Congress in Section 5(2) (c) of the Act.[42] Although as indicated previously the Commission must afford recognition to the policy underlying the antitrust laws, neither Section 5 nor any other provision of the I.C. Act contains an antitrust requirement or criterion to be applied by the Commission in railroad merger proposals. In fact, the 1940 Act eliminated the specific provisions of the 1920 Act requiring the preservation of competition. This notwithstand-

---

[34]*Erie R. Co. Merger,* 312 I.C.C. 185, 247. See also *Toledo P. & W. R. Co. Control,* 295 I.C.C. 523, 536.

[35]*Detroit, Toledo & Ironton R. Co. Control,* 275 I.C.C. 455, 488.

[36]*Maintenance Empl. v. United States,* 366 U.S. 169, 172-73.

[37]*McLean Trucking Co. v. United States, supra,* at 84-85.

[38]*Minneapolis & St. Louis R. Co. v. United States, supra.*

[39]*New York Central Securities Corp. v. United States, supra,* at p. 26.

[40]*Brown Shoe Co. v. United States,* 370 U.S. 294, 346.

[41]*Minneapolis & St. Louis R. Co. v. United States, supra,* at p. 186.

[42]Cf. *St. Joe Paper Co. v. Atlantic Coast R. Co., supra.*

ing, the effect of a proposed merger on the continuance of competition, both intra- and intermodal, is one of the elements directly related to the protection of the public interest and must be considered.[43] There, however, is no provision in the Act which expressly or by implication prohibits the merger of financially strong railroads. The Act draws no distinction as between the strong and the weak, or between competitive and noncompetitive railroads. There is no requirement in either the statute or judicial precedent which limits the Commission's authority to approve mergers to those involving carriers which are insolvent or on the brink of bankruptcy.[44] Under the Act, the primary test is whether the proposed merger will be consistent with the public interest under the standards prescribed by Section 5(2) (c), and otherwise meets the test of justice and reasonableness.

The Clayton Act

In 1914 the Congress enacted the Clayton Act, Section 7 of which[45] provided, in part:

> No corporation engaged in commerce shall acquire, directly or indirectly, the whole or any part of the stock or other share capital of another corporation engaged also in commerce, where the effect of such acquisition may be to substantially lessen competition between the corporation whose stock is so acquired and the corporation making the acquisition, or to restrain such commerce in any section or community, or tend to create a monopoly of any line of commerce.

Concurrent jurisdiction to enforce the provisions of this section of the Clayton Act was vested in the Department of Justice,[46] and "in the Interstate Commerce Commission where applicable to common carriers."[47]

The impact of the Transportation Act of 1920 upon the application of the antitrust laws to railroad mergers can best be illustrated by the Southern Pacific's control of Central Pacific. In *United States v. Southern Pac. Co.,*[48] the Supreme Court held that such control "constituted a combination in restraint of trade because it fetters the free and normal flow of competition in interstate traffic and tends to monopolization" in vio-

---

[43]See *McLean Trucking Co. v. United States, supra.*
[44]See *Norfolk & W. Ry. Co. Merger,* 307 I.C.C. 401, and *Louisville & N. R. Co. Merger,* 295 I.C.C. 457.
[45]38 Stat. 731; 15 U.S.C. 18.
[46]38 Stat. 736; 15 U.S.C. 25.
[47]38 Stat. 734; 15 U.S.C. 21.
[48]259 U.S. 214, 229.

lation of the Sherman Act. However, within a few weeks of the Supreme Court's decision, the Commission authorized such control under the terms of the newly enacted Transportation Act of 1920. In *Control of Central Pacific by Southern Pacific,*[49] the Commission said:

> Carriers affected by any order made by us pursuant to paragraph (2) of Section 5 are under the provisions of paragraph (8) relieved from the operation of "antitrust laws," and all other restraints or prohibitions by law, State or Federal, insofar as may be necessary to enable them to do anything authorized or required by such order. Under paragraph (2) we are given broad power to consider the questions of public interest involved in an acquisition of control by one carrier of another, and are given authority by order to approve and authorize such acquisition, under such rules and regulations, and for such consideration and on such terms and conditions, as shall be found by us to be just and reasonable in the premises.
>
> While the Sherman law has not been repealed, carriers affected by any order made by us under paragraphs (1) to (7) of Section 5 of the Act are relieved from its operation. How far our discretion in any particular case should be influenced by consideration of the evils which the Sherman law was designed to prevent is a question necessarily involved in every case where a carrier seeks to acquire control of a competing line. There is nothing in Section 5, however, indicating that the Congress intended that we should refuse to accept jurisdiction upon the ground, solely, that a proposed acquisition of control would violate the Sherman law. Full effect must be given to the provisions of paragraph (8). When by our order based upon broad considerations of the public interest we in effect grant relief against antitrust laws, and other restraints and prohibitions by law, we are exercising a power which the statute gives to us alone. Evidence as to public benefits to be derived from common control of competing carriers, which would be immaterial in a prosecution under the Sherman Act, might be entirely pertinent in a proceeding before us under paragraph (2). There is, therefore, an essential dissimilarity in the issues and in the nature of the proceeding which in our opinion makes it proper for us to pass upon the application, while giving full effect to the adjudication of the Supreme Court.

This view of the legislation was reiterated in the Supreme Court's decision of 20 years later in *McLean Trucking Co. v. United States, supra.*

In 1950 the Congress amended the Clayton Act by making it applicable to asset acquisitions as well as to stock acquisitions and, insofar as is pertinent, by adding the following express exemption:

> Nothing contained in this section shall apply to transactions duly consummated pursuant to authority given by the . . . Interstate Commerce Com-

---

[49]76 I.C.C. 508, 515-16; sustained, *United States v. Southern Pac. Co.,* 290 F. 443.

mission . . . under any statutory provision vesting such power in such Commission. . . .[50]

The legislative history of the quoted provision discloses that it merely accorded legislative recognition to the existing practice relating to the policy underlying the antitrust laws, and was enacted to remove any doubt that the Congress by the reenactment of the pertinent section of the Clayton Act thereby sought to change that practice.[51]

In amending the Clayton Act in 1950, the Congress did not repeal the provisions of Section 11, "That authority to enforce compliance with Sections 2, 3, 7, and 8 of this Act by the persons respectively subject thereto is hereby vested in the Interstate Commerce Commission where applicable to common carriers subject to the Interstate Commerce Act, as amended." In speaking of this grant of authority, the Supreme Court in *Georgia v. Pennsylvania R. Co.*,[52] said:

> Congress by § 11 of the Clayton Act entrusted the Commission with authority to enforce compliance with certain of its provisions "where applicable to common carriers" under the Commission's jurisdiction. It has the power to lift the ban of the antitrust laws in favor of carriers who merge or consolidate (*New York Central Securities Corp. v. United States* 287 U.S. 12, 25-26) and the duty to give weight to the anti-trust policy of the nation before approving mergers and consolidations. *McLean Trucking Co. v. United States*, 321 U.S. 67.

The Commission sought to exercise its authority under Section 11 of

---

[50]64 Stat. 1125.

[51]The last paragraph of Section 7 is new. It simply provides that provisions of the bill should not apply to corporations coming under the jurisdiction of I.C.C., CAB, FCC, FPC, SEC, and the Secretary of Agriculture. These agencies already have jurisdiction over these corporations, and there is no disposition to change the present arrangement regarding them. [H. Rep. No. 1191, 81st Cong., 1st sess. 6 (1949).]

See also. H. Rep. No. 596, 80th Cong., 1st sess. 5 (1947); H. Rep. 1820, 79th Cong., 2d sess. 4 (1946); S. Doc. No. 35, 77th Cong., 1st sess. 40 (1941); S. Doc. No. 95, 76th Cong., 1st sess. 21 (1939).

Commenting on one of the predecessor bills, Commissioner Walter M. W. Splawn, Chairman of the Legislative Committee of the Commission, on March 17, 1947, wrote the Chairman of House Committee on the Judiciary:

So far as this Commission is concerned, the foregoing provision would have only declaratory effect, as the Clayton Act is now made inapplicable to transactions governed by Section 5 of the Interstate Commerce Act. Its inclusion, however, would do no harm. [*Hearings on H.R. 515 Before a Subcommittee of the House Committee on the Judiciary*, 80th Cong., 1st sess. 272 (1947)].

See, also, *Hearings on H.R. 2357. Before a Subcommittee of the House Committee on the Judiciary*, 79th Cong., 1st sess. 359 (1945).

[52]324 U.S. 439, 456.

the Clayton Act in *Interstate Commerce Commission v. Pennsylvania R. Co.*,[53] in which it said:

> While it is true that the Transportation Act, 1920, marked a substantial departure from previous governmental policy in the matter of competition between railroad companies, we are unable to close our eyes to the fact that Congress required that in the administration of that act competition should be preserved as fully as possible, and to that end it left the Clayton Act in full force and effect, providing, however, in Section 5(8) of the interstate commerce act, that its operation might be suspended by us in order to authorize acquisitions of control of one carrier by another where, in our judgment, such acquisition would be in the public interest. The respondents, in full knowledge of these provisions, have proceeded without coming to us for such authority.

Similarly, in *Interstate Commerce Commission v. Baltimore & O. R. Co.*,[54] the Commission noted, "At the time of the acquisitions of Western Maryland stock by the respondent no application for such relief had been sought or obtained." Also in *Interstate Commerce Commission v. Baltimore & O. R. Co.*,[55] the Commission said, "No such approval has been given or sought in this case."

In each of these Clayton Act cases, the Commission ordered the respondent railroad to divest itself on the stock unlawfully acquired.[56] The Commission was without authority directly to order the divestiture of stock giving one railroad control of another without Commission authorization under Section 5(2) until 1933 when the powers now conferred by Section 5(8) were added by the Emergency Railroad Transportation Act, 1933. There is no indication that the Commission had attempted to enforce the provisions of Section 7 of the Clayton Act since that time.

While Section 11 of the Clayton Act continues on the books, and presumably would authorize the Commission to require the divestiture of control effectuated without Commission authorization in violation of Section 7 of the Clayton Act, as an alternative remedy to ordering divestiture under Section 5(8) of the I.C. Act, Section 11 cannot be read so as to require the enforcement of the provision of Section 7 when an appli-

---

[53]169 I.C.C. 618, 642, rev'd on other grounds, *Pennsylvania R. Co., v. Interstate Commerce Commission*, 66 F. 2d 37.

[54]160 I.C.C. 785, 791.

[55]152 I.C.C. 721, 723.

[56]*Interstate Commerce Commission v. Pennsylvania R. Co., supra*, at 643; *Interstate Commerce Commission v. Baltimore & O. R. Co., supra*, at 792; *Interstate Commerce Commission v. Baltimore & O. R. Co., supra*, at 737.

cation for Commission authorization is before the Commission under Section 5(2) of the I.C. Act.[57]

Three Supreme Court cases,[58] though involving the relationship between the antitrust laws and other regulatory statutes, confirm the view that an exemption such as is afforded by Section 5(12) of the I.C. Act cuts across the antitrust laws and avoids the necessity of their enforcement by the agency exercising regulatory jurisdiction. Thus, in a case brought under the Clayton Act to enjoin a proposed bank merger approved by the Comptroller of the Currency under the Bank Merger Act,[59] the Supreme Court, contrasting the exemption provisions of the I.C. Act, noted, at 374 U.S. 350, "No express immunity is conferred by the Act." On the other hand, in the *Pan American* case, the Supreme Court held that the questions of the joint control of Panagra have been entrusted to the Civil Aeronautics Board, which is authorized to approve consolidations, mergers, and the like, the participants of which are granted antitrust immunity as under the Interstate Commerce Act.

Exclusive and Plenary Character of Section 5(12)

"Exclusive and plenary" means nothing less than primary and complete. *Thompson v. Texas Mexican R. Co.*[60] Therefore, under Section 5(12), State laws conflicting with the exercise by the Commission of the powers given it by Congress cease to be effective in relation to the parties to the transaction involved. The early case of *Texas v. United States*,[61] establishes that carriers are to be relieved of State restraints and prohibitions which conflict with the exercise of power by the Commission under Section 5. The single point in controversy in the *Texas* case was with respect to the authority of the Commission to approve the acquisition of control by a lease which permits the lessee to abandon, or to remove from the State, the general offices, shops, etc. of the lessor. State law confined to Texas corporations the right to own or maintain any railway within the State. The law required railroad companies chartered by the State to keep and maintain general offices within the State and prohibited the changing of the location of general offices, shops, etc. without the consent and approval of the Railroad Commis-

---

[57]*Minneapolis & St. Louis R. Co. v. United States, supra.*

[58]*United States v. Philadelphia Nat. Bank,* 374 U.S. 321; *Pan American World Airways v. United States,* 371 U.S. 296; *California v. Federal Power Comm.,* 369 U.S. 482.

[59]12 U.S.C. 1828.

[60]328 U.S. 134, 146-50.

[61]292 U.S. 522.

sion. In discussing the purpose of Section 5, the Supreme Court said (at pp. 530-531):

> These broadening provisions of the Emergency Railroad Transportation Act, 1933, confirm and carry forward the purpose which led to the enactment of Transportation Act (February 28), 1920. . . . We found that Transportation Act, 1920, introduced into the federal legislation a new railroad policy, seeking to insure an adequate transportation service. To attain that end, new rights, new obligations, new machinery, were created. . . . It is a primary aim of that policy to secure the avoidance of waste. That avoidance, as well as the maintenance of service, is viewed as a direct concern of the public. . . . The authority given to the Commission to authorize consolidation purchases, . . . leases, operating contracts, and acquisition of control, was given in aid of that policy. . . . The criterion to be applied by the Commission in the exercise of its authority to approve such transactions — a criterion reaffirmed by the amendments of Emergency Railroad Transportation Act, 1933 — is that of the controlling public interest. And that term as used in the statute is not a mere general reference to public welfare, but, as shown by the context and purpose of the Act, "has direct relation to adequacy of transportation service, to its essential conditions of economy and efficiency, and to appropriate provision and best use of transportation facilities.

The Supreme Court held (p. 533) that there was no ground for concluding that approval of the lease by the Commission with the abandonment, etc. provision was beyond its authority. It pointed out (p. 534) that Section 5 carried "its own provision as to immunity from State requirements which would stand in the way of the execution of the policy of the Congress through the Commission's orders." It then said:

> The view that, by reference to the context, this immunity should be regarded as limited as those "restraints or prohibitions by or imposed under authority of law" which fall within the general description of "antitrust" legislation, is too narrow. The rule of "ejusdem generis" is applied as an aid in ascertaining the intention of the legislature, not to subvert it when ascertained. . . . The scope of the immunity must be measured by the purpose Congress had in view and had constitutional power to accomplish. As that purpose involved the promotion of economy and efficiency in interstate transportation by removal of the burden of excessive expenditure, the removal of such burdens when imposed by state requirements was an essential part of the plan. . . . But while railroad corporations were left under state charters, they were still instrumentalities of interstate commerce, and, as such, were subject to the paramount federal obligation to render the efficient and economical service required in the maintenance of an adequate system of interstate transportation. . . .

The court below in *State of Texas v. United States*,[62] had said:

[62]6 F. Supp. 63, 66.

Again the so-called general words of the paragraph — "all other restraints or prohibitions," in effect are interpreted by the very context in which they appear. The carriers are to be relieved of the operation of such restraints and prohibitions "insofar as may be necessary" to enable them to do anything authorized or required by such order" (i.e., order of the Commission). This is a description of the restraints and prohibitions aimed at. They are any such as would interfere with the doing of things authorized or required. The description negatives the contention that something less was intended than the description would include.

The Commission in *Seaboard Air Line Ry. Co. Receivership,*[63] after noting that the provisions of Section 5 of the Transportation Act of 1920 were further amended by the Transportation Act of 1940, commented that the provisions as to relief from restraints, limitations, and prohibitions of State laws which would stand in the way of the execution of Congressional policy were clarified and strengthened. It said (pp. 720-21):

> In administering the provisions of Section 5 and other provisions of the Act, we must do so with a view to carrying out the declared policy of Congress, including the promotion of economical and efficient service and the fostering of sound economic conditions in transportation. Corporate simplification wherever possible is in accord with this policy.

Schwabacher v. United States,[64] tells us that by reason of Sections 5(12) and 203(7) the "jurisdiction of the Commission under both Section 5 and Section 20(a) is made plenary and exclusive and independent of all other state or federal authority." The case also tells us (at p. 188) that the Commission must look for standards in passing on a voluntary merger only to the I.C. Act. "In matters within its scope it is the supreme law of the land. Its purpose to bring within its scope everything pertaining to the capital structures of such mergers could hardly be made more plain. . . ."

In *Pacific Greyhound Lines — Control and Merger,*[65] the Commission said:

> By Section 5(11) of the Act (which was not considered in the *Baggett* case), the Commission is granted "exclusive and plenary" authority over transactions involving control or acquisition of the operations of carriers subject to Part II of the Act. Approval of such a transaction relieves such carriers from the operation of State laws insofar as necessary to the exercise of the authority granted. . . . This includes the exercise of any franchises acquired through such a transaction. . . .

---

[63]261 I.C.C. 689, 720.
[64]334 U.S. 182, 197.
[65]56 M.C.C. 415, 434.

Seaboard Air Line R. Co. v. Daniel,[66] held that the Commission may, in approving the acquisition by a railroad corporation of one State of railroad lines in another, relieve such corporation of the necessity of becoming incorporated under the laws of such other State the constitution and statutes of which provide that railroad lines within the State may be owned and operated only by State-created corporations.

The facts in the *Seaboard* case are as follows: The Constitution and statutes of South Carolina provided that railroad lines within that State could be owned and operated only by State created corporations; a railroad corporation chartered only under the laws of another State was forbidden under heavy penalties to exercise such power within South Carolina. There was a way, however, in which a foreign corporation could, under South Carolina statutes, indirectly exercise some powers over its South Carolina operations. It could organize a South Carolina subsidiary. In addition, it could, under South Carolina law, consolidate that corporation with itself. In that event, so far as South Carolina statutes governed, the consolidated result would be a corporation both of South Carolina and of another State.

Seaboard, with Commission approval, succeeded to the ownership of a railroad system operating in six Southern States. 736 miles of its line traversed South Carolina connecting with its lines in adjoining States. Seaboard was a Virginia corporation, had no South Carolina subsidiary, and had effected no consolidation with a South Carolina created corporation. It, therefore, was subject to the penalties provided by South Carolina if that law was applicable.

Seaboard brought action in South Carolina Supreme Court to enjoin the State from attempting to collect statutory penalties or to enforce statutory provisions against it. The answer to the complaint did not challenge the constitutional power of Congress to relieve Seaboard of compliance with South Carolina's requirements of State incorporation. It took the position that insofar as the Commission's order could be interpreted as an attempt to override State laws it was void. The State court held that the Commission lacked power under Section 5 to enter such an order.

In reversing the State court, the Supreme Court said (pp. 124-126):

Congress has long made the maintenance and development of an economical and efficient railroad system a matter of primary national concern. Its legislation must be read with this purpose in mind. In keeping with this purpose Congress has often recognized that the nation's railroads should have sound corporate and financial structure and has taken appro-

[66]333 U.S. 118.

priate steps to this end. The purchase of this very railroad by appellant resulted from extensive reorganization proceedings conducted by the Interstate Commerce Commission and federal district courts in accordance with congressional enactments applicable to railroads. In furtherance of this congressional policy these agencies approved reorganization plans which called for the purchase and operation of these properties, including the portion in South Carolina, by appellant, as a Virginia corporation.

This court has previously approved a Commission order entered in a Section 5 consolidation proceeding which granted a railroad relief from State laws analogous to the State requirements here. *Texas v. United States,* 202 U.S. 522. . . . Most of the reasons which justified the Commission's order in that case are equally applicable here. Furthermore, since that case was decided Congress has given additional proof of its purpose to grant adequate power to the Commission to override State laws which may interfere with efficient and economical railroad operation. By . . . Section 5(11), Congress granted the Commission "exclusive and plenary" authority in refusing or approving railroad consolidations, mergers, acquisitions, etc. The breadth of this grant of power can be understood only by reference to Section 5(2) (b) which authorizes the Commission to condition its approval "upon such terms and conditions and such modifications as it shall find to be just and reasonable." All of this power can be exercised in accordance with what the Commission may find to be "consistent with the public interest." The purchaser of railroad property with Commission approval is authorized by Section 5(11) "to own and operate any properties . . . acquired through said transaction without invoking any approval under State authority;" and such an approved owner, according to that paragraph, is "relieved from the operation of the antiturst laws and of all other restraints, limitations, and prohibitions of law, Federal, State, or municipal, insofar as may be necessary to enable them to carry into effect the transaction so approved . . . and to hold, maintain, and operate any properties . . . acquired through such transaction."

The Supreme Court said (p. 126) that the language in Section 5(12) "very clearly reposes powers in the Commission to exempt railroads under a Section 5 proceeding from State laws which bar them from operating in the State or impose conditions upon such operation."

Consideration was given by the Supreme Court to the last sentence of Section 5(12) which reads, "Nothing in this section shall be construed to create or provide for the creation, directly or indirectly, of a Federal corporation, and any power granted by this section to any carrier or corporation shall be deemed to be in addition to and in modification of its powers under its corporate charter or under the laws of any State." The Supreme Court commented (p. 126):

> . . . We see nothing in this sentence that detracts from the broad powers granted the Commission by Section 5. In fact, the language of the sentence appears to support Commission's power here exercised. Although the sentence bars creation of a federal corporation, it clearly authorizes

a railroad corporation to exercise the powers therein granted over and above those bestowed upon it by the state of its creation. These federally conferred powers can be exercised in the same manner as though they had been granted to a federally created corporation. . . .

However, in *City of Palestine, Texas v. United States,*[67] it was held that the Commission's power only extends to setting aside State restraints of the effectuation of an approved Section 5(2) transaction and no further. The court said:

> In its grant of approval authority, Congress did not issue the ICC a hunting license for state laws and contracts that limit a railroad's efficiency unless those laws or contracts interfered with carrying out an approved merger. *See Schwabacher v. United States, supra,* 334 U.S. at 207, 68 S. Ct. 958 (Frankfurter, J., dissenting). *Cf. Texas & New Orleans Railroad Co. v. Brotherhood of Railroad Trainmen,* 307 F.2d 151, 158-60 (5th Cir. 1962) (ICC exceeded authority when [it] dictated labor contract as part of approval of yard agreement between railroads). Section 5(11)'s description of the freedom enjoyed by carriers in an approved merger recognizes that the carriers' immunity from state law extends only *"insofar as may be necessary to enable them to carry into effect the* transaction so approved or provided for . . . ." 49 U.S.C. § 5(11) (1970) (emphasis supplied). These words express a practical limitation on the power of the ICC. The ICC's pursuit of the public interest focuses on its approval of railroad mergers, consolidations, acquisitions, and other section 5(2) transactions. Actions taken by the ICC in connection with those transactions but not necessary to them exceed the scope of its authority. In section 5(11) Congress clearly expresses a sensitivity to state law: the ICC's approval and may overturn state law only where "necessary to carry into effect" the transaction. The ICC has shown little sensitivity in this case.

Jurisdiction under Section 5 Involving Issues of Interpretation of State Laws and Involving Interpretation and Enforcement of Contracts

Schwabacher v. U.S.,[68] described in detail the Commission's functions under Section 5(2) and their relationship to determination of ordinary stockholders rights — other than the nature of the vote required to approve the transaction. In the proceeding below, a merger involving the Michigan Central and the C. & O., the Commission had held that the transaction, on the terms if specified, was just and reasonable but indicated that it would be left to the parties and the dissenting stockholders to work out between them by agreement or by resort to the courts the amount to be received by the dissenting common stockholders if they

[67]Nos. 762689 and 763507, 5 Cir., September 19, 1977.
[68]334 U.S. 182.

were not satisfied with the provision made by the Commission, since under State law they had the right of appraisal. The contention was made that because Section 5(12) gives the Commission plenary powers the Commission's order should finally determine the amount to be received by the dissenting stockholders, thereby taking precedence over the state law. In affirming this contention, the court first reviewed the Commission's functions relative to voluntary mergers under Section 5(2). In footnote 1, page 185, the court summarized the provisions making up the Commission's jurisdiction and included Section 5(2) (a), (b), (c) and (e) and Section 5(5), together with Section 5(12). In this connection, it should be noted that Section 5(2) (b) provides in part as follows:

> If the Commission finds that, subject to such terms and conditions and such modifications as it shall find to be just and reasonable, the proposed transaction is within the scope of subdivision (a) and will be consistent with the public interest, it shall enter an order approving and authorizing such transaction, upon the terms and conditions, and with the modifications so found to be just and reasonable. . . .

After summarizing the history leading to the present posture of the statute, the court stated, "The Act does not specify every consideration to which the Commission must give weight in determining whether or not any plan meets the tests." Upon indicating certain of the statutorily prescribed specific tests, the court summarized the Commission's function as follows (page 193-194):

> This court has recently and unanimously said in reference to this Act, "Congress has long made the maintenance and development of an economical and efficient railroad system a matter of primary national concern. Its legislation must be read with this purpose in mind." *Seaboard Airline R. Co. v. Daniel*, 330 U.S. 118, ante 580, 60 S. Ct. 426.

> So reading the legislation relevant to this merger, we find that approval of a voluntary railroad merger which is within the scope of the Act is dependent upon three, and upon only three, considerations: First, a finding that, it "will be consistent with the public interest." (Second 5(2) (b).) Second, a finding that, subject to any modification made by the Commission, it is "just and reasonable." (Section 5(2) (b).) Third, assent of the "majority, unless a different vote is required under applicable State law, in which case the number so required shall assent, of the votes of the holders of the shares entitled to vote." (Section 5 (11).) When these conditions have been complied with, the Commission-approved transaction goes into effect without need for invoking the approval under State authority, and the parties are relieved of "restraints, limitations and prohibitions of law, Federal, State, or municipal, insofar as may be necessary to enable them to carry into effect the transactions so approved or provided for in accordance with the terms and conditions, if any, imposed by the Commis-

sion, and to hold, maintain, and operate any properties and exercise any control or franchise acquired through such transaction."

It is to be noted that the court assigned the first two of these considerations to the jurisdiction of the Commission; in other words, the Commission has to make the findings constituting compliance with these two considerations. The third, however, is stated as a requirement which is not a Commission determination, but one determined by State law, and this requirement is not one which the plenary effect of Section 5(12) can eliminate.

In *Levin v. Mississippi River Corp.*,[69] it was held that Section 5(12) "bows in the direction of State law." Accordingly, it is clear that the right of successful applicants in voluntary merger proceedings to consummate the transaction by stockholder approval is to be measured in accordance with the State law. The court also noted the separateness of its function dealing with that issue and the Commission's function in stating, "We do not, of course, reach the merits of the proposed plan which is the concern of the Commission in the first instance. Any reference to the effect of the plan is not to be construed as in any way passing upon its merit."

It may well be that the Commission has exclusive jurisdiction over the function of passing initially on the merits of the plan of voluntary merger, and the courts have exclusive jurisdiction of determining whether the State law requires simply a one class or a multi-class vote. But whether their jurisdictions are mutually exclusive or whether this separation finds its genesis in the doctrine of primary jurisdiction, Commission decisions make it quite clear that it would not suspend consideration of those issues which constitute its primary jurisdiction and attempt to separately consider and finally decide a matter which falls within the primary jurisdiction of the courts.

The Commission recognizes that in determining whether each stockholder receives an equivalent of what he turns in, it is its duty to see that minority interests are protected, especially when there is an absence of arms-length bargaining by the terms of the merger having been imposed by management interest adverse to any class of stockholders.[70]

In *Missouri K-T R. Co. Consolidation*,[71] in finding that constitutional and statutory provisions of the State of Texas otherwise applicable to the merger therein under review would, pursuant to Section 5(12)

[69]386 U.S. 162.
[70]*Southern Railway Company*, *Purchase*, 275 I.C.C. 724. See also, *Kansas City S. Ry. Co.*, 84 I.C.C. 113, 116-17.
[71]312 I.C.C. 13.

no longer have application, the Commission said in relieving the surviving company of requirements to remain a corporation of the State and various other requirements:

> Therefore our specific approval of the second proviso of Article X of the consolidation agreement is granted. The provisions of Section 5(11) are self-executing, and we do not deem it necessary that any condition on this subject be attached to our order.

Further evidence of the Commission's determination to exercise its functions without deciding what steps might be required by State law to be taken to effect consumation is set forth in *Pittston Co. — Merger — Brink's Armored, Inc.*[72] There, intervenors opposed approval of the proposed merger on the grounds, among others, that the provisions of Section 5(12) had not been satisfied, citing particularly the requirement of Section 5(12) for approving vote by stockholders of the majority "unless a different vote is required under applicable state law." Dealing with this contention, the Commission said, at page 643:

> Whether the assent or vote by Pittston as owner of over 90% of the Common Stock of Brink's, Illinois, in favor of the unification plan here proposed, including the elimination of intervenors' minority stock interest, would be null and void under the Illinois law as argued, is not a matter controlling the exercise of this Commission's exclusive and plenary authority under the Act. By obtaining our approval of the transaction, however, applicants do not avoid the statutory requirements of lawful assent. For, the legality of the steps here assailed by intervenors is a matter for determination under the applicable State laws by courts of competent jurisdiction.

In *Cleveland C., C. & St. L. Ry. Co. — Operating Agreement,*[73] the application under Section 5(2), which included a non-carrier company in control of an applicant, sought extension of an agreement for operating the properties of the Peoria and Eastern Railway Company. The proceeding involved a request by applicants that a determination be made that the proceeding involved an extension of an operating agreement, rather than a lease. There was also a request by a "Protective Committee" for the State of New York as to whether the extension was properly ratified by or on behalf of Peoria. The Commission considered and disposed of these issues as follows, pages 432-433:

> The Central and Big Four state that it is within the province of this Commission to rule as to whether the agreement subject to the application is an operating agreement or a lease. They argue that confirmation of the nature of the agreement is clearly within the Commission's jurisdiction and competence, and that regardless of whether such a ruling by the

[72]87 M.C.C. 637.
[73]320 I.C.C. 430.

Commission would be binding upon the courts, it would serve as an advisory opinion to aid the courts in their determination. It is not necessary for us to make the determination since either as a lease or a contract to operate, the agreement falls within the purview of Section 5 and our plenary exclusive jurisdiction thereunder to rule whether its terms are just, reasonable, and consistent with the public interest. The exercise of that jurisdiction in this case is in no way dependent upon whether the agreement is a lease or a contract to operate, notwithstanding that, under the laws of Illinois, the distinction may have special significance.

It is enough for our purposes to acknowledge that the transaction involves an agreement among carriers, short of a complete consolidation, for the operation of the Peoria by another. The terms of the agreement have been bared on the record enabling us to view, in the light of the federal law, the rights, privileges, duties and obligations established thereby as between the parties and as between them and the public. By passing upon the substantive features of the agreement, we fully discharge our function under the statutory plan of Congress. Our findings herein leave for determination under State law nothing affecting the validity of the unified operations approved herein.

By obtaining our approval of the transaction, however, applicants do not escape any applicable statutory requirements for obtaining stockholder assent. Moreover, since any authority granted under Section 5(2) is permissive, our order cannot prejudice rights which intervenors may desire to assert in the courts, and whether the authority granted herein is ultimately exercised is for the parties to determine. Compare *Raymond Bros. Motor Transp., Inc. – Purchase – Berzel*, 15 M.C.C. 477.

The same reluctance or unwillingness of the Commission to be drawn into an interpretation of State law in the exercise of its own duties is illustrated in a number of parallel situations. In *New York, C. & St. L. R. Co. – Control*,[74] the issue was whether a trust proposed to avoid violation of Section 5(5) was valid under State law. The Commission's summary of the matter and decision as to it, page 716, was:

Intervenors argue, on the basis of testimony submitted by attorneys practicing in the States of New York and Illinois, that any trust agreement broad enough in scope to accomplish its purpose would be invalid under State laws. Counsel for the applicant is of the opinion that the trust, as proposed, if approved by the Commission, would be valid, and trustee is willing to accept the trust. It is not our duty in a case like this to interpret or enforce State law. If we find that the trust will accomplish the purpose, we should not require more.

In *Standard Time Zone Investigation*,[75] involving the Commission's statutory authority to fix time zones under the Standard Time Act,[76]

[74] 295 I.C.C. 703.
[75] 309 I.C.C. 780, 784.
[76] 15 U.S.C. 261-265.

the particular issue, was the consideration, if any, which should be accorded to actions of the General Assembly of Kentucky in fixing time zones for the State, certain statutes of which had been declared unconstitutional by the Court of Appeals of Kentucky. The Commission said:

> It is not our responsibility to interpret State statutes or court decisions respecting them. However, in view of the holding of the court that the language of the 1952 Act, which was incorporated in the 1958 legislation, evinced a legislative intention to adopt whatever boundary line the Commission may prescribe in the future, we are persuaded that the legislative intent is not incompatible with any appropriate change in that line which may be made as a result of this proceeding.

In *Feather River Ry. Co. Abandonment, Acquisition,*[77] the issues involved possible consideration of the provisions of the State Water Code which required the substitution of new railroad facilities for those taken and destroyed as the result of the construction of a dam. The Commission noted, page 426, that the statute had never been enforced and that its constitutionality was being questioned in the courts. It then said:

> It is not within our province to determine the constitutionality of the disputed provisions of the Water Code or to interpret or enforce them. However, we take official notice of a decision and order handed down on November 26, 1963, Decision No. 66386, by the Public Utilities Commission of the State of California, finding that Sections 11590 to 11592 of the Water Code are valid and that if the Feather River's line is relocated thereunder, the route of such relocation will be designated by that Commission. The Public Utilities Commission provided for the modification of its order in the event the State's application in these proceedings is granted. Its decision is subject to review by the California Supreme Court. Our findings herein contemplated that the new line proposed by the railway would be provided by the State either under the provisions of the Water Code, or under whatever other authority may be resorted to by the State to provide the new line.

There are a number of analogous cases. In *Greyhound Corp Stock,*[78] a petition was filed by Greyhound requesting the Commission to reopen a stock issue proceeding and revoke that portion of the authority granted which authorized the exchange of Greyhound shares of common stock for 54,000 shares of common stock of Horne's Enterprises, Inc., owned by Robert I. Horne. The purpose of the stock issue was to enable Greyhound to acquire all of Horne's outstanding common stock. Under the terms of an agreement entered into between the parties, Greyhound was required to exchange shares of its common stock for 54,000 retained

[77]320 I.C.C. 417.
[78]101 M.C.C. 606.

shares of common stock of Horne's owned by Robert I. Horne, its then President, the retained shares to be held in escrow, and to be exchanged in specified future periods extending ten years from the closing date. The exchange ratio applicable to these particular shares would be subject to change depending on the market value of Greyhound stock, and should any future shift in the market value of the stock necessitate an additional number of shares in order to effectuate the exchanges Greyhound was prepared and would be required to seek additional authorization for the issuance of the stock.

In its petition to reopen the proceeding and revoke the authority granted to exchange Greyhound stock for the retained shares of Horne, Greyhound alleged the revocation was required in order to protect Greyhound from the consequence of alleged fradulent misrepresentations made to it and the Commission by Robert I. Horne, and to protect it from the willful failure of Robert I. Horne to perform his obligations under the employment agreement. Greyhound claimed that the alleged misrepresentation and misconduct were relied upon by it and the Commission, and worked a fraud upon the Commission and caused a partial failure of consideration Greyhound expected and was entitled to receive. The Commission denied Greyhound's petition,[79] stating (p. 609):

> Greyhound in this proceeding stood in the relation of an applicant to the Commission. Its allegations establish only that there has been a change in circumstances since the application was approved. By approving the application the Commission did not place itself under the requirement of continuing jurisdiction to enforce the underlying contracts of the application on the basis of which the stock was to be issued. Relief from the consequences of alleged fraud in a contract can only be determined and resolved in a court of law and cannot be granted by an administrative tribunal. Mr. Horne has sued Greyhound and Horne's in a Florida court to compel, among other things, the authorized exchange of the retained shares, and Horne's has counterclaimed for damages. That court is a proper forum, as we see it, for disposition of the matter.
>
> The authority granted by the Commission in this proceeding is permissive only under Section 214 of the Act. The Commission is not empowered to compel performance by the parties to contemplated or authorized action pursuant to any plan of acquisition or exchange of stock. Under the view consistently taken by the Commission such a determination is properly for the parties themselves. . . ."

In the *Central Freight* case, *supra*, the Commission gave consideration to the scope of its responsibility to resolve an issue involving the

---

[79]The Commission in *Greyhound* relied on *Central Freight Lines, Inc. — Control — Alamo Express, Inc.*, 90 M.C.C. 96, aff'd in *Walker v. United States*, 208 F. Supp. 388, aff'd 372 U.S. 526.

enforceability of a contract between the parties covering the purchase of stock including the legal effect of an assignment of the contract by one of the parties to a third party. The Commission said (p. 101):

> Our authority is permissive only. We cannot force consummation of any transaction approved by us under Section 5. In our view, the fact that the transaction conceivably may not be consummated under the modified terms does not inhibit our authority to approve the transaction on the revised terms proposed by applicants. For, as division 4 stated in *Baltimore & A. R. Co. — Purchase — Bison Lines, Inc.*, 60 M.C.C. 509 at page 517:
>
>> All matters involving interpretation of contracts and enforcement of the terms thereof must be left for settlement between the parties themselves or by the courts. Upon presentation of a properly filed application presenting a transaction subject to Section 5, we may not properly assume that authority to consummate the proposed transaction, if granted, would be futile. Compare *Hays Freight Lines. Inc. — Purchase — Bowman*, 58 M.C.C. 655, and *Marion Trucking Co., Inc. — Purchase — Harwood Trucking Co.*, 45 M.C.C. 377, and the cases therein cited. The transaction if authorized, could be lawfully consummated only upon the terms and conditions approved.

On review by a three-judge court in *Walker v. United States, supra,* consideration was given to the issue of whether there is statutory responsibility on the Commission to determine questions of legal enforceability of contracts. The court made the following comments (pp. 395-396):

> . . . The Commission's responsibility is not that of a court sitting to enforce a contract. Its responsibility is to determine whether, on the statutory standards relating to public interest, it will approve acquisition on the proposed or modified terms and conditions and such modifications as it shall find to be just and reasonable . . . § 5(2) (b). Its order, therefore, is permissive only. . . . It does not compel action by either the applicant or the carrier-to-be-acquired. The Commission's power to grant a § 5 approval for acquisition is not limited to the existence of a legally enforceable contract. If that were so, the Commission as a condition precedent to the exercise of its statutory responsibility would have to determine the threshold question of legal enforceability of the contract. That, of course, would put the Commission in the business which the Commission and the courts have long recognized to be a matter for the courts. Apart from the question of Commission approval for consumation of a contract, legal validity of such a contract presents a judicial question for judicial determination by the courts, not the Commission. . . .

In *Co-Operative Transit Co. Securities,*[80] a petition was filed requesting that orders previously entered by the Commission be further amended or modified so as to authorize the issuance of debenture bonds to the

---

[80]282 U.S. 63.

widows, heirs and legatees of deceased former employee who, if living, would have been entitled to receive shares of first-series stock issued under the orders, and to issue shares of first-series stock in an amount equal to the bonds issued to the widows, heirs and legatees of deceased former employees for the purpose of selling such shares to qualified officers and employees as freely as though these shares had been issued to the decreased former employees and had been reacquired through the issue of debenture bonds. A protest against the granting of the relief sought was filed by representatives of certain individuals who held shares of first-series stock and debenture bonds by the petitioner. The petitioner had been organized to acquire properties of a traction company which was being operated by a receiver. The employees had purchased the properties at a public sale using for such purpose funds which they had accumulated by contributing a portion of their wages into a trust fund. It was their purpose that the properties be owned and operated by the employees. Under the plan presented in a prior application filed with the Commission, the petitioner would issue shares of first-series stock, to be distributed pro-rata to the employees who had participated in the trust fund. As these employees died or left the services of the company, the corporation would reacquire the stock, at the book value thereof, and issue in exchange therefor debenture bonds. The series of stock thus reacquired would be sold to officers and employees who were eligible to own these share and the funds thus obtained would be used to retire the debenture bonds.

Certain questions respecting the rights and interests of the beneficiaries under the trust agreements were addressed to the Commission; however, the Commission said (p. 67) that it was "not the proper forum to decide such issues and we do not undertake to decide them here." A number of other issues were raised concerning matters of contracts between the corporation and the security holders, the terms of which contract were printed on the stock certificates and debenture bonds. Issues also were raised concerning certain provisions of petitioner's articles of incorporation. The Commission disposed of the issues raised by stating (p. 67), "This Commission is not the proper forum to which these interviewers should apply for the relief which they seek with respect to such matters, and we do not undertake to decide such issues."

Another analogous situation is provided in *New York Central S. Corp. v. United States*,[81] which involved an order of the Commission authorizing the New York Central to acquire control, by lease, of the "Big

[81]287 U.S. 12.

Four" and Michigan Central, and a later order permitting the assumption by the lessee of obligation and liability in respect of certain securities of the lessors. A minority stockholder of each of the lessors, and of the lessee, sought to set aside these orders upon the ground that the Commission had exceeded its authority. The stockholder contended that the provisions of the then Section 5(8) of the Act referring to "restraints or prohibitions by law, State or Federal," should be construed as limited to those restrictions which are of the same general character as the antitrust laws and not as applying to specific limitations imposed by State laws upon corporate powers with respect to the making of leases. The stockholders invoked the laws of the states of incorporation in relation to leases of competing lines, and especially the laws of Ohio upon that subject and with respect to minimum rental and security for payment and the preservation of property. The Supreme Court held that this contention "cannot, in any event, avail the appellant," stating (p. 26-27):

> . . . The order of the Commission under § 5(2) is permissive, not mandatory. There is no warrant for concluding that the Congress intended to fetter the exercise of the Commission's authority by requiring that the Commission before making its order must determine whether the acquisition is within the corporate powers ofthe carrier under State laws. The Commission has given its approval in the exercise of the authority conferred and the question of corporate powers cannot properly be raised in this suit to set aside the Commission's order. . . .

> Nor is there ground for a different conclusion with respect to the Commission's order under § 20(a) authorizing the assumption of obligations. Appellant points to the requirement in that section that the Commission shall make such an order only if it finds that the assumption by the carrier is "for some lawful object within its corporate purposes." But that this provision does not refer to state limitations upon corporate powers, but rather to the general field of corporate purposes, sufficiently appears from the context and from the legislative history of the clause. In creating federal supervision of the issue of securities by interstate carriers, the Congress, so far from making it necessary for the Commission to determine whether there had been compliance with State requirements, expressly provided in subdivision (7) of § 20(a) that the jurisdiction of the Commission should be exclusive and plenary and that approval, other than as specified in that section, should not be necessary.

An analogous case is *O. C. Wiley & Sons v. United States*,[82] where the court said:

> Wiley contends that the Commission should not have entered the order in question approving the transfer by Stuart of its operating rights to

[82]85 F. Supp. 542, 544.

Fleming until a determination of the rights, if any, of Wiley under the contract between Wiley and Stuart. The Commission has repeatedly held that the orders approving such transfers are permissive only, that the Commission is not a court and must leave to the courts the determination of such alleged conflicting rights between parties. . . .

Other analogous cases include *Texas & N. O. R. Co. v. Brotherhood of Rai'road Trainmen,*[83] where the court said that the Commission "has been unwilling to take upon itself questions of either the interpretation or enforceability of contracts submitted with respect to a transaction;" and *Watson Bros. Transp. Co. v. Jaffa,*[84] where the court said that the "Commission remains an administrative board exercising administrative power, and is not a court, and has no judicial power," and pointed out that in early case reported in the first volume of its reports, the Commission declared, "The power to enforce contracts is not one which has been confided to us."[85]

Criteria Used in Testing Proposals

Under the Transportation Act of 1940, since it has repudiated the concept of a plan for nationwide railroad combinations, every proposal to purchase, lease, merge, consolidate, or otherwise acquire control of rail properties is to be examined on its own merits in the light of certain criteria specified by Congress, without reference to a general consolidation plan.[86]

The statutory criteria which govern the Commission in cases involving control of one railroad by another are contained in Section 5(2) (c),[87] which reads as follows:

In passing upon any proposed transaction under the provision of this paragraph (2), the Commission shall give weight to the following considerations, among others: (1) The effect of the proposed transaction upon adequate transportation service to the public; (2) the effect upon the public interest of the inclusion, or failure to include, other railroads in the territory involved in the proposed transaction; (3) the total fixed charges resulting from the proposed transaction; and (4) the interest of the carrier employees affected.

Section 5(2)(b) directs the Commission to approve mergers and related transactions, subject to appropriate terms and conditions, if it finds the

[83]307 F. 2d 151, 159.
[84]143 F. 2d 340, 346.
[85]See also *Benton v. United States,* 114 F. Supp. 37, 43.
[86]*Ibid.*
[87]49 U.S.C. 5(2) (c).

proposed transaction "will be consistent with the public interest." Thus, public interest is made the fundamental touchstone for the decisional process in merger cases. The four statutory criteria noted reflect major phases of the public interest, and the phrase "among others" indicates that additional criteria, as appropriate, should be utilized by the I.C.C. in merger cases.

In deciding cases under Section 5(2) the Commission has considered a broad range of individual elements. These include the criteria spelled out in Section 5(2) (c), i.e.; effect on adequate transportation service to the public; effect on public interest of including or failing to include other railroads in the proposal; total fixed charges; and interest of carrier employees. These also include other criteria bearing on the underlying standard of public interest such as competitive impact.[88]

Certain guidelines used by the Commission in administering Section 5(2) (c) have been supplied by the courts.[89]

The *New York Central Securities* case was decided by the Supreme Court in 1932. In rail merger cases since 1940, the guides to public interest established in that case have often been used by the Commission in conjunction with the statutory criteria. From 1920 to 1940, when the Transportation Act of 1920 was controlling, the main criterion for mergers under Section 5(2) of the I.C. Act was simply "public interest," as the more specific criteria were not added to the I.C. Act until 1940. The Supreme Court, in the *New York Central Securities* case, rejected

---

[88]See *Chesapeake & Ohio Ry. Co. — Control — Baltimore & Ohio Railroad Co.,* 317 I.C.C. 261; *Chesapeake & Ohio Ry. Co. and Baltimore & Ohio Railroad Co. — Control — Western Maryland Ry. Co.,* 328 I.C.C. 684; *Seaboard Air Line Railroad Co. — Merger — Atlantic Coast Railroad Co.,* 320 I.C.C. 122; *Pennsylvania Railroad Co. — Merger — New York Central Railroad Co.,* 327 I.C.C. 475, 328 I.C.C. 304, 330 I.C.C. 328, 331 I.C.C. 754; *Illinois Central Gulf Railroad Co. — Acquisition — Gulf, Mobile & Ohio Railroad Co. et al.,* 338 I.C.C. 805; *Southern Ry. Co. — Control — Central of Georgia Ry. Co.,* 317 I.C.C. 557; *Missouri Pac. R. Co. — Control — Chicago & E.I.R. Co.,* 327 I.C.C. 279, 334 I.C.C. 273, 348 I.C.C. 414; *Norfolk and Western Ry. Co. and New York, Chicago and St. Louis Railroad Co. — Merger, Etc.* 324 I.C.C. 1, 330 I.C.C. 780; *St. Louis Southwestern Ry. — Pur. — Alton and Southern R.,* 342 I.C.C. 498; *Great Northern Pacific & Burlington Lines Inc., — Merger, Etc., — Great Northern Railway Co.,* 328 I.C.C. 460, 311 I.C.C. 228; *Chicago & North Western Railway Co. — Control — Chicago, Rock Island and Pacific Railroad Co.,* 347 I.C.C. 556; *Chicago & North Western Ry. Co. — Merger — Chicago Great Western Ry. Co.,* 330 I.C.C. 13, 333 I.C.C. 236; *Fort Worth & Denver Ry. Co. and Chicago, Rock Island & Pacific Railroad Co. Joint Ownership and Use — Burlington — Rock Island Railroad Co.,* 324 I.C.C. 561; *North Western Employees Transportation Corp. — Purchase — Chicago and North Western Ry. Co.,* 342 I.C.C. 58.

[89]49 U.S.C. 5(2) (b); see *Louisville & Nashville Railroad Company et. al., Merger,* 295 I.C.C. 457, 502-3; *New York Central Securities Corp. v. United States,* 287 U.S. 12, 25.

(at pp. 24-5) the assumption of appellant in the case that the criterion of "public interest" was uncertain:[90]

> . . . It is a mistaken assumption that this [public interest] is a mere general reference to public welfare without any standard to guide determinations. The purpose of the Act, the requirements it imposes, and the context of the provision in question to show the contrary. Going forward from a policy mainly directed to the prevention of abuses, particularly those arising from excessive or discriminatory rates, Transportation Act, 1920, was designed better to assure adequacy in transportation service. This Court, in *New England Division Case*, 261 U.S. 184, 189, 190, adverted to that purpose, which was found to be expressed in unequivocal language; "to attain it, new rights, new obligations, new machinery, were created." The court directed attention to various provisions having this effect, and to the criteria which the statute had established in referring to "the transportation needs of the public," "the necessity of enlarging transportation facilities," and the measures which would "best promote the service in the interest of the public and the commerce of the people. . ."

As judicially construed, the phrase "consistent with the public interest" means the same as compatible with the public interest or not contradictory or hostile to the public interest.[91] In order to further assure that there will be full protection of the public interest, Section 5 expressly confers upon the Commission broad authority to impose conditions to its approval of merger transactions.[92]

The Commission today cannot authorize a merger unless it has found the same to be consistent with the public interest. The language is broad enough to comprehend every public interest and the interest of every group or element of the public. There is provided no limitation upon the factors that may be and are considered by the Commission in determining whether a proposed merger "will be consistent with the public inter-

---

[90]The Commission has held that it is guided primarily by consideration for adequacy of transportation service; essential conditions of economy and efficiency; and appropriate provision for and best use of transportation facilities. These are the primary elements affecting the public interest with which the transaction must be consistent. *Louisville & Nashville Railroad Company et al., Merger*, 295 I.C.C. 457, 502-3.

[91]In Re *Chicago, R. I. & P. Ry. Co.*, 168 F. 2d 587; *Scott Bros., Inc., Collection and Delivery Service*, 2 M.C.C. 155, 164; *Merchant's Dispatch, Inc. — Purchase — Smathers*, 25 M.C.C. 407, 409; *Chesapeake & O. Ry. Co. — Control — Baltimore & O. R. Co.*, 317 I.C.C. 261, 285, and *Pacific Power & Light Co. v. Federal Power Comm.*, 111 F. 2d 1014, 1016; *County of Marin v. United States*, 356 U.S. 412, 416, 418; *Northern Lines Merger Cases*, 396 U.S. 491, 510-11; *United States v. Lowden*, 302 U.S. 225, 230; *Texas v. United States*, 292 U.S. 522, 531.

[92]*New York Central Securities Corp. v. United States, supra; Roy Bros. Transp. Co. Inc. — Purchase — Maliar*, 65 M.C.C. 339, 345; and *O. C. Wiley & Sons v. United States*, 85 F. Supp. 542, 545.

est." Section 5(2) (c) provides that the Commission shall give weight to certain enumerated considerations, "among others." And among these other considerations are those recited in the national transportation policy.[93]

In determining whether a proposed transaction is consistent with the public interest, consideration must be given to the public affected by the transaction and the effect of the proposal upon adequate transportation service to all parts of the public which would be so affected.[94]

In *Detroit, Toledo & Ironton R. Co. Control*,[95] the Commission pointed out:

> The provisions of Section 5(2) are to be administered and enforced with a view of carrying out the declared national transportation policy of the Congress, one objective of which is to promote sound economic conditions in transportation and among the several carriers, all to the end of developing, coordinating and preserving a national transportation system adequate to meet the needs of the commerce of the United States, of the postal service, and of the national defense.

The purpose of Section 5(2) is to "foster and promote the voluntary union of carriers into a sound and adequate transportation system.[96] Thus, if public benefits outweigh the adverse effects on protestants, the Commission will approve.[97]

It is not essential that the acquired carrier be financially weak or in need of rehabilitation. As pointed out in the *Detroit, Toledo & Ironton* case, *supra:*

> The provisions of Section 5(2) of the act do not contemplate the unification of only those railroads that no longer can continue under separate ownership. The purpose of the law is to foster and promote the voluntary union of carriers into a sound and adequate transportation system for the future, and such is permissible if it is otherwise consistent with the public interest. In the past we have authorized the acquisition of control through stock ownership of prosperous carriers, and in instances by two of the three protesting interveners herein.[98]

---

[93]*McLean Trucking Co. v. United States*, 321 U.S. 67.

[94]*Chicago, B. & O. R. Co. Control*, 271 I.C.C. 63, 146.

[95]275 I.C.C. 455, 488.

[96]*Detroit, Toledo & Ironton R. Co. Control, supra*, at p. 489; *Spokane International R. Co. Control*, 295 I.C.C. 425, 438; *St. Joe Paper Co. v. Atlantic Coast Line R. Co.*, 347 U.S. 298, 310.

[97]*Quinn Freight Lines, Inc. — Control and Merger*, 85 M.C.C. 271, 279, 282.

[98]See *Chicago Junction Case*, 71 I.C.C. 631; *Wheeling & L. E. Ry. Co. Control*, 267 I.C.C. 163; *Niagara Junction Ry. Co. Control*, 267 I.C.C. 649; *Toledo, Peoria & Western R. Co. Control*, 295 I.C.C. 523, 542; *Spokane International R. Co. Control, supra*, 438.

Nor is it essential that there be far-reaching economies.[99] As the Commission pointed out in *Control of Virginia Ry., supra.*[100]

> Reduction in the cost transportation is a matter of public interst. It is not, however, of controlling importance, but is to be considered and weighed in connection with all other matters affecting the public interest.

The Commission in Section 5(2) cases has often considered favorably the inherent advantages accruing to the public under single-line service. In *Chicago & N.W. Ry. Co. Purchase, Minneapolis & St. L. Ry. Co.,*[101] the Commission held:

> The single-line haul makes available a wider source of supply for transit shippers in the service area, reduces time consuming and costly interchanges, and provides greater flexibility in ratemaking — all to the benefit of the public generally.

See also *Florida East Coast Ry. Co. Reorganization,*[102] where the Commission held:

> Obstructions to the efficient flow of commerce to and from the section of the Florida peninsula served by the Florida East Coast would be lessened by the acquisition of this carrier by the Coast Line. Factors which would contribute to this end include the substitution of through movements for interchange arrangements, single-line instead of joint hauls on much traffic, more efficient use of fixed facilities, and more complete service to shippers in the matter of providing better reconsignment service, tracing, rate information, and market information services. . . .

The Commission has also recognized the inherent economy in a single-line service, vis-a-vis joint-line service, because joint-line movements require more accounting and switching than do single-line movements. *Industrial Silica Corp. v. Baltimore & O. R. Co.*[103] Such inherent economies in operation have been recognized as matters in the public interest. In *Albree v. B. & M. R. R.,*[104] the Commission held:

> It is for the public interest that every transportation service should be performed by the most economical method, since that must ultimately result in the lowest transportation charge.[105]

In *Norfolk & W. Ry. Co. Merger,*[106] the Commission found an improve-

---

[99]*Toledo, Peoria & Western R. Co. Control, supra,* at p. 546.
[100]117 I.C.C. at 75.
[101]312 I.C.C. 285, 294.
[102]282 I.C.C. 81, 125.
[103]226 I.C.C. 173, 177.
[104]22 I.C.C. 303, 316.
[105]See also *Control of Virginian Ry.,* 117 I.C.C. 67, 75.
[106]307 I.C.C. 401, 427.

ment in car fleet as a result of the merger under consideration to be a distinct advantage and in the public interest. To the same effect are *Toledo P. & W. R. Co. Control*[107] and *South Georgia Ry. Co. Control*.[108] A reduction in interchange time has also been found to be in the public interest.[109] The Commission, in *Louisville & N. R. Co. Merger*[110] recognized the improved service and the ability to recapture traffic is a commendable objective in a Section 5(2) case. There, after discussing the subsidies granted competing forms of transportation, it held (p. 468):

> The foregoing reflects how imperative it is for the railroads to do everything in their power to enhance their competitive situation through all possible economies and efficient operations. The proposed merger is designed to accomplish that result.

Benefits reflected in other cases include preservation of existing traffic relationships with all connecting lines;[111] protection of the traffic of connections;[112] insuring continuing neutrality of operation and service;[113] securing for the public continued access to local management;[114] insuring stability and continuity of management;[115] assuring the availability of greater resources, service and personnel in the event of special need;[116] permitting the acquired carrier to obtain capital from its owner;[117] and the availability of research and engineering assistance, of operating experience, and of an industrial development staff.[118]

Where permanency of operation of the controlled railroad's properties can be effected through substantial economies realized in the reduction of overhead transportation expenses, the cost of maintenance, and general expenses, and in the use of labor-saving devices, the acquisi-

---

[107]295 I.C.C. 523, 546.
[108]290 I.C.C. 281, 297.
[109]*Chicago & N.W. Ry. Co. Purchase, Minneapolis & St. L. Ry. Co.*, 312 I.C.C. 285, 294; *Florida East Coast Ry. Co., Reorganization*, 282 I.C.C. 81, 125.
[110]295 I.C.C. 457.
[111]*Wheeling & L. E. Ry. Co. Control*, 267 I.C.C. 163.
[112]*Niagara Junction R. Co. Control*, 267 I.C.C. 649, 661; *Chicago Junction Case*, 71 I.C.C. 631; *Detroit, T. & I. R. Co. Control*, 275 I.C.C. 455, 491-2.
[113]*Niagara Junction R. Co. Control, supra*, p. 663.
[114]*Ibid.*, p. 660.
[115]*Ibid.*, p. 660.
[116]*Spokane International R. Co. Control*, 295 I.C.C. 425, 440.
[117]*Niagara Junction R. Co. Control, supra*, p. 660.
[118]*Wheeling & L. E. R. Co. Control, supra*, 183; *Niagara Junction R. Co. Control, supra*, 660; *Toledo, Peoria & Western R. Co. Control, supra*, 545-46.

tion of control may be found to be consistent with the public interest.[119]

The fact that the lines of the railroads involved in the proposed transaction may be parallel to some extent is recognized as affording opportunities for elimination of duplicate and unneeded facilities by utilization of portions of each line and combination of yards, shop facilities and headquarters.[120]

Imposition of Conditions

Under Section 5, the Commission's authority to impose conditions on the basis of which the transaction may properly be found to be consistent with the public interest is broad.[121] In *Roy Bros. Transp. Co., Inc. — Purchase — Maliar*,[122] the Commission, in recognizing its broad power under Section 5 to impose conditions, held:

> Under Section 5 of the Act, our authority to impose conditions, on the basis of which the transaction may properly be found to be consistent with the public interest, is broad. *O. C. Wiley & Sons, Inc. v. United States*, 85 F. Supp. 542, and *Elliott Bros. Trucking Co., Inc. v. United States*, 59 F. Supp. 328. . . .

Conditions are frequently imposed because, without such conditions the application would have to be denied.[123] The authority thus conditionally granted is permissive, and the conditions are not transactions,

---

[119]*Brotherhood of Maintenance of W. Emp. v. U.S.*, 189 F. Supp. 942, 365 U.S. 801, 809; 366 U.S. 169; *Seaboard Air Line R. Co. v. Daniel*, 333 U.S. 118, 124; *United States v. Lowden*, 308 U.S. 225, 230, 232-233; *Texas v. United States*, 292 U.S. 522 530-531; *Chicago & Eastern Illinois R. Co. Merger*, 312 I.C.C. 564, 568; *Chicago & N.W. Ry. Co. Purchase, Minneapolis & St. L. Ry. Co.*, 312 I.C.C. 285, 297; *Erie R. Co. — Merger*, 312 I.C.C. 185; *Atlantic Coast Line R. Co. Merger*, 307 I.C.C. 614; *Norfolk & W. Ry. Co. Merger*, 307 I.C.C. 401; *Louisville & N. R. Co. Merger*, 295 I.C.C. 457, 468, 505; *Spokane International R. Co. Control*, 295 I.C.C. 425, 440; *Detroit, T. & I. R. Co. Control*, 275 I.C.C. 455, 488; *Bessemer & L. E. R. Co. Merger*, 275 I.C.C. 167, 179; *Great Northern Pac. Ry. Co. Acquisition*, 162 I.C.C. 37, 49; *Gulf, M. & O. R. Co. Merger*, 236 I.C.C. 61, 92-93; *Buffalo, R. & P. Ry. Co. Control*, 180 I.C.C. 14; *Associated Transport, Inc. — Control and consolidation*, 38 M.C.C. 133, 146.

[120]*Chicago & N.W. Ry. Co. Purchase, Minneapolis & St. L. Ry. Co.*, 312 I.C.C. 285, 297; *Erie R. Co. Merger*, 312 I.C.C. 185, 231-2; 244-5; *Norfolk & W. Ry. Co. Merger*, 307 I.C.C. 401, 417-418; *Louisville & N.R. Co., Merger*, 295 I.C.C. 457, 478-479, 488, 502-505; *Gulf, M. & O. R. Co. Merger*, 236 I.C.C. 61, 83, 92-93; *Control of International — Great Northern R. R.*, 90 I.C.C. 262, 267; *Construction of Cut-off for I.C.R.R.* 86 I.C.C. 371, 373-374.

[121]*O. C. Wiley & Sons, Inc. v. United States*, 85 F. Supp. 542, 45, aff'd 338 U.S. 902; *Elliot Bros. Trucking Co., Inc. v. United States*, 59 F. Supp. 328.

[122]65 M.C.C. 339.

[123]*Roy Bros. Transp. Co. Inc. — Purchase — Maliar*, 65 M.C.C. 339; *Cook Motor Lines, Inc. — Control and Merger*, 80 M.C.C. 560.

since the parties have the option whether or not to consummate the transaction.[124]

Consistent recognition of the Commission's broad power under Section 5 has been given by the courts. In *M. & M. Transportation Company v. United States*,[125] the district court held:

> The courts have continually asserted that the discretion of the Commission in a Section 5 proceeding is sweeping, Congress intending that the Commission exercise its expert knowledge in assuring consistency with the public interest. . . .

In *O. C. Wiley & Sons v. United States*,[126] the court wrote:

> . . . It has been often recognized that Section 5 confers broader authority and greater administrative discretion than most any other section of the Act and that the legislative history of the recent amendments to this section of the Act show congressional intent to broaden the authority of the Commission. . . .[127]

The Commission has not only the power, but also the duty to impose conditions which satisfy the public interst.[128] In *Atlantic Coast Line R. Co. v. United States*,[129] after quoting from the pertinent portion of Section 5(2), the court said:

> It will be noted that the Commission was authorized, by the section quoted, to approve the acquisition by one carrier of the control of another by lease or otherwise on such terms and conditions as shall be found by the Commission to be just and reasonable in the premises. *It is not only the right but the duty of the Commission to impose such conditions as will make the acquisition in the public interest;* for, unless the acquisition is found to be in the public interest, the Commission cannot authorize it. Chicago Junction Case, 264 U.S. 258, 265, 44. S. Ct. 317, 68 L. Ed. 667. In this case the Commission found that the lease would not be in the public interest unless the conditions in question were imposed; and consequently without them the lease could not have been authorized. . . . (Emphasis supplied.)

See also *Camp Lejeune R. Co. Securities and Operation*,[130] wherein the Commission held:

> Under Section 5(2) (b) of the Act, it is our duty to find, among other things, that the proposed transaction is consistent with the public in-

---

[124]*Plains Motor Exp. — Purchase — C. & G. Truck Lines*, 87 M.C.C. 489, 494
[125]128 F. Supp. 296, 298, affirmed 350 U.S. 857.
[126]85 F. Supp. 542, 545.
[127]Holding to the same effect is *Virginia Stage Lines v. United States*, 48 F. Supp. 79, 82.
[128]*Cook Motor Lines, Inc. — Control and Merger, supra.*
[129]48 F. 2d 239, 244, affirmed 284 U.S. 288.
[130]295 I.C.C. 511, 517.

terest, and, as we deem necessary, we may make our approval subject to whatever modifications of proposed terms and conditions we find just and reasonable.[131]

The Commission, in Section 5 cases, has exercised its broad powers in various ways to impose conditions which are in the public interest. Even prior to the enactment of Section 5(2) (f) the Commission imposed labor protective conditions.[132] The Commission has required, in a control case, that the applicant acquire another or other railroads,[133] and it has also required inclusion of segments of other railroads.[134] It has required an applicant for control to share control with another or other railroads, both before the enactment or Section 5(2) (d),[135] and after it.[136] In *Valdosta S. R. Purchase*,[137] the Commission granted the application on condition that the applicant tender a ten-year option for purchase of the acquired carrier to any of the railroads connecting with that carrier. In *Lease of Panhandle by Pennsylvania R. R.*,[138] the approval of an application to acquire control by lease was conditioned upon the applicant's not divesting itself of its stock interest in the leased road without the Commission's consent. In *Kingsport R. Co. Operation*,[139] involving an application to operate a line under lease, a condition was imposed affording two carriers connecting with the line in question an opportunity to acquire joint and equal control of the applicant, or, in the alternative, to operate the line jointly under a lease.

The Commission has approved Section 5 applications on condition that certain employment contracts be eliminated.[140] The Commission said in the *Pittston* case that continuance in office under contract of any acquired carrier's directors after consummation of control would tend to impair any necessary or desirable changes in operation and organization and would be contrary to the public interest; therefore, approval would be conditioned to require the elimination of any contract providing for continuance in office of any such director. The Commission also held in another case that an employment contract for

---

[131]See also *Roy Bros., Transport Co., Inc. — Purchase — Maliar, supra*, at page 345.

[132]*United States v. Lowden*, 308 U.S. 225.

[133]*Buffalo, R. & P. Ry. Co. Control*, 158 I.C.C. 779, 790.

[134]*New York Central Unification*, 150 I.C.C. 278, 322.

[135]*Control of Central California Traction Co.*, 131 I.C.C. 125.

[136]*Detroit T. & I. R. Co. Control*, 275 I.C.C. 455.

[137]282 I.C.C. 705. See also *Conemaugh & B. L. R. Co. Operation*, 94 I.C.C. 443; *Twin Branch R. Co. Acquisition*, 117 I.C.C. 165; *Trans Florida Central R. Co. Acquisition*, 124 I.C.C. 745; *Algers, W. & W. Ry. Construction*, 145 I.C.C. 123.

[138]72 I.C.C. 128.

[139]271 I.C.C. 479.

[140]*Pittston Co. — Control — Brinks, Inc.*, 80 M.C.C. 179.

the employment of a carrier's president for a period of time to liquidate its operations was not shown to be intended as an indirect means of increasing the purchase price of the carrier's stock; therefore, the provisions were not part of the terms of the transaction which must be found to be just and reasonable.[141] The Commission also held that duplicate operating rights be cancelled.[142] The Commission has even recognized that conditions may concern corporations not parties to the proceeding.[143]

In *Richmond-Greyhound Line, Inc. — Control*,[144] the entire Commission conditioned its approval of control of Peninsula Transit Corporation by Richmond-Greyhound by requiring applicant to renew its offer to sell to either, or both, of two intervener bus lines that portion of Peninsula Transit's or Richmond-Greyhound's, operating rights between Richmond and Norfolk, Virginia. These operating rights were, in fact, sold to Carolina Coach, one of the interveners, upon approval of that sale given by the Commission in a subsequent Section 5(2) application filed by Carolina Coach. The Commission's orders under Section 5(2) are merely permissive. The successful applicant is simply give a choice of accepting a condition or rejecting it. If the conditions are accepted, it would then become mandatory, as in the case of all conditions imposed by the Commission. This is clearly shown in *Cook Motor Lines, Inc. — Control and Merger*,[145] wherein the Commission held:

> . . . The authority thus conditionally granted is permissive, and the parties may or may not, in their discretion, elect to exercise the authority. . . .[146]

In *United States v. Lowden*,[147] it was pointed out that the Commission's imposition of protective labor conditions furthers "the Congressional policy of consolidation and of the efficient operation of the industry itself." While the *Lowden* case held that the Commission had authority to prescribe protective conditions,[148] Congress directed the Commission in the Transportation Act of 1940 "to require a fair and

---

141*Dealers Transit, Inc. — Control and Merger*, 87 M.C.C. 571, 575, 581-2.
142*Earl Bray, Inc. — Control — Wright Motor Lines, Inc.*, 80 M.C.C. 25.
143*Plains Motor Exp., Inc. — Purchase — C. & G. Truck Line, Inc.*, 87 M.C.C. 489, 495.
14436 M.C.C. 747, 752. See *Carolina Coach Company of Va. — Purchase — Richmond-Greyhound*, 38 M.C.C. 347, order affirmed in *Virginia Stage Lines v. United States*, 48 F. Supp. 79.
14580 M.C.C. 560, 564.
146See also *Roy Bros. Transport Co., Inc. — Purchase — Maliar*, 65 M.C.C. 339, 345.
147308 U.S. 225, 233.
148*Ibid.*

equitable arrangement to protect the interests of the railroad employees affected." Section 5(2) (f) of the Act[149] provides:

> As a condition of its approval, under this paragraph (2), of any transaction involving a carrier or carriers by railroad subject to the provisions of this part, the Commission shall require a fair and equitable arrangement to protect the interests of the railroad employees affected. In its order of approval the Commission shall include terms and conditions providing that during the period of four years from the effective date of such order such transaction will not result in employees of the carrier or carriers by railroad affected by such order being in a worse position with respect to their employment, except that the protection afforded to any employee pursuant to this sentence shall not be required to continue for a longer period, following the effective date of such order, than the period during which such employee was in the employ of such carrier or carriers prior to the effective date of such order. Notwithstanding any other provisions of this Act, an agreement pertaining to the protection of the interests of said employees may hereafter be entered into by any carrier or carriers by railroad and the duly authorized representative or representatives of its or their employees.

The Commission developed protective conditions in *Oklahoma Ry. Co. Abandonment*.[150] The *Oklahoma* conditions, which are based on the second sentence of Section 5(2) (f), require that dismissed employees be paid a monthly allowance equal to 100 percent of their average monthly earnings. Such allowance continues for a period equal in length to the employee's service prior to the effective date of the order, but not beyond four years following such effective date

It was apparent from the *Oklahoma* case that the Commission believed that it did not possess authority to prescribe protective provisions for any period beyond four years. However, in *Railway Labor Executives' Association v. United States*[151] it was held that under Section 5(2)(f) the four year protective period was a minimum and not the maximum protective period that could be imposed by the Commission.[152] Later the

---

[149] 49 U.S.C. 5(2) (f).

[150] 257 I.C.C. 177. Accord. *New Orleans Union Passenger Terminal Case,* 267 I.C.C. 763. A three-judge district court in *Baggett Transportation Company v. U.S. and I.C.C.* 206 F. Supp. 835, upheld the Commission's power to modify a Section 5 order approving the purchase of operating rights by the imposition of protective labor conditions under Section 5(2)(c) (4) after the consummation of the transaction and the issuance of a certificate to the vendee, where the applicants failed to comply with voluntary respresentations made in their application regarding employees affected by the transaction. The Commission proceeding is entitled *Baggett Transportation Company Purchase — Hunt Freight Lines, Inc.,* Docket No. MC-F-6034. See also *R. L. E. Assoc. v. United States,* 216 F. Supp. 101.

[151] 339 U.S. 142.

[152] See *Norfolk & Western Ry. Co. v. Nemitz,* 404 U.S. 37, 42.

Commision in *New Orleans Union Passenger Terminal Case*[153] provided additional protection for employees in accordance with the so-called Washington Job Protection Agreement[154] (a labor-management agreement providing job protection in consolidations) because it was concerned that some employees might need protection after the first four year period.

In *New York Central Unification,*[155] the Commission conditioned its order of approval of the proposed unification on the acquistion of certain shortline railroads which intervened and sought inclusion in the unification. Likewise, in *Bonhomie & H. S. R. Co. Acquisition,*[156] the Commission said that acquisition of a line may be conditioned on the granting of trackage rights over the acquired line. At that time, the I.C. Act did not specifically authorize the Commission to condition its order approving a unification upon the inclusion of another railroad, but the Supreme Court held in *New York Central Securities Corp. v. United States*[157] that the Commission was so authorized pursuant to its general authority under Section 5(2) to impose just and reasonable conditions.

In a number of other unification proposals, the Commission, acting under the same general authority, conditioned its approval of the transaction upon the inclusion of intervening short-line railroads at a value to be determined in ancillary proceedings.[158] Of course, the short-line railroads ordered to be included in these transactions had not only intervened but had also requested inclusion.

The Transportation Act of 1940 contained in an amendment to the I.C. Act authorizing the Commission, in certain instances, to require the inclusion in proposed unifications of another railroad or other railroads in the territory involved. This authority is set forth in Section 5(2) (d) of the I.C. Act, which provides as follows:

> The Commission shall have authority in the case of a proposed transaction under this paragraph (2) involving a railroad or railroads, as a prerequisite to its approval of the proposed transaction, to require, upon equitable terms, the inclusion of another railroad or other railroads in the territory involved, *upon petition by such railroad or railroads requesting such inclusion,* and upon a finding that such inclusion is consistent with the public interest. (Emphasis added.)

---

[153]282 I.C.C. 271.

[154]The Washington Job Protection Agreement has figured importantly in Commission decisions.

[155]150 I.C.C. 278.

[156]90 I.C.C. 448; 94 I.C.C. 355.

[157]287 U.S. 12, 28.

[158]See. e.g., *Union Pacific R. Co. Unification,* 189 I.C.C. 357, 363; *Rock Island System Consolidation,* 193 I.C.C. 395, 401-402; *Southern Pacific (Texas and Louisiana Lines) Consolidation,* 199 I.C.C. 47, 54-55.

It is clear from the explicit language of Section 5(2) (d) that regardless of what the Commission's authority may have been to require the inclusion of other carriers in a transaction under Section 5 prior to the adoption of this amendment, it now has no authority to require inclusion unless there is a petition by the railroad requesting inclusion. In *Chicago, M. St. P. & P. R. Co. Trustees Operation and Construction,*[159] the Monon Railroad, without filing a petition, suggested that, if in the future public convenience and necessity so required, it should be accorded the right to conduct trackage rights operations over the line involved. The Commission rejected this request, saying:

> Inasmuch as no such petition has been filed, we have no occasion to consider further the imposition of a condition of the nature suggested. Id. at 7.

Other Applicable Principles and Conditions

In other cases, the following conclusions, which have a bearing on Section 5(2) cases, were arrived at by the Commission. In the event of a dispute between the parties as to the terms of the purchase, the parties' contractual rights and obligations are for determination by the courts rather than by the Commission;[160] that public regulation is not obliged or intended to restore values, "even if promised by charter terms, if they have been lost through the operation of economic forces;[161] holders of shares not tendered are entitled to receive equal, but not more favorable treatment, than that afforded stockholders who have already tendered;[162] the price for stock should not exceed the highest price paid by applicants for stock acquired to date, plus commissions;[163] there is no basis for limiting the number of shares which may be purchased by applicant;[164] no fixed purchase price for stock is required;[165] authority to buy stock without a maximum price limitation cannot be granted;[166] that an acquisition of a line may be conditioned on continuance of service in accordance with existing contract;[167] that there be compliance with

---

[159]247 I.C.C. 1.
[160]*Service Transport Co. — Purchase — F. E. Kerr Co.,* 59 M.C.C. 481, aff'd 60 M.C.C. 112.
[161]*Schwabacher v. United States,* 334 U.S. 182, 199.
[162]*Pittston Co. — Control — Brink's Inc.,* 75 M.C.C. 345, 351, 375.
[163]*Ala. & V. Ry. Co. — Control,* 290 I.C.C. 36, 39.
[164]*Ibid.*
[165]*Middlewest Freightways, Inc. — Lease — Brashear,* 58 M.C.C. 647, 653.
[166]*United N. J. R. & Canal Co. Control,* 282 I.C.C. 737, 738-9.
[167]*Western Maryland Ry. Co. Acquisition,* 131 I.C.C. 599.

the Commission's specified accounting requirements;[168] imposition of a condition which might interfere with a plan of reorganization to the extent of preventing the lifting of a receivership would not be in the public interest;[169] and that imposition on purchase by one railroad of all properties and assets of another, of a condition that no line or service be substantially discontinued as a result of the proposal is neither necessary nor desirable, and insofar as the Commission has jurisdiction of such future proposal, it must be reserved for consideration in a proceeding in which such authority is sought.[170] In *Erie R. Co. Merger*,[171] the Commission said:

> . . . it is concluded that the magnitude of the diversion of revenues and net income from the interveners would not exceed the amounts estimated by the applicants. It is not intended to belittle the disadvantages to the interveners, but the injuries from which they seek to be insulated are part of the risk involved in the daily business of railroading within areas where strong railroad competition exists. It is not contended, and it cannot be found, that the effect of the merger of the Erie and the Lackawanna upon the volume of interchange traffic at the Buffalo gateway would jeopardize the capacity of the Nickel Plate and the Wabash to maintain adequate transportation service to the public. See *Toledo, P. & W.R. Co. Control*, 295 I.C.C. 523 (536).

In *C. & E. I. Merger*,[172] the Commission said:

> The potential adverse effect of unification on competing carriers is only one factor to be weighed, of course, and it is not in the public interest to protect them artificially, particularly where a unification would result in the provision of improved service to the shipping public by the surviving corporation. *Erie R. Co. Merger*, 312 I.C.C. 185, 191.

Consideration of Stock Values for the Purpose of Determining the Fairness of Exchange Values

The Commission has given consideration to stock values for the purpose of determining the fairness of exchange ratios in a number of acqui-

---

[168]*Gulf, M. & N. R. Co. Acquisition*, 154 I.C.C. 479; *Atlanta B. & C. R. Co. v. United States*, 28 F. 2d 885; *Missouri Pacific R. R. Co. Acquisition*, 131 I.C.C. 389; *Southern Pacific Co. Acquisition*, 131 I.C.C. 726; *C. M. & St. P. & P. R. Co. Acquisition*, 158 I.C.C. 770.

[169]*Savannah & A. Ry. Co. Acquisition*, 162 I.C.C. 771.

[170]*Chicago & N.W. Ry. Co. Purchase — Minneapolis & St. L. Ry. Co.*, 312 I.C.C. 285, 295.

[171]312 I.C.C. 185, 247.

[172]312 I.C.C. 564, 569.

sition cases.[173] In the *Brinks* case the Commission said (at 644) that it "has a duty to safeguard the rights of minority stockholders, especially when there is an absence of arm's length bargaining or when merger terms are imposed by a management whose interests are adverse to that of its minority stockholders," citing *Schwabacher v. United States*.[174] Under the principle laid down in *Schwabacher*, the predominant factor in determining the fairness of exchange ratios is the earnings of the properties to be merged. From past decisions, it is well established that book value and market prices, though proper for consideration, are entitled to far less weight in computing the rate of exchange than earning power.[175] Similarly, as noted in *Louisville & N. R. Co. Merger, supra*, physical values of the railroad proporties are not controlling, for under the *Schwabacher* principle, the predominant factor is the earnings of the properties rather than their values.

Acquisition of Control by Non-Carriers

Section 5(2) (a) of the I.C. Act provides that it shall be lawful, with the approval and authorization of the Commission, "for a person which is not a carrier to acquire control of two or more carriers through ownership of their stock or otherwise; or for a person which is not a carrier and which has control of one or more carriers to acquire control of another carrier through ownership of its stock or otherwise."

In *United States v. Marshall Transport Co.*,[176] Section 5(2) has been interpreted to require a non-carrier to file an application with the Commission not only when it is directly seeking to acquire control of a carrier or carriers, but also when it is seeking to acquire control indirectly through a subsidiary. The Supreme Court said (pp. 41-2):

> The control over the non-carrier contemplated by Section 5(3) can be acquired only if the non-carrier subjects itself to the jurisdiction of the Commission by filing its application with the Commission for its approval of such non-carrier control as is provided by Section 5(2) (b). The purpose of Section 5(3) to subject the non-carrier, thus acquiring control, to specified provisions of the Act would be defeated if the non-carrier were

[173]See *Pittston Co. — Control — Brink's Armored, Inc.*, 87 M.C.C. 637; *Yellow Transit, Inc. — Merger — Wilson, Inc.* 104 M.C.C. 737; *Illinois Cent. Gulf R. — Acquisition — G. M. & O.*, 338 I.C.C. 805; *Seaboard Air Line R. Co. — Merger — Atlantic Coast Line*, 320 I.C.C. 122; and *Erie R. Co. Merger*, 312 I.C.C. 185.
[174]334 U.S. 182, 201.
[175]See *Schwabacher v. United States, supra, Louisville & N. R. Co. Merger*, 295 I.C.C. 457 and *Erie R. Co. Merger, supra*.
[176]322 U.S. 31.

not to become subject to the Commission's order. That is avoided by making it unlawful to acquire non-carrier control save on the non-carrier's application to the Commission in conformity to Section 5(2) (b). As appellees' application to the Commission involved the acquisition of non-carrier control of Marshall by Union, Union was a person seeking authority for such control and as such was required by Section 5(2) (b) to make application to the Commission. To approve the transaction involving such non-carrier control without the application of the non-carrier would be to authorize Union's non-carrier control of Marshall without subjecting the former to the Commission's jurisdiction as required by Section 5(3).

The Commission rightly concluded that it was without authority to approve such control unless Union, the non-carrier, filed its application with the Commission, and since Union failed to do so within the time allowed by the Commission's order, the Commission properly dismissed the pending application in which Union had failed to join. It was therefore error for the District Judge to set aside the Commission's order, and the judgment of the District Court is reversed.

No authorization by the Commission is required for a non-carrier to control a single carrier. Nor does the Commission have jurisdiction over acquisition of control of an established system.[177] The Commission has held that the ownership of a majority of one carrier's stock by another does not in itself effect the control necessary to establish a system relationship, but to attain such a relationship the control must be manifested in such manner as to indicate that the purpose is the unification of management and operation.[178]

In resolving the question of system status, the Commission has given weight to evidence establishing that the operations of the property of the one line were so conducted as to promote the interests of the other line, and the latter was in position at all times to enforce compliance with its direction; that the one line was treated by the other as a part of its system in the arrangement of routes, rates and fares and schedules; that joint use was made of facilities wherever practicable; that joint agencies were maintained for soliciting freight and passenger business; that tariffs of any importance were submitted to the traffic department of one line for approval by the other line before being adopted and put into effect; that divisions of freight revenues, after conferences between representatives of the two roads, were finally determined by one; that at meetings with traffic representatives of other railroads one traffic department represented both roads; that in dealing with national organizations of employees, officers of one line represented both lines; that in

---

[177]*Louisville & J. B. & R. Co. Merger*, 295 I.C.C. 11, 17.
[178]*Live Oak, Perry & Gulf Railroad Company Excess Income*, 187 I.C.C. 485, 492-3.

traffic matters of common interest the policy was determined by one line; and that the president, comptroller, treasurer, and several other officials were the same for both lines.[179]

Section 5(2) does not on its face address itself to the question of whether a corporation which is an integrated carrier system, made up of two or more carrier entities, is to be considered one carrier or as many carriers as there are separate carrier entities.

Prior to 1955 it had been the consistent view of Division 4 of the Commission that acquisition of an already integrated system of separately existing carriers required its approval.[180] This view was expressed by Division 4 in its opinion with respect to Alleghany's application for authority to merge one of NYC's subsidiaries, *Louisvil'e & Jeffersonvi'le Bridge and Railroad Co.*[181] The entire Commission departed from this position and held to the contrary in *Louisville & Jeffersonville Bridge and Railroad Co. Merger.*[182] The Commission held (at p. 17) that because at the time Alleghany acquired control of NYC the latter was a single established system. Alleghany's acquisition of control was not a transaction which required Commission approval under Section 5(2).

In that case, the Commission in considering whether Alleghany Corporation, a non-carrier, had acquired control of New York Central and its various subsidiary railroads in violation of Section 5 of the I.C. Act, stated (at p. 17):

> . . . As Central, at the time of such acquisition of control was recognized as a single established system, we conclude that the transaction was not within the scope of the above stated provisions of Section 5(2) of the Act and that our approval was not necessary.

After the decision of the Commission in the *Jeffersonvil'e Bridge* case, two minority stockholders of Alleghany brought an action in court for an injunction requiring the Commission to set aside its orders in that case to the extent that it granted the application of Alleghany to be considered as a carrier subject to regulation. Later the scope of the action was enlarged to include a prayer for an injunction against enforcement of the orders of the Commission approving Alleghany's preferred stock issue.

---

[179]*Lease of Louisville, H. & St. L. Ry.*, 150 I.C.C. 741, 742; *Louisville, Henderson & St. Louis Railway Co. Excess Income*, 189 I.C.C. 529, 531-2; *Seaboard Air Line Railway v. Carolina & Northwestern Railway Company*, 204 I.C.C. 416, 420; *Birmingham Slag Company v. Blue Ridge Railway Company*, 201 I.C.C. 554, 555.

[180]See, e.g., *Arkansas & L. M. Ry. Co. – Control*, 282 U.C.C. 254; *Weinstein – Control – Capital Transit Co. and Montgomery*, 56 M.C.C. 127; and *Seaboard Air Lines Ry. Co. – Receivership*, 261 I.C.C. 689.

[181]290 I.C.C. 725, 733-34.

[182]295 I.C.C. 11.

There are four decisions by the district court and two by the Supreme Court relating to this litigation.[183]

In *Breswick & Co. v. United States*,[184] the district court disagreed with the Commission's determination in the *Jeffersonville Bridge* case, stating (at 144):

> . . . We believe that where a non-carrier acquires control of the parent corporation of a railroad system it acquires control of the subsidiaries and consequently of two or more carriers so as to require I.C.C. approval. . . .

In 134 F. Supp. 132 the plaintiffs first moved for a preliminary injunction vacating the Commission orders determining that Alleghany be considered as a carrier, and enjoining the enforcement of its orders approving the issuance of preferred stock. The preliminary injunction was granted. The district court then had a hearing on the merits and granted a permanent injunction in 138 F. Supp. 123 setting aside the Commission's orders on a number of grounds similar to those on which it had granted preliminary relief.

The Supreme Court in *Alleghany Corp. v. Breswick & Co.*,[185] reversed the district court on other grounds and expressly reserved decision (at p. 161) on the question of whether Commission approval is required where a non-carrier acquires control of a parent corporation of an integrated railroad system.

On remand the district court in 156 F. Supp. 227 again granted judgment to the plaintiffs. It sustained the preferred stock issue against attacks on its basic fairness. However, it set aside the Commission order approving the issue on the ground that, while the Commission had jurisdiction over Alleghany under the Supreme Court decision, it had not been asked for or given approval to the acquisition by Alleghany of control over the NYC system. The district court went on to say that validation of such control by the Commission was a prerequisite to authorization by the Commission of the Alleghany preferred stock issue, and absent such validation the Commission could not give such authorization. The district court said (at p. 232):

> Without going into the question of whether our previous determination in this regard remains the law of the case we express afresh our conclusion that such approval is required. The statute unequivocally requires

---

[183]*Breswick & Co. v. United States*, 134 F. Supp. 132, 138 F. Supp. 123, (per curiam), rev'd sub. non. *Alleghany Corp. v. Breswick & Co.*, 353 U.S. 151; 156 F. Supp. 227, rev'd per curiam sub nom *Alleghany Corp. v. Breswick & Co.*, 355 U.S. 415; 160 F. Supp. 754.

[184]134 F. Supp. 132.

[185]353 U.S. 151.

Commission approval for the acquisition of two or more carriers by any person.

Its language does not suggest any exceptions and certainly none on the basis of common control by someone else having been previously authorized. It seems to us that as long as the carriers remain unmerged and unconsolidated, the Commission has full power and the duty to decide whether control of them all or any of them by the proposed new person is in the public interest. This was the unchallenged prior consistent administrative interpretation by the Commission. The full reasons for our holding were expressed in our earlier opinion at 134 F. Supp. 132, 142, and in Appendix II to our per curiam opinion at 138 F. Supp. 123, 137. We reaffirm them. We believe our view is strengthened by the emphasis in the Supreme Court's opinion upon the importance of keeping sight of the individual entities within the system. 353 U.S. at page 170, 77 S. Ct. at page 774.

If our conclusion in this regard is to stand, subdivision 4 of Section 5 provides in emphatic terms that Alleghany's unauthorized seizure of control of the Central and its subsidiaries was unlawful and that its continued control of these carriers is unlawful as well. (Footnotes omitted.)

On appeal the Supreme Court, *per curiam* in 355 U.S. 415, again reversed the district court and remanded the case for consideration of what it said was the only claim left open by its prior decision — whether the preferred stock issue as approved by the Commission was in violation of the I.C. Act.

On the second remand from the Supreme Court the district court in 160 F. Supp. 754 vacated the injunction previously issued and dismissed the complaint on the merits.

As a part of the history of the Breswick case it is interesting to consider *Neisloss v. Bush*.[186] This case involved a suit filed by two common stockholders of Alleghany in the district court seeking declaratory and mandatory relief against the action taken by the Commission with respect to Alleghany's acquisition of control of NYC. There was a summary dismissal of the complaint by the district court.

In the suit, the two stockholders raised two objections to the Commission action. First, they said that the Commission erred in holding that Alleghany was not required under Section 5(2) to obtain Commission approval of its acquisition of control of the NYC system. This is the question the Supreme Court found it unnecessary to decide in upholding the Commission's approval of the merger. The second contention was that improper influence was brought to bear on members of the Commission in rendering their decision.

[186]293 F. 2d 873.

The court said (at p. 878) that it was not altogether clear whether the action was intended as one for judicial review of agency proceedings or as an original action to enforce a statutory right, but if intended as the latter the complaint must be dismissed for failure to assert a justiciable cause. The court said that there is nothing in the statute or its history to indicate that Congress in enacting Section 5(2) meant to authorize an original action in the district court, and that it took the extraordinary step of by-passing its expert agency in the matters involved in the case.

The court held (at p. 879) that the two stockholders had failed to show that they had exhausted their administrative remedies open to them, and therefore affirmed the decision of the district court.

It was also held that under Section 5(2) Commission approval was required of the merger of the subsidiaries of NYC and that Alleghany was a necessary party to the merger proceedings. Section 5(2) provides that the Commission must approve whenever a non-carrier already controlling one or more carriers acquires control of another carrier; and the merger of one NYC subsidiary into another was deemed the acquisition of control of the merged carrier by Alleghany, a non-carrier already controlling a carrier (NYC). Having authorized this acquisition by Alleghany under Section 5(2), the Commission was empowered by Section 5(4), formerly 5(3), to establish its exclusive jurisdiction by declaring that Alleghany should be considered a carrier, and the Commission did so.

In *Woods Industries, Inc. — Control — United Transports, Inc.*,[187] an application filed by Woods Industries, Inc. for authority to acquire control of a motor common carrier, motor contract carriers, two companies engaged in the storage and servicing of automobiles, and a company engaged principally in the exploration of oil and gas and the drilling of oil and gas wells, was dismissed by the Commission. In the same proceeding an application of Woods Industries to issue not exceeding 2,000,000 shares of common capital stock was also dismissed. The companies had the same president and the same chairman of the board of directors, and in addition all of the stock of the companies was owned by one family. Woods Industries was not a carrier but its charter authorized it to engage in the business of transportation by motor vehicle. Under the proposal, there would be no change in the control by the family of the companies. The carriers which were commonly controlled as a system would remain under common control as a system, under direct control of Woods Industries, a non-carrier person.

[187] 85 M.C.C. 672.

Division 4 of the Commission held (p. 675) that the factual situation presented, so far as jurisdiction under Section 5 is concerned, is no different than that considered in *Louisville & J. B. & R. Co., Merger*.[188] The Commission also said that the same conclusion was arrived at in *Lease Plan International Corporation — Control — Food Transportation, Inc.*,[189] and *Bangor & Aroostook Corp. — Control — Bangor & A. R. Co.*[190] After determining that the Commission had no jurisdiction over the transaction proposed under Section 5, Division 4 held that it therefore could not subject Woods Industries to the provisions of Section 214 under authority of Section 5(4). This left for consideration the question of whether Woods Industries issuance of capital stock for which it sought authority under Section 214 of the I.C. Act required Commission approval of that Section. Section 214 requires that prior approval by the Commission be obtained for the issuance of securities by "common or contract carriers, by motor vehicle corporations organized for the purpose of engaging in transportation as such carriers, and corporations authorized by order of the Commission, to acquire control of any such carrier, or of two or more such carriers." Division 4 said (pp. 675-6) that Woods Industries clearly was not a common or contract carrier by motor vehicle as defined in the I.C. Act, and that this portion of the quoted phrase need not be further considered, and that it was not a corporation that had been authorized by Commission order to acquire control of any carrier; hence, this portion also need not be further considered. The portion of the quoted provisions that required consideration, Division 4 said, relates to "corporations organized for the purpose of engaging in transportation as such carriers." In this regard, Division 4 held (pp. 676-7):

Under its certificate of incorporation, Industries may engage in numerous business enterprises, some connected with transportation and some unrelated thereto. Included among its corporate purposes is authority to conduct operations as a motor common or contract carrier, a railroad, water carrier, or air carrier, or to purchase, operate, maintain, construct, or repair all facilities necessary to conduct such business. In response to a letter from our Bureau of Finance concerning Industries' intent respecting operations as a carrier, counsel advised that the charter included authority to transport property by motor vehicle "because of the specific intent, at some future time, of the corporation itself engaging in such business."

In *Atlantic Coast Line Co. Stock*, 131 I.C.C. 345, decided October 15, 1927, hereinafter called the *Atlantic Coast Line* case, the Atlantic Coast Line Co., a holding company, filed an application under Section 20a for authority to issue $2,940,000 in capital stock, if authority was required.

[188]295 I.C.C. 11.
[189]Docket No. MC-F-7194 (order entered June 22, 1959).
[190]85 M.C.C. (Not printed in full.)

That company owned stock of the Atlantic Coast Line Railway Company, a carrier by railroad subject to the act, as well as other assets not connected with transportation. Among other things, its charter specifically authorized it "to acquire, build, aid in building, own, sell, convey, equip, lease, or maintain and operate, by steam or other power, any railroads street railways, tramways, telegraph lines, telephone lines," et cetera, and also provided that it "may obtain, carry, and transport passengers, baggage, mails, express materials, freight, and other articles." The Company contended that its charter provisions were not controlling of the jurisdictional question, that it did not propose to operate as a railroad, that it was not organized for the purpose of engaging in interstate commerce, and that, under its charter, it had no power without special legislative authority to use or occupy any highway or public grounds in the State of its incorporation for railroad purposes. The report did not find that the applicant controlled any railroad. It found, however, that—

> the applicant is a corporation organized for the purpose of engaging in transportation by railroad subject to the Interstate Commerce Act and is, therefore, subject to our jurisdiction under the provisions of Section 20a.

The report also concluded with the statutory finding that its proposed issuance of securities was "necessary and appropriate for and consistent with the proper performance by it of service to the public as a common carrier." When the *Atlantic Coast Line* case was decided, the act contained no provision similar to present Section 5(3) under which the Commission is empowered to subject to the provisions of Sections 20a and 214 noncarrier corporations authorized by its order to acquire control of carriers. Such a provision was first added by the act of June 16, 1933, as paragraph (5) of Section 5 and this paragraph was subsequently reenacted as present paragraph (3) of Section 5 by the Transportation Act of 1940.

While the *Atlantic Coast Line* case has been cited in a few subsequent decisions, (See *Greyhound Corp. — Change in Terms of Common Stock,* 1 M.C.C. 77, *Northland Greyhound Lines, Inc. — Common Stock,* 1 M.C.C. 364, and *Hollis & E.R. Co. Acquisition and Operations,* 307 I.C.C. ——— (not printed in full), decided February 3, 1959) in none of those decisions was our assumption of jurisdiction over the issuance of securities by a noncarrier corporation based solely upon the fact that the charter of the corporation authorized it to engage in carrier operations. In each of the cases cited in the footnote, the securities involved were proposed to be issued either as an incident to, or in immediate contemplation of, a transaction whereby the applicant corporation would become a carrier.

Notwithstanding the views expressed in the *Atlantic Coast Line* case, we are of the opinion that the mere inclusion in a corporation's charter of the power to engage in such operations does not constitute the corporation one "organized for the purpose of engaging in transportation as a common or contract carrier by motor vehicle" within the purview of Section 214 or a "corporation organized for the purpose of engaging in transportation by railroad" subject to part I within the purview of Section 20a(1).

In the organization of corporations, it is common practice for the incorporators to describe the corporate purposes and powers in very broad terms, encompassing many objects beyond the existing primary purpose of the organization. Doubtless, there are numerous manufacturing and business corporations whose charters are broad enough to authorize general transportation operations, including operations as a common or contract carrier by motor vehicle. Exercise by us of jurisdiction over the issuance of securities by such corporations would be foreign to and would serve none of the general purposes of the Interstate Commerce Act. Moreover, if this Commission has jurisdiction over the subject matter, the jurisdiction thereover of State bodies is superseded by reason of the provisions of Section 20a(7), and securities issued under our authorization are exempt from registration under the Securities Act of 1933. It is not reasonable to conclude that Congress intended that such results flow merely from the election of incorporators to include provisions of the indicated nature in a corporate charter.

An expression by the Commission (Division 3) on this subject is found in its order of April 17, 1968 F.D. No. 24911, *Texas Gas Transmission Corp — Control — American Commercial Lines, Inc., et al.* (embracing F.D. No. 24951, *Texas Gas Transmission Corp. et al — Stock*). In this proceeding the Commission dismissed an application filed under Section 5 of the I.C. Act by Texas Gas Transmission, a non-carrier corporation, whose principal business is the transmission of natural gas by pipeline subject to regulation by FPC, and , in its security issues, by SEC, to acquire control of an integrated system of separately existing carriers. Texas Gas Transmission sought to acquire control of American Commercial Lines, also a non-carrier, by acquisition of its capital stock, and, in turn, through such control to acquire control of American Commercial Carriers, Inc. and Terminal Transport, Inc., both motor common carriers subject to Part II of the I.C. Act, and American Commercial Barge Line Co., a water common carrier subject to Part III of the I.C. Act. Control by American Commercial Lines of the carriers had been authorized by the Commission in *American Commercial Lines, Inc. — Control — American Commercial Barge Line Co. — Purchase — American Commercial Lines, Inc.*[191]

The Commission (Division 3) held that the above-named carriers comprised a single established system of common carriers within the purview of *Louisville & J. B. & R. Co. Merger,*[192] and *Woods Industries,*

[191]330 I.C.C. 664.
[192]295 I.C.C. 11.

Inc. — Control — United Transports, Inc.,[193] and therefore a transaction within the scope of Section 5(2) (a) had not been presented.

The Commission has consistently followed the ruling in the *Louisville & J. B. & R. Co.* case.[194] An exception to the line cases of following *Louisville & J. B. & R. Co.* is *New York Central R. Co. (Delaware) Merger,*[195] where Division 4 held that Alleghany Corporation's acquisition of control of a newly formed Delaware corporation, New York Central, which was acquiring Old New York Central's subsidiaries was a transaction within Section 5(2) subject to Commission jurisdiction.

Section 5(4) of the I.C. Act provides in part: "Whenever a person which is not a carrier is authorized, by an order entered under paragraph (2), to acquire control of any carrier or of two or more carriers, such a person thereafter shall, to the extent provided by the Commission in such order, be considered as a carrier subject to" any of the following provisions as are applicable to any carrier involved in such acquisition of control: Section 20(1) to (10), inclusive, of Part I, Sections 204(a) (1) and(2) and 220 of Part II, and Section 313 of Part III (which relate to reports, accounts, etc. of carriers), and Section 20(a) (2) to (11) of Part I, and Section 214 of Part II (which relate to issues of securities and assumptions of liability of carriers), including in each case the penalties applicable for violations of such provisions.[Parts I and II only are referred in Section 5(3) insofar as issues of securities and assumptions of liability are concerned.] Jurisdiction under Section 5(4) is triggered by an order entered under Section 5(2).

The extent to which "a person which is not a carrier" will be considered as a carrier subject to the securities' provisions is a determination within the discretion of the Commission. In the past it has been the practice of the Commission to subject to these provisions investment or holding companies dealing principally in carrier securities or enterprises, but not companies whose primary investments and interests are unrelated to transportation. The Commission has refrained from imposing securities' jurisdiction in a number of proceedings.[196]

---

[193]85 M.C.C. 672.

[194]See, e.g., *Katy Industries, Inc. — Control — Missouri — K. T. R. Co.,* 331 I.C.C. 405, 411; *Kansas City Southern Industries, Inc. Control,* 317 I.C.C. 1, 4; *Delaware & Hudson Co. Merger,* 317 I.C.C. 177, 179; *Canal Randolph Corp. Control,* 312 I.C.C. 513, 515; *United Buckingham Freight Line, Inc. — Control — Nortruk* 104 M.C.C. 367, 369; and *Transcontinental Bus System, Inc. — Control — American,* 87 M.C.C. 795, 797-98.

[195]312 I.C.C. 417.

[196]See, e.g., *Missouri Pac. R. Co. — Control — Chicago, & E. I. R. Co.,* 327 I.C.C. 279; *Sea-Land Frt. Service, Inc. — Pur. — Alaska Frt. Lines, Inc.,* 104 M.C.C. 28; *Wells Fargo Armored Service Corp. — Control — Armored,* 75 M.C.C.

In the *Sea-Land* decision, Division 3 said, at page 44:

> As indicated herein, Industries is considered a water carrier subject to the provisions of Section 313 of the Act. Its revenues have been derived from water carrier operations performed under regulation by both this Commission and the Federal Maritime Commission. The additional revenue to be derived from the motor carrier operations involved herein would comprise a small part of the family of companies total revenues, and subjecting Industries to the securities provision of the Act is not warranted.

Similarly, the Commission has on occasions seen fit not to subject "a person which is not a carrier" to the reporting and accounting provisions where the primary interest is in activities unrelated to transportation.[197]

Increased Control

The Commission has stated that an increase in a carrier's proportionate ownership of stock of another carrier, already controlled through majority stock ownership, which results in the ownership of a proportion of the total stock required by applicable state statute for approval of corporate action by the controlled carrier, constitutes an acquisition over which the Commission has jurisdiction under Section 4 of the I.C. Act.[198] The effectuation of control over a carrier through stock ownership which results from the acquisition by the carrier of its own stock, has been found to be a transaction with the scope of Section 5(2) of the I.C. Act.[199] It has also been found that an increase in a carrier's propor-

---

285; F.D. No. 24911, *Texas Gas Transmission Corp. — Control — American Commercial Lines, Inc., et al.*, and F.D. No. 29451, *Texas Gas Transmission Corp. et al. — Stock* (order dated April 17, 1968). See other cases, e.g., *Arkansas & L. M. Ry. Co. Control*, 282 I.C.C. 254; *Warrior & Gulf Nav. Co. Control*, 250 I.C.C. 26; *Ohio Barge Lines, Inc. Control*, 250 I.C.C. 57, 61; *Weinstein — Control — Capital Transit Co. and Montgomery*, 56 M.C.C. 127, 136; *Pittston Co. Control — Brinks Inc.*, 80 M.C.C. 179, 190; *Rockdale, S. & R. Co. Operation and Control*, 282 I.C.C. 297, 302; *Cambria & I. R. Co. Control*, 275 I.C.C. 360, 367; *Cuyahoga Valley Ry. Co. Control*, 252 I.C.C. 683, 690; *Valdosta S. R. Purchase*, 282 I.C.C. 705, 712; *Contract Cartage Co. — Lease — Automatic Convoy Co.*, 45 M.C.C. 518, 519; *Edward Hines Lumber Co. Merger*, 312 I.C.C. 364, 368; *Missouri — K-T R. Co. Consolidation*, 312 I.C.C. 13, 29; *Consolidated Copperstate Lines — Pur. — Sunset M. Lines*, 85 M.C.C. 113, 116, M. 4.

[197]See, e.g., *B. F. Walker, Inc. — Purchase — Pittman*, 75 M.C.C. 706, 711; *Merritt-Chapman & Scott Corp. — Control — Savin Const.*, 70 M.C.C. 362, 364; *Warrior & Gulf Navigation Co. Control*, 250 I.C.C. 26, 31-32; *Contract Cartage Co. — Lease — Automobile Convoy Co., supra.*

[198]*Arkansas & L. M. Ry. Co. Control*, 290 I.C.C. 750; *Peoria & E. Ry. Co. Control*, 236 I.C.C. 749.

[199]*McCormick — Control — A.C.E. Transp. Co., Inc.*, 80 M.C.C. 401.

tionate ownership of stock of another carrier, already controlled through majority stock ownership, which results in the ownership of a proportion of the total stock required by applicable state statute for approval of certain corporate actions by the controlled carrier, constitutes an acquisition of further control over which the Commission has jurisdiction under Section 5 of the I.C. Act.[200]

The question of whether increased domination of the affairs of a carrier by its controlling corporation is an acquisition of control which requires the participation of the controlling corporation in a Commission proceeding was considered, as shown above, by the Supreme Court in *Alleghany Corp. v. Breswick & Co.*[201]

Considering the provisions of the laws of Pennsylvania and Ohio requiring the approval of not less than two-thirds of a carrier's stockholders for the consummation of corporate mergers, leases, purchases and charter amendments, Division 3 of the Commission said in *New York Central Railroad Company and Alleghany Corporation — Control — Pittsburgh & Lake Erie Railroad Company,*[202] that it was clear that the increase in Central's proportionate holdings to two-thirds of the Pittsburgh's outstanding stock would serve to "accomplish a significant increase in the power of one [Central and Alleghany] over the other [Pittsburgh], for example . . . the ability to accomplish financial transactions or operations changes with greater legal ease." Accordingly, the Commission held that the proposal involved a transaction subject to its jurisdiction under Section.

The majority report of Division 1 was attacked in a dissenting opinion which is set forth following because of the interesting comparisons made between cases and the problems raised:

> The majority cite three decisions in support of assuming jurisdiction over the purchase of capital stock here involved. Two are decisions of the Commission where jurisdiction was not questioned and the third is the decision of the Supreme Court in *Alleghany Corp. v. Breswick & Co.,* 353 U.S. 151, where the facts involved were so different from those here that the majority's application of the court's language constitutes an unwarranted "reaching" for jurisdiction.

> The issue which the court was considering in the case cited was whether the Alleghany Corporation, a holding company which already controlled the two railroads seeking approval of merger, was a necessary party applicant within the meaning of court's opinion in *United States v. Marshall*

---

[200]*Peoria & E. Ry. Co. — Control,* 236 I.C.C. 749; *Arkansas & L. M. Ry. Co., Control,* 290 I.C.C. 750.
[201]353 U.S. 151.
[202]Docket No. F.D. No. 22167.

Transport Co., 322 U.S. 31. That the Commission had jurisdiction over the proposed merger under Section 5 was not in question. See *Standard Freight Lines, Inc. — Merger,* 40 M.C.C. 41. Not mentioned by the majority is our decision in *Transcontinental Bus System, Inc., — Control — American,* 87 M.C.C. 795, decided December 29, 1961, where Transcontinental, a carrier, proposed to increase its percentage of stock ownership in two carriers from 66⅔ and 70 per cent, respectively, to 100 per cent in each instance. In sustaining a motion to dismiss for lack of jurisdiction, it was stated:

> At most, if it is an "acquisition of control" at all, it is an acquisition of control of a single established system for which, under the views of the *Louisville* case, [295 I.C.C. 11], authority under Section 5 is not required.

Here also, if the purchase of additional stock is an acquisition of control, it is acquisition of control of a railroad already in the established system.

Statutes should be so interpreted as to give them a reasonable application. Not only is the view of the majority a stretching of the court's language to cover a factual situation which the court could not have foreseen or intended; but it results in an attempt to assume jurisdiction over transactions which it will be well nigh impossible to police. One such transaction, involving the increase in stock ownership from 66⅓ per cent to 66⅔ per cent will, under this interpretation, be subject to Section 5, because of the provisions of State law under which the carrier was chartered, but an identical increase by owner of 66⅓ per cent of a competing carrier, chartered in an adjoining state, will not require our prior approval under that Section, because the laws of the latter state do not make certain corporate acts dependent upon the ownership and vote of two-thirds of the outstanding stock.

In my opinion, the power to control Pittsburgh within the meaning of Section 5 is already held by Central, the two carriers are already controlled and managed in a common interest, and the proposed increase in the percentage of stock to be held by Central is not a transaction within the scope of Section 5(2) (a), and would not be in violation of Section 5(4). The application should be dismissed for lack of jurisdiction.

In *Bekins Van & Storage Co. (California) — Control — Bekins Van & Storage Co., Inc. (Texas),*[203] the question of the Commission's jurisdiction over a proposal to purchase additional stock in an already-controlled company was presented. *Bekins (California)* represented that, by controlling *Bekins (Texas)* as a wholly owned subsidiary, it would be able to accomplish operational, financial, and management transactions with greater ease. Under the laws of Texas in which the controlled company was chartered certain actions by business corporations such

[203]Docket No. MC-F-8453.

as voluntary dissolutions, mergers, and consolidations required the approval of four-fifths of the outstanding shares entitled to vote. Amendments to articles of incorporation, a corporation's purchase of its own shares, distributions of assets with corresponding reductions of surplus, and partial liquidations required an affirmative vote of two-thirds of a corporation's outstanding stock. The Commission citing the *P & L. E.* case, *supra*, held that the transaction was within the scope of Section 5(2) (a) requiring prior approval of the Commission.

Motor Carriers — Consolidation or Merger

TRANSFER OF RIGHTS

Under Section 212(b) of the I.C. Act[204] it is stated that except as provided in Section 5, "any certificate or permit may be transferred, pursuant to such rules and regulations as the Commission may prescribe." Provisions for notice, hearing, deferment of effectiveness, stay, and other statutory procedural steps required by other sections of the I.C. Act are not applicable to transfers of operating rights of small motor carriers where the aggregate gross operating revenues of such carriers have not exceeded $300,000 for a period of twelve consecutive months preceding the date of the agreement of the parties covering the transaction.[205]

Section 212(b) is intended to permit the Commission to provide a simple and expeditious procedure for the transfer of certificates in situations in which Congress felt there would be a minor effect on competition.[206] The Commission has promulgated transfer rules in keeping with the intent of Congress.[207]

JURISDICTION OVER TRANSACTION COVERED BY SECTION 5(2)(a)

To confer jurisdiction upon the Commission, Section 5(2)(b) requires only that a transaction covered by Section 5(2)(a) be proposed.

---

[204]49 U.S.C. 312(b). Comparable provisions — Sec. 312, 410(g).

[205]49 U.S.C. 5(11).

[206]It was stated in the Senate that these transfers of certificates did not warrant "a great deal of red tape with the Commission." 79 Cong. Rec. 5655 (1935). See *Chemical Leaman Tank Lines, Inc. v. United States,* 251 F. Supp. 269, 272; *United States v. Resler,* 313 U.S. 56; *Atwood's Transport Lines — Lease — Clarke,* 52 M.C.C. 97, 107.

[207]49 CFR Part 1132. The transfer rules were upheld in *Chemical Leaman Tank Lines, Inc. v. United States,* 251 F. Supp. 269, 273-74; *A. L. Root Transportation, Inc. v. United States,* 280 F. Supp. 152, 157; *Monumental Motor Tours, Inc. v. United States,* 316 F. Supp. 663, 667. *Cf. Pfizer, Inc. v. Richardson,* 434 F. 2d. 536, 542-43.

If the application involves such a transaction the Commission has jurisdiction, and it has recognized and exercised that jurisdiction in numerous cases. See *Marion Trucking Co., Inc. — Purchase — Harwood Trucking, Inc.*,[208] where the Commission explained the meaning of these provisions of the statute:

> "Any carrier" referred to in subparagraph (a) is the same carrier referred to in subdivision (b) as the one seeking approval of a transaction coming within the purview of subparagraph (a). The person required by the statute to present an application is the purchasing carrier. When these requirements have been met, it is mandatory on the Commission to consider the application on its merits, even though presented only by the purchasing carrier, when there is a transaction within the scope of section 5(2)(a) presented for approval.

There have been a number of cases holding that the validity of a contract between the parties is not determinative of the Commission's jurisdiction under Section 5. In *Yellow Coach Corporation — Purchase — Darnel¹*,[209] two applicants each claimed to possess a contract for the purchase of the same operating rights. Yellow Coach moved to dismiss Tri-State's application, contending that it had a binding contract with the seller, that its contract and application preceded those of Tri-State by some months, and, therefore, that the seller had no operating rights which could be made the subject of a sale to Tri-State. In denying the motion, the Commission said (at 193-94):

> As will be noted, the contracts here involved are executory contracts, and both require our prior approval under section 5 of the act before they lawfully may be consummated. Where, as here, we have two contracts to purchase identical operating rights of a carrier and separate applications have been filed for appropriate authority to effect the purchases, it is our duty under the law to determine those applications on their merits. The priority of one contract over the other in point of time does not relieve us of our obligation to consider and decide the merits of both. The legal rights or obligations which might flow from the timing of the contracts as between the parties is for the courts to decide.

The Commission in the past has entertained unilateral applications under Section 5 for authority to control carriers or purchase carrier

---

[208]50 M.C.C. 613, 620.

[209]59 M.C.C. 185. See *Marion Trucking Co., Inc. — Purchase — Harwood Trucking, Inc., supra.* In *Raymond Bros. Motor Transportation, Inc. — Purchase — Berzel*, 15 M.C.C. 477, the Commission also pointed out that, "applicant having proceeded in the required manner to request permission to effect the transaction, it is not for us to assume that authority therefor, if granted, would be futile." (at p. 477) To the same effect is *C & H Transportation Co., Inc. — Purchase (Portion) — Combs Truck Line, Inc.*, 80 M.C.C. 317. See also *Walker v. United States*, 208 F. Supp. 388, 396, aff'd 372 U.S. 526.

properties subject to the I.C. Act, and such applications have often been considered while the applications of other prospective controllers or purchasers were pending. See *Central Freight Lines, Inc. — Control — Alamo Express, Inc.,*[210] where the Commission said:

> An acquisition of control transaction may be proposed under section 5 unilaterally. Opponents of a proposed acquisition of control sometimes present counter proposals, and all are heard and decided in a consolidated proceeding. The existence of a contract between the applicants and the carriers, or stockholders of such carriers, which the applicants seek to control is not determinative of the result. The public interest is the prime consideration, and in reaching our determination we must have regard for all alternative transactions seriously proposed by the parties.

Overall Jurisdiction

In *Interstate M. Frt. System — Pur. — Capital Frt. Lines, Inc.,*[211] the Commission made the following comment about its overall jurisdiction in transactions under Section 5 of the I.C. Act:

> We have repeatedly stated that, when a transaction is subject to our jurisdiction under Section 5, such jurisdiction extends to the entire transaction and to all the operating rights, interstate and intrastate, and to all the properties involved, and not alone to the purchase of the bare rights to operate in interstate or foreign commerce; and that no part of such a transaction, when it is subject to our prior approval under Section 5, may lawfully be consummated without our prior approval. *Alamo Motor Lines — Pur. — Inter-City Motor Exp., Inc.*, 45 M.C.C. 495, and cases therein cited, one of which was decided in 1940. In this same connection, it was stated in *Raymond Bros. M. Transp., Inc. — Purchase — North American*, 37 M.C.C. 431, decided in 1941:

> "To find that a transaction subject to Section 5 might lawfully be accomplished without our authority, insofar as it involves purchase of physical properties and intrastate rights, leaving for our consideration only that part of the transaction involving purchase of the interstate rights, would not permit proper consideration of the issues involved under Section 5, such as reasonableness of the terms, manner of payment of the total consideration, the effect on the purchaser's financial stability, the effect on adequate and economical transportation in the territory, and other matters affecting the public interest."

[210]90 M.C.C. 96, 101, aff'd *Walker v. United States*, 208 F. Supp. 388, aff'd 372 U.S. 526. See also *Beaver, M. & E. R. Co. Control*, 158 I.C.C. 219, 220, 232, 170 I.C.C. 556; *Toledo, P. & W. R. Co. Control*, 295 I.C.C. 523, *aff'd, Minneapolis & St. L. Ry. Co. v. United States*, 165 F. Supp. 893; *aff'd*, 361 U.S. 173; and *St. Johnsbury & Lamoille County R. Co. Control*, F. D. No. 19453 (May 2, 1958; not printed), reversed on other grounds, *Salzberg v. United States*, 176 F. Supp. 867.
[211]65 M.C.C. 37, 54.

APPLICABLE CRITERIA

The same statutory criteria found in Section 5(2) (c) and applicable to rail carriers are applied to motor carriers regulated by the Commission, thus "consistency with the public interest" is the basic criterion applying to both modes of transportation. This is demonstrated by the various motor carrier cases decided by the Commission and the courts. It has been decided that improvement in the economic position of the parties to the transaction at the expense of competitors, without a showing of benefits to be derived from the transaction to the public, was not consistent with the public interest;[212] that the elimination of circuitous operations and the rendering of through service by reason of a proposed transaction would be desirable in the public interest;[213] that substantial savings in terminal operations at common points and other economies to be effected would be desirable in the public interest;[214] that freedom from labor difficulties by the purchaser had a bearing on whether the transaction would be consistent with the public interest;[215] enhanced financial stability was desirable in the public interest;[216] that where the operations of the acquired carrier would have changed substantially under the proposal, no economies would result, and where there was adequate service available in the area, the benefits to the public would be too scant to offset the substantial disadvantage to protesting carriers from traffic diversion;[217] that the aims of the national transportation policy would not be furthered where public benefits to be expected from a proposal were outweighed by the acquiring carrier's numerous instances of unauthorized operations and violations of regulations;[218] and that there was a public interest in the approval of a purchase involving economies which outweighed potential adverse effects to carrier employees.[219]

ACTIVE OPERATIONS

The requirements for approval of a transaction in regard to past traffic participation are that vendor's operations be active rather than

---

[212]*Mushroom Transp. Co., Inc. − Control − Smith & Howell,* 87 M.C.C. 584; *New Dixie Line, Inc. − Control − Jocie,* 75 M.C.C. 659; *Ashworth Transfer, Inc. − Purchase − Willcoxon and Fowkes,* 90 M.C.C. 107.

[213]*Navajo Freight Lines, Inc. v. United States,* 186 F. Supp. 377, 383.

[214]*Bowman Transp., Inc. − Control & Merger,* 80 M.C.C. 363, 365, 367.

[215]*Byers Transp. Co., Inc. − Pur. − Ralston's Truck Lines, Inc.,* 85 M.C.C. 633, 634.

[216]*Burlington Truck Lines, Inc. − Purchase − Piernie,* 85 M.C.C. 363, 366.

[217]*McCormick − Control − A.C.E. Transp. Co., Inc.,* 80 M.C.C. 401, 417-18.

[218]*Strickland Transport Co., Inc. − Control − England Transp. Co.,* 85 M.C.C. 549, 555-7.

dormant and that vendor and vendee be shown to be competitive in the territory affected, within the limits of their financial and competitive abilities. Proof of the latter element may be shown through evidence of past interchange of traffic with one another or with other carriers. There is no requirement that either vendor or vendee show proof of operation to and from all points authorized, particularly if the authorities involved are irregular in nature.[220]

TRAFFIC DIVERSION

In the absence of a showing of how much traffic will be lost because of a transaction and the manner in which the loss will be incurred, any testimony about potential traffic loss will be accorded only little weight in the disposition of issues presented. The burden of supporting a contention that it will be adversely affected by a transaction is on the protestant. Mere apprehension of loss of traffic and revenues does not constitute a sufficient basis to warrant disapproval of a transaction. In substance the evidence in regard to traffic loss cannot be general in nature.[221] In *North American Van Lines, Inc. — Pur. — Fort Smith Furniture Transp. Co.,*[222] it was stated:

> . . . In numerous cases, where protestants have failed to show with some particularity how much traffic they would lose or how their operations would be harmed, the Commission has accorded little weight to mere apprehension that their services would be adversely affected. . . .[223]

Commission decisions on the issue of injury to carriers require protestants to show with particularity just how much traffic they allegedly would lose and to what degree their operations allegedly would be harmed. Applicable precedents include *Navajo Freight Lines, Inc. — Controls & Merger — Fleetways, Inc.,*[224] where the Commission adopted

---

[219]*Houff — Control — Elliott Bros. Trucking Co., Inc.,* 80 M.C.C. 637, 651, 653-4.
[220]*Consolidated Cooperative Lines — Purchase — Sunset M. Lines,* 85 M.C.C. 113, 131-2.
[221]*Hart Motor Express, Inc. — Pur. — Lake Superior Motor Fgt., Inc.,* Docket No. MC-F-7875, dec. April 5, 1962, sheet 9.
[222]15 Fed. Carrier Cases 35,504. See also *R. A. Young, Jr. — Control — The Arkansas Motor Freight Lines, Inc. — Pur. — Memphis — Arkansas Exp., Inc.,* 9 Fed. Carrier Cases 32, 687, 10 Fed. Carrier Cases 32,888.
[223]See *Watkins Motor Lines, Inc. — Pur. — John A. Seib,* Docket No. MC-F-7854.
[224]59 M.C.C. 801.

a proposed report of the hearing officer stating the general rule as follows:

> It is well established that opposing carriers in Section 5 proceedings cannot sustain their claims of anticipated serious injury without evidence pertaining to the volume of traffic they handle in the general area, the results of their entire operations, estimates of tonnage or revenue which they expect to be diverted from them, and approximations of the freight or revenue the loss of which might impair their service to the public. *Holland Transp. Co., Inc. — Purchase — Apicella, supra,* and *Vinci's Exp., Inc. — Purchase — B. Clayman & Sons,* 57 M.C.C. 434. The supporting evidence of record is fragmentary and insufficient to support a conclusion that interveners would sustain serious loss of traffic or revenue as a result of the proposed unification.

In *Mid-Continent Freight Lines, Inc. — Purchase — Hanson Motor Express,*[225] the Commission said:

> Protestants generally are apprehensive that if the proposed transaction is approved and consummated they would lose some of their traffic to vendee. Their fears are based upon the opinion expressed by their representatives, and there is no evidence of record such as Exhibits or statistics supporting these opinions. The extent to which these carriers claim that their operations would be affected is speculative and conjectural and, in the absence of a showing with some particularity how much traffic they would lose or to what extent their operations would be harmed, their apprehensions may be accorded little weight in determining the issues here presented.

In *Dennis Trucking Co., Inc. — Control — Johnson's Transfer, Inc.,*[226] the Commission authorized the acquisition without the imposition of conditions requested by protestants pointing out that, although vendee is a stronger carrier than vendor, and their coordinated operations would, no doubt, offer increased competition to the protestants, "The measurement of potential loss and the consequent impairment of the service of protestants can be determined only from the evidence adduced." In summarizing the evidence offered by protestants, the Commission stated:

> Evidence of carrier protestants was limited principally to a description of their operating rights and showing the adequacy of their facilities with the general observation that competition for traffic in the particular territory is keen. None adduced evidence of its financial condition, revenues, earnings, tonnage transported, by a reasonable estimate of the prospective loss of tonnage and revenues to the competition of the coordinated service of Trucking and Transfer. It does not appear, therefore, that approval of the stock control without the modifying condition would result in appreciable injury to the protestants.

[225] 65 M.C.C. 312.
[226] 75 M.C.C. 171.

The Commission has held that it "may not properly assume, in the absence of proof, that a carrier is providing a complete and satisfactory service, under its authority."[227] In *D. C. Hall Company — Purchase — David C. Hall and D. C. Hall Transport, Inc.,*[228] the Commission commented on *Ringsby Truck Lines, Inc. — Control — Northern Transp. Co.*[229] and *Pacific — Intermountain Exp. Co., Inc. — Control and Purchase,*[230] as follows:

> In our opinion, where, as here, both Braswell and Transport have interline traffic with each other and with other carriers, it would be just as inequitable to withhold approval, or to subject the operating rights involved to burdensome restrictions solely because the carriers may not have interlined a substantial volume of traffic with each other for movement in numerous directions over routes permitting innumerable combinations, as it would be to "pulverize" the operating authorities of general-commodity carriers who perform substantial operations but do not serve each and every point on all possible combination of routes. See *Mid-Continent Frt. Lines, Inc. — Purchase — Hanson M. Exp.,* 65 M.C.C. 312. We believe that the public benefits, as would result from approval herein, outweigh any potential adverse impact on the protestants. As was stated in the *Ringsby* case, in distinguishing the decision in *Pacific Intermountain Exp. Co., Inc. — Control and Purchase, supra.*
>
> "We do not consider the views expressed in the PIE case as necessarily requiring denial of every Section 5 application, merely because a single-line through service would result, and because competing carriers contend that they would be adversely affected by such a service. The right to perform single-line through service results from every physical unification of rights where a common point is served. Each case can and must be determined on the basis of the evidence of record, and where, as here, the record affirmatively establishes that the proposed plan of operations would meet a public need and that the public interest would best be served by the proposed common control, the application may properly be approved, especially where the competing carriers have failed to establish that their operations or services would be prejudiced to any material degree."

In *Mid-Continent Frt. Lines, Inc. — Purchase — Hanson M. Exp.,*[231] the Commission said:

> Protestants generally are apprehensive that if the proposed transaction is approved and consummated they would lose some of their traffic to

---

[227]*Trans-American Freight Lines, Inc. — Control & Merger — The Cumberland Motor Exp. Corp.,* 75 M.C.C. 423.

[228]70 M.C.C. 233; embracing *Braswell Motor Frt. Lines, Inc. — Control — D. C. Hall Company* (MC-F-6154).

[229]58 M.C.C. 594.

[230]57 M.C.C. 341, aff'd 57 M.C.C. 467.

[231]65 M.C.C. 312, 329.

vendee. Their fears are based upon the opinion expressed by their representatives, and there is no evidence of record such as exhibits or statistics supporting those opinions. The extent to which these carriers claim that their operations would be affected is speculative and conjectural and, in the absence of a showing with some particularity how much traffic they would lose or to what degree their operations would be harmed, their apprehensions may be accorded little weight in determining the issues here presented. It is probably true that the transaction will cause (and the operations under the temporary authority no doubt have already caused) some readjustments in competitive relations of carriers, and an intensification of competition between points in the territory of vendor. This almost always occurs, to a greater or lesser degree, when the purchasing carrier is stronger financially, and from the standpoint of equipment and facilities, than the selling carrier; but we are not convinced that any of the protestant carriers would be unable to meet the added competition without serious impairment of their existing services. The record generally shows that their operations are profitable and that their traffic and revenues have increased each year since . . . including those years in which vendor's operations were at the height of their activity. This evidence demonstrates the growth of protestants' operations and that they have sufficient financial strength to make the necessary adjustments and meet the competition which will result without difficulty. *Merchants Motor Freight, Inc. — Purchase — Bridgeways, Inc.,* 60 M.C.C. 229. Under the circumstances presented, we are of the opinion that the proposed transaction would be consistent with the public interest.

Consistency With the Public Interest Compared With Public Convenience and Necessity

Section 5 does not include a specific requirement that public convenience and necessity be established. The determination involved is whether the transaction is consistent with the public interest. In *County of Marin v. United States,*[232] the Supreme Court discussed the purpose of Section 5, stating that it "was to facilitate merger and consolidation in the national transportation system" and that it "expresses clearly the desire of Congress that the industry proceed toward an integrated national transportation system through substantial corporate simplification."

In *M & M Transportation Company v. United States,*[233] certain motor carriers that were protestant parties before the Commission challenged the validity of a Commission order approving under Section 5 of the I.C. Act a transaction in which one carrier would acquire a portion of the operating rights of another carrier. Specifically, it was alleged that

---

[232]356 U.S. 412. See *Brotherhood of Maintenance Way Employees v. United States,* 366 U.S. 169; *Detroit, T. & I. R. Co., Control,* 275 I.C.C. 455.
[233]128 F. Supp. 296.

the Commission failed to make basic findings underlying the ultimate statutory findings and that such basic findings that were made were not supported by substantial evidence. It was asserted that no findings were made that a public need existed for the unified service, that the existing service was inadequate, and that a new service would be created by the acquisition. In affirming the action of the Commission the court concluded that Congress by implication has indicated that the finding, public convenience and necessity need not be made in an acquisition proceeding involving only motor carriers. The court stated (p. 301) that "It is not possible here to hold that the statute's 'consistent with the public interest' requires the basic findings urged by petitioners." The court added:[234]

> The distinction between Sec. 5's "consistent with the public interest" and Sec. 207's "public convenience and necessity" disposes of the contention as to a finding of public need. And even within Sec. 5, it is evident that Congress intended a distinction between "public interest" and "public advantage." Petitioner's argument that the Commission must find the existing service inadequate in a Sec. 5 proceeding has been rejected by the Supreme Court. *McLean Trucking Co. v. United States,* 1944, 321 U.S. 67, 86-87, 64 S. Ct. 370, 88 L.Ed. 544. Lastly, it would not seem that the creation of a new service would be inconsistent with the public interest — on the contrary, it might greatly benefit the public. If petitioners' argument were to prevail, acquisitions would be limited to those involving non-contiguous carriers, or carriers which substantially interchanged all through traffic with one another.

Another series of cases would seem to indicate, however, that the line of distinction between the words "public convenience and necessity" and "consistency with the public interest" is very thin.[235]

---

[234]*Ibid.,* footnote 4. See also *Baltimore Transfer Co. v. Interstate Commerce Commission,* 114 F. Supp. 558, where a district court upheld an order authorizing merger of two motor common carriers despite the fact that the Commission found "no evidence of any dissatisfaction with or deficiency in the service of the opposing carriers and also that they are capable of handling additional traffic." And see *Consolidated Copperstate Lines — Purchase — Sunset Motor Lines,* 85 M.C.C. 113.

[235]*Ratner v. United States,* 162 F. Supp. 518, aff'd 356 U.S. 368. The decision is in accord with prior court affirmances of similar Commission denials. See *Super Service Motor Freight Co. v. United States,* 10 Fed. Carrier Cases, par. 80, 995, sustaining *Super Service Motor Freight Co., Inc. — Purchase — (Portion) Hayes Freight Lines, Inc.,* 60 M.C.C. 389; *Kulp & Gordon, Inc. — Purchase — Silva Bros.,* 57 M.C.C. 517; *Herrin Transp. Co. v. United States,* 108 F. Supp. 89, aff'd 344 U.S. 925, sustaining *Herrin Transp. Co. — Purchase — Mobile Exp., Inc.,* 58 M.C.C. 59; *Shein v. United States,* 102 F. Supp. 320, aff'd 343 U.S. 944, sustaining *Shein's Exp. — Purchase (Portion) — Stilwell,* 59 M.C.C. 807. The rule of decision embodied in the foregoing Commission and court decisions has also been followed since the *Ratner* decision. See *Navajo Freight Lines, Inc. v. United States,* 186 F. Supp. 377.

In *Shein v. United States, supra,* the court held (at p. 326):

It is so well established that the citation of authorities is unnecessary, that if Shein had applied to the Commission for a certificate of convenience and necessity to operate over a regular route in this territory that the burden would have been upon it (Shein) to prove, by competent evidence to the satisfaction of the Commission, that the public interst required such service. May it then attempt to attain this end result indirectly by the purchase proposed here without carrying the burden of proof incumbent upon it if it was attempted directly? We think not and we think that the Commission applied the right rule of law in reaching its conclusions.

☼　☼　☼

We, therefore, conclude that the Commission applied the right rule of law and had substantial evidence to support its ruling; that there would be a radical change in the pattern of the operations; that there would be a probably adverse effect which this would have on competing carriers; that there was a lack of evidence to show that the transaction would supply any need of the public not now being adequately met by other carriers; and therefore concluding that the granting of the transfer would not be consistent with the public interest. . . .

RESTRICTIONS

Section 208(a) of the I.C. Act authorizes the Commission to attach to a certificate issued under Sections 206 or 207 "such reasonable terms, conditions and limitations as the public convenience and necessity may from time to time require," and Section 5(2) (b) authorizes the Commission if it finds that a proposal under Section 5(2) (a) "will be consistent with the public interest" to approve the transaction "subject to terms and conditions and such modifications as it shall find to be just and reasonable." From time to time pursuant to the statutory authority expressed in Sections 208(a) and 5(2) (b), the Commission has been requested to impose restrictions of one character or another on certificates to be issued following proceedings instituted under Section 207(a) or Section 5(2) (a). The obvious purpose of requesting restrictions is to assure protection or survival of existing authorized carriers and ultimately to assure continuance of an economically stable transportation system. The Commission has exercised its authority to impose restrictions on occasions, but has expressed opposition to the imposition of the so-called "no-tacking" restriction.

During the early administration of the Motor Carrier Act, the Commission recognized that independent motor common carriers should be permitted to participate in through movement of traffic via a common point of service from origin to destination.[236] In the *Keeshin* case, which was the first major decision of the Commission involving the right of an acquiring carrier to conduct unrestricted direct operations between points on the authority sought to be acquired and the authority presently held, it was stated:

> . . . counsel for protestants further argue that the approval of this application would permit the extension of routes and the establishment of new routes without any regard to the public convenience and necessity for such new operations. This raises the question whether acquisition by one carrier of the operating rights of another gives such purchaser or lessee authority to render a through or unified service. The contention of protestants, apparently is that, in addition to procuring approval of an application to acquire properties and operating rights, applicant should also procure, upon proof of public convenience and necessity, specific authority for such through or unified service. We cannot subscribe to an interpretation which would require such authority in addition to that which results from those operating rights which motor common carriers individually preserve or obtain as a result of applications for certificates of public convenience and necessity. The right of motor common carriers to establish through routes over which through service is conducted is recognized by Section 216 of the Motor Carrier Act, 1935. It would be inconsistent to hold that such through service may not be rendered, without special proof of public convenience and necessity, after any such carriers are merged or otherwise unified. It is our understanding, indeed, that through service by interchange has heretofore been rendered by the carriers involved in the present proceeding.

The Commission's conclusion in *Keeshin, supra,* later led to the establishment of the rule permitting motor common carriers to "tack" or "use in combination" newly acquired authority with existing franchises so long as operation conducted over the two authorities was through a point common to each certificate. Under the foregoing rule there are two classes of cases: The first class[237] is where an existing carrier seeks to extend its operating authority under Section 207 of the I.C. Act by proof of public convenience and necessity; the second class[238] of case is through application under Section 5(2) (a) where two existing franchises are being merged or consolidated.

As shown by its decisions, the Commission has been reluctant to impose restrictions against the movement of traffic between an existing

---

[236]*Keeshin Motor Express Co., Inc. — Leases,* 1 M.C.C. 373; *Century-Matthews Motor Freight, Inc. v. Thrun,* 173 F. 2d 454.

[237]*Aetna Freight Lines, Inc., Interpretation of Certificate,* 48 M.C.C. 611; *Transport Corp. of Virginia — Ext. — Md.,* 43 M.C.C. 716.

[238]*Powell Bros. Truck Lines, Inc. — Purchase — Bryan,* 39 M.C.C. 11; *Days Transfer, Inc. — Purchase — Haner,* 39 M.C.C. 339; *Carolina Freight Carriers Corp., Purchase — Edmunds,* 36 M.C.C. 259.

authority and a later acquired authority, whether the authority was obtained pursuant to proof of public convenience and necessity under Section 207(a) or by proof of consistency with the public interest under Section 5(2) (a). When the Commission has made an exception to its general rule against imposing no-tacking restrictions, it has do so only where the evidence established that other existing carriers would suffer a material adverse effect which, in turn, would threaten their ability to continue to render services to the shipping public.

In application proceedings instituted under Section 207a where the applicant has existing authority and seeks to extend such authority beyond existing territorial limits, the Commission has generally refused to restrict against the through movement of freight between points on the existing authority and points on the authority sought in the absence of a compelling need to do so.[239] In the *Ecoff* case, the Commission concluded not to impose the restriction requested with the following observation, at 762, that "upon a review of the record, we agree that the restriction against tacking imposed by the prior report is inappropriate in this instance. The record is devoid of evidence that protestants or any other carrier will be seriously affected by an unrestricted grant of authority. In the absence of a showing of sufficient reason for imposition of a restriction against tacking, no such limitation should be imposed." In *Commercial Oil Transport, Extension — Jacksonville, Illinois*,[240] the Commission stated in refusing to impose a restriction against tacking that "Generally, we are reluctant to localize and isolate grants of common carrier authority by encumbering them with restrictions against tacking except for good cause shown."

In *Pacific Intermountain Express Co. — Control — West Coast Fast Freight, Inc.*,[241] it was requested that certain of the routes involved be restricted to prevent single-line service based upon the limited volume or absence of past interline between the two carriers involved. It was demonstrated that common control would produce substantial operating savings, that the amount of traffic interchanged by the vendor with protestants was only a very small percentage of the protestants' traffic, that vendor had no intention of diverting interline traffic from such carriers and even if it were to divert it, it would not materially affect those carriers. In denying the requests for a restriction and in granting

---

[239]*Rawlings Extension — Emporia*, 78 M.C.C. 636; *Eldon Miller, Inc., Ext. — Liquid Chemicals*, 73 M.C.C. 538; *Liquid Transporters, Inc., Ext .— Columbia Park, Ohio*, 76 M.C.C. 685; *Ecoff Trucking, Inc., Ext. — Ironton, O.*, 77 M.C.C. 759.

[240]77 M.C.C. 771, 773; see also *Hogan Storage & Transfer Co. — Ext. — Williamson, W. Va.*, 92 M.C.C. 63.

[241]60 M.C.C. 301.

the application, the Commission stated that "Generally, restrictions in operating rights create undesirable operating complications, and should not be imposed except where the record conclusively shows that they are necessary in the public interest. The restriction here proposed would preclude interline between the two commonly-controlled carriers at common gateway points."

Even where the parties to a Section 5(2) (a) application agree to a restriction, the Commission has refused to impose the restriction. In *Viking Freight Company — Control — Cook Truck Lines, Inc.,*[242] vendor and vendee had been interchanging traffic for a number of years at one interchange point, but had not interchanged at another point. At the hearing, applicants entered into a stipulation with protestants agreeing to accept the restriction against interchange at that second point. The Commission refused to abide by the stipulation and granted the application without restriction, stating:

> In our opinion the Examiner in his proposed report properly finds that the service restrictions mentioned, which the parties agreed upon at hearing, should not be imposed.
>
> Unless unusual circumstances are present, restrictions of such a nature are not conducive to efficient operations of service to which shippers are entitled, complicates the operating authority, particularly since [they] would apply as to these named carriers, but would not apply to their interline with other carriers. Any subsequent change in the control of either, or portions of the operating rights of either, would require a further examination to determine whether the prohibited interline between them should again be allowed. Whether particular carriers of property interline traffic with certain carriers and not with others is for them to decide, except perhaps, where shipments are specifically routed by the shipper.

The Commission reaffirmed its position on no-tacking restrictions in *Cope — Purchase — Buckner.*[243] There the Commission in refusing to impose a restriction at the request of a carrier stated as follows:

> Cope operates primarily as a connecting carrier, interlining with numerous other carriers at Asheville, and also with one carrier at Murphy, and another at Bryson. Issuance of a certificate to Cope free of restriction would not have any material effect upon the nature and scope of the operation he conducts in connection with interlined traffic received at Asheville. The most significant result would be the expanded services which could be performed in connection with interchanged traffic received at Murphy and Bryson. By a joinder of his regular and irregular-route

[242]258 M.C.C. 679. See also *Holmes — Control — Newburg Transfer, Inc.,* 70 M.C.C. 804.
[243]80 M.C.C. 723.

rights at common points of service within the Asheville base area, Cope could transport, in through single-line operations, shipments received at Murphy and Bryson to authorized points in his irregular-route territory located outside of the Asheville base area. The record shows that Cope's operations are an important adjunct to his numerous connecting carriers and are essential to the many communities he serves. In operations under the unified rights, unrestricted as to a joinder thereof, he would be enabled to provide a more adequate and efficient service carried on with increased economy, and without any apparent serious impact on the services of other carriers.

The Commission's establishment and its application of the no-tacking restriction rule is, as stated, an exception or departure from its general rule against restricting certificates. The Commission quite properly has narrowly limited the circumstances in which a restriction will be imposed. When the issue has been presented, the Commission has consistently held that the burden of proving the necessity for imposing a restriction is that of opposing carriers.[244]

DORMANCY

The core of dormancy is that once a carrier intentionally permits his operating authority to fall into disuse he may not transfer it. The result would be the authorization of a new service without a showing of public convenience and necessity.[245] There need not be a total cessation of activity for a carrier's operating rights to be dormant. A "lack of substantial service" under the carrier's authority may result in dormancy.[246] The concept of dormancy is "rooted in the well-developed common law of the I.C.C."[247] There are no mechanical rules for determining when rights have become dormant.[248] Factors considered are the commodities shipped, points served, and volume compared with the nature and scope of the carriers operating rights, the carrier's intent to perform services, the degree to which the carrier operated commensurate with his abilities and the demands for his services, and whether the proposed service is new or merely a combination or consolidation of existing services.[249]

[244]*Rawlings, supra; Hennepin Transp. Co., Inc. — Purchase — Oligney Motor Exp. Co.*, 80 M.C.C. 655, 658 cited with approval in *Spector Freight System, Inc. — Control & Merger*, 85 M.C.C. 461, 576.

[245]*Arrow Transportation Co. v. United States*, 300 F. Supp. 813, 817.

[246]*Houff Transfer, Inc. v. United States*, 291 F. Supp. 831, 835.

[247]*Atkinson Lines, Inc. v. United States*, 381 F. Supp. 39, 41.

[248]*Cedar Rapids Steel Transportation, Inc. v. ICC*, 391 F. Supp. 181, 185.

[249]*John Novak Contract Carrier Application*, 103 M.C.C. 555, 557; *Richard Dahn, Inc. v. ICC*, 335 F. Supp. 337, 339; *Houff Transfer, Inc. v. United States*, 291 F.S. at 835; *Alabama Highway Express, Inc. v. United States*, 241 F. Supp. 290, 293; *Arrow Transportation Co. v. United States*, 300 F. Supp. at 818.

In *Hilt Truck Line v. U.S. and I.C.C.*,[250] the court discussed the concept of dormancy as follows:

> In a long series of cases, the Commission has consistently held that harm to protesting carriers is a necessary prerequisite to a finding of dormancy. As early as 1958, it held that the concept of dormancy was formulated to protect "other carriers which have been required to expand their carrier facilities in order to take up the vacuum" created by the loss of service of the dormant authority. *King's Van & Storage, Inc. — Pur. — Millard*, 75 M.C.C. 582, 585 (1958). This concept was approved in *Arrow Transportation Co. v. United States*, 300 F. Supp. 813 (R.I. 1969), where dormancy was defined as "an abandonment or termination of services the reactivation of which will result in damages either to the public interest or to intervening or protesting carriers who conducted operations during the interruption of said services." At 818. This definition has been accepted by the Commission and applied in numerous cases. *Holme Freight Lines, Inc. — Control*, 116 M.C.C. 874, 880 (1975); *Roadway Exp. Inc. — Control and Merger — Atlas*, 122 M.C.C. 333, 335 (1976). Under these cases, the Commission must find that: (1) there has been an abandonment or termination of services; and (2) the reactivation of service will damage either the public interest or protesting carriers who conducted operations during the interruption of service . . .

Once a determination is made that the authority is dormant the applicant for the new service must show it is within the public convenience and necessity. A showing of shipper preference for the proposed new service is not sufficient. The applicant must prove that existing service is inadequate.[251]

In the case of dormant rights, the situation is in practical effect no different from that in which a vendee seeks to acquire operating rights so broad as to permit the vendee to furnish service different from that furnished by vendor. In such cases the Commission has also required a showing that shippers need the new service and existing motor carriers are not capable of supplying it. *LaMere and Conroy — Purchase — Ziffrin*,[252] is in point. The Commission there denied the application of one motor carrier to purchase a portion of the operating rights of another motor carrier on the ground that the service proposed by the vendee was so much more extensive than that presently furnished by the vendor as

---

[250]No. 76-1371, decided January 25, 1977.

[251]*Richard Dahn, Inc. v. ICC*, 335 F. Supp. at 339-340; *Tri-State Motor Transit Co. v. United States*, 369 F. Supp. at 1244; *Lester C. Newton Trucking Co. v. United States*, 264 F. Supp. at 885; *Robbins v. United States*, 204 F. Supp. at 82.

[252]55 M.C.C. 501. See also *John Duff — Control: Vollmer Transportation, Inc. — Purchase (Portion) — B. Clayman & Sons*, 55 M.C.C. 599, 607; *Joseph E. Faltin — Purchase (Portion) — Clyde B. Gray*, 50 M.C.C. 364, 370; *Willard Sulzberger — Control; F. D. McKay, Inc. — Purchase (Portion) — Howard G. Mathews*, 45 M.C.C. 697, 702.

to constitute it a new and different service, and that the record did not disclose need for the proposed service. The Commission said (p. 514):

> It is deemed sufficient to point out that vendor, for all practical purposes, has not been a competitor for traffic moving between those points, or between Milwaukee, and points served by the partnership (vendee) for some time, and that the revival of a service which has no present real going-concern value, in conjunction with the partnership's own operations, would be equivalent to the establishment of a new competitive operation between the points involved, thus tending further to aggravate the existing highly competitive condition. Considering the territory affected and the existing available service, this record does not show the need for the proposed service by the partnership. . . . To permit a revival of the service in this highly competitive area by the partnership would not foster sound economic conditions among the existing carriers, and would not be consistent with the public interest.[253]

HOUSEHOLD GOODS CARRIERS

While it is recognized that household-goods operations are highly specialized and are dissimilar from general commodity operations, particularly in that there is no regularity of movement between the same points or continuity of service to particular shippers, applicants, nevertheless, must submit satisfactory evidence to enable the Commission to find that the vendor has rendered an active operation under its rights or that the service it has performed has, at least, been commensurate with its resources and facilities.[254] In this connection the Commission in *Evanston Fireproof Whse. — Control — Allied Van Lines*,[255] stated:

> Competition among household-goods carriers differs from competition among general-commodity haulers. Usually, competition for household-goods traffic is encountered at the domicile of the carrier, and to a much minor extent at other points. Because of the nonrepetitive character of the traffic involved, competition does not exist to any great extent between large centers in the same way as it does between carriers handling steady volumes of traffic between industrial areas. Except in the case of national accounts, which are likely to have shipments moving between the same points because their branches are so located, individual shippers may make a long-distance move only once or twice in a lifetime. This factor causes the greatest difference between competition among household-goods carriers and other carriers.

---

[253]The ruling in the *LaMera* case has been followed in *Terminal Freight Transport, Pur. — United Freight,* 87 M.C.C. 535, 540; *Newsom Trucking Co., Inc. — Pur. — Crutcher Bros. Co.,* 85 M.C.C. 230, 233; *Dallas & Mavis Forwarding Co., Inc. — Pur. — Billy Baker Co.,* 85 M.C.C. 521, 531.

[254]*Von Der Ahe Lines, Inc., — Lease and Purchase — Bee Line,* 87 M.C.C. 53, 59; *Myers Transfer & Storage Co. — Purchase — Pioneer Storage Co.,* 85 M.C.C. 264, 268.

[255]40 M.C.C. 557, 588-9.

INTERMEDIATE POINTS

The question occasionally arises as to whether the Commission should authorize the transfer of authority to serve intermediate points on the route involved in the transaction because vendor does not serve all of those points or has interchanged shipments to other carriers for service at such points. The Commission reviewed this issue in *The Mason and Dixon Lines, Inc. — Control — The Silver Fleet Motor Express, Inc.*,[256] where it said at page 28:

> Although it has, with increasing frequency, used other carrier for service at intermediate points, we have consistently found that where a carrier has been conducting comparatively substantial operations throughout its system, it is not compelled to submit evidence of operations to and from every intermediate point or in connection with all combinations of its routes in order to show that its operations, as a whole, have been of substantial and continuous nature. Compare *New Dixie Lines, Inc.–Control–Jocie Motor Lines, Inc.*, 75 M.C.C. 659, citing, with approval, *Mid-Continent Frt. Lines, Inc. — Purchase — Hanson M. Exp.*, 65 M.C.C. 312.

In *Mid-Continent Frt. Lines, Inc. — Purchase — Hanson M. Exp.*,[257] the Commission said:

> We have found in a number of prior cases that where a carrier has been conducting comparatively substantial operations over its entire system it is not compelled to submit evidence of operations to and from every intermediate point or in connection with all combinations of its routes to show that its operations have been of a substantial character and continuous, although where operations have not been conducted over a particular route for a long period we have required the cancellation of these portions of rights as a condition precedent to approval for their transfer. Although vendor did not transport a large volume of traffic between Indianapolis and Cleveland and between Indianapolis and Akron, there was a substantial volume of traffic moving, for example, between Chicago and Ohio points, and the failure of vendor to secure a large volume for movement to and from a particular point in the same general area does not justify the cancellation of this carrier's rights to and from a particular point or points in the center of the operations as a whole.

SEPARATE CARRIER ENTITIES

In *Best Transport, Inc., Contract Carrier Application*,[258] the Commission voiced disapproval of the creation of a large number of sepa-

---

[256]Docket No. MC-F-7577, January 21, 1963.
[257]65 M.C.C. 312, 328-9.
[258]88 M.C.C. 147. See also *Schwerman Trucking Co. of Ala., Inc. Contr. Car. Applic.*, 88 M.C.C. 495.

rate carrier entities under common control of one or more persons or corporations to conduct interstate motor carrier operations, finding that the increased administrative burden and added regulatory problems created by such organization was not in the public interest.

INTRASTATE PROVISO OPERATIONS

In an early case *Baggett Transportation Co. — Purchase — Bishop*,[259] where intrastate proviso operations were being sold, the Commission held it did not have jurisdiction to approve the transaction. The Commission stated, l.c. 663:

> It necessarily follows that one who falls within the terms of the exception does not possess any "right" to operate in interstate commerce which is transferable as an interstate operating authority. What he has by way of interstate operating authority is neither "properties or franchises" within the contemplation of Section 5, nor a "certificate or permit" within Section 212(b). An exemption, or an exempt status, is not properly subject to transfer. . . .

> It is clear from the foregoing that when one subject to the exception of the proviso transfers his State certificate and possibly motor vehicles theretofore used in the operations conducted thereunder to another not subject to the exception, no interstate operating authority passes. All that does or can pass is a right to conduct an intrastate business and title to the motor vehicles, if any, involved in the transaction. . . . Such transactions, therefore, do not require our approval either under Section 5 or Section 212(b), and, falling without the intendment of these provisions, we have no authority under either of them to approve.

The Commission later reversed the *Baggett* holding in *C & D Motor Delivery Co. — Purchase — Eliott*,[260] on the grounds first that even a proviso operator was a "motor carrier" under the I.C. Act and consequently within the terms of Section 5, and second that the Commission had amended its rules to permit consideration of matters of public convenience and necessity directly related to the Section 5 issue. The *C & D* case held that proviso operations were in themselves evidence of public convenience and necessity. The Commission stated, l.c. 553-4:

> It is apparent that, where, as here and in similar cases, the operations proposed to be covered by the certificate of public convenience and necessity to be issued already are lawfully in existence, the problems presented are not identical with those where entirely new operations are proposed under Section 207. These operations have been conducted for some time in interstate commerce. Where such is the case and the operations

[259]36 M.C.C. 659.
[260]38 M.C.C. 547.

were instituted lawfully, the past continued performance of the transportation is itself evidence of public need for continuance thereof. It is true that competing carriers will be affected to some extent by the advent of vendee into the territory as a result of purchase of these operations; but the degree to which they would be affected is not substantially different from that in the ordinary acquistion case arising under Section 5. That is to say, it is not the same as if a completely new and additional operation were proposed, and the degree to which competitors would be affected would not be any different whether vendor operates under the statutory exemption or under a certificate issued by this Commission. Nevertheless, in our opinion, competing carriers in the territory concerned are entitled to notice that, in the event the Section 5 application can be approved, a certificate of public convenience and necessity will be issued covering the acquired operations, and are entitled to introduce such evidence as they may see fit concerning adequacy of existing service and the possible effect which the proposed transaction, inclding issuance of the certificate, may have on them. Such opportunity has been afforded here.

In *Pacific Greyhound Lines — Control and Merger*,[261] the contention was made that jurisdiction over the acquisition of operating rights of proviso carriers rests with the authority which granted the rights, that is the state commission. The I.C.C. denied the contention and stated, l.c. 433-4:

The Interstate Commerce Commission has long asserted jurisdiction over the acquisition of State operating rights in transactions involving . . . interstate carriers, holding that consummation of such transactions as to State rights is unlawful without its approval. *Wilson Storage & Transfer Co. — Purchase — Dakota Transp.*, 36 M.C.C. 221, *Bruce Motor Freight, Inc. — Purchase — Bruce*, 39 M.C.C. 489, 491, and *Raymond Bros. M. Transp., Inc. — Purchase — North American*, 37 M.C.C. 431, 433. And this applies to carriers operating solely within one State, as well as to those operating physically interstate, since Section 5 contains no provisions exempting the former class of carriers. *Alamo Motor Lines — Purchase — Inter-City Motor Exp., Inc.*, 45 M.C.C. 495, 504. By electing to conduct operations under the proviso, an intrastate carrier voluntarily enlarges the scope of its business to include operations in interstate or foreign commerce. The provisions of Section 5 are only incidentally concerned with the "transfer" of a "certificate," neither of which words appears in that section. Those provisions are primarily and fundamentally concerned with the control of operations as going concerns. *Adkins — Purchase — Star Transit, Inc.*, 38 M.C.C. 240, 243.

By Section 5(11) of the Act (which was not considered in the *Baggett* case), the Commission is granted "exclusive and plenary" authority over transactions involving control or acquisition of the operations of carriers subject to part II of the act. Approval of such a transaction relieves such carriers from the operation of State laws insofar as necessary to the exercise of the authority granted. Compare *Seaboard R. Co. v. Daniel*, 333 U.S. 118. This includes the exercise of any franchises acquired through such a transaction. *Seaboard Air Line Ry. Co. Receivership*, 261 I.C.C. 689, 721.

Intermodal Acquisition: Rail-Motor*

The applicable provisions of Section 5(2) are clear and unambiguous. Subdivision (2) (a) authorizes specified forms of unification, acquisition or lease arrangement by two or more carriers, and subdivision (2) (b) provides for Commission approval and authorization if "the proposed transaction" is within the scope subdivision (2) (a) "and will be consistent with the public interest." The proviso portion of subdivision (2) (b), however, requires that if the applicant is a carrier by railroad or is controlled by or affiliated with a carrier by railroad within the meaning of Section 5(7), formerly 5(8), and the transaction involves a motor carrier, then the Commission shall not enter the order of approval and authorization "unless it finds that the transaction proposed will be consistent with the public interest and will enable such carrier to use service by motor vehicle to public advantage in its operations and will not unduly restrain competition."

In addition to the showing which Section 5 requires of all carriers, Congress saw fit to impose upon railroads the further burden of showing that the transaction will benefit the public — that it will promote or advance the interest of the public.

Referring to the Motor Carrier Act of 1935, we find that Section 213 thereof,[262] as originally framed, provided for approval and authorization by the Commission of acquisitions of control of motor carriers when such transactions were shown to be consistent with the public interest. A proviso to that section, however, required that in the case of an applicant who was "a carrier other than a motor carrier," the Commission was precluded from approving the transaction unless if found that it would: (a) "promote the public interest by enabling such carrier other than a motor carrier to use service by motor vehicle to public advantage in its operations," and (b) "not unduly restrain competition." Under this proviso, therefore, neither railroads nor water carriers were permitted to acquire a motor carrier without a finding by the Commis-

---

*This subject and that relating to intermodal acquisition: rail-water are based on an article by the author entitled "Intermodal Acquisition Under The Interstate Commerce Act" appearing in the January, 1970 issue of *The Transportation Law Journal*, Vol. 2, No. 1, published by the Motor Carrier Lawyers Association. With permission.
[262] 49 Stat. 555.

sion that the public interest would be promoted by enabling such rail or water carrier to use service by motor vehicle to public advantage in their operations and would not unduly restrain competition.

Section 213 of the Motor Carrier Act was substantially re-enacted into Section 5(2) (b) of the Interstate Commerce Act when the Transportation Act of 1940 was enacted.[263] In the substantial re-enactment of Section 213 into Section 5(2) (b) only the railroads continue to have the added burden of showing in a transaction to acquire a motor carrier that the public interest will be promoted and that competition will not be unduly restrained. Water carriers, under Section 5(2) (b), are required only to show that the transaction to acquire a motor carrier will be consistent with the public interest. They are relieved of the requirements of Section 213.

Under Section 202 of the Motor Carrier Act of 1935, the policy of Congress was expressed to require the regulation of transportation by motor carriers in such manner as to recognize and preserve the inherent advantages of, and foster sound economic conditions in, such transportation and among such carriers in the public interest. This policy was not changed by the enactment of the Transportation Act of 1940. The Commission has followed this Congressional policy consistently through the years beginning with *Pennsylvania Truck Lines, Inc. — Control — Barker Motor Freight, Inc.*[264] In 1938, the Commission concluded in *Kansas City S. Transport Co., Inc. Com. Car. Application*[265] that the standards contained in Section 213 (later Section 5(2) (b)) should be followed as a general rule in other situations particularly in applications for certificates of public convenience and necessity under Section 207.

In Section 207 proceedings, the Commission as a rule will impose restrictions in certificates issued to railroads. These restrictions are imposed to insure that the service rendered under the certificate will be no more than that which is auxiliary to or supplemental of rail services. Not only the administrative, but also the judicial, current has run in favor of auxiliary and supplemental restrictions. The Supreme Court in *Interstate Commerce Commission v. Parker,*[266] revealed its understanding of the Commission's obligation to consider railroad applications under Section 207 as limited to service "truly supplementary or auxiliary to the rail traffic."

[263]See *American Trucking Associations v. United States,* 355 U.S. 14.
[264]1 M.C.C. 101.
[265]10 M.C.C. 221.
[266]326 U.S. 60. See *American Trucking Associations v. United States,* 364 U.S. 1. See also *Rock Island M. Transit Co. — Purchase — White Line M. Frt.,* 40 M.C.C. 457, aff'd *United States v. Rock Island Motor Transit Co.,* 340 U.S. 419.

As the Supreme Court said in *United States v. Rock Island M. Trans. Co.*[267]

The practice of the Commission from the beginning of motor-carrier regulation has been to restrict motor-carrier operations both geographically and functionally. The same was true of railroad motor carrier affiliates. We think that at the time of issuance of the certificate, if the Commission reasonably deems the restriction useful in protecting competition, or for other statutory purposes, the Commission may require the railroad affiliated motor carrier to perform only those services that are auxiliary and supplemental to the rail service . . . Such a restriction is a logical method to insure the maximum development of the two transportation agencies — rails and motors — as coordinate transportation services in accordance with the Declaration of Policy . . . Specific statutory authority is found in the requirements of . . . Section 5 of the Interstate Commerce Act . . . Railroad operations as motor carriers are forbidden by that acquisition section except to enable a railroad "to use service by motor vehicle to public advantage in its operations."

The guiding principles which have been established are best expressed in *American Trucking Assoc. v. United States,*[268] where the Supreme Court said (pp. 6-11):

Both the Commission and this court have recognized that Congress has expressed a strong general policy against railroad invasion of the motor carrier field. This policy is evidenced in a general way in the preamble to the 1940 amendments to the Interstate Commerce Act — the National Transportation Policy, 54 Stat 899 — which articulates the congressional purpose that the Act be "so administered as to recognize and preserve the inherent advantages" of "all modes of transportation." More particularly, Congress' attitude is reflected by a proviso to Section 5(2) (b) of the Act, which enjoins the Commission to withhold approval of an acquisition by a railroad of a motor carrier "unless it finds that the transaction proposed will be consistent with the public interest and will enable such carrier to use service by motor vehicle to public advantage in its operations and will not unduly restrain competition."

The Commission long ago concluded that the policy of the transportation legislation requires that the standards of Section 5(2) (b) — then Section 213(a) of the Motor Carrier Act of 1935, 49 Stat 555 — be followed as a general rule in other situations, notably in applications for common carrier certificates of convenience and necessity under Section 207. Kansas City Southern Transport Co., Common Carrier Application, 10 MCC 221 (1938). And this court has confirmed the correctness of the Commission's conception of its responsibilities under both Section 5(2) (b) and Section 207. See United States v. Rock Island Motor Transit Co. 340 U.S. 419, 95 L. ed. 391, 71 S Ct 382; United States v. Texas & P. Motor Transport Co. 340 U.S. 450, 95 L. ed. 409, 71 S Ct 422; Interstate Com-

[267]340 U.S. 419, 430-431.
[268]364 U.S. 7. *See Pacific M. T. Ext.,* 92 M.C.C. 774.

merce Com. v. Parker, 326 U.S. 60, 89 L. ed. 2051, 65 S Ct 1490. The court has also taken cognizance of the congressional confirmation of the Commission's policy by the 1940 re-enactment in Section 5(2) (b) of the provisions of Section 213(a), after some of the pertinent Commission decisions had been specifically called to Congress' attention. See United States v. Rock Island Motor Transit Co., supra (340 U.S. at 432). And although the instant proceeding involves contract carrier applications and hence falls under Section 209, the Commission in its opinion recognized that, for purposes of the relevance of the Section 5(2) (b) standards, there is no distinction between this type of case and proceedings arising under Section 207. 77 MCC 621-622. Nor can we discern any grounds for differentiation.

Thus it is evident that the policy of opposition to railroad incursions into the field of motor carrier service has become firmly entrenched as a part of our transportation law. Moreover, this general policy fortunately has not been implemented by way of a more or less unguided suspicion of railroad subsidiaries, but rather has evolved through a series of Commission decisions from embryonic form into a set of reasonably firm, concrete standards. The Commission's opinion in the case at bar describes these standards as follows:

> The restrictions usually imposed in common-carrier certificates issued to rail carriers or their affiliates in order to insure that the service rendered thereunder shall be no more than that which is auxiliary to or supplemental of train service are: (1) the service by motor vehicle to be performed by rail carrier or by a rail-controlled motor subsidiary should be limited to service which is auxiliary to or supplemental of rail service, (2) applicant shall not serve any point not a station on the railroad, (3) a keypoint requirement or a requirement that shipments transported by motor shall be limited to those which it receives from or delivers to the railroad under a through bill of lading at rail rates covering, in addition to the movement by applicant, a prior or subsequent movement by rail, (4) all contracts between the rail carrier and the motor carrier shall be reported to the Commission and shall be subject to revision if and as the Commission finds it to be necessary in order that such arrangements shall be fair and equitable to the parties, and (5) such further specific conditions as the Commission, in the future, may find it necessary to impose in order to insure that the service shall be auxiliary to, or supplemental of, train service. . . .

The key phrase in this summary is obviously "auxiliary to or supplemental of train service." If a trucking service can fairly be so characterized, it is clear enough that there is compliance with the mandate of Section 5(2) (b) that the carrier should be able "to use service by motor vehicle to public advantage *in its operations.*" But if, on the other hand, the motor transportation is essentially unrelated to rail service, the railroad parent is invading the field of trucking, and, under normal circumstances, the National Transportation Policy is thereby offended.

It is this "auxiliary to or supplemental of" verbalization of the policy of Section 5(2) (b), as applied to Section 207, that has found favor in this court. See American Trucking Assoc. v. United States, 355 US 141, 2 L. ed. 2d 158, 78 S Ct 165; United States v. Rock Island Motor Transit Co. 340 US 419, 95 L. ed. 391, 71 S Ct 382; supra; United States v. Texas & P. Motor Transport Co. 340 US 450, 95 L. ed. 409, 71 S Ct 422, supra; Interstate Commerce Com. v. Parker, 326 US 60, 89 L. ed. 2051, 65 S Ct 1490, supra. Moreover, while the court has not specified the more particularized restrictions which it might regard as essential constituents of the "auxiliary to or supplemental of" concept, it is significant that the court in Rock Island apparently accepted the Commission's view that the phrase implies a limitation of function, i.e., type of trucking service, and not merely a geographical limitation, i.e., place where the service is performed. 340 US, at 436-444.

But while the judicial and administrative current has run strongly in favor of auxiliary and supplemental restrictions on motor carrier subsidiaries of railroads, the Commission has determined, and this court has agreed, that the public interest may sometimes be promoted by not imposing such limitations. A prime example is American Trucking Assoc. v. United States, 355 US 141, 2 L. ed. 2d 158, 78 S Ct 165, supra, where the trucking service was not being performed adequately by independent motor concerns. We there observed that the mandatory provisions of Section 5(2) (b) do not appear in Section 207, and approved the Commission's policy of not attaching auxiliary and supplemental restrictions where "special circumstances" prevail. We concluded:

We repeat . . . that the underlying policy of Section 5(2) (b) must not be divorced from proceedings for new certificates under Section 207. Indeed, the Commission must take "cognizance" of the National Transportation Policy and apply the Act "as a whole." But . . . we do not believe that the Commission acts beyond its statutory authority when in the public interest it occasionally departs from the auxiliary and supplementary limitations in a Section 207 proceeding. 355 US at 151, 152.

Water Carriers — Consolidation or Merger

The transfer of certificates and permits of water carriers when not subject to jurisdiction under Section 5 of the I.C. Act, are governed by Section 312,[269] and the rules and regulations prescribed thereunder. Section 5(2) (b) provides, among other things, that the Commission shall approve proposed transactions within the scope of that section when it finds such transactions will be consistent with the public interest. Section 312, relating to the transfer of certificates and permits of water carriers, reads as follows:

[269]49 U.S.C. 912. Comparable provisions — Sec. 212(b), 410(g).

Except as provided in this part, any such certificate or permit may be transferred in accordance with such regulations as the Commission shall prescribe for the protection of the public interest and to insure compliance with the provisions of this part.

The legal import of the aforementioned provisions and the rules was discussed in some detail in the report of the Commission on reconsideration in *Pittsburgh Towing Co. — Certificate Transfer — Zubik.*[270]

In the *Zubik* case, the Commission observed that Sections 312 and 212(b) were similar in language and reasoned that their intent (Section 312 provides that except as provided in Section 5, any certificate or permit may be transferred, pursuant to such rules and regulations as the Commission may prescribe), namely to facilitate transfers not subject to Section 5, was likewise similar. The Commission also pointed to the similarity between the transfer regulations under Section 312 and those under Section 212(b)[271] and emphasized that approval or disapproval of transfers of operating rights under Sections 312 or 212(b) depends solely upon the conformance or nonconformance with the appurtenant transfer rules and regulations and not upon the stricter criteria set out under Section 5, citing cases.[272] Significantly, the Commission found for the proposition that operating rights might be freely transferred under Section 312 or Section 212(b) "so long as the public interest was not harmed thereby."

Among the factors to be considered in determining the question of consistency with the public interest are the immediate and prospective traffic requirements in the affected territory, the needs of the shippers, the ability of the prospective purchaser to provide the proposed service, the adequacy of the service of the existing carriers, whether the proposed service would divert traffic from them and impair their ability to serve the shipping public, and whether unsound economic conditions in the water-carrier industry would result from approval of the proposed transaction. *Upper Columbia River Towing Co. Purchase.*[273]

Pursuant to the foregoing section, the Commission adopted and prescribed rules and regulations governing transfers of certificates and permits to operate as a water carrier in interstate or foreign commerce. Section 306.9 thereof[274] reads as follows:

[270]324 I.C.C. 460.
[271]See 49 CFR 179.
[272]*Virginia Stage Lines, Inc., v. United States,* 48 F. Supp. 79; *Stearn and Hartman v. United States,* 87 F. Supp. 96; *United States v. Resler,* 313 U.S. 57; *County of Marin v. United States,* 356 U.S. 412; and *Wooton — Purchase — Columbia Truck Exp.,* 49 M.C.C. 586.
[273]265 I.C.C. 759, 769.
[274]49 CFR 306.9.

The transfer of any certificate or permit under which operations are not being conducted at the time of the proposed transfer will be approved only upon a showing that the suspension of the operations was caused by circumstances over which the holder of the certificate or permit had no control, and that the water-carrier operations authorized under the certificate or permit sought to be transferred will be consistent with the public interest.

The transfer regulations insofar as they govern the transfer of dormant operating rights were derived almost verbatim from a former motor carrier transfer rule under Section 212(b) which, as it now stands, still provides that dormant operating rights may be transferred — only upon a showing that the cessation of operations was caused by circumstances over which the holder of such operating rights had no control.[275]

In *Pan Atlantic S.S. Corp. — Purchase — Ogwilines, Inc.*,[276] the Commission held that since vendor, a non-operating water-carrier, continued to be a carrier within the meaning of Section 5(13) so long as its certificate remained outstanding, purchase of its certificate by an active water carrier fell squarely within the scope of Section 5(2) (a), and the rules prescribed under Section 312 governing transfer of water-carrier authority were inapplicable.

Intermodal Acquisition: Rail-Water

The I.C. Act contains no special requirements which water carriers must satisfy in order to acquire a motor carrier. The Commission has ruled that the ordinary standards of Section 5(2) will apply. This is made clear from *TTC Corp. — Purchase — Terminal Transport Co., Inc.*,[277] where the Commission and the reviewing court determined upon the basis of a literal reading of Section 5(2) and after giving consideration to a Congressional policy, that a water carrier acquiring a motor carrier is not required by the I.C. Act to make affirmative proof that the proposed transaction will promote, further, or advance the public interest. All that is required is that the water carrier show that the transaction is consistent with the public interest — compatible and not contradictory or hostile to the public interest.

The basic statutory provisions to railroad-water carrier common

---

[275]See 49 CFR 1132.5.

[276]85 M.C.C. 485, 489.

[277]97 M.C.C. 380 (see also order of November 12, 1965); Sustained *sub nom. Atlantic Coast Line R. Co. v. United States*, 265 F. Supp. 549.

ownership are set forth in Sections 5(15)-(17), formerly 5(14)-(16), of the I.C. Act.[278] Section 5(17) provides:

Notwithstanding the provisions of paragraph (15), the Commission shall have authority, upon application of any carrier, as defined in Section 1(3), and after hearing, by order to authorize such carrier to own or acquire ownership of, to lease or operate, to have or acquire control of, or to have or acquire an interest in, a common carrier by water or vessel, not operated through the Panama Canal, with which the applicant does or may compete for traffic, if the Commission shall find that the continuance or acquisition of such ownership, lease, operation, control, or interest will not prevent such common carrier by water or vessel from being operated in the interest of the public and with advantage to the convenience and commerce of the people, and that it will not exclude, prevent, or reduce competition on the route by water under consideration: *Provided,* That if the transaction or interest sought to be entered into, continued, or acquired is within the scope of paragraph (2) (a), the provisions of paragraph (2) shall be applicable thereto in addition to the provisions of this paragraph. . . .

Section 5(16) confers jurisdiction on the Commission over applications filed for the purpose of determining whether existing service is in violation of Section 5(15), for the continuance of service, or for authorization under Section 5(17) of ownership, lease, operation, or control.

Section 5(17) is based on the Panama Canal Act of 1912. The underlying rationale of that Act generally is set forth in *Lake Line Applications Under Panama Canal Act.*[279] In that proceeding, several rail carriers, owning or having an interest in one or more boat lines plying the Great Lakes, sought extensions of time during which their ownership or interest in the operation of such boat lines could be continued. Although it was concluded that the applicants did or might compete for traffic with the lake lines in which they had an interest, the Commission pointed out that a mere finding that competition, actual or potential, did exist did not, ipso facto, require the separation of the petitioning railroads from the boat lines in which they were interested. In that proceeding the petitioners stated that the increased powers of the Commission under the Act, as amended, conferred full jurisdiction to regulate and control the lake line situation; therefore, the railroads

[278]For the underlying rationale of statutory provisions see *Lake Line Applications under Panama Canal Act,* 33 I.C.C. 700; *Southern Pac. Co. Operation, Pacific Mail S.S. Co.,* 32 I.C.C. 690; *Southern Pac. Co. Ownership of Atlantic S.S. Lines,* 43 I.C.C. 168; *Missouri Pac. R. Co. and T. & P. Ry. Co., Service by Water,* 245 I.C.C. 143; *Investigation of Seatrain Lines, Inc.,* 206 I.C.C. 328; *Direct Navigation Co.,* 46 I.C.C. 378; *Southern Pac. Co. Ownership of Atlantic Steamship Lines,* 77 I.C.C. 124.

[279]33 I.C.C. 700.

in the future could not use the boat lines to stifle competition on the Great Lakes. The Commission rejected the argument and concluded that none of the boat lines involved were being operated in the interest of the public, or with advantage to the convenience and commerce of the people within the meaning of the Act. In pointing out the purpose of the Panama Canal Act, the Commission stated at page 712 of the report:

> . . . From an examination of the congressional debate from which the act emerged, it is at once clear that the spirit which undoubtedly prompted this legislation was a desire to preserve to the common interest of the people, free and unfettered, the "water roadbed" via the Panama Canal, which was nearing completion. Coupled as it is, the legislative purpose of the other parts of the amendment with respect to waters "elsewhere" must necessarily have been to restore all the water routes of the country to the same condition of freedom from any domination that would reduce their usefulness.

> For any case to be within the spirit of this proviso it is necessary to show a situation in which are present all the elements which prevail, or would prevail, were the water service independently operated. On a watercourse where the boats and boat lines are free from domination or control by the railroads, and where they are left to survive as their merit or the ingenuity of their owners make possible, there will be, and always is, a healthy rivalry and striving between such boat lines themselves and with paralleling railroads for all suitable and available traffic. There is competition. . . .

In *Application S. P. Co. In Re Operation S. S. Co.*,[280] the Commission considered the phrase "does or may compete for traffic," which appears in Section 5(17), and it was stated at page 694:

This section of the Panama Canal Act indicates, among other things, a clear, unmistakable policy, adopted by Congress, to separate from railroad ownership, control, or influence such common carrier water lines, and such vessels, as may, when thus separated, compete with the present owning or controlling companies, except where, upon investigation, it is found by the Commission that the existing service by water, other than through the Panama Canal, is being operated in the interest of the public, is of advantage to the convenience and commerce of the people, and that its continuance will neither exclude, nor reduce competition on the route by water. This being so, a construction of the act must be adopted which will properly and effectively carry out the purpose of Congress. The Commission may not nullify or weaken the force of the plain intendment of the act for any reasons, however, plausible they may appear to be. The words "may compete for traffic" do not mean a vague, possible through improbable competition, but mean a probable, potential competition, as when

---

[280] 32 I.C.C. 690.

the water line is entirely divorced from the railroad. We must, therefore, look at the conditions as they will exist if this divorce is effected. From a practical view the question is, will the steamship company, when free to consult only its own interests, compete for traffic with the railroad line? . . .

In *S. P. Co. Ownership of Atlantic Steamship Lines,*[281] involving an application of Southern Pacific to continue in control of Atlantic Steamship Lines, also known as the Morgan line, the Commission found that the rail and water carrier did or might compete for traffic between certain points, but concluded that an extension of time during which the railroad might continue to operate or have an interest in the water carrier would neither exclude, prevent, nor reduce competition on the routes by water under consideration. In reaching that conclusion, it was noted at page 172:

> While the above circumstances tend to show that the petitioner's interest in these steamship lines excludes, prevents, or reduces competition on these water routes, yet the record leads us to conclude that a severance of the joint ownership might have a still greater tendency to reduce competition. Of the large number of shipping interests represented at the hearing, not a single one advocated the divorcement of the Morgan line from the Southern Pacific system. Many disinterested witnesses, who have had years of familiarity with transportation conditions, expressed the conviction that a severance of the Morgan line from the Southern Pacific Company would be a calamity. This view was founded on the belief that if these lines were separated the steamships would be transferred to the other service and the Sunset-Gulf route would be temporarily, if not permanently, disrupted. . . .

In the report of the Commission on further hearing, which involved a request by the Southern Pacific to add to the service of the water carrier between New York City and points in Texas, the right to serve the added ports of Norfolk, Newport News, and Portsmouth, Va., the Commission in approving the request stated that (pp. 433-4):

> Applicant contends that the establishment of this proposed service will create rather than reduce or prevent competition on the routes by water. This contention seems warranted by the fact that services have been inaugurated by the two independent lines. It is shown, furthermore, that independent lines have for years operated successfully in competition with the applicant under rates from Atlantic seaboard territory to the Southwest that are equalized through New York, Philadelphia, and Baltimore. The Southern Pacific has no rails of its own paralleling its water lines between the ports here under consideration. While it has been found in the prior reports herein that applicant, together with its rail connections, forms all-rail routes, and, in connection with its steamship lines, also forms rail-water routes which may compete for traffic with

[281]43 I.C.C. 168; further hearing, 206 I.C.C. 427.

its all-rail routes within the meaning of the act, the fact should not be overlooked that its water lines are, in practical effect, supplements to its rail lines, acting as feeders to gather up and distribute traffic, and their coordination makes possible the fullest development of water transportation and improved service to the shipper.

Section 5 of the act was not intended to forbid railroad ownership, operation, or control of steamship lines, but to forbid the use of such ownership or control in a manner which will restrict the movement of interstate commerce in the interest of that railroad's competing rail lines. Such a condition is not here presented.

In the report of the Commission on further hearing, in *Investigation of Seatrain Lines, Inc.*,[282] the question was presented whether there was competition between the Missouri Pacific and Texas & Pacific and Seatrain Lines, in which the two rail carriers had an interest, and whether the interest of the rail carriers came within the provisions contemplated by Section 5(19) of the 1920 Act. There the two railroads only had a combined voting power in Seatrain Lines equal to 15.45 percent of its outstanding capital stock; they did not individually or jointly control Seatrain Lines or own, lease, or operate its vessels; and neither were they operated under a common management or control with Seatrain.

The evidence showed, however, that each had a member on Seatrain's board of directors, that Seatrain's operations were designed for the movement of railroad cars in non-break-bulk transportation, that Seatrain depended upon the rail carriers for its supply of rail cars, and that the operations of Seatrain afforded the two rail carriers through routes by water between points in the Southwest and points on the Atlantic Seaboard. The Commission therefore concluded that the two rail carriers had a vital interest in Seatrain and that such interest came within the purview of Section 5(19) of the 1920 Act. The rail carriers and Seatrain, however, did not have executive, operating, traffic, or other officials in common, and Seatrain had its own complete organization. The Commission thus concluded that notwithstanding the interest of the rail carriers and the competition between such carriers and Seatrain, the operation of the latter was in the public interest and with advantage to the convenience and commerce of the people, and would not exclude, prevent, or reduce competition on the route by water under consideration. In respect to the competition, the Commission stated at page 336.

The competition that is not to be excluded, prevented, nor reduced as a result of a continuing interest in the route by water of the applicant rail carriers is competition on the route by water under consideration. Seatrain

[282]206 I.C.C. 328.

has provided a service that has created additional competition on the route by water, and in so doing has received the active cooperation and assistance of applicants. The more cooperation and support Seatrain receives from applicants the more effective the competition it can offer. . . .

In the report of the Commission on further hearing in *Missouri Pac. R. Co. and T. & P. Ry. Co., Service by Water*,[283] a proposal of Seatrain was involved to extend its service between Hoboken, N. J., and Texas City, Tex. The applicant railroads also were seeking reconsideration of the prior conclusion that their interest in Seatrain was such an interest as contemplated by then existing Section 5(19). In the interim, the 1940 amendments of the I.C. Act had been made and former paragraphs (19), (20) and (21) were replaced by present paragraphs (15), (16) and (17). The Commission concluded that the basis for the prior conclusion had not changed in any material respect, that essentially Section 5(15) was the same as former Section 5(19), and that applicants' interest was contemplated by Sections 5(14). The Commission stated that the revisions of the I.C. Act made it clear that paragraph (17), like paragraph (15), was directed primarily to interests by railroad companies in competing water lines. This was the matter to be brought under control. It was not the operation of the water line in and of itself. The Commission further noted at page 150 of the report:

> The facts contained in the record as a whole show that Seatrain is independently operated, and that applicants are not in a position to dominate its operations. There is no evidence to show that applicants' minority stock ownership (amounting to less than 16 percent of the voting power) tends to have an adverse effect on the public interest, which the provisions of Section 5(14)-(16) were designed to protect. The record warrants the conclusion that, if applicants divested themselves of their interest in Seatrain, the latter's operations would continue as they have been, and that the extent and character of the competition between applicants and Seatrain and between Seatrain and competing water carriers would be unchanged.

In *Illinois Central R. Co. — Control — John I. Hay Co.*,[284] the Commission denied the authority sought by two railroads under Section 5(2) of the I.C. Act to acquire control of Hay, a water carrier, and also to acquire control of that carrier under Section 5(17). Although the railroads represented that the water carrier would be operated independently, the Commission found not only that Hay would be controlled by the railroads, but also that Hay's all-water service would be managed in

---

[283] 245 I.C.C. 143.
[284] 317 I.C.C. 39.

such a way as to serve the interests of the controlling railroads and to enhance the movement of traffic over all-rail routes. The Commission thus could not make the statutory findings under Section 5(17) that the proposed acquisition of control would not prevent the water carrier from being operated in the interest of the public and with advantage to the convenience and commerce of the people. The special burden imposed by Section 5(7) is applicable only to railroads.

In the *Hay* case, the Commission found that the competitive advantage accruing to the water carrier because of railroad backing would be substantial, and foresaw possible complete elimination of competition on the water routes involved. It also found that the fears of protestants that Hay's acquired advantages would be so great as to jeopardize their competitive position, and the continuance of independent water operations, were well-founded. It, therefore, concluded that it could not find that the transaction proposed, if approved, would not exclude, prevent, or reduce competition on the water routes under consideration, or that it would be consistent with the public interest.

In *Southern Ry. Co. Section 5(15) Application*,[285] Southern Railway organized a subsidiary barge line known as Southern Region Coal Transport, Inc. (SRCT) for the purpose of transporting coal from Illinois and Kentucky mine fields down the Ohio and Tennessee Rivers to a transloader owned by Southern at Sheffield, Alabama, and thence by Southern's own rail system to landlocked power plants at various points in the Southeast. Southern filed an application under Section 5(16) requesting the Commission to find that its operation of SRCT as a barge subsidiary would not violate Section 5(15) and even if it did, that it be authorized under Section 5(17). Southern's application was referred to a hearing officer who found Southern neither did nor would tend to compete with its barge subsidiary under Section 5(15) if the application were granted. Although it was unnecessary for the hearing officer to pursue his inquiry, he found that if the Section 5(15) ban were applicable, Section 5(16) would not save the arrangement. The Commission accepted the hearing officer's findings and conclusions of no competition under Section 5(15), but rejected those under Section 5(17) finding instead that the arrangement could be sanctioned under the latter provision notwithstanding a finding of competition under the former.

---

[285] 342 I.C.C. 416, aff'd *sub nom. American Waterways Operators, Inc. v. United States,* 386 F. Supp. 799.

Freight Forwarders — Consolidation or Merger

Section 410(g)[286] provides that any "permit, or any right to engage in service subject to this part pending disposition of any application made to the Commission for a permit, and any right to a permit when issued, may be transferred, in accordance with such rules and regulations as the Commission shall prescribe to insure compliance with the provisions of this part, if the Commission finds that, with respect to the service covered by such right or permit, the transferee thereof satisfies the conditions prescribed in subsection (c) with respect to the original issuance of permits: *Provided*, However, that if the proposed transfer would affect the interests of employees of a freight forwarder, the Commission shall require, as a prerequisite thereto, a fair and equitable arrangement to protect the interests of the employees affected."

Congressional policy of promoting the development of different modes of transportation independent of conflicting interests has been carried forward into Part IV of the I.C. Act. The pertinent provisions in Part IV are:

Section 410(c). The Commission shall issue a permit to any qualified applicant therefor. . . . No such (freight forwarder) permit shall be issued to any common carrier subject to Part I, II, or III of this Act; but no application made under this section by a corporation controlled by, or under common control with, a common carrier subject to Part I, II, or III of this Act, shall be denied because of the relationship between such corporation and such common carrier.

Section 411(a) (1). It shall be unlawful for a freight forwarder, or any person controlling, controlled by, or under common control with a freight forwarder, to acquire control of a carrier subject to Part I, II, or III of this Act; except that this subsection shall not limit the right of any carrier subject to Part I, II, or III of this Act to acquire control of any other carrier subject to Part I, II, or III of this Act in accordance with the provisions of Section 5 of Part I of this Act.

Section 411(c). After the expiration of six months from the date of the enactment of this part it shall be unlawful for any director, officer, employee, or agent of any common carrier subject to Part I, II, or III of this Act or of any person controlling, controlled by, or under common control with such a common carrier, in his or their own personal pecuniary interest, to own, lease, control, or hold stock in, any freight forwarder, directly or indirectly; but this subsection shall not forbid or preclude the holding of a director's qualifying shares of stock from which no personal pecuniary benefit is derived by the holder.

---

[286] 49 U.S.C. 1010(g). Comp. provisions — Sec. 5(2), 212(b), 312 as to transfer of operating rights; Sec. 5(2) (c), (f) as to protection of employees; and Sec. 17(11) as to intervention by employees' representatives.

Section 411(g). Nothing in this Act shall be construed to make it unlawful for any common carrier subject to Part I, II, or III of this Act, or any person controlling such a common carrier, to have or acquire control of a freight forwarder or freight forwarders; and in any case where such control exists, no rate, charge, classifications, rule, regulation, or practice of the common carrier or of any freight forwarder controlled by such common carrier or under common control with such common carrier, shall be held unlawful under any provision of this Act because of the relationship between such common carrier and such freight forwarder.

Under Section 410(c) no freight forwarder permit "shall be issued to any common carrier subject to Part I, II, or III" of the I.C. Act. However, if an application is made under Section 410(c) "by a corporation controlled by, or under common control with, a common carrier subject to Part I, II, or III" it shall not be denied "because of the relationship between such corporation and such common carrier."

Section 411(g) has been construed as allowing a person to directly control both freight forwarders and a carrier or carriers under Parts I, II, and III of the I.C. Act, notwithstanding the prohibition in Section 411(c). This construction implies that the controlling person's interest in a freight forwarder or forwarders would not be adverse to the other carriers within the apparent intent of Section 411(c).

In *Ownership of Stock in Freight Forwarders*,[287] Sections 411(c) and 411(g) were said to have been intended to allow a carrier to conduct forwarder operations through a subsidiary but that the carrier's control of the forwarder must be direct rather than indirect through common officers. In *Ownership of Stock in Freight Forwarders*, the proceeding was dismissed against respondent Bacon, who had control of two motor carriers and a minority stock interest in a freight forwarder, after he acquired a controlling interest in the freight forwarder. Bacon's acquisition of the controlling interest in the freight forwarder was considered to have rectified what had previously been an unlawful situation. In considering the provisions in Part IV of the I.C. Act, the Commission stated:

> In the case of seeming conflict in the provisions of a statute, the construction should be such that both provisions, if possible, may stand. *United States v. Moore*, 95 U.S. 760, 763. Repugnancy in a statute should, if practicable, be avoided, and if the natural import of the words contained in the respective provisions tends to establish such a result, resort may be had to construction for the purpose of reconciling the inconsistency, unless it appears that the difficulty cannot be overcome without doing violence to the language of the lawmaker. *Lamp Chimney Co. v. Brass & Copper Co.*, 91 U.S. 656, 663. And in *United States v. Louisville & N. R. Co.*, 235

[287]265 I.C.C. 75.

U.S. 314, the court, at page 326, recognized "the rule which requires that a practice which is permitted by one section should not be prohibited on the theory that it is forbidden by another."

It is to be noted that Section 411(g) provides a rule of construction with respect to provisions of the Act concerning certain forwarder relations. Where in an Act it is declared that it shall receive a certain construction, the courts are bound by that construction, though otherwise the language would have been held to mean a different thing. *Smith v. State*, 28 Ind. 321, 325. See also *United States v. Gilmore*, 75 U.S. (8 Wall.) 330, wherein the court impliedly considered as binding upon it a provision in an Act of Congress that said Act should not be construed in a certain designated manner. . . .

From the foregoing it follows that Section 411(g) is to be observed as the controlling rule of construction in ascertaining the meaning of Section 411(c), and in the event the conflict between these paragraphs is irreconcilable, the provisions of Section 411(c) must yield to those of Section 411(g). *Farmer's Bank v. Hale*, 59 N. Y. (14 Sickels) 53.

An examination of the first clause of the language found in Section 411(a) (1) shows that it constitutes an absolute prohibition against "a freight forwarder, or any person controlling, controlled by, or under common control with a freight forwarder" acquiring control of a carrier subject to Part I, II, or III of the I.C. Act. The second clause, however, constitutes an exception to the absolute prohibition. The language states that Section 411(a) (1) "shall not limit the right of any carrier subject to Part I, II, or III" "to acquire control of any other carrier subject to Part I, II, or III" under provisions of Section 5.

Section 411, according to its legislative history, was drafted to guard against freight forwarder direct domination of other carriers. The exception to 411(a) (1), however, which is similar to that adopted in the passage of the Panama Canal Act, appears to be intended to make inapplicable the prohibition in the first part of 411(a) (1), where the transaction falls within the limits provided therein. In construing this statutory language, the Commission has used the same construction applied by it in determining the meaning of Section 411(c). While bearing in mind that a freight forwarder may not acquire control of a carrier, it has construed Section 411(g) and the exception in Section 411(a) (1) together and observed the former section as the controlling rule of construction in ascertaining the meaning of what would appear to be conflicting sections. Under this construction it has determined that a Part I, II, or III carrier, which is under common control with a freight forwarder, may properly acquire control of a Part I, II, or III carrier.

The Commission gave consideration to the language of Section 411

(a) (1) in *Howard Term. — Control — Eldorado Motor Transp. Co.*,[288] where it is stated that the exception in Section 411(a) (1) is a saving clause. There the vendee, which was a freight forwarder and motor carrier, was authorized to purchase the operating rights of another motor carrier after the vendee had transferred its freight forwarder authority to a subsidiary corporation newly created to receive such authority, and the stockholders of the vendee authorized to assume control of the vendor, another motor carrier. In a subsequent proceeding the merger of the vendor and vendee motor carrier was authorized. It was the view in that proceeding that, although authority might not be given to a freight forwarder to acquire direct control of a motor carrier because of the prohibition in Section 411(a) (1), the Commission was free to authorize a motor carrier which controls a freight forwarder to acquire control of another motor carrier and to authorize the controlling stockholders of the parent company to gain control of the acquired motor carrier. This same approach was followed in *Calore Exp. Co., Inc. — Control and Merger.*[289] There it is stated, "Since Calore (R.I.) already controls Calore (Mass.) and Joseph C. Calore already controls both motor carriers and a freight forwarder, and since all three carriers are the alter ego of Joseph C. Calore, we do not believe the interest of Joseph C. Calore in the freight forwarder is or will be adverse to that of the motor carriers as contemplated by the statute."[290]

In Ex Parte 266, *Investigation Into The Status of Freight Forwarders,*[291] the Commission discussed the right of forwarder to control, and be controlled by, other modes and non-related transportation interests as follows (sheets 136-38):

> Sections 410(c) and 411 of the act govern the relationship that may exist between persons controlling and controlled by forwarders. Thus, forwarders may not acquire control of common carriers subject to parts I, II, and III of the act. Nor can such carriers obtain freight forwarder permits. Common carriers subject to parts I, II, and III, and persons controlling such common carriers, however, may obtain control of forwarders. The general tenor of the above provisions is that: (a) common carriers by rail, motor, and water, do not need, and therefore will not receive, freight forwarding permits to operate within the lawful scope of their authorities, *Continental Dispatch, Inc., Common Carrier Application*, 95 M.C.C. 483 (1964); (b) forwarders should not be allowed to control underlying modes of transportation, see *Glendenning Motorways, Inc. — Pur. — Moland Bros.*

[288]70 M.C.C. 494.
[289]87 M.C.C. 379.
[290]See also Docket No. MC-F-8505, *Lasham Cartage Co. — Control — Seatrain Lines, Inc.*, recommended report and order of Examiner, served August 31, 1964.
[291]Report served January 25, 1977.

Trucking, 93 M.C.C. 174 (1963); and (c) the underlying carrier modes may control forwarders.

In other words, the provisions of sections 411(g), when taken together, lead to the following confusing results: a person who initially gains control of a common carrier subject to parts I, II, or III of the act may subsequently acquire control of a forwarder, but a person cannot first acquire control of a common carrier; a person who acquires control of a common carrier and a forwarder, in that order, cannot later acquire control of another common carrier, although the common carrier controlled by such person can acquire control of another common carrier.

The act also prohibits any person whose principal business is manufacturing or selling, and whose business operations are such that freight forwarders are commonly used, from engaging in service subject to part IV. This appears to be in general conformity with this Commission's attitude about the users of a common carrier service having such control of that service that their traffic may be preferred over that of other shippers. Cf. *Alter Trucking and Terminal Corporation Extension,* 107 M.C.C. 644 (1967), affd. *Alter Trucking and Terminal Corp. v. United States,* 299 F. Supp. 819 (S.D. Iowa, 1969). Such a person may, however, receive a freight forwarding permit if, in addition to the other criteria, a specific finding it made that the proposed service will be consistent with the public interest and with the national transportation policy. Cf. *Encinal Terminals — Control — Shippers Express Co.,* 109 M.C.C. 536 (1970).

It appears that legislative efforts to preclude forwarder control of common carriers have been largely unsuccessful. The statutory language does not actually proscribe such control; rather, it prohibits a forwarder from acquiring control of an underlying carrier. This requirement has been readily circumvented by having the motor carrier first obtain a certificate under part II, and then having the motor carrier obtain control of the forwarder.

49

Trackage Rights

Commission Vested with Authority to Prescribe Terms and Conditions

By the Transportation Act of 1940 the Interstate Commerce Commission received new, explicit power over trackage rights. Section 5(2) (a) (ii) of the Interstate Commerce Act[1] provides: "It shall be lawful, with the approval and authorization of the Commission . . . for a carrier by railroad to acquire trackage rights over, or joint ownership in or joint use of, any railroad line or lines owned or operated by any other such carrier, and terminals incidentally thereto." Section 5(5) of the I.C. Act[2] makes it unlawful to acquire trackage rights other than as provided for in Section 5(2) (a) (ii). Joint ownership or joint use of spur, industrial, team, switching or side tracks is exempt from Commission approval and authorization under the provisions of Section 1(18) of the I.C. Act.[3]

Section 5(2)(a) of the I.C. Act vests in the Commission, not the courts, authority to prescribe terms and conditions under which trackage rights may be acquired. The jurisdiction of the Commission is exclusive. As pointed out in *Thompson v. Texas Mexican R. Co.*,[4] it is for the Commission to determine the terms and conditions under which trackage rights are acquired. If it were otherwise and parties were allowed to bypass the Commission and litigate the question in the courts, the power to fix the rental under trackage agreements would be shifted from the Commission to the courts and juries, which would mean that verdicts or settlement would take the place of the expert and informed judgment of the Commission. The Supreme Court pointed out (p. 148) that the

[1] 49 U.S.C. 5(2) (a) (ii).
[2] 49 U.S.C. 5(5).
[3] 49 U.S.C. 1(18).
[4] 328 U.S. 134, 147-8.

989

major concern of Congress in dealing with this problem was that neither inadequate rentals nor exorbitant nor unreasonable exactions would be made for trackage rights.[5] "Those questions intimately relate to the financial strength of carriers. And it is one of the Commission's high functions to protect the public interest against unfair or oppressive financial practices which in the past led to such great havoc and disaster." (p. 148)

Transactions under Section 5(2) (a) Resulting in Extensions

Acquisition of trackage rights as well as other transactions coming within the scope of Section 5(2) (a) frequently result in an extension of an applicant's service into areas not theretofore served. Such transaction for the acquisition of trackage rights, however, is not an extension requiring a certificate of public convenience and necessity. Under the provisions of Section 5(2), as decided in *Chicago, B & Q. R. Co. Control*,[6] the Commission need find only that a proposed transaction is within the scope of Section 5(2) (a) and will be consistent with the public interest. It is not necessary for the Commission to find that the present and future public convenience and necessity require or will require the transaction. As provided by subparagraph (c) of Section 5(2), weight must be given by the Commission to the following considerations, among others: The effect of the proposed transaction upon adequate transportation service to the public; the effect upon the public interest of the inclusion, or failure to include, other railroads in the territory involved in the proposed transaction; the total fixed charges resulting from the proposed transaction; and the interest of the carrier employees affected. The Commission must also administer the provisions of Section 5(2) with a view to carrying out the national transportation policy as announced in the Transportation Act of 1940.

The ruling of the Commission in *Chicago B. & Q. R. Co. Control* that under the provisions of Section 5(2) it is not necessary that the present and future public convenience and necessity require or will require the transaction was followed in *International-G. N. R. Co. Trustee Trackage Rights*.[7] There applicant applied not only under Section 5(2) but prayed relief in the alternative under Section 1(18) if this section should be found applicable. Inasmuch as the transaction proposed related to operation by the applicant over a track already in place and operated by

[5]See also *Transit Commission v. United States*, 289 U.S. 121, 128.
[6]271 I.C.C. 63, 67.
[7]275 I.C.C. 27, 282 I.C.C. 30.

another carrier, the Commission held (p. 33) that it was governed by Section 5(2) and not by Section 1(18).

Judicial Questions

The question of what constitutes a spur, industrial, team, switching, or side track within the meaning of Section 1(18) was determined by the Commission in *Central R. Co. of New Jersey Trustees Acquisition.*[8] In that case an application had been filed for authority to acquire trackage rights for switching purposes only over certain segments of track which the owning railroads considered parts of their main lines. The application was dismissed on the ground that the trackage operation involved came within the exemption provided in Section 1(18). At page 348 of the report, the Commission said "our jurisdiction over acquisitions of trackage rights is controlled by the use to be made by the applicant of the tracks involved, and not by the use made thereof, or the classification thereof, by the carrier or carriers which own the tracks."

Similar conclusions were reached by the Commission in *Texas & P. Ry. Co. Operation,*[9] wherein it was held that approval was not necessary for the operation by the Texas & Pacific, for switching purposes only, over 1,340 feet of tracks owned by the Illinois Central Railroad forming a connection with the Public Belt Railroad and New Orleans Terminal Railroad, and seven miles of track of the latter; in *Kansas City S. Ry. Co. Purchase,*[10] wherein it was held that approval was not necessary for use by the Kansas City Southern, for switching purposes only, of certain tracks of the Louisiana & Arkansas, one of which tracks in addition to use by the latter for switching purposes was used also for several of its scheduled trains; and *St. Louis S. F. & T. Ry. Co. Trackage Rights,*[11] wherein it was held approval was not necessary for use by the Frisco, for switching purposes only, of certain tracks of the Gulf, Colorado & Santa Fe Ry. Co.

The operations involved in *St. Louis, S. F. & T. Ry. Co. Trackage Rights* and *Central R. Co. of New Jersey Trustee Acquisition* in general consisted of yard operations at inland cities ordinarily performed in the movement of cars to, from, or over certain interchange tracks preliminary to the beginning of the final journey. Where an operation, however, envisioned the movement either of several passenger cars together or

[8] 254 I.C.C. 344.
[9] 247 I.C.C. 285.
[10] 252 I.C.C. 113.
[11] 267 I.C.C. 30.

complete passenger trains not as a preliminary movement but in continuation of their through journey, the movement of freight cars not as a preliminary switching movement for the purpose of sorting or assembling cars to prepare them for a through continuous journey but as a part of that journey itself, and applicant admitted that the track involved was a part of the main line of railroad, the Commission held in *International-G. N. R. Co. Trustee Trackage Rights, supra,* that the track, insofar as the use to be made of it by applicant was concerned, was not a switching track within the meaning and intention of Section 1(18).

The Commission viewed the track as "something more than an ordinary switching track such as was intended to be placed within the exemption" provision of the I.C. Act, and stated that it was "unable to conclude that the only track leading to an international boundary line over which all the traffic of two carriers moving in foreign commerce through an important port or gateway is handled, is a switching track which never could be subject, under any circumstances, to our jurisdiction." (p. 38)

Determination of Reasonableness of Rental

Although the Commission has not adopted any particular formula for determining the reasonableness of a proposed rental for the use of a line of another carrier, and trackage rights have been approved upon varying bases it is noted that in many cases the element of value was a principal factor[12] and the Commission undoubtedly was convinced that the valuation of the property, together with the terms and conditions relating to the use thereof, under the circumstances there shown was just and reasonable. In *Gulf, M. & O. R. Co. Trackage Rights*[13] the Commission stated that its duty under Section 5(2) is to approve

[12]Interest charge of 2.5 percent annually on the reproduction cost less depreciation of the joint property, *Texas & N. O. R. Co. Abandonment,* 267 I.C.C. 819; one-half of 4 percent annually on the agreed value of joint property, *Atlantic & D. Ry. Co. Trackage Rights,* 271 I.C.C. 820; one-third of 6 percent annually on the agreed value of the joint property as of a certain date, plus additions, betterments, and improvements, *Northern Pac. Ry. Co. Operation,* 261 I.C.C. 819; 3 percent on agreed valuation of joint property, *Chicago, B. & Q. R. Co. Operation,* 261 I.C.C. 819; one-half of 6 percent annually on agreed value of joint property, *Great Northern Ry. Co. Operation,* 261 I.C.C. 819; 2 1/2 percent annually on agreed value of joint property less additions and betterments, *New Orleans, T. & M. Ry. Co., Trustee Trackage Rights,* 254 I.C.C. 841; 2 1/2 percent annually on the book value of the joint property plus additions and betterments, *Chicago, R. I. & P. R. Co. Construction,* 282 I.C.C. 802; 50 percent of 4.5 percent interest annually on the original principal amount of the owning carrier's outstanding bonds, *Chicago, B. & Q. R. Co. Trackage Rights,* 271 I.C.C. 675.

[13]282 I.C.C. 689, 693.

and authorize trackage agreements if it finds that, subject to such terms and conditions and such modifications as are found to be just and reasonable; the proposed transaction is within the scope of subparagraph (a) of Section 5(2) and will be consistent with the public interest; and that the words "just and reasonable" imply the application of good judgment and fairness, of common sense, and a sense of justice to the facts of record. In determining the reasonableness of the proposed rental of tracks in the *Gulf* case the Commission considered the value of the trackage rights to the applicant from an operating standpoint, together with the indicated value of the property itself as measured by its availability for the applicant's use, the cost of reproduction new thereof, and the cost which would have been incurred in constructing a similar line.

Trackage Rights Include an Operating Right

The trackage rights referred to in Section 5(2) (a) (ii) necessarily include an operating right. This was held to be so in *Chicago & E. I. R. Co. Trackage Rights*.[14] There the C&EI applied for authority to acquire trackage rights over the line of another railroad under an agreement which provided that the owner of the tracks would furnish all necessary locomotives and crews to transport cars, both loaded and empty, of the C&EI over the tracks involved. The joint tracks were to be maintained and kept in a good state of repair by the owner, and the management, maintenance, and operation were to be in that carrier's sole control. All cars, while being switched and handled by the owner of the tracks for the applicant, would remain in the account of and were deemed to be in possession of the latter. The applicant assumed per diem charges and was responsible for any demurrage accruing in the future, also liability for death or injury to persons, or for loss of or damage to any property, including its own cars and their contents.

In denying the application for authority to acquire trackage rights, the Commission stated at page 605 of its report:

> The agreement under consideration permits the applicant to extend its freight service to the mine, not by the operation of its own trains, but through the medium of the Milwaukee, and although it purports to grant trackage rights, the fact is that its very terms deprive the applicant of

---

[14]254 I.C.C. 603; See also *Louisiana, A & T. Ry. Co. Operation,* 170 I.C.C. 602, 611, where the Commission said that there is some question whether Section 1(18) contemplates the issuance of a certificate of public convenience and necessity where actual operation is not involved.

the right to operate. The terms and conditions of an agreement such as this do not appear to satisfy the requirements of the provision of section 5(2), referred to above.

In exceptions to the proposed report, the applicant contends, among other things, that the operating arrangement in question was made in lieu of the construction of an industrial spur to serve the mine, which could have been constructed without first obtaining our approval, inasmuch as it would be a spur track located wholly within one State. Determination of whether a line is a spur track or an extension is governed by the facts in each particular case. See *Marion & E. R. Co. v. Missouri Pac. R. Co.*, 149 N. E. 492, in which the court held under somewhat similar circumstances that the line under consideration was an extension and that approval of the construction by us was therefore required.

If the trackage right agreement provides that one railroad shall handle another railroad's traffic in line haul service at an unpublished charge per car or at a contract rate, it, in effect, excludes the right to operate, and the Commission, whose approval under Section 5(2) of the I.C. Act is necessary before the arrangement can be put in operation, will not approve.[15] The end result of a nonoperating trackage right arrangement, which in fact is not a trackage right arrangement at all, can be accomplished by an interchange of traffic between the two connecting railroads.

Trackage Rights Operation Involving Relocation of Line

The Commission has taken jurisdiction in proceedings where carriers applied for permission to abandon portions of their own lines and for authority to provide substitute operations under trackage rights over lines of other carriers, and to construct connecting tracks where necessary, even though there would be no change in the transportation service to the public.[16]

Revision of Trackage Agreements

By Section 5(10) of the I.C. Act,[17] the Commission may, for good cause shown, make such orders, supplemental to any order made under Section 5(2) as it deems necessary or appropriate. Thus, upon a proper showing, it might be found that the Commission has authority to revise a trackage

---

[15]*St. Louis & O'Fallon Ry. Co. v. East St. Louis & Suburban Ry. Co.*, 81 I.C.C. 538; *L. A. & T. Ry. Co. Operations*, 170 I.C.C. 602; *Chicago & E. I. R. Co. Trackage Rights*, 254 I.C.C. 603

[16]*Sacramento No. Ry. Trackage Rights*, 290 I.C.C. 145, 147.

[17]49 U.S.C. 5(10).

rights contract which has been approved under Section 5(2) as the parties are placed on notice on the Commission's continuing power in the premises.[18] However, Section 5(2) cannot be given retroactive effect so that the powers conferred the Commission may be used to interfere with a validly existing contract entered into previous to the enactment of that legislation and prior to the lawful termination of that agreement.[19]

Authority to Compel Granting of Trackage Rights

Although the Commission held in prior decisions that it was without power to compel one carrier to grant trackage rights over its line to another carrier,[20] it decided in *Fresno Passenger Terminal Case*[21] that it did not construe the language in Section 5(2) (b) as limiting the approval and authorization of trackage rights to applications of participating carriers to the exclusion of a state highway authority having a proper interest in the subject matter. In this proceeding the city of Fresno, California, sought an issuance of a certificate to the appropriate carrier permitting or authorizing the abandonment and construction of lines, and the entering of an order under Section 5(2) approving and authorizing proposed trackage and joint operations of terminal facilities. Both the certificate and order, if issued, would be permissive and not mandatory.

Motions to dismiss were filed by the carriers involved on the grounds that the prime objective of the application was a consolidation or partial consolidation of railroad facilities and operations under Section 5(2) which, they contended, could be approved and authorized by the Commission only when it was a carrier initiated voluntary plan and then solely upon application of the interested carriers or persons in control of or affiliated with such carriers; and that the city of Fresno was not a proper party applicant because it was neither a carrier nor a person in control or affiliated with either of the carriers involved and was not otherwise qualified either by applicable statutory provisions or by request or consent of the interested carriers to file the application. The specific question raised by the motions to dismiss was whether the Commission was empowered to improve and authorize trackage rights acquisition and joint operations of terminal facilities under Section 5(2)

---

[18]*Delaware & H. R. Corp. Trackage Agrement Modification,* 290 I.C.C. 103, 110.
[19]*Ibid.*
[20]*Baltimore & O. R. Co. Operation,* 261 I.C.C. 535, 544; *Construction by Alabama, Tennessee & Northern R.R.,* 124 I.C.C. 114, 115.
[21]290 I.C.C. 753, 763. See also *City of Erie, Pa. Trackage Rights,* 328 I.C.C. 331.

upon the application of a municipal government in a proceeding adverse to the participating carriers and over their protests. The contentions of the carriers were considered by the Commission and disposed of in the following language (pp. 756-8):

> In support of their contentions that our authority to approve and authorize that portion of the applicant's proposal under Section 5(2) is to be exercised only with respect to voluntary plans of carriers or plans initiated by them, and that the city of Fresno is not a proper party applicant, the carriers rely on the legislative history of the 1940 amendments to the Interstate Commerce Act; on various court cases, including *Thompson v. Texas Mexican Ry. Co.*, 328 U.S. 134 (1946), *Schwabacher v. United States*, 334 U.S. 182 (1948), and *St. Joe Paper Co. v. Atlantic Coast Line R. Co.*, 347 U.S. 298 (1954); and on decisions of this Commission which exemplify voluntary transactions contemplated by Section 5(2) as distinguished from compulsory measures. It is the carriers' argument that it was the congressional intent, as shown by the legislative history, to provide a voluntary plan of consolidation in lieu of the prior existing law authorizing us to prepare and adopt a plan for the consolidation of railway properties; that Section 5(2) of the 1940 Transportation Act, provides for such voluntary plans of consolidation; and that trackage rights are consensual agreements since they are now incorporated under Section 5(2).

The reason for the change in the trackage-rights provisions from Section 1(18) to Section 5(2) is explained in the following extract from a Senate report on legislation considered in the enactment of the 1940 law:

> A further change to be observed is in the treatment of trackage rights. The Commission now considers trackage rights under Section 1(18) dealing with certificates of convenience and necessity for the extension of lines of railroad. . . . Trackage rights represent one aspect of the general subject of unification and it seems proper to deal with them as such, rather than in connection with the matter of certificates of convenience and necessity.

The carriers contend that under the *Texas Mexican Ry Case, supra,* our authority to approve plans of merger of consolidation under Section 5(2) is to be exercised only respecting "carrier-initiated voluntary plans," and quoted that portion of the opinion where the court said that prior to the Transportation Act of 1940, we had some jurisdiction over trackage agreements, but that by that act we had received "new, explicit powers over trackage rights." In the *Schwabacher case, supra,* which involved a merger of railway companies, the court said insofar as it might have some relevancy here, that the 1940 Transportation Act relieved us of formulating a nationwide plan of consolidation and that, instead, it authorizes approval by us of carrier-initiated voluntary plans of merger or consolidation.

The court held in the *St. Joe Paper Co.* case, *supra,* that we had no power to include a forced merger of railway properties in a plan of reorganization under Section 77 of the Bankruptcy Act. It was stated therein by the court that only mergers voluntarily initiated by the participating carriers are encompassed by that statute (49 U.S.C. Sec. 5) and sanctioned by it, that our role has traditionally been confined to approving or disapproving mergers proposed by the railroads to be merged, and that the very heart of Section 5 is that a merger of 2 carriers may be approved by us only if it originates as a voluntary proposal by the merging carriers. The carriers concede that the Supreme Court was there dealing with complete consolidations or mergers, but assert that the principles laid down are equally applicable to partial consolidations, such as those represented by the acquisition of trackage rights and the joint use of tracks and terminal facilities, for the reason that since 1940 complete consolidations and partial consolidations have rested upon common ground, and our power to authorize either derives from Section 5(2) of the act. We do not find that these court cases hold or convey the impression that a trackage right is to be considered the same as a merger or consolidation of railway properties, as contended. In not one of the cases relied upon by the carriers was the court or Commission confronted with the question as to whether we are empowered under Section 5(2) of the act to approve and authorize trackage rights acquisitions and joint operation of terminal facilities where such operations are initiated by a State authority without the participating carriers' consent, as is the case here. Those cases are not controlling, and neither does the legislative history lend much support to the carriers' contentions.

Interest of Carrier Employees

In proceedings under Section 5(2), the Commission is required to give consideration to "the interest of the carrier employees affected."[22]

---

[22]See Section 5(2)(c).

50

Unauthorized Acquisition

The Applicable Statutory Provisions

In it broadest terms,[1] Section 5(5) makes it unlawful, without Commission approval, to enter into any transaction within the scope of such approval, or to accomplish or effectuate, or to participate in accomplishing or effectuating, the control or management in a common interest of any two or more carriers, however such result is attained, whether directly or indirectly, by use of common directors, officers or stockholders, a holding or investment company or companies, a voting trust or trusts, or in any other manner whatsoever. As used in paragraphs (5) and (6) of Section 5, the words "control or management" shall be construed to include the power to exercise control or management. Section 5(6) provides that various transactions involving persons affiliated with a carrier "shall be deemed to accomplish or effectuate the control or management in a common interest of two carriers," such as a transaction by a person affiliated with a carrier, if the effect of such transaction is to place such carrier and persons affiliated with it, taken together, in control of another carrier. Section 5(7) provides that a person shall be held to be affiliated with a carrier if, by reason of the relationship of such person to such carrier, it is reasonable to believe that the affairs of any carrier of which control may be acquired by such person will be managed in the interest of such other carrier. Relationship may be by reason of the method of, or circumstances surrounding organization or operation, or whether established through common directors, officers or stockholders, a voting trust or trusts, a holding or investment company or companies, or any other direct or indirect means.

[1]*United States v. Marshall Transport Co.*, 322 U.S. 31, 38.

Under paragraph (7) of Section 5, affiliation between carriers exists if it is reasonable to believe that the affairs of one carrier will be managed in the interest of another in any material degree.[2] An ultimate finding of "affiliation" may be drawn from all the facts and circumstances of the case which establish that one will act in behalf of a carrier.[3]

Improper Advantage

When a merger or acquisition is subject to the Commission's jurisdiction, the carriers cannot be permitted to evade its jurisdiction by consummating in advance of approval certain segments of the transaction; this would be against the public interest.[4]

Unlawful control has been acquired in the past for the purpose of circumventing restrictions in existing operating rights. On occasions unlawful control of dormant companies has been attempted to expand operations. Sometimes the violations have occurred after denial of an application by the Commission; however, if the facts are uncovered, the Commission will not give any weight whatsoever to so called benefits which arise out of the unlawful control.[5]

[2]*Central of Georgia R.R. — Control*, 307 I.C.C. 39, 42-43; *Commercial Transport Corp. — Control — Commercial*, 65 M.C.C. 127, 153; *Greyhound Corp. — Investigation of Control — Southern Ltd.*, 45 M.C.C. 59, 77.

[3]*Nigro Freight Lines, Inc. — Purchase — Coady Trucking Co.*, 90 M.C.C. 113, 119-20.

[4]*Von Der Ahe Van Lines, Inc. — Lease and Purchase — Bee Line*, 87 M.C.C. 53, 60; *Interstate M. Frt. System — Purchase — Capital Frt. Lines, Inc.* 65 M.C.C. 37, 54; *Texas, N. Mex. & Okla. Coaches, Inc. — Purchase — Aaron*, 55 M.C.C. 269, 275.

[5]*Smithsons Holdings — Control — Ontario Frt. Lines Corp.*, 70 M.C.C. 628; *Coldway Food; Dorn's Transportation, Inc. — Purchase — Phillips Exp., Inc.*, 87 M.C.C. 111, 112, 116; *Congdon — Purchase — Watkins*, 50 M.C.C. 781, 784; *Krapf — Purchase — Altemose*, 85 M.C.C. 441, 443, 445; *Houff — Control — Elliott Bros. Trucking Co., Inc.*, 80 M.C.C. 637, 648; *Black — Investigation of Control*, 75 M.C.C. 275, 279; *Stacks — Investigation of Control*, 75 M.C.C. 625, 627, 637; *Von Der Ahe Van Lines*, 87 M.C.C. 53, 59; *Exley Express, Inc. — Purchase — Olsen*, 85 M.C.C. 396, 397, 399; *Houff Transfer v. United States*, 105 F. Supp. 851, 855; *Shein v. United States*, 102 F. Supp. 320, 324-326, aff'd 343 U.S. 944; *Falwell v. United States*, 69 F. Supp. 71, aff'd 330 U.S. 807; *Deaton Truck Line, Inc. — Purchase — Capitol Freight Lines, Inc.*, 70 M.C.C. 355, 360; *Cortland Fast Freight, Inc. — Purchase — H. J. Korten, Inc.*, 60 M.C.C. 321, 329; *Pacific Greyhound Lines — Control and Merger*, 56 M.C.C. 415, 438-439. The supplying of funds to allegedly independent third party purchasers is a type of informal practice the Supreme Court has cited as covered by Section 5(4) of the I.C. Act, and, thus requiring prior approval under Section 5(2). *Gilbertville Trucking Co. v. United States*, 371 U.S. 115, 125-6.

Control Is Measured under Various Standards

"Control" as used in the I.C. Act means actual as well as legal control whether obtained by direct or indirect means, and includes the existence of the power to control whether or not exercised.[6] The term "control" has been defined as follows by the Commission:[7]

> Control is generally defined to be the power or authority to manage, direct, superintend, restrict. regulate, govern, administer, or oversee. *Colletti — Control — Comet Freight Lines*, 38 M.C.C. 95. The existence of control is an issue of fact to be determined, not by artificial tests but by the circumstances of each case. *Rochester Telephone Corp. v. United States*, 307 U.S. 125. Control does not necessarily require ownership of a majority of a corporation's voting stock. On the other hand, ownership of less than a majority would not necessarily constitute control, unless such minority also commanded substantial influence and power over the corporation. *Compare Electric Bond & Share Co. v. Securities & Exc. Comm.*, 92 F. (2d) 580, wherein the court said:
>
> > practical control is often exercised, and retained, through ownership by those who are already in managerial control of a substantial minority of the voting power.

In *Colletti — Control — Comet Freight Lines*,[8] the Commission said:

> Section 5 is remedial in character and should be liberally construed. It is clear that the section was intended to cover acquisitions of control by any means and irrespective of whether or not the person holding control might legally enforce such control.

⁂ ⁂ ⁂

> It is obvious that there may, and do exist different types of control. For instance, there may be absolute control, which would imply complete dominion over the subject matter; or there may be joint control, as where two persons have equal power thereover; there may be direct or indirect control; or there may be actual as distinguished from legal control. The words "control or management" as used in Section 5 embrace all forms and types of control or management. Compare *Cleveland, Columbus & Cin. Highway, Inc. — Purchase — Reo*, 5 M.C.C. 479. The existence of legal control in one person does not prevent concurrent existence of actual control in another through acquiescence of, or a management contract with, the former.

---

[6]49 U.S.C. 1(3) (b) and 5(4).
[7]*New York, Chicago and St. Louis Railroad Co. Control*, 295 I.C.C. 703, 713-14. See also *Atlas Corporation et al — Application*, 248 I.C.C. 373, 375; *Masten Transportation, Inc. — Merger — Masten Trucking Co., Inc.*, 70 M.C.C. 421, 427.
[8]38 M.C.C. 95, 97.

In *Detroit Edison Co. v. S.E.C.*,[9] the court said that control could be exercised in the following ways:

(1) through complete ownership of capital stock, (2) a majority ownership, (3) through a legal device without majority ownership, such as pyramiding through holding companies or a large issue of nonvoting stock with a comparatively small issue of stock with voting rights, or voting trusts, (4) minority control, which exists when comparatively few shares of corporate stock are in the hands of one group and the remainder widely scattered, (5) management control, which exists where all the stock is so widely distributed that no stockholder takes sufficient interest in the affairs of the corporation to influence or control it, (6) proxy control through committees, (7) through interlocking corporate officers or directors.

There is no one factor which is considered decisive in itself in establishing unlawful control. Factors mentioned by the Commission in arriving at a determination of control include blood relationship, sharing of terminals and offices, sharing of telephone numbers and communications systems, performance of services by one carrier for the others, leasing and interchange activities, and an increase in the interlining of freight.[10]

Violation of Section 5(5) as an Element in the Consideration of the Public Interest Question

In *Central of Georgia Ry. Co. Control*,[11] the Commission said that unlawful control is an important consideration in determining the public interest issue. The Commission said that "public interest is concerned not only with improvements in transportation service, but also with maintenance of respect for and observance of the law." The willfulness of the violation of Section 5(5) is considered in deciding the issue of public interest as disregard and disrespect for the law should not be

[9]119 F. 2d 730, 739. The case was in connection with the Public Utility Holding Company Act (15 U.S.C. 79).

[10]*Ratner — Control of Midwest*, 56 M.C.C. 59; *Gate City Transport Co. — Control — Square Deal Cartage*, 87 M.C.C. 591, 594; *Nigro Freight Lines, Inc.*, 90 M.C.C. 113, 118-119; *Coldway Food Express, Inc. — Control and Merger*, 87 M.C.C. 123, 128-129; *Dorn's Transportation, Inc.*, 87 M.C.C. 111, 115; *Kenosha Auto Transport Corp. — Investigation of Control*, 80 M.C.C. 59, 69-72; *Black — Investigation of Control*, 75 M.C.C. 275, 281; *Cortland Fast Freight, Inc. — Purchase — H. J. Korten, Inc.*, 60 M..C. 321, 325-6; *Exley Express, Inc. — Purchase — Olsen*, 85 M.C.C. 396, 400.

[11]307 I.C.C. 39, 43. See also *Sellers — Control — Huckabee Transport Co.*, 80 M.C.C. 429. The Commission's policy is followed by other agencies as demonstrated by *Sherman, Control and Interlocking Relationship*, 15 CAB 876, 881. Action by the agency is not limited by reason of the fact that less drastic measures were taken in the past. *F.C.C. v. WOKO, Inc.*, 329 U.S. 223.

approved in the absence of clear and forceful evidence that substantial benefits would result.[12]

Divestiture

Divestiture may be ordered by the Commission where a violation is found to exist under Section 5(5),[13] and it may include all those respondents who participated therein.[14]

Section 5(8) expressly states that the Commission is charged with choosing the proper remedy in an unauthorized acquisition case. Judicial review, therefore, is limited and extends no further than to ascertain whether the Commission made an allowable judgment in its choice of remedy.[15] Moreover, prerequisite to such review is evidence that a judgment was in fact made, that the parties were heard on the issue, that the proper standards were applied.[16]

Stockholdings

The law does not forbid one carrier to purchase a minority stock interest in another. In *New York, C & St. L. R. Co. Control*,[17] the Commission made it clear that the purchase of the stock of a carrier by another does not, standing alone, constitute unlawful control. In *New York, N. H. & H. R. Co. Investigation*[18] and *St. Louis S. W. Ry. Co. — Control*,[19] the

---

[12]*Houff — Control — Elliot Bros. Trucking Co.*, 80 M.C.C. 637, 650; *Kenosha Auto Transport Corp. — Control — U.S.A.C. Transport, Inc.*, 85 M.C.C. 731, 736; *Dorn's Transportation, Inc. — Purchase*, 87 M.C.C. 111, 116; *Nigro Freight Lines, Inc. — Purchase — Coady Trucking Co.*, 90 M.C.C. 113, 121; *E. C. McCormick, Jr. — Control — A.C.E. Transportation Co.*, 80 M.C.C. 401, 414; *Taken Bros. Freight Line, Inc. — Control — Iowa — Nebr. Transp.*, 75 M.C.C. 236, 240-241; *Von Der Ahe Lines, Inc — Lease and Purchase — Bee-Line*, 87 M.C.C. 53, 60; *Dorn's Transportation, Inc., supra*, 87 M.C.C. 111, 116; *Houff — Control*, 80 M.C.C. 637, 650-51, 654; *Lombard Bros., Inc. v. United States*, C.A. No. 9911, U.S. D.C. Conn.

[13]*Nigro Freight Lines, Inc. — Purchase — Coady Trucking Co.*, 90 M.C.C. 113, 121; *Kenosha Auto Transport Corp. — Investigation of Control*, 80 M.C.C. 59, 77-79; *Black — Investigation of Control*, 75 M.C.C. 275, 282-283; *Houff — Control — Elliott Bros. Trucking Co.*, 70 M.C.C. 177, 194, affirmed 80 M.C.C. 637.

[14]*Sellers — Control — Huckabee Transport Corp.*, 80 M.C.C. 429, 450-451; *Kenosha Auto Transport Corp. — Investigation of Control*, 80 M.C.C. 59; *Stacks — Investigation of Control*, 75 M.C.C. 625, 638-639; *Coldway Food Express, Inc. — Control and Merger*, 87 M.C.C. 123, 130-131; *Black — Investigation of Control*, 75 M.C.C. 274, 281-282.

[15]*Jacob Siegel Co. v. F.T.C.*, 237 U.S. 608, 612.

[16]*Gilbertville Trucking Co., Inc. v. United States*, 371 U.S. 115.

[17]295 I.C.C. 131.

[18]220 I.C.C. 505.

[19]180 I.C.C. 175.

Commission stated that whether stock ownership constitutes illegal control is a question of fact to be resolved separately in each case and does not depend upon ownership of any given amount of stock. For rulings by the Commission see *Purchase of Stock of C. & A. R. R.* by *Rock Island*[20] (ownership of 25.8 percent of the capital stock of Alton by Rock Island was held not to constitute control); *Greyhound Corp., Control — Cincinnati & L. E. Transport Co.*[21] (19.87 percent stock interest increased to 30.57 percent was held not to be control); *Greyhound Corp. — Investigation of Control-Southwestern*[22] (40 percent purchase without I.C.C. approval was held not to be in violation of Section 5).

In *New York, C. & St. L. R. Co. — Control,*[23] Nickel Plate contended that if the Delaware, Lackawanna & Western Railroad, owning about 15 percent of Nickel Plate's stock, elected two or three strong directors on its Board, they could sway the less strong directors, and that their influence would be supported since they represent the holders of the largest single block of stock. After recognizing that there is always some likelihood that strong directors might sway the thinking of directors not so strong, the Commission said it is extremely doubtful that two or three strong directors could overcome the opposition or hostility of twelve or fifteen directors of the caliber normally holding such position with a major railroad. On these facts the Commission concluded at page 741 that:

> The ownership of the applicant of approximately 15 percent of Nickel Plate stock and the possibility of placing two or three of applicant's representatives on Nickel Plate's Board of Directors do not constitute control within the purview of Section 5(2) of the Interstate Commerce Act.

Other decisions of the Commission clearly demonstrate that minority stock interests, coupled with minority participation, is neither control nor the power to control. See *McCormick — Control — A.C.E. Transp., Inc.*[24] (40 percent stock ownership and participation as one of the directors on the board was not control); *Transcontinental Bus System, Inc. — Control — Continental*[25] (39 percent and 30 percent stock ownership in two bus companies coupled with a directorship in each case was held not to be control); *Greyhound Corp. — Investigation of Control — Southeastern*[26] (40 percent stock ownership and one director out of

[20]72 I.C.C. 273.
[21]40 M.C.C. 388.
[22]50 M.C.C. 709.
[23]295 I.C.C. 703.
[24]80 M.C.C. 401, 411-414.
[25]50 M.C.C. 193, 216, 217.
[26]50 M.C.C. 709, 715.

four was held not to be control); *Cleveland, Columbus & Cin. Highway, Inc. — Purchase — Reo*[27] (Erie Railroad's 19.24 percent stock ownership and one director was not control); *Northland — Greyhound Lines, Inc. — Purchase Liederback*[28] (40 percent stock interest by Great Northern Railway Company and minority company representation on the board of directors and executive committee was not control); and *J. P. Boak — Control — Rocket Freight Lines, Inc.*[29] (25.5 percent stock ownership, coupled with representation among officials and directors, was not control.

As a parallel to Section 5(2) cases, *Western Mary'and Ry. Co. Securities Modification*[30] states that the fact that certain people "may control enough of the applicant's stock to defeat any plan under section 20b for alteration or modification of its stock, as argued by intervener, does not constitute 'control of the carrier' as that term is used in the last sentence of paragraph (3) of section 20b."

Voting Trust Agreements

Section 5(5) does not preclude the use of voting trusts in proceedings wherein the acquisition of control or management was obtained without prior Commission approval, because it has been determined in a number of cases that creation of an independent voting trust for stock, the prior control of which without Commission approval constituted a Section 5(5) violation, was effective to avoid the violation and the Commission was authorized to give it that effect.[31]

The Commission has pointed out that trusts have long been accepted as a means by which one railroad might lawfully hold stock in another. In *New York C. & St. L. R. Co. Control*,[32] it said:

> Voting-trust agreements have long been accepted by the Commission as a means of effecting compliance with the law in connection with holdings of stock in one railroad by another and without which the continued ownership of the stock might be considered unlawful and contrary to the public interest. See *Interstate Commerce Commission v. Baltimore & O. R. Co.*,

---

[27]36 M.C.C. 325, 328.

[28]25 M.C.C. 109, 110.

[29]No. MC-F-4968, not printed.

[30]290 I.C.C. 445, 470.

[31]See *B. F. Goodrich Co. v. Northwest Industries, Inc.*, 303 F. Supp. 53, 61, aff'd 424 F. 2d 1349, cert. denied, 400 U.S. 822. This and other decisions make it clear that the wording of Section 5(5) does not prohibit voting trusts so long as the trustee is truly independent of the acquiring carrier settlor. See, *Illinois Central R.R. Co. v. United States*, 293 F. Supp., 421-429, aff'd *per curiam* 385 U.S. 457.

156 I.C.C. 607; 183 I.C.C. 165; *Wabash R. Co. Control*, 247 I.C.C. 365 and 252 I.C.C. 319; *Chesapeake & O. Ry. Co. Purchase, supra; Hancock Truck Lines, Inc. — Purchase — Motor Freight Corp.*, 5 M.C.C. 405.

The Commission made it clear in *Chesapeake and Ohio Railway Purchase*[33] that an appropriate trust would operate to insulate a carrier from a charge of having unlawful control of another. It said:

> By depositing in trust its holdings of Pittston stock, Alleghany would effectively divest itself of control of U. S. Trucking without sacrificing intrinsic values which at present inure to its own stockholders and without depriving minority Pittston stockholders of whatever rights they have incident to the control of U.S. Trucking by Pittston.

In the *Missouri Pacific* case, *supra*, the Commission set forth (at 319-20) what it considered the essential elements of a valid voting trust effective to accomplish avoidance of control. These are:

> The trustee must be entirely independent of the beneficiary of the trust.
> The trustee must exercise its voting power in such a way as not to cause any dependence or intercorporate relationship between the beneficiary and the carrier trusteed.

> The trust must be irrevocable for a stated period of time.

In some proceedings involving Section 5(2) control acquisitions have been complicated by the improper use of voting trusts by the settlor. The voting trusts were established after the acquiring carrier had purchased a sufficient amount of the target carrier's publicly held voting securities to be considered in control of such carrier. Additionally, the voting trusts were frequently found not to have been administered independently from the control of the settlor, but were conduits through which the settlor continued in control of the publicly held carrier. These conditions led to a number of instances where the Commission determined that the settlor had violated Section 5(5), that is, acquired control of a carrier without Commission approval. Commission policy does not require the Section 5(2) application to be denied merely because Section 5(5) has been found to have been violated, though it is a factor to be

---

[32]295 I.C.C. 703, 715. See also *Interstate Commerce Commission v. Baltimore & O. R. Co.*, 156 I.C.C. 156; *Hancock Truck Lines, Inc. — Purchase — Motor Freight Corp.*, 5 M.C.C. 405; *Wabash R. Co. Control*, 247 I.C.C. 365, 252 I.C.C. 319; *New York, C. & St. L. R. Co. Control*, 295 I.C.C. 703.

[33]261 I.C.C. 239, 243. In *Missouri Pac. R. Co. — Control — Chicago & E. I. R. Co.*, 327 I.C.C. 279 aff'd *sub nom I. C. R. Co. v. U.S.*, 263 F. Supp. 421; aff'd 875 S. Ct. 612, the Commission went even so far as to accept a voting-trust agreement as effective after an initial violation of Section 5(5). See also, *Brinks Express Company of Canada — Control — Direct*, 101 M.C.C. 639, in which, as in the *Missouri Pac. R. Co.* case, the trust was entered into to cure an existing violation.

considered. In several cases, notwithstanding Section 5(5) violations involving improper usage of voting trusts, the Commission has granted approval of the Section 5(2) applications where, in each instance, the evidence of record demonstrated that overriding public benefits would be derived from the resulting control to warrant a finding that the public should not be deprived of those benefits because of the Section 5(5) violation.[34]

Voting on Matters Pertaining to the Intrinsic Investment Value of Securities

In *Greyhound Corp. — Investigation of Control — Southeastern*,[35] Atlantic Greyhound acquired 40 percent of the stock in Southeastern under a purchase agreement with the sellers providing:

> . . . that Southeastern shares, to the extent controlled by the sellers (50 percent of the outstanding stock which when coupled with the Atlantic's 40 percent totalled 90 percent stock ownership) would not be voted without Atlantic's consent, to amend the charter of Southeastern to create a new class of stock, or to increase the shares outstanding, and would be voted to renew its charter before termination of its corporate existence in 1953. (Parentheses supplied.)

The Commission concluded:

> It is clear that neither Greyhound nor Atlantic has actually controlled or managed the affairs of Southeastern, and this record does not support a finding that Atlantic has the power to control Southeastern.

The Commission held in *Chesapeake & O. Ry. Co. Purchase*,[36] that there is compliance with Section 5 when a corporation owning stock has divested itself of all rights in connection with its stockholdings except the right to vote on those matters normally pertaining to the intrinsic investment value of the stocks, such as mergers, consolidation, sale or sales of all or substantially all of the assets, changes, in the terms of priorities of stocks and matters of similar import. In other words, it is perfectly permissible to have rights of this nature because they do not constitute control. In *Western Maryland Ry. Co. Securities Modification*,[37] the power to defeat any plan for alteration or modification of stock was held not to constitute control.

---

[34]See *East Texas Motor Frt. — Control — Consolidated*, 109 M.C.C. 213; *Alleghany Corporation — Control and Purchase*, 109 M.C.C. 333; and *Eastern Freight Ways, Inc. — Invest. of Control*, 122 M.C.C. 143.
[35]50 M.C.C. 709, 714.
[36]261 I.C.C. 239.
[37]290 I.C.C. 445.

A similar question arose in *Wood v. United States*,[38] where the Commission had ordered the Baltimore & Ohio to divest itself of control of the Western Maryland, and in compliance with that order the Baltimore & Ohio had trusteed its stock, retaining only the right to sell the stock and the right to vote on any plan of alteration or modification of Western Maryland's outstanding stock. The Commission approved this trust agreement and found it in substantial compliance with Section 5. The court, on page 595 of its opinion, stated, "The Commission passed upon the trust agreement . . . and apparently it was satisfied that its terms would prevent the Baltimore & Ohio from exercising control over the operations of a competing line, the Western Maryland."

Provisions of this nature, protective of minority interests and ownerships in corporation, are recognized and distinguished by the Commission from powers amounting to control. In *Pacific Greyhound Lines — Control — Oregon Motor Stages*,[39] the Greyhound Lines bought 25 percent of the stock in Stages, and the purchase agreement provided that Stages (1) could not sell, transfer, pledge its assets, disburse cash, and incur any liability except in the ordinary course of business; (2) could not commit itself to purchase materials and supplies other than for current purposes; (3) could not dispose of or impair its operating rights; (4) could not pay dividends, special compensations, bonuses or pensions, or pay to the sellers compensation in excess of a fixed amount per month, and (5) could not issue securities, modify its capitalization or amend its articles or incorporation and bylaws, except in conformity with the purchase agreement.

The agreement also obligated Stages (1) to amend its articles and bylaws to increase its board from three to five and for cumulative voting; (2) to require a unanimous approval of the board for the payment of salaries and bonuses, transfer of property, loans, or other transactions in excess of a fixed amount; (3) to grant all stockholders preemptive rights and (4) to require not less than 80 percent of the stockholders' voting power to amend the articles and bylaws. On this set of facts the Commission concluded, at page 331:

> Provisions like those described are something over and above those which might normally be expected in agreements to purchase minority interests in corporations . . . It is therefore evident that in consequence of the afore-mentioned restrictions, Pacific would acquire the power to control Stages with respect to the exercise by the latter of essential corporate functions to the same effect as if it held the power through stock owner-

[38]132 F. Supp. 586.
[39]55 M.C.C. 321.

ship alone. . . . In view of the terms of this agreement, the jurisdictional question here presented is clearly distinguishable from that considered in *Greyhound Corp. — Control — Cincinnati & L. E. Transp. Co.*, 40 M.C.C. 388. The restrictive scope of the terms of this agreement also goes beyond those which were in the agreement considered in *Greyhound Corp. — Investigation of Control — Southeastern*, 50 M.C.C. 709.

Where the terms of a contract of purchase places in an applicant under Section 5(2) the power of disposition of the considered rights notwithstanding the denial of the application this has been held to be in violation of the I.C. Act.[40]

---

[40]See *Atlantic Greyhound Corp. — Purchase — Pan American Bus*, 25 M.C.C. 551, 553; *Capitol Greyhound Lines — Purchase — Peninsula Transit*, 15 M.C.C. 459, 461; *Atlantic Greyhound Corp. — Purchase — Independence Bus*, 25 M.C.C. 1, 2-3.

51

Consolidation, Merger, and Acquisition of Control of Air Carriers

The Applicable Statutory Provisions

Section 408(a) of the Federal Aviation Act[1] provides it shall be unlawful, unless approved by the Board, (1) for "two or more air carriers, or for any air carrier and any other common carrier or any person engaged in any other phase of aeronautics to consolidate or merge their properties, or any part thereof, into one person for the ownership, management, or operation of the properties theretofore in separate ownerships"; (2) for "any air carrier, any person controlling an air carrier, any other common carrier, or any person engaged in any other phase of aeronautics, to purchase, lease, or contract to operate the properties, or any substantial part thereof, of any air carrier"; (3) for "any air carrier or person controlling an air carrier to purchase, lease, contract to operate the properties, or any substantial part thereof, of any person engaged in any phase of aeronautics otherwise than as an air carrier"; (4) for "any foreign air carrier to acquire control, in any manner whatsoever, of any citizen of the United States engaged in any phase of aeronautics"; (5) for "any air carrier or person controlling an air carrier, any other common carrier, any person engaged in any other phase of aeronautics, or any other person to acquire control of any air carrier in any manner whatsoever: Provided, That the Board may by order exempt any such acquisition of a non-certificated air carrier from this requirement to the extent and for such periods as may be in the public interest"; (6) for "any air carrier or person controlling an air carrier to acquire control, in any manner whatsoever, of any person engaged in any phase of aeronautics otherwise than as an air carrier";

[1] 49 U.S.C. 1378(a). Under Section 413 (49 U.S.C. 1383) "whenever reference is made to control, it is immaterial whether such control is direct or indirect."

or (7) for "any person to continue to maintain any relationship established in violation of the Section."

The Board is empowered by Section 408(e),[2] upon complaint or upon its own initiative, to investigate, and, after notice and hearing, to determine whether Section 408(a) is being violated. If a violation is determined, the Board "shall by order require such person to take such action, consistent with the provisions of this act, as may be necessary, in the opinion of the Board, to prevent further violation of such provision." The provisions of Section 408, as well as Section 409,[3] dealing with interlocking relationships, do not apply with respect to the acquisition or holding by any air carrier, or any officer or director thereof, of (1) any interest in any ticket office, landing area, hangar, or other ground facility reasonably incidental to the performance by such air carrier of any of its services, or (2) any stock or other interest or any office or directorship in any person whose principal business is the maintenance or operation of any such ticket office, landing area, hangar, or other ground facility. Section 408(a) is not retroactive thus does not apply to a relationship existing prior to the passage of the Act in 1938.[4]

Under Section 408(b)[5] it is provided that any person seeking approval of a consolidation, merger, purchase, lease, operating contract, or acquisition of control, shall present an application to the Board, and the Board shall notify the persons involved in the transaction, and others known to have a substantial interest, of the time and place of the hearing. Section 408(b) provides further that unless, "after hearing," the Board finds that the consolidation, merger, purchase, lease, operating contract, or acquisition of control will not be consistent with the public interest or that the conditions of the section will not be fulfilled, it shall by order approve such consolidation, merger, purchase, lease, operating contract, or acquisition of control, upon such terms and conditions as it shall find to be just and reasonable and with such modifications as it may prescribe."

The Board cannot approve a transaction which "would result in creating a monopoly or monopolies and thereby restrain competition or

---

[2]49 U.S.C. 1378(e).

[3]49 U.S.C. 1379.

[4]*Railroad Control of Northeast Airlines,* 4 CAB 379, 386; *National Air Freight Forward Corp. v. CAB,* 197 F. 2d 384, 389.

[5]49 U.S.C. 1378(b), Section 401(h) of the Act (49 U.S.C. 1371(h)) provides that "No certificate may be transferred unless such transfer is approved by the Board as being consistent with the public interest"; and Section 402(g) of the Act (49 U.S.C. 1371(g) provides that "No permit may be transferred unless such transfer is approved by the Board as being in the public interest."

jeopardize another air carrier not a party to the consolidation, merger, purchase, lease, operating contract, or acquisition of control."

Section 408(f)[6] provides for "the purposes of this section, any person owning benificially 10 per centum or more of the voting securities or capital, as the case may be, of an air carrier shall be presumed to be in control of such air carrier unless the Board finds otherwise. As used herein, beneficial ownership of 10 per centum of the voting securities of a carrier means ownership of such amount of its outstanding voting securities as entitles the holder thereof to cast 10 per centum of the aggregate votes which the holders of all the outstanding voting securities of such carrier are entitled to cast."

Any person affected by an order made under Section 408 is, by Section 414,[7] relieved from the operation of the antitrust laws.

Criteria Used in Deciding Cases

Consistency with the public interest is the basic criterion in consolidation, merger, and acquisition of control cases under Section 408(b). Public interest is construed not as a mere reference to public welfare, but as related to statutory objectives in the Act, which are set forth in Section 102.[8] This Section provides that in the exercise of its powers and duties the Board shall consider, among other things, as being in the public interest, and in accordance with the public convenience and necessity (a) the "encouragement and development of an air-transportation system properly adapted to the present and future needs of the foreign and domestic commerce of the United States, of the Postal Service, and of the national defense"; (b) the "regulation of air transportation in such manner as to recognize and preserve the inherent advantages of, assure the highest degree of safety in, and foster sound economic conditions in, such transportation, and to improve the relations between, and coordinate transportation by, air carriers"; (c) the "promotion of adequate, economical, and efficient service by air carriers at reasonable charges, without unjust discriminations, undue preferences or advantages, or unfair or destructive competitive practices"; (d) competition "to the extent necessary to assure the sound development of an air-transportation system properly adapted to the needs of the foreign and domestic commerce of the United States, of the Postal Service, and of the national defense"; (e) the "promotion of safety in air commerce"; and

[6]49 U.S.C. 1378(f).
[7]49 U.S.C. 1384.
[8]49 U.S.C. 1302.

(f) the "promotion, encouragement, and development of civil aeronautics."

The Board has pointed out that the determination of where the public interest lies involves the process of balancing all known factors without assigning controlling force to any single one.[9] Public interest aspects include the elimination of the acquired carrier as a competitor;[10] the price to be paid for the acquisition;[11] improved service;[12] unlawful acquisition or control of the carrier involved;[13] the integration of routes;[14] savings to be realized;[15] effect on other carriers;[16] traffic estimates;[17] financial arrangements of the carriers involved;[18] the size and competitive position of the acquiring carrier;[19] degree of control of interchange traffic;[20] development of connecting service;[21] availability of higher standards of operational procedure and maintenance;[22] availability of higher standards of financial policy;[23] the sale of a carrier in failing circumstances;[24] and the effect of the transaction on employees.[25]

In *Airline Pilots Association v. CAB*,[26] the court affirmed a CAB order authorizing the merger of two carriers, holding that the Board properly found the merger to be consistent with the public interest. The court rejected contentions that the CAB order would prejudice the petitioner's interests in certain labor disputes with one of the carriers, or that the merger was contrived for the purpose of circumventing the

---

[9]*Mackey-Midet Acquisition Case*, 24 CAB 51.
[10]*Ibid*.
[11]*Ibid*.
[12]*Ibid*.
[13]*Colonial Eastern Acquisition Case*, 23 CAB 500.
[14]*Delta-Chicago & Southern Merger Case*, 16 CAB 647.
[15]*Ibid*.
[16]*Ibid*.
[17]*Ibid*.
[18]*Arizona-Monarch Merger Case*, 11 CAB 246.
[19]*American Airlines, Inc., Acquisition of Control of Mid-Continent*, 7 CAB 365.
[20]*Ibid*.
[21]*Ibid*.
[22]*Western Air Lines, Inc., Acquisition of Inland Air Lines, Inc.*, 4 CAB 654.
[23]*Ibid*.
[24]*United-Capital Merger Case*, 33 CAB 307. Here the Board applied the failing business doctrine as expressed by the Supreme Court in *International Shoe Co. v. Federal Trade Commission*, 280 U.S. 291.
[25]Standardized labor protective provisions developed over the years have been imposed by the Board in *United-Western Transfer of Route*, 11 CAB 701, aff'd *Western Airlines, Inc., v. CAB*, 194 F. 2d 211; *North Atlantic Route Transfer Case*, 12 CAB 124; *Braniff-Mid-Continent Merger Case*, 15 CAB 708; *Delta-Chicago and Southern Merger Case*, 16 CAB 647; *Flying Tiger-Slick Merger Case*, 18 CAB 326; *Continental-Pioneer Acquisition Case*, 20 CAB 323, *Colonial-Eastern Acquisition Case*, 23 CAB 500; *Mackey-Midet Acquisition Case*, 24 CAB 51.
[26]360 F. 2d 837.

requirement of Presidential approval of the transfer of a transatlantic certificate.

In *Air Line Employees Association v. Civil Aeronautics Board*,[27] the CAB had approved the merger of Lake Central Airlines into Allegheny Airlines but, although imposing certain labor protective conditions on its approval of the merger, had refused to require assumption of Lake Central's collective bargaining agreement with the Air Lines Employees Association as a condition of the merger. The Air Line Employees Association contended that refusal to impose such a condition invalidated the Board's order of approval and that the labor protective conditions were insufficient. The court sustained the CAB's order, holding that the Board's duty in airline merger cases is to impose conditions that make the mergers consistent with the public interest and that the CAB is not obligated to pass on every question of labor law which may arise out of a merger.

Reservation of Jurisdiction Condition under Section 408(b)

Foreign Study League v. C.A.B.[28] involved a board order requiring Transamerica Corporation, the owner of Trans International, to divest itself of a newly acquired subsidiary, the Foreign Study League. In affirming the Board's order the court concluded that the Board possessed jurisdiction under Section 408(b) by virtue of a reservation of jurisdiction condition on its earlier approval of the Transamerica-Trans International acquisition, and properly found the Transamerica-FSL acquisition to be contrary to the public interest because of its anticompetitive potential.

Participation of Surface Carriers in the Air Transport Field

Section 408(b) of the Federal Aviation Act[29] provides in part that "if the applicant is a carrier other than an air carrier, or a person controlled by a carrier other than an air carrier or affiliated therewith" within the meaning of Section 5(7) of the Interstate Commerce Act,[30] as amended, "such applicant shall for the purposes of this section be

[27]413 F. 2d 1092.
[28]475 F. 2d 865.
[29]49 U.S.C. 1378(b).
[30]Section 5(7) provides that "a person shall be held to be affiliated with a carrier if, by reason of the relationship of such person to such carrier . . . it is reasonable to believe that the affairs of any carrier of which control may be acquired by such person will be managed in the interests of such other carrier."

considered an air carrier and the Board shall not enter such an order of approval unless it finds that the transaction proposed will promote the public interest by enabling such carrier other than an air carrier to use aircraft to public advantage in its operation and will not restrain competition."

In the past, the Board has vigorously carried out the Congressional policy expressed in Section 408(b). This is demonstrated by *American Export Lines, Control-American Export Airlines, Inc.*[31] where the Board held:

> Thus a construction of the (Federal Aviation Act) which rigidly limits the participation of a surface carrier in the air transport field to cases where the surface carrier is enabled to use aircraft in its own operation to public advantage is in harmony with the well established pre-existing congressional policy.

> The legislative policy thus developed had a background of experience. New modes of transportation had rarely been pioneered and developed by those engaged in the older forms of transportation. The older transportation agencies had generally resisted the new, and had entered the new field only after its commercial possibilities had been demonstrated and the new transportation had come to be regarded as a competitive threat to the old. Congress, in adopting the restrictive provisions of Section 408 of the Federal Aviation Act evidently intended that air carriers should be free to act independently of conflicting interests and feared that in the absence of strict public control these air carriers might become economic captives of financial interests whose primary concern would be the protection of their investments in other forms of transportation. Hence, that section of the Act requires a showing not merely that the proposed control is consistent with the public interest, but that it will actively promote the public interest in a particular manner, that is by enabling the acquiring carrier "to use aircraft to public advantage in its operation."

> The present application must fail because the record will not support a finding that the control of Airlines by the Steamship Company will promote the public interest by enabling the Steamship Company to use aircraft to public advantage in its operation.

In *Northeast Airlines, et al., North Atlantic Routes,*[32] *Latin American Air Service,*[33] *Hawaiian Case,*[34] and *American Overseas, et al., South Atlantic Routes,*[35] the Board in the evaluation of the comparative public interest rejected the selection of surface carriers to operate the air routes. Thus as interpreted by the Board, Section 408(b) clearly reveals a statu-

[31] 3 CAB 619.
[32] 6 CAB 319.
[33] 6 CAB 857.
[34] 7 CAB 83.
[35] 7 CAB 285.

tory intent to regulate carefully the participation of surface carriers in air transportation, and the principle it contains must be given proper consideration in any determination of public convenience and necessity. That Congress was aware of the potential dangers to the full development of air transportation that could result from the control of air by surface transportation interests, and was resolved to afford protection against them is evidenced not only by Section 408(b) but also by those provisions of the Act requiring Board approval of interlocking relationships between air carriers and other common carriers, and the provisions requiring disclosure of stock or other interests held by an officer or director of an air carrier in any common carrier. The strictness of the policy insofar as interlocking relationships are concerned is demonstrated by *Lehman v. CAB.*[36]

Section 408(a) (5) declares it unlawful unless approved by the Board: "For any air carrier or person controlling an air carrier, any other common carrier, any person engaged in any other phase of aeronautics, or any other person to acquire control of an air carrier in any manner whatsoever. . . ." Although the section literally speaks in terms of acquisitions of control "of an air carrier," the Board, ever since the *Air Freight Forwarder Case,*[37] has construed it to apply to acquisitions by air carriers of common carriers (or persons controlling common carriers) or to the unified control of air carriers and common carriers.

Where jurisdictional tests are met under Section 408(a), an acquisition of control must then satisfy the substantive standards of Section 408(b). First, the Board is permitted to approve an acquisition unless it finds that the acquisition of control will not be consistent with the public interest or that the conditions of the section will not be fulfilled. However, two provisos are added. The Board may not approve an acquisition of control which would result in creating a monopoly or monopolies and thereby restrain competition or jeopardize another air carrier not a party to the acquisition. If the applicant is a carrier other than an air carrier, or a person controlled by a carrier other than an air carrier or affiliated therewith, such applicant shall be considered an air carrier and the Board shall not enter such an order of approval unless it finds that the transaction proposed will promote the public interest by enabling such carrier other than an air carrier to use aircraft to public advantage in its operation and will not restrain competition.

In *American Export Airlines, Trans-Atlantic Service,*[38] the Board

[36]209 F. 2d 289, cert. denied 347 U.S. 916.
[37]9 CAB 473, 504.
[38]2 CAB 16, 46-47.

ordered issuance of a certificate to a newly-organized subsidiary of an ocean common carrier, and dismissed an application under Section 408 which had been simultaneously filed. The dismissal was grounded on the fact that applicant was not an air carrier at the time control of applicant through stock ownership was acquired by the steamship company, and it necessarily followed that since the acquired company was not an air carrier at the time such an acquisition of it took place, Section 408(a) (5) did not apply. The Board's action was reversed in *Pan American World Airways v. Civil Aeronautics Board*,[39] the court stating:

> This seems to us an unduly literal interpretation of subdivision (5). In our opinion "to acquire control of any air carrier in any manner whatsoever" is to take all steps involved in obtaining control which in this case would consist of supplying a subsidiary corporation, organized for air carriage and possessing adequate financial resources, with a certificate authorizing operation. Any other interpretation would enable a steamship company, by organizing a subsidiary for air carriage, to escape the requirement of Section 408(b) that "the (Board) shall not enter . . . an order of approval unless it finds that the transaction proposed will promote the public interest by enabling such carrier other than an air carrier to use aircraft to public advantage in its operation and will not restrain competition."

Section 408(a) (5) has been construed to apply to acquisitions by air carriers as well as of air carriers because of the plain policy of the section to make unlawful, in the absence of Board approval, acquisitions which may give rise to conflicts of interest.[40] Such conflicts may be present regardless of whether a surface carrier acquires an air carrier, or the latter acquires a surface carrier. Moreover, the surface carrier interests frequently could be the dominant ones notwithstanding that the form of the acquisition was one by which the air carrier controlled the surface carrier. Section 408(a) (5) in terms forbids acquisitions of control of any air carrier "in any manner whatsoever," and Section 413 specifies that "whenever reference is made to control it is immaterial whether such control is direct or indirect." Thus, Section 408 is directed to common control relationships, and the Board would be exalting form over substance were it to hold that the acquisition of an air carrier by a person controlling a surface carrier was within its jurisdiction, but that the acquisition of a surface carrier by a person controlling an air carrier was not. The Board, therefore, has construed the jurisdictional provisions of Section 408(a) in such fashion as to permit it to assert jurisdiction

---

[39] 121 F. 2d. 810, 815.
[40] See *Air Freight Forwarder Case, supra.*

over all common control situations between the various types of carriers so that it may apply the public interest standards of the section in accordance with the policy of the Act. The first proviso of Section 408(b) is plainly applicable both in terms and in spirit to common control relationships irrespective of whether the technical acquisition is by the air carrier or the surface carrier.

With respect to the second proviso of Section 408(b), the situation is different. This is not a jurisdictional provision which must be construed broadly in order to effect the intent of the Act. It is, instead, a substantial barrier to approval of relationships over which the Board has already asserted jurisdiction. The Board has held that the policy of the second proviso should be considered in certification proceedings under Section 401 of the Act although not technically applicable.[41]

There is apparently no legislative history specifically directed to the second proviso of Section 408(b). However, this void is filled by reference to the history of a similar proviso in Section 213(a) (1) of the Motor Carrier Act of 1935,[42] from which the second proviso was borrowed. A fair summary of this legislative history is reflected in the following excerpt:

> Carriers by rail, express, or water are permitted to consolidate or merge with motor carriers or to obtain control in any of the ways indicated above, but only on a showing that "the transaction proposed will promote the public interest and enable such a carrier other than a motor carrier to use service by motor vehicle to public advantage in its operations and will not unduly restrain competition." With this limitation, it will be possible for the Commission to allow acquisitions which will make for coordinated or more economical service and at the same time to protect the public against the monopolization of highway carriage by rail, express, or other interests.[43]

And the Supreme Court has stated that both the "Commission and this Court have recognized that Congress has expressed strong general policy against railroad invasion of the motor carrier field," as particularly reflected by the proviso.[44] The policy behind the corresponding proviso in the Motor Carrier Act is to severely limit and restrict incursion into motor vehicle common carriage by other transportation modes, particularly railroads. It was not specifically designed, on the other hand, to be applicable to acquisitions by motor carriers of other modes. Therefore,

---

[41]American President Lines, *et al.*, Petition, 7 CAB 799.
[42]49 Stat. 556.
[43]Senator Wheeler at 79 Cong. Rec. 5655, April 15, 1935. See also 79 Cong. Rec. 12205-12206.
[44]American Trucking Assns. v. U.S., 364 U.S. 1, 6.

the engraftment of the proviso on the Federal Aviation Act, and its plain terms persuasively indicates a policy restricted to curtailing the invasion by other modes of transportation into common carriage by air. There may be situations where in form the acquisition is that of a surface carrier by an air carrier, but where the economic or operational result of the transaction would be that the acquiring or dominant entity was the surface carrier. In such case, the fact that the second proviso was not technically applicable would not bar the Board from carrying out the policy of the Act and applying the second proviso.

52

Interlocking Relationships
by Air Carriers

The Applicable Statutory Provisions

Section 409(a)[1] provides that it shall be unlawful, unless such relationship shall have been approved by the Board upon due showing that the public interest will not be adversely affected (1) for "any air carrier to have and retain an officer or director who is an officer, director, or member, or who as a stockholder holds a controlling interest, in any other person who is a common carrier or is engaged in any phase of aeronautics"; (2) for "any air carrier, knowingly and willfully, to have and retain an officer or director who has a representative or nominee who represents such officer or director as an officer, director, or member, or as a stockholder holding a controlling interest, in any other person who is a common carrier or is engaged in any phase of aeronautics"; (3) for "any person who is an officer or director of an air carrier to hold the position of officer, director, or member, or to be a stockholder holding a controlling interest, or to have a representative or nominee who represents such person as an officer, director, or member, or as a stockholder holding a controlling interest, in any other person who is a common carrier or is engaged in any phase of aeronautics"; (4) for "any air carrier to have and retain an officer or director who is an officer, director, or member, or who as a stockholder holds a controlling interest, in any person whose principal business, in purpose or in fact, is the holding of stock in, or control of, any other person engaged in any phase of aeronautics"; (5) for "any air carrier, knowingly and willfully, to have and retain an officer or director who has a representative or nominee who represents such officer or director as an officer, director, or

[1] 49 U.S.C. 1379(a).

member, or as a stockholder holding a controlling interest in any person whose principal business, in purpose or in fact, is the holding of stock in, or control of, any other person engaged in any phase of aeronautics"; (6) for "any person who is an officer or director of an air carrier to hold the position of officer, director, or member, or to be a stockholder holding a controlling interest, or to have a representative or nominee who represents such person as an officer, director, or member, or as a stockholder holding a controlling interest, in any person whose principal business, in purpose or in fact, is the holding of stock in, or control of, any other person engaged in any phase of aeronautics." Section 409(b)[2] provides that "it shall be unlawful for any officer or director of any air carrier to receive for his own benefit, directly or indirectly, any money or thing of value in respect of negotiation, hypothecation, or sale of any securities issued or to be issued by such carrier, or to share in any of the proceeds thereof."

Interpretation of the Statute

In *Lehman v. C.A.B.*[3] several applications for approval of interlocking relationships, arising from directors of air carriers also serving as directors of another type of common carrier, had been filed with the Board and, after a hearing, the Board held that the interlocking relationships should be disapproved. This was based on findings that the air carrier and surface carrier were in competition to a consequential degree in that they competed for tourist travel between the United States and certain vacation travel areas. In the court of appeals, petitioners urged that the difference between a leisurely sea voyage via a trip eliminated the element of competition. To this argument, the court replied (pp. 291-2) that in the case of surface transportation "the vacationing is principally in the travelling" and in the case of air transportation "it is principally at the place to which the traveler is air-borne. The general area traversed, however, is largely the same; and each carrier offers its own type of service in the effort to obtain the custom."

The court said that competition "exists between types of vacationing in, and in traveling to and from, the same area, and therefore between the carriers which seek the traffic." The court said further (p. 292) that "there was an 'opposition of interest between competitors for traffic.' This being so, the public interest might suffer through the restraint which such conflict might exert upon one who is a director of both

[2]49 U.S.C. 1379(b).
[3]209 F. 2d 289, cert. denied 347 U.S. 916.

companies and responsible for decisions, in the conduct of their affairs." The Congress seeks to avoid this by "encouraging the development of aviation free of such impediments to competition." In any event, the court said "the situation outlined demonstrates that it is within the competence of the Board to conclude that there had been no due showing that the potential restraint upon freedom of action would not adversely affect the public interest." To hold otherwise, the court said, "would be inconsistent with a statutory scheme which contemplates prior approval of the regulated relationship. The purpose of the Act is preventive. Furthermore, the Board's action does not depend upon the personal integrity of the director, which is unquestioned in these cases."

The second part of the Board's order under review in the *Lehman* case involved different men in different directorships rather than one man in two positions. There was a community of interest due to membership in a partnership, an investment banking group. The court said (p. 295) that in enacting Section 409(a), "Congress deemed the public interest to require that the industry be free of the conflicting interests of interlocking relationships which might prevent unimpeded choice of action on the part of directors." Even though the record was devoid of any indication that the directors had used the partnership relations to the detriment of companies of which they were directors, the court said that "in furthering the public policy embodied in the statutory provisions Congress has seen fit to prevent relationships deemed unhealthy without requiring proof that the directors have engaged in specific acts of a detrimental character. It is the relationship itself which is prevented unless approved, because harm might occur to the industry and to the public. The regulations, as we have said, are preventive, as well as curative should the latter be necessary."

53

Carrier Finance

Valuation of Property of Carriers

Section 19a (a) of the Interstate Commerce Act[1] provides:

"That the Commission shall, as hereinafter provided, investigate, ascertain, and report the value of all the property owned or used by every common carrier subject to the provisions of this part, except any street, suburban, or interurban electric railway which is not operated as a part of a general steam railroad system of transportation; but the Commission may in its discretion investigate, ascertain, and report the value of the property owned or used by any such electric railway subject to the provisions of this part whenever in its judgment such action is desirable in the public interest. To enable the Commission to make such investigation and report, it is authorized to employ such experts and other assistants as may be necessary. The Commission may appoint examiners who shall have power to administer oaths, examine witnesses, and take testimony. The Commission shall, subject to the exception hereinbefore provided for in the case of electric railways, make an inventory which shall list the property of every common carrier subject to the provisions of this part in detail, and show the value thereof as hereinafter provided, and shall classify the physical property, as nearly as practicable, in conformity with the classification of expenditures for road and equipment, as prescribed by the Interstate Commerce Commission."

Section 19a (b)[2] provides:

"First. In such investigation said Commission shall ascertain and report in detail as to each piece of property, other than land, owned or used by said common carrier for its purposes as a common carrier, the original cost to date, the cost of reproduction new, the cost of reproduction less deprecia-

---

[1] 49 U.S.C. 19a (a). Goodwill, earning power, and operating certificates excluded as elements of value. Sections 216(k), 307(c), 406(c). Determination and certification of value in railroad reorganization proceedings, 11 U.S.C. 205(e).

[2] 49 U.S.C. 19a (b).

tion, and an analysis of the methods by which these several costs are obtained, and the reason for their differences, if any. The Commission shall in like manner ascertain and report separately other values, and elements of value, if any, of the property of such common carrier, and an analysis of the methods of valuation employed, and of the reasons for any differences between any such value and each of the foregoing cost values.

"Second. Such investigation and report shall state in detail and separately from improvements the original cost of all lands, rights of way, and terminals owned or used for the purposes of a common carrier, and ascertained as of the time of dedication to public use, and the present value of the same. "Third. Such investigation and report shall show separately the property held for purposes other than those of a common carrier, and the original cost and present value of the same, together with an analysis of the methods of valuation employed.

"Fourth. In ascertaining the original cost to date of the property of such common carrier the Commission, in addition to such other elements as it may deem necessary, shall investigate and report upon the history and organization of the present and of any previous corporation operating such property; upon any increases or decreases of stocks, bonds, or other securities, in any reorganization; upon moneys received by any such corporation by reason of any issues of stocks, bonds, or other securities; upon the syndicating, banking, and other financial arrangements under which such issues were made and the expense thereof; and upon the net and gross earnings of such corporations; and shall also ascertain and report in such detail as may be determined by the Commission upon the expenditure of all moneys and the purposes for which the same were expended.

"Fifth. The Commission shall ascertain and report the amount and value of any aid, gift, grant of right of way, or donation, made to any such common carrier, or to any previous corporation operating such property, by the Government of the United States or by any State, county, or municipal government, or by individuals, associations, or corporations; and it shall also ascertain and report the grants of land to any such common carrier, or any previous corporation operating such property, by the Government of the United States, or by any State, county, or municipal government, and the amount of mony derived from the sale of any portion of such grants and the value of the unsold portion thereof at the time acquired and at the present time, also, the amount and value of any concession and allowance made by such common carrier to the Government of the United States, or to any State, county, or municipal government in consideration of such aid, gift, grant, or donation."

The Commission said in the *Fifteen Percent Case*[3] that the consideration of the need of the carriers for sufficient revenues to enable them to provide such transportation as is contemplated by the I.C. Act requires that the fair value of their property be taken into account. The Commission said that it is necessary to inquire into the question of value of prop-

[3]226 I.C.C. 41, 60.

erty employed in performing service because of its bearing upon the economic cost of performing the service and also because of the duty the Commission is under to avoid establishing rates upon a basis which would compel the use of property without just compensation, although the Constitution does not protect against all business hazards.

While the statute leaves valuation of railroad property to the Commission without judicial participation, the Commission's valuation must be made in accordance with the statutory requirements, and whether the Commission's valuation conforms to these statutory requirements and is based on material evidence are the only matters subject to judicial review.[4] The judicial function is to see to it that the Commission's "estimate" is not a mere "guess" but rests upon an informed judgment based upon an appraisal of all facts relevant primarily, but not exclusively, to future earning capacity, and is not at variance with the statutory command.[5]

Issuance of Securities

Section 20a (1) of the Interstate Commerce Act[6] provides:

"That as used in this section, the term 'carrier' means a common carrier by railroad (except a street, suburban, or interurban electric railway which is not operated as a part of a general steam railroad system of transportation) which is subject to this part, or any corporation organized for the purpose of engaging in transportation by railroad subject to this part, or a sleeping-car company which is subject to this part."

Section 20a (2)[7] provides:

"From and after one hundred and twenty days after this section takes effect it shall be unlawful for any carrier to issue any share of capital stock or any bond or other evidence of interest in or indebtedness of the carrier (hereinafter in this section collectively termed 'securities') or to assume any obligation or liability as lessor, lessee, guarantor, indorser, surety, or otherwise, in respect of the securities of any other person, natural or artificial, even though permitted by the authority creating the carrier corporation, unless and until, and then only to the extent that, upon application by the carrier, and after investigation by the Commission of the purposes and uses of the proposed issue and the proceeds thereof, or of the proposed assumption of obligation or liability in respect of the securities

---

[4]*Freeman v. Mulcahy,* 250 F. 2d 463, 472-3.
[5]*Ibid.*
[6]U.S.C. 20a(1). Applicability of provisions for authorization of securities to railroad reorganization proceedings, Bankruptcy Act, 11 U.S.C., Sec. 205; to voluntary adjustments provisions, Section 20b (1), (2), (7), (8), (11).
[7]49 U.S.C. 20a (2).

of any other person, natural or artificial, the Commission by order authorizes such issue or assumption. The Commission shall make such order only if it finds that such issue or assumption: (a) is for some lawful object within its corporate purposes, and compatible with the public interest, which is necessary or appropriate for or consistent with the proper performance by the carrier of service to the public as a common carrier, and which will not impair its ability to perform that service, and (b) is reasonably necessary and appropriate for such purpose."

Common or contract carriers by motor vehicle, corporations organized for the purpose of engaging in transportation as such carriers, and corporations authorized by the Commission to acquire control of any such carrier, or of two or more such carriers, are, by Section 214,[8] made subject with certain exemptions to the provisions of paragraphs (2) to (11), inclusive, of Section 20a.

The mere inclusion in a corporation's charter of power to engage in railroad operations does not constitute it a corporation "organized for the purpose of engaging in transportation by railroad" subject to part I within the purview of Section 20a (1).[9] The Commission in the *Woods Industries* case said that if it had jurisdiction over issuance of securities by corporations merely because the corporate charters gave them the power to engage in railroad operations, the jurisdiction of State bodies thereover would be superseded under Section 20a (7), and further, securities issued under the Commission's authorization would be exempt from registration under the Securities Act; it is not reasonable to conclude that Congress intended that such results should flow merely from election of incorporators to include provisions of that nature in a corporate charter.

One of the canons of statutory construction which has been recognized and followed by the courts is that legislation of Congress, unless a contrary intent appears, is meant to apply only within the territorial jurisdiction of the United States; and there is nothing in Section 214 and related provisions of Section 20a, or in the I.C. Act as a whole, to overcome the presumption that Congress does not intend to give its enactments an extra-territorial effect.[10] In the *Overland Express* case, the Commission said that although a Canadian corporation operating in this country is subject to certificate and other requirements of the I.C. Act respecting actions performed in the United States, it does not follow that Congress intended to give the Commission jurisdiction over acts of such

[8]49 U.S.C. 314.
[9]*Woods Industries, Inc. — Control — United Transports, Inc.*, 85 M.C.C. 672, 677.
[10]*Overland Exp. Limited Stock*, 85 M.C.C. 354, 356.

corporations which take place outside the boundaries of the United States; the Commission's exercise of jurisdiction over the issuance of securities by applicant in Canada obviously could not be "exclusive and plenary" as contemplated by Section 20a (7), nor could the provisions of paragraph (11) thereof be made effective, as the validity of the stock would be governed by the law of Canada, where issued.

Under Section 214 the issuance of securities is exempt for motor carriers where the value of the issuance, together with the value of other securities outstanding, does not exceed $1,000,000; notes having a maturity date of two years or less and aggregating not more than $200,-000 are also exempt. No such exemptions are provided railroads in the issuance of securities and the assumption of obligations. The exemption of $200,000 is allowed in addition to the $1,000,000 exemption only where the $1,000,000 includes no short-term notes; a carrier may issue without Commission approval short-term notes in any amount if that amount and the total of all other securities do not exceed $1,000,000; a carrier under Section 20a (9) may issue short-term notes in a larger amount than $200,000 without Commission approval but the total amount of such notes including those outstanding may not exceed five percent of the par value of the carrier's outstanding securities; and a carrier may utilize up to the $1,000,000 exemption in issuing long-term securities or capital stock but in computing the exemption for that purpose the total of all short-term notes outstanding must be included.

In *Securities of Louisville & Nashville R. R.,*[11] the Commission discussed fully the criteria to be applied in reaching a determination on the issuance of securities. In that case the Commission said that only assets of a carrier which are dedicated to use in transportation service may be capitalized. Such capitalizable assets would include working capital, investments in operating property, improvements in property used by a carrier, and investments in controlled affiliates who are owners of carrier property. The Commission will examine the capital assets available to the carrier and consider the capitalization resulting from the proposed issue. Total capitalization is compared with capitalizable assets to determine whether a proposed issue is supported adequately.[12] A proposed issue ordinarily will not be authorized if there is an overcapitalization unless there are circumstances justifying the issuance.

Securities issued, or respecting which obligation or liability is as-

---

[11]76 I.C.C. 718.

[12]Long-term obligations and advances are included along with capital stock in the total capitalization. Notes payable are not included but are placed in current liabilities.

sumed, without the Commission's prior authorization when required are void and no means are provided for their validation.[13] In making the statutory findings prerequisite to a grant of authority, the Commission must examine applicant's financial structure and condition with regard to the need and effect of the authority requested, and if the need or effect is not consistent with the required findings the application must be denied.[14]

Restrictive Construction of Section 20a in the Past

In the past the Commission's construction of Section 20a has been restrictive. This is reflected by the following discussion.

The Commission has said that securities as used in the I.C. Act includes any share of capital stock or any bond or other evidence of interest in or indebtedness of a carrier.[15] It has said that a credit agreement with a bank, under which a carrier may request loans in future, does not constitute an evidence of indebtedness of a carrier and is not a security within the meaning of Sections 20a and 214 when the agreement itself does not evidence that loans have been made or provide for a sum to be paid to the bank at a fixed or determinable future time, and no promissory notes would be executed and delivered either in connection with the agreement or when the funds are actually received; nor would it be a security when funds are advanced thereunder.[16] The Commission has held that a contract for the purchase of operating rights, although the only instrument representing vendee's indebtedness to vendor for the unpaid balance of the purchase price, is not a security within Section 214.[17]

Under prior Commission decisions a mortgage, per se, was held not to be a security within the meaning of the I.C. Act.[18] However, it was held that this did not mean that a mortgage may not constitute an assumption of obligation in respect of securities of others for such an assumption may be made in a formal or informal manner and need not

[13]*McCormack — Control — A.C.E. Transp. Co., Inc.,* 80 M.C.C. 401, 418; *Chemical Tank Lines, Inc., Securities,* 87 M.C.C. 386, 388; *Indianhead Truck Line, Inc., Securities,* 75 M.C.C. 596, 600.

[14]*Hall's Motor Transit Co. Securities,* 85 M.C.C. 692, 695.

[15]*Chemical Tank Lines, Inc., Securities,* 87 M.C.C. 386, 387.

[16]*Bruce Motor Freight, Inc. — Control and Merger,* 87 M.C.C. 436, 438-9.

[17]*Transcon Lines — Purchase — Missouri — Oklahoma Exp., Inc.,* 80 M.C.C. 79, 80. See *T. & P. Ry. Co.,* 271 I.C.C. 230.

[18]*Hayes Freight Lines, Inc. — Securities,* 39 M.C.C. 576, *Illinois-California Exp., Inc. — Control and Merger,* 75 M.C.C. 671, *Illinois Term. R. Co. Consolidation and Securities,* 221 I.C.C. 676.

be undertaken in one instrument or at the time the debt is incurred. The Commission will look to the substance of the entire transaction.[19]

A chattel mortgage of itself was held not to be a security within Section 214; and a bank loan agreement without notes or evidence of indebtedness other than a chattel mortgage likewise required no authority under that section.[20] Equipment obligations evidenced by chattel mortgages, unaccompanied by promissory notes or other evidences of the indebtedness, were held not to be securities within the meaning of Section 214[21] Conditional-sale agreements not evidenced by notes were considered securities within the meaning of Section 20a, and no authority was needed for assumption of obligation and liability thereon.[22] In substance, loan agreements, credit agreements, and conditional sales contracts were not regarded as securities if no notes accompanied them; if the instruments amended, modified or affected the provisions of securities authorized to be issued the Commission would have jurisdiction.[23]

Interpretations in the Past of Transactions Subject to Section 20a

In order to invoke the provisions of Section 20a it is not necessary that the instrument for effecting the proposed transaction constitute a security within purview of that section, for the Commission's jurisdiction attaches if what is done affects an issued security, regardless of the means utilized to achieve the result.[24] In the *Boston Terminal* case, the Commission said that while neither the execution nor amendment of a mortgage constitutes an issue of securities within the purview of Section 20a, a mortgage and the note which it secures are interrelated both financially

---

[19]*Federal Barge Lines, Inc. — Assumption of Obligation*, 320 I.C.C. 600, 604; *Pennsylvania R. Co. — Assumption of Obligation*, 320 I.C.C. 111.

[20]*Gateway Transp. Co. — Purchase — Northern Transp. Co.* 85 M.C.C. 59, 66; *Commercial Motor Freight, Inc. — Control and Merger*, 75 M.C.C. 615, 617. Loan agreements, however, which are definite as to terms and certain as to purposes constitute securities. *Expanded Definition of Term "Securities,"* 340 I.C.C. 817, 824.

[21]*Illinois — California Exp., Inc. — Control and Merger*, 75 M.C.C. 671, 677.

[22]*Atlantic Coast Line R. Co. Merger*, 309 I.C.C. 614, 617.

[23]*Lehigh Valley R. Co. Conditional Sale Contract*, 233 I.C.C. 359; *Capital Transit Co. — Securities*, 40 M.C.C. 17; *Hancock Truck Lines, Inc. — Control and Merger*, 56 M.C.C. 276; *Davidson Transfer & Storage Co. First Mortgage*, 282 I.C.C. 521; *Consolidated Frt. Lines, Inc. (Del. Corp.) — Consolidation*, 80 M.C.C. 495; *Gateway Transp. Co. — Purchase — Northern Transp. Co.* 85 M.C.C. 59; *Bruce Motor Freight, Inc. — Control and Merger*, 87 M.C.C. 436; *Transcontinental Bus System, Inc., Notes*, 80 M.C.C. 54; *Davidson Transfer & Storage Co. Securities*, 271 I.C.C. 168; *United States v. New York, N. H. & H. R. Co.*, 276 F. 2d 525, cert. denied 362 U.S. 959.

[24]*Boston Term. Co. Reorganization*, 312 I.C.C. 373, 384.

and legally, and the provisions of either may, and usually do, have a substantial impact on the other; thus, the Commission said, since terminal company's first-mortgage note is a security within Section 20a, whether the Commission's approval is required for the proposed amendments of the first-mortgage deed, incidental to the sale of the terminal building covered by the mortgage deed, depends on whether such amendments alter the note.[25] The alteration which invokes the provisions of Section 20a need not be physical. The Commission said that the proposed enlargement of the scope of the default provisions of the mortgage would have a material impact on a substantive provision of the note; and an amendment whereby, if a liability of the buyer should become a lien on the station building, the terminal company would be required either to pay such liability or to repay the first-mortgage note in full would likewise constitute a material alteration of the note. A proposal producing such material and substantive effects on a security previously approved, the Commission said, likewise requires approval.[26] Similarly, the provision of the supplemental mortgage for pledging the buyer's second mortgage and second note as part of the mortgaged property under the mortgage deed materially affects the security for the first-mortgage note and hence operates to alter a substantive characteristic of the note.[27]

In *Federal Barge Lines, Inc., Assumption of Obligation*,[28] the Commission held that a transaction under which a carrier applicant proposed to execute its mortgage as security for promissory notes of its noncarrier parent company was subject to approval. Applicant had contended that the transaction was similar to those in *Texas & P. Ry. Co. Assumption of Obligation*,[29] and *West Jersey & S. R. Co. Bonds*,[30] in which applications for authority to assume obligation and liability in respect of the securities of others were dismissed where it was shown that applicants were not parties to any agreement between the security holder and the obligor.[31] The lessee applicants in each of those proceedings had agreed with the lessors, in leasing properties, to make rental payments in an amount sufficient to pay the principal and interest of the obligation

[25]*Ibid.*
[26]*Ibid.*, p. 385.
[27]*Ibid.*, p. 385.
[28]320 I.C.C. 600.
[29]271 I.C.C. 230.
[30]295 I.C.C. 380.
[31]See *Illinois Term. R. Co. Consolidation and Securities*, 221 I.C.C. 676, *Notes of Wabash Ry.*, 99 I.C.C. 55, *St. Louis S. W. Ry. Co. Securities*, 184 I.C.C. 233, *Ryder System Inc., Stock*, 80 M.C.C. 747, *Greyhound Corp. — Control — Toronto Greyhound Lines*, 35 M.C.C. 599, *C. & R. Trans., Inc., — Control — Keeshin Freight Lines, Inc.*, 60 M.C.C. 173.

to the lessor. In the event of their default under the lease agreements, the lenders or holders of the securities would have no recourse to those applicants. The Commission disagreed with the applicant's contention in the *Federal Barge* case, stating (at p. 605):

> The transaction under which applicant proposes to execute its mortgage as security for the notes of Shipbuilding is unlike the proposals in the *Texas* and *West Jersey* cases, *supra*, since applicant here is no stranger to the transaction. It is unquestionable that its failure to lend the value of its property as security would affect the consummation of the transaction. The fact that applicant's mortgage does not specifically contain provisions for repayment by it is not controlling. Moreover, the second subsection (b) of Section 16 of the proposed mortgage provides that, in the event of default by the parent company, the mortgagee may bring suit to recover judgment for any and all amounts due thereunder, "and collect the same out of any and all property of the owner [the applicant] whether covered by this mortgage or otherwise." There can be no doubt that by such provision the applicant would subject its entire property to liability for the notes of its parent company just as completely as if it were to specifically agree "to pay or assume" the notes. Although applicant's obligation is contingent, the liability of a party as indorser, guarantor, surety, or otherwise is also ordinarily contingent. The result intended or the substance of the transaction, rather than the form, controls. *Delaware and Hudson Co. Merger*, 317 I.C.C. 177, *Boston Term. Co. Reorganization*, 312 I.C.C. 373, 384.

> We find that the transaction whereby applicant would execute and deliver its mortgage as security for the notes of its parent company falls within the purview of Section 20a of the Act as an assumption of obligation and liability in respect of the notes to be issued by its parent. Applicant's motion to dismiss will be denied.

In *United States v. New York, N. H. & H. R. Co.*,[32] the court said that an agreement between a carrier and a banking group under which, subject to certain conditions, the banking group agreed to, and did, purchase a large block of the carrier's outstanding preferred stock from specified sellers at an agreed price, and the carrier agreed to repurchase such stock at a higher price constituted an unauthorized issue of securities within Section 20a (2). This, the court said, is under the Commission's settled administrative construction that it has jurisdiction over changes in the terms of securities already "issued"; and the fact that the agreement was executory was not controlling. The court said that the applicability of Section 20a to a substantial change in rights and obligations of a carrier and its stockholders does not depend on the method employed to effect the change; and the fact that neither the

---

[32] 276 F. 2d 525, 528-9, 531-2, 536, 546.

Commission nor the courts had previously applied Section 20a to such a transaction was not controlling. The court said that the word "issue" having been broadened by unquestioned administrative construction to include "alter" or "amend," it must be concluded that the words used are sufficient to express that desire and give fair warning to those who read them.

The essential provisions of Sections 20a and 214 provide that "it shall be unlawful for any carrier to issue any share of capital stock . . . unless and until, and only then to the extent that . . . the Commission by order authorizes such issue." As interpreted and applied by the Commission in a number of cases the term "issue" includes "reissue." Included among Commission decisions so holding are *McLean Trucking Company Stock*,[33] and *Consolidated Freightways Inc. Stock*.[34]

Expanded Definition of Term "Securities"

In Ex Parte No. 275, *Expanded Definition of Term "Securities,"*[35] the I.C.C. interpreted the term "securities" as found in Section 20a of the I.C. Act to include, among other things, "those instruments specifically enumerated in section 20a(2) as well as other evidences of interest in or indebtedness of carriers, which include, but are not limited to advances payable to an affiliated company, loan agreements, credit agreements, mortgages, chattel mortgages, deeds of trust, equipment trusts, security agreements, and purchase agreements of property having a useful life in excess of 1 year whose terms provide for other than full payment at the time of consummation." The I.C.C. stated that the term "shall not at this time be interpreted to include agreements entered into for the sole purpose of acquiring motor carrier equipment."[36] The I.C.C. also said that the term "assume any obligation or liability" in Section 20a shall include "advance of funds to an affiliated company."

Issuance of Stocks and Bonds

When stock is not actively traded the Commission may consider book value after issue, earnings of the carrier, and other factors in arriving at fair market value.[37] Warrants are not securities under the I.C. Act, but stock

---

[33]282 I.C.C. 70.
[34]36 M.C.C. 721.
[35]344 I.C.C. 114, 348 I.C.C. 288, 354 I.C.C. 10.
[36]49 CFR, Part 1115.
[37]*Chemical Tank Lines, Inc., Securities,* 87 M.C.C. 386.

issued in satisfaction of the warrants would be viewed as securities.[38] In order to bring about a change in control of a carrier voting and non-voting stock may be issued. Where preferred stock is convertible into common stock authority may be requested to issue common stock to be reserved for future conversion; if too much preferred stock is issued conditions may be prescribed giving preferred stockholders the right to elect a majority of directors should there be a default in payment of dividends for a long period of time; various classes of stock may be issued to give the public a preference on earnings distributed.[39]

Carriers should advise the public when offering securities that the Commission has not passed upon their quality from the standpoint of investment or on the accuracy of the facts stated in the prospectus.[40] To come within the purview of the I.C. Act, a non-carrier corporation which is not a common carrier but controls one is required to be subjected to the I.C. Act by order of the Commission. Thus to issue securities the non-carrier corporation would have to be subjected to the I.C. Act. In determining whether a non-carrier corporation should be subject to the I.C. Act consideration is given to its investments — to be subject to the I.C. Act the non-carrier corporation's investments would have to be largely in transportation.[41]

In *Illinois Terminal R. Co. Bonds,*[42] authority was granted for an issue of bonds by the Illinois Terminal Railroad Company which contained restrictions preventing the call of the bonds for an initial five-year period. In that, and several other cases containing similar call restrictions, which were approved, the carriers justified such restrictions by pointing out that they are frequently used in connection with the sale of industrial and utility issues and that the carriers must compete for their funds in the same money market. Also, that institutional investors, who form the largest market for such bonds, do not care to devote the time and study required in deciding whether to purchase bonds if the bonds are

[38]*Consolidated Freightways Corp. of Delaware Bonds,* 85 M.C.C. 697; *Norwalk Truck Lines, Inc., Securities,* 85 M.C.C. 376; *Cooper-Jarrett Inc., Stock,* 295 I.C.C. 230.
[39]*Complete Auto Transit, Inc., Stock,* 295 I.C.C. 28; *Akers Motor Lines, Inc., Stock,* F. D. No. 19306, July 20, 1956; *Navajo Freight Lines, Inc., Stock,* 87 M.C.C. 8; *Eazor Express, Inc.,* 90 M.C.C. 235.
[40]*Navajo Freight Lines, Inc., Stock,* 87 M.C.C. 8.
[41]*Woods Industries, Inc. — Control — United Transports, Inc.,* 85 M.C.C. 672; *Lease Plan International Corp. Stock,* 80 M.C.C. 451; *Roush — Control — Southern California Freight Lines,* 80 M.C.C. 573; *American Transp. Enterprises — Control — Del. Bus. Co.,* 80 M.C.C. 18; *Pittston Co. — Control — Brink's, Inc.,* 80 M.C.C. 179; *Wells Fargo Armored Service Corp. — Control — Armored,* 75 M.C.C. 285.
[42]317 I.C.C. 595; cf. *Southern Ry. Co. Bonds,* 295 I.C.C. 782, 784.

subject to call at an early date. These decisions represent some relaxation of the view expressed in *Southern Ry. Co. Bonds*, that, as a general rule, bonds should be redeemable at any time upon payment of a reasonable redemption premium. In *Southern Ry. Co. Bonds*, the Commission said that it did not look with favor upon inclusion of provisions in bonds and the indentures under which they are issued, which restrict a carrier's right to redeem them at any time upon payment of a reasonable premium. Except in cases involving stock dividends, the Commission has no jurisdiction over the declaration of dividends on capital stocks of carriers subject to the Act; that matter is entirely within the control of the management of the carriers.[43] In numerous decisions the Commission has authorized the issuance of contingent-interest debentures to be exchanged for preferred stock, and in some of those cases it authorized the issuance of stock in exchange for arrearages with the arrearage security holder becoming a corporate investor rather than receiving the full amount of his arrears in cash.[44] The Commission looks with disfavor on carrier's reacquisition of stock at costs so substantial as to create debit balances in, or to reduce substantially, their earned surplus; this is especially undesirable where the carrier is large, as support is removed, or weakened, for credit, emergency needs, and the replacement and betterment of its properties.[45]

That a transportation corporation has capitalizable assets sufficient to support an increase in securities does not in itself justify such increase; necessity for the proposed issue must be demonstrated and the terms on which it is to be sold must be found reasonable.[46] Confidence of public investors in securities would not be fostered, and is likely to be impaired if securities subject to unusual and speculative features are distributed among the public.[47] A carrier should not be permitted to issue and sell stock for the purpose of augmenting its working capital, alleged to be sufficient, when it proposes immediately to reduce its funds by payment of a cash dividend; and in effect a portion of the proceeds of the stock sold would be used immediately to pay a dividend on that and other stock.[48]

In considering the assets of a carrier which properly may be capitalized, a reasonable amount should be allowed as working capital, limited to cash, material and supplies, and pre-payments, excluding interest;

[43]*Maine Central R. Co. Debentures*, 307 I.C.C. 47, 56.
[44]*Ibid*, p. 57.
[45]*McCormick — Control — A.C.E. Transp. Co., Inc.*, 80 M.C.C. 401, 418.
[46]*Norwalk Truck Lines, Inc., Securities* 85 M.C.C. 235, 242.
[47]*Navajo Freight Lines, Inc., Stock*, 85 M.C.C. 592, 595.
[48]*Ibid.*, p. 596.

where the sum of these accounts is more than the excess of current assets over current liabilities, the amount to be capitalized should not be more than such excess.[49] Authority under Sections 5 and 20(a) may be granted to a corporation not in existence; as, upon consolidation, applicants will automatically pass out of existence, the consolidated company must have authority under Section 20(a) to issue securities and assume certain liabilities and obligations of the consolidating companies.[50]

In *Bi-State Development Agency of Mo.-Ill. Met. Dist., Bonds, supra,* the Commission granted for lack of jurisdiction, applicant's motion to dismiss its application for authority to issue transit bonds. Applicant is a bi-State agency, created as a "body corporate and politic," governed by a board of commissioners under a compact between the States of Missouri and Illinois, approved by Congress, with powers to plan and develop the St. Louis bi-State metropolitan district; own and operate various types of public works projects, including passenger transportation facilities; and borrow money and issue securities upon prescribed terms. In creating a public passenger transit system, the applicant proposed to issue revenue bonds, a portion of the proceeds of which were to be used in the purchase of properties of companies providing local transit service in the district, including several which are subject to the jurisdiction of the Commission. The Commission found that the applicant was not a "carrier" by railroad or motor vehicle, and issuance of securities by it prior to its engaging in transportation as such a carrier did not require approval of the Commission, because it could not be considered as a "corporation organized for the purpose of engaging in transportation," subject to part II of the I.C. Act with in the meaning of Section 214 relating to issuance of securities.

Stock option plans will be approved by the Commission if restricted.[51] Normally, the number of shares to be issued under an employee stock option plan should not exceed 10 percent of the number of shares actually outstanding prior to such issuance; and in absence of a definite proposal for use of the proceeds, they should be applied to investment in carrier operating property.[52]

---

[49]*Dixie Highway Exp., Inc. — Control and Merger,* 80 M.C.C. 473, 481.

[50]*Missouri — K.-T. R. Co. Consolidation,* 312 I.C.C. 13, 19. See also *Bi-State Development Agency of Mo. — Ill. Met. Dist., Bonds,* 317 I.C.C. 641.

[51]*Atchison, T. & S. F. Ry. Co. Stock,* 295 I.C.C. 298; *Cooper-Jarrett, Inc., Stock,* 85 M.C.C. 719; *American Commercial Barge Line Co., Stock,* 87 M.C.C. 19.

[52]*Cooper-Jarrett, Inc., Stock* 85 M.C.C. 719, 721.

Issuance of Securities for Noncarrier Purposes

In *Greyhound Corporation Stock*,[53] the ICC said that securities may be issued for the purpose of investment in noncarrier business enterprises if the ICC finds that the investment is judicious and not adverse to the public interest.[54] In *K. W. McKee, Inc. Stock*,[55] the ICC said:

> In the *Greyhound* case, the Commission found that the issuance of stock by a carrier to obtain funds to invest in nontransportation activities might properly be approved where it is a lawful object, compatible with the public interest, where it will not impair, in any respect, the carrier's ability, financially or otherwise, to perform service to the public, and where the proposal is not 'improvident.' In effect, it was found that such proposals could be approved where they are judicious investments, which will improve the carrier's financial condition and ability to serve the public.

The ICC distinguished the *Greyhound* case in *Redwing Carriers, Inc., Securities*,[56] as follows:

> The use to which applicant intends to put the proceeds from the proposed note and stock issuance varies from its ordinary corporate purposes. The objective here is to permit a subsidiary to clear up expenses and obligations involved in the acquisition of a pipeline. The operation of such type of transportation is not the primary transportation concern of the applicant and the diversion of applicant's credit to the stated ends is not consistent with applicant's welfare as a motor carrier. See *Louisville & N. R. Co., Securities*, 76 I.C.C. 718, 720: *Detroit, T. & I. Investment Certificates*, 82 I.C.C. 411.

> Applicant points to the fact that the diversion of its credit to the extent of the 23,000 shares of additional stock would represent only 2.5 percent of its total outstanding stock. Applicant cites *Greyhound Corp. Stock*, 90 M.C.C. 215, in support of this use of proceeds. The cited case, however, involved investment in a going concern of very substantial character whereas, in the present instance, the corporation being indirectly acquired does not have an active operating history or seasoned earnings power. The prudency of the investment herein is questionable from such standpoint alone.

In *Pittsburgh & W. Va. R. Trust Certificate*,[57] the following appears:

> Applicant acknowledges that the Commission has traditionally tested the propriety of a proposed stock issue by determining the carrier's capitaliz-

---

[53]90 M.C.C. 215.

[54]See *California Parlor Car Tours Co. — Pur. — Greyhound*, 93 M.C.C. 392, where Greyhound became a holding company transferring its operating rights and certain properties to a subsidiary carrier. The subsidiary carrier was given authority under Section 214 to assume obligation and liability in respect of outstanding secured promissory notes of Greyhound.

[55]93 M.C.C. 643, 647.

[56]101 M.C.C. 764, 767-68.

[57]336 I.C.C. 530, 534-35.

able assets and the amount of uncapitalized surplus remaining after the issue. See *Denver & R. G. W. R. Co. Stock*, 290 I.C.C. 178 (1953); *Chesapeake & O. Ry. Co. Stock*, 254 I.C.C. 653 (1943). Applicant argues that this standard was developed and is applicable to operating carriers and that it should not be applied here because it is not an operating carrier. The objective of the capitalizable assets standards, applicant contends, was to insure that operating carriers would not unduly divert their resources into noncarrier investments and thus impair their ability to render public service. Applicant denotes itself as a real estate investment trust whose present function is solely rent collection.

In support of its contention that acquisitions by a carrier of noncarrier property have been approved as part of a diversification program designed to stabilize earnings, applicant cites *Greyhound Corp. Stock*, 90 M.C.C. 215, 223 (1962) (at that time a carrier), and *Pennsylvania Co. Stock*, 324 I.C.C. 275 (1964) (a holding company).

The difference herein lies in the fact that applicant, a nonoperating carrier, would become substantially overcapitalized, by the accounting standards applied by this Commission to carriers, in order to issue securities and assume obligation with respect to securities in connection with the acquisition of noncarrier properties. We have held that decisions should be based upon the facts involved in the individual case under consideration. See *Securities of La. Ry. & Nav. Co. of Tex.*, 99 I.C.C. 357 (1925). The nonoperating character of applicant herein is, in our opinion, sufficient reason for an exception to the strict application of the rule relating to capitalization of a carrier. It is further noted that applicant will obtain $400,000 in cash upon consummation of the proposed transaction and this cash need not be distributed to the holders of shares of beneficial interest since it is not income and consequently does not come within the mandatory distribution provisions of the trust. The proposed transaction should enhance the ability of the applicant to perform its duties or obligations under the lease or under a reversion of the properties in the event the lease is terminated.

We find that (1) the proposed issue of not exceeding 370,000 shares of beneficial interest, and (2) the assumption of obligation and liability in respect of not exceeding $3,275,402 principal amount of notes, as shown in the appendix hereto, plus interest, by the Pittsburgh & West Virginia Railroad, (a) are for lawful objects within the purposes of the trust and compatible with the public interest, which are necessary and appropriate for and consistent with the proper performance by it of service to the public, and which will not impair its ability to perform that service, and (b) are reasonably necessary and appropriate for such purposes.

Modification of Railroad Financial Structures

Section 20(b) of the I.C. Act[58] provides, among other things, that a carrier, as defined in Section 20(a) (1), with the approval and authorization of the Commission as therein provided, may lawfully alter or modify

---

[58]49 U.S.C. 20(b).

any provision of any class or classes of its securities as defined in Section 20(a) (2), or any provision of any mortgage, indenture, deed of trust, corporate charter, or other instrument pursuant to which any class of its securities shall have been issued, by obtaining assets to such alterations or modifications from the holders of at least 75 percent of the securities affected thereby. It further provides that before the Commission shall cause a plan of alteration or modification to be submitted to affected security holders for acceptance or rejection, it must find, in addition to the findings required by paragraph (2) of Section 20(a) in cases involving the issuance of securities, that, subject to such terms and conditions and with such amendments as it shall determine to be just and reasonable, the proposed alteration or modification (a) is within the scope of paragraph (1) of Section 20(b); (b) will be in the public interest; (c) will be in the best interest of the carrier, of each class of its stockholders, and of the holders of each class of its obligations affected by such modification or alteration; and (d) will not be adverse to the interests of any creditor of the carrier not affected by such modification or alteration.[59]

The Commission said in the *Western Maryland* case that "Congress in enacting Section 20(b) declared it to be in aid of the transportation policy as set forth in the preamble of the Interstate Commerce Act, among other things, to enhance the marketability of railroad securities impaired by large and continuing accumulations of . . . dividends on preferred stock. . . . One of the ends to be accomplished through enhancing the marketability of such securities in the promotion of the public interest in increased stability of values of railroad securities with resulting greater confidence therein of investors."

Public Offerings

For the purpose of insuring adequate disclosure of information to the public in connection with public offerings issued by carriers pursuant to Section 20a or Section 214 of the I.C. Act, the I.C.C. held in *Securities Regulations — Public Offerings*[60] that an offering circular ("prospectus") should be required conforming to standards generally patterned after Securities and Exchange Commission requirements, except in the following instances:

1. Philadelphia plan equipment trust certificates. This plan is used to secure payment of the purchase price in equipment acquisitions. Usually, upon issuance of the certificates, the carrier makes a downpay-

---

[59]*Western Maryland Ry. Co., Securities Modification*, 290 I.C.C. 445, 454-5.
[60]344 I.C.C. 168.

ment of 20 percent of the purchase price, and thereafter makes regular payments of principal and interest pursuant to a trust indenture over a period of 10 to 15 years commencing within 1 year of the issuance of the certificates. The practical result is that the collateral backing the certificates — equipment depreciation notwithstanding — normally retains a value greater than the amount of the obligation on the certificates outstanding. Moreover, the certificates are usually purchased on the basis of competitive bids by financial institutions which because of the nature of their business are (as a matter of due course) well informed on the quality of the certificates, and do not require a prospectus with the detailed information necessary for the protection of the general public.

2. Notes, loan agreements, and other securities transactions between carriers and financial institutions wherein the terms are negotiated and the institutions normally impose their own requirements or conditions. These do not involve a sale to the public.

3. Commercial paper provided the paper is a note, draft, bill of exchange, or banker's acceptance which arises out of a current transaction or the proceeds of which have been or are to be used for current transactions and which has a maturity at the time of issuance of not exceeding nine months. Such paper is often issued on a daily basis precluding, as a practical matter, the use of a prospectus. The usual purchaser is a large, knowledgeable institutional investor who does not need a prospectus for the information governing his day to day business judgments.

4. Government guaranteed securities. A prospectus is unnecessary in this instance for protection of the general public, in that the Government stands as an insurer against loss by the purchaser or investor. Adequate disclosure of relevant information is made to the Government or can be demanded at the time of a guarantee sought.

5. Stock dividend or stock split. The former is a judgment matter wholly within the prerogative of the issuing carrier's board of directors; and the latter requires in most instances affirmative action by stockholders who have available corporate records.

6. Stock option or purchase plans involving only directors and/or officers of the issuer. These individuals, by virtue of their positions as executives, presumably know or have access to the information which a prospectus is intended to disclose.

Security for the Protection of the Public

Section 215 of the I.C. Act[61] provides:

[61]49 U.S.C. 315. Comparable provision — Section 403(c), (d).

"No certificate or permit shall be issued to a motor carrier or remain in force, unless such carrier complies with such reasonable rules and regulations as the Commission shall prescribe governing the filing and approval of surety bonds, policies of insurance, qualifications as a self-insurer or other securities or agreements, in such reasonable amount as the Commission may require, conditioned to pay, within the amount of such surety bonds, policies of insurance, qualifications as a self-insurer or other securities or agreements, any final judgment recovered against such motor carrier for bodily injuries to or the death of any person resulting from the negligent operation, maintenance, or use of motor vehicles under such certificate or permit, or for loss or damage to property of others.

"The Commission may, in its discretion and under such rules and regulations as it shall prescribe, require any such common carrier to file a surety bond, policies of insurance, qualifications as a self-insurer, or other securities or agreements, in a sum to be determined by the Commission, to be conditioned upon such carrier making compensation to shippers and/or consignees for all property belonging to shippers and/or consignees, and coming into the possession of such carrier in connection with its transportation service. Any carrier which may be required by law to compensate a shipper and/or consignee for any loss, damage, or default for which a connecting motor common carrier is legally responsible shall be subrogated to the rights of such shipper and/or consignee under any such bond, policies of insurance, or other securities or agreements, to the extent of the sum so paid."

The section provides further, that the "Commission may prescribe, with respect to motor carriers operating within the United States in the course of engaging in transportation between places in a foreign country or between a place in one foreign country and a place in another foreign country, such reasonable regulations concerning security for the protection of the public as the Commission is authorized, by this section, to prescribe for other motor carriers."

The Commission has held that carriers performing service under interim applications are required to comply with the provisions of the Act and rules and regulations thereunder, including insurance regulations promulgated under Section 215. Failure to do so leaves the public unprotected, contrary to the intent of Congress, and that cease and desist order will be entered against those carriers which are not in compliance.[62]

Bankruptcy Act

Section 77 of the Bankruptcy Act[63] was originally enacted in 1933. It was passed because of the recognition by Congress that railroad reorganizations require special treatment in that the operations of the

---

[62]*Insurance Compliance,* 79 M.C.C. 213, 214.
[63]11 U.S.C. 205.

debtor company are inevitably clothed with the public interest. Not only must the interests of the estate and the creditors be considered in dealing with railroad reorganization, but it is of vital importance that these private interests be balanced against the public interest in the continuation of essential rail transportation services.[64]

The need for the consideration of the public interest in the maintenance of continued rail service is still the same as it was in 1933 when the Bankruptcy Act was passed. Concern with this problem is demonstrated by the passage of the Regional Reorganization Act of 1973 and the 4R Act. These acts provide for an extensive government sponsored reorganization procedure in order to maintain essential rail service which was threatened with termination because of the bankruptcy of the Penn Central and several other major railroads of the Northeast. Congress then followed up that procedure with federal aid programs designed to preserve and improve needed rail services on a nationwide basis.

Section 77 of the Bankruptcy Act provides an efficient and speedy method of reviving sick and ailing railroads; it seeks to reorganize the roads, place them on a sound financial footing, so that they may continue to operate and serve the nation's needs.[65] It was intended to do away with an evil prevalent in equity receivership proceedings, that is, the practice of submitting to the court a plan already consented to by a large proportion of the old security holders, exerting pressure to approve it against objections of minorities.[66]

Lack of solvency which justifies initiation of reorganization is inability to meet debts as they become due.[67] It is the purpose of Section 77 that the court shall so reorganize the debtor as not to result in an excessively over-capitalized financial structure, in order that income may meet fixed charges and costs of operation.[68] The Commission has the responsibility for formulating a plan compatible with the public interest subject to a degree of participation by the court.[69] It is the sole responsibility of the Commission to develop the capitalization of the reorganized company. The federal court must approve or disapprove a plan in its entirety; the court alone cannot correct a plan but may suggest improvement to the Commission.[70]

---

[64] *New Haven Inclusion Cases*, 339 U.S. 392, 491-92.

[65] *In re Denver & RGW R. Co.*, 150 F. 2d 28, 34.

[66] *In re New York, N. H. & H. R. Co.*, 147 F. 2d 40, 49.

[67] *St. Louis-S. W. Ry. Co. v. Henwood*, 157 F. 2d 337, 398.

[68] *In re Chicago, R. I. & P. Ry. Co.*, 155 F. 2d 889, 891.

[69] *In re Boston Term. Co.*, 71 F. Supp. 472, 474.

[70] *Chicago, R. I. & P. Ry. Co. v. Fleming*, 157 F. 2d 241, 244; *Benton v. Callaway*, 165 F. 2d 877, 884.

The Bankruptcy Act deals with financial reorganization, not with transportation as such, and though a major purpose of Section 77 proceedings is to assure continuance of transportation service required by public convenience and necessity, the statute presupposes that financial adjustments are an adequate means to that end.[71] It is noted in this regard that in *St. Joe Paper Co. v. Atlantic Coast Line Railroad Co.*,[72] the Supreme Court held that a reorganization plan under Section 77 could not provide for the merger of the debtor with another railroad against the will of a majority of the debtor's stockholders.

[71]*Passengers Fares, New York, N. H. & H. R. Co.*, 313 I.C.C. 411, 426.
[72]347 U.S. 298.

54

Transportation Costing and Cost Base for Calculating Depreciation and Rate of Return

Uniform Cost and Revenue Accounting and Reporting System

Section 20(3)[1] of the Interstate Commerce Act, as amended by the 4R Act, provides as follows:

"(a) The Commission shall, not later than June 30, 1977, issue regulations and procedures prescribing a uniform cost and revenue accounting and reporting system for all common carriers by railroad subject to this part. Such regulations and procedures shall become effective not later than January 1, 1978. Before promulgating such regulations and procedures, the Commission shall consult with and solicit the views of other agencies and departments of the Federal Government, representatives of carriers, shippers, and their employees, and the general public.

"(b) In order to assure that the most accurate cost and revenue data can be obtained with respect to light density lines, main line operations, factors relevant in establishing fair and reasonable rates, and other regulatory areas of responsibility, the Commission shall identify and define the following items as they pertain to each facet of rail operations:

"(i) operating and nonoperating revenue accounts;
"(ii) direct cost accounts for determining fixed and variable cost for materials, labor, and overhead components of operating expenses and the assignment of such costs to various functions, services, or activities, including maintenance-of-way, maintenance of equipment (locomotive and car), transportation (train, yard and station, and accessorial services), and general and administrative expenses; and
"(iii) indirect cost accounts for determining fixed, common, joint, and constant costs, including the cost of capital, and the method for the assignment of such costs to various functions, services, or activities.

---

[1] 49 U.S.C. 20(3). Comparable provisions, Section 204(a)(1), (2); Section 313 (c); Section 412(a).

"(c) The accounting system established pursuant to this paragraph shall be in accordance with generally accepted accounting principles uniformly applied to all common carriers by railroad subject to this part, and all reports shall include any disclosure considered appropriate under generally accepted accounting principles or the requirements of the Commission or of the Securities and Exchange Commission. The Commission shall, notwithstanding any other provision of this section, to the extent possible, devise the system of accounts to be cost effective, nonduplicative, and compatible with the present and desired managerial and responsibility accounting requirements of the carriers, and to give due consideration to appropriate economic principles. The Commission should attempt, to the extent possible, to require that such data be reported or otherwise disclosed only for essential regulatory purposes, including rate change requests, abandonment of facilities requests, responsibility for peaks in demand, cost of service, and issuance of securities.

"(d) In order that the accounting system established pursuant to this paragraph continue to conform to generally accepted accounting principles, compatible with the managerial responsibility accounting requirements of carriers, and in compliance with other objectives set forth in this section, the Commission shall periodically, but not less than once every 5 years, review such accounting system and revise it as necessary.

"(e) There are authorized to be appropriated to the Commission for purposes of carrying out the provisions of this paragraph such sums as may be necessary, not to exceed $1,000,000, to be available for—

"(i) procuring temporary and intermittent services as authorized by section 3109(b) of title 5, United States Code, but at rates for individuals not to exceed $250 per day plus expenses; and
"(ii) entering into contracts or cooperative agreements with any public agency or instrumentality or with any person, firm, association, corporation, or institution, without regard to section 3709 of the Revised Statutes of the United States (41 U.S.C. 5)."

ASCERTAINING THE COST OF TRANSPORTATION

Cost Formulas

The following cost formulas have been developed and published by the Commission:

Rail Form A, "Formula for Use in Determining Rail Freight Service Costs."

Rail Terminal Form F, "Formula for Use in Determining Rail Terminal Freight Service Costs."

Highway Form A, "Formula for the Determination of the Costs of Motor Carriers of Property."

Highway Form B, "Simplified Procedure for Determining Cost of Handling Freight by Motor Carriers."

Highway Form F, "Formula for Determining the Cost of Transporting Freight in Motor Carrier Tank Vehicles."

Barge Form C, "Formula for Determining the Cost of Transporting Freight by Barge Lines."

Rail Form A — This formula has been used by the Commission for determining rail territorial costs. Although Rail Form A has principally been designed and used for the purpose of developing costs for large groups of carriers, it is said to be also adaptable to small groups of carriers and to individual railroads. It is suggested that individual carriers should make every possible effort to develop their own operating factors for use in applying this formula to their expenses and statistics. Where this course is unduly burdensome, the territorial factors developed by the Commission in special studies which are included in the appendices to the formula may be used, though it is preferable that a carrier apply its own specific factors.

Stated briefly, Rail Form A provides for separating the expenses among the various services, i.e., yard switching, train switching, running, station, special services, and general overhead, with a further separation of each of these services to the various types of operations performed within each service. It also determines the related revenue units of service, such as, car-miles, gross-ton-miles, net-ton-miles, and tons originated and terminated. The formula further provides for developing the unit costs for each service and, combining such unit costs based on the services performed on the various type movements, produces cost scales for various weight shipments moving in the different types of cars by lengths of haul. The costs include an allowance for return on investment with provisions for Federal income tax. The cost scales are based on both the variable and the fully allocated cost levels, with the constant costs distributed in connection with the latter on a pro rata ton and ton-mile basis.

Basically, the figures relating to expenses and statistics used in the formula are taken from the reports filed with the Commission by class I rail carriers and class I switching and terminal companies. These data are supplemented by special studies which develop factors used in processing the expenses and statistics throughout the various schedules, forms, and summaries which are components of Rail Form A.

Rail Terminal Form F — This formula provides a method for determining both the time consumed and the cost involved in handling each rail car in a terminal.

The formula is constructed to permit various degrees of refinement in developing terminal switching studies, depending upon the needs of each particular case. However, the formula is to be used for individual yards or terminals and is not applicable to system or territorial use. It also provides for dividing the terminal into zones, so that costs may be developed for handling traffic in a specific zone within the terminal area. The cost per car includes, in addition to the expenses involved in switching service, the cost of repairs of locomotives and equipment, of yard tracks and buildings, applicable depreciation charges, station expense, an apportionment of general overhead costs, and taxes. It is also possible to compute through the use of this formula the cost of the terminal services required for originating and terminating line-haul shipments, for switching shipments, for interchange service, and for moving cars through the terminal.

Form F provides for several levels of costs, based upon the distribution of the carrier's operating expenses, rents, taxes, and return on investment to the movement of the traffic under study. Consideration is given to all or part of the following factors, which may affect each class of switching under study: (1) number of yard locomotive minutes; (2) the extent and relative use of the trackage; (3) the number of car-miles operated; (4) the number of active car-days consumed; (5) class of locomotives used; and (6) special services received, if any.

This formula provides for the computation of costs for various classes of switching, such as carrier terminal switching, connection terminal switching, intermediate switching, intraterminal switching, interterminal switching, interchange switching, intra- and inter-train switching. Certain of these classes of switching may be further separated as to traffic handled for each connecting line, as to industries or by groups of industries. The cost for each class of switching may be computed on the basis of loaded cars handled or on the basis of the total cars handled, loaded or empty.

Apportionment factors directly relating to the individual carrier's operation are to be developed wherever possible. Thus, apportionment factors shown throughout the formula should be used only in the absence of data permitting direct assignment. It is also indicated that it is desirable that adjustments for any abnormal expenses be incorporated in the cost study.

The formula permits for the computation of unit costs per freight car, per hundredweight of freight, per total cars handled, or per loaded car by specified class of switching service, without considering the variable and constant costs separation or a specified return on investment. Accordingly, such unit costs relate to the concept of full expense level costs. However, provisions are also made for the development of service unit costs at other cost levels.

A form is provided in the introductory part of the formula for the application of a rate of return on investment when this information is required. This form suggests no particular rate of return nor any specific percentage variability factor, but requires merely an explanation of the procedure used in developing out-of-pocket costs.

Highway Form A — This formula, sometimes called the long formula, has been used for determining territorial or regional costs for motor carriers of general commodities. Although Highway Form A is principally designed for the purpose of developing costs for large groups of carriers, it is said to be also adaptable for application to individual carriers or small groups of carriers.

Highway Form A provides for separating the expenses among (1) the various services, i.e., line-haul, pickup and delivery, terminal platform, and billing and collecting, (2) expenses unrelated to the study, and (3) general overhead. It also provides for determining the related revenue units of service, such as vehicle-miles, ton-miles, tons given pickup and delivery service, tons given platform handling, shipments billed, etc. The formula further provides for separating the expenses in each service between weight brackets (sizes of shipment) and develops unit costs for each service, which are combined based upon the services performed on the shipments, producing cost scales by weight of shipment and length of haul.

The cost scales are developed separately for single-line hauls, two-line hauls, and for the weighted average of single-line and inter-line movements. These scales reflect the variable portion of operating expenses, rents, and taxes (other than income taxes) and a 5-percent allowance for return on depreciated investment. Although the mileage cost scales and most of the other schedules and summaries in the formula are limited to the variable expenses, the total revenue needs or fully allocated costs have been calculated and are shown in the aggregate.

Basically, the figures relating to expenses and statistics used in this formula are to be obtained from the annual reports filed with the Commission by class I and class II motor common carriers of general freight. The formula is designed to accommodate the accounts and statistics of such carriers which derive an average of 75 percent or more of their revenues from the intercity transportation of general commodities and which have average annual gross revenues of a fixed amount or more. Carriers whose operations fit within these limitations are required to separate certain of their major accounts between line-haul and pickup and delivery work and to report certain supplemental statistics. Their accounts and statistics lend themselves more readily to cost finding procedures than is the case with carriers that are not required to follow such procedures.

In applying Highway Form A the annual reports of the carriers involved are supplemented by special studies and working forms, as follows: (1) a field report dealing with certain accounting information; (2) a 4-day analysis of freight bills, according to weight of shipment and type of movement (local or interline); (3) a time report covering city pickup and delivery trips for one day; (4) a trip report covering speed and load on all intercity trips for two days; (5) a platform report showing the extent of platform handling for various sizes of shipments for two days; and (6) an analysis of peddle trip operations for use in separating peddle expenses between line-haul and pickup and delivery operations. While the test periods indicated above have been used by the Commission in certain regional studies, they may be expanded where a longer period is deemed essential to obtain typicality.

The factors developed from these special studies are used in processing the expenses and statistics through the various schedules, forms, and summaries which are component parts of Highway Form A in developing costs for rate making purposes.

Highway Form B — The purpose of this motor carrier cost formula is to provide a simplified or shortened procedure whereby there can be readily developed unit costs by services and variable costs for specific hauls, without the necessity of making the extensive special studies which are required as a part of the more refined Highway Form A. As previously noted, Highway Form A contains numerous schedules, forms, and summaries which are used in processing special studies and developing apportionment factors for distributing costs to various size shipments. The shortened procedure followed in Highway Form B is intended primarily to indicate ways and means whereby those who do not have the need for extensive refinements can eliminate these special studies and still develop unit costs sufficiently accurate to be useful in costing out specific hauls. In lieu of these special studies, the allocation of costs among various sizes of shipments is achieved by applying cost relationships, developed in past territorial studies through the application of Highway Form A, to the average cost for all shipments. Highway Form B consists of and is limited to one schedule, one form, and one summary. Since no consideration is given therein to interline expenses, density of commodity, circuity, and costs other than single-line, Highway Form

A, the long formula, has to be used when these matters are significant.

Highway Form F — This formula is designed for the purpose of determining individual carrier or regional average costs, for transporting products in tank vehicles by motor carriers. It is intended to serve the same purpose for tank truck carriers as Highway Form B does for general commodity motor carriers. It provides a procedure by which carriers or others having access to certain operating data may develop: (1) unit costs by services; (2) cost scales per gallon or per 100 pounds, for both short-line miles and actual miles traversed; and (3) costs for specific point-to-point movements, at both the variable and the fully allocated cost levels. While accounts of class I carriers are shown in the formula, those of class II carriers may be substituted therefor.

Although basic data for the application of the formula are obtained from annual reports filed with the Commission by the carriers, certain additional "test data" are required. Such additional information is obtained from the carriers. The former provides expense breakdowns of various annual report items and statistical data, and the latter is a report of round-trip vehicle operations during specified test periods, including information on drivers' wages, vehicle movements, commodities carried, mileages and time factors. The data obtained by means of these reports are required in order to develop mileage cost scales for actual and short-line blocks, and for the computation of costs for point-to-point movements of specific commodities.

Highway Form F, like Highway Form B, consists of one schedule, one form, and a summary schedule.

Barge Form C — The purpose of this formula is to develop costs for bargeload traffic based on the expenses and statistics of individual water carriers. The various component schedules are used to compute unit costs which are combined in a summary schedule to arrive at the total costs per ton for a particular traffic movement.

Barge Form C contains several important cost finding features consisting of a functional breakdown of accounts to services, provisions for adjustment of the annual expenses for abnormalities, costs for individual ports and river districts, and a new service unit, the equivalent barge-mile. This formula can presently be applied only by a carrier which maintains certain subaccounts and statistics specified therein, or by those which have access thereto, the expenses required to be shown by the uniform system of accounts being insufficient.

In addition, a water carrier will be obliged to accumulate a number of service units which at present are not reportable to the Commission, such as tug and towboat hours; barge-days; barge-miles;

equivalent barge-miles; numbers of barges originated, terminated, and interchanged; and number of tons handled or given special services. These service units are necessary for the proper measurement of the work performed in barge transportation and for association with the expenses of each function.

Two bases of cost are provided. The first basis, which must be computed for each movement, comprises total operating expenses, plus a 6-percent allowance (after provisions for Federal income taxes) for return on investment and on working capital. Essentially, this first basis is the equivalent of fully allocated cost, with the constant expense distributed among services on the same basis as the variable expenses. A variable level of cost may be computed separately if desired, but only when the variable percentage to be applied to total expenses and to the allowance for return on investment has been ascertained. However, since no general studies have been made of barge lines, similar to those for rail and motor carriers, to determine a standard percentage of variability, a variable cost level is not specifically set forth in Barge Form C. The absence of such a percentage figure should not be construed to mean that the expenses and return on investment of a water carrier are, therefore, 100 percent variable.

The second but an optional basis is comprised of total operating expense and an allowance for profit. It is produced, in a similar manner as in the case of motor carriers, by dividing the total operating expense by an operating ratio. This basis may be computed when a carrier desires to show its total revenue need or fully allocated costs based on an operating ratio. It has principal significance for water carriers with little or no investment in operating property.

In *Rules to Govern the Assembling and Presenting of Cost Evidence,*[2] the Commission instituted a proceeding to determine whether the approval and adoption of certain cost formulas would result in general improvement of the quality of cost evidence presented in formal proceedings, eliminate controversies concerning admissibility of data prepared in an approved manner, and obviate or shorten cross-examination. As a necessary adjunct thereto, a thorough review of cost estimating methods and theories was undertaken. However, it was not its intention to prescribe strict limits within which cost evidence must be confined in particular proceedings.

In its discussion, the Commission said (pp. 324-26):

The cost formulas.—The specific formulas considered herein have in the past, and will in the future, continue to serve as valuable tools in esti-

[2]337 I.C.C. 298; interim report, 321 I.C.C. 238.

mating carrier costs. Our reluctance to adopt the formulas with a view toward giving prima facie validity to formula-based costs is motivated primarily by our unwillingness to encourage any form of rigidity or to impose stagnation in the field of cost ascertainment, and because of the absence of evidence of tangible benefits to be derived from such adoption at this time. Nevertheless, parties to Commission proceedings may continue to rely on formula-based costs, as modified, so long as the method of allocating expenses and the variable factors utilized are appropriate for the carrier's services for which the costs are presented.

Changes in cost terminology.—The terms "variable costs" and "fully allocated costs," describe the cost levels now respectively identified as as "out-of-pocket costs" and "fully distributed costs," with the exception of the elements excluded therefrom by our findings herein. As previously indicated, we agree with the examiner's recommendation that these terms be changed.

The term "out-of-pocket costs," although used by us for many years in the rate field, is nevertheless somewhat confusion. The term seems to imply that it refers to the immediately avoidable or direct level of expense which rekuires an additional out-of-pocket outlay of funds, or that additional amount of expense which must be paid out of the carrier's pocket in order to accomplish a particuar movement. However, the term actually represents a level of expense which includes, among other things, an apportionment of joint or common expenses which, in fact, are not necessarily incurred as a direct result of a particular movement. Therefore, while it may be entirely reasonable to charge a given movement with its fair share of such common costs, it does not necessarily follow that such costs are, strictly speaking, an out-of-pocket outlay of funds required directly as a result of the particular movement. In our view, the term "veriable costs," although ont entirely free from possible misinterpretation, is nevertheless more descriptive of all the unit expenses properly associated with particular changes in output.

The term "fully distributed costs" includes all costs, both variable and constant. It also includes, however, overall carrier revenue requirements, and as such, is not, strictly speaking, descriptive of a level of true costs. Instead, it represents a blend of costing and rate making. Revenue need, of course, is a relevant consideration in rate making, but we believe that the distinction between costing and rate making should be maintained. Accordingly, henceforth the term "fully allocated costs" will be used in place of "fully distributed costs" and the noncost elements of profit, income taxes, and the passenger and less-than-carload deficits will be excluded therefrom.

Imputed interest.—Imputed interest on equity capital is undeniably a cost to the carrier, and the rate of such return is a factual matter to be determined in light of the contemporary financial and economic conditions. The question of what portion of such cost should be considered as variable, depends (as is the case with variability generally) on the relevant time period considered. This, in turn, requires a determination which can only be made in the light of specific facts concerning the nature of the carrier's operations and the relevant transportation performed.

It should be understood that the determination of estimated variable costs (including an appropriate portion of imputed interest on equity capital) is not necesarily determinative of the exclusively rate making issue of what level of expenses must be recovered before a rate can be considered as reasonable for the transportation servics performed. Such issue can only be resolved in light of all relevant circumstances, including the nature of the traffic and the competitive situation with respect to carriers as well as shippers.

Costs in rate making.—Rate proceedings before the Commission generally require consideration of the relationship of relevant carrier costs to the rates. The focal point is the determination of what are the "relevant" costs. Certain levels of carrier expenses have general utility for specific purposes in transportation regulation, and may, in appropriate circumstances, be used by parties to Commission proceedings as representative of viable rate making indicators, as set forth in our findings herein. We do not here rule out the application of any reasonable method of estimating carrier costs. On the contrary, we wish to encourage a continuing search for improved methods of transportation costing.

Upon consideration of the matters presented, the Commission found:

(1) Approval and adoption of specific cost formulas, with a view toward giving prima facie validity to formula based costs, are not shown to be necesary or desirable.

(2) The terms "out-of-pocket costs" and "fully distributed costs," as used in Commission proceedings, should be changed to "variable costs" and "fully allocated costs," respectively, and the noncost elements of profit, income taxes, and for railroads, the passenger and less-than-carload deficits, should be excluded therefrom.

(3) The determination of a variability factor for particular services requires the selection of an appropriate time period which is sufficiently long to reflect adequately those changes in operations resulting in expenses which can reasonably be expected to vary with the performance of the particular service or services rendered.

(4) The allocation of constant costs to particular services, for rate making purposes, should result in the assignment of an equitable portion of such expenses to the particular services, and no single method can be considered as universally applicable to all transportation services.

(5) There is no universally acceptable method of apportioning joint or common costs, and any method of apportionment utilized for rate making purposes should be designed to reasonably reflect the specific circumstances attending the transportation performed.

(6) In appropriate circumstances, (a) "fully allocated costs" are representative of the full expense level assignable to particular services;

(b) relevant "variable costs" are indicative of the minimum level of expenses which must normally be recovered by a carrier in providing particular services; and (c) "incremental" or "marginal" costs, in appropriate shortrun situations, may be utilized as indicative of a minimum expense level for rate making purposes.

(7) A task force of Commission employees will be established for the purpose of conferring with shipper, carrier, and other government agency representatives to consider the feasibility and practicability of additional research projects into specific areas of transportation cost ascertainment.

(8) Other relief sought and proposals advanced, to the extent inconsistent with any of the conclusions and findings made herein, are denied and disapproved as unjustified or inappropriate.

The following are various types of costs in railroad costing. Variable costs are those which over a fairly long period of time vary with changes in traffic. These include approximately 75 percent to 80 percent of freight operating expenses, rents and taxes, excluding federal income taxes, plus an allowance for cost of capital on 50 percent of the railroad property and 100 percent of equipment used in carrying freight. Constant costs cover the remaining freight operating expenses, rents, about 20 percent to 25 percent of the taxes, and all allowance for capital costs on 50 percent of the railroad property. These costs are not variable with traffic volume changes. They arise out of the total operation of the railroad. They are not chargeable to a specific kind or class of traffic. Apportionment of constant costs to particular kinds or classes of traffic are based on judgment. Fully allocated costs are the sum of the variable costs plus an apportionment of constant costs on a statistical or arbitrary basis.

Cost Base for Use in Calculating Depreciation and Return

The Commission has held in numerous decisions that the proper method of computing rate of return in rate proceedings is to use original cost as base value.[3] The Commission was persuaded in *Chicago, Burlington & Quincy R. Co. v. N. Y. Susquehanna & Western R. Co.*,[4] that in the determination of depreciation to be considered in passing upon the compensatory character of per diem charges, the basis should be the undepreciated reproduction value. There was a contrast, how-

---

[3]See e.g., *Increased Freight Rates, 1947*, 269 I.C.C. 33; 270 I.C.C. 93; 270 I.C.C. 403; *Increased Freight Rates, 1948*, 276 I.C.C. 9; *Increased Freight Rates, E. W. & S. Territories, 1956*, 300 I.C.C. 633; *Utah Intrastate Freight Rates & Charges*, 309 I.C.C. 149; *Increased Freight Rates, 1951*, 280 I.C.C. 179, 281 I.C.C. 557.

[4]297 I.C.C. 291.

ever, between the result reached by the Commission and the statement made regarding the proper method of determining depreciation. The Commission said (p. 302), "We realize that in determining depreciation the prevailing accounting practice is to use the ledger value, and we are not here concerned with the propriety of that practice." The Commission also made it clear that there are a number of deficiencies in the use of reproduction costs by referring to its decision in *Telephone and Railroad Depreciation Charges,*[5] where the following comment was made:

> When depreciation accounting is employed, a further and important objection to the cost of replacement or present value method is that retirement and replacement of the unit do not occur when the depreciation change is made, and may not occur until many years in the future. If depreciation charges, therefore, are made each year on the basis of the current replacement cost or present value, they may prove to be quite out of line with this cost or value at the time when retirement actually takes place. In view of the constant shift of such cost and values this would, indeed, normally be the case, with the result that the depreciation reserve would be either too large or too small. No very satisfactory method of adjusting these irregularities has been suggested. It would also be necessary for us to exercise constant supervision over the depreciation charges for the determination of current replacement cost or present value is so controversial a matter that it could not safely be left to the discretion of the carriers.

The extreme contrast between the actual result reached by the Commission and its statement drew from the reviewing court in *Boston & Maine R. Co. v. United States,*[6] which set aside the order of the Commission, the following comment "by way of warning":

> Depreciation, the second largest element of the *per diem* charge, was calculated by the trial examiner on the basis of the undepreciated ledger value, that is the cost, of the freight car equipment in use which he said was "in accordance with the generally accepted accounting theory." The Commission, however, disagreed. It held that the basis should be "undepreciated reproduction value." We think that this holding is open to the very serious question.

✿ ✿ ✿

> If depreciation is an element, and not a minor one, of the *per diem* charge, we fail to see why accounting practices for determining depreciation should be cast aside as irrelevant. Moreover, as the trial examiner pointed out, ledger value is a known figure whereas the cost of reproduction can

[5] 177 I.C.C. 351, 377-78.
[6] 162 F. Supp. 289, 296. See later decision of Commission in *Chicago, B & Q. R. R. v. New York, S. & Western R. R.* 332 I.C.C. 176, aff'd 297 F. Supp. 615, 300 F. Supp. 318, motion to affirm granted 396 U.S. 27.

at best only be estimated and the process is inherently difficult because it involves many assumptions which are at least open to question. Furthermore, there is persuasive evidence that with ever faster freight trains and ever more efficient use of cars, present frieght car requirements are met with fewer cars than were formerly needed with the result that in all probability many cars now in use will never actually be replaced so that on the Commission's basis car users in paying *per diem* will in part be compensating car owners for expenses they will never incur.

The Supreme Court accepts the original cost base for use in calculating both depreciation and return. Original cost was accepted as base value in *Lindheimer v. Illinois Bell Tel, Co.*,[7] and in *Federal Power Comm'n v. Hope National Gas Co.*[8] In this latter case, the Supreme Court said:

> Moreover this Court recognized in *Lindheimer v. Illinois Bell Tel. Co.*, *supra*, the propriety of basing annual depreciation on cost. By such a procedure the utility is made whole and the integrity of the investment maintained. No more is required. We cannot approve the contrary holding of *United Railway Co. v. West*, 280 U.S. 234, 253-54.

In not approving the contrary holding of *United Railway Co. v. West*,[9] the Supreme Court followed the views expressed by Justice Brandeis in a dissenting opinion in that case, where he said (pp. 264, 266):

> The depreciation charge is an allowance made pursuant to a plan of distribution of the total net expense of plant retirement. It is a bookkeeping device introduced in the exercise of practical judgment to serve three purposes. It preserves the integrity of the investment. . . . It serves to distribute equitably throughout the serveral years of service life the only expense of plant retirement which is capable of reasonable ascertainment— the known cost less the estimated salvage value. And it enables those interested, through applying that plan of distribution, to ascertain, as nearly as possible, the actual financial results of the year's operation.
>
> ✿ ✿ ✿
>
> The replacement theory substitutes for something certain and definite, the actual cost, the cost of reproduction which is highly speculative and conjectural and requiring frequent revision. It, moreover, seeks to establish for one expense a basis of computation fundamentally different from that used for the other expenses of doing business.

The F.C.C. accepts the calculation of both depreciation and return on an original cost basis. In *United States v. New York Tel. Co.*,[10] the Supreme Court sustained action of the F.C.C. in 10 F.C.C. 271, where

---

[7]292 U.S. 151.
[8]320 U.S. 591, 606-607.
[9]280 U.S. 234.
[10]326 U.S. 638.

the agency found the accounting practices of New York Telephone with respect to certain property transferred from AT&T to be improper and, therefore, required elimination of what it said were inflationary write-ups. The F.C.C. made the following comment to contentions made by New York Telephone in support of the inflationary write-ups (pp. 281-82):

> Accounting, for purposes of efficient regulation of public utilities, must be firmly grounded on the cost principle, and if the investment recorded in the accounts is to have some relationship to actual investment dedicated to the public use by an affiliated group of companies, such agreed "value" must not be allowed to exist as a distortive element. . . . Certainly, such "values" cannot be represented by an estimate of such an inherently speculative nature as reproduction cost less depreciation, or "structural value." Otherwise, transfers of property between affiliated companies would provide a device to establish write-ups to any desired "structural value. . . ."

The F.P.C., in considering base value, has rejected the use of reproduction cost. In *Safe Harbor Water Power Corp.,*[11] the F.P.C. held that the rate base was to be grounded on net investment or actual legitimate original cost. Original cost of construction was considered in *City of Los Angeles v. Nev.-Cal. Electric Corp.,*[12] to be the best evidence of the amount to be used as a rate base. The use of reproduction cost was characterized by F.P.C. in *Chicago District Generating Corp.,*[13] as a "long, tortuous, and essentially meaningless process" of attempting first to determine the amount of an extremely speculative element and then attempting to determine the equally speculative factor of how much weight should be given to the first speculation. F.P.C. added that the present reproduction cost of old equipment which is no longer manufactured can be computed only by some sort of legerdemain. In contrast with this, F.P.C. said (p. 420), the determination of original books and records with expedition and accuracy. In *City of Pittsburgh v. Pittsburgh & West Virginia Gas Co.,*[14] reproduction cost evidence was characterized by F.P.C. as synthetic, conjectural and illusory. In *Cities of Cleveland & Akron v. Hope Natural Gas Co.,*[15] Hope sought either a reproduction cost new base which was nearly double the actual legitimate cost of the property or a trended original cost estimate which would reflect changes in price levels. F.P.C. rejected

[11]5 F.P.C. 221, aff'd *Safe Harbor Water Power Corp. v. F.P.C.,* 179 F. 2d 179, cert. denied 339 U.S. 957.
[12]2 F.P.C. 104, 116.
[13]2 F.P.C. 412, 418-19.
[14]7 F.P.C. 112, 116.
[15]44 P.U.R. (N.S.) 1, 8-9, rev'd *Hope Natural Gas Co. v. F.P.C.,* 134 F. 2d 287 (4 Cir.), rev'd 320 U.S. 591.

both as hypothetical conjectures which have plagued rate regulation, and added that "asumption upon assumption as to material and labor costs, and magnified imagination as to overheads was indulged in lavishly."

The position of CAB in the consideration of base value is set forth in *General Passenger Fare Investigation*,[16] where it held that depreciation should be based on the conventional straight-line method. S.E.C. regulations promulgated pursuant to the Securities Act of 1933 show that registrants of securities are required to report assets at cost.

Owner-Operator Costs

In *Motor Carrier Rates — Owner-Operators*,[17] the Commission gave consideration to whether new cost criteria should be formulated for use in evaluating the lawfulness of rates published by motor carriers of property where the underlying transportation service is performed by so-called owner-operators, in contrast to carriers owning and operating their own equipment. The proceeding emanated from the decisions of the district court in *Eastern Central Motor Carriers Ass'n v. United States*,[18] which reversed the findings of the Commission in *Drugs and Related Articles, New Jersey to Chicago*[19] pertaining to cost evidence required of motor carriers employing owner-operators in proceedings involving proposed changed rates.

The background leading up to the proceeding in *Motor Carrier Rates — Owner-Operators* was discussed by the Commission as follows (pp. 30-33):

> The use by authorized motor carriers of owner-operators, which antedates passage of the Motor Carrier Act of 1935, has created special and complex problems in the regulation of the motor carrier industry. The nature of these problems was disclosed in the nationwide investigation instituted in 1948 in *Lease and Interchange of Vehicles by Motor Carriers*, 52 M.C.C. 675 (1951). Therein, it was concluded, among other things, that the use of owner-operators was imperiling regulation because (1) the leases were usually on a single-trip basis, which produced a transitory relationship too short to orient properly the nonregulated owner-operators into the regulated motor carrier's operation (frequently, the trip lease constituted a lease of the carrier's operating certificate to a non-carrier without Commission approval); and (2) the practice of paying the owner-operator on the basis of a split or division of the revenues made it difficult to determine carrier

[16]32 CAB 291.
[17]341 I.C.C. 28.
[18]239 F. Supp. 591, 251 F. Supp. 483.
[19]322 I.C.C. 734, 326 I.C.C. 6.

costs for transportation services for ratemaking purposes. In an attempt to remedy these problems, the Commission prescribed rules requiring equipment leases to be of at least 30 days' duration, and prohibiting the carriers from splitting or dividing revenues with the owner-operators. Subsequently, in a supplemental report in *Lease and Interchange of Vehicles by Motor Carriers,* 68 M.C.C. 553, 556 (1956), the prior leasing regulations were modified as they presently appear in 49 CFR 1057, and therein the prohibition against authorized carriers splitting revenues with owner-operators was eliminated, and the practice has continued.

In 1958, in *Class Rates and Ratings, Malone Freight Lines, Inc.,* 304 I.C.C. 395, proposed rates of a carrier utilizing owner-operators were approved on the basis of favorable rate comparisons, but it was stated:

> While not important in this proceeding for the reasons just given, we deem it advisable, for future guidance, to make some observations with respect to the cost data presented by the respondent. The only costs of record for Malone are its average cost of 27.2 cents a truck-mile for 1955; its direct line-haul cost for that year of 22.7 cents a truck-mile, divided 3.7 cents for Malone and 19 cents for purchased transportation; and its operating ratio in the same year of 92.4 percent. There is some merit to protestant's argument that the data thus shown do not reflect the full, actual cost for performing the whole service, in the sense that they do not include the actual operating costs incurred by the owner-operators. In future cases in the interest of obtaining an adequate cost picture, particularly when main reliance is placed upon cost evidence, it would be helpful for Malone, and other similarly situated carriers, to show in more detail the actual costs incurred for the movement of the traffic involved. Data for representative owner-operator movements should not be difficult of collection or submission, and certainly they would facilitate determination of the compensativeness question.

Three years later, division 2, in *Floor Coverings or Related Articles from East to South,* 313 I.C.C. 530 (1961), called the *Floor Coverings* case, disapproved other proposed rates of that same carrier, stating:

> The cost data of record do not include the full actual cost for performing the entire service. Purchased-transportation agreements premised upon a percentage of revenue afford no sound basis for a determination of the compensativeness of rates. Here, Malone holds itself out under the proposed rates as performing a complete transportation service from origin to destination, and thus, in the absence, as here, of acceptable rate comparisons, the compensativeness of these rates requires a determination of the full costs of the service thereunder, including representative costs of the owner-operators.

The conclusions and findings in that proceeding were sustained in *Malone Freight Lines, Inc. v. United States,* 204 F. Supp. 745 (N.D. Ala., April 1962). However, subsequently that proceeding was reopened for reconsideration solely with respect to the matter of presentation of owner-operator cost. Thereafter, the Commission, in *Iron or Steel Scrap from Conn., Mass., and R.I. to Pa.,* 318 I.C.C. 567 (December 1962), hereinafter called the

Scrap case, set forth new criteria for determining such costs, and concurrently with issuance of that report, the order reopening the *Floor Coverings* case was vacated and set aside. In that report, the Commission emphasized the difficulty of obtaining reliable cost data for representative owner-operator movements, and the inability of the Commission to verify such data because of its lack of direct regulation over the owner-operators who are not required to maintain accounts and records in any particular form. In lieu of requiring the costs of the owner-operators, as in the *Floor Coverings* case, two new criteria were adopted for determining the compensativeness of rates where a motor carrier, utilizing owner-operators to perform the line-haul service, attempts to justify its rates solely or principally on a cost basis. It was concluded that the carrier must show (1) that the revenue retained by it, after payment of the owner-operator, fully covers the costs incurred by the carrier itself and yields a reasonable profit, and (2) that the revenue paid to the owner-operators is sufficient to acquire or retain the services of owner-operators for the movement of the traffic to which the rate is applicable. The case was not appealed.

Later, an action was brought in the Federal District Court in *Eastern Central Motor Carriers Ass'n v. United States*, 239 F. Supp. 591, 601 (D.D.C. 1965), challenging the criteria of the *Scrapp* case, as applied in *Drugs and Related Articles, New Jersey to Chicago*, 322 I.C.C. 734 (1963). The court rejected the *Scrap* case principle on the ground that it was not supported by a rational basis, and that it discriminated against carriers owning and operating their own equipment which are required to show actual cost of service in connection with proposed rate changes. The court there stated:

> The sole reason given by the Commission for changing the requirements of evidence in *Floor Coverings*, was that "it is virtually impossible for carriers to collect and to submit reliable cost data for representative owner-operators movements." The majority base this conclusion on the fact that "owner-operators are not subject to direct regulation by the Commission" and consequently they are not required to maintain accounts and records or to file annual reports. But this overlooks the complete power of the Commission to require the submission of these data by the certificated carriers who can exact this information from their sub-contractors who are their alter-ego in the actual carriage of commodities.
>
> ❈   ❈   ❈
>
> Under the criterion of the Iron or Steel Scrap case, applicable here, the same standard is not applied to carriers using owner-operators. They have only to prove that part of the revenue, the part they retain, exceeds their costs. The other costs are not examined. This part not examined ❈❈❈ comprises approximately 60-70 percent of the cost of operation.

In this manner, the real carrier of the goods (the owner-operator) goes unregulated in a regulated industry and the purpose and design of the Interstate Commerce Act is circumvented. Unequal treatment is accorded on the one hand to the carriers who own and operate the equipment and who are required to submit refined and detailed costs data to assure compensativeness and, on the other hand, to the carriers who lease the equipment and crew and submit a lump sum covering the cost of rental equipment and crew and add to that only administrative and overhead costs and profit. This, in our opinion, is unjust discrimination against the self-sustaining carrier, as prohibited by the National Transportation Policy.

Upon remand, in a report on reconsideration, *Drugs and Related Articles, New Jersey to Chicago,* 326 I.C.C. 6 (1965), we attempted to comply with the court's opinion by providing a more detailed explanation for the principle applied in *Iron and Steel Scrap.* On appeal from that decision, in *Eastern Central Motor Carriers Ass'n v. United States,* 251 F. Supp. 483, 484 (D.C.C. 1966), the court held that we had failed to supply "additional reasons" to justify the *Scrap* criteria. No appeal from that decision was taken.

The following conclusion was arrived at by the Commission in *Motor Carrier Rates — Owner-Operators* (p. 38):

Upon further review and reflection, we conclude that, since no particular criteria or requirements are formally published to be observed by conventional carriers in presenting evidence regarding the compensativeness of proposed individual rates (in contrast to those published in regard to general rate increases, see Ex Parte No. MC-82, *New Procedures in Motor Carrier Rev. Proc.,* 340 I.C.C. 1), there is no warrant for publishing criteria in the form of specific rules with respect to carriers operating with owner-operators. As in the case of conventional carriers, any creditable method of showing the costs of the service performed by the owner-operator may hereafter be used, including the use of regional costs if the latter are shown to be appropriate. Payments made by carriers to owner-operators will not be acceptable. The selection of the costing method, or other method (such as comparisons of rates), to be followed in showing that rates in question are lawful, will be left to the discretion of the parties in each proceeding, and the evidence presented will be accorded the weight warranted by the circumstances. Our determination herein comports with our ultimate finding, among others, in *Rules to Govern Assembling & Presenting Cost Evidence, supra,* that:

Approval and adoption of specific cost formulas, with a view toward giving prima facie validity to formula based costs, are not shown to be necessary or desirable.

We find that it is not shown to be necessary or desirable to formulate new cost criteria for use in determining the compensativeness of rates published by motor carriers employing owner-operators, and that the general principles referred to herein, which have been followed in the case of conventional carriers, shall be applied.

55

Practice and Procedure before the Interstate Commerce Commission

The Rules of Practice

In addition to General Rules of Practice, the Commission has adopted rules of practice governing procedures in certain suspension and fourth-section matters (R. 200); governing procedures of the Motor Carrier Board, the Finance Board, the Operations Boards, the Special Permission Board, the Released Rates Board, and the Tariff Rules Board (R. 225); governing the applications by motor carriers of property or passengers under Sections 5(2) and 210a (b) of the I.C. Act (Rule 240); pertaining to proceedings for the discontinuance or change of train or ferry service (R. 246); governing notice of filing of applications by motor carriers of property or passengers and brokers under Section 206 (except Section 206(a) (6) relating to certificate of registration), 209 and 211, by water carriers under Sections 302(e), 303, and 309, and by freight forwarders under Section 410, and certain other procedural matters with respect thereto (R. 247); relating to the implementation of Public Law 91-375, Postal Reorganization Act — motor carrier licensing provisions (R. 248); and governing the filing of motor carrier mail transportation service orders or determinations under subsection (f) of Section 5203 of title 39, U.S.C. (R. 249).

Application of Rules of Practice

In the application of the rules of practice, the Commission looks primarily to the substance rather than the form.[1] However, while the rules of practice are liberally construed, the ends of justice do not require

---

[1]*Belle City Malleable Iron Co. v. Chesapeake & O. Ry. Co.*, 308 I.C.C. 499; *King Midas Flour Mills v. Northern Pac. Ry. Co.*, 306 I.C.C. 723, 725.

that the Commission be liberal with complainants who without justification fail to produce a complete and adequate record at time of hearing.[2]

Informal Complaints Not Seeking Damages

Informal complaint may be by letter or other writing. If the informal complaint appears to be susceptible of informal adjustment, a copy or a statement of the substance thereof will be transmitted by the Commission to each person complained of in an endeavor to have it satisfied by correspondence and thus obviate the filing of a formal complaint. A proceeding thus instituted on the informal docket is without prejudice to complainant's right to file and prosecute a formal complaint, in which event the proceeding on the informal docket will be discontinued. (R. 22)

Informal Complaints Seeking Damages

An informal complaint seeking damages, when permitted under the I.C. Act, must be filed within the statutory period, and should contain such data as will serve to identify with reasonable definiteness the shipments or transportation services in respect of which damages are sought. Such complaint should state: (1) that complainant makes claim for damages, (2) the name of each individual seeking damages, (3) the names of defendants against which claim is made, (4) the commodities, the rate applied, the date when the charges were paid, by whom paid, and by whom borne, (5) the period of time within which or the specific dates upon which the shipments were made, and the dates when they were delivered or tendered for delivery, (6) the points of origin and destination, either specifically or, where they are numerous, by definite indication of a defined territorial or rate group of the points of origin and destination and, if known, the routes of movement, and (7) the nature and amount of the injury sustained by each claimant.

Where the I.C. Act provides for an award of damage for violation thereof and a carrier is willing to pay them, or to waive collection of undercharges, petition for appropriate authority should be filed by the carrier on the special docket in the form prescribed by the Commission. If the petition is granted an appropriate order will be entered. Such petition, when not filed in connection with an informal complaint pending before the Commission, must be filed within the statutory period and will be

[2]*American Stores Co. v. Akron, C. & Y. R. Co.*, 310 I.C.C. 127.

deemed the equivalent of an informal complaint and an answer thereto admitting the matters stated in the petition. If a carrier is unable to file such petition within the statutory period and the claim is not already protected from the operation of the statute by informal complaint, a statement setting forth the facts may be filed by the carrier within the statutory period. Such statement will be deemed the equivalent of an informal complaint filed on behalf of the shipper or consignee and sufficient to stay the operation of the statute.

If an informal complaint seeking damages cannot be disposed of informally, or is denied, or is withdrawn by complainant from further consideration, the parties affected will be so notified in writing by the Commission. The matter in such complaint will not be reconsidered unless, within six months after the date such notice is mailed, either a formal complaint as to such matter is filed, or it is informally resubmitted on an additional basis.

Such filing or resubmission will be deemed to relate back to the date of the original filing, but reference to that date and the Commission's file number must be made in such resubmission or in the formal complaint filed. If the matter is not so resubmitted, or included in a formal complaint, complainant will be deemed to have abandoned the complaint and no complaint seeking damages based on the same cause of action will thereafter be placed on file or considered unless itself filed within the statutory period. (R. 23)

Formal Complaints; Allegations Generally

A formal complaint should be so drawn as fully and completely to advise the parties defendant and the Commission in what respects the provisions of the I.C. Act have been or are violated or will be violated, and should set forth briefly and in plain language the facts claimed to constitute such violation. If two or more sections or subsections of the Act or requirements established pursuant thereto are alleged to be violated, the facts claimed to constitute violation of one section, subsection, or requirement should be stated separately from those claimed to constitute a violation of another section, subsection, or requirement whenever that can be done by reference or otherwise without undue repetition. (R. 26)

Formal Complaints; When Damages Sought

A formal complaint that includes a request for an award of damages should contain the information specified for an informal complaint seeking damages. (R. 27)

Formal Complaints; Discrimination, Preference, and Prejudice

A complaint that alleges the I.C. Act is violated because of an undue or unreasonable preference or advantage, undue or unreasonable prejudice or disadvantage, or unjust discrimination should specify clearly the particular elements stated in the I.C. Act as constituting such violation, and the facts which complainant relies upon to establish it. Such elements may include a special rate, rebate, drawback, or other device; and a particular person, company, firm, association, port, port district, gateway, transit point, locality, region, district, territory, or description of traffic.

A complaint that brings in issue any rate, fare, charge, classification, regulation, or practice, made or imposed by authority of any State, upon the ground that it violates provisions of the I.C. Act which prohibit undue or unreasonable advantage, preference, or prejudice as between persons or localities in intrastate commerce and persons or localities in interstate or foreign commerce, or any undue, unreasonable or unjust discrimination against interstate or foreign commerce, should bring in issue the justness and reasonableness of the rate, fare, charge, classification, regulation, or practice applicable to the interstate or foreign commerce involved in such complaint. Such complaint should also bring in issue the question as to what should be the rate, fare, or charge, or the maximum or minimum, or maximum and minimum, thereafter to be charged, and the classification, regulation, or practice that should be established so as to remove any such advantage, preference, prejudice, or such unjust discrimination. (R. 28)

Formal Complaints; Prayers for Relief

A formal complaint in which relief for the future is sought should contain a detailed statement of the relief desired. Relief in the alternative or of several different types may be demanded, but the issues raised in the formal complaint should not be broader than those to which complainant's evidence is to be directed at the hearing.

Except under unusual circumstances, and for good cause shown, damages will not be awarded upon a complaint unless specifically prayed for, or upon a new complaint by or for the same complainant which is based upon any finding in the original proceeding. (R. 30)

Amended and Supplemental Formal Complaints

An amended or supplemental complaint may be tendered for filing by a complainant against a defendant or defendants named in the original complaint, stating a cause of action alleged to have accrued within the statutory period immediately preceding the date of such tender, in favor of complainant and against the defendant or defendants. (R. 31)

Under Section 13(1) a complainant, without regard to the nature of its interests, has a right to complain of anything done or attempted to be done in contravention of provisions of the I.C. Act, and to have its complaint considered on its merits.[3] Proceedings before the Commission are not in the nature of private litigation but are matters of public concern in which the whole body of shippers and carriers is interested.[4] The burden is upon the complainant to establish the Commission's jurisdiction over a matter before a complaint with respect thereto may receive its consideration, and the absence of any defense in no way relieves complainant of its burden of proof.[5]

Answers and Cross Complaints to Formal Complaints

An answer may simultaneously be responsive to a formal complaint and to any amendment or supplement thereof. It must be drawn so as fully and completely to advise the parties and the Commission of the nature of the defense, including, if a departure, from the requirements of Section 4(1) is involved, the number of the particular application or order, if any, which protects such departure; and must admit or deny specifically and in detail each material allegation of the pleading answered. An answer may embrace a detailed statement of any counterproposal which a defendant may desire to submit. Unless the issue is such that separate answers are required, answer for all defendants may be filed on their behalf by one defendant in one document, in which event the answer must show clearly the names of all defendants joining therein, and their concurrence.

A cross complaint, alleging that other persons, parties to the proceeding, have violated the I.C. Act or requirements established pursuant thereto, or seeking relief against them under the I.C. Act, may be tendered for filing by a defendant with its answer. (R.33)

Motions to Dismiss or to Make More Definite and Certain

As to complaint. Defendant may file with his answer, or with his statement under modified procedure, a motion that the allegations in

---

[3]*Shaw Warehouse Co. v. Southern Ry. Co.*, 308 I.C.C. 609, 612.
[4]*Ibid.; Southern Ry. Co. v. United States*, 186 F. Supp. 29, 40.
[5]*A. G. Bartlett v. Missouri Pac. Ry. Co.*, 308 I.C.C. 527, 528.

the complaint be made more definite and certain, such motion to point out the defects complained of and details desired. Defendant may also file with his answer a motion to dismiss a complaint because of lack of legal sufficiency appearing on face of such complaint.

As to answer. No replication to the answer shall be filed, but any party may file, within 10 days after the filing of an answer, or, in the case of modified procedure, complainant may file with his statement in reply, a motion that the answer, or defendant's statement, as the case may be, be made more definite and certain, such motion to point out the defects complained of and the details desired. (R. 34)

Satisfaction of Complaint

If a defendant satisfies a formal complaint, either before or after answering, a statement to that effect signed by the opposing parties must be filed (original only need be filed), setting forth when and how the complaint has been satisfied. This action should be taken as expeditiously as possible. (R. 35)

Applications, Forms and Instructions

An application filed with the Commission shall be prepared in accord with and contain the information called for in the form of application, if any, prescribed by the Commission, or any instructions which may have been issued by the Commission with respect to the filing and service of an application. (R. 36)

Protests against Applications

Content. A protest against the granting of any application shall set forth specifically the grounds upon which it is made and contain a concise statement of the interest of protestant in the proceeding. (R. 38)

Schaeffer Rule

Applications by motor carriers for authority to transport property must be accompanied by certificates from supporting shippers.[6] Addi-

---

[6]*Schaeffer Ext. — New York City,* 106 M.C.C. 100. See *Carolina Transit Lines, Common Carrier Application,* 111 M.C.C. 630 regarding applications for authority to transport passengers. See also *Carl Subler Trucking, Inc., Ext. — Canned Goods,* 111 M.C.C. 624 regarding proceedings handled under modified procedure. (Procedures in *Schaeffer* apply from the date the application is filed to service date of modified procedure order, and not thereafter.)

tional supporting shippers, which are not known at the time the application is filed, must be identified before hearing on the application.

Multiple-Application Proceedings

Where multiple-applications have been filed seeking similar motor carriers authority, the following criteria, none of which is solely determinative, and each of which must be construed in the light of the evidence adduced, will be considered by the Commission:[7]

(1) The availability of applicants' motor vehicle equipment, including the quantum operated and the type necessary for the proposed operations, within an area in reasonable proximity to the point of origin;

(2) Coupled with the availability of equipment, the present certificated operations of the applicants within the territory sought in their respective applications;

(3) The location and the proximity of each applicant's terminal facilities to the proposed origin;

(4) The consideration of the shipper's present and future needs — volume, frequency of movements, type of service, et cetera — to specified regions of the county and the availability of existing services in determining the quantum and scope of new authority required in individual States;

(5) The extent of the respective applicants' participation and experience in transporting the involved commodities;

(6) Priority in the filing of the respective applications;

(7) Shipper support of the respective applications; and

(8) The extent and nature of the opposition to the respective applications.

The emphasis on certain criteria in the selection of successful applicants is necessary as such selection cannot be accomplished in a vacuum, but must be premised on the facts in each proceeding.

Protests in Valuation Proceedings

A protest of a tentative valuation shall contain a concise statement of the essential elements of protest with particular reference to the matters in the tentative valuation concerning which protest is made and shall include a statement of the changes therein desired by protestant. When practicable, each object of protest should be set up as a separate item in a separately numbered paragraph. Each item of protest against land values or areas must state the valuation section and zone on the Com-

[7]*Southwest Freight Lines, Inc., Extension — Colorado Origins,* 1968 F. C. cases, para. 36, 236. See also *Mayfield,* 108 M.C.C. 651, 657; *Motor Freight Corp.,* 106 M.C.C. 654, 657; *Kroblin,* 95 M.C.C. 233, 237; *H. C. Gabler,* 86 M.C.C. 447, 469-70.

mission's maps in which the land is located. When protestant claims that property owned or used has been omitted, a full description of such property and its location must be included in the protest. (R. 39)

Protests against Tariffs or Schedules

The protested tariff or schedule sought to be suspended should be identified by making reference to the name of the publishing carrier, freight forwarder, or agent, to the Commission number, and to the specific items or particular provisions protested and to the effective date of the tariff or schedule. Reference should also be made to the tariff or schedule, and the specific provisions thereof, proposed to be superseded. The protest should state the grounds in support thereof, indicate in what respect the protested tariff or schedule is considered to be unlawful, and state what protestant offers by way of substitution. Such protests will be considered as addressed to the discretion of the Commission. Should a protestant desire to proceed further against a tariff or schedule which is not suspended, or which has been suspended and the suspension vacated, a separate later formal complaint or petition should be filed.

Protests against, and requests for suspension of, tariffs of schedules filed by rail carriers or the publishing agents that result in revisions of rates or charges shall also include a verified complaint containing specific facts showing: (a) that without suspension the protested tariffs or schedules will cause substantial injury to the complainant or the party represented by the complainant, (b) that it is likely that complainant or the party represented by the complainant will prevail on the merits pursuant to any applicable provisions of the act, and (c) where protestants allege that a rate is unreasonably high in violation of Section 1(5)(b), they must submit evidence relating to market dominance as set forth at 49 CFR §1109.1. Replies to verified complaints filed under this section shall be verified. (R. 40)

Service of Investigation Order; Default Where Failure to Comply

An order instituting an investigation will be served by the Commission upon respondents. If within the time period stated in that order a respondent fails to comply with any requirement specified therein, respondent shall be deemed in default and to have waived any further hearing. Thereafter the investigation may be decided without further proceedings. (R. 41)

It is the Commission's duty to investigate any operation which may be so conducted as to circumvent and evade, and thus violate, the provision of the I.C. Act that it is charged with administering, and the mere possibility that the practices investigated may be found not unlawful does not preclude reasonable investigation.[8] *Pacific Diesel Rental* demonstrates the extent of the power of the Commission to investigate. There the Commission said that by Section 204(c) of the I.C. Act[9] it is authorized, upon its initiative, and without complaint, to investigate whether "any motor carrier or broker" has failed to comply with provisions of Part II or requirements established pursuant thereto, and Section 204(a)(3)[10] requires that "motor carrier" be construed to include private carriers of property by motor vehicle in the administration of Section 204(c). The Commission said that its power, therefore, to investigate under Section 204(c) extends to all motor-carrier operations and the brokerage thereof, and whether the investigated operation is conducted by one person or by a number of persons in concert.

Another case showing the extent of the Commission's power of investigation is *Wilson — Investigation of Operations*.[11] There, as the basic purpose of investigation was to determine whether respondent's transportation of sugar in buy-and-sell operations was private or for-hire carriage, and there was no difference in, or separation of, his sugar operations in the States named in the order of investigation and in nearby States not enumerated therein, the Commission said that its right of inquiry should not be construed so narrowly as to confine the investigation strictly to the geographical scope of the order instituting it, particularly as the order sufficiently referred to his entire sugar transportation operation.

Petitions Seeking Institution of Rulemaking Proceedings

Any person may file a petition requesting the Commission to institute a proceeding for the purpose of issuing statements, rules, or regulations of general applicability and significance designed to implement or interpret law, or to formulate general policy for future effect. No reply to such a petition may be filed. Whether a proceeding shall be instituted as requested is within the discretion of the Commission and the ruling on the petition will be final. In the event a rulemaking proceeding is instituted by the Commission, the procedure to be employed for the taking of evidence or the receipt of views and comments will be designated by Commission order. (R. 42)

---

[8] *Pacific Diesel Rental Co. — Investigation of Operations,* 78 M.C.C. 161, 165.
[9] 49 U.S.C. 304 (c).
[10] 49 U.S.C. 304(a) (3).
[11] 82 M.C.C. 651, 657.

Declaratory Orders

Under the Administrative Procedure Act,[12] an "agency, with like effect as in the case of other orders, and in its sound discretion, may issue a declaratory order to terminate a controversy or remove uncertainty."

The Commission's authority under 5 U.S.C. 554(e) to issue declaratory orders is discretionary.[13] It is, therefore, the practice of the Commission, when requested to do so, to assist the courts by declaratory findings or orders.[14] The Commission may, under its general and discretionary powers to clarify questions arising in the administration of the Act, entertain petitions seeking interpretative rulings and opinions, and has in the past issued reports answering hypothetical questions.[15] However, the Commission said in the *Mississippi Valley Barge* case that it is not in public interest to entertain and issue decisions on hypothetical questions posed by a relatively small segment of those who would be affected, and in absence of compelling circumstances petitions of that type will be dismissed.

Rule Making Procedure

A notice of proposed rule making is neither an adjudication nor a finding but only a starting point for further discussion, a mere proposal promulgated for the purpose of study.[16] Its aim is to give notice and invite arguments by interested parties on the wisdom and desirability of the proposed rule, and for orderly presentation thereof the matter may be set for formal hearing. When such procedure has been followed, the issues are considered de novo.[17]

---

[12]5 U.S.C. 554(e).

[13]*Frozen Cooked Vegetables — Status* 81 M.C.C. 649, 655; *United States v. Northern Pac. Ry. Co.* 299 I.C.C. 545; *American Red Ball Transit Co., Inc. v. McLean Trucking*, 67 M.C.C. 305, 311.

[14]*United States v. Beaumont, S. L. & W. Ry. Co.*, 299 I.C.C. 477, 478; *Central Montana Stockyards v. Chicago, M. St. P. & P. R. Co.*, 299 I.C.C. 110, 111.

[15]*Jet Fuel by Pipeline within the State of Idaho*, 311 I.C.C. 439; *Mississippi Valley Barge Line Co. Exemption*, 311 I.C.C. 103, 105; *Houston and North Texas Motor Freight Lines, Inc.*, 78 M.C.C. 269, 270; *American Red Ball Transit Co., Inc. v. McLean Trucking*, 67 M.C.C. 305, 311.

[16]*Philadelphia, Pa., Commercial Zone*, 74 M.C.C. 633, 635.

[17]The courts have recognized the Commission's rulemaking authority under Sections 12, 204(a) (6), 304(a), and 403(a). See, for example, *Assigned Car Cases*, 27 U.S. 564, 575; *American Trucking Assns. v. United States*, 344 U.S. 298, 308-13: and *United States v. Pennsylvania R. Co.*, 323 U.S. 612, 616.

Applicability of Sections 556 and 557 of the Administrative Procedure Act to Rule Making Proceedings

In *United States v. Allegheny-Ludlum Steel Corp.*,[18] the Supreme Court discussed the question of when Sections 556 and 557 of the Administrative Procedure Act are applicable to rule making proceedings. It said:

> This Court has held that the Administrative Procedure Act applies to proceedings before the Interstate Commerce Commission. *Minneapolis & St. Louis R. Co. v. United States*, 361 U.S. 173, 192 (1959). Appellees claim that the Commission's procedure here departed from the provisions of 5 U.S.C. §§ 556 and 557 of the Act. Those sections, however, govern a rulemaking proceeding only when 5 U.S.C. § 553 so requires. The latter section, dealing generally with rulemaking, makes applicable the provisions of §§ 556 and 557 only "when rules are required by statute to be made on the record after opportunity for an agency hearing . . . ." The Esch Act, authorizing the Commission "after hearing, on complaint or upon its own initiative without complaint, [to] establish reasonable rules, regulations, and practices with respect to car service . . . ." 49 U.S.C. § 1 (14) (a), does not require that such rules "be made on the record." 5 U.S.C. § 553. That distinction is determinative for this case. "A good deal of significance lies in the fact that some statutes do expressly require determinations on the record." 2 K. Davis, Administrative Law Treatise, § 13.08 p. 225 (1958). Sections 556 and 557 need be applied "only where the agency statute, in addition to providing a hearing, prescribes explicitly that it be 'on the record.'" *Siegel v. Atomic Energy Commission*, 400 F. 2d 778, 785 (CADC 1968); *Joseph E. Seagram & Sons Inc. v. Dillon*, 344 F. 2d 497, 500 n. 9 (CADC 1965). Cf. *First National Bank v. First Federal Savings and Loan Assn.*, 225 F. 2d 33 (CADC 1955). We do not suggest that only the precise words "on the record" in the applicable statute will suffice to make §§ 556 and 557 applicable to rulemaking proceedings, but we do hold that the language of the Esch Car Service Rules Act is insufficient to invoke these sections.

> Because the proceedings under review were an exercise of legislative rulemaking power rather than adjudicatory hearings as in *Wong Yang Sung. v. McGrath*, 339 U.S. 33 (1950), and *Ohio Bell Telephone Co. v. Public Utilities Comm'n*, 301 U.S. 292 (1937); and because 49 U.S.C. § 1 (14) (a) does not require a determination "on the record" the provisions of 5 U.S.C. §§ 556, 557, were inapplicable.

> This proceeding therefore, was governed by the provisions of 5 U.S.C. § 553 of the Administrative Procedure Act, requiring basically that notice of proposed rulemaking shall be published in the Federal Register, that after notice the agency give interested persons an opportunity to participate in the rulemaking through appropriate submissions, and that after consideration of the record so made the agency shall incorporate in the rules adopted a concise general statement of their basis and purpose . . .

[18]S. Ct. No. 71-227, decided June 7, 1972, slip opinion, pp. 14-16.

Rules Promulgated by an Administrative Agency Are
Required to be Scrupulously Observed

Once an agency exercises its discretion and creates the procedural rules under which it desires to have its actions judged, it denies itself the right to violate these rules.[19] If an agency in its proceedings violates its rules and prejudices the results, any action taken as a result of the proceedings cannot stand.[20] As was stated in *Mississippi Valley Barge Line Co. v. United States:*[21]

> . . . Legislative regulations, created by a Federal agency pursuant to Congressional authority, have the force of law. *Columbia Broadcasting System v. U.S.,* 316 U.S. 407, 417-419, 62 S. Ct. 1194 86 L. Ed. 1563 (1942). The agency which promulgates the rule is as bound by its terms as is the general public. *Columbia Broadcasting System v. United States,* 316 U.S. 422, 62 S. Ct. 1194; *McKay v. Wahlenmaier,* 96 U.S. App. D.C. 313, 226 F. 2d 35, 43. The Commission has itself held that it is bound by its rules. United States Lines Co., Cerificate Transfer, 260 I.C.C. 355, 358. Therefore, any action taken by the Commission is invalid unless the rules pertaining to the action are followed.

The Commission, in *Akron, C. & Y. R. Co. v. Atchison, T. & S. F. Ry. Co.,*[22] has made it plain that it is bound by its own rules. There the Commission affirmed a ruling by its hearing officers in refusing to mark an exhibit in a situation where the special rules of procedure were not being followed. In their ruling, the officers said:[23]

> The defendants would have the Commission base its decision in part on purported facts discussed in their briefs but not proved as required by its General Rules of Practice and the Administrative Procedure Act. Not through witnesses but by tender of counsel they sought to introduce in evidence such matter as working papers collected by their cost analysts, a motion-picture film, and clippings of unsigned articles in trade journals. (In this course counsel departed from the ground rule agreed upon in prehearing conference under which evidence was reduced to writing and copies thereof with accompanying exhibits furnished to opposing counsel in advance of the hearing at which such evidence was offered.) The consideration of this evidence by the Commission would be in violation of its General Rule of Practice 1.74, providing that "witnesses will be orally examined under oath before the officer unless . . ." [exceptions not pertinent here]. It would also be contrary to the following sentence in Section 7(c) of the Administrative Procedure Act which provides *inter alia:*

[19]*United States ex rel. Accardi v. Shaughnessy,* 347 U.S. 260; *Service v. Dulles,* 354 U.S. 363.

[20]*Sangamon Valley Television Corp. v. United States,* 269 F. 2d 211, cert. denied 376 U.S. 915.

[21]252 F. Supp. 162, 166.

[22]321 I.C.C. 17, 35.

[23]Docket No. 31503, report, Appendix C.

> . . . Every party shall have the right to present his case or defense by oral or documentary evidence, to submit rebuttal evidence, and to conduct such cross-examination as may be required for a full and true disclosure of the facts.

The following comment on this section in the Attorney General's Manual on the Administrative Procedure Act, p. 77, is significant:

> As here used "documentary evidence" [28 U.S.C. 695] does not mean affidavits and written evidence of any kind. Such a construction would flood agency proceedings with hearsay evidence. In the last sentence of the subsection, there appears the phrase "evidence in written form," thus indicating that the Congress distinguished between "written evidence" and "documentary evidence." Against this background, it is clear that the "right to present his case or defense by oral or documentary evidence" does not extend to presenting evidence in affidavit or other written form so as to deprive the agency or opposing parties, of opportunity for cross-examination. . . . Thus, technical and statistical data may be introduced in convenient written form subject to adequate opportunity for cross-examination and rebuttal. . . . Any evidence may be admitted by agreement or if no objection is made.

(Under the circumstances specified in the last sentence above quoted so-called counsel's exhibits are sometimes received but not otherwise). The objectionable evidence for the most part was offered in the course of cross-examination of opposing witnesses for the purpose of controverting facts stated by those witnesses. Its exclusion by the examiners was not an interference with cross-examination, as argued, for it is well-settled that a party cannot introduce incompetent evidence in cross-examining an adversary witness. Nor were defendants entitled to demand that the objectionable material be numbered as an exhibit and incorporated in the record as permitted by Rule 1.84(e), which applies "in case exhibit has been identified" etc. An exhibit is a substitute for oral testimony "and should be limited to statements of fact." (Rule 1.84(a)). It receives its evidentiary status through identification by witness and not by denomination of counsel.

Doctrine of Stare Decisis

Stare Decisis is an important principle in dealing with statutory law; however, the Supreme Court has not been reluctant to reverse its own erroneous interpretations of an Act of Congress.[24] As was said in a dissenting opinion in *Canada Packers v. A., T. & S. F.*:[25]

> Moreover, we need not be slaves to a precedent by treating it as standing for more than it actually decided nor by subtly eroding it in sophis-

---

[24]See, e.g., *Helvering v. Hallock*, 309 U.S. 106; *Nye v. United States*, 313 U.S. 33, *Toucey v. New York Life Ins. Co.*, 314 U.S. 118; *Commissioner of Internal Revenue v. Estate of Church*, 355 U.S. 632; *James v. United States*, 366 U.S. 213; *Smith v. Evening News Assn.*, 371 U.S. 195; *Local No. 438, Construction & General Laborers' Union v. Curry*, 371 U.S. 542, 552; *Fay v. Noia*, 372 U.S. 391, 435.
[25]385 U.S. 182.

ticated ways. See . . . 32 Cornell L. Q. 137, 143 (1946). It is enough that we do not approve "of the doctrinal generalization which the previous court used" *(ibid.)* and confine the precedent to what it actually decided. Certainly we should not extend the range of a precedent beyond its generating reason, especially when another policy, here the plain words of an Act of Congress, will be impaired by doing so.

In the *Canadian Packers* case, the dissent in condemning a too rigid adherence to precedent, considered the approach to this matter in England and said (footnote 1):

> The House of Lords no longer regards the reasoning in previous cases as sacrosanct. Witness its striking departure in *Public Trustee v. Inland Revenue Commissioners* [1960] A. C. 398, and *Midland Silicones Ltd. v. Scruttons Ltd.* [1962] A. C. 446. Those cases show that the House will not treat as absolutely binding any line of reasoning in a previous case which was not necessary to the decision: but will regard itself as at liberty to depart from it if convinced that it was wrong. *Penn-Texas Corp. v. Murat Anstalt* (1964) 2 Q. B. 647, 661.

> And see (1966) 7 C. L. 251a:
> The Lord Chancellor made the following statement on July 26, 1966, on behalf of himself and the Lords of Appeal in Ordinary:

> Their Lordships regard the use of precedent as an indispensable foundation upon which to decide what is the law and its application to individual cases. It provides at least some degree of certainty upon which individuals can rely in the conduct of their affairs, as well as a basis for orderly development of legal rules.

> Their Lordships nevertheless recognize that too rigid adherence to precedent may lead to injustice in a particular case and also unduly restrict the proper development of the law. They propose therefore to modify their present practice and, while treating former decisions of this House as normally binding, to depart from a previous decision when it appears right to do so.

> In this connection they will bear in mind the danger of disturbing retrospectively the basis on which contracts, settlements of property and fiscal arrangements have been entered into and also the especial need for certainty as to the criminal law.

> This announcement is not intended to affect the use of precedent elsewhere than in this House.

> See generally, State Decisis in Contemporary England, 82 L. Q. Rev. 203 (1966).

The doctrine of stare decisis has no ironclad application to Commission decisions. In *Shein's Express v. United States*,[26] the court said:

---

[26]102 F. Supp. 320, 323. An administrative finding need not be consistent with findings in other cases. *Georgia Public Service Commission v. United States*, 283 U.S. 765, 775; *Bowman Transportation Co. v. United States*, 308 F. Supp. 1342, 1345; *Anderson Motor Service v. United States*, 151 F. Supp. 577, 581-582.

The plaintiffs also argue that the Commission's holding in the present case is inconsistent with its ruling in what is known as the *Powell* case and consequently unlawful. We disagree with plaintiffs in the application of the *Powell* case here on both the facts and the law. Firstly, in the *Powell* case it was determined that the vendor was possessed of operating rights over two separate but connected regular routes, and therefore the purchaser was not planning or proposing to furnish a service any greater in scope than the vendor had the right to do pursuant to its grant, under the grandfather clause. In the case now before the court, the Commission found that the vendee, Shein, proposed a radical change in the pattern of operations conducted by vendor, Stillwell. Secondly it has been established that the Commission's ruling need not be consistent in all respects. See *Beard-Laney v. United States,* supra at page 33:

> "This Court has no concern with the correctness of the Commission's reasoning, with the soundness of its conclusions, or with the alleged inconsistency with findings made in other proceedings before it." *Virginia Ry. Co. v. United States,* 272 U.S. 658; and *Interstate Commerce Commission v. Union Pacific R. Co.,* 222 U.S. 541.

> This is but a statement of the well recognized rule that the doctrine of *stare decisis* has no application to the administrative process.

It is well established that the Commission should not be precluded from reexamining questions theretofore determined by it in earlier decisions, nor be foreclosed thereby from arriving at different decisions. In *United States v. American Sheet & Tin Plate Co.,*[27] it was so stated:

> The Commission, so it is said, has approved allowances in instances such as those under review and by a long course of decision has sanctioned the practice; and the claim is that carriers have relied upon the Commission's action in doing plant spotting or making allowance for the performance of that service by industries. We cannot agree either that the Commission has so decided or that if it had it would be precluded from

---

[27] 301 U.S. 402, 407-8. In *William N. Feinstein & Co., Inc. v. United States, et al.,* 209 F. Supp. 613, aff'd 317 F. 2d 509, a district court sustained a Commission report and order in *William N. Feinstein & Co., Inc. v. New York Central Railroad Co.,* 313 I.C.C. 783, where the Commission had found unloading charges assessed and collected by the New York Central and other railroads at New York on past carload shipments of vegetables having origins in numerous States when "considered by themselves or as a part of the total transportation charges . . . are not shown to have been unjust, unreasonable, or otherwise unlawful." The primary contention of plaintiff was that the Commission's decision was erroneous because it was in conflict with the decision of the Supreme Court in *Secretary of Agriculture v. United States,* 347 U.S. 645, and was not in accord with the decision of the Supreme Court in *Adams v. Mills,* 286 U.S. 397.

The district court, in sustaining the action said that the Commission "is not required to deal with a particular case as it has dealt with a prior case that seems similar since diverse factors may be present in the second determination which the Commission feels, in the exercise of its specialized experience justify a different result," and the court is not obliged to reconcile its conclusions with decisions in earlier proceedings involving the same subject because the court may consider only the record in the proceeding under review.

reexamining the question in the light of existing conditions. The Commission has repeatedly dealt with the matter. In numerous instances, upon application of an industry for the performance of spotting service on its plant track system, or for an allowance from the carrier for itself performing the service, the Commission, in the view that like service was performed or an allowance paid for it at other similar plants, has ordered the removal of discrimination as between shippers. On the other hand, in some cases the Commission has held that the service demanded was not a service of transportation and has refused to order the carrier to perform it. But whatever may have been decided in the past, it is evident that the growth of the practice of making allowances for plant switching and the lack of uniformity in the practice of the carriers with respect to this service properly called for an investigation of the entire situation and the promulgation of appropriate orders to regulate the practice and prevent performance of a service not within the carrier's transportation obligation. The investigation and the consequent orders of the Commission were not foreclosed by its earlier decisions.

While an agency is free to make reasoned changes in its policies, it is an "equally essential proposition that, when an agency decides to reverse its course, it must provide an opinion or analysis indicating that the standard is being changed and not ignored, and assuring that it is faithful and not indifferent to the rule of law."[28] The courts thus require that an administrative agency adhere to its own precedents or explain any deviation therefrom.[29]

Modified Procedure, How Initiated

The Commision may, in its discretion, order that a proceeding be heard under modified procedure if it appears that substantially all important issues of material fact may be resolved by means of written materials and that the efficient disposition of the proceeding can be made without oral hearing. (R. 43)

Modified Procedure; Content of Pleadings

A statement filed under the modified procedure after that procedure has been directed shall state separately the facts and arguments and

[28]*Columbia Broadcasting System, Inc. v. F.C.C.*, 454 F. 2d 1018, 1026.

[29]*Greater Boston Television Corp. v. F.C.C.*, 444 F. 2d 841, cert. denied, 403 U.S. 923; *F.T.C. v. Crowther*, 430 F. 2d 510; *Port Terminal R. Assn. v. United States*. No. 75-3677, 5 Cir., May 12, 1977; *McCormack Trucking Co. Inc. v. United States*, 251 F. Supp. at 539-40; *Collette Travel Service, Inc. v. United States*, 236 F. Supp. 302; *Parkhill Truck Co. v. United States*, No. 75-1882 (D.C. Cir. June 22, 1977); *Marine Space Enclosures, Inc. v. F.M.C.*, 420 F. 2d 577, as stated in *Mary Carter Paint Co. v. FTC*, 333 F. 2d 654, an agency should not have one rule for Monday and one for Tuesday.

include the exhibits upon which the party relies. Only facts contained in the verified statement of facts can be used in argument. If no answer has been filed, defendant's statement must admit or deny specifically and in detail each material allegation of the complaint. In addition defendant's statement and complainant's statement in reply shall: specify those statements of fact and arguments of the opposite party to which exception is taken, and include a statement of the facts and arguments in support of such exception. Complainant's statement of reply shall be confined to rebuttal of the defendant's statement.

If an award of damages is sought the paid freight bills or properly certified copies thereof should accompany the original of complainant's statement when there are not more than 10 shipments, but otherwise the documents should be retained. (R. 47)

The Commission held in *Berman and Specter v. Atchison, T. & S. F. Ry. Co.*[30] that verifications of complainants' statement of facts by partners of the complainants or their employees, whose knowledge of the facts in issue was not seriously disputed (the facts themselves being undisputed), constitute substantial compliance with the rules of practice. In *Sinclair Pipe Line Co. v. Transamerican Freight Lines,*[31] the Commission said that while it was not affirmatively shown that complainant's auditor had knowledge of facts asserted, his verified statement was in substantial accord with provisions of the rules of practice since it consisted mainly of tariff references and decisions which were matters within the knowledge of defendants and relevant facts pertaining to the involved shipment were not in dispute.

Modified Procedure; Hearings

If cross examination of any witness is desired the name of the witness and the subject matter of the desired cross examination shall, together with any other request for oral hearing, including the basis therefor, be stated at the end of defendant's statement or complainant's statement in reply as the case may be. Unless material facts are in dispute, oral hearing will not be held for the sole purpose of cross examination. (R. 51)

Modified Procedure; Subsequent Procedure

Procedure subsequent to that provided in the modified procedure rules shall be the same as that in proceedings not handled under modified procedure. (R. 52)

---

[30] 308 I.C.C. 254, 256.
[31] 305 I.C.C. 772, 773.

Intervention; Petitions

A petition for leave to intervene must set forth the grounds of the proposed intervention, the position and interest of the petitioner in the proceeding, and whether petitioner's position is in support of or opposition to the relief sought. If the proceeding be by formal complaint and affirmative relief is sought by petitioner, the petition should conform to the requirements for a formal complaint. (R. 70)

Participation without Intervention

In an investigation proceeding, or in a proceeding under Section 1a, of the I.C. Act, and in a proceeding heard on a consolidated record with a complaint proceeding, but in no other proceeding, an appearance may be entered at the oral hearing, or in any proceeding in which the justness or reasonableness of any rate, rule, charge, or other provision of a tariff is at issue and the Commission has ordered that the proceeding be heard under modified procedure, without filing a petition in intervention or other pleading, if no affirmative relief is sought, if there is full disclosure of the identity of the person or persons in whose behalf the appearance is to be entered, if the interest of such person in the proceeding and the position intended to be taken are stated fairly, and if the contentions will be reasonably pertinent to the issues already presented and any right to broaden them unduly is disclaimed. A person in whose behalf an appearance is entered in this manner becomes a party to the proceeding. (R. 71)

Subpoena

Unless directed by the Commission upon its own motion, a subpoena to compel a witness to produce documentary evidence will be issued only upon petition showing general relevance and reasonable scope of the evidence sought, which petition must also specify with particularity the books, papers, or documents desired, and the facts expected to be proved thereby; Provided, however, That for good cause shown, in lieu of a petition, the request for such a subpoena may be made orally upon the record to the officer presiding at the hearing. A request for issuance of a subpoena other than to compel the production of documentary evidence may be made either by letter (original only need be filed with the Commission) or orally upon the record to the officer presiding at the hearing. A showing of general relevance and reasonable scope of the evidence sought may be required and the subpoena will be issued or denied accordingly. (R. 54)

Section 12(1)[32] specifically gives the Commission the power to require by subpoena the attendance and testimony of witnesses and the production of documents relating to any matter under investigation. The statute permits the Commission to investigate, by obtaining testimony and other evidence which is germaine to its investigation. The testimony and the documents sought need not necessarily even be admissible as evidence any more than is any other discoverable material under the Federal Rules of Civil Procedure. It need only to relate to the matter under investigation. This does not mean that the Commission has the unlimited authority to inquire into the business affairs of a person or company not under investigation. Its authority is limited by the wording of the statute itself. That limitation is that the Commission may require, by subpoena, the testimony and the production of documents in relation only to things relating to the matter under investigation. If the things sought by the subpoena do not relate to the business under investigation, then the Commission does not have the right to obtain them. It has the right to obtain evidence from anyone whomsoever of things relating to the matter properly under its investigation.[33]

Discovery

Unless otherwise available under the I.C. Act or other applicable statutes, parties may obtain discovery pursuant to the rules regarding any matter, not privileged, which is relevant to the subject matter involved in the pending proceeding, provided that, discovery procedures (except for written interrogatories and requests for admissions) may be used only when the Commission, upon its own motion, or upon a verified petition filed by a party, and upon good cause shown, shall have entered an order approving such use. Such petitions, where required, must be filed in sufficient time to allow for the filing of replies and for consideration by the Commission without requiring the postponement of any established date for hearing or for submission of initial statements under modified procedure. Likewise, the use of discovery in those circumstances in which no petition is required must be accomplished without requiring the postponement of any established date for hearing or for

---

[32]49 U.S.C. 12(1).
[33]See *Servitron, Inc. et al. v. I.C.C.*, C.A. No. 73-1, M.D. La., opinion filed September 5, 1974. See also *Interstate Commerce Commission v. Baird*, 194 U.S. 25; *Interstate Commerce Commission v. Brimson*, 154 U.S. 447.

submission of initial statements under modified procedure. It is not ground for objection that the information sought will be inadmissible as evidence if the information sought appears reasonably calculated to lead to the discovery of admissible evidence. (R. 55)

Depositions

The testimony of any person including a party, may be taken by deposition upon oral examination.

A petition requesting an order to take a deposition and perpetuate testimony or to produce documents and materials (1) shall set forth the facts it desires to establish and the substance it expects to elicit; (2) shall be served upon all parties to the proceeding and upon the person sought to be deposed and/or the custodian of the documents or materials sought to be produced; (3) shall set forth the name and address of the witness, the place where, the time when, the name and office of the officer before whom, and the cause or reason why such deposition should be taken; and (4) shall specify with particularity the documents and materials which the deponent is requested to produce.

If the Commission is convinced on its own initiative or by the petition requesting an order to take a deposition that the deposition will prevent a failure or delay of justice, it will serve an order upon the parties and the witness, naming the witness whose deposition is to be taken, specifying the time when, the place where, and the officer before whom the deposition is to be taken, and specifying the subject matter of the examination and whether the depositions shall be taken upon oral examination or written interrogatories. (R. 56)

WRITTEN INTERROGATORIES TO PARTIES

Any party may serve upon any other party written interrogatories to be answered by the party served. (R. 60)

REQUEST FOR ADMISSION

A party may serve upon any other party a written request for the admission, for purposes of the pending proceeding only, of the truth of any matters set forth in the request, including the genuineness of any documents described in the request for admission. (R. 61)

Depositions, Requests for Admission, Written Interrogatories, and Responses Thereto: Inclusion in Record

At the oral hearing, or upon the submission of statements under the modified procedure, depositions, requests for admission and written interrogatories, and respective responses may be offered in evidence by the party at whose instance they were taken. If not offered by such party, they may be offered in whole or in part by any other party. If only part of a deposition, request for admission or written interrogatory, or response thereto is offered in evidence by a party, any other party (where the matter is being heard orally) may require him to introduce all of it which is relevant to the part introduced, and any party may introduce any other parts. Such depositions, requests for admission and written interrogatories, and responses thereto shall be admissible in evidence subject to such objections as to competency of the witness, or competency, relevancy, or materiality of the testimony as were noted at the time of their taking or are made at the time they are offered in evidence. (R. 62)

Production of Documents and Things and Entry Upon Land for Inspection and Other Purposes

Any party may be ordered and directed (1) to produce and permit the petitioning party to inspect any designated documents, (including writings, drawings, graphs, charts, photographs, phonograph records, tapes, and other data compilations from which information can be obtained, translated, if necessary, with or without the use of detection devices into reasonably usable form), or to inspect and copy, test, or sample any tangible things which constitute or contain matters which are in the possession, custody, or control of the party upon whom the order is served; or (2) to permit, subject to appropriate liability releases and safety and operating considerations, entry upon designated land or other property in the possession or control of the party upon whom the order is served for the purpose of inspection and measuring, surveying, photographing, testing, or sampling the property or any designated object or operation thereon. (R. 64)

Quorum

Section 17(3) of the I.C. Act provides that a majority of the Commission, or of a division or board, shall constitute a quorum for the transaction of business. Thus, the court said in *Northern Valley Transfer, Inc. v.*

Interstate Commerce Commission,[34] a motor carrier was not deprived of a full hearing on complaint against it because one of three Commissioners constituting a division was absent from the proceeding and did not participate in the decision. Final action of the Commission by majority vote of a division rather than by vote of the entire division thus in no way impaired the validity of the vote. A decision quite in point is *Sisto v. Civil Aeronautics Board*[35] where it was held that, under a statute providing that the Board could "hear or receive" argument, opportunity for oral argument was adequate where less than a quorum of the Board presided. The court said:

> Finally petitioner contends that the order of the Board is void for lack of jurisdiction due to the fact that a statutory quorum did not hear oral argument. The statute provides that "three members shall constitute a quorum of the Board." . . . A quorum either heard or received argument either by being physically present or by reading the record and transcript. The statutory requirement was satisfied. Petitioner cannot complain of this practice.
>
> A careful reading of the record brings us to the conclusion that petitioner was afforded a full and fair hearing.

The law is well settled that where a quorum of a deliberate body, such as a division of the Commission, is present, a proposition is carried by a majority of the votes cast, although some of the members present do not vote[36]

Administrative Law Judges — Qualifications

Hearing officers presiding over certain administrative hearings[37] must be qualified pursuant to procedures of the Civil Service Commission.[38] An analysis of the court decisions on this question leads to the conclusion that the issue of the qualification of the officer should be brought forward, before the hearing officer himself prior to the close of the hearings, and that the raising of the question for the first time on a petition for reconsideration or before the court may be untimely.[39]

---

[34]192 F. Supp. 600, 603.

[35]179 F. 2d 47, 53-4.

[36]*United States v. Ballin,* 144 U.S. 1, 6; *WIBC, Inc. v. Federal Communications Commission,* 259 F. 2d 941, 943; *Frischer & Co. v. Bakelite Corporation,* 39 F. 2d 247, 155.

[37]5 U.S.C. 553 and 554.

[38]5 U.S.C. 556(a), (b); 5 U.S.C. 3105.

[39]*Monumental Tours, Inc. v. United States,* 110 F. Supp. 929, 932; *United States v. Tucker Truck Lines,* 344 U.S. 33. See also *Magnet Cove Barium Corp. v. United States,* 175 F. Supp. 473, aff'd 361 U.S. 32.

The opinion of the Supreme Court in the *Tucker* case had been preceded by the opinion of the court in *Wong Yang Sung v. McGrath*,[40] where it was held that hearing officers in deportation proceedings must be qualified under the Administrative Procedure Act even though the statute governing those proceedings did not expressly provide for hearings. The decision in the *Wong* case seems to have been predicated primarily on the necessity for a hearing in such cases and the danger of commingling the judicial and prosecuting functions of the same agency in these particular proceedings. The opinion in the *Tucker* case had been preceded also by *Riss & Co., Inc. v. United States*,[41] where it was established that hearings on applications for certificates of public convenience and necessity under Section 207(a) of the Interstate Commerce Act[42] are subject to the provisions of the Administrative Procedure Act.

The decision in the Tucker case was followed in *Wales v. United States*,[43] in which the court held that an objection by plaintiffs to the qualification of the officer came too late when raised for the first time in a petition for rehearing after the report and order of the Commission had been issued. The hearing officer question was also involved in *Dillner Transfer Co. v. United States*,[44] in which a court held that the objection to the officer's qualification came too late when raised for the first time in the complaint filed in court.

In *Reliance Steel Products Co. v. United States*,[45] the court said that when a party aggrieved elects to pursue its cailm for reparation before the Commission, the hearing required by the I.C. Act is one that should be adjudicated pursuant to the Administrative Procedure Act, i.e., one to be determined on the record after opportunity for an agency hearing, and must be made initially by a qualified officer[46] in conformity with the Administrative Procedure Act.[47] Where a proceeding was referred to a nonhearing officer, and the Commission followed his recommendations against the shipper, holding that certain demurrage and penalty charges assessed by the carrier were applicable, the Commission's action, the court said in the *Reliance Steel* case, was unlawful.

---

[40]339 U.S. 33.
[41]341 U.S. 907.
[42]49 U.S.C. Sec. 307(a).
[43]108 F. Supp. 928, aff'd per curiam 345 U.S. 954.
[44]101 F. Supp. 506, aff'd 344 U.S. 883.
[45]150 F. Supp. 118, 122.
[46]5 U.S.C. 556(a) (b); 5 U.S.C. 3105.
[47]5 U.S.C. 553 and 554.

Assignment of Hearing Officers

The assignment of hearing officers for hearings is within the discretion of the Commission.[48] Such assignments must be made in rotation so far as practicable. It is assumed therefore that the Commission makes such assignments in rotation unless contingencies make such assignments impracticable.

The Supreme Court in *Ramspeck v. Federal Trial Examiners Conference*[49] upheld the above discretionary powers. This case was brought to determine the validity of regulations pertaining to hearing officers among which was the regulation requiring that officers be assigned to cases in rotation insofar as practicable. The officers contended that they must be assigned to cases in mechanical rotation without regard to the difficulty or importance of particular cases or the competence or experience of particular officers. The Supreme Court held that such mechanical rotation was not contemplated by the Administrative Procedure Act or Civil Service rules promulgated thereunder. In its opinion the Court stated:

> The (Civil Service) Commission gave to Section 11's requirement of assignment of cases in rotation "so far as practicable" consideration beyond the mere mechanics of bringing the next case on the docket opposite the top name on the register of available examiners. It gave consideration to the kind of case involved as well as the kind of examiner available. The (Civil Service) Commission had classified the examiners on that basis, and it considered it was practicable to assign cases to examiners who were, according to their classification, qualified to handle the case at hand, having regard to the complexity and difficulty thereof, together with the experience and ability of the examiner available. If assigned by mechanical rotation, the value and use of such classification, which Congress had authorized, would be lost. To use the classification, it was not practicable to use mechanical rotation. Congress did not provide for the classification of examiners by the (Civil Service) Commission, and then provide for the (Civil Service) Commission to ignore such classification by a mechanical rotation. The rotation for practical reasons was adjusted to the classifications. This was an allowable judgment by the (Civil Service) Commission as to what was practicable.

Staff Assistants

The Commission's staff assistants are not required to be qualified under the Administrative Procedure Act.[50] The Commission's practice

---

[48]5 U.S.C. 556(a), (b); 5 U.S.C. 3105.
[49]345 U.S. 128, 139-40.
[50]*T. S. C. Motor Freight Lines, Inc. v. United States*, 186 F. Supp. 777, 788.

of having staff attorneys, who have not taken part in the proceeding before the hearing officer, review the record and make recommendations does not violate the Administrative Procedure Act. Staff attorney-advisors are not required to qualify as hearing officers, and it is not necessary that their recommendations be served upon the parties or that parties have an opportunity to file exceptions thereto.[51] In *Grouping-Louisville with Jeffersonville*,[52] the Commission said that members of the Board of Suspension are employees eligible to serve on boards of employees to which the Commission may delegate work, business, or functions, as provided in Section 17(2). Therefore, the Commission said, there was no merit to respondent's contention that the order of suspension was unlawfully issued because members of the board were not hearing examiners.

Joint Boards

Section 205(a) of the Interstate Commerce Act[53] provides:

"The Commission shall, when operations of motor carriers or brokers conducted or proposed to be conducted involve not more than three States, and the Commission may, in its discretion, when operations of motor carriers or brokers conducted or proposed to be conducted involve more than three States, refer to a joint board for appropriate proceedings thereon, any of the following matters arising in the administration of this part with respect to such operations as to which a hearing is required or in the judgment of the Commission is desirable: Applications for certificates, permits, or licenses; the suspension, change, or revocation of such certificates, permits, or licenses; applications for the approval and authorization of consolidation, mergers, and acquisitions of control or operating contracts; complaints as to violations by motor carriers or brokers of the requirements established under Section 204(a); and complaints as to rates, fares, and charges of motor carriers or the practices of brokers: *Provided, however,* That if the Commission is prevented by legal proceedings from referring a matter to a joint board, it may determine such matter as provided in Section 17.

"The Commission, in its discretion, may also refer to a joint board any investigation and suspension proceeding or other matter not specifically mentioned above which arise under this part. The joint board to which any such matter is referred shall be composed solely of one member from each State within which the motor-carrier or brokerage operations involved in such matter are or are proposed to be conducted: *Provided,* That the Commission may designate an examiner or examiners to advise with and assist the joint board under such rules and regulations as it may prescribe. In act-

[51]*Ibid.*, pp. 789-90
[52]305 I.C.C. 713, 716.
[53]49 U.S.C. 305(a).

ing upon matters so referred, joint boards shall be vested with the same rights, duties, powers, and jurisdiction as are hereinbefore vested in members or examiners of the Commission to whom a matter is referred for hearing and the recommendation of an appropriate order thereon: *Provided, however,* That a joint board may, in its discretion, report to the Commission its conclusions upon the evidence received, if any, without a recommended order. Orders recommended by joint boards shall be filed with the Commission, and shall become orders of the Commission and become effective in the same manner, and shall be subject to the same procedure, as provided in the case of orders recommended by members or examiners under Section 17. If a joint board to which any matter has been referred shall report its conclusions upon the evidence without a recommended order, such matter shall thereupon be decided by the Commission, giving such weight to such conclusions as in its judgment the evidence may justify."

The provisions of Section 205(a) relative to reference of motor carrier applications to joint boards are directory and procedural.[54] Thus a court will not interfere with the procedural acts of the Commission in referring or in not referring a matter to a joint board. Injunctive interference with procedural acts of a duly constituted administrative body is an extreme and extraordinary remedy and will not be exercised in the absence of a clear showing of impairment of constitutional or statutory rights and the probability of irreparable damage.[55]

The scope of a proposed operation must be determined from the application. Thus in *Northern Tank Line Extension*[56] an application which stated that applicant proposed to traverse the two States named for operating convenience only was, upon that basis, determined to be a proceeding which should be heard by an examiner. Although protestant asserted that the purpose of such statement was to deprive a joint board of jurisdiction, the Commission said that such a conclusion could not be assumed from the application itself, therefore referral to an examiner was proper. Failure of a member of a joint board to participate in a hearing does not affect the duty and power of the remaining member or members; under Section 205(b) when only one member participates, such member constitutes a quorum and has full authority to consider an application.[57] In *Viking Freight Co. Extension,*[58] the Commission said that a joint board's recommended report and order were not invalidated by the fact that one of two members subscribing thereto had not attended the entire hearing. No objection was made to the

[54]*De Camp Bus Lines v. United States,* 185 F. Supp. 336, 340-1.
[55]*Ibid.,* p. 343
[56]77 M.C.C. 35, 37.
[57]*Willis,* 82 M.C.C. 257, 258.
[58]82 M.C.C. 57, 58-9.

partial attendance, but even if that member should not have participated in the decision, it would be no basis for a further hearing or issuance of another recommended report and order. The other member alone could have issued a valid report, and none of the parties was prejudiced by the fact that both members signed it.

In *Kaw Transport Co. Extension*[59] when the sole member of the joint boards to whom applications were referred, and who presided at the consolidated hearing, had left the State commission and was not available to submit the boards' recommendations to the Commission, it was held that the signing and submission of the recommended orders by another State commission member was correct procedure, designation of a hearing officer in lieu of the one no longer available was a proper exercise of the State commission's functions, and there was no indication that applicant was in any way prejudiced, nor was any other method of resolving the problem suggested. Moreover, the Commission said, the hearing officer's recommendations were not binding on the Commission, and the conclusions in the case were the result of a de novo consideration.

Under Section 205(b) it is not mandatory for a joint board to act within a specified period of time; the statute merely empowers the Commission to act in the event a board fails to do so, and it is within the Commission's discretion to serve a report and recommended order entered by the board at any reasonable time after conclusion of the hearing.[60]

Hearings

AUTHORITY OF OFFICERS

An officer may grant leave to amend or to file any pleadings, or to intervene, upon request tendered at the hearing, but in no event shall an officer grant leave to amend if thereby the issues would be so changed as to make a referred matter one which should properly be referred to a different officer. An officer shall have power to decide any motion to dismiss the proceeding or other motion which involves final determination of the merits ofthe proceeding. The officer shall regulate the procedure in the hearing before him, and shall have authority to take all measures necessary or proper for the efficient performance of the duties assigned him. (R. 66)

[59]83 M.C.C. 207, 209-10.
[60]*Willis,* 82 M.C.C. 257, 258-9.

Unavailability of Hearing Officer

In *National Labor Relations Board v. Stocker Manufacturing Co.*[61] the court in upholding an order made by the National Labor Relations Board upon a recommended decision said:

> Before the Labor Management Relations Act made statutory provision for intermediate reports in proceedings under the National Labor Relations Act, the Administrative Procedure Act regulated all administrative proceedings of this type. Section 5 (c) of that Act resolves the problem of this case by stipulating that "The same officers who preside at the reception of evidence . . . shall make the recommended decision . . . except where such officers become unavailable to the agency." 5 U.S.C.A. 1004 (c). We read this language as plain authority for the submission of recommendations by a person other than the examiner who presides at the hearing and has subsequently become unavailable because of death.

Prehearing Conferences

Upon written notice by the Commission in any proceeding, or upon written or oral instruction of an officer, parties or their attorneys may be directed to appear before an officer at a specified time and place for a conference, prior to or during the course of a hearing, or in lieu of personally appearing, to submit suggestions in writing, for the purpose of formulating issues and considering:

(1) The simplification of issues;

(2) The necessity of desirability of amending the pleadings either for the purpose of clarification, amplification, or limitation;

(3) The possibility of making admissions of certain averments of fact or stipulations concerning the use by any or all parties of matters of public record, such as annual reports and the like, to the end of avoiding the unnecessary introduction of proof;

(4) The procedure at the hearing;

(5) The limitation of the number of witnesses;

(6) The propriety of prior mutual exchange between or among the parties of prepared testimony and exhibits; and

(7) Such other matters, including disposition of requests for discovery, as may aid in the simplification of the evidence and disposition of the proceeding. (R. 67)

The binding effect of matters decided upon at prehearing conferences is demonstrated by *General Motors Corp. v. New York Central R. Co.*[62] There defendant's motion to dismiss a complaint except as to shipments from two origins on the ground that the evidence was directed only to

---

[61]185 F. 2d 451, 454.
[62]306 I.C.C. 345, 345-6.

the applicability of the tariffs from those origins, was overruled by the Commission. Complainant had complied with an agreement reached at a prehearing conference to supply defendants, prior to the hearing, with a record of 30 representative shipments, 10 to each destination territory, and with detailed evidence regarding two types of shipments to each territory. The proceeding was concerned with application of tariff provisions which were substantially the same in all territories involved, as admitted by defendants' witness at the hearing.

Stipulations

The parties may in the discretion of the officer, by stipulation in writing filed with the Commission at any stage of the proceeding, or orally made at the hearing, agree upon any pertinent facts in the proceeding. (R. 68)

Evidence; Admissibility Generally

Any evidence which is sufficiently reliable and probative to support a decision under the provisions of the Administrative Procedure Act, or which would be admissible under the general statutes of the United States, or under the rules of evidence governing proceedings in matters not involving trial by jury in the courts of the United States, shall be admissible in hearings before the Commission. The rules of evidence shall be applied in any proceeding to the end that needful and proper evidence shall be conveniently, inexpensively, and speedily produced, while preserving the substantial rights of the parties. (R. 73)

Evidence; Prepared Statements

With the approval of the officer, a witness may read into the record, as his testimony, statements of fact or expressions of his opinion prepared by him, or written answers to interrogatories of counsel. A prepared statement of a witness who is present at the hearing also may be received as an exhibit, provided that the statement shall not include argument; that before any such statement is read, or admitted in evidence the witness must deliver to the officer, the reporter, and to opposing counsel as may be directed by the officer, a copy of such statement or of such interrogatories and his written answers thereto; and that the admissibility of the evidence contained in such statement is subject to the same rules as if such testimony were produced in the usual manner, including the right of cross-examination of the witness. Such approval ordinarily will be denied when in the opinion of the officer the memory or demeanor of the witness may be of importance. (R. 75)

EVIDENCE; OFFICIAL RECORDS

An official record or an entry therein, when admissible for any purpose, may be evidenced by an official publication thereof or by a copy attested by the officer having the legal custody of the record, or by his deputy, and accompanied with a certificate that such officer has the custody. If the officer in which the record is kept is within the United States or within a territory or insular possession subject to the dominion of the United States, the certificate may be made by a judge of a court of record of the district or political subdivision in which the record is kept, authenticated by the seal of the court, or may be made by any public officer having a seal of office and having official duties in the district or political subdivision in which the record is kept, authenticated by the seal of his office.

If the office in which the record is kept is in a foreign state or country, the certificate may be made by a secretary of embassy or legation, consul general, consul, vice consul, or consular agent or by any officer in the foreign service of the United States stationed in the foreign state or country in which the record is kept, and authenticated by the seal of his office. A written statement signed by an officer having the custody of an official record or by his deputy that after diligent search no record or entry of a specified tenor is found to exist in the records of his office, accompanied by a certificate as above provided, is admissible as evidence that the records of his office contain no such record or entry. This does not prevent the proof of official records or of entry or lack of entry therein or official notice thereof by a method authorized by any applicable statute or by the rules of evidence. (R. 76)

EVIDENCE; ENTRIES IN REGULAR COURSE OF BUSINESS

Any writing or record, whether in the form of an entry in a book or otherwise, made as a memorandum or record of any act, transaction, occurrence, or event, will be admissible as evidence thereof if it appears that it was made in the regular course of business, and that it was the regular course of business to make such memorandum or record at the time such record was made or within a reasonable time thereafter.[63] (R. 77)

---

[63]See 28 U.S.C. 1732, Business Records Act.

EVIDENCE; DOCUMENTS CONTAINING MATTER NOT MATERIAL

When material and relevant matter offered in evidence are in a document containing other matter not material or relevant, the offering party must produce the document at the hearing, plainly designate the matter so offered, and accord to the officer and to participating counsel an opportunity to inspect it. Unless it is desired to read such matter into the record, and the officer so directs, true copies in proper form of the material and relevant matter taken from the document may be received as an exhibit, but other parties must be afforded an opportunity to produce in evidence, in like manner, other portions of such document if found to be material and relevant. The document itself will not be received. (R. 78)

EVIDENCE; DOCUMENTS IN COMMISSION FILES

In any matter contained in a report or other document, not a tariff or schedule, open to public inspection in the files of the Commission is offered in evidence such report or other document need not be produced. If any matter contained in a tariff or schedule on file with the Commission is offered in evidence, such tariff or schedule need not be produced or marked for identification, but the matter so offered must be specified with particularity in such manner as to be readily identified and may be received in evidence subject to check by reference to the original tariff or schedule. Official notice will be taken without offer or production of that portion of any tariff or schedule which is the subject matter of an order of investigation and suspension. (R. 79)

EVIDENCE; RECORDS IN OTHER COMMISSION PROCEEDINGS

If any portion of the record before the Commission in any proceeding other than the one on hearing is offered in evidence, a true copy of such portion must be presented for the record in the form of an exhibit unless (1) the party offering the same agrees to supply such copy later at his own expense, if and when required by the Commission; (2) the portion is specified with particularity in such manner as to be readily identified; (3) the parties represented at the hearing stipulate upon the record that such portion may be incorporated by reference, and that any other portion offered by any other party may be incorporated by like reference; and (4) the officer directs such incorporation. Any such portion so offered, whether in the form of an exhibit or by reference, is subject to objection. (R. 80)

It has long been recognized that the technical rules of evidence should not be strictly applied in administrative cases.[64] As stated by the Supreme Court in *Opp Cotton Mills v. Administrator:*[65]

> . . . it has long been settled that the technical rules for the exclusion of evidence applicable in jury trials do not apply to proceedings before federal administrative agencies in the absence of a statutory requirement that such rules are to be observed.

The Administrative Procedure Act[66] provides that "Any oral or documentary evidence may be received, but the agency as a matter of policy shall provide for the exclusion of irrelevant, immaterial, or unduly repetitious evidence." The courts have held that the function of the Commission is largely one of investigation and it should not be hampered in its inquiries by the narrow rules of evidence which prevail in trials at common law,[67] nor should the Commission be hampered by the technical rules governing the weight of evidence. "The mere admission of matter which under the rules of evidence applicable to judicial proceedings would be deemed incompetent does not invalidate its order.[68]

The administrative process would be stultified if proceedings were handled in a strict or hypertechnical sense. This was vividly pointed out in *Terminal Charge on Order Bills of Lading Shipments,*[69] where the Commission was concerned with the question of burden of proof. The Commission said (pp. 329-31):

> Section 216(g) of the act imposes a statutory burden of proof upon the proponents of changed rates or tariff rules. Where a charge, such as that now under consideration, becomes effective prior to the institution of an investigation by the Commission, there is no "changed rate" in issue. Accordingly, the proponents of such a charge do not have the statutory burden of proof. In such cases, the statutory burden of proof is imposed upon those who assail the rates, not by the terms of Section 15(7) or Section 216(g) of the act, but by Section 7(c) of the Administrative Procedure Act which provides: "Except as statutes otherwise provide, the proponent of a rule or order shall have the burden of proof." We must determine, therefore, whether the protestants met their statutory burden of proof even though the evidence which they adduced, standing alone, fails to establish by any clear, preponderant weight the unjustness and unreasonableness of the assailed charges.

---

[64]*Spiller v. A., T. & S.F. R.R. Co.,* 353 U.S. 117; *Interstate Commerce Commission v. Baird,* 194, U.S. 25, 44.
[65]312 U.S. 126, 155.
[66]U.S.C. 556(d).
[67]*Interstate Commerce Commission v. Baird,* 194 U.S. 25.
[68]*Western Paper Makers Chemical Co. v. United States,* 271 U.S. 268, 271.
[69]315 I.C.C. 327.

Administative agencies must guard against the tendency of rules of evidence and procedure to become talismanic formulas for the disposition of cases involving the public inteerst. In most proceedings before the Commission, the burden of proof is primarily a rule of evidence to insure orderly procedure. Its principal effect is to require the party who asserts the affirmative of an issue — that is, the party who would fail if no evidence were offered — to go forward in the proof. Cf. *Pacific Portland Cement Co. v. Food Mach. & Chem. Corp.*, 178 F. 2d 541 (9th Cir., 1949). However, the other parties who are proponents of a different result then must proceed to sustain their burden of going forward. *Att'y. Gen. Manual on the APA* 75 (1947).

Burden of proof becomes the master rather than the servant of the administrative process when it is viewed solely in quantitative terms. Proof by a clear preponderance of the evidence may be an appropriate requirement in most civil actions where only the rights of private parties are involved. That is not the sense in which the Congress used "burden of proof" in the Interstate Commerce and Administrative Procedure Acts. The public interest, which is necessarily involved in the Commission's quasi-legislative function of rate regulation cannot be determined merely on the basis of who proved what by a clear preponderance of the evidence. The instant proceeding is an excellent example. . . .

Although there have been a few unfortunate exceptions, the Commission has refused to subordinate common sense to any abstract view of burden of proof. For example, in *Great Northern Ry. Co. Discontinuance of Service*, 307 I.C.C. 59, the carrier contended that the protestants had the burden of proving that public convenience and necessity required the continuance of certain passenger train operations. That was clearly the protestants' burden in the sense that if no evidence at all had been offered, discontinuance of service would have followed as a matter of course. However, the Commission pointed out that "the question (of who has the burden of proof) is of more theoretical than practical importance," 307 I.C.C. at page 61. The Commission said:

> Regardless of where the burden of proof lies, a carrier subject to our regulation is expected to aid in the disposition of proceedings to which it is a party by making available all pertinent facts within its knowledge. (307 I.C.C. at page 61.)

We shall expect carriers involved in rate controversies to be equally cooperative, regardless of where the burden of proof lies. And, in fact, the respondents in this proceeding have made a conscientious effort to justify the charges in question. We are not required to view the evidence adduced by the protestants in a vacuum. Even if they had offered no evidence, we would have been obliged to supplement the record rather than to permit the anomalous and discriminatory situation which would develop as a result of condemning and condoning identical charges. The following statement . . . is well known but it cannot be repeated too often:

> They (administrative agencies) are not expected merely to call balls and strikes, or to weigh the evidence submitted by the parties and

let the scales tip as they will. The agency does not do its duty when it merely decides upon a poor or nonrepresentative record. As the sole representative of the public, which is a third party in these proceedings, the agency owes the duty to investigate all the pertinent facts, and to see that they are adduced when the parties have not put them in. . . . The agency must always act upon the record made, and if that is not sufficient, it should see the record is supplemented before it acts. It must always preserve the elements of fair play, but it is not fair play for it to create an injustice, instead of remedying one, by omitting to inform itself and by acting ignorantly when intelligent action is possible. . . .

Jencks Rule

In *Jencks v. United States*, the Supreme Court held that the prosecution must make available to the defense *all* reports and memoranda made by a government witness contemporaneously with the events described in his testimony so that the defense may decide whether to use such material for impeaching the witness. The court made clear that the reason for this rule is that "time dulls treacherous memory,"[70] and that consequently, the witness' revelations at the trial should be tested against those statements, notes, and other memoranda which he made at the time of the events to which he testified. Thus, the *Jencks* rule does not impugn the witness' veracity, but is primarily a check on the reliability of his memory. A succession of decisions by Courts of Appeals has made it clear that this rule is applicable to administrative hearings such as those of the Commission.[71]

The Commission (Division 1) in applying the Jencks rule in *Empire Truck U-Drive It, Inc., — Investigation*,[72] stated the following general rules:

> The requirement of the *Jencks* rule that the government make available to the defense reports and memoranda prepared by the government's witness recording the events which are the subject of the witness' testimony, for possible use by the defense in impeaching the witness, is an absolute requirement. It leaves nothing to the discretion of the judge or the hearing officer to deny inspection when the witness does not use his memoranda in the hearing room. Only the defense is adequately equipped to determine the effective use of these reports and memoranda for the purpose of discrediting the government's witness and thereby further the defense. It, therefore, has the right to see the reports and memoranda in order to determine what use may be made of them. 353 U.S. at 668, 669.

[70]353 U.S. 657.
[71]353 U.S. at p. 667. See *National Labor Rel. Bd. v. Adhesive Products Corp.,* 258 F. 2d 403, and *Great Lakes Airlines, Inc. v. CAB,* 291 F. 2d 354.
[72]96 M.C.C. 29.

The statement of the law remains correct and has not been modified by the courts in any manner. In *Zuzich Truck Line, Inc. v. United States,*[73] it was concluded that the *Jencks* rule was inapplicable but the court specifically noted that the respondent there sought to obtain records and reports not for use in cross-examination of a witness, as required by the *Jencks* rule, but as a means of obtaining information which it sought to use for other purposes in the conduct of its case.[74] Thus, the court did not hold the *Jencks* rule to be inapplicable in administrative proceedings before the Commission, but to be inapplicable in that particular proceeding solely because it was not invoked at the time the records and reports were requested and was not pertinent to the use to which Zuzich sought to put them. Moreover, in *Zuzich* the court specifically noted that the *Jencks Act* which provides a procedure for in camera inspection of memoranda where the *Jencks* rule is invoked applies only to criminal proceedings. The pertinence of the *Jencks* decision in administrative proceedings was not overruled by *Zuzich*, nor was it repealed by the Jencks Act which applies only to criminal cases.

In the circumstances presented, in *Barnes Truck Line, Inc., — Investigation & Revocation,*[75] the Commission (Division 1) concluded that the failure of its Bureau of Enforcement to make available to respondent those reports and memoranda made by the witness to record the events to which he testified rendered a district supervisor's testimony inadmissible. The record provided no practical basis for retaining any part of his testimony. Although it might have been feasible to cure the Bureau's refusal to provide the reports if a foundation had been laid to show that they were destroyed in accordance with routine administrative practice as in *Ogden v. United States,*[76] no such foundation had been provided. This oversight, coupled with the failure to provide the missing report of investigation, required exclusion of the testimony of this witness. Consequently, none of his testimony was considered. Moreover, with the exception of certain exhibits of which Division 1 took official notice, the exhibits sponsored by the witness were so closely tied to his testimony that they were also excluded.

Official Notice

A principal case on this point is *Interstate Commerce Comm. v. Louisville & N.R. Co.*[77] In that case, the Government insisted (at p. 93)

---

[73]224 F. Supp. 457.
[74]224 F. Supp. at 461.
[75]102 M.C.C. 281.
[76]323 F. 2d 818.
[77]227 U.S. 88.

that the Interstate Commerce Act "requires the Commission to obtain information necessary to enable it to perform the duties and carry out the objects for which it was created; and having been given legislative power to make rates it can act, as could Congress, on such information, and therefore its finding must be presumed to have been supported by such information, even though not formally proved at the hearing." The Supreme Court rejected the contention of the Government, stating (pp. 93-94):

> . . . But such a construction would nullify the rights to a hearing, — for manifestly there is no hearing when the party does not know what evidence is offered or considered, and is not given an opportunity to test, explain, or refuse. . . . The Commission is an administrative body, and, even where it acts in a quasi-judicial capacity, is not limited by the strict rules as to the admissibility of evidence, which prevail in suits between private parties.

> . . . But the more liberal the practice of admitting testimony, the more imperative the obligated to preserve the essential rules of evidence by which rights are asserted or defended. In such cass, the Commissioners cannot act upon their own information, as could jurors in primitive days. All parties must be fully apprised of the evidence submitted or to be considered, *and must be given opportunity to cross-examine witnesses, to inspect documents, and to offer evidence of explanation or rebuttal.* In no other way can a party maintain its rights or make its defense. In no other way can it test the sufficiency of the facts to support the finding; or otherwise, even though it appeared that the order was without evidence, the manifest deficiency could always be explained on the theory that the Commission had before it extraneous, unknown, but presumptively sufficient information to support the finding. . . . (Emphasis supplied.)

In *United States v. Abilene & S.R. Co.*,[78] the Commission entered an order relating to the division of joint rates after an investigation into the financial needs of one of the carriers involved. A number of respondents participated in the investigation undertaken by the Commission, and supplied certain statistical information requested of them. But they introduced no evidence before the Commission, and the case was submitted without argument. The respondents contended (p. 286) that the order was void because it rested upon evidence not legally before the Commission. It was conceded by the Commission (pp. 286-87) that its finding rested in part upon data taken from the annual reports filed with the Commission by the respondents pursuant to law;[79] that these reports

---

[78]265 U.S. 274.
[79]See *Junk over the Santa Fe Trail*, 44 M.C.C. 309 regarding carrier's annual reports.

were not formally put in evidence; that the parts containing the data relied upon were not put in evidence; that attention was not otherwise specifically called to them; and objection to the use of reports, under these circumstances, was seasonably made by the carriers and was insisted upon. The contention of the Commission was (p. 287-88) that, because the officer gave notice that "no doubt it will be necessary to refer to the annual report of all these carriers," it was therefore, permitted under its rules of practice to use the matter in the report as freely as if the data had been formally introduced in evidence. The Supreme Court invalidated the order, stating (p. 288) that "a finding without evidence is beyond the power of the Commission," and "Nothing can be treated as evidence which is not introduced as such." The court stated further (p. 288-89):

> . . . If the proceeding had been, in form, an adversary one, commenced by the Orient system, that carrier could not, under Rule xiii, have introduced the annual reports as a whole. For they contain much that is not relevant to the matter in issue. By the terms of the rule it would have been obligated to submit copies of such portions as it deemed material, or to make specific reference to the exact portion to be used. The fact that the proceeding was technically an investigation instituted by the Commission would not relieve the Orient, if a party to it, from this requirement. Every proceeding is adversary in substance, if it may result in an order in favor of one carrier as against another. Nor was the proceeding under review any the less an adversary one because the primary purpose of the Commission was to protect the public interest though making possible the continued operation of the Orient system. The fact that is was on the Commission's own motion that use was made of the data in the annual reports is not of legal significance.
>
> It is sought to justify the procedure followed by the clause followed in Rule xiii, which declares that the "Commission will take notice of items in tariffs and annual or other periodical reports of carriers properly on file." But this clause does not mean that the Commission will take judicial notice of all the facts contained in such documents. Nor does it purport to relieve the Commission from introducing, by specific reference, such parts of the reports as it wishes to treat as evidence. It means that as to those items there is no occasion for the parties to serve copies. The objection to the use of the data contained in the annual reports is not lack of authenticity or untrustworthiness. It is that the carriers were left without notice of the evidence with which they were, in fact, confronted, as later disclosed by the finding made. The requirement that, in an adversary proceeding, specific reference be made, is essential to the preservation of the substantial rights of the parties.

In *Ohio Bell Telephone Co. v. Public Utilities Com.*,[80] the Public Utilities Commission of Ohio, in determining valuation for rate making

[80]301 U.S. 292.

purposes, travelled outside the record for statistics concerning price trends in order to up-date the figures in the record. The Supreme Court held that this was improper stating that even though a depression or decline in market values may be judicially noticed, still the extent of the decline is beyond the scope of judicial notice. The court held (p. 300) that "The fundamentals of a trial were denied to the appellant when rates previously collected were ordered to be refunded upon the strength of evidential facts not spread upon the record." The appellant had asked for disclosure of the documents indicative of price trends, and for an opportunity to examine, analyze, explain, and rebut them. The response by the State Commission was a curt refusal. Upon the strength of the unknown documents refunds were ordered for sums mounting into millions, the State Commission reporting its conclusion, but not the underlying proofs. The court said (p. 300) that "This is not the fair hearing essential to due process. It is condemnation without trial." An attempt was made by the State Commission to uphold its decision without evidence as an instance of judicial notice. Decisions of the Supreme Court were cited as giving support to the proposition that values of land, labor, buildings, and equipment, with all their yearly fluctuations, no longer call for evidence. The Supreme Court replied to this contention in the following manner (pp. 301-302):

> . . . Our opinions have been misread if they have been thought to point that way. Courts take judicial notice of matters of common knowledge. . . . They take judicial notice that there has been a depression, and that a decline of market values is one of its concomitants. . . . How great the decline has been for this industry or that, for one material or another, in this year or the next, can be known only to the experts, who may even differ among themselves. For illustration, a Court takes judicial notice of the fact that Confederate money depreciated in value during the war between the states . . . , but not of the extent of the depreciation at a given time and place. . . . The distinction is the more impotant in cases where as here the extent of the fluctuations is not collaterally involved but is the very point in issue. Moreover, notice even when taken has no other effect than to relieve one of the parties to a controversy of the burden of resorting to the usual forms of evidence. Wigmore, Evidence § 2567; 1 Greenleaf, Evidence, 16th ed. p. 18. "It does not mean that the opponent is prevented from disputing a matter by evidence if he believes it disputable." Ibid., Cf. *Shapleigh v. Mier*, 299 U.S. 468, ante, 355, ...

The Supreme Court made it plain (at p. 302) that to press the doctrine of official notice to the extent attempted in the *Ohio Bell* case and to do it retroactively after the case had been submitted "would be to turn the doctrine into a pretext for dispensing with a trial." The court, noting that there was an extension of the concept of notoriety by the State Commission beyond reasonable limits, said (pp. 302-303):

> . . . From the standpoint of due process — the protection of the individual against arbitrary action — a deeper vice is this, that even now we do not know the particular or evidential facts of which the Commission took judicial notice and on which it rested its conclusion. Not only are the facts unknown; there is no way to find them out. When price lists or trade journals or even government reports are put in evidence upon the trial, the party against whom they are offered may see the evidence or hear it and parry its effect. Even if they are copied in the findings without preliminary proof, there is at least an opportunity in connection with a judicial review of the decision to challenge the deductions made from them. The opportunity is excluded here. The Commission, withholding from the record the evidential facts that it had gathered here and there, contents itself with saying that in gathering them it went to journals and tax lists, as if a judge were to tell us, "I looked at the statistics in the Library of Congress, and they teach me thus and so." This will never do if hearing and appeals are to be more than empty forms.

The court noted that regulatory commissions have been invested with broad powers within the sphere of duty assigned to them by law and that even in quasi-judicial proceedings their informed and expert judgment exacts and receives a proper deference from courts when it has been reached with due submission to constitutional restraints. The court also noted that much that commissions do within the realm of administrative discretion is exempt from supervision if those restraints have been obeyed. However, the court added (pp. 304-305):

> . . . All the more insistent is the need, when power has been bestowed so freely, that the "inexorable safeguard" (*St. Joseph Stock Yards Co. v. United States*, 298 U.S. 38, 73) of a fair and open hearing be maintained in its integrity. . . . The right to such a hearing is one of "the rudiments of fair play" (*Chicago, M. & St. P. R. Co. v. Polt*, 232 U.S. 165, 168) assured to every litigant oby the Fourteenth Amendment as a minimal requirement. . . . There can be no compromise on the footing of convenience or expediency, or because of a natural desire to be rid of harrassing delay, when that minimal requirement has been neglected or ignored.

There has been a marked consistency by the Supreme Court in its approach to the doctrine of official notice.[81] There was no change in the Supreme Court's position in its decisions in *Market Street R. Co. v. Railroad Com. of Cal.*,[82] and *United States v. Pierce Auto Freight Lines*,[83] which cases might erroneously be construed as being inconsistent with the court's decision in the *Ohio Bell* case. *Market Street* involved two separate attacks on an order of the Railroad Commission of California

---

[81]See *Garner v. Louisiana*, 368 U.S. 157, 173 and *Joint Anti-Facist Refugee Com. v. McGrath*, 341 U.S. 123, 165, note 10.
[82]324 U.S. 548.
[83]327 U.S. 515.

reducing passenger fares. The first attack was made on the ground that the State Commission engaged in speculation and conjecture by predicting the effect of the reduction in fares in stimulating passenger traffic after an evaluation on the company's experience without the aid of expert testimony, subject to cross-examination, explanation and rebuttal. The court distinguished the *Ohio Bell* case, stating (p. 560):

> . . . The basis for a judgment is here in the record. The company itself put in evidence decisions by the Commission in which by cautious steps it permitted an advance of the rates from five to seven cents. Traffic records before and after each advance are in evidence. Also in the record is the traffic experience of the competing municipal line, which did not increase its fares and did not suffer declines in traffic and revenues comparable to those which followed this Company's increase of fares. This is not a case where the data basic to a judgment have been withheld from the record. . . .

The second attack was on the ground that the Commission's order was invalid under the due process clause because it was based on matters outside the record. The Commission had used certain monthly reports of the Company which had been filed with the Commission after the close of the hearing, showing operating revenues. The Company made no showing that, if a re-hearing were held to introduce its own reports, it would gain much by cross-examination, rebuttal, or impeachment of its own auditors for the reports filed. Further, the State Commission contended that even if it was an error to refer to such reports, the error was harmless, since the record without the figures supported the reasonableness of the established fare and it was therefore immaterial if the Commission used some additional figures. No contention was made that the information was erroneous or was misunderstood by the Commission, and no contention was made that the company could have disproved it or explained away its effect for the purpose for which the Commission used it. The most that could be said was that the Commission in making its predictive findings went outside of the record to verify its judgment by reference to actual traffic figures that became available only after the hearing closed. The Supreme Court said (p. 562):

> . . . Due process, of course, requires that commissions proceed upon matters in evidence and that parties have opportunity to subject evidence to the test of cross-examination and rebuttal. But due process deals with matters of substance and is not to be trivialized by formal objections that have no substantial bearing on the ultimate rights of parties. The process of keeping informed as to regulated utilities is a continuous matter with commissions. We are unwilling to say that such an incidental reference as we have here to the party's own reports, although not formally marked

in evidence in the proceeding, in the absence of any showing of error or prejudice constitutes a want of due process.

The *Pierce Auto* case involved two separate applications for motor carrier certificates of public convenience and necessity which were separately heard before two joint boards. Because the applications were so closely related in their common features, the hearings were held at the same time and place and one application was heard immediately after the other. Each applicant intervened in the proceeding on the other's application, and the same parties appeared in opposition in both proceedings. The parties stipulated that much of the evidence presented in the one hearing should be introduced by reference into the record of the other proceeding. This included all of the affirmative evidence of the protestant-appellee in opposition to the two applications. The hearings thus were substantially coordinated, though not technically consolidated, for the common features of the applications. An examiner submitted separate reports in which he recommended a denial of both applications. A division of the Commission dealt with both in a single report, reversing the examiner in both cases and ordering that each application be granted. The lower court held the Commission's order invalid on the ground that evidence that appeared only in one record was used by the Commission to support general findings in both cases. The Supreme Court upheld the Commission stating (p. 528):

> . . . The principal cause of the complaint in these respects is that the Commission did not consider each case exclusively on its own record but looked to the evidence in both proceedings in forming a judgment. If this is true and if it has resulted in substantial prejudice to the appellees, as might occur, for example, if the Commission were shown prejudicially to have considered the evidence bearing on one case which did not affect it and which was presented in the other, and which appellees were given no opportunity to meet, the orders, or one of them, would be improperly grounded.

> But no showing of this sort has been made. It is to be recalled that all the appellees, as well as both of the applicants, were parties to both proceedings; were represented at all of the hearings which were conducted at substantially the same time and places and were given full opportunity to present all evidence they considered pertinent, to cross-examine the witnesses, and otherwise to protect their interest. Moreover, large portions of the evidence applied as much to one application as to another. This was true, for example, of the proofs relating to traffic conditions, shipper demands, the need for fasted service and mechanical refrigeration, and other items. In the circumstances it is difficult to say how appellees could have substantial prejudice from the Commission's consideration of the evidence upon matters as closely related as those in issue in these two proceedings.

That the power to take official notice does not extend to records in other proceedings is established also by cases in the lower courts. In *Kline v. United States*,[84] the district court held that there was a denial of due process for the Commission to take notice of materials in its own record in deciding an application proceeding. The record on review showed that after the Commission had set forth in its report the extraneous information used, Kline filed a petition for further hearing, and for oral argument because of the foreign matter contained in the findings. The Commission denied the petition. The court was of the opinion that the refusal of the request for a chance to meet the extraneous matter was a denial of a fair hearing, stating (p. 583) that Kline "was deprived of his right to cross-examination, and of a testing of the truth of the statements appearing" in the extra records. In *Paridy v. Caterpillar Tractor Co.*,[85] the court said, "It is true that a court will take notice of its own records, but it cannot travel for this purpose out of the record relating to the particular case; it cannot take notice of the proceedings in another case, even between the same parties and in the same court, unless such proceedings are put in evidence." The court said (p. 169) that the reason for the rule "is that the decision of a cause must depend upon the evidence introduced." It added (p. 169) that "If the courts should recognize judicially facts adjudicated in another case, it makes those facts, though unsupported by evidence in the case in hand, conclusive against the opposing parties; while if they had been properly introduced they might have been met and overcome by them."

The Commission is in accord with the court cases. Its General Rules of Practice provide that if any portion of the record before the Commission in any proceeding other than the one on hearing is offered in evidence a true copy of such portions shall be presented in the form of an exhibit. This is the procedure which must be followed unless the party offering the portion of the record agrees to supply such copy later, if and when required by the Commission; the portion is specified with particularity in such manner as to be readily identified; the parties stipulate on the record that such portion may be incorporated by reference, and that any portion offered by any other party may be incorporated by like reference; and the officer directs such incorporation. Any portion of the record so offered, whether in the form of an exhibit or by reference, shall be subject to objection. Its decisions in cases in which requests

[84] 41 F. Supp. 577.
[85] 48 F. 2d 166, 168.

have been made to take official notice of records in other proceedings are in harmony with the court cases.[86]

In the *Krapf* case, Division 1 denied a request that it take official notice of a portion of the applicant's testimony in a prior proceeding, stating that the "General Rules of Practice provide a method whereby transcripts of testimony at previous hearings may be introduced in a subsequent proceeding, and we will not correct protestants' failures to follow the rules by taking official notice of the materials to which they refer." In the *Watson* case, the Commission was requested in a purchase case to take official notice of a transcript of the hearing and the examiner's proposed report in a prior proceeding. Division 4 said, "We may not properly take judicial notice of the evidence which protestants request we consider. The Commission's Rules of Practice contain adequate provision for the incorporation of the record made at one proceeding into evidence at another."

As a final comment, the Administrative Procedure Act provides that "When an agency decision rests on official notice of a material fact not appearing in the evidence in the record, a party is entitled, on timely request, to an opportunity to show the contrary."[87]

Timely Objections

The courts have recognized that, in order for a party to take advantage of a defect in procedure as a means for setting aside an agency's determination, it is necessary that that party must have clearly brought to the administrative body's attention at the appropriate time the defect and had given that body an opportunity to correct the invalid procedure.[88] In *United States v. Tucker Truck Lines,* the appellee had successfully made the contention in the district court that the Commission's action in granting a certificate was invalid for want of jurisdiction because the examiner had not been appointed pursuant to the Administrative Procedure Act. The Supreme Court held that the district court had committed error since the appellee had not raised the issue of

---

[86]See *St. Johnsbury Trucking Co., Inc., Extension — Heavy Hauling,* 53 M.C.C. 277, 289; *Krapf Extension — Cinders,* 76 M.C.C. 103, 105; *Watson Bros. Transp. Co., — Purchase — S. & C. Transport,* 70 M.C.C. 317, 318; *Motor Fuel Carriers, Inc., Ext. — Northern Alabama,* 86 M.C.C. 411, 414; *New York Central R. Co. Abandonment,* 312 I.C.C. 271, 274.

[87]5 U.S.C. 556(e). See *New York Central R. Co. Abandonment,* 312 I.C.C. 271, 274.

[88]*United States v. Tucker Truck Lines,* 344 U.S. 33; *Monumental Motor Tours v. United States,* 110 F. Supp. 929; *Nowinsky Trucking Co. v. United States,* 195 F. Supp. 748, 751; *Gateway Transp. Co. v. United States,* 173 F. Supp. 822, 828.

defective procedure at an appropriate time before the Commission. The Supreme Court indicated that simple fairness required that the Commission be informed of any defective procedure which it was following, and thus be put on notice of the possibility of wholesale reversals being incurred by its persistence in the defective procedure. The Supreme Court stated (pp. 36-8):

> In *Riss & Co. v. United States*, 341 U.S. 907, this court held that officers hearing applications for certificates of convenience and necessity under 207(a) of the Interstate Commerce Act are subject to the provisions of the Administrative Procedure Act. *But timeliness of the objection was not before us, because in that case the examiner's appointment had been twice challenged in the administrative proceedings, once, as it should have been, before the examiner at the hearings and again before the Commission on a petition for rehearing.* That decision established only that a litigant in such a case as this who does make such demand at the time of hearing is entitled to an examiner chosen as the Act prescribes.

> *We have recognized in more than a few decisions, and Congress has recognized in more than a few statutes, that orderly procedure and good administration require that objections to the procedings of an administrative agency be made while it has opportunity for correction in order to raise issues reviewable by the courts.* It is urged in this case that the Commission had a predetermined policy on this subject which would have required it to overrule the objection if made. While this may well be true, the Commission is obliged to deal with a large number of like cases. Repetition of the objection in them might lead to a change of policy, or, if it did not, the Commission would at least be put on notice of the accumulating risks of wholesale reversals being incurred by its persistence. *Simple fairness to those who are engaged in the tasks of administration, and to litigants, requires as a general rule that courts should not topple over administrative decisions unless the administrative body not only has erred but has erred against objection made at the time appropriate under its practice.*

> It is argued, however, that this case falls outside of this general rule and the result below is technically compelled because, if the appointment of the hearing examiner was irregular, the Commission in some manner lost jurisdiction and its order is totally void. This inference is drawn from our decision in *Wong Yang Sung v. McGrath*, 339 U.S. 33, for it is contended that we could not have sustained a collateral attack by writ of habeas corpus in that case unless we found the defect in that examiner's appointment to be one of jurisdictional magnitude. We need not inquire what should have been the result upon that case had the Government denied or the Court considered whether the objection there sustained was taken in time. The effect of the omission was not there raised in briefs or argument nor discussed in the opinion of the court. Therefore, the case is not binding precedent on this point. Even as to our own judicial power or jurisdiction, this Court has followed the lead of Mr. Chief Justice Marshall who held that this Court is not bound by a prior exercise of jurisdiction in a case where it was not questioned and it was passed *sub silentio*.

The question not being foreclosed by precedent, we hold that the defect in the examiner's appointment was an irregularity which would invalidate a resulting order if the Commission had overruled an appropriate objection made during the hearings. But it is not one which deprives the Commission of power or jurisdiction, so that even in the absence of timely objection its order should be set aside as a nullity. (Emphasis supplied.)

In *Monumental Motor Tours v. United States, supra,* the district court dismissed a complaint which charged not only that an order of the Commission granting a certificate of public convenience and necessity was defective because the hearing officer was not qualified in accordance with the provisions of the Administrative Procedure Act, but also that that fact had been brought to the Commission's attention by the plaintiff in the petition for reconsideration, which was filed shortly after the entry of the Commission's final order. In holding that the objection to the procedure was not timely made, the district court stated (page 932):

> In the Tucker case the objection to the examiner's qualification was not made until after the filing of the action in the District Court, while in the present case, as we have above pointed out, the objection was first made . . . when the plaintiff here filed a petition for reconsideration of the Commission's order . . ., in which the entire Commission approved the action of Division 5 on a petition for reconsideration filed by both Monumental and Safeway. It thus appears on the question of timeliness that the objection was not made before the Commission until after the hearings had been entirely concluded and a final decision had been made by the Commission. On the reasoning of the opinion in the Tucker case we think that the holding in this case must be that the objection was not timely made and therefore does not warrant a remand of the case to the Commission for another hearing.

ORAL ARGUMENT BEFORE THE HEARING OFFICER

At the discretion of the hearing officer and upon reasonable notice to the parties, oral argument may be made at the close of testimony before him as an alternative to the filing of written briefs. (R. 86)

Oral argument under the Commission's rules of practice is not granted as a matter of right but is discretionary. Neither the Interstate Commerce Act nor the Administrative Procedure Act provides the circumstances under which·oral argument shall be granted. Due process of law under the Fifth Amendment does not necessarily require that oral argument be granted. Actually, all that the Administrative Procedure Act or procedural due process requires are procedures by which the parties may be fully informed of the issues and proposed grounds for decision and be afforded a full opportunity to be heard by presentation of evidence and argument upon the issues.[89] In *Federal Communications Commission v. WJR, supra,* radio station WJR petitioned the F.C.C. for a hearing to reconsider the granting to another party of the right to construct a radio station. The F.C.C. denied the petition without affording the petitioner the opportunity for oral argument. The court of appeals held that the opportunity for oral argument is essential to a fair hearing and set aside the Commission's order. The Supreme Court reversed the court of appeals. The court said:

> On the contrary, due process of law has never been a term of fixed and invariable content. This is as true with reference to oral argument as with respect to other elements of procedural due process. For this Court has held in some situations that such argument is essential to a fair hearing. *Londoner v. Denver,* 210 U.S. 373, in others that argument submitted in writing is sufficient. *Morgan v. United States,* 298 U.S. 468, 481. See also *Johnson & Wimsatt v. Hazen,* 69 App. D. C. 151; *Mitchell & Reichelderfer,* 61 App. D. C. 50.

> The decisions cited are sufficient to show that the broad generalization made by the Court of Appeals is not the law. Rather it is in conflict with this Court's ruling, in effect, that the right of oral argument as a matter of procedural due process varies from case to case in accordance with differing circumstances, as do other procedural regulations. Certainly the Constitution does not require oral argument in all cases where only insubstantial or frivolous questions of law, or indeed even substantial ones, are raised. Equally certainly it has left wide discretion to Congress in creating the procedures to be followed in both administrative and judicial proceedings, as well as in their conjunction.

Administrative Appeals — Non-Rail Proceedings

Exceptions may be filed to an initial or tentative decision of an individual Commissioner, an administrative law judge, a joint board, or an examiner, and shall detail the assailed findings, with supporting citations to the record and authorities.

Exceptions shall be confined to factual and legal issues which are essential to the ultimate and just determination of the proceeding and shall be based on the following grounds:

(i) That a necessary finding of fact is omitted, erroneous, or unsupported by substantial evidence of record;

(ii) That a necessary legal conclusion or finding is contrary to law, Commission precedent or policy;

[89]*New England Divisions Case,* 261, at p. 200; *Western Union Division, C.T.U. v. United States,* 87 F. Supp. 324; *Federal Communications Commission v. W.J.R.* 337 U.S. 265, 275-6. See also *McGraw Electric Co. v. United States,* 120 F. Supp. 354, 358.

(iii)   That in important question of law, policy or discretion is involved which is without governing precedent; or

(iv)   That prejudicial procedural error has occurred.

Unless the division or Commission, as the case may be, reverses, changes or modifies the prior decision, order, or requirement or unless the decision, order or requirement is issued by the division or Commission in the first instance, or unless the decision, order, or requirement is issued by an employee board, no further administrative appeal shall lie.

Except when no further administrative appeal shall lie, any party may file a petition for administrative review, which shall detail in what respects further hearing, rehearing, reargument or reconsideration is sought and the reasons therefor.

A party shall not be permitted to file a second administrative appeal unless the division or Commission, as the case may be, shall have reversed, changed or modified the prior decision, order or requirement, or where the decision, order, or requirement is issued by the division or Commission in the first instance, in which event the petition shall be limited to the reversal, change or modification, and successive administrative appeals upon substantially the same grounds shall not be entertained.

The right to apply to the entire Commission for rehearing, reargument, or reconsideration of a decision, order, or requirement of a division of the Commission in any proceeding shall be limited and restricted to those proceedings in which the entire Commission, on its own motion, determines and announces that an issue of general transportation importance is involved. In proceedings in which no such announcement has been made, but in which a division reverses, changes, or modifies a prior decision by a hearing officer or where the initial decision is made by a division, a petition to the same division for rehearing, reargument, or reconsideration of its decision will be permitted and will be considered and disposed of by such division in an appellate capacity and with administrative finality.

In any proceeding which has involved the taking of evidence at oral hearing or by modified procedure in which the Commission has not noted the presence of an issue of general transportation importance, any party may, within 15 days after the service of a final decision, order, or requirement of a division or appellate division, as to which the filing of a petition for rehearing, reargument, or reconsideration is not permitted, file a petition requesting the Commission to find on its own motion that the proceeding is one involving an issue of general transportation importance.

In *Arco Auto Carriers, Inc., Extension,*[90] the Commission held that while protestants' exceptions did not conform with the requirements of the rules of practice since the Commission was able to follow the arguments contained therein they would be allowed to stand. However, the Commission admonished that the rules of practice must be observed strictly.

Administrative Appeals — Rail Proceedings

Any party may appeal from any decision which is issued in the first instance unless such an appeal is precluded by the time constraints of the Railroad Revitalization and Regulatory Reform Act of 1976. Appeals shall detail the assailed findings, with supporting citations to the record and authorities. Appeals shall be confined to factual and legal issues which are essential to the ultimate and just determination of the proceeding and shall be based on the following grounds:

(i) That a necessary finding of fact is omitted, erroneous, or unsupported by substantial evidence of record;

(ii) That a necessary legal conclusion or finding is contrary to law, Commission precedent or policy;

(iii) That an important question of law, policy or discretion, is involved which is without governing precedent;

(iv) That prejudicial procedural error has occurred.

Any party may file a petition for administrative review of the decision, order, or requirement of the division or Commission, subject to the following requirements:

(i) That the petition shall detail in what respects the proceeding involves a matter of general transportation importance or new evidence or changed circumstances exist which would materially affect the prior decision, order or requirement, and include a request that the Commission make such determination.

(ii) That, to the extent further hearing, rehearing, reargument or reconsideration is sought, the petition shall detail in what respects such relief is requested and the reasons therefor. (R. 98)

---

[90]81 M.C.C. 131, 139-140. See also *Pacific Diesel Rental Co. Investigation of Operations,* 78 M.C.C. 161, 163.

The rule that petitions for rehearings[91] before administrative bodies are addressed to their own discretion is uniformly accepted and is universally applied in the federal courts.[92] It is well settled that the granting or denying of petition for rehearing and reconsideration by the Commission and its divisions is within their sound discretion and should not be set aside except upon a showing of the clearest abuse of discretion.[93] Reversing the judgment of a district court that set aside an order of the Commission denying a rehearing, the Supreme Court said in *United States v. Pierce Auto Lines*[94] that "it has been held consistently that rehearings before administrative bodies are addressed to their own discretion," and that, "Only a showing of the clearest abuse of discretion could sustain an exception to that rule."

The rule that petitions for rehearing (or reopening) are addressed to the discretion of the Commission was stated as follows in *Interstate Commerce Commission v. Jersey City*,[95]

> . . . One of the grounds of resistance to administrative orders throughout federal experience with the administrative process has been the claims of private litigants to be entitled to rehearing to bring the record up to date and meanwhile to forestall the enforcement of the administrative order. Administrative consideration of evidence — particularly where the evidence is taken by an examiner, his report submitted to the parties, and a hearing held on their exceptions to it — always creates a gap between the time the record is closed and the time the administrative decision is promulgated. This is especially true if the issues are difficult, the evidence intricate, and the consideration of the case deliberate and careful. If upon the coming down of the order litigants might demand rehearings as a matter of law because some new circumstance has arisen, some new trend had been observed, or some new fact discovered, there would be little hope that the administrative process could ever by consummated. . . . It has been almost

---

[91]Section 17(6) of the Act provides that after a decision or order of the Commission or of a division has been made, "any party thereto may at any time, subject to such limitations as may be established by the Commission as hereinafter authorized, make application for rehearing, reargument, or reconsideration of the same, or of any matter determined therein. Such applications shall be governed by such general rules as the Commission may establish." The Commission's rules of practice provide procedure for the taking of additional evidence on rehearing and for reconsideration on the record already made.

[92]*United States ex rel. Maine Potato Growers Assn. v. Interstate Commerce Commission,* 88 F. 2d 780, 784, cert. denied 300 U.S. 684; *Mississippi Valley Barge Line Co. v. United States,* 4 F. Supp. 745; *Union Stock Yards Co. v. United States,* 9 F. Supp. 864, 873; *American C. Co. v. United States,* 11 F. Supp. 965, 972; *R.C.A. Communications v. United States,* 43 F. Supp. 851, 858.

[93]*Shein v. United States,* 102 F. Supp. 320, 326; *Lang Transp. Corp. v. United States,* 75 F. Supp. 915; *Gardner v. United States,* 67 F. Supp. 203, 232; *Eck-Miller Transfer Co. v. United States,* 143 F. Supp. 409, 411.

[94]327 U.S. 515, 535.

[95]322 U.S. 503, 514.

a rule of necessity that rehearings were not matters of right, but were pleas to discretion. And likewise it has been considered that the discretion to be invoked was that of the body making the order, and not that of a reviewing body.

In *Carolina Scenic Coach Lines v. United States*,[96] a complaint requesting that an order of the Commission denying a rehearing be set aside was dismissed. The court stated that the discretion of the Commission to deny rehearings was so complete as not to require it to give any reason for its action. The court said:

> Whether the Commission should grant a rehearing in a case which it has decided is a matter resting in its sound discretion. *Interstate Commerce Commission v. Jersey City*, 322, U.S. 503, 517, 64 S. Ct. 1129, 88 L. Ed. 1420. The discretion here was exercised, and there is nothing to show that it was abused. . . . There is nothing before us upon which we would be justified in saying that in denying the rehearing the Commission did not give full consideration to all these matters; and, for aught that appears, its denial of the rehearing may well have been based upon the view that, assuming the matters urged in the petition to be true, they could not affect its decision. To one who has denied many petitions for rehearing and seldom given a reason therefor, it comes as a matter of mild surprise that anyone should think it incumbent on a court or Commission to give reasons for denying a petition merely because a party urges grounds that he claims to have discovered recently.

In *North-South Freightways v. United States*,[97] the court said (p. 698):

> The plaintiff insists, however, that it was not given a fair and adequate opportunity to prove that its operations other than in the carriage of household goods were substantial before June 1, 1935. We cannot agree. At various hearings it had an ample opportunity to present whatever pertinent evidence it desired. The plain fact is that it did offer all that it then saw fit. If it refrained from making more or better proof because of the expense and difficulty in obtaining it or because it became conscious of a need to put in more only after the hearings were at long length finally closed and it was faced with an adverse decision, it has no just grievance. It has made no showing of newly discovered evidence, and the refusal of the Commission to grant the rehearing requested was plainly no abuse of discretion and should not be disturbed.

In *United States v. Northern Pacific Ry.*,[98] the railroad sought to set aside a rate order of the Commission on the ground that economic conditions had so changed between the time that the record was closed and the time that the order was to become effective, that the Com-

[96] 59 F. Supp. 336, 337.
[97] 55 F. Supp. 696.
[98] 288 U.S. 490.

mission erred in refusing to grant a rehearing in order that evidence respecting the changed conditions could be pointed out. In rejecting the position of the railroad, the Supreme Court emphasized the fact that it was not until after the final report and order of the Commission were entered that the carrier brought to the Commission's attention the changed economic conditions, even though such evidence was readily available to it prior to that time. Consequently, the Supreme Court held that the carrier was estopped from complaining of the Commission's refusal to grant the rehearing and stated (page 494):

> Though the order substantially reduced the carriers' revenues, we do not consider the merits of the application for rehearing, as we think the carriers' lack of diligence in bringing this matter to the Commission's attention deprived them of any equity to complain of the refusal of their petition. They sat silent and took the chance of a favorable decision on the record as made. They should not be permitted to reopen the case for the introduction of evidence long available and susceptible of production months before the Commission acted. The denial of a rehearing, in view of this delay, was not such an abuse of discretion as would warrant setting aside the order.

In *Lang Transp. Corporation v. United States*,[99] one of the grounds that the plaintiff relied upon in the court to upset the action of the Commission in granting a certificate was the fact that the ruling was based upon a stale record, in that between the date the hearing before the Commission was closed and the date when the order was issued conditions had materially changed and transportation requirements had substantially lessened. In rejecting this contention, the court stated:

> . . . but no effort was made, apparently, in the interim, by the Lang Transportation Corporation, to call the Commission's attention to this alleged change until a report adverse to the said plaintiffs had been received, and the plaintiffs were content to take a chance on a decision favorable to them. This constitutes a fatal lack of diligence. *United States v. Northern Pac. R. Co.*, 288 U.S. 490, 494, 53 S. Ct. 406, 77 L. Ed. 914.
>
> ✿ ✿ ✿
>
> Assuming, for the moment, that the plaintiffs herein could have brought themselves originally within the scope of the ruling of *Atchison, Topeka & Santa Fe R. Co. et al. v. United States et al.*, 1932, 284 U.S. 248, 52 S. Ct. 146, 76 L. Ed. 273, *supra*, and would thereby have become entitled to a rehearing because of *radically changed conditions*, again assuming conditions to have changed radically meanwhile, the plaintiffs herein have, nevertheless, prejudiced their position by not having called these so-called radically changed conditions to the attention of the Commission between November 18, 1944, and June of 1946, and so, because of lack of diligence,

---

[99]75 F. Supp. 915, 929-30.

come squarely within the rule enunciated by the Supreme Court in *United States v. Northern Pacific R. Co.*, 288 U.S. 490, 53 S. Ct. 406, 77 L. Ed. 914 *(supra)* a later case.

In *Shein, et al. v. United States*,[100] the argument that the Commission, having reported favorably upon the evidence in its earlier proceedings, could not upon reconsideration reverse its position and deny the application without new evidence was held to be without merit. In support thereof, the court in the *Shein* case cited *Beard-Laney, Inc. v. United States*,[101] where the court said:

> The rules to be applied in reviewing the order of the Commission are not different because that order resulted from a reversal of a prior decision of the hearing division upon a petition for rehearing. The fact that a rehearing was granted shows that the questions involved were carefully considered and the ultimate decision of the division, which received the approval of the Commission, was the final and definitive action of the Commission, which is what we are authorized to review; and it is to be reviewed in the same way and under the same limitations as other reviewable orders. We may not substitute our judgment for that of the Commission because upon a rehearing and fuller consideration of the facts it has arrived at a different conclusion from that which its hearing division had first expressed. *Lang Transportation Corp. v. United States*, (1948) 75 F. Supp. 915, 925.

In *Atlanta-New Orleans Motor Freight Co. v. United States*,[102] the court reiterated that the granting or denying of a petition for further hearing is discretionary with the *Commission*, and its decision will not be disturbed upon judicial review unless there is a clear showing of abuse of this discretion. The court said that denial of a petition for further hearing in an application proceeding, on grounds that new evidence proffered by opposing motor carrier would not necessitate a different decision, did not amount to abuse of its discretion. In *Yourga v. United States*,[103] the court said that a petition for rehearing or reconsideration on the ground of newly discovered evidence is addressed to the sound discretion of the Commission, and reversal of the Commission's ruling thereon can be based on only a clear showing of abuse of discretion. The court said that in order to grant such a petition, the record must show that the evidence was discovered since the hearing; the facts must indicate reasonable diligence on the part of petitioner; and it must appear that the evidence is material and not merely cumulative or impeaching, and that it would produce a different result. The court then

[100]102 F. Supp. 320.

[101]83 F. Supp. 27, 33.

[102]197 F. Supp. 364, 371. See *Kroblin Refrigerated Xpress, Inc. v. United States*, 197 F. Supp. 39, 44.

[103]191 F. Supp. 373, 377.

held that in denying plaintiff's petitions for reconsideration and for rehearing, the Commission used appropriate standards with respect to evaluating the newly discovered evidence. In *Convoy Co. v. United States*,[104] the court said that in passing on a petition for rehearing, based on claimed radical change in facts and circumstances since the original hearing, the Commission had a right to consider whether the facts were discovered since the hearing or whether they could have been discovered at or before time of such hearing, whether such facts were material, and whether matters mentioned in the petition would probably produce a different result. The court said that the Commission, having the benefit of informed experience within its particular field, should know of any drastic economic changes in the field of its experience thus the court would not substitute its own judgment and conclude that a different result should have been reached by the Commission. Since no drastic change occurred, reversal of the Commission for refusing to grant rehearing on the contention that the record was stale was not warranted. The Commission, the court said, did not abuse its discretion in denying the petition. In *Allen v. United States*,[105] the court said that the Commission's order denying reconsideration did not violate the Administrative Procedure Act because it stated only that the findings of the division were in accordance with the evidence and applicable law, when the order referred back to a full and detailed record of the decisions and reasons therefor. Reiteration of all facts, all prior findings, and applicable law would be useless and wasteful when the Commission's reasons for denial of rehearing were the same as those for making the decision at the outset.

Control of Procedure

In *T.S.C. Motor Freight Lines, Inc. v. United States*,[106] the court said that action of a division of the Commission, in certifying directly to the entire Commission, without issuance of a formal report, motor carrier application proceedings which had been submitted to the division "for action thereon," complies in all substantial respects with the Commission's organizational rules, whether viewed as a request by the division for "advice and counsel" or as assignment of additional Commissioners to consider the case. The Commission's action in accepting the certification, the court said, in effect amounts to a recall of the matter from the

---

[104]200 F. Supp. 10, 14-15.
[105]187 F. Supp. 625, 630.
[106]186 F. Supp. 777, 783-4, aff'd 366 U.S. 419.

division; whether the initiating force for such a consideration came from the division or the Commission seems unimportant. The court said further that although the vote to refer the proceedings directly to the entire Commission was recorded only in a memorandum prepared by a clerk of the division, which was not publicly recorded or served on the parties, the certification of the proceedings to the Commission did not violate Section 17(3) of the Act.

The court said that the purpose of the statute is to insure that parties have an opportunity to know of any action which may affect their rights; plaintiffs were not prejudiced by failure to record the referral action of the division, nor injured by failure of the division to issue a formal report, since the proceedings were considered by the entire Commission. In the absence of prejudice, the court said, the action of the Commission must stand. The court also said (pp. 785-6) that the Commission's report and orders granting the motor carrier operating authority were not invalid because adopted through voting by notation rather than at a conference at which members of the Commission were physically assembled. The court said that when a meeting of the Commissioners assembled together is held, as specified in the Act, a majority shall constitute a quorum; but in view of the Commission's broad authority to control its proceedings, it may select notation voting procedure as an aid in dealing with its tremendous workload. The court said that the statute does not specifically provide that administrative action be taken concurrently by the deciding members in a formal meeting, and that it would decline to impose such a requirement.

The Commission has authority under the Administrative Procedure Act to omit a recommended report and issue an order.[107]

Section 17(6) of the Interstate Commerce Act[108] provides in pertinent part that "the Commission may, from time to time, make or amend general rules or orders establishing limitations upon the right to apply for rehearing, reargument, or reconsideration of a decision, order, or requirement of the Commission or of a division so as to confine such right to proceedings, or classes of proceedings, involving issues of general transportation importance." It is clear, therefore, that the Commission possesses specific statutory authority to restrict the right to file petitions for reconsideration of division action.

A challenge to the Commission's procedures established under authority of Section 17(6) was presented in *City of Philadelphia v. United*

---

[107]*Watson Bros. Transp. Co. v. United States,* 180 F. Supp. 732, 741.
[108]49 U.S.C. 17(6).

States,[109] wherein the plaintiffs argued that the failure of the entire Commission to consider their petition for reconsideration of a division report and order permitting the discontinuance of a passenger train was violative of the law. Plaintiffs contended that rejection of their petition for reconsideration of a division report adopting the report of an examiner on the ground that it was not permitted under the rules of procedure was alleged to be an unfair denial of their rights. The court, at page 834, replied:

> Plaintiffs have also argued (for the first time before this Court) that the failure of the full Commission to consider plaintiffs' petition was contrary to law and prejudicial to the plaintiffs. As we indicated above, the full Commission now considers petitions only when the Commission has, on its own motion, decided that the matter is one of general transportation importance. . . . All other matters are decided finally by divisions of the Commission. Plaintiffs here contend that nowhere in the Commission's Rules of Practice is there a provision for a petitioner to request the full Commission to first decide whether a particular matter is, indeed, one of general transportation importance. The absence of such a provision, together with the inability of a petitioner to obtain the consideration of the full Commission of the merits of his petitions, constitutes, in the plaintiffs' view, an unfair denial of their rights.
>
> We cannot agree with this contention. There is no doubt but that the Commission has the right to prescribe its rules of practice with an eye to limiting consideration by the full Commission to those matters which are of general transportation importance. But even more pertinent is the fact that nowhere in this record is there even an allegation, much less any evidence, that this matter is in fact one of general transportation importance which would have warranted consideration by the full Commission. Therefore, the failure of the full Commission to consider the merits of plaintiffs' petition can in no way have prejudiced the plaintiffs.

Similarly, in *Malone Freight Lines, Inc. v. United States,*[110] the plaintiff challenged the validity of the Commission's rules of practice, alleging that it had the right to have its petition for reconsideration of the report and order of a division considered by the entire Commission. In the *Malone* case, like the *City of Philadelphia* case, the Commission's rules became effective while the proceeding was pending. The court rejected plaintiff's contention, and at page 754 said:

> In recognition of the consistent holdings of the courts that rehearing before administrative bodies are addressed to their own discretion (*United States v. Pierce Auto Lines,* 327 U.S. 515, 535 (1946); *I.C.C. v. Jersey City,* 322 U.S. 503, 517 (1944); and *Shein v. United States,* 102 F. Supp.

[109]197 F. Supp. 832.
[110]204 F. Supp. 745.

320 (D.C. N.J. 1951).), the Congress in Section 17(6) of the Act invested the Commission with authority to adopt rules regulating applications for rehearing. Under the rules adopted . . . the Commission purported to clothe the orders under the attack with administrative finality.

Consolidated Hearings and Decisions

Because of practical necessities, administrative agencies may consolidate hearings involving a common subject matter, or may, under certain circumstances, dispose of several cases in a single decision. A very clear statement of the Supreme Court's approval on the practice of filing a consolidated report is found in *United States v. Pierce Auto Freight Lines*.[111] This case involved a situation in which the Commission, in a single report, disposed of two separate applications for a certificate of public convenience and necessity to operate through service between points in Oregon and San Francisco. Separate hearings had been held on the two applications, though they involved many similar factors and considerations. A division of the Commission disposed of the two separate recommendations by the examiner in one consolidated report. In disposing of the contention that it was inherently improper for the Commission to dispose of both cases in a single report, the Supreme Court made the following statement at page 523:

> Obviously the court's objection was not to the manner in which the proceedings were conducted prior to the time when the hearings ended and the Commission took the cases under consideration. Up to this point no fault is found with what was done. The difficulty lay altogether, in the court's view, with the way in which it thought the Commission had considered the cases and reached its conclusions. And this arose entirely from the fact that the Commission disposed of them in a single report, rather than in separate ones for each case; and from the further fact that it concluded that both applications should be granted rather than that both should be denied or one denied and one granted. Obviously it was no sufficient ground for suspending the Commission's order that it chose to write one report rather than two, especially in matters as closely related as these, if the single report together with the findings and the evidence was sufficient to sustain the action taken in each case. It is not uncommon judicial practice to follow this course.

In *United States v. Pierce Auto Freight Lines*, it was stated (pp. 529-530):

> In the absence of any showing of specific prejudice, the claim comes down to the highly technical objection that the Commission, in the final stage of forming its judgment, could not in either case take account of

[111]327 U.S. 515.

what had been done in the other, notwithstanding the closely related character and objects of the applications and the prior proceedings. The contention in its farthest reach amounts to a legal version of the scriptural injunction against letting one's right hand know what one's left hand may be doing.

Obviously it would be consistent neither with good sense nor, we think, with the type of hearing assured by the statute to force the Commission to put on such complete blinders. Whatever may be the limits outside which it cannot go in looking beyond the record in the particular proceeding at the state of formulating its judgment, none certainly would go so far. And, given that the report contains all the essential findings required, cf. *Florida v. United States*, 282 U.S. 194, the Commission is not compelled to annotate to each finding the evidence supporting it. It is true that ordinarily an administrative agency will act appropriately, in a proceeding of this sort, upon the record presented and such matters as properly may receive its attention through "official notice." It is also true that this Court, in appropriate instances, has limited the use of the latter implement in order to assure that the parties will not be deprived of a fair hearing. See *United States v. Abilene & Southern R. Co.*, 265 U.S. 274, 286-290; *Interstate Commerce Commission v. Louisville & Nashville R. Co.*, 227 U.S. 88, 93-94. But in doing so it has not undertaken to make a fetish of sticking squarely within the four corners of the specific record in administrative proceedings or of pinning down such agencies with reference to fact determinations, even more rigidly that the courts in strictly judicial proceedings. On the contrary, in the one case as in the other, the mere fact that the determining body has looked beyond the record proper does not invalidate its action unless substantial prejudice is shown to result. *Market Street R. Co. v. Railroad Comm'n*, 324 U.S. 548, 561-562; cf. *Opp Cotton Mills v. Administrator*, 312 U.S. 126, 154-155. In these cases no more is necessary than to apply that rule.

Likewise, in *American Trucking Association v. United States*,[112] the Supreme Court had before it a situation in which the Commission had disposed of a number of separate hearings involving applications by the Seaboard Air Lines Railroad to carry on trucking operations in a number of localities. The localities were widely scattered and there were various protestants at the different hearings. The Supreme Court approved the single report by the Commission disposing of the whole set of hearings with one stroke.

In *AA Auto Delivery, Inc.*,[113] the Commission said that as each applicant in the proceeding proposed operations substantially similar to those of the others, despite variations in the methods of operations, the applications were properly consolidated; there was no substantial prejudice in considering the concerned applications together, nor was such a pro-

---

[112]226 U.S. 77.
[113]77 M.C.C. 365 (footnote, p. 367).

cedure in any way unreasonable. In *Ryder Tank Line, Inc. Extension,*[114] the Commission said that the considered proceedings presented related, if not virtually identical, issues, and in such circumstances, it has been the Commission's practice to consolidate the proceedings. Such procedure is within its discretion where several applications involve related issues including, among others, the need for service from the same origin. The Commission held in *Arco Auto Carriers, Inc. Extension*[115] that orderly procedure and a clear understanding of the transportation situation at that origin required the consideration of the applications simultaneously.

The Commission has consistently declined to consolidate merger proceedings not involving an identity of parties to a Section 5(2) transaction.[116] The courts have upheld the Commission in these determinations, holding that there is no legal requirement that merger cases in the same region should be consolidated,[117] and that whether or not such cases should be consolidated rests within the sound discretion of the Commission.[118]

Recognizing the extreme delays and confusion that could result from an inter-mixture of already complex merger proceedings, the Commission to date has exercised its discretion consistently to deny consolidation even where "cross-over" problems were clearly foreseen,[119] or where weak lines admittedly required protection in the face of a merger of directly competing railroads.[120]

In *Great Northern Pac. & B. Lines, Merger — Great Northern, supra,* at page 287, the Commission stated:

> As to whether the Western railroad realignment should be handled on a consolidated record or on an ad hoc basis, we have consistently adhered to the latter approach. Our experience makes it clear that a consolidation of the records of these cases would have been unworkable. On the other

[114]78 M.C.C. 409, 418.

[115]81 M.C.C. 131, 132.

[116]*Chesapeake & Ohio Ry. Co. — Control — Baltimore & R. Co.,* 317 I.C.C. 261, 263-67; *Norfolk & W. Ry. Co. and New York, C. & St. L. R. Co. Merger,* 324 I.C.C. 1, 18-19; *Pennsylvania R. Co. — Merger — New York Central R. Co.,* 327 I.C.C. 475, 531; *Chicago & North Western Ry. Co. and Chicago Great Western Ry. Co. — Merger, Etc.,* 330 I.C.C. 13, 333 I.C.C. 236 (see order dated August 17, 1966); *Great Northern Pac. & B. Lines — Merger — Great Northern,* 331 I.C.C. 228, 287; and *Chicago, Milwaukee & North Western Transportation Co. — Consolidation — Chicago & North Western Ry. Co., et al.,* F. D. 24182, Order of May 23, 1967.

[117]*Soo Line Railroad Company v. United States,* 280 F. Supp. 907, 909-13.

[118]*Broth. of Maint. of Way Employees v. United States,* 221 F. Supp. 19, 29-30, aff'd without opinion, 375 U.S. 216, affirming *Chesapeake & Ohio Ry. Co. — Control — Baltimore & R. Co., supra.*

[119]*Great Northern Pac. & B. Lines — Merger — Great Northern, supra.*

[120]*Pennsylvania R. Co. — Merger — New York Central R. Co., supra.*

hand, were we to process each case separately but withhold final decisions until the last proceeding would be ripe for decision, the carrier interests and the public interest would be caught in a treadmill of litigation.

In the *Norfolk & Western* case, *supra*, at page 19, the Commission refused to consolidate that proceeding with the *Penn Central* proceeding, stating:

> Accordingly, inasmuch as the applicants have developed a record herein sufficient to establish the finding of consistency with the public interest which we have already made, and have chosen to rely solely on such record, and in view of the adverse effect which could very easily result from a delayed determination of the issues here presented and of the adequate safeguards for the public interest being established through the conditions imposed by our order herein, we conclude that the public interest does not require the consolidation of these proceedings for decision with the Pennsylvania-Central merger case. Inasmuch as we are here ruling against consolidating these proceedings with the Pennsylvania-Central case for single decision or simultaneous decisions, and since, as stated above, the record before us is sufficiently well developed to permit a separate determination of the issues herein, we also conclude that the public interest does not require the reopening of these proceedings for further hearing.

Similarly, in the *Penn Central* decision, the Commission refused to consolidate the two proceedings for decision, saying (p. 531):

> We have consistently refused to consolidate the various eastern consolidation proceedings for decision, although urged to do so by substantially the same parties in each proceeding. See *Chesapeake & O. Ry. Co. — Control — Baltimore & O. Ry. Co.*, 317 I.C.C. 261, 266, and *N&W merger* case, page 19. As in the two cited proceedings, the applicants, after exhaustive public hearings at which all interested parties were permitted to appear and present their cases, have established a record completely adequate for us to make a finding with respect to the public interest as to their proposal, and to provide appropriate conditions regarding inclusion of E-L, B&M and D&H. Accordingly, we find that, with the reservations hereinafter discussed to protect E-L, D&H, and B&M, it would not be in the public interest to deprive the applicants of the immediate benefits of the merger or their shippers, of the improved service the merger will provide. Therefore, we shall not consolidate this proceeding with that of N&W merger for decision of the petitions for inclusion, nor shall we require a delay in the consummation of the merger until such time as the petitions are decided.

The refusal of the Commission to consolidate the proceedings was upheld on appeal in *Erie-Lackawanna Railroad v. United States*.[121] The court stated at page 972 of its opinion:

---

[121]259 F. Supp. 964.

Decision whether to handle all these consolidations in one giant proceeding or in several rests in the sound judgment of the Commission subject only to its management of the various proceedings so as to promote an ultimate solution fair to the carriers and consistent with the public interest, a task in which it has displayed considerable ingenuity.

This finding was not disturbed by the Supreme Court, which initially remanded the *Penn Central* case to the Commission for further consideration of the need it had found of certain carriers for more adequate protection or inclusion,[122] and later affirmed the Commission's decision approving the merger in *Penn Central Merger and N&W Inclusion cases.*[123] Thus, even in a situation where the Commission found that certain carriers were entitled to additional protection or inclusion and the Supreme Court directed that the case be remanded to the Commission for further consideration of such claims, consolidation of the related proceedings by the Commission for disposition was not required.

Modification of Orders

Under Section 16(6) of the Act,[124] the Commission ". . . may modify its orders upon such notice and in such manner as it shall deem proper." The Commission's authority to modify or amend its previous orders to remove an ambiguity without further hearing, however, is limited to instances in which the subject matter was within the scope of the previous proceeding.[125]

---

[122]*B. & O. R. Co. v. United States*, 386 U.S. 372.
[123]389 U.S. 489.
[124]49 U.S.C. 16(6).
[125]*Pennsylvania Railroad Co. v. United States*, 288 F. 88.

56

Practice and Procedure before the Civil Aeronautics Board

The rules of practice in economic proceedings of the Civil Aeronautics Board are found in 14 C.F.R., Part 302.

Procedure Generally

The rules of general applicability are found in 14 C.F.R. 302.3-302.40) Some of these rules are discussed below.

Consolidation of Proceeding

The Board, upon its own initiative or upon motion, may consolidate for hearing or for other purposes or may contemporaneously consider two or more proceedings which involve substantially the same parties, or issues which are the same or closely related, if it finds that such consolidation or contemporaneous hearing will be conducive to the proper dispatch of its business and to the ends of justice and will not unduly delay the proceedings. (14 C.F.R. 302.12)

Joinder of Complaints or Complainants

Two or more grounds of complaints involving substantially the same purposes, subject or state of facts may be included in one complaint even though they involve more than one respondent. Two or more complainants may join in one complaint if their respective causes of complaint are against the same party or parties and involve substantially the same purposes, subject or state of facts. The Board may separate or split complaints if it finds that the joinder of complaints, complainants, or respondents will not be conducive to the proper dispatch of its business or the ends of justice. (14 C.F.R. 302.13)

Participation in Hearing Cases by Persons Not Parties

Any person, including any State, subdivision thereof, State aviation commission, or other public body, may appear at any hearing, other than in an enforcement proceeding, and present any evidence which is relevant to the issues. With the consent of the administrative law judge or the Board, if the hearing is held by the Board, such person may also cross-examine witnesses directly. Such persons may also present to the administrative law judge a written statement on the issues involved in the proceeding. (14 C.F.R. 14)

Formal Intervention in Hearing Cases

Petitions for leave to intervene as a party will be entertained only in those cases that are to be decided upon an evidentiary record after notice and hearing. Any person who has a statutory right to be made a party to such proceeding shall be permitted to intervene. Any person whose intervention will be conducive to the ends of justice and will not unduly delay the conduct of such proceeding may be permitted to intervene. The Board does not grant formal intervention, as such, in non-hearing matters, and any interested person may file authorized documents without first obtaining leave.

In passing upon a petition to intervene, the following factors, among other things, will be considered: (1) The nature of the petitioner's right under the statute to be made a party to the proceeding; (2) the nature and extent of the property, financial or other interest of the petitioner; (3) the effect of the order which may be entered in the proceeding on petitioner's interest; (4) the availability of other means whereby the petitioner's interest may be protected; (5) the extent to which petitioner's interest will be represented by existing parties; (6) the extent to which petitioner's participation may reasonably be expected to assist in the development of a sound record; and (7) the extent to which participation of the petitioner will broaden the issue or delay the proceeding. (14 C.F.R. 302.15)

Motions

An application to the Board or an administrative law judge for an order or ruling not otherwise specifically provided for shall be by motion.

After the assignment of an administrative law judge to a proceeding and before the issuance of a recommended or initial decision, or the certification of the record to the Board, all motions shall be addressed to the administrative law judge. At all other times motions shall be addressed to the Board. All motions shall be made at an appropriate time depending upon the nature thereof and the relief requested therein. (14 C.F.R. 302.18)

SUBPENA

An application for a subpena requiring the attendance of a witness or the production of documentary evidence at a hearing may be made without notice by any party to the administrative law judge designated to preside at the reception of evidence or, in the event that an administrative law judge has not been assigned to a proceeding or the administrative law judge is not available, to the chief administrative law judge, for action by himself or by a member of the Board.

A subpena for the attendance of a witness shall be issued on oral application at any time.

An application for a subpena for documentary or tangible evidence shall be in writing except that if it is made during the course of a hearing, it may be made orally on the record with the consent of the administrative law judge. All such applications, whether written or oral, shall contain a statement or showing of general relevance and reasonable scope of the evidence sought. (14 C.F.R. 302.19)

DEPOSITIONS

For good cause shown, the Board, or any member or administrative law judge assigned as a hearing officer in a proceeding may order that the testimony of a witness be taken by deposition and that the witness produce documentary evidence in connection with such testimony. Ordinarily an order to take the deposition of a witness will be entered only if (1) the person whose deposition is to be taken would be unavailable at the hearing, or (2) the deposition is deemed necessary to perpetuate the testimony of the witness, or (3) the taking of the deposition is necessary to prevent undue and excessive expense to a party and will not result in an undue burden to other parties or in undue delay.

Any party desiring to take the deposition of a witness shall make application therefor in writing to a member of the Board or administrative law judge designated to preside at the reception of evidence or, in the event that a hearing officer has not been assigned to a proceeding or is not available, to the Board, setting forth the reasons why such deposition should be taken, the name and residence of the witness, the time and place proposed for the taking of the deposition, and a general description of the matters concerning which the witness will be asked to testify. If good cause be shown, the Board or the hearing officer (member or administrative law judge) may, in its or his discretion, issue an order authorizing such deposition and specifying the witness whose deposition is to be taken, the general scope of the testimony to be taken, the time when, the place where, and the designated officer (authorized to take oaths) before whom the witness is to testify, and the number of copies of the deposition to be supplied.

Depositions may also be taken and submitted on written interrogatories in substantially the same manner as depositions taken by oral examination. Ordinarily such procedure will only be authorized if necessary to achieve the purposes of an oral deposition and to serve the balance of convenience of the parties. (14 C.F.R. 302.20)

Administrative Law Judges

An administrative law judge shall have the following powers, in addition to any others specified in this part:

(1) To give notice concerning and to hold hearings;

(2) To administer oaths and affirmations;

(3) To examine witnesses;

(4) To issue subpenas and to take or cause depositions to be taken;

(5) To rule upon offers of proof and to receive relevant evidence;

(6) To regulate the course and conduct of the hearing;

(7) To hold conferences, before or during the hearing, for the settlement or simplification of issues;

(8) To rule on motions and to dispose of procedural requests or similar matters;

(9) To make initial or recommended decisions;

(10) To take any other action authorized by this part, by the Administrative Procedure Act, or by the Federal Aviation Act.

The administrative law judge's authority in each case will terminate either upon the service of a recommended decision, or upon the certification of the record in the proceeding to the Board, or upon the expiration of the period within which petitions for descretionary review of his initial decision may be filed, or when he shall have withdrawn from the case upon considering himself disqualified. (14 C.F.R. 302.22)

PREHEARING CONFERENCES

Prior to any hearings there will ordinarily be a prehearing conference before an administrative law judge, although in economic enforcement proceedings where the issues are drawn by the pleadings such conference will usually be omitted. Written notice of the prehearing conference shall be sent by the chief administrative law judge to all parties to a proceeding and to other persons who appear to have an interest in such proceeding. The purpose of such a conference is to define and simplify the issues and the scope of the proceeding, to secure statements of the positions of the parties with respect thereto and amendments to the pleadings in conformity therewith, to schedule the exchange of exhibits before the date set for hearing, and to arrive at such agreements as will aid in the conduct and disposition of the proceeding. For example, consideration will be given to: (1) Matters which the Board can consider without the necessity of proof; (2) admissions of fact and of the genuineness of documents; (3) requests for documents; (4) admissibility of evidence; (5) limitation of the number of witnesses; (6) reducing of oral testimony to exhibit form; (7) procedure at the hearing, etc. The administrative law judge may require further conference, or responsive pleadings, or both. If a party refuses to produce documents requested by another party at the conference, the administrative law judge may compel the production of such documents prior to hearing by subpena. Applications for the production prior to hearing of documents in the Board's possession shall be addressed to the administrative law judge. The administrative law judge may also on his own motion or on motion of any party direct any party to the proceeding (air carrier or non-air carrier) to prepare and submit exhibits setting forth studies, forecasts, or estimates on matters relevant to the issues in the proceeding. (14 C.F.R. 302.23)

EVIDENCE

Evidence presented at the hearing shall be limited to material evidence relevant to the issues as drawn by the pleadings or as defined in the report of prehearing conference, subject to such later modifications of the issues as may be necessary to protect the public interest or to prevent injustice and shall not be unduly repetitious. Evidence shall be presented in written form by all parties wherever feasible, as the administrative law judge may direct. (14 C.F.R. 302.24)

Argument Before the Administrative Law Judge

The administrative law judge shall give the parties to the proceeding adequate opportunity during the course of the hearing for the presentation of arguments in support of or in opposition to motions, and objections and exceptions to rulings of the administrative law judge.

When, in the opinion of the administrative law judge, the volume of the evidence or the importance or complexity of the issues involved warrants, he may, either of his own motion, or at the request of a party, permit the presentation of oral argument. He may impose such time limits on the argument as he may determine, having regard for other asignments for hearing before him. Such argument shall be transcribed and bound with the transcript of testimony and will be available to the Board for consideration in deciding the case. (14 C.F.R. 302.25)

Proposed Findings and Conclusions Before the Administrative Law Judge or the Board

Within such limited time after the close of the reception of evidence fixed by the administrative law judge, any party may, upon request and under such conditions as the administrative law judge may prescribe, file for his consideration briefs to include proposed findings and conclusions of law which shall contain exact references to the record and authorities relied upon. This is also applicable to proceedings in which the record is certified to the Board without the preparation of an initial or recommended decision by the administrative law judge. (14 C.F.R. 302.26)

Petitions for Discretionary Review of Initial Decisions; Review Proceedings

Review by the Board is not a matter of right but of the sound discretion of the Board. Any party may file and serve a petition for discretionary review by the Board of an initial decision.

Petitions for discretionary review shall be filed only upon one or more of the following grounds:

(i) A finding of a material fact is erroneous;

(ii) A necessary legal conclusion is without governing precedent or is a departure from or contrary to law, Board rules, or precedent;

(iii) A substantial and important question of law, policy or discretion is involved; or

(iv) A prejudicial procedural error has occurred. (14 C.F.R. 302.28)

Tentative Decision of the Board

Whenever the administrative law judge certifies the record in a proceeding directly to the Board without issuing an initial or recommended decision in the matter, the Board shall, after consideration of any proposed findings and conclusions submitted by the parties, prepare a tentative decision and serve it upon the parties. (14 C.F.R. 302.29)

Exceptions to Recommended Decisions of Administrative Law Judges or Tentative Decisions of Board

An party to a proceeding may file exceptions to recommended decisions of an administrative law judge or tentative decisions of the Board. (14 C.F.R. 302.30)

Briefs before the Board

Any party to a proceeding may file a brief addressed to the Board in support of his exceptions or in opposition to exceptions. (14 C.F.R. 302.31)

Oral Argument Before the Board

If any party desires to argue a case orally before the Board, he shall request leave to make such argument in his exceptions or brief. (14 C.F.R. 302.32)

Waiver of Procedural Steps After Hearing

The parties to any proceeding may agree to waive any one or more of the following procedural steps:

Oral argument before the administrative law judge, the filing of proposed findings and conclusions for the administrative law judge or for the Board, a recommended decision of the administrative law judge, a tentative decision of the Board, exceptions to a recommended decision of the administrative law judge or a tentative decision of the Board, a petition for discretionary review of an initial decision, the filing of briefs with the Board, or oral argument before the Board. (14 C.F.R. 302.33)

Shortened Procedure

In cases where a hearing is not required by law, rules relating to prehearing, hearing, and post-hearing procedures, shall not be applicable except to the extent that the Board shall determine that the application of some or all of such rules in the particular case will be conducive to the proper dispatch of its business and to the ends of justice. (14 C.F.R. 302.35)

Final Decision of the Board

When a case stands submitted to the Board for final decision on the merits, the Board will dispose of the issues presented by entering an appropriate order which will include a statement of the reasons for its findings and conclusions. Such orders shall be deemed "final orders." (14 C.F.R. 302.36)

Petitions for Reconsideration

Unless an order or a rule of the Board specifically provides otherwise, and party to a proceeding may file a petition for reconsideration, rehearing or reargument of (1) a final order issued by the Board or (2) an interlocutory order issued by the Board which institutes a proceeding or defines the scope and issues of a proceeding or suspends a provision of a tariff on file with the Board. (14 C.F.R. 302.37)

Petitions for Rule Making

Any interested person may petition the Board for the issuance, amendment, modification, or repeal of any regulation. (14 C.F.R. 302.38)

Economic Enforcement Proceedings

Rules applicable to economic enforcement proceedings are provided in 14 C.F.R. 302.200-302.218. Some of these rules are discussed below.

Informal Complaints

Informal complaints may be made in writing with respect to anything done or omitted to be done by any person in contravention of any provision of the Act or any requirement established pursuant thereto. Matters so presented may, if their nature warrants, be handled by the Board by correspondence or conference with the appropriate persons.

Any matter not disposed of informally may be made the subject of a formal proceeding pursuant to this subpart. The filing of an informal complaint shall not bar the subsequent filing of a formal complaint. (14 C.F.R. 302.200)

Formal Complaints

Any person may make a formal complaint to the Board with respect to anything done or omitted to be done by any person on contravention of any economic regulatory provisions of the Act, or any rule, regulation, order, limitation condition or other requirement established pursuant thereto. The submission of a formal complaint by a person other than an enforcement attorney (hereinafter called a third party) shall not in itself result in the institution of a formal economic enforcement proceeding and a hearing with respect to the complaint unless and until the Director of the Bureau of Enforcement dockets a petition for enforcement with respect to such complaint, or a portion thereof. A formal complaint, whether filed by a third party or an enforcement attorney, may be amended at any time prior to the service of an answer to a complaint. Thereafter, such amendment may be filed only upon the grant of a motion, except that permission to amend a third-party complaint after the filing of an answer but before the docketing of a petition for enforcement must be obtained from the Director of the Bureau of Enforcement. (14 C.F.R. 302.201)

Docketing of Petition for Enforcement

Whenever in the opinion of the Director of the Bureau of Enforcement there are reasonable grounds to believe that any provision of the act or any rule, regulation, order, limitation, condition or other requirement established pursuant thereto, has been or is being violated, that, in the case of third-party complaints, efforts to satisfy a complaint have failed, and that investigation of any or all of the alleged violations is in the public interest, the Director of the Bureau of Enforcement may institute an economic enforcement proceeding by docketing a petition for enforcement. (14 C.F.R. 302.206)

Answer

All answers shall fully and completely advise the parties and the Board as to the nature of the defense and shall admit or deny specifically and in detail each allegation of the complaint unless the person complained of is without knowledge, in which case, his answer shall so state and the statement shall operate as a denial. Allegations of fact not denied or controverted shall be deemed admitted. Matters alleged as affirmative defenses shall be separately stated and numbered and shall, in the absence of a reply, be deemed to be controverted. (14 C.F.R. 302.207)

DEFAULT

Failure of a respondent to file and serve an answer within the time and in the manner prescribed shall be deemed to authorize the Board, in its discretion, to find the facts alleged in the petition to be true and to enter such order as may be appropriate without notice or hearing, or, in its discretion, to proceed to take proof, without notice, of the allegations or charges set forth in the complaint or order, provided that the Board or administrative law judge may permit late filings of an answer for good cause shown. (14 C.F.R. 320.208)

Mail Rate Proceedings

Rules applicable to mail rate proceedings are provided in (14 C.F.R. 302.300-302.321)

Exemption Proceedings

Rules applicable to mail rate proceedings are provided in (14 C.F.R. 302.400-302-410. The rule relating to the contents of an application is discussed below.

An application for exemption shall set forth the section or sections of the Act, or the rule, regulation, term, condition, or limitation prescribed thereunder from which exemption is desired and shall state in detail the facts relied upon to establish that the enforcement of the provisions from which exemption is sought, is or would be an undue burden upon the applicant by reason of the limited extent of, or unusual circumstances affecting, the operations of such applicant and that enforcement of such provision is not in the public interest.

The application shall be accompanied by a statement of economic data or other matters which the applicant desires the Board to notice, and by affidavits establishing such other facts as the applicant desires to the Board to rely upon. Applications of air carriers for temporary route authority shall contain at least the following economic and operating data on an annual basis:

(1) Present and proposed schedules, by type of aircraft;

(2) Number of departures, plane-miles, passengers and passenger-miles;

(3) Estimate of self-diversion or diversion from other carriers, if applicable;

(4) Anticipated operating revenues; and

(5) Estimate of impact of proposal on operating expenses;

In addition, for local service carriers the following:

(6) Estimate of allowance for return on investment and taxes, computed according to Subpart K of this part;

(7) Increase or decrease in subsidy requirements; and

(8) Increase or decrease in subsidy payments under the applicable class rate formula. (14 C.F.R. 302.402)

Proceedings with Respect to Rates, Fares and Charges

Rules applicable to proceedings with respect to rates, fares and charges are set forth in (14 C.F.R. 302.500-302.508) Some of these rules are discussed below.

INSTITUTION OF PROCEEDINGS

A proceeding to determine rates, fares, or charges for the transportation of persons or property by aircraft, or the lawful classification, rule, regulation, or practice affecting such rates, fares or charges, may be instituted by the filing of a petition or complaint by any person, or by the issuance of an order by the Board. (14 C.F.R. 302.500)

ORDER OF INVESTIGATION

The Board on its own initiative, or if it is of the opinion that the facts stated in a petition or complaint warrant it, may issue an order instituting an investigation of the lawfulness of any present or proposed rates, fares, or charges for the transportation of persons or property by aircraft or the lawfulness of any clasification, rule, regulation, or practice affecting such rates, fares, or charges, and assigning the proceeding for hearing before an administrative law judge. (14 C.F.R. 302.504)

Burden of Going Forward With the Evidence

At any hearing involving a change in a rate, fare, or charge for the transportation of persons or property by aircraft, or the lawful classification, rule, regulation, or practice affecting such rate fare, or charge, the burden going forward with the evidence shall be upon the person proposing such change to show that the proposed changed rate, fare, charge, classification, rule, regulation or practice is just and reasonable, and not otherwise unlawful. (14 C.F.R. 302.506)

Adequacy of Service Petitions

Rules applicable to the adequacy of service petitions are set forth in 14 C.F.R. 302.700-302.705. Some of these rules are discussed below.

Institution of Proceedings

A proceeding to determine the adequacy of the service, equipment and facilities being provided by a certificated air carrier at a duly authorized point may be instituted by the filing of a petition or complaint, or by the issuance of an order by the Board on its own initiative. (14 C.F.R. 302.701)

Contents of Petition

If a petition or complaint is filed, it shall state the reason why the service, equipment or facilities complained of are inadequate and shall support such reasons with a full factual analysis. (14 C.F.R. 302.702)

Parties to the Proceeding

The parties to the proceeding shall be the person filing the petition or complaint, the air carrier or carriers whose service is being challenged, bureau counsel and any other person whom the Board permits to intervene. (14 C.F.R. 302.703)

Action on Petition or Complaint

If the Board is of the opinion that a petition or complaint does not state facts which warrant an investigation or action on its part, it may dismiss such petition or complaint without hearing. If the air carrier complained against shall not satisfy the complaint and there shall appear to be any reasonable ground for investigating the complaint, the Board shall investigate the matter complained of. (14 C.F.R. 302.704)

Compromise of Civil Penalties and Seizure of Aircraft

Special rules are established pursuant to Section 901(a)(2) of the Federal Aviation Act of 1958, as amended, for the compromise of civil penalties provided for in Section 901(a)(1), for the violation of any provision of Title IV (Air Carrier Economic Regulation) of the Act, or any rule, regulation or order issued thereunder; under Section 1002(i) Power to establish Through Air Transportation Service; or any term, condition or limitation of any permit or certificate issued under Title IV; and pursuant to Section 903(b) of the Act applicable to the seizure of aircraft involved in a violation and subject to a lien, pursuant to Section 901(b) of the Act, for penalties for which the owner or person in command of such aircraft may be liable for any of the foregoing violations. (14 C.F.R. 302.800-302.808)

Route Proceedings under Sections 401 and 402 of the Federal Aviation Act of 1958

Special rules are applicable to proceedings for conferment and/or modification of route authority under Sections 401 and 402 of the Federal Aviation Act of 1958. These relate to the renewal of fixed-term route authorizations granted by exemption, and the dismissal of certain stale applications filed pursuant to Section 401. (14 C.F.R. 302.901-302.930)

Supplemental Air Carriers

Procedural rules are established specifically applicable to certain proceedings involving supplemental air carriers. (14 C.F.R. 302.1001-1027)

Standardized Methods for Costing Proposed Changes in the Authorized Operations of Local Service Carriers

Specific rules are established for the preparation of cost estimates submitted by any party or nonparty in hearing or nonhearing proceedings which involve proposed changes in the authorized operations of local service air carriers. The rules also apply to the preparation of the estimated cost of operating an existing route or route segment as to which no change in authority is currently proposed, where this information is required in a proceeding. The rules are not applicable to proceedings involving rates and fares. (14 C.F.R. 302.1101-302.1109)

Procedure for the Processing of Undocketed Section 412 Contracts and Agreements

Specific rules are applicable to the processing of Section 412 contracts and agreements which have not been docketed. (14 C.F.R. 302.1201-302.1209)

Expedited Procedure for Modifying or Removing Certain Limitations on Nonstop Operations Contained in Certificates of Public Convenience and Necessity of Local Service Carriers

Special rules are applicable to proceedings on applications for amendments of certificates of public convenience and necessity of local service carriers to remove or modify certificate provisions which require local service carriers to serve one or more points between particular pairs of points. (14 C.F.R. 302.1301-302.1315)

Expedited Procedures for Modifying or Removing Nonstop and Long-Haul Restrictions Contained in Certificates of Public Convenience and Necessity of Trunkline Air Carriers

Special rules are applicable to proceedings on applications for amendment of certificates of public convenience and necessity of trunkline carriers to remove or modify provisions which restrict the authority of the holder to provide service between a specified pair of certificated points within the 48 contiguous States by requiring that one or more intermediate stops be made, or that the flight serving such pair of points originate and/or terminate at a point or points beyond the specified pair of points. The rules are further limited to cases where (a) the applicant is already providing single carrier service; (b) the applicant is carrying 20 percent or more of the passengers transported between those points as shown in the Board's competition surveys; (c) the new authority requested is not directly in issue in a pending proceeding and (d) it does not appear that the grant of the application will increase significantly the subsidy needs of any subsidized carrier. (14 C.F.R. 302.1401-302.1415)

Procedure for Processing Contracts for Transportation of Mail by Air

Rules are established which are applicable between the Postal Service and certificated air carriers for the transportation of mail by air entered into pursuant to 39 U.S.C. 5402(a), 84 Stat. 772. Such contracts must be for the transportation of at least 750 pounds of mail per flight, and no more than 10 percent of the domestic mail transported under any such contract or 5 percent, based on weight, of the international mail transported under any such contract may consist of letter mail. Any such contract is required by the statute to be filed with the Board not later than 90 days before its effective date, and unless the Board disapproves the contract not later than 10 days prior to its effective date, the contract automatically becomes effective. (14 C.F.R. 302.1501-302.1508)

Procedure for Processing Section 412 Contracts and Agreements Submitted for Prior Approval

Particular rules are applicable to the processing of Section 412 contracts or agreements which are, by their terms, to become effective only upon or after the Board's approval. The rules do not apply to traffic conference resolutions of the International Air Transport Association. (14 C.F.R. 302.1507-302.1608)

57

Practice and Procedure before the Federal Maritime Commission

The rules of practice of the Federal Maritime Commission are set forth in 46 C.F.R., Part 502. The rules in part govern procedure before the FMC under the Shipping Act, 1916, Merchant Marine Act, 1920, Intercoastal Shipping Act, 1933, Merchant Marine Act, 1936, Administrative Procedure Act, and related Acts. They are to be construed to secure the just, speedy, and inexpensive determination of every proceeding.

Rule Making

PETITION FOR ISSUANCE, AMENDMENT, OR REPEAL OF RULE

Any interested party may file with the Commission a petition for the issuance, amendment, or repeal of a rule designed to implement, interpret, or prescribe law, policy, organization, procedure, or practice requirements of the Commission. The petition shall set forth the interest of petitioner and the nature of the relief resired, shall include any facts, views, arguments, and data deemed relevant by petitioner, and shall be verified. (46 C.F.R. 502.51)

PARTICIPATION IN RULE MAKING

Interested persons will be afforded an opportunity to participate in rule making through submission of written data, views, or arguments, with or without opportunity to present the same orally in any manner. Where the proposed rules are such as are required by statute to be made on the record after opportunity for a hearing, such hearing shall be conducted pursuant to the Administrative Procedure Act.

In those proceedings in which respondents are named, interested persons who wish to participate therein shall file a petition to interevne. (46 C.F.R. 502.53)

Contents of Rules

The Commission will incorporate in any rules adopted a concise general statement of their basis and purpose. (46 C.F.R. 502.41)

Proceedings; Pleadings; Motions; Replies

Proceedings

Proceedings are commenced by the filing of a complaint, or by order of the Commission upon petition or upon its own motion, or by reference by the Commission to the formal docket of a petition for a declaratory order. (46 C.F.R. 502.61)

Complaints

The complaint shall contain the name and address of each complainant, the name and address of complainant's attorney or agent, the name and address of each carrier or person against whom complaint is made, a concise statement of the cause of action, and a request for the relief or other affirmative action sought. When reparation is sought and the nature of the proceeding so requires, the complaint shall set forth the ports or origin and destination of the shipments, consignees, or real parties in interest where shipments are on "order" bill of lading, consignors, date of receipt by carrier or tender of delivery to carrier, names of vessels, bill of lading number (other identifying reference), description of commodities, weights, measurement, rates, charges made or collected, when, where, by whom and to whom rates and charges were paid, by whom the rates and charges were borne, the amount of damage, and the relief sought. Except under unusual circumstances and for good cause shown, reparation will not be awarded upon a complaint in which it is not specifically asked for, nor upon a new complaint by or for the same complainant which is based upon a finding in the original proceeding. Wherever a rate, fare, charge, rule, regulation, classification, or practice is involved, appropriate reference to the tariff should be made, if possible. If complaint fails to indicate the sections of the acts alleged to have been violated or clearly to state facts which support the allegations, the Commission may, on its own initiative, require the complaint to be amended to supply such further particulars as it deems necessary. The complaint should designate the place at which hearing is desired. (46 C.F.R. 502.62)

REPARATION, STATUTE OF LIMITATIONS

Complaints seeking reparation shall be filed within two years after the cause of action accrues (Section 22, Shipping Act, 1916). The Commission will consider as in substantial compliance with the statute of limitations a complaint in which complainant alleges that the matters complained of, if continued in the future, will constitute violations of the shipping acts in the particulars and to the extent indicated and prays for reparation accordingly for injuries which may be sustained as a result of such violations. Notification to the Commission that a complaint may or will be filed for the recovery of reparation will not constitute a filing within the two year period. (46 C.F.R. 502.63)

ANSWER TO COMPLAINT

Respondent shall file with the Commission an answer to the complaint and shall serve it on complainant.

Such answer shall give notice of issues controverted in fact or law. Recitals of material and relevant facts in a complaint, amended complaint, or bill of particulars, unless specifically denied in the answer thereto, shall be deemed admitted as true, but if request is seasonably made, a competent witness shall be made available for cross-examination on such evidence. In the event that respondent should fail to file and serve the answer within the time provided, the Commission may enter such rule or order as may be just, or may in any case require such proof as to the matters alleged in the complaint as it may deem proper. The Commission or Chief Judge may permit the filing of a delayed answer after the time for filing the answer has expired, for good cause shown. (46 C.F.R. 502.64)

REPLIES TO ANSWERS NOT PERMITTED

Replies to answers will not be permitted. New matters set forth in respondent's answer will be deemed to be controverted.

Order to Show Cause

The Commission may institute a proceeding against a person subject to its jurisdiction by order to show cause. (46 C.F.R. 502.66)

PROCEEDINGS UNDER SECTION 3 OF THE INTERCOASTAL ACT

Protests against proposed changes in tariffs, invoking the provisions of Section 3 of the Intercoastal Shipping Act, 1933, may be made by letter, telegram, or radiogram, and shall be filed with the Director, Bureau of Compliance.

Every protest shall clearly identify the tariff in question, give specific reference to the items opposed, set forth the grounds for opposition to the change, including a reference to the section or sections of the shipping acts alleged to be violated, shall be subscribed and verified, and shall be served upon each carrier whose tariff is protested or the issuing agent. Protests sent by telegraph or radiogram shall be confirmed promptly by letter signed by the person making the protest or by someone in his behalf, and shall be subscribed and verified. (46 C.F.R. 502.67)

DECLARATORY ORDERS

The Commission may issue a declaratory order to terminate a controversy or to remove uncertainty. Petitions for the issuance thereof shall state clearly and concisely the controversy or uncertainty, shall name the persons and cite the statutory authority involved, shall include a complete statement of the facts and grounds prompting the petition, together with full disclosure of petitioner's interest, and shall be served upon all parties named therein. (46 C.F.R. 502.68)

Petitions — General

All claims for relief or other affirmative action by the Commission in petitions shall state clearly and concisely the petitioner's grounds of interest in the subject matter, shall state the facts relied upon and the relief sought, and shall cite by appropriate reference the statutory provisions or other authority relied upon for relief. (46 C.F.R. 502.69)

Amendments or Supplements to Pleadings

Amendments or supplements to any pleading will be permitted or rejected in the discretion of the Commission if the case has not been assigned for hearing, otherwise they will be allowed or refused in the discretion of the officer designated to conduct the hearing. After a case is assigned for hearing. No amendment shall be allowed which would broaden the issues without opportunity to reply to such amended pleading and to prepare for the broadened issues. The presiding officer may direct a party to state his case more fully and in more detail by way of amendment. (46 C.F.R. 502.70)

Bill of Particulars

After date of service of the complaint, respondent may file with the Commission for service upon complainant a motion for a bill of particulars. After date of service of such motion complainant shall file with the Commission and serve upon respondent either the bill of particulars requested or a reply to such request. (46 C.F.R. 502.71)

Petition for Intervention

A petition for leave to intervene may be filed in any proceeding before the Commission. The petition will be granted if the proposed intervener shows in his petition a substantial interest in the proceeding and the grounds for intervention are pertinent to the issues already presented and do not unduly broaden them. (46 C.F.R. 502.72)

Motions

All motions and requests for ruling by the Commission or the presiding officer shall state clearly and concisely the purpose of and the relief sought by the motion, the statutory or principal authority relied upon, and the facts claimed to constitute the grounds requiring the relief requested. (46 C.F.R. 502.73)

Replies

A reply to a reply is not permitted. Any party may file a reply to any written motion, pleading, petition application, etc., permitted to be filed. When time permits, replies also may be field to protests seeking suspension of tariffs, applications for enlargement of time and postponement of hearing and motions to take depositions, Replies shall be so drawn as fully and completely to advise the parties and the Commission as to the nature of the defense, shall admit or deny specifically and in detail each material allegation of the pleading answered, and shall state clearly and concisely the facts and matters of law relied upon. (46 C.F.R. 502.74)

Settlement; Prehearing Procedure

OPPORTUNITY FOR INFORMAL SETTLEMENT

Where time, the nature of the proceeding, and the public interest permit, all interested parties shall have the opportunity for the submission and consideration of facts, argument, offers of settlement, or proposal of adjustment, without prejudice to the rights of the parties. No stipulation, offer, or proposal shall be admissible in evidence over the objection of any part in any hearing on the matter. (46 C.F.R. 502.91)

SPECIAL DOCKET APPLICATIONS

Common carriers by water in foreign commerce, or conferences of carriers may file application for permission to refund a portion of freight charges collected from a shipper or to waive collection of a portion of freight charges from a shipper where it appears that there is an error in a tariff of a clerical or administrative nature or an error due to inadvertence in failing to file a new tariff and that such refund or waiver will not result in discrimination among shippers. Such application must be filed with the Commission within 180 days from the date of the involved shipment. Prior to application, the applicant must file with the Commission an effective tariff setting forth the rate on which such refund or waiver would be based.

If permission is granted, the Commission will issue an order authorizing refund or waiver. The applicant must agree to publish notice of same in the appropriate tariff and to take such other actions as the Commission may require to give notice of the rate on which the refund or waiver is based. Additional refunds or waivers on other similar shipments will be made in the manner prescribed in the Commission's order.

Common carriers by water in interstate or intercoastal commerce, or conferences of such carriers, may file application for permission to refund a portion of freight charges collected from a shipper or waive collection of a portion of freight charges from a shipper. All such applications shall be filed within the 2-year statutory period.

If allowed, an order for payment or waiver will be issued by the Commission. (46 C.F.R. 502.92)

Satisfaction of Complaint

If a respondent satisfies a complaint either before its answer thereto is due or after answering, a statement to that effect, setting forth when and how the complaint has been satisfied, shall be filed. Satisfied complaints will be dismissed in the discretion of the Commission. (46 C.F.R. 502.93)

Prehearing Conference

Prior to any hearing the Commission or presiding officer may direct all interested parties, by written notice, to attend a prehearing conference for the purpose of considering any settlement, formulating the issues in the proceeding and determining other matters to aid in its disposition. In addition to any offers of settlement or proposals of adjustment, the following may be considered:

(1) Simplification of the issues;

(2) The necessity of desirability of amendments to the pleadings;

(3) The possibility of obtaining admission of facts and of documents which will avoid unnecessary proof;

(4) Limitations on the number of witnesses;

(5) The procedure at the hearing;

(6) The distribution to the parties prior to the hearing of written testimony and exhibits;

(7) Consolidation of the examination of witnesses by counsel;

(8) Such other matters as may aid in the disposition of the proceeding.

The presiding officer may require, prior to the hearing, exchange of exhibits and any other materials which may expedite the hearing. He shall assume the responsibility of accomplishing the purposes of the notice of prehearing conference so far as this may be possible without prejudice to the rights of any party.

The presiding officer shall rule upon all matters presented for his decision, orally upon the record when feasible, or by subsequent ruling in writing. If a party determines that a ruling made orally does not cover fully the issue presented, or is unclear, he may petition for a further ruling thereon after receipt of the transcript.

The presiding officer may call the parties together for an informal conference prior to the taking of testimony, or may recess the hearing for such a conference. (46 C.F.R. 502.94)

Subpoenas

REQUESTS; ISSUANCE

Subpoenas for the attendance of witnesses or the production of evidence shall be issued upon request of any party, without notice to any other party. Requests for subpoenas for the attendance of witnesses may be made orally or in writing; requests for subpoenas for the production of evidence shall be in writing.

Where it appears to the presiding officer that the subpoena sought may be unreasonable, oppressive, excessive in scope, or unduly burdensome, he may in his discretion, as a condition precedent to the issuance of the subpoena, require the person seeking the subpoena to show the general relevance and reasonable scope of the testimony or other evidence sought. (46 C.F.R. 502.131)

Motions to Quash or Modify

After service of a subpoena for attendance of a witness or a subpoena for production of evidence, the person to whom the subpoena is directed may, by motion with notice to the party requesting the subpoena, petition the presiding officer to quash or modify the subpoena.

If served at the hearing, the person to whom the subpoena is directed may, by oral application at the hearing, petition the presiding officer to revoke or modify the subpoena.

A court in *Federal Maritime Commission v. E. G. Caragher,*[1] held that FMC subpoenas were fully enforceable were issued by the Commission in an investigation to determine whether certain ocean freight rates were in violation of Section 18(b) (5) of the Shipping Act, 1916, or certain practices of ocean carriers were in violation of Sections 14, 16, or 17 of the Act. The appellate court disagreed with the district court's holding that an investigation commenced pursuant to Section 18(b) (5) of the Act is not an investigation into alleged violations of the Act. The court stated: "Investigations brought to enforce this type of regulatory provision are brought pursuant to Section 22 of the Act; they quite clearly concern matters that might have been made the object of complaint. It follows that, unless there is strong countervailing evidence of a contrary intent, Congress intended that the Commission could exercise its Section 27 suppoena power in furtherance of such investigations."[2]

In *Federal Maritime Commission and Ludlow Corporation v. A. T. De Smedt,*[3] an appellate court affirmed an order of a district court to enforce subpoenas duces tecum issued pursuant to Section 27 of the Shipping Act, 1916. The subpoenas had been issued against officers and agents of certain common carriers by water, members of the Calcutta,

[1]364 F. 2d 709.
[2]364 F. 2d at 717.
[3]366 F. 2d 464.

East Coast of India and East Pakistan/U.S.A. Conference serving the inbound trade from East India and Pakistan ports to United States Atlantic and Gulf of Mexico ports. Under this landmark decision, the Commission's subpoena power to compel production of evidence located outside of United States' borders was upheld. The court found that the cost data and revenue information sought by the Commission were relevant to the investigation to determine whether certain freight rates were so unreasonably high as to be detrimental to the commerce of the United States and the public interest, and in violation of Sections 14(b), 15, and 18(b), of the Shipping Act. It should be noted, however, that in upholding the subpoena power the court was not unmindful of the problem of enforcing compliance with an order of production. The court was concerned with the effect of the statutes of certain foreign governments that prohibit their nationals from producing documents located abroad. Thus, when the matter was returned to the district court for enforcement of the order of production, the court found that, in fact, foreign law prohibited the production of the documents and, therefore, it could not impose contempt sanctions on the individual respondents for noncompliance. But, the matter of noncompliance was submitted to the Commission and it issued an order requiring the conference to show cause why its agreement should not be canceled in view of their refusal to comply with Section 27 of the Shipping Act, 1916. The Commission found that the conference by not complying with Section 27 had not fulfilled the requisites of Section 15 of the Shipping Act, 1916, and the Commission ordered the conference agreements canceled.

Hearings; Presiding Officers; Evidence

HEARINGS NOT REQUIRED BY STATUTE

The Commission may call informal public hearings, not required by statute, to be conducted for the purpose of rule making or to obtain information necessary or helpful in the determination of its policies or the carrying out of its duties, and may require the attendance of witnesses and the production of evidence. (46 C.F.R. 502.141)

HEARINGS REQUIRED BY STATUTE

In complaint and answer cases, investigations on the Commission's own motion, and in other rule making and adjudication proceedings in which a hearing is required by statute, formal hearings shall be conducted pursuant to the Administrative Procedure Act. (46 C.F.R. 502.142)

Notice of Nature of Hearing, Jurisdiction, and Issues

Persons entitled to notice of hearings, except those notfied by complaint, will be duly and timely informed of the nature of the proceeding, the legal authority and jurisdiction under which the proceeding is conducted, and the terms, substance, and issues involved, or the matters of fact and law asserted, as the case may be. (46 C.F.R. 502.143)

Presiding Officer

The administrative law judges will be designated by the Chief Judge to preside at hearings required by statute, in rotation so far as practicable, unless the Commission or one or more members thereof shall preside; and also at hearings not required by statute when designated to do so by the Commission. If the presiding officer assigned to a proceeding becomes unavailable to the Commission, the Commission or the Chief Judge shall designate a qualified officer to take his place. (46 C.F.R. 502.145)

Functions and Powers

The officer designated to hear a case shall have authority to arrange and give notice of hearing; sign and issue subpoenas authorized by law; take or cause depositions to be taken; rule upon proposed amendments or supplements to pleadings; delineate the scope of a proceeding instituted by order of the Commission by amending, modifying, clarifying or interpreting with order, except with regard to that portion of any order involving the Commission's suspension authority set forth in Section 3, Intercoastal Shipping Act, 1933; hold conferences for the settlement or simplification of issues by consent of the parties; regulate the course of the hearing; prescribe the order in which evidence shall be presented; dispose of procedural requests or similar matters; hear and rule upon motions, administer oaths and affirmations; examine witnesses; direct witnesses to testify or produce evidence available to them which will aid in the determination of any question of fact in issue; rule upon offers of proof and receive relevant, material, reliable and probative evidence; act upon petitions to intervene; permit submission of facts, arguments, offers of settlement, and proposals of adjustment; hear oral argument at the close of testimony; fix the time for filing briefs, motions, and other documents to be filed in connection with hearings and the examiner's decision thereon, except as otherwise provided by the rules in this part; act upon petitions for enlargement of time to file such documents including answers to formal complaints; and dispose of any other matter that normally and properly arises in the course of proceedings. (46 C.F.R. 502.147)

Consolidation of Proceedings

The Commission, the Chief Judge (or his designee) may order two or more proceedings which involve substantially the same issues consolidated and heard together. (46 C.F.R. 502.148)

Further Evidence Required By Presiding Officer During Hearing

At any time during the hearing the presiding officer may call for further evidence upon any issue, and require such evidence where available to be presented by the party or parties concerned, either at the hearing or adjournment thereof. (46 C.F.R. 502.150)

Exceptions to Rulings of Presiding Officer Unnecessary

Formal exceptions to rulings of the presiding officer are unnecessary. It is sufficient that a party, at the time the ruling of the presiding officer is made or sought, makes known the action which he desires the presiding officer to take or his objection to an action taken, and his grounds therefor. (46 C.F.R. 502.151)

Offer of Proof

An offer of proof made in connection with an objection taken to any ruling of the presiding officer rejecting or excluding proffered oral testimony shall consist of a statement of the substance of the evidence which counsel contends would be adduced by such testimony; and, if the excluded evidence consists of evidence in documentary or written form or of reference to documents or records, a copy of such evidence shall be marked for identification and shall constitute the offer of proof. (46 C.F.R. 502.152)

Appeal from Ruling of Presiding Officer Other Than Orders of Dissmissal in Whole or in Part

Rulings of the presiding officer may not be appealed prior to, during the course of the hearing, or subsequent thereto if the proceeding is still before the presiding officer except where the presiding officer shall find it necessary to allow an appeal to the Commission to prevent substantial delay, expense, or detriment to the public interest, or undue prejudice to a party. (46 C.F.R. 502.153)

Rights of Parties as to Presentation of Evidence

Every party shall have the right to present his case or defense by oral or documentary evidence, to submit rebuttal evidence, and to conduct such cross-examination as may be required for a full and true disclosure of the facts. The presiding officer shall, however, have the right and duty to limit the introduction of evidence and the examination and cross-examination of witnesses when in his judgment such evidence or examination is cumulative or is productive of undue delay in the conduct of the hearing. (46 C.F.R. 502.154)

Burden of Proof

At any hearing in a suspension proceeding under Section 3 of the Intercoastal Shipping Act, 1933, the burden of proof to show that the suspended rate, fare, charge, classification, regulation, or practice is just and reasonable shall be upon the respondent carrier or carriers. In all other cases, the burden shall be on the proponent of the rule or order. (46 C.F.R. 502.155)

Evidence Admissible

In any proceeding, all evidence which is relevant, material, reliable and probative and not unduly repetitious or cumulative shall be admissible. All other evidence shall be excluded. (46 C.F.R. 502.156)

Written Evidence

The use of written statements in lieu of oral testimony shall be resorted to where the presiding officer in his discretion rules that such procedure is appropriate. The statements shall be numbered in paragraphs, and each party in his rebuttal shall be required to list the paragraphs to which he objects, giving an indication of his reasons for objecting. Statistical exhibits shall contain a short commentary explaining the conclusions which the offeror draws from the data. Any portion of such testimony which is argumentative shall be excluded. Where written statements are used, copies of the statement and any rebuttal statement shall be furnished to all parties, as shall copies of exhibits. The presiding officer shall fix respective dates for the exchange of such written rebuttal statements and exhibits in advance of the hearing to enable study by the parties of such testimony. Thereafter the parties shall endeavor to stipulate as many of the facts set forth in the written testimony as they may be able to agree upon. Oral examination of witnesses shall thereafter be confined to facts which remain in controversy, and a reading of the written statements at the hearing will be dispensed with unless the presiding officer otherwise directs.

Where a formal hearing is held in a rule making proceeding, interested persons will be afforded an opportunity to participate through submission of relevant, material, reliable and probative written evidence properly verified. Such evidence submitted by persons not present at the hearing will not be made a part of the record if objected to by any party on the ground that the person who submits the evidence is not present for cross examination. (46 C.F.R. 502.157)

Documents Containing Matter Not Material

Where written matter offered in evidence is embraced in a document containing other matter which is not intended to be offered in evidence, the party offering shall present the original document to all parties at the hearing for their inspection, and shall offer a true copy of the matter which is to be introduced unless the presiding officer determines that the matter is short enough to be read into the record. Opposing parties shall be afforded an opportunity to introduce in evidence, in like manner, other portions of the original document which are material and relevant. (46 C.F.R. 502.158)

Records in Other Proceedings

When any portion of the record before the Commission in any proceeding other than the one being heard is offered in evidence, a true copy of such portion shall be presented for the record in the form of an exhibit unless the parties represented at the hearing stipulate upon the record that such portion may be incorporated by reference. (46 C.F.R. 502.160)

Files

Where any matter contained in a tariff, report, or other document on file with the Commission is offered in evidence, such document need not be produced or marked for identification, but the matter so offered shall be specified in its particularity, giving tariff number and page number of tariff, report, or document in such manner as to be readily identified, and may be received in evidence by reference, subject to comparison with the original document on file. (46 C.F.R. 502.161)

STIPULATIONS

The parties may, by stipulation, agree upon any facts involved in the proceeding and include them in the record with the consent of the presiding officer. (46 C.F.R. 502.162)

RECEIPT OF DOCUMENTS AFTER HEARING

Documents or other writings to be submitted for the record after the close of the hearing will not be received in evidence except upon permission of the presiding officer. (46 C.F.R. 502.163)

ORAL ARGUMENT AT HEARINGS

Oral argument at the close of testimony may be ordered by the presiding officer in his discretion. (46 C.F.R. 502.164)

OBJECTION TO PUBLIC DISCLOSURE OF INFORMATION

Upon objection to public disclosure of any information sought to be elicited during a hearing, the presiding officer may in his discretion order that the witness shall disclose such information only in the presence of those designated and sworn to secrecy by the presiding officer.

After such testimony is given, the objecting party shall file with the presiding officer a verified written motion to withhold such information from public disclosure, setting forth sufficient identification of same and the basis upon which public disclosure should not be made. (46 C.F.R. 502.167)

Shortened Procedure

SELECTION OF CASES FOR SHORTENED PROCEDURE; CONSENT REQUIRED

By consent of the parties and with approval of the Commission or presiding officer, a complaint proceeding may be conducted under shortened procedure without oral hearing. A hearing may be ordered at the request of any party prior to initial or recommended decision or upon the Commission's motion at any stage of the proceeding. (46 C.F.R. 502.181)

COMPLAINT AND MEMORADUM OF FACTS AND ARGUMENTS

A complaint filed with the Commission shall have attached a memorandum of the facts, subscribed and verified, and of arguments separately stated, upon which it relies. (46 C.F.R. 502.182)

RESPONDENT'S ANSWERING MEMORANDUM

Each respondent shall, if he consents to the shortened procedure, serve upon complainant an answering memorandum of the facts, subscribed and verified, and of arguments, separately stated, upon which it relies. (46 C.F.R. 502.183)

COMPLAINANT'S MEMORANDUM IN REPLY

Each complainant may file a memorandum in reply, subscribed and verified. (46 C.F.R. 502.184)

CONTENTS OF MEMORANDA

The memorandum should contain concise arguments and fact, the same as would be offered if a formal hearing were held and briefs filed. If reparation is sought, paid freight bills should accompany complainant's original memorandum. (46 C.F.R. 502.186)

PROCEDURE AFTER FILING OF MEMORANDA

An initial, recommended, or tentative decision will be served upon the parties. Thereafter, the procedure will be the same as that in respect to proceedings after formal hearing. (46 C.F.R. 502.187)

Depositions, Written Interrogatories, and Discovery

SCHEDULE FOR USE

After commencement of a proceeding, any party may, upon reasonable notice take the testimony of any person, including a party, by deposition upon oral examination or written interrogatories for the purpose of discovery or for use as evidence in the proceeding or for both purposes.

Unless otherwise ordered by the presiding officer, the use of deposition or interrogatory procedures shall be completed prior to a hearing. The presiding officer may at any time order the parties or their attorneys to appear at a conference at which he may direct the proper use of such procedures or the time to be allowed for such use, and shall do so whenever he considers it desirable to prevent delay or undue inconvenience. (46 C.F.R. 502.201)

Scope of Examination

Persons and parties may be examined regarding any matter, not privileged, which is relevant to the subject matter involved in the proceeding, whether it relates to the claim or defense of the examining party or to the claim or defense of any other party, including the existence, description, nature, custody, condition, and location of any books, documents, or other tangible things, and the identity and location of persons having knowledge of relevant facts. It is not ground for objection that the testimony will be inadmissible at the hearing if the testimony sought appears reasonably calculated to lead to the discovery of admissible evidence. (46 C.F.R. 502.201)

Persons Before Whom Depositions May Be Taken

Within the United States or within a territory or insular possession subject to the dominion of the United States, depositions shall be taken before an officer authorized to administer oaths by the laws of the United States or of the place where the examination is held.

In a foreign country, depositions may be taken (1) on notice before a person authorized to administer oaths in the place in which the examination is held, either by the law thereof or by the law of the United States, or (2) before a person commissioned by the Commission, and a person so commissioned shall have the power by virtue of his commission to administer any necessary oath and take testimony, or (3) pursuant to a letter rogatory. A commission or a letter rogatory shall be issued on application and notice and on terms that are just and appropriate. It is not requisite to the issuance of a commission or a letter rogatory that the taking of the deposition in any other manner is impracticable or inconvenient; and both a commission and a letter rogatory may be issued in proper cases. A notice or commission may designate the person before whom the deposition is to be taken either by name or descriptive title.

If the parties so stipulate in writing, deposition may be taken before any person, at any time or place, upon any notice, and in any manner and when so taken may be used like other depositions.(46 C.F.R. 502.202)

Use of Depositions at Hearings

At the hearing, any part or all of a deposition, so far as admissible under the rules of evidence, may be used against any party who was present or represented at the taking of the deposition or who had due notice thereof in accordance with any one of the following provisions:

(1) Any deposition may be used by any party for the purpose of contradicting or impeaching the testimony of deponent as a witness.

(2) The deposition of a party or of anyone who at the time of taking the deposition was an officer, director, or duly authorized agent of a public or private corporation, partnership, or association which is a party, may be used by any other party for any purpose.

(3) The deposition of a witness, whether or not a party, may be used by any party for any purpose if the presiding officer finds: (i) That the witness is dead; or (ii) that the witness is out of the United States unless it appears that the absence of the witness was procured by the party offering the deposition; or (iii) that the witness is unable to attend or testify because of age, sickness, infirmity, or imprisonment; or (iv) that the party offering the deposition has been unable to procure the attendance of the witness by subpoena; or (v) upon application and notice, that such exceptional circumstances exist as to make it desirable, in the interest of justice and with due regard to the importance of presenting the testimony of witnesses orally in open hearing, to allow the deposition to be used.

(4) If only part of a deposition is offered in evidence by a party, any other party may require him to introduce all of it which is relevant to the part introduced, and any party may introduce any other parts.

(5) Substitution of parties does not affect the right to use depositions previously taken; and, when a proceeding in any hearing has been dismissed and another proceeding involving the same subject matter is afterward brought between the same parties or their representatives or successors in interest, all depositions lawfully taken and duly filed in the former proceeding may be used in the latter as if originally taken therefor.

Objection may be made at the hearing to receiving in evidence any deposition or part thereof for any reason which would require the exclusion of the evidence if the witness were then present and testifying.

Objections to the competency of a witness or to the competency, relevancy, or materiality of testimony are not waived by failure to make them before or during the taking of the deposition, unless the ground of the objection is one which might have been obviated or removed if presented at that time.

Errors and irregularities occurring at the oral examination in the manner of taking the deposition, in the form of the questions or answers, in the oath or affirmation, or in the conduct of parties and errors of any kind which might be obviated, removed, or cured if promptly presented, are waived unless reasonable objection thereto is made at the taking of the deposition.

Objections to the form of written interrogatories are waived unless served in writing upon the party propounding them within the time allowed for serving the succeeding cross interrogatories.

A party shall not be deemed to make a person his own witness for any purpose by taking his deposition. The introduction in evidence of the deposition or any part thereof for any purpose other than that of contradicting or impeaching the deponent makes the deponent the witness of the party introducing the deposition.

At the hearing, any party may rebut any relevant evidence contained in a deposition whether introduced by him or by any other party. (46 C.F.R. 502.03)

Depositions Upon Oral Examination

A party desiring to take the deposition of any person upon oral examination shall, unless otherwise agreed to by all parties or otherwise ordered by the presiding officer, give at least a 20-day notice in writing to such person and to every other party to the action. The notice shall state the time and place for taking the deposition and the name and address of each person to be examined, if known, and, if the name is not known, a general description sufficient to identify him or the particular class or group to which he belongs. The notice shall also contain a statement of the matters concerning which each witness will testify. All errors and irregularities in the notice for taking a deposition are waived unless written objection is promptly served upon the party giving the notice. (46 C.F.R. 502.204)

Production of Documents and Things and Entry Upon Land for Inspection and Other Purposes

Scope. Any party may serve on any other party a request (1) to produce and permit the party making the request, or someone acting on his behalf, to inspect and copy any designated documents (including writings, drawings, graphs, charts, photographs, phono-records, and other data compilations from which information can be obtained, translated, if necessary, by the respondent through detection devices into reasonably usable form), or to inspect and copy, test, or sample any tangible things which constitute or contain matters within the scope of the discovery rules and which are in the possession, custody or control of the party upon whom the request is served; or (2) to permit entry upon designated land or other property in the possession or control of the party upon whom the request is served for the purpose of inspection and measuring, surveying, photographing, testing, or sampling the property or any designated object or operation thereon, within the scope of the discovery rules. (46 C.F.R. 502.207)

Requests for Admission

A party may serve upon any other party a written request for the admission, for purposes of the pending action only, of the truth of any matters (relevant to the subject matter of the proceeding) set forth in the request that relate to statements or opinions of fact or of the application of law to fact, including the genuineness if any documents described in the request. Copies of documents shall be served with the request unless they have been or are otherwise furnished or made available for inspection and copying. (46 C.F.R. 502.208)

Depositions of Witnesses Upon Written Interrogatories

A party desiring to take the deposition or any person upon written interrogatories shall serve them upon every other party with a notice stating the name and address of the person who is to answer them and the name or descriptive title and address of the officer before whom the deposition is to be taken. A party so served may serve cross interrogatories upon the party proposing to take the deposition. All errors and irregularities in the notice are waived unless written objection is promptly served upon the party giving the notice. (46 C.F.R. 502.205)

Interrogatories to Parties

Any party may serve upon any other party written interrogatories to be answered by the party served or, if the party served is a public or private corporation or a partnership or association, by any officer or agent, who shall furnish such information as is available to the party. (46 C.F.R. 502.206)

Briefs; Requests for Findings; Decisions; Exceptions

Briefs; Requests for Findings

Unless otherwise ordered by the presiding officer, opening or initial briefs shall contain the following matters in separately captioned sections: introductory section describing the nature and background of the case, proposed findings of fact in serially numbered paragraphs with reference to exhibit numbers and pages of the transcript, argument based upon principles of law with appropriate citations of the authorities relied upon, and conclusions. (46 C.F.R. 502.221)

Decisions—Contents

All initial, recommended, tentative, and final decisions will include a statement of findings and conclusions, as well as the reasons or basis therefor, upon all the material issues of fact, law, or discretion presented on the record, and the appropriate rule, order, sanction, relief, or denial thereof. (C.F.R. 502.225)

Decision Based on Official Notice; Public Documents

Official notice may be taken of such matters as might be judicially noticed by the courts, or of technical or scientific facts within the general knowledge of the Commission as an expert body.

Where a decision or part thereof rests on the official notice of a material fact not appearing in the evidence in the record, the fact of official notice shall be so stated in the decision, and any party, upon timely request, shall be afforded an opportunity to show the contrary.

Whenever there is offered in evidence (in whole or in part) a public document, such as an official report, decision, opinion, or published scientific or economic statistical data issued by any of the executive departments (or their subdivisions), legislative agencies or committees, or administrative agencies of the Federal government (including government-owned corporations), or similar document issued by a state or its agencies, and such document (or part thereof) has been shown by the offeror to be reasonably available to the public, such document need not be produced or marked for identification, but may be offered in evidence as a public document by specifying the document or relevant part thereof. (46 C.F.R. 502.226)

EXCEPTIONS TO DECISIONS OR ORDERS OF DISMISSAL OF ADMINISTRATIVE LAW JUDGES; REPLIES THERETO; AND REVIEW OF DECISIONS OR ORDERS OF DISMISSAL BY COMMISSION

After date of service of the initial, recommended, or tentative decision, any party may file a memorandum excepting to any conclusions, findings or statements contained in such decision, and a brief in support of such memorandum. Such exceptions and brief shall constitute one document, shall indicate with particularity alleged errors, and shall indicate the pages of the transcript and the exhibit numbers when referring to the record. In the absence of ascertained error or exceptions, a recommended or tentative decision will be taken by the Commission as the basis of its decision. Whenever the officer who presided at the reception of the evidence, or other qualified officer, makes an initial decision, such decision shall become the decision of the Commission unless request for review is made in exceptions filed, or notice of review is served. Upon the filing of exceptions to, or review of, an initial decision, such decision shall become inoperative until the Commission determines the matter. Where exceptions are filed to, or the Commission reviews, an initial decision, the Commission, except as it may limit the issues upon notice or by rule, will have all the powers which it would have in making the initial decision. An adverse party may file and serve a reply to exceptions. (46 C.F.R. 502.227)

CERTIFICATION OF RECORD BY PRESIDING OR OTHER OFFICER

The presiding or other officer shall certify and transmit the entire record to the Commission when exceptions are filed or the time therefor has expired, when notice is given by the Commission that the initial decision will be reviewed on its own initiative, or when the Commission requires the case to be certified to it for initial decision. (46 C.F.R. 502.229)

Reopening By Presiding Officer or Commission

At any time after the conclusion of a hearing in a proceeding, but before issuance by the presiding officer of a recommended or initial decision, any party to the proceeding may file with the presiding officer a petition to reopen the proceeding for the purpose of receiving additional evidence. A petition to reopen shall set forth the grounds requiring reopening of the proceeding, including material changes of fact or of law alleged to have occurred since the conclusion of the hearing. Replies may be filed.

At any time prior to filing his decision, the presiding officer upon his own motion may reopen a proceeding for the reception of further evidence.

Where a decision has been issued by the presiding officer or where a decision by the presiding officer has been omitted, but before issuance of a Commission decision, the Commission may, after petition and reply, or upon its own motion, reopen a proceeding for the purpose of taking further evidence.

Nothing shall preclude the Commission from remanding a proceeding to the presiding officer for the taking of additional evidence or determining points of law. (46 C.F.R. 502.230)

Oral Argument; Submission for Final Decision

Oral Argument

If oral argument before the Commission is desired on exceptions to an initial, recommended, or tentative decision, or on a motion, petition, or application, a request therefor shall be made in writing. Any party may make such request irrespective of his filing exceptions. If a brief on exceptions is filed, the request for oral argument shall be incorporated in such brief. Requests for oral argument on any motion, petition, or application shall be made in such pleadings. Applications for oral argument will be granted or denied in the discretion of the Commission, and, if granted, the notice of oral argument will set forth the order of presentation. (46 C.F.R. 502.241)

Submission to Commission for Final Decision

A proceeding will be deemed submitted to the Commission for final decision as follows: (1) If oral argument is had, the date of completion thereof, or if memoranda on points of law are permitted to be filed after argument, the last date of such filing; (2) if oral argument is not had, the last date when exceptions or replies thereto are filed, or if exceptions are not filed, the expiration date for such exceptions; (3) in the case of an initial decision, the date of notice of the Commission to review the decision, if such notice is given. (46 C.F.R. 502.242)

Reparation

PROOF ON AWARD OF REPARATION

If many shipments or points of origin or destination are involved in a proceeding in which reparation is sought, the Commission will determine in its decision the issues as to violations, injury to complainant, and right to reparation. If complainant is found entitled to reparation, the parties thereafter will be given an opportunity to agree or make proof respecting the shipments and pecuniary amount of reparation due before the order of the Commission awarding reparation is entered. In such cases, freight bills and other exhibits bearing on the details of all shipments, and the amount of reparation on each, need not be produced at the original hearing unless called for or needed to develop other pertinent facts. (46 C.F.R. 502.251)

REPARATION STATEMENTS

When the Commission finds that reparation is due, but that the amount cannot be ascertained upon the record before it, the complainant shall immediately prepare a statement showing details of the shipments on which reparation is claimed. This statement shall not include any shipments not covered by the findings of the Commission. Complainant shall forward the statement, together with the paid freight bills on the shipments, or true copies thereof, to the carrier or other person who collected the charges for checking and certification as to accuracy. Statements so prepared and certified shall be filed with the Commission for consideration in determining the amount of reparation due. Disputes concerning the accuracy of amounts may be assigned for conference by the Commission or in its discretion referred for further hearing. (46 C.F.R. 502.252)

Reconsideration of Proceedings

PETITIONS

After issuance of a final decision or order by the Commission, any party may file a petition for reconsideration. The petition shall state concisely the alleged errors in the Commission decision or order. If a petition seeks to vacate, revere, or modify a Commission decision or order by reason of matters that have arisen since the decision or order, or by reason of a consequence that would result from compliance with a decision or order, the petition shall state concisely the matters relied upon by the petitioner. A petition shall be verified if verification of original pleading is required. A petition for reconsideration shall not operate as a stay of any rule or order of the Commission or of an Administrative Law Judge if the proceeding is before him. (46 C.F.R. 502.261)

REPLY

Any party may file a reply to a petition for reconsideration.

In *Alaska Steamship Company v. Federal Maritime Commission,*[4] an appellate court affirmed an order of the Commission denying a petition to reopen a rate case which had been pending before the Commission for a number of years. The court held that the Commission had broad discretion in disposing of petitions to reopen evidentiary records, and that there was no abuse of the discretion in this case.

Nonadjudicatory Investigation

Procedures are established for the conduct of investigation by the Commission. (46 C.F.R. 502.281-502.291)

Informal Procedure for Adjudication of Small Claims

POLICY

Claims against common carriers subject to the Shipping Act, 1916, as amended and the Intercoastal Shipping Act, 1933, as amended, in the amount of $5,000 or less, for the recovery of damages (not including claims for loss of or damage to property), or for the recovery of overcharges, will with the written consent of all parties, be determined by the Commission's Settlement Officers. (46 C.F.R. 502.301)

LIMITATIONS OF ACTIONS

Claims may be filed with the Commission within 2 years from the time the cause of action accrues. The cause of action shall be deemed

---

[4] 356 F. 2d 59.

to accrue (a) for overcharges upon delivery of the property or the payment of the charges, whichever is later, (b) for damages on the date on which the act which is the basis of the claim occurred. (46 C.F.R. 502.302)

OVERCHARGES AND DAMAGES DEFINED

The term "overcharges" means charges for transportation services in excess of those applicable under tariffs lawfully on file with the Commission. The term "damages" means such violations of the Shipping Act, 1916, as amended, or the Intercoastal Shipping Act, 1933, as amended, other than overcharges for which reparation may be granted. (46 C.F.R. 502.303)

PROCEDURE

A sworn claim shall be filed. Copies of tariff pages need not be filed; reference to such tariffs or to pertinent parts thereof will be sufficient. Supporting documents may consist of affidavits, correspondence, bills of lading, paid freight bills, export declarations, dock or wharf receipts, or of such other documents as, in the judgment of the claimant, tend to establish the claim. The Settlement Officer may, if deemed necessary, request additional documents or information from claimants. Claimant may attach a memorandum, brief or other document containing discussion, argument, or legal authority in support of its claim. If a claim involves any shipment which has been the subject of a previous claim filed with the Commission, formally or informally, full reference to such previous claim must be given.

The carrier shall file with the Commission its response to the claim, together with an indication as to whether the informal procedure is consented to. Failure of the carrier to indicate refusal or consent in its response will be conclusively deemed to indicate such consent. The response shall consist of documents, arguments, legal authorities, or precedents, or any other matters considered by the carrier to be a defense to the claim. The Settlement Officer may request the carrier to furnish such further documents or information as he deems necessary, or he may require the claimant to reply to the defenses raised by the carrier.

If the carrier refuses to consent to the claim being informally adjudicated the claim will be considered a complaint.

Both parties shall promptly be served with the Settlement Officer's decision which shall state the basis upon which the decision was made.

This decision shall be final, unless the Commission exercised its discretionary right to review. (46 C.F.R. 502.304)

Formal Procedure for Adjudication of Small Claims

APPLICABILITY

In the event that a carrier elects not to consent to determination of a claim under the informal procedure it shall be adjudicated under the formal procedure. (46 C.F.R. 502.311)

ANSWER TO COMPLAINT

The carrier shall file with the Commission an answer to the complaint and shall serve a copy of the answer upon complainant. The answer shall admit or deny each matter set forth in the complaint. Matters not specifically denied will be deemed admitted. Where matters are urged in defense, the answer shall be accompanied by appropriate affidavits, other documents and memoranda. (46 C.F.R. 503.312)

REPLY OF COMPLAINANT

Complainant may file a reply memorandum accompanied by appropriate affidavits and supporting documents. (46 C.F.R. 503.313)

ADDITIONAL INFORMATION

The Administrative Law Judge may require the submission of additional affidavits, documents, or memoranda from complainant or carrier. (46 C.F.R. 503.314)

REQUEST FOR ORAL HEARING

No oral hearing will be held; however, the Administrative Law Judge in his discretion may order such hearing. A request for oral hearing may be incorporated in the answer or in complainant's reply to the answer. Requests for oral hearing will not be entertained unless they set forth in detail the reasons why the filing of affidavits or other documents will not permit the fair and expeditious disposition of the claim, and the precise nature of the facts sought to be proved at such oral hearing. The Administrative Law Judge shall rule upon a request for oral hearing. (46 C.F.R. 502.315)

INTERVENTION

Intervention will ordinarily not be permitted. (46 C.F.R. 502.316)

ORAL ARGUMENT

No oral argument will be held, unless otherwise directed by the Administrative Law Judge. (46 C.F.R. 502.317)

DECISIONS

The decision of the Administrative Law Judge shall be final unless either party requests review of the decision by the Commission asserting as grounds therefor that a material finding of fact or a necessary legal conclusion is erroneous or that prejudicial error has occurred, or unless the Commission exercises its discretionary right to review the decision. (46 C.F.R. 502.318)

Conciliation Service

POLICY

It is the policy of the Commission:

(a) To offer its good offices and expertise to parties to disputes involving matters within its jurisdiction, so as to permit resolution of such disputes with dispatch and without the necessity of costly and time-consuming formal proceedings;

(b) To facilitate and promote the resolution of problems and disputes by encouraging affected parties to resolve differences through their own resources;

(c) To create a forum in which grievances, interpretations, problems, and questions involving the waterborne commerce of the United States may be aired, discussed and, hopefully, resolved to the mutual advantage of all concerned parties.

PERSONS ELIGIBLE FOR SERVICE

Request for conciliation service may be made by any shipper, merchant, carrier, conference of carriers, freight forwarder, terminal operator, government agency, or any other person affected by or involved in the transportation of goods by common carrier in the waterborne domestic offshore or foreign commerce of the United States. (46 C.F.R. 502.403)

OPINIONS

The conciliator will write an advisory opinion, although not binding, by approval of all parties. If the advisory opinion, or revision thereof requested by one or more of the parties, is not unanimously agreed upon, then the conciliation will stop without prejudices to any of the parties involved. If unanimity is not reached, the conciliatory will note in a report to the Commission, which he shall serve on all parties, that the parties failed to reach agreement. (46 C.F.R. 502.406)

Judicial Review of Orders
of the Interstate Commerce Commission

Tests of Federal Jurisdiction

The tests of federal jurisdiction to be applied in determining whether a case arises "under the Constitution or laws of the United States" have been enumerated as follows: (1) It should be kept in mind that federal courts are courts of limited jurisdiction; (2) a right claimed must be one which will succeed on one construction of federal laws but will fail on another; (3) there must be necessity for construction of a federal statute and a genuine controversy between the parties as to meaning and effect of federal law asserted to be involved; (4) the asserted federal question must be real, substantial, and meditorious, not foreclosed by previous court decisions; (5) the right itself must be federal in nature, not merely in its source or origin; (6) the presentation of a federal question must be determined from plaintiff's own statement of his cause of action, of which the claimed federal right must be an essential element; and (7) matters pleaded by plaintiff in anticipation or avoidance of defenses, or matters appearing in such pleadings subsequent to plaintiff's complaint and defendant's answer or petition for removal, are immaterial and cannot be considered in determining whether a federal question is presented.[1]

The Applicable Statutory Provisions

Judicial review of action by the Interstate Commerce Commission is provided by specific statutory authority.

---

[1]*Pan American Petroleum Corp. v. Cities Service Gas Co.*, 182 F. Supp. 439, 440-1.

Section 1336(a) of Title 28, U.S.C., as amended by P.L. 93-584, 88 Stat. 1917, provides:

"Except as otherwise provided by Act of Congress, the district courts shall have jurisdiction of any civil action to enforce, in whole or in part, any order of the Interstate Commerce Commission, and to enjoin or suspend, in whole or in part, any order of the Interstate Commerce Commission for the payment of money or the collection of fines, penalties, and forfeitures."

Section 1398(a) of Title 28, U.S.C., as amended by P.L. 93-584, 88 Stat. 1917, provides:

"(a)   Except as otherwise provided by law, a civil action brought under section 1336(a) of this title shall be brought only in a judicial district in which any of the parties bringing the action resides or has its principal office."

Section 2321 of Title 28, U.S.C., as amended by P.L. 93-584, 88 Stat. 1917, provides:

"(a)   Except as otherwise provided by an Act of Congress, a proceeding to enjoin or suspend, in whole or in part, a rule, regulation, or order of the Interstate Commerce Commission shall be brought in the court of appeals as provided by and in the manner prescribed in chapter 158 of this title.
"(b)   The procedure in the district courts in actions to enforce, in whole or in part, any order of the Interstate Commerce Commission other than for payment of money or the collection of fines, penalties, and forfeitures, shall be as provided in this chapter.
"(c)   The orders, writs, and process of the district courts may, in the cases specified in subsection (b) . . . be served and be returnable anywhere in the United States."

Section 2323 of Title 28, U.S.C., as amended by P.L. 93-584, 88 Stat. 1917, provides:

"The Attorney General shall represent the Government in the actions specified in section 2321 of this title . . .."

Section 2341(3) of Title 28, U.S.C., as amended by P.L. 93-584, 88 Stat. 1917, provides:

"As used in this chapter—

"(3) 'agency' means—

"(A)   The Commission, when the order sought to be reviewed was entered by the Federal Communications Commission, the Federal Maritime Commission, the Interstate Commerce Commission, or the Atomic Energy Commission, as the case may be; ***"

Section 2342 of Title 28, U.S.C., as amended by P.L. 93-584, 88 Stat. 1917, provides:

"The court of appeals has exclusive jurisdiction to enjoin, set aside, suspend (in whole or in part), or to determine the validity of—

* * *

(5) all rules, regulations, or final orders of the Interstate Commerce Commission made reviewable by section 2321 of this title."

Section 2343 of title 28, U.S.C. provides:

"The venue of a proceeding under this chapter is in the judicial circuit in which the petitioner resides or has its principal office, or in the United States Court of Appeals for the District of Columbia Circuit."

Section 2344 of Title 28, U.S.C. provides:

"On the entry of a final order reviewable under this chapter, the agency shall promptly give notice thereof by service or publication in accordance with its rules. Any party aggrieved by the final order may, within 60 days after its entry, file a petition to review the order in the court of appeals wherein venue lies. The action shall be against the United States. The petition shall contain a concise statement of—

(1)   the nature of the proceedings as to which review is sought;
(2)   the facts on which venue is based;
(3)   the grounds on which relief is sought; and
(4)   the relief prayed.

The petitioner shall attach to the petition, as exhibits, copies of the order, report, or decision of the agency. The clerk shall serve a true copy of the petition on the agency and on the Attorney General by registered mail, with request for a return receipt."

Section 2346 of title 28, U.S.C. provides:

"Unless the proceeding has been terminated on a motion to dismiss the petition, the agency shall file in the office of the clerk the record on review as provided by section 2112 of this title."

Section 2347 of title 28, U.S.C. provides:

"(a)   Unless determined on a motion to dismiss, petitions to review orders reviewable under this chapter are heard in the court of appeals on the record of the pleadings, evidence adduced, and proceedings before the agency, when the agency has held a hearing whether or not required to do so by law.
"(b)   When the agency has not held a hearing before taking the action of which review is sought by the petition, the court of appeals shall determine whether a hearing is required by law. After that determination, the court shall—

(1)   remand the proceedings to the agency to hold a hearing, when a hearing is required by law;
(2)   pass on the issues presented, when a hearing is not required by

law and it appears from the pleadings and affidavits filed by the parties that no genuine issue of material fact is presented; or

(3) transfer the proceedings to a district court for the district in which the petitioner resides or has its principal office for a hearing and determination as if the proceedings were originally initiated in the district court, when a hearing is not required by law and a genuine issue of material fact is presented. The procedure in these cases in the district court is governed by the Federal Rules of Civil Procedure.

"(c) If a party to a proceeding to review applies to the court of appeals in which the proceeding is pending for leave to adduce additional evidence and shows to the satisfaction of the court that—

(1) the additional evidence is material; and

(2) there were reasonable grounds for failure to adduce the evidence before the agency;

the court may order the additional evidence and any counterevidence the opposite party desires to offer to be taken by the agency. The agency may modify its findings of fact, or make new findings, by reason of the additional evidence so taken, and may modify or set aside its order, and shall file in the court the additional evidence, the modified findings or new findings, and the modified order or the order setting aside the original order."

Section 2348 of title 28, U.S.C. provides:

"The Attorney General is responsible for and has control of the interests of the Government in all court proceedings under this chapter. The agency, and any party in interest in the proceeding before the agency whose interests will be affected if an order of the agency is or is not enjoined, set aside, or suspended, may appear as parties thereto of their own motion and as of right, and be represented by counsel in any proceeding to review the order. Communities, associations, corporations, firms, and individuals, whose interests are affected by the order of the agency, may intervene in any proceeding to review the order. The Attorney General may not dispose of or discontinue the proceeding to review over the objection of any party or intervenor, but any intervenor may prosecute, defend, or continue the proceeding unaffected by the action or inaction of the Attorney General."

Section 2349 of title U.S.C. provides:

"(a) The court of appeals has jurisdiction of the proceeding on the filing and service of a petition to review. The court of appeals in which the record on review is filed, on the filing, has jurisdiction to vacate stay orders or interlocutory injunctions previously granted by any court, and has exclusive jurisdiction to make and enter, on the petition, evidence, and proceedings set forth in the record on review, a judgment determining the validity of, and enjoining, setting aside, or suspending, in whole or in part, the order of the agency.

"(b) The filing of the petition to review does not of itself stay or suspend the operation of the order of the agency, but the court of appeals in its discretion may restrain or suspend, in whole or in part, the operation of the order pending the final hearing and determination of the petition. When the petitioner makes application for an interlocutory injunction restraining or suspending the enforcement, operation, or execution of, or setting aside, in whole or in part, any order reviewable under this chapter, at least 5 days' notice of the hearing thereon shall be given to the agency and to the Attorney General. In a case in which irreparable damage would otherwise result to the petitioner, the court of appeals may, on hearing, after reasonable notice to the agency and to the Attorney General, order a temporary stay or suspension, in whole or in part, of the operation of the order of the agency for not more than 60 days from the date of the order pending the hearing on the application for the interlocutory injunction, in which case the order of the court of appeals shall contain a specific finding, based on evidence submitted to the court of appeals, and identified by reference thereto, that irreparable damage would result to the petitioner and specifying the nature of the damage. The court of appeals, at the time of hearing the application for an interlocutory injunction, on a like finding, may continue the temporary stay or suspension, in whole or in part, until decision on the application. The hearing on an application for an interlocutory injunction shall be given preference and expedited and shall be heard at the earliest practicable date after the expiration of the notice of hearing on the application. On the final hearing of any proceeding to review any order under this chapter, the same requirements as to precedence and expedition apply."

Section 2350 of title 28, U.S.C. provides:

"(a) An order granting or denying an interlocutory injunction under section 2349(b) of this title and a final judgment of the court of appeals in a proceeding to review under this chapter are subject to review by the Supreme Court on a writ of certiorari as provided by section 1254(1) of this title. Application for the writ shall be made within 45 days after entry of the order and within 90 days after entry of the judgment, as the case may be. The United States, the agency, or an aggrieved party may file a petition for a writ of certiorari.

(b) The provisions of section 1254(3) of this title, regarding certification, and of section 2101(f) of this title, regarding stays, also apply to proceedings under this chapter."

Section 17(10) of the Interstate Commerce Act[2] provides that "When an application for rehearing, reargument, or reconsideration of any decision, order, or requirement of a division, an individual Commissioner, or a board with respect to any matter assigned or referred to him or it shall have been made and shall have been denied, or after rehearing, reargument, or reconsideration otherwise disposed of, by the Commission, or an appellate division, a suit to enforce, enjoin, suspend, or set aside such decision, order, or requirement, in whole or in part, may be

---

[2] 49 U.S.C. 17(10). See also Section 205(g).

brought in a court of the United States under those provisions of law applicable in the case of suits to enforce, enjoin, suspend, or set aside orders of the Commission, but not otherwise."

The Administrative Procedure Act[3] provides:

Sec. 702. Right of Review. — A person suffering legal wrong because of agency action, or adversely affected or aggrieved by agency action within the meaning of any relevant statute, shall be entitled to judicial review thereof.

Sec. 703. Form and Venue of Proceeding. — The form of proceeding for judicial review is the special statutory review proceeding relevant to the subject matter in a court specified by statute or, in the absence or inadequacy thereof, any applicable form of legal action, including actions for declaratory judgments or writs of prohibitory or mandatory injunction or habeas corpus, in a court of competent jurisdiction. Except to the extent that prior, adequate, and exclusive opportunity for judicial review is provided by law, agency action is subject to judicial review in civil or criminal proceedings for judicial enforcement.

Sec. 704. Actions Reviewable. — Agency action made reviewable by statute and final agency action for which there is no other adequate remedy in a court are subject to judicial review. A preliminary, procedural, or intermediate agency action or ruling not directly reviewable is subject to review on the review of the final agency action. Except as otherwise expressly required by statute, agency action otherwise final is final for the purposes of this section whether or not there has been presented or determined an application for a declaratory order, for any form of reconsideration, or, unless the agency otherwise requires by rule and provides that the action meanwhile is inoperative, for an appeal to superior agency authority.

Sec. 705. Relief Pending Review. — When an agency finds that justice so requires, it may postpone the effective date of action taken by it, pending judicial review. On such conditions as may be required and to the extent necessary to prevent irreparable injury, the reviewing court, including the court to which a case may be taken on appeal from or on application for certiorari or other writ to a reviewing court, may issue all necessary and appropriate process to postpone the effective date of an agency action or to preserve status or rights pending conclusion of the review proceedings.

Sec. 706. Scope of Review. — To the extent necessary to decision and when presented, the reviewing court shall decide all relevant questions of law, interpret constitutional and statutory provisions, and determine the meaning of applicability of the terms of an agency action. The reviewing court shall—

(1) compel agency action unlawfully withheld or unreasonably delayed; and

[3] 5 U.S.C. 702-706.

(2) hold unlawful and set aside agency action, findings, and conclusions found to be—

(A) arbitrary, capricious, an abuse of discretion, or otherwise not in accordance with law;

(B) contrary to constitutional right, power, privilege, or immunity;

(C) in excess of statutory jurisdiction, authority, or limitations, or short of statutory right;

(D) without observance of procedure required by law;

(E) unsupported by substantial evidence in a case subject to Sections 556 and 557 of this title or otherwise reviewed on the record of an agency hearing provided by statute; or

(F) unwarranted by the facts to the extent that the facts are subject to trial de novo by the reviewing court.

In making the foregoing determinations, the court shall review the whole record or those parts of it cited by a party and due account shall be taken of the rule of prejudicial error.

Judicial Review and Enforcement under the Interstate Commerce Act and Related Statutes

A. *Single-judge United States district courts.*

1. All cases arising under the Interstate Commerce Act involving fines, penalties or civil forfeitures and cases involving reparation or other orders for the payment of money.[4]

Appeals in these cases are heard by the United States courts of appeal whose decisions are reviewable in the Supreme Court by a write of certiorari.

2. Civil enforcement cases arising under the Expediting Act and the Elkins Act. Appeals in these cases go directly to the Supreme Court.

B. *Court of Appeals.*

1. Appeals from all final judgments and orders of the Commission arising under Section 17(10) of the Interstate Commerce Act.[5] Review in the Supreme Court is by petition for certiorari.

C. *Court of Claims.*

1. Suits by carriers against the United States for reparation or other matters involving damages under the Interstate Commerce Act. The Commission does not participate in these cases unless the mat-

[4]28 U.S.C. 1336, 1398.
[5]28 U.S.C. 2321(a), 2341(3), 2342(5).

ter is referred to the Commission by the court under 28 U.S.C. 1398(b). In those cases where an appeal is permitted, appeal is direct to the Supreme Court.

The courts of appeal are not vested with any more jurisdiction than was previously exercised by three-judge district courts. The courts of appeal handle actions brought to enjoin or suspend Commission order while single-judge district courts retain jurisdiction to enjoin or suspend Commission orders for the payment of money or collection of fines.[6] Actions for review of orders relating to monetary matters only are adjudicated under 28 U.S.C. 1336(a) by single-judge district courts.[7] The validity of Commission orders are to be filled in a court of appeals pursuant to 28 U.S.C. 2321(a) and 2342(5).

Reviewable Order

An order may be reviewable even though technically it might not be an "order" in that it does not require anybody to do anything. For example, where the Commission, after investigating the lawfulness of a rate, finds it lawful — it does not affirmatively do anything; it just lets the rate go into effect, and such rate proceedings have long been held reviewable. This is closely analogous to discontinuance cases. Strictly speaking, the only order the Commission issues in a Section 13a(1) case, if after a hearing it decides not to vote on the discontinuance, is an order discontinuing the proceeding. Technically that might not be an "order" in that it does not require anybody to do anything.

In *The People of the State of California, et al. v. United States,*[8] a district court assumed jurisdiction to review a report and order of the Commission discontinuing its investigation of a proposed reduction in train service, and, finding no abuse of the Commission's discretion, the court sustained the Commission's actions, by unreported per curiam order, entered April 6, 1961. However, a contrary articulation on judicial review of reports and orders, decided upon the investigations authorized by Section 13a (1) of the Act, may be found in *State of New Hampshire v. Boston and Maine Corp., et al.*[9] The district court in that case determined that it was without jurisdiction to review the report and order of the Commission finding that the public convenience and necessity did not require the continued operation of certain trains sought to be dis-

---

[6]*Southern Railway Co. v. United States,* 412 F. Supp. 1122, 1126 n.1.
[7]*Carothers v. Western Transportation Co.,* 412 F. Supp. 1158.
[8]C.A. No. 38915, N.D. Calif.
[9]C.A. No. 2570, D. N.H.

continued by the railroad. The suggestion that the court was without power to review the Commission's actions did not come from the Commission. The court, in its unreported opinion, acknowledged that "[t]he Commission argues for jurisdiction in this case." It did so by reasoning by analogy to the judicial review of reports and orders of the Commission finding assailed rates not shown to be unjust and unreasonable. Moreover, as the court said, "The Commission has directed our attention to two unreported per curiam decisions affirming Commission orders terminating investigations under Section 13(a) (1). *Rhodes, et al. v. United States, Civil Action* No. 63-472, U.S.D.C., W.D. Pa., October 15, 1963, *California v. United States,* Civil Action No. 38915, U.S.D.C., N.D. Cal. April 6, 1961."

In *Public Service Board of the State of Vermont v. United States,*[10] the Commission reiterated its view before a district court that its final report and order under Section 13a(1), discontinuing its investigation of a railroad's train discontinuance proposal, would be reviewable by the district court. In its pleading of July 13, 1966, the Commission stated flatly, "[A]fter issuance of a final Report and Order and ruling upon petition for reconsideration, the matter [will] be ripe for review." The three-judge court in that case, while denying a preliminary injunction because the State failed to prove irreparable injury, agreed that the Commission's action would be reviewable when it was administratively final. The Commission had urged that the district court was without jurisdiction to review the particular order of the Commission, Division 3, entered July 6, 1966, then before it. That order though declaring that continued operations of the trains would not be required, was not ripe for judicial review[11] because it was unaccompanied by a report announcing the reasons or findings and conclusions for the Commission's actions and it was not yet the subject of petitions for reconsideration, which the Commission's General Rules of Practice allow the parties to file as a matter of right.

In *Parkhill Truck Co. v. United States,*[12] Parkhill brought suit in a district court to set aside an order on reconsideration in an application proceeding, and to enjoin issuance of a certificate to a motor carrier, C. & H. Before the court, the Commission took the position that the determination of the scope of Parkhill's authority in the prior report was an advisory opinion only, and that, because no order actually ran against Parkhill, the determination was not reviewable, and the complaint should

[10]C.A. No. 4611, D. Vt.
[11]See *Eastern Airlines v. CAB,* 271 F. 2d 752, 757.
[12]198 F. Supp. 362.

be dismissed. The court accepted the suggestion that the determination was merely advisory, but did not agree that this in turn called for dismissal of the complaint. Instead, the court stated that the scope of Parkhill's authority could be "determined effectively only in plenary proceedings which result in an appealable order," and it remanded the proceeding to the Commission. The Commission felt impelled to comment upon the district court's holding, and the suggestion made to the court that the interpretation of the scope of a protestant's operating authority in an application proceeding constitutes merely an advisory opinion and is not judicially reviewable. The Commission said that an error was made in advancing this argument as representing the position of this Commission. It is very frequently necessary, in determining whether a grant of motor common or contract carrier authority is required by the public convenience and necessity or is consistent with the public interest, for the Commission to make the preliminary determination whether a particular carrier is already authorized to transport the pertinent traffic. The effective administration of the Act depends upon as prompt as possible a disposition of pending application proceedings. The Commission said that it would be a burden on everybody were it to delay making necessary determinations of protestants' authorities to transport given traffic or to serve given points, and to await the institution and final determination of formal investigations into the scope of their operating rights.

At the same time the Commission agreed with the court that it is hardly consistent with the dictates of "fair treatment and due process"[13] to make such a determination and then to take the position that it is immune from judicial review. A finding of this kind necessarily puts a carrier on notice that if it continues to perform certain transportation it may be subject to civil and criminal penalties, and such a finding is unquestionably justiciable.[14]

In *Worster Motor Lines, Inc. v. United*,[15] the court said:

> It is believed that necessarily the scope of a protestant's authority is subject to interpretation when it protests an application which is pending before the Commission. The Commission must find that the public convenience and necessity require the requested operating rights. An important factor for the Commission to consider is whether the operating rights which are applied for are already covered by the certificates of the protestants. . . . In the opinion of the Court this, of necessity, requires

[13]198 F. Supp. at p. 364.
[14]Cf. *Frozen Food Exp. v. United States*, 351 U.S. 40, 44; *National Van Lines, Inc. v. United States*, 326 F. 2d 362.
[15]226 F. Supp. 603, 607.

the Commission to review the scope of the authority of each competing carrier who protests an application.

It is true, of course, that no actual order runs against a protestant whose authority is interpreted in an application proceeding. Should such a carrier continue to perform service found to be unauthorized, the Commission could order it to cease and desist from conducting such operations only in an appropriate formal proceeding — either an investigation instituted upon own motion or a complaint brought by a competitor. This factor, however, in no way diminishes the effect of a necessary interpretation made in the course of disposing of an application proceeding.

Previously there was conflict among the courts on the question of whether Commission decisions terminating investigations under Section 13a(1) were or were not "orders" within the meaning of 28 U.S.C. 1336(a).[16] The conflict was resolved by the Supreme Court in *City of Chicago v. United States*[17] where it held that such orders are reviewable. In discussing this matter the Supreme Court said:

> Section 13a in its present form came into the Act in 1958 and was designed to superside the prior confused and delayed procedure under which the States supervised the discontinuance of passenger trains. Accordingly, Congress provided a uniform federal scheme to take the place of the former procedure. A single federal standard was to govern train discontinuances whether interstate or intrastate, though the procedure of § 13a (1) for discontinuance of an interstate train was made somewhat different from the procedure for discontinuance of intrastate trains. But the Commission is to have the final say in each case and "precisely the same substantive standard" now governs discontinuance of either interstate or intrastate operations. *Southern R. Co. v. North Carolina*, 376 U.S. 93, 103.
>
> Whether the Commission should make an investigation of a § 13a(1) discontinuance is of course within its discretion, a matter which is not reviewable. *State of New Jersey v. United States*, 168 F. Supp. 324, affirmed, 359 U.S. 27. But when the Commission undertakes to investigate, it is under a statutory mandate:
>
> > Whenever an investigation shall be made by said Commission, it shall be its duty to make a report in writing in respect thereto, which shall state the conclusions of the Commission, together with its decision, order, or requirement in the premises . . . " 49 U.S.C. § 14(1).

[16]See *Minnesota v. United States,* 238 F. Supp. 107, and *New Hampshire v. Boston & Maine Corp.,* 251 F. Supp. 421, holding that the decisions terminating investigations under Section 13a(1) are not "orders" within the meaning of 28 U.S.C. 1336(a). See contra *Vermont v. Boston & Maine Corp.,* 269 F. Supp. 80, and *New York v. United States,* 299 F. Supp. 989. See also *City of Williamsport v. United States,* 273 F. Supp. 899, 282 F. Supp. 46, aff'd 392 U.S. 642.

[17]24 L. ed. 2d 340.

A decision to investigate indicates that a substantial question exists under the statutory standards. The Commission's report therefore deals with the merits. We cannot say that an answer that discontinuance should not be allowed is agency "action," while an answer saying the reverse is agency "inaction." The technical form of the order is irrelevant. In each case the Commission is deciding the merits. The present cases are kin to the "negative orders" which we dealt with in *Rochester Telephone Corp. v. United States*, 307 U.S. 125, 142-143:

> An order of the Commission dismissing a complaint on the merits and maintaining the status quo is an exercise of administrative function, no more and no less, than an order directing some change in status. The nature of the issues foreclosed by the Commission's action and the nature of the issues left open, so far as the reviewing power of courts is concerned, are the same. . . .

> We conclude, therefore, that any distinction, as such, between "negative" and "affirmative" orders, as a touchstone of jurisdiction to review the Commission's orders, serves no useful purpose, and insofar as earlier decisions have been controlled by the distinction, they can no longer be guiding.

The district court reasoned that since "the statute is self-implementing" only an "order" requiring action is reviewable. 294 F. Supp., at 1106. But that theory is of the vintage we discarded in *Rochester Telephone*.

Ripeness Doctrine

The methodology for applying the ripeness doctrine to particular cases was delineated by the Supreme Court in the *Abbott Laboratories* cases.[18] Specifically, the Supreme Court enunciated two factors to be assessed in determining whether a reviewing court should exercise its equitable discretion and entertain a challenge: "The problem is best seen in a twofold aspect, requiring us to evaluate both the fitness of the issues for judicial decision and the hardship to the parties of withholding court consideration."[19] As recognized in *Continental Air Lines, Inc. v. Civil Aeronautics Board*,[20] "determinations of ripeness are necessarily imprecise and very much a matter of practical common sense."

The courts have generally determined that agency decisions are fit for judicial review where the issues presented are "purely legal" and

---

[18]*Abbott Laboratories, Inc. v. Gardner*, 387 U.S. 136; *Toilet Goods Association v. Gardner*, 387 U.S. 158; *Gardner v. Toilet Goods Association*, 387 U.S. 167.

[19]387 U.S. at 149.

[20]522 F. 2d 107, 124. "[T]he problem of finality is often rooted in considerations of fairness and practicality." *Puget Sound Traffic Ass'n. v. CAB*, 536 F. 2d 437, 439.

where the agency action to be reviewed is final.[21] If further factual developments would not sharpen the issues and if further court consideration at this stage would not in any way usurp the agency's fact-finding prerogatives, then the issues presented by an appeal are deemed to be "purely legal."[22] Also, a "final" agency decision is one which imposes an obligation, denies a right, or fixes some legal relationship.[23] An administrative agency's procedural or evidentiary rulings during the course of a proceeding do not constitute a final order justifying judicial review except in extreme cases where the action constitutes an effective deprivation of an appellant's rights.[24]

The second aspect of determining the ripeness of administrative action for judicial review is to ascertain whether withholding judicial review would result in hardship to the parties, and the Supreme Court limits hardship to those situations where the challenged agency action has a "sufficient direct and immediate" impact on the complaining party to require "immediate and significant change" in the day-to-day conduct of such party's business.[25] Thus, even where the issues were fit for review because the challenged agency action is final and the appeal involves purely legal questions, the Supreme Court withheld review for want of ripeness where the complaining party failed to demonstrate "irremediable adverse consequences" would result from postponing review until the agency decision had been applied and its effects actually measured.[26] As the Court stated, "judicial appraisal of these factors is likely to stand on a much surer footing in the context of a specific application of this regulation than could be the case in the framework of the generalized challenge made here."[27]

Administrative Finality and the Scope of Judicial Review

The scope of judicial review by courts of the decisions of independent administrative bodies has evolved over a period of years into the policy

[21]*Bethlehem Steel Corp. v. U.S. Environmental Protection Agency,* 536 F. 2d 156, 160-163; *A. O. Smith Corp. v. Federal Trade Commission,* 530 F. 2d 515, 521.

[22]*A. O. Smith Corp. v. Federal Trade Commission, supra,* at 521-22.

[23]*Puget Sound Traffic Association v. Civil Aeronautics Board,* 536 F. 2d 437, 439, citing, *Chicago & Southern Air Lines, Inc. v. Waterman Steamship Corp.,* 333 U.S. 103. However, it has been stated that to invoke the abstract "rights and duties" criterion as the test of a reviewable order has "the hollow ring of another era." *Marine Terminal v. Raederi Transatlantic,* 400 U.S. 62, 71.

[24]*Thermal Ecology Must Be Preserved v. Atomic Energy Commission,* 433 F. 2d 524; *National Airlines, Inc. v. Civil Aeronautics Board,* 392 F. 2d 504.

[25]387 U.S. at 139, 152.

[26]387 U.S. at 164-67.

[27]387 U.S. 164.

that findings of permissible conclusions of facts based upon substantial evidence of record are final, conclusive and binding upon the courts as well as upon the parties. It is the exclusive province and function of the authorized administrative officer or agency to draw legitimate inference of fact, to make the findings and conclusions of fact, to appraise the conflicting testimony or other evidence, to judge the credibility of witnesses and evidence adduced by the parties, and to determine the weight of the evidence.[28] In *Scripps-Howard Radio v. Comm'n.,*[29] an action involving the Federal Communications Commission, the Supreme Court succinctly stated the scope of judicial review:

> Generally speaking, judicial review of administrative orders is limited to determining whether errors of law have been committed. *Rochester Telephone Co. v. United States,* 307 U.S. 125, 139-140. Because of historical differences in the relationship between administrative bodies and reviewing courts and that between lower and upper courts, a court of review exhausts its power when it lays bare a misconception of law and compels correction.

Thus it is axiomatic that the scope of judicial review of an order of the Interstate Commerce Commission is very limited. The reviewing court will not set aside an order of the Commission entered in the ambit of its statutory authority if the order is based upon adequate findings, founded on substantial evidence, or is a rational conclusion of the matter involved in the light of the entire record.[30]

As stated in *Rochester Tel. Corp. v. United States:*

> From these general considerations the court evolved two specific doctrines limiting judicial review of orders of the Interstate Commerce Commission. One is the primary jurisdiction doctrine, firmly established in Texas &

---

[28]*Consolidated Freightways v. United States,* 83 F. Supp. 811.

[29]316 U.S. 4, 10.

[30]*Interstate Commerce Commission v. Union Pacific R. Co.* 222 U.S. 541, 547; *Mississippi Valley Barge Line v. United States,* 292 U.S. 282, 286; *Rochester Telephone Corp. v. United States,* 307 U.S. 125, 139-140; *Universal Camera Corp. v. Labor Board,* 340 U.S. 474, 488; *Lang Transportation Co. v. United States,* 75 F. Supp. 915; *De Camp Bus Lines v. United States,* 185 F. Supp. 336, 342-3; *Illinois Central Railroad v. Interstate Commerce Commission,* 206 U.S. 441, 454-5; *United States v. Pierce Auto Freight Lines,* 327 U.S. 515, 536-6; *N.L.R.B. v. Columbian Enameling and Stamping Co.,* 306 U.S. 292,300.

The agency must articulate a "rational connection between the facts found and the choice made." *Burlington Truck Lines v. United States,* 371 U.S. 156, 168. While the court may not supply a reasoned basis for the agency's action that the agency itself has not given, *SEC v. Chenery Corp.,* 332 U.S. 194, 196, the court will uphold a decision of less than ideal clarity if the agency's path may reasonably be discerned. *Colorado Interstate Gas Co. v. FPC,* 324 U.S. 581, 595. See *Bowman Transportation, Inc. v. Arkansas-Best Freight System, Inc.,* 419 U.S. 281, 285-86; *Warren Transport, Inc. v. United States,* 525 F. 2d 148, 151.

Pacific Ry. Co. vs. Abilene Cotton Oil Co., 204 U.S. 426. Thereby matters which call for technical knowledge pertaining to transportation must first be passed upon by the Interstate Commerce Commission before a court can be invoked. The other is the doctrine of administrative finality. Even when resort to courts can be had to review a Commission's order, the range of issues open to review is narrow. Only questions affecting constitutional power, statutory authority and the basic prerequisites of proof can be raised. If these legal tests are satisfied, the Commission's order becomes incontestable. *Interstate Commerce Comm'n. v. Illinois Central R. Co.,* 215 U.S. 452, 470; *Interstate Commerce Comm'n v. Union Pacific R. Co.,* 222 U.S. 541.

Another principle of the scope of judicial review universally recognized by courts is that the administrative determinations should remain undisturbed unless they are unsupported by substantial evidence on the record as a whole or are arrived at in an arbitrary and capricious manner.[31] This is true even though the court believes that the decision of the Commission lacks wisdom; though the court would weigh evidence differently from that of the agency; or even though the final decision is inconsistent with prior or future determinations arising under analogous or similar basic circumstances. The Commission's judgment is to be exercised in the light of each individual case, and the courts have no concern with the consistency of decisions it has rendered.[32] Further there is a presumption that the Commission has properly performed its official duties, and this presumption supports its acts in the absence of clear evidence to the contrary.[33]

As stated in *Interstate Commerce Commission v. Union Pacific R. Co.:*[34]

> In determining these mixed questions of law and fact, the court confines itself to the ultimate question as to whether the Commission acted within its power. It will not consider the expediency or wisdom of the order, or whether, on like testimony, it would have made a similar ruling. "The findings of the Commission are made by law *prima facie* true, and this

---

[31]*Atchison, T. and S. F. Ry. v. Wichita Board of Trade,* 412 U.S. 800. In *Warren Transport, Inc. v. United States,* 525 F. 2d 148, 151, it was held that "a petition for review of a Commission's order will be denied on a summary basis when the order is based on the evidence and supported by a rational judgment of the Commission." See also *Midwest Coast Transport, Inc., v. Interstate Commerce Commission,* 536 F. 2d 256, 259.

[32]*Virginia Ry. v. United States,* 272 U.S. 658, 663-6; *Western Paper Makers' Chemical Corp. v. United States,* 271 U.S. 268, 271; *Bowman Transportation, Inc. v. Arkansas-Best Freight System, Inc.,* 419 U.S. 281, 285; *United States v. Pierce Auto Freight Lines, Inc.,* 327 U.S. 515, 536; *Mobile Home Express, Ltd. v. United States,* 354 F. Supp. 701, 707; *Accelerated Transport-Pony Express, Inc. v. United States,* 227 F. Supp. 815, 821.

[33]*Interstate Commerce Commission v. Jersey City,* 322 U.S. 503, 512; *Baltimore & Ohio R.R. v. United States,* 298 U.S. 349, 358-9.

[34]222 U.S. 541, 547.

court has ascribed to them the strength due to the judgment of a tribunal appointed by law and informed by experience." *Ill. Cent. v. I.C.C.* 206 U.S. 441. Its conclusion, of course, is subject to review, but when supported by evidence is accepted as final; not that its decision, involving as it does so many and such vast public interests, can be supported by a mere scintilla of proof — but the courts will not examine the facts further than to determine whether there was substantial evidence to sustain the order.

In *United States v. Pierce Auto Freight Lines, Inc.,*[35] the Supreme Court reiterated the principles of the scope of judicial review by courts of administrative functions when it stated:

> We think the court misconceived not only the effects of the Commission's action in these cases but also its own function. It is not true, as the opinion stated, that ". . . the courts must be in a litigated case, be the arbiters of the paramount public interest." This is rather the business of the Commission, made such by the very terms of the statute. The function of the reviewing court is much more restricted. It is limited to ascertain whether there is warrant in the law and the facts for what the Commission has done. Unless in some specific respect there has been prejudicial departure from requirements of the law or abuse of the Commission's discretion, the reviewing court is without authority to intervene. It cannot substitute its own view concerning what should be done, whether with reference to competitive considerations or others, for the Commission's judgment upon matters committed to its determination, if that has support in the record and the applicable law.

In the case of *Illinois Cent. R. Co. v. United States,*[36] plaintiff alleged that an order of the Commission fixing rates for the shipment of new automobiles was arbitrary and not supported by substantial evidence. The court found that the record disclosed that the Commission had before it substantial evidence upon the question involved and had considered it carefully. In dismissing the complaint the court, at page 322, stated:

> . . . We are not concerned with the weight of the evidence except to ascertain from an examination of the entire record whether it supports the Commission's findings in this respect. After such examination we do not feel at liberty to announce that the finding is not supported by the record as a whole. In *Mississippi Valley Barge Line v. United States,* 292 U.S. 282, 286, 287, 54 S. Ct. 692, 694, 78 L. Ed. 1260, the court said: ". . . The judicial function is exhausted when there is found to be a rational basis for the conclusions approved by the administrative body." We believe that such a rational basis existed.

[35] 327 U.S. 515, 534-6.
[36] 101 F. Supp. 317.

Further, at page 327, in discussing the function of a reviewing court, it was stated:

Our function is well defined. Thus, if an order lies within the scope of the statute, which the Commission is empowered to administer and enforce and is based upon adequate findings which, in turn, are supported by substantial evidence, we may not set it aside or modify it, even though we would have decided otherwise originally and even though it is against the weight of the evidence. *United States v. Illinois Central R. Co.*, 263 U.S. 515, 524, 44 S. Ct. 189, 68 L. Ed. 417. ". . . To consider the weight of the evidence before the Commission, the soundness of the reasoning by which its conclusions were reached, or whether the findings are consistent with those made by it in other cases, is beyond our province" *Virginian Railway Co. v. United States*, 272 U.S. 658, 663, 47 S. Ct. 222, 224, 71 L. Ed. 463.

In *A. B. & C. Motor Transport Co. v. United States*,[37] the court declared:

It was left to the Commission by Congress to find the facts and in the exercise of reasonable judgment to determine whether additional motor service would service public convenience and necessity and if its decision is supported by substantial evidence the finding must stand in the absence of any mistake of law.

See also *General Transp. Co. v. United States*,[38] where the court said:

Since it does not appear that the Commission overstepped any limit expressly placed by Congress upon its discretion, and since its conclusion has ample support in the evidence — in fact the plaintiffs' argument on this point, upon analysis, is only that the Commission erroneously weighed conflicting evidence — we see nothing to warrant further consideration of this point.

In this connection "the court must sustain the Commission if its findings are supported by substantial evidence on the record considered as a whole."[39]

In *Brooks Transp. Co., Inc. v. United States*,[40] a three-judge court, in dismissing a complaint brought to set aside an order of the Commission denying an application for a certificate of public convenience and necessity, posed this question at page 248:

Turning to a consideration of the application as one for an extension of service, it is well settled that the question on review is not whether the court would have made the same findings as the Commission on the record

[37]69 F. Supp. 166, 169.
[38]65 F. Supp. 981, 984. See also *C. E. Hall & Sons v. United States*, 88 F. Supp. 596.
[39]*St. Johnsbury Trucking Co. v. United States*, 99 F. Supp. 977.
[40]108 F. Supp. 244, aff'd 344 U.S. 804. See also *Ayshire Corp. v. United States*, 335 U.S. 573, 592-3.

before it, but is: Was there a rational basis for the finding made by the Commission?

In *Riss & Co., Inc. v. United States*,[41] the court, in acknowledging the distinction between the duties of the Commission and the function of the courts on review of Commission decisions, said at page 483:

> The Commission is the fact-finding body. The court does not make findings of fact, but simply determines whether or not the Commission's findings are supported by substantial evidence. Although the court and the Commission might differ with respect to the weight of evidence, or what the evidence reveals, yet that does not give the court the right to decide whether or not the Commission is mistaken in its findings, if there is substantial evidence upon which to base those findings. In reviewing the evidence there may be instances where our finding would be different from that of the Commission, but we have no authority to substitute our opinion for that of the Commission, any more than an appellate court has the right to substitute its views as to the facts for that of a trial court or jury.

In *Sites Freightlines, Inc. v. United States*,[42] the court said that if the Commission has acted within the scope of its statutory authority; has not arbitrarily or capriciously abused its discretion and has proceeded in accordance with essential requirements of due process; has acted upon adequate findings; and, if in the record considered as a whole there is substantial evidence and a rational basis to support the findings, then the orders of the Commission are entitled to finality and may not be disturbed, set aside or modified by the court. In *Navajo Freight Lines, Inc. v. United States*,[43] the court said that the scope of judicial review is limited, particularly in proceedings involving purchase of motor-carrier operating rights, since by statute the Commission has the responsibility of determining whether a transaction presented under 5(2) (b) is consistent with public interest. Because of its expertise, the Commission is equipped to resolve all factors and reach a conclusion that conforms to the national transportation policy; and where it has not exceeded its statutory limits and its findings are adequate and supported by convincing evidence, they must be sustained.

The scope of judicial review is, as shown above, delineated in the Administrative Procedure Act.[44] In comparing the scope of review of

---

[41]100 F. Supp. 468, aff'd 342 U.S. 937.

[42]158 F. Supp. 909, 912. See also *Burlington-Chicago Cartage, Inc. v. United States*, 178 F. Supp. 857, 862; *Arrow Trucking Co. v. United States*, 181 F. Supp. 775, 777-8.

[43]186 F. Supp. 377, 383.

[44]5 U.S.C. 706.

agency decisions before and after the pasage of the Administrative Procedure Act, it was stated in *Olin Industries v. National Labor Relations Board*,[45] as follows:

> Both the terms of this section, and its legislative history, make it clear that Section 10 is merely declaratory of the existing law of judicial review and that it neither confers jurisdiction on this court above and beyond that which it already has, nor grants to aggrieved parties any right they did not have under the National Labor Relations Act.

Passing upon the judicial review, the Supreme Court said in *Universal Camera Corp. v. Labor Board*:[46]

> . . . The substantiality of evidence must take into account whatever in the record fairly detracts from its weight. This is clearly the significance of the requirement in both statutes that courts consider the whole record. To be sure, the requirement of canvassing, "the whole record" in order to ascertain substantially does not furnish a calculus of value by which a reviewing court can assess the evidence. Nor was it intended to negative the function of the Labor Board as one of those agencies presumably equipped or informed by experience to deal with a specialized field of knowledge, whose findings within that field carry the authority of an expertness which courts do not possess and therefore must respect. Nor does it mean that even as to matters not requiring expertise a court may displace the Board's choice between two fairly conflicting views, even though the court would justifiably have made a different choice had the matter been before it *de novo*. Congress has merely made it clear that a reviewing court is not barred from setting aside a Board decision when it cannot conscientiously find that the evidence supporting that decision is substantial, when viewed in the light that the record in its entirety furnishes, including the body of the evidence opposed to the Board's view.

Courts heeding the Administrative Procedure Act have applied it consistently, and elaborated upon it, stating that the Commission alone is to weigh the evidence, and that a court must sustain the Commission if its findings are supported by "substantial evidence," or if there is found to be a "rational basis" for the conclusions, and its rulings and decisions are found to be in accord with the applicable law.[47] The *State Corporation Commission of Kansas* case stated, l.c. 696:

> Administrative orders entered by the Commission in the exercise of its power *are not to be overturned* on judicial review *unless* they exceed constitutional limits, *are based upon a mistake of law*, are made without

---

[45]72 F. Supp. 225, 228.
[46]340 U.S. 474, 488.
[47]*Yourga v. United States*, 191 F. Supp. 373, 375; *State Corporation Commission of Kansas v. United States*, 184 F. Supp. 691, 696; *Mississippi Valley Barge Line Co. v. United States*, 292 U.S. 282, 286-7; *Rochester Telephone Corp. v. United States*, 307 U.S. 125, 146.

a hearing, *are unsupported by the evidence,* or for some other reason amount to an abuse of power. (Emphasis added).

In *McLean Trucking v. United States,*[48] the Supreme Court in approving an order of the Commission which authorized the consolidation of several motor carriers, said:

> Resolving these considerations is a complex task which requires extensive facilities, expert judgment and considerable knowledge of the transportation industry. Congress left that task to the Commission "to the end that the wisdom and experience of that Commission may be used not only in connection with this form of transportation, but in its coordination of all other forms." 79 Cong. Rec. 12207.

> "The wisdom and experience of that commission," not of the courts, must determine whether the proposed consolidation is "consistent with the public interest." Cf. *Interstate Commerce Commission v. Illinois Central R. Co.,* 215 U.S. 452; *Pennsylvania Co. v. United States,* 236 U.S. 351; *United States v. Chicago Heights Trucking Co.,* 310 U.S. 344; *Purcell v. United States,* 315 U.S. 381. If the Commission did not exceed the statutory limits within which Congress confined its discretion and its findings are adequate and supported by evidence, it is not our function to upset its order.

In *Virginia Stage Lines v. United States,*[49] wherein the court was considering the purcase of operating rights by one motor carrier from another, it was said:

> It would be difficult to conceive of a statute which confers broader authority and greater administrative discretion than Section 5 of the Interstate Commerce Act. Under that section, the Commission may approve any merger, purchase, consolidation, lease or contractual arrangement affecting motor carriers which it finds will be "consistent with the public interest." Moreover, except where rail carriers are involved, transactions within the scope of Section 5 may be approved by the Commission without a hearing. In the instant case, however, a public hearing was held at which the parties exercised the rights given to them to introduce testimony and to examine witnesses.

> With regard to judicial review of the decisions and orders of the Commission, it is well settled that the Court's function is exhausted where there is found to be a rational basis for the conclusions reached by that administrative body. Mississippi Valley Barge Line Co. v. United States, 292 U.S. 282, 54 S. Ct. 692, 78 L. Ed. 1260; *Rochester Telephone Corp. v. United States,* 307 U.S. 125, 59 S. Ct. 754, 83 L. Ed. 1147. As was stated by the Supreme Court in *Alton Railroad Company v. United States,* 315 U.S. 15, 23, 62 S. Ct. 432, 437, 86 L. Ed. 586:

> The weighing of such evidence involves in part a judgment based on the characteristics of the highly specialized transportation service involved.

[48]321 U.S. 67, 87-8.
[49]48 F. Supp. 79, 82.

Thus, as we have said, the function is peculiarly one for the Commission not the courts.

In *O. C. Wiley & Sons v. United States,*[50] the court said:

It has been often recognized that Section 5 confers broader authority and greater administrative discretion than most any other section of the Act and that the legislative history of the recent amendments to this section of the Act show congressional intent to broaden the authority of the Commission. We are, accordingly, of the opinion that the Commission's report and order, approving the transfer upon terms and conditions found to be just and reasonable and consistent with the public interest, should not be set aside.

In *Watson Bros. Transp. Co. v. United States,*[51] the court said that its review of the Commission's action was limited by the Administrative Procedure Act to a determination of whether that action was arbitrary, capricious, an abuse of discretion, or otherwise not in accordance with law; contrary to constitutional rights, power, privilege, or immunity; in excess of statutory jurisdiction, or short of statutory right; without observance of procedure required by law; unsupported by substantial evidence; or so unwarranted by the facts as to be subject to trial de novo; the exercise of the Commission's discretion will not be overturned even though the reviewing court might on the same record have arrived at a different conclusion.

The limited scope of review is especially applicable to rate proceedings. The Supreme Court pointed out in *Mississippi Valley Barge Line v. United States.*[52]

The structure of a rate schedule calls in peculiar measure for the use of that enlightened judgment which the Commission by training and experience is qualified to form. *Florida v. United States. ante* p. 1. It is not the province of a court to absorb this function to itself. *I.C.C. v. Louisville & Nashville R. Co.*, 227 U.S. 88, 100; *Western Paper Makers' Chemical Co. v. United States*, 271 U.S. 268, 271; *Virginian Ry. Co. v. United States*, 272 U.S. 658, 663. The judicial function is exhausted when there is

---

[50]85 F. Supp. 542, 545.

[51]338 U.S. 902.

[52]292 U.S. 286-7. The courts may not exercise an administrative function such as, fixing rates, making joint rates, making divisions, and granting relief from the long-and-short haul clause. *Federal Power Commission v. Pacific Co.*, 307 U.S. 156, 160; *Federal Power Commission v. Idaho Power Companies*, 344 U.S. 17; *Ford Motor Co. v. Labor Board*, 305 U.S. 364, 773-4; *State of New Jersey v. United States*, 168 F. 324, aff'd 359 U.S. 27; *M. P. & St. L. Express, Inc. v. United States*, 165 F. Supp. 677; *Piek v. Chicago N.W.R. Co.*, 94 U.S. 164; *Reagan v. Farmers' Loan & T. Co.*, 154 U.S. 362; *Simpson v. Sheppard (Minnesota Rate Case)*, 230 U.S. 352; *Louisville & N. R. Co. v. Garrett*, 231 U.S. 298; *Loomis v. Lehigh Valley R. Co.*, 240 U.S. 43; *Terminal R. Assn. v. United States*, 232 U.S. 199, 221.

found to be a rational basis for the conclusions approved by the administrative body . . . .

In *Board of Trade v. United States*,[53] the Supreme Court stated:

> The process of rate making is essentially empiric. The stuff of the process is fluid and changing — the resultant of factors that must be valued as well as weighed. Congress has therefore delegated the enforcement of transportation policy to a permanent expert body and has charged it with the duty of being responsive to the dynamic character of transportation problems.

In regard to the issue of reasonableness of rates and undue preference and prejudice, the Supreme Court said in *Virginia Ry. v. United States*:[54]

> The finding of reasonableness, like that of undue prejudice, is a determination of a fact by a tribunal "informed by experience." *Illinois Central R. R. Co. v. Interstate Commerce Commission*, 206 U.S. 441, 454. This court has no concern with the correctness of the Commission's reasoning, with the soundness of its conclusions, or with the alleged inconsistency of findings made in other proceedings before it . . . .

Exhaustion of Administrative Remedies

Exhaustion of administrative remedies is a conditioned precedent to judicial review, as evidenced by numerous authorities. In *Aircraft & Diesel Equipment Co. v. Hirsch*,[55] the Supreme Court said:

> Where the intent of Congress is clear to require administrative determination, either to the exclusion of judicial action or in advance of it, a strong showing is required, both of inadequacy of the prescribed procedure and of impending harm to permit short-circuiting the administrative process. Congress' commands for judicial restraint in this respect are not likely to be disregarded.

To emphasize the necessity of exhausting prescribed administrative remedies the Supreme Court further said:

> Where Congress has clearly commanded that administrative judgment be taken initially or exclusively, the courts have no lawful function to anticipate the administrative decision with their own, whether or not when it has been rendered they may intervene either in presumed accordance with Congress' will or because, for constitutional reasons, its will to exclude them has been exerted in an invalid manner. To do this not only would contravene the will of Congress as a matter of restricting or deferring judicial action, it would nullify the Congressional objection in providing the administrative determination.

[53]314 U.S. 534, 536.
[54]272 U.S. 658, 663.
[55]331 U.S. 752, 772.

Even though the question of the Commission's jurisdiction to so act may be involved, exhaustion of administrative remedies still must be completed previous to judicial review unless the prescribed administrative remedies are insufficient and irreparable injury may occur by delay in following the prescribed procedure. The principle was enunciated in the case of *Macauley v. Waterman S. S. Corp.,*[56] in which the plaintiff alleged that irreparable injury would occur in being forced to exhaust administrative remedies previous to judicial action. The court in commenting upon this allegation said:

> Even if one or all of these things might possibly occur in the future, that possibility does not affect the application of the rule, requiring exhaustion of administrative remedy. The district court had no power to determine in this proceeding and at this time issues that might arise because of these future contingencies. Its judgment dismissing the complaint was correct.

The principle is further emphasized in the case of *Myers v. Bethlehem Corp.,*[57] in which the court said with reference to the contention that to exhaust administrative remedies would subject the plaintiff to irreparable damage:

> This contention is at war with the long settled rule of judicial administration that no one is entitled to judicial relief for a supposed or threatened injury until the prescribed administrative remedy has been exhausted. The rule has been repeatedly acted upon in cases where, as here, the contention is made that the administrative body lacked power over the subject matter. Obviously, the rule requiring exhaustion of administrative remedy cannot be circumvented by asserting that the charge on which the complainant rests is groundless and that the mere holding of the prescribed administrative hearing would result in irreparable damage.

In the case of *Refrigerated Transport, Inc. v. United States,*[58] the court said:

> To put it more bluntly, the Commerce Act does not give an allegedly aggrieved party the right to sue the United States until such administrative remedies as is afforded in the Act shall have been exhausted . . . . The academic rule of law is supported by many decisions and particularly by decisions of the Supreme Court upon other statutes.

In *National Water Carriers Assoc. v. United States,*[59] the court said that since the plaintiffs failed to comply with the statutory condition precedent to judicial review of the Commission's order, there was lack of jurisdiction in the court to annul such order. The court said:

[56]327 U.S. 540.
[57]303 U.S. 41, 50.
[58]101 F. Supp. 95.
[59]126 F. Supp. 87.

If Division 2 was in error in setting aside the . . . order on the record before it, and we do not suggest that it was, the plaintiffs' remedy was to apply for rehearing, reargument or reconsideration of the decision. 49 U.S.C.A. 17(9). They made no such application. Their brief, it is true, asserts "compliance with the statutory requirement" of 17(9). This assertion appears to be based on the contention that their telegram . . . should be deemed a request for the reconsideration of the order . . . as well as of the refusal by the Board of Suspensions to suspend the rates proposed to become effective . . . . We do not think this telegram can reasonably be interpreted as referring to the order . . . . Moreover, if it could be so interpreted, it was filed too late . . . .

A district court in *Michigan P.S.C. v. United States*[60] dismissed for lack of jurisdiction an action by a State regulatory body seeking to restrain the Commission from proceeding further with administrative action with respect to the proposed abandonment of a rail operation which lay within a single State. The plaintiff contended that it had sole jurisdiction over the proposed abandonment. The court held that the Commission had taken only preliminary or procedural steps in the abandonment proceeding and had issued no final reviewable order therein, and that the State body had not exhausted its administrative remedies before the Commission prior to bringing the suit. A court in *Salvatore Territo v. United States*[61] dismissed for lack of jurisdiction a review proceeding by two respondents, named in investigations instituted under Section 204(c) of the Act,[62] to determine whether such respondents were operating as motor common carriers or as private carriers of property by motor vehicle. The plaintiffs sought an injunction to restrain the holding of hearings in the investigation proceedings, alleging that the Commission had no power to investigate their activities. The court held it had no jurisdiction to review the Commission's merely procedural order until final disposition had been made of the investigation proceedings. In the *Camp Bus Lines v. United States*,[63] the court said that until completion of motor carrier application proceedings before the Commission, there was no justification for judicial intervention. The Commission's orders which the court was asked to review were adminis-

---

[60]162 F. Supp. 670.

[61]49 U.S.C. 304(c).

[62]170 F. Supp. 855, appeal dismissed, 358 U.S. 279, rehearing denied, 359 U.S. 963. Mandamus will not lie to direct a public official or agency to perform discretionary acts. *I.C.C. v. United States*, 206 U.S. 32; *Wilbur v. United States*, 281 U.S. 206; *Chicago Great Western Ry. Co. v. I.C.C.*, 294 U.S. 50; *United States v. Helvering*, 301 U.S. 540; *Work v. Rives*, 267 U.S. 175; *Panama Canal Co. v. Grace Line, Inc.*, 356 U.S. 309.

[63]185 F. Supp. 336, 339-40.

trative and procedural, they did not impose an obligation, deny a right, or fix some legal relationship as consummation of administrative process.

Parties Entitled to Challenge Commission Orders

The mere fact that carrier was permitted to intervene before the Commission did not entitle such carrier to institute an independent suit to set aside the Commission's order in the absence of resulting actual or threatened legal injury to it.[64] Owners of trucks leased with drivers were not entitled to attack, as confiscatory, an order of the Commission requiring leasing on minimum number of days on the theory that such owners were not "interested parties," hence not entitled to intervene before the Commission, when no showing was made that any plaintiff or any one in their position attempted to intervene before the Commission and was denied that right.[65]

The Supreme Court said in *American Trucking Assns. v. United States*[66] that under the "person suffering legal wrong . . . or adversely affected or aggrieved" criterion of the Administrative Procedure Act,[67] and the "party in interest" criterion of Section 205(g) of the Interstate Commerce Act,[68] three associations of motor carriers and six motor carriers had standing to maintain their action to set aside order of the Commission granting certain contract-carrier authority. In *National Motor Freight Traffic Associations, Inc. v. United States, supra*, the Supreme Conurt held that a classification or rate making association of motor carriers had standing to sue in the district court to challenge an order of the Commission. The court said:

> The appellants are associations of motor carriers, authorized under 49 U.S.C. 5b, and perform significant functions in the administration of the Interstate Commerce Act, including the representation of member carriers in proceedings before the Commission. Since individual member carriers of appellants will be aggrieved by the Commission's order, and since appellants are proper representatives of the interests of their members, appellants have standing to challenge the validity of the Commission's

[64]*Seatrain Lines, Inc. v. United States*, 152 F. Supp. 619, 622. A party cannot claim a grievance, assuming one exists, which does not belong to it. *Chicago, St. P. & O. Ry. Co. v. United States*, 50 F. Supp. 249, 253-4, aff'd 322 U.S. 1. Cf. *Sprunt & Son v. United States*, 281 U.S. 249; *Edward Hines Trustees v. United States*, 263 U.S. 143; *Dept of Public Works of Washington v. United States*, 55 F. 2d 392.

[65]*Christian v. United States*, 152 F. Supp. 561, 569.

[66]364 U.S. 18. See also *National Motor Freight Association, Inc. v. United States*, 9 L. ed. 2d 709.

[67]5 U.S.C. 702.

[68]49 U.S.C. 305(g).

order in the District Court. See Administrative Procedure Act, 5 U.S.C. § 1009(a); *Federal Communications Com. v. Sanders Bros Radio Station,* 309 U.S. 470, 84 L. ed. 869, 60 S. Ct. 693; *NAACP v. Alabama,* 357 U.S. 449, 459, 2 L. ed. 1488, 1497, 78 S. Ct. 1163.

Shareholders are sharply limited in their ability to challenge orders of the Commission which affect their companies. A minority stockholder may not do so where his interest in the order is one shared by all other investors in the company — i.e., where the "injury feared is the indirect harm which may result to every stockholder from harm to the corporation."[69] The shareholder has standing to use only where the Commission's order threatens him with an independent injury, not common to all securityholders.[70]

The decision in *New York Central Securities Corp. v. United States,*[71] well illustrates the applicable principles. There, a minority stockholder of three carriers, New York Central, Big Four and Michigan Central, sought to challenge a Commission order which, among other things, approved a lease to New York Central of the properties of its partly-owned subsidiaries, Big Four and Michigan Central. The leasing arrangements provided that the minority stockholders of the lessor corporations (Big Four and Michigan Central) were to be paid "dividend rentals" by New York Central as lessee. No rental payments were to be made to New York Central as majority stockholder of the lessors. The district court held that the plaintiff in its capacity as a minority stockholder of the lessee (New York Central) had no standing to challenge the order, since any injury to plaintiff in that capacity was a derivative injury suffered by the corporation and common to all of its stockholders. The plaintiff was permitted to sue, however, in its capacity as a minority stockholder of the lessor corporations, because the provision for the payment of dividend rentals to the minority, as a special class, gave them "a new interest of a substantially independent character" which was not shared by the other stockholders.[72]

Due Process

Initially, it should be pointed out that a claim of constitutional rights cannot be raised as a subterfuge where the actual question involved is merely whether regulatory authority has been validly exercised.[73]

---

[69]*Pittsburgh & West Va. Ry. Co. v. United States,* 281 U.S. 479, 487.
[70]*Alleghany Corporation v. Breswick & Co.,* 353 U.S. 151.
[71]54 F. 2d 122, aff'd 287 U.S. 12.
[72]54 F. 2d, at p. 126.
[73]*Baltimore & Ohio R. Co. v. United States,* 305 U.S. 507, 526; *Trans-American Freight Lines v. United States,* 51 F. Supp. 405, 409.

The Supreme Court has pointed out many times that the exercise of the federal commerce power is not dependent on the maintenance of the economic status quo. The Fifth Amendment is no protection against a congressional scheme of business regulation otherwise valid merely because it disturbs the profitability of methods of the interstate concerns affected.[74]

In *American Trucking Associations, Inc. v. United States,*[75] the Supreme Court said:

> . . . They attack an order which is valid even if its effect is to drive some operators out of business. As we have indicated, the rule-making power is rooted in and supplements Congress' regulatory scheme, which in turn derives from the commerce power. The fact that the value of some going concerns may be affected, therefore, does not support a claim under the Fifth Amendment, if the rules and the Act be related, as we have said they are, to evils in commerce which the federal power may reach. This being the case appellants had not constitutional claim in support of which they are entitled to introduce evidence *de novo*, and the court did not err in sustaining the objection thereto.

In *Capital Transit Co. v. United States,*[76] the court stated:

> . . . And any gaps in Capital Transit's case are chargeable to it and not to the Joint Board or to the Commission. The latter bodies, after all, are basically concerned with protecting the public interest. They must, of course, consider and give due weight to the position of existing carriers serving the public along the routes in question. *I.C.C. v. Parker*, 326 U.S. 60, 65 S. Ct. 1490, 89 L. Ed. 2051; *American Trucking Assn's v. United States*, 326 U.S. 77, 65 S. Ct. 1499, 89 L. Ed. 2065. But under the Motor Carrier Act, 49 U.S.C.A., Sec. 301 et. seq., there is no vested right in the public highways or in any transportation business conducted on those highways.

In *Watson Bros. Transportation Co., Inc. v. United States,*[77] the court said:

> In the proceedings before the Commission the basic facts were definitely established. The parties had received notice; were given the opportunity to be heard and to present evidence; to know and contest the claims of the opposing parties; and to submit argument. The plaintiff was accorded all the requirements of due process.

---

[74]*Labor Board v. Jones & Laughlin S. Corp.*, 301 U.S. 1, 43-45; *Currin v. Wallace*, 306 U.S. 1, 13-15; *United States v. Rock Royal Co-operative, Inc.* 307 U.S. 533, 572-573; *North American Co. v. Securities & Exchange Comm'n.* 327 U.S. 686, 707-10; *American Power & Light Co. v. Securities & Exchange Comm'n.* 329 U.S. 90, 106-108.

[75]344 U.S. 208, 322.

[76]97 F. Supp. 614, 620.

[77]180 F. Supp. 732, 738. See also *New England Divisions Case*, 261 U.S. 184, 200.

Establishing the Validity of Agency
Rules as Promptly as Possible

Insofar as administrative agency rules are concerned it is generally deemed desirable that the validity of such rules be established as promptly as possible to permit either implementation or revision.[78]

Change or Modification of Order

Upon reversal of an administrative order, the courts may not usurp the administrative function and rewrite the order; the cause must be remanded to the administrative body for further proceedings consistent with the court decision.[79]

Presumption of Regularity That Attends and Supports
Acts of Administrative Body

In *Peninsula Corp. v. United States*,[80] where the allegation was made that the Commission was improperly influenced in performing its administrative functions, the court stated:

> We find nothing in the record, nor was anything elicited at the hearing before us other than mere assertion, to support either the conclusion or the inference that the Commission was unduly influenced in the performance of its administrative function and in taking the action it did. The allegations to the contrary in the complaint are mere conclusions, unsupported by any facts pleaded and are, therefore, insufficient. *Isbrandtsen-Moller Co., Inc. v. United States*, 300 U.S. 139, 145, 57 S. Ct. 407, 81 I. Ed. 562.

> Again, and for reasons as cogent as they are obvious, there is a presumption of regularity that attends and support "the official acts of public officers, and, in the absence of clear evidence to the contrary, courts will

---

[78]These include the following: *United States v. Storer Broadcasting Co.*, 351 U.S. 192, where the Supreme Court upheld review of a rule which prescribed limits applicable in future proceedings for licenses for television broadcast stations; *FPC v. Texaco, Inc.*, 417 U.S. 380, reviewing a rule providing that large producers could be held responsible in the future for unreasonably high prices to consumers with respect to gas purchased from small producers; *Industrial Union Dept., AFL-CIO v. Hodgson*, 499 F. 2d 467, involving standards for exposure to asbestos dust under the Occupational Safety and Health Act; *Kennecott Copper Corp. v. EPA*, 462 F. 2d 846, challenging secondary air quality standards; and *City of Chicago, Illinois v. FPC*, 458 F. 2d 731, involving a challenge to a rule governing valuing of gas for ratemaking purposes despite the availability of subsequent individualized inquiry. See 28 U.S.C. 2344.

[79]*Burlington-Chicago Cartage, Inc. v. United States*, 178 F. Supp. 857, 860.

[80]60 F. Supp. 174, 180.

presume that they have properly discharged their official duties." *United States v. Chemical Foundation, Inc.*, 272 U.S. 1, 14, 15, 47 S. Ct. 1, 6, 71 L. Ed. 131.

In *Salzberg v. United States*,[81] the court stated:

The exercise of authority and discretion of the I.C.C. to condition its approval of applications upon such reasonable and just terms as it deems necessary to protect the public interest is subject to review by the courts. . . . This review, however, as the Supreme Court has stated "is limited to ascertaining whether there is warrant in the law and the facts for what the Commission has done. Unless in some specific respect there has been prejudicial departure from requirements of the law or abuse of the Commission's discretion, the reviewing court is without authority to intervene." (Citing United States v. Pierce Auto Freight Lines, Inc., 327 U.S. 515, 536.)

As the Supreme Court stated in *Interstate Commerce Commission v. Jersey City*,[82] "the Commission's order does not become suspect by reason of the fact that it is challenged. It is the product of expert judgment which carries a presumption of validity." And as a lower court said in *Southern Ry. Co. v. United States*,[83] there is a presumption that the Commission has properly performed its official duties, and this presumption supports its acts in absence of clear evidence to the contrary. The burden of proof to establish the invalidity of the order is on the party urging improper action.[84]

The Record Made before the Commission Should Be Filed with the Court

It is fundamental, of course, that the court have before it the record made before the Commission before it can enter upon a review to determine if the findings made by the Commission are supported by substantial evidence. It is well established that lacking such record, or portions thereof containing the evidence upon which any of the issues turn, the court must accept the findings made by the Commission. In *Mississippi Valley Barge Line v. United States*,[85] the court stated:

[81]176 F. Supp., at p. 869.

[82]322 U.S. 503, 512.

[83]186 F. Supp. 29, 40. See also *United States v. Chemical Foundation*, 272 U.S. 1, 14-15; *Carolina Scenic Coach Lines v. United States*, 59 F. Supp. 336, 337-8, aff'd 326 U.S. 680.

[84]*Watson Bros. Transp. Co. v. United States*, 59 F. Supp. 762, 769.

[85]292 U.S. 282, 286-7. See also *Lubetich v. United States*, 315 U.S. 57; *United States v. Northern Pacific R. Co.*, 288 U.S. 490, 499; *Falwell v. United States*, 69 F. Supp. 71, 76, aff'd 330 U.S. 807.

The settled rule is that the findings of the Commission may not be assailed upon appeal in the absence of the evidence upon which they were made.

In *Louisiana & P. B. Ry. Co. v. United States,*[86] the court said:

> In a suit to enjoin the enforcement of and annul, an order of the Interstate Commerce Commission, it could not be claimed that the order was unsupported by evidence, where only a part of the evidence taken before the Commission was introduced.

It is also well to re-emphasize here even though discussed heretofore that once it is ascertained that the findings of the Commission have substantial support in the evidence and provide a rational basis for the conclusion reached, they are unassailable in a proceeding of this type;[87] the weight and value of the evidence and the inferences to be drawn therefrom are matters for the Commission to determine;[88] and the court "has no concern with the correctness of the Commission's reasoning, with the soundness of its conclusions, or with the alleged inconsistency with findings made in other proceedings before it."[89] As was said in *Lang Transportation Corp. v. United States:*[90]

> They (the courts) cannot, under the guise of exerting judicial powers, usurp merely administrative functions by setting aside a lawful administrative order of the Interstate Commerce Commission upon their own conception of whether the administrative power has been wisely exercised. *Interstate Commerce Commission v. Illinois C. R. Co.,* 1910, 215 U.S. 452 . . . stated by the Court in *Rochester Telephone Co. v. United States:*[91]

> Having found that the record permitted the Commission to draw the conclusion it did, a court travels beyond its province to express concurrence therewith as an original question. "The judicial function is exhausted when there is found to be a rational basis for the conclusions approved by the Administrative body." *Mississippi Barge Line Co. v. United States,* 292 U.S. 282, 286-287; *Swayne & Hoyt, Ltd. v. United States,* 300 U.S. 297, 303, et seq.

---

[86]257 U.S. 114.

[87]*Interstate Commerce Commission v. Union Pacific Railroad Co.,* 222 U.S. 541, 547; *Virginian R. Co. v. United States,* 272 U.S. 658, 665; *Mississippi Valley Barge Line v. United States,* 292 U.S. 282, 286, 287; *Rochester Tel. Corp. v. United States,* 307 U.S. 125, 146; *United States v. Carolina Freight Carriers Corp.,* 315 U.S. 475, 482, 490.

[88]*United States v. Carolina Freight Carriers Corp.,* 315 U.S. 475, 482, 490; *United States v. Pan American Petroleum Corp.,* 304 U.S. 156, 158; *Merchants' Warehouse Co. v. United States,* 283 U.S. 501, 508.

[89]*Virginian R. Co. v. United States,* 272 U.S. 658, 665; *Interstate Commerce Commission v. Union Pacific Railroad Co.,* 222 U.S. 541, 547.

[90]75 F. Supp. 915, 926.

[91]307 U.S. 125, 146.

It is noted that review proceedings must be confined to the record made in the Commission proceedings. Evidence *de hors* the record is inadmissible.[92] Objections not presented to the Commission may not be raised for the first time on review.[93]

Trial De Novo

The Senate Judiciary Committee's report[94] on the bill leading to the enactment of the Administrative Procedure Act explains the purpose of Section 706[95] in the following manner:

The sixth category, respecting the establishment of facts upon trial de novo, would require the reviewing court to determine the facts in any case of adjudication not subject to Sections 7 and 8 or otherwise required to be reviewed exclusively on the record of a statutory agency hearing. It would also require the judicial determination of facts in connection with rule making or any other conceivable form of agency action to the extent that the facts were relevant to any pertinent issues of law presented. For example, statutes providing for "reparation order," in which agencies determine damages and award money judgments, usually state that the money orders issued are merely prima facie evidence in the courts and the parties subject to them are permitted to introduce evidence in the court in which the enforcement action is pending. In other cases, the test is whether there has been a statutory administrative hearing of the facts which is adequate and exclusive for purposes of review. Thus, adjudications such as tax assessments not made upon a statutory administrative hearing and record may involve a trial of the facts in the Tax Court or the United States district courts. Where administrative agencies deny parties money to which they are entitled by a statute or rule, the claimants may sue as for any other claim and in so doing try out the facts in the Court of Claims or United States district courts as the case may be. Where a court enforces or applies an administrative rule, the party to whom it is applied may for example offer evidence and show the facts upon which he bases a contention that he is not subject to the terms of the rule. Where for example an affected party claims in a judicial proceeding that a rule issued without an administrative hearing (and not required to be issued after such hearing) is invalid for some relevant reason of law, he may show the facts upon which he predicates such invalidity. In short, where a rule or order is not required by statute to be made after opportunity for agency hearing and to be reviewed solely upon the record thereof, the facts pertinent to any relevant question of law must be tried and determined de novo by the reviewing court respecting either the validity or application of such rule or

---

[92]*American Trucking Assns. v. United States,* 344 U.S. 298, 320-23; *Tagg Bros. v. United States,* 280 U.S. 420, 423-24.

[93]*United States v. Tucker Truck Lines,* 344 U.S. 33, 37; *United States v. Hancock Truck Lines,* 324 U.S. 774, 779.

[94]Sen. Doc. No. 248, 79th Cong., 2d sess. (1946), pp. 279-280.

[95]5 U.S.C. 706.

orders — because facts necessary to the determination of any relevant question of law must be determined of record somewhere and, if Congress has not provided that an agency shall do so, then the record must be made in Court.

Thus, finding of fact of an administrative agency which go to the jurisdiction of the agency and which affect constitutional rights are not conclusive and may be tried by the courts *de novo*. Where only statutory rights are involved, the findings of fact are final if substantially supported by evidence before the agency.[96] In *Watson Bros. Transp. Co. v. United States*,[97] wherein the carrier sought to set aside an order of the Commission denying rights under the "grandfather" clause, the court stated at page 768:

> In a case of this character the inquiry of the court is limited. Controlling judicial decisions have defined its boundaries, beyond which this court must not venture. This proceeding invites neither a trial de novo of the plaintiff's original demand nor a judicial review after the manner of an equity appeal of the Commission's determination. In the exercise of the jurisdiction committed to them . . . "the courts will not review determinations of the Commission made within the scope of its powers or substitute their judgment for its findings and conclusions."

In *Luckenbach S. S. Co. Inc. v. Lowe*,[98] plaintiff sought to set aside an award of the deputy commissioner of the U. S. Employees Compensation Commission, and requested a trial de novo on the issues of jurisdiction, i.e., the place of injury and whether there was a master-servant relationship. The court dismissed the complaint stating (p. 919):

> It appears that the evidence upon the so-called questions of jurisdictional fact has been fully and completely presented before the Deputy Commissioner and the plaintiff does not allege that he has new or different evidence to present to the court; nor does the Plaintiff advance any other valid reason why there should be a new record. On the contrary, he merely claims a trial de novo as of right. This court is unwilling to hear de novo the same testimony already offered before the Deputy Commissioner. An examination of the record reveals that there is adequate support for all of the Deputy Commissioner's finding, and his order is in accordance with the law.

In considering an order of the Secretary of Agriculture under the Packers & Stockyards Act, the Supreme Court in *Tagg Bros. v. United States*[99] stated:

---

[96]*Cox v. United States*, 157 F. 2d 787, aff'd 322 U.S. 442; *South Chicago Co. v. Bassett*, 309 U.S. 251; *St. Joseph Stockyards Co. v. United States*, 298 U.S. 38.
[97]59 F. Supp. 762.
[98]96 F. Supp. 918.
[99]280 U.S. 420, 443.

The validity of an order of the Secretary, like that of an order of the Interstate Commerce Commission, must be determined under the record of the proceedings before him, — save as there may be an exception of issues presenting claims of constitutional right, a matter which need not be considered or decided now . . . . On all other issues his findings must be accepted by the court as conclusive, if the evidence before him was legally sufficient to sustain them and there was no irregularity in the proceeding. To allow his findings to be attacked or supported in court by new evidence would substitute the court for the administrative tribunal as the rate making body.

Harmless Error

Section 706 of the Administrative Procedure Act[100] provides that "In making the foregoing determination, the court shall review the whole record or such parts of it cited by a party and due account shall be taken of the rule of prejudicial error." This provision sets forth the "harmless error" rule applied by the courts in the review of lower court decisions namely that errors which have no substantial bearing on the ultimate rights of the parties will be disregarded.[101] The provision which requires the courts to take due account of the rule of prejudicial error, thus means that unless an error is deemed prejudicial the action of an administrative agency should not be set aside merely because a harmless error was committed by it.[102]

In the *Market Street* case, the Supreme Court said (pp. 561-2), that "due process deals with matters of substance and is not to be trivialized by formal objections that have no substantial bearing on the ultimate rights of the parties."

In *United States v. Watkins*,[103] the district court said (p. 225):

> . . . The court understands this provision [5 U.S.C. 1009(e)] to mean that unless an error is deemed prejudicial, the action of the administrative agency should not be set aside merely because an error was committed by it.

In *Canadian Pacific Railway Co. v. United States*,[104] the court dismissed the complaint attacking an order of the Commission because of alleged procedural defects, stating:

[100]5 U.S.C. 706.

[101]*Market Street Ry. v. Commission*, 324 U.S. 548, 561-2.

[102]*United States v. Watkins*, 73 F. Supp. 216, 219, 225; *ABC Freight Forwarding Corp. v. United States*, 169 F. Supp. 403, 409; *Columbia Transportation Co. v. United States*, 167 F. Supp. 5, 11; *Yale Transportation Co. v. United States*, 185 F. Supp. 96, 107; and *Sisto v. CAB*, 179 F. 2d 47, 51.

[103]73 F. Supp. 216, reversed on other grounds, 164 F. 2d 457.

[104]158 F. Supp. 248, 256.

The due process clause of the Fifth Amendment protects substantial rights of litigants, and it does not require any particular or technical procedures. *Inland Empire Dist. Council, etc. v. Millis,* 1945, 325 U.S. 697, 710, 65 S. Ct. 136, 89 L. Ed. 1877; *Morgan v. United States,* 1936, 298 U.S. 468, 481, 56 S. Ct. 906, 80 L. Ed. 1288. The Morgan case makes it clear that due process is satisfied when a party receives notice and is given opportunity to be heard and to present evidence and to know and contest the claims of the opposing party and to submit an argument.

Conclusions of Law

Conclusions of law by the Commission, while entitled to consideration by the courts, do not have the same finality as the Commission's findings of fact.[105]

Findings of Fact

Section 14(1) of the Act[106] does not require the Commission to make "formal and precise findings" except in actions to enforce its order awarding damages. All that is necessary is that basic or quasi-jurisdictional findings are made. The Supreme Court in *Alabama Great Southern R. Co. v. United States*[107] had occasion to discuss the adequacy of the findings of the Commission. At pp. 227-228, the Supreme Court said:

> As to the contention of appellants that the Commission's order is not supported by essential findings of fact, Section 14(1) of the Interstate Commerce Act, 49 U.S.C. 14(1), does not require the Commission to make detailed findings of fact except in a case where damages are awarded. *Manufacturers R. Co. v. United States,* 246 U.S. 457, 477, 489, 490, 62 L. Ed. 831, 846-848, 38 S. Ct. 383. The statute requires the Commission only to file a written report, stating its conclusions, together with its decision and order. This the Commission did, and the essential basis of its judgment is sufficiently disclosed in its report. Of course, Section 14(1) does not relieve the Commission of the duty to make the "basic" or "quasi-jurisdictional" findings essential to the statutory validity of an order. *Florida v. United States,* 282 U.S. 194, 215, 75 L. Ed. 291, 304, 51 S. Ct. 119; *United States v. Baltimore & O. R. Co.,* 293 U.S. 454, 464, 465, 79 L. Ed.

[105]*Chicago M., St. P. & P. R. Co. v. Aloquette Peat Products,* 253 F. 2d, 449, 454 (Citing *Levinson v. Spector Motor Co.,* 330 U.S. 649).

[106]49 U.S.C. 14(1); comparable provisions — Sections 204(d), 316(c), and 417(c). See *Watson Bros. Transp. Co. v. United States,* 59 F. Supp. 762, 777.

[107]340 U.S. 216, 227-8. See also *Yonkers v. United States,* 320 U.S. 685, 689. 694-5; *United States v. Louisiana,* 290 U.S. 70, 76, 78-90; *Manufacturers Ry. Co. v. United States,* 246 U.S. 457, 489-90; *Cantlay & Tanzola, Inc. v. United States,* 115 F. Supp. 72; *Illinois Central R. Co. v. United States,* 101 F. Supp. 317, 322; *United States v. Pierce Auto Freight Lines,* 327 U.S. 515, 531-2; *Minneapolis & St. Louis Ry. v. United States,* 361 U.S. 173, 193-4.

587, 594, 595, 55 S. Ct. 268. And the basic findings essential to the validity of a given order will vary with the statutory authority invoked and the context of the situation presented. (citing cases). Here the Commission found, in conformity to the statute invoked, supra, note 2, that the differentials prescribed are "justified as reasonable" and "necessary and desirable in the public interest." And "the report, read as a whole, sufficiently expresses the conclusion of the Commission based upon supporting data . . . ." *United States v. Louisiana*, 290 U.S. 70, 80, 78 L. Ed. 181, 188, 54 S. Ct. 28. Enough has been "put on record to enable us to perform the limited task which is ours." *Eastern-Central Motor Carriers Assoc. v. United States*, 321 U.S. 194, 212, 88 L. Ed. 668, 680, 64 S. Ct. 499.

When the Commission's order is subject to judicial review, the accompanying report required by Section 14(1) must contain "basic" or "quasi-jurisdictional" findings responsive to the statutory provision under which the order is made. In turn those findings must be supported by adequate subordinate findings of fact. Looking to substance the court does not require that findings be set forth in any particular form; but it does require that they be stated clearly and with sufficient precision to enable the court charged with the duty of adjudicating the validity of the order to determine the meaning with reasonable certainty.[108]

A full discussion of the adequacy of findings in a Commission report is contained in *Chicago, B. & O. R. Co. v. United States*[109] where the court said:

> The principal problems with which we are confronted are whether the order of the Commission is supported by an adequate finding in respect to the basic or quasi-jurisdictional fact upon which the expercise of its statutory power depends and, if so, whether or not such essential finding rests upon a rational basis and is supported by substantial evidence of record.
>
> In *United States v. B & O. R. Co.*, 293 U.S. 454, 464, 55 S. Ct. 268, 79 L. Ed. 587, after pointing out the single primary question of fact upon which a finding by the Commission was essential to the exercise of its statutory power, the court commented upon the distinction between findings of fact which are indispensable and others which are not essential and after referring to *State of Florida v. United States*, 282 U.S. 194, 51 S. Ct. 119, 75 L. Ed. 291, said: "In the Florida case the legal distinction was pointed out between what may be termed quasi-jurisdictional findings, there held to be indispensable, and the 'complete statement of the grounds of the Commission's determination' which was declared in *Beaumont, S. L. & W. Ry. Co. v. United States*, 282 U.S. 74, 86, 51 S. Ct. 1, 75 L. Ed. 221, to be desirable for a proper consideration of the case in the courts. The lack of such a complete statement, while always regrettable, because un-

[108]*United States v. Chicago, M. St. P. & P. R. Co.*, 294 U.S. 499, 505.
[109]60 F. Supp. 580, 583. See also *Beaumont, Sour Lake & W. Ry. Co. v. United States*, 282 U.S. 74.

necessarily increasing the labor of the reviewing court (compare *Virginian Ry. v. United States*, 272 U.S. 658, 675, 47 S. Ct. 222, 71 L. Ed. 463), is not fatal to the validity of the order. It is true that formal and precise findings are not required, under Section 14(1) of the Interstate Commerce Act . . . which declares that the report 'shall state the conclusions of the Commission together with its decision.' . . . That provision relieves the Commission from making comprehensive findings of fact . . . . But Section 14(1) does not remove necessity of making, where orders are subject to judicial review, quasi-jurisdictional findings essential to their constitutional or statutory validity." . . .

. . . It appears that a finding of the ultimate basic fact is all that is indispensable to the Commission's exercise of the statutory power invoked in this proceeding. As a prerequisite to the validity of its order, the Commission is not compelled to report special findings as to the underlying or subordinate facts . . . .

Agency action taken with fair exposition of the grounds supporting the action is not immune to judicial scrutiny, but when the Commission's report fairly and understandably sets forth the basis of its conclusions and the reasoning upon which it proceeded, minor deficiencies in form should not invalidate its order. Thus where there is no room for serious doubt as to basis upon which the Commission acted or that its conclusions were so lacking in rationality as to warrant judicial interference, injunctive relief sought must be denied.[110] It is not the function of the court to reverse the Commission for minor errors nor is it authorized to reject the Commission's findings even though, if the original finders of fact, the court might have reached a different conclusion on the evidence.[111] In *Newtex S. S. Corp. v. United States*,[112] the court said:

> In examining the report we bear in mind that the Commission is not required to make formal or detailed findings of fact. It has not done so; on the contrary, its findings are quite informally incorporated in a discussion of a technical transportation problem, and commingled with factual summary, statement of issue and exposition and evaluation of conflicting evidence. A piece-meal, hypercritical reading to extract the requisite findings, while it can be done, may lead to the dangerous possibility of distorting the meaning otherwise conveyed by works not divorced from the significance lent by context . . . . It is not meant, however, that findings may be undiscernible, vague or nonexistent, abdicating their function to some generalized impression said to be conveyed by the whole report. The question is whether "the essential basis of (the Commission's) judg-

---

[110]*Southern Ry. Co. v. United States*, 180 F. Supp. 189, 195.

[111]*Sites Freightlines, Inc., v. United States*, 158 F. Supp. 909, 912.

[112]107 F. Supp. 388, aff'd 344 U.S. 901. See *Beard-Laney, Inc. v. United States*, 83 F. Supp. 27, 31, aff'd 338 U.S. 803, where the court said that findings of the Commission may not be ignored because they were made in the form of a narrative order rather than in separately numbered paragraphs.

ment is sufficiently disclosed in its report" and whether "the report, read as a whole, sufficiently expressed the conclusion of the Commission, based upon supporting data . . . . "*Alabama Great Southern R. Co. v. United States*, 340 U.S. 216, 228, 71 S. Ct. 264, 272, 95 L. Ed. 225. Reading the report as a whole, we think that the essential findings clearly appear.

On the question of the findings required to support a Commission order, the law was stated as follows in *Inland Navigation Co. v. United States*.[113]

> The Commission is not required to make formal or detailed findings of fact. The Interstate Commerce Act provides that the Commission shall make a report in writing, which shall state its "conclusions" and "its decision, order, or requirement in the premises." The Act does not direct that findings of fact be made except where damages are awarded 49 U.S.C.A. Sec. 14(1). All that is required of the Commission in a case such as the present one, wher damages are not involved, is that its report, in writing, contain a statement of quasi-jurisdictional or basic findings, sufficient to enable a reviewing Court to determine whether the statutory standards, prescribed by Congress, and essential to the validity of the Commission's order, have been applied. *United States v. Baltimore & Ohio Railroad Co.*, 293 U.S. 454, 463, 464, 465, 55 S. Ct. 268, 79 L. Ed. 587; *United States v. Carolina Freight Carriers Corp.*, 315 U.S. 475, 488, 489, 62 S. Ct. 722, 86 L. Ed. 971.

The orders of the Commission not supported by proper findings cannot be sustained was held by the Supreme Court in *Florida v. United States*,[114] where it said that in the absence of such findings, "we are not called upon to examine the evidence in order to resolve opposing contentions as to what it shows or to spell out and state such conclusions of fact at it may permit." A finding without evidence is arbitrary and baseless and is beyond the power of the Commission.[115]

The Administrative Procedure Act,[116] does not require detailed findings of every subsidiary evidentiary fact. So long as the agency makes clear the factual basis upon which it has proceeded, there can be no ground for complaint.[117] In *County Board of Arlington County, Va. v. United States*,[118] certain exceptions were filed by the county board to

---

[113]76 F. Supp. 567, 571.

[114]282 U.S. 194, 215. See also *United States v. Chicago, Milwaukee, St. Paul & Pacific R. Co.* 294 U.S. 499.

[115]*Interstate Commerce Commission v. Louisville & Nashville R. Co.*, 227 U.S. 88; *United States v. Abilene & Southern Ry.*, 265 U.S. 274, 288.

[116]5 U.S.C. 557(c).

[117]*Capital Transit Co. v. United States*, 97 F. Supp. 614, 621; *Norfolk Southern Bus Corp. v. United States*, 96 F. Supp. 756, 759-60, aff'd 340 U.S. 802; *Meeker v. Lehigh Valley R. Co.*, 236 U.S. 412, 427.

[118]101 F. Supp. 328.

the report of the hearing officer. With reference to the exceptions filed in that case, division 2 said in its report that requested findings and exceptions not discussed in the report or reflected in the findings or conclusions had been given consideration and found not justified. In denying the county board's petition for reconsideration of the report of Division 2, the Commission stated that "the evidence of record adequately supports the findings of Division 2." This was deemed sufficient by the court and it sustained the action of the Commission, stating at page 329:

> Although the reasons for these rulings are thus unequivocably stated, the County Board insists that Division 2, as well as the Commission, failed to comply with Section 8 of the Administrative Procedure Act, by not adding findings and conclusions to support its action in refusing requested findings and (by) its actions in overruling exceptions and refusing reconsideration. The contention is obviously meritless.

Similarly in *National Labor Rel. Bd. v. State Center Wrhse. & C.S. Co.*[119] a protest was made that the Board did not observe the requirements of the Administrative Procedure Act by failing to make a ruling or finding on each exception of the respondent to the officer's intermediate report. The court ruled that the Board's decision and order, which, save for certain specified particulars, adopted the findings and conclusions of the officer, unmistakably informed respondent of its ruling on exceptions, and that further particularity was not required. In overruling a contention to the same effect, the court in *Carolina Scenic Coach Lines v. United States*[120] made the following statement:

> . . . There is nothing before us upon which we would be justified in saying that in denying the rehearing the Commission did not give full consideration to all these matters; and, for aught that appears, its denial of the rehearing may well have been based upon the view that, assuming the matters urged in the petition to be true, they could not affect its decision. To one who has denied many petitions for rehearing and seldom given a reason therefor, it comes as a matter of mild surprise that anyone should think it incumbent on a court or commission to give reasons for denying a petition merely because a party urges grounds that he claims to have discovered recently. Orders of the Commission are presumed to be valid. *Baltimore & O. R. Co. v. United States*, 298 U.S. 349, 56 S. Ct. 797, 80 L. Ed. 1209. It was proper for it to deny the petition for rehearing, if of opinion that the fact alleged as ground for rehearing would not, if true, cause a change of decision. We certainly cannot say that the fact relied on by Scenic would require the Commission to change its decision;

---

[119]193 F. 2d 156.
[120]59 F. Supp. 336, 337, aff'd 326 U.S. 680.

and, this being true, we cannot say that there was any abuse of discretion in denying the rehearing.

Moreover, the Commission is not compelled to annotate to each required finding the evidence supporting it.[121] It was stated in *Chicago & E.I.R. Co. v. United States*[122] that while the Commission is not required to make detailed findings of facts as required of a trial court "it is not relieved of the duty to make basic or quasi-jurisdictional findings essential to the validity of the order." Additionally it was stated in *Securities & Exchange Commission v. Chenery Corporation*[123] "the grounds upon which an administrative order must be judged are those upon which the record discloses that its action was based." Further, l.c. 95, it is stated: "We merely hold that an administrative order cannot be upheld unless the grounds upon which the agency acted in exercising its powers were those upon which its action can be sustained."

In *Baltimore & Ohio R. Co. v. United States*[124] the court stated:

> The purpose of findings in such cases is to enable the courts to discharge their proper functions, which is to make sure that the Commission in the discharge of its highly specialized and technical duties, has followed the statute . . . .

In *Inter-City Transportation Co. v. United States,*[125] the court said:

> On that comprehensive report, as a matter of common justice to the Commission, we must hold that its decision makes sense. . . . While another fact finding tribunal might possibly arrive at a different conclusion from the facts, the Commission's decision is at least understandable.

In *Southern Ry. Co. v. United States,*[126] the court said that although it may not essay the role of fact finder, it is its duty to canvass the whole record in determining whether there is a rational basis for the Commission's ultimate conclusions.

Failure to Follow the Recommendations of the Hearing Officer and Disagreement with Prior Decision

The fact that the Commission did not follow the recommendation of its hearing officer does not make its decision suspect. In *Shein's Express*

---

[121]*United States v. Pierce Auto Freight Lines, Inc.* 327 U.S. 515, 529; *Michigan Motor Freight Lines, Inc. v. United States,* 113 F. Supp. 812.
[122]107 F. Supp. 118, 124.
[123]318 U.S. 80, 87.
[124]22 F. Supp. 533, 536.
[125]89 F. Supp. 441.
[126]186 F. Supp. 29, 36.

v. United States,[127] where the Commission had disagreed not only with its subordinate officer but with its own prior decision, the court said:

> Plaintiff argues that the Commission having reported favorably on the application, upon the evidence before it and the examiner, cannot upon reconsideration reverse its position and deny the application without any new evidence. We hold this argument to be without merit.

> The very nature of our American practice has been that an aggrieved party may always have opportunity to say, "You make a mistake." If upon deeper research, fuller reflection and consideration the judicial or quasi-judicial body would see a mistake but persist in it, this would amount to mere obstinacy or stubbornness and foster the highest form of injustice.

This view was expressed by Chief Justice Parker of the Fourth Circuit in the matter of *Beard-Laney, Inc. v. United States,* 83 F. Supp. 27, at page 33 where he said:

> "The rules to be applied in reviewing the Order of the Commission are not different because that Order resulted from a reversal of a prior decision of the hearing division upon a petition for rehearing. The fact that a rehearing was granted shows that the questions involved were carefully considered and the ultimate decision of the division which received the approval of the Commission was the final and definitive action of the Commission which is what we are authorized to review; and it is to be reviewed in the same way and under the same limitations as other reviewable orders. We may not substitute our judgment for that of the Commission because upon a rehearing and fuller consideration of the facts it has arrived at a different conclusion from that which its hearing division had first expressed."

As was also said in *Board of Trade of Kansas City v. United States:*[128]

> That the Commission itself was of divided mind in the successive stages of this controversy emphasizes that the problem is enmeshed in difficult judgments of economic and transportation policy. Neither rule of thumb, nor formula, nor general principles provide a ready answer. We certainly have neither technical competence nor legal authority to pronounce upon the wisdom of the course taken by the Commission. It is not for us to tinker with so sensitive an organism as the grain rate structure, only a minor phase of which is caught in the record before us.

In *Hall & Sons v. United States,*[129] a case in which the Commission disagreed with the recommendation of its hearing officer, the court said:

> . . . The Commission of course was not bound by the examiner's finding, and was not obliged to accept the examiner's recommendation. (Citing *Federal Radio Commission v. Nelson Brothers Bond & Mortgage Co.,* 289 U.S. 266.)

[127]102 F. Supp. 320, 323.
[128]314 U.S. 534, 548.
[129]88 F. Supp. 596, 598.

The courts have many times held that the findings of the Commission may not be attacked because they are inconsistent with findings made in other cases.[130]

The Weight to Be Accorded Evidence Is within the Discretionary Power of the Commission

The weight to be accorded the evidence offered and the inference to be drawn therefrom are within the province of the Commission to decide.[131] The hearing of evidence is an exclusive function of the Commission. It may disbelieve or disregard any evidence if it seems unconvincing, and it may give as much or as little weight to the evidence as it deems proper.[132] As to those matters entrusted to the Commission, its determinations are final and conclusive if founded upon substantial evidence and if made free from arbitrary and capricious conduct. There may be difference of opinion concerning the weight accorded certain factors by the Commission in reviewing the evidence, nevertheless, the courts may not usurp the administrative function of the Commission by overruling and substituting their own appraisal of those factors.[133] The reviewing court should not substitute its judgment for that of the Commission as to findings or conclusions of fact, even though the court may be of the opinion that they are wrong; this is in accordance with the doctrine of administrative finality.[134]

The Administrative Procedure Act precisely defines the formal requirements to be followed and lays down the standards to be adhered to in considering evidence. A decision, under the requirements of the Administrative Procedure Act must be rendered upon consideration of the whole record and supported by reliable, probative, and substantial

---

[130]*Georgia Public Service Commission v. U.S.* 283 U.S. 765, 775; *Virginian Ry. Co. v. U.S.*, 272 U.S. 658, 663; *Western Paper Makers Chemical Co. v. U.S.*, 271 U.S. 268, 271; *Interstate Commerce Commission v. Consolidated Freightways*, 41 F. Supp. 651, 655.

[131]*Assigned Car Cases*, 274 U.S. 564, 580; *Merchants Warehouse Co. v. United States*, 283 U.S. 501, 508; *United States v. Louisville & Nashville R. Co.*, 235 U.S. 314, 320; *Interstate Commerce Commission v. Louisville & Nashville R. Co.*, 227 U.S. 88, 92; *Callaghan & Co. v. Federal Trade Commission*, 163 F. 2d, 359; *Warehouse Co. v. United States*, 283 U.S. 501, 508; *United States v. Carolina Carriers Corp.*, 315 U.S. 475, 484; *Hanna Furnace Corporation v. United States*, 53 F. Supp. 341 aff'd 323 U.S. 667.

[132]*Loving v. United States*, 32 F. Supp. 464, aff'd 310 U.S. 609.

[133]*Interstate Commerce Commission v. Illinois Central R. Co.*, 215 U.S. 452, 471; *Skinner & Eddy Corp. v. United States*, 249 U.S. 557, 562; *United States v. New River Co.*, 265 U.S. 533, 542; *New York v. United States*, 331 U.S. 284, 349.

[134]5 U.S.C. 702-706.

evidence. Administrative agencies, in appraising the evidence, may not rely on suspicion, surmise, implication or plainly incredible evidence. The legislative history of the Administrative Procedure Act indicates the legislators were well aware that in some instances administrative agencies were mistakenly accepting that type of evidence. The Senate Judiciary Committee's report[135] on the bill which became the Administrative Procedure Act, in defining the substantial evidence rule, stated:

> . . . The "substantial evidence" rule set forth in Section 10(e) is exceedingly important. As a matter of language, substantial evidence would seem to be an adequate expression of law. The difficulty comes about in the practice of agencies to rely upon (and of courts to tacitly approve) something less — to rely upon suspicion, surmise, implications or plainly incredibly evidence. It will be the duty of the courts to determine in the final analysis and on the exercise of their independent judgment, whether on the whole record the evidence in a given instance is sufficiently substantial to support a finding, conclusion, or other agency action as a matter of law. In the first instance, however, it will be the function of the agency to determine the sufficiency of the evidence upon which it acts — and the proper performance of its public duties will require it to undertake this inquiry in a careful and dispassionate manner. Should these objectives of the bill as worded fail, supplemental legislation will be required.

That the Administrative Procedure Act does not require that findings of the Commission be based on more than substantial evidence is shown by *Universal Camera Corp. v. Labor Board*[136] where, in speaking of the judicial review provisions of the Act, the Supreme Court expressly stated that "Retention of the familiar 'substantial evidence' terminology indicates that no drastic reversal of attitude was intended." Substantial evidence means only such evidence as a reasonable mind might accept as adequate to support a conclusion.[137]

In *Lang Transp. Corp. v. United States*,[138] the court said:

> It is well settled, under established principles of judicial review, that it is the task of the Commission, and not of the courts, to pass upon the weight and credibility of evidence.

In *Merchants Warehouse Company v. United States*,[139] the Supreme Court said:

> . . . The credibility of witnesses and weight of evidence are for the Commission and not for the courts, and its findings will not be reviewed here if supported by evidence. See *Interstate Commerce Commission v.*

---

[135]Sen. Doc. No. 248, 79th Cong. 2d sess. (1946), pp. 216-217.
[136]340 U.S. 474, 489.
[137]*Edison v. Labor Board*, 305 U.S. 197, 229.
[138]75 F. Supp. 915, 925 (footnote 8).
[139]283 U.S. 501, 508.

Louisville & Nashville R. Co., 227 U.S. 88, 92, 100; *United States v. Louisville & Nashville R. Co.,* 235 U.S. 314, 320; *Assigned Car Cases,* 274 U.S. 564, 580, 581.

In *Akin v. United States*,[140] the court sustained an order of the Commission denying an application of a motor carrier for a certificate, saying (p. 305):

> Like a jury in a case at law, the Commission is the judge of the credibility of the witnesses and the weight of the evidence and we cannot disturb its findings of fact, if supported by substantial proof.

Likewise in *Fish Transport Co., Inc. v. United States*,[141] the court, in dismissing a complaint to set aside a portion of the Commission's order which denied plaintiff's application for a certificate, said (p. 648):

> In any event, the question of the credibility of a witness is one that belongs to the Commission and is not open to consideration by this court. *Alton R. Co. v. United States,* 315 U.S. 15, 62 S. Ct. 432, 86 L. Ed. 586. It was considered judgment of the Commission that the evidence presented to it by the plaintiff failed to sustain the plaintiff's burden of proving that it was entitled to a certificate for all commodities, with exceptions, under the "grandfather" clause . . . .

As the Supreme Court stated in *Illinois Commerce Commission v. United States:*[142]

> But as we have already said it was for the Commission to determine whether the cost study was adequate or whether it was necessary to refine or supplement it in order to make it dependable evidence for the purpose of rate making. The study itself afforded evidence of the reasonableness of the rate fixed, and upon the whole record there was abundant support for the Commission's finding, which was carefully and thoroughly considered in its report. There is no basis upon which the courts, not authorized to weigh evidence, could re-examine or disregard its conclusion.

Thus where an order of the Commission is attacked as being contrary to the evidence, the judicial function is exhausted when there is found to be a rational basis for the Commission's conclusions. Even if the court disagreed with the Commission on the issues raised, it would not be free to return the Commission's decision where, upon review of the record, the Commission's findings are found to be supported by substantial evidence.[143] The court's reviewing function is limited to whether the finds of the Commission are supported by substantial evi-

---

[140]62 F. Supp. 391, aff'd 327 U.S. 766. See also *Southern Ry. Co. v. United States,* 186 F. Supp. 29, 40.

[141]75 F. Supp. 647.

[142]292 U.S. 474, 484.

[143]*Southern Ry. Co. v. United States,* 186 F. Supp. 29, 40.

dence in the record as a whole, and whether there is rational basis for inferences and conclusions of the Commission.[144]

Moot Questions

A federal court is without power to decide moot questions or give advisory opinions which cannot affect rights of litigants in the case before it.[145] Thus, the court said in the *Cargill* case, where the cause of any controversy has been terminated by dismissal, to lay down rules of practice for future guidance of the Commission would be nothing more than substitution of judicial for executive administration; action seeking an injunction of a temporary Fourth Section order and a declaratory judgment condemning the Commission's practice in permitting the establishment of rates pending hearing on Fourth Section applications was dismissed, as withdrawal of the carriers' applications and cancellation of the temporary order had rendered moot the issues involved.

The Commission Promulgates, Interprets and Enforces Its Own Decrees

Since it is the Commission's task to frame the language of certificates conferring operating authority as well as to determine when and to whom they shall be issued, the construction of such certificates is primarily a task for the Commission, falling peculiarly within its technical judgment and administrative expertise. The courts hold that Commission decisions in such matters are entitled to great weight and should be set aside only if clearly erroneous or arbitrary.[146]

In *Southwest Freight Lines, Inc. v. Interstate Commerce Commission*,[147] the court said:

> In the G. & M. Transfer Co. case, *supra*, (64 F. Supp. 304) the Commission made a formal interpretation of its certificate on the application of the holder. The court held that the Commission's interpretation of its certificate was conclusive on the court. In the circumstances of the present case, the Commission's interpretation of its certificate though less formal is no less effective.

---

[144]*Malone Freight Lines, Inc. v. United States,* 159 F. Supp. 952, 954.

[145]*Cargill, Inc. v. United States,* 188 F. Supp. 386, 389.

[146]*Norwegian Nitrogen Co. v. United States,* 288 U.S. 294, 315; *United States v. American Trucking Assns.,* 310 U.S. 534, 549; *Adirondack Transit Lines, Inc. v. United States,* 59 F. Supp. 503; *Boulevard Transit Lines, Inc. v. United States,* 77 F. Supp. 594; *United States v. Seatrain Lines, Inc.,* 329 U.S. 424; *Rochester Telephone Corp. v. United States,* 307 U.S. 125, 146.

[147]184 F. 2d 149.

As a three-judge district court held in *Coastal Tank Lines, Inc. v. United States*:[148]

> The Commission promulgates, interprets and enforces its own decrees. It is the duty of the Court, rather, to determine whether or not there have been inconsistencies in the application of the Commission's rulings such as to constitute abuse of administrative discretion . . . .
>
> It is our opinion that there has been neither abuse of discretion nor arbitrary action on the part of the Commission.

In *Converse v. United States*,[149] a three-judge court held:

> We cannot say that under all the circumstances, the Commission was not justified in concluding that the phrase "machinery and machinery parts" had a special and limited meaning different from the broad all-inclusive meaning of the words as defined in the dictionary.

The court further stated (pp. 803-809):

> The court's function in deciding this case does not involve a de novo construction of the certificate or a reevaluation of the undisputed facts relating to the services being performed under the pretended warrant of its authority. The scope of our review is limited by Section 10(e) of the Administrative Procedure Act 1946, 5 U.S.C.A. 1001 et seq., and the principle of limited judicial review heretofore applied in the decided case. We may not substitute our judgment for that of the Interstate Commerce Commission unless its judgment is clearly erroneous or arbitrary. *United Truck Lines v. Interstate Commerce Commission*, 9 Cir., 1951, 189 F. 2d 816, certiorari denied 342 U.S. 830, 72 S. Ct. 54, 96 L. Ed. 628; *Adirondack Transit Lines v. United States*, D. C. 1944, 59 F. Supp. 503, affirmed 324 U.S. 824, 65 S. Ct. 688, 89 L. Ed. 1393. The Commission is familiar with the ordinary usage and common understanding of the industry. The administrative agency's judgment in a field where it has expert knowledge and experience should be deferred to unless clearly erroneous or arbitrary. . . .

Again in *Dart Transit Co. v. Interstate Commerce Commission*,[150] a three-judge district court held:

> It is our opinion that in an action such as this, a court may not substitute its judgment for that of the Commission with respect to the question of the scope or coverage of a permit which the Commission has issued to a motor carrier, if that question is at all doubtful. In *Noble v. United States*, 319 U.S. 88, 93, 63 S. Ct. 950, 952, 87 L. Ed. 1277, the Supreme Court said that "The precise delineation of an enterprise which seeks the protection of the 'grandfather' clause has been reserved for the Commission." By the same token, we think that within reasonable limits it is for the

---

[148] 9 Fed. Carrier Cases 80, 838.
[149] 109 F. Supp. 807, 809.
[150] 110 F. Supp. 876, 880-1.

Commission to determine the scope of the "delineation." The meaning of words may be a question of law or a question of fact. This was made plain in *Great Northern Railway Co. v. Merchants Elevator Co.*, 259 U.S. 285, 291-296, 42 S. Ct. 477, 66 L. Ed. 943. See also, *Standard Oil Co. (Indiana) v. United States,* 283 U.S. 235, 238-240, 51 S. Ct. 429, 75 L. Ed. 999. Words may have one meaning when used in industry or in the regulation of industry and another meaning when used in common speech. We are not convinced that in the interpretation of Dart's permit the Commission misapplies the law or exceeded its jurisdiction. For instance, we are not prepared to say that as a matter of law the term "canned goods" used in Dart's permit covered "canned beer" or every sort of canned materials. In the interest of uniformity in the regulation of policing of the motor carrier industry, it is of course essential that the Commission be subject to as little judicial interference as the law will permit.

Some of the findings of the Commission in the instant case were, in our opinion, clearly right. We are not convinced that any finding of the Commission was clearly wrong. We think the inferences the Commission drew from the evidence were permissible. The evidence relative to Dart's shipments of commodities to or for corporations which were apparently not in any way engaged in the packing-house, dairy or canning industries was, we think, sufficiently persuasive to call for an explanation from Dart. For instance, one reasonably may believe that a "Biscuit Company" is not a packing-house, dairy or canning industry. In the absence of any explanation indicating that these questioned shipments were of commodities covered by Dart's permit, the Commission was, we think, warranted in inferring that Dart had exceeded its authority with respect to the transportation of such shipments.

But if it be assumed that some of the findings of the Commission were based upon a wrongful inference as to the nature of the business of a shipper for whom or to whom goods were transported, we would still be of the opinion that the order of the Commission directing Dart to abstain from transporting commodities not authorized by its permit as construed by the Commission was a valid order.

In an action to enjoin and set aside a Commission order holding that "grandfather" certificates authorizing transportation of petroleum products were not intended to authorize transportation of petroleum or crude oil, the court in *Devine-Chicago Transport Co. v. United States*[151] said that the Commission construction of such certificates is binding on the courts unless clearly erroneous since there was substantial evidence to sustain the Commission's construction; its determination of its own intent could not be said to be clearly erroneous; that intent was consistent with the literal meaning of the language used.

[151]183 F. Supp. 785, 789.

Statutory Construction

The purpose of statutory construction is to harmonize the law and save apparently conflicting statutes from ineffectiveness.[152] The courts have repeatedly held that the contemporaneous and long-settled construction of an Act by the agency charged with its enforcement is entitled to great weight.[153] Thus, in *United States v. American Trucking Associations, supra,* the court, in upholding the Commission's construction of Section 204(a) of the Motor Carrier Act, stated (p. 549):

> In any case such interpretations are entitled to great weight. This is peculiarly true here where the interpretations involve "contemporaneous construction of a statute by the men charged with the responsibility of setting its machinery in motion, of making the parts work efficiently and smoothly while they are yet untried and new." Furthermore, the Commission's interpretation gains much persuasiveness from the fact that it was the Commission which suggested the provisions' enactment to Congress.

In *United States v. Mo. Pac. R. Co., supra,* the Supreme Court stated (p. 280):

> It has been held in many cases that a definitely settled administrative construction is entitled to the highest respect; and, if acted on for a number of years, such construction will not be disturbed except for cogent reasons. See, e.g., *Logan v. Davis*, 233 U.S. 613, 627.

In *United States v. Alabama Railroad Co., supra,* the Supreme Court stated (p. 621):

> We think the contemporaneous construction thus given by the executive department of the government, and continued for nine years through six different administrations of that department — a construction which, though inconsistent with the literalism of the act, certainly consorts with the equities of the case — should be considered as decisive in this suit. It is a settled doctrine of this court that, in case of ambiguity, the judicial department will lean in favor of a construction given to a statute by the department charged with the execution of such statute, and, if such construction be acted upon for a number of years, will look with disfavor upon any sudden change, whereby parties who have contracted with the government upon the faith of such construction may be prejudiced.

---

[152]*Musselman Hub-Brake Co. v. Commissioner of Internal Revenue*, 139 F. 2d 65, 67.

[153]*United States v. American Trucking Associations*, 310 U.S. 534, 549; *United States v. Mo. Pac. R. Co.*, 278 U.S. 269, 280; *United States v. Alabama Railroad Co.*, 142 U.S. 615; *United States v. Leslie Salt Co.*, 350 U.S. 383; *Helvering v. Winmill* 305 U.S. 79; *Atchison, T. & S. F. Ry. Co. v. United States*, 209 F. Supp. 35.

In *Brooks Transp. Co. v. United States*,[154] the court said:

> Though the question here involved is one of law, it is well settled that the courts should give great weight to the Commission's interpretation of the Act. Thus, in *Levinson v. Spector Motor Co.*, 330 U.S. 649, 672, 67 S. Ct. 931, 943, 91 L. Ed. 1158, Mr. Justice Burton said: "As conclusion of law, these do not have the same claim to finality as do the findings of fact made by the Commission. However, in the light of the Commission's long record of practical experience with this subject and its responsibility for the administration and enforcement of this law, these conclusions are entitled to special consideration." . . . .

The Supreme Court announced in *United States v. Johnston*:[155]

> In view of the foregoing facts the case comes fairly within the rule often announced by this court, that the contemporaneous construction of a statute by those charged with its execution, especially when it has long prevailed, is entitled to great weight, and should not be disregarded or overturned except for cogent reasons, and unless it be clear that such construction is erroneous. *Edwards v. Darby*, 12 Wheat. 206, 210; *United States v. Moore*, 95 U.S. 760; *Hahn v. United States*, 107 U.S. 402; *United States v. Philbrick*, 120 U.S. 52, 59.

In *United States v. Chicago, St. P., M. & O. Ry. Co.*,[156] the court said:

> If the meaning of this statute were in doubt the practical construction given it through all these years should be presumed to be the correct one, and this is particularly true where there has been a contemporaneous construction of the statute by those charged with its execution and application. We should be reluctant to overturn a long standing departmental construction, presumably known to the legislative department which has made no amendments to the act, seeking to make it applicable to the practice now challenged in this action.

Thus, in the foregoing cases and in other decisions it has been held that the interpretations placed on a statute by the administrative agency are entitled to the greatest consideration.[157] The weight attributed to the administrative agency's interpretation is even greater in those instances where the agency has over a period of years followed a consistent construction of the statute with the knowledge and acquiescence of Congress.[158] In the *Kocmond* case, the court held that, "The numer-

---

[154] 93 F. Supp. 517, 522, aff'd 340 U.S. 925.

[155] 124 U.S. 236, 253.

[156] 43 F. 2d 300, 305-6.

[157] See *Boutell v. Walling*, 148 Fed. 329, 332, affirmed 327 U.S. 463, 471.

[158] Where cogent reasons and the public interest compel it, even a consistent and generally unchallenged administrative practice may be overturned. Cf. *Norwegian Nitrogen Co. v. United States*, 288 U.S. 294, 311, 315. See also *Skidmore v. Swift & Co.*, 323 U.S. 134, 140; *United States v. Kocmond*, 200 F. 2d 370, 373. See also *Arrow Trucking Co. v. United States*, 181 F. Supp. 775, 778.

ous administrative interpretations of the statute to the same effect are entitled to great weight, inasmuch as they have persisted for years without congressional interference." The Supreme Court has repeatedly held that great weight must be given to interpretations of an administrative body. Thus in *Overnight Motor Co. v. Missel*[159] it held that the interpretative bulletins of the Administrator of the Fair Labor Standards Act were entitled to great weight, even though they were not regulations issued under statutory authority. The court said (pp. 580-581, footnote 17):

> While the interpretative bulletins are not issued as regulations under statutory authority, they do carry persuasiveness as an expression of the view of those experienced in the administration of the Act and acting with the advice of a staff specializing in its interpretation and application. Cf. *United States v. American Trucking Assns.*, 310 U.S. 534, 549; *United States v. Darby*, 312 U.S. 100, 118, n. 2; *Graves v. Armstrong Creamery Co.*, 154 Kan. 365, 370, 118 P. 2d 613, 616. Even negative construction may be significant. *Trade Comm'n v. Bunte Bros.*, 312 U.S. 349, 351, 352.

In the absence of any ambiguity in the language of the statute, there is no warrant to seek for other meanings in legislative history. As stated in *United States v. Go'denberg*,[160] "The primary and general rule of statutory construction is that the intent of the lawmaker is to be found in the language that he has used." It is established that resort to aids to construction is improper where the language of the statute is unambiguous.[161] In the *Van Camp* case (at 253-54), the Supreme Court said:

> . . . The words being clear, they are decisive. There is nothing to construe. To search elsewhere for a meaning either beyond or short of that which they disclose is to invite the danger, in the one case, of converting what was meant to be open and precise, into a concealed trap for the unsuspecting, or, in the other, of relieving from the grasp of the statute some whom the legislature definitely means to include. . . .

Court Review of Fourth Section Orders

A district court set aside a Commission order which found rates on crude sulphur from Louisiana and Texas to Virginia to be lawul and granted Fourth Section relief. The court held that the Commission failed

---

[159]316 U.S. 572.
[160]168 U.S. 95, 102-3.
[161]See *United States v. Missouri P. R. Co.*, 278 U.S. 269, 276-77; *United States v. Shreveport Grain & E. Co.*, 287 U.S. 77, 83; *Gemsco v. Walling*, 324 U.S. 244, 260; *Van Camp & Sons Co. v. American Can Co.*, 278 U.S. 245, 253-54; *Helvering v. City Bank Farmers Trust Co.*, 296 U.S. 85, 89; *Packard Motor Co., v. National Lab. Rel. Bd.*, 330 U.S. 485, 492.

to make basic findings essential to the validity of its conclusion that the authorized long-haul rate was reasonably compensatory, and that it failed to give sufficient reasons for concluding that of the two cost studies submitted in the transportation of sulphur, the rail carriers' study more accurately reflected the cost of handling the sulphur traffic.[162] In another district court case it was held that the Commission was not required to hold an adversary hearing on the Fourth Section applications or on a petition for their denial. The court also held that Fourth Section orders were reviewable to the extent necessary to determine whether the procedure followed was lawful and whether on their face they disclose sufficient basis for their issuance to comply with the limited requirements of Section 4. However, plaintiffs must exhaust their remedies under Sections 13 and 15, the court said, on the issue that the proposed rates are unduly discriminatory.[163]

Review by a One-Judge Court

While a mere abstract declaration on some issue by the Commission may not be judicially reviewable, an order that determines a right or obligation so that legal consequences will flow from it is reviewable. Such review is equally available whether the order relates to past or future rates, or whether its proceeding follows referral by a court or originates with the Commission.[164] In the *Pennsylvania* case, the Supreme Court said that where the Commission found, upon referral from the Court of Claims, that plaintiff railroad's domestic rates charged on certain war-blocked export shipments of the United States were unreasonable as to some shipments to the extent they exceeded the corresponding export rates, the order issued was not a mere advisory opinion. Its legal consequences were obvious, for if valid it foreclosed the railroad's right to recover its domestic rates, the General Accounting Office having deducted from other bills due it the difference between the higher and the lower rates on those shipments. The railroad was therefore entitled to have the Commission's order judicially reviewed. The order was

---

[162]*Marine Transport Lines, Inc. and National Water Carriers Association v. United States,* 173 F. Supp. 326.

[163]*Seatrain Lines, Inc. v. United States,* 168 F. Supp. 819.

[164]*Pennsylvania R. Co. v. United States,* 363 U.S. 202, 203, 205-6. See *Parkhill Truck Co. v. United States,* 198 F. Supp. 362; *C. &H. Transp. Co., Inc. Extension — Denison, Tex.,* 94 M.C.C. 711; *Frozen Food Exp. v. United States,* 351 U.S. 40, 44; and *National Van Lines, Inc. v. United States,* 326 F. 2d 362 (7 Cir.); regarding judicial review of a determination by the Commission of a protestant's scope of authority in an application proceeding.

properly reviewable by a one-judge court because it was essentially one for the payment of money within the terms of 28 U.S.C. 2321, 2325.

Review of Orders of the Interstate Commerce Commission in Judicial Reference Cases

The Judicial Code was amended in 1964 with respect to the jurisdiction and venue of actions brought to enforce, enjoin, set aside or annul orders of the Commission in judicial reference cases. 28 U.S.C. 1336 was amended to provide that when a district court or the Court of Claims refers a question to the Commission for determination, the referring court shall have exclusive jurisdiction of a civil action to enforce, enjoin, set aside, or annul the order of the Commission arising out of the referral. 28 U.S.C. Sec. 1398 was also amended in substantially the same way. The result was to provide a more streamlined procedure for judicial review of questions that involve the primary jurisdiction of the Commission and are referred to it for a preliminary determination.[165]

The 1964 amendments made no changes in the substantive law, except to fix venue and jurisdiction in the referring court, thus the prerequisites for judicial review remain the same. Once an issue has been referred to the Commission, the matter must be prosecuted there until a final order is issued; only after administrative remedies have been exhausted may the case proceed to judgment in the court.

It was argued in *McLean Trucking Co. v. United States*,[166] that the words "civil action," as used in 28 U.S.C. Sec. 1336 and 28 U.S.C. Sec. 1398, created a requirement that the party challenging the Commission's order institute an entirely new action by filing a separate petition against the Commission in the Court of Claims and by pursuing the new action to a conclusion before the original case is reopened. Thus, plaintiff contended that defendant's use of a motion to attack the Commission's decision was a failure to comply with the law. The court held that the acceptance of plaintiff's view "would require the adoption of a procedure almost as burdensome as that which the amended statutes were designed to supplant. Pointless duplication and needless expense would be entailed, because both the suspended action and the newly instituted one would be docketed in the same forum where only one final judgment is required to dispose of both suits." The court said that it could not agree that Congress intended to cure one procedural difficulty

---

[165]*Shipbuilding Corp.*, 303 U.S. 41, 50-51. *Myers v. Bethlehem.*
[166]Ct. of Cls. No. 305-64.

by creating another as cumbersome as the old. "A more sensible reading of the statute shows that Congress used the term 'civil action' simply to distinguish it from a 'criminal action' and that nothing more is to be inferred from the term. In a case in which there are already several pleadings, it would be redundant at best to require anything more of a party challenging the Commission's order than a pleading setting forth the action he requests of this court and stating specifically the grounds therefor."

Prior to the 1964 amendments, a suit in a district court to set aside an order of the Commission in judicial reference cases was, as a matter of general practice, ordinarily filed against the United States and the Commission. When the United States brought an action to set aside an order of the Commission, that agency was customarily named as defendant in the suit. Since this was the first case brought under the new statutory pattern, the Court of Claims invited the Commission to file a brief and it did no. The Court of Claims said, "We think the Commission is a necessary party whenever its decision on a referred case is attacked. Therefore, the court will not entertain a motion or other action to set aside an order of the Commission unless it is made a party to the suit, duly served, and thus given an opportunity to defend its decision."

Temporary Stay and Interlocutory Injunction

By 28 U.S.C. 2349(b) the courts of appeals in their discretion may restrain or suspend, in whole or in part, the operation of agency orders pending final hearing and determination of a petition for review.

Under Rule 18 of the Federal Rules of Appellate Procedure, application for a stay of a decision or order of an agency pending direct review in the court of appeals shall ordinarily be made in the first instance to the agency. A motion for such relief may be made to the court of appeals or to a judge thereof, but the motion shall show that application had been made to the agency and denied, with the reasons given by it for denial, or that the action of the agency did not afford the relief which the applicant had requested. The motion shall also show the reasons for the relief requested and the facts relied upon, and if the facts are subject to dispute the motion shall be supported by affidavits or other sworn statements or copies thereof. With the motion shall be filed such parts of the record as are relevant to the relief sought. Reasonable notice of the motion shall be given to all parties to the proceeding in the court of appeals. The court may condition relief under this rule upon the filing of a bond or other appropriate security. The motion shall be filed with the clerk and normally will be considered by a panel or division of the court, but in exceptional cases where such procedure would be impracticable due to the requirements of time, the application may be made to and considered by a single judge of the court.

A request for temporary stay and interlocutory injunction must satisfy the factors set forth in Virginia *Petroleum Jobbers Ass'n. v. Federal Power Commission*[167] before relief will be granted by the court. These factors are:

(1) Has the petitioner made a strong showing that it is likely to prevail on the merits of its appeal?
(2) Has the petitioner shown that without such relief, it will be irreparably injured?
(3) Would the issuance of a stay substantially harm other parties interested in the proceedings?
(4) Where lies the public interest?

Timely Objections

It is established that in reviewing the validity of an order of the Commission a court is confined to considering only those errors that were specifically relied upon by the plaintiff before the Commission. Matters not deemed of sufficient significance to be brought to the attention of the administrative body and relied on there may not be raised for the first time in court.[168] In *United States v. Tucker Truck Lines*,[169] where the district court set aside a Commission order on the ground that there was a lack of jurisdiction over the subject matter since the hearing had been held before an officer not appointed in compliance with the requirements of Section 11 of the Administrative Procedure Act, the Supreme Court reversed, holding that the district court had erred in considering a matter not raised at an appropriate time before the Commission.[170]

---

[167]259 F. 2d 921. See *Washington Metropolitan Area, Etc. v. Holiday Tours*, 559 F. 2d 841, which moves away from adherence to a strict probability requirement of prevailing on the merits of appeal. See also *Leland v. Morin*, 104 F. Supp. 401; *Acme Fast Freight, Inc. v. United States*, 135 F. Supp. 823; *Atlantic & Gulf West Coast v. United States*, 90 F. Supp. 554; *Arkansas & O. Ry. Corp.* 185 F. Supp. 36, 42.

[168]*Vajtauer v. Comm'r of Immigration*, 273 U.S. 103, 113.

[169]344 U.S. 33, 36-7.

[170]For other decisions on this point see *Spiller v. Atchison, T. & S. F. R. Co.*, 253 U.S. 117, 130; *United States v. Northern Pacific R. Co.*, 288 U.S. 490, 494; *Unemployment Compensation Commission of Alaska v. Aragon*, 329 U.S. 143, 155. For *Congressional* requirements see Section 9(a) of the Securities Act of 1933, 15 U.S.C. Section 77i; Section 25(a) of the Securities Exchange Act of 1934, 15 U.S.C. Section 78y; Section 24 of the Public Utility Holding Company Act, 15 U.S.C. Section 79x; Section 10 of the Fair Labor Standards Act, 29 U.S.C. Section 210; Section 10(e) of the National Labor Relations Act, 29 U.S.C. Section 160(e).

In *United States v. Capital Transit Co.,*[171] the Supreme Court held that a point not raised before the Commission could not be relied upon in courts as a ground for setting aside the Commission's action, stating, "It is also argued here that the orders should be set aside because they are confiscatory. But the record fails to show that this issue was properly presented to the Commission for its determination. Therefore the question of confiscation is not ripe for judicial review." In *Carolina Scenic Coach Lines v. United States,*[172] a district court rejected the argument that the administrative body which heard the matter did not have jurisdiction, stating that "even if there had been error in the matter, the record does not show that Scenic raised any objection thereto either before the Board or before the Commission, and it is too late to object for the first time in this court."

Similarly, in *McGraw Electric Co. v. United States,*[173] the court rejected certain arguments made by the plaintiffs, stating (at p. 359), "The short answer to this is that the plaintiffs made no such contentions before the Commission and should not be heard to make them for the first time before this court." In *General Transp. Co. v. United States,*[174] the court refused to consider an alleged error that had not been urged before the Commission, stating (p. 984):

> Their second point was not made before the Commission but is made for the first time here. Therefore, upon the authority of *United States v. Hancock Truck Lines,* 324 U.S. 774, 779, 780, 65 S. Ct. 1003, 89 L. Ed. 1357, we rule that it is not properly before us for consideration . . . the plaintiffs here, when appearing as protestants before the Commission, did not expressly waive the point they now make, and in this respect the case at bar differs from the Hancock case. Nevertheless the reasoning of that case is applicable, and furthermore, although strictly speaking we are not an appellate court, we in reality are called upon to exercise appellate functions, and from this we think it follows that we should apply general principles applicable on review.

The principle that a party must have relied on the alleged error before the Commission in order to be able to raise it in court as a ground for setting aside the Commission's order is based essentially on the doctrine of exhaustion of administrative remedies, and, insofar as the Interstate Commerce Act is concerned, on Section 17(9), which is a statutory expression of that doctrine. A party thus is in no position

[171]338 U.S. 286, 291.
[172]56 F. Supp. 801, 804-5, aff'd 323 U.S. 678.
[173]120 F. Supp. 354, aff'd 348 U.S. 804. See *General Transp. Co. v. United States,* 65 F. Supp. 981, 984.
[174]65 F. Supp. 981, aff'd 329 U.S. 668.

to have a court set aside an order of the Commission if it has failed to pursue its administrative remedies before that agency. The Supreme Court has repeatedly recognized as shown herein that the principle of exhaustion of administrative remedies must be applied, and that a party may not circumvent the administrative process by seeking judicial relief prior to recourse to the administrative body.[175]

---

[175]See, for example, *Macauley v. Waterman S.S. Corp.*, 327 U.S. 540; *Federal Power Commission v. Edison Co.*, 304 U.S. 375; *Myers v. Bethlehem Corp.*, 303 U.S. 41. Where the period for pursuing the administrative remedy has expired, the Supreme Court has held that the administrative questions could not be passed upon by a court. *Lichter v. United States*, 334 U.S. 742, 791.

59

Judicial Review of Orders of the Civil Aeronautics Board and Judicial Enforcement

The Applicable Statutory Provisions

Section 1006(a) of the Federal Aviation Act[1] provides "any order, affirmative or negative, issued by the Board or Administrator under this Act, except any order in respect of any foreign air carrier subject to the approval of the President as provided in Section 801 of this Act, shall be subject to review by the courts of appeals of the United States or the United States Court of Appeals for the District of Columbia upon petition, filed within sixty days after the entry of such order, by any person disclosing a substantial interest in such order."

Section 1006(a) also states that after the expiration of sixty days a petition may be filed only by leave of court upon a showing of reasonable grounds for failure to file the petition theretofore. The petition must "be filed in the court for the circuit wherein the petitioner resides or has his principal place of business or in the United States Court of Appeals for the District of Columbia."[2] A copy of the petition, when filed, must forthwith be transmitted by the cleark of court to the Board, and the latter "shall thereupon certify and file in the court a transcript of the record, if any, upon which the order complained of was entered."[3] Section 1006(d)[4] provides that "upon transmittal of the petition to the Board or Administrator, the court shall have exclusive jurisdiction to affirm, modify, or set aside the order complained of, in whole or in part, and if need be, to order further proceedings by the Board or Administrator." Section 1006(d) provides further that upon "good cause shown, interlocutory relief may be granted by stay of the order or by such man-

[1]49 U.S.C. 1486.
[2]Section 1006(b) of the Act, 49 U.S.C. 1486(b).
[3]Section 1006(c) of the Act, 49 U.S.C. 1486(c).
[4]49 U.S.C. 1486(d).

datory or other relief as may be appropriate: *Provided,* That no interlocutory relief may be granted except upon at least five days' notice to
the Board or Administrator." A judgment and decree of the court affirming, modifying or setting aside an order of the Board is subject to
review by the Supreme Court upon certification or certiorari as provided in 28 U.S.C. 1254.[5]

Public Interest Factor

Those seeking court review under provisions such as Section 1006
of the Act are primarily vindicating the public and not private interest.[6]
Thus in court reviews of administrative orders the public interest looms
large.[7] As the court said in *United Air Lines v. CAB,*[8] "the purpose
of the Act is not primarily to advance the private interests of carriers,
but the public interest in an adequate transportation system." The court
added, "When conflicts between private and public interests occur, the
private interests of the certificate holder should yield to the broader
interests of the public embodied in the copcept of public convenience
and necessity."

Substantial Interest Required to Seek Review

Although the judicial review section of the Federal Aviation Act is
broadly phrased so as to authorize review of "any order, affirmative or
negative, issued by the Board or Administrator," it also provides that
review must be at the behest of "any person disclosing a substantial interest in such order."

Reviewable Orders

The Supreme Court has said that the courts have "by self-denying
constructions" limited the word "any" as used in Section 1006(a) of
the Act ("any order, affirmative or negative") so as to exclude orders
which "are inappropriate for review."[9] The court also has said that administrative orders are not reviewable "unless and until they impose

---

[5]Section 1006(f) of the Act, 49 U.S.C. 1486(f).
[6]*Scripps-Howard Radio, Inc. v. F.C.C.,* 316 U.S. 4, 14.
[7]*Ibid.*
[8]198 F. 2d 100, 107.
[9]*Chicago & Southern Air Lines v. Waterman S.S. Corp.,* 333 U.S. 103, 106.

an obligation, deny a right or fix same legal relationship as a consummation of the administrative process."[10]

Finality of Action

Although the Act does not expressly require that the order be final before it may be reviewed, the requirement of finality has been read into the Act by the courts.[11] While making judicial review available without a petition for reconsideration, the Administrative Procedure Act[12] does not operate to repeal the law with respect to finality. The legislative history of 5 U.S.C. 1009(c) indicates that it was adopted to achieve harmony with the holding in *Levers v. Anderson*[13] to the effect that a petition for rehearing is not necessary to exhaust administrative remedies.

Where a petition for rehearing is filed, however, there is no final action until the rehearing is denied. Where rehearing is sought there is always the possibility that the order complained of will be modified in a way which renders judicial review unnecessary; practical considerations, therefore, dictate that when a petition for rehearing is filed, review may properly be deferred until this has been acted upon.[14]

Findings of Fact

Under Section 1006(e)[15] the findings of fact of the Board, if supported by substantial evidence, are conclusive. No objection to an order of the Board "shall be considered by the court unless such objection shall have been urged before the Board" or, if not so urged, "unless there were reasonable grounds for failure to do so."

Granting of a Stay of an Order

The Act authorizes a court to grant a stay "upon good cause shown." Section 10(d) of the Administrative Procedure Act also provides for

---

[10]Id., p. 113. See also *Seaboard & Western Airlines v. C.A.B.*, 181, F. 2d. 777, 181 F. 2d 515, cert. denied 339 U.S. 963.

[11]*McManus v. CAB*, 286 F. 2d 414, 417, cert. denied 366 U.S. 928, rehearing denied 366 U.S. 978; *Eastern Airlines v. CAB*, 243 F. 2d 607; *Western Air Lines v. CAB*, 184 F. 2d 545.

[12]5 U.S.C. 1009(c).

[13]326 U.S. 219.

[14]*Braniff Airways, Inc. v. CAB*, 147 F. 2d 152; *Outland v. CAB*, 284 F. 2d 224, 227-8. Cf. *Consolidated Flowers Ship. v. CAB*, 205 F. 2d 449.

[15]49 U.S.C. 1486(e).

a stay. The stay of an order of an administrative agency may be granted where petitioner is likely to prevail on the merits of its appeal, where the petitioner has shown that without a stay it will suffer irreparable injury, where there is no substantial harm to other interested persons, and where the public interest will not be harmed.[16]

Matters Subject to Approval of the President

Section 801 of the Federal Aviation Act[17] provides that the "issuance, denial, transfer, amendment, cancellation, suspension, or revocation of, and the terms, conditions, and limitations contained in, any certificate authorizing an air carrier to engage in overseas or foreign air transportation, or air transportation between places in the same Territory or possession, or any permit issuable to any foreign air carrier under Section 402 shall be subject to the approval of the President." Section 801 also provides that copies "of all applications in respect of such certificates and permits shall be transmitted to the President by the Board before hearing thereon, and all decisions thereon by the Board shall be submitted to the President before publication thereof."

Board action under Section 801 is not subject to judicial review.[18] Since there is extraordinary power visited in the Executive by this statute, the Supreme Court said in the *Waterman* case (p. 111) that the statute should not be expanded beyond the needs of the foreign relations considerations which have been relied upon to justify the grant. Thus in *Pan American World Airways v. CAB,*[19] the court of appeals held that an exemption grant under Section 416(b), which for a limited period authorized a carrier to transport overseas mail between points already receiving certified cargo service from the same carrier, although having operative effects not unlike an amendment of a certificate, should not be subject to Section 801 and is subject to review by the court. The court said (p. 756):

> These factors — the uniqueness of the statutory provision, its drastic impact, the precise definition of the statute, and the Board's interpretation fortify the conclusion that Congress did not intend to include exemptions in Section 801. The enduring and continuing character of the operation under a certificate as contrasted with the temporary and limited character of the exemption supply the most important basis for distinction.

[16]*Eastern Air Lines v. CAB*, 261 F. 2d 830; *Yakus v. United States*, 321 U.S. 414, 440; *Air Line Pilots Ass'n v. CAB*, 215 F. 2d 122, 125.
[17]49 U.S.C. 1461.
[18]*Chicago & Southern Air Lines v. Waterman S.S. Corp.*, 333 U.S. 103.
[19]261 F. 2d 754, 756, cert. denied 359 U.S. 912.

Judicial Enforcement

Section 1007(a)[20] provides that if "any person violates any provision of this Act, or any rule, regulation, requirement, or order thereunder, or any term, condition, or limitation of any certificate or permit issued under this Act, the Board or Administrator, as the case may be, their duly authorized agents, or, in the case of a violation of Section 401(a) of this Act, any party in interest, may apply to the district court of the United States, for any district wherein such person carriers on his business or wherein the violation occurred for the enforcement of such provision of this Act, or of such rule, regulation, requirement, order, term, condition, or limitation; and such court shall have jurisdiction to enforce obedience thereto by a writ of injunction or other process, mandatory or otherwise, restraining such persons, his officers, agents, employees, and representatives, from further violation of such provision of this Act or of such rule, regulation, requirement, order, term, condition, or limitation, and requiring their obedience thereto."

Where a non-certificated carrier gave service in violation of its authorization as an irregular carrier, the Board, under Section 1007(a) of the Act, was permitted by the court in *CAB v. Modern Air Transport*[21] to obtain a preliminary injunction prohibiting the carrier from engaging in air transportation in violation of the Act. The carrier attacked the granting of the injunction on the ground that so long as its authorization to operate as an irregular carrier had not been suspended by the Board, its exemption from Section 401(a) was absolute and complete, and the court had no jurisdiction to enjoin its unauthorized regular service until the Board had first proceeded to take action to suspend or revoke. The court said (p. 626) that although it expressed no opinion as to the jurisdiction of a court to issue an injunction at the suit of a private party,[22] where "the Board is the petitioner seeking restraint of a violation of law, we find no judicial barrier to granting the swift remedy accorded it by Congress." The decision of the lower court to issue a preliminary injunction was, therefore, affirmed.

In the lower court case, *CAB v. Modern Air Transport*,[23] it was

---

[20]49 U.S.C. 1487.

[21]179 F. 2d 622.

[22]Such jurisdiction has been denied in *Trans-Pacific Airlines, Ltd. v. Hawaiian Airlines, Ltd.*, 174 F. 2d 63; and *American Airlines, Inc. v. Standard Airlines, Inc.*, 80 F. Supp. 135. Cf. *Pacific Northern Airlines v. Alaska Airlines*, 80 F. Supp. 592.. Although expressing no opinion, the court in the *Modern Air Transport* case said that there may be an understandable reluctance on the part of a court to control the activities of an air carrier without action by the agency entrusted with its regulation.

[23]81 F. Supp. 803, 806.

pointed out that Section 1007(a), authorizing the Board to apply to the district courts to enforce the provisions of the Act, is in very much the same language of Section 222(b) of the Interstate Commerce Act, and that in *Interstate Commerce Comm. v. Fordham Bus Corp.*[24] the Commission was said to have full authority to institute suit and for the court to exercise jurisdiction. The court said that the language of the *Fordham* case was equally applicable to Section 1007(a).

---

[24]38 F. Supp. 739, 740.

60

Judicial Review of Orders of the Federal Maritime Commission and Judicial Enforcement

The Applicable Statutory Provisions

The Administrative Orders Review Act[1] provides for the review of orders of the Federal Maritime Commission. Under 5 U.S.C. 1032 the courts of appeals "shall have exclusive jurisdiction to enjoin, set aside, suspend (in whole or in part), or to determine the validity of, all final orders" of the Federal Maritime Commission. The venue of any proceeding is placed by 5 U.S.C. 1033 "in the judicial circuit wherein is the residence of the party or any of the parties filing the petition for review, or wherein such party or any of such parties has its principal office, or in the United States Court of Appeals for the District of Columbia."

Under 5 U.S.C. 1034 a party may within 60 days after entry of an order file in the court of appeals a petition for review; the action in court "shall be brought against the United States"; the petition "shall contain a concise statement of (a) the nature of the proceedings as to which review is sought, (b) the facts upon which venue is based, (c) the grounds on which relief is sought, and (d) the relief prayed." Under 5 U.S.C. 1036 provision is made for the filing of the record on review; and the petition for review by 5 U.S.C. 1037(a), unless determined on a motion to dismiss, "shall be heard in the court of appeals upon the record of the pleadings, evidence adduced, and proceedings before the agency." Under 5 U.S.C. 1040 review by the Supreme Court is provided by writ of certiorari of the action by the court of appeals.

---

[1] 5 U.S.C. 1031 et seq. The Hobbs Act, as the Administrative Orders Review Act is known, applies also to certain orders of the Federal Communications Commission, Secretary of Agriculture, Maritime Administration, and the Atomic Energy Commission.

Section 31 of the Shipping Act[2] provides that the venue and procedure in suits to enforce, suspend, or set aside any order of the Federal Maritime Commission shall, "except as otherwise provided," be the same as in similar suits in regard to orders of the Interstate Commerce Commission. The relevant statutory provisions regarding orders of Interstate Commerce Commission are contained in 28 U.S.C. 1336, 2321-2325. Section 1336 of Title 28 states that except as otherwise provided, "the district courts shall have jurisdiction of any civil action to enforce, enjoin, set aside, annul or suspend, in whole or in part, any order of the Interstate Commerce Commission." Section 1336 gives the district courts broad jurisdiction to set aside Interstate Commerce Commission orders. The procedure for review of Federal Maritime Commission orders has been similar to that followed in the review of Interstate Commerce Commission orders by virtue of Section 31; however, the jurisdiction to set aside final orders of the Federal Maritime Commission formerly possessed by the district courts has been transferred to the courts of appeals by the Hobbs Act.[3]

Pendency of Review

Pendency of a review petition does not automatically bar reopening of an administrative proceeding.[4] However, "when an agency seeks to reconsider its action, it should move the court to remand or to hold the case in abeyance pending reconsideration by the agency."[5]

Finality

On the question of the finality of an order, the court of appeals said in *Isbrandtsen Co. v. United States:*[6]

> Whether or not the statutory requirements of finality are satisfied in any given case depends not upon the label affixed to its action but rather upon a realistic appraisal of the consequence of such action. "The ultimate test of reviewability is not to be found in an overrefined technique, but in the need of the review to protect from the irreparable injury threatened in the exceptional case by administrative rulings which attach

---

[2]46 U.S.C. 830.

[3]5 U.S.C. 1031 et seq. See *Flota Mercante Grancolombiana v. F.M.C.*, 302 F. 2d 887.

[4]*Wrather-Alvarez Broadcasting, Inc. v. F.C.C.*, 259 F. 2d 808; *WORZ, Inc. v. F.C.C.*, 268 F. 2d 889.

[5]*Anchor Line Limited v. F.M.C.*, 299 F. 2d 124 cert. denied 370 U.S. 922.

[6]211 F. 2d 51, cert. denied sub nom. *Japan-Atlantic & Gulf Conference v. United States*, 347 U.S. 990.

legal consequences to action taken in advance of other hearings and adjudications that may follow, the results of which the regulations purport to control." Thus, administrative orders are ordinarily reviewable when "they impose an obligation, deny a right, or fix some legal relationship as a consummation of the administrative process." Under this test, a final order need not necessarily be the very last order.

In *Trans-Pacific Freight Conf. of Japan v. F.M.B.,*[7] the court of appeals said that where the Commission sought by order to deny a conference the right to assess or collect any fines, the issuance of the order was thus intended to deprive the conference of its most important means of enforcement of the conference agreement. An "order which so threatens, for an indefinite period of time, to undermine the very function of the conference is 'final' for purposes of the Review Act."

Findings

The requirement for a full hearing and evidence adequate to support pertinent and necessary findings of fact, which is applied in matters calling for administrative determination,[8] is applicable also to the Federal Maritime Commission.[9] A reviewing court, therefore, is charged with setting aside action unsupported by substantial evidence.[10] The Commission must conform to the requirements of Section 8(b) of the Administrative Procedure Act[11] whereby parties are afforded an opportunity to propose findings and to note exceptions to decisions or recommended decisions.[12] As stated in *Commonwealth of Puerto Rico v. F.M.B.,*[13] the Administrative Procedure Act requires all decisions to state not only findings and conclusions, but also the reasons or basis therefor, upon all the material issues of fact, law or discretion presented on the record; the agency should make the basis of its action reasonably clear.

A general conclusion stated in the order, which is phrased in the language of the statute, does not conform to the requirements of the Administrative Procedure Act, nor does it satisfy the rule respecting the necessity of findings.[14] The requirement of specific, definite and basic

---

[7]302 F. 2d 875, 878. See also *Lee v. F.M.B.*, 284 F. 2d 577.
[8]*Morgan v. United States*, 298 U.S. 468, 480.
[9]*Isbrandtsen Co. v. United States*, 211 F. 2d 51.
[10]*Universal Camera Corp. v. N.L.R.B.*, 340 U.S. 474.
[11]5 U.S.C. 1007(b).
[12]*Baltimore & O. R. Co. v. United States*, 201 F. 2d 795.
[13]288 F. 2d 419. See also *Sec'y of Agriculture v. United States*, 347 U.S. 645; *Erie R. Co. v. United States*, 59 F. Supp. 748 64 F. Supp. 162; *United States v. Chicago M., St. P. & P. R.R. Co.*, 294 U.S. 499.
[14]*Florida v. United States*, 282 U.S. 194, 213.

findings, is well settled; it is settled doctrine in the federal courts.[15] Thus in *Colorado-Wyoming Co. v. Commission*,[16] the court said, "But we must first know what the 'finding' is before we can give it that conclusive weight. We have repeatedly emphasized the need for clarity and completeness in the basic or essential findings on which administrative orders rest."

In *Saginaw Broadcasting Co. v. F.C.C.*,[17] the court of appeals, after noting the necessity for findings of fact by administrative agencies and the reasons for the requirement, said that "In discussing the necessary content of findings of fact, it fill be helpful to spell out the process which a commission properly follows in reaching a decision. The process necessarily includes at least four parts: (1) evidence must be taken and weighed, both as to its accuracy and credibility; (2) from attentive consideration of this evidence a determination of facts of a basic or underlying nature must be reached; (3) from these basic facts the ultimate facts, usually in the language of the statute, are to be inferred, or not, as the case may be; (4) from this finding the decision will follow by the application of the statutory criterion." In the *Saginaw* case, the court noted further (p. 563) that the absence of required findings is fatal to the validity of the administrative decision regardless of whether there may be in the record evidence to support proper findings. The court, therefore, is not required to inquire as to what evidence there is which might support adequate findings.[18]

In *Commonwealth of Puerto Rico v. F.M.B.*,[19] the court of appeals was asked to review a Commission ruling that certain large rate increases for carriage of cargo between Puerto Rico and ports on the Atlantic and Gulf coasts were just and reasonable. The Commission had acted under Section 18 of the Shipping Act and Section 3 of the Intercoastal Shipping Act. In its report, the Commission merely stated that it found that the value of the vessels on the domestic market, with adjustments to eliminate short term peaks in vessel values, was the proper method for determining the value of the property being used for the public. The Commission did not say why it adopted market value as a rate base or why it rejected Puerto Rico's contention that the base was grossly excessive and rates should be based on prudent investment less depreciation. The court of appeals said (p. 420) that the

---

[15]*Anglo-Canadian Shipping Co. v. F.M.C.*, 310 F. 2d 606, 615.
[16]324 U.S. 626, 634.
[17]796 F. 2d 554, 559.
[18]*Anglo-Canadian Shipping Co., Ltd. v. F.M.C.*, 310 F. 2d 606, 617.
[19]288 F. 2d 419.

rate base question could not be resolved on the record. The court said that the Administrative Procedure Act[20] requires all decisions to state not only findings and conclusions but also the reasons or basis therefor, upon all the material issues of fact, law or discretion presented on the record. The court said that the Commission should make the basis of its action reasonably clear, and "We cannot find that it did so here."[21]

The courts have recognized the desirability of enabling regulatory agencies to exercise broad discretion in the selection of a rate base, but as pointed out in the *Puerto Rico* case, the administrative agency should state the reasons for adopting a particular rate base. In *F.P.C. v. Natural Gas Pipeline Co.*,[22] the Supreme Court held that the Constitution does not bind rate-making bodies to the use of any single formula or combination of formulas. Also in *F.P.C. v. Hope Natural Gas Co.*,[23] the court held that it was not the theory but the impact of the rate order which counts; if the total effect of the rate order cannot be said to be unjust and unreasonable, judicial inquiry is at an end. The fact that the method employed to reach that result may contain infirmities is not then important.

Reparation Orders

In *Flota Mercante Grancolombiana v. F.M.C.*,[24] the court said (p. 894) that the Hobbs Act was meant "to clarify and simplify the review situation as much as possible, rather than to perpetuate distinctions, between awards, denial of awards" and other actions;[25] and that even though the Act in terms does not give the court of appeals authority to render a money judgment based on a Commission order awarding reparation or to enforce any order of the Commission, Congress intended the court of appeals to review reparation orders at least to the extent necessary to determine the validity of such orders on appropriate petition. The court of appeals pointed out, however, that if a carrier chose not to obey an order of the Commission for payment of reparation, even after affirmance by the court of appeals, "it may

---

[20]U.S.C. 557(c).

[21]See *Radio Station KFH Co. v. F.C.C.*, 247 F. 2d 570, 572; *Pacific Far East Line, Inc. v. F.M.B.* 275 F. 2d 184. Cf. *Secretary of Agriculture v. United States*, 347 U.S. 645, 654.

[22]315 U.S. 586.

[23]320 U.S. 602.

[24]302 F. 2d 887.

[25]Cf. *Pennsylvania R. Co. v. United States*, 363 U.S. 202; *D. L. Piazza Co. v. West Coast Line, Inc.*, 210 F. 2d 947, cert. denied 348 U.S. 839.

be that to obtain enforcement, the complainant would be forced to go into the district court in a suit under Section 30 of the Shipping Act," and that the defendant in such a suit would be free to ask for a jury trial and to introduce evidence not previously before the Commission.

Section 29 of the Shipping Act of 1916[26] provides that in case of violation of any order of the Commission, "other than an order for the payment of money," the Commission "or any party injured by such violation, or the Attorney General, may apply to a district court having jurisdiction of the parties; and if, after hearing, the court determines that the order was regularly made and duly issued, it shall enforce obedience thereto by a writ of injunction or other proper process, mandatory or otherwise." Section 30[27] provides that in case of violation of any order of the Commission for the "payment of money the person to whom such award was made may file in the district court for the district in which such person resides, or in which is located any office of the carrier or other person to whom the order was directed, or in which is located any point of call on a regular route operated by the carrier, or in any court of general jurisdiction of a State, Territory, District, or possession of the United States having jurisdiction of the parties, a petition or suit setting forth briefly the causes for which he claims damages and the order of the board in the premises." In the district court the findings and order of the Commission "shall be prima facie evidence of the facts therein stated, and the petitioner shall not be liable for costs, nor shall he be liable for costs at any subsequent stage of the proceedings unless they accrue upon his appeal. If a petitioner in a district court finally prevails, he shall be allowed a reasonable attorney's fee, to be taxed and collected as part of the costs of the suit." All parties in whose favor the Commission "has made an award of reparation by a single order may be joined as plaintiffs, and all other parties to such order may be joined as defendants, in a single suit in any district in which any one such plaintiff could maintain a suit against any one such defendant. Service of process against any such defendant not found in that district may be made in any district in which is located any office of, or point of call on a regular route operated by, such defendant. Judgment may be entered in favor of any plaintiff against the defendant liable to that plaintiff." Section 30 provides further that no "petition or suit for the enforcement of an order for the payment of money shall be maintained unless filed within one year from the date of the order."

[26]46 U.S.C. 828.
[27]46 U.S.C. 829.

61

Implementation
of National Environmental Policy
by Administrative Agencies

The National Environmental Policy Act of 1969 (NEPA)[1] declares—

> that it is the continuing policy of the Federal Government, in cooperation with State and local governments, and other concerned public and private organizations, to use all practicable means and measures, including financial and technical assistance, in a manner calculated to foster and promote the general welfare, to create and maintain conditions under which man and nature can exist in productive harmony, and fulfill the social, economic, and other requirements of present and future generations of Americans.

To implement this policy the Congress, in the same statute, authorized and directed, among other things, that, to the fullest extent possible: (1) the policies, regulations, and public laws of the United States shall be interpreted and administered in accordance with the policies set forth in this Act, and (2) all agencies of the Federal Government shall—

> (B) identify and develop methods and procedures, in consultation with the Council on Environmental Quality . . . , which will insure that presently unquantified environmental amenities and values may be given appropriate consideration in decision-making along with economic and technical considerations;

> (C) include in every recommendation or report on proposals for legislation and other major Federal actions significantly affecting the quality of the human environment, a detailed statement by the responsible official on—

>> (i) the environmental impact of the proposed action,
>> (ii) any adverse environmental effects which cannot be avoided should the proposal be implemented,
>> (iii) alternatives to the proposed action,

[1]Public Law 91-224, 42 U.S.C. 4321, 4331-35, 4341-47.

(iv) the relationship between local short term uses of man's environment and the maintenance and enhancement of long-term productivity, and

(v) any irreversible and irretrievable commitments of resources which would be involved in the proposed action should it be implemented.

Prior to making any detailed statement, the responsible Federal official shall consult with and obtain the comments of any Federal agency which has jurisdiction by law or special expertise with respect to any environmental impact involved. Copies of such statement and the comments and views of the appropriate Federal, State, and local agencies, which are authorized to develop and enforce environmental standards shall, be made available to the President, the Council on Environmental Quality and to the public as provided by section 552 of title 5, United States Code, and shall accompany the proposal through the existing agency review processes; . . .

The policies and goals set forth in the NEPA are made supplementary to those set forth in existing authorizations of Federal agencies, and all such agencies, are required to review their present statutory authority, administrative regulations, and current policies and procedures for the purpose of determining whether there are any deficiencies or inconsistencies therein which prohibit full compliance with the purposes and provisions of that act.

The I.C.C.'s environmental rules, adopted in 1972,[2] were in response to interim guidelines promulgated by the Council on Environmental Quality in 1970. These rules, codified at 49 CFR 1100.250, require, among other things, that all initial papers filed with the I.C.C. by a party indicate whether the requested I.C.C. action would have an effect on the quality of the human environment. If an effect is alleged to be present, all parties must submit statements concerning the five factors which NEPA requires to be considered under Section 102(2)(C). When the proposed action is determined to have a significant environmental impact a detailed environmental impact statement is made as part of the initial determination which will become final (with or without modification) when the I.C.C. enters its final order. Those rules do not contemplate the holding of hearings prior to the issuance of a draft EIS.

Since the promulgation of the I.C.C.'s NEPA guidelines in 1972, a number of court decisions have raised numerous questions about the adequacy of its NEPA, procedures. In *Greene County Planning Board v. Federal Power Commission*,[3] the NEPA guidelines prepared by FPC were declared invalid because the agency had substituted an environmental impact statement prepared by an applicant as its own and had

---

[2]See *Implementation — Natl. Environmental Policy Act, 1969,* 340 I.C.C. 431.
[3]455 F. 2d 412.

failed to make the draft statement available prior to the holding of formal hearings. Conforming to the *Greene County* decision, CEQ revised its interim guidelines at 40 CFR 1500. The revised CEQ guidelines suggest that no public hearings be held until at least 15 days after issuance of a draft EIS. In addition, the guidelines recognize that agencies must depend on applicants to provide initial environmental information in some situations. Consequently, agencies are advised to assist applicants by outlining the types of information required,[4] but, in all cases, the agency should make its own evaluation of the environmental issues and take responsibility for the scope and content of draft and final impact statements.

In *Harlem Valley Transportation Association v. Stafford*,[5] the court expressly followed its earlier holding in *Greene County* and found, among other things, that the I.C.C.'s environmental guidelines as applied to rail abandonment proceedings did not comply with NEPA, in that evaluation of environmental issues must take place prior to any hearings and the impact statement must be the product of an independent staff investigation rather than a reliance on applicant's assertions.

Based on the *Gren County* and *Harlem Valley* interpretation of NEPA, the I.C.C. concluded that its enviromental rules were deficient in a number of aspects. Consequently, a rulemaking proceeding was instituted in Ex Parte No. 55 (Sub-No. 4), *Revised Guidelines for the Implementation of the National Environmental Policy Act of 1969*, for the purposes of examining and evaluating the existing environmental rules in light of the above-mentioned judicial interpretations, and for the purpose of proposing new environmental rules.

At approximately the same time that the rulemaking was instituted, the Supreme Court issued its decision in *Aberdeen & Rockfish Procedures (SCRAP II)*.[6] The *SCRAP II* case represents the first major decision by the Supreme Court interpreting the substantive aspects of NEPA. One of the main thrusts of the decision is the recognition of a basic distinction between actions which are initiated by federal agencies and actions proposed by private parties for which feredal license or permit is required. In reviewing the environmental procedures employed by the I.C.C. in authorizing a general rate increase proposal filed by the Nation's railroads, the Court concluded, among other things, that the timing of environmental impact statements is determined by the provision in NEPA which requires that the impact statement be included in recom-

---

[4]The CEQ Guidelines recognize the need for agencies, which must rely on applicants to submit initial environmental information, to assist applicants by outlining the types of information required.

[5]500 F. 2d 328, affirming 360 F. Supp. 1057.

[6]422 U.S. 289.

mendations or reports "on proposals." The Court noted that there is no statutory duty to prepare a final impact statement until a federal proposal is made, and when a proposal is initiated by a private applicant for which a federal license or permit is required, the earliest time at which an impact statement is required is at the time the agency issues a report on the proposal. This is in contrast to the situation where an agency initiates a federal action by publishing a proposal on its own.

The Court also concluded that the nature and scope of an environmental analysis is related to the scope of the agency proceeding for which the impact statement is prepared. It would appear, therefore, that a limited environmental impact statement is permissible as long as the action to which it relates is likewise limited in nature.

SCRAP II recognizes that the only statutory requirement of NEPA is that a detailed impact statement be filed. The Court concluded that the statement referred to in NEPA must be the final statement because no other statement is mentioned in the statute.

In *SCRAP II* the Court also recognized the need for agencies to consult with other agencies prior to preparation of the final impact statement.[7] It found that the I.C.C. had prepared and circulated a draft statement and received substantive comments. At the very least, tacit approval was given to the draft statement and comment process, and the Court seemed to agree that this, as a practical matter, satisfied the consultation requirement of NEPA.

Although no specific reference to an environmental threshold assessment survey or negative declaration is contained in NEPA, this has been required in borderline proceedings where there is generally a potential for environmental impacts, but due to particular circumstances, the impacts are not significant. In these instances courts have required the agency to substantiate any conclusion not to prepare an impact statement.[8] The environmental threshold assessment survey represents a reviewable record of this determination, and will enable a reviewing

[7]To fulfill this consultation requirement, CEQ developed a two-stage impact statement process (i.e., draft and final). Under this procedure, the purpose of the draft statement is to inform other agencies and the public of the proposed action, potential impacts, and available alternatives, thereby providing the necessary information for consultation. The draft statement is important in the NEPA process inasmuch as outside views can enhance objectivity and minimize any bias in the draft statement. The final statement generally receives only "in-house" review. It is supposed to present to the decisionmaker an objective analysis of environmental impacts.

[8]*First National Bank v. Richardson*, 7th Cir. 1973, 5 ERC 1830; *Hanly v. Kleindienst*, 471 F. 2d 823. The CEQ guidelines specifically recommend that each agency should review the typical classes of actions that it undertakes and develop specific criteria and methods for identifying those actions likely to require environmental impact statements.

court to determine whether the decision not to prepare an EIS was arbitrary or capricious.[9] The preparation of a negative declaration has become a widely accepted procedure for federal agencies.

The I.C.C. has assessed the environmental impact statements for the following general revenue proceedings: Ex Parte 281, *Increased Freight Rates and Charges, 1972* and Ex Parte 295 (Sub-No. 1), *Increased Freight Rates and Charges, 1973 — Recyclable Materials.* In both of these proceedings it concluded that there would be no significant environmental impacts resulting from approval of the proposed rate increases. Additionally, a single environmental impact statement was prepared for Ex Parte No. 270 (Sub-No. 5), *Investigation of Railroad Freight Rate Structure — Iron Ore,* and Ex Parte 270 (Sub-No. 6), *Investigation of Railroad Freight Rate Structure — Scrap Iron and Steel.* The purpose of this impact statement was to consider the environmental impacts of various possible I.C.C. actions regarding changes in the rates charged for the transportation of iron and steel scrap in comparison with iron ores. Based on an extensive environmental investigation, it was concluded that inasmuch as the consumption of the purchased scrap is inelastic to changes in the transportation rate charged, changes in the rate for scrap iron and steel have very little impact upon the consumption of scrap, and as a consequence, changes in the transportation rate have a negligible effect on the environment.

Since the preparation of the above-mentioned environmental impact statements, the I.C.C. had occasion to investigate the environmental impacts associated with additional general revenue proceedings. In all of these proceedings an impact statement was not prepared inasmuch as the same conclusion was reached as in Ex Parte Nos. 281, 295 (Sub-No. 1), and 270 (Sub-Nos. 5 and 6), i.e., that granting of the requested rate increases would not result in any significant environmental impacts. To substantiate this conclusion, the I.C.C. prepared an environmental threshold assessment survey for Ex Parte No. 299, *Increased Freight Rates and Charges to Offset Retirement Tax Increases, 1973,* and Ex Parte No. 303, *Increased Freight Rates and Charges,* 1974. Finally, it concluded in Ex Parte No. 310, *Increased Freight Rate and Charges, 1975, Nationwide,* that neither the immediate nor cumulative effect of the proposed increase would have a significant effect on the environment.

The I.C.C. also has conducted detailed environmental investigations in general revenue proceedings, and in every instance it has concluded that the rate increase proposals either individually or cumulatively would not result in significant environmental impacts.

[9]*Maryland Planning Commission v. Postal Service,* 487 F. 2d 1029.

Appendix A: Master Disposition Table—Interstate Commerce Act

This table shows the disposition of provisions of the Interstate Commerce Act and related laws according to the United States Code Citation under Public Law 95-473, 95th Congress, October 17, 1978, an act to revise, codify, and enact without substantive change to the Interstate Commerce Act and related laws as subtitle IV of Title 49, United States Code, "Transportation".

TABLE I-A—UNITED STATES CODE

United States Code		United States Code Revised	
Title	Section	Title	Section
45	715(a) (words after the comma in the 2d sentence).	49	10362
	715(a) (less words after the comma in the 2d sentence).	49	10361
	715(b)	49	10363
	715(c) (first 2 sentences)	49	10363
	715(c) (less first 2 sentences)	49	10364
	715(d)	49	10362
	715(e)	49	10362
	744(j)	49	10504
	793	49	10710
49	1(1)	49	10501
	1(2)	49	10501
	1(3)	49	10102
	1(4) (related to standards)	49	10701
	1(4) (2d sentence last cl.)	49	10702
	1(4) (1st sentence related to through routes and 2d sentence less last cl.)	49	10703
	1(4) (1st sentence 14th—23d words)	49	11101
	1(5)(a)	49	10701
	1(5)(b) (7th and 8th sentences)	49	10709
	1(5)(b) (less 7th and 8th sentences)	49	10701
	1(5)(c)(i)	49	10709
	1(5)(c)(ii)	49	10102

1235

TABLE I-A—UNITED STATES CODE—Continued

United States Code		United States Code Revised	
Title	Section	Title	Section
49	1(5)(d)		
	1(5½)	49	10749
	1(6) (last sentence)	49	10750
	1(6) (less last sentence)	49	10702
	1(7) (1st sentence, 32 words before 8th semicolon-9th semicolon).	49	10721
	1(7) (1st sentence words before 2d semicolon, words between 5th semicolon and 21st word after 7th semicolon, 1st-18th words after 9th semicolon, 1st proviso (words before semicolon), 2d, and 3d provisos).	49	10722
	1(7) (1st sentence 1st-4th and 13th-20th words after 2d semicolon and words between 3d and 5th semicolons).	49	10723
	1(7) (1st sentence 5th-12th and 21st-29th words after 2d semicolon and last 11 words before 1st proviso).	49	10723
	1(7) (1st sentence 1st proviso, words between semicolon and colon).	49	10724
	1(7) (less 1st sentence)	49	11905
	1(8)	49	10746
	1(9)	49	11104
	1(10)	49	10102
	1(11)	49	11121
	1(12) (3d sentence)	49	11902
	1(12) (less 3d sentence)	49	11126
	1(13)	49	11121
	1(14)(a)	49	11122
	1(14)(b)	49	11105
	1(15) (related to car service less last sentence)	49	11123
	1(15) (last sentence)	49	11128
	1(15) (related to service less last sentence)	49	11127
	1(16) (related to traffic less (b))	49	11124
	1(16) (related to service less (b))	49	11127
	1(16)(b)	49	11125
	1(17)(a)(1st sentence)	49	11121
	1(17)(a) (last sentence less proviso)	49	11703
	1(17)(a) (last sentance proviso)	49	10501
	1(17)(b)	49	11907
	1(18)(a)	49	10901
	1(18)(b)	49	10901
	1(18)(c)	49	10902
	1(18)(d)	49	10907
	1(18)(e) (related to action by the Attorney General)	49	11703
	1(18)(e) (related to Commission action)	49	11702
	1(18)(e)	49	11901
	1(18)(e) (related to State enforcement)	49	11505
	1(19)-(22)		
	1a(1) (1st sentence)	49	10903
	1a(1) (less 1st and last sentences)	49	10904
	1a(1) (last sentence)	49	10907
	1a(2)	49	10904
	1a(3)	49	10904
	1a(4)	49	10903
	1a(5)	49	10904
	1a(6)	49	10905
	1a(7)	49	10905
	1a(8)		
	1a(9) (related to Commission action)	49	11702
	1a(9) (related to action by the Attorney General)	49	11703
	1a(9) (last sentence)	49	11901
	1a(9) (related to State enforcement)	49	11505
	1a(10)	49	10906
	1a(11)	49	10905
	2	49	10741
	3(1)	49	10741
	3(1a)		
	3(2) (1st sentence)	49	10743
	3(2) (less 1st sentence)	49	10744
	3(3)	49	10744
	3(4) (1st sentence 2d cl., 2d sentence related to standards).	49	10701
	3(4) (less 1st sentence 2d cl., and 2d sentence related to facilities).	49	10742
	3(5)	49	11103
	4	49	10726
	5(1) (words between semicolon and 1st colon)	49	11914
	5(1) (less words between semicolon and 1st colon)	49	11342
	5(2)(a)	49	11343
	5(2)(b)-(e)	49	11344
	5(2)(f)	49	11347
	5(2)(g)	49	11345

1236

TABLE I-A—UNITED STATES CODE—Continued

United States Code		United States Code Revised	
Title	Section	Title	Section
49	5(2)(h)	49	11345
	5(3)(a)-(e)	49	11346
	5(3)(f) (last sentence)	49	11346
	5(3)(f) (less last sentence)	49	11350
	5(3)(g)	49	11346
	5(4)	49	11348
	5(5)	49	11343
	5(6)	49	11343
	5(7)	49	11343
	5(8) (last sentence)	49	11912
	5(8) (less last sentence)	49	11701
	5(9)	49	11702
	5(10)	49	11701
	5(11)	49	11343
	5(12)	49	11341
	5(13)		
	5(14)	49	11343
	5(15) (words after semicolon)	49	11914
	5(15) (less words after semicolon)	49	11321
	5(16)	49	11321
	5(17)	49	11321
	5a	49	10706
	5b	49	10706
	5c	49	10762
	6(1)	49	10765
	6(2)	49	10762
	6(3)	49	10762
	6(4)	49	10764
	6(5)	49	10762
	6(6)	49	10761
	6(7)	49	11128
	6(8)	49	10762
	6(9)	49	11901
	6(10)	49	10503
	6(11)	49	10765
	6(12)	49	10745
	7	49	11705
	8	49	11705
	9	49	11914
	10(1)	49	11904
	10(2)-(4)	49	10301
	11	49	10321
	12(1)(a) (less 2d sentence words after semicolon and last sentence words after 1st semicolon and before last semicolon)		
	12(1)(a) (words after semicolon in 2d sentence)	49	10311
	12(1)(a) (last sentence less words before 1st semicolon and after last semicolon)	49	11703
	12(1)(b)	49	10505
	12(2)-(7)	49	10321
	13(1)	49	11701
	13(2) (last sentence)	49	11502
	13(2) (less last sentence)	49	11701
	13(3)	49	11502
	13(4)	49	11501
	13(5)	49	11501
	13(6)	49	10326
	13a(1)	49	10908
	13a(2)	49	10909
	14(1)	49	10310
	14(2)	49	10310
	14(3) (last sentence)	49	10311
	14(3) (less last sentence)	49	10310
	15(1)	49	10704
	15(2)	49	10324
	15(3)	49	10705
	15(4)	49	10705
	15(5)	49	10748
	15(6)	49	10748
	15(7)	49	10708
	15(8) [1]	49	10707
	15(9)	49	10709
	15(10)	49	10763
	15(11)	49	11710
	15(12)	49	10763
	15(13)	49	11910
	15(14)	49	11910
	15(15)	49	10747
	15(16)	49	10321
	15(17)	49	10727

See footnotes at end of table.

TABLE I-A—UNITED STATES CODE—Continued

United States Code		United States Code Revised	
Title	Section	Title	Section
49	15(18)	49	10728
	15(19)	49	10729
	15a(1)–(5)	49	10704
	15a(6)		
	15b		
	16(1)	49	11705
	16(2)	49	11705
	16(3)(c)	49	11705
	16(3)(g)	49	11705
	16(3)(h)		
	16(3) (less (c), (g), and (h))	49	11706
	16(4)	49	11705
	16(5)	49	10329
	16(6)	49	10324
	16(7)	49	11914
	16(8)	49	11901
	16(9)	49	11901
	16(10)	49	11901
	16(11)	49	10301
	16(12) (related to Commission action)	49	11702
	16(12) (related to action by the Attorney General)	49	11703
	16(12) (related to action by private person)	49	11705
	16(12) (enforcement of money award)	49	11705
	16(13)	49	10303
	16a		
	17(1)	49	10302
	17(2) (1st sentences 80th–98th words and 2d sentence)	49	10304
	17(2) (less 80th–90th words in 1st sentence, less 2d sentence).	49	10305
	17(3) (less 2d sentence and last 42 words of 3d sentence).	49	10306
	17(3) (2d sentence)	49	10301
	17(3) (last 42 words of 3d sentence)	49	10321
	17(4) (1st and 3d sentences)	49	10305
	17(4) (2d sentence)	49	10303
	17(5)	49	10322
	17(6)	49	10323
	17(7)	49	10323
	17(8)	49	10324
	17(9)(j)	49	10310
	17(9) (less (j))	49	10327
	17(10)	49	10325
	17(11)	49	10305
	17(11)	49	10305
	17(12)	49	10328
	17(13)	49	10339
	17(14)(a)	49	11701
	17(14)(b)		
	17(15)	49	10309
	18(1) (1st and 3d sentences)	49	10301
	18(1) (2d sentence)	49	10303
	18(1) (4th sentence)	49	10307
	18(1) (last sentence)	49	10321
	18(2)	49	10301
	19	49	10307
	19a(a) (1st and last sentences)	49	10781
	19a(a) (2d and 3d sentences)	43	10331
	19a(b)	49	10782
	19a(c)	49	10781
	19a(d)		
	19a(e)	49	10783
	19a(f)	43	10781
	19a(g)	49	10784
	19a(h)	49	10785
	19a(i)	49	10785
	19a(j)	49	10785
	19a(k) (1st sentence)	49	10786
	19a(k) (less 1st sentence)	49	11901
	19a(l)	49	11703
	20(1)	49	11145
	20(2)	49	11145
	20(3) (less (e)) [2]	49	11142
	20(3)(e)		
	20(4)	49	11143
	20(5)	49	11144
	20(6) (2d sentence, 1st cl.)	49	11144
	20(6) (2d sentence, 2d cl.)	49	11145
	20(6) (less 2d sentence)	49	11144
	20(7)(a)	49	11901
	20(7)(b) (proviso)	49	11144

See footnotes at end of table.

TABLE I–A—UNITED STATES CODE—Continued

United States Code		United States Code Revised	
Title	Section	Title	Section
49	20(7)(b) (less proviso)	49	11909
	20(7)(c)	49	11901
	20(7)(d)	49	11901
	20(7)(e)	49	11901
	20(7)(f)	49	11910
	20(8)	49	11141
	20(9)	49	11703
	20(10)	49	10301
	20(11) (2d sentence, 1st proviso)	49	10103
	20(11) (less 1st sentence 2d proviso related to released value, 2d sentence less words before 2d provisio).	49	11707
	20(11) (1st sentence 2d proviso related to released value), 2d sentence (less 1st–5th provisos).	49	10730
	20(12)	49	11707
	20a(1)–(10)	49	11301
	20a(11) (2d and 3d sentences)	49	11709
	20a(11) (less 2d, 3d, and 4th sentences)	49	11301
	20a(11) (last sentence)	49	11911
	20a(12) (last sentence)	49	11911
	20a(12) (less last sentence)	49	11322
	20b(1)	49	11361
	20b(2) (1st–3d sentences, 4th sentence less words between 8th comma and period, 9th sentence).	49	11362
	20b(2) (4th sentence, words between 8th comma and period, 8th comma and period, 8th sentence).	49	11363
	20b(2) (5th and 7th sentences)	49	11364
	20b(2) (less 1st–9th sentences)	49	11365
	20b(3) (1st and last sentences)	49	11362
	20b(3) (less 1st and last sentences)	49	11363
	20b(4)	49	11365
	20b(5)	49	11361
	20b(6)	49	11366
	20b(7)		
	20b(8)	49	11362
	20b(9)	49	11367
	20b(10)	49	11321
	20b(11)	49	11367
	20b(12)		6
	20b(13)	49	1131
	20c	49	11303
	21	49	10311
	22(1) (1st sentence 1st 26th and 62d-76th words)	49	10721
	22(1) (1st sentence 77th–86th words and 2d proviso, 2d–4th sentences).	49	10722
	22(1) (1st sentence words between 2d and 4th semi-colons).	49	10722
	22(1) (1st sentence words between 4th and 5th semi-colons).	49	10722
	22(1) (1st sentence 27th–61st words and words between 1st and 2d semicolons).	49	10723
	22(1) (1st sentence words between 6th semicolon and 1st proviso).	49	10723
	22(1) (last 2 sentences)	49	10724
	22(1) (1st sentence words between 5th and 6th semicolons).	49	10103
	22(1) (1st proviso 1st sentence)		
	22(2) (less 1st sentence proviso)	49	10721
	22(2) (1st sentence proviso)		
	23	49	11703
	25		
	26 ³		
	26a	49	11504
	26b	49	10381–10388
	26c	49	11503
	29		
	41(1) (1st sentence)	49	11915
	41(1) (less 1st sentence)	49	11903
	41(2) (related to corporate violations)	49	11903
	41(2) (related to corporate violations)	49	11915
	41(2) (last sentence)	49	11916
	41(3)	49	11902
	42		
	43	49	11703
	44		
	45		
	46	49	11913
	49 ⁴	49	
	50 (related to notice)	49	10329
	50 (related to process)	49	10330

See footnotes at end of table.

TABLE I–A—UNITED STATES CODE—Continued

United States Code		United States Code Revised	
Title	Section	Title	Section
49	51 (related to ownership)	49	11321
	51 (related to 49:6(11))	49	10503
	52	49	10783
	53		
	54		
	55		
	56		
	57		
	58		
	59		
	60	49	11507
	61–64		
	65	49	10721
	65a	49	10721
	66		
	67 [6]		
	71		
	72		
	73		
	74		
	75		
	76		
	77		
	78		
	79		
	80		
	81–124 [6]		
	141		
	142		
	143		
	151–157		
	250		
	251		
	252		
	253–263		
	264		
	265–268		
	301		
	302(a)	49	10521
	302(b)(1)	49	10521
	302(b) (less (1))	49	11506
	302(c)	49	10523
	303(a)(1)	49	10102
	303(a)(2)	49	10342
	303(a)(3)		
	303(a)(4)	49	10341
	303(a)(5)		
	303(a)(6)		
	303(a)(7)		
	303(a)(8)	49	10102
	303(a)(9)	49	10102
	303(a)(10) (proviso)	49	10522
	303(a)(10) (less proviso)	49	10521
	303(a)(11)	49	10521
	303(a)(12)	49	10102
	303(a)(13)	49	10102
	303(a)(14) (words before 2d comma)	49	10102
	303(a)(14) (words after 2d comma)	49	10502
	303(a)(15)	49	10102
	303(a)(16)	49	10102
	303(a)(17)	49	10102
	303(a)(18)	49	10102
	303(a)(19)	49	10102
	303(a)(20)		
	303(a)(21)		
	303(a)(22) [3]		
	303(a)(23) [3]		
	303(b)	49	10526
	303(c) (words between 6th and 7th commas)	49	10521
	303(c) (words before "nor", less words between 6th and 7th commas)	49	10921
	303(c) (less words before "nor")	49	10524
	304(a) (matter preceding (1))	49	10321
	304(a)(1) (related to service)	49	11101
	304(a)(1) (related to accounts)	49	11142
	304(a)(1) ("qualifications" through period) [3]		
	304(a)(2) ("qualifications" through period) [3]		
	304(a)(2) (less "qualifications" through period)	49	11142
	304(a)(3) [3]		
	304(a)(3a) [3]		

See footnotes at end of table

TABLE I–A—UNITED STATES CODE—Continued

United States Code		United States Code Revised	
Title	Section	Title	Section
49	304(a)(4)	49	11142
	304(a)(4a)	49	10525
	304(a)(5) ³		
	304(a)(6)	49	10321
	304(a)(7) (words after semicolon)	49	10311
	304(a)(7) (less words after semicolon)	49	10321
	304(b)	49	11102
	304(c)	49	11701
	304(d) (related to administration matters)	49	10303
	304(d) (related to reports)	49	10310
	304(d)	49	10311
	304(e)	49	11107
	304(f)	49	11101
	304a(1)	49	11706
	304a(2)	49	11706
	304a(3)	49	11706
	304a(4)	49	11706
	304a(5)	49	11705
	304a(6)	49	11705
	304a(7)		
	304a(8)	49	11706
	305(a) (1st and 2d sentences)	49	10341
	305(a) (3d sentence less proviso)	49	10342
	305(a) (3d sentence proviso)	49	10344
	305(a) (less 1st–3d sentences)	49	10343
	305(b) (2d sentence, 1st 12 words)	49	10344
	305(b) (1st, 3d, 5th, and 12th sentences)	49	10342
	305(b) (2d sentence 13th–37th words)	49	10341
	305(b) (4th and 6th sentences)	49	10342
	305(b) (7th sentence)	49	10343
	305(b) (8th sentence)	49	10343
	305(b) (9th sentence)	49	10343
	305(b) (10th sentence)	49	10342
	305(b) (11th sentence)	49	10344
	305(b) (less 1st–12th sentences)	49	10342
	305(c) (related to the Commission)	49	10307
	305(c) (related to joint boards)	49	10344
	305(d) (related to Commission and employee board subpena power).	49	10321
	305(d) (related to joint boards)	49	10344
	305(d) (related to liability)	49	11913
	305(e)	49	10328
	305(f) (4th sentence)	49	10344
	305(f) (less 4th sentence)	49	11502
	305(g) (proviso)		
	305(g) (less proviso)	49	11705, 11706
	305(h)	49	10301–10306, 10308, 10309. 10321–10325, 10328.
	305(i) (related to members of Commission)	49	10301
	305(i) (related to joint board)	49	10344
	305(i) (related to examiner)	49	10306
	305(j)	49	10301
	305a		
	306(a)(1) (word before proviso)	49	10921
	306(a)(1) (words after colon)		
	306(a)(2)	49	10932
	306(a)(3)		
	306(a)(4)		
	306(a)(5)		
	306(a)(6)	49	10931
	306(a)(7)	49	10932
	306(b)	49	10922
	307	49	10922
	308 (a), (b)	49	10922
	308 (c), (d)	43	10332
	309(a)(1) (words before 1st proviso)	49	10321
	309(a)(1) (words between 1st and last colons)		
	309(a)(1) (last proviso)	49	10526
	309(a)(2)	49	10932
	309(a)(3)		
	309(a)(4)		
	309(a)(5)		
	309(b) (last proviso)	49	10932
	309(b) (less last proviso)	49	10923
	310	49	10930
	310a(a)	49	10928
	310a(b)	49	11349
	310a(c)	49	10928
	310a(c)	49	11349

See footnotes at end of table.

1241

TABLE I-A—UNITED STATES CODE—Continued

United States Code		United States Code Revised	
Title	Section	Title	Section
49	311(a) (words before 1st proviso)	49	10921
	311(a) (words after 1st colon)	49	10924
	311(b)	49	10924
	311(c) (words before 2d comma)	49	10924
	311(c) (words after 2d comma)	49	10927
	311(d)	49	11144
	312(a)	49	10925
	312(b)	49	10926
	312(c)		
	313	49	11304
	314 (related to securities)	49	11302
	314 (related to penalties)	49	11911
	315	49	10927
	316 (related to standards)	49	10701
	316(a) (1st–24th, 45th–59th words)	49	10703
	316(a) (60th–143d words)	49	10702
	316(a) (25th–44th words)	49	11101
	316(b) (related to standards)	49	10701
	316(b) (16th–33d words)	49	11101
	316(b) (less 16th–33d words)	49	10702
	316(c) (less 2d sentence)	49	10703
	316(c) (2d sentence)	49	10702
	316(d) (1st sentence)	49	10701
	316(d) (less 1st sentence)	49	10741
	316(e) (2d sentence 2d cl.)	49	10705
	316(e) (2d sentence less 2d cl. and less proviso)	49	10704
	316(e) (proviso)	49	10521
	316(e) (less 2d sentence)	49	11701
	316(f)	49	10705
	316(g) (less proviso)	49	10708
	316(g) (proviso)		
	316(h)	49	10701
	316(i)	49	10704
	316(j)	49	10103
	317(a)	49	10762
	317(b) (proviso)	49	10103, 10721–10724
	317(b) (less proviso)	49	10761
	317(c)	49	10762
	317(d)	49	10761
	318(a) (1st sentence related to standards)	49	10701
	318(a) (1st and 4th sentences, and 7th sentence proviso related to relief).	49	10702
	318(a) (2d, 5th, and 6th sentences, and 7th sentence proviso related to general requirements).	49	10762
	318(a) (3d sentence, 7th sentence less proviso, and 7th sentence proviso related to relief).	49	10761
	318(b)	49	10704
	318(c) (proviso)		
	318(c) (less proviso)	49	10708
	319	49	11701
	319	49	10730
	320(a) (1st and 2d sentences)	49	11145
	320(a) (less 1st and 2d sentences)	49	10764
	320(b)	49	11145
	320(c)	49	11143
	320(d)	49	11144
	320(e)	49	11141
	320(f) ³		
	320(g)	49	11144
	321(a)	49	10329
	321(b)	49	10324
	321(c)	49	10330
	321(d) (related to orders)	49	10324
	321(d) (related to notice)	49	10329
	321(d) (related to process)	49	10330
	322(a)	49	11914
	322(b)(1)	49	11702
	322(b) (less (1))	49	11708
	322(c) (related to rate violations)	49	11904
	322(c) (related to evasion of regulation)	49	11906
	322(d)	49	11910
	322(e)	49	11910
	322(f)	49	11910
	322(g)	49	11909
	322(h)	49	11901
	323 (1st sentence)	49	10743
	323 (less 1st sentence)	49	10744
	324	49	11106
	324a	49	10747
	325 ³		

TABLE I-A—UNITED STATES CODE—Continued

United States Code		United States Code Revised	
Title	Section	Title	Section
49	325a	49	11504
	326		
	327		
	901		
	902(a)	49	10102
	902(b)		
	902(c)	49	10102
	902(d) (less exception)	49	10102
	902(d) (words after 1st comma)	49	10502
	902(e) (1st and 2d sentences)	49	10102
	902(e) (3d–5th sentences)	49	10544
	902(f)	49	10102
	902(g)	49	10102
	902(h)	49	10102
	902(i)	49	10541
	902(j)–(m)	49	10102
	903(a)	49	10541
	903(b)	49	10542
	903(c)	49	10542
	903(d)	49	10542
	903(e)(1)	49	10544
	903(e)(2) (last sentence)		
	903(e)(2) (less last sentence)	49	10544
	903(e)(3)	49	10544
	903(f)	49	10543
	903(g)	40	10544
	903(h)	49	10544
	903(i)	49	10721
	903(j)	49	10541
	903(k)	48	10541
	903(l)	49	10929
	904(a)	49	10321
	904(b) (words after last semicolon)	49	10311
	904(b) (less words after last semicolon)	49	10321
	904(c)	49	11102
	904(d)	49	11108
	904(e)	49	11701
	905(a) (1st sentence related to standards and 2d sentence)	49	10701
	905(a) (1st sentence 1st cl.)	49	11101
	905(a) (less 1st sentence 1st cl. and last sentence)	49	10702
	905(b) (4th sentence)	49	10701, 10702
	905(b) (less 4th sentence)	49	10703
	905(c)	49	10741
	905(d) (1st sentence 2d cl., 2d sentence related to facilities)	49	10701
	905(d) (less 1st sentence 2d cl., 2d sentence related to standards)	49	10742
	906(a)	49	10762
	906(b)	49	10762
	906(c) (proviso)	49	10103, 10721–10724
	906(c) (less proviso)	49	10761
	906(d) (1st sentence)	49	10761
	906(d) (less 1st sentence)	49	10762
	906(e) (1st sentence related to standards)	49	10701
	906(e) (1st sentence and 7th sentence proviso related to relief)	49	10702
	906(e) (2d, 4th, 5th, and 6th sentences, and 7th sentence provision, related to general requirements)	49	10762
	906(e) (3d sentence, and 7th sentence less proviso, and 7th sentence proviso related to relief)	49	10761
	907(a)	49	11701
	907(b)	49	10704
	907(c)	49	10701
	907(d)	49	10705
	907(e)	49	10705
	907(f)	49	10704
	907(g) (proviso)	49	10708
	907(g) (less proviso)	49	10704
	907(h)		
	907(i) (proviso)		10708
	907(i) (less proviso)	49	11705
	908(a)–(e)	49	11705
	908(f)(4)	49	11706
	908(f) (less (4))	49	11706
	908(g)	49	11705
	908(g) (words before 1st proviso)	49	10921
	908(g) (words after 1st colon)	49	10922
	908(h)	49	10922
	908(c)	49	10922
	908(d)	49	10922

TABLE I-A—UNITED STATES CODE—Continued

United States Code		United States Code Revised	
Title	Section	Title	Section
49	909(e)	49	10922
	909(f) (words before 1st proviso)	49	10921
	909(f) (words after 1st colon)		
	909(g)	49	10923
	910	49	10930
	911(a)	49	10928
	911(b)	49	11349
	912	49	10926
	912a	49	10925
	913(a)	49	11145
	913(b)	49	10764
	913(c)	49	11142
	913(d)	49	11143
	913(e)	49	11144
	913(f)	49	11144
	913(g)	49	11144
	913 (less (a)–(g))	49	11141
	914	49	10747
	915(a)	49	10329
	915(b)	49	11701
	915(c)	49	10324
	915(d)	49	10324
	915(e)	49	11914
	916(a)	49	10301–10306, 10308, 10309, 10321–10325, 10328, 11703, 11913.
	916(b) (related to Commission action)	49	11702
	916(b) (related to action by the Attorney General)	49	11703
	916(b) (related to action by private person)	49	11705
	916(c)	49	10310
	916(d)	49	10303
	917(a)	49	11914
	917(b)	49	11904
	917(c)	49	11904
	917(d)	49	11909
	917(e)	49	11910
	917(f) (1st and 2d sentences)	49	11910
	917 (less (a)–(e) and (f) (1st and 2d sentences))	49	11910
	918 (1st sentence)	49	10743
	918 (less 1st sentence)	49	10744
	919	49	10301
	920		
	921		
	922		
	922a	49	11303
	922b	49	11504
	923		
	1001		
	1002(a)(2)		
	1002(a) (1), (3), (4), (5), (8)	49	10102
	1002(a) (6), (7)	49	10561
	1002(b)	49	10562
	1002(c)	49	10562
	1003(a)	49	10321
	1003(b)	49	11101
	1003(c)	49	10927
	1003(d)	49	10927
	1003(e) (words after last semicolon)	49	10311
	1003(e) (less words after last semicolon)	49	10321
	1003(f)	49	11701
	1004(a) (1st cl.)	49	11101
	1004(a) (related to standards)	49	10701
	1004(a) (related to carrier authority)	49	10702
	1004(b)	49	10741
	1004(c)	49	10741
	1004(d)	49	10766
	1005(a)	49	10762
	1005(b)	49	10762
	1005(c) (proviso)	49	10103, 10721–10724
	1005(c) (less proviso)	49	10761
	1005(d)	49	10762
	1005(e)	49	10761
	1006(a)	49	11701
	1006(b)	49	10704
	1006(c)	49	10701
	1006(d)	49	10704
	1006(e) (proviso)		
	1006(e) (less proviso)	49	10708
	1006(f) (2d and 3d sentences)	49	10502
	1006(f) (less 2d-last sentences)	49	11502
	1006(f) (4th and last sentences)	49	11501

TABLE I-A—UNITED STATES CODE—Continued

United States Code		United States Code Revised	
Title	Section	Title	Section
49	1006a (5), (6)	49	11705
	1006a (less (5), (6), (7))	49	11706
	1006a(7)		
	1007	49	10725
	1008	49	10725
	1009	49	10766
	1010(a)(1) (words before semicolon)	49	10921
	1010(a) (less words before semicolon in par. (1))		
	1010(b)	49	10923
	1010(c) (less 2d sentence, words before semicolon)	49	10923
	1010(c) (2d sentence, words before semicolon)	49	10930
	1010(d)	49	10923
	1010(e)	49	10923
	1010(f)	49	10925
	1010(g)	49	10926
	1010(h)	49	10930
	1010(i) (1st sentence)	49	10933
	1010(i) (less 1st sentence and 2d sentence words before semicolon).	49	11908
	1010(i) (related to Commission action)	49	11702
	1010(i) (related to enforcement by the United States)	49	11703
	1010(i) (related to private enforcement)	49	11704
	1010(i) (related to State enforcement)	49	11505
	1011(a)	49	11323
	1011(b) (last proviso)		
	1011(b) (less last proviso)	49	10930
	1011(c)	49	11323
	1011(d)	49	11701
	1011(e)	49	11702
	1011(f)	49	11701
	1011(g)	49	11323
	1012(a) (1st and 2d sentences)	49	11145
	1012(a) (3d sentence)	49	11142
	1012(a) (last sentence)	49	10764
	1012(b)	49	11145
	1012(c)	49	11144
	1012(d)	49	11144
	1012(e)	49	11144
	1012(f)	49	11141
	1013 (1st sentence related to released value)	49	10730
	1013	49	11707
	1014	49	10743
	1015	49	10747
	1016(a)	49	10329
	1016(b)	49	10324
	1016(c)	49	10324
	1016(d)	49	11914
	1017(a)	49	10301-10306, 10308, 10309, 10311, 10321-10325, 10328, 11703, 11705, 11913.
	1017(b)(1) (related to Commission action)	49	11702
	1017(b)(1) (related to action by the Attorney General)	49	11703
	1017(b)(1) (related to action by private person)	49	11705
	1017(b) (less (1))	49	11708
	1017(c)	49	10310
	1017(d)	49	10303
	1018	49	10749
	1019		
	1020 (related to service)	49	11127
	1020 (related to penalties)	49	11901
	1021(a)	49	11914
	1021(b)	49	11904
	1021(c)	49	11901
	1021(d)	49	11909
	1021(a)	49	11910
	1021(f)	49	11910
	1021 (less (a)-(f))	49	11703
	1022		
	1231-1240		

[1] Section 15(8)(b) and (c) repealed effective February 5, 1978.
[2] Repeal effective January 1, 1978.
[3] Scheduled for future codification in subtitle II of title 49.
[4] Previously transferred to sec. 23 of title 49.
[5] Previously transferred to sec. 66 of title 49 that is transferred to title 31 by this codification.
[6] Scheduled for future codification in subtitle V of title 49.

Appendix B: Revised Interstate Commerce Act

Public Law 95-473
95th Congress

An Act

To revise, codify, and enact without substantive change the Interstate Commerce Act and related laws as subtitle IV of title 49, United States Code, "Transportation".

Oct. 17, 1978

[H.R. 10965]

Be it enacted by the Senate and House of Representatives of the United States of America in Congress assembled, That certain general and permanent laws of the United States, related to transportation, are revised, codified, and enacted as title 49, United States Code, "Transportation", as follows:

Interstate
Commerce Act
and related laws.
Enactment as title
49, Subtitle IV.
U.S. Code.

TITLE 49—TRANSPORTATION

SUBTITLE   Sec.

I. [RESERVED—DEPARTMENT OF TRANSPORTATION]
II. [RESERVED—TRANSPORTATION PROGRAMS]
III. [RESERVED—AIR TRANSPORTATION]
IV. INTERSTATE COMMERCE _____ 10101
V. [RESERVED—MISCELLANEOUS]

SUBTITLE IV—INTERSTATE COMMERCE

CHAPTER 101—GENERAL PROVISIONS

§ 10101. Transportation policy

49 USC 10101.

(a) To ensure the development, coordination, and preservation of a transportation system that meets the transportation needs of the United States, including the United States Postal Service and national defense, it is the policy of the United States Government to provide for the impartial regulation of the modes of transportation subject to this subtitle, and in regulating those modes—

(1) to recognize and preserve the inherent advantage of each mode of transportation;

(2) to promote safe, adequate, economical, and efficient transportation;

(3) to encourage sound economic conditions in transportation, including sound economic conditions among carriers;

(4) to encourage the establishment and maintenance of reasonable rates for transportation without unreasonable discrimination or unfair or destructive competitive practices;

(5) to cooperate with each State and the officials of each State on transportation matters; and

(6) to encourage fair wages and working conditions in the transportation industry.

(b) This subtitle shall be administered and enforced to carry out the policy of this section.

49 USC 10102.

§ 10102. Definitions

In this subtitle—

(1) "broker" means a person, other than a motor carrier or an employee or agent of a motor carrier, that as a principal or agent sells, offers for sale, negotiates for, or holds itself out by solicitation, advertisement, or otherwise as selling, providing, or arranging for, transportation by motor carrier for compensation.

(2) "carrier" means a common carrier and a contract carrier.

(3) "car service" includes (A) the use, control, supply, movement, distribution, exchange, interchange, and return of locomotives, cars, other vehicles, and special types of equipment used in the transportation of property by a rail carrier, and (B) the supply of trains by a rail carrier.

(4) "common carrier" means an express carrier, a pipeline carrier, a rail carrier, a sleeping car carrier, a motor common carrier, a water common carrier, and a freight forwarder.

(5) "contract carrier" means a motor contract carrier and a water contract carrier.

(6) "control", when referring to a relationship between persons, includes actual control, legal control, and the power to exercise control, through or by (A) common directors, officers, stockholders, a voting trust, or a holding or investment company, or (B) any other means.

(7) "express carrier" means a person providing express transportation for compensation.

(8) "freight forwarder" means a person holding itself out to the general public (other than as an express, pipeline, rail, sleeping car, motor, or water carrier) to provide transportation of property for compensation and in the ordinary course of its business—

(A) assembles and consolidates, or provides for assembling and consolidating, shipments and performs or provides for break-bulk and distribution operations of the shipments;

(B) assumes responsibility for the transportation from the place of receipt to the place of destination; and

(C) uses for any part of the transportation a carrier subject to the jurisdiction of the Interstate Commerce Commission under subchapter I, II, or III of chapter 105 of this title.

Post, pp. 1359, 1361, 1365.

(9) "highway" means a road, highway, street, and way in a State.

(10) "motor carrier" means a motor common carrier and a motor contract carrier.

(11) "motor common carrier" means a person holding itself out to the general public to provide motor vehicle transportation for compensation over regular or irregular routes, or both.

(12) "motor contract carrier" means a person, other than a motor common carrier, providing motor vehicle transportation for compensation under continuing agreements with a person or a limited number of persons—

(A) by assigning motor vehicles for a continuing period of time for the exclusive use of each such person; or

(B) designed to meet the distinct needs of each such person.

(13) "motor private carrier" means a person, other than a motor carrier, transporting property by motor vehicle when—

(A) the transportation is as provided in section 10521(a) (1) and (2) of this title;

Post, p. 1361.

(B) the person is the owner, lessee, or bailee of the property being transported; and

(C) the property is being transported for sale, lease, rent, or bailment, or to further a commercial enterprise.

(14) "motor vehicle" means a vehicle, machine, tractor, trailer, or semitrailer propelled or drawn by mechanical power and used on a highway in transportation, or a combination determined by the Commission, but does not include a vehicle, locomotive, or car operated only on a rail, or a trolley bus operated by electric power from a fixed overhead wire, and providing local passenger transportation similar to street-railway service.

(15) "person", in addition to its meaning under section 1 of title 1, includes a trustee, receiver, assignee, or personal representative of a person.

(16) "pipeline carrier" means a person providing pipeline transportation for compensation.

(17) "rail carrier" means a person providing railroad transportation for compensation.

(18) "railroad" includes—

(A) a bridge, car float, lighter, and ferry used by or in connection with a railroad;

(B) the road used by a rail carrier and owned by it or operated under an agreement; and

(C) a switch, spur, track, terminal, terminal facility, and a freight depot, yard, and ground, used or necessary for transportation.

(19) "rate" means a rate, fare, or charge for transportation.

(20) "sleeping car carrier" means a person providing sleeping car transportation for compensation.

(21) "State" means a State of the United States and the District of Columbia.

(22) "tariff", when used in reference to a contract carrier, means a schedule.

(23) "transportation" includes—

(A) a locomotive, car, vehicle, motor vehicle, vessel, warehouse, wharf, pier, dock, yard, property, facility, instrumentality, or equipment of any kind related to the movement of passengers or property, or both, regardless of ownership or an agreement concerning use; and

(B) services related to that movement, including receipt, delivery, elevation, transfer in transit, refrigeration, icing, ventilation, storage, handling, and interchange of passengers and property.

(24) "United States" means the States of the United States and the District of Columbia.

(25) "vessel" means a watercraft or other artificial contrivance that is used, is capable of being used, or is intended to be used, as a means of transportation by water.

(26) "water carrier" means a water common carrier and a water contract carrier.

(27) "water common carrier" means a person holding itself out to the general public to provide water transportation for compensation.

(28) "water contract carrier" means a person, other than a water common carrier, providing water transportation for compensation under an agreement with another person, including transportation on a vessel provided to a person other than a carrier subject to the jurisdiction of the Commission under this subtitle when the vessel is used to transport only the property of the other person.

49 USC 10103.   **§ 10103. Remedies as cumulative**

The remedies provided under this subtitle are in addition to remedies existing under another law or at common law.

CHAPTER 103—INTERSTATE COMMERCE COMMISSION

SUBCHAPTER I—ORGANIZATION

SUBCHAPTER II—ADMINISTRATIVE

SUBCHAPTER III—JOINT BOARDS

SUBCHAPTER IV—RAIL SERVICES PLANNING OFFICE

SUBCHAPTER V—OFFICE OF RAIL PUBLIC COUNSEL

SUBCHAPTER I—ORGANIZATION

§ 10301. General

49 USC 10301.

(a) The Interstate Commerce Commission is an independent establishment of the United States Government.

(b) The Commission is composed of 11 members appointed by the President, by and with the advice and consent of the Senate. The President shall designate one of the members as Chairman. Not more than 6 members may be appointed from the same political party.

Membership.
Chairman.

(c) The term of each member of the Commission is 7 years and begins when the term of the predecessor of that member ends. An individual appointed to fill a vacancy occurring before the expiration of the term for which the predecessor of that individual was appointed, is appointed for the remainder of that term. When the term of office of a member ends, the member may continue to serve until a successor is appointed and qualified. The President may remove a member for inefficiency, neglect of duty, or malfeasance in office.

Term.

(d) A member of the Commission may not have a pecuniary interest in, hold an official relation to, or own stock in or bonds of, a carrier providing transportation by any mode and may not engage in another business, vocation, or employment.

(e) A vacancy in the membership of the Commission does not impair the right of the remaining members to exercise all of the powers of the Commission. The Commission may designate a member to act as Chairman during any period in which there is no Chairman designated by the President.

(f) Subject to the general policies, decisions, findings, and determinations of the Commission, the Chairman is responsible for administering the Commission. The Chairman may delegate the powers granted under this subsection to an officer, employee, or administrative unit of the Commission. The Chairman shall—

Responsibilities.

(1) appoint and supervise, other than regular and full time employees in the immediate offices of another member, the officers and employees of the Commission, including attorneys to provide legal aid and service to the Commission and its members, to represent the public interest in investigations and proceedings of the Commission, and to represent the Commission in any case in court;

(2) appoint the heads of major administrative units with the approval of the Commission;

(3) distribute Commission business among officers and employees and administrative units of the Commission;

(4) prepare requests for appropriations for the Commission and submit those requests to the President and Congress with the prior approval of the Commission; and

(5) supervise the expenditure of funds allocated by the Commission for major programs and purposes.

(g) The Commission shall have a seal that shall be judicially recognized.

(h) The expenses of the Commission shall be paid after presentation and approval by the Chairman of itemized vouchers.

49 USC 10302.

§ 10302. Divisions of the Commission

(a) The Interstate Commerce Commission may establish and assign Commissioners to serve on as many divisions as may be necessary and may designate any division as an appellate division. Each division shall be composed of at least 3 Commissioners. The Commission may assign a Commissioner to serve on more than one division.

(b) Unless otherwise directed by the Commission—

(1) the Commissioner senior in service of the Commissioners on a division is chairman of the division; and

(2) the Chairman of the Commission, or another Commissioner designated by the Chairman, may serve on a division temporarily, when there is a vacancy in the membership of the division or when another Commissioner is absent or unable to serve.

(c) The Commission shall designate each division numerically or by a term descriptive of the function of that division.

49 USC 10303.

§ 10303. Secretary of the Commission; public records

(a) The Chairman of the Interstate Commerce Commission, with its approval, shall appoint the Secretary of the Commission.

(b) The Secretary is the custodian of public records filed with the Commission. Copies of classifications, tariffs, and all arrangements filed with the Commission under this subtitle, and the statistics, tables, and figures contained in reports made to the Commission under this subtitle, are public records. A public record, or a copy or extract of it, certified by the Secretary under the seal of the Commission is competent evidence in a proceeding of the Commission and in a judicial proceeding.

49 USC 10304.

§ 10304. Employee boards

The Interstate Commerce Commission may establish employee boards composed of at least 3 employees. An employee who is a director or assistant director of a bureau, a chief of a section, an employee designated by the Commission, or an attorney may serve on a board.

49 USC 10305.

§ 10305. Delegation of authority

(a) The Interstate Commerce Commission may delegate to a division, an individual Commissioner, an employee board, or an employee appointed under section 3105 of title 5, a matter before the Commission for action, including a matter referred to it by either House of Congress or by Congress. However, the Commission may not delegate a matter required to be referred to a joint board under section 10341 of this title, or a function vested in the Commission under this chapter. The Commission may change or rescind a delegation under this subsection at any time. When a Commissioner or employee cannot act on a matter delegated under this section because of absence or another reason, the Chairman of the Commission may designate another Commissioner or employee, as the case may be, to serve temporarily until the Commission otherwise orders.

(b) Delegation to a division of a matter related to the validity of rates shall be made according to the character of regulation exercised.

The delegation of any such matter may not be made according to the kind or class of carrier involved or to the form or mode of transportation in which that carrier may be engaged.

(c) A division, individual Commissioner, employee board, or an employee may act on a matter delegated under subsection (a) of this section. When acting under this section, a division, individual Commissioner, board, or an employee has the same power and authority and is subject to the same duties and obligations as the Commission. Action taken under this section has the same force and is taken in the same manner as if taken by the Commission.

§ 10306. Conduct of proceedings

49 USC 10306.

(a) A majority of the Interstate Commerce Commission, a division, or an employee board is a quorum for the transaction of business. A Commissioner, the Secretary of the Commission, a member of an employee board, or an employee delegated to act under section 10305 of this title may administer oaths.

(b) A party may appear and be heard before the Commission, a division, an individual Commissioner, a board, or an employee delegated to act under section 10305 of this title in person or by an individual admitted to practice under section 10308 of this title. A hearing before the Commission, a division, an individual Commissioner, a board, or an employee shall be made public on the request of an interested party.

(c) The Commission shall conform its forms for giving notice and their manner of service, to the extent practical, to those used by the courts of the United States.

(d) Votes and other official acts of the Commission, a division, an individual Commissioner, an employee board, or an employee delegated to act under section 10305 of this title shall be recorded and shall be made public on the request of an interested party.

(e) A member of a board and an employee delegated to act under section 10305 of this title may not have a pecuniary interest in, hold an official relation to, or own securities of a carrier providing transportation by any mode.

(f) The Commission shall review at least once every 3 years and revise as necessary the rules of practice for matters related to rail carriers adopted under section 305(c) of the Railroad Revitalization and Regulatory Reform Act of 1976 (90 Stat. 53).

Rail carriers practice rules, review.
49 USC 17 note.

§ 10307. Office and sessions

49 USC 10307.

(a) The principal office of the Interstate Commerce Commission is in the District of Columbia. Until otherwise provided by law, the Commission may obtain suitable offices for its use and may procure all necessary office supplies.

(b) General sessions of the Commission are held at its principal office. However, the Commission may hold special sessions in any part of the United States, for the convenience of the public or the parties and to avoid delay and expense. The Commission, an individual Commissioner, an employee board, or an employee delegated to act under section 10305 of this title may conduct proceedings under this subtitle in any part of the United States for the convenience of the parties.

§ 10308. Admission to practice

49 USC 10308.
Fee.

Subject to section 500 of title 5, the Interstate Commerce Commission may regulate the admission of individuals to practice before it and may impose a reasonable admission fee.

§ 10309. Access to records by congressional committees

(a) When the Committee on Interstate and Foreign Commerce of the House of Representatives or the Committee on Commerce, Science, and Transportation of the Senate makes a written request for a record in the possession or under the control of the Interstate Commerce Commission related to a matter involving a rail carrier providing transportation subject to this subtitle, the Commission shall send that record or a copy to the committee by the 10th day after the date of receipt of the request. If the record is not sent, the Commission shall send a written report to that committee within the 10-day period stating the reason why the record has not been sent and the anticipated date on which it will be sent. If the Commission transfers a record in its possession or under its control to another department, agency, or instrumentality of the United States Government, or to a person, it must condition the transfer on the guaranteed return of the record by the transferee to the Commission so that the Commission can comply with this subsection.

(b) Subsection (a) of this section does not apply to a record obtained by the Commission from a person subject to regulation by it if the record contains trade secrets or commercial or financial information of a privileged or confidential nature. Subsection (a) of this section does not limit other authority of Congress, either House of Congress, or a committee or subcommittee of either House, to obtain a record.

§ 10310. Reporting official action

(a) The Interstate Commerce Commission shall make a written report of each proceeding conducted on complaint or on its own initiative and furnish a copy to each party to that proceeding. The report shall include the findings, conclusions, and the order of the Commission and, if damages are awarded, the findings of fact supporting the award. The Commission may have its reports published for public use. A published report of the Commission is competent evidence of its contents.

(b)(1) When action of the Commission in a matter related to a rail carrier is taken by the Commission, a division, a group of Commissioners, an individual Commissioner, an employee board, an employee delegated to act under section 10305 of this title, or another individual or group of individuals designated to take official action for the Commission, the written statement of that action (including a report, order, decision and order, vote, notice, letter, policy statements, or regulation) shall indicate—

(A) the official designation of the individual or group taking the action;

(B) the name of each individual taking, or participating in taking, the action; and

(C) the vote or position of each participating individual.

(2) If an individual member of a group taking an official action referred to in paragraph (1) of this subsection does not participate in it, the written statement of the action shall indicate that the member did not participate. An individual participating in taking an official action is entitled to express the views of that individual as part of the written statement of the action. In addition to any publication of the written statement, it shall be made available to the public under section 552(a) of title 5.

§ 10311. Annual report

49 USC 10311.
Submittal to
Congress.

The Interstate Commerce Commission shall prepare and send to Congress an annual report before April 3 of each year. The Commission shall include in the annual report information that may be of value in answering questions related to regulation of transportation and the names and pay of individuals employed by the Commission. The Commission may include in its annual report, or send to Congress at any time, recommendations for additional legislation related to regulation of transportation.

SUBCHAPTER II—ADMINISTRATIVE

§ 10321. Powers

49 USC 10321.

(a) The Interstate Commerce Commission shall carry out this subtitle. Enumeration of a power of the Commission in this subtitle does not exclude another power the Commission may have in carrying out this subtitle. The Commission may prescribe regulations in carrying out this subtitle.

Regulations.

(b) The Commission may—

(1) inquire into and report on the management of the business of carriers providing, and brokers for, transportation and service subject to this subtitle;

(2) inquire into and report on the management of the business of a person controlling, controlled by, or under common control with those carriers or brokers to the extent that the business of that person is related to the management of the business of that carrier or broker; and

(3) obtain from those carriers, brokers, and persons information the Commission decides is necessary to carry out this subtitle.

(c) (1) The Commission, an individual Commissioner, an employee board, and an employee delegated to act under section 10305 of this title may subpena witnesses and records related to a proceeding of the Commission from any place in the United States, to the designated place of the proceeding. If a witness disobeys a subpena, the Commission, or a party to a proceeding before the Commission, may petition a court of the United States to enforce that subpena.

Subpenas.

(2) Subpenas may be signed by a Commissioner, the Secretary of the Commission, or a member of a board when the subpena relates to a matter delegated to the board under section 10305 of this title.

(3) The district courts of the United States have jurisdiction to enforce a subpena issued under this section. Trial is in the district in which the proceeding is conducted. The court may punish a refusal to obey a subpena as a contempt of court.

(d) (1) In a proceeding, the Commission may take the testimony of a witness by deposition and may order the witness to produce records. A party to a proceeding pending before the Commission may take the testimony of a witness by deposition and may require the witness to produce records at any time after a proceeding is at issue on petition and answer.

Depositions.

(2) If a witness fails to be deposed or to produce records under paragraph (1) of this subsection, the Commission may subpena the witness to take a deposition, produce the records, or both.

(3) A deposition may be taken before a judge of a court of the United States, a United States magistrate, a clerk of a district court, or a chancellor, justice, or judge of a supreme or superior court, mayor

or chief magistrate of a city, judge of a county court, or court of common pleas of any State, or a notary public who is not counsel or attorney of a party or interested in the proceeding.

(4) Before taking a deposition, reasonable notice must be given in writing by the party or the attorney of that party proposing to take a deposition to the opposing party or the attorney of record of that party, whoever is nearest. The notice shall state the name of the witness and the time and place of taking the deposition.

(5) The testimony of a person deposed under this subsection shall be taken under oath. The person taking the deposition shall prepare, or cause to be prepared, a transcript of the testimony taken. The transcript shall be subscribed by the deponent.

(6) The testimony of a witness who is in a foreign country may be taken by deposition before an officer or person designated by the Commission or agreed on by the parties by written stipulation filed with the Commission. A deposition shall be filed with the Commission promptly.

(e) Each witness summoned before the Commission or whose deposition is taken under this section and the individual taking the deposition are entitled to the same fees and mileage paid for those services in the courts of the United States.

49 USC 10322.

§ 10322. Initial decisions—nonrail proceedings

(a) When testimony is taken at a public hearing, an individual Commissioner, an employee board, or an employee delegated to act under section 10305 of this title shall issue an initial decision that

Filing.

includes a statement of reasons for the decision and an order. The decision and order shall be filed with the Interstate Commerce Commission. An initial decision becomes an action of the Commission on the 20th day after the initial decision is served on the interested parties, including persons referred to in section 10328(b) of this title if the proceeding involves a motor carrier, unless—

(1) an exception to the initial decision is filed by an interested party during that 20-day period or by the end of an extended period if authorized by the Commission, or a division or board designated by the Commission; or

(2) the Commission, or a division or board designated by the Commission, stays or postpones the initial decision.

Review.

(b) Before an initial decision of an individual Commissioner, a board, or an employee becomes an action of the Commission, a division or board designated by the Commission, or the Commission, may review the initial decision on its own initiative and shall review the initial decision if exception to it is filed under subsection (a)(1) of this section. An initial decision may be reviewed on the record on which it is based or by a further hearing. If an initial decision is reviewed, it is stayed or postponed pending final determination of the matter, and it is an action of the Commission only after the final determination is made.

49 USC 10323.

§ 10323. Rehearing, reargument, and reconsideration—nonrail proceedings

(a) The Interstate Commerce Commission may grant rehearing, reargument, or reconsideration of a decision that has become an action of the Commission. A party to the proceeding may apply for rehearing, reargument, or reconsideration under Commission regulations. Except as provided in subsection (b)(2) of this section, the Commission may limit the right to apply for rehearing, reargument, or reconsideration of a decision of the Commission or a division to a proceeding or class of proceedings involving issues of general transportation importance.

(b)(1) An application for rehearing, reargument, or reconsideration shall be considered and acted on—

(A) by the Commission if the action of the Commission was taken by it; or

(B) by the Commission, or by an appellate division designated by the Commission, if the initial decision was made by a division, individual Commissioner, board, or employee.

(2) An application for rehearing, reargument, or reconsideration shall be granted and referred to an appellate division for action if—

(A) the matter was delegated for an initial decision to an individual Commissioner, board, or employee;

(B) the application is filed by the 20th day after the date the initial decision became an action of the Commission under section 10322(a) of this title; and

(C) the matter has not been previously reviewed under section 10322(b) of this title.

(c) The Commission or an appellate division may change a decision of a division, an individual Commissioner, board, or employee if the decision appears unreasonable after rehearing, reargument, or reconsideration. However, the subsequent decision is subject to rehearing, reargument, or reconsideration under this section.

§ 10324. Commission action

49 USC 10324.

(a) Unless otherwise provided in this subtitle, the Interstate Commerce Commission may determine, within a reasonable time, when its actions, other than an action ordering the payment of money, take effect. However, an action of the Commission in a proceeding involving a motor carrier, a broker, a water carrier, or freight forwarder may not take effect for 30 days.

(b) An action of the Commission remains in effect under its own terms or until superseded. The Commission may change, suspend, or set aside any such action on notice. Notice may be given in a manner determined by the Commission. A court of competent jurisdiction may suspend or set aside any such action.

(c) An action of the Commission is enforceable unless—

(1) application for rehearing, reargument, or reconsideration is made under section 10323 of this title before the effective date of the action; or

(2) the Commission stays or postpones the action.

§ 10325. Judicial review—nonrail proceedings

49 USC 10325.

A civil action to enforce, enjoin, suspend, or set aside an action of the Interstate Commerce Commission taken by a division, individual Commissioner, employee board, or employee delegated to act under section 10305 of this title may be started in a court of the United States only—

(1) on denial of an application for rehearing, reargument, or reconsideration; or

(2) if the application is granted, after a rehearing, reargument, reconsideration or other disposition by the Commission or an appellate division under section 10323 of this title.

49 USC 10326.

§ 10326. Limitations in rulemaking proceedings related to rail carriers

Petitions.

(a) When, under section 553(e) of title 5, an interested person (including a governmental authority) petitions the Interstate Commerce Commission to begin a rulemaking proceeding in a matter related to a rail carrier providing transportation subject to this subtitle, the Commission, or a division, an individual Commissioner, an employee board, an employee delegated to act under section 10305 of this title, or another person authorized to act on behalf of the Commission for any part of the proceeding, shall grant or deny that petition by the 120th day after receiving it. If the petition is granted, the Commission, or its delegate, shall begin an appropriate proceeding as soon as practicable. If the petition is denied, the reasons for the denial shall be published in the Federal Register.

Publication in Federal Register.
Civil action.

(b)(1) If a petition is denied or action is not taken within the 120-day period under subsection (a) of this section, the petitioner may begin a civil action in an appropriate court of appeals of the United States for an order directing the Commission to begin a proceeding to take the action requested in the petition. A civil action under this subsection must be filed by the 60th day after the date of the denial or by the 60th day after the end of the 120-day period, whichever is appropriate.

(2) The court of appeals shall order the Commission to begin the action requested in the petition to the Commission if the court finds that the action requested in that petition is necessary and failure to take that action will result in the continuation of practices that are not consistent with the public interest or are not in accordance with this subtitle. The finding of the court must be based on a preponderance of the evidence in the record before the Commission or its delegate, or, if the civil action is based on a petition on which action was not taken, in a new proceeding before the court. The court may not require the Commission to take action under this subtitle other than to begin a rulemaking proceeding.

49 USC 10327.

§ 10327. Commission action and appellate procedure in rail carrier proceedings

(a) Notwithstanding sections 10322, 10323, and 10324(c) of this title, this section applies to a matter before the Interstate Commerce Commission involving a rail carrier providing transportation subject to the jurisdiction of the Commission under subchapter I of chapter 105 of this title. However, other sections of this subtitle related to action of the Commission in proceedings involving rail carriers supersede this section to the extent that they are inconsistent with the provisions of this section related to deadlines.

Initial decisions.

(b) A division, individual Commissioner, employee board, or employee delegated under section 10305 of this title to make an initial decision in a matter related to one of those rail carriers shall complete all evidentiary proceedings related to the matter by the 180th day after assignment of the matter. The initial decision shall be submitted to the Commission in writing. If evidence is submitted in writing or testimony is taken at a public hearing, the initial decision shall be submitted to the Commission in writing by the 120th day after completion of all evidentiary proceedings and shall include—

(1) specific findings of fact;

(2) specific and separate conclusions of law;

(3) an order; and

(4) justification of the findings of fact, conclusions of law, and order.

(c) The Commission, or a division designated by the Commission, may void the requirement of an initial decision under subsection (b) of this section and may require the matter to be considered by the Commission or that division on finding that the matter involves a question of Commission policy, a new or novel issue of law, or an issue of general transportation importance, or that it is required for the timely execution of its functions.

(d) In a proceeding under this section, after the parties have had at least an opportunity to submit evidence in written form, the Commission shall give them an opportunity for briefs, written statements, or conferences of the parties. A conference of the parties must be chaired by a division, an individual Commissioner, an employee board, an employee delegated to act under section 10305 of this title, or an employee designated by the Commission.

(e) Copies of an initial decision under subsection (b) of this section shall be served on the interested parties. An initial decision becomes an action of the Commission on the 20th day after it is served on the interested parties, unless—

(1) an interested party files an appeal during the 20-day period, or by the end of an additional period of not more than 20 days, if authorized by the Commission or division designated by the Commission; or

(2) the Commission stays or postpones the initial decision under subsection (g)(2) or (j) of this section within the period or additional period referred to in clause (1) of this subsection.

(f)(1) Before an initial decision becomes an action of the Commission, the Commission, or a division or board designated by the Commission, may review the initial decision on its own initiative, and shall review an initial decision if an appeal is filed under subsection (e)(1) of this section. However, a board may not decide an appeal from an initial decision if the appeal may be further appealed to the Commission. **Review.**

(2) An initial decision may be reviewed on the record on which it is based or by a further hearing. If an initial decision is reviewed, it shall be stayed pending final determination of the matter, and it is an action of the Commission only after the final determination is made. If an appeal is filed under subsection (e)(1) of this section, the final determination shall be made by the 180th day after the appeal is filed.

(3) Review of, or appeal from, an initial decision shall be conducted under section 557 of title 5. The Commission may prescribe rules limiting and defining the issues and pleadings on review under section 557 (b) of that title. **Rules.**

(g)(1) The Commission may, at any time on its own initiative because of material error, new evidence, or substantially changed circumstances—

(A) reopen a proceeding;

(B) grant rehearing, reargument, or reconsideration of an action of the Commission; and

(C) change an action of the Commission.

An interested party may petition to reopen and reconsider an action of the Commission under this paragraph under regulations of the Commission. **Petition.**

(2) The Commission may grant a rehearing, reargument, or reconsideration of an action of the Commission that was taken by a division designated by the Commission if it finds that—

    (A) the action involves a matter of general transportation importance; or

    (B) the action would be affected materially because of clear and convincing new evidence or changed circumstances.

Petition. An interested party may petition for rehearing, reargument, or reconsideration of an action of the Commission under this paragraph under regulations of the Commission. The Commission may stay an action pending a final determination under this paragraph. The Commission shall complete reconsideration and take final action by the 120th day after the petition is granted.

(h) An action of the Commission under this section and an action of a designated division under subsection (c) of this section is effective on the 30th day after service on the parties to the proceeding unless the Commission provides for it to become effective on an earlier date.

(i) Notwithstanding this subtitle, an action of the Commission under this section and an action of a designated division under subsection (c) of this section is final on the date on which it is served, and a civil action to enforce, enjoin, suspend, or set aside the action may be filed after that date.

Extensions. (j) The Commission may extend a time period established by this section for a period of not more than 90 days. The extension shall be granted if a majority of the Commissioners agree to it by public vote. Annual report to Congress. The Commission shall send a written annual report to each House of Congress about extensions granted under this subsection. The report shall specify each extension granted (classified by the type of proceeding involved) together with the reasons for and duration of each extension.

(k) If an extension granted under subsection (j) of this section is not sufficient to allow for completion of necessary proceedings, the Commission may grant a further extension in an extraordinary situation if—

    (1) at least 7 Commissioners agree to the further extension by public vote; and

    (2) not later than the 15th day before expiration of the extension granted under subsection (j) of this section, the Commission submits a written report to the Congress that a further extension has been granted. The report shall include—

        (A) a full explanation of the reasons for the further extension;

        (B) the anticipated duration of the further extension;

        (C) the issues involved in the matter before the Commission; and

        (D) the names of personnel of the Commission working on the matter.

49 USC 10328. § 10328. Intervention

(a) Designated representatives of employees of a carrier may intervene and be heard in a proceeding arising under this subtitle that affects those employees.

(b) Under regulations of the Interstate Commerce Commission, reasonable notice of, and an opportunity to intervene and participate in, a proceeding under this subtitle related to transportation subject to the jurisdiction of the Commission under subchapter II of chapter 105 of this title that is, or is proposed to be, provided in a State shall be given to interested persons and to the authority of that State having jurisdiction to regulate transportation by motor vehicles in intrastate commerce on the highways of that State, or, if there is no such authority, to the chief executive officer of the State.

§ 10329. Service of notice in Commission proceedings   49 USC 10329.

(a) (1) A common carrier providing transportation subject to the Agent jurisdiction of the Interstate Commerce Commission under subchapter designation. I of chapter 105 of this title shall designate an agent in the District of Columbia, on whom service of notices in a proceeding before, and of actions of, the Commission may be made.

(2) A motor carrier, a broker, a water carrier, or a freight forwarder providing transportation or service subject to the jurisdiction of the Commission under subchapter II, III, or IV of chapter 105 of this title shall designate an agent by name and post office address on whom service of notices in a proceeding before, and of actions of, the Commission may be made.

(b) A designation under subsection (a) of this section shall be in writing and filed with the Commission. A motor carrier or broker providing transportation under a certificate or permit issued under this subtitle shall also file the designation with the authority of each State in which it operates having jurisdiction to regulate transportation by motor vehicle in intrastate commerce on the highways of that State. The designation may be changed at any time in the same manner as originally made.

(c) Except as otherwise provided, notices of the Commission shall be served as follows:

(1) A notice of the Commission to a rail, express, sleeping car, or pipeline carrier is served on its designated agent at the office or usual place of residence in the District of Columbia of that agent. A notice of action of the Commission shall be served immediately on the agent or in another manner provided by law. If that carrier does not have a designated agent, service may be made by posting the notice in the office of the Secretary of the Commission.

(2) A notice to a motor carrier or broker is served personally or by mail on the motor carrier or broker or its designated agent. Service by mail on the designated agent is made at the address filed for the agent. When notice is given by mail, the date of mailing is considered to be the time when the notice is served. If a motor carrier or broker does not have a designated agent, service may be made by posting a copy of the notice in the office of the secretary or clerk of the authority having jurisdiction to regulate transportation by motor vehicle in intrastate commerce on the highways of the State in which the carrier or broker maintains headquarters and in the office of the Secretary of the Commission.

(3) A notice to a water carrier or freight forwarder is served personally or by mail on the water carrier or freight forwarder or its designated agent. Service by mail on the designated agent is made at the address filed for the agent. When notice is given by mail, the date of mailing is considered to be the time when notice is served. If a water carrier or freight forwarder does not have a designated agent, service may be made by posting the notice in the office of the Secretary of the Commission.

(d) In a proceeding involving the lawfulness of classifications, rates, or practices of (1) a rail, express, sleeping car, or pipeline carrier that has not designated an agent under this section, or (2) a **freight forwarder**, service of notice of the Commission on an attorney in fact who filed the tariff for the carrier constitutes service of notice on the carrier.

(e) In a proceeding involving the lawfulness of classifications, rates, or practices—

   (1) service of notice of the suspension of a tariff on an attorney **in fact of a carrier** or broker, except a freight forwarder, constitutes service of notice on the carrier or broker if that attorney filed the tariff and, if the carrier is a water carrier, the notice specifies the classifications, rates, or practices involved; and

   (2) service of notice of the suspension of a joint tariff or schedule on a carrier or a broker, except a freight forwarder, that filed that tariff or schedule to which another carrier or broker is a party and, if the carrier is a water carrier, the notice specifies the classifications, rates, or practices involved, constitutes service of notice on all carriers or brokers that are parties to the joint tariff.

Service of notice under this subsection may be made by mail on that attorney or carrier at the address shown in the tariff.

49 USC 10330.
Agent
designation.

§ 10330. Service of process in court proceedings

(a) A common carrier providing transportation subject to the jurisdiction of the Interstate Commerce Commission under subchapter I of chapter 105 of this title shall designate an agent in the District of Columbia on whom service of process in an action before a district court may be made. Except as otherwise provided, process in an action before a district court shall be served on the designated agent of that carrier at the office or usual place of residence in the District of Columbia of that agent. If the carrier does not have a designated agent, service may be made by posting the notice in the office of the Secretary of the Commission.

(b) A motor carrier or broker providing transportation subject to the jurisdiction of the Commission under subchapter II of chapter 105 of this title, including a motor carrier or broker operating within the United States while providing transportation between places in a foreign country or between a place in one foreign country and a place in another foreign country, shall designate an agent in each State in which it operates by name and post office address on whom process issued by a court with subject matter jurisdiction may be served in an action brought against that carrier or broker. The designation shall be in writing and filed with the Commission and with the authority of each State in which the motor carrier or broker operates having jurisdiction to regulate transportation by motor vehicle in intrastate commerce on the highways of that State. If a designation under this subsection is not made, service may be made on any agent of the carrier or broker within that State.

(c) A designation under this section may be changed at any time in the same manner as originally made.

SUBCHAPTER III—JOINT BOARDS

49 USC 10341.

§ 10341. Jurisdiction

(a) The Interstate Commerce Commission may refer a matter related to motor carriers providing, or brokers for, transportation subject to the jurisdiction of the Commission under subchapter II of chapter 105 of this title, to a joint board established under section 10342 of this title for action. When the operation of a motor carrier or broker involves not more than 3 States, the Commission shall refer the following matters to a joint board for action when an opportunity for a proceeding is required or when the Commission finds that it is desirable:

(1) an application for a certificate, permit, or license.

(2) a suspension, change, or revocation of a certificate, permit, or license.

(3) an application for approval and authorization of a consolidation, merger, or acquisition of control or of an operating contract.

(4) a complaint about a violation by a motor carrier or broker of a requirement established under section 10321(a), 10525, 11101 (b), or 11142(b) of this title.

(5) a complaint about rates of motor carriers or practices of brokers.

Post, pp. 1419, 1425.

(b) Notwithstanding subsection (a) of this section, if the Commission is prevented by legal proceedings from referring a matter to a joint board, the Commission may determine the matter under subchapter II of this chapter.

§ 10342. Establishment

49 USC 10342.

(a) The Interstate Commerce Commission may establish and abolish joint boards as necessary to carry out section 10341 of this title. Except as provided in this section, a joint board is composed of a member from each State in which transportation subject to the jurisdiction of the Commission under subchapter II of chapter 105 of this title is, or is proposed to be, provided. The Commission may appoint an individual nominated under subsection (b) of this section as a member of a joint board.

Membership.

(b) The member of a joint board from a State shall be nominated by the State authority having jurisdiction to regulate intrastate transportation by motor vehicle on the highways of that State. If there is no such authority in that State or if that authority does not nominate a member when requested by the Commission, the chief executive officer of the State may nominate the member. If both that State authority and the chief executive officer of that State do not nominate a member when requested, the board is constituted without a member from that State if the Commission has appointed members for at least 2 other States to the board.

(c) When a matter required to be referred to a joint board involves the operation of a motor carrier in or through a place outside the United States, if only one State is involved or if only one State nominates an individual to be a member of the joint board, that State may nominate and the Commission may appoint not more than 3 members to the board.

(d) A substitution in the membership of a joint board may be made at any time in the same manner as an initial nomination and appointment under this section.

§ 10343. Powers

49 USC 10343.

(a) When conducting a proceeding involving a matter referred under section 10341 of this title, a joint board may make an initial decision under section 10322 of this title. Subchapter II of this chapter applies to an initial decision of a joint board. However, a joint board may report to the Interstate Commerce Commission its conclusions on evidence received without making an initial decision. When a joint board makes a report instead of an initial decision, the Commission

Report.

shall decide the matter. The Commission may consider the conclusions of the joint board in making its decision.

(b) A joint board may make an initial decision or report of its conclusions only by a majority vote. However, if only one member of the board participates in the proceeding, that member shall make the initial decision alone.

Waiver.
(c) When a member of a joint board does not participate in a proceeding referred to that board, after notice of the proceeding, the State from which that member was appointed waives its right to act in that proceeding. The waiver does not affect the duty or power of remaining members of the board to continue the proceeding and make an initial decision.

(d) In addition to decisions made under subsection (a) of this section, the Commission shall decide a matter referred to a joint board when—

(1) the authority of each State from which a member of the board may be appointed waives action on a matter referred to that board;

(2) a joint board does not act, or cannot agree, on a matter referred to it in 45 days after the matter is referred to it (or in another period authorized by the Commission); or

(3) a member is nominated for only one State, except as provided in section 10342(c) of this title.

49 USC 10344.
§ 10344. Administration

(a) Meetings and procedures of joint boards shall be conducted under regulations of the Interstate Commerce Commission. The Commission may designate an employee appointed under section 3105 of title 5 to advise and assist a joint board.

(b) When practicable and when directed by the Commission, a proceeding involving a matter referred to a joint board shall be held at a place in the United States that is convenient to the parties to the proceeding.

(c) The members of joint boards and employees designated to advise and assist them under subsection (a) of this section may administer oaths, subpena witnesses and the production of records, and take depositions under section 10321 of this title related to matters referred to the boards.

Travel expenses.
(d) When carrying out this subtitle, members of joint boards shall receive an allowance for travel and subsistence expenses as the Commission shall provide.

Conflict of interest, prohibition.
(e) A member of a joint board may not have a pecuniary interest in, hold an official relation to, or own securities of, a carrier providing transportation by any mode.

Facilities.
(f) The Administrator of General Services shall assign space and facilities in the Interstate Commerce Commission building not required by the Commission for the use of the national organization of the State commissions and their representatives. The space and facilities shall be available for the use of joint boards and for members and representatives of those boards cooperating with the Commission or with another department, agency, or instrumentality of the United States Government. If suitable space is not available in the Interstate Commerce Commission building, the Administrator shall assign space in another building in convenient proximity to it.

SUBCHAPTER IV—RAIL SERVICES PLANNING OFFICE

§ 10361. Organization

The Rail Services Planning Office is an office in the Interstate Commerce Commission.

§ 10362. Duties

(a) In this section—

(1) "avoidable costs of providing transportation", "reasonable management fee", "reasonable return on the value", and "revenue attributable to the rail properties" have the same meanings as they have when used in section 744 of title 45.

(2) "avoidable cost of providing rail freight transportation" has the same meaning as it has when used in section 10905(b)(2)(A) of this title.

(b) The Rail Services Planning Office shall—

(1) assist the Interstate Commerce Commission in studying and evaluating proposals, submitted to the Commission under subchapter III of chapter 113 of this title for a merger, consolidation, unification, or coordination project, joint use of tracks or other facilities, or acquisition or sale of assets involving a rail carrier subject to this subtitle;

(2) assist the Commission in developing, with respect to economic regulation of transportation, policies likely to result in a more competitive, energy-efficient, and coordinated transportation system using each mode of transportation to its maximum advantage to meet the transportation needs of the United States;

(3) assist States and local and regional transportation authorities in deciding whether to provide rail transportation continuation subsidies to continue in operation particular rail properties, by establishing criteria for determining whether particular rail properties are suitable for rail transportation continuation subsidies;

(4) conduct continuously an analysis of the national rail transportation needs, evaluate the policies, plans, and programs of the Commission on the basis of the analysis, and advise the Commission of the results of the evaluation;

(5) maintain regulations that contain—

(A) standards for the computation of subsidies for rail passenger service (except passenger transportation compensation disputes subject to the jurisdiction of the Commission under section 562(a) of title 45) that are consistent with the compensation principles described in the final system plan established under the Regional Rail Reorganization Act of 1973 (87 Stat. 985), as amended, and which avoid cross-subsidization among commuter, intercity, and freight rail transportation; and

(B) standards for determining emergency commuter rail passenger transportation operating payments under section 1613 of this title;

(6) maintain, and from time to time revise and republish after a proceeding under section 553 of title 5, standards for determining the revenue attributable to the rail properties, the avoidable costs of providing transportation, a reasonable return on the value, and a reasonable management fee;

(7) maintain regulations that—

---

49 USC 10361.

49 USC 10362.
Definitions.

Post, p. 1406.
Assistance.

Post, p. 1434.

Criteria.

Analysis and evaluation.

Regulations.

45 USC 701 note.

49 USC 1613.

(A) develop an accounting system permitting the collection and publication by the Consolidated Rail Corporation or by profitable rail carriers providing transportation over lines scheduled for abandonment, of information necessary for an accurate determination of the attributable revenues, avoidable costs, and operations of light density lines as operating and economic units; and

(B) determine the avoidable cost of providing rail freight transportation; and

(8) carry out other duties conferred on the Office by law.

(c) The criteria referred to in subsection (b) (3) of this section shall provide that rail properties are suitable for rail transportation continuation subsidies if the cost of the required subsidy to the taxpayers for the properties each year is less than—

(1) the cost of termination of rail transportation over the properties measured by increased fuel consumption and operational costs for alternative modes of transportation;

(2) the cost to the gross national product in terms of reduced output of goods and services;

(3) the cost of relocating or assisting, through unemployment, retraining, and welfare benefits, individuals and firms adversely affected if the rail transportation is terminated; and

(4) the cost to the environment measured by damage caused by increased pollution.

(d) The Office may at any time revise and republish the standards and regulations required by this section to incorporate changes made necessary by the accounting system developed under subsection (b)(7) of this section.

§ 10363. Director

49 USC 10363.

(a) The Director is the head of the Rail Services Planning Office and is responsible for administering and carrying out the duties of the Office.

(b) The Director is appointed for a term of 6 years by the Chairman of the Interstate Commerce Commission with the concurrence of at least 5 members of the Commission. The Director may be removed by the Commission only for cause.

(c) The Director is appointed without regard to those provisions of title 5 governing appointments in the competitive service and is paid without regard to chapter 51 and subchapter III of chapter 53 of title 5. However, the annual rate of basic pay of the Director may not exceed the rate for GS–18.

5 USC 5101 et seq., 5331.

(d) The Director is subject to the direction of, and shall report to, a Commissioner or the Chairman, as designated by the Chairman.

§ 10364. Powers

49 USC 10364.

(a) With the concurrence of the Commissioner designated under section 10363(d) of this title or, if the Director of the Rail Services Planning Office and the Commissioner disagree (and that Commissioner is not the Chairman), with the concurrence of the Chairman of the Commission, the Director may enter into agreements or other transactions necessary to carry out the duties of the Office. The transactions may be entered into with any person, including a governmental authority, and without regard to section 5 of title 41.

(b) On written request of the Director for assistance, each department, agency, and instrumentality of the United States Government shall consider the request, and may furnish assistance the Director considers necessary to carry out the duties of the Office. Assistance may be furnished on a reimbursable or nonreimbursable basis. Assistance includes the transfer of an officer or employee, with the consent, and without prejudice to the position and rating, of the officer or employee.

SUBCHAPTER V—OFFICE OF RAIL PUBLIC COUNSEL

§ 10381. Organization

49 USC 10381.

The Office of Rail Public Counsel is an independent office affiliated with the Interstate Commerce Commission.

§ 10382. Duties; standing

49 USC 10382.

(a) The Office of Rail Public Counsel—

(1) may petition the Interstate Commerce Commission to begin a proceeding on a matter within the jurisdiction of the Commission involving a rail carrier subject to this subtitle;

(2) may seek judicial review of Commission action on a matter involving a rail carrier providing transportation subject to this subtitle, to the extent, and on the same basis, that a person may seek judicial review;

(3) shall solicit, study, evaluate, and present before an informal or formal proceeding of the Commission, the views of those communities and users of rail transportation affected by a proceeding begun by, or pending before, the Commission, when the Director of the Office determines, for whatever reason (such as size or location), that any such community or user might not otherwise be represented adequately at the proceeding;

(4) shall—

(A) before the Commission and other departments, agencies, and instrumentalities of the United States Government when the policies and activities of any such department, agency, or instrumentality affect rail transportation subject to the jurisdiction of the Commission, evaluate and represent the public interest in safe, efficient, reliable, and economical rail transportation; and

(B) assist in constructively representing that public interest by other means;

(5) in carrying out its duties under clauses (1)–(4) of this subsection, shall assist the Commission in developing a public interest record in proceedings before the Commission; and

(6) shall carry out other duties conferred on the Office by law.

(b) The Office has standing as a party to any informal or formal proceeding that is pending or begun before the Commission involving a rail carrier providing transportation subject to this subtitle.

§ 10383. Director

49 USC 10383.

(a) The Director is the head of the Office of Rail Public Counsel and is responsible for administering and carrying out the duties of the Office.

(b) The Director is appointed by the President, by and with the advice and consent of the Senate, for a term of 4 years.

(c) The Director is paid without regard to chapter 51 and subchapter III of chapter 53 of title 5. However, the annual rate of basic pay of the Director may not exceed the rate for GS–18.

5 USC 5101 *et seq.*, 5331.
5 USC 5332 note.

§ 10384. Office staff

The Director of the Office of Rail Public Counsel may—
(1) appoint and fix the pay of employees of the Office; and
(2) procure under section 3109 of title 5 the temporary or intermittent services of experts and consultants.

§ 10385. Powers

(a) Without regard to section 5 of title 41, the Director of the Office of Rail Public Counsel may enter into agreements or other transactions necessary to carry out the duties of the Office.

(b) On request of the Director for information, each department, agency, and instrumentality of the United States Government may furnish the information requested.

§ 10386. Reports

The Director of the Office of Rail Public Counsel shall submit each month to the Chairman of the Interstate Commerce Commission a report on the activities of the Office for the preceding month. In its annual report to Congress, the Commission shall include its evaluation and recommendations with respect to the activities, accomplishments, and shortcomings of the Office.

§ 10387. Budget requests and estimates

The Office of Rail Public Counsel shall submit its budget requests and budget estimates concurrently to Congress and to the President.

§ 10388. Authorizations of appropriations

Not more than $1,000,000 may be appropriated to the Office of Rail Public Counsel for the fiscal year ending September 30, 1978, to carry out this subchapter.

CHAPTER 105—JURISDICTION

SUBCHAPTER I—RAIL, RAIL-WATER, EXPRESS, AND PIPELINE CARRIER TRANSPORTATION

SUBCHAPTER II—MOTOR CARRIER TRANSPORTATION

SUBCHAPTER III—WATER CARRIER TRANSPORTATION

SUBCHAPTER IV—FREIGHT FORWARDER SERVICE

SUBCHAPTER I—RAIL, RAIL-WATER, EXPRESS, AND
PIPELINE CARRIER TRANSPORTATION

§ 10501.   General jurisdiction

49 USC 10501.

(a) Subject to this chapter and other law, the Interstate Commerce Commission has jurisdiction over transportation—

    (1) by rail carrier, express carrier, sleeping car carrier, water common carrier, and pipeline carrier that is—

        (A) only by railroad;

        (B) by railroad and water, when the transportation is under common control, management, or arrangement for a continuous carriage or shipment; or

        (C) by pipeline or by pipeline and railroad or water when transporting a commodity other than water, gas, or oil; and

    (2) to the extent the transportation is in the United States and is between a place in—

        (A) a State and a place in another State;

        (B) the District of Columbia and another place in the District of Columbia;

        (C) a State and a place in a territory or possession of the United States;

        (D) a territory or possession of the United States and a place in another such territory or possession;

        (E) a territory or possession of the United States and another place in the same territory or possession;

        (F) the United States and another place in the United States through a foreign country; or

        (G) the United States and a place in a foreign country.

(b) The Commission does not have jurisdiction under subsection (a) of this section over—

    (1) the transportation of passengers or property, or the receipt, delivery, storage, or handling of property, entirely in a State (other than the District of Columbia) and not transported between a place in the United States and a place in a foreign country except as otherwise provided in this subtitle; or

    (2) transportation by a water common carrier when that transportation would be subject to this subchapter only because the water common carrier absorbs, out of its port-to-port water rates or out of its proportional through rates, a switching, terminal, lighterage, car rental, trackage, handling, or other charge by a rail carrier for services in the switching, drayage, lighterage, or corporate limits of a port terminal or district.

(c) This subtitle does not affect the power of a State, in exercising its police power, to require reasonable intrastate transportation by carriers providing transportation subject to the jurisdiction of the Commission under this subchapter unless the State requirement is inconsistent with an order of the Commission issued under this subtitle or is prohibited under this subtitle.

49 USC 10502.

§ 10502. Express carrier transportation

The Interstate Commerce Commission has jurisdiction under this subchapter, and not under subchapter II or III of this chapter, over transportation of an express carrier—

> (1) by motor vehicle, to the extent the transportation was subject to the jurisdiction of the Commission on September 18, 1940, under part I of the Interstate Commerce Act (24 Stat. 379), as amended; and

49 USC prec. 1 note.

> (2) by water in providing express transportation.

49 USC 10503. Jursidiction.

§ 10503. Railroad and water transportation connections and rates

(a) When a rail carrier and a water common carrier may or do provide jointly, transportation, not entirely in one State from a place in the United States to another place in the United States, even if part of the transportation is outside the United States, the Interstate Commerce Commission has the following jurisdiction over that transportation:

> (1) To establish a physical connection between the railroad lines of the rail carrier and the dock at which an interchange is to be made, the Commission may—
>
> > (A) require the rail carrier to make a suitable connection between its lines and tracks that have been constructed from the dock to the limits of the railroad right-of-way;
> >
> > (B) subject to the same restrictions on findings of public convenience and necessity and other matters that are imposed on construction under sections 10901, 10902, and 10907 of this title, require the rail carrier or water common carrier, or both, to construct to the dock at least one track connecting with the lines of the rail carrier;

Post, pp. 1402, 1403, 1407.

> > (C) determine and prescribe the conditions under which a connecting track is to be operated; and
> >
> > (D) in the construction or operation of the track, determine the sum to be paid to, or by, either carrier.
>
> (2) The Commission may—
>
> > (A) prescribe proportional rates, maximum proportional rates, minimum proportional rates, or maximum and minimum proportional rates, of a rail carrier to and from the ports to which the passengers or property is transported by the water common carrier; and
> >
> > (B) determine the passengers, property, vessels, and on which conditions those rates apply.

"Proportional rates."

In this paragraph, "proportional rates" means those rates that differ from the corresponding local rates to and from a port and apply only to passengers or property brought to the port or carried from the port by a water common carrier.

Hearing.

(b) The Commission may act under this section only after a full hearing. An order entered as the result of an action may be conditioned on giving security for the payment of an amount of money or the discharge of an obligation that is required to be paid or discharged under that order.

49 USC 10504.

§ 10504. Exempt rail mass transportation

(a) In this section—

> (1) "local public body"—

"Local public body."

> > (A) has the same meaning given that term by section 1608 (c) (2) of this title; and

(B) includes a person or entity that contracts with the local public body to provide transportation services.

(2) "rail mass transportation" means transportation services described in section 1608(c)(5) of this title that are provided by rail.

Rail mass transportation. 49 USC 1608.

(b) The Interstate Commerce Commission does not have jurisdiction under this subtitle over rail mass transportation provided by a local public body if—

Jursidiction.

(1) the Commission would have jurisdiction but for this section; and

(2) the fares of the local public body, or its authority to apply to the Commission for changes in those fares, is subject to the approval or disapproval of the chief executive officer of the State in which the transportation is provided.

§ 10505. Authority to exempt rail carrier transportation

49 USC 10505.

(a) In a matter related to a rail carrier providing transportation subject to the jurisdiction of the Interstate Commerce Commission under this subchapter, the Commission shall exempt a person, class of persons, or a transaction or service because of the limited scope of the transaction or service, when the Commission finds that the application of a provision of this subtitle—

(1) is not necessary to carry out the transportation policy of section 10101 of this title;

Ante, p. 1337.

(2) would be an unreasonable burden on a person, class of persons, or interstate and foreign commerce; and

(3) would serve little or no useful public purpose.

(b) The Commission may begin a proceeding under this section on its own initiative or on application by the Secretary of Transportation or an interested party. The Commission may specify the period of time during which the exemption is effective.

(c) The Commission may revoke an exemption, to the extent it specifies, when it finds that application of a provision of this subtitle to the person, class, or transportation is necessary—

Revocation.

(1) to carry out the transportation policy of section 10101 of this title;

(2) to achieve effective regulation by the Commission; and

(3) to serve a useful public purpose.

(d) The Commission may act under this section only after an opportunity for a proceeding.

SUBCHAPTER II—MOTOR CARRIER TRANSPORTATION

§ 10521. General jurisdiction

49 USC 10521.

(a) Subject to this chapter and other law, the Interstate Commerce Commission has jurisdiction over transportation by motor carrier and the procurement of that transportation to the extent that passengers, property, or both, are transported by motor carrier—

(1) between a place in—

(A) a State and a place in another State;

(B) a State and another place in the same State through another State;

(C) the United States and a place in a territory or possession of the United States to the extent the transportation is in the United States;

(D) the United States and another place in the United States through a foreign country to the extent the transportation is in the United States; or

(E) the United States and a place in a foreign country to the extent the transportation is in the United States; and

(2) in a reservation under the exclusive jurisdiction of the United States or on a public highway.

(b) This subtitle does not—

(1) affect the power of a State to regulate intrastate transportation provided by a motor carrier;

(2) authorize the Commission to prescribe or regulate a rate for intrastate transportation provided by a motor carrier;

(3) allow a motor carrier to provide intrastate transportation on the highways of a State; or

Post, p. 1446.

(4) except as provided in section 11504(b) of this title, affect the taxation power of a State over a motor carrier.

49 USC 10522.

§ 10522. Exempt transportation between Alaska and other States

To the extent that transportation by a motor carrier between a place in Alaska and a place in another State under section 10521 of this title is provided in a foreign country—

(1) the Interstate Commerce Commission does not have jurisdiction to impose a requirement over conduct of the motor carrier in the foreign country conflicting with a requirement of that country; but

(2) the motor carrier, as a condition of providing transportation in the United States, shall comply, with respect to all transportation provided between Alaska and the other State, with the requirements of this subtitle related to rates and practices applicable to the transportation.

49 USC 10523.

§ 10523. Exempt motor vehicle transportation in terminal areas

(a)(1) The Interstate Commerce Commission does not have jurisdiction under this subchapter over transportation by motor vehicle provided in a terminal area when the transportation—

(A) is a transfer, collection, or delivery;

(B) is provided by—

(i) a rail carrier subject to the jurisdiction of the Commission under subchapter I of this chapter;

(ii) a water carrier subject to the jurisdiction of the Commission under subchapter III of this chapter; or

(iii) a freight forwarder subject to the jurisdiction of the Commission under subchapter IV of this chapter; and

(C) is incidental to transportation provided by the carrier or service provided by the freight forwarder that is subject to the jurisdiction of the Commission under any of those subchapters.

(2) Transportation exempt from the jurisdiction of the Commission under paragraph (1) of this subsection is subject to the jurisdiction of the Commission under subchapter I of this chapter when provided by such a rail carrier, under subchapter III of this chapter when provided by such a water carrier, and under subchapter IV of this chapter when provided by such a freight forwarder.

(b)(1) Except to the extent provided in paragraph (2) of this subsection, the Commission does not have jurisdiction under this subchapter over transportation by motor vehicle provided in a terminal area when the transportation—

(A) is a transfer, collection, or delivery; and

(B) is provided by a person as an agent or under other arrangement for—

    (i) a rail carrier or express carrier subject to the jurisdiction of the Commission under subchapter I of this chapter;

    (ii) a motor carrier subject to the jurisdiction of the Commission under this subchapter;

    (iii) a water carrier subject to the jurisdiction of the Commission under subchapter III of this chapter; or

    (iv) a freight forwarder subject to the jurisdiction of the Commission under subchapter IV of this chapter.

(2) Transportation exempt from the jurisdiction of the Commission under paragraph (1) of this subsection is considered transportation provided by the carrier or service provided by the freight forwarder for whom the transportation was provided and is subject to the jurisdiction of the Commission under subchapter I of this chapter when provided for such a rail carrier or express carrier, under this subchapter when provided for such a motor carrier, under subchapter III of this chapter when provided for such a water carrier, and under subchapter IV of this chapter when provided for such a freight forwarder.

§ 10524. Transportation furthering a primary business

49 USC 10524.

The Interstate Commerce Commission does not have jurisdiction under this subchapter over the transportation of property by motor vehicle when—

    (1) the property is transported by a person engaged in a business other than transportation; and

    (2) the transportation is within the scope of, and furthers a primary business (other than transportation) of the person.

§ 10525. Exempt motor carrier transportation entirely in one State

49 USC 10525.

(a) The Interstate Commerce Commission shall exempt transportation of a motor carrier subject to the jurisdiction of the Commission under this subchapter from compliance with this subtitle when—

    (1) the motor carrier provides transportation entirely in one State; and

    (2) the Commission finds that the nature or quantity of transportation provided by the motor carrier does not substantially affect or impair uniform regulation by the Commission of motor carrier transportation in carrying out the transportation policy of section 10101 of this title.

Ante, p. 1337.
Proceedings.

(b) The Commission may begin a proceeding under this section on its own initiative or on application of a motor carrier, a State authority having jurisdiction to regulate intrastate transportation by motor vehicle on the highways of that State, or an interested party. An application must be under oath and must contain information required by Commission regulation. The Commission may exempt the transportation by motor carrier or class of motor carriers. When an exemption is granted, the Commission shall issue a certificate of exemption describing the conditions required by the public interest under which the certificate is issued.

Exemption certificate.

(c) When an application for exemption is accompanied by a certificate of the authority of the State in which the applicant provides transportation stating the finding of the State authority that the applicant is entitled to a certificate of exemption under this section, the exemption is effective on the 60th day after the application is filed with the Commission unless the Commission denies the application before that date. If not denied before that date, the exemption remains effective until the Commission thereafter denies or revokes it.

Revocation.

(d) The Commission may revoke any part of an exemption granted under this section when it finds that the nature or quantity of the transportation by the motor carrier or class of motor carriers is, or is likely substantially to affect or impair uniform regulation by the Commission of motor carrier transportation in carrying out the trans-

Ante, p. 1337.

portation policy of section 10101 of this title. If the exemption is revoked, the Commission shall restore without further proceedings the authority any such motor carrier had to provide transportation subject to the jurisdiction of the Commission under this subchapter at the time the exemption was effective.

(e) State regulation of the operations of a motor carrier covered by an exemption under this section is not a burden on interstate or foreign commerce.

49 USC 10526.

§ 10526. Miscellaneous motor carrier transportation exemptions

(a) The Interstate Commerce Commission does not have jurisdiction under this subchapter over—

(1) a motor vehicle transporting only school children and teachers to or from school;

(2) a motor vehicle providing taxicab service and having a capacity of not more than 6 passengers and is not operated on a regular route or between specified places;

(3) a motor vehicle owned or operated by or for a hotel and only transporting hotel patrons between the hotel and the local station of a common carrier;

(4) a motor vehicle controlled and operated by a farmer and transporting—

(A) the farmer's agricultural or horticultural commodities and products; or

(B) supplies to the farm of the farmer;

(5) a motor vehicle controlled and operated by a cooperative association (as defined by section 1141j(a) of title 12) or by a federation of cooperative associations if the federation has no greater power or purposes than a cooperative association, except that if the cooperative association or federation provides transportation for compensation between a place in a State and a place in another State, or between a place in a State and another place in the same State through another State—

(A) for a nonmember that is not a farmer, cooperative association, federation, or the United States Government, the transportation (except for transportation otherwise exempt under this subchapter)—

(i) shall be limited to transportation incidental to the primary transportation operation of the cooperative association or federation and necessary for its effective performance;

(ii) may not exceed in each fiscal year 15 percent of the total transportation of the cooperative association or federation between those places, measured by tonnage; and

(iii) shall be provided only after the cooperative association or federation notifies the Commission of its intent to provide the transportation; and

(B) the transportation for all nonmembers may not exceed in each fiscal year, measured by tonnage, the total transportation between those places for the cooperative association or federation and its members during that fiscal year;

(6) a motor vehicle carrying, for compensation, only property and that property consists of —

(A) ordinary livestock;

(B) agricultural or horticultural commodities (other than manufactured products thereof);

(C) commodities listed as exempt in the Commodity List incorporated in ruling numbered 107, March 19, 1958, Bureau of Motor Carriers, Interstate Commerce Commission, other than frozen fruits, frozen berries, frozen vegetables, cocoa beans, coffee beans, tea, bananas, or hemp, or wool imported from a foreign country, wool tops and noils, or wool waste (carded, spun, woven, or knitted); and

(D) cooked or uncooked fish, whether breaded or not, or frozen or fresh shellfish, other than fish or shellfish that have been treated for preserving, such as canned, smoked, pickled, spiced, corned, or kippered products;

(7) a motor vehicle used only to distribute newspapers;

(8) transportation by motor vehicle incidental to transportation by aircraft; or

(9) the operation of a motor vehicle in a national park or national monument.

(b) Except to the extent the Commission finds it necessary to exercise jurisdiction to carry out the transportation policy of section 10101 of this title, the Commission does not have jurisdiction under this sub-chapter over—   *Ante,* p. 1337.

(1) transportation provided entirely in a municipality, in con-tiguous municipalities, or in a zone that is adjacent to, and com-mercially a part of, the municipality or municipalities, except—

(A) when the transportation is under common control, management, or arrangement for a continuous carriage or shipment to or from a place outside the municipality, munici-palities, or zone; or

(B) that in transporting passengers over a route between a place in a State and a place in another State, or between a place in a State and another place in the same State through another State, the transportation is exempt from the jurisdic-tion of the Commission only if the motor carrier operating the motor vehicle also is lawfully providing intrastate transportation of passengers over the entire route under the laws of each State through which the route runs;

(2) transportation by motor vehicle provided casually, oc-casionally, or reciprocally but not as a regular occupation or busi-ness, except when a broker or other person sells or offers for sale passenger transportation provided by a person authorized to transport passengers by motor vehicle under an application pend-ing, or certificate or permit issued, under this subtitle; or

(3) the emergency towing of an accidentally wrecked or dis-abled motor vehicle.

SUBCHAPTER III—WATER CARRIER TRANSPORTATION

§ 10541. General jurisdiction   49 USC 10541.

(a) Subject to this chapter and other law, the Interstate Com-merce Commission has jurisdiction over transportation insofar as water carriers are concerned—

(1) by water carrier between a place in a State and a place in another State, even if part of the transportation is outside the United States;

(2) by water carrier and rail carrier or motor carrier from a place in a State to a place in another State, except that if part of the transportation is outside the United States, the Commission only has jurisdiction over that part of the transportation provided—

(A) by rail carrier or motor carrier that is in the United States; and

(B) by water carrier that is from a place in the United States to another place in the United States; and

(3) by water carrier or by water carrier and rail carrier or motor carrier between a place in the United States and a place outside the United States, to the extent that—

(A) when the transportation is by rail carrier or motor carrier, the transportation is provided in the United States;

(B) when the transportation is by water carrier to a place outside the United States, the transportation is provided by water carrier from a place in the United States to another place in the United States before transshipment from a place in the United States to a place outside the United States; and

(C) when the transportation is by water carrier from a place outside the United States, the transportation is provided by water carrier from a place in the United States to another place in the United States after transshipment to a place in the United States from a place outside the United States.

(b) If transportation by a carrier would be subject to the jurisdiction of the Commission under both subsection (a) of this section and subchapter I of this chapter, then that transportation is subject to the jurisdiction of the Commission under subsection (a) of this section. However, that transportation is also subject to the jurisdiction of the Commission under subchapter I of this chapter to the extent that this subtitle imposes requirements on transportation by carriers subject to the jurisdiction of the Commission under subchapter I that are not imposed on transportation by carriers subject to the jurisdiction of the Commission under subsection (a) of this section.

(c) This subtitle does not—

(1) affect the power of a State to regulate intrastate transportation provided by a water carrier; or

(2) authorize the Commission to prescribe or regulate a rate for intrastate transportation by a water carrier.

49 USC 10542.   § 10542. Exempt bulk transportation

(a)(1) The Interstate Commerce Commission does not have jurisdiction under this subchapter over transportation by a water carrier of commodities in bulk that, under an existing custom of the trade in the handling and transportation of commodities in bulk as of June 1, 1939—

(A) are loaded and carried without wrappers or containers; and

(B) are received and delivered by the carrier without transportation mark or count.

(2) This subsection does not apply to transportation subject to chapter 23A of title 46 on September 18, 1940.

46 USC 843 *et seq.*

(b) The Commission does not have jurisdiction under this subchapter over transportation by a water contract carrier of commodities in bulk in a non-oceangoing vessel on a normal voyage during which—

(1) the cargo space of the vessel is used for carrying not more than 3 commodities in bulk; and

(2) the vessel passes in or through waters that are international for navigational purposes by a treaty to which the United States is a party.

(c) The Commission does not have jurisdiction under this subchapter over transportation by water carrier of liquid cargoes in bulk in tank vessels—

(1) designed exclusively for transporting such a cargo; and

(2) certified under regulations of the Secretary of Transportation under section 391a of title 46.

§ 10543. Exempt incidental water transportation

49 USC 10543.

(a)(1) The Interstate Commerce Commission does not have jurisdiction under this subchapter when the transportation—

(A)(i) is provided in a terminal area and is a transfer, collection, or delivery; or

(ii) is flotage, car ferrying, lighterage, or towage;

(B) is provided by—

(i) a rail carrier subject to the jurisdiction of the Commission under subchapter I of this chapter; or

(ii) a motor carrier subject to the jurisdiction of the Commission under subchapter II of this chapter; and

(C) is incidental to transportation provided by the carrier subject to the jurisdiction of the Commission under either of those subchapters.

(2) Transportation exempt from the jurisdiction of the Commission under paragraph (1) of this subsection is subject to the jurisdiction of the Commission under subchapter I of this chapter when provided by such a rail carrier and under subchapter II of this chapter when provided by such a motor carrier.

(b)(1) Except to the extent provided in paragraph (2) of this subsection, the Commission does not have jurisdiction under this subchapter over transportation by water when the transportation—

(A)(i) is provided in a terminal area and is a transfer, collection, or delivery; or

(ii) is flotage, car ferrying, lighterage, or towage; and

(B) is provided by a person as an agent or under other arrangement for—

(i) a rail carrier or express carrier subject to the jurisdiction of the Commission under subchapter I of this chapter;

(ii) a motor carrier subject to the jurisdiction of the Commission under subchapter II of this chapter; or

(iii) a water carrier subject to the jurisdiction of the Commission under this subchapter.

(2) Transportation exempt from the jurisdiction of the Commission under paragraph (1) of this subsection is considered transportation provided by the carrier for whom the transportation was provided and is subject to the jurisdiction of the Commission under subchapter I of this chapter when provided for such a rail carrier

or express carrier, under subchapter II of this chapter when provided for such a motor carrier, and under this subchapter when provided for such a water carrier.

49 USC 10544.

§ 10544. Miscellaneous water carrier transportation exemptions

(a) Except to the extent the Interstate Commerce Commission finds it necessary to exercise jurisdiction to carry out the transportation

Ante, p. 1337.

policy of section 10101 of this title, the Commission does not have jurisdiction under this subchapter over transportation by water carrier when the transportation is provided—

(1) entirely in one harbor or between places in contiguous harbors, other than transportation under common control, management, or arrangement for a continuous carriage or shipment to or from a place outside the limits of the harbor or the contiguous harbors;

(2) by a vessel of not more than 100 tons carrying capacity or 100 indicated horsepower;

(3) by a vessel carrying only passengers and equipped to carry not more than 16 passengers;

(4) by a ferry;

(5) by a water carrier transporting equipment of contractors used, or to be used, in construction or repair for the water carrier; or

(6) to carry out salvage operations.

(b) The Commission may exempt from its jurisdiction under this subchapter the transportation of passengers between places in the United States through a foreign port when the Commission finds its jurisdiction is not necessary to carry out the transportation policy of section 10101 of this title. The Commission may begin a proceeding

Proceeding.

under this subsection on its own initiative or on application of an interested party.

(c) The Commission shall exempt from its jurisdiction under this subchapter the transportation of commodities by water contract carrier when the Commission finds that the transportation is not actually and substantially competitive with transportation provided by a carrier subject to the jurisdiction of the Commission under subchapter I or II of this chapter because of the inherent nature of the commodities transported, their requirement of special equipment, or their shipment

Conditions.
Proceeding.

in bulk. The Commission may prescribe conditions applicable to an exemption under this subsection. The Commission may begin a proceeding under this subsection on application of a water contract carrier.

(d) (1) The Commission does not have jurisdiction under this subtitle over transportation by a water common carrier provided between the 48 contiguous States and Alaska if, before January 3, 1959—

(A) the carrier provided that transportation, was also a motor common carrier, and has continued to provide the transportation since before that date; and

(B) the transportation was subject to chapters 23 and 23A of

46 USC 801 *et seq.,* 843 *et seq.*

title 46.

(2) The transportation remains subject to the jurisdiction of the Federal Maritime Commission.

(e) The Commission shall exempt the transportation of property on a vessel furnished by a water contract carrier to a person not a carrier providing transportation or service subject to the jurisdiction of the Commission under this subtitle when the person uses the vessel to transport its own property and the Commission finds its jurisdiction is not necessary to carry out the transportation policy of section 10101 of this title. The Commission may begin a proceeding under this section on its own initiative or on application of an interested party. The Commission may exempt the transportation by person or class of persons. The Commission shall specify the period of time during which the exemption is effective. The Commission may revoke the exemption when it finds that its jurisdiction over the transportation of the property is necessary to carry out the transportation policy of section 10101. The Commission may deny or revoke an exemption only after an opportunity for a proceeding.

Ante, p. 1337.
Proceeding.

(f) (1) The Commission shall exempt the transportation of property by a water carrier under this subchapter when the Commission finds that the carrier is transporting only the property of a person owning substantially all of the voting stock of the carrier. When an exemption is granted, the Commission shall issue a certificate of exemption. The Commission may begin a proceeding under this subsection on its own initiative or on application of an interested party.

Exemption
certificate.
Proceeding.

(2) The Commission may revoke an exemption granted under this subsection when it finds the water carrier is no longer entitled to the exemption. If the exemption is revoked, the Commission shall restore without further proceedings the authority the water carrier had to provide transportation subject to the jurisdiction of the Commission under this subchapter at the time the exemption became effective.

Revocation.

SUBCHAPTER IV—FREIGHT FORWARDER SERVICE

§ 10561. General jurisdiction

49 USC 10561.

(a) Subject to this chapter and other law, the Interstate Commerce Commission has jurisdiction over service that a freight forwarder—

(1) undertakes to provide; or

(2) is authorized or required under this subtitle to provide;

to the extent transportation is provided in the United States and is between—

(A) a place in a State and a place in another State, even if part of the transportation is outside the United States;

(B) a place in a State and another place in the same State through a place outside the State; or

(C) a place in the United States and a place outside the United States.

(b) The Commission does not have jurisdiction under subsection (a) of this section over service undertaken by a freight forwarder using transportation—

(1) of an air carrier subject to chapter 20 of this title; or

(2) by motor vehicle exempt under section 10526(a)(8) of this title.

49 USC 1301 et
seq.

§ 10562. Exempt freight forwarder service

The Interstate Commerce Commission does not have jurisdiction under this subchapter over—

(1) service provided by, or under the direction of, a cooperative association (as defined by section 1141j(a) of title 12) or by a federation of cooperative associations if the federation has no greater power or purposes than a cooperative association;

(2) service subject to the jurisdiction of the Commission and provided with respect to only one of the following categories:

(A) ordinary livestock;

(B) fish (including shellfish);

(C) agricultural or horticultural commodities (other than manufactured products thereof); or

(D) used household goods;

(3) the service of a shipper or a group of shippers in consolidating or distributing freight on a nonprofit basis, for the shipper or members of the group to secure carload, truckload, or other volume rates; or

(4) the service of an agent of a shipper in consolidating or distributing pool cars when the service is provided for the shipper only in a terminal area in which the service is performed.

CHAPTER 107—RATES, TARIFFS, AND VALUATIONS

SUBCHAPTER I—GENERAL AUTHORITY

SUBCHAPTER II—SPECIAL CIRCUMSTANCES

SUBCHAPTER III—LIMITATIONS

SUBCHAPTER IV—TARIFFS AND TRAFFIC

SUBCHAPTER V—VALUATION OF PROPERTY

SUBCHAPTER I—GENERAL AUTHORITY

§ 10701. Standards for rates, classifications, through routes, rules, and practices

49 USC 10701.

(a) A rate, classification, rule, or practice related to transportation or service provided by a carrier subject to the jurisdiction of the Interstate Commerce Commission under chapter 105 of this title must be reasonable. A through route established by such a carrier must be reasonable. Divisions of joint rates by those carriers must be made without unreasonable discrimination against a participating carrier and must be reasonable.

(b)(1) A rate for transportation provided by a rail carrier subject to the jurisdiction of the Commission under subchapter I of chapter 105 of this title that contributes, or would contribute, to the going concern value of that carrier does not violate subsection (a) of this section because it is below a reasonable minimum rate for the service rendered or to be rendered. This subsection does not prohibit increasing a rate to a level that contributes to the going concern value of a rail carrier if the increase is otherwise reasonable. The increased rate is presumed reasonable if it does not exceed the incremental costs of rendering the transportation to which the increase applies.

Rate increases.

(2)(A) A rate for transportation by a rail carrier that equals or exceeds the variable costs of providing the transportation is presumed to contribute to the going concern value of the rail carrier proposing the rate. However, the presumption may be rebutted by clear and convincing evidence.

(B) Variable and incremental costs shall be determined under formulas prescribed by the Commission. However, when making a determination of variable costs, the Commission shall, on application of the rail carrier proposing the rate, determine only the costs of that carrier and only those costs of the specific service in question unless the specific information is not available. The Commission may not include in variable costs an expense that does not vary directly with the level of transportation provided under the proposed rate.

(c) A common carrier providing transportation subject to the jurisdiction of the Commission under subchapter I or III of chapter 105 of this title may not discriminate in its rates against a connecting line of another carrier providing transportation subject to the juris-

Nondiscrimination.

diction of the Commission under either of those subchapters or unreasonably discriminate against that line in the distribution of traffic that is not routed specifically by the shipper.

(d) In a proceeding to determine whether a rate for transportation or service provided by a common carrier subject to the jurisdiction of the Commission under subchapter II, III, or IV of chapter 105 of this title complies with subsection (a) of this section, the good will, earning power, or certificate or permit under which that carrier is operating may not be considered or admitted as evidence of the value of the property of that carrier. When the carrier receives a certificate or permit under chapter 109 of this title, it is considered to have agreed to this subsection for itself and for all transferees of that certificate or permit.

Post, p. 1402.

§ 10702. Authority for carriers to establish rates, classifications, rules, and practices

(a) A common carrier providing transportation or service subject to the jurisdiction of the Interstate Commerce Commission under chapter 105 of this title shall establish—

    (1) rates, including divisions of joint rates, and classifications for transportation and service it may provide under this subtitle; and

    (2) rules and practices on matters related to that transportation or service, including rules and practices on—

        (A) issuing tickets, receipts, bills of lading, and manifests;

        (B) carrying of baggage;

        (C) the manner and method of presenting, marking, packing, and delivering property for transportation; and

        (D) facilities for transportation.

Filing.

(b) A contract carrier providing transportation subject to the jurisdiction of the Commission under chapter 105 of this title shall establish, and file with the Commission, actual and minimum rates for the transportation it may provide under this subtitle and rules and practices related to those rates. However, this subsection does not require a motor contract carrier to maintain the same rates and rules related to those rates for the same transportation provided to shippers served by it. The Commission may grant relief from this subsection when relief is consistent with the public interest and the transportation policy of section 10101 of this title. The Commission may begin a proceeding under this subsection on application of a contract carrier or group of contract carriers or on its own initiative for a water contract carrier or group of water contract carriers.

Relief.

Ante, p. 1337.
Proceeding.

49 USC 10703.

§ 10703. Authority for carriers to establish through routes

(a) A carrier providing transportation subject to the jurisdiction of the Interstate Commerce Commission under chapter 105 of this title shall establish through routes as follows:

    (1) Rail, express, sleeping car, and pipeline carriers shall establish through routes with each other and shall establish rates and classifications applicable to those routes.

    (2) Rail and water common carriers shall establish through routes with each other and shall establish rates and classifications applicable to those routes.

    (3) A motor common carrier of passengers shall establish through routes with other carriers of the same type and shall establish individual and joint rates applicable to them.

(4)(A) A motor common carrier of property may establish through routes and joint rates and classifications applicable to them with other carriers of the same type, with rail and express carriers, and with water common carriers, including those referred to in subparagraph (D) of this paragraph.

(B) A motor common carrier of passengers may establish through routes and joint rates applicable to them with rail carriers or water common carriers, including those referred to in subparagraph (D) of this paragraph, or both.

(C) Water common carriers shall establish through routes with each other and shall establish rates and classifications applicable to those routes and may establish—

(i) through routes and rates and classifications applicable to them with motor common carriers; and

(ii) through routes and joint rates and classifications applicable to them with water common carriers referred to in subparagraph (D)(ii) of this paragraph.

(D) A through route or joint rate or classification authorized to be established with a carrier referred to in this subparagraph may be established with a water common carrier providing transportation subject to—

(i) the jurisdiction of the Commission under subchapter III of chapter 105 of this title; or

(ii) section 801 or sections 843–848 of title 46 (including persons holding themselves out to transport goods by water but not owning or operating vessels) and providing transportation of property between Alaska or Hawaii and the other 48 States.

A through route and a rate, classification, rule, or practice related to a through route with a water common carrier referred to in this subparagraph is subject to the provisions of this subtitle governing the type of carrier establishing the rate, classification, rule, or practice.

(b) A carrier providing transportation subject to the jurisdiction **Operating rules.** of the Commission under subchapter I or III of chapter 105 of this title that establishes a through route with another carrier under this section shall establish rules for its operation and provide—

(1) reasonable facilities for operating the through route; and

(2) reasonable compensation to persons entitled to compensation for services related to the through route.

§ 10704. Authority and criteria: rates, classifications, rules, and practices prescribed by Interstate Commerce Commission

49 USC 10704.

(a)(1) When the Interstate Commerce Commission, after a full **Violations.** hearing, decides that a rate charged or collected by a carrier for transportation subject to the jurisdiction of the Commission under subchapter I of chapter 105 of this title, or that a classification, rule, or practice of that carrier, does or will violate this subtitle, the Commission may prescribe the rate (including a maximum or minimum rate, or both), classification, rule, or practice to be followed. The Commission may order the carrier to stop the violation. When a rate, classification, rule, or practice is prescribed under this subsection, the affected carrier may not publish, charge, or collect a different rate and shall adopt the classification and observe the rule or practice prescribed by the Commission.

Revenue levels,
standards and
procedures.

(2) The Commission shall maintain standards and procedures for establishing revenue levels for rail carriers providing transportation subject to its jurisdiction under that subchapter that are adequate, under honest, economical, and efficient management, to cover total operating expenses, including depreciation and obsolescence, plus a reasonable and economic profit or return (or both) on capital employed in the business. The Commission shall make an adequate and continuing effort to assist those carriers in attaining revenue levels prescribed under this paragraph. However, a rate, classification, rule, or practice of a rail carrier may be maintained at a particular level to protect the traffic of another carrier or mode of transportation only if the Commission finds that the rate or classification, or rule or practice related to it, reduces or would reduce the going concern value of the carrier charging the rate. Revenue levels established under this paragraph should—

(A) provide a flow of net income plus depreciation adequate to support prudent capital outlays, assure the repayment of a reasonable level of debt, permit the raising of needed equity capital, and cover the effects of inflation; and

(B) attract and retain capital in amounts adequate to provide a sound transportation system in the United States.

(b)(1) When the Commission decides that a rate charged or collected by—

(A) a motor common carrier for providing transportation subject to its jurisdiction under subchapter II of chapter 105 of this title by itself, with another motor common carrier, with a rail, express, or water common carrier, or any of them;

(B) a water common carrier for providing transportation subject to its jurisdiction under subchapter III of chapter 105 of this title; or

(C) a freight forwarder for providing service subject to its jurisdiction under subchapter IV of chapter 105 of this title;

or that a classification, rule, or practice of that carrier, does or will violate this chapter, the Commission shall prescribe the rate (including a maximum or minimum rate, or both), classification, rule, or practice to be followed.

(2) When prescribing a rate, classification, rule, or practice for transportation or service by common carriers other than by rail carrier, the Commission shall consider, among other factors, the following:

(A) the effect of the prescribed rate, classification, rule, or practice on the movement of traffic by that carrier; and

(B) the need for revenues that are sufficient, under honest, economical, and efficient management, to let the carrier provide that transportation or service.

(3) If the carrier is a motor or water common carrier or a freight forwarder, the Commission shall also consider the need, in the public interest, of adequate and efficient transportation or service by that carrier at the lowest cost consistent with providing that transportation or service.

(4) If the carrier is a motor common carrier or a freight forwarder, the Commission shall also consider the inherent advantages of transportation by motor common carrier or the inherent nature of freight forwarding, respectively.

(c)(1) When the Commission finds that a minimum rate of a contract carrier for transportation subject to the jurisdiction of the Commission under subchapter II or III of chapter 105 of this title, or a rule or practice related to the rate or the value of the service under it, violates this chapter or the transportation policy of section 10101 of this title, the Commission may prescribe the minimum rate, rule, or practice for the carrier that is desirable in the public interest and will promote that policy. In prescribing the rate, the Commission may not give a motor or water contract carrier an advantage or preference in competition with a motor or water common carrier, respectively, if an advantage or preference is unreasonable or inconsistent with the public interest and the transportation policy of section 10101 of this title.

Ante, p. 1337.

(2) When prescribing a minimum rate, or rule or practice related to a rate, for a contract carrier, the Commission shall consider—

(A) the cost of the transportation provided by the carrier; and

(B) the effect of a prescribed minimum rate, or rule or practice, on the movement of traffic by that carrier.

(d) In a proceeding involving competition between carriers of different modes of transportation subject to this subtitle, except rail carriers, the Commission, in determining whether a rate is less than a reasonable minimum rate, shall consider the facts and circumstances involved in moving the traffic by the mode of carrier to which the rate is applicable. Subject to the transportation policy of section 10101 of this title, rates of a carrier may not be maintained at a particular level to protect the traffic of another mode of transportation.

Proceedings.

(e) In a proceeding involving a proposed increase or decrease in rail carrier rates, the Commission shall specifically consider allegations that the increase or decrease would (1) change the rate relationships between commodities, ports, places, regions, areas, or other particular descriptions of traffic (without regard to previous Commission consideration or approval of those relationships), and (2) have a significant adverse effect on the competitive position of shippers or consignees served by the rail carrier proposing the increase or decrease. The Commission shall investigate to determine whether the change or effect violates this subtitle when it finds that those allegations are substantially supported on the record. The investigation may be made either before or after the proposed increase or decrease becomes effective and either in that proceeding or in another proceeding.

Investigation.

(f) The Commission may begin a proceeding under this section on its own initiative or on complaint. A complaint under subsection (a) of this section must be made under section 11701 of this title, but the proceeding may also be in extension of a complaint pending before the Commission. A complaint under subsection (c) of this section must contain a full statement of the facts and the reasons for the complaint and must be made under oath.

Post, p. 1449.

§ 10705. Authority: through routes, joint classifications, rates, and divisions prescribed by Interstate Commerce Commission

49 USC 10705.

(a)(1) The Interstate Commerce Commission may, and shall when it considers it desirable in the public interest, prescribe through routes, joint classifications, joint rates (including maximum or minimum rates or both), the division of joint rates, and the conditions under which those routes must be operated, for a common carrier providing transportation subject to the jurisdiction of the Commission under subchapter I, II (except a motor common carrier of property), or III of chapter 105 of this title. When one of the carriers on a through route is a water carrier, the Commission shall prescribe a differential between an all-rail rate and a joint rate related to the water carrier if the differential is justified.

(2) The Commission may require a rail carrier to include in a through route substantially less than the entire length of its railroad and any intermediate railroad operated with it under common management or control if that intermediate railroad lies between the terminals of the through route only when—

Post, p. 1419.   (A) required under section 10741–10744 or 11103 of this title;

(B) one of the carriers is a water carrier;

(C) inclusion of those lines would make the through route unreasonably long when compared with a practicable alternative through route that could be established; or

(D) the Commission decides that the proposed through route is needed to provide adequate, and more efficient or economic, transportation.

The Commission shall give reasonable preference, subject to this subsection, to the rail carrier originating the traffic when prescribing through routes.

Prohibition.   (3) The Commission may not prescribe—

(A) a through route, classification, practice, or rate between a street electric passenger railway not engaged in the general business of transporting freight in addition to its passenger and express business and (i) a rail carrier of a different character, or (ii) a water common carrier; or

(B) a through route or joint rate applicable to it to assist a participating carrier to meet its financial needs.

(b) The Commission shall prescribe the division of joint rates to be received by a carrier providing transportation subject to its jurisdiction under chapter 105 of this subtitle when it decides that a division of joint rates established by the participating carriers under section 10703 of this title, or under a decision of the Commission under subsection (a) of this section, does or will violate section 10701 of this title. When prescribing the division of joint rates of a rail or water carrier under this subsection, the Commission shall consider—

(1) the efficiency with which the carriers concerned are operated;

(2) the amount of revenue required by the carriers to pay their operating expenses and taxes and receive a fair return on the property held and used for transportation;

(3) the importance of the transportation to the public;

(4) whether a particular participating carrier is an originating, intermediate, or delivering line; and

(5) other circumstances that ordinarily, without regard to the mileage traveled, entitle one carrier to a different proportion of a rate than another carrier.

(c) If a division of a joint rate prescribed under a decision of the Commission is later found to violate section 10701 of this title, the Commission may decide what division would have been reasonable and order adjustment to be made retroactive to the date the complaint was filed, the date the order for an investigation was made, or a later date that the Commission decides is justified. The Commission may make a decision under this paragraph effective as part of its original decision.

(d) When the Commission suspends, for investigation, a rail or water common carrier tariff that would cancel a through route, joint rate, or classification without the consent of all carriers that are parties to it or without authorization of the Commission, the carrier proposing the cancellation has the burden of proving that cancellation is consistent with the public interest without regard to subsection (a) (2) of this section. In determining whether a cancellation involving a rail carrier is consistent with the public interest, the Commission shall, to the extent applicable—

> (1) compare the distance traveled and the average transportation time and expense required using (A) the through route, and (B) alternative routes, between the places served by the through route;
>
> (2) consider any reduction in energy consumption that may result from cancellation; and
>
> (3) consider the overall impact of cancellation on the shippers and carriers that are affected by it.

(e)(1) The Commission may begin a proceeding under subsection (a) or (b) of this section on its own initiative or on complaint and may take action only after a full hearing. The Commission must complete all evidentiary proceedings to adjust the division of joint rates for transportation by rail carrier within one year after the complaint is filed if the proceeding is brought on complaint or within 2 years after the commencement of a proceeding on the initiative of the Commission and must take final action by the 270th day after completion of the evidentiary proceedings. The Commission may decide to extend such a proceeding to permit its fair and expeditious completion, but when the Commission cannot meet those time limits, it must report its reasons to Congress. *[margin: Hearing and proceeding.]* *[margin: Extension, report to Congress.]*

(2) When a carrier begins a proceeding to adjust the division of joint rates for transportation by a rail carrier under this section by filing a complaint with the Commission, the carrier must also file all of the evidence in support of its position with the complaint and, during the course of the proceeding may only file rebuttal or reply evidence unless otherwise ordered by the Commission.

(3) When the Commission receives a notice of intent to begin a proceeding to adjust the division of joint rates for transportation by a rail carrier under this section, the Commission shall allow the party filing the notice the same right to discovery that a party would have on filing a complaint under this section. *[margin: Discovery.]*

(f) When there is a shortage of equipment, congestion of traffic, or other emergency declared by the Commission, it may prescribe temporary through routes that are desirable in the public interest on its own initiative or on application without regard to subsection (e) of this section, subchapter II of chapter 103 of this title, and subchapter II of chapter 5 of title 5. *[margin: Emergency.]* *[margin: Ante, p. 1345. 5 USC 5311 et seq.]*

§ 10706. Rate agreements: exemption from antitrust laws

[margin: 49 USC 10706. Definitions.]

(a)(1) In this subsection—

> (A) "affiliate" means a person controlling, controlled by, or under common control or ownership with another person and "ownership" refers to equity holdings in a business entity of at least 5 percent.
>
> (B) "single-line rate" refers to a rate or allowance proposed by a single rail carrier that is applicable only over its line and for which the transportation (exclusive of terminal services by

switching, drayage or other terminal carriers or agencies) can be provided by that carrier.

Approval.

(2) (A) A rail carrier providing transportation subject to the jurisdiction of the Interstate Commerce Commission under subchapter I of chapter 105 of this title that is a party to an agreement of at least 2 rail carriers or an agreement with a class of carriers referred to in subsection (c) (1) (B)–(E) of this section, that relates to rates (including charges between rail carriers and compensation paid or received for the use of facilities and equipment), classifications, divisions, or rules related to them, or procedures for joint consideration, initiation, or establishment of them, shall apply to the Commission for approval of that agreement under this subsection. The Commission shall approve the agreement only when it finds that the making and carrying out of the agreement will further the transportation policy of section 10101 of this title and may require compliance with conditions necessary to make the agreement further that policy as a condition of its approval. If the Commission approves the agreement, it may be made and carried out under its terms and under the conditions required by the Commission, and the Sherman Act (15 U.S.C. 1, et seq.), the Clayton Act (15 U.S.C. 12, et seq.), the Federal Trade Commission Act (15 U.S.C. 41, et seq.), sections 73 and 74 of the Wilson Tariff Act (15 U.S.C. 8 and 9), and the Act of June 19, 1936, as amended (15 U.S.C. 13, 13a, 13b, 21a) do not apply to parties and other persons with respect to making or carrying out the agreement. However, the Commission may not approve or continue approval of an agreement when the conditions required by it are not met or if it does not receive a verified statement under subparagraph (B) of this paragraph.

Verified statement, filing.

(B) The Commission may approve an agreement under subparagraph (A) of this paragraph only when the carriers applying for approval file a verified statement with the Commission. Each statement must specify for each rail carrier that is a party to the agreement—

(i) the name of the carrier;

(ii) the mailing address and telephone number of its headquarter's office; and

(iii) the names of each of its affiliates and the names, addresses, and affiliates of each of its officers and directors and of each person, together with an affiliate, owning or controlling any debt, equity, or security interest in it having a value of at least $1,000,000.

Final disposition.

(3) (A) An organization established or continued under an agreement approved under this subsection shall make a final disposition of a rule or rate docketed with it by the 120th day after the proposal is docketed. Such an organization may not—

(i) permit a rail carrier to participate in agreements related to, or to vote on single-line rates proposed by another rail carrier, or on rates related to a particular interline movement unless that rail carrier can practicably participate in that movement; or

(ii) permit, provide for, or establish a procedure for joint consideration or joint action to protest or seek the suspension of a rate or classification filed by a rail carrier under section 10707 of this title when that rate or classification is established by independent action.

(B) Subparagraph (A) (i) and (ii) of this paragraph does not apply to—

(i) general rate increases or decreases if the agreement gives shippers, under specified procedures, at least 15 days' notice of the proposal and an opportunity to present comments on it before a tariff containing the increases or decreases is filed with the Commission; or

Notice and comments.

(ii) broad tariff changes that are of at least substantially general application throughout the area where the changes will apply.

(C) In any proceeding in which a party alleges that a rail carrier voted or agreed on a rate or allowance in violation of this subsection, that party has the burden of showing that the vote or agreement occurred. A showing of parallel behavior does not satisfy that burden by itself.

(b) A common carrier providing transportation or service subject to the jurisdiction of the Commission under chapter 105 of this title (except a rail carrier) that is a party to an agreement of at least 2 carriers related to rates (including charges between carriers and compensation paid or received for the use of facilities and equipment), allowances, classifications, divisions, or rules related to them, or procedures for joint consideration, initiation, or establishment of them, may apply to the Commission for approval of that agreement under this subsection. The Commission shall approve the agreement only when it finds that the making and carrying out of the agreement will further the transportation policy of section 10101 of this title and may require compliance with conditions necessary to make the agreement further that policy as a condition of approval. If the Commission approves the agreement, it may be made and carried out under its terms and under the conditions required by the Commission, and the antitrust laws, as defined in section 12 of title 15, do not apply to parties and other persons with respect to making or carrying out the agreement.

Ante, p. 1358.

Ante, p. 1337.

(c) (1) In this subsection, carriers are classified as follows:

Carrier classification.

(A) Rail, express, and sleeping car carriers are a class.
(B) Pipeline carriers are a class.
(C) Motor carriers are a class.
(D) Water carriers are a class.
(E) Freight forwarders are a class.

(2) The Commission may not approve an agreement under this section.

Unapprovable agreements.

(A) between or among carriers of different classes unless, in addition to the finding required under subsection (a) or (b) of this section, the Commission finds that the agreement is limited to matters related to transportation under joint rates or over through routes;

(B) related to a pooling, division, or other matter to which subchapter III of chapter 113 of this title applies; or

Post, p. 1434.

(C) establishing a procedure for determination of a matter through joint consideration unless the Commission finds that each party to the agreement has the absolute right under it to take independent action before or after a determination is made under that procedure.

(d) The Commission may require an organization established or continued under an agreement approved under this section to maintain records and submit reports. The Commission, or its delegate, may inspect a record maintained under this section.

Records maintenance.

Review.

(e) The Commission may review an agreement approved under subsection (a) or (b) of this section and shall change the conditions of approval or terminate it when necessary to comply with (1) the

Postponement.

public interest and subsection (a), or (2) subsection (b). The Commission shall postpone the effective date of a change of an agreement under this subsection for whatever period it determines to be reasonably necessary to avoid unreasonable hardship.

Proceeding.

(f) The Commission may begin a proceeding under this section on its own initiative or on application. Action of the Commission under this section (1) approving an agreement, (2) denying, ending, or changing approval, (3) prescribing the conditions on which approval is granted, or (4) changing those conditions, has effect only as related to application of the antitrust laws referred to in subsection (a) or (b) of this section.

Review.

(g) The Commission shall review each agreement approved under subsection (a) of this section periodically, but at least once every 3 years (1) to determine whether the agreement or an organization established or continued under one of those agreements still complies with the requirements of that subsection and the public interest, and (2) to evaluate the success and effect of that agreement or organization on the consuming public and the national rail freight transportation system. If the Commission finds that an agreement or organization does not conform to the requirements of that subsection, it shall end or suspend its approval. The Commission shall report to the President

Report to
President and
Congress.
Ante, p. 1345.

and Congress the results of the review as a part of its annual report under section 10311 of this title.

Assessment
report by FTC,
publication.

(h)(1) The Federal Trade Commission, in consultation with the Antitrust Division of the Department of Justice, shall prepare periodically an assessment of, and shall report to the Commission on—

(A) possible anticompetitive features of—

(i) agreements approved or submitted for approval under subsection (a) of this section; and

(ii) an organization operating under those agreements; and

(B) possible ways to alleviate or end an anticompetitive feature, effect, or aspect in a manner that will further the goals of this subtitle and of the transportation policy of section 10101 of this title.

(2) Reports received by the Commission under this subsection shall be published and made available to the public under section 552(a) of title 5.

49 USC 10707.

§ 10707. Investigation and suspension of new rail carrier rates, classifications, rules, and practices

(a) When a new individual or joint rate or individual or joint classification, rule, or practice related to a rate is filed with the Interstate Commerce Commission by a rail carrier providing transportation sub-

Ante, p. 1359.

ject to its jurisdiction under subchapter I of chapter 105 of this title, the Commission may begin a proceeding, on its own initiative or on complaint of an interested party, to determine whether the proposed

Notice.

rate, classification, rule, or practice violates this subtitle. The Commission must give reasonable notice to interested parties before beginning a proceeding under this subsection but may act without allowing an interested party to file an answer or other formal pleading in response to its decision to begin the proceeding.

(b) (1) The Commission must complete a proceeding under this section and make its final decision by the end of the 7th month after the rate, classification, rule, or practice was to become effective. However, if the Commission reports to Congress by the end of the 7th month that it cannot make a final decision by that time and explains the reason for the delay, it may take an additional 3 months to complete the proceeding and make its final decision. If the Commission does not reach a final decision within the applicable time period, the rate, classification, rule, or practice— Extension, report to Congress.

   (A) is effective at the end of that time period; or
   (B) if already in effect at the end of that time period, remains in effect.

(2) If an interested party has filed a complaint under subsection (a) of this section, the Commission may set aside a rate, classification, rule, or practice that has become effective under this section if the Commission finds it to be in violation of this chapter.

(c) (1) Pending final Commission action in a proceeding under subsection (a) of this section, the Commission may suspend the proposed rate, classification, rule, or practice for 7 months after the time it would otherwise go into effect or, if a report is made under subsection (b) of this section, for 10 months after the time it would otherwise go into effect. However, the Commission may suspend a rate under this subsection only if it appears from specific facts shown by the verified complaint of a person that—

   (A) without suspension, the proposed rate change will cause substantial injury to the complainant or the party represented by the complainant; and
   (B) it is likely that the complainant will prevail on the merits.

(2) The burden is on the complainant to prove the facts required under paragraph (1) (A) and (B) of this subsection.

(d) If the Commission does not suspend a proposed rate increase that is the subject of a proceeding under this section, the Commission shall require the rail carriers involved to account for all amounts received under the increase until the Commission completes the proceeding or until 7 months after the increase becomes effective, whichever occurs first, or, if the proceeding is extended under subsection (b) of this section, until the Commission completes the proceeding or until 10 months after the increase becomes effective, whichever occurs first. The accounting must specify by whom and for whom the amounts are paid. When the Commission takes final action, it shall require the carrier to refund to the person for whom the amounts were paid that part of the increased rate found to be unjustified, plus interest at a rate equal to the average yield (on the date the proposed increase is filed) of marketable securities of the United States Government having a duration of 90 days. When any part of a proposed rate decrease is suspended and later found to comply with this subtitle, the rail carrier may refund any part of the portion of the decrease found to comply with this subtitle if the carrier makes the refund available equally to the shippers who participate in the rate according to the relative amounts of traffic shipped at that rate. Accounting. Refund requirement.

(e) In a proceeding under this section, the burden is on the carrier proposing the changed rate, classification, rule, or practice to prove that the change is reasonable. The Commission shall specifically consider proof that the proposed rate, classification, rule, or practice will have a significantly adverse effect (in violation of section 10701, 10741–

10744, or 11103 of this title) on the competitive posture of shippers or consignees affected by the proposed rate, classification, rule, or practice. The Commission shall give proceedings under this section preference over all other proceedings related to rail carriers pending before it and make its decision at the earliest practical time.

§ 10708. **Investigation and suspension of new nonrail carrier rates, classifications, rules, and practices**

(a) (1) The Interstate Commerce Commission may begin a proceeding to determine the lawfulness of a proposed rate, classification, rule, or practice immediately, on its own initiative or on application of an interested party when—

(A) a new individual or joint rate or individual or joint classification, rule, or practice affecting a rate is filed with the Commission by a common carrier, other than a rail carrier, under this subtitle; or

(B) a new or reduced rate or rule or practice that causes a reduction of a rate is filed with the Commission by a contract carrier under this subtitle.

Notice.

(2) The Commission must give reasonable notice before beginning a proceeding under this section but may act without allowing an interested carrier to file an answer or other formal pleading in response to its decision to begin the proceeding. The Commission may take whatever final action on a rate, classification, rule, or practice under this section, after a full hearing (whether completed before or after the rate, classification, rule, or practices goes into effect), as it could in a proceeding begun after a rate, classification, rule, or practice became effective.

(b) Pending final Commission action in a proceeding under subsection (a) of this section, the Commission may suspend the proposed rate, classification, rule, or practice at any time for not more than 7 months beyond the time it would otherwise go into effect by (1) delivering to each affected carrier, and (2) filing with the proposed rate, classification, rule, or practice, a statement of reasons for the suspension. If the Commission does not take final action during the suspension period, the proposed rate, classification, rule, or practice is effective at the end of that period. However, if an increase in a rate for, or related to, transportation of property by an express, sleeping car, or pipeline carrier becomes effective under this subsection, the Commission may require the interested carrier to account for all amounts received under it and specify by whom and on whose behalf those amounts were paid. When the Commission takes final action, it may require the carrier to refund, with interest, to the persons on whose behalf those amounts were paid, the part of the increased rate found to be in violation of this subtitle.

Accounting.

Refund requirement.

(c) In a proceeding under this section, the burden is on the carrier proposing the changed rate, classification, rule, or practice to prove that the change is reasonable. The Commission shall give proceedings under this section preference over all other proceedings related to that type of carrier pending before it and make its decision at the earliest practical time.

49 USC 10709.

§ 10709. **Determination of market dominance in rail carrier rate proceedings**

"Market dominance."

(a) In this section, "market dominance" means an absence of effective competition from other carriers or modes of transportation for the transportation to which a rate applies.

(b) When a rate for transportation by a rail carrier providing transportation subject to the jurisdiction of the Interstate Commerce Commission under subchapter I of chapter 105 of this title is challenged as being unreasonably high, the Commission shall determine, within 90 days after the start of a proceeding under section 10707 of this title to investigate the lawfulness of that rate, whether the carrier proposing the rate has market dominance over the transportation to which the rate applies. The Commission may make that determination on its own initiative or on complaint. A finding by the Commission that the carrier does not have market dominance is determinative in a proceeding under this subtitle related to that rate or transportation unless changed or set aside by the Commission or set aside by a court of competent jurisdiction.

Ante, p. 1359.

(c) When the Commission finds in any proceeding that a rail carrier proposing or defending a rate for transportation has market dominance over the transportation to which the rate applies, it may then determine that rate to be unreasonable if it exceeds a reasonable maximum for that transportation. However, a finding of market dominance does not establish a presumption that the proposed rate exceeds a reasonable maximum. This subsection does not limit the power of the Commission to suspend a rate under section 10707(c) of this title. However, if the Commission has found that a carrier does not have market dominance over the transportation to which the rate applies, the Commission may suspend an increase in that rate as being in excess of a reasonable maximum for that transportation only if it specifically changes or sets aside its prior determination of market dominance.

Suspension.

§ 10710. Elimination of discrimination against recyclable materials

49 USC 10710.

The Interstate Commerce Commission shall maintain regulations that will eliminate discrimination against the transportation of recyclable materials in rate structures and in other Commission practices where discrimination exists.

§ 10711. Effect of certain sections on rail rates and practices

49 USC 10711.

Sections 10701 (a) and (b), 10707, 10709, 10727, and 10728 of this title, related to rail carriers, do not—

(1) modify the application of sections 10701(c), 10726, 10741–10744, or 11103 of this title in determining whether a rate or practice complies with this subtitle;

(2) make a competitive practice that is unfair, destructive, predatory, or otherwise undermines competition that is necessary in the public interest comply with this subtitle;

(3) affect a law in existence on February 5, 1976, or the authority of the Interstate Commerce Commission related to rate relationships between ports; or

(4) affect the authority and responsibility of the Commission to guarantee the equalization of rates in the same port.

SUBCHAPTER II—SPECIAL CIRCUMSTANCES

§ 10721. Government traffic

49 USC 10721.

(a)(1) Except as provided in this section, the full applicable commercial rate shall be paid for transportation for the United States Government by a common carrier providing transportation or service subject to the jurisdiction of the Interstate Commerce Commission under this subtitle. Section 5 of title 41 does not apply when transportation for the United States Government can be obtained from a common carrier lawfully operating in the area where the transportation

Increased
revenues.

will be provided. When prescribing rates for transportation or service by those common carriers, the Commission shall consider increased revenues those carriers receive under this subsection to reflect those increases in appropriate readjustments of their rates.

(2) Paragraph (1) of this subsection does not apply, and the law related to compensation for transportation for the United States Government in effect immediately before September 18, 1940, applies to a rail carrier if that carrier, or its predecessor in interest, received a grant of land from the United States to aid in constructing the railroad it operates but did not file a release with the Secretary of the Interior before September 18, 1941, of claims against the United States Government to, or arising out of, lands that were granted, claimed to have been granted, or claimed should have been granted to that carrier or its predecessor in interest. This paragraph does not require a rail carrier to reconvey to the United States land patented or certified to it or prevent the patent of land that the Secretary of the Interior found was sold by the carrier to an innocent purchaser for value or as preventing the patent of land listed or selected by the carrier and finally approved by the Secretary of the Interior to the extent that issuance of those patents is authorized by law.

(b)(1) A common carrier providing transportation subject to the jurisdiction of the Commission under subchapter I, II, or III of chapter 105 of this title may transport individuals for the United States Government without charge or at reduced rates. The carriers may transport custom inspectors and immigration officers without charge. A common carrier providing transportation or service subject to the jurisdiction of the Commission under chapter 105 of this title shall provide transportation for the United States Postal Service under chapters 50 and 52 of title 39, and may transport property for the United States Government, a State, or municipal government without charge or at reduced rates.

Ante, pp. 1359,
1361, 1365.

Ante, p. 1358.

39 USC 5001 et
seq., 5201 et seq.

Quoted or
tendered rate,
filing.

(2) Unless a carrier is advised by the United States Government that disclosure of a quotation or tender of a rate established under paragraph (1) of this subsection for transportation provided to the United States Government would endanger the national security, the carrier shall file the quoted or tendered rate, including a retroactive rate made after the transportation has been provided, concurrently, with the Commission and the department, agency, or instrumentality of the United States Government for which the quotation or tender was made or for which the proposed transportation is to be provided. A carrier may quote or tender a rate established under an agreement made and approved under section 10706 of this title, but the exemption from the antitrust laws provided by that section applies only when the filing requirements of this paragraph are met.

(c) A different policy, rule of rate making, system of accounting, method of determining costs of transportation, value of property, or rate of return may not be applied to a water carrier owned or controlled by the United States Government than is applied to a water carrier providing transportation subject to the jurisdiction of the Commission under subchapter III of chapter 105 of this title.

49 USC 10722.

§ 10722. Special passenger rates

(a) A common carrier providing transportation subject to the jurisdiction of the Interstate Commerce Commission under subchapter I,

II, or III of chapter 105 of this title may establish mileage, excursion, and commutation passenger rates including joint interchangeable 5,000 mile passenger rates with the privilege of carrying an amount of baggage without charge for at least 1,000 miles. A carrier that establishes a rate under this subsection may issue tickets reflecting that rate. A carrier that establishes a joint interchangeable 5,000 mile passenger rate shall also establish rules related to that rate specifying the amount of baggage that may be carried without charge under it. *Ante,* pp. 1359, 1361, 1365.

Ticket issuance. Baggage charge, rules.

(b) A common carrier providing transportation subject to the jurisdiction of the Commission under one of those subchapters may establish reduced rates for individuals when the cost of that transportation is an expense of an individual who—

(1) is a member of the armed forces of the United States or another country when that individual is traveling in uniform on official leave, furlough, or pass; or

(2) has been released from the armed forces of the United States not more than 30 days before beginning that transportation and is traveling home or to a prospective place of abode.

(c) A common carrier providing transportation subject to the jurisdiction of the Commission under one of those subchapters may provide transportation without charge for an individual who is—

(1) a necessary caretaker of livestock, poultry, milk, or fruit;

(2) an executive officer, general chairman, or counsel of an employee organization authorized to represent employees of that carrier under chapter 8 of title 45; 45 USC 151 *et seq.*

(3) an employee in charge of the mails when working or traveling to or from work;

(4) a newsboy on a train;

(5) a baggage agent; or

(6) a witness attending a legal investigation in which that carrier has an interest.

(d) (1) In this subsection— Definitions.

(A) "employee of a carrier" includes an individual who—

(i) is furloughed, pensioned, or not on active duty because of advanced age or infirmity that occurred while the individual was employed by that carrier;

(ii) is being transported for purposes of reemployment by that carrier; or

(iii) was killed while employed by a carrier.

(B) "family" refers to the family of an individual named in clause (A) of this paragraph and includes the widow or minor child of an employee who died while employed by a carrier.

(2) A common carrier providing transportation subject to the jurisdiction of the Commission under subchapter I, II, or III of chapter 105 of this title may provide transportation without charge for officers and employees (and their families) of that carrier, another carrier (by exchange of passes or tickets), or a telegraph, telephone, or cable company. A freight forwarder providing service subject to the jurisdiction of the Commission under subchapter IV of that chapter may provide services related to movement of property for those individuals without charge. However, transportation of, or service provided for, household goods must be due to a change in the place of employment of an officer or employee while employed by that carrier.

§ 10723. Charitable purposes 49 USC 10723.

(a) (1) A common carrier providing transportation subject to the jurisdiction of the Interstate Commerce Commission under subchapter

Ante, pp. 1359, 1361, 1365.
I, II, or III of chapter 105 of this title may provide transportation without charge for—

(A) an indigent or homeless individual (including an individual transported by a hospital, charitable organization, or municipal government and the necessary agents employed in that transportation);

(B) an individual who is confined to or about to enter or return home after discharge from a—

(i) Veterans' Administration facility;

(ii) State home for disabled volunteer soldiers; or

(iii) soldiers' and sailors' home, under an arrangement with the board of managers of that facility;

(C) a minister of religion; and

(D) an individual who is confined to a hospital or charitable facility.

(2) A common carrier providing transportation or service subject to the jurisdiction of the Commission under chapter 105 of this title may provide transportation for property without charge or at a reduced rate for—

(A) a charitable purpose, including transportation referred to in paragraph (1) of this subsection; or

(B) use in a public exhibition.

(b)(1) A common carrier subject to the jurisdiction of the Commission under subchapter I, II, or III of that chapter may provide transportation without charge to an individual who is—

(A) engaged only in charitable work;

(B) injured in an accident (together with the physicians and nurses attending that individual); or

(C) a traveling secretary of a railroad Young Men's Christian Association.

(2) That carrier may also establish a rate and related rule equal to the rate charged for the transportation of one individual when that rate is for the transportation of—

(A) a totally blind individual and an accompanying guide or a dog trained to guide the individual; or

(B) a disabled individual and accompanying attendant when required because of the disability.

49 USC 10724.
§ 10724. Emergency rates

(a) A common carrier providing transportation subject to the jurisdiction of the Interstate Commerce Commission under subchapter I, II, or III of chapter 105 of this title may transport passengers without charge to provide relief during general emergencies.

(b)(1) The Commission may authorize a common carrier providing transportation or service subject to its jurisdiction under chapter 105 *Ante,* p. 1358. of this title to give reduced rates for service and transportation of property to or from an area in the United States to provide relief during emergencies. When the Commission takes action under this subsection, it must—

(A) define the area of the United States in which the reduced rates will apply;

(B) specify the period during which the reduced rates are to be in effect; and

(C) define the class of persons entitled to the reduced rates.

(2) The Commission may specify those persons entitled to reduced rates by reference to those persons designated as being in need of relief by the United States Government or by a State government authorized

to assist in providing relief during the emergency. The Commission may act under this subsection without regard to subchapter II of chapter 103 of this title and subchapter II of chapter 5 of title 5.

§ 10725. Special freight forwarder rates

(a) A common carrier providing transportation subject to the jurisdiction of the Interstate Commerce Commission under subchapter I, II, or III of chapter 105 of this title may establish—

    (1) assembling rates and related classifications and rules for transportation of less-than-carload or less-than-truckload shipments to a place for further movement as part of a carload or truckload shipment; and

    (2) distribution rates and related classifications and rules for transportation of less-than-carload or less-than-truckload shipments moving from a place to which those shipments have moved as a part of a carload or truckload shipment.

(b) A rate and related classification and rule established under subsection (a) of this section applies to freight forwarders and other persons using common carrier transportation under like conditions and may differ from other rates and related classifications and rules that contemporaneously apply to the same common carrier transportation when the difference is justified by a difference in the respective conditions under which that transportation is used. A rate referred to in subsection (a) (1) or (2) of this section may not be established to cover the line-haul transportation between the principal concentration place and the principal break-bulk place.

(c) When establishing a rate, classification, rule, or practice, a motor common carrier providing transportation subject to the jurisdiction of the Commission under subchapter II of chapter 105 of this title may consider the type of property tendered to it by a freight forwarder for transportation when the property is in parcels that do not exceed 70 pounds in weight or 100 inches in length and girth combined. The carrier may establish the lowest rate for the transportation that allows it to receive adequate compensation for transporting the property.

§ 10726. Long and short haul transportation

(a)(1) A carrier providing transportation subject to the jurisdiction of the Interstate Commerce Commission under subchapter I or III of chapter 105 of this title (except an express carrier) may not charge or receive more compensation for the transportation of property of the same kind or of passengers—

    (A) for a shorter distance than for a longer distance over the same line or route in the same direction (the shorter distance being included in the longer distance); or

    (B) under a through rate than under the total of the intermediate rates it may charge or receive under this chapter.

This paragraph does not authorize a carrier to charge or receive equal compensation for transportation over a shorter distance than a longer distance.

(2) Notwithstanding paragraph (1) of this subsection, a carrier operating over a circuitous line or route to or from a place in competition with another carrier of the same type that operates over a more direct line or route may establish a rate (otherwise complying with this chapter) for that transportation to meet the rate of the carrier operating over the more direct line or route. A rate established for transportation over a circuitous route under this subsection is not evidence of the compensatory character of rates in other proceedings.

Ante, p. 1345.
5 USC 551.
49 USC 10725.

Ante, pp. 1359, 1361, 1365.

49 USC 10726.

(b) In special cases, the Commission may authorize a carrier to charge less for transportation over a longer distance than it charges for transportation over a shorter distance. The Commission may prescribe the extent to which a carrier authorized to charge less under this subsection may be granted relief from subsection (a) of this section. However, the Commission may not authorize a rate—

Relief.

(1) to or from the more distant place unless it is reasonably compensatory; or

(2) because of potential water competition not actually in existence.

(c) A rail carrier that reduces a rate for the transportation of property in competition with a water route to or from competitive places may increase the rate only if, after a proceeding, the Commission finds that the increase is proposed because of a change in conditions other than the elimination of water competition.

Proceeding.

(d) The Commission shall begin a proceeding under subsection (b) of this section on application of a carrier. A carrier may file a proposed rate with its application, and if the application is approved, the Commission shall allow the rate to become effective one day after the approval becomes effective.

49 USC 10727.
Standards and procedures.

§ 10727. Demand-sensitive rates

(a) The Interstate Commerce Commission shall maintain standards and procedures to permit seasonal, regional, or peak-period demand rates for transportation by rail carrier subject to its jurisdiction under subchapter I of chapter 105 of this title, that—

(1) provide sufficient incentives to shippers, through rescheduling and advance planning, to reduce peak-period shipments;

(2) generate additional revenue for rail carriers;

(3) make better use of the national supply of freight cars;

(4) improve—

(A) the transportation of property by rail carriers;

(B) the level of employment by rail carriers; and

(C) the financial stability of markets served by rail carriers.

Annual report to Congress, legislative recommendations.

(b) The Commission shall submit to Congress an annual report on the implementation of rates under this section and shall include recommendations for additional legislation needed to make it easier to establish those rates.

49 USC 10728.

§ 10728. Separate rates for distinct rail services

(a) A rail carrier providing transportation subject to the jurisdiction of the Interstate Commerce Commission under subchapter I of chapter 105 of this title may, on its own initiative or at the request of a shipper or receiver of property, establish separate rates for distinct rail services to—

(1) encourage competition;

(2) promote increased reinvestment by rail carriers; and

(3) encourage and make easier increased non-railroad investment in the production of rail services.

Expeditous procedures.

(b) The Commission shall maintain expeditious procedures to permit separate rates for distinct rail services to—

(1) encourage those services to be priced in accordance with the cash-outlay incurred by the carrier and the demand for them; and

(2) enable shippers and receivers to evaluate transportation and related rates and alternatives.

§ 10729. Rail carriers; incentive for capital investment

49 USC 10729.

(a) A proposed rate, classification, rule, or practice for transportation by a rail carrier subject to the jurisdiction of the Interstate Commerce Commission under subchapter I of chapter 105 of this title requiring a total capital investment of at least $1,000,000 to implement shall be established and become effective under this section. This section applies whether the investment is made individually or collectively by the carrier or by a shipper, receiver, or agent for any of them, or by a third party.

Ante, p. 1359.

(b) A rail carrier may file a notice of intent to establish a rate, classification, rule, or practice under subsection (a) of this section with the Commission. The notice must include a sworn affidavit detailing the anticipated capital investment. Unless the Commission after holding a proceeding under subsection (c) of this section, decides by the 180th day after the notice is filed that the proposed rate, classification, rule, or practice would violate this subtitle, the carrier may establish that rate, classification, rule, or practice at any time during the next 180 days, and it may become effective 30 days after it is established. Once a rate, classification, rule, or practice becomes effective under this section, the Commission may not, for 5 years, suspend or set it aside as violating section 10701, 10726, 10741-10744, or 11103 of this title. However, the Commission may order the rate, classification, rule, or practice to be revised to a level equal to the variable costs of providing the transportation when the Commission finds the level then in effect reduces the going concern value of the carrier.

Notice of intent, filing.

(c) On request of an interested person, the Commission shall hold a proceeding to investigate and determine whether the rate, classification, rule, or practice proposed to be established under this section complies with this subtitle. The Commission must give reasonable notice to interested parties before beginning a proceeding under this subsection but may act without allowing an interested party to file an answer or other formal pleading.

Proceeding.

Notice.

§ 10730. Rates and liability based on value

49 USC 10730.

The Interstate Commerce Commission may require or authorize a carrier providing transportation or service subject to its jurisdiction under subchapter I, II, or IV of chapter 105 of this title, to establish rates for transportation of property under which the liability of the carrier for that property is limited to a value established by written declaration of the shipper, or by a written agreement, when that value would be reasonable under the circumstances surrounding the transportation. A rate may be made applicable under this section to livestock only if the livestock is valuable chiefly for breeding, racing, show purposes, or other special uses. A tariff filed with the Commission under subchapter IV of this chapter shall refer specifically to the action of the Commission under this section.

Ante, pp. 1361, 1365.

§ 10731. Investigation of discriminatory rail rates for transportation of recyclable or recycled materials

49 USC 10731.

(a) In this section—

Definitions.

(1) "recyclable material" means material collected or recovered from waste for a commercial or industrial use whether the collection or recovery follows end usage as a product.

(2) "virgin material" means raw material, including previously unused metal or metal ore, woodpulp or pulpwood, textile fiber or material, or other resource that, through the application

of technology, is or will become a source of raw material for commercial or industrial use.

(b) When appropriate, the Interstate Commerce Commission shall—

(1) investigate the rate structure for the transportation of recyclable or recycled materials and competing virgin material by rail carriers providing transportation subject to the jurisdiction of the Commission under subchapter I of chapter 105 of this title and the manner in which that rate structure has been affected by successive general rate increases approved by the Commission for those carriers;

Ante, p. 1359.

(2) determine whether those rate increases affect any part of the rate structure in violation of section 10701 or 10741 of this title and order the rate found to be in violation of either of those sections removed from the rate structure; and

Proceedings, report to President and Congress.

(3) report to the President and Congress, in each of the annual reports of the Commission for 1978 and 1979, and in other appropriate reports, all proceedings started or completed under this subsection.

Public hearing.

(c) A determination under subsection (b)(2) of this section may be made only after a public hearing. During the hearing, the rail carriers have the burden of proving that rate increases that affect the rate structure applicable to the transportation of those competing materials comply with sections 10701 and 10741 of this title.

Research program, cooperation with Treasury Secretary.

(d) In cooperation with the Commission, the Secretary of Transportation shall maintain a research, development, and demonstration program to develop and improve transport terminal operations, transport service characteristics, transport equipment, and collection and processing methods to facilitate the competitive and efficient transportation of recyclable or recycled materials by rail carriers providing transportation subject to the jurisdiction of the Commission under subchapter I of chapter 105 of this title.

SUBCHAPTER III—LIMITATIONS

49 USC 10741.

§ 10741. Prohibitions against discrimination by common carriers

(a) A common carrier providing transportation subject to the jurisdiction of the Interstate Commerce Commission under subchapter I of chapter 105 of this title may not charge or receive from a person a different compensation (by using a special rate, rebate, drawback, or another means) for a service rendered, or to be rendered, in transportation the carrier may perform under this subtitle than it charges or receives from another person for performing a like and contemporaneous service in the transportation of a like kind of traffic under substantially similar circumstances. A common carrier that charges or receives such a different compensation for that service unreasonably discriminates.

Ante, p. 1358.

(b) A common carrier providing transportation or service subject to the jurisdiction of the Commission under chapter 105 of this title may not subject a person, place, port, or type of traffic to unreasonable discrimination. However, subject to subsection (c) of this section, this subsection does not apply to discrimination against the traffic of another carrier providing transportation by any mode.

(c) A common carrier providing transportation subject to the jurisdiction of the Commission under subchapter I, II, or III of that chapter may not subject a freight forwarder providing service subject to the jurisdiction of the Commission under subchapter IV of that chapter to unreasonable discrimination whether or not the freight forwarder is controlled by that carrier.

Ante, pp. 1359, 1361, 1365.
Ante, p. 1369.

(d) Differences between the rates, classifications, rules, and practices of water and rail common carriers in effect for their respective types of transportation do not constitute a violation of this section or an unfair or destructive competitive practice under this subtitle.

§ 10742. Facilities for interchange of traffic

49 USC 10742.

A common carrier providing transportation subject to the jurisdiction of the Interstate Commerce Commission under subchapter I or III of chapter 105 of this title shall provide reasonable, proper, and equal facilities that are within its power to provide for the interchange of traffic between, and for the receiving, forwarding, and delivering of passengers and property to and from, its respective line and a connecting line of another common carrier under either of those subchapters.

§ 10743. Payment of rates

49 USC 10743.

(a) Except as provided in subsection (b) of this section, a common carrier (except a pipeline or sleeping car carrier) providing transportation or service subject to the jurisdiction of the Interstate Commerce Commission under this subtitle shall give up possession at destination of property transported by it only when payment for the transportation or service is made.

(b) (1) Under regulations of the Commission governing the payment for transportation and service and preventing discrimination, those carriers may give up possession at destination of property transported by them before payment for the transportation or service. The regulations of the Commission may provide for weekly or monthly payment for transportation provided by motor common carriers and for periodic payment for transportation provided by water common carriers.

(2) Such a carrier (including a motor common carrier being used by a freight forwarder) may extend credit for transporting property for the United States Government, a State, a territory or possession of the United States, or a political subdivision of any of them.

§ 10744. Liability for payment of rates

49 USC 10744.

(a) (1) Liability for payment of rates for transportation for a shipment of property by a shipper or consignor to a consignee other than the shipper or consignor, is determined under this subsection when the transportation is provided by a rail, motor, or water common carrier under this subtitle. When the shipper or consignor instructs the carrier transporting the property to deliver it to a consignee that is an agent only, not having beneficial title to the property, the consignee is liable for rates billed at the time of delivery for which the consignee is otherwise liable, but not for additional rates that may be found to be due after delivery if the consignee gives written notice to the delivering carrier before delivery of the property—

(A) of the agency and absence of beneficial title; and

(B) of the name and address of the beneficial owner of the property if it is reconsigned or diverted to a place other than the place specified in the original bill of lading.

(2) When the consignee is liable only for rates billed at the time of delivery under paragraph (1) of this subsection, the shipper or consignor, or, if the property is reconsigned or diverted, the beneficial

owner, is liable for those additional rates regardless of the bill of lading or contract under which the property was transported. The beneficial owner is liable for all rates when the property is reconsigned or diverted by an agent but is refused or abandoned at its ultimate destination if the agent gave the carrier in the reconsignment or diversion order a notice of agency and the name and address of the beneficial owner. A consignee giving the carrier, and a reconsignor or diverter giving a rail carrier, erroneous information about the identity of the beneficial owner of the property is liable for the additional rates.

(b) Liability for payment of rates for transportation for a shipment of property by a shipper or consignor, named in the bill of lading as consignee, is determined under this subsection when the transportation is provided by a rail or express carrier under this subtitle. When the shipper or consignor gives written notice, before delivery of the property, to the line-haul carrier that is to make ultimate delivery—

(1) to deliver the property to another party identified by the shipper or consignor as the beneficial owner of the property; and

(2) that delivery is to be made to that party on payment of all applicable transportation rates;

that party is liable for the rates billed at the time of delivery and for additional rates that may be found to be due after delivery if that party does not pay the rates required to be paid under clause (2) of this subsection on delivery. However, if the party gives written notice to the delivering carrier before delivery that the party is not the beneficial owner of the property and gives the carrier the name and address of the beneficial owner, then the party is not liable for those additional rates. A shipper, consignor, or party to whom delivery is made that gives the delivering carrier erroneous information about the identity of the beneficial owner, is liable for the additional rates regardless of the bill of lading or contract under which the property was transported. This subsection does not apply to a prepaid shipment of property.

(c)(1) A rail carrier may bring an action to enforce liability under subsection (a) of this section. That carrier must bring the action during the period provided in section 11706(a) of this title or by the end of the 6th month after final judgment against it in an action against the consignee, or the beneficial owner named by the consignee or agent, under that section.

Post, p. 1452.

(2) A water common carrier may bring an action to enforce liability under subsection (a) of this section. That carrier must bring the action by the end of the 2d year after the claim accrues or by end of the 6th month after final judgment against it in an action against the consignee or beneficial owner named by the consignee by the end of that 2-year period.

(3) A rail or express carrier may bring an action to enforce liability under subsection (b) of this section. That carrier must bring the action during the period provided in section 11706(a) of this title or by the end of the 6th month after final judgment against it in an action against the shipper, consignor, or other party under that section.

49 USC 10745. ## § 10745. Continuous carriage of freight

A carrier providing transportation or service subject to the jurisdiction of the Interstate Commerce Commission under subchapter I of chapter 105 of this title may not enter a combination or arrangement to prevent the carriage of freight from being continuous from the place of shipment to the place of destination whether by change of time schedule, carriage in different cars, or by other means. The car-

Ante, p. 1359.

riage of freight by those carriers is considered to be a continuous carriage from the place of shipment to the place of destination when a break of bulk, stoppage, or interruption is not made in good faith for a necessary purpose, and with the intent of avoiding or unnecessarily interrupting the continuous carriage or of evading this subtitle.

§ 10746. Transportation of commodities manufactured or produced by a rail carrier

49 USC 10746.

A rail carrier providing transportation subject to the jurisdiction of the Interstate Commerce Commission under subchapter I of chapter 105 of this title may not transport from a State or territory or possession of the United States to another State, territory, or possession or a foreign country, an article or commodity that—

Ante, p. 1359.

    (1) is manufactured, mined, or produced by the carrier or under its authority; or

    (2) is owned by the carrier or in which it has an interest.

However, a rail carrier may transport such an article or commodity when it is necessary and intended for use in the business of that carrier. This section does not apply to timber and products manufactured from timber.

Timber products, exemption.

§ 10747. Transportation services or facilities furnished by shipper

49 USC 10747.

A carrier providing transportation or service subject to the jurisdiction of the Interstate Commerce Commission under chapter 105 of this title may publish in a tariff filed with the Commission under subchapter IV of this chapter a charge or allowance for transportation or service for property when the owner of the property, directly or indirectly, furnishes a service related to or an instrumentality used in the transportation or service. The Commission may prescribe the maximum reasonable charge or allowance a carrier subject to its jurisdiction may pay for a service or instrumentality furnished under this section. The Commission may begin a proceeding under this section on its own initiative or on application.

Ante, p. 1358.

Maximum charge or allowance.

Proceeding.

§ 10748. Transportation of livestock by rail carrier

49 USC 10748.

(a) Transportation entirely by railroad of ordinary livestock in carload lots to public stockyards shall include necessary services of unloading and reloading in route, delivery of inbound shipments at those stockyards into suitable pens, and receiving and loading outbound shipments at those stockyards. A rail carrier providing transportation subject to the jurisdiction of the Interstate Commerce Commission under subchapter I of chapter 105 of this title may charge a shipper, consignee, or owner an extra amount for those services only if, under Commission regulations, the unloading or reloading in route is at the request of the shipper, consignee, or owner, to try an intermediate market, or to comply with quarantine regulations.

(b) Subsection (a) of this section does not affect the duties and liabilities of a rail carrier in existence on February 28, 1920, under a law related to the transportation of other than ordinary livestock or the duty of providing transportation for shipments other than shipments to or from public stockyards.

§ 10749. Exchange of services and limitation on use of common carriers by freight forwarders

49 USC 10749.

(a) A common carrier providing transportation or service subject to the jurisdiction of the Interstate Commerce Commission under chapter 105 of this title may contract with a telephone, telegraph, or cable company to exchange services.

Ante, p. 1369.

(b) A freight forwarder providing service subject to the jurisdiction of the Commission under subchapter IV of chapter 105 of this title may use a carrier, including a carrier referred to in this subsection, to transfer, collect, or deliver in a terminal area. However, to provide other services, a freight forwarder may only use—

(1) a rail, express, motor, or water common carrier providing transportation subject to the jurisdiction of the Commission under chapter 105 of this title including—

Ante, pp. 1363, 1365.

(A) a motor common carrier providing exempt transportation under section 10525 or 10526(a)(8) of this title; or

Ante, p. 1366.

(B) a water common carrier providing exempt transportation under section 10542(a) of this title or transportation between places in Alaska or Hawaii and between those places and other places in the United States;

49 USC 1301 et seq.

(2) an air carrier subject to the jurisdiction of the Civil Aeronautics Board under chapter 20 of this title; or

(3) the Alaska Railroad.

49 USC 10750.

§ 10750. Demurrage charges

Rules.

A rail carrier providing transportation subject to the jurisdiction of the Interstate Commerce Commission under subchapter I of chapter 105 of this title shall compute demurrage charges, and establish rules related to those charges, in a way that fulfills the national needs related to—

Ante, p. 1359.

(1) freight car use and distribution; and

(2) maintenance of an adequate supply of freight cars to be available for transportation of property.

SUBCHAPTER IV—TARIFFS AND TRAFFIC

49 USC 10761.

§ 10761. Transportation prohibited without tariff

(a) Except as provided in this subtitle, a carrier providing transportation or service subject to the jurisdiction of the Interstate Commerce Commission under chapter 105 of this title shall provide that transportation or service only if the rate for the transportation or service is contained in a tariff that is in effect under this subchapter. That carrier may not charge or receive a different compensation for that transportation or service than the rate specified in the tariff whether by returning a part of that rate to a person, giving a person a privilege, allowing the use of a facility that affects the value of that transportation or service, or another device.

Relief.

(b) The Commission may grant relief from subsection (a) of this section to contract carriers when relief is consistent with the public interest and the transportation policy of section 10101 of this title.

Ante, p. 1337.
Proceeding.

The Commission may begin a proceeding under this subsection on application of a contract carrier or group of contract carriers and on its own initiative for a water contract carrier or group of water contract carriers.

49 USC 10762.

§ 10762. General tariff requirements

Rates, publication and filing.

(a)(1) A carrier providing transportation or service subject to the jurisdiction of the Interstate Commerce Commission under chapter 105 of this title (except a motor common carrier) shall publish and file with the Commission tariffs containing the rates and (A) if a common carrier, classifications, rules, and practices related to those rates, and (B) if a contract carrier, rules and practices related to those rates, established under this chapter for transportation or service it may provide under this subtitle. A motor common carrier shall publish and file with the Commission tariffs containing the rates for transportation it may provide under this subtitle. The Commission may prescribe other information that motor common carriers shall include in their tariffs. A motor contract carrier that serves only one shipper and has provided continuous transportation to that shipper for at least one year may file only its minimum rates unless the Commission finds that filing of actual rates is required in the public interest.

(2) Carriers that publish tariffs under paragraph (1) of this subsection shall keep them open for public inspection. A rate contained in a tariff filed by a common carrier providing transportation or service subject to the jurisdiction of the Commission under subchapter II, III, or IV of chapter 105 shall be stated in money of the United States. A tariff filed by a motor or water contract carrier or by a freight forwarder providing transportation or service subject to the jurisdiction of the Commission under subchapter II, III, or IV of that chapter, respectively, may not become effective for 30 days after it is filed.

Public inspection.

Ante, pp. 1361, 1365, 1369.

(b) (1) The Commission shall prescribe the form and manner of publishing, filing, and keeping tariffs open for public inspection under this section. The Commission may prescribe specific charges to be identified in a tariff published by a common carrier providing transportation or service subject to its jurisdiction under subchapter I, III, or IV of that chapter, but those tariffs must identify plainly—

Charges, identification.

Ante, p. 1359.

   (A) the places between which property and passengers will be transported;

   (B) terminal, storage, and icing charges (stated separately) if a carrier providing transportation subject to the jurisdiction of the Commission under subchapter I of that chapter;

   (C) terminal charges if a common carrier providing transportation or service subject to the jurisdiction of the Commission under subchapter III or IV of that chapter;

   (D) privileges given and facilities allowed; and

   (E) any rules that change, affect, or determine any part of the published rate.

(2) A joint tariff filed by a carrier providing transportation subject to the jurisdiction of the Commission under subchapter I of that chapter shall identify the carriers that are parties to it. The carriers that are parties to a joint tariff, other than the carrier filing it, must file a concurrence or acceptance of the tariff with the Commission but are not required to file a copy of the tariff. The Commission may prescribe or approve what constitutes a concurrence or acceptance.

Joint tariffs, concurrence or acceptance.

(c) (1) When a common carrier providing transportation or service subject to the jurisdiction of the Commission (A) under subchapter I of chapter 105 of this title proposes to change a rate, or (B) under another subchapter of that chapter proposes to change a rate, classification, rule, or practice, the carrier shall publish, file, and keep open for public inspection a notice of the proposed change as required under subsections (a) and (b) of this section.

Proposed changes, notice.

(2) When a contract carrier providing transportation subject to the jurisdiction of the Commission under subchapter II or III of chapter 105 of this title proposes to establish a new rate or to reduce a rate, directly or by changing a rule or practice related to the rate or the value of service under the rate, the carrier shall publish, file, and keep open for public inspection a notice of the new or reduced rate as required under subsections (a) and (b) of this section.

New or reduced rates, notice.

(3) A notice filed under this subsection shall plainly identify the proposed change or new or reduced rate and indicate its proposed effective date. A proposed change and a new or reduced rate may not become effective for 30 days after the notice is published, filed, and held open as required under subsections (a) and (b) of this section.

(d)(1) The Commission may reduce the 30-day period of subsections (a) and (c) of this section if cause exists. The Commission may change the other requirements of this section if cause exists in particular instances or as they apply to special circumstances.

Tariff simplification, regulations.

(2) The Commission may prescribe regulations for the simplification of tariffs by carriers providing transportation subject to its jurisdiction under subchapter I of chapter 105 of this title and permit them to change rates, classifications, rules, and practices without filing complete tariffs that cover matter that is not being changed when the Commission finds that action to be consistent with the public interest. Those carriers may publish new tariffs that incorporate changes or plainly indicate the proposed changes in the tariffs then in effect and kept open for public inspection. However, the Commission shall require that all rates of rail carriers and rail rate-making associations be incorporated in their individual tariffs by the end of the 2d year after initial publication of the rate, or by the end of the 2d year after a change in a rate becomes effective, whichever is later. The Commission may extend those periods if cause exists, but if it does, it must send a notice of the extension and a statement of the reasons for the extension to Congress. A rate not incorporated in an individual tariff as required by the Commission is void.

Extensions, statement to Congress.

Rejections.

(e) The Commission may reject a tariff submitted to it by a common carrier under this section if that tariff violates this section or regulation of the Commission carrying out this section.

Relief.

(f) The Commission may grant relief from this section to contract carriers when relief is consistent with the public interest and the transportation policy of section 10101 of this title. The Commission may begin a proceeding under this subsection on application of a contract carrier or group of contract carriers and on its own initiative for a water contract carrier or group of water contract carriers.

Ante, p. 1337.
Proceeding.

49 USC 10763.

§ 10763. Designation of certain routes by shippers or Interstate Commerce Commission

(a)(1) When a person delivers property to a rail carrier for transportation subject to the jurisdiction of the Interstate Commerce Commission under subchapter I of chapter 105 of this title, the person may direct the carrier to transport the property over an established through route. When competing rail lines constitute a part of the route, the person shipping the property may designate the lines over which the property will be transported. The designation must be in writing. A carrier may be directed to transport property over a particular through route when—

Ante, p. 1359.

(A) there are at least 2 through routes over which the property could be transported;

(B) a through rate has been established for transportation over each of those through routes; and

(C) the carrier is a party to those routes and rates.

(2) A carrier directed to route property transported under paragraph (1) of this subsection must issue a through bill of lading containing the routing instructions and transport the property according to the instructions. When the property is delivered to a connecting carrier, that carrier must also receive and transport it according to

the routing instructions and deliver it to the next succeeding carrier or consignee according to the instructions.

(b) If no direction is made under subsection (a) of this section, the Commission may designate the route over which the property may be transported after arrival at the end of the route of one carrier or at a junction with the route of another carrier when the property is to be delivered to another carrier for further transportation. The Commission may act under this subsection when the public interest and a fair distribution of traffic require that action.

(c) The Commission may prescribe exceptions to the authority of a person to direct the movement of traffic under subsection (a) of this section. Exceptions.

§ 10764. Arrangements between carriers: copy to be filed with Interstate Commerce Commission 49 USC 10764.

(a)(1) A common carrier providing transportation subject to the jurisdiction of the Interstate Commerce Commission under subchapter I of chapter 105 of this title shall file with the Commission a copy of each arrangement related to transportation affected by this subtitle that the carrier has with another common carrier. The Commission may require other carriers and brokers subject to its jurisdiction under chapter 105 to file a copy of each arrangement related to transportation or service affected by this subtitle that they have with other persons. *Ante,* p. 1359.

(2) When the Commission finds that filing a class of arrangements by a carrier subject to its jurisdiction under subchapter I of that chapter is not necessary in the public interest, the Commission may except the class from paragraph (1) of this subsection. Exception.

(b) The Commission may disclose the existence or contents of an arrangement between a contract carrier and a shipper filed under subsection (a) of this section only if the disclosure is—

(1) limited to those parts of the arrangement that are necessary to indicate the extent of its failure to conform to a tariff then in effect under section 10762 of this title; or

(2) consistent with the public interest and made as a part of the record in a formal proceeding.

§ 10765. Water transportation under arrangements with certain other carriers 49 USC 10765.

(a) The Interstate Commerce Commission may require a common carrier providing transportation or service subject to its jurisdiction under chapter 105 of this title that makes an arrangement with a water carrier (whether or not subject to its jurisdiction under this subtitle) providing transportation from a port in the United States to another country for the through transportation of property from a place in the interior of the United States to another country to make similar arrangements with steamship lines that provide transportation from that port to that country.

(b) A carrier providing transportation subject to the jurisdiction of the Commission under subchapter I of chapter 105 of this title that transports property from a place in the United States through another country to a place in the United States shall publish and keep open for public inspection tariffs as required under section 10762 of this title. The tariffs shall identify the through rate established for that transportation to the United States from another country to which the carrier accepts property for shipment from the United States. Unless the through rates are available for public inspection under that section, Tariffs,
publication and
public inspection.

the property is subject to customs duties applicable to property produced in another country before the property may be admitted to the United States.

§ 10766. Freight forwarder traffic agreements

(a) A freight forwarder providing service subject to the jurisdiction of the Interstate Commerce Commission under subchapter IV of chapter 105 of this title may agree with another freight forwarder to load traffic jointly between places served under this subtitle. However, the Commission may cancel, suspend, or require changes in the agreement when the Commission finds the agreement is inconsistent with the transportation policy of section 10101 of this title.

(b) A freight forwarder providing service subject to the jurisdiction of the Commission under that subchapter may contract with motor common carriers providing transportation subject to the jurisdiction of the Commission under subchapter II of that chapter, to provide transportation for the forwarder. A copy of that contract must be filed with the Commission. The contract may govern use by the freight forwarder of the services and instrumentalities of the motor common carrier and the compensation to be paid for the transportation. However, the parties to a contract must establish reasonable conditions and compensation that are consistent with the transportation policy of section 10101 of this title and do not unreasonably discriminate against a party or another freight forwarder. When a contract under this subsection governs line-haul transportation of property for a total distance of at least 450 highway miles in truckload lots between concentration and break-bulk places, the compensation paid to a motor common carrier under the contract may not be less than the rate for that transportation established under this chapter. When the Commission finds that a contract, or its conditions or compensation, under this subsection is or will be inconsistent with this subsection, the Commission shall prescribe consistent conditions and compensation.

(c) The Commission may begin a proceeding under this section on its own initiative or on complaint.

SUBCHAPTER V—VALUATION OF PROPERTY

§ 10781. Investigation and report by Interstate Commerce Commission

(a) The Interstate Commerce Commission shall investigate, establish, and report the value of all property owned or used by each carrier providing transportation subject to its jurisdiction under subchapter I of chapter 105 of this title, except a street, suburban, or interurban electric rail carrier not operated as a part of a general railroad system of transportation. However, the Commission may investigate, establish, and report the value of property owned or used by such an electric rail carrier when the Commission decides that action is desirable in the public interest. When the Commission makes an investigation required to be made under this section, it must—

(1) inventory and list the property of that carrier in detail;

(2) indicate the value established under section 10782 of this title for that property; and

(3) classify the physical property under classifications that conform, as nearly as practicable, to the classification of expenditures prescribed by the Commission for railroads and equipment.

(b) Except as provided in subsection (a) of this section, the Commission may prescribe—

(1) the procedure to be followed when conducting an investigation under this subchapter;

(2) the form in which to submit the results of the valuation; and

(3) the classification of the elements that make up the established value.

The report for each investigation conducted under this subchapter shall indicate the value of the property of each common carrier as a whole and separately identify the value of its property in each State and territory and possession of the United States in which the property is located.

§ 10782. Requirements for establishing value

49 USC 10782.

(a) In carrying out an investigation of a common carrier required under section 10781 of this title, the Interstate Commerce Commission shall—

(1) establish, for each piece of property except land owned or used by the carrier as a common carrier, the original cost to date, cost of reproduction new and cost of reproduction less depreciation, and analyze the methods used to establish those costs and the reasons for differences among them;

(2) establish other values, and elements of value, of that property and analyze the methods used to establish them and the reasons for differences between them and the cost values established under clause (1) of this subsection;

(3) establish separately from improvements, the original cost on the date of dedication to public use, of all lands, rights of way, and terminals owned or used by the carrier as a common carrier and establish their current value;

(4) identify property not held by the carrier as a common carrier, its original cost, and current value and analyze the methods of valuation used;

(5) establish the amount and value of assistance or grant of right of way made to the carrier, or to a previous corporation that operated its property, by the United States Government or by a State, county, or municipal government, or by an individual, association, or corporation and the amount and value of any concession and allowance made by the United States Government or another of those governments in consideration of that assistance; and

(6) identify the grants of land to that carrier, or to a previous corporation that operated its property, by the United States Government, or by a State, county, or municipal government, the amount of money derived from the sale of part of those grants, the value of the unsold parts (established as of the date acquired and currently), and the amount and value of any concession and allowance made by the carrier to the United States Government, or another of those governments, in consideration of that assistance or grant of land.

(b) The Commission may prescribe elements to consider in establishing the cost to date of property owned or used by a carrier. However, in establishing that cost, the Commission shall investigate and include in those elements—

(1) the history and organization of the corporation that currently operates the property and of previous corporations that also operated that property;

(2) increases or decreases of securities during reorganization of that corporation or such a previous corporation;

(3) money received through the issuance of securities by that corporation or such a previous corporation;

(4) syndicating, banking, and other financial arrangements under which those securities were issued and the expenses thereof;

(5) the net and gross earnings of those corporations; and

(6) the expenditure of all money and the purposes of those expenditures in as much detail as the Commission determines to be necessary.

49 USC 10783.

§ 10783. Cooperation and assistance of carriers

(a) Each common carrier providing transportation subject to the jurisdiction of the Interstate Commerce Commission under subchapter I of chapter 105 of this title shall cooperate with and assist the Commission in valuing property under this subchapter. The Commission may order those carriers to—

Ante, p. 1359.

(1) give to the Commission maps, profiles, contracts, engineering reports, and other records to assist it in investigating and establishing the value of that carrier's property; and

(2) assist the Commission in valuing property under this subchapter in other ways, including giving its agents free access to its right-of-way, property, and records on request.

(b) A rail carrier whose property is being valued under this subchapter shall—

(1) transport employees of the United States Government who are making surveys and other examinations of the physical property of that carrier in the course of that valuation when reasonably required by them in the actual discharge of their duties;

(2) transport and store the cars of the United States Government that are used to house and maintain those employees when reasonably required during the valuation; and

(3) transport supplies necessary to maintain those employees and the property of the United States Government actually used on the railroad during the valuation.

Special service, compensation and accounting.

(c) The transportation required to be provided under subsection (b) of this section is considered a special service for which the Commission may prescribe the compensation to be paid. A rail carrier shall give the Commission an accurate accounting of the transportation provided under this section when required by the Commission.

Records inspection.

(d) The Commission shall keep records compiled under this subchapter open for public inspection. However, the Commission may order those records closed to the public but must state its reasons for closing them.

49 USC 10784.

§ 10784. Revision of property valuations

(a) When the Interstate Commerce Commission completes an initial valuation of property under this subchapter, it shall thereafter correct, revise, and supplement that valuation, including previous inventories and classifications, by keeping itself informed of new construction, changes in condition, quantity, use, and classification of property on which an initial valuation was made and the cost of all improvements to, and changes in investment, in that property. The Commission may keep itself informed of current changes in costs and values of railroad property to carry out this section.

(b) The Commission may order a carrier providing transportation subject to the jurisdiction of the Commission under subchapter I of chapter 105 of this title to give it reports and information needed to carry out this section.

Reports.
Ante, p. 1359.

§ 10785. Finality of valuation: notice, protest, and review

49 USC 10785.

(a) The Interstate Commerce Commission shall notify the carrier, the Attorney General, and the chief executive officer of each State in which property being valued under this subchapter is located, of the completion of a tentative valuation of that property. The Commission may also notify other parties. The notice must be sent by certified mail and must indicate the valuation established for each of that carrier's classes of property. A valuation of property under this subchapter becomes final if a protest is not filed within 30 days after notice of the tentative valuation of that property is given. When the tentative valuation becomes final under this subsection, the effective date is the date of the tentative valuation.

(b) When a carrier files a protest of a tentative valuation, the Commission shall begin a proceeding to consider the protest. If the Commission decides that a tentative valuation should be changed, it may make the necessary changes. The tentative valuation, as changed, becomes final and is effective on the date of the final action of the Commission under this subsection.

Proceeding.

(c) The Commission shall publish final valuations and classifications of property established under this subchapter. A final valuation or classification that has become effective under this subchapter is prima facie evidence of the value of the property in a proceeding under this subtitle and in a judicial proceeding to enforce, enjoin, set aside, annul, or suspend an action of the Commission.

Publication.

(d) When evidence is introduced at the trial of an action involving a final valuation of property established by the Commission and found by the court to be different from the evidence offered to the Commission during a proceeding under subsection (b) of this section or in addition to that evidence and substantially affecting the valuation, the court shall send a copy of that evidence to the Commission and stay further proceedings in the action. The court may determine the duration of the stay of proceedings. The Commission shall consider the evidence and may change the final valuation established under this subchapter. The Commission shall complete its action and report to the court in the time determined by the court. If the Commission changes the valuation, the court must substitute the valuation as changed for the original valuation and give its judgment on the substituted valuation. If the Commission does not change the original valuation, the court must give judgment on the original valuation.

New evidence.

§ 10786. Applicability

49 USC 10786.

In addition to common carriers providing transportation subject to the jurisdiction of the Interstate Commerce Commission under subchapter I of chapter 105 of this title, this subchapter applies to receivers and operating trustees of those carriers.

CHAPTER 109—LICENSING

SUBCHAPTER I—RAILROADS AND FERRIES

SUBCHAPTER II—OTHER CARRIERS AND MOTOR CARRIER BROKERS

SUBCHAPTER I—RAILROADS AND FERRIES

49 USC 10901.

§ 10901. Authorizing construction and operation of railroad lines

Ante, p. 1359

(a) A rail carrier providing transportation subject to the jurisdiction of the Interstate Commerce Commission under subchapter I of chapter 105 of this title may—

(1) construct an extension to any of its railroad lines;

(2) construct an additional railroad line;

(3) acquire or operate an extended or additional railroad line; or

(4) provide transportation over, or by means of, an extended or additional railroad line;

only if the Commission finds that the present or future public convenience and necessity require or will be enhanced by the construction or acquisition (or both) and operation of the railroad line.

Application, filing.

(b) A proceeding to grant authority under subsection (a) of this section begins when an application is filed. On receiving the application, the Commission shall—

(1) send a copy of the application to the chief executive officer of each State that would be directly affected by the construction or operation of the railroad line;

Publication in newspaper.

(2) send an accurate and understandable summary of the application to a newspaper of general circulation in each area that would be affected by the construction or operation of the railroad line;

Publication in Federal Register.

(3) have a copy of the summary published in the Federal Register;

(4) take other reasonable and effective steps to publicize the application; and

(5) indicate in each transmission and publication that each interested person is entitled to recommend to the Commission that it approve, deny, or take other action concerning the application.

(c)(1) If the Commission—

    (A) finds public convenience and necessity, it may—

        (i) approve the application as filed; or

        (ii) approve the application with modifications and require compliance with conditions the Commission finds necessary in the public interest; or

    (B) fails to find public convenience and necessity, it may deny the application.

(2) On approval, the Commission shall issue to the rail carrier a certificate describing the construction or acquisition (or both) and operation approved by the Commission.

Certificate issuance.

§ 10902. Authorizing action to provide adequate, efficient, and safe facilities

49 USC 10902.

The Interstate Commerce Commission may authorize a rail carrier providing transportation subject to the jurisdiction of the Commission under subchapter I of chapter 105 of this title to take action necessary to provide adequate, efficient, and safe facilities to enable the rail carrier to perform its obligations under this subtitle, including extension of any of the carrier's railroad lines after issuance of a certificate under section 10901 of this title. The Commission may authorize a rail carrier to act under this section only if it finds that the expense involved will not impair the ability of the carrier to perform its obligations to the public. The Commission may conduct a proceeding on its own initiative or on application of an interested party.

Ante, p. 1359.

Proceeding.

§ 10903. Authorizing abandonment and discontinuance of railroad lines and rail transportation

49 USC 10903.

(a) A rail carrier providing transportation subject to the jurisdiction of the Interstate Commerce Commission under subchapter I of chapter 105 of this title may—

    (1) abandon any part of its railroad lines; or

    (2) discontinue the operation of all rail transportation over any part of its railroad lines;

only if the Commission finds that the present or future public convenience and necessity require or permit the abandonment or discontinuance. In making the finding, the Commission shall consider whether the abandonment or discontinuance will have a serious, adverse impact on rural and community development.

Adverse impact.

(b)(1) A proceeding to grant authority under subsection (a) of this section begins on application filed with the Commission. Subject to sections 10904–10906 of this title, if the Commission—

Proceeding.

    (A) finds public convenience and necessity, it shall—

        (i) approve the application as filed; or

        (ii) approve the application with modifications and require compliance with conditions that the Commission finds are required by public convenience and necessity; or

    (B) fails to find public convenience and necessity, it shall deny the application.

Certificate.

(2) On approval, the Commission shall issue to the rail carrier a certificate describing the abandonment or discontinuance approved by the Commission. Each certificate shall also contain provisions to protect the interests of employees. The provisions shall be at least as beneficial to those interests as the provisions established under section 11347 of this title and section 565(b) of title 45.

Post, p. 1439

(c) Except as provided in sections 10905 and 10906 of this title—

(1) if a certificate is issued without an investigation under section 10904(c) of this title, the abandonment or discontinuance may take effect under the certificate on the 30th day after the issuance of the certificate; or

(2) if a certificate is issued after an investigation under section 10904(c) of this title, the abandonment or discontinuance may take effect under the certificate on the 120th day after the issuance of the certificate.

49 USC 10904.

§ 10904. Filing and procedure for applications to abandon or discontinue

(a)(1) An application for a certificate of abandonment or discontinuance under section 10903 of this title, and a notice of intent to abandon or discontinue, must be filed with the Interstate Commerce Commission at least 60 days before the day on which the abandonment or discontinuance is to become effective.

(2) When a rail carrier providing transportation subject to the jurisdiction of the Commission under subchapter I of chapter 105 of this title files an application and notice of intent, the notice shall include—

(A) an accurate and understandable summary of the rail carrier's application and the reasons for the proposed abandonment or discontinuance; and

(B) a statement indicating that each interested person is entitled to recommend to the Commission that it approve, deny, or take other action concerning the application.

(3) The rail carrier shall—

(A) send by certified mail a copy of the notice of intent to the chief executive officer of each State that would be directly affected by the proposed abandonment or discontinuance;

(B) post a copy of the notice in each terminal and station on each portion of a railroad line proposed to be abandoned or over which all transportation is to be discontinued;

(C) publish a copy of the notice for 3 consecutive weeks in a newspaper of general circulation in each county in which each such portion is located;

(D) mail a copy of the notice, to the extent practicable, to all shippers that have made significant use (as designated by the Commission) of the railroad line during the 12 months preceding the filing of the application; and

(E) attach to the notice filed with the Commission an affidavit certifying the manner in which clauses (A)–(D) of this paragraph have been satisfied.

(b) The burden is on the person applying for the certificate to prove that the present or future public convenience and necessity require or permit the abandonment or discontinuance.

(c)(1) During the period between the date the application is filed through the day immediately before the date proposed in the application that the abandonment or discontinuance become effective, the Commission shall, on petition, and may, on its own initiative, begin an investigation to assist it in determining what disposition to make of the application. The order to conduct the investigation must be served on any affected rail carrier not later than the 5th day before the proposed effective date of the abandonment or discontinuance. An investigation may include public hearings at any location reasonably adjacent to the railroad line involved in the abandonment or discontinuance. The hearing may be held on the request of an interested party or on the initiative of the Commission.

(2) If an investigation is not conducted, the Commission shall act under section 10903(b) of this title by the last day of the period referred to in paragraph (1) of this subsection. If an investigation is to be conducted, the Commission shall postpone the proposed effective date of any part of the abandonment or discontinuance. The postponement shall be for a reasonable period of time necessary to complete the investigation.

(d)(1) In this subsection, "potentially subject to abandonment" has the meaning given the term in regulations of the Commission. The regulations may include standards that vary by region of the United States and by railroad or group of railroads. "Potentially subject to abandonment."

(2) Each rail carrier shall maintain a complete diagram of the transportation system operated, directly or indirectly, by the carrier. The carrier shall submit to the Commission and publish amendments to its diagram that are necessary to maintain the accuracy of the diagram. The diagram shall—

(A) include a detailed description of each of its railroad lines potentially subject to abandonment; and

(B) identify each railroad line for which the carrier plans to file an application for a certificate under subsection (a) of this section.

(3) If an application for a certificate is opposed by—

(A) a shipper or other person that has made significant use (as determined by the Commission) of the railroad line involved in the proposed abandonment or discontinuance during the 12-month period before the filing of the application for a certificate; or

(B) a State or political subdivision of a State in which any part of the railroad line is located;

the Commission may issue a certificate under section 10903 of this title only if the railroad line has been described and identified in the diagram or amendment to the diagram of the rail carrier that was submitted to the Commission at least 4 months before the date on which the application was filed.

§ 10905. Offers of financial assistance to avoid abandonment and discontinuance 49 USC 10905.

(a) In this section—

(1) "avoidable cost" means all expenses that would be incurred by a rail carrier in providing transportation that would not be incurred if the railroad line over which the transportation was provided were abandoned or if the transportation were discontinued. Expenses include cash inflows foregone and cash outflows incurred by the rail carrier as a result of not abandoning or discontinuing the transportation. Cash inflows foregone and cash outflows incurred include— "Avoidable cost."

(A) working capital and required capital expenditure;

(B) expenditures to eliminate deferred maintenance;

(C) the current cost of freight cars, locomotives, and other equipment; and

(D) the foregone tax benefits from not retiring properties from rail service and other effects of applicable Federal and State income taxes.

"Reasonable return."

(2) "reasonable return" means—

(A) if a rail carrier is not in reorganization, the cost of capital to the rail carrier, as determined by the Interstate Commerce Commission; and

(B) if a rail carrier is in reorganization, the mean cost of capital of rail carriers not in reorganization, as determined by the Commission.

Publication in Federal Register.

(b) When the Commission finds under section 10903 of this title that the present or future public convenience and necessity require or permit abandonment or discontinuance, it shall publish the finding in the Federal Register. If, within 30 days after the publication, the Commission finds that—

(1) a financially responsible person (including a governmental authority) has offered financial assistance to enable the rail transportation to be continued over that part of the railroad line to be abandoned or over which all rail transportation is to be discontinued; and

(2) it is likely that the assistance would be equal to—

(A) the difference between the revenues attributable to that part of the railroad line and the avoidable cost of providing rail freight transportation on the line, plus a reasonable return on the value of the line; or

(B) the acquisition cost of that part of the railroad line; the Commission shall postpone the issuance of a certificate authorizing abandonment or discontinuance for a reasonable time, not to exceed 6 months, to enable the person or governmental authority to enter into an agreement with the rail carrier to provide the assistance or to buy that part of the railroad line and to continue to provide rail transportation over the line. Thereafter, the Commission shall determine the extent to which the avoidable cost of providing rail transportation plus a reasonable return on the rail properties involved exceed the revenues attributable to the railroad line or the rail transportation proposed to be abandoned or discontinued. On notice to the Commission that such an agreement has been executed, the Commission shall further postpone the issuance of the certificate as long as the agreement, or an extension or modification of the agreement, is in effect.

(c) The rail carrier shall provide promptly to a party considering offering financial assistance under subsection (b) of this section—

(1) its most recent reports on the physical condition of that part of the railroad line involved in the proposed abandonment or discontinuance; and

(2) traffic, revenue, and other data necessary to determine the amount of financial assistance that would be required to continue rail transportation over that part of the railroad line.

49 USC 10906.

§ 10906. Offering abandoned rail properties for sale for public purposes

When the Interstate Commerce Commission finds under section 10903 of this title that the present or future public convenience and necessity require or permit abandonment or discontinuance, the Commission shall find further whether the rail properties that are involved in the proposed abandonment or discontinuance are suitable for use for public purposes, including highways, other forms of mass transportation, conservation, energy production or transmission, or recreation. If the Commission finds that the rail properties proposed to be abandoned are suitable for public purposes, the properties may be sold, leased, exchanged, or otherwise disposed of only under conditions provided in the order of the Commission. The conditions may include a prohibition on any such disposal for a period of not more than 180 days after the effective date of the order, unless the properties have first been offered, on reasonable terms, for sale for public purposes.

§ 10907. Exceptions

49 USC 10907.

(a) Notwithstanding sections 10901 and 10902 and subchapter III of chapter 113 of this title, and without the approval of the Interstate Commerce Commission, a rail carrier providing transportation subject to the jurisdiction of the Commission under subchapter I of chapter 105 of this title may enter into arrangements for the joint ownership or joint use of spur, industrial, team, switching, or side tracks.

Ante, p. 1359.

(b) The Commission does not have authority under sections 10901–10906 of this title over—

(1) the construction, acquisition, operation, abandonment, or discontinuance of spur, industrial, team, switching, or side tracks if the tracks are located, or intended to be located, entirely in one State; or

(2) a street, suburban, or interurban electric railway that is not operated as part of a general system of rail transportation.

§ 10908. Discontinuing or changing interstate train or ferry transportation subject to State law

49 USC 10908.

(a) When a discontinuance or change in any part of the transportation of a train or ferry operating between a place in a State and a place in another State—

(1) is proposed by a carrier providing transportation subject to the jurisdiction of the Interstate Commerce Commission under subchapter I of chapter 105 of this title; and

(2) is subject to the law of a State, or to a regulation or order of, or proceeding pending before, a court or other authority of a State;

the carrier, notwithstanding that law, regulation, order, or proceeding, may discontinue or change the transportation—

(A) if it files a notice of the proposed discontinuance or change with the Commission at least 30 days before the discontinuance or change is intended to be effective and carries out the discontinuance or change under that notice;

(B) if it mails a copy of the notice to the chief executive officer of each State in which the train or ferry is operated and posts a copy of the notice at each station, depot, or other facility served by the train or ferry; and

(C) except as otherwise provided by the Commission under this section.

(b) On petition or on its own initiative, the Commission may conduct a proceeding on the proposed discontinuance or change if it begins the proceeding between the date the carrier files the notice under subsection (a) of this section and the date on which the discontinuance or change is intended to be effective. After the proceeding begins, the Commission may order the carrier proposing the discontinuance or change to continue any part of the transportation pending completion of the proceeding and the decision of the Commission if the Commission serves a copy of its order on the carrier at least 10 days before the date on which the carrier intended the discontinuance or change to be effective. However, the Commission may not order the transportation continued for more than 4 months after the date on which the carrier intended the discontinuance or change to be effective.

(c) If, after a proceeding completed either before or after the proposed discontinuance or change has become effective, the Commission finds that any part of the transportation is required or permitted by present or future public convenience and necessity and will not unreasonably burden interstate or foreign commerce, the Commission may order the carrier to continue or restore that transportation for not to exceed one year from the date of the Commission order. On expiration of the Commission order, the jurisdiction of each State involved in the discontinuance or change is no longer superseded except to the extent this section is again invoked.

49 USC 10909.

§ 10909. Discontinuing or changing train or ferry transportation in one State

(a) When a carrier providing transportation subject to the jurisdiction of the Interstate Commerce Commission under subchapter I

Ante, p. 1359.

of chapter 105 of this title has proposed a discontinuance or change of any part of the transportation of a train or ferry operated by it entirely in one State and—

    (1) the law of the State prohibits the discontinuance or change;

    (2) the carrier has requested the State authority having jurisdiction over the discontinuance or change for permission to discontinue or change the transportation and the request has been denied; or

    (3) the State authority has not acted finally by the 120th day after the carrier made the request;

the carrier may petition the Commission for permission to discontinue or change the transportation.

Notification.

(b) When a petition is filed under subsection (a) of this section, the Commission shall notify the chief executive officer of the State in

Hearing opportunity.

which the train or ferry is operated concerning the petition. Before acting on the petition, the Commission shall give interested parties a full hearing. If such a hearing is requested, the Commission shall give all interested parties at least 30 days notice of the hearing and shall hold the hearing in the State in which the train or ferry is operated. The Commission may cooperate with, and use the services, records, and facilities of, the State in carrying out this section.

(c) The Commission may grant permission to the carrier to discontinue or change any part of the transportation if the Commission finds that—

    (1) the present or future public convenience and necessity require or permit the discontinuance or change to be authorized by the Commission; and

    (2) continuing the transportation, without the proposed discontinuance or change, will constitute an unreasonable burden on the interstate operations of the carrier or on interstate commerce.

SUBCHAPTER II—OTHER CARRIERS AND MOTOR CARRIER BROKERS

§ 10921. Requirement for certificate, permit, or license

Except as provided in this subchapter or another law, a person may provide transportation or service subject to the jurisdiction of the Interstate Commerce Commission under subchapter II, III, or IV of chapter 105 of this title or be a broker for transportation subject to the jurisdiction of the Commission under subchapter II of that chapter, only if the person holds the appropriate certificate, permit, or license issued under this subchapter authorizing the transportation or service.

49 USC 10921.

Ante, pp. 1361, 1365, 1369.

§ 10922. Certificates of motor and water common carriers

49 USC 10922.

(a) Except as provided in this section and section 10930(a) of this title, the Interstate Commerce Commission shall issue a certificate to a person authorizing that person to provide transportation subject to the jurisdiction of the Commission under subchapter II or III of chapter 105 of this title as a motor common carrier or water common carrier, respectively, if the Commission finds that—
  (1) the person is fit, willing, and able—
    (A) to provide the transportation to be authorized by the certificate; and
    (B) to comply with this subtitle and regulations of the Commission; and
  (2) the transportation to be provided under the certificate is or will be required by the present or future public convenience and necessity.

(b) A person must file an application with the Commission for a certificate to provide transportation as a motor common carrier or water common carrier. The Commission may approve any part of the application or deny the application. The application must—
  (1) be under oath;
  (2) contain information required by Commission regulations; and
  (3) be served on persons designated by the Commission.

Applications.

(c)(1) Subject to section 10927(a) of this title, each certificate issued to a person to provide transportation as a motor common carrier shall specify—
    (A) the transportation to be provided by the carrier;
    (B) any of the regular routes over which, any of the places between which, and off-route places at which, the carrier may provide transportation; and
    (C) if transportation is not over regular routes or between specified places, the area in which the carrier may provide transportation.
  (2) Under regulations of the Commission, a motor common carrier may occasionally deviate from the regular routes, or the places specified in the certificate, or both.
  (3) If a motor common carrier transports passengers, the Commission may authorize transportation of the passengers only over a regular route and between specified places, except to the extent the carrier is authorized to provide special or charter transportation.

(4) A certificate of a motor common carrier to transport passengers may include authority to transport—

(A) newspapers, baggage of passengers, express, or mail in the same motor vehicle with the passengers; and

(B) baggage of passengers in a separate motor vehicle.

(d) Each certificate issued to a person to provide transportation as a water common carrier shall specify each route over which, and each port between which, the carrier may provide transportation.

(e)(1) A motor common carrier may provide transportation under a certificate only if the carrier complies with conditions the Commission finds are required by public convenience and necessity, including conditions—

(A) on extending routes of the carrier; and

(B) to carry out requirements established by the Commission under this subtitle.

(2) The Commission may prescribe necessary conditions under which a water common carrier provides transportation, including conditions on extending routes of the carrier.

(3) The Commission may prescribe conditions when the certificate is issued and at any time thereafter. The Commission may not prescribe a condition preventing—

(A) a motor common carrier or water common carrier from adding to its equipment and facilities or its transportation within the scope of the certificate to satisfy business development and public demand; or

(B) a water common carrier, if the carrier has authority to provide transportation over completed parts of a waterway project authorized under law, from extending its transportation over the uncompleted parts of the project when opened for navigation to satisfy business development and public demand.

(f) A certificate issued under this section does not confer a proprietary or exclusive right to use the public highways or public waterways.

49 USC 10923.

§ 10923. Permits of motor and water contract carriers and freight forwarders

(a) Except as provided in this section and section 10930 of this title, the Interstate Commerce Commission shall issue a permit to a person authorizing the person to provide transportation subject to the jurisdiction of the Commission under subchapter II or III of chapter 105 of this title as a motor contract carrier or water contract carrier, respectively, or to provide service subject to that jurisdiction under subchapter IV of chapter 105 as a freight forwarder, if the Commission finds that—

Ante, pp. 1361, 1365.
Ante, p. 1369.

(1) the person is fit, willing, and able—

(A) to provide the transportation or service to be authorized by the permit; and

(B) to comply with this subtitle and regulations of the Commission; and

(2) the transportation or service to be provided under the permit is or will be consistent with the public interest and the transportation policy of section 10101 of this title.

Ante, p. 1337.
Applications.

(b)(1) A person must file an application with the Commission for a permit to provide transportation as a contract carrier or to provide service as a freight forwarder. The Commission may approve any part of the application or deny the application. The application must—

(A) be under oath;

(B) contain information required by Commission regulations; and

(C) be served on persons designated by the Commission.

(2) In deciding whether to approve the application of a person for a permit as a motor contract carrier, the Commission shall consider—

(A) the number of shippers to be served by the carrier;

(B) the nature of the transportation proposed to be provided;

(C) the effect that granting the permit would have on the transportation of carriers protesting the granting of the permit; and

(D) the effect that denying the permit would have on the person applying for the permit, its shippers, or both, and the changing character of the requirements of those shippers.

(3) The Commission may not deny any part of an application for a freight forwarder permit filed by a corporation controlled by, or under common control with—

(A) a common carrier providing transportation subject to the jurisdiction of the Commission under subchapter I, II, or III of chapter 105 of this title, because of the relationship between the corporation and that carrier; and *Ante, pp. 1359, 1361, 1365.*

(B) a common carrier providing transportation subject to the jurisdiction of the Commission under subchapter I of chapter 105 only because the service to be provided by the corporation will compete with service provided by another freight forwarder subject to subchapter IV of that chapter. *Ante, p. 1369.*

(c) Each permit issued to a person—

(1) to provide transportation as a motor contract carrier is subject to section 10927(a) of this title and shall specify the transportation to be provided by the carrier;

(2) to provide transportation as a water contract carrier shall specify the transportation to be provided by the carrier; and

(3) to provide service as a freight forwarder shall specify the nature or general description about which the service is to be provided, the area in which, and the areas between which, the service may be provided by the freight forwarder.

(d)(1) The Commission may prescribe necessary conditions under which a contract carrier or freight forwarder provides transportation or service. The Commission may prescribe the conditions when the permit is issued and at any time thereafter.

(2) The permit for a motor contract carrier shall specify necessary conditions, including each person or number or class of persons for which the carrier may provide transportation—

(A) to ensure that the carrier provides transportation as a motor contract carrier and within the scope of the permit; and

(B) to carry out requirements established by the Commission under this subtitle.

(3) Subject to the permit and its conditions, a motor contract carrier may substitute or add to its equipment and facilities as requests for its transportation develop. The Commission may not prescribe a condition preventing—

(A) a water contract carrier from substituting or adding contracts within the scope of the permit to satisfy the requirements of business development and public demand; and

(B) a water contract carrier or freight forwarder from adding to its equipment and facilities, and transportation or service, as the case may be, within the scope of the permit to satisfy the requirements of business development and public demand.

49 USC 10924.

§ 10924. Licenses of motor carrier brokers

(a) The Interstate Commerce Commission shall issue, subject to section 10927(b) of this title, a license to a person authorizing the person to be a broker for transportation subject to the jurisdiction of the Commission under subchapter II of chapter 105 of this title, if the Commission finds that—

Ante, p. 1361.

(1) the person is fit, willing, and able—
(A) to be a broker for transportation to be authorized by the license; and
(B) to comply with this subtitle and regulations of the Commission; and
(2) the transportation for which the person is to be a broker will be consistent with the public interest and the transportation policy of section 10101 of this title.

Ante, p. 1337.

(b)(1) The broker may provide the transportation itself only if the broker also has been issued a certificate or permit to provide the transportation under this subchapter. A broker may use only the transportation of a motor carrier holding a certificate or permit issued under this subchapter.

(2) This subsection does not apply to a motor carrier having a certificate or permit issued under this subchapter or to an employee or agent of the motor carrier to the extent the transportation is to be provided entirely by the motor carrier, with other motor carriers holding certificates or permits, or with rail, express, or water common carriers.

(c) A person must file an application with the Commission for a license to be a broker for motor carrier transportation. The Commission may approve the application or any part of it, or deny the application.

(d) Commission regulations shall provide for the protection of travelers and shippers by motor vehicle, to be observed by brokers.

49 USC 10925.

§ 10925. Effective periods of certificates, permits, and licenses

(a) Each certificate, permit, and license issued under section 10922, 10923, or 10924 of this title is effective from the date specified in it and remains in effect except as otherwise provided in this section.

(b) On application of the holder of a certificate, permit, or license, the Interstate Commerce Commission may amend or revoke any part of the certificate, permit, or license. On complaint or on its own initiative and after notice and an opportunity for a proceeding, the Commission may suspend, amend, or revoke any part of a certificate, permit, or license—

(1) if a motor carrier, broker, or freight forwarder, for willful failure to comply with this subtitle, a regulation or order of the Commission, or a condition of its certificate, permit, or license; and

Ante, p. 1370.

(2) if a water carrier, for willful failure to comply with section 10701(a) or 11101(a) of this title, a regulation or order of the Commission, or a condition of its certificate or permit.

(c)(1) Except on application of the holder, the Commission may revoke a certificate or permit of a motor carrier or freight forwarder, or a license of a broker, only after the Commission has issued an order to the holder under section 11701 of this title requiring compliance with this subtitle, a regulation of the Commission, or a condition of the

Post, p. 1449.

certificate, permit, or license of the holder, and the holder willfully does not comply with the order.

(2) Except on application of the holder, the Commission may suspend, amend, or revoke a certificate or permit of a water carrier only after the Commission has issued an order to the holder under section 11701 of this title requiring compliance with section 10701(a) or 11101(a) of this title, and the holder willfully does not comply with the order. *Post*, p. 1449. *Ante*, p. 1370.

(3) The Commission may act under paragraph (1) or (2) of this subsection only after giving the holder of the certificate, permit, or license at least 30 days to comply with the order.

(d)(1) Without regard to subchapter II of chapter 103 of this title and subchapter II of chapter 5 of title 5, the Commission may suspend a certificate of a motor carrier, a permit of a freight forwarder, or a license of a broker— *Ante*, p. 1345. *Ante*, p. 1383.

(A) if a motor carrier or broker, for failure to comply with section 10701, 10702, 10761, 10762, 10924(d), or 10927 (b) or (d) of this title, or an order or regulation of the Commission prescribed under those sections; and *Ante*, pp. 1371, 1372, 1394.

(B) if a freight forwarder, for failure to comply with section 10762 or 10927 (c) or (d) of this title, or an order or regulation of the Commission prescribed under those sections.

(2) The Commission may suspend the certificate, permit, or license only after it gives notice of the suspension to the holder at least 15 days before the date the suspension is to begin. The suspension remains in effect until the holder complies with those applicable sections.

§ 10926. Transfers of certificates and permits   49 USC 10926.

Except as provided in this subtitle, a certificate or permit issued under section 10922 or 10923 of this title—

(1) if a certificate or permit of a motor carrier, may be transferred under regulations of the Interstate Commerce Commission;

(2) if a certificate or permit of a water carrier, may be transferred under regulations prescribed by the Commission to protect the public interest and to ensure compliance with this subtitle; and

(3) if a permit of a freight forwarder, may be transferred under regulations prescribed by the Commission to ensure compliance with this subtitle, if the Commission finds that the person to whom the permit is to be transferred satisfies section 10923 (a) and (b) of this title. However, if the proposed transfer would affect the interests of employees of a freight forwarder, the Commission shall require a fair and equitable arrangement to protect the interests of those employees before the transfer is effective.

§ 10927. Security of motor carriers, brokers, and freight forwarders   49 USC 10927.

(a)(1) The Interstate Commerce Commission may issue a certificate or permit to a motor carrier under section 10922 or 10923 of this title only if the carrier files with the Commission a bond, insurance policy, or other type of security approved by the Commission. The security must be sufficient to pay, not more than the amount of the security, for each final judgment against the carrier for bodily injury to, or death of, an individual resulting from the negligent operation, maintenance, or use of motor vehicles under the certificate or permit, or for loss or damage to property (except property referred to in paragraph (3) of this subsection), or both. A certificate or permit remains in effect only as long as the carrier satisfies the requirements of this paragraph.

(2) A motor carrier operating in the United States when providing transportation between places in a foreign country or between a place in one foreign country and a place in another foreign country shall comply with the requirements of sections 10329 and 10330 that apply to a motor carrier providing transportation subject to the jurisdiction of the Commission under subchapter II of chapter 105 of this title. To protect the public, the Commission may require any such motor carrier to file the type of security that a motor carrier is required to file under paragraph (1) of this subsection.

Ante, pp. 1351, 1352.

(3) The Commission may require a motor common carrier providing transportation under a certificate to file with the Commission a type of security sufficient to pay a shipper or consignee for damage to property of the shipper or consignee placed in the possession of the motor common carrier as the result of transportation provided under this subtitle. A carrier required by law to pay a shipper or consignee for loss, damage, or default for which a connecting motor common carrier is responsible is subrogated, to the extent of the amount paid, to the rights of the shipper or consignee under any such security.

(b) The Commission may issue a broker's license to a person under section 10924 of this title only if the person files with the Commission a bond, insurance policy, or other type of security approved by the Commission to ensure that the transportation for which a broker arranges is provided. The license remains in effect only as long as the broker complies with this subsection.

(c)(1) The Commission may require a freight forwarder providing service under a permit issued under section 10923 of this title to file with the Commission a bond, insurance policy, or other type of security approved by the Commission. The security must be sufficient to pay, not more than the amount of the security, for each final judgment against the freight forwarder for bodily injury to, or death of, an individual, or loss of, or damage to, property (other than property referred to in paragraph (2) of this subsection), resulting from the negligent operation, maintenance, or use of motor vehicles by or under the direction and control of the freight forwarder when providing transfer, collection, or delivery service under this subtitle.

(2) The Commission may require a freight forwarder providing service under a permit to file with the Commission a bond, insurance policy, or other type of security approved by the Commission sufficient to pay, not more than the amount of the security, for loss of, or damage to, property for which the freight forwarder provides service under this subtitle.

(d) The Commission may determine the type and amount of security filed with it under this section.

§ 10928. Temporary authority for motor and water carriers

49 USC 10928.

Without regard to subchapter II of chapter 103 of this title and subchapter II of chapter 5 of title 5, the Interstate Commerce Commission may grant a motor carrier or water carrier temporary authority to provide transportation to a place or in an area having, respectively, no motor carrier or water carrier capable of meeting the immediate needs of the place or area. Unless suspended or revoked, the Commission may grant the temporary authority for not more than 180 days. A grant of temporary authority does not establish a pre-

5 USC 551.

sumption that permanent authority to provide transportation will be granted under this subchapter.

§ 10929. Temporary authority for previously exempt water transportation

49 USC 10929.

When transportation exempt from the jurisdiction of the Interstate Commerce Commission under section 10544(a)–(c) of this title becomes subject to the jurisdiction of the Commission, the water carrier may continue to provide the transportation without a certificate or permit issued under this subchapter for a period of 120 days beginning on the day the transportation becomes subject to the jurisdiction of the Commission. If the carrier applies to the Commission within that period for a certificate or permit to provide the transportation previously exempt, the Commission shall issue to the carrier the appropriate certificate or permit authorizing the transportation. The Commission shall issue each such certificate and permit without regard to subchapter II of chapter 103 of this title and subchapter II of chapter 5 of title 5.

Ante, p. 1368.

Ante, p. 1345.
Ante, p. 1361.

§ 10930. Limitations on certificates and permits

49 USC 10930.

(a) Except when the Interstate Commerce Commission finds good cause consistent with the public interest and the transportation policy of section 10101 of this title—

Ante, p. 1337.

(1) a person may not hold both a certificate of a motor common carrier and a permit of a motor contract carrier issued under this subchapter, or both a certificate of a water common carrier and a permit of a water contract carrier issued under this subchapter, to transport property over the same route or in the same area; and

(2) if a person controls, is controlled by, or is under common control with, another person—

(A) one of them may not hold a certificate of a motor common carrier, while the other holds a permit of a motor contract carrier, to transport property over the same route or in the same area; and

(B) one of them may not hold a certificate of a water common carrier, while the other holds a permit of a water contract carrier, to transport property over the same route or in the same area.

(b)(1) A person may not hold a permit of a freight forwarder issued under this subchapter if the person is a common carrier providing transportation subject to the jurisdiction of the Commission under subchapter I, II, or III of chapter 105 of this title.

Ante, pp. 1359, 1365.

(2) Except for motor vehicle transportation subject to the jurisdiction of the Commission under subchapter IV of chapter 105 of this title by section 10523(a)(2) of this title, a permit may not authorize a freight forwarder to conduct direct rail, water, or motor carrier transportation subject to the jurisdiction of the Commission under subchapter I, II, or III of that chapter.

Ante, p. 1369.
Ante, p. 1362.

(3) Except when the Commission finds that service to be provided as a freight forwarder is consistent with the public interest and the transportation policy of section 10101 of this title, a person may not hold a permit of a freight forwarder when—

(A) the principal business of the person is manufacturing and selling, or buying and selling, or both manufacturing and selling and buying and selling articles or commodities, and the service of a freight forwarder (or similar assembling, consolidating, and shipping service is provided by the person for its own business) is commonly used to transport the articles or commodities; or

(B) the person controls, is controlled by, or is under common control with, a person referred to in clause (A) of this paragraph.

49 USC 10931.

§ 10931. Motor common carriers providing transportation entirely in one State

(a) A motor common carrier may provide transportation subject to the jurisdiction of the Interstate Commerce Commission under subchapter II of chapter 105 of this title without a certificate issued by the Commission under section 10922 of this title, when—

Ante, p. 1361.

(1) the carrier provides transportation entirely in one State;

(2) the carrier is not controlled by, controlling, or under common control with a carrier providing transportation outside the State;

(3) the carrier has applied for, and has been issued, a certificate of public convenience and necessity by the State authority having jurisdiction to issue such a certificate, permitting the carrier to provide intrastate transportation by motor vehicle; and

(4) the intrastate certificate was issued after, and the certificate states that—

Publication in Federal Register.

(A) notice was given to interested parties through publication in the Federal Register of the filing of the application by the carrier and the desire of the carrier to provide transportation otherwise under the jurisdiction of the Commission within the limits of the certificate issued by the State authority;

(B) reasonable opportunity to be heard was given; and

(C) the State authority considered and found that the public convenience and necessity require that the carrier be permitted to provide transportation under the jurisdiction of the Commission within limits that do not exceed the scope of the certificate issued by the State authority.

Petitions.

(b) An interested party that opposed issuing the certificate to a motor common carrier in a proceeding before a State authority may petition the Commission for reconsideration of a decision of the State authority. On reconsideration, the Commission, based on the record before the State authority, may affirm, reverse, or change that decision, but only with respect to the transportation subject to Commission jurisdiction.

(c) The Commission may require, before a motor common carrier provides transportation authorized under this section, that—

(1) a certified copy of the carrier's intrastate certificate and other appropriate information be filed with the Commission; and

(2) the carrier comply with applicable requirements established by the Commission.

Certificates of registration.

(d)(1) The Commission shall issue a certificate of registration to a motor common carrier authorizing the carrier to provide transportation under this section. The authority granted under the certificate is subject to all other applicable provisions of this subtitle. Except as otherwise provided in this subsection and subchapter III of chapter 113 of this title, the certificate of registration may be transferred if it is transferred with the intrastate certificate. Transfer of the intrastate certificate without the certificate of registration revokes the certificate of registration.

(2) The certificate of registration issued by the Commission is valid as long as the motor common carrier provides transportation entirely in the State from which it received its intrastate certificate and is not controlled by, controlling, or under common control with, a carrier providing transportation outside the State.

(e)(1) On the 180th day after the termination, restriction in scope, or suspension of the intrastate certificate, the authority granted under this section to provide transportation is revoked or likewise restricted unless the intrastate certificate is renewed or reissued or the restriction is removed by that 180th day.

(2) Transportation authorized under this section may be suspended or revoked by the Commission under section 10925 of this title.

§ 10932. Motor carrier savings provisions

49 USC 10932.

(a) Except as specifically provided in a certificate or permit, the holder of a motor carrier certificate or permit issued as the result of an application filed before September 2, 1950, authorizing the carrier to provide transportation in the United States or between the United States and a foreign country (to the extent the transportation is in the United States), may provide the transportation between a place in the United States and a place in a territory or possession of the United States—

(1) without being authorized to do so by the Interstate Commerce Commission; and

(2) to the same extent and subject to the same conditions of the certificate or permit of the carrier.

(b)(1) A motor common carrier providing transportation under an intrastate certificate issued by a State and under a certificate of registration issued by the Commission under section 206(a)(7) of the Interstate Commerce Act (76 Stat. 912) that has been in effect since October 15, 1962, may continue to provide transportation otherwise subject to the jurisdiction of the Commission under subchapter II of chapter 105 of this title—

Ante, p. 1361.

(A) if the certificate of the State authorizing intrastate transportation is limited to a specified period of time, only for that period;

(B) subject to all other applicable provisions of this subtitle;

(C) as long as the carrier provides transportation only in the State issuing the intrastate certificate; and

(D) as long as the carrier is not controlled by, controlling, or under common control with, a carrier providing transportation outside the State.

(2) Except as provided in subchapter III of chapter 113 of this title, the certificate of registration issued by the Commission may be transferred if it is transferred with the intrastate certificate. Transfer of the intrastate certificate without the certificate of registration revokes the certificate of registration.

(3) On the 180th day after the termination, restriction in scope, or suspension of the intrastate certificate, the authority granted under the certificate of registration is revoked or likewise restricted unless the intrastate certificate is renewed or reissued or the restriction is removed by that 180th day. The certificate of registration may be suspended or revoked by the Commission under section 10925 of this title.

(c) Under regulations of the Commission, a motor common carrier transporting passengers under a certificate issued by the Commission as the result of an application filed before January 2, 1967, or under a reissuance of the operating authority provided in the certificate, may provide transportation to any place subject to the jurisdiction of the Commission under subchapter II of chapter 105 of this title for special and chartered parties.

(d) The Commission may not prescribe a condition for a motor contract carrier permit issued before August 23, 1957, that restricts the authority of the carrier—

(1) to substitute similar contracts within the scope of the permit; or

(2) to add contracts within the scope of the permit, unless the Commission, on its own initiative or on petition of an interested carrier, finds that the scope of the transportation to be provided by the motor contract carrier under any such additional contract is not confined to transportation provided by a motor contract carrier as defined after August 21, 1957.

§ 10933. Authorizing abandonment of freight forwarder service

When a freight forwarder is controlled by, or under common control with, a common carrier providing transportation subject to the jurisdiction of the Interstate Commerce Commission under subchapter I, II, or III of chapter 105 of this title, the freight forwarder may abandon any part of the service it provides subject to the jurisdiction of the Commission under subchapter IV of chapter 105, only if the Commission finds the abandonment is consistent with the public interest and the transportation policy of section 10101 of this title. On making the finding, the Commission shall issue to the freight forwarder a certificate describing the abandonment authorized by the Commission.

Ante, pp. 1359, 1361, 1365.
Ante, p. 1369.

Ante, p. 1337.

CHAPTER 111—OPERATIONS OF CARRIERS

SUBCHAPTER I—GENERAL REQUIREMENTS

SUBCHAPTER II—CAR SERVICE

SUBCHAPTER III—REPORTS AND RECORDS

SUBCHAPTER I—GENERAL REQUIREMENTS

§ 11101. Providing transportation and service

49 USC 11101.

(a) A common carrier providing transportation or service subject to the jurisdiction of the Interstate Commerce Commission under chapter 105 of this title shall provide the transportation or service on reasonable request. In addition, a motor common carrier shall provide safe and adequate service, equipment, and facilities.

Ante, p. 1358.

(b) The Commission may prescribe requirements for continuous and adequate transportation and service provided by motor common carriers and freight forwarders subject to the jurisdiction of the Commission under subchapters II and IV of chapter 105 of this title and for transportation of baggage and express by such motor common carriers of passengers.

Ante, pp. 1361, 1369.

(c) The Commission may not regulate the duration of, or the amount of compensation payable under, an arrangement between a motor carrier and another party to use, with a driver, a motor vehicle not owned by that carrier to transport property when—

(1) the motor vehicle—

(A) to be used is that of a farmer or a cooperative association or a federation of cooperative associations under section 10526(a) (4) or (5) of this title or a motor private carrier;

(B) is used regularly in the transportation of (i) property referred to in section 10526(a) (6) of this title, or (ii) perishable products manufactured from perishable property referred to in that section; and

Ante, p. 1364.

(C) is to be used by the carrier in a single movement or in one or more of a series of movements, loaded or empty, in the general direction of the general area where the motor vehicle is based; or

(2) the motor vehicle to be used has completed a movement exempt under section 10526(a) (6) of this title and is next to be used by that carrier in a loaded movement in any direction or in a movement referred to in clause (1) (C) of this subsection, or both.

§ 11102. Classification of carriers

49 USC 11102.

The Interstate Commerce Commission may classify and maintain requirements for groups of carriers included in the terms "motor common carrier", "water common carrier", "motor contract carrier", or "water contract carrier" and for brokers, when required because of the special nature of the transportation provided by them.

§ 11103. Use of terminal facilities

49 USC 11103.

(a) The Interstate Commerce Commission may require terminal facilities, including main-line tracks for a reasonable distance outside of a terminal, owned by a rail carrier providing transportation subject to the jurisdiction of the Commission under subchapter I of chapter 105 of this title, to be used by another rail carrier if the Commission finds that use to be practicable and in the public interest without substantially impairing the ability of the rail carrier owning the facilities or entitled to use the facilities to handle its own business. The carriers are responsible for establishing the conditions and compensation for use of the facilities. However, if the carriers cannot agree, the

Ante, p. 1359.

Commission may establish conditions and compensation for use of the facilities under the principle controlling compensation in condemnation proceedings. The compensation shall be paid or adequately secured before a carrier may begin to use the facilities of another carrier under this section.

(b) A rail carrier whose terminal facilities are required to be used by another carrier under this section is entitled to recover damages from the other carrier for injuries sustained as the result of compliance with the requirement or for compensation for the use, or both, as appropriate, in a civil action, if it is not satisfied with the conditions for use of the facilities or if the amount of the compensation is not paid promptly.

49 USC 11104.

§ 11104. Switch connections and tracks

(a) On application of the owner of a lateral branch line of railroad, or of a shipper tendering interstate traffic for transportation, a common carrier providing transportation subject to the jurisdiction of the Interstate Commerce Commission under subchapter I of chapter 105 of this title shall construct, maintain, and operate, on reasonable conditions, a switch connection to connect that branch line or private side track with its railroad and shall furnish cars to move that traffic to the best of its ability without discrimination in favor of or against the shipper when the connection—

    (1) is reasonably practicable;
    (2) can be made safely; and
    (3) will furnish sufficient business to justify its construction and maintenance.

Ante, p. 1359.

Filing of complaints.

(b) If a common carrier fails to install and operate a switch connection after application is made under subsection (a) of this section, the owner of the lateral branch line of railroad or the shipper may file a complaint with the Commission under section 11701 of this title. The Commission shall investigate the complaint and decide the safety, practicability, justification, and compensation to be paid for the connection. The Commission may direct the common carrier to comply with subsection (a) of this section only after a full hearing.

Ante, p. 1371.

Hearing.

49 USC 11105.

§ 11105. Protective services

A rail or express carrier providing transportation subject to the jurisdiction of the Interstate Commerce Commission under subchapter I of chapter 105 of this title may arrange for a person to furnish to or for the carrier a protective service against heat or cold for property transported by it subject to that jurisdiction only when the Commission finds the arrangement to be reasonable and in the public interest.

49 USC 11106.

§ 11106. Identification of motor vehicles

(a) The Interstate Commerce Commission may—

    (1) issue and require the display of an identification plate on a motor vehicle used in transportation subject to its jurisdiction under subchapter II of chapter 105 of this title; and
    (2) require the carrier to pay the reasonable cost of the plate.

(b) A carrier may use an identification plate only as authorized by the Commission.

Ante, p. 1361.

49 USC 11107.

§ 11107. Leased motor vehicles

Except as provided in section 11101(c) of this title, the Interstate Commerce Commission may require a motor carrier providing transportation subject to the jurisdiction of the Commission under subchapter II of chapter 105 of this title that uses motor vehicles not owned by it to transport property under an arrangement with another party to—

Ante, p. 1361.

(1) make the arrangement in writing signed by the parties specifying its duration and the compensation to be paid by the motor carrier;

(2) carry a copy of the arrangement in each motor vehicle to which it applies during the period the arrangement is in effect;

(3) inspect the motor vehicles and obtain liability and cargo insurance on them; and

(4) have control of and be responsible for operating those motor vehicles in compliance with requirements prescribed by the Secretary of Transportation on safety of operations and equipment, and with other applicable law as if the motor vehicles were owned by the motor carrier.

§ 11108. Water carriers subject to unreasonable discrimination in foreign transportation

49 USC 11108.

(a) The Interstate Commerce Commission may relieve a water carrier providing transportation subject to the jurisdiction of the Commission under subchapter III of chapter 105 of this title, from the requirements of this subtitle when a rate, rule, or practice established by a person providing water transportation to or from a port in a foreign country in competition with that carrier unreasonably discriminates against that carrier. The Commission may relieve that carrier to the extent and for the period of time necessary to end or ease the discrimination if the relief is in the public interest and consistent with the transportation policy of section 10101 of this title.

Ante, p. 1365.

Ante, p. 1337.
Proceedings.

(b) The Commission may begin a proceeding under this section on its own initiative or on application.

SUBCHAPTER II—CAR SERVICE

§ 11121. Criteria

49 USC 11121.

(a) A rail carrier providing transportation subject to the jurisdiction of the Interstate Commerce Commission under subchapter I of chapter 105 of this title shall furnish safe and adequate car service and establish, observe, and enforce reasonable rules and practices on car service. The Commission may—

Ante, p. 1359.

(1) require a rail carrier to file its car service rules with the Commission; and

(2) require that carrier to incorporate those rules in its tariffs.

(b) The Commission may designate and appoint agents and agencies to make and carry out its directions related to car service and matters under sections 11123–11125, 11127, and 11128(a)(1) of this title.

§ 11122. Compensation and practice

49 USC 11122.
Regulations.

(a) The regulations of the Interstate Commerce Commission on car service shall encourage the purchase, acquisition, and efficient use of freight cars. The regulations may include—

(1) the compensation to be paid for the use of a locomotive, freight car, or other vehicle;

(2) the other terms of any arrangement for the use by a rail carrier of a locomotive, freight car, or other vehicle not owned by the rail carrier using the locomotive, freight car, or other vehicle, whether or not owned by another carrier, shipper, or third person; and

(3) sanctions for nonobservance.

(b)(1) The rate of compensation to be paid for each type of freight car shall be determined by the expense of owning and maintaining that type of freight car, including a fair return on its cost giving consideration to current costs of capital, repairs, materials, parts, and labor. In determining the rate of compensation, the Commission shall consider the transportation use of each type of freight car, the national level of ownership of each type of freight car, and other factors that affect the adequacy of the national freight car supply.

(2) The Commission may increase a rate of compensation determined under paragraph (1) of this subsection by an incentive element only when the Commission finds that the supply of a type of freight car is inadequate and an incentive element will compensate freight car owners, contribute to sound car service practices (including efficient utilization and distribution of cars), and encourage the acquisition and maintenance of a car supply adequate to meet the needs of commerce and national defense. The Commission may exempt that incentive element from the compensation to be paid by a carrier or group of carriers when the Commission finds that exemption is in the national interest.

49 USC 11123.

§ 11123. Situations requiring immediate action

(a) When the Interstate Commerce Commission considers that a shortage of equipment, congestion of traffic, or other emergency requiring immediate action exists in a section of the United States, the Commission may—

(1) suspend any car service rule or practice;

(2) take action during the emergency to promote service in the interest of the public and of commerce regardless of the ownership (as between carriers) of a locomotive, car, or other vehicle on terms of compensation the carriers establish between themselves subject to subsection (b)(2) of this section;

(3) require joint or common use of terminals, including mainline tracks for a reasonable distance outside of those terminals, on terms of compensation the carriers establish between themselves, subject to subsection (b)(2) of this section, when that action will best meet the emergency and serve the public interest; and

(4) give directions for preference or priority in transportation, embargoes, or movement of traffic under permits.

(b)(1) Except as provided in paragraph (2) of this subsection, the Commission may act under this section on its own initiative or on application without regard to subchapter II of chapter 103 of this title and subchapter II of chapter 5 of title 5.

Ante, p. 1345.
Ante, p. 1361.

(2) When the carriers do not agree on terms of compensation under subsection (a)(2) of this section or on terms for joint or common use of terminals under subsection (a)(3) of this section, the Commission may establish for them in a later proceeding terms of compensation the Commission finds to be reasonable.

49 USC 11124.

§ 11124. Rerouting traffic on failure of rail carrier to serve the public

Ante, p. 1359.

(a) When the Interstate Commerce Commission considers that a rail carrier providing transportation subject to the jurisdiction of the Commission under subchapter I of chapter 105 of this title cannot transport the traffic offered to it in a manner that properly serves the public, the Commission may direct the handling, routing, and movement of the traffic of that carrier and its distribution over other railroad lines to promote commerce and service to the public. Subject to subsection (b)(2) of this section, the carriers may establish the terms of compensation between themselves.

(b)(1) Except as provided in paragraph (2) of this subsection, the Commission may act under this section on its own initiative or on application without regard to subchapter II of chapter 103 of this title and subchapter II of chapter 5 of title 5.

Ante, p. 1345.
Ante, p. 1361.

(2) When the carriers do not agree on the terms of compensation under this section, the Commission may establish the terms for them in a later proceeding.

§ 11125. Directed rail transportation

49 USC 11125.

(a) When a rail carrier providing transportation subject to the jurisdiction of the Interstate Commerce Commission under subchapter I of chapter 105 of this title cannot transport the traffic offered to it because—

Ante, p. 1359.

    (1) its cash position makes its continuing operation impossible;

    (2) transportation has been discontinued under court order; or

    (3) it has discontinued transportation without obtaining a required certificate under section 10903 of this title;

the Commission may direct the handling, routing, and movement of the traffic available to that carrier and its distribution over the railroad lines of that carrier by another carrier to promote service in the interest of the public and of commerce. Subject to subsection (b) of this section, the Commission may act without regard to subchapter II of chapter 103 of this title and subchapter II of chapter 5 of title 5.

(b)(1) Action of the Commission under subsection (a) of this section may not remain in effect for more than 60 days. However, the Commission may extend that period for an additional designated period of not more than 180 days if cause exists.

(2) The Commission may not take action that would—

    (A) cause a directed carrier to operate in violation of section 421 of title 45; or

45 USC 421.

    (B) impair substantially the ability of a directed carrier to serve its own patrons adequately, or to meet its outstanding common carrier obligations.

(3) A directed carrier is not responsible, because of the direction of the Commission, for the debts of the other carrier.

Debts.

(4) A directed carrier shall hire the employees of the other carrier, to the extent that they previously provided that transportation for the other carrier, and assume the existing employment obligations and practices of the other carrier for those employees including agreements governing rate of pay, rules and working conditions, and employee protective conditions for the period during which the action of the Commission is effective.

(5) A directed carrier may apply to the Commission for payment of an amount equal to the amount by which (A) the total expenses of that carrier incurred in or attributable to the handling, routing, and moving the traffic over the lines of the other carrier for the period during which the action of the Commission is effective, including renting or leasing necessary equipment and an allocation of common expenses, overhead, and a reasonable profit, exceed (B) the direct revenues from handling, routing, and moving that traffic over the lines of the other carrier during that period. The carrier must submit a current record of those total expenses to the Commission. The Commission shall certify promptly, to the Secretary of the Treasury, the amount to be paid. The Secretary shall pay that amount by the 90th

Audit.

49 USC 11126.

Ante, p. 1359.

Ante, pp. 1338,
1359, 1371,
1372, 1380,
1383–1386,
1390, 1391,
1393, 1394,
1402, 1403, *Post,*
pp. 1444, 1448,
1455, 1457,
1459, 1464.
"Unit train
Service."

49 USC 11127.

day after the end of the period during which the direction of the Commission is effective, and funds are authorized to be appropriated for that payment. The Commission may audit any such record.

§ 11126. Distribution of coal cars

(a) Subject to subsection (b) of this section, a rail carrier providing transportation subject to the jurisdiction of the Interstate Commerce Commission under subchapter I of chapter 105 of this title shall make a reasonable distribution of cars for transportation of coal among the coal mines served by it whether the mines are located on its line or are customarily dependent on it for car supply. If the supply of available cars does not equal the requirements of the mines, the carrier shall maintain and apply reasonable ratings of the mines and count each car furnished to or used by a mine for transportation of coal against that mine. However, coal cars supplied by shippers or receivers are deemed not to be a part of the carrier's fleet and are not counted in determining a question about distribution or car count under subsection (b) of this section or section 10102, 10501, 10701–10703, 10707, 10721(b), 10722 (c)–(d), 10723(a)–(b)(1), 10724(a), 10741–10744, 10746, 10749, 10750, 10901, 10902, 10907, 11101, 11103–11105, 11121–11125, 11127, 11128(a) (1), 11501(c), 11505(a), 11702(a)(1), 11703, 11901(d)–(e)(2), 11902, 11903, 11905, 11907, 11915, or 11916 of this title.

(b)(1) In this subsection, "unit-train service" means the movement of a single shipment of coal of at least 4,500 tons, tendered to one carrier, on one bill of lading, at one origin, on one day, and destined to one consignee, at one plant, at one destination, over one route.

(2) Unit-train service and non-unit-train service are deemed to be separate and distinct classes of service. A distinction shall be made between them and between the cars used in each class of service. A question about the reasonableness of, or discrimination in, the distribution of cars shall be determined within each class and not between them, notwithstanding a section referred to in subsection (a) of this section.

§ 11127. Service of freight forwarders

(a)(1) When the Interstate Commerce Commission considers that a shortage of equipment, congestion of traffic, or other emergency requires immediate action at a place in the United States, the Commission may—

(A) suspend any service, equipment, or facilities requirement applicable to a freight forwarder under the jurisdiction of the Commission under subchapter IV of chapter 105 of this title;

(B) take action to promote transportation in the interest of the public and of commerce; and

(C) give directions for preference or priority in transportation, embargoes, or movement of traffic under permits.

(2) When the Commission considers that any such freight forwarder cannot properly serve the public by providing service for the traffic offered it, the Commission may require the handling, routing, and movement of that traffic in another manner to promote commerce and service to the public. When the equipment or facilities of another freight forwarder are required to be used, the freight forwarders may establish terms of compensation between themselves subject to subsection (b)(2) of this section.

(b)(1) Except as provided in paragraph (2) of this subsection, the Commission may act under this section on its own initiative or on

application without regard to subchapter II of chapter 102 of this title and subchapter II of chapter 5 of title 5. *Ante*, p. 1345.
Ante, p. 1361.

(2) When the freight forwarders do not agree on the terms of compensation under this section, the Commission may establish the terms for them in a later proceeding.

§ 11128. War emergencies; embargoes imposed by carriers

(a) (1) When the President, during time of war or threatened war, certifies to the Interstate Commerce Commission that it is essential to the defense and security of the United States to give preference or priority to the movement of certain traffic, the Commission shall direct that preference or priority be given to that traffic under sections 11123 (a) (4) and 11127 (a) (1) (C) of this title.

(2) When the President, during time of war or threatened war, demands that preference and precedence be given to the transportation of troops and material of war over all other traffic, all carriers providing transportation subject to the jurisdiction of the Commission under subchapter I of chapter 105 of this title shall adopt every means within their control to facilitate and expedite the military traffic. *Ante*, p. 1359.

(b) An embargo imposed by any such carrier does not apply to shipments consigned to agents of the United States Government for its use. The carrier shall deliver those shipments as promptly as possible.

SUBCHAPTER III—REPORTS AND RECORDS

§ 11141. Definitions 49 USC 11141.

In this subchapter—
(1) "carrier", "broker", and "lessor" include a receiver or trustee of a carrier (except a freight forwarder), broker, and lessor, respectively.

(2) "lessor" means a person owning a railroad, water line, or a pipeline that is leased to and operated by a carrier providing transportation subject to the jurisdiction of the Interstate Commerce Commission under subchapter I of chapter 105 of this title, and a person leasing a right to operate as a motor carrier or water carrier to another.

(3) "association" means an organization maintained—
(A) by or in the interest of a group of carriers (except water carriers) or brokers providing transportation or service subject to the jurisdiction of the Commission under chapter 105 of this title that performs a service, or engages in activities, related to transportation under this subtitle; or *Ante*, p. 1358.

(B) only by water carriers providing transportation subject to the jurisdiction of the Commission under subchapter III of chapter 105 of this title that engages in activities related to the fixing of rates, publication of classifications, or filing of tariffs by water carriers. *Ante*, p. 1365.

§ 11142. Uniform accounting systems 49 USC 11142.

(a) The Interstate Commerce Commission shall prescribe, for rail carriers providing transportation subject to this subtitle, a uniform cost and revenue accounting and reporting system (1) under generally accepted accounting principles uniformly applied to those carriers and (2) after consideration of appropriate economic principles. To the extent possible, the system shall be cost effective, without duplication, and compatible with the present and desired managerial and responsibility accounting requirements of those carriers. The Commission may prescribe a uniform accounting system for classes of carriers providing, and brokers for, transportation subject to the jurisdiction of the Commission under subchapters II, III, and IV of chapter 105 of this title.

Ante, pp. 1361, 1365, 1369.

(b)(1) To obtain the most accurate cost and revenue information about light density railroad lines, main line operations, factors used to establish rates, and other regulatory areas of responsibility, the Commission shall identify and define, for each facet of rail transportation—

(A) operating and nonoperating revenue accounts;

(B) direct cost accounts for determining fixed and variable costs for materials, labor, and overhead components of operating expenses and the assignment of those costs to various functions, services, or activities, including maintenance-of-way, maintenance of equipment (locomotive and car), transportation (train, yard and station, and accessorial services), and general and administrative expenses; and

(C) indirect cost accounts for determining fixed, common, joint, and constant costs, including the cost of capital, and the method for the assignment of those costs to various functions, services, or activities.

(2) Reports required under the rail accounting system must include information considered appropriate for disclosure under generally accepted accounting principles or the requirements of the Commission or of the Securities and Exchange Commission. To the extent possible, the Interstate Commerce Commission should require that information be reported or disclosed only for essential regulatory purposes including rate change requests, abandonment of facilities requests, responsibility for peaks in demand, cost of service, and issuance of securities.

Review.

(3) The Commission shall review the rail accounting system periodically, but at least once every 5th year after 1977, and revise the system as necessary to conform it to generally accepted accounting principles compatible with the managerial and responsibility accounting requirements of those carriers and to keep it in compliance with this section.

49 USC 11143.

§ 11143. Depreciation charges

The Interstate Commerce Commission shall, for a class of carriers providing transportation subject to its jurisdiction under subchapter I or III of chapter 105 of this title, and may, for a class of carriers

Ante, p. 1359.

providing transportation subject to its jurisdiction under subchapter II of that chapter, prescribe, and change when necessary, those classes of property for which depreciation charges may be included under operating expenses and a rate of depreciation that may be charged to a class of property. The Commission may classify those carriers for purposes of this section. A carrier for whom depreciation charges and rates of depreciation are in effect under this section for any class of property may not—

(1) charge to operating expenses a depreciation charge on a class of property other than that prescribed by the Commission;

(2) charge another rate of depreciation; or

(3) include other depreciation charges in operating expenses.

49 USC 11144.

§ 11144. Records: form; inspection; preservation

(a) The Interstate Commerce Commission may prescribe the form of records required to be prepared or compiled under this subchapter—

(1) by carriers, brokers, and lessors, including records related to movement of traffic and receipts and expenditures of money; and

(2) by persons furnishing cars or protective service against heat or cold to or for a rail or express carrier providing transportation subject to the jurisdiction of the Commission under subchapter I of chapter 105 of this title to the extent related to those cars or that service.

Ante, p. 1359.

(b) The Commission, or an employee designated by the Commission, may on demand and display of proper credentials—

(1) inspect and examine the lands, buildings, and equipment of a carrier, broker, or lessor; and

(2) inspect and copy any record of—

(A) a carrier, broker, lessor, or association;

(B) a person controlling, controlled by, or under common control with a carrier if the Commission considers inspection relevant to that person's relation to, or transaction with, that carrier; and

(C) a person furnishing cars or protective service against heat or cold to or for a rail or express carrier if the Commission prescribed the form of that record.

(c) The Commission, or an employee designated by the Commission, may, during normal business hours, inspect and copy any record related to motor vehicle transportation of a cooperative association or federation of cooperative associations required to notify the Commission under section 10526(a)(5) of this title. However, the Commission may not prescribe the form of records to be maintained by a cooperative association or federation of cooperative associations.

Ante, p. 1364.

(d) The Commission may prescribe the time period during which operating, accounting, and financial records must be preserved by carriers, brokers, lessors, and persons furnishing cars or protective services.

§ 11145. Reports by carriers, lessors, and associations

49 USC 11145.

(a) The Interstate Commerce Commission may require—

(1) carriers, brokers, lessors, and associations, or classes of them as the Commission may prescribe, to file annual, periodic, and special reports with the Commission containing answers to questions asked by it; and

(2) a person furnishing cars or protective services against heat or cold to a rail or express carrier providing transportation subject to this subtitle, to file reports with the Commission containing answers to questions about those cars or services.

(b)(1) An annual report shall contain an account, in as much detail as the Commission may require, of the affairs of the carrier, broker, lessor, or association for the 12-month period ending on the 31st day of December of each year. However, when an annual report is made by a motor carrier, a broker, or a lessor or an association maintained by or interested in one of them, the person making the report may elect to make it for the 13-month period accounting year ending at the close of one of the last 7 days of each calendar year if the books of the person making the report are kept by that person on the basis of that accounting year.

Annual report.

(2) An annual report shall be filed with the Commission by the end of the 3d month after the end of the year for which the report is made unless the Commission extends the filing date or changes the period covered by the report. The annual report and, if the Commission requires, any other report made under this section, shall be made under oath.

CHAPTER 113—FINANCE

SUBCHAPTER I—CARRIER SECURITIES, EQUIPMENT TRUSTS, AND SECURITY INTERESTS

SUBCHAPTER I—CARRIER SECURITIES, EQUIPMENT TRUSTS, AND SECURITY INTERESTS

49 USC 11301.

§ 11301. Authority of certain carriers to issue securities and assume obligations and liabilities

(a) In this section—

"Carrier."

Ante, p. 1359.

(1) "carrier" means a rail or sleeping car carrier providing transportation subject to the jurisdiction of the Interstate Commerce Commission under subchapter I of chapter 105 of this title

(except a street, suburban, or interurban electric railway not operated as a part of a general railroad system of transportation), and a corporation organized to provide transportation by rail carrier subject to that subchapter.

(2) "security" means a share of capital stock, a bond, or other evidence of interest in, or indebtedness of, a carrier. "Security."

(b)(1) Subject to subchapter I of chapter 2A, chapter 2B, and subchapter I of chapter 2D of title 15, the Commission has exclusive jurisdiction to approve the issuance of securities by a carrier and the assumption of an obligation or liability related to the securities of another person by a carrier. A carrier may not issue securities or assume those obligations or liabilities without the approval of the Commission. No other approval is required. A security issued or obligation or liability assumed by a carrier in violation of this subsection or in violation of a condition prescribed by the Commission under subsection (d) of this section is void. However, a security or obligation issued or assumed under authority of this section is not void for failure to comply with a procedural requirement of this section or other matter preceding entry of the order of the Commission.

Issuance of securities.
15 USC 77a, 78a, 80a-1.

(2) Paragraph (1) of this subsection does not apply to notes issued by a carrier if the notes mature not more than 2 years after their date of issue and total (with all then outstanding notes having a maturity of not more than 2 years) not more than 5 percent of the par value of the then outstanding securities of that carrier. If the securities do not have a par value, the par value of those securities is the fair market value on the date of issue. Paragraph (1) of this subsection applies to a subsequent funding of notes referred to in this paragraph.

(c)(1) A carrier issuing notes referred to in subsection (b)(2) of this section shall file a certificate of notification with the Commission by the end of the 10th day after they are issued. That notification must include substantially the same matter required by the Commission for an application for authority to issue other securities.

(2) A carrier that pledges, repledges, or otherwise disposes of a security referred to in an application for authority or a certificate of notification under this section as pledged or held unencumbered in the treasury of that carrier shall file a certificate of notification with the Commission by the end of the 10th day after it disposes of the security.

(d)(1) The Commission may begin a proceeding under this section on application of a carrier. Before taking final action, the Commission must investigate the purpose and use of the securities issue or assumption and the proceeds from it. The Commission may approve any part of the application and may require the carrier to comply with appropriate conditions. After an application is approved under this section, the Commission may change a condition previously imposed or use that may be made of the securities or proceeds for good cause shown subject to the requirements of this section. The Commission may approve an application under this section only when it finds that the securities issue or assumption—

Proceedings.

(A) is for a lawful object within the corporate purpose of the carrier and reasonably appropriate for that purpose;

(B) is compatible with the public interest;

(C) is appropriate for or consistent with the proper performance by the carrier of service to the public as a common carrier; and

　　　(D) will not impair the financial ability of the carrier to provide the service.

　　(2) An application or certificate must be made under oath and signed and filed for the carrier by a designated executive officer who knows the matters stated in the application or certificate. On receipt of an application of a carrier under this section, the Commission shall have a copy of the application served on the chief executive officer of each State in which that carrier operates. The appropriate authorities of those States are entitled to be admitted as parties to a proceeding under this section to represent the rights and interests of their people and States.

Reports to Interstate Commerce Commission.

　　(e) The Commission shall require a carrier that issues securities, including notes, under this section to submit reports to it. The reports must identify the disposition of those securities and the application of the proceeds from their disposition.

　　(f) This section does not imply a guaranty or obligation of those securities by the United States Government. This section does not apply to securities issued or obligations or liabilities assumed by the United States Government, a State, or an instrumentality or political subdivision of one of them.

49 USC 11302.

§ 11302. Issuance of securities and assumption of obligations and liabilities by motor carriers

　　(a) Except as provided in this section, section 11301 of this title applies to—

Ante, p. 1361.

　　　　(1) motor carriers providing transportation subject to the jurisdiction of the Interstate Commerce Commission under subchapter II of chapter 105 of this title;

　　　　(2) corporations organized to provide transportation as carriers subject to the jurisdiction of the Commission under that subchapter; and

　　　　(3) corporations authorized by the Commission to acquire control of at least one motor carrier subject to its jurisdiction under that subchapter.

　　(b) Section 11301 of this title does not apply when the total value of capital stock (or principal amount of other securities to be issued) and the value of capital stock and principal amount of other securities then outstanding is not more than $1,000,000, or to notes of a maturity of not more than 2 years that aggregate not more than $200,000. Notes that, with other outstanding notes of a maturity of not more than 2 years, aggregate that amount may be issued without regard to the percentage limitations applicable under section 11301 (b)(2) of this title. The value of capital stock having no par value is the fair market value on the date of issue of that stock, and the value of capital stock that has a par value is the fair market value on the date of issue or the par value, whichever is greater.

　　(c) This section does not apply to the United States Government, a State, or an instrumentality or political subdivision of one of them.

49 USC 11303.

§ 11303. Equipment trusts: recordation; evidence of indebtedness

　　(a) A mortgage (other than a mortgage under the Ship Mortgage Act, 1920), lease, equipment trust agreement, conditional sales agreement, or other instrument evidencing the mortgage, lease, conditional sale, or bailment of railroad cars, locomotives, or other rolling stock or vessels, intended for a use related to interstate commerce may be filed with the Interstate Commerce Commission. An assignment of a right or interest under one of those instruments and an amendment to that instrument or assignment including a release, discharge, or satisfaction of any part of it may also be filed with the Commission. The instrument, assignment, or amendment must be in writing, executed by the parties to it, and acknowledged or verified under Commission regulations. When filed under this section, that document is notice to, and enforceable against, all persons. A document filed under this section does not have to be filed, deposited, registered, or recorded under another law of the United States, a State (or its political subdivisions), or territory or possession of the United States, related to filing, deposit, registration, or recordation of those documents. This section does not change the Ship Mortgage Act, 1920.

46 USC 984.

(b) The Commission shall maintain a system for recording each document filed under subsection (a) of this section and mark each of them with a consecutive number and the date and hour of their recordation. The Commission shall maintain and keep open for public inspection an index of documents filed under that subsection. That index shall include the name and address of the principal debtors, trustees, guarantors, and other parties to those documents and may include other facts that will assist in determining the rights of the parties to those transactions.

Record system.

§ 11304. Security interests in certain motor vehicles

(a) In this section—

Definitions.

(1) "motor vehicle" means a truck of rated capacity (gross vehicle weight) of at least 10,000 pounds, a highway tractor of rated capacity (gross combination weight) of at least 10,000 pounds, a property-carrying trailer or semitrailer with at least one load-carrying axle of at least 10,000 pounds, or a motor bus with a seating capacity of at least 10 individuals.

(2) "lien creditor" means a creditor having a lien on a motor vehicle and includes an assignee for benefit of creditors from the date of assignment, a trustee in bankruptcy from the date of filing of the petition in bankruptcy, and a receiver in equity from the date of appointment of the receiver.

(3) "security interest" means an interest (including an interest established by a conditional sales contract, mortgage, equipment trust, or other lien or title retention contract, or lease) in a motor vehicle when the interest secures payment or performance of an obligation.

(4) "perfection", as related to a security interest, means taking action (including public filing, recording, notation on a certificate of title, and possession of collateral by the secured party), or the existence of facts, required under law to make a security interest enforceable against general creditors and subsequent lien creditors of a debtor, but does not include compliance with requirements related only to the establishment of a valid security interest between the debtor and the secured party.

(b) A security interest in a motor vehicle owned by, or in the possession and use of, a carrier having a certificate or permit issued under section 10922 or 10923 of this title and owing payment or performance of an obligation secured by that security interest is perfected in all jurisdictions against all general, and subsequent lien, creditors of, and all persons taking a motor vehicle by sale (or taking or retaining a security interest in a motor vehicle) from, that carrier when—

Ante, pp. 1409, 1410.

(1) a certificate of title is issued for a motor vehicle under a law of a jurisdiction that requires or permits indication, on a

certificate or title, of a security interest in the motor vehicle if the security interest is indicated on the certificate;

(2) a certificate of title has not been issued and the law of the State where the principal place of business of that carrier is located requires or permits public filing or recording of, or in relation to, that security interest if there has been such a public filing or recording; and

(3) a certificate of title has not been issued and the security interest cannot be perfected under paragraph (2) of this subsection, if the security interest has been perfected under the law (including the conflict of laws rules) of the State where the principal place of business of that carrier is located.

(c) This section does not affect a security interest perfected before January 1, 1959.

SUBCHAPTER II—OWNERSHIP

§ 11321. Limitation on ownership of certain water carriers

(a)(1) Notwithstanding sections 11343 and 11344 of this title, a carrier, or a person controlling, controlled by, or under common control with a rail, express, sleeping car, or pipeline carrier providing transportation subject to the jurisdiction of the Interstate Commerce Commission under subchapter I of chapter 105 of this title may not own, operate, control, or have an interest in a water common carrier or vessel carrying property or passengers on a water route with which it does or may compete for traffic.

Ante, p. 1359.

(2) The Commission may decide, after a full hearing, questions of fact related to competition or the possibility of competition under this subsection on application of a carrier. A carrier may file an application to determine whether an existing service violates this subsection and may request permission to continue operation of a vessel or that action be taken under subsection (b) of this section. The Commission may begin a proceeding under this subsection on its own initiative or on application of a shipper to investigate the operation of a vessel used by a carrier providing transportation subject to the jurisdiction of the Commission under subchapter I of that chapter if the carrier has not applied to the Commission and had the question of competition or the possibility of competition determined under this subsection.

Hearing.

(b) Notwithstanding subsection (a) of this section, the Commission may authorize a carrier providing transportation subject to the jurisdiction of the Commission under that subchapter to own, operate, control, or have an interest in a water common carrier or vessel that is not operated through the Panama Canal and with which the carrier does or may compete for traffic when the Commission finds that ownership, operation, control, or interest will still allow that water common carrier or vessel to be operated in the public interest advantageously to interstate commerce and that it will still allow competition, without reduction, on the water route in question. However, section 11343 of this title also applies to a transaction or interest under this subsection if the transaction or interest is within the scope of that section. The Commission may begin a proceeding under this subsection on application of a carrier. An authorization under this subsection is not necessary for a carrier that obtained an order of extension before

September 18, 1940, under section 5(21) of the Interstate Commerce Act (37 Stat. 567), as amended, if the order is still in effect.

49 USC 5.

(c) The Commission may take action under this section only after a full hearing. An order entered as a result of the action may be conditioned on giving security for the payment of an amount of money or the discharge of an obligation that is required to be paid or discharged under that order.

§ 11322. Restrictions on officers and directors

49 USC 11322.

(a) A person may hold the position of officer or director of more than one carrier as defined in section 11301(a)(1) of this title only when authorized by the Interstate Commerce Commission. The Commission may authorize a person to hold the position of officer or director of more than one of those carriers when public or private interests will not be adversely affected.

(b) An officer or director of a carrier referred to in subsection (a) of this section may not—

(1) receive, for the benefit of that officer or director, a thing of value in relation to the negotiation, hypothecation, or sale of a security issued or to be issued by that carrier;

(2) share in the proceeds from the negotiation, hypothecation, or sale of a security issued or to be issued by that carrier; or

(3) participate in making or paying dividends of an operating carrier from funds included in a capital account.

§ 11323. Limitation on ownership of other carriers by freight forwarders

49 USC 11323.

(a) A freight forwarder, or a person controlling, controlled by, or under common control with a freight forwarder, providing service subject to the jurisdiction of the Interstate Commerce Commission under subchapter IV of chapter 105 of this title, may not acquire control of a carrier providing transportation subject to the jurisdiction of the Commission under subchapter I, II, or III of that chapter. However, this subsection does not prohibit a carrier providing transportation under subchapter I, II, or III of chapter 105 from acquiring control of another such carrier under subchapter III of this chapter but subject to section 11321.

Ante, p. 1369.

Ante, pp. 1359, 1361, 1365.

(b) A director, officer, employee, or agent of a common carrier providing transportation subject to the jurisdiction of the Commission under subchapter I, II, or III of chapter 105 of this title or a person controlling, controlled by, or under common control with one of those carriers, may not, for that person's pecuniary benefit, own, lease, control, or hold stock in a freight forwarder providing service subject to the jurisdiction of the Commission under subchapter IV of that chapter. However, this subsection does not prohibit the holding of a director's qualifying shares of stock from which no personal pecuniary benefit is derived by the holder.

(c) This subtitle does not prohibit a common carrier providing transportation subject to the jurisdiction of the Commission under subchapter I, II, or III of chapter 105 of this title or a person controlling, controlled by, or under common control with one of those carriers from controlling a freight forwarder. When that control exists, a rate, classification, rule, or practice of one of those carriers may not be found to be unlawful because of the relationship.

SUBCHAPTER III—COMBINATIONS

49 USC 11341.

§ 11341. Scope of authority

(a) The authority of the Interstate Commerce Commission under this subchapter is exclusive. A carrier or corporation participating in or resulting from a transaction approved by the Commission under this subchapter may carry out the transaction, own and operate property, and exercise control or franchises acquired through the transaction without the approval of a State authority. A carrier, corporation, or person participating in that transaction is exempt from the antitrust laws and from all other law, including State and municipal law, as necessary to let that person carry out the transaction, hold, maintain, and operate property, and exercise control or franchises acquired through the transaction. However, if a purchase and sale, a lease, or a corporate consolidation or merger is involved in the transaction, the carrier or corporation may carry out the transaction only with the assent of a majority, or the number required under applicable State law, of the votes of the holders of the capital stock of that corporation entitled to vote. The vote must occur at a regular meeting, or special meeting called for that purpose, of those stockholders and the notice of the meeting must indicate its purpose.

(b) A power granted under this subchapter to a carrier or corporation is in addition to and changes its powers under its corporate charter and under State law. Action under this subchapter does not establish or provide for establishing a corporation under the laws of the United States.

49 USC 11342.

§ 11342. Limitation on pooling and division of transportation or earnings

(a) A common carrier providing transportation subject to the jurisdiction of the Interstate Commerce Commission under subchapter I, II, or III of chapter 105 of this title may not agree or combine with another of those carriers to pool or divide traffic or services or any part of their earnings without the approval of the Commission under this section or sections 11124 and 11125 of this title. The Commission may approve and authorize the agreement or combination if the carriers involved assent to the pooling or division and the Commission finds that a pooling or division of traffic, services, or earnings—

Ante, pp. 1359, 1361, 1365.

(1) will be in the interest of better service to the public or of economy of operation; and

(2) will not unreasonably restrain competition.

(b) The Commission may impose conditions governing the pooling or division and may approve and authorize payment of a reasonable consideration between the carriers.

(c) This section affects an agreement or combination filed with the Commission before March 19, 1941, to which a water common carrier providing transportation subject to the jurisdiction of the Commission under subchapter III of chapter 105 of this title is a party only when the Commission determines that the agreement or combination does not meet the requirements for approval and authorization under subsection (a) of this section.

Proceedings.

(d) The Commission may begin a proceeding under this section on its own initiative or on application.

49 USC 11343.

§ 11343. Consolidation, merger, and acquisition of control

(a) The following transactions involving carriers providing transportation subject to the jurisdiction of the Interstate Commerce Commission under subchapter I (except a pipeline carrier), II, or III of chapter 105 of this title may be carried out only with the approval and authorization of the Commission:

Ante, pp. 1359, 1361, 1365.

(1) consolidation or merger of the properties or franchises of at least 2 carriers into one corporation for the ownership, management, and operation of the previously separately owned properties.

(2) a purchase, lease, or contract to operate property of another carrier by any number of carriers.

(3) acquisition of control of a carrier by any number of carriers.

(4) acquisition of control of at least 2 carriers by a person that is not a carrier.

(5) acquisition of control of a carrier by a person that is not a carrier but that controls any number of carriers.

(6) acquisition by a rail carrier of trackage rights over, or joint ownership in or joint use of, a railroad line (and terminals incidental to it) owned or operated by another rail carrier.

(b) A person may carry out a transaction referred to in subsection (a) of this section or participate in achieving the control or management, including the power to exercise control or management, in a common interest of more than one of those carriers, regardless of how that result is reached, only with the approval and authorization of the Commission under this subchapter. In addition to other transactions, each of the following transactions are considered achievements of control or management:

(1) A transaction by a carrier has the effect of putting that carrier and persons affiliated with it, taken together, in control of another carrier.

(2) A transaction by a person affiliated with a carrier has the effect of putting that carrier and persons affiliated with it, taken together, in control of another carrier.

(3) A transaction by at least 2 persons acting together (one of whom is a carrier or is affiliated with a carrier) has the effect of putting those persons and carriers and persons affiliated with any of them, or with any of those affiliated carriers, taken together, in control of another carrier.

(c) A person is affiliated with a carrier under this subchapter if, because of the relationship between that person and a carrier, it is reasonable to believe that the affairs of another carrier, control of which may be acquired by that person, will be managed in the interest of the other carrier.

(d) (1) Approval and authorization by the Commission are not required if the only parties to a transaction referred to in subsection (a) of this section are motor carriers providing transportation subject to the jurisdiction of the Commission under subchapter II of chapter 105 of this title and the aggregate gross operating revenues of those carriers were not more than $300,000 during a period of 12 consecutive months ending not more than 6 months before the date of the agreement of the parties covering the transaction. However, the approval and authorization of the Commission is required when a motor carrier that is controlled by or affiliated with a carrier providing transportation subject to the jurisdiction of the Commission under subchapter I of that chapter is a party to the transaction.

(2) The approval and authorization of the Commission are not required if the only parties to a transaction referred to in subsection (a) of this section are street, suburban, or interurban electric railways

that are not controlled by or under common control with a carrier that is operated as part of a general railroad system of transportation.

§ 11344. Consolidation, merger, and acquisition of control: general procedure and conditions of approval

(a) The Interstate Commerce Commission may begin a proceeding to approve and authorize a transaction referred to in section 11343 of this title on application of the person seeking that authority. When an application is filed with the Commission, the Commission shall notify the chief executive officer of each State in which property of the carriers involved in the proposed transaction is located and shall notify those carriers. If a motor carrier providing transportation subject to the jurisdiction of the Commission under subchapter II of chapter 105 of this title is involved in the transaction, the Commission must notify the persons specified in section 10328(b) of this title. The Commission shall hold a public hearing when a rail carrier providing transportation subject to the jurisdiction of the Commission under subchapter I of that chapter is involved in the transaction unless the Commission determines that a public hearing is not necessary in the public interest.

(b) In a proceeding under this section, the Commission shall consider at least the following:

(1) the effect of the proposed transaction on the adequacy of transportation to the public.

(2) the effect on the public interest of including, or failing to include, other rail carriers in the area involved in the proposed transaction.

(3) the total fixed charges that result from the proposed transaction.

(4) the interest of carrier employees affected by the proposed transaction.

(c) The Commission shall approve and authorize a transaction under this section when it finds the transaction is consistent with the public interest. The Commission may impose conditions governing the transaction. When the transaction contemplates a guaranty or assumption of payment of dividends or of fixed charges or will result in an increase of total fixed charges, the Commission may approve and authorize the transaction only if it finds that the guaranty, assumption, or increase is consistent with the public interest. When a rail carrier, or a person controlled by or affiliated with a rail carrier, is an applicant and the transaction involves a motor carrier, the Commission may approve and authorize the transaction only if it finds that the transaction is consistent with the public interest, will enable the rail carrier to use motor carrier transportation to public advantage in its operations, and will not unreasonably restrain competition. When a rail carrier is involved in the transaction, the Commission may require inclusion of other rail carriers located in the area involved in the transaction if they apply for inclusion and the Commission finds their inclusion to be consistent with the public interest.

§ 11345. Consolidation, merger, and acquisition of control: rail carrier procedure

(a) If a rail carrier providing transportation subject to the jurisdiction of the Interstate Commerce Commission under subchapter I of chapter 105 of this title is involved in a proposed transaction under section 11343 of this title, this section and section 11344 of this title also apply to the transaction. The Commission shall publish notice of the application in the Federal Register by the end of the 30th day after the application is filed with the Commission and after a certified copy of it is furnished to the Secretary of Transportation. However, if the application is incomplete, the Commission shall reject it by the end of that period. The order of rejection is a final action of the Commission under section 10327 of this title.

Ante, p. 1348.
Filing comments.

(b) Written comments about an application may be filed with the Commission within 45 days after notice of the application is published under subsection (a) of this section. Copies of those comments shall be served on the Secretary of Transportation and the Attorney General, each of whom may decide to intervene as a party to the proceeding. That decision must be made by the 15th day after the date of receipt of the written comments, and if the decision is to intervene, preliminary comments about the application must be sent to the Commission by the end of the 15th day after the date of receipt of the written comments.

(c) The Commission shall require that applications inconsistent with an application, notice of which was published under subsection (a) of this section, and applications for inclusion in the transaction, be filed with it and given to the Secretary of Transportation by the 90th day after publication of notice under that subsection.

(d) The Commission must conclude evidentiary proceedings by the 240th day after the date of publication of notice under subsection (a) of this section. However, if the application involves the merger or control of at least 2 class I railroads, as defined by the Commission, it must conclude evidentiary proceedings by the end of the 24th month after the date of publication of notice under subsection (a) of this section. The Commission must issue a final decision by the 180th day after the date it concludes the evidentiary proceedings. If the Commission does not issue a decision that is a final action under section 10327 of this title, it shall send written notice to Congress that a decision was not issued and the reason why it was not issued.

Evidentiary proceedings.

(e) The Commission may waive the requirement that an initial decision be made under section 10327 of this title and make a final decision itself when it determines that action is required for the timely execution of its functions under this subchapter or that an application governed by this section is of major transportation importance. The decision of the Commission under this subsection is a final action under section 10327 of this title.

Waiver.

(f) The Secretary of Transportation may propose changes in transactions governed by this section when a rail carrier is involved. The Secretary may appear before the Commission to support those changes.

§ 11346. Consolidation, merger, and acquisition of control: expedited rail carrier procedure

49 USC 11346.

(a) A rail carrier providing transportation subject to the jurisdiction of the Interstate Commerce Commission under subchapter I of chapter 105 of this title or the Secretary of Transportation may apply, before January 1, 1982, for authority for and approval of a merger, consolidation, unification or coordination project (as described in section 1654(c) of this title), joint use of tracks or other facilities, or acquisition or sale of assets involving one of those rail carriers, under this section instead of sections 11344 and 11345 of this title. The Secretary may apply under this section only when the parties to the application that are rail carriers providing transportation subject to the jurisdiction of the Commission under subchapter I of that chapter consent to an application by the Secretary. A rail carrier may apply under

Ante, p. 1359.

this section only if it sent the proposed transaction to the Secretary for a report under section 11350 of this title at least 6 months before applying under this section.

Notice.

(b) When the Commission notifies persons required to receive notice that an application has been filed under this section, the Commission must include in the notice a copy of the application, a summary of the proposed transaction, and the applicant's reasons and public interest justification for the transaction. When the Commission notifies the Secretary of Transportation that an application has been filed under this section, the Commission shall also request the report of the Secretary prepared under section 11350 of this title. By the 10th day after receiving an application under this section, the Commission shall send notice of the proposed transaction to—

(1) the chief executive officer of each State that may be affected by the execution or implementation of the proposed transaction;

(2) the Attorney General;

(3) the Secretary of Labor; and

(4) the Secretary of Transportation (unless the Secretary is the applicant under subsection (a) of this section).

Panel;
recommended
decisions.

(c) The Commission shall designate a panel of the Commission to make a recommended decision on each application under this section. The panel must begin a proceeding by the 90th day after the date the Commission receives the application, complete the proceeding by the 180th day after the application is referred to it, and give its recommended decision and certify the record to the entire Commission by the 90th day after the proceeding is completed. The panel may use employees appointed under section 3105 of title 5 and the Rail Services Planning Office in conducting the proceeding, evaluating the application and comments received about it, and determining whether it is in the public interest to approve and authorize the transaction under the last sentence of subsection (d) of this section. To carry out this subsection, the panel may make rules and rulings to avoid unnecessary costs and delay. In making its recommended decision, the panel shall—

(1) request the views of the Secretary of Transportation about the effect of the transaction on the national transportation policy, as stated by the Secretary, and consider the report submitted under section 11350 of this title;

(2) request the views of the Attorney General about the effect of the transaction on competition; and

(3) request the views of the Secretary of Labor about the effect of the transaction on rail carrier employees, particularly whether the proposal contains adequate employee protection provisions.

Written views to
the panel.
Availability to
public.

The Secretaries and the Attorney General shall send their written views to the panel. Those statements are available to the public under section 552(a) of title 5.

(d) When the recommended decision and record of a proceeding under this section are certified to the entire Commission, it must hear oral argument on the matter certified to it and make a final decision by the 120th day after receiving the recommended decision and record. The Commission may extend a time period under subsection (c) of this section or under this subsection but must make its final decision by the end of the 2d year after receipt of the application by the Commission. The Commission shall consider the report of the Secretary of Transportation under section 11350 of this title in making its final decision. The final decision must be accompanied by a written opinion stating the reasons for the Commission action. The Commission may—

(1) approve the transaction if the Commission determines the transaction is in the public interest;

(2) approve the transaction with conditions and modifications that it determines are in the public interest; or

(3) disapprove the transaction if it determines the transaction is not in the public interest.

§ 11347. Employee protective arrangements in transactions involving rail carriers

49 USC 11347.

When a rail carrier is involved in a transaction for which approval is sought under sections 11344 and 11345 or section 11346 of this title, the Interstate Commerce Commission shall require the carrier to provide a fair arrangement at least as protective of the interests of employees who are affected by the transaction as the terms imposed under this section before February 5, 1976, and the terms established under section 565 of title 45. Notwithstanding this subtitle, the arrangement may be made by the rail carrier and the authorized representative of its employees. The arrangement and the order approving the transaction must require that the employees of the affected rail carrier will not be in a worse position related to their employment as a result of the transaction during the 4 years following the effective date of the final action of the Commission (or if an employee was employed for a lesser period of time by the carrier before the action became effective, for that lesser period).

§ 11348. Interstate Commerce Commission authority over non-carrier that acquires control of carrier

49 USC 11348.

(a) When the Interstate Commerce Commission approves and authorizes a transaction under sections 11344 and 11345 of this title in which a person not a carrier providing transportation subject to the jurisdiction of the Commission under chapter 105 of this title acquires control of at least one carrier subject to the jurisdiction of the Commission, the person is subject, as a carrier, to the following provisions of this title that apply to the carrier being acquired by that person, to the extent specified by the Commission: section 10764, subchapter III of chapter 111, and sections 11301, 11302, 11709, 11711, 11901(f), (h)(1), 11909(a)(1), (b), and 11911(a).

Ante, p. 1397.

(b) When a person subject to sections 11301, 11302, 11322, 11709, and 11911 of this title because of acquiring control of a carrier, applies to the Commission for authority to issue securities or assume obligations or liabilities under those sections, the Commission may authorize the issue or assumption only when it finds the issue or assumption—

(1) is consistent with the proper performance of public transportation by the carrier that is controlled by that person;

(2) will not impair the ability of the carrier to provide public transportation; and

(3) is consistent with the public interest in other respects.

§ 11349. Temporary operating approval for transactions involving motor and water carriers

49 USC 11349.

(a) Pending determination of an application filed with the Interstate Commerce Commission under this subchapter for approval of a consolidation or merger of the properties of at least 2 motor carriers or at least 2 water carriers, or of a purchase, lease, or contract to operate the properties of at least one motor carrier or at least one water carrier, the Commission may approve, for a period of not more than 180 days, the operation of the properties sought to be acquired by the person proposing in the application to acquire those properties. The Commission may approve operation of motor carrier properties when it appears that failure to grant the approval may result in destruction of or injury to those motor carrier properties the person is seeking to acquire, or substantially interfere with their future usefulness in providing adequate and continuous service to the public. The Commission may approve the operation of water carrier properties only for good cause shown.

Ante, p. 1345.
5 USC 551.

(b) The Commission may take action under subsection (a) of this section without regard to subchapter II of chapter 103 of this title and subchapter II of chapter 5 of title 5. Transportation provided by a motor carrier under a grant of approval under this section is subject to this subtitle.

49 USC 11350.

§ 11350. Responsibility of the Secretary of Transportation in certain transactions

Publication in
Federal Register.
Ante, p. 1359.

(a) When a rail carrier providing transportation subject to the jurisdiction of the Interstate Commerce Commission under subchapter I of chapter 105 of this title sends a proposed transaction to the Secretary of Transportation under section 11346(a) of this title or the Secretary develops a proposed transaction for submission to the Commission under that section, the Secretary shall publish a summary and a detailed account of the transaction in the Federal Register and give notice of the transaction to the Attorney General and to the chief executive officer of each State in which property of a rail carrier involved in the transaction is located. The Secretary shall initiate an informal proceeding on the proposed transaction under section 553 of title 5.

Study.

(b) By the 10th day after an application is submitted to the Commission under section 11346 of this title, the Secretary shall complete and send to the Commission a study of the proposed transaction about—

(1) the needs of rail transportation in the geographical area affected by the transaction;

(2) the effect of the transaction on competition in rail transportation and other modes of transportation in the geographical area affected by the transaction;

(3) the environmental impact of the transaction and of alternative choices of action;

(4) the effect of the transaction on employment;

(5) the cost of rehabilitation and modernization of track, equipment, and other facilities, with a comparison of the potential savings or losses from other possible choices of action;

(6) the rationalization of the rail system;

(7) the impact of the transaction on shippers, consumers, and rail carrier employees;

(8) the effect of the transaction on communities in the geographical area affected by the transaction and on geographical areas contiguous to the affected areas; and

(9) whether the proposed transaction will improve rail service.

SUBCHAPTER IV—FINANCIAL STRUCTURE

§ 11361. Scope of authority: changes in financial structure

49 USC 11361.

(a) The authority of the Interstate Commerce Commission to act under this subchapter is exclusive. The Commission may approve and authorize a carrier, as defined in section 11301(a)(1) of this title, to change (1) a part of a class of its securities, as defined in section 11301 (a)(2) of this title, or (2) a part of an instrument under which a class of its securities is issued or a class of its obligations is secured. When a change is approved and authorized by the Commission under this subchapter, the carrier may carry out the change notwithstanding an express provision in the affected instrument or a State law and without getting other approval from the Commission or from a State authority. A person participating in carrying out a change that is approved and authorized under this subchapter is exempt from all other law, including State and municipal law, as necessary to let that person carry out the change.

(b) The Commission may not approve an application filed under this section by a carrier that is in equity receivership or reorganization under section 205 of title 11.

(c) A power granted to a carrier under this subchapter changes its powers under its corporate charter and under State law.

(d) This subchapter does not affect the negotiability of a security of a carrier or of the obligation of a carrier that assumed liability related to a security. This subchapter does not apply to an equipment-trust certificate under which a carrier is obligated, to an evidence of indebtedness of a carrier the payment of which is secured solely by equipment, or to another instrument under which that equipment-trust certificate or evidence of indebtedness was issued or by which either of them is secured.

§ 11362. Criteria for approval and authority

49 USC 11362.

(a) A carrier may apply to the Interstate Commerce Commission for approval and authority to make a change under this subchapter. To approve a proposed change, the Commission must find that the proposed change—

(1) is within the scope of section 11361 of this title;

(2) will be in the public interest;

(3) will be in the best interests of the carrier, of each class of its stockholders, and of the holders of each class of the carrier's obligations that are affected by the change; and

(4) will not be against the interests of a creditor of the carrier who is not affected by the change.

If the change involves an issuance of securities, the Commission must also make the findings required under section 11301(d)(1) of this title.

(b)(1) The Commission shall begin a proceeding under this section on receipt of an application but may require an applicant to get assurances of assent to the change from the holders of the outstanding shares of the securities that will be affected by the change before continuing with the proceeding. The Commission may determine the percentage of the principal amount or number of those shares needed to establish assurance of assent to the change. A class of securities is considered to be affected by a proposed change only if the change is proposed to a part of that class or to a part of an instrument under which that class was issued or by which it is secured. However, if a proposed change is to an instrument under which at least 2 classes of securities were issued and are outstanding or secured by that instrument, only those classes to which the change is related are considered to be affected. The Commission shall divide the securities to be affected by a proposed change under this subchapter into reasonable classes for purposes of this subchapter.

(2) On receipt of an application of a carrier under this section the Commission shall notify, and file a copy of the application with, the chief executive officer of each State in which that carrier operates. The appropriate authorities of those States are entitled to be admitted as parties to a proceeding under this section to represent the rights and interests of their people and States.

Notice.

(c) The carrier must give notice of the proceeding to the holders of the class of securities affected. The Commission may direct the carrier to give notice to other persons the Commission determines to have an interest in the proceeding. The carrier may give notice under this subsection only after it gets assurances of assent when they are required under this section.

(d) The Commission may impose conditions governing the proposed change. The Commission may determine the effective date for a change it approves and authorizes under this subchapter and may allow it to become effective on publication of a declaration to that effect by the carrier. After an application is approved, the Commission may change a condition imposed and impose supplemental requirements for good cause shown subject to the requirements of this subchapter.

49 USC 11363.

§ 11363. Assent of holders of securities and certain other instruments

(a)(1) After making the findings required under section 11362(a) of this title, the Commission may approve and authorize the change if it is assented to by the holders of at least 75 percent of the aggregate principal amount or number of outstanding shares of each class of securities affected by the change. The Commission may increase the percentage required for assent under this subsection for a class of shares when an increase is in the public interest and—

(A) 75 percent of the shares in that class are held by less than 25 security holders; or

(B) that class is entitled to vote for the election of directors of the carrier and the Commission determines that the assent of at least 25 percent of the security holders of that class are controlled by the carrier or a person controlling the carrier.

(2) The carrier may withdraw its application after the Commission makes the findings required under section 11362(a) of this title. If the application is not withdrawn, the Commission must require the carrier to submit the proposed change, with conditions imposed by the Commission, to the holders of each class of its securities affected by the change for their assent or rejection.

(b)(1) In determining the percentage of outstanding securities when making a finding under section 11362(a) of this title, a security that secures an evidence of indebtedness of the carrier or of a company controlling or controlled by the carrier is considered to be outstanding unless the Commission determines that the proposed change does not materially affect the interest of the holder of that evidence of indebtedness. When that security is considered to be outstanding, assent to a proposed change may be given, notwithstanding another instrument, only—

(A) if the security is pledged as security under an instrument under which an evidence of indebtedness was issued and is outstanding, by the holder of a majority of the principal amount of the evidence of indebtedness; or

(B) if the security secures an evidence of indebtedness not issued under an instrument under which an evidence of indebtedness was issued, by the holder of the evidence of indebtedness.

(2) In addition to a submission required under subsection (a) of this section, the Commission shall require the carrier to submit a proposed change to a security referred to in this subsection, with requirements imposed by the Commission, to the holder of the evidence of indebtedness referred to in paragraph (1) (A) and (B) of this subsection as appropriate, for assent or rejection. A carrier is not required to submit the change to the trustee of the instrument referred to in that paragraph.

(c) If the Commission determines that the assent of the holder of a security not entitled to vote for the election of directors of the carrier or an evidence of indebtedness is in the control of the carrier or of a person controlling the carrier, that security or evidence of indebtedness is not considered to be outstanding.

§ 11364. Procedure

49 USC 11364.

(a) The Commission may prescribe the manner in which assents, assurances of assent, or rejections of the security holders may be solicited whether the solicitation is made before or after the Commission approves and authorizes the proposed change.

(b) The Commission may approve a bank or trust company, incorporated under the law of the United States or a State, that is a member of the Federal Reserve System and has a capital and surplus of at least $2,000,000, to receive assents and revocations of assents from security holders. The Commission may require the security holders to send those assents and revocations to that bank or trust company. That bank or trust company shall certify the result of the submission to the Commission. The Commission may rely on that certification as conclusive evidence in determining the result of that submission.

§ 11365. Effect of change on other persons

49 USC 11365.

(a) When a change becomes effective under this subchapter, the change is binding on, and changes the rights of—

(1) each holder of a security of the carrier of each class affected by the change; and

(2) a trustee or other party to an instrument under which a class of securities has been issued or by which it is secured.

(b) An authorization and approval of a change under this subchapter is authority for, and approval of, a corresponding change of the obligation of another carrier that assumed liability related to that class of securities if that carrier consents to the change in writing. When consent is given, the corresponding change becomes effective when the change of the class of securities or instrument becomes binding. A person who is liable or obligated on a class of securities issued by a carrier is a carrier with respect to that class for the purposes of this subchapter.

§ 11366. Reports

49 USC 11366.

A carrier receiving approval and authorization to make a change under this subchapter shall report the action taken by it in making that change to the Interstate Commerce Commission. The Commission may require periodic or special reports.

49 USC 11367.

§ 11367. Application of other laws

(a) Section 78n(a) of title 15 does not apply to a solicitation related to a proposed change under this subchapter.

(b) If the Interstate Commerce Commission finds an issuance of a security, that is an interest in a railroad equipment trust as defined in section 77c(a)(6) of title 15, under this subchapter complies with section 11301 of this title, it is considered to be an issuance subject to section 11301 within the meaning of section 77c(a)(6) of title 15. Section 77e of that title does not apply to the issuance, sale, or exchange of certificates of deposit representing securities of, or claims against, a carrier that are issued by committees in proceedings under this subchapter. Those certificates and transactions under this subchapter are exempt from subchapter I of chapter 2A of title 15.

15 USC 77a.

CHAPTER 115—FEDERAL-STATE RELATIONS

49 USC 11501.

§ 11501. Interstate Commerce Commission authority over intrastate transportation

(a)(1) The Interstate Commerce Commission shall prescribe the rate, classification, rule, or practice for transportation or service provided by a carrier subject to the jurisdiction of the Commission under subchapter I or IV of chapter 105 of this title when the Commission finds that a rate, classification, rule, or practice of a State causes—

Ante, pp. 1359, 1369.

(A) between persons or localities in intrastate commerce and in interstate and foreign commerce, unreasonable discrimination against those persons or localities in interstate or foreign commerce; or

(B) unreasonable discrimination against or imposes an unreasonable burden on interstate or foreign commerce.

(2) The Commission may make a finding under this subsection involving a carrier providing transportation subject to its jurisdiction under subchapter I of chapter 105 of this title without separating interstate and intrastate property, revenues, and expenses, and without considering the total operations, or their results, of a carrier or group of carriers operating entirely in one State.

(b)(1) The Commission has exclusive authority to prescribe an intrastate rate for transportation provided by a rail carrier subject to the jurisdiction of the Commission under subchapter I of chapter 105 of this title when—

(A) a rail carrier files with an appropriate State authority a change in an intrastate rate, or a change in a classifiction, rule, or practice that has the effect of changing an intrastate rate, that adjusts the rate to the rate charged on similar traffic moving in interstate or foreign commerce; and

(B) the State authority does not act finally on the change by the 120th day after it was filed.

(2) When a rail carrier files an application with the Commission under this subsection, the Commission shall prescribe the intrastate rate under the standards of subsection (a) of this section. Notice of the application shall be served on the State authority.

(c) The Commission may take action under this section only after a full hearing. Action of the Commission under this section supersedes State law or action taken under State law in conflict with the action of the Commission.

§ 11502. Conferences and joint hearings with State authorities

(a)(1) In carrying out this subtitle as it applies to a class of persons providing transportation or service subject to the jurisdiction of the Interstate Commerce Commission under subchapter I, III, or IV of chapter 105 of this title, the Commission may—

(A) confer and hold joint hearings with the State authorities having regulatory jurisdiction of that class when the conference or hearing is related to an investigation of the relationship between rate structures and practices of carriers providing transportation or service subject to the jurisdiction of the State authorities and of the Commission, and the Commission may take action as a result of the investigation that may affect the rate-making authority of a State; and

(B) cooperate with and use the services, records, and facilities of the State authorities.

(2) In carrying out this subtitle as it applies to motor carriers and brokers providing transportation subject to the jurisdiction of the Commission under subchapter II of chapter 105 of this title, the Commission may—

(A) confer and hold joint hearings with State authorities;

(B) cooperate with and use the services, records, and facilities of State authorities; and

(C) make cooperative agreements with a State to enforce the economic laws and regulations of a State and the United States concerning highway transportation.

(b) When an investigation under this subtitle involving a common carrier providing transportation or service subject to the jurisdiction of the Commission under subchapter I or IV of chapter 105 of this title, is about a rate, classification, rule, or practice of a State, the Commission shall notify the interested State of the proceeding before disposing of the issue.

(c) When a representative of a State authority sits with the Commission in an investigation about a carrier subject to the jurisdiction of the Commission under subchapter I or III of chapter 105 of this title, the representative may be given an allowance for travel and subsistence expenses. The Commission may determine the amount of the allowance.

§ 11503. Tax discrimination against rail transportation property

(a) In this section—

(1) "assessment" means valuation for a property tax levied by a taxing district.

(2) "assessment jurisdiction" means a geographical area in a State used in determining the assessed value of property for ad valorem taxation.

(3) "rail transportation property" means property, as defined by the Interstate Commerce Commission, owned or used by a rail carrier providing transportation subject to the jurisdiction of the Commission under subchapter I of chapter 105 of this title.

(4) "commercial and industrial property" means property, other than transportation property and land used primarily for

---

Margin notes:

Hearing.

49 USC 11502.

Ante, pp. 1359, 1365, 1369.

Ante, p. 1361.

Travel and subsistence allowances.

49 USC 11503. Definitions.

agricultural purposes or timber growing, devoted to a commercial or industrial use and subject to a property tax levy.

(b) The following acts unreasonably burden and discriminate against interstate commerce, and a State, subdivision of a State, or authority acting for a State or subdivision of a State may not do any of them:

(1) assess rail transportation property at a value that has a higher ratio to the true market value of the rail transportation property than the ratio that the assessed value of other commercial and industrial property in the same assessment jurisdiction has to the true market value of the other commercial and industrial property.

(2) levy or collect a tax on an assessment that may not be made under clause (1) of this subsection.

(3) levy or collect an ad valorem property tax on rail transportation property at a tax rate that exceeds the tax rate applicable to commercial and industrial property in the same assessment jurisdiction.

(4) impose another tax that discriminates against a rail carrier providing transportation subject to the jurisdiction of the Commission under subchapter I of chapter 105 of this title.

(c) Notwithstanding section 1341 of title 28 and without regard to the amount in controversy or citizenship of the parties, a district court of the United States has jurisdiction, concurrent with other jurisdiction of courts of the United States and the States, to prevent a violation of subsection (b) of this section. Relief may be granted under this subsection only if the ratio of assessed value to true market value of rail transportation property exceeds by at least 5 percent, the ratio of assessed value to true market value of other commercial and industrial property in the same assessment jurisdiction. The burden of proof in determining assessed value and true market value is governed by State law. If the ratio of the assessed value of other commercial and industrial property in the assessment jurisdiction to the true market value of all other commercial and industrial property cannot be determined to the satisfaction of the district court through the random-sampling method known as a sales assessment ratio study (to be carried out under statistical principles applicable to such a study), the court shall find, as a violation of this section—

(1) an assessment of the rail transportation property at a value that has a higher ratio to the true market value of the rail transportation property than the assessed value of all other property subject to a property tax levy in the assessment jurisdiction has to the true market value of all other commercial and industrial property; and

(2) the collection of an ad valorem property tax on the rail transportation property at a tax rate that exceeds the tax ratio rate applicable to taxable property in the taxing district.

49 USC 11504.

§ 11504. **Withholding State and local income tax by certain carriers**

(a)(1) In this subsection, an employee is deemed to have earned more than 50 percent of pay in a State or subdivision of a State if the employee—

(A) performs regularly assigned duties on a locomotive, car, or other track-borne vehicle in at least 2 States and the mileage traveled in one State or subdivision of that State is more than 50 percent of the total mileage traveled by the employee while employed during the calendar year; or

(B) is engaged principally in maintaining roadways, signals, communications, and structures or in operating motortrucks from railroad terminals in at least 2 States and the percent of the time worked by the employee in one State or subdivision of that State is more than 50 percent of the total time worked by the employee while employed during the calendar year.

(2) A rail, express, or sleeping car carrier providing transportation subject to the jurisdiction of the Interstate Commerce Commission under subchapter I of chapter 105 of this title shall withhold from the pay of an employee referred to in paragraph (1) of this subsection only income tax required to be withheld by the laws of a State, or subdivision of that State— *Ante,* p. 1359.

(A) in which the employee earns more than 50 percent of the pay received by the employee from the carrier; or

(B) that is the residence of the employee (as shown on the employment records of the carrier), if the employee did not earn in one State or subdivision more than 50 percent of the pay received by the employee from the carrier during the preceding calendar year.

(b)(1) In this subsection—

(A) "State" includes a State, territory, or possession of the United States, and the Commonwealth of Puerto Rico. "State."

(B) an employee is deemed to have earned more than 50 percent of pay in a State or subdivision of a State in which the mileage traveled by the employee in that State or subdivision is more than 50 percent of the total mileage traveled by the employee while employed during the calendar year.

(2) A motor carrier providing transportation subject to the jurisdiction of the Commission under subchapter II of chapter 105 of this title and a motor private carrier shall withhold from the pay of an employee having regularly assigned duties on a motor vehicle in at least 2 States, only income tax required to be withheld by the laws of a State, or subdivision of that State— *Ante,* p. 1361.

(A) in which the employee earns more than 50 percent of the pay received by the employee from the carrier; or

(B) that is the residence of the employee (as shown on the employment records of the carrier), if the employee did not earn in one State or subdivision more than 50 percent of the pay received by the employee from the carrier during the preceding calendar year.

(c)(1) In this subsection, an employee is deemed to have earned more than 50 percent of pay in a State or subdivision of that State in which the time worked by the employee in the State or subdivision is more than 50 percent of the total time worked by the employee while employed during the calendar year.

(2) A water carrier providing transportation subject to the jurisdiction of the Commission under subchapter III of chapter 105 of this title or a water carrier or class of water carriers providing transportation on inland or coastal waters under an exemption under this subtitle shall file income tax information returns and other reports only with— *Ante,* p. 1365.

(A) the State and subdivision of residence of the employee (as shown on the employment records of the carrier); and

(B) the State and subdivision in which the employee earned more than 50 percent of the pay received by the employee from the carrier during the preceding calendar year.

(3) This subsection applies to pay of a master, officer, or seaman who is a member of the crew on a vessel engaged in foreign, coastwise, intercoastal or noncontiguous trade or in the fisheries of the United States.

(d) A rail, express, sleeping car, motor, and motor private carrier withholding pay from an employee under subsection (a) or (b) of this section shall file income tax information returns and other reports only with—

(1) the State and subdivision of residence of the employee; and

(2) the State and subdivision in which withholding of pay is required under subsection (a) or (b) of this section.

49 USC 11505.

§ 11505. State action to enjoin rail carriers from certain actions

(a) The attorney general of a State or transportation regulatory authority of a State or area affected by a violation of sections 10901–10907 of this title, may bring a civil action to enjoin a rail carrier from violating those sections.

Ante, pp. 1402-1407.

(b) A transportation regulatory authority of a State affected by an abandonment of service by a freight forwarder in violation of section 10933 of this title may bring a civil action to enjoin the abandonment.

Ante, p. 1418.

49 USC 11506.

§ 11506. Registration of motor carriers by a State

"Standards," and "amendments to standards."

(a) In this section, "standards" and "amendments to standards" mean the specification of forms and procedures required by regulations of the Interstate Commerce Commission to prove the lawfulness of transportation by motor carrier referred to in section 10521(a) (1) and (2) of this title by—

Ante, p. 1361.

(1) filing and maintaining certificates and permits issued to the motor carrier by the Commission;

(2) registering motor vehicles operating under the certificates and permits;

(3) filing and maintaining proof of required insurance coverage or qualification as a self-insurer; and

(4) filing the name of a local agent for service of process.

(b) The requirement of a State that a motor carrier, providing transportation subject to the jurisdiction of the Commission under subchapter II of chapter 105 of this title and providing transportation in that State, register the certificate or permit issued to the carrier under section 10922 or 10923 of this title is not an unreasonable burden on transportation referred to in section 10521(a) (1) and (2) of this title when the registration is completed under standards of the Commission under subsection (c) of this section. When a State registration requirement imposes obligations in excess of the standards, the part in excess is an unreasonable burden.

Ante, p. 1361.

Ante, pp. 1409, 1410.

Ante, p. 1361.

(c) (1) The Commission shall maintain standards and amendments to standards (A) prepared and certified to it by the national organization of the State Commissions, and (B) prescribed by the Commission. If the national organization determines to withdraw entirely standards prescribed by the Commission, the Commission shall prescribe new standards by the end of the first year after the national organization determines to withdraw the standards.

(2) An amendment to the standards prepared and certified by the national organization and prescribed by the Commission is effective

when the amendment is prescribed or at another time as determined by the national organization.

(d) The national organization shall consult with the Commission and representatives of motor carriers subject to the State registration requirement when preparing amendments to the standards. Different amendments may be prescribed for each class of motor carriers as warranted by the differences in the operations of each class.

(e) This section does not—

(1) authorize standards in conflict with regulations of the Commission; or

(2) affect the authority of the Commission to interpret its regulations and certificates and permits issued under section 10922 or 10923 of this title.

Ante, pp. 1409, 1410.

§ 11507. Prison-made property governed by State law

49 USC 11507.

Goods, wares, and merchandise produced or mined in a penal institution or by a prisoner not on parole or probation and transported into and used, sold, or stored in a State or territory or possession of the United States, is subject to the laws of that State, territory, or possession. This section does not apply to commodities produced in a penal institution of the United States Government for its use.

CHAPTER 117—ENFORCEMENT: INVESTIGATIONS, RIGHTS, AND REMEDIES

§ 11701. General authority

49 USC 11701.

(a) The Interstate Commerce Commission may begin an investigation under this subtitle on its own initiative or on complaint. If the Commission finds that a carrier or broker is violating this subtitle, the Commission shall take appropriate action to compel compliance with this subtitle. The Commission may take that action only after giving the carrier or broker notice of the investigation and an opportunity for a proceeding.

Investigations.

Notice.

(b) A person, including a governmental authority, may file with the Commission a complaint about a violation of this subtitle by a carrier providing, or broker for, transportation or service subject to the jurisdiction of the Commission under this subtitle. The complaint must state the facts that are the subject of the violation and, if it is against a water carrier, must be made under oath. The Commission may dismiss a complaint it determines does not state reasonable grounds for investigation and action. However, the Commission may not dismiss a complaint made against a common carrier providing transportation subject to the jurisdiction of the Commission under subchapter I of chapter 105 of this title because of the absence of direct damage to the complainant.

Complaints.

Ante, p. 1359.

(c) A formal investigative proceeding begun by the Commission under subsection (a) of this section related to a rail carrier is dismissed automatically unless it is concluded by the Commission with administrative finality by the end of the 3d year after the date on which it was begun.

49 USC 11702.

§ 11702. Enforcement by the Interstate Commerce Commission

(a) The Interstate Commerce Commission may bring a civil action—

Ante, pp. 1409, 1410, 1418.

(1) to enjoin a rail carrier from violating section 10901-10907 or 10933 of this title, or a regulation prescribed or certificate issued under any of those sections;

Ante, p. 1415, 1433, 1434.

(2) to enforce section 10930 or 11323 of this title, or subchapter III of chapter 113 of this title and to compel compliance with the order of the Commission under any of those sections and that subchapter;

(3) to enforce an order of the Commission, except a civil action to enforce an order for the payment of money, when it is violated by a carrier providing transportation subject to the jurisdiction of the Commission under subchapter I of chapter 105 of this title;

(4) to enforce this subtitle (except a civil action under a provision of this subtitle governing the reasonableness and discriminatory character of rates), or a regulation or order of the Commission or a certificate or permit issued under this subtitle when violated by a motor carrier or broker providing transportation subject to the jurisdiction of the Commission under subchapter II

Ante, p. 1361.

of chapter 105 of this title;

(5) to enforce this subtitle (except a civil action under a provision of this subtitle governing the reasonableness and discrimitory character of rates), or a regulation or order of the Commission or a certificate or permit issued under this subtitle, except a civil action to enforce an order for the payment of money, when violated by a carrier providing transportation subject to the jurisdiction of the Commission under subchapter III of chapter

Ante, p. 1365.

105 of this title; and

Ante, p. 1369.

(6) to enforce this subtitle, or a regulation or order of the Commission or permit issued under this subtitle when violated by a carrier providing service subject to the jurisdiction of the Commission under subchapter IV of chapter 105 of this title.

(b) In a civil action under subsection (a) (4) of this section—

(1) trial is in the judicial district in which the motor carrier or broker operates;

(2) process may be served without regard to the territorial limits of the district or of the State in which the action is instituted; and

(3) a person participating with a carrier or broker in a violation may be joined in the civil action without regard to the residence of the person.

49 USC 11703.

§ 11703. Enforcement by the Attorney General

(a) The Attorney General may, and on request of the Interstate Commerce Commission shall, bring court proceedings to enforce this subtitle or a regulation or order of the Commission or certificate or permit issued under this subtitle and to prosecute a person violating this subtitle or a regulation or order of the Commission or certificate or permit issued under this subtitle.

(b) The United States Government may bring a civil action on behalf of a person to compel a common carrier providing transportation or service subject to the jurisdiction of the Commission under

Ante, p. 1359.

chapter 105 of this title to provide that transportation or service to that person in compliance with this subtitle at the same rate charged, or on conditions as favorable as those given by the carrier, for like traffic under similar conditions to another person.

§ 11704. Action by a private person to enjoin abandonment of service

An interested person may bring a civil action to enjoin an abandonment of service in violation of section 10933 of this title or a certificate issued under that section.

49 USC 11704.

Ante, p. 1418.

§ 11705. Rights and remedies of persons injured by certain carriers

49 USC 11705.

(a) A person injured because a carrier providing transportation or service subject to the jurisdiction of the Interstate Commerce Commission under chapter 105 of this title does not obey an order of the Commission, except an order for the payment of money, may bring a civil action to enforce that order under this subsection.

Ante, p. 1359.

(b)(1) A common carrier providing transportation or service subject to the jurisdiction of the Commission under chapter 105 of this title is liable to a person for amounts charged that exceed the applicable rate for transportation or service contained in a tariff filed under subchapter IV of chapter 107 of this title.

Ante, p. 1394.

(2) A common carrier providing transportation subject to the jurisdiction of the Commission under subchapter I or III of chapter 105 of this title is liable for damages sustained by a person as a result of an act or omission of that carrier in violation of this subtitle.

Ante, pp. 1359, 1365.

(3) A common carrier providing transportation or service subject to the jurisdiction of the Commission under subchapter II or IV of chapter 105 of this title is liable for damages resulting from the imposition of rates for transportation or service the Commission finds to be in violation of this subtitle.

Ante, pp. 1361, 1369.

(c)(1) A person may file a complaint with the Commission under section 11701(b) of this title or bring a civil action under subsection (b)(1) or (2) of this section to enforce liability against a common carrier providing transportation subject to the jurisdiction of the Commission under subchapter I or III of chapter 105 of this title. A person may begin a proceeding under section 10704 or 10705 of this title to enforce liability under subsection (b)(3) of this section by filing a complaint with the Commission under section 11701(b) of this title.

(2) When the Commission makes an award under subsection (b) of this section, the Commission shall order the carrier to pay the amount awarded by a specific date. The Commission may order a carrier providing transportation subject to the jurisdiction of the Commission under subchapter I or III of chapter 105 of this title to pay damages only when the proceeding is on complaint. The person for whose benefit an order of the Commission requiring the payment of money is made may bring a civil action to enforce that order under this paragraph if the carrier does not pay the amount awarded by the date payment was ordered to be made.

(d)(1) When a person begins a civil action under subsection (b) of this section to enforce an order of the Commission requiring the payment of damages by a common carrier providing transportation subject to the jurisdiction of the Commission under subchapter I or III of chapter 105 of this title, the text of the order of the Commission must be included in the complaint. In addition to the district courts of the United States, a State court of general jurisdiction having jurisdiction of the parties has jurisdiction to enforce an order under this paragraph. The findings and order of the Commission are competent evidence of the facts stated in them. Trial in a civil action brought in a district court of the United States under this paragraph is in the judicial district (A) in which the plaintiff resides, (B) in which the principal operating office of the carrier is located, (C) if a rail carrier, through which the railroad line of that carrier runs, or (D) if a water carrier, in which a port of call on a route operated by that carrier is located. In a civil action under this paragraph, the plaintiff is liable for only those costs that accrue on an appeal taken by the plaintiff.

(2) All parties in whose favor the award was made may be joined as plaintiffs in a civil action brought in a district court of the United States under this subsection and all the carriers that are parties to the order awarding damages may be joined as defendants. Trial in the action is in the judicial district in which any one of the plaintiffs could bring the action against any one of the defendants. Process may be served on a defendant at its principal operating office when that defendant is not in the district in which the action is brought. A judgment ordering recovery may be made in favor of any of those plaintiffs against the defendant found to be liable to that plaintiff.

(3) The district court shall award a reasonable attorney's fee as a part of the damages for which a carrier is found liable under this subsection. The district court shall tax and collect that fee as a part of the costs of the action.

49 USC 11706.

§ 11706. Limitation on actions by and against common carriers

(a) A common carrier providing transportation or service subject to the jurisdiction of the Interstate Commerce Commission under chapter 105 of this title must begin a civil action to recover charges for transportation or service provided by the carrier within 3 years after the claim accrues.

Ante, p. 1359.

(b) A person must begin a civil action to recover overcharges under section 11705(b)(1) of this title within 3 years after the claim accrues. If that claim is against a common carrier providing transportation subject to the jurisdiction of the Commission under subchapter I or III of chapter 105 of this title and an election to file a complaint with the Commission is made under section 11705(c)(1), the complaint must be filed within 3 years after the claim accrues.

(c)(1) A person must file a complaint with the Commission to recover damages under section 11705(b)(2) of this title within 2 years after the claim accrues.

(2) A person must begin a civil action to recover damages under section 11705(b)(3) of this title within 2 years after the claim accrues.

(d) The 3-year period under subsection (b) of this section is extended for 6 months from the time written notice is given to the claimant by the carrier of disallowance of any part of the claim specified in the notice if a written claim is given to the carrier within that 3-year period. The 3-year period under subsection (b) of this section and the 2-year period under subsection (c)(1) of this section are each extended for 90 days from the time the carrier begins a civil action under subsection (a) of this section to recover charges related to the same transportation or service, or collects (without beginning a civil action under that subsection) the charge for that transportation or service if that action is begun or collection is made within the appropriate period.

(e) A person must begin a civil action to enforce an order of the Commission against a carrier for the payment of money within one year after the date the order required the money to be paid.

(f) This section applies to transportation for the United States Government. The time limitations under this section are extended, as related to transportation for or on behalf of the United States Government, for 3 years from the date of (1) payment of the rate for the transportation or service involved, (2) subsequent refund for overpayment of that rate, or (3) deduction made under section 244 of title 31, whichever is later.

(g) A claim related to a shipment of property accrues under this section on delivery or tender of delivery by the carrier.

§ 11707. Liability of common carriers under receipts and bills of lading

49 USC 11707.

(a) (1) A common carrier providing transportation or service subject to the jurisdiction of the Interstate Commerce Commission under subchapter I, II, or IV of chapter 105 of this title shall issue a receipt or bill of lading for property it receives for transportation under this subtitle. That carrier and any other common carrier that delivers the property and is providing transportation or service subject to the jurisdiction of the Commission under subchapter I, II, or IV are liable to the person entitled to recover under the receipt or bill of lading. The liability imposed under this paragraph is for the actual loss or injury to the property caused by (1) the receiving carrier, (2) the delivering carrier, or (3) another carrier over whose line or route the property is transported in the United States or from a place in the United States to a place in an adjacent foreign country when transported under a through bill of lading and applies to property reconsigned or diverted under a tariff filed under subchapter IV of chapter 107 of this title. Failure to issue a receipt or bill of lading does not affect the liability of a carrier. A delivering carrier is deemed to be the carrier performing the line-haul transportation nearest the destination but does not include a carrier providing only a switching service at the destination.

Ante, pp. 1359, 1361, 1369.

Ante, p. 1394.

(2) A freight forwarder is both the receiving and delivering carrier. When a freight forwarder provides service subject to this subtitle and uses a motor common carrier providing transportation subject to the jurisdiction of the Commission under subchapter II of chapter 105 of this title to receive property from a consignor, the motor common carrier may execute the bill of lading or shipping receipt for the freight forwarder with its consent. With the consent of the freight forwarder, a motor common carrier may deliver property for a freight forwarder on the freight forwarder's bill of lading, freight bill, or shipping receipt to the consignee named in it, and receipt for the property may be made on the freight forwarder's delivery receipt.

(b) The carrier issuing the receipt or bill of lading under subsection (a) of this section or delivering the property for which the receipt or bill of lading was issued is entitled to recover from the carrier over whose line or route the loss or injury occurred the amount required to be paid to the owners of the property, as evidenced by a receipt, judgment, or transcript, and the amount of its expenses reasonably incurred in defending a civil action brought by that person.

(c) (1) A common carrier may not limit or be exempt from liability imposed under subsection (a) of this section except as provided in this subsection. A limitation of liability or of the amount of recovery or representation or agreement in a receipt, bill of lading, contract, rule, or tariff filed with the Commission in violation of this section is void.

(2) If loss or injury to property occurs while it is in the custody of a water carrier, the liability of that carrier is determined by its bill of lading and the law applicable to water transportation. The liability of the initial or delivering carrier is the same as the liability of the water carrier.

(3) A common carrier of passengers may limit its liability under its passenger rate for loss or injury of baggage carried on passenger trains, boats, or motor vehicles, or on trains, or boats, or motor vehicles carrying passengers.

Ante, p. 1389.

(4) A common carrier may limit its liability for loss or injury of property transported under section 10730 of this title.

(d) A civil action under this section may be brought against a delivering carrier in a district court of the United States or in a State court. Trial, if the action is brought in a district court of the United States is in a judicial district, and if in a State court, is in a State, through which the defendant carrier operates a railroad or route.

(e) A carrier may not provide by rule, contract, or otherwise, a period of less than 9 months for filing a claim against it under this section and a period of less than 2 years for bringing a civil action against it under this section. The period for bringing a civil action is computed from the date that person receives written notice from the carrier that it has disallowed any part of the claim specified in the notice.

49 USC 11708.

§ 11708. Private enforcement: motor carrier and freight forwarder licensing

(a) If a person provides transportation by motor vehicle or service of a freight forwarder in clear violation of section 10921–10924, 10927, 10930–10932, or 11323 of this title, a person injured by the transportation or service may bring a civil action to enforce any such section. In a civil action under this subsection, trial is in the judicial district in which the person who violated that section operates.

Ante, pp.
1409–1412,
1413,
1415–1417,
1333.

(b) A copy of the complaint in a civil action under subsection (a) of this section shall be served on the Interstate Commerce Commission and a certificate of service must appear in the complaint filed with the court. The Commission may intervene in a civil action under subsection (a) of this section. The Commission may notify the district court in which the action is pending that it intends to consider the matter that is the subject of the complaint in a proceeding before the Commission. When that notice is filed, the court shall stay further action pending disposition of the proceeding before the Commission.

Notification.

(c) In a civil action under subsection (a) of this section, the court may determine the amount of and award a reasonable attorney's fee to the prevailing party. That fee is in addition to costs allowable under the Federal Rules of Civil Procedure.

49 USC 11709.

§ 11709. Liability for issuance of securities by certain carriers

A carrier issuing a security or assuming an obligation or liability that is void under section 11301 of this title and its directors, officers, attorneys, and other agents who participate in authorizing, issuing, hypothecating, or selling that security, or in authorizing the assumption of that obligation or liability, are jointly and severally liable for the damages sustained by a person who acquires for value, in good faith, and without notice that the issue or assumption is void (1) that security, or (2) a security under which an assumption or liability is void. If a security void under that section is acquired directly from the carrier issuing it, the holder may rescind the transaction and recover

Ante, p. 1428.

the consideration given for the security when it is surrendered to that carrier.

§ 11710. Liability when property is delivered in violation of routing instructions

49 USC 11710.

(a) (1) When a carrier providing transportation subject to the jurisdiction of the Interstate Commerce Commission under subchapter I of chapter 105 of this title diverts or delivers property to another carrier in violation of routing instructions in the bill of lading, both of those carriers are jointly and severally liable to the carrier that was deprived of its right to participate in hauling that property for the total amount of the rate it would have received if it participated in hauling the property.

Ante, p. 1359.

(2) A carrier is not liable under paragraph (1) of this subsection when it diverts or delivers property in compliance with an order or regulation of the Commission.

(3) A carrier to whom property is transported is not liable under this subsection if it shows that it had no notice of the routing instructions before transporting the property. The burden of proving lack of notice is on that carrier.

(b) The court shall award a reasonable attorney's fee to the plaintiff in a judgment against the defendant carrier under subsection (a) of this section. The court shall tax and collect that fee as a part of the costs of the action.

CHAPTER 119—CIVIL AND CRIMINAL PENALTIES

§ 11901. General civil penalties

49 USC 11901.

(a) Except as otherwise provided in this section, a common carrier providing transportation subject to the jurisdiction of the Interstate Commerce Commission under subchapter I of chapter 105 of this title, an officer or agent of that carrier or a receiver, trustee, lessee, or agent of one of them, knowingly violating an order of the Commission under this subtitle is liable to the United States Government for a civil penalty of $5,000 for each violation. Liability under this subsection is incurred for each distinct violation. A separate violation occurs for each day the violation continues.

(b) A common carrier providing transportation subject to the jurisdiction of the Commission under subchapter I of chapter 105 of this title, or a receiver or trustee of that carrier, violating a regulation or order of the Commission under section 10761, 10762, 10764, 10765, or

Ante, pp. 1394, 1397.

Ante, p. 1425.

11128(a)(2) or (b) of this title is liable to the United States Government for a civil penalty of $500 for each violation and for $25 for each day the violation continues.

Ante, p. 1398.

(c) A carrier, receiver, or trustee violating subchapter V of chapter 107 of this title, or a regulation under that subchapter, is liable to the United States Government for a civil penalty of $500 for each violation. A separate violation occurs each day the violation continues.

Ante, pp. 1402-1407.

(d) A person knowingly authorizing, consenting to, or permitting a violation of sections 10901-10907 of this title or of a condition of a certificate or a regulation under any of those sections, is liable to the United States Government for a civil penalty of not more than $5,000.

Ante, pp. 1422-1425.

(e)(1) A carrier, receiver, or operating trustee violating an order or direction of the Commission under section 11123, 11124, 11125, 11127, or 11128 (a)(1) of this title is liable to the United States Government for a civil penalty of at least $100 but not more than $500 for each violation and for $50 for each day the violation continues.

Ante, p. 1424.

(2) A rail carrier, receiver, or operating trustee violating section 11126 of this title is liable to the United States Government for a civil penalty of $100 for each violation. A separate violation occurs for each car not counted when a car count is required under that section.

Ante, p. 1425.

Ante, p. 1359.

(f)(1) A person required under subchapter III of chapter 111 of this title to make, prepare, preserve, or submit to the Commission a record concerning transportation subject to the jurisdiction of the Commission under subchapter I of chapter 105 of this title that does not make, prepare, preserve, or submit that record as required under that subchapter, is liable to the United States Government for a civil penalty of $500 for each violation.

Ante, p. 1426.

(2) A carrier providing transportation subject to the jurisdiction of the Commission under subchapter I of chapter 105 of this title, and a lessor, receiver, or trustee of that carrier, violating section 11144 (b)(1) of this title, is liable to the United States Government for a civil penalty of $100 for each violation.

(3) A carrier providing transportation subject to the jurisdiction of the Commission under subchapter I of chapter 105 of this title, a lessor, receiver, or trustee of that carrier, a person furnishing cars or protective services against heat or cold, and an officer, agent, or employee of one of them, required to make a report to the Commission or answer a question that does not make the report or does not specifically, completely, and truthfully answer the question, is liable to the United States Government for a civil penalty of $100 for each violation.

(4) A separate violation occurs for each day a violation under this subsection continues.

Ante, p. 1361.

Ante, p. 1409.

(g) A person required to make a report to the Commission, answer a question, or make, prepare, or preserve a record under this subtitle concerning transportation subject to the jurisdiction of the Commission under subchapter II of chapter 105 of this title, or an officer, agent, or employee of that person that (1) does not make the report, (2) does not specifically, completely, and truthfully answer the question, (3) does not make, prepare, or preserve the record in the form and manner prescribed by the Commission, or (4) does not comply with section 10921 of this title, is liable to the United States Government for a civil penalty of not more than $500 for each violation and for not more than $250 for each additional day the violation continues.

(h)(1) Trial in a civil action under subsections (a)-(f) of this section is in the judicial district in which the carrier has its principal operating office or in a district through which the railroad of the carrier runs.

(2) Trial in a civil action under subsection (g) of this section is in the judicial district in which (A) the motor carrier or broker has its principal office, (B) the motor carrier or broker was authorized to provide transportation under this subtitle when the violation occurred, (C) the violation occurred, or (D) the offender is found. Process in the action may be served in the judicial district of which the offender is an inhabitant or in which the offender may be found.

§ 11902. Civil penalty for accepting rebates from common carrier

49 USC 11902.

A person (1) delivering property to a common carrier providing transportation or service subject to the jurisdiction of the Interstate Commerce Commission under chapter 105 of this title for transportation under this subtitle or for whom that carrier will transport the property as consignor or consignee for that person from a State or territory or possession of the United States to another State or possession, territory, or to a foreign country, and (2) knowingly accepting or receiving by any means a rebate or offset against the rate for transportation for, or service of, that property contained in a tariff filed with the Commission under subchapter IV of chapter 107 of this title, is liable to the United States Government for a civil penalty in an amount equal to 3 times the amount of money that person accepted or received as a rebate or offset and 3 times the value of other consideration accepted or received as a rebate or offset. In a civil action under this section, all money or other consideration received by the person during a period of 6 years before an action is brought under this section may be included in determining the amount of the penalty, and if that total amount is included, the penalty shall be 3 times that total amount.

Ante, p. 1394.

§ 11903. Rate, discrimination, and tariff violations

49 USC 11903.

(a) A person that knowingly offers, grants, gives, solicits, accepts, or receives by any means transportation or service provided for property by a common carrier subject to the jurisdiction of the Interstate Commerce Commission under chapter 105 of this title (1) at less than the rate in effect under chapter 107 of this title, or (2) by practicing discrimination, shall be fined at least $1,000 but not more than $20,000, imprisoned for not more than 2 years, or both.

Ante, p. 1359.
Ante, p. 1371.

(b) A carrier providing transportation or service subject to the jurisdiction of the Commission under chapter 105 of this title or an officer, director, receiver, trustee, lessee, agent, or employee of a corporation that is subject to the jurisdiction of the Commission under that chapter, that willfully does not file and publish its rates or tariffs as required under chapter 107 of this title or observe those tariffs until changed under law, shall be fined at least $1,000 but not more than $20,000, imprisoned for not more than 2 years, or both.

(c) When acting in the scope of their employment, the actions and omissions of persons acting for or employed by a carrier or shipper that is subject to subsection (a) or (b) of this section are considered to be the actions and omissions of that carrier or shipper as well as that person.

(d) Trial in a criminal action under this section is in the judicial district in which any part of the violation is committed or through which the transportation is conducted.

§ 11904. Additional rate and discrimination violations

49 USC 11904.

(a)(1) A common carrier providing transportation subject to the jurisdiction of the Interstate Commerce Commission under sub-

Ante, p. 1359.
chapter I of chapter 105 of this title, and when that carrier is a corporation, an officer, employee, or agent of the corporation, that by any means knowingly and willfully assists a person in getting, or willingly permits a person to get, transportation provided under this subtitle for property at less than the rate in effect for that transportation under *Ante*, p. 1371. chapter 107 of this title, shall be fined not more than $5,000, imprisoned for not more than 2 years, or both.

(2) A person, or officer or agent of the person, that (A) delivers property for transportation under this subtitle to a common carrier providing transportation subject to the jurisdiction of the Commission under subchapter I of chapter 105 of this title, or for whom that carrier transports property as consignor or consignee, and (B) knowingly and willfully by any means gets or attempts to get that property transported at less than the rate in effect for that transportation under chapter 107 of this title, shall be fined not more than $5,000, imprisoned for not more than 2 years, or both.

(3) A person, or an officer or agent of a corporation or company that by payment of anything of value, solicitation, or in any other way, induces or attempts to induce a common carrier providing transportation subject to the jurisdiction of the Commission under subchapter I of chapter 105 of this title, or any of its officers or agents, to discriminate unreasonably against another consignor or consignee in the transportation of property shall be fined not more than $5,000, imprisoned for not more than 2 years, or both.

(b) A person, or an officer, employee, or agent of that person, that (1) knowingly offers, grants, gives, solicits, accepts, or receives a rebate, concession, or discrimination in violation of a provision of this subtitle related to motor carrier transportation subject to the *Ante*, p. 1361. jurisdiction of the Commission under subchapter II of chapter 105 of this title, or (2) by any means knowingly and willfully assists or permits another person to get transportation that is subject to the jurisdiction of the Commission under that subchapter at less than the rate in effect for that transportation under chapter 107 of this title, shall be fined at least $200 but no more than $500 for the first violation and at least $250 but not more than $2,000 for a subsequent violation.

(c) (1) A water carrier providing transportation subject to the jurisdiction of the Commission under subchapter III of chapter 105 of this *Ante*, p. 1365. title, or an officer, agent, or employee of that carrier, that knowingly and willfully by any means offers, grants, or gives, or intentionally permits a person to get, transportation provided under that subchapter at less than the rate in effect for that transportation under chapter 107 of this title, shall be fined not more than $5,000.

(2) A person that knowingly and willfully by any means solicits, accepts, or receives transportation provided under subchapter III of chapter 105 of this title at less than the rate in effect for that transportation under chapter 107 of this title, shall be fined not more than $5,000.

(3) Trial in a criminal action under this subsection is in the judicial district in which any part of the violation is committed.

(d) (1) A freight forwarder providing service subject to the jurisdiction of the Commission under subchapter IV of chapter 105 of this *Ante*, p. 1369. title, or an officer, agent, or employee of that freight forwarder, that knowingly and willfully assists a person in getting, or willingly permits a person to get, service provided under that subchapter at less

than the rate in effect for that service under chapter 107 of this title, *Ante,* p. 1371.
shall be fined not more than $500 for the first violation and not more
than $2,000 for a subsequent violation.

(2) A person that knowingly and willfully by any means gets, or
attempts to get, service provided under subchapter IV of chapter 105 *Ante,* p. 1369.
of this title at less than the rate in effect for that service under chapter
107 of this title, shall be fined not more than $500 for the first violation
and not more than $2,000 for a subsequent violation.

§ 11905. Transportation of passengers without charge   49 USC 11905.

A common carrier providing transportation subject to the jurisdiction of the Interstate Commerce Commission under subchapter I,
II, or III of chapter 105 of this title that provides transportation of *Ante,* pp. 1359,
passengers without charge except as provided in section 10721(b), 1361, 1365.
10722 (c) and (d) (if the transportation is for its employees on sleep- *Ante,* p. 1383.
ing and express cars or linemen of telegraph and telephone companies), *Ante,* p. 1384.
10723(a)(1) (other than paragraph (1)(A) of that subsection when *Ante,* p. 1385.
transportation is arranged by a municipal government), or 10724(a) *Ante,* p. 1386.
of this title, shall be fined at least $100 but not more than $2,000. An
individual who uses a free ticket for, or accepts transportation subject to the jurisdiction of the Commission under those subchapters,
except as provided in those sections, shall be fined at least $100 but not
more than $2,000.

§ 11906. Evasion of regulation of motor carriers and brokers   49 USC 11906.

A person, or an officer, employee, or agent of that person that by any
means knowingly and willfully tries to evade regulation provided
under this subtitle for motor carriers or brokers shall be fined at least
$200 but not more than $500 for the first violation and at least $250 but
not more than $2,000 for a subsequent violation.

§ 11907. Interference with railroad car supply   49 USC 11907.

(a) A person that offers or gives anything of value to another person acting for or employed by a rail carrier providing transportation
subject to the jurisdiction of the Interstate Commerce Commission
under subchapter I of chapter 105 of this title intending to influence
an action of that other person related to supply, distribution, or movement of cars, vehicles, or vessels used in the transportation of property, or because of the action of that other person, shall be fined not
more than $1,000, imprisoned for not more than 2 years, or both.

(b) A person acting for or employed by a rail carrier providing
transportation subject to the jurisdiction of the Commission under
subchapter I of chapter 105 of this title that solicits, accepts, or receives anything of value (1) intending to be influenced by it in an
action of that person related to supply, distribution, or movement of
cars, vehicles, or vessels used in the transportation of property, or (2)
because of the action of that person, shall be fined not more than
$1,000, imprisoned for not more than 2 years, or both.

§ 11908. Abandonment of service by freight forwarder   49 USC 11908.

A freight forwarder controlled by or under common control with
a common carrier providing transportation subject to the jurisdiction of the Interstate Commerce Commission under subchapter I, II,
or III of chapter 105 of this title, or a director, officer, receiver,
operating trustee, lessee, agent, or employee of that freight forwarder
or common carrier, that knowingly authorizes or permits a violation
of section 10933 of this title, shall be fined not more than $5,000. *Ante,* p. 1418.

49 USC 11909.

§ 11909. Record keeping and reporting violations

(a) A person required to make a report to the Interstate Commerce Commission, or make, prepare, or preserve a record, under sub-
Ante, p. 1425. chapter III of chapter 111 of this title about transportation subject to the jurisdiction of the Commission under subchapter I of chap-
Ante, p. 1359. ter 105 of this title that knowingly and willfully (1) makes a false
entry in the report or record, (2) destroys, multilates, changes, or by
another means falsifies the record, (3) does not enter business related
facts and transactions in the record, (4) makes, prepares, or preserves
the record in violation of a regulation or order of the Commission, or
(5) files a false report or record with the Commission, shall be fined
not more than $5,000, imprisoned for not more than 2 years, or both.

(b) A person required to make a report to the Commission, answer
a question, or make, prepare, or preserve a record under this subtitle
about transportation subject to the jurisdiction of the Commis-
Ante, p. 1361. sion under subchapter II of chapter 105 of this title, or an officer,
agent, or employee of that person, that (1) willfully does not make
that report, (2) willfully does not specifically, completely, and truthfully answer that question in 30 days from the date the Commission requires the question to be answered, (3) willfully does not make, prepare, or preserve that record in the form and manner prescribed by the
Commission, (4) knowingly and willfully falsifies, destroys, mutilates,
or changes that report or record, (5) knowingly and willfully files a
false report or record with the Commission, (6) knowingly and willfully makes a false or incomplete entry in that record about a business related fact or transaction, or (7) knowingly and willfully makes,
prepares, or preserves a record in violation of a regulation or order
of the Commission, shall be fined not more than $5,000.

(c) A person required to make a report to the Commission, answer
a question, or make, prepare, or preserve a record under this subtitle
about transportation subject to the jurisdiction of the Commission
Ante, p. 1365. under subchapter III of chapter 105 of this title, or an officer, agent,
or employee of that person, that (1) willfully does not make that
report, (2) willfully does not specifically, completely and truthfully answer that question in 30 days from the date the Commission
requires the question to be answered, (3) willfully does not make,
prepare, or preserve that record in the form and manner prescribed by
the Commission, (4) willfully falsifies, destroys, mutilates, or
changes that report, or record, (5) willfully makes a false or
incomplete entry in the record about a fact or transaction required
under this subtitle, (6) willfully makes, prepares, or preserves a
record in violation of a regulation or order of the Commission, or
(7) knowingly and willfully files a false report or record with the
Commission, shall be fined not more than $5,000. Trial in a criminal
action under this subsection is in the judicial district in which any
part of the violation is committed.

(d) A freight forwarder, or an officer, agent, or employee of that
freight forwarder, required to make a report to the Commission,
answer a question, or make, prepare, or preserve a record under this
subtitle about transportation subject to the jurisdiction of the Com-
Ante, p. 1369. mission under subchapter IV of chapter 105 of this title that (1)
willfully does not make that report, (2) willfully does not specifically,
completely, and truthfully answer that question in 30 days from the
date the Commission requires the question to be answered, (3) willfully does not make, prepare, or preserve that record in the form and
manner prescribed by the Commission, (4) knowingly and willfully

falsifies, destroys, mutilates, or changes that report or record, (5) knowingly and willfully files a false report or record with the Commission, (6) knowingly and willfully makes a false or incomplete entry in that record about a fact or transaction related to the business of that freight forwarder, or (7) knowingly and willfully makes, prepares, or preserves a record in violation of a regulation or order of the Commission, shall be fined not more than $5,000.

§ 11910. Unlawful disclosure of information

49 USC 11910.

(a) (1) A common carrier providing transportation subject to the jurisdiction of the Interstate Commerce Commission under subchapter I of chapter 105 of this title, or an officer, agent, or employee of that carrier, or another person authorized to receive information from that carrier, that knowingly discloses to another person, except the shipper or consignee, or a person who solicits or knowingly receives (A) information about the nature, kind, quantity, destination, consignee, or routing of property tendered or delivered to that carrier for transportation provided under this subtitle without the consent of the shipper or consignee, and (B) that information may be used to the detriment of the shipper or consignee or may disclose improperly, to a competitor the business transactions of the shipper or consignee, shall be fined not more than $1,000.

Ante, p. 1359.

(2) A motor carrier or broker providing transportation subject to the jurisdiction of the Commission under subchapter II of chapter 105 of this title or an officer, receiver, trustee, lessee, or employee of that carrier or broker, or another person authorized by that carrier or broker to receive information from that carrier or broker may not knowingly disclose to another person, except the shipper or consignee, and another person may not solicit, or knowingly receive, information about the nature, kind, quantity, destination, consignee, or routing of property tendered or delivered to that carrier or broker for transportation provided under this subtitle without the consent of the shipper or consignee if that information may be used to the detriment of the shipper or consignee or may disclose improperly to a competitor the business transactions of the shipper or consignee.

Ante, p. 1361.

(3) A common carrier providing transportation subject to the jurisdiction of the Commission under subchapter III of chapter 105 of this title, or an officer, receiver, trustee, lessee, agent, or employee of that carrier, or another person authorized by that carrier or person to receive information from that carrier, that knowingly and willfully discloses to another person, except the shipper or consignee, or a person that solicits or knowingly and willfully receives (A) information about the nature, kind, quantity, destination, consignee, or routing of property tendered or delivered to that carrier for transportation provided under that subchapter without the consent of the shipper or consignee, and (B) that information may be used to the detriment of the shipper or consignee or may disclose improperly, to a competitor, the business transactions of the shipper or consignee, shall be fined not more than $2,000. Trial in a criminal action under this paragraph is in the judicial district in which any part of the violation is committed.

Ante, p. 1365.

(4) A freight forwarder providing service subject to the jurisdiction of the Commission under subchapter IV of chapter 105 of this title, or an officer, agent, or employee of that freight forwarder, or another person authorized by that freight forwarder, or person to receive information, who knowingly and willfully discloses to another person, except the shipper or consignee, or a person that solicits or knowingly and willfully receives (A) information about the nature,

Ante, p. 1369.

kind, quantity, destination, consignee, or routing of property tendered or delivered to that forwarder for service provided under that subchapter without the consent of the shipper or consignee, and (B) that information may be used to the detriment of the shipper or consignee or may disclose improperly, to a competitor the business transactions of the shipper or consignee, shall be fined not more than $100 for the first violation and not more than $500 for a subsequent violation. A separate violation occurs each day the violation continues.

Ante, p. 1359.

(b) This subtitle does not prevent a carrier or broker providing transportation subject to the jurisdiction of the Commission under chapter 105 of this title from giving information—

    (1) in response to legal process issued under authority of a court of the United States or a State;

    (2) to an officer, employee, or agent of the United States Government, a State, or a territory or possession of the United States; or

    (3) to another carrier or its agent to adjust mutual traffic accounts in the ordinary course of business.

Ante, p. 1426.

(c) An employee of the Commission delegated to make an inspection or examination under section 11144 of this title who knowingly discloses information acquired during that inspection or examination, except as directed by the Commission, a court, or a judge of that court, shall be fined not more than $500, imprisoned for not more than 6 months, or both.

49 USC 11911.

§ 11911. Issuance of securities; disposition of funds; restriction on ownership

Ante, p. 1428.
Ante, p. 1430.

(a) A director, officer, attorney, or agent of a carrier defined in section 11301(a)(1) of this title or of a person to which that section is made applicable by section 11302(a) of this title that knowingly agrees to or concurs in (1) an issue of securities or assumption of obligations or liability in violation of section 11301 of this title, (2) a disposition of securities in violation of an order of the Interstate Commerce Commission, or (3) an application not authorized by the Commission of the funds derived by the carrier through a disposition of securities shall be fined at least $1,000 but not more than $10,000, imprisoned for at least one year but not more than 3 years, or both.

Ante, p. 1433.

(b) A person that violates section 11322 of this title shall be fined at least $1,000 but not more than $10,000, imprisoned for at least one year but not more than 3 years, or both.

49 USC 11912.

§ 11912. Consolidation, merger, and acquisition of control: violation by a person not a carrier

Ante, pp.
1434–1439.

A person, other than a common carrier, that violates section 11343, 11344, 11345, 11346, or 11347 of this title shall be fined not more than $5,000.

§ 11913. Disobedience to subpenas

49 USC 11913.

A person not obeying a subpena or requirement of the Interstate Commerce Commission to appear and testify or produce records shall be fined at least $100 but not more than $5,000, imprisoned for not more than one year, or both.

§ 11914. General criminal penalty when specific penalty not provided

49 USC 11914.

(a) When another criminal penalty is not provided under this chapter, a common carrier providing transportation subject to the jurisdiction of the Interstate Commerce Commission under subchapter I of chapter 105 of this title, and when that carrier is a corporation, Ante, p. 1359. a director or officer of the corporation, or a receiver, trustee, lessee, or person acting for or employed by the corporation that, alone or with another person, willfully violates this subtitle or an order prescribed under this subtitle, shall be fined not more than $5,000. However, if the violation is for discrimination in rates charged for transportation, the person may be imprisoned for not more than 2 years in addition to being fined under this subsection. A separate violation occurs each day a violation of section 11321(a) or 11342 of this title continues. Ante, pp. 1432, 1434.

(b) When another criminal penalty is not provided under this chapter, a person that knowingly and willfully violates a provision of this subtitle or a regulation or order prescribed under this subtitle, or a condition of a certificate or permit issued under this subtitle related to transportation that is subject to the jurisdiction of the Commission under subchapter II of chapter 105 of this title, shall be fined Ante, p. 1361. at least $100 but not more than $500 for the first violation and at least $200 but not more than $500 for a subsequent violation. A separate violation occurs each day the violation continues.

(c) When another criminal penalty is not provided under this chapter, a person that knowingly and willfully violates a provision of this subtitle or a regulation or order prescribed under this subtitle, or a condition of a certificate or permit issued under this subtitle related to transportation that is subject to the jurisdiction of the Commission under subchapter III of chapter 105 of this title, shall be fined Ante, p. 1365. not more than $500. A separate violation occurs each day the violation continues. Venue in a criminal action under this subsection is in the judicial district in which any part of the violation was committed.

(d) When another criminal penalty is not provided under this chapter, a person that knowingly and willfully violates a provision of this subtitle or a regulation or order prescribed under this subtitle or a condition of a permit issued under this subtitle related to service that is subject to the jurisdiction of the Commission under subchapter IV of chapter 105 of this title, shall be fined not more than $100 for the Ante, p. 1370. first violation and not more than $500 for a subsequent violation. A separate violation occurs each day the violation continues.

49 USC 11915.

§ 11915. Punishment of corporation for violations committed by certain individuals

An act or omission that would be a violation of this subtitle if committed by a director, officer, receiver, trustee, lessee, agent, or employee of a common carrier providing transportation or service subject to the jurisdiction of the Interstate Commerce Commission under chapter 105 of this title that is a corporation is also a violation of this subtitle by that corporation. The penalties of this chapter apply to that violation. When acting in the scope of their employment, the actions and omissions of individuals acting for or employed by that carrier are considered to be the actions and omissions of that carrier as well as that individual.

Ante, p. 1359.

49 USC 11916.

§ 11916. Conclusiveness of rates in certain prosecutions

Ante, p. 1371.

When a carrier files with the Interstate Commerce Commission or publishes a particular rate under chapter 107 of this title or participates in one of those rates, the published or filed rate is conclusive proof against that carrier, its officers, and agents that it is the legal rate for that transportation or service in a proceeding begun under section 11902 or 11903 of this title. A departure, or offer to depart, from that rate is a violation of those sections.

CONFORMING AND TECHNICAL PROVISIONS

Sec. 2. (a) (1) Title 18, United States Code, is amended—
(A) by striking out of the first definition of section 831 "common, contract, or private carrier, or freight forwarder as those terms are used in the Interstate Commerce Act, as amended" and substituting "common, contract, or motor private carrier, as those terms are defined in section 10102 of title 49"; and
(B) by striking out of section 835(c) "by the Interstate Commerce Act" and substituting "under subtitle IV of title 49".
(2) The Internal Revenue Code of 1954 (26 U.S.C. 1) is amended—

26 USC 48.

(A) by striking out of section 48(a)(2)(B)(ii) "subject to part I of the Interstate Commerce Act" and substituting "providing transportation subject to subchapter I of chapter 105 of title 49";

26 USC 185.

(B) by striking out of section 185(e)(3)(B) "section 19a of part I of the Interstate Commerce Act (49 U.S.C. 19a)" and "such section 19a" and substituting "subchapter V of chapter 107 of title 49" and "such subchapter V", respectively;

26 USC 250.

(C) by striking out of section 250(a)(1) "common carrier by railroad (as defined in section 1(3) of the Interstate Commerce Act (49 U.S.C. 1(3)))" and substituting "rail carrier (as defined in section 10102(17) of title 49)";

26 USC 281.

(D) by striking out of section 281(d)(1)(A) "subject to part I of the Interstate Commerce Act (49 U.S.C. 1 and following)" and substituting "providing transportation subject to subchapter I of chapter 105 of title 49";
(E) by striking out of section 281(d)(1)(B) "subject to part I of the Interstate Commerce Act" and substituting "providing transportation subject to subchapter I of chapter 105 of title 49";

(F) by striking out of section 354(c) "section 20b of the Inter-   26 USC 354.
state Commerce Act" and substituting "subchapter IV of chapter
113 of title 49";

(G) by striking out of section 3231(g) "express company,   26 USC 3231.
sleeping-car company, or carrier by railroad, subject to part I of
the Interstate Commerce Act (49 U.S.C., chapter 1)" and substituting "express carrier, sleeping car carrier, or rail carrier providing transportation subject to subchapter I of chapter 105 of title
49"; and

(H) by striking out of section 6362(f)(9) "26, 226A, or 324 of   26 USC 6362.
the Interstate Commerce Act" and substituting "section 11504 of
title 49".

(3) Title 28, United States Code, is amended—

(A) by striking out of section 1445(b) "section 20 of Title 49"
and substituting "section 11707 of title 49";

(B) by striking out of section 2321(c) "the cases and proceedings under section 20 of the Act of February 4, 1887, as amended
(24 Stat. 386; 49 U.S.C. 20), section 23 of the Act of May 16,
1942, as amended (56 Stat. 301; 49 U.S.C. 23), and section 3 of the
Act of February 19, 1903, as amended (32 Stat. 848; 49 U.S.C.
43)" and substituting "enforcement actions and actions to collect
civil penalties under subtitle IV of title 49"; and

(C) by striking out of section 2323 "actions under section 20
of the Act of February 4, 1887, as amended (24 Stat. 386; 49
U.S.C. 20), section 23 of the Act of May 16, 1942, as amended (56
Stat. 301; 49 U.S.C. 23), and section 3 of the Act of February 19,
1903, as amended (32 Stat. 848; 49 U.S.C. 43)" and substituting
"enforcement actions and actions to collect civil penalties under
subtitle IV of title 49".

(4) Title 39, United States Code, is amended—

(A) by striking out of section 5201(2) "motor carrier, or an
express company" and substituting "motor common carrier, or express carrier";

(B) by striking out section 5201(5) and substituting the
following:

"(5) 'motor common carrier' means a motor common carrier,
except a passenger-carrying motor vehicle of such a carrier, within the meaning of section 10102(11) of title 49, that holds a certificate of public convenience and necessity issued by the Commission;";

(C) by striking out of section 5201(6) "company" and "section 1(3) of title 49" and substituting "carrier" and "section
10102(7)", respectively;

(D) by striking out of section 5203 "motor carrier" each time
it appears and substituting "motor common carrier" in each
place; and

(E) by striking out of section 5215(a) "motor carrier" and substituting "motor common carrier".

(5) Section 308(c)(1) of title 44, United States Code, is amended by striking out "section 66 of title 49" and substituting "section 244 of title 31".

49 USC 11503
note.

(b) Section 11503 of title 49, as stated in the first section of this Act, is effective after February 4, 1979.

LEGISLATIVE PURPOSE AND CONSTRUCTION

49 USC prec.
10101 note.
Ante, pp. 1337,
1464.

SEC. 3. (a) Sections 1 and 2 of this Act restate, without substantive change, laws enacted before May 16, 1978, that were replaced by those sections. Those sections may not be construed as making a substantive change in the laws replaced. Laws enacted after May 15, 1978, that are inconsistent with this Act are considered as superseding it to the extent of the inconsistency.

(b) A reference to a law replaced by sections 1 and 2 of this Act, including a reference in a regulation, order, or other law, is deemed to refer to the corresponding provision enacted by this Act.

(c) An order, rule, or regulation in effect under a law replaced by sections 1 and 2 of this Act continues in effect under the corresponding provision enacted by this Act until repealed, amended, or superseded.

(d) An action taken or an offense committed under a law replaced by sections 1 and 2 of this Act is deemed to have been taken or committed under the corresponding provision enacted by this Act.

(e) An inference of a legislative construction is not to be drawn by reason of the location in the United States Code of a provision enacted by this Act or by reason of the caption or catchline thereof.

(f) If a provision enacted by this Act is held invalid, all valid provisions that are severable from the invalid provision remain in effect. If a provision of this Act is held invalid in any of its applications, the provision remains valid for all valid applications that are severable from any of the invalid applications.

REPEALS

49 USC prec.
10101 note.

SEC. 4. (a) The repeal of a law by this Act may not be construed as a legislative inference that the provision was or was not in effect before its repeal.

(b) The laws specified in the following schedule are repealed except as provided in subsection (c) of this section and except for rights and duties that matured, penalties that were incurred, and proceedings that were begun before the date of enactment of this Act:

Schedule of Laws Repealed

Statutes at Large

Date	Chapter or Public Law	Section	Statutes at Large Volume	Page
1887 Feb. 4	104	(less 25, 203(a) (22), (23), 204(a)(1) ("qualifications" through period), (a)(2) ("qualifications" through period), (a)(3), (a)(3a), (a)(5), 220(f), 226).	24	379.
1889 Mar. 2	382		25	855.
	411	1 (proviso)	25	954.
1891 Feb. 10	128		26	743.
1893 Feb. 11	83		27	443.
1895 Feb. 8	61		28	643.
1903 Feb. 19	708		32	847.
1906 Mar. 7	P. R. 8		34	823.
Mar. 21	P. R. 11		34	824.
June 29	3591		34	584.
1908 Apr. 13	143		35	60.
1909 Feb. 25	193		35	648.
1910 June 18	309		36	539.
1912 Aug. 24	390	11 (less last par. on p. 567)	37	566.
1913 Mar. 1	92		37	701.
Oct. 22	32	1 (last full par. on p. 219 and all language before the heading "United States Courts" on p. 221).	38	219, 221.
1914 Aug. 1	223	1 (5th full par.)	38	627.
1915 Mar. 4	176		38	1196.
1916 Aug. 9	301		39	441.
29	417	1 (2d full par.)	39	604.
1917 May 29	23		40	101.
Aug. 9	50		40	270.
10	51		40	272.
1920 Feb. 28	91	(less 1, 213, 441 "Sec. 26," 500)	41	456.
May 8	172	1 (1st par.)	41	590.
1921 Feb. 26	72		41	1145.
27	81		41	1149.
June 10	20		42	27.
1922 Feb. 24	70		42	393.
June 7	210		42	624.
Aug. 18	280		42	827.
Sept. 22	413		42	1025.
1923 Mar. 3	233		42	1443.
1924 June 7	325		43	633.
1925 Jan. 30	120		43	801.
1926 July 3	761		44	835.

Statutes at Large

Date	Chapter or Public Law	Section	Statutes at Large	
			Volume	Page
1927				
Feb. 26	217		44	1247.
Mar. 4	510	(less 6)	44	1446.
1929				
Jan. 19	79		45	1084.
1930				
Apr. 23	208		46	251.
1932				
Mar. 15	78		47	65.
1933				
Feb 28	136		47	1368.
June 16	91		48	211.
1934				
June 13	498		48	954.
19	648	1 (2d full par.)	48	1056.
	652	602(b)	48	1102.
1935				
Feb. 2	3	3	49	19.
May 23	136		49	287.
June 14	247		49	376.
July 16	383		49	481.
Aug. 9	498	(less 1 "Sec. 204(a)(1) ('qualifications' through period), (a)(2) ('qualifications' through period), (a)(3), (a)(5), 225")	49	543.
12	509		49	607.
1937				
July 5	432		50	475.
Aug. 25	776		50	809.
1938				
June 23	601	1107(j)	52	1029.
29	811		52	1236.
1940				
Jan. 7	938		54	1226.
Sept. 18	722	(less 14(b), 20(b)(4), 24 "Sec. 220 (f)", 322, 331)	54	898.
1942				
Mar. 27	199	101–103 (title I)	56	176.
May 16	318		56	284.
Aug. 7	552		56	746.
1943				
Nov. 12	299		57	590.
1944				
Sept. 27	423		58	751.
1945				
May 16	128		59	169.
Dec. 12	573		59	606.
1946				
Feb. 20	32		60	21.
1948				
Apr. 9	180	(less 3)	62	162.
June 3	386		62	295.
12	457		62	386.
17	491		62	472.
24	622		62	602.
1949				
May 24	139	133	63	108.
June 29	272		63	280.
July 26	361		63	479.
Aug. 2	379		63	485.
1950				
Sept. 1	835		64	574.
Dec. 20	1140		64	1113.
1952				
June 27	477	402(g)	66	277.
July 3	570	1(a)(25), (26)	66	332.
9	599		66	479.
10	648		66	542.
16	881		66	724.
1953				
June 30	165		67	115.
July 31	292		67	244.

Statutes at Large

Date	Chapter or Public Law	Section	Statutes at Large	
			Volume	Page
1954 July 22	563		68	526.
1956 July 27 Aug. 3	759 928		70 70	702. 983.
1957 July 11 Aug. 13 14 16 22 28 31 Sept. 7	85–99 85–124 85–135 85–150 85–163 85–176 85–246 85–309	 4	71 71 71 71 71 71 71 71	292. 343. 352. 369. 411. 452. 564. 631.
1958 Aug. 12 23 26 Sept. 2	85–625 85–728 85–762 85–857	 1 13(a)	72 72 72 72	568. 812. 859. 1264.
1960 June 11 July 12	86–507 86–615	1(38)	74 74	202. 382.
1961 Apr. 1 Sept. 14	87–16 87–247		75 75	41. 517.
1962 Aug. 24 Sept. 27 Oct. 15	87–595 87–707 87–805		76 76 76	397. 635. 911.
1963 Dec. 17	88–208		77	402.
1965 July 24 27 Sept. 6	89–86 89–93 89–170		79 79 79	263. 284. 643.
1966 May 26 Oct. 15 Nov. 10	89–430 89–670 84–804	 8(d)	80 80 80	168. 943. 1521.
1968 July 26 Oct. 17	90–433 90–586	 1	82 82	448. 1149.
1970 Oct. 15 Dec. 23 28	91–452 91–569 91–590	243–245 1–3	84 84 84	931. 1499. 1587.
1972 July 7 13	92–338 92–348	 5, 6	86 86	423. 463.
1973 July 10 Dec. 27	93–69 93–201	201–202 (title II)	87 87	166–168. 838.
1974 Jan. 2 Feb. 8 Oct. 28 Dec. 21	93–236 93–249 93–496 93–528	205, 601(e) 14 6(b)	87 88 88 88	993, 1021. 11. 1532. 1709.
1975 Jan. 2 Feb. 28	93–585 94–5	9 3	88 89	1918. 7.
1976 Feb. 5	94–210	201, 202 (less (f)), 203–212, 301–307, 308(a)(3), 309, 310, 312, 402, 403, 801, 802, 804 "Sec. 304(j)", 809(c).	90	34–38, 39–56, 57–60, 62–66, 125–130, 139, 146.
Apr. 21 Oct. 19	94–273 94–555	11(4) 206, 218, 220(i)–(o)	90 90	378. 2621, 2628, 2630.
1978 Feb. 15	95–231		92	29.

Reorganization Plans

Year	Plan No.	Section	Statutes at Large	
			Volume	Page
1969....	1	---	83	859.

49 USC prec. 10101 note.
(c) The laws specified in the schedule in subsection (b) of this section, as they existed on October 1, 1977, are not repealed to the extent—

(1) those laws (A) vested functions in the Interstate Commerce Commission, or in the chairman or members of the Commission, related to the transportation of oil by pipeline, and (B) vested functions and authority in the Commission, or an officer or component of the Commission, related to the establishment of rates or charges for the transportation of oil by pipeline or the valuation of any such pipeline; and

(2) those functions and authority were transferred by sections 306 and 402(b) of the Department of Energy Organization Act (91 Stat. 581, 584, 42 U.S.C. 7155, 7172(b)).

Effective date.
49 USC prec.
10101 note.
49 USC 1 note,
1020 note.
(d) The repeals, by subsection (b) of this section, of section 1(a) (25), (26) of the Act of July 3, 1952, chapter 570, the Act of June 30, 1953, chapter 165, and the Act of July 31, 1953, chapter 169, are effective on September 14, 1978.

Approved October 17, 1978.

LEGISLATIVE HISTORY:

HOUSE REPORT No. 95-1395 (Comm. on the Judiciary).
CONGRESSIONAL RECORD, Vol. 124 (1978):
    Sept. 19, considered and passed House.
    Sept. 25, considered and passed Senate, amended.
    Sept. 26, House concurred in Senate amendment.
WEEKLY COMPILATION OF PRESIDENTIAL DOCUMENTS, Vol. 14, No. 42:
    Oct. 18, Presidential statement.

O

Appendix C: Airline Deregulation Act of 1978

Public Law 95-504
95th Congress

An Act

To amend the Federal Aviation Act of 1958, to encourage, develop, and attain an air transportation system which relies on competitive market forces to determine the quality, variety, and price of air services, and for other purposes.

Oct. 24, 1978
[S. 2493]

Be it enacted by the Senate and House of Representatives of the United States of America in Congress assembled,

Airline
Deregulation
Act of 1978.

SHORT TITLE

SECTION 1. This Act may be cited as the "Airline Deregulation Act of 1978".

49 USC 1301
note.

DEFINITIONS

SEC. 2. (a) Section 101 of the Federal Aviation Act of 1958 (49 U.S.C. 1301) is amended—
> (1) by inserting after paragraph (13) the following new paragraphs:

"(14) 'Charter air carrier' means an air carrier holding a certificate of public convenience and necessity authorizing it to engage in charter air transportation.

"(15) 'Charter air transportation' means charter trips, including inclusive tour charter trips, in air transportation, rendered pursuant to authority conferred under this Act under regulations prescribed by the Board.";
> (2) by inserting after paragraph (32) the following new paragraph:

"(33) 'Predatory' means any practice which would constitute a violation of the antitrust laws as set forth in the first section of the Clayton Act (15 U.S.C. 12).";
> (3) by inserting after paragraph (35) the following new paragraph:

"(36) 'State agency' means that department, agency, officer, or other entity of a State government which has been designated according to State law as—
> "(A) the recipient of any notice required under title IV of this Act to be given to a State agency; or
> "(B) the representative of the State in any matter about which the Board is required, under such title IV, to consult with or consider the views of a State agency."; and
> (4) by striking out paragraphs (36) and (37).

(b) Section 101 of such Act is amended by renumbering the paragraphs of such section, including all references thereto, as paragraphs (1) through (41), respectively.

DECLARATION OF POLICY

SEC. 3. (a) Section 102(a) of the Federal Aviation Act of 1958 (49 U.S.C. 1302(a)) is amended to read as follows:

"FACTORS FOR INTERSTATE AND OVERSEAS AIR TRANSPORTATION

"SEC. 102. (a) In the exercise and performance of its powers and duties under this Act with respect to interstate and overseas air transportation, the Board shall consider the following, among other things, as being in the public interest, and in accordance with the public convenience and necessity:

"(1) The assignment and maintenance of safety as the highest priority in air commerce, and prior to the authorization of new air transportation services, full evaluation of the recommendations of the Secretary of Transportation on the safety implications of such new services and full evaluation of any report or recommendation submitted under section 107 of this Act.

Post, p. 1709.

"(2) The prevention of any deterioration in established safety procedures, recognizing the clear intent, encouragement, and dedication of the Congress to the furtherance of the highest degree of safety in air transportation and air commerce, and the maintenance of the safety vigilance that has evolved within air transportation and air commerce and has come to be expected by the traveling and shipping public.

"(3) The availability of a variety of adequate, economic, efficient, and low-price services by air carriers without unjust discriminations, undue preferences or advantages, or unfair or deceptive practices, the need to improve relations among, and coordinate transportation by, air carriers, and the need to encourage fair wages and equitable working conditions.

"(4) The placement of maximum reliance on competitive market forces and on actual and potential competition (A) to provide the needed air transportation system, and (B) to encourage efficient and well-managed carriers to earn adequate profits and to attract capital.

"(5) The development and maintenance of a sound regulatory environment which is responsive to the needs of the public and in which decisions are reached promptly in order to facilitate adaption of the air transportation system to the present and future needs of the domestic and foreign commerce of the United States, the Postal Service, and the national defense.

"(6) The encouragement of air service at major urban areas through secondary or satellite airports, where consistent with regional airport plans of regional and local authorities, and when such encouragement is endorsed by appropriate State entities encouraging such service by air carriers whose sole responsibility in any specific market is to provide service exclusively at the secondary or satellite airport, and fostering an environment which reasonably enables such carriers to establish themselves and to develop their secondary or satellite airport services.

"(7) The prevention of unfair, deceptive, predatory, or anticompetitive practices in air transportation, and the avoidance of—

"(A) unreasonable industry concentration, excessive market domination, and monopoly power; and

"(B) other conditions;

that would tend to allow one or more air carriers unreasonably to increase prices, reduce services, or exclude competition in air transportation.

"(8) The maintenance of a comprehensive and convenient system of continuous scheduled airline service for small communities and for isolated areas, with direct Federal assistance where appropriate.

1382

"(9) The encouragement, development, and maintenance of an air transportation system relying on actual and potential competition to provide efficiency, innovation, and low prices, and to determine the variety, quality, and price of air transportation services.

"(10) The encouragement of entry into air transportation markets by new air carriers, the encouragement of entry into additional air transportation markets by existing air carriers, and the continued strengthening of small air carriers so as to assure a more effective, competitive airline industry.".

(b) Section 102 of such Act is amended by adding at the end thereof   49 USC 1302.
the following new subsection:

"FACTORS FOR FOREIGN AIR TRANSPORTATION

"(c) In the exercise and performance of its powers and duties under this Act with respect to foreign air transportation, the Board shall consider the following, among other things, as being in the public interest, and in accordance with the public convenience and necessity:

"(1) The encouragement and development of an air transportation system properly adapted to the present and future needs of the foreign and domestic commerce of the United States, of the Postal Service, and of the national defense.

"(2) The regulation of air transportation in such manner as to recognize and preserve the inherent advantages of, assure the highest degree of safety in, and foster sound economic conditions in, such transportation, and to improve the relations between and coordinate transportation by air carriers.

"(3) The promotion of adequate, economical, and efficient service by air carriers at reasonable charges, without unjust discriminations, undue preferences or advantages, or unfair or destructive competitive practices.

"(4) Competition to the extent necessary to assure the sound development of an air transportation system properly adapted to the needs of the foreign and domestic commerce of the United States, of the Postal Service, and of the national defense.

"(5) The promotion of safety in air commerce.

"(6) The promotion, encouragement, and development of civil aeronautics.".

(c) That portion of the table of contents contained in the first section of such Act which appears under the side heading

"SEC. 102. Declaration of Policy: The Board."

is amended by striking out

"(a) General factors for consideration.
"(b) Factors for all-cargo air service."

and inserting in lieu thereof

"(a) Factors for interstate and overseas air transportation.
"(b) Factors for all-cargo air service.
"(c) Factors for foreign air transportation.".

FEDERAL PREEMPTION

SEC. 4. (a) Title I of the Federal Aviation Act of 1958 (49 U.S.C. 1301 et seq.) is amended by adding at the end thereof the following new section:

"FEDERAL PREEMPTION

"PREEMPTION

49 USC 1305.

"SEC. 105. (a) (1) Except as provided in paragraph (2) of this subsection, no State or political subdivision thereof and no interstate agency or other political agency of two or more States shall enact or enforce any law, rule, regulation, standard, or other provision having the force and effect of law relating to rates, routes, or services of any air carrier having authority under title IV of this Act to provide interstate air transportation.

49 USC 1371.

"(2) Except with respect to air transportation (other than charter air transportation) provided pursuant to a certificate issued by the Board under section 401 of this Act, the provisions of paragraph (1) of this subsection shall not apply to any transportation by air of persons, property, or mail conducted wholly within the State of Alaska.

49 USC 1371.

"PROPRIETARY POWERS AND RIGHTS

"(b) (1) Nothing in subsection (a) of this section shall be construed to limit the authority of any State or political subdivision thereof or any interstate agency or other political agency of two or more States as the owner or operator of an airport served by any air carrier certificated by the Board to exercise its proprietary powers and rights.

"(2) Any aircraft operated between points in the same State (other than the State of Hawaii) which in the course of such operation crosses a boundary between two States, or between the United States and any other country, or between a State and the beginning of the territorial waters of the United States, shall not, by reason of crossing such boundary, be considered to be operating in interstate or overseas air transportation.

"EXISTING STATE AUTHORITY

"(c) When any intrastate air carrier which on August 1, 1977, was operating primarily in intrastate air transportation regulated by a State receives the authority to provide interstate air transportation, any authority received from such State shall be considered to be part of its authority to provide air transportation received from the Board under title IV of this Act, until modified, suspended, amended, or terminated as provided under such title.

"DEFINITION

"(d) For purposes of this section, the term 'State' means any State, the District of Columbia, the Commonwealth of Puerto Rico, the Commonwealth of the Northern Mariana Islands, Guam, the Virgin Islands, and any territory or possession of the United States.".

(b) That portion of the table of contents contained in the first section of such Act which appears under the center heading

"TITLE I—GENERAL PROVISIONS"

is amended by adding at the end thereof

"Sec. 105. Federal preemption.
    "(a) Preemption.
    "(b) Proprietary powers and rights.
    "(c) Existing State authority.
    "(d) Definition.".

REPORT ON SUBSIDY COST-SHARING, STUDY OF LEVEL OF AIR SAFETY,
AND REPORT ON AIR CARRIER MARKETING OF TOURS

SEC. 5. (a) Title I of the Federal Aviation Act of 1958 (49 U.S.C. 1301 et seq.) is further amended by adding at the end thereof the following new sections:

"REPORT ON SUBSIDY COST-SHARING

"SEC. 106. Not later than January 1, 1980, the Board and the Secretary of Transportation, shall, separately or jointly, submit a comprehensive report to the Congress on the feasibility and appropriateness of devising formulas by which States and their political subdivisions could share part of the costs being incurred by the United States under sections 406 and 419 of this Act. Such report shall include any recommendations of the Board and the Secretary for the implementation of such cost-sharing formulas.

49 USC 1306.

49 USC 1376.
Post, p. 1732.

"SAFETY STUDY

"POLICY

"SEC. 107. (a) The Congress intends that the implementation of the Airline Deregulation Act of 1978 result in no diminution of the high standard of safety in air transportation attained in the United States at the time of the enactment of such Act.

49 USC 1307.

"REPORT

"(b) Not later than January 31, 1980, and each January 31 thereafter, the Secretary of Transportation shall prepare and submit to the Congress and the Board a comprehensive annual report on the extent to which the implementation of the Airline Deregulation Act of 1978 has affected, during the preceding calendar year, or will affect, in the succeeding calendar year, the level of air safety. Each such report shall, at a minimum, contain an analysis of each of the following:

Ante, p. 1705.

"(1) All relevant data on accidents and incidents occurring during the calendar year covered by such report in air transportation and on violations of safety regulations issued by the Secretary of Transportation occurring during such calendar year.

"(2) Current and anticipated personnel requirements of the Administrator with respect to enforcement of air safety regulations.

"(3) Effects on current levels of air safety of changes or proposals for changes in air carrier operating practices and procedures which occurred during the calendar year covered by such report.

"(4) The adequacy of air safety regulations taking into consideration changes in air carrier operating practices and procedures which occurred during the calendar year covered by such report.

Based on such report, the Secretary shall take those steps necessary to ensure that the high standard of safety in air transportation referred to in subsection (a) of this section is maintained in all aspects of air transportation in the United States.

"(c) Not later than January 31, 1980, and each January 31 thereafter, the Secretary of Transportation shall submit to the Congress and the Board recommendations with respect to the level of surveillance necessary to enforce air safety regulations and the level of staffing necessary to carry out such surveillance. The Secretary of Transportation's recommendations shall include proposals for any legislation needed to implement such recommendations.

"REGULATIONS AND INSPECTION PROCEDURES

Review and
report to
congressional
committees.

49 USC 1371.

"(d) Not later than July 1, 1979, the Secretary of Transportation shall complete a thorough review, and submit a report thereon to the appropriate authorizing committees of the Congress and to the Administrator, of the safety regulations and inspection procedures applicable to each class of air carriers subject to the provisions of title IV of this Act, in order to ensure that all classes of air carriers are providing the highest possible level of safe, reliable air transportation to all the communities served by those air carriers. Based on such review, the Administrator shall promulgate such safety regulations and establish such inspection procedures as the Administrator deems necessary to maintain the highest standard of safe, reliable air transportation in the United States.

"REPORT ON AIR CARRIER MARKETING OF TOURS

49 USC 1308.

"SEC. 108. Not later than May 1, 1979, the Board shall prepare and submit a report to the Congress which sets forth the recommendations of the Board on whether this Act and regulations of the Board should be amended to permit air carriers to sell tours directly to the public and to acquire control of persons authorized to sell tours to the public. The report shall evaluate the effects on the following groups of allowing air carriers to sell tours:
    "(1) The traveling public.
    "(2) The independent tour operator industry.
    "(3) The travel agent industry.
    "(4) The different classes of air carriers.".
(b) That portion of the table of contents contained in the first section of such Act which appears under the center heading

"TITLE I—GENERAL PROVISIONS"

is amended by adding at the end thereof

"Sec. 106. Report on subsidy cost-sharing.
"Sec. 107. Safety study.
        "(a) Policy.
        "(b) Report.
        "(c) Recommendations.
        "(d) Regulations and inspection procedure.
"Sec. 108. Report on air carrier marketing of tours.".

APPLICATION FOR CERTIFICATE

SEC. 6. Section 401(b) of the Federal Aviation Act of 1958 (49 U.S.C. 1371(b)) is amended—
    (1) by striking out "and shall be so verified"; and
    (2) by inserting ", and upon any community affected" immediately before the period.

ROUTE APPLICATIONS

SEC. 7. (a) Section 401(c) of the Federal Aviation Act of 1958 (49 U.S.C. 1371(c)) is amended to read as follows:

"ROUTE APPLICATIONS

"(c)(1) Upon the filing of any application pursuant to subsection (b) of this section, the Board shall give due notice thereof to the public by posting a notice of such application in the office of the secretary of the Board and to such other persons as the Board may by regulation determine. The Board shall—

Public notice.

"(A) set such application for a public hearing;

"(B) begin to make a determination with respect to such application under the simplified procedures established by the Board in regulations pursuant to subsection (p); or

"(C) dismiss such application on the merits;

not later than ninety days after the date the application is filed with the Board. Any interested person may file with the Board a protest or memorandum of opposition to or in support of the issuance of the certificate requested by such application. Any order of dismissal of an application issued by the Board without setting such application for a hearing or beginning to make a determination with respect to such application under such simplified procedures, shall be deemed a final order subject to judicial review in accordance with the provisions of section 1006 of this Act.

49 USC 1486.

"(2) If the Board determines that any application should be set for a public hearing under clause (A) of the second sentence of paragraph (1) of this subsection, an initial or recommended decision shall be issued not later than one hundred and fifty days after the date of such determination by the Board. Not later than ninety days after the initial or recommended decision is issued, the Board shall make its final order with respect to such application. If the Board does not act within such ninety-day period—

Final order.

"(A) in the case of an application for a certificate to engage in interstate or overseas air transportation, the initial or recommended decision shall become the final decision of the Board and shall be subject to judicial review in accordance with the provisions of section 1006 of this Act; and

"(B) in the case of an application for a certificate to engage in foreign air transportation, the initial or recommended decision shall be transmitted to the President pursuant to section 801 of this Act.

49 USC 1461.

"(3) Not later than the one-hundred-eightieth day after the Board begins to make a determination with respect to an application under the simplified procedures established by the Board in regulations pursuant to subsection (p) of this section, the Board shall issue its final order with respect to such application.

"(4) If an applicant fails to meet the procedural schedule adopted by the Board in a particular proceeding, the applicable period prescribed in paragraph (2) or (3) of this subsection may be extended by the Board for a period equal to the period of delay caused by the applicant. In addition to any extension authorized by the preceding sentence, in extraordinary circumstances, the Board may, by order delay an initial or recommended decision for not to exceed thirty days beyond the final date on which the decision is required to be made.".

(b) The amendments made by subsection (a) of this section shall

49 USC 1371 note.

apply to any application filed under section 401(b) of the Federal Aviation Act of 1958 on or after the one-hundred-eightieth day after the date of enactment of this Act.

(c) That portion of the table of contents contained in the first section of such Act which appears under the side heading

"Sec. 401. Certificate of public convenience and necessity."

is amended by striking out

"(c) Notice of application."

and inserting in lieu thereof

"(c) Route applications."

ISSUANCE OF CERTIFICATE

SEC. 8. Paragraphs (1), (2), and (3) of section 401(d) of the Federal Aviation Act of 1958 (49 U.S.C. 1371(d)(1)-(3)) are amended to read as follows:

"(d)(1) The Board shall issue a certificate authorizing the whole or any part of the transportation covered by the application, if it finds that the applicant is fit, willing, and able to perform such transportation properly and to conform to the provisions of this Act and the rules, regulations, and requirements of the Board hereunder, and that such transportation—

"(A) in the case of interstate or overseas air transportation, is consistent with the public convenience and necessity; and

"(B) in the case of foreign air transportation, is required by the public convenience and necessity;
otherwise such application shall be denied.

"(2) In the case of an application for a certificate to engage in temporary air transportation, the Board may issue a certificate authorizing the whole or any part thereof for such limited periods—

"(A) in the case of an application for interstate or overseas air transportation, as is consistent with the public convenience and necessity; and

"(B) in the case of an application for foreign air transportation, as may be required by the public convenience and necessity;
if it finds that the applicant is fit, willing, and able properly to perform such transportation and to conform to the provisions of this Act and the rules, regulations, and requirements of the Board hereunder.

"(3) In the case of an application for a certificate to engage in charter air transportation, the Board may issue a certificate to any applicant, not holding a certificate under paragraph (1) or (2) of this subsection on January 1, 1977, authorizing interstate air transportation of persons, which authorizes the whole or any part thereof—

"(A) in the case of an application for interstate or overseas air transportation, for such periods, as is consistent with the public convenience and necessity; and

"(B) in the case of an application for foreign air transportation, for such periods, as may be required by the public convenience and necessity;
if it finds that the applicant is fit, willing, and able properly to perform the transportation covered by the application and to conform to the provisions of this Act and the rules, regulations, and requirements of the Board hereunder.".

THROUGH SERVICE AND JOINT FARES

SEC. 9. Paragraph (4) of section 401(d) of the Federal Aviation Act of 1958 (49 U.S.C. 1371(d)(4)) is amended to read as follows:

"(4)(A) Notwithstanding any other provision of this Act, any citizen of the United States who undertakes, within any State, the carriage of persons or property as a common carrier for compensation or hire with aircraft capable of carrying thirty or more persons pursuant to authority for such carriage within such State granted by the appropriate State agency is authorized—

"(i) to establish services for persons and property which includes transportation by such citizen over its routes in such State and transportation by an air carrier or a foreign air carrier in air transportation; and

"(ii) subject to the requirements of section 412 of this title, to enter into an agreement with any air carrier or foreign air carrier for the establishment of joint fares, rates, or services for such through services.   49 USC 1382.

"(B) The joint fares or rates established under clause (ii) of subparagraph (A) of this paragraph shall be the lowest of—

"(i) the sum of the applicable fare or rate for service in the State approved by the appropriate State agency, and the applicable fare or rate for that part of the through service provided by the air carrier or foreign air carrier;

"(ii) a joint fare or rate established and filed in accordance with section 403 of this Act; or   49 USC 1373.

"(iii) a joint fare or rate established by the Board in accordance with section 1002 of this Act.".   49 USC 1482.

UNUSED AUTHORITY

SEC. 10. (a) Section 401(d) of the Federal Aviation Act of 1958 (49 U.S.C. 1371(d)) is amended by adding at the end thereof the following new paragraph:

"(5)(A) Except as provided in subparagraphs (B) and (G)(i) of this paragraph, if an air carrier is authorized by its certificate to provide round trip service nonstop each way between any two points in the forty-eight contiguous States or between any two points in overseas air transportation and if such air carrier fails to provide such service pursuant to published flight schedules at a minimum of five round trips per week for at least thirteen weeks during any twenty-six-week period (other than such a period during which service was interrupted by a labor dispute which lasted more than six weeks) the last day of which ends on or after the date of enactment of this paragraph and if such service, at a minimum of five round trips per week, has been provided between such points for at least thirteen weeks during such twenty-six-week period, pursuant to published flight schedules, by no more than one other air carrier, then the Board shall issue a certificate to the first applicant who, within thirty days after the last day of such twenty-six-week period, submits an application which certifies that its aircraft meet all requirements established by the Secretary of Transportation for the carriage by aircraft of persons or property as a common carrier for compensation or hire or the carriage of mail by aircraft in commerce and that it is able to conform to the rules, regulations, and requirements of the Board promulgated pursuant to this Act.

"(B) Except as provided in subparagraph (G)(ii) of this paragraph, if an air carrier is authorized to provide seasonal round trip service nonstop each way between any two points in the forty-eight contiguous States in interstate air transportation or between any two points in overseas air transportation and if such air carrier fails to provide such service pursuant to published flight schedules at a minimum of five round trips per week during half of the weeks during such season (other than such a season during which service was interrupted by a labor dispute which lasted more than 25 per centum of such season) the last day of which ends on or after the date of enactment of this paragraph and if such service, at a minimum of five round trips per week, has been provided between such points for at least half of the weeks during such season, pursuant to published flight schedules, by no more than one other air carrier, then the Board shall issue a certificate to the first applicant who, within thirty days after the last day of such season, submits an application which certifies that its aircraft meet all requirements established by the Secretary of Transportation for the carriage by aircraft of persons or property as a common carrier for compensation or hire or the carriage of mail by aircraft in commerce and that it is able to conform to the rules, regulations, and requirements of the Board promulgated pursuant to this Act.

Final order.

"(C) With respect to any application which is submitted pursuant to subparagraph (A) or (B) of this paragraph, except as provided in subparagraph (G), the Board shall issue a final order granting such certificate within fifteen days of the date of such application.

"(D) Except as provided in subparagraphs (E) and (G)(i) of this paragraph, if an air carrier is authorized by its certificate to provide round trip service nonstop each way between any two points in the forty-eight contiguous States or between any two points in overseas air transportation and if such air carrier fails to provide such service pursuant to published flight schedules at a minimum of five round trips per week for at least thirteen weeks during any twenty-six-week period (other than such a period during which service was interrupted by a labor dispute which lasted more than six weeks) the last day of which ends on or after the date of enactment of this paragraph and if such service, at a minimum of five round trips per week, has been provided between such points for at least thirteen weeks during such twenty-six-week period, pursuant to published flight schedules, by two or more other air carriers, then the Board, subject to subparagraph (F) of this paragraph, shall issue a certificate to the first applicant who, within thirty days after the last day of such twenty-six-week period, submits an application which certifies that its aircraft meet all requirements established by the Secretary of Transportation for the carriage by aircraft of persons or property as a common carrier for compensation or hire or the carriage of mail by aircraft in commerce and that it is able to conform to the rules, regulations, and requirements of the Board promulgated pursuant to this Act.

"(E) Except as provided in subparagraph (G)(ii) of this paragraph, if an air carrier is authorized to provide seasonal round trip service nonstop each way between any two points in the forty-eight contiguous States in interstate air transportation or between any two points in overseas air transportation and if such air carrier fails to provide such service pursuant to published flight schedules at a minimum of five round trips per week during half of the weeks during such season (other than such a season during which service was interrupted by a labor dispute which lasted more than 25 per centum of such season) the last day of which ends on or after the date of enactment of this paragraph and if such service, at a minimum of five round trips per week, has been provided between such points for at least half of the weeks during such season, pursuant to published flight schedules, by two or more other air carriers, then the Board, subject to subparagraph (F) of this paragraph, shall issue a certificate to the first applicant who, within thirty days after the last day of such season, submits an application which certifies that its aircraft meet all requirements established by the Secretary of Transportation for the carriage by aircraft of persons or property as a common carrier for compensation or hire or the carriage of mail by aircraft in commerce and that it is able to conform to the rules, regulations, and requirements of the Board promulgated pursuant to this Act.

"(F)(i) Except as provided in subparagraph (G) of this paragraph, with respect to any application which is submitted pursuant to subparagraph (D) or (E) of this paragraph, the Board shall issue a final order granting such certificate within sixty days of the date of such application, unless the Board finds that the issuance of such certificate is inconsistent with the public convenience and necessity. Prior to issuing such final order, the Board shall afford adequate notice and opportunity for interested persons to file appropriate written evidence and argument, but the Board need not hold oral evidentiary hearings. Notice.

"(ii) For purposes of clause (i) of this subparagraph, there shall be a rebuttable presumption that any transportation covered by an application for a certificate submitted pursuant to subparagraph (D) or (E) of this paragraph is consistent with the public convenience and necessity.

"(G)(i) If, after the failure of any air carrier to provide the minimum level of service between any pair of points for the period of time specified in subparagraph (A) or (D) of this paragraph and before the Board receives an application from any applicant for a certificate under such subparagraph to provide air transportation between such points, the Board receives notice from such air carrier that it intends to commence service within thirty days of such notice and to provide a minimum of five round trips per week for thirteen consecutive weeks between such points and the Board has not previously received notice from such air carrier with respect to such points, the Board shall not approve such application for a certificate to provide service between such points during such thirteen-week period based upon such failure, unless such air carrier fails to provide such service during such thirteen-week period. Notice.

"(ii) If, after the failure of any air carrier to provide the minimum level of service between any pair of points for the period of time specified in subparagraph (B) or (E) of this paragraph and before the Board receives an application from any applicant for a certificate under such subparagraph to provide air transportation between such points, the Board receives notice from such air carrier that it intends to commence service within fifteen days of the first day of the next season and to provide a minimum of five round trips per week for the first half of such season between such points and the Board has not previously received notice from such air carrier with respect to such points, the Board shall not approve such application for a certificate to provide service between such points during the first half of such period based upon such failure, unless such air carrier fails to provide such service during the first half of such period.

"(H)(i) Whenever the Board issues a certificate pursuant to subparagraph (A) or (D) of this paragraph, the air carrier receiving such certificate shall commence service pursuant to such certificate within forty-five days of such issuance. If such air carrier fails to commence service within such period, the Board shall revoke such certificate.

Revocation of certificate.

"(ii) Whenever the Board issues a certificate pursuant to subparagraph (B) or (E) of this paragraph to provide seasonal service, the air carrier receiving such certificate shall commence service pursuant to such certificate within fifteen days after the beginning of the first such season which begins on or after the date of such issuance. If such air carrier fails to commence service within such period, the Board shall revoke such certificate.

Revocation of certificate.

"(I) Not more than one certificate shall be issued under this paragraph for round trip nonstop service between two points in interstate air transportation based upon the failure of the same air carrier to provide such service between such points.

"(J) Whenever the Board issues a certificate pursuant to subparagraph (A) of this paragraph based upon the failure of any air carrier to provide the round trip service described in such subparagraph, the Board shall suspend the authority of such air carrier to provide such service, and suspend the authority of any other air carrier which failed to provide such service during the same twenty-six-week period for twenty-six weeks after the date of issuance of such certificate pursuant to subparagraph (A), or until such time within such twenty-six weeks as the air carrier to which a certificate is issued under such subparagraph fails to provide such service at a minimum of five round trips per week for at least thirteen weeks, whichever first occurs, except that the Board shall not suspend the authority of such air carriers under this subparagraph if the Board finds that such suspension is not necessary to encourage continued service between such points by the air carrier which received a certificate under subparagraph (A).".

(b) Section 401(f) of such Act is amended by striking out "hereinafter provided" and inserting in lieu thereof "provided in this section".

FILL-UP RIGHTS

Sec. 11. Section 401(d) of the Federal Aviation Act of 1958 (49 U.S.C. 1371(d)) is further amended by adding at the end thereof the following new paragraph:

"(6) Any air carrier holding a valid certificate to engage in foreign air transportation is authorized, on any scheduled flight in foreign air transportation, to transport persons, property, and mail between points in the United States between which it is authorized to operate during such flight. The authority described in the preceding sentence shall be limited to one round-trip flight per day between any such pair of points, unless the Board authorizes more than one round-trip flight per day between any such pair of points.".

AUTOMATIC MARKET ENTRY PROGRAM

Sec. 12. Section 401(d) of the Federal Aviation Act of 1958 (49 U.S.C. 1371(d)) is further amended by adding at the end thereof the following new paragraph:

"(7)(A) After the first business day of each of the calendar years 1979, 1980, and 1981 and before the thirtieth day of such calendar year—

"(i) any air carrier which (I) has operated during the preceding calendar year in accordance with a certificate issued by the Board under this section which has been in force during such entire preceding calendar year, and (II) has provided air transportation of persons during such calendar year; and

"(ii) any intrastate air carrier which has a valid certificate or license issued by a State regulatory authority to engage in intrastate air transportation and which has operated more than one hundred million available seat-miles in intrastate air transportation in the preceding calendar year;

may apply to the Board for a certificate under this subparagraph to engage in nonstop service between any one pair of points in interstate or overseas air transportation (other than a pair of points either point of which is in the State of Hawaii) in addition to any pair of points authorized by any existing certificate or license held by such air carrier or intrastate air carrier, except that no air carrier may apply to engage in nonstop service between such pair of points if any air carrier has filed written notice to the Board pursuant to subparagraph (C) of this paragraph with respect to such pair of points. Not later than the sixtieth day after the date on which the Board receives an application from an applicant under this subparagraph, the Board shall issue a certificate to such applicant for the nonstop service specified in such application, unless within such sixty-day period the Board determines that the applicant is not fit, willing, and able to provide such nonstop service and to conform to the provisions of this Act and the rules, regulations, and requirements of the Board issued under this Act.

"(B) Not later than the one-hundred-twentieth day of calendar year 1979, 1980, or 1981, any air carrier which submitted an application to the Board in accordance with subparagraph (A) of this paragraph in such calendar year and—

"(i) which did not receive a certificate to provide service between the pair of points set forth in the application because of a determination by the Board under such subparagraph (A); or

"(ii) which received a certificate to provide service between such pair of points, but was not the only air carrier to receive a certificate under such subparagraph (A) during such calendar year to provide nonstop service between such pair of points;

may reapply to the Board for a certificate to engage in nonstop service between any one pair of points in interstate or overseas air transportation (other than the pair of points specified in the first application submitted to the Board by such air carrier in such calendar year and other than a pair of points either point of which is in the State of Hawaii) in addition to any pair of points authorized by any existing certificate or license held by such air carrier or intrastate air carrier, except that no air carrier may apply to engage in nonstop service between such pair of points if any air carrier has filed written notice to the Board pursuant to subparagraph (C) of this paragraph with respect to such pair of points. Not later than the sixtieth day after the date on which the Board receives an application under this subparagraph, the Board shall issue a certificate to the applicant for such nonstop service, unless within such sixty-day period the Board makes a determination with respect to the issuance of such certificate in accordance with the second sentence of subparagraph (A) of this paragraph. If the Board issues a certificate to an applicant under this subparagraph, it shall revoke any authority in any certificate which it granted to such applicant in the same calendar year under subparagraph (A) of this paragraph.

Written notice.
Ante, p. 1712.
"(C) (i) Subject to clause (ii) of this subparagraph, any air carrier which is authorized pursuant to paragraph (1) or (2) of this subsection to engage in nonstop service between any pair of points in interstate or overseas air transportation on the first business day of calendar year 1979, 1980, or 1981 and which wants to preclude any other air carrier from obtaining authority under subparagraph (A) or (B) of this paragraph to engage in nonstop service between such pair of points during such calendar year may, on such day, file written notice to the Board which sets forth such pair of points. Upon receipt of any written notice under the preceding sentence, the Board shall make such notice available to the public.

Public
availability.

"(ii) No air carrier may file a written notice under clause (i) of this subparagraph during any calendar year with respect to more than one pair of points in interstate or overseas air transportation.

Program
modification.

"(D) (i) The Board shall, on an emergency basis, by rule, modify the program established by this paragraph, if the Board finds that—

"(I) the operation of such program is causing substantial public harm to the national air transportation system, or a substantial reduction in air service to small and medium sized communities in any region of the country;

"(II) the modification proposed by the Board is required by the public convenience and necessity in order to alleviate such harm or reduction; and

"(III) such harm or reduction identified by the Board cannot be rectified by any reasonably available means other than the modification proposed by the Board.

Any emergency modification proposed by the Board under this subparagraph shall modify such program only to the minimum extent necessary to rectify the harm or reduction identified by the Board. Any emergency modification of such program may be limited to any pair of points.

"(ii) The findings of fact by the Board in any proceeding held pursuant to this subparagraph, if supported by substantial evidence, shall be conclusive. No objection to a modification of the program proposed by the Board under this subparagraph shall be considered by a court unless such objection shall have been submitted to the Board, of if it was not so submitted, unless there were reasonable grounds for failure to do so.

Study of
procedure.

"(E) The Board shall conduct a study of the procedure for certification of air carriers and intrastate air carriers set forth in subparagraphs (A) and (B) of this paragraph to evaluate—

49 USC 1302.

"(i) whether such procedure is consistent with the criteria set forth in section 102 of this Act; and

"(ii) the relative effectiveness of such procedure as compared with other procedures for certification set forth in this Act, including but not limited to, the procedures set forth in paragraphs (5) and (6) of this subsection and in subsection (p) of this section.

Not later than December 31, 1980, the Board shall complete such study and report the results of such study to the Congress.".

EXPERIMENTAL CERTIFICATES

SEC. 13. Section 401(d) of the Federal Aviation Act of 1958 (49 U.S.C. 1371(d)) is further amended by adding at the end thereof the following new paragraph:

Ante, p. 1712.

"(8) The Board may grant an application under subsection (d) (1), (2), or (3) of this section (whether the application be for permanent or temporary authority) for only a temporary period of time whenever the Board determines that a test period is desirable in order to determine if projected services, efficiencies, methods, rates, fares, charges, or other projected results will in fact materialize and remain for a sustained period of time, or to assess the impact of the new services on the national air route structure, or otherwise to evaluate the proposed new services. In any case where the Board has issued a certificate under any one of such subsections on the basis that the air carrier holding such certificate will provide innovative or low-priced air transportation under such certificate, the Board, upon petition, or its own motion, may review the performance of such air carrier, and may alter, amend, modify, suspend, or revoke such certificate or authority in accordance with the procedures prescribed in section 401(g) of this title, on the grounds that such air carrier has not provided, or is not providing, such air transportation.".

49 USC 1371.

DETERMINATIONS FOR ISSUANCE OF CERTIFICATES

SEC. 14. Section 401(d) of the Federal Aviation Act of 1958 (49 U.S.C. 1371(d)) is further amended by adding at the end thereof the following new paragraph:

"(9)(A) In any determination as to whether or not any applicant is fit, willing, and able to perform properly the air transportation specified in the application for a certificate described in paragraph (1)(A), (2)(A), or (3)(A) of this subsection and to conform to the provisions of this Act, the applicant shall have the burden of showing that it is so fit, willing, and able.

Ante, p. 1712.

"(B) In any determination as to whether the air transportation specified in any application for a certificate described in paragraph (1)(A), (2)(A), or (3)(A) of this subsection is or is not consistent with the public convenience and necessity, an opponent of the application shall have the burden of showing that such air transportation is not consistent with the public convenience and necessity.

"(C) Transportation covered by any application for a certificate described in paragraph (1)(A), (2)(A), or (3)(A) of this subsection shall, for the purposes of such paragraphs, be deemed to be consistent with the public convenience and necessity, unless the Board finds based upon a preponderance of the evidence that such transportation is not consistent with the public convenience and necessity.".

TERMS AND CONDITIONS OF CERTIFICATES

SEC. 15. (a) Paragraph (3) of section 401(e) of the Federal Aviation Act of 1958 (49 U.S.C. 1371(e)(3)) is amended by striking out "supplemental air transportation" and inserting in lieu thereof "foreign charter air transportation".

(b) Paragraph (4) of section 401(e) of such Act is amended by striking out the semicolon and all that follows down through the period and inserting in lieu thereof a period.

(c) Paragraph (6) of section 401(e) of such Act is amended by striking out "supplemental air carrier" and inserting in lieu thereof "charter air carrier".

REMOVAL OF RESTRICTIONS

SEC. 16. Section 401(e) of the Federal Aviation Act of 1958 (49 U.S.C. 1371(e)) is further amended by adding at the end thereof the following new paragraph:

"(7) (A) On and after the date of enactment of this paragraph, the Board shall not attach a closed-door restriction to any certificate issued under this section. Any closed-door restriction attached to any certificate issued before such date shall, on and after such date, have no force or effect. This subparagraph shall not apply to (i) a closed-door restriction applicable to air transportation between two points both of which are in the State of Hawaii, or (ii) a closed-door restriction in effect on such date which resulted from a sale, exchange, or transfer by any air carrier of its authority to provide air transportation to another air carrier.

"(B) Upon application of any air carrier seeking removal or modification of a term, condition, or limitation attached to a certificate issued under this section to engage in interstate, overseas, or foreign air transportation, the Board shall, within sixty days after the filing of such application, set such application for oral evidentiary hearings on the record or begin to consider such application under the simplified procedures established by the Board in regulations pursuant to subsection (p) of this section for purposes of eliminating or modifying any such term, condition, or limitation which it finds is inconsistent with the criteria set forth in section 102 of this Act. Applications under this paragraph shall not be subject to dismissal pursuant to section 401(c) (1) of this Act.

"(C) For purposes of this paragraph, the term 'closed-door restriction' means any condition attached to a certificate to provide interstate or overseas air transportation issued to any air carrier under this section which prohibits such air carrier from providing local passenger service between any pair of points between which it is authorized to operate pursuant to such certificate.".

49 USC 1302.

Ante, p. 1711.
"Closed-door restriction."

EFFECTIVE DATE AND DURATION OF CERTIFICATE

SEC. 17. Section 401(f) of the Federal Aviation Act of 1958 (49 U.S.C. 1371(f)) is amended by striking out "ceased:" and all that follows down through the period and inserting in lieu thereof "ceased.".

AUTHORITY TO MODIFY, SUSPEND, OR REVOKE

SEC. 18. The first sentence of section 401(g) of the Federal Aviation Act of 1958 (49 U.S.C. 1371(g)) is amended by inserting "or pursuant to the simplified procedures under subsection (p) of this section" after "notice and hearings".

TERMINATIONS, REDUCTIONS, AND SUSPENSIONS OF SERVICE

SEC. 19. (a) Section 401(j) of the Federal Aviation Act of 1958 is amended to read as follows:

"TERMINATIONS, REDUCTIONS, AND SUSPENSIONS OF SERVICE

"(j) (1) No air carrier holding a certificate issued under this section shall—

"(A) terminate or suspend all air transportation which it is providing to a point under such certificate; or

"(B) reduce any such air transportation below that which the Board has determined to be essential air transportation for such point;

unless such air carrier has first given the Board, any community Notice.
affected, and the State agency of the State in which such community
is located, at least 90 days notice of its intent to so terminate, suspend,
or reduce such air transportation. The Board may, by regulation
or otherwise, authorize such temporary suspension of service as may
be in the public interest.

"(2) If an air carrier holding a certificate issued pursuant to section
401 of this Act proposes to terminate or suspend nonstop or single-   49 USC 1371.
plane air transportation between two points being provided by such
air carrier under such certificate, and such air carrier is the only air
carrier certificated pursuant to such section 401 providing nonstop
or single-plane air transportation between such points, at least sixty
days before such proposed termination or suspension, such air carrier
shall file with the Board and serve upon each community to be directly
affected notice of such termination or suspension.".

(b) That portion of the table of contents contained in the first
section of such Act which appears under the side heading

"Sec. 401. Certificate of public convenience and necessity."

is amended by striking out

"(j) Application for abandonment."

and inserting in lieu thereof

"(j) Terminations, reductions, and suspensions of service.".

ADDITIONAL POWERS AND DUTIES OF BOARD WITH RESPECT TO CHARTER AIR CARRIERS

SEC. 20. (a) The center heading for section 401(n) of the Federal   49 USC 1371.
Aviation Act of 1958 is amended by striking out "SUPPLEMENTAL" and
inserting in lieu thereof "CHARTER".

(b) Paragraphs (1) through (4) of section 401(n) of such Act are
amended to read as follows:

"(n)(1) No air carrier providing air transportation under a certificate issued under this section shall commingle, on the same flight,
passengers being transported in interstate or overseas charter air
transportation with passengers being transported in scheduled interstate or overseas air transportation, except that this subsection shall
not apply to the carriage of passengers in air transportation under
group fare tariffs.

"(2) No rule, regulation, or order issued by the Board shall restrict
the marketability, flexibility, accessibility, or variety of charter trips
provided under a certificate issued under this section except to the
extent required by the public interest, and shall in no event be more
restrictive than those regulations regarding charter air transportation
in effect on October 1, 1978.

"(3) Notwithstanding any other provision of this title, no certificate
issued under this section shall authorize the holder thereof to provide
charter air transportation between two points within the State of
Alaska unless, and then only to the extent to which, the Board, in issuing or amending such certificate, may authorize after determining
that such charter air transportation is required by the public convenience and necessity. This subsection shall not apply to a certificate
issued under this section to a person who, before July 1, 1977, maintained its principal place of business within the State of Alaska and
conducted air transport operations between points within the State
of Alaska with aircraft having a certificated gross takeoff weight of
more than 40,000 pounds.

"(4) No certificate issued under this section shall permit a charter air carrier to sell or offer for sale an inclusive tour in air transportation by selling or offering for sale individual tickets directly to members of the general public, or to do so indirectly by controlling, being controlled by, or under common control with, a person authorized by the Board to make such sales.".

49 USC 1371.

(c) Paragraph (5) of section 401(n) of such Act is amended—
    (1) in the first sentence, by striking out "a supplemental air carrier to comply with the provisions of paragraph (1), (3), or (4) of this subsection" and inserting in lieu thereof "a charter air carrier to comply with the provisions of subsection (q) or (r) of this section"; and
    (2) in the last sentence, by striking out "paragraphs (1), (3), and (4) of this subsection" and inserting in lieu thereof "subsections (q) and (r) of this section".

(d)(1) Section 401 of such Act is amended by adding at the end thereof the following new subsections:

"INSURANCE AND LIABILITY

"(q)(1) No certificate shall be issued or remain in effect unless the applicant for such certificate or the air carrier, as the case may be, complies with regulations or orders issued by the Board governing the filing and approval of policies of insurance or plans for self-insurance in the amount prescribed by the Board which are conditioned to pay, within the amount of such insurance, amounts for which such applicant or such air carrier may become liable for bodily injuries to or the death of any person, or for loss of or damage to property of others, resulting from the operation or maintenance of aircraft under such certificate.

"(2) In order to protect travelers and shippers by aircraft operated by certificated air carriers, the Board may require any such air carrier to file a performance bond or equivalent security arrangement, in such amount and upon such terms as the Board shall prescribe, to be conditioned upon such air carrier's making appropriate compensation to such travelers and shippers, as prescribed by the Board, for failure on the part of such carrier to perform air transportation services in accordance with agreements therefor.

"CONTINUING REQUIREMENT

"(r) The requirement that each applicant for a certificate or any other authority under this title must be found to be fit, willing, and able to perform properly the transportation covered by its application and to conform to the provisions of this Act and the rules, regulations, and requirements of the Board under this Act, shall be a continuing requirement applicable to each such air carrier with respect to the transportation authorized by the Board. The Board shall by order, entered after notice and hearing, modify, suspend, or revoke such certificate or other authority, in whole or in part, for failure of such air carrier to comply with the continuing requirement that the air carrier be so fit, willing, and able, or for failure to file such reports as the Board may deem necessary to determine whether such air carrier is so fit, willing, and able.".

Notice and hearing.

(2) That portion of the table of contents contained in the first section of such Act which appears under the side heading

"Sec. 401. Certificates of public convenience and necessity."

is amended—

> (A) by striking out

>> "(n) Additional powers and duties of Board with respect to supplemental air carriers."

> and inserting in lieu thereof

>> "(n) Additional powers and duties of Board with respect to charter air carriers.";

and

> (B) by adding at the end thereof

>> "(q) Insurance and liability.
>> "(r) Continuing requirement.".

PROCEDURES FOR PROCESSING APPLICATIONS

Sec. 21. (a) (1) Section 401 of the Federal Aviation Act of 1958 (49 U.S.C. 1371) is amended by adding at the end thereof the following new subsection:

"PROCEDURES FOR PROCESSING APPLICATIONS FOR CERTIFICATES

"(p)(1) The Board shall promulgate rules establishing simplified procedures for—

Rules.

> "(A) the disposition of applications for a certificate to engage in air transportation pursuant to subsection (d) (1), (2), or (3) of this section; and

Ante, p. 1712.

> "(B) the alteration, amendment, modification, suspension, or transfer of all or any part of any certificate pursuant to subsection (f), (g), or (h) of this section.

49 USC 1371.

Such rules shall provide for adequate notice and an opportunity for any interested person to file appropriate written evidence and argument, but need not provide for oral evidentiary hearings. Such rules may provide that such written evidence and argument shall be filed by such person as part of a protest or memorandum filed with respect to such application under subsection (c) of this section.

"(2) The Board may use such simplified procedures in any case if the Board determines that the use of such simplified procedures is in the public interest. The rules adopted by the Board pursuant to this subsection shall, to the extent the Board finds it practicable, set forth the standards it intends to apply in determining whether to employ such simplified procedures, and in deciding cases in which such procedures are employed.".

(2) That portion of the table of contents contained in the first section of such Act which appears under the side heading

"Sec. 401. Certificate of public convenience and necessity."

is amended by inserting at the end thereof

> "(p) Procedures for processing applications for certificates.".

(b) (1) Section 402 of the Federal Aviation Act of 1958 (49 U.S.C. 1372) is amended by adding at the end thereof the following new subsection:

Rules.

"(h) The Board shall promulgate rules establishing simplified procedures for—

"(1) the disposition of applications for a permit to engage in foreign air transportation pursuant to this section; and

"(2) the alteration, amendment, modification, suspension, or transfer of all or any part of any permit pursuant to subsection (f) of this section.

Notice.

Such rules shall provide for adequate notice and an opportunity for all interested persons to file appropriate written evidence and argument, but need not provide for oral evidentiary hearings.".

(2) That portion of the table of contents contained in the first section of such Act which appears under the side heading

"Sec. 402. Permits to foreign air carriers."

is amended by inserting at the end thereof

"(h) Procedures for processing applications for permits.".

NOTICE OF TARIFF CHANGES

SEC. 22. Section 403(c) of the Federal Aviation Act of 1958 (49 U.S.C. 1373(c)) is amended to read as follows:

"NOTICE OF TARIFF CHANGES

"(c)(1) Except as provided in paragraph (2) of this subsection, no change shall be made in any rate, fare, or charge, or any classification, rule, regulation, or practice affecting such rate, fare, or charge, or the value of the service thereunder, specified in any effective tariff of any air carrier until thirty days after notice of the proposed change has been filed, posted, and published in accordance with subsection (a) of this section, except the Board may establish an alternative notice requirement, of not less than twenty-five days, to allow an air carrier to match the fares or charges specified in another air carrier's proposed tariff. Any notice specified under this subsection shall plainly state the change proposed to be made and the time such change will take effect.

"(2) If the effect of any proposed tariff change would be to institute a fare that is outside of the applicable range of fares specified in subparagraphs (A) and (B) of section 1002(d)(4) of this Act, or specified by the Board under section 1002(d)(7) of this Act, or would be to institute a fare to which such range of fares does not apply, then such proposed change shall not be implemented except after sixty days' notice filed in accordance with regulations prescribed by the Board.

49 USC 1482.

"(3) In exercising its power to suspend tariffs under sections 1002(g) and 1002(j) of this Act, the Board shall file and deliver a statement in writing of its reasons for such suspension, as required under section 1002(g), at least thirty days before the date on which the affected tariff would otherwise go into effect.".

RATES OF CARRIAGE FOR PERSONS AND PROPERTY

SEC. 23. Section 404(a)(1) of the Federal Aviation Act of 1958 (49 U.S.C. 1374(a)(1)) is amended by inserting "authorized to engage in scheduled air transportation by certificate or by exemption under section 416(b)(3) of this title" immediately before the first semicolon.

49 USC 1386.

MAIL AND COMPENSATION

Sec. 24. (a)(1) Clause (3) of the second sentence of section 406(b) of the Federal Aviation Act of 1958 (49 U.S.C. 1376(b)) is amended to read as follows: "(3) the need of each such air carrier (other than a charter air carrier) for compensation for the transportation of mail sufficient to insure the performance of such service, and—

"(A) during the period beginning on the date of enactment of this clause and ending on January 1, 1983, both dates inclusive, together with all other revenue of the air carrier from the service for which the compensation is being paid; and

"(B) after January 1, 1983, together with all other revenue of the air carrier;

to enable such air carrier under honest, economical, and efficient management, to provide (except for modifications with respect to an individual point determined after January 1, 1983, to be required by the public interest, after giving interested parties an opportunity for an evidentiary hearing with respect to air transportation for such individual point) air transportation of at least the same extent, character, and quality as that provided during the year ending December 31, 1977, to maintain and continue the development of air transportation to the extent and of the character and quality required for the commerce of the United States, the Postal Service, and the national defense.".

(2) Section 406(b) of the Federal Aviation Act of 1958 is amended by inserting after the second sentence the following new sentences: "Notwithstanding any other provision of this section, rates of compensation paid to any carrier under this section for service performed between the date of enactment of this sentence and January 1, 1983, shall be based on the subsidy need of such carrier with respect to service performed to points for which such carrier was entitled to receive compensation for serving during calendar year 1977. In the case of any local service carrier, such subsidy need shall be based on the adjusted eligible need of such carrier determined in a matter consistent with the provisions of Local Service Class Subsidy Rate VIII, with technical adjustments, and in the case of any other carrier receiving compensation during the twelve months ended June 30, 1978, such subsidy need shall be determined pursuant to the method in effect during the twelve months ended June 30, 1978. Any air carrier receiving compensation from the Board pursuant to this section which, before January 1, 1986, terminates service to a point for which such compensation is paid shall not, if such service is resumed by such air carrier, be eligible for compensation from the Board under this section for such service. Nothing in this subsection shall be construed as prohibiting any air carrier specified in the preceding sentence from applying for and receiving compensation for such service under section 419 of this title.".

(b) Subsection (c) of such section 406 (49 U.S.C. 1376(c)) is amended by adding at the end thereof the following new sentence: "The Board shall make no payments under this section for any services performed after January 1, 1986.".

LOCAL SERVICE AIR CARRIER COMPENSATION

Sec. 25. (a) The last sentence of section 406(b) of the Federal Aviation Act of 1958 (49 U.S.C. 1376(b)) is amended as follows:

(1) By striking out "the year 1966" and inserting in lieu thereof "the years 1964, 1965, and 1966".

(2) By striking out "Rate III-A" and inserting in lieu thereof "Rates III and III-A".

(3) By striking out "order E-23850 (44 CAB 637 et seq.)" and inserting in lieu thereof "orders E-21311 and E-23850 (41 CAB 138 et seq. and 44 CAB 637 et seq.)".

49 USC 1376
note.
(b) Section 12(b) of Public Law 95-163, Ninety-fifth Congress, approved November 9, 1977, is amended by striking out "the year 1966" and inserting in lieu thereof "the year 1964, 1965, or 1966".

MERGERS AND CONTROL

SEC. 26. (a) Section 408 of the Federal Aviation Act of 1958 (49 U.S.C. 1378) is amended as follows:

(1) Subsection (a) of such section 408 (49 U.S.C. 1378(a)) is amended to read as follows:

"ACTS PROHIBITED

"SEC. 408. (a) Except as provided in subsection(b) of this section, it shall be unlawful—

"(1) for two or more air carriers, or for any air carrier and any other common carrier or any person substantially engaged in the business of aeronautics, to consolidate or merge their properties, or a substantial portion thereof, into one person for the ownership, management, or operation of the properties previously in separate ownerships;

"(2) for any air carrier, any person controlling an air carrier, any other common carrier, or any person substantially engaged in the business of aeronautics, to purchase, lease, or contract to operate all or a substantial portion of the properties of any air carrier;

"(3) for any air carrier or person controlling an air carrier to purchase, lease, or contract to operate all or a substantial portion of the properties of any person substantially engaged in the business of aeronautics otherwise than as an air carrier;

"(4) for any foreign air carrier or person controlling a foreign air carrier to acquire control in any manner whatsoever of any citizen of the United States substantially engaged in the business of aeronautics;

"(5) for any air carrier or person controlling an air carrier, any other common carrier, or any person substantially engaged in the business of aeronautics to acquire control of any air carrier in any manner whatsoever;

"(6) for any air carrier or person controlling a certificated air carrier to acquire control, in any manner whatsoever, of any person substantially engaged in the business of aeronautics other than as an air carrier; or

"(7) for any person to continue to maintain any relationship established in violation of any of the foregoing paragraphs of this subsection.".

(2) Subsection (b) of such section 408 (49 U.S.C. 1378(b)) is amended to read as follows:

"POWER OF BOARD

"(b)(1) In any case in which one or more of the parties to a consolidation, merger, purchase, lease, operating contract, or acquisition of control, specified in subsection (a) of this section is an air carrier holding a valid certificate issued by the Board under section 401(d) of this section to engage in interstate or overseas air transportation, a foreign air carrier, or a person controlling, controlled by, or under common control with, such an air carrier or a foreign air carrier, the person seeking approval of such transaction shall present an application to the Board, and, at the same time, a copy to the Attorney General and the Secretary of Transportation, and thereupon the Board shall notify the persons involved in the transaction and other persons known to have a substantial interest in the proceeding, of the manner in which the Board will proceed in disposing of such application. Unless, after a hearing, the Board finds that the transaction will not be consistent with the public interest or that the conditions of this section will not be fulfilled, it shall, by order, approve such transaction, upon such terms and conditions as it shall find to be just and reasonable and with such modifications as it may prescribe, except the Board shall not approve such transaction—

Ante, p. 1712.

"(A) if it would result in a monopoly or would be in furtherance of any combination or conspiracy to monopolize or to attempt to monopolize the business of air transportation in any region of the United States; or

Monopolization.

"(B) the effect of which in any region of the United States may be substantially to lessen competition, or to tend to create a monopoly, or which in any other manner would be in restraint of trade, unless the Board finds that the anticompetitive effects of the proposed transaction are outweighed in the public interest by the probable effect of the transaction in meeting significant transportation conveniences and needs of the public, and unless it finds that such significant transportation conveniences and needs may not be satisfied by a reasonably available alternative having materially less anticompetitive effects.

Competition.

The party challenging the transaction shall bear the burden of proving the anticompetitive effects of such transaction, and the proponents of the transaction shall bear the burden of proving that it meets the significant transportation conveniences and needs of the public and that such conveniences and needs may not be satisfied by a less anticompetitive alternative.

"(2) In any case in which the Board determines that the transaction which is the subject of the application does not affect the control of an air carrier directly engaged in the operation of aircraft in air transportation, and determines that neither the Attorney General, nor the Secretary, nor any other person disclosing a substantial interest in the transaction then currently is requesting a hearing, the Board, no sooner than 30 days after publication in the Federal Register of notice of the Board's intention to dispose of such application without a hearing (a copy of which notice shall be furnished by the Board to the Attorney General and the Secretary not later than the day following the date of such publication), may determine that the public interest does not require a hearing and, in accordance with the standards set forth in subparagraphs (A) and (B) of paragraph (1) of this subsection, by order, approve or disapprove such transaction.

Notice.
Publication
in Federal
Register.

"(3)(A) In any case in which none of the parties to a consolidation, merger, purchase, lease, operating contract, or acquisition of control, specified in subsection (a) of this section. is an air carrier holding a valid certificate issued by the Board under section 401(d) of this title to engage in interstate or overseas air transportation, a foreign air carrier, or a person controlling, controlled by, or under common control with, such an air carrier or a foreign air carrier, any person seeking approval of such transaction shall file with the Board not later than the forty-fifth day before the effective date of such transaction, a statement of its intent to enter into any of the prohibited acts set forth in **Application filing.** subsection (a) of this section. The Board may, within forty-five days after the date of such filing, require such person to file an application for approval pursuant to the requirements of paragraph (1) of this subsection if it finds either that the proposed transaction may monopolize, tend to monopolize, or otherwise restrain competition in air transportation in any section of the country or that the person may not be fit, willing, and able to properly perform the transportation authorized by any license which is a part of such transaction and to conform to the provisions of this Act and the rules, regulations, and requirements of the Board issued pursuant to this Act. Subject to subparagraph (B) of this paragraph, if the Board fails to require such person to file an application pursuant to such paragraph (1) within such forty-five days, the proposed transaction shall not be subject to subsection (a) of this section.

"(B) If the Board determines that any transaction is not subject to subsection (a) of this section as a result of the last sentence of subparagraph (A) of this paragraph and such transaction received such statutory exemption due to any fraud, misrepresentation, or omission of relevant and material facts, the Board may, pursuant to rules which it is authorized to prescribe, make such transaction subject to subsection (a) of this section.".

49 USC 1378. (b) Section 408(c) of such Act is amended by inserting "any person controlling such air carrier," after "air carrier," the first place it appears in such subsection.

INTERLOCKS

Sec. 27. (a) Section 409 of the Federal Aviation Act of 1958 (49 U.S.C. 1379) is amended by striking out the center heading of such section and the center heading for subsection (a) of such section and inserting in lieu thereof the following section center heading:

"INTERLOCKING RELATIONSHIPS".

(b) Section 409 of the Federal Aviation Act of 1958 is also amended by striking out "Sec. 409. (a)" and inserting in lieu thereof "Sec. 409.".

(c) Section 409 (as amended by subsections (a) and (b) of this section) is amended as follows:

(1) Paragraphs (1), (2), and (3) are each amended by striking out "is engaged in any phase of" and inserting in lieu thereof "is substantially engaged in the business of".

(2) Paragraphs (4), (5), and (6) are each amended by striking out "engaged in any phase of" and inserting in lieu thereof "substantially engaged in the business of".

Repeal. (d) Section 409(b) of the Federal Aviation Act of 1958 (49 U.S.C. 1379(b)) is hereby repealed.

(e) That portion of the table of contents contained in the first section of the Federal Aviation Act of 1958 which appears under the center heading

"TITLE IV—AIR CARRIER ECONOMIC REGULATION"

is amended by striking out

"Sec. 409. Prohibited interests.
    "(a) Interlocking relationships.
    "(b) Profit from transfer of securities."

and inserting in lieu thereof

"Sec. 409. Interlocking relationships.".

SEC. 28. (a) Section 412(a) of the Federal Aviation Act of 1958 (49 U.S.C. 1382(a)) is amended—
    (1) by inserting in the subsection center heading "AFFECTING FOREIGN AIR TRANSPORTATION" immediately after "AGREEMENTS"; and
    (2) by inserting "foreign" immediately after "affecting".
  (b) Section 412(b) of such Act is amended by inserting "affecting foreign air transportation" immediately after "agreement" each place it appears in such section.
  (c) Section 412 of such Act is further amended by adding at the end thereof the following new subsections:

"FILING AND APPROVAL OF AGREEMENTS AFFECTING INTERSTATE OR OVERSEAS AIR TRANSPORTATION

  "(c)(1) Any air carrier may file with the Board a true copy, or, if oral, a true and complete memorandum, of any contract or agreement (whether enforceable by provisions for liquidated damages, penalties, bonds, or otherwise), or a request for authority to discuss possible cooperative working arrangements, affecting interstate or overseas air transportation and in force on the effective date of this subsection, or thereafter entered into, or any modification or cancellation thereof, between such air carrier and any other air carrier, foreign air carrier, or other carrier.
  "(2)(A) The Board shall by order disapprove any contract, agreement, or request filed pursuant to paragraph (1) of this subsection, whether or not previously approved by it, that it finds to be adverse to the public interest or in violation of this Act, and shall by order approve any contract, agreement, or request, or any modification or cancellation thereof, that it does not find to be adverse to the public interest, or in violation of this Act, except that—
    "(i) the Board may not approve or, after periodic review, continue its approval of any such contract, agreement, or request, or any modification or cancellation thereof, which substantially reduces or eliminates competition, unless it finds that the contract, agreement, or request is necessary to meet a serious transportation need or to secure important public benefits and it does not find that such need can be met or such benefits can be secured by reasonably available alternative means having materially less anticompetitive effects;
    "(ii) the Board may not approve any contract or agreement between an air carrier not directly engaged in the operation of aircraft in air transportation and a common carrier subject to the Interstate Commerce Act, as amended, governing the compensation to be received by such common carrier for transportation services performed by it; and
    "(iii) the Board may not approve any such contract or agreement, or any modification or cancellation thereof, that limits the level of capacity among air carriers in markets in which they compete, that fixes rates, fares, or charges between or among air carriers (except for joint rates, fares, or charges).
  "(B) In any proceeding before the Board involving the application of the standards set forth in subparagraph (A)(i) of this paragraph, the party opposing the proposed contract, agreement, or request shall have the burden of proving the reduction or elimination of competition, and the availability of alternative means having less anticompeti-

tive effects, and the party defending the proposed contract, agreement, or request shall have the burden of proving transportation need or public benefits.

"(C) The findings required by subparagraph (A)(i) of this paragraph, shall be included in any order of the Board approving or disapproving any contract or agreement, or any memorandum of any contract or agreement, or any modification or cancellation thereof, or any request.

"PROCEEDINGS UPON FILING

Written
notice.

"(d) Upon the filing of any contract or agreement, or any modification or cancellation thereof, or any request for authority to discuss possible cooperative working arrangements, pursuant to subsection (a) or (c) of this section, the Board, in accordance with regulations which it prescribes, shall provide to the Attorney General and the Secretary of Transportation written notice of, and an opportunity to

Hearings.

submit written comments on, the filed document. The Board may, upon its own initiative or if requested by the Attorney General or such Secretary, hold a hearing, in accordance with regulations prescribed by the Board, to determine if a contract or agreement, or request for discussion authority, whether or not previously approved, is consistent with the provisions of this Act.".

(d) That portion of the table of contents which appears under the side heading

"Sec. 412. Pooling and other agreements."

is amended by striking out

"(a) Filing of agreements required.
"(b) Approval by Board."

and inserting in lieu thereof

"(a) Filing of agreements affecting foreign air transportation required.
"(b) Approval by Board.
"(c) Filing and approval of agreements affecting interstate or overseas air transportation.
"(d) Proceedings upon filing.".

MUTUAL AID AGREEMENTS

SEC. 29. (a) Section 412 of the Federal Aviation Act of 1958 (49 U.S.C. 1382) is amended by adding at the end thereof the following new subsection:

"MUTUAL AID AGREEMENTS

"(e)(1) Notwithstanding any other provision of law, any mutual aid agreement between air carriers which was approved by the Board before the date of enactment of this subsection and which is in effect on such date of enactment shall be deemed disapproved and not in effect on and after such date of enactment.

"(2) No air carrier shall enter into any mutual aid agreement with any other air carrier, unless such air carrier files a true copy of such agreement with the Board and the Board approves such agreement pursuant to the provisions of this section. Notwithstanding subsection (c) of this section, the Board shall not approve any such agreement unless such agreement provides (A) that any air carrier will not receive payments for any period which exceed 60 per centum of the direct operating expenses during such period, (B) that benefits under the agreement are not payable for more than eight weeks during any labor strike, and that such benefits may not be for losses incurred

1406

during the first thirty days of any labor strike, and (C) that any party to such agreement will agree to submit the issues causing any labor strike to binding arbitration pursuant to the Railway Labor Act if the striking employees request such binding arbitration.

45 USC 151.

"(3) For purposes of this subsection, the term—

"(A) 'mutual aid agreement' means any contract or agreement between air carriers which provides that any such air carrier will receive payments from the other air carriers which are parties to such contract or agreement for any period during which such air carrier is not engaging in air transportation, or is providing reduced levels of service in air transportation, due to a labor strike; and

"Mutual aid agreement."

"(B) 'direct operating expenses' includes interest expenses but does not include depreciation or amortization expenses.".

"Direct operating expenses."

(b) That portion of the table of contents contained in the first section of the Federal Aviation Act of 1958 which appears under the side heading

"Sec. 412. Pooling and other agreements."

is amended by inserting at the end thereof

"(e) Mutual aid agreements.".

ANTITRUST EXEMPTION

Sec. 30. (a) Section 414 of the Federal Aviation Act of 1958 (49 U.S.C. 1384) is amended to read as follows:

"ANTITRUST EXEMPTION

"Sec. 414. In any order made under section 408, 409, or 412 of this Act, the Board may, as part of such order, exempt any person affected by such order from the operations of the 'antitrust laws' set forth in subsection (a) of the first section of the Clayton Act (15 U.S.C. 12) to the extent necessary to enable such person to proceed with the transaction specifically approved by the Board in such order and those transactions necessarily contemplated by such order, except that the Board may not exempt such person unless it determines that such exemption is required in the public interest.".

49 USC 1378, 1379, 1382.

(b) That portion of the table of contents contained in the first section of such Act which appears under the center heading

"TITLE IV—AIR CARRIER ECONOMIC REGULATION"

is amended by striking out

"Sec. 414. Legal restraints."

and inserting in lieu thereof

"Sec. 414. Antitrust exemption.".

EXEMPTION AUTHORITY

Sec. 31. (a) Section 416(b)(1) of the Federal Aviation Act of 1958 (49 U.S.C. 1386(b)(1)) is amended to read as follows:

"EXEMPTIONS

"(b)(1) Except as provided in paragraph (2) of this subsection, the Board, from time to time and to the extent necessary, may exempt from the requirements of this title or any provision thereof, or any rule, regulation, term, condition, or limitation prescribed thereunder, any person or class of persons if it finds that the exemption is consistent with the public interest.

49 USC 1386.

(b) Section 416(b) of such Act is amended by adding at the end thereof the following new paragraph:

"(3) The Board may by order relieve foreign air carriers who are not directly engaged in the operation of aircraft in foreign air transportation from the provisions of this Act to the extent and for such periods as such relief may be in the public interest.".

COMMUTER EXEMPTION

SEC. 32. Section 416(b) of the Federal Aviation Act of 1958 (49 U.S.C. 1386(b)) is further amended by adding at the end thereof the following new paragraphs:

"(4) Subject to paragraph (5) of this subsection, any air carrier in air transportation which provides (A) passenger service solely with aircraft having a maximum passenger capacity of less than fifty-six passengers, or (B) cargo service in air transportation solely with aircraft having a maximum payload capacity of less than eighteen thousand pounds, shall be exempt from the requirements of subsection

49 USC 1371.

(a) of section 401 of this title, and of such other sections of this Act as may be prescribed in regulations promulgated by the Board, if such air carrier conforms to such liability insurance requirements and such other reasonable regulations as the Board shall from time to time adopt in the public interest. The Board may by regulation increase the passenger or property capacities specified in this paragraph when the public interest so requires.

"(5) The exemption from section 401 of this title or any other requirement of this Act shall not apply to any air transportation by any air carrier between points both of which are in the State of Alaska, or one of which is in the State of Alaska and the other in Canada, unless such air carrier also holds authority to provide such air transportation from the State of Alaska.

"(6) Any air carrier operating within the State of Alaska pursuant to the exemption from section 401 of this title shall not be subject to any limitation, promulgated by the Board, on the number or location of points to be served by such air carrier, or any limitation on the frequency of service by such air carrier to points within such State, unless the Board, after a hearing, finds that the operation of such air carrier substantially impairs the ability of a certificated air carrier to provide the service authorized by its certificate, including but not limited to, the minimum service requirement for such State specified

Infra.

in section 419(c)(2) of this title.".

SMALL COMMUNITY AIR SERVICE

SEC. 33. (a) Title IV of the Federal Aviation Act of 1958 is amended by adding at the end thereof the following new section.

"SMALL COMMUNITY AIR SERVICE

"GUARANTEED ESSENTIAL AIR TRANSPORTATION

"Eligible point."
49 USC 1389.

"SEC. 419. (a)(1) For purposes of this subsection, the term 'eligible point' means any point in the United States to which, on the date of enactment of this section, any air carrier—

"(A) is providing service pursuant to a certificate issued to such carrier under section 401 of this title; or

"(B) is authorized pursuant to such certificate to provide such service, but such service is suspended on such date of enactment.

"(2)(A) With respect to each eligible point which on the date of enactment of this section is served by not more than one air carrier holding a certificate issued under section 401 of this title, not later than the last day of the one-year period beginning on such date of enactment, the Board, after considering the views of any interested community and the State agency of the State in which such community is located, shall determine what is essential air transportation for such point.

49 USC 1371.

"(B) With respect to any eligible point which on the date of enactment of this section is served by more than one air carrier holding a certificate issued under section 401 of this title and which thereafter receives service by not more than one such air carrier, not later than the last day of the six-month period beginning on the date on which the Board receives notice that service to such point will be provided by not more than one such air carrier, the Board, after considering the views of any interested community and the State agency of the State in which such community is located, shall determine what is essential air transportation to such point.

"(C) The Board shall periodically review the determination of what is essential air transportation to each eligible point, and may, based upon such review and consultations with any interested community and the State agency of the State in which such community is located, make appropriate adjustments as to what is essential air transportation to such point.

Review.

"(3) No air carrier shall terminate, suspend, or reduce air transportation to any eligible point below the level of essential air transportation established by the Board under paragraph (2) unless such air carrier—

"(A) if such air carrier—

"(i) holds a certificate issued under section 401 of this title, or

"(ii) does not hold such a certificate, but is receiving compensation pursuant to paragraph (5) of this subsection for service to such eligible point,

has given the Board, the appropriate State agency or agencies, and the communities affected at least ninety days notice prior to such termination, suspension, or reduction; and

"(B) if such air carrier does not hold such a certificate and is not receiving compensation pursuant to paragraph (5) of this subsection for service to such eligible point, has given the Board, the appropriate State agency or agencies, and the communities affected at least thirty days notice prior to such termination, suspension, or reduction.

"(4) Whenever the Board determines that essential air transportation will not be provided to any eligible point without compensation—

"(A) the Board shall provide notice that applications may be submitted by any air carrier which is willing to provide essential air transportation to such point for compensation under this subsection. In selecting an applicant to provide essential air transportation to such point for compensation the Board shall, among other factors, specifically consider—

"(i) the desirability of developing an integrated linear system of air transportation whenever such a system most adequately meets the air transportation needs of the communities involved;

"(ii) the experience of the applicant in providing scheduled air service in the vicinity of the communities for which essential air transportation is proposed to be provided; and

"(iii) notwithstanding the provisions of clause (ii), with respect to any eligible point in the State of Alaska, the experience of an applicant in providing scheduled air service, or significant patterns of nonscheduled air service pursuant to an exemption granted pursuant to section 416 of this title, in Alaska; and

49 USC 1386.

Compensation rate, establishment.

"(B) the Board shall establish, in accordance with the guidelines promulgated under subsection (d) of this section, a rate of compensation to be paid for providing such essential air transportation.

"(5) The Board shall make payments of compensation under this subsection at times and in a manner determined by the Board to be appropriate. The Board shall continue to pay compensation to any air carrier to provide essential air transportation to any eligible point only for so long as the Board determines it is necessary in order to maintain essential air transportation to such eligible point.

Service extension.
Ante, p. 1720.

"(6) Notwithstanding section 401(j) of this title, if an air carrier has provided notice to the Board under paragraph (3) of such air carrier's intention to suspend, terminate, or reduce service to any eligible point below the level of essential air transportation to such point, and if at the conclusion of the applicable period of notice the Board has not been able to find another air carrier to provide essential air transportation to such point, the Board shall require the carrier which provided such notice to continue such service to such point for an additional 30-day period, or until another air carrier has begun to provide essential air transportation to such point, whichever first occurs. If at the end of such 30-day period the Board determines that no other air carrier can be secured to provide essential air transportation to such eligible point on a continuing basis, either with or without compensation, then the Board shall extend such requirement for such additional 30-day periods (making the same determination at the end of each such period) as may be necessary to continue air transportation to such eligible point until an air carrier can be secured to provide essential air transportation to such eligible point on a continuing basis.

"(7)(A) If any air carrier (i) which is providing air transportation to any eligible point, and (ii) which is receiving compensation under this subsection or under section 406 of this title for providing such air transportation to such point, is required by the Board to continue service to such point beyond the date on which such air carrier would, but for paragraph (6) of this subsection, be able to suspend, terminate, or reduce service to such point below the level of essential air transportation to such point, then after such date such air carrier shall continue to receive such compensation until the Board finds another air carrier to provide essential air transportation to such point.

49 USC 1376.

Losses, compensation.
49 USC 1371.

"(B) If the Board requires an air carrier which holds a certificate issued under section 401 of this title and which is providing air transportation to any eligible point without compensation pursuant to paragraph (5) of this subsection or section 406 of this title to continue to provide essential air transportation to such point beyond the 90-day notice period after which, but for paragraph (6) of this subsection, such air carrier would be able to suspend, terminate, or reduce service to such point below essential air transportation for such point, then the Board shall compensate such air carrier for any losses that the air carrier incurs in complying with this subparagraph after the last day of such 90-day period, except that the Board shall not make any payments under this subparagraph, to any trunk air carrier for service to such point after the last day of the one-year period beginning on the date on which any payment is made to such air carrier under this subparagraph for service to such point.

"(C) If the Board requires an air carrier which does not hold a certificate issued under section 401 of this title, but which is providing air transportation to any eligible point without compensation pursuant to paragraph (5) of this subsection or section 406 of this title to continue to provide essential air transportation to such point beyond the 30-day notice period after which, but for paragraph (6) of this subsection, such air carrier would be able to suspend, terminate, or reduce service to such point below essential air transportation for such point, then the Board shall compensate such air carrier for any losses that such air carrier incurs in complying with this paragraph after the last day of such 30-day period.   49 USC 1371.

49 USC 1376.

"(9) During any period for which the Board requires any air carrier to continue providing air transportation to an eligible point which such air carrier has proposed to terminate, reduce, or suspend, the Board shall continue to make every effort to secure an air carrier to provide at least essential air transportation to such eligible point, on a continuing basis.

"(10) Unless the Board has determined what is essential air transportation for any eligible point pursuant to paragraph (2) of this subsection, the Board shall, upon petition of any appropriate representative of such point, prohibit any termination, suspension, or reduction of air transportation which reasonably appears to deprive such point of essential air transportation, until the Board has completed such determination.   Petition.

"(11)(A) After January 1, 1983, any air carrier may file an application with the Board seeking to have any compensation provided under section 406 of this title to the air carrier then serving an eligible point terminated in order to allow the applicant air carrier to provide air transportaton to that eligible point for compensation under this section. The Board shall grant such application, after notice and a hearing if requested by the air carrier receiving subsidy under section 406, taking into consideration the objectives specified in subparagraphs (A) (i) and (ii) of paragraph (5) of this subsection, if the applicant can show that termination of the compensation being paid under section 406, and that the provision of service by such applicant with compensation under this section, will result in a substantial—   Application.

Notice and hearing.

"(i) improvement in the air service being provided such eligible point; and

"(ii) decrease in the amount of compensation that will be required to continue essential air transportation to such eligible point.

"(B) After January 1, 1983, any air carrier may file an application with the Board seeking to have the compensation provided under this section to the air carrier then serving an eligible point, and which has been serving such eligible point for at least two years preceding the date on which such application is filed, terminated in order to allow the applicant air carrier to provide essential air transportation to such eligible point for compensation under this section. The Board shall grant such application, after notice and a hearing if requested by an air carrier receiving compensation under this section, taking into consideration the objectives specified in subparagraphs (A) (i) and (ii) of paragraph (4) of this subsection, if the applicant air carrier can show that termination of the compensation being provided to the air carrier   Application.

Notice and hearing.

1411

then serving such eligible point, and the provision of essential air transportation for compensation under this section by the applicant air carrier will result in a substantial—

"(i) improvement in the air transportation being provided such eligible point with no increase in the amount of compensation then being paid; or

"(ii) decrease in the amount of compensation that will be required to continue essential air transportation to that eligible point.

"(C) In disposing of each application filed under this subsection, the Board shall, in addition to considering the objectives specified in subparagraphs (A) (i) and (ii) of paragraph (4), solicit and give great weight to the opinions of the communities affected by the proposed replacement of an air carrier under this subsection.

"OTHER AIR SERVICE

"Eligible point."

"(b)(1) For purposes of this subsection, the term 'eligible point' means—

49 USC 1371.

"(A) any point in the United States which has been deleted from a certificate issued under section 401 of this title between July 1, 1968, and the date of enactment of this section, both dates inclusive, and which the Board designates pursuant to paragraph 2 of this subsection; and

"(B) any other point in the State of Alaska or Hawaii designated by the Board under paragraph 2 of this subsection.

Eligible point designation, rules.

"(2)(A) Not later than January 1, 1980, after considering the views of State agencies and other interested parties, the Board shall, by rule, establish objective criteria for designating points as eligible points. In establishing or modifying such criteria, the Board shall consider, among other factors, the level of traffic generated by the point concerned, its future traffic generating potential, the cost to the Federal Government of providing essential air transportation to such point, the alternative means of transportation available to the residents of such point for access to the national transportation system and its principal communities of interest, and the degree of isolation of such point from the national air transportation system. The Board may, from time to time, by rule, modify the criteria established by it under this subparagraph.

Review.

"(B) Not later than January 1, 1980, the Board shall begin to review each point described in paragraph (1)(A) of this subsection to determine whether such point shall be designated as an eligible point under the criteria established under subparagraph (B) of this paragraph. The review and designation of each such point shall be completed before January 1, 1982.

"(C) On or after January 1, 1982, the Board, upon application by any interested party, may designate any point an eligible point under the criteria established under subparagraph (B) of this paragraph (i) if such point is in the State of Alaska or the State of Hawaii, and (ii) if such designation would not increase the total number of points

49 USC 1376.

receiving a subsidy under this section and section 406 of this title above the total number of points receiving a subsidy under such section 406 on July 1, 1968.

Withdrawal.

"(3) The designation of any point by the Board under paragraph (2) of this subsection as an eligible point may be withdrawn if the point no longer meets the criteria for designation as an eligible point.

"(4)(A) With respect to any point which the Board designates as an eligible point pursuant to paragraph (2) of this subsection, not later than the last day of the six-month period beginning on the date on which the Board makes such designation, the Board, after considering the views of any interested community and the State agency of the State in which such community is located, shall determine what is essential air transportation to such point. Determination, consultation.

"(B) The Board shall periodically review the determination of what is essential air transportation to each eligible point, and may, based upon such review and consultations with any interested community and any State agency of the State in which such community is located, make appropriate adjustments as to what is essential air transportation to such point. Review.

"(5) Whenever the Board determines that essential air transportation will not be provided to any eligible point without compensation—

"(A) the Board shall provide notice that applications may be submitted by any air carrier which is willing to provide essential air transportation to such point for compensation under this subsection. In selecting an applicant to provide essential air transportation to such point for compensation, the Board shall, among other factors, specifically consider— Notice.
Applicant selection.

"(i) the desirability of developing an integrated linear system of air transportation whenever such a system most adequately meets the air transportation needs of the communities involved;

"(ii) the experience of the applicant in providing scheduled air service in the vicinity of the communities for which essential air transportation is proposed to be provided; and

"(iii) notwithstanding the provisions of clause (ii), with respect to any eligible point in the State of Alaska, the experience of an applicant in providing scheduled air service, or significant patterns of nonscheduled air service pursuant to an exemption granted pursuant to section 416 of this title, in Alaska; and 49 USC 1386.

"(B) the Board shall establish, in accordance with the guidelines promulgated under subsection (d) of this section, a rate of compensation to be paid for providing such essential air transportation. Compensation rate, establishment.

"(6) The Board shall make payments of compensation under this subsection at times and in a manner determined by the Board to be appropriate. The Board shall continue to pay compensation to any air carrier to provide essential air transportation to any eligible point only for so long as the Board determines it is necessary in order to maintain essential air transportation to such eligible point. Payments.

"(7) Prior to terminating, suspending, or reducing essential air transportation to any eligible point, an air carrier— Notice.

"(A) if such air carrier—

"(i) holds a certificate issued under section 401 of this title, or 49 USC 1371.

"(ii) does not hold such a certificate, but is receiving compensation pursuant to paragraph (6) of this subsection for service to such eligible point, shall give the Board, the appropriate State agency or agencies, and the communities affected at least ninety days notice prior to such termination, suspension, or reduction; and

"(B) if such air carrier does not hold such a certificate and is not receiving compensation pursuant to paragraph (6) of this subsection for service to such eligible point, shall give the Board, the appropriate State agency or agencies, and the communities affected such notice (not to exceed 30 days), as the Board shall by regulation prescribe.

Application.

"(8) (A) After January 1, 1983, any air carrier may file an application with the Board seeking to have the compensation provided under this subsection to the air carrier then serving an eligible point, and which has been serving such eligible point for at least 2 years preceding the date on which such application is filed, terminated in order to allow the applicant air carrier to provide essential air transportation to such

Notice and hearing.

eligible point for compensation under this subsection. The Board shall grant such application, after notice and a hearing if requested by an air carrier receiving compensation under this section, taking into consideration the objectives specified in subparagraphs (A) (i) and (ii) of paragraph (5) of this subsection, if the applicant can show that termination of the compensation being provided to the air carrier then serving such eligible point, and that the provision of essential air transportation for compensation under this subsection by the applicant, will result in a substantial—

"(i) improvement in the air transportation being provided such eligible point with no increase in the amount of compensation then being paid; or

"(ii) decrease in the amount of compensation that will be required to continue essential air transportation to that eligible point.

"(B) In disposing of each application filed under this paragraph, the Board shall, in addition to considering the objectives specified in subparagraphs (A) (i) and (ii) of paragraph (5), solicit and give great weight to the opinions of the communities affected by the proposed replacement of an air carrier under this subsection.

"LEVEL OF SAFETY

"Commuter air carrier."
Ante, p. 1732.
Compensation and service, conditions.

"(c) (1) For purposes of this subsection the term 'commuter air carrier' means an air carrier exempt from any requirement of this Act under section 416(b) (3) of this title.

"(2) Notwithstanding section 416(b) of this title, the Board shall not provide any compensation under this section to any commuter air carrier to provide service to any eligible point, and the Board shall prohibit any commuter air carrier from providing service to any eligible point, unless the Board determines that such commuter air carrier—

"(A) is fit, willing, and able to perform such service; and

"(B) that all aircraft which will be used to perform such service and all operations relating to such service will conform to the safety standards established by the Administrator under paragraph (3) of this subsection.

Safety standard regulations.

"(3) Not later than the one-hundred-eightieth day after the date of enactment of this paragraph, the Administrator, by regulation, shall establish safety standards (A) for aircraft being used by commuter air carriers to provide any service described in paragraph (2) of this subsection, and (B) for all operations relating to such service. Such safety standards shall become effective not later than the last day of the eighteenth month which begins after such date of enactment and shall impose requirements upon such commuter air carriers to assure that the level of safety provided to persons traveling on such commuter air carriers is, to the maximum feasible extent, equivalent to the level of safety provided to persons traveling on air carriers which provide service pursuant to certificates issued under section 401 of this title.   49 USC 1371.

"GUIDELINES FOR COMPENSATION

"(d) The Board shall, by rule, establish guidelines to be used by the   Rule.
Board in computing the fair and reasonable amount of compensation required to insure the continuation of essential air transportation to any eligible point. Such guidelines shall include expense elements based upon representative costs of air carriers providing scheduled air transportation of persons, property, and mail, using aircraft of the type determined by the Board to be appropriate for providing essential air transportation to the eligible point.

"INSURANCE

"(e) No air carrier shall receive any compensation under this section unless such air carrier complies with regulations or orders issued by the Board governing the filing and approval of policies of insurance or plans for self-insurance in the amount prescribed by the Board which are conditioned to pay, within the amount of such insurance, amounts for which such air carrier may become liable for bodily injuries to or the death of any person, or for loss of or damage to property of others, resulting from the operation or maintenance of aircraft.

"DEFINITION

"(f) For purposes of this section, the term 'essential air transporta-   "Essential air
tion' means scheduled air transportation of persons to a point provided   transportation."
under such criteria as the Board determines satisfies the needs of the community concerned for air transportation to one or more communities of interest and insures access to the Nation's air transportation system, at rates, fares, and charges which are not unjust, unreasonable, unjustly discriminatory, unduly preferential, or unduly prejudicial, and—

"(1) with respect to air transportation to any point (other than in the State of Alaska), in no case shall essential air transportation be specified as fewer than two daily round trips. 5 days per week, or the level of service provided by air carriers to such point based on the schedules of such air carriers in effect for calendar year 1977, whichever is less; and

"(2) with respect to air transportation to any point in Alaska, essential air transportation shall not be specified at a level of service less than that which existed for such point during calendar year 1976, or two round trips per week, whichever is greater. unless otherwise specified under an agreement between the Board and the State agency of the State of Alaska, after consultation with the community affected.

"DURATION OF PROGRAM

"(g) This section shall cease to be in effect after the last day of the ten-year period which begins on the date of enactment of this section.".

(b) That portion of the table of contents which appears under the center heading

"TITLE IV—AIR CARRIER ECONOMIC REGULATION

is amended by adding at the end thereof

"Sec. 419. Small community air service.
        "(a) Guaranteed essential air transportation.
        "(b) Other air service.
        "(c) Level of safety.
        "(d) Guidelines for compensation.
        "(e) Insurance.
        "(f) Definitions.
        "(g) Duration of program.".

PRESIDENTIAL REVIEW OF INTERNATIONAL ROUTE CASES

SEC. 34. Section 801(a) of the Federal Aviation Act of 1958 (49 U.S.C. 1461(a)) is amended to read as follows:

"THE PRESIDENT OF THE UNITED STATES

49 USC 1372.
Disapproval, issuance.

"SEC. 801. (a) The issuance, denial, transfer, amendment, cancellation, suspension, or revocation of, and the terms, conditions, and limitations contained in, any certificate authorizing an air carrier to engage in foreign air transportation, or any permit issuable to any foreign air carrier under section 402 of this Act, shall be presented to the President for review. The President shall have the right to disapprove any such Board action concerning such certificates or permits solely upon the basis of foreign relations or national defense considerations which are within the President's jurisdiction, but not upon the basis of economic or carrier selection considerations. Any such disapproval shall be issued in a public document, setting forth the reasons for the disapproval to the extent national security permits, within sixty days after submission of the Board's action to the President. Any such Board action so disapproved shall be null and void. Any such Board action not disapproved within the foregoing time limits shall take effect as action of the Board, not the President, and as such shall be subject to

49 USC 1486.

judicial review as provided in section 1006 of this Act.".

ASSESSMENT OF CIVIL PENALTIES

Notice and hearing.

SEC. 35. (a) Paragraph (1) of subsection (a) of section 901 of the Federal Aviation Act of 1958 (49 U.S.C. 1471(a)(1)) is amended by inserting after the fourth sentence thereof the following new sentences:

49 USC 1371.
49 USC 1482.

"The amount of any such civil penalty for any violation of any provision of title IV of this Act, or any rule, regulation, or order issued thereunder, or under section 1002(i) of this Act, or any term, condition, or limitation of any permit or certificate issued under title IV shall be assessed by the Board only after notice and an opportunity for a hearing and after written notice upon a finding of violation by the Board. Judicial review of any order of the Board assessing such a penalty may be obtained only pursuant to section 1006 of this Act.".

Compromise.

(b) Paragraph (2) of subsection (a) of such section 901 is amended to read as follows:

"(2) Any civil penalty may be compromised by the Secretary of Transportation in the case of violations of title III, V, VI, or XII

49 USC 1341,
1401, 1421,
1441.

of this Act, or any rule, regulation, or order issued thereunder, or by the National Transportation Safety Board in the case of violations of title VII of this Act, or any rule, regulation, or order issued thereunder, or by the Postmaster General in the case of regulations issued by him.

The amount of such penalty when finally determined or fixed by order of the Board, or the amount agreed upon in compromise, may be deducted from any sums which the United States owes to the person charged.".

PROCEDURES FOR CIVIL PENALTIES

SEC. 36. (a) The first sentence of subsection (b) (1) of section 903 of the Federal Aviation Act of 1958 (49 U.S.C. 1473(b) (1)) is amended by inserting "or assessed" immediately after "imposed".

(b) The second sentence of subsection (b) (1) of such section 903 is amended by inserting "with respect to proceedings involving penalties other than those assessed by the Board," immediately after "except that".

RATES

SEC. 37. (a) Subsection (d) of section 1002 of the Federal Aviation Act of 1958 (49 U.S.C. 1482(d)) is amended—

(1) in paragraph (1), by inserting "or (4)" immediately after "paragraph (2)"; and

(2) by adding at the end thereof the following new paragraphs: Unjust or
"(4) The Board shall not have authority to find any fare for inter-   unreasonable
state or overseas air transportation of persons to be unjust or unreason-   fares, findings.
able on the basis that such fare is too low or too high if—

"(A) with respect to any proposed increase filed with the Board on or after July 1, 1979 (other than any proposed increase in any fare filed by any air carrier if such proposed fare is for air transportation between any pair of points and such air carrier provides air transportation to 70 per centum or more of the persons traveling in air transportation between such points on aircraft operated by air carriers with certificates issued under section 401 of this Act), such proposed fare would not be more than 5 per centum   49 USC 1371.
higher than the standard industry fare level for the same or essentially similar class of service, except that, while no increase of any fare within the limits specified in this subparagraph may be suspended, an increase in such fare, above the standard industry fare level shall be found unlawful if that increase results in a fare which is unduly preferential, unduly prejudicial, or unjustly discriminatory; or

"(B) with respect to any proposed decrease filed after the date of enactment of this paragraph, the proposed fare would not be more than 50 per centum lower than the standard industry fare level for the same or essentially similar class of service, except that this provision shall not apply to any proposed decrease in any fare if the Board determines that such proposed fare would be predatory.

In determining whether any fare for air transportation of persons is unjust or unreasonable on the basis that it is too high, the Board shall take into consideration reasonably estimated or foreseeable future costs and revenues for a reasonably limited future period during which the fare at issue would be in effect.

"(5) In any Board proceeding under paragraph (1) of this subsection with respect to interstate or overseas air transportation of persons, the party opposing any fare or charge on the basis that it is too low shall have the burden of proving that the fare or charge is too low.

"(6)(A) For purposes of paragraph (4) of this section, 'standard   "Standard
industry fare level' means the fare level (as adjusted only in accord-   industry
ance with subparagraph (B) of this paragraph) in effect on July 1,   fare level."
1977, for each interstate or overseas pair of points, for each class of

1417

service existing on that date, and in effect on the effective date of the establishment of each additional class of service established after July 1, 1977.

Adjustments.

"(B) The Board shall, not less than semiannually, adjust each standard industry fare level specified in subparagraph (A) by increasing or decreasing such fare level, as the case may be, by the percentage change from the last previous period in the actual operating cost per available seat-mile for interstate and overseas transportation combined. In determining the standard, the Board shall make no adjustment to costs actually incurred.

Service
classes,
rules.

"(C) Not later than July 1, 1979, the Board shall issue rules modifying the rules governing those classes of service in existence on July 1, 1977, which classes provide lower fare levels during off-peak periods, so as to expand the period of availability of such classes. The Board shall allow any air carrier to establish additional classes of service in accordance with the objectives of subsection (e)(5) of this section or as may be otherwise consistent with the public interest.

Rule.

"(7) The Board may by rule increase the percentage specified in paragraph (4)(B) of this subsection.

Complaint.

"(8) Whenever a complaint is filed with the Board by a civic party under this subsection alleging that any individual or joint fare or charge demanded, charged, collected, or received for interstate or overseas air transportation is or will be unjustly discriminatory, unduly preferential, unduly prejudicial, or predatory, the Board shall grant, deny, or dismiss such complaint within ninety days after such complaint is filed.".

49 USC 1482.

(b) Subsection (e) of such section 1002 is amended to read as follows:

"RULE OF RATEMAKING

"(e) In exercising and performing its power and duties with respect to determining rates, fares, and charges described in paragraph (1) of subsection (d) of this section, the Board shall take into consideration, among other factors—

49 USC 1302.

"(1) the criteria set forth in section 102 of this Act;

"(2) the need for adequate and efficient transportation of persons and property at the lowest cost consistent with the furnishing of such service;

"(3) the effect of prices upon the movement of traffic;

"(4) the desirability of a variety of price and service options such as peak and off-peak pricing or other pricing mechanisms to improve economic efficiency and provide low-cost air service; and

"(5) the desirability of allowing an air carrier to determine prices in response to particular competitive market conditions on the basis of such air carrier's individual costs.".

Uniform
method.
49 USC 1482a.

49 USC 1371.

Notice.

(c)(1) Whenever the Board pursuant to its authority under section 1002 of the Federal Aviation Act of 1958 (49 U.S.C. 1482) prescribes a uniform method generally applicable to the establishment of joint fares, and the divisions thereof, between air carriers holding certificates issued under section 401 of such Act, it shall make such uniform method applicable to the establishment of joint fares, and the divisions thereof, between such air carriers and commuter air carriers. Any commuter air carrier which has an agreement with any air carrier to provide service for persons and property which includes transportation over its routes and transportation by such air carrier in air transportation shall provide at least ninety days notice to such air carrier and to the Board prior to modifying, suspending, or terminating such service, and if such commuter air carrier fails to provide such notice, any uniform method made applicable to the establishment of joint fares, and the divisions thereof, between air carriers and commuter air carriers in accordance with the preceding sentence shall not apply to such commuter air carrier.

(2) For purposes of this subsection—

    (A) the terms "air carrier" and "Board" have the meanings given such terms in the Federal Aviation Act of 1958; and

    (B) the term "commuter air carrier" means any air carrier operating pursuant to section 416(b)(3) of the Federal Aviation Act of 1958 (49 U.S.C. 1386(b)(3)) who operates at least five round trips per week between one pair of points, pursuant to flight schedules.

(3) Paragraph (1) of this subsection shall apply to any uniform method described in such paragraph which the Board prescribes on or after December 27, 1974.

Definitions.

49 USC 1301 note.

TIME REQUIREMENTS

SEC. 38. (a) Title X of the Federal Aviation Act of 1958 (49 U.S.C. 1481 et seq.) is amended by adding at the end thereof the following new section:

"TIME REQUIREMENTS

"SEC. 1010. In the case of any application or other written document submitted to the Board under section 408, 409, 412, or 416 of this Act on or after the one-hundred-eightieth day after the date of enactment of this section, the Board shall—

    "(1) if the Board orders an evidentiary hearing, issue a final order or decision with respect to such written document, not later than the last day of the twelfth month which begins after the submission of such document, except in the case of an application submitted under section 408 of this Act, the Board shall issue its final order or decision not later than the last day of the sixth month after submission; or

    "(2) if the Board does not order an evidentiary hearing, issue a final order or decision with respect to such document, not later than the last day of the sixth month which begins after the date of the submission of such document.".

Final order or decision, issuance.
49 USC 1490.
49 USC 1378, 1379, 1382.

(b) That portion of the table of contents contained in the first section of such Act which appears under the center heading

"TITLE X—PROCEDURE"

is amended by adding at the end thereof

"Sec. 1010. Time requirements.".

WITHHOLDING OF INFORMATION

SEC. 39. Section 1104 of the Federal Aviation Act of 1958 (49 U.S.C. 1504) is amended to read as follows:

49 USC 1504.

"SEC. 1104. Any person may make written objection to the public disclosure of information contained in any application, report, or document filed pursuant to provisions of this Act or of any information obtained by the Board, the Secretary of State, or the Secretary of Transportation pursuant to the provisions of this Act stating the grounds for such objection. Any information contained in such application, report, or document, or any such other information obtained by the Board, the Secretary of State, or the Secretary of Transportation, shall be withheld from public disclosure by the Board, the Secretary of State, or the Secretary of Transportation, as the case may be, if disclosure of such information would prejudice the formulation and presentation of positions of the United States in international negotiations and adversely affect the competitive position of any air carrier in foreign air transportation. The Board, the Secretary of State, or the Secretary of Transportation, as the case may be, shall be responsible for classified information in accordance with appropriate law, except that nothing in this section shall authorize the withholding of information by the Board, the Secretary of State, or the Secretary of Transportation from the duly authorized committees of Congress.".

SUNSET PROVISIONS

SEC. 40. (a) The Federal Aviation Act of 1958 (49 U.S.C. 1301 et seq.) is amended by adding at the end thereof the following new title:

"TITLE XVI—SUNSET PROVISIONS

"TERMINATION OF CIVIL AERONAUTICS BOARD AND TRANSFER OF CERTAIN FUNCTIONS

"TERMINATION OF AUTHORITY

49 USC 1551.

"SEC. 1601. (a) (1) The following provisions of this Act (to the extent such provisions relate to interstate and overseas air transportation of persons) and the authority of the Board with respect to such provisions (to the same extent) shall cease to be in effect on December 31, 1981:

Ante, p. 1712.

"(A) Sections 401(d) (1), (2), and (3) of this Act (insofar as such sections require a determination of consistency with the public convenience and necessity and insofar as section 401(d) (3) prohibits persons holding certificates under section 401 (d) (1) or (d) (2) from obtaining certificates to provide interstate or overseas charter air transportation of persons).

"(B) Section 401(d) (8) of this Act.

"(C) Section 401(e)(1) of this Act (insofar as such section permits the Board to specify terminal and intermediate points).

"(D) Section 401(j) of this Act (except with respect to essential air transportation).

"(E) Sections 401(n) (1) and (4) of this Act.

"(F) Section 404(a) of this Act (insofar as such section requires any air carrier to provide air transportation authorized by its certificate).

49 USC 1375.

"(G) Section 405(b) of this Act (insofar as such section requires the filing of any statement or schedule by any air carrier).

"(2) The following provisions of this Act (to the extent such provisions relate to interstate and overseas air transportation of persons) and the authority of the Board with respect to such provisions (to the same extent) shall cease to be in effect on January 1, 1983:

"(A) Section 403 of this Act.   49 USC 1373.
"(B) Section 404 of this Act (except insofar as such section   49 USC 1374.
requires air carriers to provide safe and adequate service).
"(C) Section 407 (b) and (c) of this Act.   49 USC 1377.
"(D) Sections 1002 (d)(1) and (d)(2), (e), (g), (h), and (i)
of this Act.   *Ante,* p. 1741.

"(3) The authority of the Board under sections 408 and 409 of this   49 USC 1378,
Act (relating to interstate and overseas air transportation) and the   1379.
authority of the Board under section 414 of this Act (relating to such   49 USC 1384.
sections 408 and 409) is transferred to the Department of Justice on
January 1, 1983.

"(4) Title II of this Act shall cease to be in effect on January 1, 1985.   49 USC 1321.

"(b)(1) The following authority of the Board is transferred to the following Federal departments and instrumentalities:

"(A) The authority of the Board under sections 406 (b)(3) and
(c) of this Act to provide compensation for air transportation to   *Ante,* p. 1725.
small communities and under section 419 of this Act is transferred   *Ante,* p. 1732.
to the Department of Transportation.

"(B) The authority of the Board under this Act with respect to
foreign air transportation is transferred to the Department of
Transportation which shall exercise such authority in consultation with the Department of State.

"(C) The authority of the Board under sections 408 and 409 of
this Act (relating to foreign air transportation), the authority
of the Board under section 412 of this Act, and the authority of   49 USC 1382.
the Board under section 414 of this Act (relating to such sections
408, 409, and 412) is transferred to the Department of Justice.

"(D) The authority of the Board under this Act with respect to
the determination of the rates for the carriage of mails in interstate and overseas air transportation is transferred to the Postal
Service and such authority shall be exercised through negotiations
or competitive bidding.

"(2) Any authority transferred under paragraph (1) of this subsection shall take effect on January 1, 1985.

"(c) Not later than January 1, 1984, the Board shall prepare and   Review,
submit to the Congress a comprehensive review of the Board's imple-   submittal
mentation of the provisions of this Act during the preceding initial   to Congress.
period of this Act's existence, and a comprehensive review of each of
the Board's programs under this Act. Each such review shall be made
available to the committee or committees of the Senate and House
of Representatives having jurisdiction with respect to the annual
authorization of funds for the Board and its programs for the fiscal
year beginning October 1, 1983.

"ELEMENTS OF BOARD CONSIDERATION

Review
provisions.

"(d) The comprehensive review of the Board's implementation of this Act, prepared for submission under subsection (c), shall include—

"(1) a detailed comparison of the degree of competition within the airline industry as of the year preceding enactment of this section and the final year covered by the review;

"(2) a comparison of the degree of pricing competition in the industry during those two one-year periods;

"(3) a comparison of the extent of unused authority held by the industry during those two one-year periods, with details as to the number of nonstop route segments which have been transferred from one carrier to another under section 401(d)(5) of his Act;

Ante, p. 1713.

49 USC 1382.

"(4) an assessment of the degree to which agreements approved under section 412 of this Act have affirmatively or negatively affected the degree of competition within the industry;

"(5) a comparison of the extent of air transportation service provided to small communities during the two one-year periods specified above, together with details as to the comparative subsidy costs during these two periods;

"(6) an assessment of the degree, if any, to which the administrative process has been expedited under this Act;

"(7) an assessment of the impact of the foregoing changes upon the national air transportation system in terms of benefits or detriments to the traveling and shipping public, the Postal Service, and the national defense, and the benefits and detriments to air carriers, certificated and uncertificated; and

"(8) the Board's opinion as to whether the foregoing changes in combination, have improved or harmed this Nation's domestic air transportation system and the United States-flag foreign air transportation system.

Continuation,
opinion and
recommenda-
tions.

This assessment shall be accompanied by a detailed opinion from the Board as to whether the public interest requires continuation of the Board and its functions beyond January 1, 1985, and, if it is the Board's conclusion that it should continue to exist, detailed recommendations as to how the provisions of this Act should be revised to insure continued improvement of the Nation's air transportation system beyond January 1, 1985. The Board's assessment under this subsection shall also be accompanied by a comparative analysis of procedures under section 801 of this Act before and after the date of enactment of the Airline Deregulation Act of 1978, together with the Board's opinion as to the benefits of each set of procedures.

49 USC 1461.

"ELEMENTS FOR EACH COMPREHENSIVE REVIEW

"(e) Each comprehensive review of the Board's programs under this Act, prepared for submission under subsection (c) of this section, shall include—

"(1) an identification of the objectives intended for the program, and the problem or need which the program was intended to address;

"(2) an identification of any other programs having similar or potentially conflicting or duplicative objectives;

"(3) an assessment of alternative methods of achieving the purposes of the program;

"(4) a justification for the authorization of new budget authority, and an explanation of the manner in which it conforms to and integrates with other efforts;

"(5) an assessment of the degree to which the original objectives of the program have been achieved, expressed in terms of the performance, impact, or accomplishments of the program and of the problem or need which it was intended to address, and employing the procedures or methods of analysis appropriate to the type or character of the program;

"(6) a statement of the performance and accomplishments of the program in each of the previous four completed fiscal years and in the year of submission, and of the budgetary costs incurred in the operation of the program;

"(7) a statement of the number and types of beneficiaries or persons or entities by the program;

"(8) an assessment of the effect of the program on the national economy, including, but not limited to, the effects on competition, economic stability, employment, unemployment, productivity, energy consumption and conservation, and price inflation, including costs to consumers and to businesses;

"(9) an assessment of the impact of the program on the Nation's health and safety;

"(10) an assessment of the degree to which the overall administration of the program, as expressed in the rules, regulations, orders, standards, criteria, and decisions of the officers executing the program, are believed to meet the objectives of the Congress in enacting this Act;

"(11) a projection of the anticipated needs for accomplishing the objectives of the program, including an estimate if applicable of the date on which, and the conditions under which, the program may fulfill such objectives;

"(12) an analysis of the services which could be provided and performance which could be achieved if the program were contained at a level less than, equal to, or greater than the existing level; and

"(13) recommendations for necessary transitional requirements in the event that funding for such program is discontinued, including proposals for such executive or legislative action as may be necessary to prevent such discontinuation from being unduly disruptive.".

(b) That portion of the table of contents contained in the first section of such Act is amended by inserting at the end thereof

AMENDMENTS TO THE AIRPORT AND AIRWAY DEVELOPMENT ACT OF 1970

Air carrier
airport
designation.
49 USC 1729.

SEC. 41. (a) Section 29 of the Airport and Airway Development Act of 1970 is amended—

(1) by striking out "Notwithstanding" and inserting in lieu thereof the following:

"(a) SERVICE BY INTRASTATE AIR CARRIER.—Notwithstanding"; and

(2) by inserting at the end thereof the following new subsection:

"(b) SUSPENDED OR DELETED SERVICE.—Notwithstanding any other provision of this title, any public airport which, on the date of enactment of the Airline Deregulation Act of 1978, is regularly served by an air carrier (other than a charter air carrier) certificated by the Civil Aeronautics Board under section 401 of the Federal Aviation

49 USC 1371.

Act of 1958 shall be deemed to be an air carrier airport (other than a commuter service airport) for the purposes of this title. This subsection shall cease to be in effect after September 30, 1980.".

49 USC 1711.

(b) Paragraph (1) of section 11 of the Airport and Airway Development Act of 1970 is amended by striking out "(other than a supplemental air carrier)" and inserting in lieu thereof "(other than a charter air carrier)".

GOVERNMENT GUARANTEE OF EQUIPMENT LOANS

SEC. 42. (a) (1) The first sentence of the first section of the Act entitled "An Act to provide for Government guarantee of private loans of certain air carriers for purchase of modern aircraft and equipment, to foster the development and use of modern transport aircraft by such carriers, and for other purposes", approved September 7, 1957 (49 U.S.C. 1324 note) (hereinafter in this section referred to as the "Act"), is amended by inserting "and to promote the development of local, feeder, and short-haul charter air transportation of cargo" after "and short-haul air transportation".

(2) The second sentence of the first section of the Act is amended by inserting ", charter air carriers, commuter air carriers, and intrastate air carriers" immediately after "air carriers".

Definitions.
49 USC 1324
note.

(b) Section 2 of the Act is amended to read as follows:

"SEC. 2. As used in this Act—

"(1) 'aircraft purchase loan' means any loan, or commitment in connection therewith, made for the purchase of commercial transport aircraft, including spare parts normally associated therewith;

"(2) 'air carrier' means any air carrier holding a certificate of public convenience and necessity issued by the Civil Aeronautics Board under section 401(d)(1) of the Federal Aviation Act of 1958 (49 U.S.C. 1371(d)(1));

49 USC 1301.

"(3) 'charter air carrier' has the meaning given such term in section 101(14) of the Federal Aviation Act of 1958;

"(4) 'charter air transportation' has the meaning given such term in section 101(15) of the Federal Aviation Act of 1958;

"(5) 'commuter air carrier' means any air carrier operating pursuant to section 416(b)(3) of the Federal Aviation Act of 1958 (49 U.S.C. 1386(b)(3)) who operates at least five round trip flights per week between one pair of points in accordance with published flight schedules;

"(6) 'intrastate air carrier' means any citizen of the United States who undertakes, whether directly or indirectly or by a lease or any other arrangement, to engage primarily in intrastate air transportation (as such term is defined in section 101(26) of the Federal Aviation Act of 1958) : and

49 USC 1301.

"(7) 'Secretary' means the Secretary of Transportation.".

(c) Section 3 of the Act is amended to read as follows:

Eligible lenders.
49 USC 1324 note.

"SEC. 3. The Secretary is authorized to guarantee any lender against loss of principal or interest on any aircraft purchase loan made by such lender to—

"(1) any air carrier whose certificate (A) authorizes such air carrier to provide local or feeder air service, (B) authorizes scheduled passenger operations the major portion of which are conducted within the State of Hawaii, (C) authorizes operations (the major portion of which is conducted either within Alaska or between Alaska and the forty-eight contiguous States), within the State of Alaska (including service between Alaska and the forty-eight contiguous States, and between Alaska and adjacent Canadian territory), or (D) authorizes metropolitan helicopter service,

"(2) any charter air carrier for the purchase of any all-cargo nonconvertible aircraft,

"(3) any commuter air carrier, or

"(4) any intrastate air carrier.

Such guarantee shall be made in such form, on such terms and conditions, and pursuant to such regulations, as the Secretary deems necessary and which are not inconsistent with the provisions of this Act.".

(d) Section 4 of the Act is amended to read as follows:

Restrictions.
49 USC 1324 note.

"SEC. 4. (a) Subject to subsection (b) of this section, no guaranty shall be made—

"(1) extending to more than the unpaid interest and 90 percent of the unpaid principal of any loan;

"(2) on any loan or combination of loans for more than 90 percent of the purchase price of the aircraft, including spare parts, to be purchased therewith;

"(3) on any loan whose terms permit full repayment more than 15 years after the date thereof;

"(4) wherein the total face amount of such loan, and of any other loans to the same air carrier, charter air carrier, commuter air carrier, or intrastate air carrier or corporate predecessor of such air carrier, charter air carrier, commuter air carrier, or intrastate air carrier guaranteed and outstanding under the terms of this Act exceeds $100,000,000;

"(5) unless the Secretary finds that, without such guaranty, in the amount thereof, the air carrier, charter air carrier, commuter air carrier, or intrastate air carrier would be unable to obtain necessary funds for the purchase of needed aircraft on reasonable terms;

"(6) unless the Secretary finds that the aircraft to be purchased with the guaranteed loan is needed to improve the service and efficiency of operation of the air carrier, charter air carrier, commuter air carrier, or intrastate air carrier;

"(7) unless the Secretary finds that the prospective earning power—

"(A) of the applicant air carrier or charter air carrier, together with the character and value of the security pledged, furnish (i) reasonable assurances of the applicant's ability to repay the loan within the time fixed therefor, and (ii) reasonable protection to the United States; and

"(B) of the applicant commuter air carrier or intrastate air carrier, together with the character and value of the security pledged, furnish (i) reasonable assurances of the applicant's ability and intention to repay the loan within the time fixed therefor, to continue its operations as a commuter air carrier or intrastate air carrier, and to the extent found necessary by the Secretary, to continue its operations as a commuter air carrier or intrastate air carrier between the same route or routes being operated by such applicant at the time of the loan guarantee, and (ii) reasonable protection to the United States; and

"(8) on any loan or combination of loans for the purchase of any new turbojet-powered aircraft which does not comply with the noise standards prescribed for new subsonic aircraft in regulations issued by the Secretary acting through the Administrator of the Federal Aviation Administration (14 CFR part 36), as such regulations were in effect on January 1, 1977.

"(b) No guaranty shall be made by the Secretary under subsection (a) of this section on any loan for the purchase of any all-cargo nonconvertible aircraft by any charter air carrier in an amount which, together with any other loans guaranteed and outstanding under this Act to such charter air carrier, or corporate predecessor of such charter air carrier, would result in the ratio of the total face amount of such loans to $100,000,000 exceeding the ratio of the amount of charter air transportation of such charter air carrier provided to medium, small, and non-hub airports during the twelve-month period preceding the date on which the application for such guaranty is made by such charter air carrier to the total amount of charter air transportation of such charter air carrier during such twelve-month period.".

(e) Section 8 of the Act is amended to read as follows:

Termination date. 49 USC 1324 note. *Ante*, p. 1749.

"Sec. 8. The authority of the Secretary under section 3 of this Act shall terminate five years after the date of enactment of this section.".

EMPLOYEE PROTECTION PROGRAM

Payment by Labor Secretary. 49 USC 1552.

Sec. 43. (a). General Rule.—(1) The Secretary of Labor shall, subject to such amounts as are provided in appropriation Acts, make monthly assistance payments, or reimbursement payments, in amounts computed according to the provisions of this section, to each individual who the Secretary finds, upon application, to be an eligible protected employee. An eligible protected employee shall be a protected employee who on account of a qualifying dislocation (A) has been deprived of employment, or (B) has been adversely affected with respect to his compensation.

Eligibility.

(2) No employee who is terminated for cause shall receive any assistance under this section.

(b) Monthly Assistance Computation.—(1) An eligible protected employee shall, subject to such amounts as are provided in appropriation Acts, receive a monthly assistance payment, for each month in which he is an eligible protected employee, in an amount computed by the Secretary. The Secretary, after consultation with the Secretary of Transportation, shall, by rule, promulgate guidelines to be used by him in determining the amount of each monthly assistance payment to be made to a member of each craft and class of protected employees, and what percentage of salary such payment shall constitute for each applicable class or craft of employees. In computing such amounts for any individual protected employee, the Secretary shall deduct from such amounts the full amount of any unemployment compensation received by the protected employee.

Guideline rules, consultation.

(2) If an eligible protected employee is offered reasonably comparable employment and such employee does not accept such employment, then such employee's monthly assistance payment under this section shall be reduced to an amount which such employee would have beeen entitled to receive if such employee had accepted such employment. If the acceptance of such comparable employment would require relocation, such employee may elect not to relocate and, in lieu of all other benefits provided herein, to receive the monthly assistance payments to which he would be entitled if this paragraph were not in effect, except that the total number of such payments shall be the lesser of three or the number remaining pursuant to the maximum provided in subsection (e).

Relocation.

(c) ASSISTANCE FOR RELOCATION.—If an eligible protected employee relocates in order to obtain other employment, such employee shall, subject to such amounts as are provided in appropriation Acts, receive reasonable moving expenses (as determined by the Secretary) for himself and his immediate family. In addition, such employee shall, subject to such amounts as are provided in appropriation Acts, receive reimbursement payments for any loss resulting from selling his principal place of residence at a price below its fair market value (as determined by the Secretary) or any loss incurred in cancelling such employee's lease agreement or contract of purchase relating to his principal place of residence.

(d) DUTY TO HIRE PROTECTED EMPLOYEES.—(1) Each person who is a protected employee of an air carrier which is subject to regulation by the Civil Aeronautics Board who is furloughed or otherwise terminated by such an air carrier (other than for cause) prior to the last day of the 10-year period beginning on the date of enactment of this section shall have first right of hire, regardless of age, in his occupational specialty, by any other air carrier hiring additional employees which held a certificate issued under section 401 of the Federal Aviation Act of 1958 prior to such date of enactment. Each such air carrier hiring additional employees shall have a duty to hire such a person before they hire any other person, except that such air carrier may recall any of its own furloughed employees before hiring such a person. Any employee who is furloughed or otherwise terminated (other than for cause), and who is hired by another air carrier under the provisions of this subsection, shall retain his rights of seniority and right of recall with the air carrier that furloughed or terminated him.

49 USC 1371.

(2) The Secretary shall establish, maintain, and periodically publish a comprehensive list of jobs available with air carriers certificated under section 401 of the Federal Aviation Act of 1958. Such list shall include that information and detail, such as job descriptions and required skills, the Secretary deems relevant and necessary. In addition to publishing the list, the Secretary shall make every effort to

Job list, establishment and publication.

assist an eligible protected employee in finding other employment. Any individual receiving monthly assistance payments, moving expenses, or reimbursement payments under this section shall, as a condition to receiving such expenses or payments, cooperate fully with the Secretary in seeking other employment. In order to carry out his responsibilities under this subsection, the Secretary may require each such air carrier to file with the Secretary the reports, data, and other information necessary to fulfill his duties under this subsection.

(3) In addition to making monthly assistance or reimbursement payments under this section, the Secretary shall encourage negotiations between air carriers and representatives of eligible protected employees with respect to rehiring practices and seniority.

(e) PERIOD OF MONTHLY ASSISTANCE PAYMENTS.—(1) Monthly assistance payments computed under subsection (b) for a protected employee who has been deprived of employment shall be made each month until the recipient obtains other employment, or until the end of the 72 months occurring immediately after the month such payments were first made to such recipient, whichever first occurs.

(2) Monthly assistance payments computed under subsection (b) for a protected employee who has been adversely affected relating to his compensation shall be paid for no longer than 72 months, so long as the total number of monthly assistance payments made under this section for any reason do not exceed 72.

(f) RULES AND REGULATIONS.—(1) The Secretary may issue, amend, and repeal such rules and regulations as may be necessary for the administration of this section.

(2) The rule containing the guidelines which is required to be promulgated pursuant to subsection (b) of this section and any other rules or regulations which the Secretary deems necessary to carry out this section shall be promulgated within six months after the date of enactment of this section.

(3) The Secretary shall not issue any rule or regulation as a final rule or regulation under this section until 30 legislative days after it has been submitted to the Committee on Commerce, Science, and Transportation of the Senate and the Committee on Public Works and Transportation of the House of Representatives. Any rule or regulation issued by the Secretary under this section as a final rule or regulation shall be submitted to the Congress and shall become effective 60 legislative days after the date of such submission, unless during that 60-day period either House adopts a resolution stating that that House disapproves such rules or regulations, except that such rules or regulations may become effective on the date, during such 60-day period, that a resolution has been adopted by both Houses stating that the Congress approves of them.

(4) For purposes of this subsection, the term "legislative day" means a calendar day on which both Houses of Congress are in session.

(g) AIRLINE EMPLOYEES PROTECTIVE ACCOUNT.—All payments under this section shall be made by the Secretary from a separate account maintained in the Treasury of the United States to be known as the Airline Employees Protective Account. There are authorized to be appropriated to such account annually, beginning with the fiscal year ending September 30, 1979, such sums as are necessary to carry out the purposes of this section, including amounts necessary for the administrative expenses of the Secretary related to carrying out the provisions of this section.

(h) DEFINITIONS.—For the purposes of this section—

(1) The term "protected employee" means a person who, on the date of enactment of this section, has been employed for at least 4 years by an air carrier holding a certificate issued under section 401 of the Federal Aviation Act of 1958. Such term shall not include any members of the board of directors or officers of a corporation.

(2) The term "qualifying dislocation" means a bankruptcy or major contraction of an air carrier holding a certificate under section 401 of the Federal Aviation Act of 1958, occurring during the first 10 complete calendar years occurring after the date of enactment of the Airline Deregulation Act of 1978, the major cause of which is the change in regulatory structure provided by the Airline Deregulation Act of 1978, as determined by the Civil Aeronautics Board.

49 USC 1371.

(3) The term "Secretary" means the Secretary of Labor.

(4) The term "major contraction" means a reduction by at least $7\frac{1}{2}$ percent of the total number of full-time employees of an air carrier within a 12-month period. Any particular reduction of less than $7\frac{1}{2}$ percent may be found by the Board to be part of a major contraction of an air carrier if the Board determines that other reductions are likely to occur such that within a 12-month period in which such particular reduction occurs the total reduction will exceed $7\frac{1}{2}$ percent. In computing a $7\frac{1}{2}$-percent reduction under this paragraph, the Board shall not include employees who are deprived of employment because of a strike or who are terminated for cause.

(i) TRANSFER OF AUTHORITY OF THE BOARD.—The authority of the Board under this section is transferred to the Department of Transportation on January 1, 1985.

(j) TERMINATION.—The provisions of this section shall terminate on the last day the Secretary is required to make a payment under this section.

LABOR DISPUTE

SEC. 44. Within ten days after the date of enactment of this section the President, pursuant to section 10 of the Railway Labor Act, shall create a board to investigate and report on the dispute between Wier Air Alaska, Incorporated, and the Air Line Pilots Association. Such board shall report its findings to the President within thirty days from the date of its creation.

Emergency board.
45 USC 160.

COLLECTION OF FEES, CHARGES, AND PRICES

SEC. 45. Notwithstanding any other provisions of law, neither the Secretary of Transportation nor the Administrator of the Federal Aviation Administration shall collect any fee, charge, or price for any approval, test, authorization, certificate, permit, registration, conveyance, or rating relating to any aspect of aviation (1) which is in excess of the fee, charge, or price for such approval, test, authorization, certificate, permit, registration, conveyance, or rating which was in effect on January 1, 1973, or (2) which did not exist on January 1,

Review and approval by Congress.
49 USC 1341 note.

1973, until all such fees, charges, and prices are reviewed and approved by Congress.

CONTINUITY FOR CERTAIN CERTIFICATES

49 USC 1301 note.

SEC. 46. Any reference in any law, rule, regulation, or document of the United States to a supplemental air carrier or supplemental air transportation shall be deemed to be a reference to a charter air carrier or charter air transportation, respectively.

EXISTING DETERMINATIONS

49 USC 1301 note.

SEC. 47. All orders, determinations, rules, regulations, permits, contracts, certificates, rates, and privileges which have been issued, made, or granted, or allowed to become effective, by the President, the Civil Aeronautics Board, or the Postmaster General, or any court of competent jurisdiction, under any provision of law repealed or amended by this Act, or in the exercise of duties, powers, or functions, which are vested in the Board, and which are in effect at the time this Act takes effect, shall continue in effect according to their terms until modified, terminated, superseded, set aside, or repealed by the Board, or by any court of competent jurisdiction, or by operation of law.

Approved October 24, 1978.

LEGISLATIVE HISTORY:

HOUSE REPORTS: No. 95–1211 and No. 95–1211 pt. 2, accompanying H.R. 12611
      (Comm. on Public Works and Transportation) and No. 95–1779
      (Comm. of Conference).
SENATE REPORT No. 95–631 (Comm. on Commerce, Science, and Transportation).
CONGRESSIONAL RECORD, Vol. 124 (1978):
    Apr. 19, considered and passed Senate.
    Sept. 14, 21, H.R. 12611 considered and passed House; passage vacated and
      S. 2493, amended, passed in lieu.
    Oct. 14, Senate agreed to conference report.
    Oct. 15, House agreed to conference report.
WEEKLY COMPILATION OF PRESIDENTIAL DOCUMENTS, Vol. 14, No. 43:
    Oct. 24, Presidential statement.

○

Index